RELIGION AND THE
AMERICAN MIND

FROM THE GREAT AWAKENING
TO THE REVOLUTION

RELIGION AND THE AMERICAN MIND

FROM THE
Great Awakening
TO THE
Revolution

Alan Heimert

HARVARD UNIVERSITY PRESS
CAMBRIDGE, MASSACHUSETTS
1966

TO THE MEMORY OF

Perry Miller

1905-1963

As his genius was extraordinary, so it was greatly improved by
long and hard study, by which he treasured up much useful
knowledge, both divine and human, and was thus uncommonly
prepared for the arduous and important province to which he
was called. Divinity was his favorite study, in the knowledge of
which, he had but few, if any equals, and no superior in these
provinces . . . Others of his writings likewise deserve to be mentioned with honor; it is a comfort to us, in the midst of grief, that
this ascending ELIJAH, has left behind him, the mantle of so
many valuable volumes, by which though dead, he speaks with
wisdom and warmth . . . .

Gilbert Tennent, March 28, 1758

FOREWORD

THIS book probably had its inception in Tokyo, Japan, where I served, in the early 1950's, in the army's Far East Psychological Warfare Section. While analyzing leaflets and broadcasts, and helping to compose our own propaganda, I pondered over the relationship of ideology and political commitment to modes of persuasion. In 1955 I returned to Harvard with the thought of applying some of my non-academically acquired insight to a projected study of the political thought and discourse of our early national period. After perusing nearly every utterance of this "Golden Age of American Oratory," I was, quite frankly, perplexed. For this discourse reflected—in its forms as well as in substance—assumptions that could not be comprehended in terms of what I at that time understood as the intellectual universe of the early nineteenth century.

Accordingly I began to move backward through American thought and discourse, until, in the period of Federalist-Republican confrontation and competition, the source of my perplexity was revealed. The political literature had its coordinates, not so much in "romantic" attitudes or in Enlightenment premises, as in eighteenth-century religion—its homiletics as well as its doctrines. At this point I leapt backward in time no less far than the middle of the eighteenth century, where, indeed, answers to some of my earlier questions were to be found. But, more importantly, I discovered that the religious literature of that era—of the Great Awakening and its aftermath—contained a story fascinating in its own right, one that deserved to be disentangled and disclosed.

The results of that investigation comprise the present volume. No doubt certain of my themes reflect the direction from which I originally approached the literature of the eighteenth century, and they surely attest my difficulties in overcoming standard interpretations of the relationship of religion and politics in the pre-Revolutionary era. For it has long been received historical doctrine that "Liberal" religion—the rationalism espoused by critics of Awakening enthusiasm and further developed as a counterthrust to eighteenth-century Calvinism—was comparatively humane and progressive in outlook and import, that, indeed, Liberal religion prepared the way for a Revolution of which its spokesmen were the heralds. It is my conclusion, however, that Liberalism was profoundly conservative, politically as well as socially, and that its leaders, insofar as they did in fact embrace the Revolution, were the most reluctant of rebels. Conversely, "evangelical" religion, which had as its most notable formal expression the "Calvinism" of Jonathan Edwards, was not the retrograde philosophy that many historians rejoice to see confounded in America's Age of Reason. Rather Calvinism, and Edwards, provided pre-Revolutionary America with a radical, even democratic, social and political ideology, and evangelical religion embodied, and inspired, a thrust toward American nationalism.

But these themes hardly exhaust the subject matter of my study of the eighteenth-century American mind. Nor is it, for that matter, my purpose to assign any causative explanation for rebellion or Independence. Rather I have attempted to set forth the contours of American thought in the later eighteenth century—specifically, the mind of religious America in the period between the Great Awakening and the Revolution. The era's more secular modes of thought are considered only incidentally, the primary concern being with what was thought and said by various elements of American Protestantism. However, the focus is not on formal theology as such; nor is the scope limited to, or even defined by, the traditional categories of doctrinal and ecclesiastical history. Rather this volume explores the ramifications of religious principles and practices into many realms of eighteenth-century American thought and activity, and touches on nearly all.

Some of these implications of the religious life of eighteenth-century America were developed expressly by the spokesmen of American Protestantism. Others are to be discovered, at least in their inception, only by attending to the more imaginative aspects of religious thought and discourse, as well as to stated doctrine. My manner of approaching the literature, and the premises on which my method of analysis is founded, are expounded in more detail in the Introduction. Here it should suffice to say merely that I am convinced it is only by way of "literary" analysis that the full meaning and import of discourse can be ascertained. More particularly, it is necessary to discern the rhetorical stances and strategies of the spokesmen of the various colonial religious persuasions. Eighteenth-century religious utterances do not just propound doctrine; they attempt to enforce that doctrine, and with it its moral and social imperatives, on the minds (and perhaps more importantly, in the case of evangelical discourse, on the hearts and the wills) of Americans.

What this book contains, therefore, is not simply an explication of eighteenth-century thought, but a view of that thought as part of a process, wherein competing intellectuals seek to make their ideologies efficacious in the lives of Americans, and in their communities. In this respect the two streams of thought—evangelical and rational—into which American Protestantism was divided by the Great Awakening may have considerable relevance even beyond the period in which their contrasting heritages can be distinctly traced in the life of the mind in America, and its politics. To such matters I turn briefly in the concluding pages, but such speculations are not (any more than the "causes" of the Revolution) either the burden of disquisition, or my purpose in setting forth an analysis of the eighteenth-century American mind. My primary intention was to explore, in considerably greater depth and detail than has hitherto been granted this material, a chapter of intellectual history that seems worthy of a proper understanding quite apart from any of its possible legacies.

Meanwhile, however, my original purpose of exploring nineteenth-century political thought remained unfulfilled. For this I surely owe apologies to Louis Hartz, who first undertook to guide my research, as well as gratitude for his assistance, and above all his patience, during my crab-wise progress into the colonial past. As I reached into the earlier period, it was my good fortune to receive the cordial counsel of Kenneth Murdock, from whom I had long ago gained my first introduction to the delights of early American literature. He seemed, in his wisdom, almost to have been expecting me, knowing that I and my first intellectual love could not long be parted. For his perceptive observations, at several stages in the evolution of my manuscript, I am deeply grateful.

Many others on whose time and energies I had no rightful call were likewise generous in their assistance. Twice and more Kenneth Lynn read manuscript and offered what proved to be the most invaluable of advice and admonishment. His concern greatly exceeded the obligations of friendship, as did the generosity of many who found time to read, and assess, my work. W. J. Bate and Herschel Baker provided aid and, perhaps more importantly, comfort, while Harry Levin and Oscar Handlin gave my pages the searching and thoughtful criticism that eased, and made tolerable, the last of my several revisions. To all I give thanks, as well as, of course, liberation from a burden that would not in any case be properly theirs—that is, responsibility for any of my analyses or conclusions.

Assistance was also provided by the staffs of the numerous libraries on which I relied in the course of my investigations. These included the Boston Public, New York Public, New York State, and Congressional libraries; the libraries of the American Antiquarian and American Philosophical societies, and of the Historical Society of Pennsylvania; of the Congregational, Lutheran, and Presbyterian, the Connecticut, Massachusetts, and New York historical societies; the Boston Athenaeum and the Library Company of Philadelphia; the John Carter Brown Library and the libraries of Princeton University, the University of Pennsylvania, and Harvard University. The staff of Harvard's Houghton Library, where the bulk of my research was completed, was unfailingly helpful, and to them, through the patient Miss Carolyn Jakeman, I convey my special gratitude.

An opportunity for research in the libraries of New York, New Jersey, and Pennsylvania (and for untroubled postdoctoral reconsideration of my project) was provided by the Institute for Advanced Study, which elected me a member for 1960-1961. I also wish to thank the Kendall Foundation for helping to finance preparation of the final manuscript, in which task I was aided by two students, Bruce Thomas and Barry O'Connell. There were, moreover, a number of students who had a part in this work by stimulating or helping to confirm my thinking. One deserves, I believe, special mention: David Bertelson, now of the University of California at Berkeley, whose investigations, the latest being into the mind of the colonial South, invariably provoked me to extend my own intellectual and scholarly horizons.

I am grateful also for the aid of Elizabeth Williams Miller, who, when I first set about putting my thoughts on paper, tutored me in the craft and art of using the English language. Later my wife served as my editorial advisor, blue-penciling the manuscript through several revisions. As for her contribution, I shall say only that without her assistance this book could undoubtedly have been written, but it is questionable whether it could otherwise have been read!

My greatest debt, on which there remains a considerable balance outstanding, is attested elsewhere.

Alan Heimert

Cambridge, Massachusetts
March 1966

CONTENTS

RELIGION AND THE AMERICAN MIND

FROM THE GREAT AWAKENING TO THE REVOLUTION

INTRODUCTION

IN 1790 New Jersey's Governor William Livingston, looking back on the years of the Revolution, recalled that the clergy of America had been "almost all universally good Whigs."[1] His estimate has been sustained by later historians, most of whom have likewise tended to see the "black regiment" as something of a monolithic phalanx. The exception of the northern Episcopalians is duly noted, but it is otherwise assumed that the Protestant preachers of America were indistinguishably united in resistance to tyranny and obedience to God. Actually, the clergy's involvement in the Revolution was such that not even the most exhaustive denominational roll call would do justice to the differences among them. The diversity was reflected as well in the response of the laity to the various episodes and issues of the imperial crisis. In Massachusetts, for instance, the great majority of citizens were nominally Congregationalists. Yet wide variations in political outlook were observable during the Stamp Act difficulties of 1765-1766. "The general discontent" of those years, observed one participant, was expressed quite differently within various elements of the populace, depending on what "religious principles" each espoused.[2] Similar differences were evident elsewhere in the colonies, not merely in 1765, but in the variety of reactions to most of the events and issues of the next ten years.

To comprehend the nature of Americans' intellectual differences in the years of the Revolution it is necessary to explore the progress of the American mind in the preceding generation. The divisions as to religious principles were an inheritance from one of the most critical episodes in the history of the American mind: the Great Awakening of the 1740's. Indeed the great revival with its intellectual aftermath is itself probably a more fascinating subject of inquiry than any of the ramifications of religious thought in the years of the Revolution. The intellectual division revealed in the Awakening, and codified in subsequent years by American theologians, persisted long after the Revolution, and in that perspective, the struggle for Independence may well have been only an incidental episode. The subject of this volume, however,

1

is limited to the Awakening and the Revolution, and the continuities in American thought in the decades between them. This Introduction is designed to indicate, by way of anticipatory synopsis and not as demonstration or argument, the broader intellectual contours of that period, and to indicate something of the manner of defining and interpreting the religious principles and divisions of eighteenth-century America.

The Great Awakening was the series of religious revivals which, foreshadowed in the "refreshings" in New Jersey and New England in 1734-1735, rose to intercolonial crescendo in 1740. In the estimation of the Awakening's most outspoken critic, the revivals of the 1740's caused American Protestantism to be "divided into Parties" for the first time since the Antinomian Crisis of the 1630's.[3] Actually, divisions existed within the American churches even before the Great Awakening. The Presbyterian Church, for instance, was torn by various issues throughout the 1730's. Likewise the Congregational ministers of New England differed on such questions as the standards of church membership and, though no open breach had as yet appeared, were aligning themselves into clearly identifiable groups. What the Awakening did was crystallize these differences, giving them objective form, and more importantly, expand them beyond the clergy, making partisans of the laity as well. The "two armies, separated, and drawn up in battle array" which Jonathan Edwards espied in 1742 were not clerical factions merely but hosts whose confrontation embodied a fundamental cleavage within the colonial populace itself.[4]

One way of assessing the divisive consequences of the Awakening is that which has often been followed by historians of American Christianity—by considering the manner in which the Awakening altered the denominational structure of the colonies. The two churches most directly involved in the revival were fragmented. Presbyterianism was split into the Synod of Philadelphia, dominated by the "Old Side" opposers of the Awakening, and that of New York, whose members were the "New Side" partisans of the revival. In Connecticut the Congregational Church was similarly, though not so dramatically, sundered into "Old Lights" and "New Lights." There, also, "Separate" conventicles were established in defiance of the parish system and the semi-Presbyterial Saybrook Platform. Indeed, throughout New England evangelical congregations declared their independence from the associations and consociations that had developed over the course of a century. Some defined themselves as Baptists, and a few even as Presbyterians, but most simply stood as autonomous, and disaffected, seceders from the New England Way. Moreover, the revival impulse encouraged the growth of Presbyterianism in the South, where previously the Anglican Church had enjoyed a near monopoly. In Pennsylvania and New Jersey, and eventually in New England, the Baptists rose into new prominence as the beneficiaries of the revival. Throughout the North the Church of England, whose spokesmen were almost unanimously opposed to the Awakening, grew in numbers by virtue of its appeal to citizens offended by the enthusiasm of the revival.

But such a chronicle of sectarian division and proliferation obscures the fact that the "parties" thrown up by the Awakening were hardly so numerous as any listing of denominations might suggest. The fundamental post-Awakening division of the American mind was one that transcended both the inherited denominational structure and that created by the revival. There were in substance only *two* parties on the American religious scene in the period after the Great Awakening. Generally speaking, one consisted of the opponents of the revival, the other of its advocates, each of which over the succeeding years evolved a religious philosophy consistent with its involvement in and attitude toward the Awakening. These parties were of course not organizational entities, though it is true that the tendency of the century was toward more explicit and formal alignments. The parties into which American Protestantism was divided by the Awakening are best understood, and most accurately described, in intellectual terms. Both represented a casting off from the intellectual universe of Protestant scholasticism, and each marked the independent fulfillment of one of the strains that in Puritanism had been held in precarious balance: "piety" and "reason."

Such a division within Protestantism has long been acknowledged to be the intellectual characteristic of the eighteenth century. Indeed from one perspective what happened in America seems "merely one variant of a universal occurrence in Western culture." In England and on the Continent, as well as in the colonies, the "educated classes" turned to the "generalities of eighteenth-century rationalism," and the "spiritual hungers of the lower classes" found expression in revivals, in Pietism or what is called Evangelicalism.[5] Such a division has been characterized by a recent chronicler of the Great Awakening in New England as the divergence and confrontation of the eighteenth-century forces of "Pietism" and the "Enlightenment."[6] However, the evangelical religion of the colonies differed markedly from the pietism of Europe, and the "rational religion" that arose to thwart the revival impulse was hardly identical to the faith of the Encyclopedists. The Great Awakening in America was a unique and profound crisis in the history of the "indigenous culture."

First of all, it perhaps needs to be stressed that the revival in Amer-

3

ica, unlike that promoted by the Wesleys in England, built and throve on the preaching of Calvinist doctrine. The "work of God is carried on here," George Whitefield wrote to John Wesley in early 1740, "(and that in a most glorious manner) by doctrines quite opposite to those you hold."[7] The doctrines to which Whitefield referred were those of Wesley's sermon, *Free Grace,* in which the English evangelist had propounded what, in the parlance of the day, was deemed an "Arminian" theory of salvation. "Arminianism," a name derived from that of the Dutch theologian, Jacobus Arminius (1560-1609), had originally referred to the belief that grace is not irresistible, as Calvin had argued, but conditional. By the eighteenth century, however, the term was used less rigorously, often in conjunction with the names of such Trinitarian heresies as Pelagianism and Socinianism, to refer to any of a number of vague ideas expressive of impatience with the "rigid" and "harsh" doctrines of Calvinism. It was against such an "Arminianism," more appropriately called "rationalism," that the proponents of the American revival thought they were contending.

The Arminianism of the colonies had few affinities with the warmer faith of the Wesleys. Here it was the official theology only of the Church of England, which ascribed to man the power to work out his own salvation largely through the use of his rational powers. In the first quarter of the eighteenth century, moreover, not a few Congregational and Presbyterian preachers were also suggesting that man was not so depraved, nor God quite so sovereign, as orthodox doctrine had argued. Such an undermining of Calvinism was in fact part of the inevitable working out of Puritanism's own modifications of strict Calvinist doctrine. The "covenant theology" itself had made God something less than an arbitrary and inscrutable being, and the doctrine of "preparation" had come to imply, over the course of the century, that man was capable of "willing" his own salvation.

The opening charge of the American revival was thus the sermon of 1735 in which Edwards strove to restore the reformation doctrine of "justification by faith alone" as the "principal hinge" of American Protestantism. In so challenging Arminianism, however, Edwards revealed that the two "schemes" which he contrasted—the "evangelical" and the "legal"—were hardly those traditionally identified with the terms Calvinist and Arminian. For Edwards, in presenting evidence of "God's approbation of the doctrine of justification by faith alone," pointed, not to the Pauline epistle, but to the numerous and "remarkable conversions" experienced in Northampton in 1735.[8] The focus of debate was turning from the theoretic manner of God's operations to what He was actually accomplishing, and over the next decade it moved even further away from the traditional issues of the seventeenth century. During the Great Awakening the contest of ideas was often phrased in the older terms. In 1740, for instance, the young Presbyterian revivalist, Gilbert Tennent, declared that "we may as easily reconcile Light and Darkness, Fire and Water, Life and Death, as Justification partly by Works, and partly by Grace."[9] But even for Tennent, who yielded to no man in the rigor of his Calvinism, the "principal hinge" of the "evangelical scheme" was no longer a point of doctrine. Though the issue was at first whether the Awakening was a genuine "Work of God," the challenge of criticism and the response of evangelical spokesmen were such that the focus of analysis quickly shifted from the will of God to the nature of man. In this context, the crux of Calvinism became the existential reality of the emotional conversion experience.

Similarly, the party that Edwards and Tennent opposed was not perfectly characterized as an Arminian one. The advocates of what Edwards styled the "legal scheme" eventually took to themselves, by virtue presumably of their opposition to the "oppressive" doctrines of Calvinism, the name of "Liberals." But their most distinguishing intellectual mark was the notion that man is—or should be—a rational being, one who derives his standards of virtuous behavior from an observation of the external world. A rationalist strain had of course been present in American Puritanism from the beginning. One of the classic assumptions of the Puritan mind was that the will of God was to be discerned in nature as well as in revelation. But in the late seventeenth century, and with greater boldness by the 1720's, voices had been heard in the colonies proclaiming that a knowledge of God's will was best derived, not from His word, but from His works. The articulation of such a "religion of nature," attended as it was by the reversion of several of Connecticut's more prominent young ministers to Episcopalianism, was one of the developments that prompted the attack in the 1730's on Arminianism. But with the Awakening the avowal of a rational or "reasonable" theology was no longer limited to colonial Anglicans. The notion that Christianity is pre-eminently a rational religion permeated the thinking of Old Side Presbyterianism, the Old Lights of Connecticut, and the Liberal clergy of the neighborhood of Boston.

It was in Massachusetts that the creed of reason was most conspicuously developed into a partisan ideology. There it emerged, in the decades after the Awakening, as "the instrument of a group, or of an interest"[10]—the group opposed to the "enthusiasm" of the revival and the seeming unreason of evangelical religion. The premises of rational religion were first unfolded in the criticisms of the Awakening published by the leading Boston Liberal, Charles Chauncy. But the manifesto of Congregational Liberalism was probably Ebenezer Gay's 1759

Harvard Dudleian Lecture, *Natural Religion*. Here Gay summarized the Liberal thesis that God had formed men as rational beings so they "might learn from his Works, what is good, and what is required of them." The lessons of Scripture could only confirm what man was able to discover from the "Constitution of Things, in their respective Natures and Relations."[11] That Massachusetts Liberals were not alone in evolving such a theology is indicated by the fact that the magnum opus of colonial rationalism was the *Elementa Philosophica* of the Anglican spokesman, Samuel Johnson of Connecticut. And this volume, in turn, was recommended by Benjamin Franklin to all who would properly understand the true nature and bases of morality.

In sharp contrast to this studiously rationalistic religion of nature stood the "Calvinism" evolved in the decades after the Awakening. Actually the Calvinists of eighteenth-century America were hardly subscribers to the theology of the *Institutes*. All were familiar with, and frequently quoted, Edwards' classic disclaimer of "dependence on Calvin."[12] If—as Samuel Hopkins explained of Edwards—their "Principles were *Calvinistic*," they "called no man, Father."[13] They assumed the designation of Calvinist only, as one New Jersey Presbyterian announced, because such terms were "exceeding useful" when one wished "to express Complex Ideas." Yet the idea that essentially defined American Calvinism was acknowledged to be a rather simple one—a belief in the "inward operation of the holy spirit in regeneration."[14] Herein they followed Jonathan Edwards in emphasizing the role of the "affections" in religion and in making virtue dependent on the reception of a "vital indwelling principle" from the Holy Spirit.

In truth, the partisans of evangelical and emotional religion were all in some degree under the intellectual dominion of Jonathan Edwards. Samuel Hopkins would undoubtedly have liked to consider himself Edwards' only begotten intellectual offspring. But he, like the Edwards of whom he wrote, "thought and judged for himself, and was truly very much of an Original."[15] Just as close to Edwards in idea and spirit (and perhaps closer) were the multitude of New Light and New Side preachers, Separatists and Baptists, who, despite their minor differences with Edwards, acknowledged him to be "the greatest pillar in this part of ZION'S BUILDING." Joseph Bellamy, Edwards' student and friend, invariably cited his writings as the best books "on experimental religion and vital piety since the days of inspiration." The Baptist Isaac Backus, though at one time in disagreement with Edwards over the qualifications of the ministry, was always ready to acknowledge him a writer of "pure truth" and, in later years, spoke of him as "our Edwards."[16] Ebenezer Frothingham, who was distraught when Edwards refused to accept the leadership of the Separates, continued to praise him as a defender of the revival and as a theologian and, after Edwards' death, saluted him as one who had "doubtless gone to heaven."[17] Indeed a variety of ministers and men cherished the memory of the "late divine, whose praise is in all the churches," and for all of them Edwards' legacy consisted in the "many valuable volumes" which, as Gilbert Tennent consoled himself, this "ascending ELIJAH" had left as his mantle to American Calvinism.[18] So well did they wear it, indeed, that the Calvinist ministry, averse as they were to invoking "great names" in support of ideas, were nevertheless more accurately "Edwardeans."*[19] Perhaps not until Calhoun similarly convinced two generations of Southerners that, like Edwards, he spoke with "almost superhuman wisdom,"[20] were the axioms and postulates of so broad a movement ever thus provided by one individual nor its inspiration and significance so readily discernible in his writings.

For three and more decades the Calvinists (or Edwardeans) of America debated with the Liberals the questions of the nature of man and the character of God. In this confrontation the party lines of the revival were preserved essentially intact—and even reinforced. To be sure, not all the critics of the Awakening were full-blown rationalists. But as one defender of the revival observed, "the principal and most *inveterate Opposers*" were men of "Arminian and *Pelagian* Principles." The others, those whom he styled "only Deputy or second Hand Opposers," could not, however, long deny their fundamental differences with the Liberal opponents of the Awakening.[21] Moreover, on the issues of the freedom of the human will, man's original sin, and, perhaps most importantly, the place of the emotions in religious experience, they came to acknowledge their affinities with the evangelical religion of the Awakening and of Edwards.

Of course there remained a number of American clergymen for whom the federal (or covenant) theology and its metaphysic continued to have some meaning. Generally of an older generation than either the partisans of the revival or its more vehement critics, they persisted

---

* Though some Calvinist ministers from William Tennent to David Austin considered themselves the successors of John Baptist (and dressed accordingly) and though others conceived their function as that of the apostles Paul and James, Edwards was alone in contending consistently that the Christian minister was a "type of the Messiah." The notion of a peculiar analogue between pre-Christian society and pre-Awakening America, which filled all of Edwards' speculations on the millennium, frequently led him (particularly in the heady ecstasies of the Awakening) to conclusions as to his personal role in the redemption of mankind which other Calvinists implicitly accepted. At one point Edwards privately remarked that "if it was plain to all the world of Christians that I was under the infallible guidance of Christ, and I was sent forth to teach the world the will of Christ, then I should have power in all the world." Edwards never attained to this eminence, but neither his thinking nor that of his colleagues is fully understandable without an appreciation of their lurking suspicion that he probably deserved it.

in defining the minister's role as that of "pointing out those middle and peaceable Ways, wherein the Truth generally lies, and guarding against Extreams on the right Hand and on the Left."[22] But their formulas proved untenable in the post-Awakening era, as did for the most part those of the new generation of moderates who, in an effort to straddle or avoid the central issues of the period, evolved a creed comparable to that of second-generation Puritanism.

While there were more than two theologies at work in post-Awakening America, the intellectual life of American Protestantism was clearly dominated and substantially defined by the spokesmen of rationalism and of evangelical religion. Part I of this study is devoted to an exploration and interpretation of the nature and significance of this contest of ideas. The assumption on which the analysis proceeds is that of the essential similarity of all Liberals, regardless of denominational commitment, and of the evangelicals of whatever sectarian persuasion.

To be sure, one of the bitterest debates of the period was that which came to rage between the more Liberal Presbyterians and Congregationalists and the representatives of an equally rational Episcopalianism. Likewise the Baptists of the Middle Colonies argued with New Side Presbyterians, and the New England Separates with the New Lights who remained within the Congregational Church. By the beginning of the Seven Years War, indeed, such "disputings" had, according to Isaac Backus, the leader of New England's Baptists, brought the Church "in all parts" of the colonies "into terrible circumstances." And by 1760 Gilbert Tennent was complaining that the Christian Church of America had become, "by her numerous and scandalous Divisions," a "Torment to herself, a Grief to her Friends, and the Scorn of her Enemies."[23] Backus and Tennent, as well as such Liberals as Charles Chauncy, had programs for healing these divisions. These led in some instances to a realignment of parties, but in others served only to perpetuate and further encourage division. Any analysis of the intellectual history of eighteenth-century America must necessarily concern itself with such developments, but like denominational multiplicity itself, they should not obscure—they did not at the time —the fundamental cleavage between rationalists and evangelicals.

Indeed the lack of any sharp intellectual differences among the participants in these intestine debates was testimony to the American religious mind's acceptance of the fact that in the years after the Awakening it had only two viable intellectual options. The only vehement debates within rationalism and evangelicalism were ecclesiastical, and the matter of church structure was, in the context of post-Awakening America, something of a "thing indifferent." Such contests represented efforts merely to refine, or to define somewhat more precisely, the character of the two parties between which the fundamental conflict of the era was acknowledged to lie, and to decide the institutional allegiances of Americans presumably already committed to one religious philosophy or the other.

There are many ways of looking at the division brought to America by the Awakening. One historian has concluded that the revival "cut a swath between rich and poor, stimulating the hostility that already divided them," and thus opened the way for "class conflict" in the colonies.[24] Clearly there were divisions and antagonisms among the American people in the period before the Awakening. One New England preacher, surveying the scene just before the impact of the revival had been felt, noted that New Englanders were distinguished by their "want of Brotherly Love (evident by their quarrelsome, litigious Disposition, and Law-Suits without number)."[25] In many communities, disputes had arisen over the use and control of the common lands, and for years nearly every colony was racked by debates over the relative merits of specie and paper currency. The latter issue, revolving about the needs of the merchants for a "medium of trade" and the search by farmers for solutions to the problems of inflation, indebtedness, and the declining productivity of the land, had given rise to fairly hardheaded and pragmatic partisan contests. In each community and province hostility was expressed and exacerbated by such speculative programs as the "land-bank" scheme. All these controversies, in many of which the clergy participated, reflected the difficulty Americans were experiencing in coming to terms with their environment and with the involvement of the British government and economy in their affairs.

Far from stimulating these hostilities, however, the immediate effect of the religious revivals seems to have been a tempering of the fierce social, economic and political antagonisms that had racked the colonies since the beginning of the century. One glory of the Awakening in the eyes of those who approved it was the restoration of social and political concord to the villages and towns of the colonies. In 1741, Jonathan Edwards reported, the politicians and citizens of New England ceased their usual bickerings and contentions, and whole communities enjoyed a union and social harmony greater than that known "at any time during the preceding thirty years."[26] (To many Calvinists it seemed that true concord had departed from the colonies much earlier—in the moment when God's plantations had been converted into trading enterprises and the "God Land" had become, as Roger Williams once apprehended, "as great a God" among the English "as the God Gold was with the Spaniard.")[27] The Calvinist ministry

9

welcomed the Awakening, and long remembered it, as a golden age when men were not divided, personally or as partisans, over acquisition and distribution of the New World's resources.

Even in 1740, however, it escaped no one's notice that those who possessed "a greater measure of this world's goods" were less disposed toward the Awakening, or that evangelical religion held a greater appeal for the "lower classes" of American society.[28] Yet at no time was the division between Calvinist and Liberal one merely of economic or social class—any more than the Great Awakening itself was "a revolt of the backcountry producers from the stringent controls of the mercantile aristocracy."[29] Such interpretations of the eighteenth century do as much violence to the American temper as accounts of the Great Migration that portray New England as originally a plantation of trade. The parties and debates of eighteenth-century American religion simply will not yield to the categories of Marx and Beard, for the reason that the fundamental post-Awakening division was an intellectual one—one more aesthetic, in fact, than economic or social. In the more accurate terms of H. Richard Niebuhr, the division was between those who "saw the reality of an order of being other than that walled and hemmed in existence in which a stale institutional religion and bourgeois rationalism were content to dwell," and those who did not.[30] What distinguished Americans, so far as the "great debate" of the eighteenth century was concerned, was differences not of income but, in substance, of taste.

Implicit in the "new light" of the revival was a foreswearing of the pragmatic and rather hardheaded differences in policy that before the Awakening had distinguished colonial partisanship. But from the moment when the eyes of some citizens of the colonies were taken from their "ordinary secular business" and turned to the "great things of religion," the stage was being prepared for a new kind of party struggle, but one hardly less vehement.[31] In the contest between rational and evangelical religion was embodied, indeed, one of those fundamental value disagreements which, according to many historians, America has from the beginning been free. When Edwards first challenged Arminian rationalism he proclaimed that the differences between his "scheme" and the "legal one" were multiform and irreconcilable. When the "foundation" is so different, he went on to insist, "the whole scheme becomes exceeding diverse and contrary."[32] Over the remainder of the century this contrariety was to be manifested in nearly every area of thought and behavior.

What these many contrasts between Liberalism and Calvinism were, and where they led, is the subject of this volume. The differences were perhaps even more numerous and various than the detailed analyses that follow suggest. But the sharpest differences in the realm of ideas were ones that necessarily ramified throughout American culture. The great debate of the eighteenth century focused on such questions as the nature and needs of the human personality, the pattern and tendency of history (and of American history in particular), the nature of the good society—phrased both as judgment on the social order of colonial America and as conviction as to what the civilization of the New World might and should be—and the role of the intellectual, and of ideas and expression, in translating ideals into practice.

Certain of the differences between evangelical and rational religion emerge from the express utterances of their spokesmen. Others, including some of the more important, must be inferred, or at least confirmed, by way of what amounts to a translation of theological discourse into more instrumental terms. The interpretations that follow often derive from a view of doctrinal positions and developments that does not, confessedly, adhere to the standard rubrics for a history of religious dogma. A fresh look is frequently taken at such formulations as that of the Trinity, or of God's wisdom in the permission of sin. Viewed in conjunction with other ideas, and institutional changes, such doctrines provide insight into the general intellectual pattern and tendencies of the period. Throughout, the goal of analysis has been that of discovering what was ultimately at stake, for the American mind, in a dispute that was not so much a debate between theologians as a vital competition for the intellectual allegiance of the American people.

Obviously such an intellectual history is not a narrative merely but an interpretation as well. My conclusions, however, or perhaps more accurately my hypotheses, are based on an abundance of what is, after all, the only appropriate evidence for the historian of ideas—the recorded thoughts and expression of the men who spoke to and for the people of colonial America. Nearly everything published in the colonies (and not a few items printed elsewhere, or unpublished) has been read—and read always with the hope of determining not merely what was said but what was *meant*. To discover the meaning of any utterance demands what is in substance a continuing act of literary interpretation, for the language with which an idea is presented, and the imaginative universe by which it is surrounded, often tells us more of an author's meaning and intention than his declarative propositions. An understanding of the significance of any idea, or of a constellation of ideas, requires an awareness of the context of institutions and events out of which thought emerged, and with which it strove to come to terms. But full apprehension depends finally on reading, not between the lines but, as it were, through and beyond them.

Almost any reading of the literature of pre-Revolutionary America soon yields the conclusion that many of the ideas apparently held in common by all American Protestants were not in fact shared. By virtue of the disparate intellectual universes out of which the utterances of Calvinism and Liberalism emerged, the same word as employed by each often contained and communicated a quite different meaning. As will be abundantly demonstrated two such words were among the most important in the vocabulary of eighteenth-century Americans: "liberty" and "union." Indeed, in the disparate connotations of these two words was encapsulated nearly the whole of the larger significance of the confrontation of rational and evangelical religion. The conflict between Liberalism and Calvinism was not, as is generally assumed, simply a token of the unwillingness of the latter to confess itself an anachronism in an age of reason and science. Rather the intellectual division and debate had implications for both the society of the colonies and its politics, and in such a context rational religion is not so readily identifiable as the more liberal of the two persuasions. Indeed the evidence attests that Liberalism was a profoundly elitist and conservative ideology, while evangelical religion embodied a radical and even democratic challenge to the standing order of colonial America.

From the very outset opponents of the revival sensed in the evangelical impulse a revolutionary potential. The "best of the people of all denominations," reported a Connecticut Anglican in 1742, feared that the "enthusiasts would shortly get the government into their hands and tyrannize over us."[33] Ever afterward critics of evangelical thought were unable to debate with Calvinists (the latter complained) without having "something to say about the mad men of Munster, who they tell us rebelled against their civil rulers."[34] Liberal fears seemed justified when, in the early 1760's, a New Light party took control of the Connecticut legislature. It seemed obvious that the "rigid enthusiasms and conceited notions" of the revival and evangelicalism were the sources of the "republican and mobbish principles and practices" of the insurgent party. The Calvinist ministry, "fond to a madness" of "popular forms of government," were, it was charged, responsible for Connecticut's "revolutionary" change of government.[35] And when, a decade later, America was confronted by genuine revolution, it would often be concluded that what the colonies had awakened to in 1740 was none other than independence and rebellion.

The revival impulse and the divisions it engendered were objectified in the party structure and the political process of the colonies. In 1763 a frightened Connecticut Arminian complained that the New Lights, who within his "short memory were a small Party, merely a religious one," had already "such an Influence as to be nearly the ruling part of the Government." Among his explanations for their rise and success was a "superior Attention to Civil Affairs," but to fix on the civil concerns of Calvinists is to distort both their manner of thinking and the manner in which evangelical religion impinged on colonial politics.[36] For one thing the civil issues that had most concerned the New Lights of Connecticut for two decades were the opposition of the provincial government to the Awakening and its support of the anti-revival and seemingly Arminian administration and faculty of Yale College. Even in the 1760's the reigning public issue, so far as Calvinists were concerned, was that which also first introduced a "party spirit" into the politics of Virginia: the rights of evangelical dissenters to religious liberty. It is by no means unimportant that in the Old Dominion Samuel Davies' Presbyterians learned to exact "Bonds from candidates to serve and stand by their Interests" in the House of Burgesses.[37] But such strategies are hardly the whole tale of the involvement of evangelical religion in the political life of the colonies, and it is not the purpose of this study in any case to trace institutional changes and development. The concern here is rather with the history of ideas and their impact on pre-Revolutionary America.

Some Thoughts Concerning the Present Revival of Religion, written and published by Jonathan Edwards in 1742, was in a profound sense the first national party platform in American history. Yet Edwards' thoughts seem totally divorced from all the topics of which partisan issues are presumably made. His thinking reveals the disengagement of the evangelical ministry and populace from the usual institutions and processes of government and politics. Edwards even dismisses as a relatively insignificant matter the outbreak of hostilities between Britain and Spain: "We in New England are now engaged in a more important war"—the battle between the opposition to the revival and those who wanted to encourage and forward it.[38] Three years later the "serious people" of New England refused to enlist for the expedition against Louisburg until the magistrates somehow managed to persuade George Whitefield to bless the venture.[39] Though Edwards eventually hailed the victory at Cape Breton as a Providential dispensation of momentous significance, the Calvinist mind continued to respond in the spirit of the *Thoughts on the Revival* to many of the great events of the next decades. In 1757, at the height of the French and Indian War, Samuel Davies was seeking an *"outpouring of the Spirit"* as the "grand, radical, all-comprehensive blessing" for Virginia.[40] Even on the first day of January, 1775, Calvinist spokesmen were insisting that a revival of religion was the one thing needful, the "Sum of all Blessings," for the American colonies.[41]

Nonetheless, it can be said that Edwards' judgment on the comparative importance of New England's two "wars" proved as prescient as
his views on so many other subjects. For Edwards' *Thoughts*, like the
Awakening he defended, was in a vital respect an American declaration
of independence from Europe, and the revival impulse was one toward
intercolonial union. To be sure, the Awakening was in inception a
response to the changing conditions of American life as perceived on
the level of the local community. But the Calvinist mind was such that
Edwards' vision moved quickly outward from Northampton toward
making all "New England a kind of heaven upon earth"—and from
there to all America.[42] Over the next decades evangelical thought so
progressed that Davies sought the blessings of the spirit not for Hanover parish alone, but for his "country," and by 1775 Calvinists were
looking for a gracious shower on what by then they saw as their
"Nation and Land." The evangelical impulse, promoted almost entirely within the church and through "the ordinary means," was the
avatar and instrument of a fervent American nationalism.

The Calvinist commitment to the unity of the American people—
part of the fascinating tale of the passage of the American mind out of
the theological universe of the eighteenth century into the world of
national politics—took thirty-five years to reach overt expression. It is
but one instance of what constitutes a major theme of the pages that
follow: the manner in which the Awakening, by shattering the communities and the social assumptions inherited from the seventeenth
century, allowed the evangelical ministry to offer the American people
new commitments, political as well as ethical.

Much of Calvinism's thrust, its radical and emphatic definitions of
liberty and equality, emerged more as the premises and assumptions
of doctrine than as an articulate program. Still, the Calvinist ministry
aspired to understand the times in order that they, like the men of
Issachar, might "know what Israel ought to do."[43] In this respect,
something of a watershed for the Calvinist mind was passed in 1755,
when Aaron Burr, Edwards' son-in-law, published a sermon on imperial affairs which, omitting the doctrinal section, consisted entirely
of commentary and advice on British and colonial government and
policy.[44] Over the next decades Calvinist spokesmen grew ever bolder
in proposing programs for the accomplishment of what they took to be
the general welfare. Many of their policies, indeed most of them, were
directed toward the amelioration of domestic conditions—as, for instance, their demand for a "more effectual provision for the Instruction of our Children, in our Common Schools."[45] In the Revolutionary
period, domestic and imperial issues merged, and the evangelical
scheme was translated into the political imperative that the colonial

"poor" not be "squeezed, to support the corruption and luxury of the great."[46]

As the last quotation suggests, the programmatic elements of Calvinism were invariably subordinated to, or conceived within, what the evangelical clergy considered the primary moral dimension of all activity, individual or communal. In the Revolutionary period, and before, the Calvinist mind responded to political challenge in terms of the felt obligation of both ministers and people to "fight sin always."[47] Often the evangelical ministry concluded that "Sin" was the cause of all difficulties, "civil, ecclesiastical, and domestic," and they were ever ready to describe an opposing policy as a "mere ideal project, arising from the DECEITFULNESS of sin." They also ranged rather widely in search of this "dreadful monster" and of means for overcoming and destroying sin.[48] In sum, to the thought of post-Awakening and Revolutionary Calvinism can be traced that enduring quality of the American political mind that Richard Hofstadter has characterized as an impatience with "hard politics." In this sense the American tradition —of Populists and rank-and-file Jacksonians and Jeffersonians—was hardly the child of the Age of Reason. It was born of the "New Light" imparted to the American mind by the Awakening and the evangelical clergy of colonial America.

The contribution of eighteenth-century Calvinism to the making of the American public mind has been allowed to remain unappreciated. In fact it has been for the most part ignored, possibly because its thought evolved in a context of indifference to the stuff of which politics is made. Quite clearly Calvinists were not, in the quarter century or so after the Awakening, as disposed as the Liberal clergy to "pulpit politics." In 1750, for instance, Jonathan Mayhew, the young hope of Boston rationalism, proclaimed the clergy's right to engage in the avocation of *"preaching politics."* In the same year Edwards was reminding his Northampton congregation that the "mutual concerns of ministers and their people" were of infinitely greater moment "than any of the temporal concerns of men, whether private or public"—of more importance indeed than the fate of the greatest "earthly monarchs, and their kingdoms or empires."[49] As late as the autumn of 1774 Calvinist ministers were insisting that they had a more important function than discussing "the civil rights of human nature" and just as sternly denying any but a recent interest in affairs of state.[50]

Meanwhile the Liberal ministry were preaching intermittently on what they considered to be the rights of man. Indeed history has judged the rationalist clergy of eighteenth-century America to have been ideologically and even personally heralds of the Revolution. This notion, one of the more sophisticated myths concerning the American past, seems to be largely the creature of John Adams' memory, though Peter Oliver's registering of surprise and disgust at the spectacle of "respectable" ministers hawking "sedition" has helped to reinforce it.[51] Nineteenth-century Unitarian historiography of course encouraged the thought that there is some inherent relationship between Liberal religion and the patriotism of the Revolution. Perhaps the ideas which informed the Declaration of Independence were in some way collaterally descended from those used to resist the revival and Calvinism, but the two were hardly blood relatives. Indeed, some twentieth-century historians have sensed a warmer faith at work in the "religious antecedents" of the Revolution. But they nevertheless concentrate almost exclusively on the words of the more familiar Chauncy and Mayhew. Thus is preserved the Liberal ministry's reputation as both the foremost among the Revolutionary clergy and the representatives of the mind of Protestant patriotism.

In the quarter century before 1776 the Liberal clergy did expound the ideas of the social contract and the law of nature—concepts derived from John Locke's *Second Treatise of Government*. A favored vehicle for exposition of these ideas was the New England Election Sermon. Delivered each spring in the capitals of Massachusetts and Connecticut, such sermons were intended as the ministry's edification of governor and legislature on the nature of civil government. On these occasions Liberal spokesmen articulated a nearly pure and simple Lockeanism. Passages and even whole sections of their sermons offer few hints of the speakers' clerical vocation. A paragraph like this one (from the Massachusetts Election Sermon of 1767) might as well have been composed by any American of the century who had read John Locke:

> Although there is a natural equality and independency among men yet they have voluntarily combined together, and by compact and mutual agreement, have entered into a social state, and bound themselves to the performance of a multitude of affairs, tending to the good; and to the avoiding of a multitude of injuries tending to the hurt and damage of the whole. And hence arises order and government, and a just regulation of all those matters which relate to the safety of the persons, lives, liberties, and property of individuals.[52]

To extract such a passage from a clerical utterance, is, however, to distort and obscure the full meaning of the sermon and even of the ideas of social contract and natural law as expounded by the clergy. If the discourses of the ministry were assessed only in terms of the extent to which each at some point repeated the postulates of John Locke, Liberals, and Calvinists—with several signal exceptions—would appear nearly indistinguishable. Indeed one of the earliest uses of Locke's ideas was in a pamphlet defending the revival and Separatism, which opened with "a *short sketch* of what the celebrated Mr. Lock in his *Treatise of Government* has largely demonstrated, and in which it is justly to be presumed all are agreed who understand the natural Right of Mankind."[53] (This dissenter was also an admirer of the celebrated Mr. Locke's *Letter on Toleration,* which the Connecticut authorities, likewise exponents of the idea of social contract, had forbidden to be printed or circulated by a group of Yale undergraduates who wanted freedom for evangelical religion.) Down through the years nearly every Protestant minister in America, when commenting on civil affairs, argued that though men give up "some part" of their "natural liberty" on entering into society, no government could violate their persons or property in an arbitrary manner.[54] In neither Liberal sermons nor Calvinist, however, did these echoes and expositions of Lockean theory have the same meanings as those attached to the concepts by the authors of the Declaration of Independence.

Until and unless Liberals were confronted by imperial issues, their interpretations of the social contract, particularly as they applied to the internal affairs of the provinces, were careful and methodical arguments for holding in check a populace that was by no means conceived to be a community of natural equals. Even in the Revolutionary period, when the Liberal spoke on public affairs, his ideas were so phrased, and presented in such a form, as to keep the "multitude" from involving itself in matters of state. Indeed the rationalist clergy were in the 1770's, nearly to a man, if not outright Tories, then praying that the magistrates and merchants to whose judgment they deferred would find some compromise solution to the lamentable controversy between Britain and her colonies. They preached Locke almost as a justification of the *status quo,* and even more importantly they did so by way of deploring and seeking to subdue the revolutionary enthusiasm that was, despite their hopes and efforts, arising in the American populace.

It was the more orthodox clergymen of America who infused the Lockean vocabulary with a moral significance, a severity and an urgency, and thereby translated the ideas of social contract and natural law into a spur to popular activity. In 1775, for instance, Moses Mather, latest of his illustrious name to occupy a pulpit, phrased *America's Appeal* largely in terms of Locke's defense of civil rights. But in so doing Mather eloquently affirmed the obligation of "all the members" of society to actively pursue and promote the general welfare. His appeal was not to the candid world but to the populace, who he believed already had a "right understanding" of the circumstances in which America found itself. His purpose was not to inform but to "render the exertions, the noble struggles of a brave, free and injured people, bold, rapid, and irresistible."[55] As will be demonstrated, the multitudes of sermons delivered by more evangelical Calvinists were even more clearly devised as a means of stimulating the hearts and wills of the American people.

Herein consisted the most conspicuous difference between the utterances of Calvinists and of Liberals in the Revolutionary period. A further difference, and a not unrelated one, was that the evangelical ministry were not dependent on Locke for their political and social philosophy. Even when they employed his concepts of natural law and the social contract they were offering a counterstatement to the individualistic premises of Lockean theory. Eventually the spokesmen for the evangelical scheme produced a corpus of social and political thought that stands as the American counterpart of the writings of Rousseau. Radically communitarian in its assumptions and goals, such a theory sustained not only the Calvinist pressure toward independence and revolution but subsequent efforts to secure "the most equitable, rational, natural mode of civil government" for an independent America.[56]

The Calvinist political philosophy, which centered finally not on the consent of the governed but on the general will of the community, was sustained by the equally fundamental evangelical conception that the purpose of public discourse was to activate men's wills as well as inform their minds. Whatever his particular thoughts, the Calvinist presented them in such a form and language that his political sermons were not vindications of action already taken but encouragement to further endeavor on the part of the populace. It is in this regard that our traditional view of the Revolution, its inspirations and its aspirations, may need some modification. As has been observed, a "pure rationalism" might have declared the independence of the American people, "but it could never have inspired them to fight for it."[57]

Quite apart from the question of the Revolution, the contrasts between Liberal and Calvinist social thought were possibly of less ultimate significance than the remarkable differences between their oratorical strategies and rhetorical practices. Such an assumption makes Chapter IV the principal hinge, as it were, of the present study; herein is examined the restructuring of particular churches after the Awakening and the concurrent redefinition, by both rational and evangelical ministers, of the nature and function of the sermon. It was the Calvinist conception of the pastor's role and his relationship to his people that led to the creation of an institutional framework within which men responded enthusiastically, in the 1770's, to the verbal promptings of their spiritual guides. Meanwhile, as the Calvinist clergy relied on the voluntary allegiance of their congregations and depended on what they came to call "the will of the people," the Liberals increasingly deferred to the civil authority. Within their own congregations they acquiesced in what was in effect an abandonment of the clergy's role as an intellectual force giving direction to the course of society.

The reconstitution of evangelical churches derived in part from explicit doctrine. Its profounder inspiration, however, seems to have been the radical imperative contained in Edwards' somewhat startling thesis of 1742—that God is, "as it were, under the power of his people."[58] For at the heart of the evangelical scheme was an implicit democratization of the Deity—while Liberalism, for its part, devised a God who, however reasonable and forebearing, was nonetheless a sovereign from whom the prerogatives and privileges of the clergy descended. Similarly, the intellectual premises of Calvinism were such that it reconceived and reconstituted the congregation as a vital communion of kindred spirits, its members animated by each other as well as by the minister. It was thus, often without seeming plan or direction, that Calvinism converted its ecclesiastical institutions into the bases of that "close union among themselves" to which its ultimate effectiveness "in Politicks" was attributed.[59]

Indeed, in the evangelical churches of pre-Revolutionary America was forged that union of tribunes and people that was to characterize the early American Democracy. Yet it was not by ideas alone, nor even with social imagination, that the Calvinist ministry strove to energize the American populace. They differed from nearly all other eighteenth-century spokesmen in their recognition of the peculiar potency of the spoken word, and perhaps herein lay their chief contrast with such a rational clerical agitator as John Wise. Surely Wise, despite his rationalist premises, had been something of an emotional Populist, filled as he was with resentment of priestly "conspiracies" and fiscal "monopolies." In 1721 Wise, arguing in support of "a plentiful Medium," had warned that the farmers who shared his interest in an expanded currency had it "in their Power to Remove those who stand in their Way."[60] In point of fact they did not, nor would any disaffected Americans gain such power, it would appear, until their intellectual leaders *spoke* in order to arouse them, as well as wrote on their behalf.

Obviously the evangelical clergy were not alone among Americans in making the latter half of the eighteenth century something other than an age of reasoned discourse. The pamphleteers of the 1740's and 1750's, who charged that proposals for the immediate redemption of paper money betrayed the design and desire of certain "Lords of Mammon" to make "slaves and vassals of the commonality" were as emotional in their language as in their policies.[61] So also were the numerous scriveners who in the early 1770's filled the colonial newspapers with allegations of perfidious British avarice. But their mode of discourse, if nothing else, clearly identified them with the eighteenth-century rational mind, which, to whatever degree enlightened, tended to agree with Benjamin Franklin that "Modern Political Oratory" was chiefly, and most properly, "performed by the Pen and Press."[62] John Adams, for one, came to realize that the spoken word was also an essential instrument of persuasion (and so far as the Revolution was concerned, probably the more efficacious). But along with most of the more prominent lawyer-patriots of the day, he left that task to others and confined his public efforts to the medium of the written word.

The Liberal clergy too, despite their cultivation of a literary eloquence, were equally disposed to reach men primarily through the instrument of writing. It was in this regard that the evangelical impulse, by its demurral from the standards of the eighteenth century, can be said to have inaugurated a new era in the history of American public address. Though Puritanism had of course always assumed the importance of "hearing the Word," an epoch can be dated from the arrival in the colonies of George Whitefield and a realization of the remarkable effectiveness of his preaching. In 1741 Alexander Garden sought to dismiss both Whitefield and the Awakening by bidding him "only to put the *same* words, which from his mouth produced the boasted effects, into the mouth of an *ordinary* speaker, and see whether the same *effects* would be the consequence."[63] Garden was paying unwitting and unwilling tribute to the skillful manner of address of Whitefield, the "wonder of the world" who, along with other evangelical preachers, launched an age in which oratory would be recognized as the essential instrument of moving the American public.[64]

In emphasizing the Calvinists' mastery of the science and art of the spoken word, it is not intended to deny the contribution of the Liberal clergy to the Revolutionary impulse. It would appear, however, that the utterances of Liberalism were hardly so inflammatory as has been assumed, and that indeed its ideology was more profoundly conservative than even the usual definition of the Whig mind would allow. Similarly, the political thought of Calvinism was such that in premises and implications it was an evident anticipation of what, by the early nineteenth century, emerged clearly as the more vital of American democratic traditions. So far as the Revolution is concerned, however, the thought and expression of "reasonable" Americans can hardly be dismissed as irrelevant or incidental. Indeed the likelihood entertained in this study is that it was the very competition among contending ideas, as expressed by variant voices, that made the Revolution not only possible but inevitable.

It would appear that the uprising of the 1770's was not so much the result of reasoned thought as an emotional outburst similar to a religious revival. At the time it was observed that "the minds of the people are wrought up into as high a degree of Enthusiasm by the word liberty, as could have been expected had Religion been the cause."[65] But an assessment of the quality of the spirit of 1775 is not to be construed as a diagnosis of the causes of the Revolution. Nor for that matter is it the purpose of this study to demonstrate how any event or activity was a consequence of the Awakening or of any idea espoused by either Calvinists or Liberals. What is here delineated is the sequence of ideas, and their myriad interrelationships, in the period between the Awakening and the Revolution.

Frequently the evidence cries out for some connecting of the political behavior of Americans with the ideas of one or another of its variant brands of religion. As early as 1751 it was observed that Americans were "Prone to act in *Civil*, as they stand Affected in *religious Matters*."[66] And in the 1770's Governor Martin of North Carolina reported to Lord Dartmouth that the political squabbles in that province could be understood only in light of the "distinctions and animosities" that had "immemorially prevailed" between "the people of the established Church and the Presbyterians." The "same spirit of division," Martin observed, "has entered into or been transferred to most other concernments."[67] But the governor did not explain the precise process of transference, and in the pages that follow there is likewise no pretence to any final analysis of the innermost anatomy of the American mind.

A few surmises are offered, however, if only because it is assumed that any coherent intellectual history must of necessity consider the intellectual dispositions and attitudes of the people to whom ideas are addressed. In the eighteenth century, at least, the intellectual conceived his role as not merely comprehending reality but bringing his knowledge to bear by affecting the thoughts of the populace. Thus to understand any one sermon it is necessary to analyze not only the author's ideas and his manner of expression, but his intentions, particularly with respect to influencing the conduct of his audience. Such analysis requires establishing the speaker's own attitude toward his audience, and this in turn demands an estimate of that on which any rhetorical strategy is ultimately founded: the writer's assessment of the dispositions of those he addresses. With each sermon one gains additional insight into how, and through what manner of appeal, particular groups were disposed to move or not to move. In reading hundreds of such sermons, many of them delivered nearly concurrently or focusing on the same issue or episode, one is driven to speculate as to what, at any given moment, was the state of that elusive quantity we call "the popular mind."

Of course the American mind cannot be treated as a monolith. At no point in the eighteenth century was it such, not even during the presumed unanimity of the early years of the Revolution. Indeed it is one of the major premises of this study that Americans, even when they espoused a common policy or engaged in a common enterprise, often did so from a variety of motives and with disparate intentions. It would thus be folly to declare with anything approaching assurance that any one idea was the most efficacious in any given situation. What can be assumed, however, is that the intellectual premises of any individual or group give form to an act—and indeed are very much a part of its nature. In this sense all Americans did not, in rebelling, perform the *same* act, for the acts of each individual or group partook of and were defined by the ideational framework out of which and within which action proceeded. And here once again one is thrown back— unless he holds ideas to be wholly irrelevant to the reality of history— to the basic fact of eighteenth-century American life: the conflicting ideologies which, in the period between the Awakening and the Revolution, were presented to the American people as alternative patterns of thought and behavior.

Any final assessment of the Revolutionary mind would obviously have to take into consideration many ideas that do not fall within the scope of this study. Enlightenment thought is traditionally and properly identified with the Revolution and the later eighteenth century generally. In excluding such thinkers as Thomas Jefferson from this account it is by no means suggested that the intellectual history of the period can be fully told in terms of the ideas of religious leaders. It is to be hoped only that the present study will stimulate fresh and further looks at the entire era, in order that the outlines of our history may be more clearly drawn and the various elements in the composition more accurately limned and balanced. My primary purpose has been to contribute to the portrait by giving the religious literature of the eighteenth century the careful analysis, in breadth as well as depth, it has deserved but not received.

In the course of so examining the thought and expression of post-Awakening Protestantism I have been led to certain evaluations of the two philosophies that contended for hegemony over the American mind. Though I have not been uncritical of Calvinism and have pointed indeed to what I consider its ultimate intellectual culpabilities, some readers may feel that I have been too tolerant, or less unsparing than in my assessment of Liberalism. It should be borne in mind, however, that the faith of Edwards has long carried a burden, heaped on it by historians, for sins of which it was in fact guiltless, and that in the case of Liberalism one is dealing with a philosophy almost uniformly praised for its "enlightened" principles and "liberating" tendencies. Indeed the spokesmen of Liberal religion are often celebrated personally for a heroic virtue and a generous spirit that stand in contrast to the character of the presumably benighted, unyielding, and dictatorial exponents of Calvinism.

Each of these assumptions I hold to be in error, but it has not been my purpose to judge the personal merits of either the Liberals or the Calvinists, or of any of their number. In general the sort of biographical data without which such personality judgments are impossible is omitted from the following account. The facts of an individual's life are introduced only when they seem helpful to a fuller appreciation of the nature and import of his ideas, and the thought of any one figure is contemplated, for that matter, only as it is part of a larger configuration of ideas. A few thinkers necessarily loom large in this account, but for the most part even the names of characters are introduced only as as assistance to the spectator in following the intellectual drama of the age.* In sum, my theme is not the personal virtue of any individual but the life of the mind in which all participated.

It is a concern for the intellectual life of America that has inspired the most substantial value judgments implicit in the pages that follow. I register disappointment with the Calvinists' profounder self-deceptions because they represent an ironic denial of Calvinism's first principle—the need for continuous and relentless self-assessment. I also regret the disposition of the evangelical mind toward action that is merely symbolic, or toward taking refuge, when confused or threatened, in outmoded formulas, or withdrawing into the securities of ecclesiasticism. Hereby were confounded expressed ideals as to the role and responsibility of intelligence in human affairs. A similar concern underlies my undisguised impatience with the Liberals' smug self-approbation and their resistance to the play of ideas either within the mind of the intellectual or among the populace. A comparative judgment of Calvinism and Liberalism undoubtedly reflects one's convictions as to the proper definitions of American democracy and the function of the intellectual in its processes, but my more immediate interest

* Brief biographies of figures frequently mentioned are provided in the Biographical Glossary.

has been with the failure of either to fulfill, in the eighteenth century, the whole of its intellectual promise. As the following pages will, however, attest, there can be no question that both contributed prodigiously to an exciting chapter in the history of the American mind.

PART ONE

AWAKENING

We have seldom any news on our side of the globe that can be entertaining to you or yours. All our affairs are *petit*. They have a miniature resemblance only, of the grand things of Europe.

—Benjamin Franklin, July 4, 1744

I

THE NATURE AND NECESSITY OF THE NEW BIRTH

THE "great and general awakening" that in 1740 spread from Georgia to New England and, as it seemed, through every element of the populace, was not wholly unexpected. For three quarters of a century the ministers of New England had periodically arraigned their people for "declension" from the virtues of their fathers and called for that "reformation" which alone could hold back the calamities an outraged God would surely visit on a backsliding "covenant" people. The earthquake of 1727 appeared to be just such a divine judgment, and for the moment there was considerable religious "concern." "But Alas!" cried a Boston preacher only a few years later,

> as tho' nothing but the most amazing Thunders and Lightnings, and the most terrible Earthquakes could awaken us, we are at this time, fallen into as dead a sleep as ever.

As the impressions of the earthquake year "dyed away," the formula of the jeremiad was slowly abandoned.[1] In the 1730's ministers began to call, not for a reformation merely, but for the "reviving" of the vital Christian spirit of an earlier day.

One such spiritual quickening had already been witnessed in 1721, in Windham, Connecticut, among a group of Quakers. More noteworthy were the series of "harvests" in Northampton, Massachusetts, in the congregation of Solomon Stoddard, the "pope" of western New

England. With Stoddard's death in 1729 his grandson, Jonathan Edwards, succeeded to the pulpit, and within five years Northampton enjoyed a spiritual refreshing more remarkable than any yet witnessed in America. This revival was both prelude to the Awakening and in a sense one of its causes. Edwards' account of the revival, soon published to the world as *A Narrative of Surprising Conversions,* alerted both Old England and New to God's working, not through the processes of the covenant, but by way of the "divine and supernatural light" imparted directly to the minds of men by the Holy Spirit.

Concurrently with the revival in Northampton the Scotch-Irish Presbyterians of New Jersey and Pennsylvania also enjoyed a spiritual "refreshing." There the revival had its antecedents in the efforts of Theodorus Frelinghuysen, who for a decade had been encouraging religious concern among the Dutch Reformed through the strategy of restricting admission to the sacraments. But the chief instrument of the Middle Colony revival was the party that formed around William Tennent, with three of his sons as leading figures. Shortly after arriving in America Tennent had founded the "Log College" for the education of ministers to serve the immigrants from Ulster who had been flooding into the area around Philadelphia. Though the Scotch-Irish had been in the New World less than a generation there were heard among them bewailings of a falling off from the first spirit. Encouraged by Frelinghuysen's example and advice, the Log College men proclaimed the need for a "revival" through the agency of the Holy Spirit.

Here they went beyond many of the older Presbyterians of the Middle Colonies who held to a somewhat more prosaic interpretation of orthodox Calvinism. The Scotch Presbyterians had already provoked a controversy within the church by proposing in 1729 that all ministerial candidates "subscribe" to the tenets of the Westminster Confession and Catechisms. In the "subscription controversy" they were opposed by another distinctive element within American Presbyterianism, the New Englanders of northern New Jersey and Long Island. This group, whose acknowledged leader was Jonathan Dickinson, displayed its background in New England "Independency" by resisting all efforts to impose such centralized and intellectually rigid control on the church. Dickinson had also spoken for the Puritan churches of America generally in arguing, as against an increasingly vocal Anglicanism, the validity of non-Episcopal ordination. In so doing, Dickinson aligned himself intellectually with the Log College men, for at the heart of the Episcopal controversy lay the spread of Arminian rationalism into areas once dominated by Puritan Calvinism.

The growth and appeal of the Church of England, dramatically witnessed earlier in the century when several young Yale tutors and graduates took Episcopal orders, was but one symptom of the attractiveness of a more "reasonable" Christianity. Nearly every young minister of the period was, it would seem, to some degree and in some way tempted, or bewildered at least, by the new intellectual currents. For instance, Jonathan Parsons was, like his mentor Edwards, in his early years more than ready to entertain the possibility that men could, and should, will their own salvation. One form in which Parsons' perplexity was expressed was that of a visit to Dean Berkeley, who was then residing in Rhode Island. Though Parsons quickly decided against Episcopal ordination, his torment was not so readily overcome. On the day of his installation at Lyme, Connecticut, he renounced the Saybrook Platform, which stipulated that a Connecticut minister should give evidence of his doctrinal orthodoxy. Over the next years Parsons and his congregation debated the "Half-Way Covenant," under the terms of which the children and later descendants of Puritan "saints" were accorded nearly the full privileges of church membership. In the 1730's the question was again raised whether any but those who could personally profess a "saving faith" were to be admitted to the sacraments.[2] In each of these issues was embodied the torment of a community puzzled over the possibility that an inherited orthodoxy did not appropriately define the way to salvation.

When in 1735 Edwards arraigned the "legal scheme" he did so without explicitly proclaiming his belief that many occupants of New England's Congregational pulpits were disposed to "loose" doctrine. The same was true of the Log College graduates, who throughout the revival of 1734-1735 declaimed in general terms against the prophets of an easier salvation:

> If so, then a smooth Scene opens, then these men have found out a new and easy Way to Heaven; but they must shew their Authority before we believe them, their great Names, blustering Figures, and bold saysoes will hardly gain our implicit Assent, or gull us out of our Senses, tho' they were as much renown'd for Piety and Learning as the old Pharisees their Predecessors.[3]

In the next year, however, Edwards was fighting to prevent a young minister suspected of Arminianism from being installed in the Springfield pulpit, and the Tennent party were beginning to turn their thunder against certain of the Presbyterian ministers of New Jersey and Pennsylvania.

The latter challenge reflected a struggle for power in the Synod of Philadelphia, which had refused to ordain the Log College graduates. The older Presbyterians, nearly all of whom had been born and educated in Scotland, insisted that a university degree was necessary for

admission to the ministry. The Tennent party began to license ministers without the synod's approval and to send them into "vacant" parishes. When rebuked, the Log College men insisted that formal training was less important than warm piety. The test of true faith lay not
in subscription to the propositions of orthodoxy but in the experience
of grace. And finally the Tennents assumed the offensive by charging
their tormenters with "deadness" and proclaiming that their preaching
of an "easy" Christianity revealed them to be no Calvinists at all.

When the Log College men also charged that certain "pharisee-
preachers" were too tolerant of the "sins" of the age, they disclosed
something of the social import of the assault on Arminianism. As
preached by the younger Presbyterians, Calvinism stood in judgment
on the increasingly acquisitive and indulgent spirit of the America of
the 1730's. In sermon after sermon men were rebuked for pursuing
sensual pleasure and profit, and the fulness of Christ was contrasted
with the emptiness of all the world could offer. In this the Tennent
group was joined by the New Englanders. The Harvard-trained Ebenezer Pemberton, pastor of a Presbyterian Church in New York City,
discoursed on the pointlessness of men's immoderate grasping after
wealth:

> And what can all this World afford us beyond a competent supply
> of our bodily wants, and a suitable provision for the comforts and
> conveniences of life? And these, if our desires be moderate, and we
> do not give the reins to an ungovern'd fancy, may be easily provided
> for. Every thing else is burdensom and unprofitable.[4]

Such a scale of values embodied something more than a mere restatement of the Puritan ideal of weanedness from the world. Implicit in it
were assumptions as to the American social malaise that, no less than
the evangelical counterattack on Arminianism, signified a departure
from the intellectual premises of the seventeenth century.

For generations the social analyses of the clergy had proceeded
within a framework in which all problems were definable as "vices"
needful of reforming. In New England, where the rubrics of social
commentary had been set forth by the Synod of 1679, the clergy had
long concerned themselves more with the sensual indulgences of their
people than with their economic behavior. Since the beginning of the
century the latter concern had emerged largely in complaints about an
"extravagance" which, according even to those who chided the gentry
for showing a poor example to their inferiors, was seen to abound
among the lower orders of society. For the same number of years the
generality of the clergy had also explained that God "requires and

expects, that every Man should *abide in his Calling*."[5] In sum, those ambitions and endeavors were frowned upon that seemed to disturb the tranquil social and economic order of the commonwealth.

In the late 1720's a handful of ministers began to assess their culture in terms not of manners that had to be reformed but of the need, as one put it, for New Englanders to make "a covenant with their eyes" so that the goods of this world would not be so appealing or distracting. The very clergy who in the 1730's began to call for a "reviving" of religion were also disposed to arraign the age, not for its vices but for its acquisitive spirit. Samuel Wigglesworth, son of the Puritan poet whose "God's Controversy with New England" had fixed the formula of the jeremiad, delivered before the Massachusetts legislature in 1733 a sermon that he entitled *An Essay for the Reviving of Religion*. New Englanders, he observed, were to all appearances decent, churchgoing folk, and far from being slaves to their senses, they were sober and industrious. In fact they were far too industrious, for the single source of New England's spiritual deadness was the "Exorbitant Reach after Riches" that had come to be "the reigning Temper in Persons of all Ranks in our Land."[6] According to Wigglesworth, the only solution to this situation was such an inner change of "heart" as could come only through a conversion by the Holy Spirit, and this in turn required of the ministers a return to the rigors of pure Calvinist doctrine.

Though Wigglesworth reproved New Englanders for their greed, he also assumed that many citizens of Massachusetts were inwardly dissatisfied with a life given over solely to the pursuit of wealth. This had long been the theme of Joseph Morgan, the patriarch of New England-born Presbyterianism. In his popular allegory of Puritan doctrine, *The History of the Kingdom of Basaruah,* Morgan had implicitly exposed the emotional sterility of what Americans had come over the course of a century to assume was their appointed errand—a competitive conquest of the wilderness. In his sermons too, Morgan dealt with the impossibility of finding happiness in what the world calls wealth. By defining "the true nature of riches" in terms of an inner composure that could not come from any outward circumstance, Morgan broke through the intellectual vise of the covenant theology.

That internal felicity could be achieved only through "unseen things" became in the 1730's the nearly incessant theme of the younger Presbyterians, and, of course, of such New England sermons as Edwards' *The Peace which Christ Gives His True Followers.* Like Edwards, the Log College men proclaimed a Calvinism that focused less on the divine sovereignty than on the soul's need to realize the supreme "excellency of Christ." In neither instance, however, was the evangelical scheme otherworldly or even churchly in the usual sense.

Gilbert Tennent was expressly disdainful of "the talking, praying parts of Religion," because, as he observed, many professing Christians made "a blazing appearance" in this regard for the simple reason that the duties of the first table of the Decalogue were "cheap, and touch not the Pocket."[7] What the young Calvinists were after, in their preaching of the majesty of God and the glory of Christ, was a thorough reconsideration of the Christian ethic as it had come to be understood and practiced in the America of the 1730's. And as Tennent's summons to acts of Christian charity attests, the selfish ethic was as troubling for the economic inequities it produced as for the spiritual iniquity it embodied.

Tennent was not deceived into seeing wickedness as a total monopoly of the rich. But he pointed in his sermons to the peculiar and enormous worldliness of "the *Grandees*." Men, he observed, "grow in Wickedness in Proportion to the Increase of their Wealth."[8] Edwards' sermons of the 1730's were also charged with a special animus against what seemed the worst of the era's sinful tempers—an ambition for honor, position, or wealth that would sustain man's desire to look down on other men. Precisely here, according to Edwards, appeared one of the more remarkable "excellencies" of Christ: the contrast between His character and the contrary disposition of men who came to occupy a "high station" on earth:

> If one worm be a little exalted above another, by having more dust, or a bigger dunghill, how much does he make of himself! What a distance does he keep from those that are below him![9]

Only one additional thought was needed to complete the circle of the evangelical scheme, and that was provided when, in the late 1730's, Tennent began to declaim against the manner in which "reasonable" preachers indulged the acquisitiveness or the lavish displays of their more favored parishioners.

The evangelical mind was responding to the emergence in colonial America of disparities of wealth, as well as ways of life, unknown to earlier, and presumably purer, generations. In the uneven prosperity of the early century a few merchants and larger landowners fattened, and meanwhile mechanics and smaller farmers were subjected to what was, in effect, a recurring cycle of indebtedness and inflation. At the same time the more prosperous colonials were seizing the opportunity to emulate what they took to be the culture of Augustan England. In Boston, as well as in tidewater Virginia, they had begun to affect a way of life which, if not quite so cavalier as Nathaniel Tucker was to imagine, stood in sharp and sorry contrast to the more Hogarthian recreations of their less successful brethren. Nor were such distinctions lacking in the smaller towns of the colonies. When in the late 1730's Edwards examined the society of Northampton, he discovered some citizens who through success in their farms or "merchandize" had "more plentiful accommodations" than their neighbors. They could "sit down at a full table" and even indulge themselves in what Edwards styled "fashionable living." There were also many who had a "much smaller part of the good things of this life," some of whom were obliged, Edwards observed, to wear coarse clothes, eat mean fare, and sometimes even be "pinched with hunger."[10]

A few of the latter indulged themselves in an irrational extravagance, Edwards allowed, but most were given, insofar as they sinned openly, to the commoner and more traditional sins of the flesh: "tippling" and "chambering." However, Edwards' analysis of his society went well beyond the standard rubrics of vices. In his diagnosis too he moved ahead of many of his contemporaries by discovering at the heart of New England's illness the commercial frenzy of the period. To this Edwards attributed men's "dishonesty" in their dealings with one another. Much the same complaint was being voiced by other ministers, as for instance Edward Holyoke, who in early 1741 painted a summary portrait of the eighteenth-century New England character. Through the dishonesty of many of her merchants, Holyoke observed, New England had been "made to stink in the Nostrils of the People of other Countries." But such conduct was not limited to the metropolis, for a similar spirit was manifest

among those who call themselves very good Christians, in all our Towns, in Dealing and Commerce one with another, even in smaller Things. If they abstain from Drunkenness, Theft and Fornication, and the like open and scandalous Crimes, nevertheless they look upon . . . their Extortion, their private Cheats, and their secret Covetousness, and defrauding both GOD and the poor of their Dues, to support their own Pride and Vanity; I say, they seem to look upon these things as little and trivial Things.[11]

Where Edwards went further was in tracing to "covetousness" the "envy" and the "backbitings" that were the bane of nearly every New England town, and also the land and currency disputes that divided many a community against itself. And most importantly, he saw the situation (as Holyoke surely did not) in terms of the "false scheme of religion" that gave men both an undue sense of their own importance and an errant definition of the way to wealth.

Edwards' sociology derived in part from his recognition that the fundamental economic fact of the early 1700's was the "changing of the course of trade and the supplying of the world with its treasures from America."[12] He saw the basic cultural phenomenon of the age, on the other hand, as the importation of not only the colonies' government, but their "books" and "learning," from England. Together the two impressed Edwards as comprising a highly unfavorable balance of trade—one that put Americans in something of a double jeopardy. First they were encouraged to a furious exploitation of the New World's resources, and at the same time they were in danger of having their society "assimilated" and "likened" to that of England. Since according to Edwards "wickedness of almost every kind" had "well nigh come to the utmost extremity" in Britain, the restlessly acquisitive Americans were threatened with an inundation of the Old World's sottish and selfish ways.[13] The source of England's corruption, Edwards concluded, was the Arminianism that had insinuated itself into Protestantism. As it infiltrated the colonies in the 1730's, the American people were confronted with the awesome possibility that God's favor would be finally and irrevocably withdrawn. Only through the preaching of the evangelical scheme, he decided, could the New World be purified and redeemed.

In 1739 Edwards delivered a series of sermons in which, over the course of thirty-nine weeks, he introduced his congregation to the knowledge that the redeeming work of the Holy Spirit concerned not individuals merely but society. He examined the course of Christian history from the beginning, and discovered among other things, that the times of most terrible darkness in the affairs of men invariably were followed by remarkable and surprising outpourings of the Spirit. The "revivals" of 1734-1735, he declared, were, despite the impermanency of their effects, compelling evidence that God was about to perform a great work of redemption, in which the sinful dispositions of men would be more thoroughly overcome. Indeed there were many reasons to believe that an extraordinary dispensation of grace was about to descend wherever the gospel was preached in its purity and its power.

II

When the anticipated "work of God" occurred in 1740 its apparent instrument, ironically enough, was one who had left the depravations of England to carry his message to the provinces. George Whitefield arrived in America in the autumn of 1739, and over the next months the path of the Awakening seemed to follow his progress through the colonies. Yet Whitefield can hardly be said to have "caused" the revival. The American mind was profoundly prepared for the day of his coming, and he served only as the catalyst of a spiritual and social ferment that had been brewing for more than a decade. Whitefield had visited America briefly once before, but this time he was preceded by his reputation as an instrument of the "revival" in England and as a spokesman for evangelical religion within and against an Arminian and decadent Church of England. He served as an incarnate symbol of what, in the colonies, had for some time been recognized as the problems and the issues of the age. His dramatic impact testified to nothing so much as the need of the American people to find salvation from somewhere outside the experiences and circumstances by which they felt confined.

Before Whitefield appeared, many of his sermons—among them his celebrated discourse on *The Nature and the Necessity of Our New Birth*—had been reprinted in America. The young evangelist, who had preached to thousands in the fields of England and Wales, was also reputed to be one of the most outstanding orators "since the days of the apostles." His reputation was amply substantiated during the first weeks in America. In the late months of 1739 he preached to crowds of as many as 6000 in the Philadelphia area. Reports of his ever larger and increasingly enthusiastic audiences led Whitefield to be expected, as Benjamin Colman put it on December 3, "with much Desire" elsewhere in the colonies.[14] After a brief stay in the Middle Colonies, where he saluted the Log College men as "the burning and shining lights of this part of America," the itinerant moved southward. In Georgia, the site of the orphan asylum, promotion of which was the ostensible purpose of Whitefield's visit to the colonies, his preaching met with equal acclaim and success.

Just as quickly, however, Whitefield became the controversial figure he was to remain throughout the course of the Awakening. Whitefield's preaching in Georgia, and his cooperation there with "dissenting" ministers, provoked the wrath of Alexander Garden, the Bishop of London's Commissary in Charleston. (Very few of the Anglican clergy anywhere in the colonies welcomed the itinerant; nearly a lone exception was Commissary James Blair, administrative head of the Church in Virginia.) By the time Whitefield returned to Philadelphia, strictures on his conduct and preaching were being voiced, and printed, by elements of Presbyterianism.[15] In New England too, where Whitefield moved later in 1740, his visits met with mingled rejoicing and resistance.

> He is the wonder of the Age, and no one Man More employs the Pens, and fills up the Conversation of People, than he does at this Day: None more admir'd and applauded by some contemn'd and reproach'd by others. . .[16]

In the later months of the Awakening, when in fact it was generally felt that the revival impulse was spent, Jonathan Edwards referred to Whitefield as "a Person, concerning whom the Country is so much divided in their Sentiments, with Spirits so deeply, and contrarily engaged."[17] And when in 1745 Whitefield announced his intention to make another tour of the colonies, it was acknowledged that the "Parties" into which the American churches had divided were most clearly defined by the decision to welcome or prevent his second coming.[18]

For five or more years Whitefield was a center of attention and concern. Yet though he was personally applauded and attacked, his role, in the context of the Awakening, was very much a symbolic one. As Samuel Blair observed in replying to one of the more bitter Presbyterian critiques of Whitefield's preaching and behavior, the assaults on Whitefield were designed ultimately to repress the revival impulse.[19] Celebration of Whitefield was likewise an expression of faith in the progress of the Awakening and of evangelical religion. In his person and career were focused the underlying issues of the "religious Debates" spawned by the revival, and these in turn, and not "the grand Itinerant" merely, were the "common Topick of Conversation" and contention.[20] Tennent and James Davenport, also hailed and reviled, similarly served to embody the issues of the Awakening. But George Whitefield was the most evocative symbol of the divisions, intellectual and social, that the explosion of the Awakening brought to America.

One episode that immediately captured the American imagination was Whitefield's confrontation with Commissary Garden. Whitefield stormed into Charleston, where he called on Garden and upbraided him for failing to preach against the "sinful diversions" of the deep-South metropolis. Garden's response—that balls and assemblies were "innocent" amusements—was less revealing than his public dismissal of Whitefield with the announcement that he had simply never entertained the thought of criticizing the behavior of gentlemen and ladies "of the first *Figure* and *Character* in the Place." When Garden went on to observe that a far greater "Danger to *Religion*" and to the "*Peace* and *Happiness* of Society" was Whitefield's "*Mobb-Preachings*" and the assemblies of the rabble who flocked to hear him, one of the battle lines of the Awakening was squarely and clearly drawn.[21]

The ecclesiastical issues of the Awakening—"itinerancy" and religious liberty—were also raised in Charleston. Fuming at Whitefield's impertinence, Garden summoned the evangelist before a church court and forbade him to preach in the Carolina area. Since Whitefield denied Garden's jurisdiction, the ecclesiastical issue was not resolved. In any case the quarrel was, as all the participants understood, doctrinal. Whitefield had published a pamphlet with the engaging title of *A Letter wherein he Vindicates his Asserting that Archbishop Tillotson knew no more of Christianity than Mahomet.* Here Whitefield charged nearly the entire Church of England with a heretical departure from the "Calvinism" on which he contended Anglicanism had been founded. Garden replied to the tract, and to Whitefield's sermons, with a defense of Episcopal doctrine that was one of the most explicit avowals of Arminianism yet to be published in the colonies. In so doing, however, Garden disclosed that neither for him nor for Whitefield was the reigning issue that of God's sovereignty or the inefficacy of man's will. Garden's subject was the curious, and to him reprehensible, doctrine of "regeneration" that had come, through the instrumentality of Whitefield's preaching, to stand at the center of the philosophy of the revival:

> the Belief and Expectation of a certain happy *Moment,* when, by the *sole* and *specifick* Work of the *Holy Spirit,* you shall at once (as 'twere by Magic Charm) be matamorphosed. . .[22]

The issue, in sum, was that which represented Whitefield's primary contribution to the thought and vocabulary of American evangelicalism: the "New Birth."

Unquestionably Whitefield's revival sermons consisted largely of rehearsals of traditional Calvinist doctrine. All who during the Awakening remarked on Whitefield's discourses stressed his attention to such dogmas as human depravity and divine potency.[23] To be sure, Whitefield's critics were trying to convict him of inconsistency for having cooperated with the "Arminian" Wesleys, but he removed this source of guilt by association by publishing (from Georgia) his strictures against Wesley's abandonment of the cherished Calvinist doctrine of unconditional election. Moreover, Whitefield proudly insisted, in response to cavilers, that "the constant Tenour of my preaching in *America,* has been *Calvinistical.*"[24] Subsequently his critics decided that Whitefield's visit, and the "favourable Opinion" of his preaching held by the populace, had been exploited by ministers fearful for their influence and that of "the Calvinistic Principles and Doctrines of Grace." Whitefield's popular preaching, declared spokesmen for reasonableness, had been converted into an engine of counterattack on more enlightened currents of religious thought.[25]

Whitefield did not, however, give each of the five points of Calvinism equal time in his sermons. His focus and emphasis were on the irresistibility of grace, and this in turn pointed to the Pauline doctrine of justification—which itself, in Whitefield's preaching, was nearly synonymous with his doctrine of regeneration. The "Sum of the Matter," so far as Whitefield was concerned, was that none could hope to enter the Kingdom of Heaven unless he experienced the New Birth.[26] In such an emphasis Whitefield was by no means alone among the revivalists in America. One of his Charleston admirers allowed that for many years he too had insisted that without the New Birth no man, whatever his "boasted *Morality*" or however "splendid or rhetoricated upon" his seeming virtues, could hope to be saved.[27] Similarly, Jonathan Dickinson opened one of his revival sermons with the flat declaration that it was impossible for anyone to be justified who had "not experienced so great a Change of Heart, as may be aptly called a *new Birth.*"[28] Edwards and Tennent had of course preached a similar doctrine through the 1730's, but what Whitefield provided was both a slogan and an axis around which the evangelical scheme more freely revolved.

What was accomplished in the Awakening was the translation of a single precept into the quintessence of doctrine, and indeed, into an existential fact that ultimately validated the whole of evangelical doctrine. In an early report of the revival it was observed (as had for some time been suspected) that men were not converted where "dead and *Arminian* time-servers" held forth in the pulpit. Soon it was concluded that the doctrines of Calvinism and the evangelical notion of the necessity of a vital regenerative experience were inherently and inescapably related. They are "now happily combining to illustrate & confirm each other," a group of Boston ministers declared, "in so glaring and strong a Manner."[29] Furthermore, the relationship was understood less in terms of the internal logic of Calvinist thought, or the common scriptural source of doctrine and the describable characteristics of the New Birth, than of the "efficacy" of Calvinist dogma in inducing the experience. Whitefield himself defended unconditional election, as against Wesley, on the basis of the demonstrable effectiveness of the doctrine in producing conversion. The Awakening inaugurated an era in which an evangelical spokesman could proclaim, without once blinking, that St. Paul had "argued the divinity of his *doctrines* from the success and power of them."[30] The ultimate confirmation of Calvinism was the fact that the spirit had in 1740 entered the hearts of the American people.

Similarly, the point of contention with the opponents of evangelical religion was not whether God's dispensations were unconditional but that of the validity and value of man's experience of grace. In the early stages of the Awakening the revival was greeted by its partisans as a divine shower seemingly beyond human comprehension.[31] "Hence much of the effort in the first delirious months went into formulating the signs or symptoms of authentic conversion, this being still conceived as a seizure from above."[32] But almost from the beginning the revivalists were accused of exciting by artificial means the experiences they hailed as a supernatural work. Critics argued that "the *religious*

Stir" was evidence only of the ease with which demagogues and "confusion of Thought" can induce a flight from sanity.[33] Confronted by such a challenge, the pro-revivalists were compelled to expound the conversion experience in terms of their understanding of the "faculties and potentialities" of the human constitution. The "great divide that we call the Awakening forced both American parties, whether proponents or opponents, to shift the focus of analysis to the nature of man."[34] With the shift, it became easier to discover what was involved, in and for the American mind, in an experience that the revivalists encouraged and their opponents just as strenuously condemned as an abusing of human nature.

Before exploring the psychology of the revival it is probably first necessary to note that in neither the Awakening itself nor in the thought of Calvinism was the emphasis on convulsive fears of the terrible wrath of God. Indeed, in one of the first attempts to describe the revival experience, Jonathan Dickinson's sermon of May 1740, *The Witness of the Spirit*, it was observed that probably the greater number of the subjects of the revival were "reborn" without any previous terror whatever.[35] In granting validity to such a path to salvation Dickinson signaled eighteenth-century Calvinism's break with Puritanism and its emphases on "preparation" and a "true sight of sin." The doctrine of "convictions," which the leader of anti-revival Presbyterianism, John Thomson, took to be the issue in the first months of the revival, did continue to occupy a place in Calvinist thought and preaching. Yet the critics of the Awakening soon acknowledged that evangelical religion was distinguished less by its terror than by the enthusiastic delight of the moment of conversion. "Conviction" was for the revivalists merely a possible antecedent of conversion, and not a necessary one. It represented the travail pains that some men, but not all, experienced in coming to the joyful release of spiritual rebirth.

Thus to identify either the Awakening or Calvinism exclusively with such a sermon as Edwards' *Sinners in the Hands of an Angry God* is to distort the character of the entire evangelical impulse. Even in "The Future Punishment of the Wicked Unavoidable and Intolerable," which Edwards considered the most effective of his "terror" sermons, Edwards placed "hell-fire" in its fuller context: "The nature of man desires happiness; it is the nature of the soul to crave and thirst after well-being; and if it be under misery, it eagerly pants after relief."[36] Men were placed in fear of hell only that they might be rendered capable of the joy of heaven, and of this the New Birth was an earthly prelibation. Thus Edwards explained, in the first assessment of the Awakening, the ultimate purpose of the "frightening" sermons of the revivalists: "the law is to be preached only to make way for the gospel, and in order that it may be preached more effectually."[37] Nor was the typical Calvinist sermon one designed to induce a sense of terror, perhaps because, as was noted early in the Awakening, men often came to "conviction" by themselves—or under a ministry that preached neither hell-fire nor the inscrutable power of God. (As one subject of the revival observed, "I am sure they, who have tasted the Wrath of God, have no need for Hell to be represented with burning Flames.")[38] Such "convicted persons" thereupon left their ministers in the hope of enjoying the experience of grace under the ministrations of such as preached an evangelical gospel.[39] Though the Calvinist interpretation of "conviction" was, as will be noted, by no means irrelevant to the significance of the Awakening, what distinguished evangelical religion was less the manner in which men were first awakened out of their old deadness than that to which they were or hoped to be newly born.

In the first exhilaration of the Awakening the "necessity" of the New Birth was undoubtedly better appreciated than its precise "nature" was understood.[40] Had it been left to George Whitefield to explore and expound the experience, the New Birth might in fact have forever remained an ineffable mystery. "How this glorious Change is wrought in the Soul," Whitefield confessed, "cannot easily be explained."[41] Moreover, Whitefield was far from precise in his descriptions of the experience of grace; in his sermons the New Birth was only something that came instantaneously as a "feeling." In the early months of the Awakening Whitefield was often echoed by other revivalists the sum and substance of whose message was that saving faith was "felt." This language gave rise to the popular expectation (or so at least critics of the revival complained) that the Holy Spirit would be known as a physical presence, as tangible as bowel pains or a tumor.

One group of scoffers allowed (presumably in allusion to the free love it was said prevailed in revival sessions) that "it must be owned that some of the crying roaring Women among us have brought forth something that may be both seen and felt."[42] But such were no more the legitimate offspring of the revival spirit than the various other misbegotten caricatures that populated hostile accounts of the Awakening. In these descriptions, "the work of the HOLY SPIRIT" was, so far as the actual witnesses and subjects of the revival were concerned, "grievously misrepresented and defamed."[43] Where critics erred was not so much in their exaggeration and distortion of the behavior of the awakened as in failing to come to terms with the inward, or spiritual, qualities of the New Birth. Even Whitefield allowed that the experience of conversion came as a "spiritual, as well as a corporeal feeling."[44] The other spokesmen of the revival came to focus even more intently and exclusively on the spiritual character of the New Birth, as distinguished and divorced from conduct that at most represented only its attendants and attributes. According to their accounts, the Spirit operated and was known by its impact on the minds and hearts of men.

The psychology of the revival was first probed by Jonathan Dickinson in his sermon on *The Witness of the Spirit*. But here Dickinson seemed to be wresting the language of Scripture in order to make its brief descriptions of conversion experiences conform to what he considered the observable phenomena of the Awakening. Something of the same was true of the sermon Edwards delivered in New Haven in September 1741, *The Distinguishing Marks of a Work of the Spirit of God*. More empirical accounts were provided in Dickinson's frequently reprinted dialogue, *A Display of God's Special Grace*, and in Edwards' *Thoughts on the Revival*. The summary study of the revival psychology was, however, Edwards' *Treatise Concerning Religious Affections*, which, first delivered as a series of sermons in the late months of the Awakening, was reworked for publication in 1746. It is to this volume, "the most profound exploration of the religious psychology in all American literature," that one must turn for the most meaningful descriptive analyses of the revival experience.[45]

Of course it is necessary to go behind and beyond the *Religious Affections* for confirmatory evidence, but Edwards' study is surely central to any appreciation of the nature and significance of the New Birth. The centrality of Edwards' volume derives in part from the confessed failure of other Calvinist writers to characterize the experience adequately. For many it was "better felt than expressed," and its sublime "joys" were so "unspeakable" that "no words were sufficient to describe it."[46] Edwards found the words, at least to the point that others agreed that his was the most accurate and complete portrait. To be sure, the Edwardean analysis of regeneration reflected his acquaintance with and reformulations of Lockean psychology and Newtonian physics. But these concepts merely provided (except as they were used more extensively in Edwards' delineations of what regeneration *ought* to be) the vocabulary with which he described what was not so much a philosophic construct as a recognized "experimental" phenomenon. In theory grace was such that through reception of a "new simple idea" man's perceptions were reorganized and a new, transcendent, and harmonious order of being made manifest. In Edwards' telling, however, regeneration was describable, simply and more vividly, as an emotional apprehension of beauty: a *"sense of the heart"* in kind "exceeding different" from any natural sensation, attended by a felt perception of beauty (or "excellence") "infinitely diverse from all other beauty." Being reborn consisted, in sum, in a new and unwonted inner harmony achieved through the feeling discovery of a "divine excellency" wholly different from anything perceivable by the eye of mere reason.[47]

That the experience of grace consisted in a perception and sensation of beauty was attested by other evangelical accounts. Such a view filled the pages of David Brainerd's *Diary,* the most publicized spiritual pilgrimage of the age. Edwards used Brainerd's recorded experience as both substantiation and illustration of his analysis of regeneration. The facts of the revival experience were the ultimate confirmation of that theory, and not Locke and Newton. A few of Edwards' evangelical contemporaries seem also to have been familiar with the new thought, and to have reworked it, as he did, into concepts and definitions of "subjective excellency" and "objective excellence." But the philosophic framework was not absolutely essential to the central premise of eighteenth-century Calvinism: that the phenomena of regeneration were characterizable as the "idea which the saint has of the loveliness of God" and the "delight he has in that view." Of course in later years the Calvinist description of the regenerate man as perceiving "such loveliness as ravisheth his heart" invariably carried much of the meaning imparted to the psychology of conversion by Edwards.[48] For the *Religious Affections,* and the other works in which Edwards popularized its doctrines, provided two and more generations with the axioms and postulates for the "experimental religion" that was the distinctively American pietism.

III

For many Americans too young to have participated in the Great Awakening, the *Affections* and other writings of the 1740's served as manuals in which were delineated what had been "experimentally known" in the years of the revival. For a generation after the Awakening the evangelical impulse was largely defined by its belief in, and efforts to induce, such vital conversion experiences. Outraged Arminians complained that an espousal of "calvinistick Principles" was the only way for a minister to "fix" himself in "the good Graces of the Populace."[49] The Genevan reformer, however, might well have objected to the use of his name by eighteenth-century American evangelicals, for, as bears repeating, their religious scheme was distinguished above all by its insistence on the necessity and the desirability of the New Birth. There is "much vain philosophy in our land," grumbled one Connecticut "Calvinist" when the attempt was made to provide his faith with a more complex creed and metaphysic, "which some, through *Mistake,* call Divinity." "You may let all this alone," he advised his congregation, "and then it will never harm you."[50] To comprehend the full thrust of eighteenth-century Calvinism it is undoubtedly necessary to spurn his recommendation, but what cannot be ignored is the fact it was offered. For despite the variety of strategies, intellectual and otherwise, devised by American evangelicals, the inspiration and the dynamic of the impulse was the effort to satisfy a hunger for inner felicity.

As experience, expectation, or doctrine the New Birth represented the evangelical version of the pursuit of happiness. In 1760, shortly before Hermon Husband began the public career that included leadership of the North Carolina Regulators and closed with agitation during the Whiskey Rebellion, he published a tract entitled *Some Remarks on Religion*. Here Husband chronicled his spiritual travails during the 1740's, when he and other Americans "left all their livings" to wander about the countryside in the hope of hearing "the preacher, newly come from England." On the basis of his experience, Husband became and remained "fully convinced" that the New Birth was the best and surest "Way to Happiness."[51] His persuasion is not especially surprising, considering some of the conditions of eighteenth-century American life. To Edwards, who allowed it strange that men should "ever be brought to such exceeding happiness as that of heaven seems to be," it was evident that few men achieved any "great degree of happiness" in pre-revival America. The New Birth represented an existential liberation from a world where, as Edwards saw it, "everything awakens painful apprehension."[52] In the experience of grace was transcended, not the human condition merely, but the circumstances in which men felt themselves imprisoned.

Though the debate between the exponents of evangelical religion and a more reasonable faith had as its subject the matter of human salvation, its more urgent theme was how and where happiness was to be found in the American setting. The heaven of evangelical sermons was only an exaltation of the perceptions and sensations vouchsafed on earth in the "divine illumination" of inward regeneration. The "heavenly, eternal state" to which the Calvinist aspired, and in which he was to achieve "boundless felicity," was not entered through "gates of pearl." It was not even to be considered "under the notion of a place," the Calvinist clergy insisted, but to be construed, as sermon after sermon affirmed, as a "state of mind" consisting in a "sweet" and "blisful" inner "harmony." There were not "two Kinds of Happiness in God's Universe," the evangelical clergy proclaimed. The "same kind of happiness" as "saints are possessed of in heaven" could be enjoyed in this world by the subjects of the New Birth.[53]

In the controversies that issued from the Awakening, the debate between Calvinists and Liberals was often phrased in terms of human virtue. Yet it had already been made clear in the late 1730's, when the

Log College men repudiated the eudaemonism of the older Presbyterians, that any viable definition of holiness depended finally on an assessment of the nature and sources of human happiness.[54] The subsequent course of religious thought was such that both parties came to acknowledge the inseparability of virtue and felicity: "Every creature in the universe, so far as he is holy, is happy; and as far as he is unholy, he is miserable."[55] To be sure, both were able to distinguish in theory between man's happiness and his holiness, but they did so only in terms of the "faculties" of the human mind of which each was conceived to be a function.[56] The Calvinist saw happiness in terms of the "understanding," the soul's "perceiving faculty," and virtue as a function of the will, the faculty through which the soul (or "heart") expressed itself in action. The two were simply modes of what, in Calvinist thought, was a single integrated personality. Where Liberals demurred, even in their discussions of virtue, was in their conception of the capacities and needs of man's psychic constitution. It was on this matter that the post-revival divergence between evangelical and rational religion was most sharply revealed.

The criticisms of the revival rested at bottom on an objection to the evangelical evaluation of the place of the emotions in man's psychology. Once the opponents of the Awakening became fully articulate, their most repeated complaint against the preachments of the revivalists was this:

> The great *Doctrine* of *Conversion* or *Regeneration* is represented in such a Manner, consisting in great Terrours and Convulsions, succeeded by sudden and rapturous Joys, which the Gospel knows nothing of; as if to bring a Man to the most rational Acts (for such are the Acts of the Soul in Conversion) the Way was to render him capable of no rational Acts at all.[57]

Though objections to the revival psychology were often phrased in the language of the older Puritan and scholastic view of human nature, in which the "passions" were viewed as hindrances to or interferences with the "reason," the anti-revivalists, in their insistence on the "rationality" of conversion, were, no less than the preachers of Calvinism, entering on a new era in religious philosophy. For Chauncy too, Locke's *Essay on Human Understanding* was a source of psychological insight, but Chauncy used it, not as Edwards did, but as Locke had intended his epistemology to be used: to counter religious "enthusiasm." Many critics of the revival declared that enthusiasm was no substitute for, indeed it was an enemy to, that "faculty" through which all knowledge must come: "Man's reasoning and perceptive Power, by which he compares Things to form his Judgment."[58] Such an argument in effect overthrew the Puritans' twofold definition of reason, for it was now being conceived not so much as a power or faculty instrumental in judging what is true but as the whole process by which man comes to know the truth. In this respect Garden, Chauncy, and indeed almost all Old Lights and Old Side Presbyterians were announcing the eighteenth-century principle—that man is, or ought to be, pre-eminently a rational creature.

In the indictment of the revival doctrines as "contrary to reason" there was also more than a hint of the notion that the universe itself was a rational order, in which were embodied truths to which all others must be able to conform. For many critics of the revival, to be sure, the saving truths were those disclosed in Scripture. "The Holy Spirit converts and sanctifies men," explained a Connecticut Old Light in 1742, "and improves them in holiness, by opening their Understanding, and leading them to a just and *rational* View and Belief in the great Truths contained in the Scriptures."[59] In the course of the Awakening, however, the anti-revivalists came to the ever bolder assurance that the most important truths were discoverable in the "nature of things." In either case, when they spoke of "saving knowledge" they defined it propositionally, as declarative truths to which reasoned judgment gave assent. This was not the same order of truth that was imparted to the minds of men by the divine and supernatural light of Calvinism. For even Scripture truth, according to the spokesmen of the revival, had to be known "not merely in a doctrinal Way, but by an Experimental Acquaintance."[60] So known, truth for Calvinists partook of that "excellence" which it was not reason's office to perceive and which indeed the spiritually unenlightened mind could not possibly apprehend.

The emotional apprehension of beauty in which the New Birth consisted was a demurral from both the stated precepts of orthodoxy and the dictates of reason. Neither, it seems, were adequate to the circumstances of American life, for regeneration, as experienced and defined by Calvinists, represented a shattering of the continuum of human existence. The opponents of the revival, on the other hand, argued that all necessary knowledge, including that which was saving, could and must come through a process of steady and uninterrupted accumulation. Man was brought to holiness and happiness, not in the twinkling of an eye, but through "Reasoning and Study, close Care and Application, use of Helps and Time."[61] Enlightenment was not in fact, even for the most reasonable anti-revivalists, a perfectly continuous process; for they conceived man's psychology as something of a series of frequently shifted gears. Still, a critic of evangelical doctrine did insist that "we grow up to the Christian life, by insensible gradations."[62] In so doing he was arguing that human nature, in its unaided constitution, was quite capable of dealing with prevailing external circumstance. He was restricting the Christian pilgrimage to a methodical adjustment to the given norms of existence, and it was precisely this that the evangelical scheme could not and would not abide. The New Birth was an expression of displeasure with the order of reality that presented itself to the eye of unaided reason, and of a desire to make a happier world in a manner that reason would not allow.

In the decades following the Awakening both parties refined their definitions of the nature of happiness and the proper means of pursuing it. Over these years the delineations of the Liberal clergy betrayed something of an eclectic imprecision, born possibly, as was that of Benjamin Franklin, of alternating moods. Franklin tended in the middle period of his life to identify the pursuit of happiness exclusively with the way to wealth. Only in the late 1750's did he begin to conceive of happiness as a state of mind and not in terms of the material stuff of which it was made. Liberal religion was often similarly obscure as to the nature of happiness, but for the most part it accepted one of the reigning psychological postulates of the eighteenth century: that "true happiness" results from "the suitableness of the object enjoyed, to the faculty enjoying."[63] Nonetheless, the Liberal ministry in effect defined the pursuit of happiness in terms of a set of conditions. The starting point of Liberal doctrine was the objective "realities" of the "present state" of human existence—so many "confinements and limitations," Samuel Johnson called them in his *Elementa Philosophica*.[64] For the Calvinist, on the other hand, it seemed the "grossest absurdity" to define or pursue happiness without beginning with the "capacities, desires, and cravings" of the human personality.[65] The Liberal was not oblivious to man's inner nature, though here again he was more aware of limitations than needs, but happiness, as he defined it, came through accommodation to the environment in which man had been placed.

The substance of the program offered by Liberal religion was embodied in this formula: happiness was to be found through development of one's God-given faculties in accordance with a circumstance that was likewise divinely ordained. Though Liberalism tended to replace the formulas of Locke with the formulations of his Scotch "improvers," they continued to consider the understanding as the chief of these faculties. For them "the original of knowledge" was in the ideas received by the understanding and "the comparing, compounding and disposing of them, together with the perception of those operations."[66] Out of their common-sense version of sensational psychology, Liberals derived a scheme of salvation in which "time, exercise, observation, instruction" and the improvement of one's original "capacities" were the means of grace.[67]

Since in theory knowledge was available even "to the meanest capacity" in the nature and constitution of things, Liberal religion seemed to open to all men the way to holy felicity.[68] Indeed it was just such a doctrine that Chauncy developed and published—after two decades of dissimulation and furtive circulation of his manuscript. As Chauncy expounded his theory of universal salvation, "all intelligent moral beings" were shown "going on, while they suitably employ and improve their original faculties, from one degree of attainment to another; and, hereupon, from one degree of happiness to another, without end."[69] For all its seeming liberalism, however, Chauncy's universalism was perhaps more illiberal than the Calvinist creed which he despised. Chauncy's heaven—a sort of glorified Harvard graduate school—appealed to Chauncy because he fully expected to serve as its dean, to his colleagues because they had already received their doctorates on earth, and to other Liberals because such a heaven would be an extension—not a reorganization—of the best of all possible worlds: the Boston of the mid-eighteenth century.

Liberals so qualified their rationalism as in fact to provide a new definition of the elect. Casting off the trammels of Calvinism meant for them a rejection of the revivalists' presumptuous claim that salvation might come to anyone regardless of his intellectual abilities. Though Mayhew admitted that every man had "the power of judging in *some degree*" the wisdom that is of God, he implied rather strongly that some men were far more likely to be cleansed of sin:

> It is not intended in this assertion, that all men have *equal abilities* for judging what is true and right . . . Those of the lower class can get but a little ways in their inquiries into the natural and moral constitution of the world.

If none of the Liberals had the audacity to guarantee entrance into the fold, they were seldom unwilling to declare who would finally appear among the goats. In passing such a judgment Mayhew preferred another barnyard metaphor, one which he often found useful in describing "the most dull and stupid of the human species"—a category which at times seemed to include nearly everyone in creation less intelligent than Jonathan Mayhew. "He that was born like the *wild asses-colt*," was Mayhew's reassuring observation, "must needs continue to be so; or, at best come to maturity, and grow up into an ass himself."[70] When Arminianism first appeared on the American scene it perhaps at least theoretically offered happiness to more than the wise

and discerning few. Certainly as the creed evolved, however, rationalism was clearly disposed to abandon to an unhappy existence whoever
suffered from "ignorance, or weakness of the understanding" or to
enforce the presumed welfare of the incompetent multitude through
the compulsion and restraints of the law.[71]

The wisdom effective in gaining and securing earthly happiness
would also earn the Liberal student entrance into a heaven which was,
to William Smith, for instance, practically a grander Philadelphia in
the sky. He who was happy would in time be holy too, either because,
as the Liberal ministry argued, it was by knowledge that man conformed his will to the reasonable dictates of the divine lawgiver, or, as
Franklin summarized his learning in the *Autobiography,* because the
nature of things was such that it was "every one's interest to be virtuous
who wish'd to be happy." Both aspects of the rational creed offended
Calvinist sensibilities: its Arminianism, and its suggestion, which
Edwards flayed, that virtue was not *bonum formosum* but *bonum utile.*
But perhaps what chiefly offended Calvinists was the Liberals' sense of
timing. Despite considerable evasion and obfuscation, it was quite
clear that the Liberal formula tolerated and even encouraged men to
pursue earthly happiness in the easy knowledge that salvation might
be reached for at some later time.

The greater energy of Liberal theoreticians of happiness was spent
in ridiculing those who reversed the Liberal order of worship by insisting that "man must be first born anew, and from above, before he
can be holy here, or happy hereafter."[72] Setting themselves to exposing
the philosophic "fallacies" of Calvinism, they derided as flagrantly
absurd, and presumably anti-intellectual, the notion that happiness
could and must come from a knowledge "in kind and species, so pure,
sublime and glorious" that not even the most "penetrating genius"
with all the "comprehension of human literature" could acquire it
without the intervention and assistance of the Holy Spirit. Calvinists
were neither as "irrational" or as "unphilosophic" as their critics
claimed, but they were perhaps "sick-brained" by Liberal standards in
holding that God did "not stand in need of great abilities or acquired
knowledge" in order to grant salvation.[73] When Liberals complained
that the Calvinist God behaved in a manner "which would be unbecoming and even shocking to the Mind, in the Character of a wise
and good Man," they always came around to remarking on the absurdities of a theory which held that the "least beam" of light of God's
glory and beauty was "worth more than all the human knowledge that
is taught in all the most famous colleges and universities of the
world."[74]

The Calvinist ministry was not in fact anti-intellectual. They contended only that no amount of human wisdom—not even the "knowledge," as Nathaniel Whitaker explained, "of a Solomon, a Newton, or an Edwards"—could by itself make men either holy or happy.[75] Nor were they hostile to "humane learning." They objected not to education as such, but to the manner in which it was used, and flaunted, by the Augustan heralds of the Liberal faith. Education, particularly that of the common schools, was one plank in the Calvinist platform for promoting the happiness of the American people. Yet even Samuel Davies, who succeeded Edwards as president of the College of New Jersey, never wavered from his assured belief that "the divine excellency" offered more felicity than all the "present pleasure" men might "receive from present things"—among which he listed not only "riches, honors, sensual gratifications," but "learning, and intellectual improvements."[76]

Such a faith was more easily sustained in Davies' Virginia, for there, if not necessarily at Princeton, the Liberal program for achieving happiness seemed quite unreasonable. It appeared less reasonable still in Litchfield County, Connecticut, where Joseph Bellamy's people wondered if the earth could actually sustain the saintly host he expected to inhabit it in the millennial era, considering the difficulties a comparatively sparse agricultural population had in providing themselves with "food and raiment"—and in supporting, by their taxes and otherwise, the armies, lawyers, colleges and ecclesiastical establishments that reasonable men deemed necessary to human felicity.[77] For any number of reasons the Arminian paradise of whitened sail, stately mansions and collegiate commencements seemed to most Americans not within reach this side of the grave.

In the decades after the Awakening the appeal of evangelical religion remained most enduring in those parts of the colonies that suffered economic difficulty: the great valley of Pennsylvania and Virginia, the Northern Neck and the Carolina highlands, south Jersey, inland Connecticut and Rhode Island, southeast and central Massachusetts, the Berkshire hills, and the villages of Essex and Middlesex counties. In these areas Calvinist expatiation on the "universal emptiness" of the "enjoyments and pleasures of this world" and insistence that man's vocation was to lay up treasures safe from moth and rust made sufficient sense that it was still possible, in the midst of the Revolutionary War for Calvinists to argue convincingly that those who sought "satisfaction and happiness in the things of the world" were engaged in "a vain pursuit!"[78] There also it was possible to believe in the imminence of another Awakening as great as the first. "Who shall limmit our God," asked Samuel Buell during the Long Island revival of 1764, "saying such a Degree of the Earnest of heavenly Happiness shall be given upon Earth, and no more?"[79] When at last the supremacy of "things unseen" waned even in these regions, it was not because the evangelical faith had been undermined by a barrage of enlightened criticism, nor that events made it possible for men to aspire to the goodly estate here or hereafter that rational religion offered. It was rather that an opportunity was provided, in part by the efforts of the Calvinist ministry itself, for men to experience an earnest of heavenly happiness while pursuing more earthly satisfaction.

Calvinism was not, however, simply the "frontier religion" of the hypotheses of William Warren Sweet; it was on Boston Common that Whitefield gathered in 1740 the largest audience seen in America before Webster's performances on Bunker Hill. In the decades after the Awakening Calvinists filled pulpits in Philadelphia, New York, and Boston with such notable itinerants and partisans of the Awakening as Gilbert Tennent, Andrew Croswell, and Ebenezer Pemberton. They formed on the outskirts of the smaller trading towns such imposing congregations as the "Separate" church of Samuel Bird in White Haven, Connecticut, and that of Jonathan Parsons in Newbury, Massachusetts, which, by the 1770's, was probably "the most numerous on the continent."[80] By 1770 Calvinism was represented in Newport by the notable theologian Samuel Hopkins, in Philadelphia and Charleston by such powerful younger preachers as the New Light Presbyterian George Duffield and the "Independent" William Tennent III, and in Savannah by the *émigré* Swiss friend of Whitefield and the orphan asylum, Johann Joachim Zubly. Whitefield's death in 1770 in fact inspired as many commemorative sermons in the "principal cities of America" as in the areas where he had but recently preached to expectant thousands in the rural fields.[81]

Despite such evidence of Calvinism's urban appeal, it is probably true that evangelical religion was, as Liberals believed it to be, a faith highly congenial to the more "clownish and rustic part" of the colonies.[82] Among such people, Liberal religion seemed no "more a-kin to the apostle's doctrine than the bible is to the *alcoran*."[83] Not that Oliver Wendell Holmes was fully accurate in presenting the "village folk" of America as alone in their admiration for Edwards' masterpieces. But especially after the earthquake years of the 1750's the Calvinists' belief in the impermanency of artifice and their faith in things unseen was undoubtedly more difficult to sustain in the cities and larger commercial depots. Conspicuous in the roll of rationalist ministers by 1765 were the Anglicans of Charleston and Philadelphia, a number of Yale graduates scattered among the Congregational churches of the southern New England ports and the Connecticut Valley, and the leading ministers of that "corner of the land" which Edwards had singled out as the headquarters of American Arminianism—the metropolis and nearby towns of Massachusetts Bay.

In the decade of economic opportunity that accompanied the French and Indian War the Liberal way to wealth held particular appeal for city dwellers. Still, Philadelphians were not the only people whom Tennent in 1760 found guilty of "immoderate Desires, Fears, and Cares about Earthly Things."[84] Indeed it was on the basis of his observations throughout plantation Virginia that Davies sardonically asked the Anglican parson and historian, William Stith, whether men really needed to be offered "such comfortable Doctrine" as that of the Church of England in order "to moderate their excessive concern about eternal Things, & to check their over-eager Career towards Heaven?"[85] Nor was it merely in the Boston area that New England Anglican clergymen boasted that their congregations consisted "chiefly of families of Property." Even Litchfield County eventually spawned its counterparts to the clergy who served the nabobs of tidewater Virginia.[86] Old Side Presbyterianism and Liberal Congregationalism attracted the wealthier citizens of many rural counties—if not the well-born, then the successful *arriviste*.

From the Awakening onward it seldom escaped notice that the "most substantial and sensible people" inclined to the churches of rational religion. During the Awakening one Boston clergyman, the Reverend William Hooper, a man "high in the Esteem of Gentlemen of Figure," was so offended by revival enthusiasm that he moved into the Church of England, taking his more "respectable" parishioners with him.[87] Three decades later it seemed that throughout the colonies Liberal religion was the preference of all who, in their "self-sufficiency," wanted to be able to proclaim, "we are rich, and increased with goods, and have need of nothing."[88] Likewise throughout the era the communions of evangelical religion remained for the most part attractive only to "the lower Sort."[89] Still, such a religious division of American society did not lead the Calvinist ministry to think that men embraced or resisted the evangelical spirit only according to their worldly substance. Though they believed that there were probably few "great men" in Heaven, and that it was peopled, as Edwards declared in 1742, "mostly with the poor of this world," they did not, on that account, rush to the conclusion that the Calvinist God elected only His proletarian children.[90]

Even when Whitefield failed to duplicate his 1740 triumphs during subsequent visits to Boston and Philadelphia, Calvinists were not persuaded that farmers, simply as farmers, were the chosen people of God. Rather they explained the religious preferences of Americans by the fact that some men were, as Bellamy explained, unfortunately afflicted with "spiritual blindness." This disease, "seated chiefly in the heart," consisted in "being stupid to that beauty and loveliness, with which the mind ought to be deeply affected."[91] Thus possibly the most sophisticated analysis of the differences in Americans' religious preferences was that offered by Nathaniel Whitaker, who in the 1770's erected a Tabernacle in central Salem as a monument to Whitefield and his religion. "A sight of *beauty*," Whitaker explained, "supposes a *taste* for that which renders the object beautiful."[92] It was the substance of what according to evangelical religion was "excellence" that made its scheme attractive to some men and yet so displeasing to the eyes and hearts of more reasonable beings.

The true nature of Calvinist excellence was fully revealed only over the course of a generation, but its essential qualities were disclosed in the Awakening—both in the form of ministerial preachments and in the very behavior of the awakened multitude. The Awakening, as indeed each of the "spiritual refreshings" that periodically overcame Calvinist communions during the remainder of the century, was something more than a mere quantity of individual conversion experiences. What made the revival "pleasant and admirable to behold" was the fact that multitudes were jointly flocking to Christ, and the joy of the New Birth itself was in part an expression of delight in one's communion with his equally delighted fellow saints.[93] And as it turned out, the beatific vision of Calvinism was an explicit objectification of aspirations for social as well as individual redemption. The "true, spiritual, original beauty" that Edwards defined as the excellency of excellency was none other than that "of a society or system of intelligent beings, sweetly united in benevolent agreement of heart."[94] In sum, men were reborn in the Great Awakening that their eyes might be turned from the things of this world to the beauties of humanity.

Over the years Calvinist leaders translated their vision of "excellence" into programs for an objective reorganization of society. Yet the evangelical scheme remained, as it was initially, primarily a means of satisfying existential needs and desires. Though the Calvinist ministry eventually strove to mobilize the American people in a variety of enterprises, they did not in doing so cease to seek that people's "subjective happiness." Programs and goals were so defined that there might be delight in the pursuit as well as in the attainment. Thus what Calvinism conceived as a "suitable object" for the "full and sufficient exercise" of man's capacious faculties was in substance the same in the Revolutionary year of 1775 as in the Awakening year of 1740.[95] Nearly all the difference lay in the attempt to hasten the day when every individual might have the "enjoyments of the heavenly state" on earth—

when the transcendent beauty of the Calvinist Deity could be immediately seen in the social arrangements of mankind.

IV

Elder John Leland, whose long career opened with participation in the last of America's colonial revivals, spent twenty years struggling to secure religious liberty for the Baptists and other evangelical dissenters of Virginia and New England. In the election year of 1800 he served as a "Jeffersonian itinerant," seeking to bring pious Americans to support of the Republican ticket. In later years he encouraged and supported the second war against Britain and, finally, the candidacy of Andrew Jackson.[96] Though in the course of these activities Leland advocated many ideas, according to him the one vital truth on which all others depended was "the doctrine of a *new birth*." If a preacher denied or failed to mention it, he deservedly (according to Leland) preached unheard—at least in the back country of Virginia or in interior New England.[97] Leland's observations are essential to any understanding of the evangelical impulse, not of the progress of piety merely, but of numerous ventures, in state as well as church, that struck the bewildered critics of Calvinism as beyond all understanding.

At the outset the evangelical pursuit of happiness seemed to the rational mind a senseless and idle dissipation. Already in the 1730's Georgia planters were complaining that Wesley's preaching and prayer meetings were beguiling the lower classes into improper endeavors, "at improper hours," detrimental to the thriving of the colony.[98] After 1740 the southern Anglican hierarchy blasted Whitefield (and, in succession, Davies) as well-nigh subversive for "holding forth on working days" and thereby encouraging "great numbers of poor people" to behave in a manner "inconsistent with the religion of labor."[99] Such complaints were by no means restricted to the South, where "idleness" was the traditional epithet for any endeavor, however energetic, which did not seem to contribute to what some considered the general welfare. In Franklin's Pennsylvania too, the awakened were castigated for contenting themselves with what seemed a perfunctory attention to their merchandise and farms and for expiring in "idle visions" of the unreal world. From Boston emerged possibly the most strident objections to the revivalists' calling off "poor deluded tradesmen and laborers" from the world's work, "to the private detriment of their families, and great damage to the public."[100]

Of course the Calvinist ministers were no more advocates of idleness than Ben Franklin. By the end of the Revolution, indeed, they were demanding that *every* citizen of the United States find a useful occupation, so that all together would compose "a mighty army" working industriously for the American commonwealth.[101] And when in 1740 they thought it to Whitefield's credit that wherever he went men "shut up their Shops, forgot their secular Business, and laid aside their Schemes for the World,"[102] they were not standing in judgment on diligence in one's calling. Rather they were voicing a demurrer from the kind of "labor" reason approved, and from the kind of "schemes" it spawned. And, in the particular instance of those whom the itinerants called the "dead drones" then clogging the Christian ministry, Calvinism expressed its explicit—and alarming—contempt for the ways in which reasonable religion allowed some Americans to consider the lily of the field in a manner which, according to the evangelical scheme, was truly inconsistent with the "religion of labor."

To be sure, many partisans of the revival sought to affirm some consensus underlying the furious controversy of the Awakening. Those who welcomed Whitefield on his first visit to Boston, for instance, protested that they were "as much for maintaining *order, peace,* and *industry*" as the "Company" of men who saluted his departure with a sigh of relief.[103] But the kind of industry which Calvinists encouraged, the peace in which they were able to find satisfaction, and the order to which they aspired turned out to be quite different from those admired by the colonial Liberals. These words held for Calvinists meanings which by no means corresponded to the standard listings in the Liberal lexicon, and the latter—despite their cries of "slothful revery"—clearly understood this. Their ultimate argument against the "spiritual contemplations and exercises" which Calvinists encouraged was that minds so idle, so detached from the real world, had time for the devil's work of plotting sedition.

The critique of the revival reproduced in substance the seeming inconsistencies of the seventeenth-century Massachusetts establishment in its arguments against the Antinomians. The latter had been charged both with divesting the Sabbath of its peculiar sanctity and with making every day, in a sense, the Sabbath. In short, they were bent on overthrowing a traditional and judicious system of social norms in order that man's entire life might be pervaded with the spirit of grace. Similarly, the Calvinists of the eighteenth century were accused of hawking antinomianism—of offering the "Flattering Hope of Happiness" to men who had "no Thot's of attempting a virtuous Life."[104] As in 1637, the issue was that of "preparation," with reason and orthodoxy both contending that man must perform his assigned moral duties as, in effect, a condition of salvation. Implicit in Calvinism's reaffirmation of the doctrine of justification by faith alone was a repudiation, not just of the notion of preparatory works, but of the kind of works approved and expected in the moral code of pre-revival America. The awakeners rejected the values (or prejudices) not of the spokesmen of the legal scheme merely, but those as well of the nominally orthodox ministers who betrayed their leanings by rejecting as unreasonable the unconditional election of the Awakening:

> They can't bear the Supposal, that GOD has not a good Esteem of those whom they think well of: that he does not proportion his special Favours to Men's External Conduct. . . They who could bear these Doctrines well enough in *Speculation,* are now embittered against them when they appear in a *practical* View. . .[105]

Yet the Calvinists of post-Awakening America were *not* antinomians, and it was because they were not that they posed a challenge to the standing order.

Calvinism did not divorce the salvational process from human conduct, but it did place Christian behavior in a new perspective. Its first and possibly most significant achievement, in this regard, lay in cutting the confusion created by those ministers who, as Tennent complained, kept "Driving, Driving to Duty, Duty."[106] The duties which such "legal" preachers urged Americans to perform were appropriate only to the more static society of the previous century. Evangelical religion divested Americans of this quasi-feudal intellectual heritage by defining virtue not as a variety of deportments that differed from class to class and calling to calling but as a "temper" essentially the same for all men, regardless of station. The new Calvinism thus made it possible for an individual to cope with the ethical problems inherent in an expanding economy and a mobile society.

In its express economic creed Calvinism was seemingly reactionary— as hopelessly reactionary indeed as recent historians have judged the faith of Jackson and Benton to have been. The Calvinist ministry proposed that every man be "Content with his Lot," and their definition of true virtue could have been upheld with ease perhaps only by such landed squires as "never seemed to aspire" beyond the competence they had inherited.[107] Indeed the spirit of Calvinism was profoundly hostile to the emerging capitalist ethic of eighteenth-century America. It was not, however, opposed either to prosperity or to success as such, but only to the motive of self-seeking which, according to certain contrary moralists, was essential to personal or social progress. What Calvinism asked—or rather demanded—was that no man use whatever worldly success he enjoyed as an occasion for looking on "the common People, with an Air of Disdain."[108] What concerned Calvinists was what men did with their new and more fluid freedom, and insofar as the Edwardean definition of virtue was enforced on the minds of men, it served as an imperative reminder that achievement was not personal but a product of that larger community to which all men were responsible.

In ultimate terms, the evangelical impulse was a response to change and seeming social chaos that bore within it a desire to make the new order satisfying to more than a handful of the people of the colonies. The revival spirit appeared on the American scene as a triumphant competitor to land-bank enthusiasms. The objection of Calvinism to such devices was not, however, quite the same as those of Thomas Hutchinson or William Douglass, the rationalist historian, who disapproved speculative fiscal schemes because they induced orgies of "unreal" prosperity, or of Benjamin Franklin, who, after an early flirtation with inflationary currency policies, became an advocate of steadier ways to wealth. The Calvinist clergy looked on the land-bank promoters as "a corrupt Designing Party," whose intention was not the social salvation of all but the aggrandizement of a few.[109]

Calvinism was opposed both to the disposition of men to place fortune above salvation, and to the heresy that seemed to sustain them in such ambitions. In 1786 Isaac Backus, addressing the followers of Daniel Shays, bemoaned the rebellion as evidence of men's forsaking more important matters in attention to "affairs of worldly gain." He went on to observe that such a concern could only have been aroused by the Arminian notion of *"self-determination* in the *will of man."*[110] He also granted, however, that the insurgents' grievances were just, and suggested that they should petition the legislature for redress. If this were not given they could use their overwhelming numbers, Backus reminded them, to remove the offending magistrates in the coming election.

Like the dithyrambs of Thomas Hart Benton on the Arcadian felicity of the Republic's golden age, the anti-entrepreneurial utterances of Calvinism embodied considerably more than a conservative nostalgia. The evangelical scheme, seemingly counterrevolutionary in its opposition to the surface tendencies of the eighteenth century, was in fact progressive in its implications and portent. The radical character of Calvinism was attested already in the Awakening by its very definition of the process of regeneration. The first step was a "conviction" that any man is "undone, helpless, and hopeless" in himself. But the next and more important, the New Birth itself, carried with it a realization that man's true happiness derived not merely from his dependence on God but from his interdependence with his fellow men.[111] In this idea, as expanded and enforced on the American mind in the decades after the Awakening, consisted the most enduring of Calvinism's contributions to American political thought and practice. For the evangelical defini-

tion of virtue was such that it inexorably worked to give the people of
the colonies what Edwards called "the capacity to act with united
strength," and in that power, to assert their wills as the ultimate
guarantors of the social good.

Obviously such developments were barely glimpsed in the ecstasies of
the 1740's. Indeed, many of the partisans of the Awakening insisted
that no new ideas were being introduced by the spokesmen of Calvinism. The "Promoters of the late Revival of Godliness," according to a
New England Presbyterian,

> pretend not to bring in any new Fashions in Religion, or to make
> any Alteration in its Principles; on the contrary, they do steadily
> adhere to the Doctrines of primitive Christianity, and the Reforma-
> tion. . .[112]

But not a few novelties were in fact brought to bear on the American
mind by the revivalists. Hardly the least of these was the notion that
it was easy to "run a Parallel" between the career of George Whitefield
and that of Jesus Christ. Whitefield himself thought it worth mentioning in his *Journal* that he had been born in an inn—though without
noting, as his critics pointed out, that his parents happened to own
the establishment. Yet though Chauncy could justifiably complain that
Whitefield's fancy had in many instances "formed a Kind of Resemblance between *your own,* and the Circumstances of *Christ Jesus,*" the
parallel drawn by the American admirers of the grand itinerant was
not personal. Whenever God wanted to revive mankind, Samuel Finley
observed in early 1740, he has "rais'd up some eminent Men" to
arouse and awaken the world.[113] From the coming of Whitefield, in
sum, could be dated an historic epoch in American affairs.

The contributions of this new era are yet to be considered, but here
it might at least be noted what the Awakening did *not* bring to
America. In his *Thoughts on the Revival* Edwards noted how during
the early months of the Awakening all classes of men gave up, "as it
were at once, those things of which they were extremely fond, and in
which they placed the happiness of their lives." All "notoriously
vicious persons" ceased drinking, whoring, and unseemly "extravagance
in apparel," and the "wealthy and fashionable"—the "great beaus and
fine ladies" of New England—likewise "relinquished their vanities."
Had American Calvinists rested here, their contribution to American
life would have been little different from that which the Wesleys and
Whitefield (in his role as the Countess of Huntingdon's chaplain) were
to make in England. But the intellectual energy of American Calvinists, in the age after the Awakening, was not spent in reproving the
rabble, in Wesleyan accents, for the vices to which they were enslaved,

nor of invading, *à la* Whitefield, resorts of fashion. The task of Edwards, of Tennent and Bellamy, and of the other young preachers whom Edwards in 1742 commissioned "captains of the host in this war" was that of making American society, in all its elements, conform to the excellency promised by the New Light of the Awakening.[114]

Edwards noted Whitefield's historic role in the *Thoughts on the Revival*, but he did so by pointing to his *"zeal* and *resolution."* The same virtues, Edwards observed, had made possible the "great things that *Oliver Cromwell* did." In almost the same breath Edwards allowed Britain only "one generation more" before it would "sink under the weight" of its vice and selfishness. And at the same time he looked forward to a future in which the people of America, having resisted the corruptions of the present, could export the "spiritual treasures" he saw as the true promise of American life. In order that America achieve its spiritual potentiality, Edwards declared, it was necessary for all the "people of God," and not their magistrates and ministers merely, to be filled with the spirit of Whitefield and of Cromwell.[115] By making such great things presently possible, Edwards led Americans, even as they contemplated their ancestors' worth, in their first steps into the age that was coming before.

II

THE WORK OF
REDEMPTION

THE watershed in American history marked by the 1740's can be understood best in terms of the degree to which, after the Great Awakening, the American populace was filled with the notion of an impending millennium. From 1740 on, American thought and expression—or, more precisely, that of the evangelical American—was above all characterized by a note of expectation. Few Calvinist utterances of the period—and almost none of Edwards'—can be fully comprehended except as proceeding from the assumption that the "unspeakably happy and glorious" period of the "prosperity" of Christ's church and people was approaching and, more significantly, that it was attainable "through the ordinary processes of propagating the gospel."[1] Edwards' *Thoughts on the Revival* was, thus, far more than the first and the best of many tracts in defense of emotional and "experimental" religion. It was inspired, Edwards reports, by the knowledge that the "people of God" were filled with "earnest desires, that the Work of God, now in the land," would be "carried on" until the Kingdom of the Messiah was established throughout the earth "as a kingdom of holiness, purity, love, peace, and happiness to mankind."[2] Edwards not only confirmed these expectations; he gave them substance by assigning tasks and duties to various elements of the people of Christ for establishing the Kingdom with the least delay and confusion. In sum, he announced confidently that the coming of the millennium might be hastened through the use of human instrumentalities.

The explosion of millenarianism in the Great Awakening was one of the symptoms of some Americans' dissatisfaction with the conditions of eighteenth-century life. Edwards described the world in which he lived as "for the most part a scene of trouble and sorrow,"[3] and, whatever the judgment of others, apocalyptic speculations persisted throughout the sixty years of American history after the Awakening.[4] Yet the revival of the 1740's also brought hope; the Great Awakening, like the revivals of 1800-1801, was preceded as well as accompanied by popular speculations and prophecies concerning "when Christ would appear and set up his true kingdom."[5] Such aspirations seem to have been fed in New England by underground Fifth Monarchy sentiments, largely unarticulated since the Revolutions of 1689 and their frustrating aftermath, and by chimney-corner traditions and recollections of New Haven colony, of Cotton, Vane, and Eliot. Perhaps they were sustained by a reading of such copies of Edward Johnson's *Wonder-Working Providence* as had survived the century; surely they were encouraged by Joseph Morgan's popular allegorical *History of the Kingdom of Basaruah* (1715), which held out the promise of the earthly Kingdom as a final solution to the intolerable hostilities of an emotionally parched New England and New Jersey.

In the first quarter of the century the Mathers had dilated on the "Universal Reign of Holiness and Righteousness" which the eighteenth century would surely see. They had predicted "horrid concussions, and wrecks in nature" as the attendants of the general judgment which, in their vision, was presumably to precede the millennium. But such chiliasm seems not to have persisted as a widely acceptable formula, at least not after the earthquake of 1727. When in 1734 a New England divine wrote of the final conflagration as occurring *before the happy State* of the Church," he acknowledged that the contrary opinion generally prevailed: the earthly Kingdom was foreseen this side of judgment and cataclysm. The Great Awakening confirmed the American disposition against premillenarianism. James Davenport, to be sure, announced during the revival that "in a very short Time all these Things would be involv'd in devouring Flames."[6] But even he soon afterward understood what other Calvinists had seen, either by the New Light of the revival itself, or by the clearer light provided them by Edwards: that a shattering of the order of nature would not be required to introduce the era of earthly felicity.

In this regard the "Fort Hill Address" of eighteenth-century Calvinism was Edwards' *History of the Work of Redemption,* the thirty-nine sermons he delivered in 1739. Although the sermons were not published until the 1770's, they contained the axioms and postulates which, as expounded and expanded in such works as *An Humble Attempt to Promote Explicit Agreement and Visible Union of God's People* and *A Dissertation Concerning the End for which God Created the World,* sustained several American generations in a belief that the millennium was not a mere possibility but an imminent and attainable reality. The theory set forth in the *Work of Redemption* was postmillennial; that is, the thousand years of earthly felicity would come *before* the General Judgment. It has been suggested that the source of Edwards' millenarian theory was the chiliasm which arose out of late seventeenth-century interpretations of Newtonian physics. But the Edwardean metaphysic—a repudiation of the premillenarianism of the previous generation—seems rather to have been made intense belief and firm conviction by the revivals and the Great Awakening itself.

The revivals of the 1730's encouraged Edwards' inquiries into the "History of the Advancement of Christ's Kingdom," and his attention to its progress in the contemporary world.[7] Edwards presumably longed for the coming of the Kingdom well before 1735, but until then his sermons considered the Kingdom only as one into which men were to press as a matter of personal rather than corporate, and deferred rather than temporal, salvation. Such, at least, were the themes of his *Pressing into the Kingdom,* a sermon which preceded the Northampton revival of 1735. (And such were the themes of its Middle Colony counterpart, Tennent's discourse on *The Necessity of Religious Violence.*) But in 1739 Edwards, defining the "Work of Redemption" anew—as he put it, "more largely"—conceived of the Kingdom as an "evangelical state of things in the church, and in the world."[8] In *A History of the Work of Redemption* Edwards declared that from the "fall of man" onward the Kingdom had been advanced chiefly by such "remarkable communications of the spirit of God" as the people of Northampton had witnessed in 1735. In 1739 Edwards was not certain whether what had "already taken place," among the pietists of Germany and the followers of Frelinghuysen and the Tennents, as well as in the Connecticut Valley, constituted the "forerunners and beginning" of the triumphant Kingdom.[9] By 1741, however, he had more extensive data by which to test his hypothesis according to the rules of the inductive philosophy.

It was the Great Awakening itself that made non-cataclysmic millenarianism "the common and vital possession" of evangelical American Christians.[10] The prodigious accomplishments of George Whitefield on his first majestic tour of the colonies inspired both Calvinist ministry and populace with a new perspective on the tendency of history. The very first experience of the revival immediately rang a high and clear note of anticipation: "It looks as if some happy period were opening." Soon the question was not what "great things" were *"at the Birth"* but when, exactly, the "glorious day"—the millennium itself—would begin.[11] Samuel Finley announced that the showers of grace which had descended on the colonies were "proof that the kingdom of Christ is come unto us this day." Edwards himself was more cautious and could not in 1741 decide "whether the present work be the beginning of that great and frequently predicted coming of Christ to set up his kingdom, or not." But a year later he publicly testified (with what proved to be embarrassingly few qualifications) that the *"New Jerusalem"* had "begun to come down from heaven" in 1740.[12] Eventually Edwards confessed his conclusion to have been not only premature, but inopportune; still, he continued to affirm the revivals of 1740-41 to have been "forerunners" of the millennium, which, he likewise insisted, must "needs be approaching."[13]

The Awakening had clearly reversed the apparent course of history. Calvinists ceased looking on the events of the past century as a tale of mournful declension. Instead *The Christian History,* the magazine in which accounts of the Awakening were assembled, in a series of articles on the religion of the seventeenth century, noted the sins and afflictions of that age, but only incidentally to what now seemed the more significant facts of the past: "Some Former Instances of the Revival of Religion in New England." In the course of the Awakening the themes of the jeremiad all but disappeared from Calvinist sermons. Thomas Foxcroft, who in 1730 had commemorated the first century of New England with a lamentation for departed spiritual glories, greeted the year 1747 with a recapitulation of Christian history in which the Reformation and the Puritan experiments loomed as forerunners of the Spirit's triumphs in the Great Revival of the 1740's.[14] No longer did the tendency of history seem toward judgment, or the thoughts of the pious bent on despair.

With the publication of Edwards' dissertations, *Will* and *God's End in Creation,* the elements of American Protestantism for whom he spoke and whom he profoundly influenced were committed, by his very postulates, to an optimistic view of history. The crux of Edwardean theology was the inherent and necessary relation of the regenerating work of the Spirit to the "erection, establishment, and universal extent of the Kingdom of the Messiah."[15] As Perry Miller has observed, Edwards' achievement in placing the millennium "on this side of the apocalypse" was to provide Calvinism with a formula in which the good society would and could be attained solely through "natural causes." But the aspect of creation involved in the Work of Redemption was, for Edwards, the "supernatural" realm—that portion of the universe which was above and beyond nature, consisting in man's "union and communion with God, or divine communications and influences of God's spirit." The earthly Kingdom of the Calvinist Messiah was not of the "natural, material" world: but "within men." It consisted not "in things external," but in happiness and the "dominion of virtue" in the minds and hearts of mankind.[16] The Work of Redemption was one with the regeneration of humanity; it depended on no awful display of Divine power, no shattering of the physical creation, but on the gradual restoration of the influences of the Holy Spirit which had been withdrawn at the Fall.

Certain of the implications of Edwards' theology may be gathered from the fact that his God, an otherwise inscrutable and arbitrary Being, unlimited by any of the variety of covenants to which He was a party in Puritan thought, was absolutely committed to the Work of Redemption. Scripture, nature, reason and all else united in Edwards' philosophy to confirm his faith in "that common prosperity and advancement, so unspeakably great and glorious, which God hath so abundantly promised to fulfill in the latter days."[17] Indeed the Edwardean Deity seemed designed as a guarantor of the millennium.*[18] The Second Person of his Trinity—"the deity generated by God's understanding"—was the substantial pattern of the millennial commonwealth; the Holy Spirit—the deity "subsisting in the act"—was the force that would accomplish such a society in time.[19] Such at least was the inference for many Calvinists from Edwards' *End in Creation:* that the divine happiness, derived from "the Propension of His Will to his own glory, and the delightful View and Enjoyment of his own infinite Excellencies," was one with the earthly felicity of mankind.[20] To be sure, the millennium was not the ultimate state in the Work of Redemption. God's end would not be fulfilled until that moment when the process of the "emanation and remanation" of the Divine personality would culminate in the restoration of the saints to unity with the Godhead. But by insisting that this moment would never fully arrive, as by refusing to tolerate the possibility that the personalities of the elect would be annihilated, Edwards not only showed himself no mystic but disclosed how his eschatology centered on and served as

---

* Nineteenth-century Unitarians mistakenly took Edwards for a Sabellian; and in the sense that he and other Calvinists conceived of Christ and the Holy Ghost as "modes" of a Godhead whose "essential" nature was indivisible, Edwardeans were perhaps heterodox. But Calvinists were not particularly interested in such traditional doctrinal questions as the nature of the Trinity. Edwards' unpublished speculations on the subject betray an impatience with the whole matter, and it was not until the 1750's—and then only in response to the first rumbling of Arianism among the New England Liberals—that any Calvinist publicly addressed himself to the offices of the persons of the Trinity and their relationships. In every case the "sublime doctrine of a *triune Deity*" was expressed by Calvinists in such a manner as to disclose that their ulterior intentions were to preserve the Edwardean eschatology. The Calvinist God was conceived as nought but "understanding and will," because, as Nathaniel Niles explained, only then would His attributes and persons be clearly seen as "all harmoniously agreeing in the most vigorous prosecution of the truly God-like plan of redemption!"

the final cause, so to speak, of the "third stage" of the Work of Redemption, the earthly Kingdom of Christ, the dominion of the Spirit.

Perhaps Edwards' most impressive achievement was to purge Calvinist millenarianism of all those seventeenth-century elements which were symptoms of cosmic despair. Reveries on God's need to "interrupt and disturb the course of nature," or to send fire from heaven as a chastening of refractory man, bespoke a lack of confidence in the capacity of the Holy Spirit, working through the ordinary means, to advance the felicity of mankind.[21] Behind this apparent indifference to matter was the principle which comprised Edwards' special contribution to American radicalism:

> God's great design in his works, is doubtless concerning his reasonable creatures, rather than brute beasts and lifeless things. The revolutions by which God's great design is brought to pass, are doubtless chiefly among them, and concern their state, and not the state of things without life or reason.[22]

Like his ideological heirs, the spokesmen of the early American democracy, Edwards conceived of "those things that more directly concern the mind" as the most appropriate avenues, as well as the truest measure, of social reorganization and progress.[23] The "inanimate and unintelligent world" had been created only for "the rational and moral world, much as a house is prepared for its inhabitants."[24] From this singular precept derived both the comparative indifference of Calvinists to institutions and their scorn for such theories as expected some mighty Divine intervention in the course of Providence.[25] The millennium was to come neither by a reconstruction of the temple nor through its destruction, but as a renewal of the nature of those who dwell within.

In sum, Edwards considered the creation of a new earth unnecessary to the inauguration of the new heaven. In his more careful delineations of cosmic history he even seemed to dismiss the prospect of consuming fire at the end of the world: "the external and transitory part of the universe" would then be disposed of "in some way or other" for the simple reason that it would be of "no further use."[26] His view that the "lower world" would be "gradually" destroyed was the corollary—aesthetically necessary if not logically—of Edwards' insistence on the constancy of what "we call the laws of nature" in the years leading to the millennium.[27] For one thing, dilation on the "dreadful element of fire" or the "universal ruins" of the latter days represented a rhetorical effort to frighten men into virtue, and this Edwards had silently abandoned after the Great Awakening. Also it confused the eternal torments of hell with physical circumstance, and this was inappropriate to a philosophy which defined heaven as a state of mind. But in the last analysis cataclysm was inconsistent with a vision of history as the progressive enlargement of the realm of the spirit. For matter to be consumed in a dazzling pyrotechnic display implied a power of resistance, an imperviously hostile force. Nature was "indifferent" and needed not to be overthrown but only brought under the control of mankind, whose wills had been altered by the Holy Spirit.

Cataclysm, providential judgment, a personal second coming—all were contrary to the high cosmic optimism of Edwards' historical vision. They represented dramatic interference in the course of history, abrupt reversals of its flow. Edwards was certain that the progress of humanity was largely consistent and continuous: all "will not be accomplished at once, as by some miracle," such as a spectacular raising of the dead, but will be *gradually* brought to pass."[28] The specific embodiment of this conviction was Edwards' conclusion that the so-called "slaying of the witnesses" was the Dark Ages preceding the Reformation. Earlier Americans, John Davenport and Increase Mather particularly, had testified to their doubts and fears by wrestling—in the years of the Restoration and the execution of the regicide judges—with this apocalyptic mystery. Edwards, however, was certain that the enemies of the Kingdom had long since reached the zenith of their power, that the anti-Christian apostasy had fallen to rise no more. In support of this interpretation of history Edwards marshaled few facts. It derived rather from the assumption that once God had brought his people out of "such a long night of dismal darkness, he will not extinguish the light, and cause them to return again to midnight darkness."[29] Such a vision European and English pietists found less compelling than American Calvinists, who, as the eighteenth century wore on, increasingly shared Edwards' pleasure in the "beautiful order" of a history which was always in process of becoming, the steady unfolding of the Kingdom of Light.[30]

Edwards' dalliance with Scripture and with the "application of the prophecies" to particular events attests the fact that history even for him consisted of something more than "remarkable effusions" of grace. Still, the latter constituted the mainstream of history, the line on which it was seen to move and which gave it unity. Only the work of the Spirit was in truth the "Work of Redemption," and this was "so much the greatest of all the works of God" that all else—the tribal battles and kingly successions of the Old Testament or the politics and warfare of the Christian era—was "to be looked upon either as parts of it, or appendages to it, or as some way reducible to it."[31] Other developments and events—the withering away of the Papacy or the Cromwellian revolution—carried no meaning except as in some sense tributary to the work of the Spirit. The course of Providence, in Edwards' telling, was most fitly compared to a number of "different streams," each with a seemingly disparate source, all traveling different channels, their various meanderings apparently confused. But "all unite at last, all come to the same issue, disgorging themselves in one into the same great ocean."[32] His very metaphor bespoke a conviction that the whole of human history was somehow connected to and inseparable from those showers of grace that impelled humanity, not so much on a prescribed course as toward a destined and predictable goal.

Thus God's grand design was embodied and confirmed likewise in the "various parts of the work of providence." But the workings of Providence were, if properly viewed, incidental and subordinate to, though ultimately one with, the work of grace. Like George Bancroft a century later, the Calvinist saw the Spirit breathing beneath, above, and around all history; in the Work of Redemption everything seemed "connected together in a regular, beautiful, and glorious scheme."[33] Here indeed was a source of the rhetorical power of Edwards, his colleagues and successors, whose enduring message was that the "design of God in all his works of creation, providence and grace" was but one —"to advance and secure" His glory through the happiness of His people.[34] Much of that beauty wherein the essential glory of the Calvinist Godhead consisted and in which the saint delighted was contained in the vision of mankind moving in nearly linear progress toward felicity.

II

Whether the millennial theory of post-Awakening Calvinism was intellectually respectable may be questioned, but what cannot be gainsaid is that the expectancy expressed in that theory controlled the mind of the period. Something of a key to the era is contained in one of Edwards' pronouncements of the 1740's:

> We are sure this day will come; and we have many reasons to think that it is approaching; from the fulfillment of almost every thing that the prophecies speak of as preceding it, and their having been fulfilled now a long time; and from the general earnest expectations of the church of God, and the best of her ministers and members, and the late extraordinary things that have appeared in the church of God, and appertaining to the state of religion.[35]

The heart and soul of Calvinism was not doctrine but an implicit faith that God intended to establish this earthly Kingdom—and to do so within the eighteenth century. The Awakening had brought history to a critical juncture, a discernible confluence which disposed the Calvinist mind to "look for the beginnings" of the millennium "from year to year."[36] And the faith of the 1740's sustained the Calvinists through dispensations of Providence which other Americans, less confident than they that Edwards had read God's plan aright, found both dark and bewildering.

In the sermons, the *Work of Redemption*, Edwards had portrayed mankind's progress as impelled by periodic impulses of the Spirit. But in the years of the Awakening, and those immediately following, he seemed to identify the beauty of history with what, in the *Notes*, he had defined as "proportion." The tempo of history in the early 1740's was seemingly such that God's purpose now promised to be fulfilled with ever-doubling acceleration, by geometric enlargement of the saintly host. But by 1747 history obviously no longer moved with its anticipated velocity, and such a vision proved untenable. It was then that Edwards adopted and announced a "cyclical" theory of history— one not of mere repetition, but of recurrence and periodically renewed and increased momentum. Outpourings of the Spirit were to be expected only in certain "times and seasons" roughly corresponding to each generation's coming of age. In such springtimes of the race, humanity's stagnant pools would once more become freshets, and the rivers of history would again be sent rushing on their way, each time etching more indelibly on the earth the courses through which they would at last hurtle to their destination.

Thus of all the "signs of the times," the most significant in the eyes of Calvinist watchmen was a "happy revival of religion." Well after Edwards himself acknowledged that the Awakening impulse was spent, his every statement continued to underscore the proposition that the "unspeakably happy" millennial era would be signaled by a "glorious day of religious revival" in which the experience of 1740-41 would be both infinitely exalted and indefinitely prolonged.[37] With the outbreak of the imperial wars, however, he began to seek other evidence of the fulfilling of God's grand design. Edwards was impressed by God's "dealings, both with Great Britain and the American plantations" in the conflict which culminated in the victory at fortress Louisburg— with its presumed consequences for the French fisheries and, thus, the revenues of the Papacy. But though he collected a body of notes on such contemporary events, and apparently planned to use them in the final version of his "History of the Work of Redemption," that history was ultimately written as *The End for which God Created the World*.[38] Battles and sieges were, after all, mere interludes in God's sublimest plot. Far from determining the course of history, their meaning—and the meaning of all temporal events—was subsumed in the grander tale of the spiritual transformation of mankind.

For many reasons Edwards' Calvinist colleagues likewise refused to attach primary significance to temporal events. Their viewpoint was in substance one derived from Edwards, whose expectant soul expressed itself in a brand of "typology" that was not confined to the traditional search for scriptural prefigurations. Typology was for Edwards—as in each of its efflorescences of Christian thought—a denial of the possibility that the universe is devoid of meaning. For Edwards it served the classic purpose of giving coherence and unity to history. Just as the events and personages of the Old Testament foreshadowed the Redeemer, so too did all that transpired in Edwards' own day strike him as somehow prophetic of the coming Kingdom. Such a reading of events and developments served, among other purposes, to insure history against discordant intrusions on its harmonious unfolding. As a "typologist," Edwards could welcome the progress of human enlightenment in the eighteenth century, despite his explicit awareness that "carnal men" could and did apply such knowledge to "wicked purposes." All the "wonderful discoveries" in arts and sciences were for Edwards not merely emblems, but prophetic tokens of the "spiritual knowledge" which mankind would enjoy in the millennial era. From such a perspective, even the most troubling and painful occurrence could be viewed optimistically, and the world visible to the eye of reason transmuted into a guarantor of Edwards' faith in the unseen but immanent glory. The present was pregnant with the future, and all that occurred in the "carnal realm" was, in the metaphor of Scripture, the "travail-pains" of a creation laboring to bring the millennium to birth.[39] All history stood on tip-toe to discern and announce the spiritual progress of humanity.

The End for Which God Created the World was Edwards' consummate effort to sustain such cosmic optimism in the dark years of the 1750's, a time of "lukewarmness" among God's people, of deaths and contention in the Church, and of natural catastrophies and imperial wars which threatened to impose on history a different, and contrary, meaning of their own. These years witnessed waverings of the Calvinist faith in certain circles, and even departures from it. In 1755 Jonathan Parsons, once Edwards' student, suffered a relapse into pre-Awakening thinking and jargon when he proposed that the Lisbon earthquake, which was felt throughout the colonies, was the beginning of "those terrible things in righteousness" that would culminate in general judgment.[40] A portion of the pious populace seemed also to be gripped by despair, for concurrently sectarians, indulging a renewed popular appetite for "millennial arithmetic," sought to fix the exact date of the Second Coming.[41] But the Calvinist mind quickly proved incapable of returning for long to premillenarianism. Indeed, by the close of the 1750's it seemed that historical pessimism was congenial only to the spokesmen of "enlightened" and rational religion.

One of the more dramatic indications of how radically the Awakening altered the American intellectual scene is the contrast between the clerical response to the earthquake of 1727 and to those which rocked the Christian world in 1755 and 1756. On the former occasion nearly every New England pulpit had thundered forth reminders of the awful retribution in store for a backsliding people. Less than thirty years later the Calvinist ministry nearly ignored the phenomena; their major contribution was the reprinting of a 1727 sermon by Thomas Prince with an appendix setting forth an "electrical" hypothesis of the nature of earthquakes. The leading Liberal clergy, however, issued what they clearly considered important pronouncements. In 1755 Jonathan Mayhew delivered a sermon, *The Expected Dissolution of All Things,* in which he dismissed Calvinist millenarianism as idle speculation. The millennium, were there to be such a thing, was a thousand, "perhaps a million," years away; the earthquake was an emblem of a cataclysm and judgment which were "still very remote in futurity." Still, Mayhew was cheerful by comparison to Chauncy, who improved the earthquake of 1756 (which shook the colonies themselves) as a rejoinder to those who thought "that these *new heavens and earth* will be formed before the *general resurrection* and judgment."[42] For the lesson Chauncy derived from the earthquake was that the tendency of history was against improvement in the human condition.

According to Chauncy, God's curse on Adam had fallen on the earth itself, changing it from a *"paradisiack"* state into one where the seasons were extreme, the climate marked by violent storms and prolonged droughts, and the ground less fruitful, full of *"thorns,* and *thistles,* and *weeds,* which are the occasion of infinite *toil* to the sons of men." The same curse had filled the earth's "bowels" with the "affluvia" that gave rise to earthquakes, themselves a striking emblem of nature's hostility to man. All evidence pointed to the necessity for a drastic change in the "external constitution of nature" prior to the millennium:

> The present constitution of nature is incompatible with unmingled happiness . . . The present heaven & earth must pass away, and a new heaven and earth rise up in their room, before any son or daughter of *Adam* can possess life without passing through a multiplied variety of inconveniences, disappointments, vexations, and sorrows.

In Chauncy's telling, it was not clear whether the human race, underfed and overworked, would end at last with a whimper, or the earth, its hostile energies unchained, would bring history to a close with a resounding bang. What he did insist on, however, was that "solid and compleat happiness" for mankind was possible only beyond the end of both earth and time.[43]

Like his Liberal ethic, Chauncy's view of history made man the creature of an environment which, in the last analysis, conspired against human felicity. In Mayhew's perspective, history is nearly static, but for Chauncy it is irredeemably retrograde. To be sure, Chauncy in 1752 publicly endorsed a program of factory construction in Boston and, in so doing, seemed to suggest that science, with its attendant command over nature, might ameliorate the human predicament. Something of this hope had informed the *Essays upon Field Husbandry* which Jared Eliot, beginning in the late 1740's, had published with a view to popularizing "scientific" attitudes and practices among the farmers of New England. Like much of the "science" of the 1740's and 1750's, Eliot's encouragement of "Skill and Industry" was at bottom negative both in its inspiration and its implication. Eliot, once a near-apostate to Episcopacy and ever a partisan of "reasonable" religion, seems to have undertaken the *Essays* with the half-conscious thought that agricultural decline was at the root of the wild nonsense of the Awakening. The Enlightenment creed, as interpreted by Eliot, was less an invocation of man's capacity for creation than a reminder of his limitations. Turning a miry swamp into "a rich Source of Supply for Man" was, according to Eliot, "as much as we, impotent Beings, can attain to." His vision of the American garden was a token of the anxieties of those for whom the barren land and "creeping Vermin" of a barbarous America were symbols of a fall from the well-drained and hedge-rowed Eden that was England.[44] In the final analysis, Eliot's *Essays* comprised a novel jeremiad, in which manure was the one thing needful to arrest New England's declension from the glory which was the fathers'.

The cosmic pessimism implicit in the Liberal theory of history carried little of the appeal inherent in Edwards' predictions of the spiritual advancement of the race. Even though Edwards conceived both prosperity and progress in terms of "spiritual enjoyments" transcending man's relationship to nature, he nevertheless also rejoiced in science and inventions. The mind's increasing command of nature was not for him, however, a tale of desperate struggle against a weedy circumstance that was man's appointed lot. It implied rather the promise of the leisure necessary for that life of the mind and the spirit which Edwards foresaw as the "saints' ordinary business" in the millennial era. So disposed were Calvinists to encouraging such "instruments of leisure" that they took the lead in introducing chemistry into the eighteenth-century American collegiate curriculum and turned, many of them, personally to invention and manufacturing. Eventually Edwards' grandson, Timothy Dwight, and Samuel Hopkins placed so much emphasis on a useful knowledge of nature as a prelude to the "moral perfection" of humanity that their millennia became paradises virtually within the reach of all men capable of pursuing the "art of husbandry" and the "mechanic arts" scientifically.[45] The Calvinist mind could never bring itself to repudiate the Edwardean proposition that historical progress was not contingent on, nor to be measured in terms of, technological mastery of external nature. But it tended, as the century moved on, to be overborne by a "science" it had once deemed but a useful servant.

Curiously enough, the Liberal mind came to pride itself on its use of scientific reason to counter what it deemed the "pessimism" of Calvinism. Herein the prized Liberal advocate was Professor John Winthrop, whose *Lecture on Earthquakes* was delivered in the Harvard chapel one week after the tremors were felt in New England. Winthrop, scion of New England's first family, was to achieve deserved fame as a major figure in the development of colonial science. In 1769 he organized the observations on the transit of Venus that constituted the most impressive pre-Revolutionary contribution to the advancement of science. But the import of his 1755 lecture was more metaphysical and moral than scientific. Winthrop espoused a "wave" theory of earthquakes, which he attributed to "explosions of subterraneous vapor." These, it would seem, loosened the earth, thus changing the courses of underground streams and releasing exhalations of "salutary air." Thus, Winthrop argued, the seemingly destructive earthquake actually served to "promote even the growth of vegetables" on the surface of the earth and, somehow, of valuable minerals beneath:

> To sum up all in a word. This is a MIX'D state; in which there is such a variety of purposes, *natural* as well as *moral*, in prosecution at the same time, that there may be nothing, perhaps, in the material world, that is simply and absolutely *evil;*—nothing, but what . . . is, in some or other of its consequences, productive of an over-balance of *good*.[46]

Winthrop was no clergyman, but his *Lecture on Earthquakes*, he privately admitted, was conceived as an assault on the premises of evangelical religion. (In 1738, when Winthrop was appointed Harvard's second Hollis Professor of Mathematics and Natural Philosophy, the college authorities wisely refrained from inquiring into his notoriously heterodox religious principles; five years later he signed the Harvard Testimony against George Whitefield.) What better contribution to the Liberal cause than to posit, in the first place, a universe in which the all-powerful forces of nature were to be thanked for whatever blessings were available, and then, in a New England where discontent with human affairs made Edwards' millenarian vision so compelling, to issue a reminder that this world, albeit far from perfect, was, after all, the best of all possible?

To be sure, Winthrop did not phrase his argument against Calvinism explicitly in terms of undermining the cosmic support of evangelical optimism. That he was not indifferent to the rhetorical implications of his doctrine was borne out, however, by his wrestling with a problem raised by his Panglossism—one which would remain to torture the Liberal mind for half a century. If the operations of nature tended, as Winthrop insisted, to a maximization of the good, then wherein did the earthquake carry a caveat against man's disobedience to Divine instructions? Both Chauncy and Mayhew interpreted the earthquake as an earnest of Divine judgment, and Winthrop, in a long footnote, acknowledged that his theory might be criticized as hostile to religion. But he went on to observe why the "favorable light" which he put on the earthquake could hardly detract seriously from the common sense of God's majesty and justice:

> the terror, which an earthquake never fails to carry with it, will be sufficient to secure the interests of religion, so far as they are to be secured by the influence of fear.[47]

Here, in substance, was what would long serve as the Liberal resolution of the dilemma posed by Winthrop's divesting the earthquake (and all nature) of its sublimer terrors. His theories, it was assumed, were too esoteric—*and should remain so*—to be embraced by the multitude, among whom uncomprehending fear would continue to have its uses. Meanwhile those few capable of Winthrop's wisdom might act in the happy assurance that God would not, and indeed could not, interpose His strong right arm of judgment.

To Winthrop's admirers among the New England illuminati of the 1750's the target of his Harvard lecture was the "Calvinist doctrine" that the earthquake was a "special Providence." In this regard, Winthrop was assumed to be refuting Prince's sermon of 1727. Actually, however, even the original text of Prince's sermon carried no suggestion that an earthquake was evidence of God's ability to manipulate nature for monitory or judicial reasons. Rather Prince had sought out what he took to be the "secondary causes" of earthquakes and ascribed causal agency to God only in the sense that He had ordained the "laws of nature" of which the tremors were a consequence. In the 1755 version Prince, far from insisting on God's immediate intercession in the process of nature, seemed rather to agree with the spokesmen of Liberalism that whatever capacity for judgment nature carried was inherent in its original endowment.

Winthrop had in fact hurled the gauntlet on an issue which was no longer an issue, except perhaps among the less-informed evangelical populace and to a handful of older Calvinist ministers who had never been able to rise to the challenge of Newtonian physics. The doubts or fears of the latter had been given expression by Joseph Morgan, author of the *History of Basaruah,* who in the 1720's warned Cotton Mather against the kind of speculations that informed the latter's *Christian Philosopher.* It was Morgan's opinion that the "unseen Design" of the "modern Philosophy" was to provide a metaphysical support for Arminianism, Arianism, and other heresies. Precisely how this intellectual conspiracy operated was beyond Morgan's comprehension, and in his unreasoning fear he simply condemned any and all investigation of the "internal constitution" of nature, arguing simply that it were better for humanity and for Christianity that the mysterious deeps of nature remain unplumbed. It is revealing, however, that Morgan's last such caveat was issued, not against such doctrine as that expressed in Wollaston's *Religion of Nature,* but in reply to a proposal, published in Franklin's *General Magazine,* which clearly bespoke the yearnings of the pious for irrefutable "scientific" evidence of the majesty of God.[48] Even more revealing was the fact that Morgan's obscurantist preference for a universe accepted on faith was easily overborne, among the Calvinist community, by the intellectual curiosity and courage of a younger generation of ministers, whose interpretation of Newton and of the "laws of nature" even Winthrop was unable, or unwilling, to answer.

The metaphysics which Winthrop chose to ignore was, of course, that which resulted from Edwards' reinterpretation of Newtonian physics. To assess its significance in the context of 1755 it is hardly necessary to recapitulate the whole of Edwards' achievement. It is enough to note that Edwards, as Perry Miller concludes, was "prepared to stake his career" on a "reading of Newton" which held it a "mistaken notion that a cause is what 'has a positive efficiency to produce a thing, or bring it to pass.' " To Edwards what others called a relationship between cause and effect was merely sequence, and one "based upon the 'divine establishment that it shall follow.' "[49] In sum, Edwards argued that the whole universe, being in a sense an idea in the mind of God, contained no independent potency of its own. The atoms of creation impinged on and impelled each other only because God, at each moment, thought it fit that they do so.

Other Calvinists, possibly without reading Newton, also thought the Liberal mind guilty of a "disastrous reading of science." Often they employed an older vocabulary, as when Samuel Davies contemptuously dismissed "the set of little, conceited, smattering philosophers," who, in their interpretation of natural occurrences, reasoned as though the author was not man but the pen that put the words on paper. Though God "makes use of secondary causes and effects," Davies explained,

> yet their efficacy depends upon his superintending influence. It is his hand that sustains the great chain of causes and effects, and his agency pervades and animates the worlds of nature and grace.[50]

More frequently, however, the eighteenth-century Calvinist ministry echoed Edwards in explaining that the *"law or constitution* of nature" by which philosophers sought to account for causal relationships was "only a certain method in which God works," that the law had no "agency of its own" but was "nothing but the continued, immediate efficiency of God."[51] They did not merely refine the Puritan distinction between "primary" and "secondary" causes. Rather they all but obviated the need for such a distinction by making the Deity the efficient cause of all phenomena.

The Calvinist questioned the Liberal cosmography, which seemed to reduce God to the role of an onlooker who, once He had set nature going, thereafter stood aside, no longer willing or able to influence the course of events. But it was not the purpose of Calvinist doctrine to vindicate the possibility of divine intervention in the order of nature, of arbitrary or violent repeal of its "laws." There were, to be sure, apparent exceptions, as when in the 1750's (and again in the 1770's), ministers attempted to console their flocks with the thought that God could and would reverse the earthly "scene" by turning "a single leaf in the volume of his decrees."[52] But such symptoms of flagging confidence represented a resignation from the abiding faith of post-Awakening Calvinism. The God of eighteenth-century evangelical Americans was not, like the one which Urian Oakes had invoked in a rapidly changing Restoration New England, disposed to providential caprice. The Calvinist, no less than the Liberal whose philosophy he despised, discerned a "pattern" in the order of nature as well as that of grace. When Edwards wrote of the "divine establishment" by which certain sequences were ordained or permitted, he was thinking, above all, of the great chain of events that constituted the Work of Redemption. That the universe was pervaded with the divine impulse was not for him a threat to an orderly succession of phenomena. Rather it provided assurance that no power was at work which operated contrary to, or even independently of, God's redeeming Will.

Edwards was probably in advance of his colleagues in granting the whole of the "natural, material world" a career according to "the laws of motion, and the course of nature" so steady and uninterrupted that it might, to the end of time, be predicted by some "very able mathematician."[53] Indeed, he had insisted that natural laws be considered immutable because he did not wish humanity to hinge its hopes for the Work of Redemption on some miraculous divine intercession. If during the terrible earthquake year a handful of Calvinists trifled with archaic philosophies, the lasting consequence of that "dispensation" was, surprisingly enough, not an undermining of Edwards' logic but its enforcement on the evangelical mind.

The late 1750's witnessed the first widespread acceptance of Edwards' notion that the "natural" order was significant chiefly as a type of the spiritual. To those who believed in this "kind of *sympathy*" between the two realms, nothing that took place in nature was primarily a sign of Divine pleasure or displeasure. Thus Samuel Davies, who argued for a "correspondence" between the physical and spiritual orders, did not improve the earthquakes as the materials of a jeremiad. Instead he interpreted the tremors as "*prognostics, or foretokens,*" of some impending occurrence in the "spiritual world"—as, indeed, a harbinger of the millennium. The reorientation of Calvinist thought was also disclosed in Thomas Prince's 1757 reprinting of William Torrey's *Brief Discourse Concerning Futurities*. The argument of this seventeenth-century New England tract was essentially postmillennial, but Torrey had focused on earthquakes as the dramatic attendants, at least, of some Final Conflict and Judgment. But Prince in his preface carefully pointed out that the word "earthquake," as used by Torrey, must not be taken literally, that Torrey had undoubtedly intended it (much as, according to Prince, had St. John) to be a metaphor for "great Changes" in society.[54] The earthquakes of the mid-1750's thus did not undermine Calvinist confidence; they rather sustained it, by confirming the evangelical mind in its use of nature as an emblem. Thereafter even the rudest shocks could be interpreted as the guarantors (and by no means the possible surrogates) of God's supernatural work of spiritual redemption.

III

So emphatic was post-Awakening Calvinist insistence on the universality of Divine influence that its language often bordered on the transcendental. The instance of Edwards is too well known to require comment, but other Calvinists also portrayed nature as alive with Divine energy. Samuel Buell concluded one such depiction with the observation "that all nature is full of God, full of his perpetual, moving, guiding, and over-ruling influence."[55] Such doctrine differed widely, however, from the Emersonian. For the Calvinist entertained no thought of the charming happenstance that Emerson was to associate with what he called the "method of nature." That the divine influence descended "even to the very minutest particles, so as to give them all their variety of modes, properties and relations of every kind," did not serve the Calvinist as an argument for miracles—except, that is, for the ultimate miracle of grace. When the Calvinist contended that God's agency was discernible throughout the "whole universe," his emphasis was on God's "conducting" power, His efficacy in guiding the worlds both of nature and of man toward the fulfillment of His purpose.[56] The Calvinist God perhaps performed His wonders in various ways, but not deviously; and His ways, after all, were no more various than His single end in the creation of the world.

In freeing Liberal religion from the snare in which Winthrop had entrapped it in 1755, William Ellery Channing found it necessary to enter a brief for "miracles." He was arguing expressly against Deism, which had formally sealed what Liberal religion had merely proposed —the exile of God from the operations of nature. But Channing's reasons for preferring a world in which God could transcend the limitations of the laws of nature represented, at bottom, a repudiation of what in Edwardeanism most offended his independent soul. To Channing the worst that could be said of a universe whose operations were ordained was that it stood seemingly indifferent to the happiness of the individual. In its relentless and unsurprising constancy, it displeasingly emphasized the fortunes of the "race." The construction of such a cosmos had been Edwards' achievement more than Paine's. As many of Channing's heirs were never to forget, Edwards' universe, though anything but mechanical, was far too impersonal.

That such was the import of Edwardeanism is perhaps most convincingly disclosed by the fact that his celebrated argument against the "freedom of the will" was set forth in a context of concern for the social salvation of mankind. "Unless God foreknows the future acts of men's wills," Edwards contended,

> all those great things which are foretold both in the Old Testament and the New, concerning the erection, establishment and universal extent of the *kingdom* of the *Messiah,* were predicted and promised while God was in ignorance whether any of these things would come to pass or no, and did but guess at them.[57]

The logic by which Edwards sustained such a predestinarianism is perhaps of less importance than the sense of urgency with which he strove to destroy the Arminian doctrines—doctrines which allowed individuals to be the initiators of action. To accept this possibility was to give the destiny of humanity over to those whose natures were so hopelessly corrupt that they sought to oppose the divine plan.

Though Edwards employed the doctrine of Divine "foreknowledge" to assure the coming of the millennium, he by no means committed Calvinism to the metaphor of the predetermined universal machine—or to the idea, implied thereby, that God was exclusively the first cause in history. His every pronouncement of the 1740's implies a belief that the future, as well as the past, is somehow a cause of the present.[58] But not until the *Freedom of the Will* did he develop a "scientific" vocabulary with which to account for the manner in which the transcendent became apparent. Employing the metaphor of the telescope, and conceiving of temporal relations in terms of distance, he concluded that it was necessary to "suppose future existences some way or another to have influence back, to produce effects beforehand."[59] Edwards' final statement of this proposition appeared, of course, in the *End in Creation*, wherein he declared that God was both "the first author" of humanity's "being and motion" and, at the same time, "the last end, the final term, to which is their ultimate tendency and aim."[60] His Deity was both the efficient and final cause of history—and, indeed, its formal and material cause as well.

Where Calvinists most commonly followed Edwards, however, was in his frequent depiction of the courses of history as a number of "large and long" rivers which "all unite at last, all come to the same issue, disgorging themselves in one into the same great ocean." In using this metaphor, Calvinists anticipated, in a sense, such social Darwinists as William Graham Sumner. "It is vain for men to attempt to turn back the stream," Edwards affirmed, "or put a stay to it."[61] But where Sumner mocked the absurdity of efforts to make the world over in defiance of the mainstream of history, Edwardeans conceived of Providence as a variety of "different streams"—all of them overturning and overturning as humanity was carried toward millennial felicity. "Not one of all the streams fail," Edwards affirmed.[62] The Calvinist Deity—both Alpha and Omega—stood not only at the beginning of history, supplying the waters and dispatching them on their downward course, but at the end of time, as an irresistible center of gravity.

The better part of Calvinist literature on the subject of causation was designed to undermine the smugness of Arminians in ascribing to "instruments" what was due only to the "efficient." It was employed in support of the ultimate truth that every being—whether a spider over a pit or a creature in the hand of God—had "nothing to support its Being, but its producing Cause."[63] But the Calvinist theory of causation was far more than a merely critical doctrine. That God was a motive force extending "to all actions of the creature—to natural, civil, supernatural . . . to all fortuitous and voluntary actions," was not, as Liberals incessantly complained, a hopeless and depressing proposition, but an optimistic and stimulating one.[64] It gave assurance that

77

God did not only "sit at the helm and steer the ship," but, as it were, blew the gale.[65] In Newtonian terms, it implied that God gave direction as well as momentum to the lines of force which He had projected. In practical terms, it promised success to all who moved into the rushing streams of history.

If the Calvinist was a pawn of fate, his fate was to triumph so long as he exerted himself to assist in the accomplishment of God's Will. Meanwhile, such human endeavors as failed to fall in with the Divine plan were doomed to futility. Thus there was profound method in Edwards' seemingly mad refusal, in the *Freedom of the Will,* to give mankind over to what he disparagingly called a "wild contingency." God's irreversible decrees guaranteed that history was not formless, that it had a pattern; they also assured the successful fulfillment of whatever Work He had projected. Unconditional election was a rebuke to the pride of men, but it was, equally importantly, a source of historical optimism:

> I think the Doctrine of Election may be a comfortable Support to exercised Christians, concerning the true Interests of the Kingdom of Christ, at this Day, when there is such fierce Opposition made against the Revival of Religion and Success of the Gospel amongst us, though it is the Doing of the Lord. Bold men set themselves with all their Might against it, and try to blacken it to the World with horrid Falshoods and odious malicious Reflections: But God will carry on his own Designs against all the feeble Attempts of Creatures.[66]

Because the efficacy of their efforts seemed guaranteed by a supreme and superintending Will, pious Americans found it possible to exert themselves on behalf of what was thought to be the ordained destiny of God's people. "God's foreknowledge and decrees," explained Thomas Allen in 1801, were "the most powerful incentives to human endeavor." That Allen, after a lifetime of battles against the "River Gods" of Western Massachusetts, against Tories and the British army, and, finally, against Federalism, could in the same year celebrate the election of Thomas Jefferson, was eloquent testimony to the practical import of Calvinist "fatalism." "If everything was entirely contingent," Allen declared, "this would cut the sinews of all our exertions."[67]

The Republican persuasion of 1800—that mankind would witness the "coming of the Lord's Kingdom with power" only when all power and authority was "considered in the body of the people"—was in a sense the supreme fulfillment of the promise of the Great Awakening.[68] Out of the Awakening emerged a Calvinism which sought not merely to understand the course of history but rather to influence and control it, or at least to add momentum to it. Had the Calvinist mind, in the years after the Awakening, merely responded to events, neither the pace nor the direction of colonial history would have been so strikingly altered in the 1740's. What actually happened is that the Calvinists of America consciously undertook to advance the Work of Redemption.

In 1742 Edwards explained so all who ran might read that the days were "coming, when the saints shall reign on earth, and all dominion and authority shall be given into their hands." But the more remarkable of his propositions, and in all respects the most radical, was one set forth three years earlier in *The History of the Work of Redemption*. A view of the divine plan for redeeming the world, he declared, helped to make history comprehensible. But it was even more valuable as a means of inspiring men to action on behalf of the Kingdom. It was both testimony and summons to God's "friends and subjects"—who, Edwards proclaimed, were "capable of actively falling in with" the divine program and indeed of "promoting it."[69] Thereafter Edwards continued to descant on the "connection of one event with another, and the beautiful order of all things that come to pass," but it was never his sole purpose, in doing so, to explain the mysteries of Providence to the bewildered saints.[70] Nor for other Calvinists was the vision of God "conducting all things" to a predetermined end primarily "calculated to give consolation" to God's people. Its purpose was to assure them of the efficacy of their own endeavors on behalf of the Kingdom.

In its purer version, the Calvinist view of history was a stirring reminder that man's own efforts, God willing and assisting, were the only means of advancing the Kingdom. The Calvinist doctrine of the "means" was of course an inheritance from seventeenth-century Puritanism. But after the Awakening all "the ordinary means of grace," long focused on mere individual conversions, were incorporated into a strategy for advancing the earthly Kingdom. Chief among these was "the preaching of the Gospel," for the Calvinist, as a worker together with the Spirit, conceived progress the task primarily of those capable of communicating ideas.[71] Other devices—such as the establishment of seminaries of learning in order to train Christian ambassadors—were inspired by the belief that preaching was by far the most efficient means of exciting that revival, "far more pure, extensive, and glorious" than the Awakening, which would usher in the millennium.[72] It was generally in the context of hastening the "glorious day" that the eighteenth-century Calvinist best understood the efficacy of the means.

More importantly, perhaps, it was generally in such terms that he offered to his people an explanation of "how means become effectual, either in the natural or moral world." Eleazar Wheelock, for instance, thought of preachers as means for the "enlargement of the church of *God*" in terms both of greater population and of more extensive territory. He was confident, moreover, that either a handful of apostles among the Six Nations or a single evangelist sent to Virginia could somehow bring about the millennium, though the "means, by which this great event is to be brought about, seem to be in themselves but weak, and to bear but a small proportion to the greatness of the effects to be produced by them."[73] The doctrine of "constant providence" on which Wheelock's confidence was based seemed to make greater sense —as it did for a Calvinist chaplain of Revolutionary troops—in a context of "God's perfect scheme of universal government."[74] Its meaning, and the conviction which it carried to Calvinist audiences, was largely dependent on the relevance of the means to the felicity, not of individuals merely, but of the larger Kingdom.

Among the Calvinist means was one which in conception and practice was both consistent with the traditional Calvinist emphasis on the Spirit and yet revealing of the novel grandeur of Calvinist eschatology: the "Concert of Prayer." These quarterly meetings for prayer by the faithful throughout the world are commonly acknowledged to be among the more impressive institutions introduced to western Protestantism by the Awakening. Official credit for the idea is commonly given a group of Scotch Presbyterians associated with the dissenter revivals in and about Cambuslang, but a similar proposal had been broached three years earlier by Edwards in the *Thoughts on the Revival.* The venture was given publicity and meaningful metaphysic, moreover, in Edwards' *Humble Attempt to Promote Explicit Agreement and Visible Union of God's People in Extraordinary Prayer, for the Revival of Religion and the Advancement of Christ's Kingdom on Earth.* Here Edwards outlined a program whereby the people of God might be induced to manifest "a great spirit of prayer," which, as it tended gradually to "spread more and more, and increase to greater degree," would induce a great and general "revival of religion." This in turn would "be the means of awakening others," all of whom would then join again in prayer, until the process culminated in the "work of God's spirit" which would inaugurate "that glorious day of religious revival, and advancement of the church's peace and prosperity"—the millennium.[75]

This argument, though it was sustained by Edwards' faith in the final cause of history, contained within itself the premise that mankind could create within itself the very desires that were to accomplish and constitute the earthly Kingdom. It was, to be sure, the nearly perfect "spirituality" of this means that allowed Edwards to conclude that history would necessarily rise to a crescendo. For the Concert of Prayer represented a re-creation of the conditions of the revival and thus a stepping, as it were, into the clearly discernible mainstream of history.

Yet Edwards' argument for the "fitness" of such a strategy can hardly disguise the truly radical notions embodied in his rationale for the Concert of Prayer. Edwards' crucial premise—that God is "at the command of the prayer of faith and in this respect, as it were, under the power of his people"—was, for all its modifications, a clear declaration that the achievement of millennial society was dependent on the collected will of God's people. Perhaps even more significantly, it depended more on the will of the multitude than on that of their pastors and leaders.

The program which Edwards outlined in the *Humble Attempt* served to chasten the "religion of the closet" which Cotton Mather had promoted in eighteenth-century New England, and even to overbear his own insistence on the value of private prayer and devotion. But despite the encouragement it gave to communal endeavor, the Concert of Prayer never fulfilled the whole of the hopes expressed in Edwards' title. It did, however, seem to induce some of the "happy *revivals* of *religion*" which Edwards expected it to accomplish.[76] The device produced its first apparent fruits in 1757, when the students of the College of New Jersey enjoyed the first revival in American history which "was not begun by the ordinary means of preaching."[77] For many years thereafter the better part of the Calvinist ministry continued to consider the Concert one of the most appropriate instruments for advancing the Kingdom. The fact that so many were in 1759 praying for the millennium gave Robert Smith the "Hope, that the Dawn of the foresaid glorious Day is not far off."[78] In 1763 and 1764 the prayers of the faithful seemed answered in an outpouring of the Spirit that spread through the colonies. The events of the next two decades altered everyone's millenarian calendar and strategy, but by 1795 Calvinists were again "calling the attention of the pious to an expectation of the introduction of this glorious day" by means of the Concert of Prayer.[79] The Congregationalists and many of the Baptists of New England were persuaded that the revival of 1799 was to be "traced, in its beginning, to these seasons for special prayer."[80] But even more significantly, the *Humble Attempt* inspired David Austin in the series of speculations and ventures by which he persuaded himself, and a large part of the dissenter population of New England and the Middle Colonies, to exert themselves on behalf of the election of Jefferson so the millennium might be inaugurated before the beginning of the nineteenth century.[81]

The curious history and consequences of the *Humble Attempt* are testimony to the fact that preaching and prayer were not, in the second half of the eighteenth century, the only Calvinist means of advancing the Work of Redemption. Nor was an outpouring of the Spirit the only goal to which they pressed. Late in 1747, indeed, Edwards himself privately confessed that he did not expect another revival until the children of the Awakening generation were "brought fully on the stage of action."[82] Thereafter he acknowledged that the progress of mankind would be forwarded only by periodic pulsations of the Spirit. Meanwhile, however, Edwards, and his Calvinist colleagues and their people with him, began to seek further instruments for forwarding the Kingdom. Their activities—educational, missionary, military, and political —took them out of the realm of the Spirit into that of Providence, from the "moral order" into what they called the "natural." In doing so, Calvinists diverted their eyes somewhat from the purely spiritual vision of millenarian progress, but whatever their more "practical" strategies for advancing the Kingdom, they remained convinced that each bore an integral relationship to the work of spiritual redemption.

Among the first ventures to which Calvinists turned in the years after the Awakening were missions among the American Indians. These represented, to be sure, something of a renewal of a Puritan endeavor. But Indian missions were given a new emphasis by the Awakening, and they subsequently became, at times, the most prominent of the many devices by which Calvinism sought to accomplish the millennium. By 1770 Calvinist spokesmen were looking on most events, however seemingly disconnected, as "openings in Providence" auguring success to the missionary enterprise.[83] Clearly one consequence of the Awakening had been a turning of American eyes westward—for the first time, securely, since the days of Edward Johnson's *Wonder-Working Providence*. The Indian missions were one result of this new spatial dimension in Calvinist millenarianism, and they also contributed to its increasing emphasis in eighteenth-century American thought.

The victory of New England's pious crusaders at Cape Breton in 1745 was surprisingly enough not interpreted by Calvinists as primarily a guarantee of security from eastern invasion. Rather it seemed to offer the opportunity for a spreading of the Kingdom throughout the continent, until God "extends his empire from the *Eastern* to the *Western* Sea, and from the River of Canada to the Ends of *America*."[84] Particularly after 1763 there arose considerable confusion in the Calvinist mind as to whether the Kingdom was to grow by a Christianizing of the heathens who had so long sat in darkness or through what Horace Bushnell was to call the outpopulating power of the Christian people. On this question Calvinists divided, first with their Liberal opponents and, when the Connecticut New Lights involved themselves in negotiation for the Wyoming lands, among themselves. In the decade of the Revolution, however, Calvinists found it unnecessary to clarify their position. They found it enough to be persuaded that for the Kingdom to come "to its perfection in America," it would have to "extend wider and wider, until it has reached the Pacific Ocean."[85] Once convinced that the lines of force projected by their God pointed in a westerly direction, Calvinists instinctively chose those "means" which seemed to move the Kingdom toward the Pacific and even on the passage to India.

As late as 1850, quite a few Americans were yet unwilling to believe that Daniel Webster had correctly divined an oceanbound Republic as the *whole* meaning of the image on the buckler of Achilles. In the eighteenth century they were even more certain that the westward course of empire did not fully embody the destiny of God's people. They assumed an integral relationship between the extension of the Kingdom and the flourishing of the Spirit, not merely among the Indians, but, even more importantly, among their white benefactors as well. Edwards' biography of Brainerd, the most famous of the Indian missionaries, developed the logical, aesthetic, and typological consistency of missions, revivals, and the Concert of Prayer. In 1764, likewise, Samuel Buell concluded his narrative of the Long Island "awakening" by relating it to the first success of the Calvinist efforts to "extend the Kingdom of our enthroned *Saviour* among the Indians."[86] To be sure, it was not until the 1830's that evangelical Americans were able to offer a full "explanation" of what they called "The Reflex Influence of Missions," but some such theory was already in splendid practice in the less self-conscious years of the eighteenth century.*[87] And unlike his successors, who at last allowed the waste places to dictate the meaning of Christian history, the earlier Calvinist, for all his glances westward, managed to keep fairly bright the happier vision of Jonathan Edwards by remembering that the virgin continent was not simply a desert to be reclaimed but an intimation of the spiritual promise and potentiality of those who had settled it.

Though the imperial wars, like the Indian missions, provided additional "means" for advancing the Work of Redemption, the Calvinist mind managed to integrate these providential occurrences into their earlier millenarian theory. The military success in "the affair of Cape Breton" was in Calvinist thinking inherently related to the "remarkable appearances of a spirit of prayer" among God's New England people in 1745. To this prayer Thomas Prince attributed the victory

---

* The crux of the latter argument was implicit in the Calvinist notion that God fostered "piety" by arranging and disposing the drama of history, thereby "raising and continuing" certain *Ideas* in the human mind. The *Humble Attempt* represented an effort to attain such results by human strategy, but missions and the prospect of settling the former French domains stretched Edwards' thinking—by "extension" as it were—and introduced what might be called "the geographic sublime" into Calvinist thinking.

at Louisburg, and from it Edwards derived additional inspiration for the mechanics of the Concert of Prayer.[88] The perspective of Calvinism was that of Gilbert Tennent, who, explicating the variety of instruments used by Nehemiah ("a type of Christ") in a comparable situation, concluded with this observation:

> From the aforesaid *Example,* may not every impartial Eye behold the sweetest *Harmony* and *Connection,* between *spiritual* and *outward* Means, between *Prayer, Watching,* a *dependence upon* GOD, and the Use of *Martial Weapons* . . .?[89]

Later in the century Calvinists would find it less easy to discern the harmony of the various instruments they employed for encouraging the Work of Redemption. Not that they ever doubted a common tendency, but the inherent connections among numerous Calvinist strategies grew increasingly obscure, until, at last, each "outward means" took on a seeming efficacy, and an independent life, of its own. Yet Tennent's conviction, uttered during the War of the Spanish Succession, remained in some degree the very heart of the Calvinist persuasion. Through years in which Calvinist policy, and Calvinist preaching, took the people of the colonies through war and social revolution, the evangelical mind preserved its faith that each of these endeavors was somehow consistent—aesthetically, if in no other way—with the design of stimulating a work of the Spirit.

IV

By far the rudest challenge to the seemingly consistent Calvinist historical vision came with the outbreak of the Seven Years' War. It was during these years that Jonathan Parsons, Edwards' friend and student, confessed the "greatest difficulty, in fixing the year of *Daniel's* prophecy."[90] By which he signified that the millenarian calendar published in the Awakening years seemed no longer consistent with the apparent course of human events. Like other Calvinists, Parsons was certain that God's "eternal Plan of Government" was not subject to repeal or amendment. But the Calvinist mind was always sufficiently inductive in method to allow that the particulars of the Divine decrees could be known only as they were revealed in "actual Administration." As Samuel Davies observed on July 4, 1755,

> Our readiest Way to know what he intended to do from Everlasting, is to enquire what he actually does in Time: & here we find obvious Facts revealed to us, or within the Sphere of human Observation.[91]

The observable facts of the 1750's were clear enough; the problem lay in their interpretation and in relating them to earlier revelations. Parsons' confusion bespoke the sense, prevalent among Calvinists after

1755, of an incongruity between the workings of Providence in the imperial war and the direction and dynamic of history discerned in the Great Awakening. Surprisingly, a Calvinism for which the earthquakes held little intellectual terror was at times confounded by the imperial struggle.

The perplexity had little to do with the fluctuating course of the Seven Years' War. Rather it derived from the very effort to identify the opposition of English and French arms with the "grand decisive conflict between the Lamb and the beast" on which apocalyptic thought had traditionally focused.[92] An underlying source of difficulty was the mixed Calvinist view of Great Britain. Presumably the bulwark of the Reformation against Popery, England had recently, it seemed, shown itself provokingly hostile to God. Not to mention its abounding vices and heresies, had not Britain in the wars of the 1740's conspicuously failed to acknowledge the dependence of its armies on Divine favor? Perhaps, suggested Aaron Burr on the fast day of 1755, Great Britain was preparing, not for imperial ascendancy, but for a fall. After all, the courses of empires "spring from *unforeseen* Causes, and turn on *such Incidents,* as the Sagacity of the wisest Politicians could not discover, nor the greatest human Power prevent!"[93] Burr's observations take on additional significance against a background of considerable evidence that the pious mind saw the imperial war as incidental, even irrelevant, to the central theme of history. It was not simply that the populace began to murmur a prophecy that the millennium might somehow be anticipated by *French* victory, nor even that pamphlets were published, during the war, inveighing against the King of England for having assumed the "popish Title" of Defender of the Faith.[94] What was revealed was not so much anti-British sentiment in the colonies as that the evangelical mind had grown indifferent to and weary with the archaic battle lines of the Reformation. The notion of an Armageddon between Protestants and "Papists" was one of the dogmas of a stormy past that proved inadequate to a stormier present.

In the 1740's Edwards had all but removed the prospect of Armageddon from Calvinist millennial theory. In the *Humble Attempt* he set himself to a lengthy refutation of the notion that "before the fulfilment of the promises relating to the church's latter-day glory, there must come a most terrible time, a time of extreme suffering and dreadful persecution of the church of Christ; wherein *Satan* and *Antichrist* are to obtain their greatest victory."[95] His argument against this "notion" or "hypothesis" was phrased, among other ways, as a demonstration that the so-called "slaying of the witnesses" had already taken place, in the Dark Ages before the Reformation, and that the downfall of the Papacy was to be dated from the era of Luther and Calvin. His belief that the Papacy had been already "much brought down" as an effective power, that it was, as it were, withering away, left no possibility of a final dramatic confrontation with a Catholic Antichrist.[96] Nonetheless, he continued to look forward to a moment in history when the Pope would be "utterly overthrown" and, in the 1740's, offered a traditional interpretation of the relevance of the French War to the progress of the Work of Redemption.[97]

Moreover, he never explicitly rebuked the concern for papal power which, in the 1750's, disposed Americans to speculate anew on the pouring out of the sixth vial. When the Seven Years' War opened, the Calvinist ministry was disposed to hinge the whole course of history on a battle with enemies whom they described as "the French King, the Pope, and the Devil."[98] Samuel Davies advised the Presbyterians of Virginia that the contest could, by its outcome, disclose whether "the period for the slaying of the witnesses is just coming" or whether "the time is past, and the time is just come" for the beginning of the millennium.[99] Still, like most of the Calvinist ministry, Davies found it necessary to be ingenious, even arbitrary, in relating the events of the French War, typologically or otherwise, to his millennial vision. Well before Wolfe's victory over Montcalm, Davies flatly declared that he would "live and die in the unshaken belief" that the "glorious days" were "not very remote."[100] His conviction had little to do with the battles then raging, which he referred to chiefly by way of noting the (to him) remarkable fact that much of the fighting had taken place in the *western* reaches of Pennsylvania. What chiefly distinguished Davies' wartime utterances—other than the clear evidence they carried of how difficult it was to arouse evangelical Virginians against the French—was his unabashed certainty that the course of history was to be decided in America.

Davies' tortured response to the French War was symptomatic of a prevailing Calvinist conviction that God's American people had more important concerns than a warfare against a distant Pope. Indeed such an Armageddon seemed nearly irrelevant to what had been discerned, in the Great Awakening, as the mainstream of history. It was not without considerable intellectual turning and winding, however, that Calvinism was restored, in the 1750's, to a clear vision of the essential continuity of history. In 1756 Aaron Burr spoke before the Synod of New York—for what must have been close to four hours—on the subject of the millennium. Noting the developments which challenged the formulas of the preceding decade, Burr reluctantly acknowledged his disagreement with his father-in-law on the matter of the "slaying of the witnesses." Yet even as Burr suggested that a period of trouble yet faced the people of God, he concluded that from all appearances they were "in the Close of this dark *Night,* and that the Morning Cometh."[101] Two years later—the very year of Edwards' death— Joseph Bellamy, in his sermon *The Millennium,* took the steps that finally purged Calvinism of those vestiges of pre-Awakening thought which, in the 1750's, had distorted its perspective on history.

To clarify the tendency of history Bellamy found it necessary to repudiate outright the theory that the historical drama of the ages and of his age turned on a duel between Catholics and Protestants. He scorned the glosses on "six-hundred and sixty-six" which Christian divines had concocted in previous centuries, and, in doing so, relegated the Pope to a stature roughly equal to that of the "muslims" and other unbelievers who hindered the Work of Redemption. He likewise unequivocally dismissed as irrelevant all "endeavors to fix the precise time when the twelve hundred and sixty years of Antichrist's reign" had begun or would end.[102] They were irrelevant because, as Bellamy reminded the people of Connecticut, they were, after all, engaged in a far more important war—the progress of the Work of Redemption depended on a "glorious triumph" over enemies of the Kingdom much nearer home.

How Bellamy wielded his doctrines in the Revolutionary decade is part of the tale, to be unfolded later, of the manner in which the streams of Providence and grace released by the Awakening were turned, finally, against domestic enemies of the people of God. It was not indeed until the late 1790's that evangelical Americans finally disabused themselves of even a remnant of the thought that the headquarters of the Antichrist were "across the Atlantic."[103] Then the surviving establishment of church and state were identified as "*mystery* Babylon the great," and the funding system, the national bank, and the Federalist clergy were seen to be the dragon, the beast, and the false prophet. The spirit of 1800, whether expressed in the great revivals on the Kentucky frontier, or in the East as political enthusiasm in support of Jefferson and Edwards' grandson, rose and throve—not on enmity to the Pope but on "indignation against the old aristocratic spirit."[104]

At last, it seemed, the "large and long" rivers which Edwards had depicted in 1739 had found their "common issue." Some had met impediments, and others had temporarily left their courses. And perhaps it was not quite true, as Edwards had proclaimed, that "not one of all the streams fails." For in the sixty years since the Great Awakening an inherited anti-Catholicism had been exorcised from the evangelical mind as inconsistent with the dynamic and the meaning of the American revival. The outmoded theory was disposed of because post-Awakening Americans could not tolerate being consigned, in effect, to an incidental role in the Work of Redemption, much less to being subjected to European contingencies over which they seemingly had little control. But the old view of Armageddon was most of all intolerable because it denied what was perhaps *the* lesson of the revival: that the forces of evil, no less than the will needed to overcome them, were most readily discoverable in the society of the New World itself.

The Great Awakening had itself seemed for a moment nearly the final conflict in the eyes of the awakened. So evident were the bitter animosities released by the revival that an Anglican, writing to the Secretary of the Society for the Propagation of the Gospel in Foreign Parts, allowed that the "year of Enthusiasm," 1741, might be "as memorable as was 1692 for witchcraft for the converted cry out upon the unregenerated, as the afflicted did then upon the poor innocent wretches that unjustly suffered."[105] Quickly the battle lines were drawn, and both converts and the evangelical ministry were disposed to consider the chief enemies of the Kingdom those who were "raging" against the Awakening. The New Side Presbyterians needed no "further Witnesses" to the identity of Antichrist than the "furious Opposition to the Work of God in the Land." Both Finley and Edwards went far toward identifying opposition to the Awakening as the "unpardonable sin against the Holy Ghost," and, by doing so, impressed their critics as intending to draw up the populace of the colonies in battle array. In the pro-revivalists' view of history, the state of affairs in 1741 was, according to critics, placed on "a Level with the State of Things in the Days of Christ," and thus designed "to make those, who are (if you will) Enemies to the present Work, and violent Opposers of it, Sinners to the same Degree of Guilt, as were those, who opposed Jesus Christ himself." By design or otherwise, it appeared, the revivalists worked to make "the holy *Furioso*'s of the present Day hate, for God's Sake, all that are not in *their* wild Scheme."[106] At the height of the Awakening the strident censoriousness of the revival leaders sounded very much like a trumpet call to battle.

Jonathan Edwards clearly participated in such attitudes and encouraged the people of God to look on the revival as a holy war. Whereas in 1739 he had been more eclectic in his characterization of "Satan and all his instruments," two years later Edwards expressly defined the archenemies of the Work of Redemption as those who would "maliciously oppose and reproach" the revival. But by 1742 Edwards was working to suppress the antagonism that he as well as others had helped to arouse. In fact, even in 1741 Edwards wanted to restrain the impetuosity of the awakened—or at least to temper their vehemence of expression. Were the evil of those who opposed the revival "ten times so great as it is," he insisted, "it would not be best to say so much about it," nor call for "fire from heaven, when the Samaritans oppose us." His precise intentions in the 1740's are not always easy to discover; in one breath he would remind the people of God that "it becomes Christians to be like lambs," in the next, that they must be "wise as serpents."[107] Whether, then, his strictures against violence of word or deed, in the *Religious Affections,* were prudent counsel or deep conviction cannot be decided with absolute assurance. Obviously Edwards disclosed a temperamental aversion to violence, especially when he had reason to regret his own impetuous arrogance. But it is also clear that he was responding to the pride and pathos inherent in the partisans of the revival calling for heavenly judgment on those whom they judged the enemies of the Kingdom. Divine fire was simply not to be expected, and the complacent self-satisfaction of the awakened provided neither the kind of weapon necessary to turn their judgment to account, nor the discipline that would make Armageddon anything but a rout of mere unaided virtue.

In a broader perspective Edwards' denial of a need for conflict seems a strategy for dispelling the fears still lingering from the pre-Awakening era. The *Humble Attempt* was an effort to strengthen the hands of those on whom Edwards knew he must count to forward the Work of Redemption. He did so by encouraging the people, at a moment in history which might otherwise have seemed discouraging, to exercise their wills. The idea that a "slaying of the witnesses" was yet to come, he argued, would have to be dismissed because, quite simply, it was *practically* "of such hurtful tendency" to the cause of the Kingdom:

> If persons expect no other, than that the more the glorious times of Christ's kingdom are hastened, the sooner will come this dreadful time, wherein the generality of God's people must suffer so extremely, and the church of Christ be almost extinguished, and blotted out from under heaven; how can it be otherwise, than a great damp to their hope, their courage and activity, in praying for, and reaching after the speedy introduction of those glorious promised times? As long as this opinion be retained, it will undoubtedly ever have this unhappy influence on the minds of those that wish well to Zion . . . So that this notion tends to discourage all earnest prayer in the church of God for that glorious coming of Christ's kingdom, till it be actually come; and that is to hinder its ever being at all.[108]

In the context of the 1740's, Edwards' declaration that a devastation of the godly was not to be expected served to instill with confident hope those on whose efforts the coming of the Kingdom depended. It would, Edwards believed, "be a great discouragement to the labours of nations, of pious magistrates and divines, to endeavour to advance Christ's kingdom, if they understood it was not to be advanced." More significantly, the hope of irreversible progress—or, more precisely, "the keeping alive such hopes"—had, as Edwards saw it, "a tendency to enliven all piety and religion in the general, amongst God's people."[109] Such a vision of unimpeded victory was for him the guarantor, because the inspiration, of the popular desires which alone could fulfill the promise of history.

It seems not to have been Edwards' purpose, at least in the years after the celebrated Enfield sermon, to frighten men into endeavors on behalf of the coming Kingdom by threatening to deprive them of its benefits. His observation in the *Thoughts,* that the magistrates and other "great men" of New England ought to assist in the Work of Redemption if they wished a share in its honors, probably carried an implicit threat. But by the late 1740's he clearly preferred to woo men into the Kingdom with the prospect of the millennium, the expectation of which should, he thought, be enough to "strongly excite" both pastors and people to be "such as God had promised to bless" in His day of earthly triumph. That Edwards was to acknowledge the failure of such methods is attested by the fact that, within two years of his dismissal from Northampton, he was reminding the Synod of New York that the world is a place of bitter conflict between "Christ's little children" and the followers of the Devil, "the chief enemy of God and Christ."[110] The emphasis on Satan and the indifference to the historical Antichrist were, of course, underscored in the next years by the polemical bitterness of Edwards' essays, *Will* and *Original Sin.* It was on the basis of the *Original Sin,* particularly, that Joseph Bellamy restored the prospect of a millennium inaugurated by an embattled host. As its captain he would lead the Church Militant to victories which seemingly overshadowed the achievements of Edwards as shepherd of the flock. But it should not be forgotten that it was Edwards, who having in the 1740's taught the pious of the colonies to behave like Christians, had given them the time and the will to acquire something of the stamina which Bellamy was able to call upon.

Throughout the second half of the eighteenth century the thought of Calvinism showed an impatience to return to the battle lines of 1742. Even in the *Humble Attempt,* Edwards quietly explained that though the spirit of prayer and the revival *might* finally spread "till the awakening reaches those that are in the *highest station,*" the redeeming Spirit would necessarily first express itself in the lower reaches of society.[111] Such a suggestion as to where the greater number of saints were enrolled and enrollable reinforced, even as it sought to suppress, the sense of social cleavage aroused by the Awakening. Though in subsequent years ideas and events did mute momentarily the animosities of those who, in the Awakening, had taken such delight in conceiving their local enemies as "particular objects of divine displeasure,"[112] neither the literature nor the history of the decades after the revival can be wholly understood except as reflecting, in some manner, a fairly constant sense of social tension.

Even the missionary enterprise, which Chauncy no less than Edwards came to support, betrayed the antagonisms of the age. It was not merely that Liberals and Calvinists disagreed, and violently, over how missions were to be conducted, or by whom and for what ultimate purpose. Rather more significant is the fact that critics of the revival saw Indian missions as a means of turning the "fiery zeal" of the awakeners away from established institutions and to the "good use" of undermining the French hold on tribal allegiances.[113] While the Calvinist by no means consciously acquiesced in such blatantly diversionary attitudes, it is clear that his commitment to the missionary enterprise was a symptom of his inability to resolve satisfactorily the internal contradictions of colonial culture.

Such also was the case of the wars with France, which the awakened in the 1740's saw, and perhaps rightly so, as something of a red herring designed to blur the battle lines of the revival. Yet in 1754 Whitefield came to Boston to preach, not on the necessity of the New Birth, but on the "imminent Gallic menace."[114] He was awarded, on this occasion, a degree from the very Harvard which but ten years earlier had denounced him as a socially dangerous demagogue. This is not, however, to say that his cooperation, or that of any Calvinist leader, was consciously purchased by the colonial authorities. It required no such prompting for many Calvinists—among them some once suspicious even of Whitefield's blessing of the Louisburg fleet—to be caught up in the "crusade" against the French. Notable among them was James Davenport, the erstwhile contemner of iniquitous minions of Satan in high places in the colonies, who in 1755 expressed the belief that a British victory at Crown Point could "bring on the latter-day glory" by causing the Pope's reign to "come to its final period!"[115] And in the 1770's this history was recapitulated when George III was identified as the Antichrist of Revelation. Though ever conscious of being divided among themselves, Americans were seldom able to resist any opportunity to postpone a final reckoning.

Such a pattern of diversion and reunion is as much a part of the story of the pre-Revolutionary American mind as the schism in colonial society opened by the Awakening. Still, it must be emphasized that any consensus, however fascinating the process by which it was reached, was something of an interlude and a point of departure for a new division along the lines of 1740. Moreover, for forty years after the Awakening, Americans of all persuasions were supremely aware of a potential for discord within colonial society. Whatever the efforts of colonial preachers—Liberal and Calvinist—to move or mollify the people of the colonies, they ordered their thoughts and chose their words in the knowledge that the revival impulse had threatened the colonies, politically as well as intellectually, with revolution.

From its first eruption the revival spirit of eighteenth-century America had judged and even threatened the standing order. The New Milford awakened of the 1720's, for instance, had disparaged and challenged the magistracy of Connecticut as "the BEAST." In the Great Awakening there were widespread verbal assaults on the occupants of the higher places in colonial society. One of the most outspoken New England evangelicals was accused of "speaking evil of Dignities—declaring that the Leaders and Rulers of this People were Opposers of the glorious Work of God in the Land."[116] In fact they were, largely because they were persuaded that the revival was hostile to all established institutions, and this even before any overt expressions of seditious sentiment. To the rational mind the mere words, "Work of God," and "millennium," seemed designed to "foment Rebellion against Authority."[117] The first colonial criticism of Whitefield, that of Alexander Garden, contained a reminder of what enthusiasm had once led to: "Look back to the *Oliverian* Days—what Ruin and Desolation *such Pretenders* brought upon the Kingdom!" Nor were Anglicans the only Americans to sense social and political danger in the emotions of the revival. In defending Harvard's testimony against Whitefield, Professor Edward Wigglesworth warned that enthusiasm could not be dismissed as "a pretty harmless Thing," for had it not given rise to the Fifth Monarchy insurgency![118]

At the very center of Liberal thought through the end of the century was a conviction that the evangelical scheme in whatever form contained a revolutionary potential. The Liberal version of Christian and American history was conceived, and perfected, as a conscious rejoinder to the ominous millenarianism of Edwards' *Thoughts on the Revival*. In his *Seasonable Thoughts* Chauncy took direct aim at Edwards for his stupidity in suggesting to "the people" that anything like a "third stage" of the Work of Redemption was possible. In Germany, Chauncy warned, at the beginning of the Reformation, "the Imagination of the Multitude" was "fired with this Notion," and

> they were soon perswaded, that the Saints were now to reign on Earth, and the Dominion to be given into their Hands: And it was under this influence of this vain Conceit, (in which they were strengthened by *Visions, Raptures,* and *Revelations*) that they took up *Arms* against the lawful Authority.

Of what the American multitude were in fact persuaded was not apparently to the point, so far as Chauncy was concerned. Since enthusiasts had once at Münster sought to "make all things common, *wives* as well as *goods*," the New England revival must also be a leveling enterprise.[119] In the circumstances rational religion emerged as most favorable, not to morality merely, but to the preservation of property rights and political stability.

By 1750 the New Light clergy had the reputation of being the "foremost in propagating the Principles of Sedition." Edwards, by virtue of his observations on the "charity" practiced in the Apostolic Church, was seemingly revealed as the grand leveler of Christian history.[120] Yet it was hardly the case that the revival or those who promoted the Work of Redemption were intent on seizing governments or despoiling fortunes. Actually, the Calvinist ministry insisted that only the reprobate sought "riches and Honors"—a "dull pursuit," Tennent affirmed, by comparison to the saint's efforts to advance the Kingdom of Christ.[121] Undoubtedly evangelical rhetoric helped to stimulate an animus within the populace against "great men," but for this, Liberal tactics—especially their oppression of the revival—must share the blame. But to the Calvinist ministry it seemed absurd to compare the awakened of the eighteenth century with the peasant revolutionaries of the Reformation. To understand the revival, Edwards advised Chauncy, one must look not at "external, accidental circumstance," but at "substances." So viewed, the Awakening would appear quite different from any of the leveling, seditious uprisings of the past, and indeed from all previous enthusiasms whatever.[122]

To Calvinists the Awakening was a revival of pure Christianity, and the crusade it launched was the perfection of God's age-old plan of redemption. Yet there may have been an unintended wisdom to Chauncy's thrust, made ironically enough as part of his effort to dispose of Calvinist millenarianism, that the "work of the SPIRIT is different now from what it was in the first days of Christianity."[123] The "spirit" at work in 1740 and after was indeed totally and essentially different from any before active on the face of the earth. To be sure, some of the avatars of the revival spirit sought to identify the Awakening with ancient causes and inherited slogans. For example, Alexander Craighead called on the Presbyterian awakened to renew the Solemn League and Covenant. But the Log College men refused to join him and, when Craighead complained that they "feared men" and lacked the courage needed to assail Episcopacy anew, answered that Craighead mistook the nature of the "cause." And indeed Craighead probably did, most particularly in thinking that the new spirit did not summon men "to leave their proper Stations in the World, such as, for Persons to run through the Country."[124] To the American revivalist, the cause was such that its goals could be achieved only through attitudes and institutions appropriate to the promise of the New World.

As waves of enthusiasm rolled against the parish hierarchies of colonial America, the true quality of the revival's millenarian aspirations was dramatically revealed. Not liberty, nor even equality, was, as it turned out, the essence of the Awakening, but fraternity. In the course of the eighteenth century many Calvinists were to be shocked as they saw the single end toward which all the streams of Providence and grace tended. But the spirit aroused in 1740 proved to be that of American nationalism.

III

THE BEAUTY AND GOOD TENDENCY OF UNION

W H A T made it possible for post-Awakening Calvinists to cling so tenaciously to a belief in the coming Kingdom was the discernible tendency of American history. Their faith was grounded, ultimately, on the fact that at nearly every point in the late eighteenth century events and circumstances seemed to demonstrate that the American people were achieving social goals conformable to the promise of the Awakening. The hope of the Awakening was for a more "affectionate union" of Christians, and toward unity Calvinists pressed, partly as an effective defense against local and provincial oppression, in part also as the most effective organization for those who would advance the Kingdom of Christ throughout the world. But the appeal of unity was far more than that of mere utility: "union," as Edwards explained, "is not only beautiful, but *profitable* too."[1] The revival and the evangelical impulse pressed to the goal of a more beautiful social order—which meant, in the New World, a union of Americans, freed from the covenant relationships of the parochial past and united by the love which God's American children bore for one another.

At first there was little more than a conviction that the clearest glimpse of Zion's glory would come first to the western hemisphere. Whitefield arrived in the colonies reciting George Herbert's stanzas about religion standing on tip-toe, waiting to leap to the American strand. But it was not until 1741 that it was first hinted that the revival revealed America's special role in millenarian history. In a preface to Jonathan Dickinson's *True Scripture-Doctrine,* Thomas Foxcroft, after hailing the "smiling Scene" of the day of grace, allowed that he did not know

> what Constructions may be put upon it; but I can't forbear, on this Occasion, transcribing some remarkable Passages, of a prophetick Aspect.[2]

What followed was the fulsome rhetoric of Cotton Mather's *Theopolis Americana,* in which it had been announced that one day America would be the seat of the Lord's Kingdom, a New Jerusalem whose streets were paved with gold.

A less ornate but hardly less compelling image of the American future emerged from Edwards' *Thoughts on the Revival.* Here Edwards authoritatively announced, on the basis of the Awakening experience, "The latter-day glory, is probably to begin in America." Edwards' argument depended on the metaphor of Scripture prophecy—particularly the passage in which it was predicted that "the Sun of righteousness" was to "rise in the west, contrary to the course of things in the old heavens and earth." But he also offered a typological reading of economic geography:

> it is probable that will come to pass in spirituals, which has taken place in temporals, with respect to America; that whereas, till of late, the world was supplied with its silver, and gold, and earthly treasures from the old continent, now it is supplied chiefly from the new; so the course of things in spiritual respects will be in like manner turned.

His theme, essentially, was that the Old World had had its chance, wasted it in seeking to destroy the Church, and that, concurrently with the Reformation, God had opened the "new world" to mankind "in order to make way for the introduction of the church's latter-day glory —which is to have its first seat in, and is to take its rise from, that new world."[3] In a sense Edwards' belief represented a revival of the Puritan idea of New England as a "city on a hill," but in fact it marked a radical departure in the thinking of American Protestantism. America was no longer committed to a merely partial role, however exemplary, in the history of the Church, but rather to the proposition, eventually ridiculed in *Roderick Hudson* by Henry James, that Northampton— the site of the first revival—was the spiritual center of Christendom.

Behind this conviction lay, among other things, the Calvinist image of Europe, and of Great Britain in particular. Their England was not the Augustan splendor which dazzled the eyes of the colonial Anglican ministry, nor even the Whiggish society triumphant in the Revolution of 1688 and so admired by provincials like Jonathan Mayhew. Rather from Doddridge, from Whitefield, and from an English pietist volume entitled *Britain's Remembrancer* (which John Witherspoon was still citing at the beginning of the Revolution)[4] they derived a view of an England as degenerate as that which Thomas Hooker had deserted in the 1630's. It was Edwards' opinion, and that of every Calvinist after him, that if Britain were in fact the bulwark of Protestantism, there was little hope for a triumph of the spirit in the European hemisphere. It is not "agreeable to God's manner," Edwards affirmed in the *Thoughts,* to "introduce a new and more excellent state of his church" in a region which had grown old and corrupt. "When God is about to turn the world into a paradise," he declared in one of the most significant assertions of the Awakening, he begins "in the wilderness."[5] America was, in a sense, a *tabula rasa* whereon the Holy Spirit might etch its new ideas.

It took many years for all the implications of Edwards' prediction of the spiritual greatness of America to be revealed, but some were disclosed in the "awakening" that occurred in 1763-64. Far more extensive than historians of the colonial church generally allow, this revival clarified for many Americans the tendency of a history badly confused by the French and Indian War. Samuel Buell, instrument of one of the more fruitful branches of the "Glory of the Lord's Work" in these years, not only relegated news of spiritual progress in Europe to a footnote but with almost Whitmanesque inclusiveness reported how the revival, which began with a "marvellous work of God's grace" in Massachusetts, spread through Connecticut and Long Island, and from there to New Jersey, Pennsylvania, and the South. "So extensive" did it seem that Buell, wondering if the "glorious Day" did not indeed "already begin to dawn," insisted that in any case it could not be far off. Although Buell's hopes were frustrated, what became known as the "outpouring of the Holy Spirit (Anno 1764)" sustained Isaac Backus through the 1770's in a belief that he could "see the day approaching!"[6] Sporadic revivals in the same years in New England and Virginia led not a few Calvinists to conclude, on the very eve of the battle of Lexington, that the millennium was impending.

On the 17th of January, 1776, Samuel Sherwood, nephew and student of Aaron Burr, and a friend of Joseph Bellamy, delivered a sermon in which he "improved" the final verses of the twelfth chapter of the Book of Revelation—the "flight of the woman into the wilderness." Sherwood's conclusion was that his text, "in its most natural, genuine construction, contains as full and absolute promise of this land, to the Christian Church as to the Jewish of the land of Canaan." Sherwood argued in terms of the "prophecies," of the "plan of God's providence so far open to view," and His "past and present dispensations," including the recent turmoils in the British Empire. His history was largely a tale of the successes of the people of God, who had departed from England in the seventeenth century, in thereafter preserving and reviving vital piety in the New World. His prophecy was little more than a spiritual version of the concept, hardly unknown to other commentators in that year of grace, of the westward course of empire. But when Sherwood turned finally to disposing of all commentators, European or colonial, who had ever surmised that the millennium would begin elsewhere than in the western world, he revealed the peculiar significance of his "natural" construction of Scripture. They had erred, he observed, because the "word WILDERNESS" suggested to their "delicate, but inattentive minds" something "frightful and shocking." In brief, the doubters had kept their eyes too long on the "civilized" world and thus had failed to appreciate the true glories of the American strand.[7] When all was said and done, the guiding light of Calvinism was a delight in the New World itself—a delight which redefined not merely the errand of the Puritans, but Calvinism's own sense of history, in terms of the wilderness to which Europeans had come.

The prevailing image of the New World among the Liberal opponents of the revival may be gathered from the fact that Charles Chauncy, in belittling Edwards' suggestion that the millennium would begin in America, reached back to the lamentations of Increase Mather before the students of Harvard College to support his point that it was "the Judgment of very learned Men, that, in the glorious Times promised to the Church on Earth, AMERICA will be HELL."[8] In the following decades a few Liberal clergymen revised their estimate of the future, but they never altered their belief that America—civilization its first need, barbarism its first danger—was no likely capital for a New Jerusalem. A few Old Lights, to be sure, held that the true city of Jerusalem had been founded in seventeenth-century New England. But in defining the perfection of the Kingdom of God in terms of the "privileges and enjoyments, civil and sacred," inherited from the Puritan fathers, they too inevitably committed themselves to a pessimistic view of American history.[9] Like Increase Mather, they were destined to cry Ichabod over the fallen glories of their plantations; for by seeking to preserve the society and institutions of pre-Awakening America they were clinging to a foredoomed program for American development.

The blueprint for the millennial age in the years after the Awakening was not the Cambridge nor the Saybrook Platform but Edwards' *Work of Redemption*. So accurately did it delineate the course which

American society would take that it might be called a scenario for American social and political history in the last half of the eighteenth century. The Calvinists' vision of the future, which they never drastically altered and to which they pressed with ever-apparent success, was a corollary of Edwards' description of the nature of the world during the thousand or more years of the prosperity and joy of the church of God:

> Then shall all the world be united in one amiable society. All nations, in all parts of the world, on every side of the globe, shall then be knit together in sweet harmony. All parts of God's church shall assist and promote the spiritual good of one another. A communication shall then be upheld between all parts of the world to that end; and the art of navigation, which is now applied so much to favour men's covetousness and pride, and is used so much by wicked debauched men, shall then be consecrated to God, and applied to holy uses.[10]

As the last sentence suggests, Edwards was looking forward to a change in the purposes of tradesmen, and a general alteration in the employment of the world's goods. His vision reflected, to some degree, a conviction that "great cities" were the "places where profaneness, sensuality, and debauchery commonly prevail to the greatest degree."[11] The Calvinist critique of urban life—always more piercing than, say, the murmurs of "Windsor Forest" that echoed through not merely poems like William Livingston's *Philosophic Solitude* but programs such as Jared Eliot's—grew increasingly strident in the course of the century. Often it was expressed in a hostility not only to foreign trade but to cityfolk generally. Eventually such a Calvinist animus would evolve into the Embargo and Henry Clay's American System. Yet the initial concern of Calvinism was not the failure of Bostonians and Philadelphians—nor even tidewater planters and Connecticut "River Gods"— to consecrate their wealth and energies. Nor was it, surely, the creation of an economically independent North America. In 1739 Edwards was envisioning no less than a restoration of Christendom to a unity it had been losing since the opening of the western hemisphere to the mercantile powers of Europe.

Still, Edwards' image of the good society stood in marked judgment on the erratic and often ruthless individualism, the divisions and contentions, of colonial American society. When Edwards informed his Northampton congregation that the saints would one day "all be one society," or that they would be "united together without any schism," he was implicitly remarking on all the local animosities which the Awakening but temporarily numbed.[12] Out of his reaction to local conditions, however, emerged a vision of the future which looked to far more than a return to the kind of social solidarity that had presumably characterized the communities of seventeenth-century Massachusetts and Connecticut. Slowly, but nonetheless surely, the vision of the *Work of Redemption* was transformed into an ideal of continental union. Throughout the last half of the century Edwards and other Calvinists would seek to temper the passions dividing man from man in the towns and parishes of the colonies. They would strive also to promote the unity of American and European Christians. But as the Calvinist mind amply proved whenever an appropriate occasion arose, both local and international schism was tolerable, even to be encouraged, so long as it brought within nearer view the union of God's people in America.

Though Calvinism did eventually embrace a policy of the millennium, as it were, in one country, it never wholly lost sight of the ultimate aim of Edwardean history. Not only the *Work of Redemption,* but Calvinist thought generally, placed American history in the broadest of historical perspectives. Unlike those who wielded the jeremiad, and unlike even Solomon Stoddard, Edwards himself conceived of land disputes and other local grievances as simply the most recent manifestations of a "discord and confusion" that had plagued mankind since the Fall. Edwards' history predicated a prelapsarian age when "all was in excellent order, peace, and beautiful harmony." With the withdrawal of the influences of the Holy Spirit came "the succession of a state of the most odious and dreadful confusion." These appalling conditions persisted into the eighteenth century, but in 1735 came an outpouring of the Spirit in sufficient strength to make it equally evident that God would, and could, bring about a restoration of the beautiful and felicitous conditions which pertained before the Fall. Just as the Calvinist God, in the Work of Creation, had formed "a confused chaos into a beautiful world," so in the Work of Redemption would He bring beauty and harmony into the social arrangements of mankind.[13]

The larger purpose of American Calvinism was preserved from 1740 even to 1801, when evangelical Americans were first able to proclaim that in the New World, at least, the Work of Redemption was nearly complete. In the latter year James Sloan, a leader of the Democratic Party in New Jersey, and soon to enter the national Congress as one of the first representatives of evangelical America in the new government saluted the election of Jefferson as a triumph of American "union." His accents suggest how far was Calvinism, even at this date, from seeking merely an amelioration of the conditions of American life. Calling on his "beloved brethren" to press on in the Work of Redemption until "Liberty, Peace, and Love, pervade the Universe,"

Sloan entered on his peroration by urging the Republicans of New Jersey to

> thank GOD, and take courage, and in full faith and confidence that He that hath helped us hitherto, will support our righteous cause, and crown it with success; let us unitedly determine to persevere in this Christian warfare . . . until the beautiful order and harmony of the Creation of GOD be restored as it was in the beginning, when the morning stars sang together, and all the Sons of GOD shouted for joy![14]

Wherever the Calvinist beliefs had been upheld with similar tenacity, wars with France and England, Stamp Acts and tea taxes, Anglican Bishops and Sedition Laws had been but incidents in a sublime historical epic that saw the larger task of Calvinism the same at its end as at its beginning.

The instruments which Calvinists selected to aid God in the achievement of this purpose led them into a variety of programs for social meliorism and even social revolution. But the ultimate goal to which they aspired was a society which, in the whole of its character and tendencies, would be as visibly excellent as the Calvinist Deity Himself. "A time approaches," Edwards declared in the *Humble Attempt,* "when this whole great society shall appear in glorious beauty." It would appear as " 'the perfection of beauty, an eternal excellency,' " and—in improvement on Scripture language—"shining with a reflection of the glory of Jehovah risen upon it, which shall be attractive and ravishing to all."[15] Whatever the other characteristics of the millennium, it would be "a time of *excellent order*" in the arrangements of mankind: "All the world shall then be as one church, one orderly, regular, beautiful society."[16] Something of the "mystery" of post-Awakening Calvinist behavior was attributable to a commitment to social goals which were ultimately aesthetic—to a desire for a society as indescribable in the terms of Liberal discourse as the essential beauty of the Calvinist God.

In Calvinist eyes, the beauty of history itself was contingent on the degree and velocity of approach to the good society. Indeed, it is quite fair to say that the burden of Edwardean theology was to guarantee the collective happiness of mankind. Although Edwards envisioned the elect, in the moment of God's fulfilled purpose, as being "one with God, brought home to him, centering most perfectly, as it were swallowed up in him," that particular moment, he insisted, could and would never come to pass.[17] The reason, as he revealed again and again in both his private and his public eschatological speculations, was a necessity that the saints continue to see and be seen. They must so persevere, Edwards indicated, in order that the events at the end of the world might bring "a great accession of happiness to the saints, who shall behold them."[18] Their happiness required a perceived relationship, not merely between the saints and the Deity, but even more significantly, among the saints themselves.*[19] The Edwardean Deity was not an undifferentiated Being—for the very reason that, as Edwards explained in his *Notes on the Mind,* "in a being that is absolutely without any plurality, there cannot be excellency."[20]

The "happy moment" of the saint's entrance into heaven supposed a perception, not in truth of the Divine beauty, but of the "sweet harmony" pertaining among the members of the body of Christ. So too was the moment of God's last purpose, a resurrection day distinguished by the "happiness" of the saints "in the society of each other." At the end of the world, both God and His elect creatures would be supremely happy, but only because all could rejoice in seeing "so great a multitude all united, all perfectly holy, all full of natural love, all fellow-citizens, all brethren!"[21] The "most perfect union" with God to which the elected tended in Edwards' sublime vision was in fact imperfect—and designedly so, as a guarantor of a more perfect union among the saints.

The millennium was and remained for most Calvinists but a type of God's end in the creation of the world. Edwards, of course, believed it "God's manner to keep things always progressive" that there was ever "a more perfect state" yet to come. Other Calvinists likewise refused to posit earthly social perfection as the final cause of history; Bellamy, for instance, once proposed that when the millennium was achieved on earth there would still be work for the saints in extending its blessings to other planets. A transcendent end and aim stood always in judgment on whatever "whole general assembly" might, in earthly terms, be otherwise deemed perfect.[22] The attitude attested to a wise unwillingness to deprive the evangelical impulse of its driving force.

Nevertheless, by the 1770's Calvinist spokesmen were all but announcing that the "glory and pleasures" of the good society on earth could provide the full equivalent, in terms of "pure felicity, and exalted beauty," of the Deity. Even in the previous thirty years the God

---

* The fundamental Edwardean proposition was his "universal definition of Excellency" as *"The Consent of Being to Being,"* or, in other words, the love of the "spiritual" beings for each other. "The more the Consent is, and the more extensive," he added, "the greater is the Excellency." In simplest terms this meant that the greatest happiness was derived from a perception of the mutual love of all the spiritual beings in the universe: "happiness strictly consists in the perception of these three things; of the consent of being, to its own being; of its own consent to being, and of being's consent to being." The first of these ingredients of happiness was, of course, the "inner harmony" of the saint; the second, however, was a perception of his love to all men, and the third, of the love of all men for each other.

of Calvinism (or, more accurately, the Christ) had been, in effect, the *"Paradise* of Beauty and Pleasure" into which the Spirit was expected to change "this disordered Earth."[23] For whoever in a Calvinist auditory panted after holy joy was always reminded, most emphatically perhaps by Edwards himself, that the happiness of the earthly Kingdom bore "a great resemblance" to what might be enjoyed thereafter.[24] Whoever aspired to deliverance "from all that obstructs and interrupts the sight and sense of divine glories" was eventually confronted with a beatific vision that was not the face of God, but a beauteous society.[25] The Calvinist pursuit of happiness was, almost by definition, a quest for the great community.

Had Edwards elaborated on his observation that "God himself is in effect being in general,"[26] the radical import of his theology might have been better understood. As it is, the primacy of a social vision in his thinking is most readily inferred from his response to what he called "The Beauty of the World." Edwards' appreciation of the beauties of nature has often been celebrated by historians of American literature, but few have observed the extent to which each of his so-called "idylls" was an explicit commentary on how the beauty "peculiar to natural things" shadowed forth the Divine intention to overcome the moral ugliness of human society.[27] Edwards turned to nature, not for refuge from the still, sad music of humanity, but because he believed that God had devised a world of natural beauty—where "one thing sweetly harmonizes with another"—to provide Christ's ambassadors and their people with a constant reminder and example of His desire that the spiritual world also be placed in "excellent order and harmony."[28]

The universe, according to Edwards, was filled with such "excellent" objects, all of them "images" or "shadows" of the Divine: "the Son of God created the world for this very end, to communicate Himself in an image of His own excellency." This created universe consisted of the "spiritual world," the world of "beings" whose beauty was an "image" of the Divine excellency, and the "natural world," or that realm of creation which, having none of the qualities of mind which distinguished angels, saints, and men, embodied only "a sort of shadow, or glimpse" of the moral beauty of the Godhead.[29] In his early sermons, Edwards defined the "highest excellency" in terms which were of course to remain explicit Calvinist doctrine:

The beauty of trees, plants and flowers, with which God has bespangled the face of the earth is delightsome, the beautiful frame of the body of men, especially in its perfection is astonishing, the beauty of the moon and stars, is wonderful, the beauty of the highest heavens, is transcendent, the excellency of angels and the saints in light, is very glorious, but it is all darkness in comparison of the higher glories and beauties of the Creator of all.[30]

Yet in his own private observations, he developed a theory of the "highest and primary beauty" which, when it finally emerged in the *True Virtue,* made not God but men—"beings that have *perception* and *will*"—the noblest object of Christian regard. "Natural beauty" remained an excellency of a "secondary and inferior kind," but delightsome because in it might be discerned something of the "peculiar beauty of spiritual and moral beings, which are the highest and first part of the universal system, for whose sake all the rest has existence." The "reason, or at least one reason," Edwards declared in the *True Virtue,* why God had made the physical world

beautiful and grateful to those intelligent beings that perceive it probably is, that there is in it some image of the true, spiritual, original beauty . . . some image of the consent of mind, of the different members of a society or system of intelligent beings, sweetly united in benevolent agreement of heart.[31]

In substance, the God of Jonathan Edwards was a supremely excellent Christian commonwealth.

The beauties of architecture and music, as well as nature, offered Edwards glimpses of "a society of so many perceiving beings sweetly agreeing together."[32] His successors, most of them less sensitive than he to the beauties of the world, were more disposed to seek excellency in Scripture, which Bellamy, for one, considered "the only sure guide we poor mortals have." Yet for Bellamy too the "visible creation" was a "designed manifestation" of the "invisible glories of the invisible God" and of the special glory of "by far the chief of all his works"— "the work of redemption." The degree to which other Calvinists retained the doctrinal framework of Edwardeanism would probably have been enough to commit them to his vision even in the absence of the kind of response to the natural world for which Edwards was preeminently distinguished in the eighteenth century. All adhered to the premise that "God's works are uniform," that some contained "in miniature the nature of the whole," and that all if properly seen blazoned forth "strong characters of His Divine Excellencies."[33] And all arrived privately as well as publicly at an approximation of the Edwardean definition of excellency, one dependent ultimately on their conviction that the "spiritual and eternal world" typified by the "material and natural" was, as Edwards had so succinctly described it, none other than "the city of God."[34]

Although it was among Edwardeans that typology chiefly throve in the eighteenth century, the millenarianism of Tennent and Davies was also ultimately dependent on a similar reading of nature. Davies actually composed a splendid series of poems—which constitute a missing link, as it were, between the meditations of Edward Taylor and the lyrics of Philip Freneau—in which this "fair harmonious world" was seen as a devised type of social felicity.[35] The implications of such thinking become evident with the merest glance at the manner in which the relationship between the natural world and the world of man was developed in evangelical political discourse.

In 1773 a somewhat obscure Massachusetts dissenter, one Ebenezer Chaplin, delivered for the benefit of the people of God a sermon in which he analyzed the nature of civil society. Though preoccupied at the time with the latest efforts of the Liberal Massachusetts authorities to harrass the dissenter population, Chaplin felt called upon, in the circumstances brought about by the recent activities of the British ministry and Parliament, to discuss the duties and obligations of rulers and citizens. His sermon was among the two or three most significant articulations of pre-Revolutionary Calvinist political theory. The underlying premise of Chaplin's sermon was peculiarly Edwardean. The people of God must never forget, he insisted, that forms of government and their administration are matters of relative unimportance. What is important is that the purpose of all institutions, and the desire of all good men, ever be a society "harmonizing together, according to the pattern God has set us in the works of nature."[36]

In New England especially the belief that the temporal and carnal was typical of things spiritual served as the foundation of a dynamic social faith. But it was in New Jersey that David Austin, looking on his farm and that of Jonathan Dayton—and at the same time considering all things "visible on the earth" as "emblems or shadows"—was led to think of the "sublime subject" of the Work of Redemption and thence to conceive a program for inaugurating the millennium that eventually took him, and perhaps a hundred thousand others, out of the Federalist Party into the "national camp" of Thomas Jefferson.[37] The nearly endemic intellectual disease of eighteenth-century America —as witnessed by the continual popularity of Flavel's *Husbandry Spiritualized*—was a desire to find sermons in, and under, stones.[38] After the Awakening, however, the evangelical mind was not disposed to see individual objects as "special providences," nor even to use them, as had Cotton Mather in his *Agricola*, as "preachers" of a variety of Christian messages. To Calvinists such "spiritualizing" betrayed, in the words of Perry Miller, "a capriciousness that used God's creation for incidental ornaments, that read meanings into things which were no more than what the fancy pretended they might mean."[39] Typology instead assumed a single and consistent meaning in the works of God, a pattern prophetic of things spiritual to come. The post-Awakening Calvinist, in contemplating nature, saw God's larger purpose, and its promised fulfillment.

In sharp contrast to the Calvinist use of nature was the Liberals' employment of the physical universe chiefly as a source of metaphor for adorning a discourse or pointing a tale. They employed the solar system, and even Newtonian physics, as something of an analogue of what they considered wise and reasonable arrangements in society and state. Seeing the heavenly orbs as components of an ingenious universal mechanism, as "numerous worlds" moving through the sky with remarkable "regular motion,"[40] they decided this to be clear evidence of the need for a similar regular order in the political and social arrangements of mankind. During the Awakening, the itinerating evangelists were thus compared to comets: "the Manner of their Motion is such, that they may give a most dreadful Shock to some Globe, that shall happen to come in their Way." In 1742 Isaac Stiles, who was considered the most accomplished orator among the Connecticut Old Lights, applied the metaphor to politics as well as to ecclesiastical affairs. The "changelings" of the revival—those "given to change"— were likened to

> the tail of some baleful, baneful, red-hot Comet. [They] kindle a destroying Fire and make a rueful Conflagration wherever they come. And were there enough such Phaetons, they would soon set the World on Fire in good earnest, not in fiction but in fact.[41]

In later years rationalist spokesmen drew less vivid pictures, in which the fiery properties of comets gave way to the equally displeasing vision of derangements in the universal machine. "As in the solar system," an election preacher intoned, so in human affairs; if the "grand design" of government is to be carried out, every man must "keep the line of his own particular department," for "every eccentric motion will introduce disorder and be productive of mischief."[42] Sustained by what they took to be Newton's meaning, Liberals were always prepared to insist that whenever men "fly off" from the "common centre of gravity" and take "an eccentric course, the coercion of law should be used, to check their irregular motions."[43] Wherefore for Liberals the construction of a constitution for Massachusetts, or for a Federal Union, was a task comparable to devising an orrery. For partisans of the legal scheme down through the years of Rufus Choate and the younger Theophilus Parsons, it seemed that checks and balances, and above all regulation and restraint, were necessary characteristics of the social machine.

Calvinists were certain that Liberals failed to understand that the Newtonian system was not mechanical nor its harmony impressed from without. The Calvinist interpretation of Newton, quite simply, was that the gravity inherent in the atoms of creation was a type of the love which alone could hold the beings of the spiritual world together. One of Edwards' many private, experimental efforts to elicit the divine meaning from nature produced this observation:

> The whole material universe is preserved by gravity or attraction, or the mutual tendency of all bodies to each other. One part of the universe is hereby made beneficial to another; the beauty, harmony, and order, regular progress, life and motion, and in short all the well-being of the whole frame depends on it. This is a type of love or charity in the spiritual world.[44]

Here is disclosed, not merely the ultimate differences between Liberals and Calvinists, but the larger import of the distinction Miller has drawn between the "trope," which, as he explained, concerns the "outward thing," and the "type" which is "the shadow or the image" of what "spiritual reality consists in itself."[45]

Calvinists also used nature metaphorically in order to convey the divine meaning to the minds of their hearers, but they sought—for the most part successfully—to distinguish rhetorical device from the search for Divine meaning. Perhaps the Liberal too saw meaning in the whirling orbs, but he was surely aware of the degree to which he spoke poetry when he invoked the world machine in political discourse. But Edwards, when he declared that "the sweet harmony between the various parts of the Universe, is only an image of mutual love,"[46] firmly believed that he was proclaiming the matter-of-fact result of a scientific, experimental confrontation with the divinity of divinity.

Throughout the century Calvinists continued to dwell on the physical propensity for union among the atoms of the universe—perhaps because Edwards' majestic hymn to the Church Triumphant (in the *End in Creation*) and its "infinite increase of nearness and union to God" was phrased in obviously Newtonian terms[47]—and, in this phenomenon, to find meanings for mankind. "Universal love," explained Samuel Eusebius McCorkle in 1795, is not merely the moral law of the 133rd Psalm; it is

> a natural law. There is a striking resemblance between that attractive influence, which binds the natural world, and that general love of benevolence which should bind the moral world together.

Among North Carolina Presbyterians appalled by the divisions and factions of the Federalist era, no less than in Northampton during the

Awakening, Calvinists knew that men had to be "full of love to one another" if mankind were to manifest the harmony of the physical creation.[48]

The ultimate tendency of Calvinist thought was away from what in the eighteenth century was called "mechanical philosophy" and toward the new science of "chymistry" for an explanation of the "affinities" they were certain inhered in the particles of matter. Nevertheless, it was in Edwards' first youthful encounter with the Newtonian universe that America's most compelling social vision, and the longest-lived, was born. For out of his observations—made long before the Awakening—that the relationship among the atoms of creation was an "image of love in all the parts of a Society, united by sweet consent and charity of heart" arose the Edwardean definition of *True Virtue*.[49] From this definition in turn arose the Calvinist insistence that *"Love"* was not merely "agreeable to" but was, indeed, the "natural law" which inhered "in the nature of things."[50]

Well before the publication of the *True Virtue,* to be sure, other Calvinists, defining love as an *"affectus unionis,"* were struggling toward the same formulation. Like the English Puritans Samuel Ward and John Preston, and Thomas Hooker and Cotton Mather in America, they sought to explain the essence of religion in terms of the properties of a magnet: "Love," explained Gilbert Tennent, "is a Kind of Loadstone."[51] Throughout the eighteenth century a favorite Calvinist account of the effects of love was one drawn from gravitation —seen, though, in more homely terms than Newton had intended. Love, according to Eleazar Wheelock, causes men to "flow" toward the beloved object "as freely, and as much without any force put upon themselves, as the waters of a full river flow down to their appointed place."[52] Even Edwards, who only occasionally used the "tendency of bodies one to another by mutual attraction" as a metaphor for the relationship of holy beings, was also fond of the image of falling water. Most commonly, however, he employed a figure general to all Calvinists: "union of heart."[53]

Underlying all this imagery, however, and indeed giving it its special meaning, was the fact that it was no mere rhetoric, but an attempt to communicate what Calvinists were fully persuaded was the very nature of things. The Calvinist message was not dependent on the kind of ingenuity to which Samuel Sewall, for instance, had been driven for a demonstration that the millennium might begin in America. Nature could no longer be manipulated—nor surely tortured as an immense cipher for the New England Way. Once Edwards had revealed the inner constitution of the universe, Calvinists, whatever their language, saw nature in a new and different light. It was now a simple, but sublime, Divine declaration, impervious to the arbitrary tampering of even the cleverest human minds, that God's people were to establish a more perfect union.

II

For the better part of a century the most urgent task of evangelical Americans, as they understood it, was to induce in humanity what Poe was to call "an appetite for Unity among the Atoms." In the years between the Awakening and the Revolution their endeavors focused on what they understood to be the happy effects of an outpouring of the Spirit. To defenders of the standing order, the revival spirit seemed "subversive of *peace, discipline,* and *government,*" and their efforts, in the same years, were directed toward discouragement and suppression of emotional religion. It was the proven consequence of a revival, the Liberals charged, and the clear intention of the revivalists, to "make a gap to let in a flood of confusion and disorder."[54] Rather, the avowed Calvinist goal was to cement all men in the bonds of mutual affection. To them it seemed "all the better" if "holy Love and Joy" arose, on earth, "even to celestial Flame and Rapture."[55] Such sharply divergent opinions derived not merely from the different meanings which Liberals and Calvinists gave "order" and "union," but from their contrasting views of the effects of grace on the human personality.

Not only Calvinist metaphysics but Calvinist psychology sustained the belief in the great community. Its first premise was a rejection— as against the variety of mysticisms and perfectionisms spawned in the Awakening—of the notion that grace enters the human mind as a direct infusion of the Divine essence.[56] As Edwards characterized grace in the *Religious Affections,* the Spirit entered the personality to be "united to the faculties of the soul."[57] To appreciate the significance of this definition of sainthood, it is necessary to touch briefly on Edwards' conception of the faculties of the human mind. The faculties, according to Edwards (who here largely followed Locke), were two: the understanding, the soul's "perceiving faculty," and the will, or that faculty "by which the soul chooses."[58] In his treatise *Will,* from which, along with the *Affections,* Calvinism derived its psychological axioms, Edwards described these two faculties as so organically related that one could speak of the entire personality in terms of its seat and center: the "heart."[59] Edwards' admission in his discussion of the faculties that "language is here somewhat imperfect"*[60] would be

---

* To the end of his days Chauncy professed bewilderment not only at this simplified psychology but at the Edwardean characterization of grace as "what some metaphysicians call a new simple idea." All Liberals, for that matter, charged Calvinists with fantastically presuming that some "new faculty" was added to the human personality in regeneration, while in fact Calvinists argued that man received no "new

repeated by other Calvinists. But it is evident that in the years after the Awakening, the "heart" came to take precedence over the "understanding" in the Calvinist conception of holiness. When Joseph Bellamy explained that in regeneration "the temper and frame of our hearts become like God's," he thought he had given all the necessary characteristics of sainthood.[61] Even for Edwards, holiness came to imply less a sight of the highest excellence and more a heart to love accordingly.

Edwardean psychology was a designed rebuke to those who, in the ecstasies of the Awakening, conceived joyful apprehension of God as the substance of holiness. Against any such antinomian notions Edwards insisted that holiness "consists not only in contemplation, and a mere passive enjoyment, but very much in action."[62] The course of Calvinism after the half-century can be gauged by its changing definition of holy action, and by the degree to which the will finally occupied the center of Calvinist attention. In the beginning, however, what Calvinism meant by the soul's action was that heartfelt expression or exercise of the mind which they called love. To a certain degree Calvinists conceived of love as an exercise of both the understanding and the will: "As to the general *Nature* of *Love*," Gilbert Tennent explained, "it is Two-fold, namely, of *Benevolence* and *Complacency*."[63] According to Edwards in the *True Virtue*, however, complacency was not truly love, or at least it was a love of an inferior order to that of benevolence. Complacency, which Edwards defined as "no other than a delight in beauty," was a function of the understanding; it was internal and subjective, the soul's "joy."[64] Benevolence was an extension of the personality outward, toward and terminating in the object of regard, seeking, like the attraction between physical bodies, to diminish the "distance" between a spiritual being and its "Beloved Object."[65] Not the joy of the understanding, but the heart's love, was the antitype of the gravity that preserved the universe in beautiful harmony; "Love, the great Cement of the Universe," Davies styled it in one of his poems, and it was likewise to Calvinists the cement of society.[66] And that which inspired "communion," or the "union of heart with others," was for Calvinists, far more than any mere delight, the "essence" of sainthood.[67]

There was a subtle shift in the purport of Edwardeanism when

---

faculties, but all his faculties are renewed." Yet Chauncy was sufficiently familiar with the metaphysician to whom Edwards referred to use whole paragraphs from Book IV, Chapter XIX, Section 8 of Locke's *Understanding* in his 1745 caveat against enthusiasm, and by 1760 the entire Liberal clergy were citing Locke and lauding his psychology as fundamental to any understanding of the human mind. When Liberals embraced the Scottish metaphysic, however, they of course accepted the longer catalogue of faculties postulated by this new scholasticism.

benevolence replaced the divine and supernatural light of the Awakening as the distinguishing quality of sainthood. Of course, the two were never separable, simply because Edwards believed that man must necessarily love whatever, "extant in the view or apprehension of the understanding," was perceived as the greatest apparent good—whatever, that is, seemed to provide or promise the greatest complacence or delight. "The choice of the mind never departs from that which, at that time, and with respect to the direct and immediate objects of that decision of the mind, appears most agreeable and pleasing, all things considered."[68] The fundamental Calvinist psychological postulate was the total integrity of the personality. The heart or will of man, Jonathan Parsons affirmed, "depends on his understanding, and can not move or chuse independently of it."[69] Just as the unregenerate mind could not perceive the excellence of "spiritual and divine things," so was it incapable of "choosing" them. "But when a man is regenerated, he chuses, and cannot but chuse spiritual objects, because he sees their glory and excellency."[70]

In the Edwardean dictionary, these concepts were further refined: "choice" was limited to the "consent of Minds toward other things," and only the "Consent of Minds toward other Minds" was precisely and properly defined as love or benevolence.[71] Love was an exercise of the mind only toward other spiritual creatures—those perceivably bearing something of the "true image" of the delightful Divine excellence. It was a question to Edwards, and remained one to other Calvinists, whether unregenerate men, mere "shadows" of the Divine beauty, could be truly loved. In theory it was only toward other saints, men with "the moral image and likeness of God in the temper of their hearts," that the heart of the saint was properly "drawn."[72] More importantly, the saint was loved only partly for his own beauty, and the greater part for his "union and consent with the great whole."[73] This was, according to Edwards, his "general beauty," which he defined as "that by which a thing appears beautiful when viewed most perfectly, comprehensively, and universally" with regard to all "its connexions with every thing to which it stands related."[74] True Christian love then was a response, not to the moral excellence of individuals, but to the excellent harmonies among them. The greater the number of saints in cordial union, of course, the greater the delight of the individual saint in perceiving their beauty, and the greater his loving participation in their union. And thus the very working of the Spirit was a guarantor of the great community, for the personality of the regenerate man would be such that he could not help being drawn into loving and lovely saintly communion.

The importance of love to the thought of the eighteenth century may be gathered from Edwards' observation that it was "generally allowed, not only by Christian divines, but by the more considerable Deists, that virtue most essentially consists in love."[75] What distinguished Edwardeanism from the moral system of his contemporaries was his definition of virtue as "love to being in general"—a definition which made heartfelt love of the beautiful society and active longing after its establishment the essence and test for Calvinists of the regenerate personality. To be sure, only in the *Two Dissertations* did Edwards bring his metaphysics and epistomology into sublime fusion. Many of his utterances, particularly those in which he identifies love or benevolence with "that great virtue of charity which is so much insisted on throughout the New Testament under the name of *agape*," appear indifferent to the larger beauty in which Christian love is to find its appropriate object. By proclaiming love as the "primary and radical virtue" to which all virtue was related and could, in fact, be reduced, other Calvinists likewise seemed to divert their eyes away from the nature of divine beauty to its essence.[76] They were emphasizing, in short, that which held together the atoms of the spiritual world to the seeming neglect of the larger harmonies into which their mutual attractions would draw them.

To appreciate the significance of such emphasis one need only compare Edwards' many hymns to light with the incantatory cadences of Samuel Davies' famous sermon, "God is Love":

> *God is love;* not only lovely and loving, but love itself; pure unmixed love, nothing but love; love in his nature and his operations; the object, source, and quintessence of all love.[77]

The accent here is on the Divine love, not the Divine beauty, and the contrast is that between a Calvinism rejoicing in the beatific vision and one preoccupied with that which held together the constituent elements of the holy communion.

Still, it cannot be said that Calvinists, as such, ever became wholly ignorant of the larger pattern that Edwards had set before them. "When supreme Love to God, and undissembled Affection to one another reign," declared Aaron Burr in 1756, "it will produce universal Harmony."[78] What can be said is that after Edwards the whole of the Calvinist message was seldom held together so perfectly in a single statement. Of all Edwards' heirs, Joseph Bellamy was probably most successful in preserving the complete vision. In 1762 he pictured for the Connecticut legislature the happy effects of the Spirit:

> And, O, behold how they love one another! Look through a province; they are united in one faith, and love and live as brethren. Yea, look through a kingdom, yea look from kingdom to kingdom;

there are no sects, no parties, no divisions . . . and we would all become brethren, united together in the most cordial love.[79]

But Bellamy introduced his sermon with an explanation that such love assumed delight in, and consent to, nothing less than the "beauty and harmony" of "the whole intellectual system."[80] It was not so much an emphasis on one or the other aspects of Edwardeanism that brought about the death of Calvinism, as a concurrent redrawing of both its psychology and its metaphysics. So long as the essence of the Calvinist God remained love, and so long as sainthood continued to mean an essential likeness to such a God, Calvinism preserved the substance of Edwards' vision, a definition of sainthood in terms that allowed no man to rest content short of all mankind's being drawn into beautiful union.

A leading instrument of the downfall of Awakening Calvinism was Samuel Hopkins, who both recast Edwards' psychology and redrew his beatific vision.*[81] Still, generally applicable to the Calvinists of pre-Revolutionary America were William Ellery Channing's recollections of Hopkins, who, he declared,

took refuge from the present state of things in the millennium. The millennium was his chosen ground. If any subject possessed him above all others, I suppose it to have been this. The millennium was

* Until Samuel Hopkins revived scholasticism in the New England theology, it was characteristic of all Calvinists to refuse to consider the Divine nature divisible save "for the sake of gaining an easy admission for the subject, into the minds of mankind." This insistence that there were "no distinctions" between the faculties, attributes, or perfections of the Divine personality was inevitably accompanied by an assertion that all the Divine "attributes and perfections, are none other than different modifications of pure love or benevolence." The essential character of God, Nathaniel Niles explained, "is called by different names," but "properly speaking, all the moral attributes of God are nothing but LOVE, called by various names, on account of the various appearances it makes as exercised towards various objects, under various circumstances, and on various occasions." Before the Revolution, regeneration consisted in the apprehension of such an "amiable" Deity, but in the 1790's Hopkins, having concluded that the human mind was "infinitely unequal to an adequate, comprehensive view of God," argued that it was possible for a true saint to "have a more affecting, pleasing sense" of some "than of other perfections." Once it was admitted that a "discerning sensibility of any thing in God, is seeing him," Calvinism was on the way to the kind of separate consideration of God's "power, knowledge, goodness, wisdom, justice, and righteousness" which had once seemed so offensive in the sermons of Jonathan Mayhew. The redivision of the divine personality (a corollary, of course, of the reintroduction of a kind of faculty psychology into the New England theology) allowed certain of the self-appointed heirs of Edwards to all but forget what Edwards, Davies, and other pre-Revolutionary divines had posited as the essence of divine holiness. "God is love," Davies had insisted. "There is an unfathomable depth in this concise laconic sentence, which even the penetration of an angel's mind cannot reach." The logic of Emmons and the younger Edwards simply fell short of this insight.

more than a belief to him. It had the freshness of visible things. He was at home in it. His book on the subject has an air of reality, as if written from observation. He describes the habits and customs of the millennium as one familiar with them.

Channing found it both heart-warming and tolerably amusing that the last notable survivor of the Awakening intelligentsia enjoyed his millennial vision "not a whit less because it was his own creation." To the greatest of American quietists it seemed obvious that Hopkins had lived "in a region of imagination, feeding on visions of a holiness and a happiness which are to make earth all but heaven."[82] Perhaps by the time Channing was privileged to know Hopkins, the Calvinist vision of the third stage of the Work of Redemption was something of a utopian escape from a confusing present. But for Edwards and Bellamy, as indeed for those latter-day Calvinists who in 1798 reluctantly broke with Hopkins over what they considered his Federalist-inspired postponement of the millennium to the end of the nineteenth century, the image of impending earthly felicity was no idle reverie.

Indeed, the key to the social dynamic of Calvinism was the certainty and confidence with which the ministry were able to discern and convey the outlines of a more perfect community that contrasted sharply with the "darkness, discord, and dissent" of the society in which they found themselves. Calvinist preachers insisted on the *reality* of the eschatological visions they portrayed. A "lively and eloquent description of many pleasant things that attend the state of the blessed in heaven" was not to be taken as an entertainment of the imagination—"a romantic description of the pleasantness of fairy land, or the like"—but rather as an effort to describe what in fact existed, though seen by mortals as through a glass darkly.[83] What made it real, of course, was a conviction that earthly society, as then organized, was most unreal: "the present state of things is not lasting; it is confusion."[84] An ability to give form and content to heaven, to the resurrection of the just, was one secret—perhaps the secret—of Calvinists' amazing rhetorical power,*[85] but some of their noblest literary achievements were depictions of the earthly Kingdom of Christ. "Nor let any think this a description of a fictitious state of things," Bellamy exclaimed in 1762 as he provided the worthies of Connecticut with "lively pictures" of millennial bliss. Similarly, a Calvinist preacher was equally sure that there was nothing "romantic" about his portrait

---

* When Edwards preached his concluding sermons on the *Work of Redemption*, the people of Northampton were convinced that the meetinghouse floor was about to open and prepare the stage for the resurrection. When Bellamy "lay open the glories of Heaven" the people of Connecticut actively sensed the "joys of the paradise of God."

of the heaven on earth that seemed impending in 1774.[86] And though evangelical preachers dared not confess it, it was by setting the beauties of Christian union before the eyes of their congregations that they hoped to remove "the interposing cloud," not simply from the eyes of the saints, but from American society itself.[87] An eloquent depiction of social beauty was their means of inducing harmonious union in the affairs of men.

The crucial premises of Calvinist rhetoric were disclosed in Edwards' argument for a concert of prayer. The central section of the *Humble Attempt*—that in which Edwards explains "The Beauty and Good Tendency of Such Union" in prayer—opens with a celebration of the beauties of union:

> How *condecent,* how *beautiful,* and of *good tendency* would it be, for multitudes of christians, in various parts of the world, by *explicit agreement,* to unite in such prayer as is proposed to us. *Union* is one of the most *amiable* things that pertains to human society; yea, it is one of the most beautiful and happy things on earth, which indeed makes earth most like heaven . . . A *civil* union, or an harmonious agreement among men in the management of their secular concerns, is amiable; but much more a pious union, and sweet agreement in the great business for which man was created, even the business of religion; the life and soul of which is LOVE.

These accents, which would continue their hold on the Calvinist mind for another half century, reveal what, essentially, Edwards means by the "good tendency" of union. In the course of defending the proposal, Edwards used arguments readily understandable to the modern mind: such union would "tend to Christians' assistance, and encouragement in their duty, and also to their mutual comfort."[88] But it was not simply Edwards' intention to overwhelm the laggard members of the church by a demonstration of what would be called, in later years, the tyranny of the majority. The Concert of Prayer differed from such other unifying devices—among them the history of the revival proposed by Edwards in the *Thoughts* and embodied in Thomas Prince's *Christian History*—which Edwards considered a means of letting God's people know "who are united with them in this affair."[89] Rather it was to Edwards self-evident that "union among God's people" was so "beautiful and amiable" that it "should be *visible*" and every member of the Church of Christ "behold it." For if, by agreement in the "two visible circumstances, time and place," it were in fact possible to convey to the minds of the faithful an image of harmonious union, the very beauty of the spectacle—"the lovely sight"—would inspire them with the "desire to perfect that union."[90] It was this possibility—that a perception of beauty would induce a taste for more exalted beauty—that persuaded Edwards the Concert of Prayer might go on, conquering and to conquer, until the millennium itself arrived.

When John Witherspoon, in the late 1760's, delivered at Princeton the first series of lectures on "Eloquence" to be given in America, he could take it as an axiom that the "excellence" of eloquence consisted "in making another perceive what I perceive, and feel towards it as I feel."[91] Yet long before European theorists had thus reduced the rhetoric of sensation to its simplest elements, the Calvinist ministry, in its delineations of the united Church, were assuming this to be the orator's role. In seeking to induce in their congregations the same love of union that filled their own souls, they assumed, of course, that those who could perceive the same beauty the preacher saw were saints indeed. In theory, regeneration was necessary before men could "perceive the highest objective evidence" of the excellency of Divine things. The unregenerate could no more see the true beauty of union "than a man who is born blind can perceive colors."[92] One need not either question this belief, nor deny the revivalists' own disclaimers of the efficacy of their preaching, in order to appreciate the Calvinist preachers' achievement. As late as 1801, pious Jeffersonians were calling on faithful Democratic audiences to "ever bear in mind, that although Paul may plant, and Apollos water, it is God that gives the increase."[93] The evolution of the American mind is comprehensible without excessive attention to the work of the Holy Spirit in illuminating the minds of Americans and thus helping even Calvinist preachers, as Samuel Buell would have it, "to discern the moral Beauty and Amiableness" of the divinity of divinity.[94] Whatever "the agency of a superior power"[95] in making Calvinist rhetoric effective, it is obvious that Calvinist eloquence had done much to prepare the way for the unification of God's people—and had done so because the evangelical preacher was consciously and intentionally a literary artist.

To be sure, it was the very transcendence of the beatific vision that gave the evangelical impulse its driving force. When the vision dimmed, or was translated into simple earthly terms, the nation was sent on that fifty years' voyage away from the great community that would find its subtlest chronicler in the author of *Moby Dick*. Such considerations need not, however, detract from the achievement of the eighteenth-century Calvinist orator. Edwards' portrayal of the Church Triumphant surely etched on the consciousness of even his "unregenerate" auditors something of an enduring image of the highest excellence:

And at that glorious appearing of the great God, and our Saviour

Jesus Christ, shall the whole elect church, complete as to every individual member, and each member with the whole man, both body and soul, and both in perfect glory, ascend up to meet the Lord in the air, to be thenceforth forever with the Lord . . . And they both shall in that relation and union, together receive the Father's blessing; and shall thenceforward rejoice together, in consummate, uninterrupted, immutable, and everlasting glory, in the love and embraces of each other, and joint enjoyment of the love of the Father.[96]

Samuel Davies was just as ravished as any New England Calvinist by the beauty and glory of the millennium. Indeed, even as Davies arraigned "those smooth-tongued Preachers, who would admit promiscuous Crowds into Heaven," he followed Whitby in predicting an era in which the saints would more overrun than inherit the earth: "how prodigious the Multitude!" But when Davies in his Virginia sermons entered "upon the majestic scene" of the General Resurrection, he feared his powers of eloquence inadequate to his theme. "But alas! what images shall I use to represent it?" Yet he knew that it was "necessary we should have such ideas" of the Day "as may affect our hearts," and described, as well as he could, "the glorious company"—"all vital, all active, all glorious, all happy."[97] The New Englanders, however, were never at a loss for such images, as witness Jonathan Parsons' eloquent celebration of the Church Triumphant:

O happy day, when the whole body shall be incorporated, and united in Christ their common Head! Happy day, when all are stamped with the same image and superscription, and influenced by the same power. O when will that day come, that all shall be knit together in the bond of love and charity, all of one heart; one in their designs and aims; one in their desires and prayers; one in love and affection, and be perfect in one.[98]

Perhaps it was simply a difference in social conditions that accounts for the ultimate divergence of southern and New England aims, and for the fact that Yankee eyes would ever be most appalled in beholding the fragmented and dissevered union. Yet one wonders whether the "reality" was all that diverse in eighteenth-century America and, beyond even this, why the disunionist visions of Hopkins and Timothy Dwight proved such conspicuous failures in New England. Eventually one returns to the possibility that Edwards had enforced on the New England mind an idea of excellence—one which even Dwight acknowledged when he called his grandfather a "moral Newton"—that could not thereafter be long resisted.

III

Though New England eyes first imagined the beauty of union and New England preachers best succeeded in communicating that beauty, it was in New England too that the Awakening seemed, often even to its adherents, the most divisive of social impulses. Throughout the colonies it was the "grand business" of the revivalists, as Chauncy reported of his region, "to persuade the People, that their Ministers are *unconverted*,"[99] and, therefore, to separate from them. The separatist impulse was epitomized in Gilbert Tennent's celebrated Nottingham sermon, *On the Dangers of an Unconverted Ministry*—an utterance which enjoyed a continuing popularity and republication throughout the eighteenth century.

Tennent's sermon was only in part a justification of leaving a "carnal" preacher. It was, as a critic pointed out, "full of divisive principles."[100] Tennent summoned men also to leave the "impure and unholy" among the laity and to cleave to the pious. It is better, he insisted, to shatter "Congregations in Pieces" than have the "sincere Servants of God" break bread with the "Servants of Satan." Once the people of the colonies began acting on Tennent's advice, and started to go "from Place to Place" in order to enjoy the "greater Good" of a new fellowship, the parochial order of early America was never again the same.[101] In the Awakening years the geographic mobility of preachers and people was extreme and often dramatic. The "itinerancy" that divided the Presbyterian Church was not limited to a few preachers. Criticisms of the revival were filled with complaints against laymen leaving the bounds of the parishes, and with epithets testifying to the horror with which defenders of the old order viewed the new dispensation: "Enthusiastic Rovers," "disorderly Ramblers," "disorderly Rovings," "Wanderers or Vagabonds." In New England too people left their communities to hear Whitefield and Tennent, and even more common was attendance at local lectures by people "belonging to other Churches & Places."[102] The mass migrations of the Awakening—Samuel Buell brought "a number of zealous people from Suffield"[103] with him when he visited Edwards in Northampton—were seldom duplicated in the subsequent ecclesiastical history of eighteenth-century America. But men and women continued to leave their parish churches to seek the joys of a goodly communion outside the relationships into which they happened to have been born.

The "dividing Spirit" of the Great Awakening was not, as one Calvinist minister observed in 1745, "confin'd to those that are Friends to what we esteem as a remarkable Work of God's Grace."[104] During and after the Awakening many Americans, affronted by the "pernicious Doctrine of Enthusiasts," renounced both the faith of their fathers and, as they grandly dismissed it, a "misleading" childhood education, and entered the Anglican communion. Seeking to keep their skirts unsoiled in the "flood of confusion" introduced by "Mr. Whitefield," his "followers and imitators," and deploring the degree to which less reasonable Americans were "taken in with the New Light," many provincials —among them the minister as well as the more "respectable" members of Boston's West Church—"fled to the Church of England for safety."[105] Rational in persuasion and urbane by self-appointment, they looked to England, to Commissaries and Bishops, for ever more elaborate protection from the barbarism of American life.

Withdrawals of either sort posed a unique challenge to the New England Way, for the simple reason that only there had the churches been organized historically on the basis of the local covenant. Liberal and Old Light opposers of the revival conceived of itineracy itself as an intrusion on the covenant relationship of minister and people.[106] But they were even more adamant in refusing to abide mobility among the members of a congregation:

> You have no liberty, no right, to forsake the communion of these churches . . . you cannot do it without breaking the covenant . . . and incurring the awful guilt of schism.[107]

In this instance the time-honored precepts of the New England Way were being invoked against those who were drifting into Anglicanism. But Old Light admonitions against defections from the covenanted churches continued to be directed toward "Separatists both upon the *New-Light* and *Episcopal* Scheme." Indeed, through most of the thirty years after the Awakening the burden of argument most often fell, for obvious reasons, on those less respectable members of society whose "*itch* for separations" took them into New Light conventicles. Even arraignments of the Church of England frequently digressed into bitter recollections of the Awakening, for the "anarchy" of which Episcopalianism, and of course the "priest" Whitefield, were held to be somehow responsible. In the literature of controversy over the place of the Church of England in the colonies, one of the worst of sins ascribed to it was the setting of a precedent—its "missionaries," Noah Hobart complained, were the "first Itinerants"—that allowed the multitude to flout the parish order.[108]

Against such separations the opposers of evangelical religion devised a battery of additional arguments. In the *Seasonable Thoughts* Chauncy declared that the "Law of Charity"—which, he insisted, "is the Law of Christianity by Way of Eminence"—forbade separations. In 1773 he was still proclaiming that the formation of "separate communities" was a violation of this law.[109] John Tucker of Newburyport added that traveling on the Sabbath affronts the Deity, and he went on to explain that the preservation of "parish lines" is necessary to maintain "order and regularity in societies." Violating them tends directly "to the confusion and detriment of societies, whether we consider them as civil or religious.*[110] The anti-revival party, however, had, as Isaac Backus complained, an even "more powerful way of reasoning" than the logic of Chauncy's *Seasonable Thoughts*.[111] In Connecticut the Old Light clergy gave the civil authorities primary responsibility for "suppressing all Disorders, frowning away Seducers, and preventing the prevailing and spreading of dangerous Errors, &c."[112] But they also worked to contain the revival impulse with the ecclesiastical machinery of the province—as did the southern Anglican hierarchy and the anti-revival ministers of Massachusetts.

The consociations of Massachusetts were used to deny the entrance of itinerant preachers into parishes and, eventually, to impose unpopular ministers on congregations and intolerable tax burdens on dissenters. In 1773 a convention of Massachusetts ministers defended the traditional system as the only means of preserving "that Union" among the towns of the province which the founders of New England "had so much at Heart, as our truest Strength and Glory."[113] An "Independent" Calvinist, speaking on behalf of the "separates and Baptists" of New England (and, in effect, for the Calvinist Congregational ministers who had long boycotted these annual meetings) observed that this was to seek "peace and harmony" on the "same terms" as those offered by "the Pope."[114] The Liberal policy, in so many respects medieval, was perfectly consistent with their view of the Newtonian universe as a contrived order, its unity impressed from without, its harmony not vital but a mechanical resistance of centrifugal tendencies.

The language in which the struggle was carried on in the mid-eighteenth century somewhat obscured the inner dynamic and ultimate purpose of the Calvinist drive for ecclesiastical liberty. In pleading their case the spokesmen of dissent sounded at times like black-letter barristers, at others like sloganeers of the Enlightenment, and at still others like the deadliest of Scriptural expositors. In debates over the qualifications of ministers and church members, the power of consociations and councils, and the relationship of church and state, they alluded to the church law set forth in the Bible, to the various ecclesiastical laws of Old and New England, even to the common law, judicial review, and nullification. They invoked the hallowed right of

---

* In all fairness to Tucker, it should be observed that he was not unalterably opposed to any and all freedom of movement. "No man is obliged by the province," he charitably observed, "to fix himself or to continue his residence in any town or parish where the minister, or anything else, is not agreeable. He is always at liberty to remove to where he can be better pleased."

private judgment and of freedom of conscience, they spoke of the religious liberties, and even the civil rights guaranteed them by the British Constitution and the New England charters.[115] Yet the partisans of the evangelical scheme were at no point bent on establishing either the common law or the Enlightenment in America. Their cry that "Christ is the only source of all power and authority in this kingdom," and their belief that the "least yielding" to the civil authorities in religious matters would let in "a flood of persecution" were all quite as irrational as the New Light imparted to the minds of men in the ecstasies of the Great Revival.[116]

The dynamic impulse of the evangelical quest for freedom was an awareness, however dim, that the old regime was an impediment to the achievement of the affectionate and beautiful society of the beatific vision. The opponents of separation argued that freedom could not be permitted except to those religions consistent "with the public safety."[117] So appalled were the Old Side Presbyterians by the "license" and "anarchy" of the Log College party that they openly questioned the ideal of toleration and demanded that the theory be refined. What men needed, it was argued, was "not an universal Toleration of all Things; but a well bounded Toleration to discharge their Duties to God and Man in their Proper Places, Callings, and Relations, without disturbing others in their proper Stations." The ecclesiastical issue of the Awakening was thus clearly focused when the Synod of Philadelphia denied Tennent's plea for Christian liberty. If his definition of "liberty of conscience" were made "a Rule for a Society," it was observed, "we must all turn Levellers."[118] To such charges evangelical spokesmen did not reply; they did, however, deny that Scripture or any other authority had imposed "*one* particular, stated, invariable *Order*" on the Christian community.[119] And as against the anti-revivalists' notion of "federal liberty" they insisted, finally, that no institution whatever could be allowed to "destroy the blessed union, or prevent the communion" of the saints.[120]

The implicit goal of evangelical liberty was stated in its simplest terms when Jonathan Parsons argued for the abolition of parish lines. Complete religious liberty—including freedom from inherited relationships—was essential if men were "to sit down with their brethren" in "good order and pleasure."[121] But the spirit of Calvinism was probably nowhere better revealed than in the brace of discourses delivered in 1759 by Gilbert Tennent. In the first sermon he defined religious liberty as absolute freedom from "*coercive* measures" or external restraint; in the second he explained that such freedom was worthless, and was not even worthy of seeking, unless such liberty were used to establish an "affectionate union" among the liberated.[122] It took some years for the Calvinist mind to appreciate the full import of this identity of liberty and union, but at no point was it the goal of any advocate of religious freedom merely to "lay open the sluices of society."[123] They sought freedom from the old order, and encouraged its withering away, in the hope of bringing a new and better order into being.

IV

In the South the struggle for religious independence, waged largely by a newly organized Presbyterian church against the Anglican establishment, preserved the lines of "rational" and "evangelical" drawn in the Awakening. Much the same was true of the Middle Colonies, where the ecclesiastical issue was drawn between the Old Side opposers of the revival and the New Side. In the synodical debates the Tennent party repudiated the "federal" notion of the church as organized only in obedience to explicit Scriptural mandate and as serving merely governmental and disciplinary purposes. When the Synod tried to suppress the "unscriptural, antipresbyterial, uncharitable, divisive Practices" of the Log College men, the latter, for their part, broached a conception of the church as an instrument of evangelism: "the Necessity of our Preaching abroad was great and urgent, from the Soul-Exercises and strong Desires of the People."[124] Thereafter, even through the reunion of 1757, the evangelical element of Presbyterianism preserved the vision of a church in which greater liberty was demanded in order to achieve the "greater Good" of the laity.

But the ecclesiastical struggles of the post-Awakening period also had their sources in what was a rift within the ranks of the evangelical party itself. During the revival, Samuel Finley recalled, New Side Presbyterians and Baptists were "jointly and amicably endeavouring to promote the main Cause of Religion, about which we were comfortably agreed."[125] But by 1745 Finley was locked in debate with the leader of the Middle Colony Baptists, and indeed as early as 1743 both Finley and Tennent were arguing with another of the sects whose growth had been stimulated by the Awakening: the Moravian followers of Count Zinzendorf. The ecclesiastical debate among these groups was not over religious liberty—all evangelicals seemed to take this so much for granted that it did not even need to be mentioned—but over the nature and structure of the church. A similar situation arose in New England, where the sectarian impulse was advanced by those "wild enthusiastical People," the Separates, whom Edwards described as renouncing both the ministers and churches of the land and seeking to set up "a *pure church*" of their own.[126] It was Edwards' task—one which Presbyterians of the Middle Colonies and the South for many reasons comparatively neglected—to recall these Separates to membership in the Calvinist communion.

Edwards' differences with the separatists were more apparent than real—or at least, as it turned out, more capable of reconciliation than any of their common differences with the partisans of rational religion and the old church polity. To begin with, Edwards never joined the critics of enthusiasm in arraigning the come-outers of New England as "trumpeters of Sedition."[127] Nor did he deny their right to ministers and churches of their own choosing or ask that the government or the church associations restrict or in any way hinder the freedom of the Separate congregations. Indeed, as against those Liberals who contended that Christian love demanded an acquiescence in one's old allegiances—to minister or church—Edwards contended that the kind of easy tolerance for which Liberals pleaded was "a bastard, mischievous charity."[128] His conception of the church, moreover, was not unlike that of the Separates, and his efforts to revise the constitution of New England's churches brought him dismissal from Northampton in 1750 under the charge that he "had fallen in with those wild people" and that he himself had become the "grand separatist" of New England.[129] So similar was his ecclesiastical theory to that of the Separates that Isaac Backus, leader of the New England Baptists that were an outgrowth of the Separatist movement, could refer to him as "our Edwards."

Yet Edwards was not, as historians of the Separates contend, simply failing to accept the inevitable conclusions of his own logic when in the 1740's he criticized their "pure" churches.[130] Like them, he wished to divest the church of those "ingenious inventions" of *human wisdom*" that seemed to deface the *excellent order*" that Christ had intended as the true constitution of His churches. His vision of a "perfectly pure" church stood in judgment on the particular visible churches of Christ, which seemed "often defiled and dishonored by one wicked man or other."[131] Even as Gilbert Tennent, Edwards believed that the Church must not be composed of "Persons of the most contrary characters" and that the presence of "carnal men" in the church could interrupt, even "destroy Brotherly Love and Christian Communion."[132] Indeed the awakening impulse, which had in many areas been stimulated by efforts to undo the "lax Method of Admission" to the church that had come to be standard practice in New England as well as within Presbyterianism, everywhere inspired renewed disdain for the moral ugliness of "mixed communions."[133] Where Edwards differed from other evangelical spokesmen was in seeking to reform the "church" without shattering the local "congregation" and, by so doing, to give both discipline and meaning to the revival-born desire to "separate the precious from the vile."

The issue between Edwards and the separatist advocates of a "pure church" was not unlike that between the Brownism and the Puritanism of an earlier era. Like the separatism which had colonized Plymouth, that of the eighteenth century throve on a fear of contamination by "unsanctified persons." In the eyes of older Calvinists, the Separates seemed to be seeking an easy way to self-purification: "How many seem more fearful of being defiled by corrupt fellow members, than by the corruptions of their own hearts!"[134] Thus it was not surprising that Edwards' arguments against the Separates of his day echoed many used by John Cotton in the early stages of his debate with Roger Williams. Was it not better, Edwards asked, to bring the unregenerate under the discipline of the saints than, by ejecting or forsaking them, to leave the world in their hands?

In his efforts to deny the sacraments to all but "visible" saints Edwards conspicuously failed. So too, eventually, did Joseph Bellamy, though his congregation quietly accepted, in the 1750's, the very repudiation of the Half-Way Covenant and Stoddardeanism that had proved Edwards' undoing. The larger purpose of making the "right to be received as a visible saint by the public" dependent on the Christian judgment of the presumptive saints in each community could not, in the circumstances of the eighteenth century, succeed.[135] Failure was predicted by Solomon Williams, who in his critique of Edwards' *Inquiry* observed that "when Persons see themselves shut out from the Ordinances of the Gospel on such Terms as they think Christ has given them a Right to them, they will be apt to go where they may enjoy them."[136] And when, in the years after the Awakening, any man was deprived of his traditional sacramental privileges (and the attendant political-ecclesiastical advantages) he could, if it were impossible to remove the minister who aggrieved him, escape—as in the case of Samuel Hopkins' outraged parishioners in Great Barrington—to a more tolerant Church of England. Or, like Timothy Pickering and the other "respectable" citizens of Salem whom Nathaniel Whitaker excommunicated in the 1770's, they founded whatever birthright congregation they could hastily organize and have approved by a Liberal consociation.

As a consequence, rigorously Edwardean congregations generally became, in the course of the century, nearly as "pure" as the churches the Separates and Baptists aspired to. Yet the issue between Edwards and the Separate-Baptists was much larger than that of simple church structure. This is immediately evident when one turns to the tracts in which Edwards argued for restricted church membership. In his *Humble Inquiry into the Qualifications for Communion* and his reply to Solomon Williams' attack on the *Humble Inquiry*, Edwards made it abundantly clear that he saw the particular church as something far more than a mere local institution. His argument focuses on the sacrament of the Lord's Supper—which he always called, significantly enough, "communion." The sacrament he took to be not a seal of the covenant nor even, in any seventeenth-century sense, a remembrance of Christ, but rather an expression of that "*peculiar* affection which gracious persons have one to another."[137] A restricted church membership was a "type," as it were, of Edwards' ideal particular church, one in which a whole congregation was "happily united" in "mutual sympathy with each other" and had "a communion in each other's prosperity and joy."[138] Indeed communion was, in a sense, an image of an image, and even more. It was a means of leading the minds of the godly, by the use of "emblems," up to that which they represented— which in Edwards' case was, as it had not been for Edward Taylor or any other pre-Awakening sacramental typologist, the larger communion of the saints.[139] In sum, the church polity into which Edwards inquired and which he sought to impose on Northampton was an image, however dim, "a faint resemblance," of the millennium and, like the Concert of Prayer, "a forerunner of that future joy" and an instrument for bringing it into being.[140]

Perhaps the failure of the Concert of Prayer helped inspire Edwards with a sense of urgency in refashioning the ecclesiastical polity of New England. It would seem more likely, however, that his desire to purify the church was testimony to the curious workings of his prophetic mind. Given Edwards' typologizing, that which was promised as coming into being in the millennium might seem, and often did seem, an instrument for bringing the millennium into being. For instance, Edwards sought, along with the Calvinist ministry generally, to reverse the emphasis on those first-table duties the performance of which he considered the "cheapest part of religion." But in urging men to "acts of charity" he was not merely invoking the moral law; rather he conceived of such exercises as a "means, as it were," of fetching God "down from His throne in Heaven."[141] The strategy, of course, was to hasten the coming of the Kingdom by duplicating something of its qualities in advance. Similarly, Edwards acknowledged that the "true government and discipline of the church" would not be "settled and put into practice" until the Kingdom had actually come.[142] Remolding the churches now might therefore be an instrument of hastening the day of a perfect constitution.

In any case, the *Humble Inquiry* was clearly cast in an eschatological

framework. Those who opposed Edwards were thrown back, not only
on a more covenant-centered orthodoxy, but on a view of history that
marked a retrogression from the insight of the Awakening. Solomon
Williams, for instance, was himself an advocate of the revival in the
1740's, but, having entered the lists with Edwards as a defender of the
Half-Way Covenant, he was by 1759 speaking in these accents:

> Tho' God did not call our Fathers in that extraordinary Manner, as
> he did Abraham, nor promise them New England, or North-
> America, as he promised Canaan to Abraham and his Seed. Yet he
> offer'd our Fathers the Call of the Gospel, and the Privileges of the
> Covenant of Grace thro' JESUS CHRIST, and by his Grace he persuaded
> them to accept his offer. So they became his People, and he became
> their God as truly, and really, as if this had been transacted by an
> immediate call from Heaven. He made them a pious and holy
> People . . . and gave them signal Tokens of his Favour from Time to
> Time, blessing their Labours, bestowing on them the good Things of
> the World, making this a pleasant Land. . .[143]

When, a few years after Williams spoke, the thunder of the jeremiad
again rolled through New England, it bellowed forth largely from
pulpits of churches where the Half-Way Covenant was still enjoyed.
Edwards' judgment of the traditional New England notion of its
special covenant with God is suggested by the fact that nowhere in his
published writing is to be found a single fast or thanksgiving sermon—
the instrument and embodiment, for more than a century, of the
notion that New Englanders were somehow a "peculiar" and specially
chosen people.

Even more interesting, however, is it that Edwards in arguing with
Williams had been driven by his very logic (or aesthetic) to exorcise
from his thinking all thoughts whatever of a special New England
history. In part this was not compatible with Edwards' view of the universal visible church:

> they are all of one kindred . . . they have a relation to other Chris-
> tians which they have not to the rest of the world; being of a distinct
> race from them, but of the same race one with another.[144]

The thought that New Englanders were somehow in special relationship with God and each other was also untenable given Edwards'
general repudiation of the covenant as a meaningful concept. But the
view of New England history that emerged from the *Humble Inquiry*
was more than anything testimony to the inherent irony of an
historiography which had, for nearly a century, understood New England's development in terms of the same parallel with the Children of
Israel that scripturally justified the Half-Way Covenant. Edwards, in

denying the scriptural basis of the Half-Way Covenant, read the Old Testament as typical, and in doing so he produced what reads like a condescending gloss on all of New England's history before the advent of Jonathan Edwards:

> The great and main end of separating one particular nation from all others, as God did *the nation* of Israel, was to prepare the way for the coming of the Messiah . . .
> That nation was a *typical nation.* There was then literally a *land,* which was a type of heaven, the true dwelling-place of God; and an *external city,* which was a type of the spiritual city of God; *an external temple of God,* which was a type of his spiritual temple. So there was an *external people and family of God,* by carnal generation, which was a type of his spiritual progeny. And the covenant by which they were made a people of God, was a type of the covenant of grace . . . God, agreeably to the nature of that dispensation, shewed a great regard to external and carnal things in those days, as types of spiritual things.[145]

Considering the perspective in which Edwards viewed the question of church government, it is not surprising that he was unsatisfied with the "pure churches" of separatism. To be sure, they shared something of the Edwardean vision, conceiving as they did of the particular church as united in mutual love. John Rogers, who early in the eighteenth century founded the movement that served as something of an inspiration to New England's subsequent separatists, insisted that his come-outers were "not Sectaries, but are united together, in a perfect Bond of Love and Unity." But according to Edwards such love, whether of the "Rogerenes" or of the post-Awakening Separates, was partial:

> There is commonly in the wildest enthusiasts a kind of union and affection . . . occasioned by their agreeing in those things wherein they greatly differ from all others, and from which they are objects of the ridicule of all the rest of mankind.[146]

A similar objection was voiced by Gilbert Tennent when, in his *Irenicum Ecclesiasticum,* he rebuked even his own followers for conceiving the New Side as a party. The love they bore for each other was inadequate, because like that of the Moravians—the *Unitas Fratrum*—it failed to extend to the universal Church.

In stressing the local communion, the Separates of New England may have embodied the primitive spirit of Congregationalism. Surely they followed the course of some New England churches, which over the century had, in their efforts to remain independent of consociations and other centralist devices, managed also to obscure their relationship to the larger saintly brotherhood. But neither Edwards nor any of the other leaders of post-Awakening Calvinism was a "Congregationalist" in the sense in which John Wise, for instance, understood the "good old way." As one of Edwards' more faithful disciples put it, Wise was proposing an absurdity when he asked that "every small town or village" be assured its ecclesiastical independence. All genuine Christians "are mutually in covenant," Nathaniel Whitaker proclaimed, "by virtue of their relationship to CHRIST, the great head of the family."[147] Whitaker was in fact no Congregationalist at all, but something of a Presbyterian; so too was Edwards, whose conception of the Church assumed the need of cooperation and even organization among the churches in order to forestall and overcome the reign of "wicked men" on earth.

In any case, the Separates erred, according to Edwards, in conceiving their churches as sanctuaries from the distress and turmoil of the world. As might be expected, the Separates—like their pietist brethren elsewhere in America as well as in Europe—were more than disposed to premillenarianism and thought that the purpose of gathering churches was to provide a place to await the coming of the Kingdom. Ebenezer Frothingham, who first set forth the "platform" of New England separatism, believed that the whole society about him was corrupt. He expressed the hope that if the separatists were allowed to thrive without hindrance from the civil authority, Christ might "rule in the Kingdom of Providence, and civil Rule in this Land, as well as in the Kingdom of Grace." But Frothingham, who lacked any program whatever for fulfilling his hope, likewise despaired of seeing society redeemed. In his writings, he took ultimate comfort in predictions that New England would soon be overwhelmed by the all-devouring flames of the Last Judgment. Throughout the 1750's the separatist mind remained disposed to visions of cataclysm.[148] It was only as Isaac Backus succeeded in converting the Separates to his redefinition of the Baptist Church that they came to the persuasion—the more "American" one, as it were—that the church was not a haven but a place to mobilize the saints and encourage their efforts to bring the Kingdom into being.

V

Edwards and other American Calvinists seldom engaged the sectarians directly on the issue of millenarianism, or even on the question of the proper form of the church. Where they did, as in the "debate" between the New Side Presbyterians and Abel Morgan, the contest was hardly distinguished by intellectual profundity. The discussion of infant baptism was one of the few which, in post-Awakening America, continued to be conducted in a scriptural and scholastic vein. If Morgan could complain of the Presbyterians' "useless Repetition of their Thread bare Arguments from *Abraham's Covenant* and *Circumcision*," Finley had an equally good case against the Baptists' piling up of scriptural evidence in support of their position. Inherent in the controversy was, to be sure, the Baptist challenge to the last vestige of covenant theology in the thought of Calvinism. But the truly vital issue in the Middle Colonies was not forms of government but what the Presbyterians took to be the Baptists' perversion of the spirit of the revival. Over the course of history, Finley observed, it seemed always to have been that sect's role to mar "the Progress of Religion, by turning the Exercises of awaken'd Souls into another Channel."[149] In part Finley was bewailing the manner in which the Baptists, like Craighead's "primitive Covenanters," restricted the revival impulse to its ecclesiastical import. But the heart of the matter was really the quality of Baptist "enthusiasm" and the Baptists' apparent encouragement of the antinomian spirit released by the Awakening.

The Calvinist challenge to the sects thus focused on the "false scheme" of religion from which all other errors, including the ecclesiastical, derived. In differing with the Separates, Edwards was not opposing a sect but a "heresy"—one that was not limited to the followers of Frothingham but bespoke a disposition seemingly inherent in the American mind, and undoubtedly present even in those awakened by Edwards himself. Both in theory and in practice separatism betrayed a distinct bias toward spiritual individualism. It assumed, according to Frothingham,

an absolute Necessity for every Person to act singly, as in the Sight of God only; and this is the Way, under God, to bring the Saints all to worship God sociably, and yet have no Dependence upon one another.[150]

It was this very "independence" that Edwards identified as *the* heresy of revival enthusiasm. The antinomianism he arraigned, like that bewailed by Tennent in the Pennsylvania Moravians, seemed just as egocentric in its implications as the Arminianism against which the revival had been mounted.

Edwards' most probing analysis of the experiences of the revival was his treatise, *Religious Affections*. Of the numerous "wrong theories" there arraigned, nearly all were some variant of the notion of "particular faith." Throughout the colonies, it seems, men awoke from the revival with the "Sweet Dream, that *Assurance* is the *Essence* of Faith." Their religion was personal, centering on a conviction that God had conspicuously revealed His "love to them in Particular."[151] Whitefield's sermons may well have encouraged such a notion of the conversion experience, and, at least in the early stages of the revival, not only the itinerants but even Jonathan Dickinson celebrated the internal and personal witness of the Spirit.

The doctrine of personal assurance had its most outspoken clerical defender in Andrew Croswell, who persistently and insistently asked, *What is Christ to me, if he is not Mine?* Solomon Williams, who answered Croswell on behalf of New England's Calvinist orthodoxy, detected a selfish principle at the very center of Croswell's faith:

> 'tis very observable, that among the Followers and Admirers of *Mr. Croswell*'s Doctrine, there is little or no Appearance of Love to any of their Fellow-Creatures. . .[152]

When Edwards condemned such notions as Croswell's he did not invoke the doctrines of Calvin (which Croswell, with some justice, claimed to be upholding). Rather Edwards rebuked the notion of "assurance" by way of proclaiming the ultimate difference between America's "evangelical scheme" and the pietism of Britain and the Continent. Writing to Thomas Gillespie, of Carnock, Scotland, Edwards refused to grant the assurance of faith and patiently explained that he did so in order to prevent a "bold, proud and stupid confidence."[153] Gillespie replied that men needed the "comfort" of an assured faith; like Croswell he considered it necessary to prevent the "discouraging" of the saints.[154] Edwards, in refusing to make this concession to the presumed psychological needs of the particular saints, was saying, in effect, that the Spirit's work is not the salvation of individuals but of society.

To appreciate Edwards' position it is necessary to recognize that *The Religious Affections* was not simply a treatise on psychology but another of his contributions to the forwarding of the Work of Redemption. It opens with a recollection that but "a little while ago" the New World had glimpsed the "fair prospect" of the earthly Kingdom. The purpose of the treatise, as set by Edwards, is to so accurately ascertain the nature of true religion that the course of history could again be set on its way.[155] To achieve his purpose Edwards first contemptuously dismisses those who would argue that the affections have no place in religion whatever. Then he proceeds to the task of overcoming antinomianism, which he does by defining gracious affections as not merely the "flowers" of the gracious experience but the "fruits" which follow after as "practical signs" of the heart's changed temper. His account of the relationship between justification and sanctification—in which several generations of Calvinists followed him—was not so much an explanation as a series of metaphors.*[156] "The tendency of grace in the heart to holy practice," he affirmed,

> is very direct, and the connexion most natural, close, and necessary . . . Godliness in the heart, has as direct a relation to practice, as a fountain has to a stream, or the luminous nature of the sun has to the beams sent forth . . .[157]

Here in part was Edwards' challenge to those who would select the membership of a "pure church" by a "spirit" of discerning, and to those who, in the New England churches, continued to accept fulfillment of the "external covenant" as sufficient for participation in the Lord's Supper.* Some "qualifications are necessary in order to communion," Edwards argued, "which have their seat *in the heart*."[158] Although certain of Edwards' opponents argued that visible sainthood was an inherited privilege never to be denied to a citizen of New England (as late as 1772 Chauncy insisted that the children of Boston's First Church are "from their first coming into existence, members of this kingdom in common with their parents"),[159] most of the defenders of Stoddardeanism and the Half-Way Covenant contended that "moral sincerity" was to be expected of applicants for church membership. Calvinists, however, insisted on "regeneration and renovation of heart."[160] Men may be "sober, serious, and conscientious," Edwards affirmed, "but if their hearts are not changed, there is no probability at all of these things continuing long."[161] The true saint, in other words, would continually manifest his altered internal dispositions by actions morally fit and becoming.

But in the *Religious Affections* the "signs" of sainthood were advanced only as secondarily useful in the judgment by others of man's

---

* A further contrast between the Liberal and Calvinist minds is suggested by the latter's use of the word "spring" in their accounts of sanctification as the equivalent of "fountain." When Liberals spoke of man's internal "spring" as the source of his motives, they implied that the personality was a mechanical device with which some artisan might tinker. An early critic of enthusiasm, for instance, saw the psychology of the revival as a breakdown in intellectual machinery—"as the stoping or breaking any necessary Constituent Part, or moving Spring in Clock-work, destroys the Regularity of the Motion, and deforms the Piece." But for Edwardeans the alteration of man's internal nature was more properly comparable to a chemical reorganization. "If there be sweet water in the fountain," Edwards observed, "sweet water will . . . flow out into those various channels; but if the water in the fountain be poisonous, then poisonous streams will also flow out into all those channels."

* Though man's internal dispositions are "not to be intuitively seen by others," Edwards argued, yet it is necessary that one's qualifications "be made so visible or audible to others, that others may rationally judge they are there." For the "eye of Christian judgment" to decide on visible sainthood, it was necessary to scan a man's "practice" as well as his "profession." Behavior was to be studied, however, only as an index to the heart from which such behavior flowed.

estate. Their chief value was as a means whereby each man tested the validity of his own experience. This was "experimental religion," for which Edwards was famous in his day and which his writings enforced on the Calvinist mind as the true American religion. Only in "practice" could men ascertain, "by *actual experience and trial,* whether they have a heart to do the will of God."[162]

Of the many signs listed by Edwards in the *Religious Affections,* the most important was the "beautiful symmetry and proportion" of them all. Like the Sun of the Godhead, or the fountain from which all divine goodness flowed,*[163] the saint was to be known not by particular emanations from his essence but by the whole of his lustrous being: there was "something of the same beautiful proportion in the image, which is in the original."[164] True sainthood was not a behavioral *imitatio Christi* but an essential likeness to God—or, even more pointedly, an inherent and personal type of the beatific vision. At the heart of all, of course, was that "excellent divine thing, charity . . . which is a prelibation and beginning of the light, sweetness, and blessedness of heaven."[165] Edwards offered several suggestions as to the acts of charity—the "sign of signs"—a saint might practice: they involved benevolence to the bodies of others as well as a general good will toward their souls. But he seemed to sum up all when he required, as part of the "profession" accompanying all Christian practice, a convincing "general benevolence to mankind" on the part of putative saints and a persuasion of "their hearts being united to the people of Jesus Christ as their people."[166] The only satisfactory evidence of sainthood, in brief, was much the same as that which Edwards would discern when, in *God's End in Creation,* he in effect tested the Deity by the principles of experimental religion. The true saint, Edwards observed, seems "greatly to exert and deny himself for the honor of Christ and to promote his Kingdom and interest in the world."[167]

The *Religious Affections* was far more than a mere exposition of the Calvinist doctrine of sanctification. It was an exhortation to Edwards' readers to be up and doing, and to the ministers of the colonies to urge their people on their way. Actually, the *Affections* represented a major homiletic departure and achievement. Conceived originally as a series of sermons, the final version saw Edwards so reworking the old Puritan sermon form that doctrine, reasons, and uses were no longer in disjunction. All were so fused that the finished volume, simply by stating the doctrine in terms so reasonable, considering the state and nature

---

* Grace, as Edwards and every Calvinist after him asserted, was "a kind of emanation of God's beauty, and is related to God as the light is to the sun," while the Calvinist saints—children of light indeed—were "so many rays of light from the light and fountain of goodness."

of mankind, became a single sustained "use of exhortation" to all who wondered what they must do in order to prove themselves saints. Edwards had even come close to defining sainthood in such a way (as he would explicitly in the essay *Original Sin*) that man's sense of having fallen short of fulfilling the will of God was a necessary induction from the observable fact that the Kingdom had not yet come:

> There are remarkable tokens of his presence still to be seen . . . as though he had a mind to carry on his work; but only was waiting for something that he expected in us, as requisite in order to it.[168]

But the message of the *Religious Affections* hardly needed to be deciphered. What was more than obvious was that no man could call his election sure, nor any rejoice that his heart had been touched, unless he were practically committed to restoring the pace of history that had flagged in the confused emotions of the 1740's.

The burden of Edwards' message was incorporated into his *Life and Diary of David Brainerd* and Joseph Bellamy's *True Religion Delineated: or Experimental Religion* (on which Edwards placed his imprimatur in 1750). In both works the "enthusiast" or "evangelical hypocrite" was advised that true religion consisted not in mere sensations and impressions but in some "act, exercise, or exertion" whereby the saint served to forward the Work of Redemption.[169] But in these works the doctrines of the *Religious Affections* were employed only incidentally as a spur to action. Edwards used Brainerd's career as confirmation of the fact that the "great change" and the "abiding change" wrought in conversion produced a life in genuine conformity to the moral law—"universal holiness of heart and practice."[170] Setting forth the truths of experimental religion was intended as instruction of the aspiring saints of the colonies in the fullness of that knowledge which, according to Edwards and Bellamy, must and should flow from a heartfelt sense of the Divine beauty. The characteristic utterance of the 1750's was not so much an exhortation designed to get the country moving again, as an insistent reminder that its goals must be fully understood.

The tutorial role of the Calvinist ministry was most commonly fulfilled in the preaching of the moral law. In name only was this the same doctrine that Thomas Shepard had used in rebuffing the Antinomians of the seventeenth century. It differed, too, from the law with the terrors of which Edwards and the Tennents had sought in the 1730's to "slay" the complacency of the unregenerate.[171] For the law which Calvinists invoked after the Awakening was one with, and in no wise distinguishable from, the first law of nature, the "royal law of love":

The whole of what the law requires, is love, with all its exercises and fruits; therefore love is the sum of all virtue; therefore, where there is no love there is no virtue; not the least degree of conformity to God's nature and laws.[172]

Bellamy believed that "were this point understood and attended to, it would put an end to more than half the disputes in the Christian world." But in fact it was this very point that involved Calvinists in nearly all the controversies to which they were parties. For such a view of the moral law made the task of determining conformity to God not, as with the Liberals, an exercise in rational comparison of behavior with standards derived from an interpretation of God's revealed Will, but one of discovering an aesthetic and essential likeness to God. The Calvinist moral law had as "its *Prototype,* or original *Copy* and *Exemplar,*" not Divine decrees, but nothing less than the *"Divine Nature"* itself.[173] It was neither codified reason nor a catalogue of duties. It was—in the words of Joseph Bellamy—no other than "a transcript of God's moral character."[174]

What such statements attested is that post-Awakening Calvinism read Scripture itself in the light of what Edwards took to be the meaning of nature. It is "pleasant to think," Tennent allowed, "that the whole *Law of Nature* is contained in, and enforced by the Gospel of CHRIST" as an absolute "Rule of Conduct."

As to the moral law, it is originally founded on the very reason and nature of things. The duties required there are required originally, because they are right in themselves . . . Thus he bids all the world love him with all their hearts . . . and love one another as brethren, because they are all children of the same common father, having the same nature.[175]

In a sense the Calvinist saint was liberated even from Scripture itself by so radical a reformulation of the law in terms of the single message of the gospel. According to Edwards, the saint decided his course of conduct, not by "a particular recourse to the express rules of God's word,"[176] but through a "spiritual taste" that led him, instinctively as it were, to recognize its peculiar fitness:

This holy relish discerns and distinguishes between good and evil, between holy and unholy, without being at the trouble of a train of reasoning. As he who has a true relish of external beauty, knows what is beautiful, he stands in no need of a train of reasoning.

Considering what the Calvinist saw as the highest beauty, what he meant—even as he referred to a Scripture*[177] that was itself an "image"

* Much of God, Bellamy explained, "is to be seen in the moral law; it is his

of the Divine nature—was that sainthood involved no less than a total commitment in deed as well as thought to the harmonious society of the beatific vision.

When the New Side and Edwardean clergy invoked the law after 1745 their target was no longer the smugness and self-content of unconcerned legalists but the delusive self-esteem of the "enthusiasts." The changing function of the moral law was attested, among other ways, by Jonathan Parsons' contrasting in 1748 of St. Paul, who addressed "demure Arminians," and St. James, who "wrote to an Antinomian Tribe." The latter folk were, in the two decades after the Awakening, the primary objects of Calvinist preaching of the law. To be sure, the evangelical preacher continued to allow that the law had its uses to both unregenerate and regenerate, and that neither were "discharged from perfect obedience."[178] But its uses to the unregenerate were, as it turned out, not conveyed primarily through the "terrors" of the Word. Generally the Calvinist sermon in the decades after the Awakening assumed—as did Edwards' Farewell Sermon—that those people of the colonies unconverted in the 1740's were beyond redemption. The Calvinist preacher no longer attempted to terrify men into virtue—except, of course, as their preaching of the moral law to the putative saints eventually did become an effective and dramatic instrument of suasion outside the churches.

In the context of the churches, however, the Calvinist preaching of the moral law was in answer to the question, not "What shall I do to be saved?" but "How shall I know I am saved?" It was to this latter question that Isaac Backus, leader of the New England Baptists, replied when in the 1750's he began to demand of the erstwhile separatists a full understanding of "the great things wherein godliness consists."[179] Backus too preached the moral law, not as a means of showing men "how to obtain the divine favor," but (as he thought the Apostle James had done) to "stir up" professing Christians and "exhort them to live agreeable to their profession."[180] For a few years the fullness of that life was not explicitly revealed in Baptist sermons, but when Backus came to explain that the moral law required nothing less than a heart and life consistent with "union and benevolence to being in general,"[181] the most painful wound of the Awakening had been healed. The "wild, enthusiastical people" of the Awakening were now —given the doctrines enforced by their leader—restored to the Edwardean fold. Whoever would be accepted as a saint in the eyes of the Baptist churches, or in his own, would have to be committed to the

image; but more of God is to be seen in the gospel; for herein his image is exhibited more to the life, more clearly and conspicuously."

whole of the Edwardean vision of the redemption of both church and society.

The teaching of the moral law represented an effort to inculcate in all for whom religion was a matter of the affections what it had been supposed the Holy Spirit itself, working in its perfection, should have achieved in the outpourings of the 1740's. No wonder that Jonathan Parsons insisted that Calvinists did not "preach the law as a matter of speculation, or as a moral philosopher would preach it." For the law as preached from Calvinist pulpits was a reminder of the beauty and blessedness of the largest possible social harmony, and that any who would be saints must commit themselves to its achievement:

> A view of God as an infinitely glorious being, and our common Creator, shows how reasonable and beautiful it is for all mankind, who are fellow-creatures, children of the same common stock, to unite together as brethren just as the divine law requires.[182]

To be sure, the preaching of the moral law represented an implicit admission, and often an explicit one, that either the beauteous vision of the Awakening had dimmed or, as had clearly been even more common, that in the ecstasies of the revival not all Americans had come up to a "full, realizing sense," as it were, of what Edwards took to be the fullness of the beatific vision. Dispensing the law was an effort to preserve and fulfill—by acts of sheer imagination and will—the hope of humanity's most perfect union.

Whether Calvinist preaching by itself inspired the people of the colonies with a desire for union is not here argued, nor can an answer to such a question ever be finally ascertained. But there is reason to believe that the spirit of 1740, wheresoever and in whomsoever poured out, was a repudiation of simplistic individualism—both that of the economic arrogance which Dr. Alexander Hamilton, on his tour from Maryland to New England, saw with genteel eyes as the most ridiculous of American traits, and that more metaphysical individualism implicit in the Arminian doctrines of spiritual self-help. Despite the criticisms of the rationalist clergy or Edwards' own admonitions, few of the awakened were ever, even in the moment of conversion, anarchic individualists. Most of them went to hear Whitefield not simply in the hope of being saved but to seek the joys of a new communion.

There is no record of any enthusiast simply de-churching himself. Rather all seemed to discover, concurrently with their awakening, that there is "a Church of Christ here upon earth."[183] The churches they quickly joined were so organized that it was evident the separatists were not antinomian anarchists but something closer to what, in the seventeenth century, had been called "Familists." From the

"Rogerenes" of the pre-Awakening years, down through the cult of Robert Sandeman (who arrived in the colonies in the 1760's with a faith distinguished by the "kiss of charity" and periodic "love feasts" not unlike those introduced to the colonies in the same years by Irish Methodist exhorters), the eighteenth-century American sectarian, though perhaps a member of an "independent" church, was by no means an independent man. Even the separatist clergy preached of a heaven that was "not a lonesome and retired, but a social state" and of a happiness of the risen saints that was to be "eminently collective and social."[184] In sum, the "evangelical hypocrite" with whom Calvinism had to deal shared something at least of Edwards' vision of the future.

Experimental religion as preached by Edwards, Bellamy, Davies, or Backus was inherently designed to expand the outlook of the affectionate religionist toward participation in ever larger communion. How precisely Calvinism worked its purpose cannot be described, much less established. Yet it is surely worth noting that the Awakening turned the American mind away from a concern with what Thomas Hooker had called "preparation" and toward what in the Christian life had most concerned John Cotton: sanctification. Only the preachers of the "legal scheme" were in this sense the heirs of the seventeenth century, and of course their sermons set out, as the appropriate path to salvation, steps and an order of proceeding that emphasized not merely the relationships of the old regime but its duties and obligations.

In the eyes of the multitude the "unconverted" minister was both one who required of them fulfillment of particular duties, and a symbol of what, in the conditions of American life, made them unable to find satisfaction in such dutiful Christianity. In a context of new economic activity and of social mobility, the revival and the evangelical church offered a seemingly simple solution to what Solomon Stoddard and the other preachers of the early eighteenth century had called "cases of conscience." To be sure, the Calvinist saint was not freed from all duties or obligations whatever, nor was he everywhere liberated from the burden of the past. Jonathan Dickinson anticipated even Edwards in making works, and not the internal witness of the Spirit, the ultimate evidence of the saint's "adoption"; but Dickinson summoned men to test themselves by this standard:

> If we have much at Heart the Flourishing and Prosperity of his Kingdom and interest in the World, and exert ourselves with Diligence in our respective Stations to promote it.[185]

But in most Calvinist pulpits of post-Awakening America it was at this point precisely that the law was preached in something other than the "legal, carnal manner" of the spokesmen of Arminianism. There it was proclaimed that the saint was entirely "delivered from the law as a covenant of works" in order to begin a "new life" as a voluntary subject of the law of love.[186] In Edwards' formulation men were told that what essentially mattered was not so much particular acts as the spirit in which they were performed. Thus was the putative saint offered and even exhorted to a social commitment that effectively served to still his doubts about his failure to fulfill what once had been his duties and allegiances.

The moral law and experimental religion, preached together with the Calvinist vision of social harmony, could only have served to relieve the anxieties of those Americans who in one way or another were protesting against the forms and even the structure of American society. In dismissing the "steps to salvation" as no longer a proper Christian concern, Edwards was not quite advising the awakened to forget their past obligations, but he was surely inviting them to forget the guilt and the anxiety—the "wrestlings" with their conscience, by which they had come finally to free themselves of some of those duties. Existentially at least the most radical message of the *Religious Affections* was this: "There is need we should forget the things that are behind, and be reaching for the things that are before." Here was an invitation to forget the past and even much of what had been conceived as Christian duties, for according to Edwards virtue consisted in far more than "mere negatives, or in universally avoiding wicked practices."[187] It is not unlikely, then, that the old sins—or at least the sense of torment attendant on a failure to perform the old duties—could be forgotten in a commitment to nothing other than the larger love of the brethren. And even forgiven; for while it was the burden of Edwards' writing to defend against all self-deception whatever, in the *Religious Affections* he was chiefly warning those who took their slaying of "beastly lusts" as an occasion or excuse for indulging that more "devilish" one, a prideful concern with self that rested short of the true virtue of charity. Not unsurprisingly, in later years even drunkenness came to be overlooked by Calvinists in those who by deed and word proved themselves otherwise zealous participants in the larger cause of forwarding the Kingdom. In sum, Calvinism made it possible for one to persuade himself that, regardless of all other behavior, he was a child of God indeed so long as he thought himself to be struggling toward and on behalf of the earthly communion of the saints.

The mental processes of most eighteenth-century Americans can only be inferred. But in one case at least it is possible to discern how a commitment to the Kingdom of God served to resolve inner doubts and perplexities about the proper behavior in the changing economic and social circumstances of the period. The mind in which the hidden dynamic of the Awakening is revealed is of course that of Jonathan Edwards. Through the 1730's Edwards recorded in his notebooks a continuing bewilderment about how to behave toward the other citizens of Northampton: the scoffers, the drunkards, and the upstart rich. Were he to condemn them too strongly, his would be the sin of pride; were he to be too courteous he would be failing to fulfill the demands of his calling. Edwards' perplexity represented something of his personal predicament as a grandson of the imperious Solomon Stoddard, but his was simply a more pointed instance of a general problem of the 1730's—that of the functional role of the clergy in a society where power was coming increasingly into the hands of secular men. The status concern of the clergy was merely an epitome of the general problem of the decade: what, in the changing circumstances of colonial America, was the proper duty of any man.

Americans resolved the problem in various ways; those for whom Benjamin Franklin composed his "Dialogues" on virtue perhaps came easily to the conclusion that self-love and social love were much the same. But Edwards, having vacillated for some time between thinking himself too prideful and fearing his social humility to be treason to God, found composure at last in discovering that there was to be a Kingdom of Christ on earth and that he had a role in bringing it into being. For a while he used his hopes for the Work of Redemption, and for his own place in the Divine strategy, as a means of reviving the inner exhilaration and peace of the 1740's. If even Edwards could be so deceived, what, we may ask, were the inner workings of those multitudes of American minds which, in the course of the eighteenth century, almost invariably responded to personal and local confusions by committing themselves increasingly to the general benevolence of the communion of the saints?

VI

Whatever its manner of working, Calvinist doctrine succeeded in breaking down the local and particular allegiances of Americans. When the revival spread through Virginia, for instance, evangelical religion was charged with destroying family relationships and even the relationship between slave and master: "Thus the very Heart-strings of these little Societies which form the greater are torn in sunder, and all their Peace destroyed."[188] Although Calvinists considered the family, and family religion, something approaching a means of grace, they were certain that family obligations and family relationships would have to give way if they conflicted with the saint's primary loyalty to the universal Church and, even more significantly, to being in general. It was not until 1776, when Calvinists severed a relationship to the most sovereign of earthly fathers, that they disclosed the ultimate implications of their primary allegiance to the communion of the brethren. The role of Calvinism in the Revolution is to be more fully unfolded in subsequent chapters, but there is some value in noting now, even before the emergence of the imperial crisis, that the aspirations and the doctrines of the Awakening foreshadowed the eventual emergence of an American union which, though not perhaps as pious as Edwards had hoped for, would be just as affectionate and nearly as amiable.

The revival itself struck a note of intercolonial as well as interdenominational sympathy and cooperation. Already in 1734 Tennent, like Edwards, was remarking on and sympathizing with the progress of the revival in other parts of America.[189] In the Great Awakening itself what was done and thought in each of the provinces was soon common knowledge everywhere, especially as the pro-revivalists came to argue the genuineness of the Work of God from its spread throughout the colonies. Whitefield, first through his published *Journals* and then by his very appearances, gave subjects of the revival a sense of joining in a common experience. A sense of affinity soon was translated into working alliances. The New England group within Presbyterianism provided from the very beginning a point of contact between the two major revival parties. On his visit to Northampton Whitefield proposed an entente; the union of Presbyterians and pro-revival Congregationalists was effectively sealed during Tennent's tour of New England.

In the larger towns of the colonies the pro-revivalists sponsored joint lecture series and began to promote free communion as a characteristic "Beauty and Strength" of the visible church.[190] Everywhere itinerants were given access to pulpits not of their own denomination; Bellamy preached to the Baptists of Wallingford, Finley to those of south Jersey.[191] Whitefield himself was of course a symbol of this indifference to denominational names, and the criticism to which he was subjected attested how dim a view the opponents of the revival took of the ecumenical spirit of the Awakening. He was reminded that he had no right to join in the celebration of the sacrament in any but his own church, and the specter was invoked of Anglicanism's traditional "priestly enmity" to nonconformists. Such attitudes, Thomas Foxcroft observed, were to be expected from men who "have got little *Party-Notions*." The goal of the revivalists was, as Samuel Finley phrased it, "to make up a party for JESUS CHRIST," and this party, as it turned out, was the first in America that not only transcended parochial allegiances but crossed provincial boundaries as well.[192]

The revival notion of Christian union was derided by such critics as the "Querists," who mockingly asked who would give up the "good

Constitutions," the order and discipline, of the inherited churches "as a Sacrifice to obtain a *golden Dream* of *supposed Union* we *know not in what?*"[193] The answer was soon forthcoming, though more by way of practice than in the statements of the revivalists. Seldom did they define the nature and basis of the new union with care or precision. All "the *Catholicism* and *Union,* that I know of, on Foot amongst us," Samuel Blair explained, consisted in one's holding in Christian love "all good Men, where-ever he finds them," and enjoying "agreeable and sweet Fellowship with them."[194] Quite rightly, however, the opponents of the revival sensed that much more was afoot in the ecumenical strivings of the Awakening, and that in the union of they knew not what lay an implicit threat to the order and stability of society as they knew it:

> Can it be supposed that this Catholicism will be brought about by a mobbish factious Rabble, by clamorous Tumults, Lies, and Exclamations, and anarchical Measures, when a Legal Establishment, and Force, and Compulsion . . . proved . . . ineffectual to establish a Catholicism in our Native Land . . . ?[195]

What the opponents of the revival feared was not so much the anarchy of the revival as the new order of unity that threatened to emerge from the liberty the revivalists were demanding. Would not others "have a very unhappy World to live in," asked the Querists, "if ever such unruly Creatures should become the more numerous Party?"[196] Like Chauncy, the Querists invoked the memory of Münster and a community of wives and goods. What they may have realized, however, is that the Awakening's "party of Christ" represented the first stirring of an impulse that would be satisfied only when the "people of God" throughout America could use their united strength to redress grievances in particular communities and provinces.

That impulse was far from satisfied in the 1740's. Indeed, insofar as the spokesmen of the revival sought to join hands—or even to carry their message—across provincial boundaries, they met with considerable difficulty. This was especially the case in Connecticut, where James Davenport was tried under the laws of 1742 and deported to Long Island. Indeed, the laws were expressly designed to prevent the intrusion of the Middle Colony Presbyterians into the affairs of New England. After Samuel Finley was called to a Connecticut pulpit, he had his career as a Presbyterian ambassador of Christ brought to an abrupt end when he was turned over to the secular arm for transportation across the Hudson. Within a decade of the Awakening it was largely the presence in the Presbytery of New York of such New Englanders as Aaron Burr (and, in effect, of Jonathan Edwards) that preserved something of the intercolonial ties of the revival.

The founding and organization of the College of New Jersey provided another focus for interprovincial Calvinist cooperation, as did the efforts of Brainerd among the Indians of New Jersey. But it was not until the late 1750's and early 1760's that the evangelical party again began to assume something of an intercolonial character. The first step—and one of the more essential—was a recognition of the common persuasion of the variety of evangelical denominations that had come to occupy the New World as an aftermath of the Great Awakening. To Isaac Backus it was the open and concerted attack on the Half-Way Covenant that convinced him of the insignificance of the differences among the "true Calvinists" of the colonies.[197] Similarly Samuel Davies began in the late 1750's to urge a *"unity of affection and design"* among all the Virginia dissenters—Presbyterians as well as Baptists. Arguing that it was not doctrine, nor logic, nor interpretation of Scripture that mattered, but "experimental and *practical Religion,"* Davies anticipated what were to be invoked as the bases of Christian union in the revival of 1763, when once more evangelical preachers came to urge their people to be *"one in heart,* one in affection," in attending "to the same great concern."[198] The one concern was, as two decades earlier, the Work of Redemption; evangelical Americans were implored to set aside their disagreements on "indifferent" matters in order to "agree in one end, which is to set forward the Work of God."[199]

In the context of the early 1760's it was more than churchly cooperation for which evangelical spokesmen were asking. To be sure, a major element in the resurgence of affectionate religion was a rediscovery, on the part of erstwhile separatists, that the Divine constitution of the Church was not merely congregational. All "particular Churches," announced John Cleaveland, once perhaps *the* grand separatist of New England, "that are true Churches, make one general Church."[200] What made churches "true," in the 1760's, was not polity but a commitment to the essentials of Calvinism—the New Birth and experimental religion. For many reasons, moreover, the leaders of American Calvinism were by this time curiously indifferent to the progress of piety or dissent in England and on the Continent. In the 1760's the commitment to the Work of Redemption had translated even the ecumenical spirit into a New World nationalism.

The tendency of the 1760's was nowhere better illustrated than by the memorial services held throughout the colonies in the autumn of 1770 for George Whitefield, the news of whose death in Newburyport affected many Americans more deeply than the report of the Boston Massacre. Within six weeks of the morning of September 30, when Whitefield died in the arms of Jonathan Parsons, scores of memorial services were held from New England to Georgia. His death was little noticed in America's Episcopal churches; most of his eulogists were ministers of denominations of which he was not even a member— Congregationalists, Presbyterians, Baptists; his mourners, they of whatever persuasion who had thronged to hear him that summer in the hope that he would promote a revival more glorious than that of 1740. Nathaniel Whitaker, for one, found this ecumenical display fitting rather than surprising and recalled that if in England Whitefield had aired his differences with the Wesleys, in America he had refused to discuss "the outward appendages of religion."[201] Perhaps the major theme of all these sermons was that with which Whitaker concluded the first of his two discourses on Whitefield's life and deeds:

> His noble, enlarged soul was so far above the little differences which divide various denominations of christians who profess the same *pure* faith, and which often become the occasions of trite and unchristian heat and animosities, that he would take no notice of the different parties, *as* such, but, by conforming in these non-essentials to all, manifested his high esteem of the liberty of conscience, while at the same time, by his practice, he nobly reproved that narrowness of spirit which imposes those things as terms of christian communion and love, which God had left indifferent.[202]

Not perhaps since the Great Awakening itself had the spokesmen of the varieties of evangelical religion in America been in such total accord on the need to put aside all "trifling things" and perfect a "blessed union" among—not merely all evangelical denominations—but among the "real and sincere Christians" of America, regardless of their denominational preference.[203]

It was most appropriate that such ecumenical sentiments were inspired by the death of the grand itinerant. The full measure of Whitefield's importance to American history cannot be taken by chronicling the nearly ten thousand sermons he delivered in the colonies in the years between September 14, 1740—when, on the day of his arrival in Newport, he had preached his first American sermon—and the day before his death, when he spoke for two hours in the fields near Exeter. Perhaps the multitude, who, having heard of his coming, implored him to deliver what would prove to be his final sermon, were consciously impressed only by the "charms of his rhetorick and oratory."[204] But his impact on the American mind was not merely that of the most eloquent of the revivalists, nor even of one of the eighteenth-century's more exemplarily benevolent men.[205]

Not the Georgia orphan asylum but the Free Church in Philadelphia, consecrated to the use of any and all denominations, was Whitefield's most suitable monument in the colonies. One of his more famous sermons had been that in which he admonished his auditors not to tell him whether they were "a Baptist, an Independent, a Presbyterian, a Dissenter; tell me who are a Christian, that is all I want."[206] Thus, according to all Whitefield's American eulogists, the heaven to which he had gone was that of the Father Abraham of his sermons,* where it was understood that "names and parties of any kind" did "much mischief and little service to the cause of vital religion."[207] Moreover, it had been Whitefield who succeeded in overcoming the mutual reservations of the New Jersey Presbyterians of New England descent and the Scotch-Irish graduates of the Log College and, finally, brought them into cooperation with the Edwardeans of New England. By his personal efforts and his example, George Whitefield had been both instrument and symbol of the intercolonial union of the people of God.

The larger significance of Whitefield's American career becomes evident only if one considers the 1770 obsequies in the light of the transformation of Christology by the Calvinists of the Awakening. Before 1740 Edwards had celebrated Christ as a personal Savior, and Tennent had verged on an erotic Jesus-mysticism.[208] Within a decade of the Awakening, however, the Second Person of the Calvinist Trinity bore little resemblance to the Christ of Francis and Fénelon, still less to the Jesus which Channing and Bushnell would subsequently imagine. By the middle 1740's Calvinists were presenting Christ "in all the Charms of his Person, Offices, and Relations."[209] Within a generation He had become, for Calvinists, the almost abstract representation of the gospel scheme of the Work of Redemption:

> JESUS CHRIST, is (if I may be indulged the humble phrase) the soul and substance, the cream, marrow and kernel of the scriptures; the foundation upon which the whole structure is built, and the grand center to which all the lines in their circumference directly tend, and in which they sweetly terminate.[210]

So Christ-centered was the gospel of Calvinists that they even attributed to Him characteristics and operations normally associated with the other persons of the Trinity; they spoke of the "Spirit of Christ" and the "Providences of Christ."[211] Such seeming lapses from dogmatic precision were of course symptoms of the Calvinist emphasis on corporate salvation, and of the degree to which their thinking drove toward the good society of which the Second Person was the "ideal" embodiment.

* "All that are here," Whitefield had the patriarch answer in reply to his question concerning the persuasion of those who occupied heaven, "are Christians."

Something of the Calvinist reconstruction of the Christ image, together with its more significant implications, can be clearly seen in the *Religious Affections*. There as elsewhere Edwards' strongest language (verging on contempt) was addressed to those of the awakened who took comfort in visions of Christ's "smiling face," His outstretched arms, His "pleasant voice," or who revelled in the gaudy pomp of a Savior occupying an ornate throne.[212] Such mystic experiences seem to have been fairly common during the Awakening. Many of the awakened, it was reported, thought they "actually saw Christ hanging on the Cross, and saw the Spear pierce his Side, and the Blood streaming out towards them." Among the Separates, visions of "an outward Christ, with open and inviting arms," were held in particularly *"high repute."*[213] The prevalence of such baroque visions was, one suspects, testimony to the kind of preaching in which Cotton Mather and Edward Taylor, among others, had indulged in the first three decades of the century.*[214] Edwards' own correspondent, Benjamin Colman, had painted the beatific vision in these words:

> He will come *enthroned.* Suppose on a radiant Cloud, fashion'd and blazon'd with all the skill of Heaven into a *great white Throne;* as if a thousand Suns were made into one vast Globe, and on it *One* out-shining what he treads on, as *Solomon's Chariot* of State did the Dust it pass'd over . . . So on a burning refulgent Cloud shall the King of Glory come: the most pompous Show the World can ever see or Heaven afford.[215]

In the 1730's Gilbert Tennent had described heaven as a pearl-studded palace, with God "seated on a blazing Throne of solemn Majesty, and unexpressable Beauty," and Christ's coming to judgment, as a spectacle of "inexpressible pomp." But a decade later Tennent was patiently explaining to his auditors that to preach Christ was not "to amuse the Ignorant" with portraits of His personal beauty or with delineations of the pageantry and trappings of the Divine Court.[216] After the Awakening every Calvinist, including those who had earlier indulged themselves in ornate sermon imagery, bewailed the attendant visions as "airy and chimerical."[217]

In the *Religious Affections* Edwards disclosed what in such imagery —beyond of course its implicit premillenarianism—was inconsistent with the thought of post-Awakening Calvinism. Such ornate language was a false delineation of the "essential beauty" of the Deity, and insofar as the awakened were fascinated by "imaginations" of this order,

---

* "Behold Him, who Sits on the Lofty Battlements of Heaven, yet stretch'd out on a Cross, until all His Bones might be told . . . Behold and be Astonished!"

they betrayed, according to Edwards, both a desire for easy assurance and an unwillingness to aspire to the true dignity—and duty—of the elected saint. They represented, Edwards suggested, a notion of sainthood as no more than a rise from beggary to participation in a feudal lord's largesse, whereas the true saint, as Edwards indicated, must recognize himself as the fully equal brother of all others engaged in the common cause of the Work of Redemption.

In the *Religious Affections* Edwards seemed only to know what Christ did *not* look like. He acknowledged the difficulty of portraying Him properly, given the limited scriptural metaphor available—language Edwards himself had used, however sparingly, in his early sermon on "The Excellencies of Christ." The "true beauty" of the Deity, Edwards did not of course clearly reveal until the *Two Dissertations,* where the Godhead was presented as a single point of light —or rather as the numerous emanations from that point which composed the Church Triumphant. Such an unadorned yet brilliant luminary was something of the epitome of the Calvinist Christ, except that no Calvinist, perhaps not even Edwards, was ready for the dazzlingly simple brightness of the Edwardean vision. For Edwards was not able, until the last dissertations, to acknowledge the possibility that social harmony, like that of the atoms, could come about simply through mutual attraction. Until then his system—and long afterwards the system of all Calvinists—required a central luminary that might serve as a center of attraction bringing the saintly planetary system into harmonious order.

In theory, of course, Calvinists' saints could have achieved union simply through perception of one another's beauty and virtue. This was nearly the import of Edwards' 1740 sermon on the social arrangements of heaven: "Each one will be perfectly excellent and lovely, and will appear so in every other's eyes." Yet Edwards and the Calvinist clergy generally continued to describe the saints as united "by virtue of their relationship to CHRIST, the great head of the family."[218] The explanation is only in part that which leaps most readily to mind—that the Calvinists of post-Awakening America were after all Christians. Something more was involved in their refusal to humanize completely the beatific vision. When they spoke of Christ as the Sun, the "most glorious sight" in the heavens, they were providing that in which the aspirations of the many could be objectified and on which the eyes of all might focus. Much the same was true of their signification of ministers as "burning and shining lights," star-like reflections, as it were, of Christ's own brightness: they were the "subordinate lights" which served in the local church the function of Christ in the universal.[219]

Of all the American Calvinists perhaps Edwards alone conceived it possible for men to find love and joy in a mere object of light. But even Edwards, who hymned light as "the most glorious thing in the material world," portrayed a sun that gave warmth as well as illumination:

There are no parts of the natural world that have so great an image of the goodness of God as the lights or luminaries of heaven; as especially the sun, who is constantly communicating his benign influences to lighten, quicken, and refresh the world by his beams.[220]

In the years after the Awakening the Calvinist image of Christ grew for a while less lustrous, more glowingly warm—and not merely in the Virginian sermons of Samuel Davies. The sun was perhaps warmest in the sermons of George Whitefield. All that "the natural sun is to the world"—Whitefield explained in one of his few attempts "to spiritualize natural things"—"Jesus Christ is, and more, to his people." Christ was the Sun who shined not on Presbyterians, Methodists, or Independents, but on "us all."[221] Neither Whitefield nor any other Calvinists were echoing Bossuet; never after the Awakening did the Calvinist Sun King have any feudal equipage whatever. Christ was, quite simply, the "Sun of righteousness," not brilliantly arrayed nor even more than warmly comforting, which would appear at last on resurrection morn, as the western sun to whom the eyes of the saints would turn.[222]

Such a sun served the function of the enlightened king in the thought and expectations of the *philosophes:* one to whom all owed allegiance, without the intervention or the intercession of a hierarchy, and who guaranteed them genuine national unity. The Calvinists of America were too egalitarian to aspire to unity except under a transcendent King. Still, in 1770 Nathaniel Whitaker did employ a particularly felicitous image in trying to convey to the Countess of Huntingdon the meaning to America of Whitefield's death. We now behold, Whitaker exclaimed, "so bright a sun descending below the horizon, whose benign beams have long enlightened and warmed so great a part of our hemisphere."[223] The grand itinerant, the one man to be known and seen in all the colonies, and known as well for the fact that he was so known, had brought to America the possibility of colonial union.

Within a decade of Whitefield's death, Americans did manage to evolve their union under a leader who impressed Calvinists as perhaps just as benevolent and enlightened as Whitefield. George Washington, known to all Calvinists through the "prophetic" sermon of Samuel Davies following Braddock's defeat, was, in the days of the Revolution, a glorious star, and then a luminary of "superior magnitude and splendor." Under Washington, Parsons' successor in Newburyport believed, the American people had been "wonderfully consolidated into one body, and became a band of brothers," and warmed by his influence they embraced the Federal Union. It was only as they discovered that the Constitution was the product of master mechanics, and that the checked and balanced government of John Adams gave off little light and less warmth, that evangelical Americans sought harmonious union around another central orb. The "convulsing clouds which darkened our political hemisphere," a dissenter spokesman noted in the early 1800's, had been "instantly scattered by the resurrection of *Jefferson, that sun of democratic glory.*"[224] Whether the enlightened sage of Monticello knew it or not, he had inherited the mantle of George Whitefield.

When the symbols of union were passed on finally to General Jackson, it was apparent that in the larger sense the leaders of American Democracy enjoyed the legacy not merely of Whitefield but of Jonathan Edwards. Already in the Revolution it was observable that the evangelical impulse bore within itself a disposition to something akin to Bonapartism. In April of 1776 Joseph Hawley, acknowledged leader of the Berkshire and Connecticut Valley dissenters, wrote to Sam Adams of his followers' impatience with the Continental Congress. The Congress, Hawley complained, seemed guilty of the unpardonable sin of *"dozing,"* and unless Congress began to act with organized vigor, "a great Mobb" was prepared to descend on Philadelphia to set up General Washington as a "Dictator."[225] By August the representatives of Liberal thought were ominously predicting that someone with "shining qualities—a Julius Caesar or an Oliver Cromwell"—could assume such a role in America, as indeed the powers of a "dictator" had already been voted to Patrick Henry by the House of Burgesses.[226] Only at the close of the war, when Washington appealed to his army to disband, were reasonable Americans disabused of their fears. But the point made by Calvinist spokesmen throughout the war was hardly limited to military action. It was no less providential, they argued at the end of the war, that heaven had provided the "services of a NEHEMIAH indeed" to overcome the lack of unity and vigor which America's "popular councils" had betrayed. In observing that "a multitude of opinions often distract, sometimes divide," Calvinist orators were echoing and perpetuating a definition of leadership set forth in more peaceful times by the least martial of all eighteenth-century Americans—that proclaimed in the Awakening by Jonathan Edwards.[227]

Both the fears of an American Cromwell and the emergence of an

Oliverian spirit had been foreshadowed in the Awakening. The opponents of the revival accused the preachers of evangelical religion of so using Christ's *"Name* as a *Charm"* that the awakened were brought to "a warm *Pitch* of *Enthusiasm"* and were "ready to die in Defence of *Stupidity* and *Nonsense.*"[228] What was actually occurring was of course a revival of the concepts of a Church Militant, dormant in the colonies since the days of Edward Johnson except perhaps for a brief moment in 1688-1689, and of a Christ who was not merely King but generalissimo. One of the first sermons delivered in 1740 by Whitefield, and among the best known in the colonies, concerned "The Necessity of Religious Society." In it Whitefield celebrated the union and communion of *"Christians* kindled by the grace of GOD," whom he urged to look on themselves as *"Soldier's* listed under CHRIST's Banner." In Whitefield's image the Church Militant was something of a saving remnant, fighting a rearguard action against the degeneracies of the age. His enlistees enjoyed the "invaluable Privilege" of having "a Company of *Fellow Soldiers"* about them, "animating and exhorting each other, to stand our ground, to keep our ranks."[229] Whitefield's rhetoric of 1740, consistent with his view of the English saints, was often echoed among the separatists of New England. But in the sermons of the American revivalists, the Militant Church quickly assumed a more aggressive aspect, particularly as Edwards, in *The Distinguishing Marks,* sounded a trumpet call to battle against the "enemies" of the Work of God. The American image of the church was fortified by the success of New England's "pious army" at Louisburg—under Whitefield's banner of *"Nil Desperandum, Christo Duce"*[230]—and apparently fixed in the Calvinist mind by the continuing warfare of the middle century. What the martial image represented was of course the evangelical aspiration for the movement of the people of God through time, and over all impediments, to history's fulfillment.

During the Awakening, invocations of a marshaled church were clearly inspired in part by fears that the "irregularities" of the revival might destroy the unity of the evangelical host. Even if extravagant enthusiasm and groundless separations did not lead men to "run over in great Numbers to the Enemies Camp,"[231] they might well give the opponents of the revival an advantage by dividing the partisans of evangelical religion on matters of small moment. This was the theme of Jonathan Parsons' celebrated and controversial Boston lecture of 1742, *Wisdom Justified of her Children,* which a critic of the Awakening considered the most dangerous of any of the "new fangled sermons that have been thunder'd out in our *Metropolis,* by *any Youth or Stranger,* these two Years." In the lecture, Parsons implored the "friends of Christ" to avoid needless disagreements:

O, if we were all united under him, what a Defence might we make, and what a Victory might we get, by his Blessing, over the Enemies of his Cause! Beautiful as *Tirzah,* comely as *Jerusalem,* and terrible as an Army with Banners, if our Forces were all united![232]

Nor was the continued use of martial imagery unrelated to the spectacle, later in the 1740's, of America's evangelical party being divided within itself by "the Contests, Wranglings, and Revilings of Professors!"[233] Indeed, in the celebration of the Church Militant was embodied and expressed the central problem of Calvinist thought and rhetoric in the 1740's. The challenge, in substance, was how to overcome the disarray of the Calvinist host without arousing in its individual members the belligerent and "unsanctified zeal" that seemed to endanger the success of "the cause."

Some Calvinists were more successful than others in resolving what was probably *the* inherent contradiction of the new evangelical impulse. Gilbert Tennent, for instance, was so appalled by the intestine quarrels of American Protestantism that he began to call in 1748 for a reunion of the Presbyterian Church. In order to do so, however, he had to overcome the conviction, still regnant within the New Side, that all who had opposed the late "Work of God" were the unforgivable enemies of Christ and His Church. Thus Tennent, in his *Irenicum Ecclesiasticum,* was forced to rewrite, in effect, the history of the early 1740's, particularly by dismissing as things indifferent the more scurrilous of attacks on the revival. Yet in his appeal for Presbyterian unity Tennent raised anew the banner of the Militant Church:

> In this glorious situation the visible Church strikes a dread, a panick, into the Hearts of all her Foes, like *an Army with Banners,* like regular veteran Troops kept under good Discipline, marshal'd in good Order, and Drawn up in *Battalia,* with their proper military Ensigns, Arms and Officers, ready to repel with Valour, Conduct, and Success any Assailants.[234]

Tennent's picture of the Church was a reminder of how mighty an army a reunited Presbyterianism would be, but it also reinforced the notion that God's people were beset by "enemies." Not surprisingly, the text of Tennent's *Irenicum* provided New Side Presbyterians with the logic and the rhetoric both to encourage Presbyterian union and, in after years, to press for continuing warfare against the opponents of "vital religion."

Jonathan Edwards also participated in the post-Awakening Calvinist dilemma. But his utterances of the 1740's suggest that he gave somewhat more thought to the question of the nature of the Church Militant, and, probably even more importantly, to the definition of Christian leadership. In *Thoughts on the Revival* he linked Whitefield's name with those of Alexander and Cromwell and described the ministers of the colonies as "captains" in the spiritual warfare of the revival. In the mid-1740's he translated this perspective into secular terms. The leaders of communities, as their qualifications were unfolded in the sermon on the death of Colonel Stoddard, were those who served as "heads of union" in their societies, holding men together so they might "act by concert, so as to concur in what shall be for the welfare of the whole."[235] The leader, in Edwards' view, was one who both unified the multitude and energized their wills in acting toward a common purpose. As it turned out, colonial society after the Awakening produced few leaders to Edwards' liking, and thus, in the sermons in which Christ was described as the transcendent leader of the Church Militant, Edwards went on to explain always that His Will could never be fulfilled unless ministers managed to "imitate" Christ.[236] Thereafter Christ's ambassadors were represented by Calvinists in the image of Cromwell—whose qualities of leadership were essential to the fulfilling of the Work of Redemption.

The American Calvinist did not find the provincial and local magistrates of the colonies particularly charismatic. For one thing, those in power seemed all too ready, from 1740 onward, to assist the clerical opponents of the revival. When repressive measures were passed by the Connecticut legislature, Benjamin Pomeroy was arrested and arraigned for charging that "great men had fallen in with those that were on the devils side, and enemies to the Kingdom of Christ."[237] Thus in late 1776, when the fortunes of war seemed to be going against the Americans, a younger Connecticut New Light explained why God might well be justified in punishing the colonies with defeat. The "spirit of God," he contended, has for thirty-five years been "called the spirit of the devil," and those who "preached the Gospel called the troublers of Israel." In the 1740's, he recalled, at the behest of those who cried "help, those that turn the world upside down are come here also," laws were enacted "to suppress the progress of the Gospel." Christ's ambassadors were carried out of the state, and "others imprisoned."[238] In those thirty-five years Calvinists, on the other hand, were certain that civil rulers were "bound in duty" to assist, and promote, whatever measures the Calvinist ministry thought necessary for forwarding the Work of God.[239] And as they rehearsed the abominations of the secular magistrates, either in sermons or in such masterworks of evangelical historiography as Benjamin Trumbull's *History of Connecticut* or Isaac Backus' *History of the New England Baptists*, it was clear where they derived their image of the true leader and his qualities of greatness.

In *Thoughts on the Revival* Edwards had appealed to the "civil authority," to the "great men" and the "rich men" of New England, to assist in forwarding the Work of Redemption. But he seemed to know already in 1742 that his call would be answered with indifference, or even—as indeed proved to be the case with most of those Edwards styled "particularly great men, or those that are high in honor and influence"—with their patronage of Chauncy's *Seasonable Thoughts* and participation in that higher logic which Backus considered characteristic of the opponents of the revival.[240] In such circumstances, Edwards' appointment of himself as the field marshal of the pro-revival forces was, however presumptuous, an act of felt necessity:

> Without order there can be no general direction of a multitude to any particular designed end, their purposes will cross and hinder one another. A multitude cannot act in union one with another without order; confusion separates and divides them, so that there can be no concert of agreement. If a multitude would help one another in any affair, they must unite themselves one to another in a regular subordination . . . by this means they will be in some capacity to act with united strength.[241]

What Edwards was seeking to provide pious America was a harmony not merely of purpose but of means. For the moment he provided them also the leadership, executive as well as symbolic, that seemed one of the more likely means of inducing and preserving their union.

In *Thoughts on the Revival* Edwards allowed that only through such concord could the saints achieve the "dominion and authority" that was their promised earthly inheritance.[242] In the *Religious Affections* he removed the prospect of earthly triumph from the immediate future, no doubt largely in revulsion from the simple and selfish secularism of many of the awakened. Too many would-be saints, he observed in the *Affections*, believed (like the Jews of old) that Christ was no more than a national liberator, bent on confiscating and distributing the property of the hierarchs of the Roman Empire. Also he thought it important in the context of the mid-1740's to remind the people of New England that while Christians must ever be ready to "withstand and counteract the enemy without," they "must more importantly suppress the enemy within." Was this merely a warning that even the dispossessed can be self-deceived, or was it Edwards' announcement of those to whom, after all, the victory would be given? The problem of the post-Awakening years, as Edwards saw it, was the readiness of nearly all the awakened to find some occasion for exalting themselves "above their fellow creatures."[243] In such circumstances, Edwards wished to make it perfectly clear that there was more to the Work of Redemption than simply liberating men from restraints in order to provide them saintly communion. For the millennium to come it was necessary that men acknowledge the fraternal working of the Spirit in all the affairs of mankind.

Or did Edwards' muting of the animosities of the Awakening in the *Religious Affections* represent no more than a wise assessment of the power structure of colonial society in the 1740's? He was by no means unaware of what he described as "wrongs done by men acting in a public character" or that the goods and things of the world were "subject to wicked men." But he came to believe that there was little that men could do to alter this situation, that God would take "a little time to put an end to it."[244] Meanwhile the true saint, he urged, would be patient, calm and steadfast amid the oppression of "this evil and unreasonable world."[245] Whatever the final explanation for Edwards' changing orders to the awakened, there was poetic (and perhaps hidden) truth in his admonitions to them: that it was best not to behave "like children, who are impatient to wait for the fruit and snatch it before it is ripe."[246] In 1746, as in 1742, Edwards' function as taskmaster of God's people was chiefly one of making it quite clear just who at any moment was committing the unpardonable error of poor timing.

Here of course was Edwards' ultimate hubris—his assumption that in all America he alone understood the destination of history, and even the precise blueprint for its fulfillment. In the *Thoughts on the Revival* Edwards defined the minister's role as ideally like that of "a wise builder or architect." In issuing his instructions and admonitions, Edwards left little room for doubt that only he had the "comprehensive view" required of the master builder—"a view of the whole frame, and all the future parts of the structure, even to the pinnacle, that all may fitly be framed together."[247] It may well be that in this Edwards was guilty (and came to consider himself so) of the very self-exaltation he condemned in the *Religious Affections* as *the* sin of the revival. According to Edwards only the prophets of the Old Testament and the seer of Patmos had been granted a full revelation of the "future Kingdom," and of its manner and its time of coming.[248] Yet it was by thinking himself privy to just such special knowledge that Edwards in 1742 assumed leadership of the partisans of the Work of God. From his commanding perspective he found it easy to arraign the awakened for censoriousness, for lay-exhorting, and for thinking "that whatever is found to be of present and immediate benefit, may and ought to be practised, without looking forward to future consequences."[249] To Edwards, for whom each moment of the present had to be viewed in terms of an ideal future, the issue was the aesthetic consistency of any action with the known pattern of history's unfolding.

Whatever Edwards' pride, or his own belated judgment on it, the fact remains that only he, of all the spokesmen of the revival, was ready to accept the role that history, or the Awakening, evidently demanded. Tennent's *Irenicum*, for example, is fascinating testimony to the young itinerant's inability to accept the crown that his New Side followers were apparently eager to offer him. His appeal for Christian unity is marked by implicit deprecation of his own earlier career and attitudes. To make his people not partisans but members of the universal Church, Tennent had to divert their eyes from his person to the transcendent glories of Christ. Other Calvinists were equally sensible of the temptations and dangers implicit in the disposition of the awakened to "glory in men," though most often they were acutely aware only of the pride of other men. For example, Solomon Williams complained that Davenport was, by his blazing career, leading men's "Thoughts from Christ, and the Gospel, to a Dependance on Man."[250] One of the worst sins ascribed to the separatists was their setting up Whitefield as a little god, and even some Calvinists objected that he "arrogated to himself a super-intendency, and the Authority of a Dictator general."[251] Possibly Edwards was also aware of his own presumption, for his downfall in Northampton—which, it has been suggested, was self-engineered—was attended by a renewed emphasis in his sermons on the supreme leadership of Christ: "He is the captain of their salvation, and it becomes soldiers to follow their captain and their leader."[252] Yet even in defeat Edwards continued to act as though the church also needed a more earthly leader, one whose special historical insight provided the intellectual guidance that was necessary to the success of any human organization.

In the controversy over qualifications for communion that led to his removal, Edwards was in effect trying to bring into being—prematurely as it turned out—what he knew to be the church of the future. What he was seeking, in his repudiation of Stoddardeanism, was to give the saints a power over the local society that, in his grandfather's day, had been granted only to the elders and the more respectable citizens, and never to the "fraternity."[253] He wanted to give the "public," the presumptive saints in his community, more than a share in the control of their society; and they were not ready. In 1750 he was dismissed, but not without advising the people of Northampton that there was possibly more than one way in which the people of God could effect concert and agreement:

> He that is an enemy to one saint as a saint, is an enemy to all. They are jointly called to resist the same powers of darkness; the church here upon earth is an army that goes forth under Jesus Christ, the Captain of their salvation, to resist the common adversary.[254]

Edwards' removal from Northampton probably did more to cement him in the affections of the multitude—New England Baptists and New Side Presbyterians—than any of his imperious instructions in the 1740's. But it was in exile that he performed those tasks of intellectual leadership that moved Tennent, among others, in 1758 to mourn the passing of the central pillar of the American church.

In his Farewell Sermon Edwards advised the people of Northampton to beware, not enthusiasm, but once again corpse-cold rationalism and the false guidance of legal preachers, overt or, as he suggested, more likely disguised. In Stockbridge he set himself to battle with what seemed, even more than the pride of the awakened, the most dangerous intellectual and spiritual tendency of the age—Arminianism. He also sought to comprehend more fully the nature and tendency of history, and though his reconstruction of the Work of Redemption never came to be written, Edwards did finally reveal what, in the larger pattern of history, had been his underlying fault, and fear, in the 1740's. The pages of the *Two Dissertations* make it clear that in the church, as in the good society, there was no lasting place for a Cromwell or even an Edwards, that the earthly leader, no matter how kindly or well-disposed, was but one more of those vestiges of the past that must in the Work of Redemption finally wither away. For in the final vision the constituents of humanity's union, being the antitypes of the atoms of the physical world, could not conceivably be other than absolutely and irreducibly equal.

What Edwards might have achieved, had he not died soon after assuming in 1758 the presidency of the College of New Jersey, and with it once more the functional leadership of American Calvinism, is an endlessly fascinating question. What is known, however, is that in earlier years Edwards used his power and prestige, not for the purpose of holding God's people to their old allegiances, but to give them the strength—even the freedom—to achieve new ones. He traveled far from Northampton for the single purpose of sustaining an oppressed seceder minister and church. Though it was Edwards' destiny to broach his differences with nearly every religious thinker and sect, it is clear where his sympathies finally lay and why the respectable people of New England so quickly and so fearfully abused him for having "fallen in" with the separatists. What Edwards was seeking to impress on the evangelical mind generally was the vision of a future that could be brought into being through the harmonious cooperation of all men. Had all quickly and fully understood his message, nothing could have divided the evangelical party—especially not the issue of infant baptism, for on this point Edwards' teaching was perfectly plain: the church is not for children. What he asked, in sum, was that the people of God in America understand both the privileges and the promise of their dawning age of maturity.

In this respect Edwards seems rightly to have discerned the pattern of the future, more accurately surely than even the most far-sighted reasonable creature of his age. One of the sharpest contrasts in the history of the American mind is that between Edwards' *Thoughts on the Revival* and another document published only a few months later: Benjamin Franklin's celebrated *Proposal for Promoting Useful Knowledge among the British Plantations in America.* Franklin too thought in 1743 that America had arrived at a critical moment in its coming-of-age. The era of settlement was over, and now the time had come for men of leisure to cooperate in the cause of asserting the dominion of mind over matter—of taking an inventory of the New World's economic resources and, finally, of converting it into the material goods, the stuff of happiness. In the *Proposal* the rude American wilderness, stretching from New Hampshire to Georgia, made the colonies seem geographically one, at least from the perspective of London. The rising glory of America, as Franklin saw it then and as he continued to see it, depended on the intelligence and skill, and above all the diligence, with which Americans responded to the task set by this vast natural domain.

Compare with this what Edwards took to be the meaning of the wilderness in his *Thoughts on the Revival,* and with his vision of the potentialities of the Spirit in America. What he there predicted was not simply the beginning of the millennium in the New World, for it was not in the *Humble Attempt* but in the *Thoughts on the Revival* that Edwards first proposed a Concert of Prayer. Whatever his commitment to the universal church, it bears recording that his earlier thoughts took him less far from home. "I have often thought it would be very desirable," he wrote in 1742,

> and very likely to be followed with a great blessing, if there could be some contrivance for an agreement of all God's people in *America,* who are well-affected to this work, to keep a day of fasting and prayer.[255]

The rational mind was totally unequipped for Edwards' unbounded fancy. Chauncy could not see any "peculiar Advantage" in such a day of prayer as Edwards proposed. "A warm imagination may conceive of great Things from such a Fast," he complained, "but I know not that it would be more acceptable to GOD, or to better Purpose, than one of less Extent."[256] Acceptable to God was not, after all, the issue; what mattered, as Edwards declared, was that such a strategy made "the union and agreement of God's people" the "more visible" to God's people themselves.[257]

Just two decades earlier John Wise had ridiculed the proponents of a New England ministerial association by showing how their principles could be extended to imply the patent absurdity of *intercolonial* affiliation. What seemed amusing to Wise struck the rational mind of the 1740's as uncomfortable and ominous, for a reason that might have induced even John Wise, advocate as he was of the power of the "fraternity," to participate, had he lived, in the Concert of Prayer. For what Edwards was summoning into being was not a ministerial directorate, nor even a confederacy of churches, but the heartfelt communion and cooperation of the people of God in America.

Not until the 1760's did those opposed to the revival think it seasonable to propose a union of American Christians. The call to cooperation was first issued in Ezra Stiles's celebrated *Discourse on the Christian Union*. The particular context of his address is here less pertinent than the fact that Stiles spoke of "universal harmony" among Christians in terms of the numerous sects of America serving as "a mutual balance upon one another."[258] When he proceded to translate his proposal into institutional terms, he called, not for a concert of prayer, but first and characteristically, for correspondence among the Old Side clergy of the Middle Colonies, the Old Lights of southern New England, and the Liberals of Boston. (A "most congenial group of scholars and divines," Carl Bridenbaugh has called them.)[259] The response, though not necessarily enthusiastic, was revealing. Jonathan Mayhew, impressed by "the great use and importance of a communion of colonies," instinctively thought of "communion of churches," or, even more significantly, of "an ecclesiastical council"—of, that is, a piece of machinery useful among other things for purposes of control. Whatever their responses, the more rational clergy all saw the proposal in the light in which Stiles had presented it: Christian union among Americans "must take the nature of a social Confederacy between and among *three* distinct, separate, and independent Bodies."[260] Such a union was hardly conceived in the new light of the Awakening. It assumed, like the Old Side proponents of the Presbyterian reunion of 1758, that ecumenicity was a function of clerical concert and not, as Gilbert Tennent hastened to point out in giving the reunion his qualified blessing, of the "brotherly love" of both *"preachers* and *professors."*[261]

Stiles's efforts to devise an American Christian union, though often lauded as farseeing and of prodigious significance, were actually light-years behind the vision of Edwards' *Thoughts on the Revival* and even what Tennent in the 1740's described as the unifying principle of "several branches" of the "one visible Kingdom of the Messiah." Not coercion, nor hierarchy, nor a constitutional confederation united the people of God, but the mutual love of the brethren. In the words of Edwards in the *Humble Attempt,* the Kingdom was "more strictly united, in many respects," than any other community on earth, certainly more so than the most rigidly disciplined church of the apostolic succession. This was not because the "Honour and Interest" of every member was "one and the same," nor even that they had "infinitely greater interests that are common to the whole, than any other society." Nor was it simply that they shared in the pursuit of a "common prosperity," but because they were "members, however dispersed" of a communion held together by the spiritual ligaments of Christian love. So far as Edwards was concerned, geography could neither separate nor by itself unite the household of faith. In Scotland or the Palatine, and more significantly, in New Hampshire or Georgia, they were citizens of "one holy society, one city, one family, one body."[262] And it was a similar love of the brethren that in a little while cemented the less extensive but equally perfect union that Edwards helped to forge in the New World.

IV

THE DANGER OF
AN UNCONVERTED
MINISTRY

T H E contrasting doctrines and visions produced by the Awakening impinged on the American mind only as they were given expression by the colonial ministry and received by their auditors and readers. Thus the most exciting drama of the post-Awakening years was the mobility of ministers and people and the realignments that provided the altered setting in which ideas were dispensed. Both Calvinism and Liberalism succeeded in redefining the role of the minister and the purpose and nature of preaching. The late 1740's and early 1750's witnessed a special concern, in ordination sermons, for homiletics. "At this time," Nathaniel Appleton observed in 1751, the most distinctive quality of New England's religious life is the "different Tastes among People as to Preaching" and a consequent "Diversity of Opinions about the Nature and Manner of true Preaching."[1] Almost concurrently Joseph Bellamy concluded that there were as many "different sorts of religion" in the colonies as there were "different sorts of preaching."[2] But there were not in fact all that many varieties of preaching in mid-eighteenth-century America. The Great Awakening had brought a rhetorical division almost totally congruent with the doctrinal opposition of evangelical and rational religion.

The manner in which a preacher delivered his message was often more revealing of his persuasion than the particular doctrines he happened to espouse. Charles Chauncy preached in 1740 on something approximating the nature and necessity of the New Birth. But even at that time he was employing the strategy that served as a prudent substitute for open criticism of the revival—that of casting suspicion on the preaching style of Whitefield and other itinerants. Chauncy's first obvious attack on the Awakening was not his sermon on enthusiasm, but one in which he examined what he called the "amazing difference in the natural make of people" that led some "to be pleased with one way of preaching, others with another still, and so on, according to the difference there is in that *relish* they bring into the world with them." Chauncy professed impartiality as among the various modes of discourse, but his commitments were clearly revealed in his defense of Boston's more "rational" preachers and in his suggestion that "eloquence"—the power Whitefield so conspicuously enjoyed—might well be "a gift less valuable than some others."[3]

It was not simply Whitefield's "Calvinism" that made him a popular and controversial figure. The "Preacher, newly come from *England*," was no teacher, nor even an ordinary speaker, but the "prince of pulpit orators," whose great talent, all agreed, was not as a theologian or dogmatist, but "undoubtedly lay in moving the affections."[4] George Whitefield had "something so peculiar in his manner" that he convinced his auditors "what he said was not only true, but of the last importance."[5] He inaugurated a new era in the history of American Christianity—an era aptly characterized in 1740 by Chauncy's First Church colleague as one in which "Evangelistic Preaching" would serve as the dynamic of American Protestantism.[6] An Old Light opponent of the revival, lamenting the preference of Americans for *"new Methods of Speech, Tone, and Gesture,"* for *"new Preachers"* as well as *"new Doctrines,"* captured something of the significance of the Awakening. Not just the old divinity, but the old homiletics, had proven "stale and unsavory" to American "palates."[7] They who flocked to hear Whitefield were not seeking merely to be edified, but to be "affected," and however the separations and the ecclesiastical controversies of the succeeding years were argued in terms of doctrine and polity, the grand ecclesiastical drama of the eighteenth century in fact expressed itself and crystallized as a resentment against the "flat and formal" preaching of the established Liberal clergy.

When Gilbert Tennent in 1740 criticized the "cold and sapless" discourses of the "Pharisee-Teachers" as "unaffecting," he proclaimed what was to be the most enduring challenge of the evangelical scheme to American religion. An "unconverted" minister, Tennent insisted, was "neither inclined to, nor fitted for Discoursing, frequently, clearly, and pathetically" on the "important Subjects of Christian doctrine."[8]

Tennent was raising questions both of doctrine and style, but as his words suggest, the underlying issue was one of character—of the inclination of the minister's heart and his fitness to his calling. To Tennent, as to the ministers who echoed him and the multitude who followed him, the unconverted minister was in his very being, as well as in his matter and manner, something of a symbol of what to Calvinists seemed the moral malaise of colonial society: an un-Christian aspiration for wealth and lordly status, and an indifference to the welfare of others.

In 1740 Tennent charged that a minister who was offended by the separation of his church members had "good Cause to grieve over his own Rottenness and Hypocrisie," since by seeking to hold them he proved a preference for his own "Credit" over their "greater Good." In what precisely this "Credit" was supposed to consist the Calvinist ministry was seldom reluctant to announce; from the moment when Tennent likened the Old Side ministry to Judas, whose eyes had been "fixed upon the Bag,"[9] through the 1760's, when Joseph Bellamy accused a Connecticut Socinian of overwhelming desires to "keep possession of the hundred pounds per annum,"[10] the standing Calvinist opinion of the anti-revival clergy was that they had come

> into the Priests Office for a Piece of Bread; they took it up as a Trade, and therefore endeavoured to make the best Market of it they could.

Whether Tennent's cry of "Shame!" was justifiably applied to every Arminian,[11] and whether every Calvinist indeed came before the people not "to get his Bread, but," as Eleazar Wheelock explained, "to be instrumental to save your Souls,"[12] cannot, of course, be determined. In fact, most Arminians were equally certain that a "mendicant turn" was behind the Calvinist efforts to augment the size of dissenter congregations and to withhold church taxes from the official parish minister.*[13]

---

* Most of the critics of the revival strongly suggested in the 1740's that Whitefield was pocketing the money he raised for the Orphan Asylum. These critics included Benjamin Franklin, whose anonymous jibes at Whitefield as a "trimmer" were hardly as artful as the better-known portrait, in the *Autobiography*, of the evangelists' money-raising gifts. The outlines of this sketch were, interestingly enough, also penned during the Awakening, and even earlier. One Massachusetts opponent of the revival recalled the career (in the late 1690's) of Samuel May and noted that this mountebank had been distinguished for his eloquence. William Cooper, who took this as an implicit slur on Whitefield, denied that May had been an orator. His opponent replied with quotations from Cotton Mather's characterization of May: "the surest Argument of the *Power of his* Oratory" is that "he *open'd the People's Pockets,* as well as mov'd *their passions.*"

The rationalist ministry did believe, however, that a Christian minister, in order to fulfill the functions of his office properly, had to be guaranteed an unfluctuating income. The Arminian clergy were characteristically defenders of the solemn obligations of contracts. When the people of a parish settle a minister, John Tucker insisted, they enter into a "Civil contract" to pay him a stated annual salary. To separate, he explained, is worse than a breaking of one's covenant with his neighbors; it is a violation of his contract with the minister.[14] So enamored was Tucker of this legal principle that during the inflation of the Revolution he evolved what was possibly the first practical substantive interpretation of the common law concept of due process. To this inflation each element of the Protestant clergy responded differently. The Calvinist ministry, willing to share with their people the misfortunes of war, arranged to reduce or forego the payments agreed upon at the time of settlement; while, if memoirs and autobiographies of the heralds of America's Liberal faith can be trusted, many of the proto-Unitarians of New England were inspired by a reduced real income to question whether they had indeed been called unto the ministerial profession.[15] But Tucker (who wondered in his declining years why a barbarous antipathy to "hireling ministers" had arisen among the American people in the course of the Revolution) developed the most remarkable system for meeting the challenge of the age. Demanding the equivalent purchasing power of his contracted salary, Tucker arranged with the civil authorities of Newburyport to have his rightful due in Continentals brought him monthly in wheelbarrows.

The Calvinists' conception of the relationship of minister and people had nothing to do with contractual obligations. Their attitude was given its consummate expression in Edwards' sermon at the installation of Samuel Buell. At the end of the sermon Edwards mentioned, as of somewhat incidental importance, the provision for a minister's "outward subsistence and comfort," not as an obligation but to be given voluntarily and cheerfully to all who manifested themselves as serving in Christ's "embassy," as cheerfully, indeed, as the services of Rebekah for Abraham's servant.[16] The major theme of the sermon, which marks a high point in Edwards' effort to revive and enforce on the mind of American Calvinism an ideal of "the great importance and high ends of the office of an evangelical pastor," was not parish finances, but the fact that a minister was to be "knit" to his people "in a spiritual and pure love, and, as it were, a conjugal tenderness." The central passage of The Church's Marriage was that in which Edwards dismissed what he considered the prevailing relationship between ministers and people, and articulated another. "The minister's heart," Edwards explained,

> is united to the people, not for filthy lucre or any worldly advantage, but with a pure benevolence to them, and desire to their spiritual welfare and prosperity, and complacence in them as children of God and followers of Christ Jesus. And, on the other hand, they love and honour him with a holy affection and esteem . . . receiving him as the messenger of the Lord of Hosts, coming to them on a divine and infinitely important errand, and with those holy qualifications that resemble the virtues of the Lamb of God.[17]

Edwards' celebration of the union of minister and people was informed, like all his thoughts, by typology.*[18] But that the Calvinist populace did receive their ministers as "Types of the Messiah" was testimony less to the brilliant consistency of Edwards' theories than to the manner in which the Calvinist ministry strove to embody the virtues of the Lamb of God. The Calvinist *Manuductio ad Ministerium* was Edwards' biography of Brainerd, in which the young missionary was represented as seeking to do nothing that was not "in some respect for the glory of God or the good of men."[19] It may be that Chauncy's complaint that Americans were being taught by Calvinists to "glory in Men" was not wholly unjustified. From the time of Tennent's following Whitefield into New England dressed in the sackcloth of John Baptist, the Calvinist ministry was accused by the Liberals of affecting a friar-like disdain for the world's goods.

Few Calvinists practiced or condoned such blatant exhibitions as James Davenport's burning of his vestments, but all insisted that it was "a wrong mercenary thing" for ministers to have "any eye to their own benefit in any thing they do."[20] Their opponents, on the other hand, were distinguished, though hardly by a selfish indifference to the glory of God and the good of mankind, yet by what L. J. Trinterud has called, in the case of the Presbyterian Old Side, "an ugly form of clericalism."[21] Such clericalism took the form of a special emphasis on the privileges and prerogatives of the clergy and an apparent unwillingness to provide the laity with what Tennent called the "greater Good." Among New England Liberals it was first expressed in a conviction that the *only* purpose of the itinerating evangelists was "to subvert the

---

* In the Edwardean formulation, the minister was characterized by a beauty, or "true excellence," essentially that of Christ. "Therefore it must needs be," Edwards explained in another ordination sermon of the 1740's, "that ministers, by being burning and shining lights, are acceptable and amiable in the sight of God, as he delights in his own image and the image of his Son: and hereby also they will be honourable and amiable in the sight of men, all such as have any sense of that which is truly excellent and beautiful."

standing Ministry." Similarly, when it became clear that men were "divided about their Teachers," the anti-revivalists saw it as their main "Duty" to "crush such Factions."[22] Eventually the rationalist attitude hardened into policies that seemed designed to maintain the clergy as a privileged class.

The contrasting evangelical conception of the ministry was in part a function of Calvinism's definition of the "law of charity." For Calvinists, natural abilities, "acquired accomplishments," and indeed any and all of "the Endowments of Nature, Improvements of Art, or Aids of Birth and Fortune" were "so many talents" to be improved and consecrated by doing "good in the world."[23] Thus in evangelical eyes the primal sin of the Liberal clergy was what seemed an "insatiable Thirst" for "that Honour which consists in an unscriptural Preheminence over their brethren."[24] In making this charge the Calvinist was only in part thinking of Liberal sacerdotalism or of the manner in which the rational clergy construed the constitution of the church. The objection was ultimately to what the Liberal minister conceived to be his place in society and to the manner in which he expressed and revealed his aspirations. The issue was indeed, at bottom, one of style.

In the years between the Awakening and the battles of Lexington and Concord, the most common complaint against dissenters, and in later years presumably an argument against their religious freedom, was that they rejected "men of learning and abilities for teachers" and altogether preferred "such as are illiterate and men of ordinary abilities." Insofar as men sought religious liberty in order to enjoy the ministrations of Parsons, Cleaveland, and Whitaker, the accusation was a patent libel, and by the 1770's even Baptists had abandoned their prejudices against an educated clergy. In fact it seems to have been the *"manners"* of the Harvard-trained ministry that succeeded in "prejudicing peoples minds" not only against the ministers themselves, but often against the "college-learning" that had presumably taught them such manners.[25]

The more substantial suspicion of a merely educated clergy was that articulated by Tennent in his sermon on an *Unconverted Ministry:*

> The old Pharisees were very proud and conceity; they loved the uppermost Seats in the Synagogues, and to be called Rabbi, Rabbi; they were masterly and positive in their Assertions, as if forsooth Knowledge must die with them; they look'd upon others that differed from them, and the common People, with an Air of Disdain; and especially any who had a Respect for JESUS and his Doctrine, and dislik'd them; they judged such accursed.[26]

Behind Tennent's opinion of the Pharisees of his own day was a belief, common to Edwards and many of the older Calvinists as well as to the itinerants, that the "greater part of learned men" in the age of Anne—as just "before Christ came" and again in the "dark times of popery, before the Reformation"—misused their education.[27] One familiar consequence of learning was described by Ebenezer Pemberton in a sermon delivered at Yale College at the invitation of the undergraduates:

> Men are apt highly to value themselves upon the account of their human Knowledge and to look down with contempt upon others, whom they esteem ignorant and unlearn'd. . .[28]

Another Calvinist complaint was a symptom of partisan sensitivity: those who possessed what Tennent called "the Learning in Fashion" were more than ready to scoff at the old faith as a ridiculous anachronism in an age of reason and science. Nor need one accept Calvinism as a superior philosophy in order to appreciate the legitimacy of its resentments of what was as much the manner of American rationalism as its matter. Thomas Foxcroft hardly erred when, in his preface to Jonathan Dickinson's *True Scripture-Doctrine,* he complained that men who "had but a little" of the wisdom of Newton and Locke used their smattering of knowledge to "run down" Calvinism "as obsolete, jejune & insipid to the refin'd Taste of the present free and thinking Age."[29] There is in eighteenth-century literature perhaps no more relentless an exposure of the intellectual arrogance, the pretension and the condescension of the Augustan mind than Edwards' characterization, in the *Dissertation on the Will,* of the manner in which the prophets of rational religion, having allowed—"in an ostentation of a very generous charity"—that Luther, Calvin, Ames, and Hooker "did pretty well for the day in which they lived," went on to plainly suggest

> that they were persons, who—through the lowness of their genius, and the greatness of the bigotry with which their minds were shackled, and their thoughts confined, living in the gloomy caves of superstition—fondly embraced, and demurely and zealously taught the most absurd, silly, and monstrous opinions, worthy of the greatest contempt of gentlemen possessed of that noble and generous freedom of thought, which happily prevails in this age of light and inquiry.[30]

The Calvinist quarrel was not with "human learning in itself," but, as Isaac Backus put it, with the "Place" some accorded it in eighteenth-century society. Those who in the colonies were most "forward to cry up Human Reason and Accomplishments," he observed, were generally possessed of a profound "spiritual ignorance."[31] For "when real or pretended knowledge," Backus explained,

> is used to keep others in ignorance, and to excite a high opinion of themselves, instead of laboring to enlighten and benefit others; that it is a certain token of such persons being ensnared by, if they are not under the full power *of,* the *wisdom* which is from beneath.[32]

The issue, at least as it was drawn by the Calvinist clergy and populace, came down finally to the "infinite importance," as Edwards put it, "to common people, as well as to ministers," of knowing "what kind of being God is."[33] So far as Calvinists were concerned the Liberal minister often used his learning, not merely to magnify himself, but to keep a knowledge of God from the people.

On the latter count the record seems to bear out the Calvinist indictment, at least to the extent that the rationalist clergy were disposed to keeping their thoughts to themselves. During the Awakening many opponents of the revival were more than reluctant to make public their opinion either of the Awakening or of the doctrines of Calvinism. Their diffidence, Chauncy explained in his *Seasonable Thoughts,* was the result of fears that open awovals of attitude might result in a minister's "being turn'd out into the wide World" by a displeased congregation. Considering the minister's dependence on his salary, could he be faulted for "behaving as might best take with the *Populace*" until such a time as was more propitious for disclosure of his true sentiments?[34] By the end of the 1740's such an argument had been translated, by ministers whose orthodoxy was suspect, into a justification of silence or equivocation where a people was "not ready" for profounder theological insights.[35] The attitude persisted well beyond the period in which Liberal religion mounted an open assault on Calvinist doctrine. As late as 1779 a younger Liberal recommended that Chauncy's speculations on *The Mystery Hid from Ages and Generations,* being "too sublime for the soaring of vulgar imaginations," remain hidden for a few more years, lest they "dazzle, if not blind, the eyes of the populace."[36] Not surprisingly many of the Liberal clergy were among the earliest patrons of English Masonry in the colonies. For the Liberal mind was clearly disposed to the classic and medieval distinction between esoteric and exoteric knowledge.

Moreover, the characteristic Liberal utterance on controverted points of doctrine was an exercise, if not in pure obfuscation, then in avoiding what Calvinists took to be the issues. In the late 1740's several rationalists, among them Lemuel Briant, whom John Adams considered the father of American Unitarianism, issued what were clearly intended as repudiations of inherited doctrine. According to orthodox critics, however, the manifestoes of rationalism were far from pointed; rather they were distinguished by "loose and general Hints only, attended with ambiguity, and conveying no distinct determinate Idea." Briant's intention in his sermon on *The Absurdity of Depreciating Moral Virtue* was abundantly clear, and even his precise meaning evident to the discerning eye. But when challenged, Briant claimed the right to put an orthodox gloss on his guarded expressions. A descendant and namesake of the Puritan intellectual, John Cotton, in expressing disgust with such evasiveness, testified both to the pride of Calvinists and their frustrations in the controversy: I "don't desire (as the Manner of some is) to muffle my self up in Shade and Obscurity, in general Terms, and ambiguous Expressions, as if ashamed of my Principles."[37] For a number of years, Calvinists refused to consider the "great debate" over doctrine to be a debate at all, since by their lights the spokesmen of the new rationalism were persistently avoiding a direct confrontation of ideas.

Nor was the imprecision of Liberal argument a mere debater's trick. Curiously enough, American rationalism seems not to have been given to logical or semantic precision. Bellamy once complained that his opponents' approach to theological discussion was to brand as "metaphysical niceties" all the "clear distinctions, and conclusive arguments" that they were "not able fairly to get rid of."[38] Whatever the justice of Bellamy's charge, the partisans of reason seemed to prefer the simplicity of faith to what struck them as Calvinism's intellectual complexity. During the Awakening Alexander Garden sought to dismiss Whitefield as a preacher of *"speculative perplexing* Notions."[39] Clearly the Anglican clergy were particularly prepared for such a response by virtue of their two centuries' battle against a logic-chopping Puritanism. Garden's protégé, the Boston-born Samuel Quincy, defined the principles of "rational religion" in this manner:

> whatever Doctrine is of Importance, it is always very plain and obvious. . . And therefore when any Doctrines are proposed to us full of Intricacy and Perplexity, we may rest assured (whatever confident Man may pretend) that they signifie very little to us whether true or false, and therefore had much better be wholly neglected by us, than that we perplex our Minds about them.[40]

A similar disposition to salutary neglect of difficult ideas was also evinced where presumably it should least have been expected—among the Congregationalists of New England. One of the first Boston assaults on the revival consisted of a compendium of extracts from Flavel, so applied as to convict Whitefield and his followers of both

"Popish credulity" *and* a vain intellectual curiosity—"an itching Desire to pry into Things unrevealed, at least above our Ability to search out and discover."[41] Indeed, one of Charles Chauncy's earliest contributions to the study of religious psychology was a declaration that the effects of the Holy Spirit on the mind were "such the less we puzzle ourselves or others about them, the better."[42] Similarly, one of Mayhew's more candid discussions of the question of the freedom of the will included the observation that "if we *exercise ourselves in these things,* I know of no valuable end it can answer."[43] Given such evidence, it might be that, in the search for the sources of anti-intellectualism in America, the place to begin is not with the revivalists*[44] but with those more reasonable Bostonians who, long before the era of the younger Holmes, thought it dangerous for one to play too much with his mind.

To the multitude, however, the more searing judgment on the letter-learned clergy was their use of knowledge for an affectation of pre-eminency. Actually, Liberals were, like Calvinists, seeking in their own way to restore the ministry to the position it seemed to have enjoyed

---

* To be sure, James Davenport did commit the ultimate anti-intellectual sin when he consigned hundreds of books (including what he thought some diabolical sermons by Jonathan Parsons) to a bonfire. But such conduct was not approved by the revival ministry generally; Gilbert Tennent quickly rebuked Davenport for this "ridiculous" episode. And Davenport himself, even before he issued his *Confession,* acknowledged that in his book-burning he had been false to the spirit of evangelical religion in that he had thereby laid a "Stress on Externals." The more typical Awakening attitude toward "dangerous" books was Isaac Chanler's "Advice to New Converts, concerning the Books they should read or avoid." This was in the nature of pastoral advice, and comparable to Edwards' suggestion, not that a gynecologic manual be banned, but that the parents of Northampton's delinquents know what their children were reading and act accordingly. Similarly, Whitefield did not ask that Tillotson and Chubb be removed from the Harvard library; he only proposed that Shepard and Stoddard were better reading. Despite the outraged cries of the Harvard and Yale faculties that Whitefield was interfering with their academic freedom, his advice was hardly of the same order as the punishment meted out to Yale students for proposing the republication of Locke's *Letter on Toleration.*

The Calvinist ministry was, if anything, rather too ingenuous in publicizing not only its knowledge but some of the implications of that knowledge. Edwards, for instance, presumably made a heedless remark to President Clap of Yale that Whitefield planned to import a battalion of regenerate young Scotsmen to replace the unconverted clergy of New England. A distorted version of this interview served the Liberal cause as handsomely as the charge that Edwards, in arguing against the Stoddardean polity, was secretly working with the separatists.

In time certain younger members of the evangelical party, believing they were victims of a persecuting conspiracy at John Witherspoon's Princeton, thought it necessary to circulate Bellamy's writings (without title pages) furtively and under a pledge of secrecy. Eventually also some of Bellamy's students deemed it advisable, in order to avoid the long arms of the Connecticut magistracy and of the Alien and Sedition Laws, to address their parishioners in a private, highly metaphorical language. But there seems to have been no instance of the Calvinist ministry's cherishing knowledge as too precious or too dangerous to be shared with the laity.

in the Puritan past and from which it had fallen to a low point in the 1720's. That decade witnessed the emergence of a variety of strategies whereby ministerial status might be regained. Some New England ministers opted simply to take Episcopal orders. They and those who followed them in this course could thereafter look down, as did Samuel Johnson, on the less favored clergy who were not dignified by history and ceremony. Others, among them Chauncy's colleague, Thomas Foxcroft, strove to impress on their people the need for order in the church, and with it "distinctions of Superior and Inferior."[45] Foxcroft was perhaps closest of all to invoking the reality of the Puritan ideal, but he happened also to be among those who welcomed the Awakening. He remained its partisan long after Chauncy began to deride and condemn the upstart progress of enthusiasm, and thus unwittingly if not unwillingly encouraged what was to be not the least of the fruits of the revival, the ascendancy in the church of the laity.

The growth of lay power took different forms in the churches of Calvinism and those of the legal scheme. Apart from purely constitutional questions, it must be observed that the Liberal clergy were prone to the temptation which Increase Mather had warned against early in the century: avoiding "such things as may be offensive to some of the Wealthiest people in the Town."[46] As Francis Alison explained in 1758 when pleading for Presbyterian reunion, the Old Side clergy was just "naturally more calm and moderate" and "not so easily, nor vehemently, moved against the errors and iniquities of the times."[47] Behind such moderation was the relation between minister and people that came to obtain in Liberal churches. The nature of the relationship is suggested by Thomas Barnard's recommendation that the laity "think and act for themselves in the Things of Religion." This meant, according to Barnard, that ministers must be "ready to receive Light" from their people "as well as give it to them."[48] Considering who among the people the Arminian clergy thought capable of discerning the light, this meant of course that Barnard expected to receive counsel from the more reasonable and respectable of his parishioners. In sum, the Liberal clergy were heir to that New England tradition, older perhaps than the Half-Way Covenant but with it written into the constitution of the churches, that made the minister by no means master in his house.

Had the Liberal clergy done no more than perpetuate the policies of Hooker and Stoddard, they might not have aroused such fervid hostility. But it seems clear that they were given to measuring the ministerial calling by "worldly" standards. In advising the youth of Boston of "the most effectual means of securing a good name amongst men," Jonathan Mayhew posed these rhetorical questions:

Which is the most to be desired, the approbation of the *few* wise and *knowing,* who judge of things according to nature, truth and propriety; or that of a vast *multitude* of *fools* and *madmen,* who are really ignorant what true worth, excellency and honor consist in? If you were painters, statuaries or architects; if you were poets, musicians or orators; and not riches, but reputation was your principal end, would you not be ambitious of pleasing the best judges, the greatest masters in these noble arts, rather than vast ignorant multitudes, who had neither skill, taste nor judgment in them?[49]

This keynote passage from Mayhew's famous sermons entitled *Christian Sobriety* helps in an understanding of Mayhew's own career. It also discloses what was ultimately at stake in the numerous *ad hominem* charges of "gross vice and impiety" leveled at various clergymen in the eighteenth century.[50] The truth of such accusations is of less significance than what the charges represented: a feeling that certain ministers were behaving in a manner unbecoming a Christian by seeking standards of conduct outside the traditional forms and conventions of American experience.

What the Liberal clergyman was seeking was of course gentility. In this pursuit he encountered more obstacles and perplexities than even the pious hungerer after salvation. As Benjamin Franklin's life and writings attest, the American experience did not provide within itself an adequate definition of the gentleman. The people of New Jersey, as Dr. Alexander Hamilton complained in 1744,

commonly held their heads higher than the rest of mankind and imagined few or none were their equals. But this I found always proceeded from their narrow notions, ignorance of the world, and low extraction, which indeed is the case with most of our aggrandized upstarts in these infant countreys of America who never had an opportunity to see, or if they had, the capacity to observe the different ranks of men in polite nations or to know what it is that really constitutes that difference of degrees.[51]

The seemingly ingrained egalitarianism of the American multitude was but one source of the perplexity of those who, in the eighteenth century, aspired to gentility in a provincial setting. The effort of the would-be gentleman of the colonies to define his character and function is perhaps *the* theme of our eighteenth-century literature.

Of particular pertinence is the degree to which the Liberal clergy played a role in defining the American gentleman. The Anglican clergy, not surprisingly, were the most outspoken in conceiving the minister as a gentleman and from that premise arguing for salary appropriate to the station. As Jonathan Boucher explained to his Virginia parishioners,

We are often by birth, and always by education and profession, gentlemen: and if the establishment of such an order of men be of moment to the welfare of society, (as it unquestionably is,) society is much concerned to see that means be provided to enable us to live in a decorous and exemplary style.[52]

Boucher differed even from his Anglican colleagues in being neither American-born nor discreet, but unquestionably the Episcopal clergy generally were identified with gentility throughout eighteenth-century America. In the early 1720's, Samuel Johnson hesitated to take Episcopal orders because he feared in himself a "want of that politeness" requisite to the office. Once he had taken the step, however, he ceased to doubt his qualifications, or at least he paraded his presumed superiority to those citizens of Connecticut who remained attached to the church of their fathers. In 1733 he addressed a letter to the dissenters of Connecticut concerning the scriptural validity of the Episcopal way. Attacked in an anonymous pamphlet, Johnson replied that he was sorry his critic had shown "himself so little of the gentleman" in his manner. Thereafter, whether admonishing Connecticut dissenters or such spokesmen of Calvinism as Jonathan Dickinson, the first president of the College of New Jersey, Johnson generally observed of his opponents that their ideas and style had "nothing of the English spirit," that their performances were "all over out-landish."[53]

This combination of a quest for gentility with strictures on the style, literary and otherwise, of less fortunate Americans came to distinguish the Liberal clergy of the colonies who did not make the journey to Lambeth. In the period after the Awakening, the attitude of the Arminian clergy toward the Anglican was generally a combination of questioning the morals of the latter and yet using them as something of a standard by which to measure their own approximation of gentility. Evidence of such ambivalence is to be seen in the reaction of recent Yale graduates to Noah Hobart's 1747 sermon at the ordination of Noah Welles. The Old Light Hobart accused the Anglican ministry of "looseness and immorality," and when Welles sent a copy of the sermon to William Livingston, the latter allowed that probably the Episcopalian clergy did "indulge themselves in a much more licentious course of Life than the Dissenting Ministers."[54] None of the three, however, was concerned merely with the qualifications of a gospel minister. In passing these observations on men of some English experience, they were struggling to ascertain the qualities of a true gentleman, or, as Livingston's *Philosophic Solitude* (1747) suggests, to evolve a concept of the gentleman more befitting American conditions.

So too the clergymen, among them Welles, who penned rhymed prefaces to Livingston's *Philosophic Solitude*. Welles' tribute—"A *second Windsor* starts in every line"—suggests both the literary standards of this circle and something of the appeal to this and the next American generations of Pope's poem. In *Philosophic Solitude* Livingston righteously foreswore a life in the metropolis that was not, in any case, a likely possibility in the New World. Yet soon after celebrating the joys of rural solitude, Livingston left the meanders of Connecticut for the bustle of New York City, where he commenced a career of publication that brought him finally into Revolutionary politics. As in the case of Benjamin Franklin, it would be hard to point to the precise moment when Livingston ceased being moved primarily by a desire for English approbation and when his motives became those of one resentful of the failure of the metropolitan mind to appreciate his endeavors. In any case, the literary endeavor of Livingston's friends among the Old Light and Old Side clergy developed not merely in imitation of English models but as an avowed and self-conscious quest for London critical plaudits. Francis Alison, for instance, writing to Ezra Stiles in 1757 of his projected *American Magazine,* proposed that this undertaking might encourage "some men of abilities" and some "young students to become literary adventurers," and thus

> promote a friendly intercourse among men of Learning in our different Colonies, & possibly produce some papers worthy the approbation of Great Britain famed for Arts & Sciences.[55]

Alison's proposal was an extension of that made in 1743 by Benjamin Franklin. Insofar as young Philadelphians were encouraged to enter on literary careers, there was set a stage for that final contest between Whigs and Tories that took as one form the struggle over definition of the American Philosophical Society. The leader of the "cultural" phalanx in Philadelphia—as opposed to the more "practical" David Rittenhouse and, eventually, Franklin himself, was the Reverend William Smith. An Anglican, Smith was the epitome of the self-conscious littérateur of pre-Revolutionary America. He published among other things a series of "original" essays entitled "The Hermit," one theme of which was the evolution of an American gentleman, and in which the hermitage was happily placed to allow for frequent visits from members of the Philosophical Society. Even more characteristic of Smith's output were some Hudibrastic verses he published in London in 1756. The volume opened with an "apology" from the author (identified as "a Gentleman in London") for not having the time

> to finish it in so correct a manner as I could wish; and yet, unfinished as it is, I dare say there are some whimsical Particularities of Sentiment and Expression, which will afford you Entertainment.[56]

The "apology," dispatched as it was to a "friend in Pennsylvania," revealed, albeit in perhaps an extreme form even for that era, one of the values of a literary career to a Liberal minister. Familiarity with the theory and practice of belles-lettres was one certificate of knowledge of the great world and its manners.

Such knowledge gave the minister a role as something of a social arbiter in colonial society. It allowed him to serve as a tutor in etiquette to his parishioners, or, as in the instance of Mayhew, to all the would-be young gentlemen of the city. No Liberal minister of the period managed this role nearly so well as would William Ellery Channing, or, for that matter, as had Benjamin Colman in the obsessively provincial Boston of the early eighteenth century. But it was the ability to monitor the conduct of even his most successful parishioners—themselves in search of standards of behavior commensurate with a new status in life—that gave the worldly-wise Liberal clergyman some of the prestige and power of an earlier day.

Although the order of advice dispensed from Liberal pulpits hardly agreed with the Calvinist ministry, the latter by no means looked on literary endeavor as entirely unworthy of a sacred calling. As has been noted, Samuel Davies wrote poems; Finley, in his memorial sermon, praised Davies' compositions for their "great degree of true poetic fire, style, and imagery."[57] But there was in this respect as in others a wide difference of taste between the rational and evangelical clergy. In his poems Davies sought to preserve, as against the "modern taste," both the reputation and something of the style of the "Divine Wit, Herbert." He praised Young's *Night Thoughts* and approvingly quoted one stanza, though adapting "to the *Preacher* what was originally applied to the Poet":

On Themes like these, 'tis *impious* to be *calm*
Passion is *Reason; Transport Temper,* here. . .

Davies also saluted Young as an excellent judge of "the *true Sublime*" and, by way of praising Thomson's *The Seasons,* objected to neoclassicism's fixation on Mediterranean shepherds and deities. The beauty and propriety of "poetical Descriptions," Davies argued, "and particularly of Invocations, consist in their Correspondence to the Sentiments, Manners and Customs of those for whom we write."[58] Such critical observations, as well as Davies' poetic practice, are evidence that in the colonies as in England there was a relationship between evangelical dissent and what the literary historian calls "preRomanticism."

But the issue between the American Calvinist and Liberal was not simply that of whether to imitate, with the rational poetaster, Butler and Pope. As Liberal sensibilities were sharpened, the sublimities of Akenside came to be appreciated, and throughout the century the rationalist mind considered Calvinism as behind the times in its appreciation of literature as in its dogmas. A New Englander who defended Whitefield against the Harvard faculty was charged with both impudence and a quaintness that was no match for the tasteful periods of the Harvard *Testimony:*

> I doubt not but it will always be esteemed by judicious and unprejudic'd Persons, as much preferable to your Defence of the *Itinerant,* as Mr. *Lock's* Works are to *John Bunyan's.*[59]

Undoubtedly most Calvinists did admire Bunyan, and surely they kept alive the memory of John Milton as "one of the finest Genius's" in English literary history. But in celebrating Milton's virtues the fundamental question, for the Calvinist, was not literary, but the moral one implied in the conviction that Milton was most to be remembered as one of "the greatest of Men that ever lived."[60] The ultimate issue was Milton's end and aim in writing, and the purpose of all literary composition whatever. Davies stated the case for American Calvinists by citing Herbert's line, "A Verse may hit him whom a Sermon flies." Poetry was not a whimsical entertainment, but a "glorious Enterprize" aimed, in the case either of Davies' verses or the hymns composed by Samuel Buell or Nathaniel Niles, at alluring men from sin (and sinful poetry). It was not one of the elements of greatness, Calvinists believed, to neglect the spiritual needs of the many in order to titillate the few.

As in the days of the Puritan assault on the preaching of Andrewes and Donne, the literary ideals of Calvinism contained both social imperative and a moral judgment on Liberal pulpit practice. The minister, according to the Calvinist, should sacrifice "such ornaments of style as might best suit the taste of men of polite literature" in order that he might better serve "the benefit of persons of a vulgar capacity."[61] The issue was clearly one of purposes and priority; a minister must be "more anxious about being understood by the Weakest, and most Unpolished, than pleasing to the Learned and Polite."[62] Whence David Bostwick, in setting forth the conditions of the New Side Synod of New York for accepting union with the Synod of Philadelphia, demanded that henceforth all Presbyterian ministers should cease producing sermons "set off with glittering toys, with figures of rhetorick, and arts of elocution." But to accomplish this, Bostwick allowed, it was necessary for the minister to "disclaim self," and this, it seemed, was the very hurdle that Liberal ministers, with their literary aspirations, were unable to overcome.[63]

There is certainly no reason to accept unquestioningly the judgment of the Calvinist ministry as to the motives of the "liberal" young men who in the decades before the Revolution entered on a career in the ministry. To James Finley it seemed evident they were *"eager* in grasping after" such a position because it seemed "not only a Genteel, but, as they may think, an *easy* employment."[64] Actually Jonathan Mayhew in 1763 included the ministry among the various learned occupations and professions in which men might engage without being "obliged to what is commonly called hard labor."[65] In any case, they who became Liberal clergymen in the second half of the eighteenth century were generally not the most vigorous or heroic figures ever to serve in the American pulpit. Perhaps some of them deserved Samuel Buell's jibe that the consequence of filling such candidates with a *"Measure* of Literature" would be a ministry of "whole Clusters of light, airy" dilettantes.[66] Possibly the development of American literature did in fact demand (as the editors of so many gentleman's magazines would contend in the last years of the century) an American leisure class. In the *Monthly Anthology* the generation of Emerson's father and of Andrews Norton would go so far as to argue the public subsidization of a literary vicarage. All this the Calvinist ministry sensed well before the Revolution, but they were not hostile to the progress of letters. They did believe that the Christian embassy demanded "men of self-denial" and that such a high calling had no place for those who aspired to "living politely."[67] They would not abide the conversion of the ministry into a mere scholar's sinecure or, even more clearly, the perversion of the sacred desk into a rostrum for the gaining of a literary reputation.

The pulpit practices of Liberalism were probably as appropriate to their urbane (or hopefully so) congregations as were those of the evangelical preacher to his. Indeed the charges and countercharges of the embattled clergy clearly evinced the reorganization of church membership consequent to the Awakening. When Samuel Davies arraigned the "polite" Anglican preachers of Virginia as "the lumber, or rather the pests of society," his audiences were already composed exclusively of men and women who had little stomach for the prescriptions of reason.[68] Likewise when Chauncy characterized the "ravings" of the evangelical clergy as "arising from Pride, Ignorance, Prejudice, Heat and Strength of Imagination,"[69] it was not too likely that many of his hearers were still particularly sympathetic to the doctrines and preachments of the Awakening. The ecclesiastical mobility of the 1740's resulted in giving each order of preaching something of a monopoly on the attention and taste of elements of the populace. Indeed one of the profounder interpretations of the effects of the Awakening was that offered by Joseph Bellamy. Taught by his own experience that Calvinism appealed more to some Americans than others, Bellamy came close to an immutable truth when he observed that men generally "cry up those ministers most" whose preaching and conduct "agree with their hearts."[70]

In this respect the Liberal clergy seem also to have learned a version of the homiletic precept that Davies considered the most essential: "It is comparatively easy to a minister, who ardently loves his people to make them sensible that he does love them and is their real friend."[71] The ardor of the rationalist clergy was most unquestionable when they inveighed against religious enthusiasm—and, especially, against the enthusiasts themselves. With the possible exception of John Thomson's *The Government of the Church of Christ*, the anti-revival literature was uniformly characterized by ill-tempered satire and personal abuse. The attacks of the Querists on Whitefield and Tennent, and "The Wandering Spirit" and other revival criticisms published in Franklin's *General Magazine* were of such an order that Finley expressed surprise to see Thomson proceeding "as tho' he were for Reasoning the Matter soberly."

> [The] other Members of the Synod, in the Queries, and Examination, and as they say Refutatation [sic] of Mr. *Tennent*'s Remarks on the Protestation, have laid aside, seemingly, all Pretence to Sobriety, and betake themselves to Outrage and Banter: They go on like Men Swallowed up in Passion; like Men that look on themselves baffled, and therefore grow desperate and care not what they say.[72]

Whatever the explanation, the evidence indicates that those who criticized the revival in the name of "reason" frequently gave way, in the heat of battle, to modes of discourse that hardly justified their lecturing Gilbert Tennent on the tastelessness of his sermon on an unconverted ministry. And long after the revival, they treated enthusiasm as a subject of derision rather than one to be examined and discussed. "There is no Argument in scornful Laughter and witty Burlesque," Samuel Blair at last wearily reminded the Old Side: "Come and let us reason together."[73]

In New England the opponents of the revival were at first content to republish the Middle Colony diatribes. But there also the spokesmen of reasonable Christianity, even as they counted the epithets in "that famous, or rather infamous, *Nottingham* Sermon," developed their own vocabulary of *ad hominem* attack and derisive condescension.[74] What was to become the prevailing tone of Liberal commentary on evangelical religion was set in Chauncy's *Seasonable Thoughts*. In his argument, Chauncy leaned heavily on Locke's *Essay Concerning Human Understanding*, but most especially on those sections in which Locke suggested enthusiasm was a sort of mental disease. Thereafter Liberal discussion of the "New Light" became ill-tempered diatribes, increasingly filled with pompous and condescending observations on the insanity rather than the heresy of the enthusiast. In the late 1740's Jonathan Mayhew, but recently come to be pastor of Boston's West Church, told his congregation that those who claimed to be "awakened" were in fact "enlightened Ideots" who

> impute all their ravings and follies and wild imaginations to the spirit of God; and usually think themselves *converted,* when the poor, unhappy creatures are *only out of their wits.*[75]

Similar sentiments filled Smith's poem of 1756, a satire of the Quakers that broadened into a derisive characterization of all who claimed direction of the *"heav'nly light"* instead of being "Slaves to Common Sense."[76] Likewise Ezra Stiles in 1760, rehearsing the history of the Great Awakening, recalled the converts of those days as being simply out of their minds, and though it is difficult to comprehend how such thoughts were to contribute to the "Christian union" for which he pleaded, it is not hard to understand why they came to be uttered even in such circumstances. For years Old Light and Liberal clergy had been speaking not *to* the advocates of emotional religion, but *about* them, to the delight if not the edification of their own parishioners.

Such habits of discourse were carried over into Liberal contributions to New England's doctrinal and ecclesiastical "debates." Isaac Backus considered the more typical of rationalists' response to his challenges was their "calling the worst names, and using the most odious comparisons, that their learning afforded."[77] It was not only the unlettered Backus, however, whom the reasonable clergy held in contempt. The "senseless Divinity" of Calvin, by whomever upheld, was conceived by Liberals to appeal only to "the tho'tless Multitude," whose ignorance they invariably contrasted with the wisdom of the favored few in whom the precepts of reason reigned.[78] By the late 1750's all defenders of such doctrines as original sin were targets for the derisive thrusts of Liberals. A typical performance in this regard was that of John Tucker, who answered a long refutation of Arminianism by observing of his critic that, among other things, his literary style might do for the "clownish and rustic" parts and classes of America, but not in enlightened and urbane Newburyport. His debater, one Aaron Hutchinson, observed in reply that "the chief beauty" of Tucker's essay seemed to be "bitterness of invective," and that a cause seemed "very suspicious, that needs such weapons to support it."[79] Suspicious or not, the cause of Liberalism was often comforted if not abetted by literary and forensic devices that were aptly characterized as *"Banter"*—not merely *"personal* Reflection" but ridicule both of what Calvinists called the "Christian experience" (a "disordered Brain") and of what they deemed "the great Soul-humbling and Christ-exalting Doctrines of the Gospel."[80] Curiously enough, the Liberal clergy all along pleaded for charity and forbearance on all doctrinal differences. Presumably the "epithets of reproach or some discriminating marks of odium" of which Calvinists complained were also the mint, anise, and cumin over which true Christians should never divide.[81]

Something of the import of Liberal "banter" may be gathered from the Harvard commencement exercises of 1771 (a time when Liberals saw a more than usual need for peace and unity among America's Christians) and from the commentary on them provided by Andrew Croswell. Croswell, himself a graduate of Harvard, was one of the more outspoken itinerants of the Great Awakening and among the few who defended James Davenport throughout his ecstatic career of the early 1740's. Contending that by virtue of his ministry to a Boston church he was entitled to a seat on the Harvard Board of Overseers, Croswell attended the annual Harvard commencements and twice published his opinions of what, on such occasions, he had overseen. The commencement of 1771 included a dramatic performance in which various professional figures—including one "Stephen the Preacher"—were portrayed in burlesque. Although the author of this American version of the life of Geoffrey Wildgoose may have had the recently deceased Whitefield in mind, it was apparent, and even admitted, that the butt of his humor was Croswell himself. Stephen was represented as "a serious but weak preacher" so desirous of the "salvation of men" that he stood over a physically injured man, expressing the hope that his groans came from "a wounded spirit" and exclaiming joyfully that he was "under convictions."[82]

Croswell analyzed this pageant as a means of making those present "think more highly" of "their own dear selves" and, by a "secret comparison" with the object of derision, of having "their vain hearts" tickled by a sense of "superiority." Such humor, he insisted, had a "natural tendency" to raise in men "a worldly jovial spirit, to make them less sensible of the one thing needful."[83] Croswell's suggestion that both pride and insecurity fed this vein of academic humor was a not imperceptive insight into a genre that would continue to find exponents in America—Washington Irving, among others, as well as the editors of the *Knickerbocker,* and the southern humorists who, as

Kenneth Lynn has shown, sought to divest Jacksonism of its terrors with an uneasy ridicule. In the pre-Revolutionary years too the lampooning of enthusiasm was a stratagem of social as well as personal reassurance:

> Composed as these sectaries of our western world in general are of a confused heterogeneous mass of infidels and enthusiasts, oddly blended and united, (most of them ignorant, and all of them shamefully illiterate,) it is not easy, in a serious discourse, to speak of them with becoming gravity.[84]

The author of these words was the Anglican parson Jonathan Boucher, and the discourse, one delivered in the 1760's, the first of those he later collected, presumably with the advantage of Tory hindsight, into a volume he entitled *A View of the Causes and Consequences of the American Revolution.*

II

Those who became Tories were not the only members of American society who stood in cavalier judgment on the Roundheads of the colonies in the years before the Revolution. In the Virginia ratifying convention of 1788, Edmund Pendleton confessed that it was only "lately" that the graduates of Virginia's "seminaries" had employed the "benefits" of their education for another purpose than that of setting themselves up as "an order of being superior to honest citizens —peasants."[85] The discovery was even more belated in Massachusetts, where, in the palmy days of 1775-1776, professional abilities were, as Theodore Sedgwick complained, "represented as dangerous, learning as a crime."[86] In the Berkshires the prejudice against learning took a not unsurprising form: "an undue jealousy and hatred" of "the makers of law, the judges of law, the pleaders of law, and the executors of law."[87] Hostility to the legal profession, like the evangelical preference for a regenerate clergy, was essentially a commentary on what the more reasonable members of colonial society took to be the place of intelligence in America. If men of abilities and learning were oppugned in pre-Revolutionary America, perhaps they had themselves, and not the Calvinist ministry, to blame.

At the outset of Shays' Rebellion the electors of the town of Braintree demanded that the Massachusetts General Court "cease grants to Harvard College" and that they "limit the number of attorneys, paying them out of the publick treasury."[88] The rebellion was triggered, according to Isaac Backus, by a series of essays, published in Boston's *Independent Chronicle,* entitled *The Pernicious Practice of the Law.*[89] In the background of the rebellion, however, were the grievances of the 1770's, especially the enforcement of the laws of the province concerning indebtedness. The manner in which the courts of western Massachusetts (generally under the control of the same Williams clan that had ousted Edwards from Northampton) enforced these laws led the Berkshire populace to commit the first act of open rebellion in New England—the closing of the provincial courts in Great Barrington on August 15, 1774. After Lexington and Concord, Berkshire declared its courts independent of the Boston government and sought, under the leadership of the Reverend Thomas Allen, to guarantee "substantial justice" to the inhabitants.[90]

Yet the Berkshire grievances against the colonial courts, as indeed the attitude of the radical Calvinist, Allen, toward law and lawyers, had profounder sources than the immediate pressure of agricultural depression or the use of the provincial legal machinery by the "River Gods" to forestall collection of debts they had incurred by "improving" their holdings in a time of high prices. It was in 1767 that a Connecticut Election Preacher first demanded, on behalf of the Calvinist populace, that the legislature make provisions "to prevent such vast Expences in Law-suits, and such oppressive Measures in collecting just Debts."[91] But New England dissenters, like the North Carolina Regulators whom they recognized as kindred spirits, and who, in the 1770's, insisted there "should be no Lawyers in the Province—they damned themselves if there should"—were heirs to a view of the law which antedated the grievances of the post-1763 economic crisis.[92] Both the Regulators and the Calvinist ministry looked on lawyers as upstarts, risen from the dung heap of oblivion to exercise lordly sway over their fellowmen, but behind it all was a conviction that the law was simply no career for an adult Christian.

At the height of the Awakening, Whitefield published this observation in his *Journal:*

> As for the *Business* of an *Attorney,* I think it *unlawful* for a Christian, at least *exceeding dangerous: Avoid it therefore,* and glorify God in some *other Station.*

This particular utterance helped secure Whitefield's reputation with the more respectable citizens of the colonies, some of whom immediately responded by proclaiming the usefulness to all men, rich and poor, of "conscientious Attornies, well versed in the Law."[93] Yet the practice of law in the colonies in the subsequent decades seems to have been such that only two lawyers were able to gain the respect and confidence of the rural dissenter population in the years before the Revolution. One of these was Patrick Henry, who, his critics confirmed, was "so infatuated" that he went about the Virginia countryside "praying and preaching amongst the common people."[94]

The other was Joseph Hawley of Northampton, who in 1750 had served as a spokesman for those who removed Edwards from his pulpit. In 1760, Hawley, having decided that his conduct in the Edwards affair was attributable to the "wicked Arminian doctrines" that he had embraced in 1750, wrote a letter to one of the ministers who had served on the council which approved Edwards' dismissal, confessing his error and shame and asking forgiveness of the Christian people of Massachusetts.[95] "This ingenuous confession," Governor Hutchinson recalled, "raised his character more than his intemperate conduct had lessened it."[96] After 1760, moreover, Hawley refused to join his colleagues at the bar in asking exorbitant fees and, like Patrick Henry, often provided his services without charge, particularly when the opportunity arose to champion the cause of religious freedom.

Yet for all this, Hawley was perhaps best known in western Massachusetts as a lawyer who, having once studied for the ministry, would on occasion order an unimpressive speaker from the pulpit and proceed himself to deliver a rousing exposition and application of Calvinist doctrines. The popular attitude toward law and lawyers among the populace whom Hawley served, as well as what the industrious poor considered most important in 1761, may be gathered from this letter to Hawley:

Sr I am grieved that your place & Character exposes you often times to engage for Clients in Such causes as I am satisfied you are Sorry for afterwards—I had conceived Such an opinion of you especially upon Seeing your public appearance in the case of the immortal (deservedly) & now Glorified Mr. Edwards as made one wish you might be Influenced & Determined to quit the Barr and resume the Pulpit—Hond Sr. if you would be advised by me a poor illiterate mechanic To Leave the Law To The Lawyers (few of whom enter into The Kingdom of Heaven here or hereafter) & come over upon the Lord Side my Heart would rejoice ever more and The church of christ I hope would rejoice with me . . .[97]

In time Hawley would leave not only the law but the government of Massachusetts to the lawyers, and for the very reason that he, like his semiliterate correspondent, considered the church of Christ a rather more important interest than the causes of the secular community.

As Peter Oliver, Tory historian of the Revolution in Massachusetts, never tired of observing, Hawley was an "enthusiast," even a mystic. But Hawley's latter-day conception of the lawyer's role had much to do with what the new light of the Awakening disclosed as the nature of the good society. In 1762 Joseph Bellamy treated the magistrates of Connecticut to the Calvinist vision of how, in the course of the Work of Redemption, courts of law would necessarily wither away. Were Connecticut to become a habitation of righteousness, Bellamy prophesied, the courts would be unfrequented, for, the people being virtuous, they would

> live in love. And while they do as they would be done by there seldom happens any affair that needs to be disputed at the bar.[98]

Informing Bellamy's opinion was not only a glimpse of the coming millennium but a memory of the Great Awakening, which all Calvinists recalled as a time when courts, as well as taverns, had little business.[99] It was in these years that Edwards himself had sternly reminded his Northampton congregation of the relationship of Christian society to the bar and barristers. Man's obligations to human laws were subordinate to those he owed "to the higher laws of God and nature." To use courts "to gain what the laws of moral honesty allow not," he explained, was "an oppression and violence" against the moral law.[100]

The Puritan conviction that legal contention was essentially sinful had been more than reinforced by the Awakening. Lawyers, Calvinists came to believe, provoked "needless law-suits" and served any cause in order to make a profit, thus encouraging men to use legal procedures to deny or circumvent their moral obligations.[101] The belief that the law and Christian religion were at cross purposes would persist in America long after the era of Edwards and Bellamy. Indeed, it would survive even Daniel Webster's eloquent effort, in the Dartmouth College case, to demonstrate that the law was not, as the clergy had so long believed, essentially hostile to the aim and design of evangelical religion. In the age of Jackson, P. W. Grayson, among others, would invoke, as against the lawyers, the fundamental evangelical insight that legal endeavors were corrupting, that the abolition of both the profession and the common law would guarantee Americans' living in love. By this time, however, the contest between the evangelical scheme and the legal would have taken another form, one which would find the ministry meeting defeat in the very moment of its greatest triumph under a converted ex-lawyer, Charles Grandison Finney, and the bar winning what proved to be a hollow victory as they acquiesced in the role of hired advocates for America's business interests.

Not until after the Revolution did the ministry discover that the lawyers, and not the Liberal clergy, were their chief competitors for control of the American mind. In pre-Revolutionary America, lawyers seemed, as they certainly were, of mere secondary importance as spokesmen for the elements of American society whom the Liberal clergy otherwise so well represented. The Calvinist clergy were not unaware of the changes in American society that were giving an increasingly important function to the legal profession. But their grievance against the lawyers was only a part of a larger complaint against the liberally educated men of the colonies.

In the 1740's the itinerants had called New England's attention to the fact that its intellectuals, and its academic institutions, had forgotten the purposes to which the founders of New England had devoted their intelligence:

> I make no Doubt but the Colleges pour forth Swarms of young Men, who have spent their Days in diverse Lusts and Vanities;—and these unhappy Men come forth to serve the Churches (but really to serve *themselves*) and after a Life spent in Pleasure, Pomp, and Worldly-mindedness, go down to the Dead, and to the *Damned,* and *their People with them.*[102]

The charge, however immoderate, was little more than a recapitulation of what Cotton Mather and Benjamin Franklin, from their differing perspectives, had said of Harvard two decades earlier. That it had some substance is suggested by the complaint of a Connecticut Arminian after New Light pressure had helped restore Yale to a semblance of orthodoxy. Longing for New Haven commencements "in the old Stile," when graduates and alumni were "allowed to dance, kiss the Girls, and drink Wine,"[103] this self-styled "man of the World" bespoke a notion of the life of the mind that is not perhaps unique to the eighteenth century. On the other hand, the style was hardly old enough to have become a New England tradition, and however noble the ideal, it met defeat at Harvard in 1774, when the Sons of Liberty imported Whitefield's friend, Samuel Langdon, from Portsmouth, New Hampshire, to serve as president. Langdon inaugurated the era known to his students and to Unitarian historians as the dark days of the Revolution.

In arraigning Harvard and Yale, the Calvinist concern was less with undergraduate follies than what seemed the administrations' hostility to the flourishing of piety among students. In this respect, the Calvinist opinion of the colleges was something of an analogue to the Wesleys' contempt for the English universities of their day. (When Yale refused to grant David Brainerd a degree, the incident was improved in Calvinist sermons in conjunction with the tale of Oxford's disciplining prayerful young Wesleyans.) Another criticism of Harvard and Yale was that they were being converted into something other than seminaries for the training of a prospective ministry. Among the programs of Edwards' *Thoughts on the Revival* was that "care should be taken, some way or other," that the colleges of New England "be so regulated, that they should, in fact be nurseries of piety."[104] Although Chauncy insisted, in his reply to Edwards, that Harvard College was still a school of prophets, Edwards continued to tell his own congregation and the people of New England that he knew, from experience, their colleges were nurturing neither piety nor prophets.

The question of the purpose of collegiate instruction had been argued, and seemingly resolved, well before the Awakening. Already early in the century, Harvard graduates had been entering on careers as merchants and in the law and politics. When Calvinists founded the College of New Jersey, it was not intended only as a place to prepare future clergymen. However, they could not agree with Benjamin Gale, who in 1755 called on Yale to so alter its curriculum as to turn it into primarily an institution for instruction of young men aspiring to a career in trade and commerce.[105] Nor did they agree with the founders of the College of Philadelphia. That institution was an indirect consequence of Franklin's *Proposals Relating to the Education of Youth in Pensilvania,* wherein he called for a remodeled curriculum designed to train worthy young Pennsylvanians in all things useful and all things ornamental, but chiefly in those areas of knowledge that would contribute to careers in practical science.

In 1751 the Anglican clergy of Philadelphia undertook the task of publicizing and getting financial support for the academy Franklin had proposed. But by virtue of their endeavors the scope and purpose of the college was radically altered. In pleading for assistance to the noble cause of education, Richard Peters described what he called "the deplorable Consequences of a low and defective Education." Notwithstanding our happy constitution, Peters declared, and

> the Fertility of the Soil, the Extent and Flourishing Condition of our Commerce; all which deservedly make us a conspicuous People; yet it does not require a more than ordinary Penetration to foresee, that if some Methods be not taken of giving a proper Education to our Youth, these very advantages and Privileges, for want of Knowledge, and a Capacity of exercising the Offices necessary for Government of so populous and indulged a Country, will run Things into Anarchy and Confusion; and, in a very little Time, perhaps some of us may live to see it, our Superiors may be forced to make Alterations in our Laws and Constitution.[106]

To the Liberal mind, the ultimate purpose of the higher learning was to produce leaders for society and government. Graduates of their colleges were expected to secure the "tranquillity" of the state both by leavening the social lump and by serving as its magistrates.[107]

Soon after the Episcopalians took over control of the College of Philadelphia, Francis Alison, who at first cooperated in the venture— seeing it as a counterfoil to the New Side seminary at Princeton—was ready to resign from its governing board. Young men educated at Philadelphia, he complained, "get a taste for high life."[108] Actually this had been the purpose of the Anglican clergy, though not necessarily in the sense in which either Alison or the undergraduates understood it. The goals and character of the College of Philadelphia had their pattern in William Smith's essay on "The College of Mirania," in which he outlined a theory of Christian nurture that respectable Philadelphians found so impressive they selected Smith as first provost of the College. Smith began by assuming that society was divisible into "two grand classes," only one of which might reasonably profit from humane studies. The more numerous part of the American population had best content themselves, for their own sakes as well as for the good of society, with the kind of mechanical training in which Benjamin Franklin showed interest.[109] Smith failed to publish his principle of selection, but he nowhere suggested any of those precautions against a class university that Jefferson included in his later scheme for Virginian education. Elsewhere Smith always betrayed a strong disposition—strong even for a Philadelphian*[110]—to account for both learning capacity and native genius as functions of good family.[111]

Smith's proposed curriculum was primarily classical. Ancient history was to be studied in such a way as to make past events "a lesson of ethics and politics, and a useful rule of conduct and manners through life." Perhaps because enough Americans had become sufficiently enlightened as to discover heterodox ethical and political rules in the private and public acts of Greeks and Romans, Smith wanted no graduate of his college to be a mere thinking machine. His ideal university was to be distinguished by an emphasis on the study of *belles-lettres,* which were supposed to develop a taste for "the pleasures of the imagination." By encouraging this taste (knowledge of which Smith had derived from Addison and from some "sentimental" English poets) the college would "improve the temper, soften the manners, [and] serene the passions" of its young men. Whenever Smith approached this question of cultivating the taste, his social biases became

---

* A similar tendency was already evident in Boston in 1760. In a eulogy of Stephen Sewall, Mayhew gave Harvard much of the credit for the judge's attainments, but he also considered it of some importance that Sewall came "of a family of distinction in New-England." Something of the significance of such "liberalizing" of theology as Mayhew pursued may be discerned in his embarrassed explanation, in the sermon on Sewall, that the phrase *"honorably descended"* was perhaps "hardly applicable, in strictness to any of the degenerate race of mankind."

more than apparent. Granting that everyone perhaps had a modicum of "understanding," Smith argued that few had more than the "rudiments" of taste. Only these few had a measure of taste worth cultivating, and cultivation, according to Smith, was that amiable quality which distinguished the true Christian and gentleman from the vulgar herd.[112]

Whatever Smith's success as an educator, he was able in after years to take pride in the fact that his Philadelphia contained not only men of "inferior stations" but others who had either been born or trained to "all the amiable qualities of the Christian and the Gentleman."[113] At Harvard the effort to remodel the curriculum to achieve such a purpose was hindered for years by a recalcitrant orthodox ministry. But Boston too had its Liberal theoreticians of the life of the mind; one of them was Jonathan Mayhew, who in 1763 defined the function of the gentleman-scientist and gentleman-clergyman:

> There are some persons, whom God has blessed at once with riches, and with large, sagacious, and contemplative minds, who may both very worthily as to themselves, and usefully to the world, devote the greater part of their time to study, to making observations on, and discoveries in, the word and works of God, and communicating their discoveries to mankind . . .[114]

At least a decade before the Revolution, something of Mayhew's spirit triumphed at Harvard, where the "liberal arts" joined Winthrop's brand of theoretical science in the catalogue of courses. The same occurred at King's College, though there the educational theories of Samuel Johnson were challenged by Presbyterians under the leadership of William Livingston, partly because they preferred a slightly more practical curriculum, but largely because they did not want New York's Anglicans to have a monopoly on gentility.

With all the bitter disputes of the pre-Revolutionary decades over control of the colleges, it is surprising how Liberals, Old Lights, and Old Side Presbyterians failed even once to confute the elitist premises of Anglican educational theory.[115] To be sure, in 1777 Smith was removed from his position at the College, and the University of Pennsylvania was established with an enlightened and Presbyterian administration and faculty. But Harvard Liberalism survived these Revolutionary years of change and storm so successfully that by 1780 the proto-Unitarians of Massachusetts had contrived the theoretical and social basis of a self-perpetuating intellectual elite in the Commonwealth. In the year of the new Massachusetts Constitution the Election Preacher, a Liberal, was ready to argue that rulers must be "men of understanding," not only because the duties of state required such capacities, but because only educated men were likely to be "patrons of letters." In their stupidity, "ignorant and illiterate men" might weaken or destroy Harvard College, now a nursery of literature as well as magistrates.[116]

Both Philadelphia Anglicans and Boston Arminians were undoubtedly sincere in their love of learning. They were presumably also enlightened and farseeing in their wish to civilize American society by training cadres of philosopher kings:

> This polished and flourishing City! what was it fourscore years ago? Even its foundations were not then laid, and in their place was one depth of gloomy wilderness! This very spot, the Seat of the Muses— where I have now the honour to stand . . . surrounded with men excelling in every valuable accomplishment, and youths rising after their great example—had I seen it then, what should I have found it? A spot rank with weeds perhaps, or the obscure retreat of some lawless and uncultivated savage!
>
> O Glorious Change! O happy day! that now beholds the Science planted where barbarity was before . . .[117]

Thus William Smith addressed a College of Philadelphia commencement in 1760. Possibly Livingston and Alison were to a degree sounding the jubilee trumpet of the enlightenment against Smith's and Johnson's more outright Augustanism, and possibly even the latter were friendly to a progressive enlargement of both human knowledge and the ranks of the knowledgeable. Yet implicit in the educational theory of the pre-Revolutionary rationalist mind would seem to have been a considerable degree of aristocratic Neoplatonism.*[118]

At the close of the Revolutionary War, Calvinist ministers were the first to enter a plea for education (and, incidentally, higher salaries for instructors) in the new republic. They supported not only the primary schools which Edwards, in the *Thoughts on the Revival,* had urged for raising up the nation's children "in common learning" as well as in piety, but the colleges of which the Liberal ministry had been so long and so exclusively enamored.[119] Yet even as they issued their appeals "for the improvement of the rising generation," Calvin-

---

* What the reasonable mind comprehended as lawless and uncultivated barbarity was by no means limited to rank weeds and savages. Beneath the surface of all such celebrations as Smith's of the rising glory of America lurked the fear that in the wilderness of the New World human nature too was threatening by virtue of its naturalness. The ultimate formulation of this attitude appeared in Samuel Peters' Loyalist history of Connecticut, which closes on a note of mingled admiration and disgust for American "nature." The "soil, the rivers, the ponds, the ten thousand landskips" of Connecticut, Peters allows, "would tempt me into the highest wonder and admiration of them, could they once be freed of the skunk, the moping-owl, and fanatic christian."

ists left no doubt as to what they considered the most necessary improvements.[120] In the spring of 1783 Charles Turner, "V.D.M.," friend and confidant of Sam Adams, appeared in Cambridge to announce to officers and students the Calvinist program for Harvard College:

> We do not censure their inclination to excel, in various arts and sciences, which are embellishing, and in a more moderate degree, useful to society; but our grand wish is to see their ambition *chiefly* engaged about *those things,* which are the most worthy, important and glorious; to see them emulous for excelling, *in divine science;* in love to God and their Country; in truly Christian, and republican sobriety and economy; in the art of being truly happy, in this world and forever; and in the noble principles, and temper of *liberty,* which may render them blessings to the Commonwealth, by disposing them to use their best endeavours, for cultivating, and perpetuating its *freedom* and felicity, in connection with *pure and undefiled religion.*[121]

That Turner urged undergraduates to cultivate a love for their country and indeed, proposed that Harvard establish a "professorship of liberty," discloses, of course, whither the Calvinist mind was tending.

It had not, however, traveled very far since the days when Samuel Davies had pointed out to the students of the College of New Jersey that they were among the fortunate few of thousands to enjoy the immense privilege of being exposed "to knowledge of every kind." Unsanctified learning, Davies had insisted in 1760, would only produce such beings as Milton's Satan or those "other sinners of great parts, fine geniuses, like fallen angels, those vast intellects."[122] Like Hawthorne, Melville, or Whittier commenting a century later on the fatal flaw of Daniel Webster, the Calvinists of pre-Revolutionary America were certain that "without holiness, wisdom would be but craft and subtilty."[123] Before 1783 Calvinists were not concerned with the problem of the godless godlike genius, for they paid none of their contemporaries so much respect. (Ironically enough, it would be the grandson of Jonathan Edwards who would first confront American Calvinists with the demonic potentialities of misdirected genius.) In the world with which they dealt, the Christian ministry were the recognized intellectuals of society, and the aim of Calvinism was to make certain that in this profession, at least, abilities and intelligence would be dedicated to the glory of God and the good of mankind.

In its initial phase, the Awakening impulse expressed itself (as enthusiasm generally had always done in its first moments) in a popular preference for self-taught gospel ministers. "It appeard plain to me that these unlarned men," explained a woman of Sturbridge, Massachusetts, in accounting for her joining a Separate conventicle in the 1740's, "ware the foolish things that God had chose to confound the wisdom of the wise."[124] Such sentiments seem even to have been encouraged by the spokesmen of the revival. The graduates of the Log College sought to impress the people of the Middle Colonies with the fact that Christ in his day had passed by the "established" clergy in favor of "Twelve unlearned, unpolished Men, most of them Fishers.[125] Isaac Backus invariably came before the Baptists of New England describing himself as "a person of no great note in the learned world" and a graduate of what he styled the "school Dr. Franck speaks of," wherein things had been "taught in an *experimental* way."[126]

Within three years of the Awakening, however, Eleazar Wheelock and Benjamin Pomeroy had withdrawn their approval of the installation of the uneducated Solomon Paine over the Canterbury Separates. By the late 1740's both Tennent and Finley, insisting that an "ignorant Minister of God is a great Absurdity, a plain Contradiction," were proposing to make Presbyterian fishers of men through the instrumentality of the College of New Jersey. The preference for what Tennent derided as "foolish preaching" represented to the Calvinist mind the same "superficial View of Things" that had seduced the awakened into thinking an easy assurance was the essence of sainthood.[127] Not unexpectedly Backus himself, who in the 1750's encouraged young New Englanders to attend the college over which Edwards, Davies, Finley and Tennent presided, was one of the guiding spirits in the founding of the College of Rhode Island.

Of anti-intellectualism Edwards was presumably always free. He devoted one of the strongest sections of *Thoughts on the Revival* to the need for fixing "some certain, visible limits" on admission to the ministry, and to proposing that the line be drawn at the level of the bachelor's degree. But his argument was in terms of not "bringing odium" on the Work of God,[128] and like all his prudential advice, it could be and was violated when circumstances seemed to point to another course.* But what most deeply troubled Calvinists was the extent to which "poisonous notions" of theology were gaining currency among the faculties of Harvard and Yale in the 1740's. "The accounts I receive from time to time," Jonathan Belcher, governor of New Jersey and patron of the New Side college, wrote to Edwards in 1748, "give

---

* Edwards approved and even participated in the ordination of ministers who lacked college degrees. The most famous, of course, was David Brainerd, who had been denied a degree from Yale for suggesting that a professor was as graceless as the college furniture. Other ministers whom Edwards and the New Side ministry recognized, even after the founding of Princeton, were the two Cleavelands, expelled from Yale for attending a Separate meeting, and Samson Occum, the first of the Indian ministers to go forth from Eleazar Wheelock's school at Lebanon.

me too much reason to fear that Arminianism, Arianism, and even Socinianism, in destruction to the doctrines of free grace, are daily propagated in the New England colleges."[129] Not only was this true, but Belcher's successor in Massachusetts, Governor Shirley, overtly urged a more classical and literary curriculum specifically as an antidote to the nonsensical, seditious, and anti-British doctrines of Calvinism.

In such a context, it might be said that even when Calvinists did battle for an "orthodox" curriculum they were trying to prevent the colonial colleges from becoming seedbeds of aristocratic, European, and profoundly unchristian sentiments. Actually, though Edwards argued, as against the seeming tendency of his age, that theology was and must remain the queen of the sciences, he was not oblivious to the propriety and utility of other subjects in the collegiate curriculum. It was only, as Edwards explained, that "divinity" was an "infinitely more useful and important science" than any other:

> There are various kinds of arts and sciences taught and learned in the schools, which are conversant about various objects; about the works of nature in general, as philosophy; or the visible heavens, as astronomy; or the sea, as navigation; or the earth, as geography; or the body of man, as physic and anatomy . . . or about human government, as politics and jurisprudence. But one science, or kind of knowledge and doctrine, is above all the rest; as it treats concerning God and the great business of religion.[130]

Edwards was far from hostile toward either theoretical or practical science; he praised "inventors and improvers of useful arts and sciences" as benefactors of the race. Other Calvinist ministers, interested like Edwards in religious psychology and likewise inclined to inductive observation, developed a thriving interest in medical science.[131] And Calvinism generally conceived scientists to be "raised beyond their species" and perhaps approaching "near to the lower ranks of angels by a superior genius."[132] But in this respect, as in all others, Calvinists were profoundly utilitarian and profoundly democratic; from Edwards onward they looked forward to the day when the burden of mankind would be lightened by "discoveries and inventions." They scorned the suggestion that the purpose of any art or science was to serve the comfort and convenience of the happy few, and not to provide "for all, a sufficiency and fulness of everything needed for the body, and for the comfort and convenience of every one."[133] From their perspective, only a full understanding of what kind of being God was would assure the proper utilization of the products of scientific genius and the nation's natural resources.

Advancement of the Work of Redemption was not a task for lawyers, nor engineers, but for those primarily who understood the true working of the Spirit. The quarrel of Calvinism was not with the Enlightenment, nor its warfare with science, but with English rationalism and "the sapless morality of the *Heathens,* so much in Vogue among carnal Teachers, who relish both the Matter and Stile of those unsanctified Philosophers."[134] Although much of the Calvinist counterattack on neoclassicism was waged in terms of the plenary inspiration of Scripture, their crucial point—made nearly a century before the full impact of Wordsworth was felt in America—was that the entire intellectual fabric of rationalism was unsound, artificial, and oblivious to the clearest available evidence as to the nature of the human personality and the natural creation. The "philosophers" against whom Calvinists inveighed did not, moreover, include Franklin—a friend of both Tennent and Whitefield—nor David Rittenhouse, a particular hero of theirs in the Revolutionary era. Nor were they hostile to any of a host of physicians, from Joseph Warren in Boston to David Ramsay, the most pious layman in the younger Tennent's Charleston congregation and the historian of South Carolina dissent. Among the Calvinists for whom Edwards spoke, the true enlightenment of the eighteenth century was "a thing to be rejoiced in," not only because any kind of knowledge was, "if duly applied, an excellent handmaid to divinity,"[135] but because learning of all sorts, properly used, was serviceable in the cause of Christ and humanity.

The Calvinist ministry was never hostile to applied science, nor to medicine, but only to what they considered fruitless speculation or, even worse, a scientism that employed a rather naïve interpretation of Newtonian physics to sustain human pride and deny human equality. In practical terms, the Calvinist ministry and their lay pupils were instrumental in introducing the science of chemistry into the American collegiate curriculum at a time when the Liberal ministry were still speculating on the delightful order of the heavenly orbs. It was thus by no means surprising that in the late 1790's, when the Liberals of Boston and Philadelphia—bewailing the latest form of infidelity—proposed that Joseph Priestley and Thomas Cooper be incarcerated or sent back where they came from, the heirs of Edwards were not only welcoming and befriending these deistic chemists, but saluting Thomas Jefferson as their "hero" of the day. The same untutored pietists who barked and jerked their way through the ecstasies of the Kentucky revival sought to cast off America's Age of Reason also by elevating Jefferson—"*the man of the People,* the patron of science" —into the Presidency.[136]

To the evangelical mind, as to the enlightened, the highest calling of intelligence and talent was that of seeking and serving the general welfare of the multitude. It was to prevent another definition of the role of the intellectual in American society that pre-Revolutionary Calvinism criticized the higher learning. For this they should hardly be accounted unfriendly either to education or the intellect. Even Andrew Croswell, who so frequently reminded the administration of Harvard College that the generality of the citizens of Massachusetts—whose taxes supported Harvard—would be content if students did not have to "learn their cunning by disputing against God,"[137] was himself an advocate of a learned clergy. They "who are Enemies to Learning," Croswell maintained, "are *so far,* whether they know it or not, Enemies to Religion."[138] As the tribune of the populace, Croswell asked only that a college maintained at the public expense use its resources for the welfare of the people.

What this implied, as likewise what was involved in the encouragement of an Arminian curriculum and pedagogy, may be gathered from Harvard's response to Croswell's criticism of the burlesque of the commencement of 1771. A self-styled friend of the college, probably the author of the lampoon, defended the performance in a mock-pious open letter to Croswell, who, he suggested, seemed to long for the good old days of the Great Awakening. In compensation for Croswell's being kept from the Board of Overseers, this wit suggested, he would arrange for Harvard to give him an honorary degree. Then, he observed, the "name before your future learned and pious volumes, may appear not with the vulgar V.D.M. but ornamented with the more graceful addition of D.D."[139] The implication that Croswell's criticism of Harvard was inspired by an envy of his betters was characteristic of the Arminian mentality. Though the Calvinist ministry may have been a rather humorless lot ("the art of buffoonery," Croswell declared in his final thrust, "is not one of the *liberal arts*"),[140] one wonders if they were any more anti-intellectual than those who looked upon "Human Learning" as the "One thing needful" and on Croswell's ideal of a regenerate clergy as but another of his "enthusiastick Notions."[141] Many Calvinists, including some who were as well entitled to list university degrees after their name as the Boston ministers who had purchased them from Aberdeen, chose to bear the simpler appellation V.D.M. or "Minister of the Word of God," not because they opposed human learning, but because they wanted to make it clear whom they served.

Not all Calvinist ministers went to such extremes in proclaiming their essential humility. But all agreed that the service of God and mankind required something other than a merely learned ministry.

Even before the outbreak of the Awakening the Log College men were arguing (as against those Presbyterians who considered a formal education and subscription to the Westminster creeds the essential qualifications) that a minister could not fulfill his calling without "vital piety." Among their reasons was of course that advanced by Tennent in his Nottingham sermon: that an "unconverted" minister could not preach effectively.*[142] The young Presbyterians were also convinced that a minister must himself be "experienced" in order to analyze and deal with the psychological states of his parishioners. "If a minister is unexperienced in the Exercises of Piety, he cannot natively and readily take up the Cases of Christians."[143] Thus the substance of the argument against the "letter-learned" was that men who misunderstood the nature of God must be equally in the dark as to the essential nature of man.

In the *Thoughts on the Revival* Edwards hedged on the question of whether unconverted ministers were to be tolerated by Christians. But his writings on qualifications for church membership, and above all his Farewell Sermon, left no doubt that he shared the radical notion that learning without piety made a minister "an extensive Mischief" in the church. Actually it was Edwards himself who most eloquently phrased the evangelical objection to the value that Liberals placed on a minister's learning:

> When there is light in a minister, consisting in human learning, great speculative knowledge, and the wisdom of this world, without a spiritual warmth and ardor in his heart, and a holy zeal in his ministrations, his light is like the light of an *ignis fatuus,* and some kinds of putrifying carcasses that shine in the dark, though they are of a stinking savour.[144]

Finally, Calvinist attitudes toward the "intellectual" must be judged in the context of Edwards' own reputation. It was a Yale alumnus, after all, who Backus was certain was wiser than any other mortal, and it was the greatest American mind of the century who all pious Americans agreed had doubtless gone to heaven. What was important to eighteenth-century Calvinists was that Edwards, like Milton, was a great man as well as a genius. The evangelical respect for the mind was, in short, of the same perverse variety that later allowed American Democrats to worship not only the Monticello philosopher, but

---

* The New Side carefully defended themselves against the charge that they held that the gospel as preached by an unconverted minister could be of no saving benefit: "This charge we deny as slanderous. God, as an absolute Sovereign, may use what Means he pleases to accomplish his Work by. We only assert this, that Success by unconverted Ministers Preaching is very improbable, and very seldom happens, so far as we can gather."

Jackson and Benton, as "deep and original thinkers" and to look on their critics as Lilliputians in thought and baying dogs in practice.

III

The image of Edwards as an immensely popular figure from New England to the Carolinas and, eventually, Kentucky has been all but effaced by the nineteenth-century Unitarian-drawn caricature of the cold logician threatening a resentful American populace with an eternity of hell torments. John Adams (writing to Jefferson in the "friendly" correspondence of their twilight years) insisted that Aaron Burr, "from the single Circumstance of his descent," was always assured of one hundred thousand votes—more than enough, by any calculation, to have accounted for the Republican victory in 1800.[145] Edwards' reputation is actually something of an unused key to the political behavior of Americans in the early nineteenth century, and the later assaults on his writings and memory were something of a political stratagem, as well as part of a continuing intellectual debate. It is at least noteworthy that as late as 1836-37 two such seemingly diverse figures as Charles Grandison Finney and George Bancroft were both trying to prove themselves in the direct line of descent from Edwards, and that each in his way paid tribute to Edwards as the profoundest thinker of America's two previous centuries of history.

Edwards' lasting and popular reputation was derived from all his writings, but in the late eighteenth century it was acknowledged that his noblest effort on behalf of the general welfare was his confutation of the notion that man's will is self-determining. In doing so Edwards confronted, first of all, the psychological postulates of Arminian rationalism, which assumed the will's independence of man's other "faculties."

> Be my Mind ever so much necessitated to assent to evident Truth, I am nevertheless free to chuse or refuse, to act or not to act, in Consequence of this Assent; for Action according to the Frame, of our Nature, ever springs from a self-exerting Power.[146]

As this quotation from the American Samuel Johnson attests, the issue as between Edwards and Arminianism was not simply that of the nature and working of the mind. The larger difference lay in Johnson's conceiving of knowledge (or salvation) in terms of the mind's *assent* to truth. Edwards insisted that the operations of the will depended ultimately on the understanding's *consent* to excellency—to a beauty, a taste for which could not be induced through education. It was not ratiocination, but an aesthetic perception of the good, that according to Edwards determined human action.

All this other Calvinists had also argued, though perhaps not so eloquently as Edwards in the *Will*. Men come, according to Jonathan Dickinson, to "a true Discovery, a realizing View and powerful Impression of what is *best* for them; and that necessarily determines their Choice."[147] Edwards systematized Calvinist psychology and refined its vocabulary. Yet in terms of popular impact the logic of his treatise was probably of less importance than the spirit in which he challenged the doctrines that seemed to him in the 1750's the principal threat to the progress of the Work of Redemption. To Edwards the ultimate iniquity of the proponents of a self-determining power in the will was a denial of the "common sense" meaning of words—indeed of what the "common people" took such words as "freedom of the will" to mean—and an "artificial deceitful management of terms, to darken and confound the mind."[148] Edwards may well have been bludgeoning a straw man in attributing such willful obfuscation to the theoreticians of free will, for the issue was actually one of how to arrive at a knowledge of the workings of the human personality. Nevertheless, Edwards was convinced that the Liberal manner of proceeding led at last to their using "pure metaphysical sounds without any ideas whatsoever in their minds to answer them." Thus his conclusion—"It is a fact, that they, and not we, have confounded things with metaphysical, unintelligible notions and phrases"—represented an ultimate demurrer from the "enlightened" intelligence of Liberalism.[149]

Edwards was committed to inductive reasoning and insisted, even while allowing that the human will might well be just as free as the Arminians proposed, that the human will had shown itself unable to act virtuously in the absence of divine grace. He upheld the doctrine of original sin as no arbitrary construct but a truth "most evident from the *Experience* of all the World." (To debate it, Jonathan Dickinson had asserted, "is even to dispute against our Senses, and against the clearest Observations that we are capable of in any case whatsoever.")[150] Given what nature and revelation disclosed as to what man *might* be (which for Edwards was also what man *should* be), humanity had proven itself depraved over thousands of years: "facts are stubborn things."[151] Liberals denied those facts by deduction from what they took to be the nature of God, by what the English Samuel Johnson called man's strong sense of his will's freedom, and with the Franklinian observation that while the doctrine of "necessity" might be true it was not very useful. Calvinism, according to the American Samuel Johnson and every other critic of Edwards,* somehow made God "the author of sin."[152]

---

* Actually, Edwards' American critics did very little to answer him in the period

The Calvinist insisted in reply that the only useful approach to the question of original sin was not "to show how we came into this condition," but to point out plainly "what that condition is which we are actually in."[153] This Calvinists did long after the publication of Edwards' treatises; in 1777, for instance, the pastor of the Second Society of Norwich, Connecticut, observed that "men will sacrifice every thing in the *universe,* to do honor, and pay obedience to the dictates of their own selfishness." These things, he continued, "are not imaginary abstruse speculations, they are real facts."[154] Such statements are testimony to the evangelical powers of observation, but it is also true that their assurance had something to do with the seeming finality of Edwards' dissertations, *Will* and *Original Sin.* Once Edwards had written, his colleagues and successors were more than prepared to deal with the notion of "the heathen Philosophers" that virtue was the "fruit of education." After he had disarmed those who would have used the "oppositions of science, falsely so-called" to impugn the common sense doctrine of original sin, Calvinists in their own way could condescend to the Liberals.[155]

Edwards' treatises of the 1750's provided Calvinism with several compelling objections to Arminianism. One was a conviction that adherence to Arminian tenets was prima-facie evidence of a minister's unregenerate nature. In the concluding section of *Original Sin,* Edwards strongly hinted that it was no mere error in judgment that led Liberals to read Scripture as they did. That the "Holy Scripture is subtilized into a mere mist," he suggested, "or made to evaporate into a thin cloud, that easily puts on any shape, and is moved in any direction, with a puff of wind, just as the manager pleases," was probably owing to "something worse" even than intellectual arrogance.[156] It is "no argument," Edwards insisted, that the "ineffable, distinguishing, evidential excellencies" of the gospel are not visible to every man, since

> the distinguishing glories of his word are of such a kind, as that the
> sin and corruption of men's hearts—which above all things alienate
> them from the Deity, and make the heart dull and stupid to any

---

before the Revolution. The Anglican Thomas Bradbury Chandler once grandly announced that he would foreswear all other activity and devote five years to the composition of a reasoned confutation of Edwards. But the time, it would seem, was not available, and Chandler proposed, as a stop-gap measure, that Edwards be answered with satire and derision. James Dana did finally publish an "answer" to Edwards, but it is worth noting that it was not only the weight of "reason" that he brought to bear against Edwards' essay *Will.* "The friends of Mr. Edwards pique themselves much on the supposed reputation of his book in England & Scotland," Dana wrote to Andrew Eliot. "If deists and rakes are the persons there by whom it is had in estimation it might serve the cause of truth to let this be published."

sense or taste of those things wherein the moral glory of the divine perfections consists—would blind them from discerning the beauties of such a book; and that therefore they will not see them, but as God is pleased to enlighten them, and restore a holy taste, to discern and relish divine beauties.[157]

Those who could or would not see the divinity of divinity where it was most clearly revealed were not just lacking in critical acumen; they were blindly and even wilfully oblivious to the Will of God.

That "unenlighten'd" men could not interpret Scripture correctly was not a belief peculiar to Calvinists. As early as 1742 Nathaniel Appleton was declaiming against those of the awakened who thought they could understand the Bible "without any help of human study and learning."[158] But the issue was not, as even Andrew Croswell was quick to point out, whether "the Labours of learned and godly Men" were needed in the exposition of the Bible.[159] Calvinists and Liberals alike agreed that "acquaintance with language" and with "nature" were necessary for an understanding of the Scripture.[160] The true difference was that Liberals read Scripture, if not as a mere historic record, then at least as a series of incidents the meaning of any of which was to be discovered by squaring the text with reason. Eighteenth-century rationalism continued to subscribe officially to the medieval principle that any portion of Scripture was to be interpreted through the "analogy of faith"—that in dealing with a particular text one must consider the "whole Current of Inspiration as to the Point under Examination." But in attending to what they called "the general Drift and Design of the Author," Edwards' Liberal contemporaries were also slowly tending to make scriptural interpretation what Channing was to conceive it as being: the analogue of Blackstone's *Commentaries on the Laws of England*.[161] On more than one occasion an eighteenth-century Liberal used the Bible as a stock of precedents, as well as of proof texts, out of which could be drawn "laws" to which conflicting or confusing texts could be made to conform. It was by such a process that Charles Chauncy came to conclude that any who construed the Book of Acts as indicating that the Church at Antioch was a commune must have had their eyes "blinded by the rise of impure mists from a grossly carnalized heart."[162]

The Calvinist, on the other hand, sought to grasp the single meaning of the whole Scripture—the "glory of the gospel"—in as aesthetic and as unitary a perception as that by which the gracious understanding apprehended the beauty of the Godhead. The Bible for Calvinists was not a chronicle of events, nor even a logical collection of doctrines, but rather a complete "image" of the Divine nature, a "type" of the Divine meaning—to use Poe's phrase, "a plot of God." Something of what Calvinists meant by a "taste for moral excellence" in reading Scripture was disclosed in Edwards' observation, in the *Religious Affections,* that *Paradise Lost* was not a series of declarative stanzas but an epic that had to be read and understood as a whole. Charles Chauncy, of course, once expressed the wish that *Paradise Lost* might be translated into prose. There is "need of uncommon force of mind," Edwards insisted, "to discern the distinguishing excellencies of the works of authors of great genius." When the author was the Holy Spirit Himself, uncommon intelligence was required, but more particularly the ineffable taste granted to the regenerate. Like "mean judges" of literature who failed to appreciate the "inimitable excellencies" of Milton, they who wrongly interpreted Scripture were guilty above all of tastelessness.[163]

As might be surmised, the Calvinist approach to Biblical interpretation was—even as the Puritan vision from which it derived—implicitly a theory of literary criticism. The evangelical perspective could be defined as a judgment on both the prosaic and historicist Liberal mind and on the new criticism in which the more radical antinomians of the day engaged. Liberals sought to convict all Calvinists of searching the "most hidden recesses" of the Bible in order "to decipher hieroglyphicks—to develop mystical allusions—to unriddle metaphors and the like," and thus to condemn the whole of the evangelical ministry as not "to be reasoned with." Yet the dismissal of every Calvinist as a "symbolical divine" was unjust, for though Calvinists did seek meanings in Scripture that the unrenewed understanding knew not of, they were quick to set themselves against the easy "spiritualizing" of Scriptures. In criticizing those who sought to turn individual passages of the Bible "into allegories, and what they call the spiritual meaning," Calvinism was continuing a battle that had begun in America in the seventeenth century, and elsewhere probably far earlier. It was not that Calvinists saw no difference between the words of the Bible and its meaning, but that Separates and Baptists conceived every verse, or at least those which they focused on, to "have a literal and carnal Sense and a mystic and spiritual Sense, hidden and wrapped up under it, as in a Riddle."[164] Such a procedure was condemned even by Solomon Paine, one of the more mystic of the New England Separates, when he arraigned enthusiasts for "perverting the Scriptures, turning all the perceptive [sic] Part into Allegory, and the allegorical Part into Precept."[165] Paine's objection suggests, however, the degree to which his kind of Calvinist was disposed to read portions of the Bible in isolation. For he did not acknowledge, as the Edwardeans did, that the nature and the glory of the gospel was such that its allegory and its precepts comprised a single meaning.

One of the more profound consequences of Edwards' writings was to provide a standard whereby were convicted of sinfulness all who offered variant readings of Scripture, whether Arminian or antinomian. Increasingly a "tasteful" reading of Scripture became for Calvinists a test of a regenerate clergyman. One of the fruits of an unrenewed heart and mind was, they were certain, a perversion of the nature and the meaning of Scripture. A natural man, being "destitute of a renewed Faculty, or Supernatural Principal [sic] to discern" portions of the Bible "in their Genuine Light," was according to James Finley "apt either to accomodate them to his own corrupt Reasoning, or to look upon them as inconsistent, weak, and enthusiastick."[166] In the 1740's those who departed from the "genuine or natural Sense" of Scripture were in the minds of "Calvinistical" citizens false guides; by 1760 those who claimed to derive from the Bible "Pelagian Arminian principles, vulgarly so called" were beyond doubt the worst of sinners. If one has grace, Joseph Bellamy explained, "the whole gospel plan will naturally open to view, and appear to contain a complete system of religious sentiments, harmonious and consistent throughout, perfect in glory and beauty."[167] If such a plan did not open to view, or if a contrary one was stubbornly upheld, then it was perfectly evident that the expositor was graceless.

The Calvinist defense of the faith once delivered to the saints was neither Biblical fundamentalism nor refractory creedalism. Curiously enough, the true "fundamentalists," in the context of eighteenth-century America, would appear to have been the Liberals. In the debate with Calvinists they accused their opponents of defining as doctrines precepts that were nowhere to be found in Scripture, and often they invoked the pure text of the Bible as the rock on which Protestantism was founded. To be sure, the Liberal defense of the centrality of Scripture—"the best and most fundamental Principle" of the Reformation—was modified by expressions of gratitude for "the great Advantages and Helps" given their own age by learned expositors. But at the same time Liberals accused the spokesmen of evangelical religion of being un-Protestant in placing "the *Divinity* of the reformed Churches," that is, of Calvin, "into a sort of Competitorship with the *Bible*."[168] On occasion, the rationalist clergy of the eighteenth century sounded as though they wished to make the Bible something of a fundamental charter of Christianity—and the Apostles, Founding Fathers whose words were to be literally understood and followed, instead of being corrupted by later commentators.

The degree to which American Calvinists actually subscribed to the doctrines of the reformers has already been indicated. Furthermore, the evangelical minister did not look on his doctrines as venerable relics; he rather conceived them as vital and instrumental truths. During the Awakening it had been noticed that the Spirit did not pour down where there was ministerial opposition to Calvinist doctrines, "or a total Absence *of them, or but a* cold *and* infrequent Glancing at them."[169] Jonathan Dickinson took the further step (in his disputes with Anglicanism in the mid-1740's) of arguing that the New Birth was unlikely unless men were told of "the Necessity of that great and important Change."[170] There seemed, in sum, an internal and integral relationship between the preaching of evangelical doctrines and the thriving, as well as the fact, of regeneration.*[171] Thus by 1750 the issue on which the doctrinal debate hinged was almost as Edwards had seen it in the 1730's: "the *good old Calvinistical Way* of Preaching up Justification by Faith" was essential were the colonies to enjoy a further experience of grace.[172]

In the 1750's Edwards too held to the possibility of another revival. But as might be expected from his reorientation of "experimental religion," his emphasis in the debate against Arminianism was on his conviction that doctrines were a *"means"* of transforming "a people in point of morality." This assumption directed the Calvinist ministry, and eventually the Calvinist populace, to action against both Arminianism and Arminians as enemies to the Kingdom.[173] The arousing of the popular mind had no little to do with the notorious fact, according to the popular folklore of the eighteenth century, that Edwards was removed from Northampton by the Arminians in his congregation and the less Calvinistic ministers of the neighboring churches. When Edwards took farewell of his people, he did not raise this issue, except to tell them to take special heed that they not choose an Arminian as his successor. More precisely, he admonished them not to install any minister until after strict examination they had established his belief in the doctrines and principles of evangelical religion.

Edwards' dismissal and his farewell advice were both part of a most complicated chapter in colonial ecclesiastical history. In the confrontation between Calvinists and Liberals in the years between the Awakening and the Revolution, both parties would seem to have been advocates of "religious liberty." Yet there was an essential difference, one disclosed most clearly by Edwards' taking it as a self-evident proposition that it was the "people's part to choose with what food they will be fed."[174] In this statement, which was delivered by way of rebuke to those who wanted to outlaw and suppress separatist preachers and

---

* Another Calvinist found—by what he called "long Observation and Experience" —that the converse was true: a prevailing experience of grace invariably exposed and overbore the "*Error,* or mistaken Opinion," on which Arminianism was based.

churches, Edwards certified his sympathy with the definition of religious freedom consistent with the principles of the Awakening—that which assumed the rights of the laity to be uppermost.

The attitude of the rationalist ministry toward religious liberty was disclosed in the resolutions passed by a 1743 convention of Massachusetts clergymen. The recent "irregularities and excesses" were condemned as having nothing in them of a genuine work of the Spirit. To prevent the recurrence of such emotions, the convention recommended, ministerial associations should take steps to prevent itinerant preachers from entering their parishes. The partisans of the revival (a more numerous group, as it turned out) issued a counterstatement attacking the decision of the convention as an interference with rights that could not be "denied, without inhumanly invading the essential rights of conscience."[175] And when in 1745 ministerial associations met and publicly announced their intentions to keep Whitefield from being heard again, lay pamphleteers were not the only New Englanders to issue reminders that the pulpit was not the minister's personal property. Whitefield's clerical defenders also declared that the decision as to what minister was to be heard in any church was one of the unalienable "Rights of the Fraternity."[176] Similarly, the separations of the same years, which critics of enthusiasm opposed as affronts to ministerial prerogative, were defended in terms of "the Liberty of the Brotherhood."[177] Even those Calvinists who were offended by the wildness of the Separates agreed that a removal was not only "warrantable" but "highly necessary" whenever a minister showed himself to be doctrinally "corrupt."[178]

Around 1750, however, as the Calvinists of New England saw Arminianism mounting a counterreformation, their definition of religious freedom took on a slightly different meaning. In the context of doctrinal debate, many Calvinists (including some who had looked unfavorably on Whitefield's 1745 tour) began urging the people of New England to "labour to get free from the dangerous Contagion of a corrupt Ministry, such as disseminates *Arminian* errors."[179] What was being recommended was not, however, separation, but dismissal of heterodox ministers. Now Calvinists worked to expose Arminians, and "Pretenders to Orthodoxy," to public view, in order to encourage their dismissal or prevent their settlement. And now, for the first time, the Liberal ministry began to flaunt as their banner that of freedom of conscience. Edwards quickly pointed to the incongruity when he observed that "though none seem to be such warm advocates as they for liberty and freedom of thought," Arminians seemed to be aroused only when anyone threatened to restrain "*their* liberties."[180]

To appreciate some of the finer differences between the Liberal and the evangelical conceptions of religious liberty it is helpful to clarify the terms in which Calvinists argued for the exclusion of the heterodox from the ministry. In the controversies that divided the Presbyterian Church after 1739 it may well be that the Log College party was at first seeking to impose its own definition of orthodoxy as a term of admission to the ministry. Yet the *"Spanish* Inquisition" they were accused of attempting was not in fact an examination of formal beliefs, but, as even John Thomson acknowledged, "a putting Men upon the Rack to declare their inward Experiences." ("No doubt it is racking enough," Samuel Finley commented, "to such as have nothing to declare that Way.")[181] Throughout the period of struggle for control of the Synod, the New Side faithfully preserved Jonathan Dickinson's disdain for "subscriptionism." Over the subsequent decades, however, the evangelical element of Presbyterianism did grow concerned with the matter of a prospective minister's doctrinal orthodoxy. In the 1750's both Tennent and Davenport argued that admitting candidates without "positive Evidences of vital Godliness" would in time flood the church with "heterodox, loose, and vicious Ministers."[182] Behind this prediction lay, of course, the premise that gracelessness and heterodoxy were related in the very nature of things. Still, when the erstwhile members of the Synod of New York in 1761 called on the united church to examine every candidate for the ministry, they did not ask for an inquiry into a man's creedal commitments. Once again the "inquisition" was intended to give the presbytery an opportunity to form "a judgment of his experimental acquaintance with religion, according to which judgment they are to receive or reject him."[183]

By 1760, moreover, the religious multiplicity of America was so taken for granted that even an examination of a candidate's "orthodoxy," or rejection on that acount, was hardly an infringement of religious liberty. A young man guilty of "heresy" in Calvinist eyes could, it was assumed, peddle his wares where he would not shame an evangelical church. Indeed, something of the same assumption seems to have been at work already in the 1730's, when Edwards participated in a council that examined a candidate who was suspected of "Arminianism." What Edwards seemed to be asking was that a candidate who disagreed with the received faith of New England display the same dignity and courage as that shown by the Yale tutors who had openly chosen to take Anglican orders. Still, it is far from impossible that Edwards understood the "Springfield case" in terms of using the semi-Presbyterian polity of western Massachusetts to suppress deviations from the established religion. The same might also be said of the post-Awakening struggles in Connecticut, where New Lights as well as Old attempted to use ministerial associations as a device for outlawing dissent in the churches of the province.

The ecclesiastical histories of both Connecticut and Massachusetts are eloquent testimony to the problems, and the temptations, inherent in a situation where one church is established and enjoys tax support. The problem in Connecticut was particularly acute by virtue of the Saybrook Platform, which designedly limited the independence of the local churches in order to maintain religious uniformity. Through the 1740's, and indeed well afterward, the platform was used to outlaw separatist conventicles. But in the 1750's "pure congregationalism" also became the battle cry of those more reasonable citizens of the colony who resented what seemed a Calvinist crusade to prevent less rigid doctrines from being preached in the Connecticut churches. In this context, Governor Fitch published a pamphlet in which he strove to demonstrate that Congregational independence was the first principle of the Saybrook Platform. That a New Light critic should then have accused him of attempting to destroy "our Constitution by explaining it in a Sense contrary to the very Design" is some indication of the alignment of Connecticut's parties on the question of ecclesiastical independence.[184]

By the 1750's, however, the New Light party of Connecticut included many who had not proclaimed the glorious Awakening and who had in fact done their best to suppress enthusiastic dissent. One such was President Thomas Clap of Yale, who in 1743 had accused Edwards of a "plot" to replace the standing ministry of New England with young Scotch evangelicals. A decade later Clap was summoning all the "Calvinists" of Connecticut to defense of the ancient faith against the "new scheme" of religion that was making inroads both in the college and in the pulpits of Connectitcut. One strategy recommended by Clap was a careful inquiry by associations into the beliefs of young men, in order to make certain, before licensing them, that they were not tainted with rationalist heresy. His most articulate critic, Thomas Darling, a former Yale tutor turned prosperous merchant, rightly accused Clap of "priestcraft." Clap was no more the libertarian in this context than he had been when, as rector of the college, he had expelled the Cleavelands for attending a Separate service.

Nevertheless, Darling himself acknowledged that the underlying premise of the "Calvinist" crusade, and to him the most appalling, was that church members had the right to insist on a minister's preaching the doctrines they believed. "This is a fine Compliment paid to the *Laity*," Darling sneeringly commented; after all, was it not the "teacher's" privilege to introduce a people to truths he understood far better than they?[185] Thomas Clap's declaration of the rights of the laity probably did not extend to allowing that if a congregation actually wanted a graceless heretic they were welcome to him. But some such premise seems to have informed the ecclesiastical practice of other, more evangelical, Calvinists. When Edwards asked that the council of ministers concerned with his case be expanded to include more than the neighboring ministers, he was not seeking to pack the jury in his favor. He assumed that the jury was the church itself and that the council's deliberations were simply a means to the people's making a better judgment. Moreover, the council that recommended Edwards' dismissal included some who were in complete agreement with him but would not vote to impose any minister on a recalcitrant congregation. And the "Presbytery of Boston," of which Jonathan Parsons was a leader, voted in the 1750's to allow a congregation to remove their minister (a protégé of Edwards') when they grew discontent with the "strictness" of his Calvinist doctrines and practices.[186]

In the most famous of Connecticut's pre-Revolutionary ecclesiastical disputes—one often pointed to as evidence of Calvinist opposition to "liberty" and even of Joseph Bellamy's "dictatorial" character— the "Wallingford controversy," a council was convened, and attempted to move against the "Arminian" James Dana, at the request of church members. Dana had professed adherence to the Westminster Confession, but later he began to voice sentiments that sounded to some of his more pious, and attentive, parishioners like monstrous heresy. When Joseph Bellamy entered the controversy as a polemicist, he made it quite clear that the issue, so far as he and the New Lights for whom he spoke were concerned, was how such duplicity might be prevented. What disturbed Bellamy was the thought of a minister who, as he put it, "uses all his art to conceal himself from the congregation in general, and in the meantime, is usually cunning to make proselytes to the Socinian scheme, in a secret, underhanded way."[187] Underhanded or not, what is clear is that Dana, long before his public "rebuttal" of Edwards' *Will*, was quietly expressing Arminian sentiments in private correspondence with the Liberals of Boston—sentiments which he there stated far more explicitly than in any sermons. What the council was seeking was first and foremost an open avowal of beliefs by Dana in order that the congregation, in voting to retain or dismiss him, would know precisely the kind of food they were arranging to receive. To Dana's sympathizers throughout Connecticut the controversy may have seemed to involve the question of religious liberty, but the more pressing question, so far as Bellamy was concerned, was whether a minister who resisted inquiries into his beliefs was not asking for the privilege of taking tax money from a people without making clear what he would offer in return.

Undoubtedly there were instances, in Connecticut as elsewhere, of evangelical members of the establishment trying to use the institutional mechanisms of the church to suppress what they considered heresy. At the heart of nearly every dispute, it must be remembered, was that which eventually led to litigation of the Calvinist-Unitarian controversy in Massachusetts: whether the power in any particular church was vested in the church or in the whole community. In such circumstances, the power of ministerial associations seemed at first glance the best way of keeping the saints from being outvoted by the graceless in communities where the latter had the majority. Of course there could have been no such controversies had not the religion of Connecticut and Massachusetts been supported, financially or otherwise, by the state—had the voluntary principle, that is, been perfectly applied in post-Awakening America. Indeed, shortly before the Revolution, spokesmen for Bellamy's party began to attest publicly their awareness that voluntarism was *the* essential ecclesiastical principle of evangelical religion, and that there was no way of making it consistent with a quest for centralized authority or with an establishment of religion.

Finally, whatever may have been the inconsistencies, actual or seeming, of the New Lights, none were nearly so flagrant as those revealed in the record of Liberals and Old Lights on the question of religious freedom. As the historian Trumbull observed, in Connecticut it was the very ministers who had been "some of the most violent opposers of the religious awakening," and who had "publicly thanked the legislature for their tyrannical, unjust, and persecuting laws," who in the 1750's became "great sticklers for liberty."[188] What liberty meant to Liberals, moreover, was something quite different from that to which evangelicals were dedicated. To the Liberal ministry religious liberty signified, not the right of any man to leave his parish church, but, above all things, the freedom of the clergy—freedom ultimately from the laity as well as from the interference of prying Calvinist associations. John Tucker, for instance, insisted that the "right of private judgment" was involved in his refusal to be fallen upon and worried "with councils." It was also involved, Tucker argued, in his reluctance and that of reasonable ministers generally to publish their fullest thoughts. According to Tucker, the reason he had decided against printing certain of his discourses was a "fear of being exposed to," and having his name blackened by, "licentious and persecuting tongues." Enlightened ministers, he complained, were always in danger of having their character blasted by the multitude as "oppressors and blasphemers of the truth."[189] To Tucker, as to Jonathan Mayhew, religious freedom meant the right of the individual to have his say without being harassed by a tyrannical majority.

Liberals were not always willing to give an equivalent freedom to spokesmen of the evangelical scheme. Yet they could, on the basis of a perhaps archaic definition, stand as advocates of religious freedom. "Such is the mild, the liberal, and catholic spirit of this government," Tucker explained, "that it pretends not to meddle with any man's conscience, but leaves everyone to possess and use it without molestation."[190] But in the controversies that racked New England after 1760, it was not freedom of conscience merely that was at stake. Tucker defined religious liberty in such a way that it consisted in the right of a man to *think* for himself. Calvinists denied neither Tucker nor any man this right, nor even the right to *speak,* for they believed, in the words of Milton several times quoted in the attacks on Tucker, that "truth is great and will prevail." What Calvinists asked, and were refused, was a right they considered just as precious—and, in the context of post-Awakening religion, perhaps more precious: the right of every man in the colonies to *hear* the minister of his choice.

One of the more revealing controversies in this regard is that which erupted at Newbury, Massachusetts, when certain of John Tucker's parishioners, complaining that he refused to preach the Calvinistic doctrines of "efficacious grace," summoned a council of ministers, including some so distant from Newburyport as Ebenezer Pemberton. Tucker greeted the committee of visitation by announcing his belief that they were "neither fit advisers nor competent judges in any difficulties of mine."[191] At the same time, however, Tucker, along with other exponents of the Congregational way, was denying relief from the tax rate to those of his disaffected parishioners who, considering the quality of his gospel, preferred the ministrations of Jonathan Parsons. A similar and even more pointed irony emerged when in one year the established clergy of Massachusetts republished John Wise's tracts in defense of congregationalism, in the hope of ousting Nathaniel Whitaker from the Salem Tabernacle, and concurrently, defended the use of the consociational system to deny the right of a congregation to remove by majority vote a minister accused of Arminianism.

The issue was not simply whose ox was being gored but, once again, the degree to which evangelical preachers seemed able to "insinuate themselves into the affections" of the people, and the manner in which, almost everywhere, the gentry were able to use the power structure of colonial society to maintain their brand of religion, or, as Isaac Backus would have it, of "civility."[192] For even in Connecticut, "independence" of Bellamy's prying examiners was but one device for maintaining the preachers of rational religion. As one enthusiastic critic of the Saybrook Platform complained, though the "converted holy men" of a town might choose a St. Paul for their minister, they could be outvoted by the "scandalous" citizens who happened to "have the Money Qualifications" for the town franchise.[193] In the decades which began with the awakening of 1763 enmities were aroused: against the Tuckers who refused either to preach Calvinism or to free men to hear it elsewhere, and against the respectable gentry who preferred removing an evangelical minister to going elsewhere for a more reasonable gospel. But everywhere the underlying issue, so far as Calvinists were concerned, was the right of "pastors and people" to achieve their "union and welfare" freely.[194]

The ultimate goal of those who demanded religious liberty in the decades before the Revolution was, in the profoundest sense, freedom of speech—the right of as many Americans as possible to hear not merely the doctrines, but the voices, of the evangelical clergy. The quest for religious freedom, involved as it came to be with the economic and political question of taxes, poured much of the energy of evangelical religion directly into the movement that became the American Revolution, and foreshadowed an era of American life in which even the people of God could be more concerned with worldly goods than with the salvation of their immortal souls. But the drive for religious liberty retained much the same purpose from 1751, when Davies informed Bellamy that the Virginia "clergy, universally, as far as my intelligence* extends, have embraced the modish system of Arminian divinity,"[195] through the 1770's, when Joseph Hawley defended a Baptist petition in the Massachusetts General Court on the simple basis "that the established religion of the country was not worth a groat."[196]

From Hawley's perspective, those who upheld the "religion in fashion" were guilty not of economic self-sufficiency merely, nor of social pretense, nor even of political tyranny, but of the ultimate sin, a failure of perception. In his view likewise the ultimate purpose of the religious liberty he and dissenters throughout the colonies demanded was the opportunity for ministers to touch their people's hearts and wills in ways that only the evangelical preacher understood. In this sense the wealthy and fashionable served themselves well, in the years just before the Revolution, by preventing the union of pastor and people that dissenters desired. For there was always the possibility

---

* Davies' remark that "universal fame has superseded my information" suggests the efficiency of the Calvinist intercolonial network of communication.

that those whom the evangelical ministry exhorted might even be aroused to a fulfillment of the will of the Calvinist God.

IV

Throughout the period of the Great Awakening men left their parish ministers, or chose new ones, for reasons that were seldom explained in terms of polity or doctrine. The most common justification of separation was that the "old Way of Preaching" had become "very *unsavoury.*"[197] Over the following decade Presbyterianism grew in Virginia, according to Davies, not as the result of some Roundhead conspiracy against Anglican ritual and liturgy but by virtue of the "*strange* Charm" of the preaching of plain evangelical doctrine.[198] By the 1760's, despite the doctrinal controversies, it was once again clear that doctrine alone could not assure a minister's appeal. Some of the most militant Calvinists of the Great Awakening were by then concerned by the degree to which men were separating even "where they cannot deny but the doctrine is sound." The complaint—that a particular minister is "not so zealous, so lively, so spiritual, so evangelical as some others"—reflected, to be sure, the fact that the laity were often the first to sense that a preacher was only nominally sound in doctrine. What they were responding to were modifications, muting, and failure to insist on the crucial precepts of evangelical doctrine.[199] But the response attested the fact that a minister was most likely to prove "unpopular" when his sermons, whatever their content, were felt to be "unanimating."[200]

Behind the desire for a regenerate clergy was a sense that doctrines could be made emotionally evocative and effective only when the minister was at heart qualified to make them so. A teacher's knowledge and command of logic was not enough; it was essential that ministers "be spiritually taught"—be "supernaturally enlightened"—if they were to preach effectively. "Can it be supposed," asked a protégé of Edwards in the summer of 1776,

> that a preacher, however rational, without a sense at heart of the beauty and importance of divine things, will, in the course of preaching, treat the great and interesting doctrines of divine revelation in so lively and affecting a strain, as another of equal genius, whose heart is ravished with the glory of divine things, and his whole soul deeply impressed with the whole weight of eternity!![201]

The central Calvinist rhetorical precept, and the crux of their social theory as well, had been articulated by Edwards in 1743: "Our people do not so much need to have their heads stored, as to have their hearts touched."[202] Herein lay the basis of the division of American Protestantism by the Great Awakening, rhetorically as well as doctrinally or socially.

Soon after the Awakening Joseph Bellamy discovered that neither his doctrine nor his delivery was designed for success in an urban setting. The First Presbyterian Church of New York, Bellamy complained, preferred a "more free and generous gospel" than he could offer, but it also desired a preacher who had shaken the country dust from his diction and delivery. "I may possibly do to be a minister out in the woods," he exclaimed in words that other evangelists would echo through the era of Charles Grandison Finney, "but am not fit for a city." Bellamy's lament—"I am not polite enough for them"—was testimony not so much to a rural-urban division in eighteenth-century America as to the profounder disparity in American taste wrought by the dividing spirit of the revival. Those in New York who objected to Bellamy's preaching delighted in a "modulation of voice, and a propriety of method, and refinement of language" in which he was thought deficient, while in Connecticut it was said that no one who had not "seen and heard" Bellamy could appreciate the consummate "force and beauty of his preaching."[203] The argument between Liberal and Calvinist was, in substance, whether the end of preaching was to entertain or to arouse, and aesthetic criteria were contingent on what was considered the purposes of the spoken word.

The rhetorical theory of rational religion was devised in conscious reaction to the enthusiasm of the Awakening. In one of his first public discussions of the revival, Chauncy allowed that it was proper for a preacher to address men's "passions" only if he made certain "that they are kept under the restraints of *reason*; for otherwise they will soon run wild, and make those in whom they reign do so too."[204] In his *Seasonable Thoughts* Chauncy (still working within the framework of Puritan psychology though he had read Locke) acknowledged that the "passions" were "planted in the human constitution *for very valuable uses.*" However, he continued, ministers should not raise them "to such a height as really to unfit" men for "the exercise of their *reasonable* powers."[205] As Chauncy developed his argument, it became clear that the only place of the "passions," either in the human soul or in pulpit practice, was "their proper place, under the government of a well inform'd understanding." Such psychological postulates were soon translated into homiletic and rhetorical precepts. According to Ebenezer Gay, the philosopher of Massachusetts rationalism, the true "evangelical preacher" sought to elicit no passionate emotions but only a "rational Devotion." What this meant in practice was speaking primarily, even exclusively, to what the seventeenth century had called the rational soul. Persuaded as they were that enthusiasm had its rise in efforts to "please the Fancy and raise the imagination," the rational clergy hesitated to practice, or to permit, any departure from the purest and flattest of expository and logical prose.[206]

Among the critics of revival enthusiasm were of course ministers who strove to preserve, in rhetoric as in doctrine, something of the old Puritan middle way. Nathaniel Appleton, for instance, explained that while a minister must always speak rationally, this did not require

> a bald, low, groveling Stile; our Reasoning should be with such Strains of Eloquence as will give the Argument its proper Force. But here we must beware of Excess, and take heed that we don't by the Power of Oratory bear too hard upon the Passions, to the Prejudice of the nobler Powers of the Soul . . .

But the experience of the revival, and the new psychologies it introduced, made it difficult to preserve a conception of eloquence that was based on a scholastic view of the personality. For the critics of the Awakening, even subdued addresses to the sensible soul were a thing of the past, for "the rugged Passions" needed to be soothed, not awakened by vivid or familiar images. Especially among ministers directly confronted by revival enthusiasm, or forced into a continuing argument with rabid separatists, the passions became something to be feared. If one's emotions were aroused, the soul would be "thrown into such a Ferment, as to Cloud the Judgment, Usurp the seat of Reason, and Distract the Man."[207] By 1750 Liberals and Old Lights were invariably seeking safety in a rhetoric, as well as a religion, of the understanding. Their sermons had little of the power of oratory and were, in fact, designedly lectures.

However, a few rationalist clergymen, most of them too young or too self-confident to have imbibed all the fears engendered by the Awakening, found a place in their religion and their preaching for the "affections." One such was Jonathan Mayhew:

> We ought not to be so fond of a rational religion, as to suppose that it consists wholly in cold dry speculation, without having any concern for the affections. Real piety necessarily supposes that the heart is touched, affected, warmed, inflamed; and not merely that we have right speculative notions concerning God.[208]

While the espousal of so warm a religion set Mayhew apart from such hardheaded specimens as Chauncy, his religious affections should not be confused with Edwards' nor his faith with the true religion of Joseph Bellamy. Mayhew himself carefully distinguished his "enthusiasm" from the holy love of Whitefield, whose "enthusiastic flights" he considered both tasteless and dangerous. Such enthusiasm, according to Mayhew, was so "contrary to sobriety of mind, and of such fatal consequence," that it was the minister's duty to keep from arousing it.[209] Whoever believed that true faith consists of "something more refined and sublime" than "solid, substantial religion"—which Mayhew defined as "a rational love of God, of mankind, and the practice of moral virtue"—was anathema to him. Calvinists, on the other hand, often observed that Mayhew's "devotion of the heart" was nothing but an exercise of the carnal, unrenewed emotions, his affection for God a thinly disguised self-love.[210]

In time even Chauncy managed to find a place for something called "sentiment" in his creed. But Liberals introduced emotion into religion or preaching not in defiance of reason or with the intention of violating the rational order, but in the hope of reinforcing both. True enthusiasm, Mayhew explained, asks and seeks nothing "besides that which *sober reason* requires."[211] Liberals often felt called upon to apologize, not only for their enthusiasm, but even for their use of the word itself. William Smith appended to a sermon dealing with "noble, manly and rational Enthusiasm" a footnote, in which he asked to be "excused" for his "use of the word, as here restricted and explained. He does not know another, that would convey his idea to substitute in its place."[212] How rationalists restricted and explained their enthusiasm is disclosed by Mayhew's discussion of "the love of God," presumably the most intense and exalted emotion the Liberal temper could sustain:

> [It] is a calm and rational thing, the result of thought and consideration. It is indeed, a passion or affection; but a passion excited by reason presenting the proper object of it to the mind.[213]

Within such limits a Liberal could be delighted, enraptured, or even ravished, but only if his object of regard was already worthy of rational approbation.

The emotionalism of these disciples of reason challenged nothing, and asked nothing more than what Chauncy, by his own more labored intellectual processes, might also come to approve. Love of God or of mankind—indeed any sort of reasonable enthusiasm—proceeded from and could be inspired only by "just and elevated notions."[214] Man might feel pleasure in the creation but only because its "wonderful order" made heaven and earth seem such eminently reasonable contrivances.[215] Any feeling which did not so arise, Liberals relentlessly insisted, came in response to self-generated and unreasonable visions. Moreover, the development or titillation of the imaginative faculty was intended, as William Smith made clear in urging tasteful studies for the students of the College of Philadelphia, to make men not less reasonable, but more. The products of his tutelage would not be purely rational men; indeed they might be—by virtue of their glowing imaginations—"enthusiasts" of a sort. But in no case would they be "unruly and turbulent."[216] True enthusiasm, in short, was vouchsafed only to men in other respects wise and discerning. It was social reliability that made Smith's and Mayhew's brand of enthusiasts so serenely superior to the ecstatic multitude—as superior indeed as were the preachers and professors of such an affective religion to the Calvinist clergy and their ecstatic converts.

Emotional religion was the effort of a generation younger than Chauncy to sustain a religion of respectability against intellectual challenge. A creed centered on sensibility served as a bulwark against the deism to which eighteenth-century rational religion so dangerously tended and, perhaps more conveniently, as a useful weapon in the struggle with evangelical piety. William Smith's creed, for instance, contained a fideistic answer to those whose speculations into the nature of God inevitably led them to ask if this were indeed the best of all possible worlds. Smith believed that God had implanted in the human soul "a natural affectation," responsive to whatever is "great" or "marvellous." Since only the Deity himself was sufficiently marvelous to be "fully commensurate" to these "more generous affections," man's emotional capacity became, for Smith, the unerring guarantor of the existence of God.[217]

Like the Liberals of New England who eventually celebrated the "theology" of Fénelon, and like such other Anglicans as Duché and Peters, whom respectable Philadelphians and other Liberals thought mad when they began to dabble in the reveries of Jacob Böhme, Smith had purposeful method in his evocation of an affective religion. The emotions served to check "vain curiosity" about the nature of God, who had "never intended the human race should throw away time, in metaphysical researches into his unsearchable Essence."[218] His brand of affectionate religion was useful in intellectual combat with American Calvinists. Smith hesitated to engage in debate with the Tennents. He preferred to accuse the revival party and its leaders of an overbearing and litigious interest in "points of controversy," of a vain insistence on "minute distinctions, party-shibboleths, perplexing definitions, and nice modes."[219]

In charging the Calvinists with hyperrationalism, Smith was well ahead of most Massachusetts Liberals, few of whom (with the exception of Mayhew) were intellectually prepared, until the advent of Channing, to defend their religion as more worthy than Calvinism because less rigorously logical. But the process had begun in pre-Revolutionary New England, if only in jibes that nearsighted revivalists, incapable of a wider and more imaginative perspective, were splitting hairs on indifferent and inessential matters. In politics as well as in religion, in Boston or in Philadelphia, Liberals always preferred the broad and sensitive view to the careful and probing examination.

The "affectionate religion" of Smith and Mayhew was of some consequence in the modeling of their sermons. Moving often at random between appeals to each stratum of their audiences, they encouraged only the chaste and temperate "affections"—since men of cultivation would surely, even if touched, choose the solid and substantial good of rational virtue—and, for greater safety, discouraged and worked to subdue the popular "passions." The effect was often more an athletic than a literary exhibition, as for instance Mayhew's effort in 1760 to deliver an American *oraison funèbre*. In eulogizing Stephen Sewall, Mayhew paused to declare that he was "so deeply touch'd, so penetrated" by the judge's death that he hardly knew "how to speak." "For alas! one, indeed, the far better part of my heart," he exclaimed, "seems torn away from me, while the other is left wounded, panting and bleeding." Mayhew's demonstrative grief, while it may have served to communicate some emotion to his audience, also served, as he himself confessed apologetically, to make his discourse "appear broken and unconnected." Unconnected to, among other things, the several solid and weighty reasons offered intermittently by Mayhew as to why Judge Sewall had not, nor reasonably need have, been particularly liberal in his benefactions to the Boston poor.[220]

Where Mayhew derived the inspiration for such a funeral sermon is a matter of speculation. But William Smith claimed to have learned from Massillon and Bossuet that emotions might be directly communicated from speaker to audience. "A good preacher," he contended, would "speak what he feels, and strive to make others feel what he speaks."[221] Though he strove to blend "French animation" with those English qualities of reasonable instruction that he, along with the New England Arminians, admired in the sermons of Tillotson, Smith's success in integrating logic and emotion is questionable. So far as Smith was concerned, however, a true "devotion of heart" could be induced in men only if the preacher himself was filled with such a feeling.

Not wishing to be accused of mimicking Gilbert Tennent, Smith carefully distinguished between his feelings and those of the revivalists, whose enthusiasm, he was convinced, was mere "uninformed Zeal." True godlike emotion came only to those ministers who had a "comprehensive knowledge" of "Religion in general." Smith expected the devotion of the comprehensive ministry to manifest itself normally only in a mild pulpit glow, but, if sufficiently ravished by his idea of God, a preacher might on extraordinary occasions rise to greater heights of emotion. Because at such a moment the preacher would seem to move on "the winged ardour of genius" and to pour forth "a torrent of sacred eloquence," he might, Smith allowed, be thought an "enthusiast." Yet whatever this exalted emotional state might be called, it was as different from revivalist enthusiasm as day from night, for it alone would be "the noble enthusiasm of Truth and Reason."[222] If Smith's ideas, like the effort of any advocate of sweet reason to deal with the question of enthusiasm, seem to lack semantic precision, they had the merit of being perfectly designed to show that certain preachers were noble geniuses and George Whitefield was not.

These samples from the sermons of Mayhew and Smith suggest why there was nothing that can be called a typical Liberal sermon. Informed as they were by the variety of imported manuals of rhetoric popular in culturally ambitious American circles, younger Liberals especially indulged themselves in the cultivation of personal and even idiosyncratic styles. Herein they seemed to follow the advice of Cotton Mather, who had observed in his *Manuductio ad Ministerium* (1726), "After all, Every man will have his own *Style*, which will distinguish him as much as his *Gate*."[223] In Mather's own case this had meant in fact *two* styles, one for use in his own church or for the people of New England generally, not far from the "plain style" of his forebears, and another, designed to impress European readers with the fact that Americans were not unread and unfashionable provincials, which he characterized as "massy" and "flowery." According to the precepts of the traditional "plain style," content was more important than form, the "substance and solidity of the frame," in the words of Thomas Hooker, of more concern than the "varnish."[224] In the years after the Awakening, however, when Liberals began to build somewhat statelier mansions for the soul, they came to give a much greater attention to the ornament of their address.

At times Liberals continued to hold the frame of the discourse most important, but at others they insisted that God's altar stood in need of no little polishing. When criticizing Calvinist "bombast," the Liberal preacher allowed that the only normally permissible departure from pure reason was "expressive diction, and tuneful cadences."[225] Otherwise, however, their own attempts to adorn truth—including those which took a form accurately if contemptuously described by Devereux Jarratt as "fine paintings of moral virtue"[226]—were among the many efforts of America's eighteenth-century provincials to come up to European standards. Buffeted by winds of fashion as well as doctrine, the Liberal rhetoric was eclectic. Like the *beaux-arts* designs that were to enjoy so great a vogue in mid-nineteenth-century America, the Liberal aesthetic represented less a substantial commitment to the known good than a negative response to the cultural deprivations of the Western wilderness. In this respect Liberal sermons are to be considered more as a chapter in the formation of polite taste than a contribution to the evolution of American oratory.

Liberal discourses, modeled on Cicero and guided by Quintilian, aspired to literary felicity and not to arouse the fierce democracy. Most of the pre-Revolutionary literati were not at ease with the arts of persuasion, if only because the faculty psychology which they persistently maintained assumed a radical disjunction between the understanding and the emotions. Consider, for instance, William Livingston's discourse on method in one of the articles in the *Independent Reflector* in which he argued against an Anglican monopoly on higher education in New York:

> Nor fancy I aim at warping your Judgment by the Illusion of Oratory, or the Fascination of Eloquence. If in the Sequel, I appear rather to declaim than prove, or seem to prefer the Flowers of Rhetoric to the Strength of Argument, it is because, by the clearest Demonstration, I have already evinced the Necessity of frustrating so injurious a Step. My Assertions have not been unsupported by Evidence; nor have I levelled at your Passions, till I had convinced your Reason. After this, you will pardon a more animated Address, intended to warm the Imagination, and excite your Activity.[227]

Livingston's essays betokened a new era in American life, one in which some of the erstwhile critics of bustle and energy would themselves seek to participate in and even encourage American activity. But having once opted for tranquillity—even so briefly as Livingston—they were hardly prepared for all that this new career entailed. As one historian of American rhetoric and oratory has concluded, the skills learned at Cambridge, New Haven, and Philadelphia in mid-eighteenth-century America were "more sought after for their ornamental than their functional persuasive values."[228] The subsequent efforts of such students to arouse audience or readers were inevitably hobbled by ambitions that could not, even in the heat of battle, be totally foresworn.

In point of fact, the rational mind preferred to achieve its social and even its ecclesiastical goals through the instrumentality of the law or, in exceptional cases, education. To many Liberal clergymen, moreover, the sacramental role was of far more importance than the pastoral. Among the higher Anglicans, such as Samuel Johnson, there was something of a studied indifference to the composition of sermons, on the assumption that the Book of Common Prayer had been happily devised as a comfort to clergymen whose gifts did not happen to fall in the area of preaching. Interestingly, even Congregationalists were provoked, by the revival, into echoes of Archbishop Laud's strictures against a pulpit-centered religion. Benjamin Colman's son-in-law, the poet Ebenezer Turrell, at first approved of the revival, but he soon had second thoughts and was one of the first Boston ministers to publish his criticisms. Among his objections to the phenomena of 1741 was what he considered an "insatiable Thirst for hearing Sermons upon Sermons, without any Time for Prayer, Meditation, and Self-Examination between."[229] Herein Turrell was presumably seeking to restore something of American Puritanism's balanced order of worship, but his thoughts were soon expanded, by other critics of the Awakening, into an explicit denigration of the sermon. "Reading, Meditation, and Prayer," one New Englander affirmed, "is a much more safe Way to labour to obtain Satisfaction . . . than *hastily running after the* Preachments of those whose Persons we know but little."[230] Such an assessment led to, among other things, the higher estimate placed by the rational mind on the written (as distinguished from the spoken) word. And in the years after the revival not a few Congregationalists (and Old Side Presbyterians) participated in what might be styled a modest liturgical movement.

Considering their different evaluations of the spoken word, variations in eighteenth-century Liberal pulpit practice were inevitable. But one generalization may surely be hazarded: the great end of preaching remained much the same for all—the younger and more ardent as well as their more circumspect elders, those disposed to liturgy as much as those who aspired to literary grace. For Johnson and Smith, just as for Chauncy, the "divine faculties of Reason and Understanding" remained the only means of "knowing and searching the Truth" and conducting one's self or others toward "true Happiness."[231] Thus the "most edifying Way of Preaching," indeed the "only Gospel Preaching," was, as according to the Anglican Henry Caner:

> informing the Minds or Understanding of the Hearers, in the great Truths and Duties of the Gospel; and endeavouring to convince their Judgments of the importance of these Duties, and of the Necessity of receiving and practicing them; and of avoiding every Thing that is inconsistent or Contrary to them.[232]

The characteristic Liberal sermon was instructional, filled with propositional truths, somewhat less concerned with what the Puritans had called "doctrine" than with "reasons," and, most importantly, designed, in its "applications" or "uses," for edification rather than for exhortation. Only in their manner of enforcing the reasonable precepts of Christian conduct did Liberals betray a distinctive gait—for some were prepared to have men march rather than amble along the paths of salvation.

The relationship between the social and literary concerns of the Liberal ministry may be gathered from a satirical essay on "the *Bombastick* and the *Grubstreet*" style, published in Boston's *American Magazine and Historical Chronicle* five years after Whitefield's first visit. The essay has been identified as the work of the illustrious Dr. Mather Byles—wit, correspondent of Alexander Pope, and eventually Boston's most prominent Tory. Although certain of Byles' critical comments foreshadowed his later observations on Calvinist preaching, his essay gave little direct attention to the issues raised by the revival. Like the articles on Ciceronian and Demosthenic oratory that would appear in such gentlemen's magazines for another seventy-five years, this piece was not a serious analysis of American literature, but an effort to ape the critical articles such publications often so generously extracted from English periodicals.*

Yet Byles' announced intention, at least, was to correct the "false Taste" prevailing in America, where, to his chagrin, "Bombast and Fustian" and an "Inundation of Sound" were mistaken for the *"true Sublime."*[233] It is difficult to read his pronouncements except as against the background of the Great Awakening and Byles' avowed displeasure with the quality of evangelical preaching. Only three years before Byles' article, Chauncy had sarcastically complained that the itinerants used "more *sublime* and *spiritual* Phrases than are common among sober and good Christians" as a means of exciting men's passions.[234] Other critics of the revival believed that the worst error of the itinerants was that of swelling "into the imaginary and false sublime, into fustian and bombast," and then sinking "into mean and low expressions." It was for the latter sort of language that the revivalists were more often criticized. John Thomson, for one, had no stomach for "such hellish Words and Expressions" as the Log College men used; they were borrowed, he was sure, "from the most profane, black guard Ruffians, Cursers and Swearers."[235] When rationalist ministers referred to the revivalists' "many horrid Expressions concerning God" they had in mind, along with the cruel fatalism presumably imputed to the Deity, the manner of Whitefield and others in personally addressing the Godhead. But whatever the offense, or the catalogue of epithets

---

* "One great Design of many of the Entertainments in our Magazine," explained the editors in introducing Byles' essay, "is to cultivate *polite* writing, and form and embellish the Style of our ingenious Countrymen."

assembled by critics of Calvinist sermons, the conclusion was always the same—that evangelical discourse was stylistically abominable:

> 'Twould be endless to mention all the Barbarism, to remark upon all the *Nonsense, Fustian* and *Bombast,* the *awkward Simile's* and *Affectation of Polite Writing,* and the *strange Jumbling of Metaphors.*[236]

It was with the tasteless literature of the revival in mind that certain Liberal clergymen set themselves the task—one which they often fulfilled in ordination sermons—of lecturing young ministers on the rudiments of style. In 1758 Byles, speaking at the ordination of his son, urged that "uncouth jargon" and "affected phrases" be "condemned," "hissed from the desk and blotted from the page."[237] Among the "uncouth Phrases" which Liberals found "rather grating and offensive, than pleasing, to a sober and judicious Ear," were, to be sure, such "party Terms" as "Arminians,"[238] but Byles had specifically in mind Samuel Davies' famous sermon, *The General Resurrection.* This sermon, as indeed all Calvinist sermons on their favorite of subjects, contained what Samuel Finley, in characterizing Davies' oratorical talent, called "thoughts sublime,"[239] and "the sublime," as Liberals had learned from experience, if not from Longinus, "not only persuades, but even throws an audience into transports."

When, in the *End for which God Created the World,* Edwards penned perhaps the sublimest passage in all colonial literature, the Liberal ministry either ignored it or refused to admit that one not of their own had succeeded in creating a work of beauty.*[240] For majestic images of the Church Triumphant were never to the Liberal taste, and particularly not when they served to persuade or to transport those whom the Liberal ministry considered of the lower class.

Perhaps the best illustrations of the differences between Liberal and Calvinist rhetoric are the responses of a leading Liberal and an outstanding Calvinist preacher to the oratory of the American Indians. Toward the end of the Revolution, William Smith, seeking to demonstrate the validity of his thesis that oratory in general (or his oratory in particular) was the consummate integration of all the liberal arts and sciences, made this observation:

> There is something in Poetry and Music admirably suited to divine

---

* The Liberal domination of organs of literary criticism and of canons of taste in the early years of the Republic helps explain the continuing reputation of such writers and preachers as Jonathan Mayhew and William Smith, and the nearly total neglect into which the superior efforts of Bellamy and Davies were to fall. As late as 1823, Channing, who acknowledged his own indebtedness to Edwards' heir, Samuel Hopkins, was to explain that Edwards himself had been "lost, in a great degree, to literature" by "vassalage to a false theology."

and lofty subjects; and it is natural for the soul of man, when struck with any thing surprisingly great, good, or marvellously new, to break forth beyond the common modes of speech, into the most rapturous strains of expression, accompanied with correspondent Attitudes of Body, and Modulations of Voice. Even the untutored savages around us, furnish striking proofs of this!

That Smith considered it somehow suprising that uneducated savages should respond and act in a manner supposedly natural to all mankind suggests the character of his fascination with the primitive. Many years earlier, Smith had published in New York and arranged to have republished in London a speech ostensibly delivered by a Creek Indian. The text of the speech reveals, even in the absence of directions for "Attitudes of Body" and "Modulations of Voice," that the only good Indian orator, so far as Smith was concerned, was one who spoke in the deadly prose that Smith and those other "curious" folk to whom he thought the speech "might, at least, be acceptable," considered poetry.[241]

The speech, "against the immoderate use of spirituous liquors," was supposedly translated from the original Creek by an acquaintance of Smith, but one can detect Smith's editorial hand in the finished product. His "Indian orator" began by begging "leave to assert, and submit to your impartiality my arguments to support this assertion, that our prevailing love, our intemperate use of this liquid, will be productive of consequences the most destructive to the welfare and glory of the public, and the felicity of every individual offender." The "desertion of all our reasonable powers," and "that barbarian madness, wherewith this liquid inspired us," he argued, "prove beyond doubt that it impairs all our intellectual faculties." He went on to observe, pathetically, that only a dry Creek could be sensitive to the "endowments" and the "charms" of womankind,* and, in his peroration (for in Philadelphia the speech appeared "to contain all the parts or members of the most perfect oration") attained these lofty strains:

Let me conjure you by all these softer ties, and inexpressible endearments;—let me conjure you too, as you yet hope to behold the Tree of Peace raise its far-seen top to the sun, and spread its odorous branches, watered by the dew of Heaven, over all your abodes, while you rejoice unmolested under its shade; and as you yet wish to behold the nations round about you, bound with the sacred Chain

* "Shall an unnatural, and unreasonable, a vicious perversity of taste be preferred to those Heaven born joys of life? . . . Will any Creek henceforth dare to approach those lovely creatures with unhallowed lips, breathing the noisome smell of this diabolical juice; or roll into their downy embrace in a state inferior to the brutes . . . ?

of Concord, every hand maintaining a link:—By all these ties, by all these hopes, I conjure you, O Creeks! hence-forward let the cup of Moderation be the crown of your festivities . . . Break not the great chain of nature; but let an honest, rational, and delicate inter-course of the sexes be the plan of social joy. Let each domestic bliss wreathe the garland of connubial life.[242]

"How is it possible," asked Brackenridge's Captain Farrago, "for men who live remote from the scene of action, to have adequate ideas of the nature of Indians" and how to "get speeches made, and interpret them so as to pass for truth"? The latter, at least, was according to Brackenridge "an easy matter" in the literary circles of Philadelphia, where Indians speeches were "nearly all alike," and men had only to talk of "brightening chains" in order to pass for Indian experts.[243] Smith, whose interest in inland America was as a propagandist for the Philadelphia land speculators who contested with the New Lights of Connecticut for the rich Wyoming Valley, understood the literary canons of his day, if not the nature of Indians. Like Thomas Jefferson and DeWitt Clinton, and the biographers of Red Jacket and the Prophet, he discovered a remarkable disposition among Indians to speak as he himself would speak.

The Calvinist ministry was probably more fortunate in approaching Indian oratory by way of living among the Indians as missionaries and of having in their very ranks at least one genuine red man. The intellectual by-products of the missionary ventures included a dissertation on the Indian language by the younger Jonathan Edwards (which Madison believed so scientific that he sent a copy to Jefferson) and the conversion of Samson Occum who, awakened in 1741, eventually became perhaps the most famous graduate of the Lebanon school. Ordained as a Presbyterian minister in 1756, Occum subsequently served as a preacher among his own people and as Calvinist ambassador to the dissenters of England. Despite his yielding occasionally "to excess in the use of intoxicating liquors,"* he was described by Samuel Buell as "the glory of the Indian nation."[244]

So impressed was Buell by Occum's preaching that he sought to assess the sources and nature of Indian "natural and free," "quick

---

* Rather than thinking it unnatural for Indian males to visit Indian maids with noisome breath, the Calvinist ministry concluded, out of their experience with Indians, that the doctrine of original sin was fully vindicated in the character of these most natural of men. Not only did Edwards, in disposing of John Taylor's arguments against original sin, suggest that those who believed man by nature virtuous might spend some time among the aborigines of America, but Brainerd found the Indians themselves quite capable of understanding that men came into this world as sinners. Indian experience with their own children, Calvinists fondly observed—by way of indirect reply to sentimental arguments against infant damnation—was sufficient evidence for them.

and powerful" eloquence. Occum, he observed, used "great plainness of speech," though, when he spoke to Indians, he made frequent use of apt and significant similitudes." This "method of conveying *Ideas*," Buell concluded, was as "pleasing as 'tis natural." Behind these observations and conclusions was the Calvinist conviction that if Occum's "Method of Preaching" was not "so pleasing to them who form a Taste" for "the Flowers of Oratory," yet it was the one "best adapted to do good to the Souls of Men," one upon which, in the case of Occum's preaching and in every other, the Lord had been "pleased to command his Blessing."[245] The greater significance of Buell's comments, however, is his critical approach; he began with the empirical fact of Occum's effectiveness in awakening and converting men, then sought the key to these results in his method of speaking.

Twenty years later another scientist, Thomas Jefferson, was to inform the savants of Europe that America had produced, in the celebrated lament of Logan the Mingo Chieftain, an oration equal to any of Demosthenes or Cicero. In Jefferson's text appeared none of the stilted diction, and none of the periphrasis, which passed for "natural" eloquence in Philadelphia, but only the simplicity of the lines which ended: "Who is there to mourn for Logan?"[246] But it had been a Calvinist minister who first took the "opportunity to Observe" that Indian eloquence, and therefore the most "natural" eloquence, derived from the most "solemn and grave simplicity."[247] In 1745 Mather Byles, after deploring and satirizing an oration which passed as the "true sublime" among the rabble of Boston, had ended on a note of hope for America: a young man who carried on in such a manner was to "be regarded as a good *Genius* run wild, for want of Cultivation from Study, and the Rules of Art." By taking the "proper Methods to improve his Mind" and "by conversing with the best Authors" he might, Byles proposed, "in the End make a chaste and excellent Writer."[248] Byles, in short, considered genius something which inevitably required training in order to attain to the orderly cultivation of Augustan England, while the Calvinist ministry, out of their concern for the souls of men, were perhaps the first to suggest what others besides Jefferson would discover: that Americans had listened too long to the courtly muse of Europe.

V

Calvinist oratory did not proceed from a preconception of the "true sublime," but from a notion of what constituted the great end of preaching. The minister's office, they believed, was "not, to play the orator, or show his hearers how gracefully he can act his part," but to be instrumental in "the Salvation of Souls."[249] Though Calvinists, as against the "Elegance of Stile" to which Liberals aspired, preferred what even Edwards called "the foolishness of preaching," they were by no means rhetorical barbarians. They were familiar with the classics and Addison, and seem to have been the first in the colonies to appreciate so advanced a rhetorician as James Fordyce of Aberdeen.[250] They knew, moreover:

> There is the SIMPLE, EASY, and FAMILIAR STYLE; the GAY and FLOWERY; the PUNGENT and PATHETIC; the LACONIC; the DIFFUSIVE; the GRAND and SUBLIME STYLE: Each of which have their particular use; and are to be varied according to the subject matter.[251]

But "subject matter" and "use" were always uppermost in the minds of the Calvinist preachers, who, purest of the Puritans as they were, refused to "recommend themselves to the Applause of Men."[252] Their rhetorical theory and practice were not determined by "Cicero, Seneca, or the *Spectator*," which, as Edwards complained, were the models for the "modern fashionable discourses" of the Liberals.[253] Their discourses, like Whitefield's—whose "preaching was analogous to that of his divine master"—were "rather practical than nicely laboured." They were such, in sum, "as might minister grace to the hearers."[254]

Though Whitefield and other evangelical preachers were in a sense "natural orators," they made use of art, at least, to conceal art. However "practical" their concerns, they developed a remarkable and largely indigenous rhetorical theory of their own.[255] The Calvinist rhetorical theory is not to be found in such works as John Witherspoon's *Lectures on Eloquence* or Timothy Dwight's essay, *The History, Poetry and Eloquence of the Bible.* Both were achievements of a higher intellectual order than anything produced in the period by any Liberal "master of Literature and Expression," but their very appearance marked a declension from the purity of evangelical pulpit theory and practice. As had the latter-day Puritan disquisitions on style, they marked a rhetorical self-consciousness, and were symptoms either of a defensive posture with respect to the standards of an old order some qualities of which now seemed appealing, or of a certain unwitting shame about a rustic and untutored past.

At the very least, extensive Calvinist disquisitions on style represented a need to inculcate in a younger generation the secrets of an art that once to some men came more naturally. So instinctive was the eloquence of the early Calvinists that even their polemical tracts betray the accents of the spoken word, and, though they appreciated that different styles were appropriate to various occasions, they glided easily into "affecting" discourse. For example, Samuel Davies, while engaging in written debate with a Virginia Anglican, suddenly announced, in the course of his argument, his decision to "drop the epistolary Style for a while, to apply myself to my Readers in general, with the expatiating and pathetic Freedoms of a popular address." Actually Davies never returned to the first style in his pamphlet, perhaps because he, having by his own admission rambled on much longer than a confutation of his adversary would have required, found himself in his true rhetorical element—that of the hortatory cadences of Demosthenes and St. Paul.[256]

It may be that evangelical orators like Davies were not made, but, as it were, reborn. Or perhaps it was that for the generation of Jonathan Edwards, Jr., Calvinism was not so much a faith as a creed. Whatever the reason, young Edwards in 1783 took particular pains to impress on his charges the "importance of a thorough application of the powers of eloquence, and all the address of oratory." To be sure, in urging the "very advantageous use" of "the beauty and force of pronunciation and gesture," young Edwards insisted that it must "be taken for granted, that by all these arts of oratory, the attention of the hearers is attracted to the *truth,* and not to the speaker, or to his ingenuity."[257] Here was a decided difference between many of the second generation and that of their awakened fathers. It was not simply that young Edwards protested overmuch, or that he believed the auditors of his era easily distracted. Rather he seems to have forgotten that communicating the truth was only one purpose, and surely not *the* purpose, of the sermon.

For thirty years the Calvinist ministry called their hearers' "closest and most careful Attention" to the various and difficult "Mysteries of Christianity." But within a decade of the Awakening there was no evangelical minister who did not understand that a minister might "live long" and "preach Truth, and nothing but Truth, as long as he lives, and yet do no real service" so long as his truths were "unaffecting."[258] The central precept of Calvinist rhetorical theory was of course the Edwardean refashioning of the rhetoric of sensation, which Perry Miller has described as a conviction that "by the word (used in the place of a thing) an idea can be engendered in the mind, and that when the word is apprehended emotionally as well as intellectually, then the idea can be more readily and accurately conceived."[259] Edwards' contemporaries and successors assumed that while one had always "a due Regard to the Information of the Mind," the understanding was addressed always with the intention to "affect the heart," for not until an idea had been so apprehended was it truly understood.[260]

In 1770 Jonathan Parsons, in attempting to account for Whitefield's eloquence, gave this as the goal of the prince of pulpit orators: "He endeavored so to place truth before his auditory, as that it might descend through the understanding, and from thence sink into the heart with the utmost influence."[261] Something of what this involved in practice was implied in a statement made by Edwards early in his preaching career:

> Reason's work is to perceive truth and not excellency. It is not ratiocination that gives men the perception of . . . beauty and excellency.[262]

Thus perhaps the highest achievement of the evangelical ministry was its ability to portray doctrine itself as something of an image of the Divine beauty. "Orthodox speculations and notions in theory concerning God, Christ, and things divine, tho' ever so exact," Samuel Buell explained, "give not those amiable apprehensions of divine objects, which the divinely enlightened soul is the subject of."[263] Precisely how the Calvinist preacher made doctrine appear beautiful cannot be readily described, nor even illustrated. Inherent in the very attempt was the Calvinist belief that *the* truth was not doctrinal, but the very quintessence of the gospel.

Something of a clue to Calvinist artistry has already been suggested in the discussion of the manner in which preachers set distinct images (or shadows) of beauty before the eyes of their auditors. But their artistry was not confined to delineating the beatific vision. It was said of Joseph Bellamy that "his talent was surprising, at painting truth, in the most lively colours, and making invisible things appear new and real."[264] The latter of these efforts yields to analysis; the former was hardly confined by any strict rhetorical rules. The stated precepts of Calvinism were for the most part echoes of the Puritan "plain style," particularly its negative injunctions, made sharper in the contest with the contrived official language of the eighteenth century. The evangelical ministry avoided learned allusions, Latin (and Latinate diction), and periphrasis. For them it was the highest praise to say (as Backus did of Tennent) that a preacher's language "is short and cutting, like Luther's formerly."[265] Like their Puritan forebears, post-Awakening Calvinists limited themselves to the homelier and more familiar images, in order that truth be made accessible to a general audience.

Evangelical preachers were also given to what was called a "free use of parabolical representation," that is, to illustrating truth, as had Christ, "by familiar parables." Many of their examples were drawn from Scripture, but in this respect their *exempla* were not quite what the Puritan had considered "similitudes," nor even what Edwards, in turning to the biographies of the Old Testament, set forth as "types."

Rather—and quite possibly this was the secret not merely of Calvinist eloquence but of the age itself—they employed Scripture, not as an authoritative source of doctrine but as a storehouse of metaphor for making "lively impressions on the human mind." One need not argue that the Calvinists doubted the plenary inspiration of Scripture; had they done so the controversies of the era would have been less intense. Had their auditors not inherited an abiding faith in the authority of Scripture, Calvinist sermons might not have wrought their effects. But the evangelical minister spoke to an audience that was apparently persuaded that the Holy Spirit was more a rhetorician than a logician: "the Scriptures speak not phylosophically, but after a popular manner."[266] In such circumstances, it is not surprising that the mark of an excellent preacher was not his careful collation of scriptural proofs but his "choice of the most rousing and awakening Texts"—to be, not expounded, but used for the conviction and awakening of an audience.[267]

The texts of Calvinist sermons offer considerable evidence of their use of the Bible as confirmation of the "excellency" of a gospel discoverable in nature and as history. Moreover, Scripture appears to function in their discourses not as a source of doctrine but as something of a verbal armory with which to make truths "affecting" and compelling. When early in the century Benjamin Colman had used Scripture as a source of metaphor with which to adorn his sermons, he had felt obliged to explain his procedure, in order to distinguish it from the usual Puritan manner of "extracting" the doctrine from the text. But the younger evangelical ministers were hardly so careful; when Gilbert Tennent wanted to "confirm the Truth" of a proposition, he began by observing that he thought his doctrine was "very evident from the various Metaphors in Scripture."[268] Often such metaphors were used more to enforce a doctrine than to confirm it, particularly as a single phrase or even word was separated from its immediate scriptural context and developed into something of an incantation. Edwards' apostrophes to light are one example of this technique; another is Tennent's invocation of "the sweet, sweet, sweet *Truths* of the *ever-blessed* LORD JESUS."[269] What the Bible provided was not merely a metaphoric vocabulary, and seeming authority to use it at will, but something of an objective correlative for the most common words and phrases in the Calvinist language. The impact of Calvinist sermons was no doubt partly the consequence of their audiences' familiarity with the language (and of course the rhythms) of the King James Version. But the rhetorical strategy of the ministers who employed it was far removed from the scholastic and scriptural world of Puritanism, of Ramus and Talon.

What the Calvinist did preserve from Puritanism was the belief that stylistic felicity should not interfere with clarity and perspicuity, for thoughts could not be emotionally apprehended unless they were clearly and distinctly *ideas*. "The heart cannot be set upon an object of which there is no idea in the understanding."[270] Herein once more the determinant of Calvinist rhetoric was its practical, utilitarian, and democratic presupposition. The minister, according to Samuel Finley,

> should study rather to speak instructively than learn'dly, and suppress a Thousand flowery Expressions for the sake of one that is pertinent, and level to the capacity of his Hearers . . . Some, perhaps, may Glory in a sublime Stile, and many more in the Affectation of it; but what is the Fruit of their Labours, while they go beyond the reach of their Audience?[271]

This is what Calvinists meant by complaining (in one of their many uses of Biblical metaphor) that it was improper for the minister to give his people "Bran instead of Bread."[272] The clearest idea was the simplest one, the product of the minister's winnowing and sifting of his own immense erudition, served up to his people in a form both palatable and nutritious. It was the duty of the Calvinist minister to fully comprehend his subject, but it was still more important that he "bring that knowledge to the ears" of the people whom he served.[273] Language might be used for many purposes, but its "original and special design," as Edwards insisted, was "to be understood."[274]

The Calvinist ministry did admit and uphold Locke's distinction between the language used in coming to a comprehension of truth and that used in communicating it. "I shall not now stand to inquire which, according to the rules of art, is the most accurate definition," Edwards said in a practical application of his resolution never to allow his metaphysics to interfere with his preaching, "but shall so define or describe it, as I think has the greatest tendency to convey a proper notion of it."[275] Calvinists believed no subject so worthy of "close consideration" as the nature of the Deity, but once they had divined the character of the Godhead, they wanted the common people, as well as themselves, to look directly into the noonday sun.*[276] The only allowable "indistinctness and obscurity" was that which Edwards, in the volume that stands as the Calvinist counterpart of Chauncy's

---

* It was by way of this very distinction between gaining a knowledge of God and communicating it that evangelical ministers disclosed the substance of their "anti-intellectualism." Isaac Backus, for instance, thought a stronger argument could be made "to prove that Men in our Land ought to learn the *Indian* Tongue, or other Languages in these Parts of the World, before they preach" than that they study "*Hebrew, Greek,* and *Latin.*" The implicit denigration of scholarship (in favor of publicism) was also, it might be noted, additional evidence of the degree to which evangelical religion represented a liberation from Scripture.

Mystery, concluded was "unavoidable, through the imperfection of language to express things of so sublime a nature" as the essential character of God.[277] Some things were by their very nature ineffable, but the Calvinist strove to pierce the veil as deeply as possible and then to reproduce something or all of what he comprehended as the precise quality of the inexpressible.

The Calvinist reading of the Divine essence was enforced above all by a commensurate unity of sermon form. The young men who promoted the Awakening, and the younger men who came into the ministry in the succeeding years, slowly but resolutely undid the sermon form once set forth in William Perkins' *The Art of Prophesying* and inherited by generations of Puritan preachers. By the 1750's they had forsworn the "antiquated multiferious [sic] Divisions" of the Puritan sermon—both its Ramistic structure of argument and its sequence of doctrine, reason, and uses. Calvinists were likewise conspicuously indifferent to the "parts" of the classical oration, and yet they had only distaste for what they called the "loose Harangue," a "mere confus'd Huddle of Words, shuffl'd together in a wild and incoherent manner." Their sermons were, as Hopkins said of Edwards', "well connected,"[278] but the connection was unique and even original. What they achieved is that which has been already pointed out in remarking on the *Religious Affections:* the fusion of truth and its enforcement into a single and, as it were, seamless entity.

Such was the obvious and inevitable imperative of the Calvinist awareness that the human personality was not to be "looked upon as several independent Principles." Even before John Lawson argued, in his 1752 *Lecture Concerning Oratory,* that the purpose of public discourse was to "affect" the "whole Soul" of an auditor, the Calvinist ministry were constructing their sermons on this assumption.[279] Such sermons were characterized, as their authors so often proudly proclaimed, "not so much indeed by a strict conformity to any rules of composition devised by men, as by a noble superiority to such rules."[280] Out of such noble superiority came the recognizably evangelical sermon, one in which understanding, affections, and will were all addressed concurrently and without interruption.

Edwards retained something of the Puritan structure in most of his published sermons, but he clearly pointed the way, and set the standard, for all who followed. "Good Order," Samuel Buell observed, "hath Power and Beauty in it," and such order, he explained, is one in which the entire production builds to one issue, in which digressions are avoided or dismissed for the purpose of attaining a single end.[281] And such an order was most majestically displayed, of course, in the consummate architectonics of the *End in Creation,* wherein Edwards, setting forth the sublimest plot of God, likewise provided American Calvinism with its model of literary excellence.

It was not of course merely language with which the Calvinist minister reached the hearts of his people. One of Edwards' arguments for preaching being God's chief instrument of advancing the Work of Redemption was his realization—vividly reinforced in 1740—that the written word could give men only a "doctrinal or speculative understanding." Only the spoken word, it seemed, had a proper "tendency" to impress truth on men's "hearts and affections."[282] As he went on to explain, "affection and earnestness in the manner of delivery" necessarily and "more truly" represented Divine truths "than a mere cold and indifferent way of speaking of them."[283] Two decades later the Irish elocutionist, Thomas Sheridan, opened fire on John Locke as the source of the "common delusion, that by help of words alone" speakers could communicate or persuade. In those two decades the American Calvinist ministry had simply assumed that not only tone of voice but "looks and gesture" were part of "the hand-writing of Nature."[284]

Thus the literary remains of the Calvinist ministry do not convey the whole of their artistry. The sermons of Whitefield, unless read aloud, now seem quite dull. Yet all contemporaries were astounded by Whitefield's ability to affect his audiences; his critics considered him unequaled in exciting "the passions of his hearers." In fact, the substance of the complaint against Whitefield was that he was no more than an "accomplished orator":

> that enchanting Sound! the *natural* and alone *Cause,* which produced all the *Passion* and *Prejudice* . . . and which would equally have produced the *same* Effects whether he had acted his Part in the *Pulpit* or on the *Stage.*

It was not Whitefield's matter, read the repeated indictment, "that *charms,* but the *air* and *Tone,* the *tuned Voice, vehement Pathos,* and *theatrical Gestures.*" Indeed, were one to trust Whitefield's critics, it would seem he cut an absurd figure in the pulpit, or that in his "extravagant Excess" of *"Voice* and *Action"* he came forward as a fulminating and flailing declaimer.[285] But many less partial observers suggest that there was in fact nothing extravagant in Whitefield's manner or delivery, and Liberal jibes must be set down as the attempts of reasonable men to explain his uncommon oratorical success.

Like most other Calvinist ministers, Whitefield seems to have been distinguished above all, by a solemnity of address. He had sufficient dignity of appearance to make most men overlook or forget his curious eyes. (These did not include Horace Walpole, whose lines remind us that Whitefield had one eye on earth, the other on heaven.) What was phenomenal about Whitefield was the range of his voice, both, as Franklin tells us, in the distance it traveled, and in its inflections, from which Franklin derived a pleasure "of much the same kind with that received from an excellent piece of musick." Here Edwards agreed with Commissary Garden, who remarked on the "charming music" of Whitefield's sermons. Edwards, howsoever in other respects wary of the effects of the musical tone on the passions, was delighted by Whitefield's "lovely song."[286]

Far from being impressed by histrionics or operatic flourishes, the Calvinist ministry and multitude received Whitefield as a "natural and unaffected" orator.[287] That they did so is in part a commentary on the studied gesture and inflection that already in 1740 characterized the established clergy. It was also apparently a tribute to Whitefield's character, for throughout the next decades "naturalness" would be looked on as somehow synonymous with sincerity and benevolence. Samuel Davies, for instance, characterized "natural" preaching in this manner:

Love has a language of its own—a language, which mankind can hardly fail to understand; and which flattery and affectation can but seldom mimic with success. Love, like the other passions, has its own look, its own voice, its own air and manner in everything, strongly expressive of itself . . . The most studied and well-managed artifices of flattery and dissimulation have something in them so stiff, so affected, so forced, so unnatural, that the cheat may often be detected, or, at least, suspected . . .[288]

Such a premise (which also obviously informed the Calvinist demand for an oral profession of faith from would-be church members)[289] was largely negative. But it is unlikely that any Calvinist minister, given such a popular attitude, could have found acceptance had he strained after oratorical effects.

What struck many observers is how little even the itinerants of 1740-1741 used any of the easier devices of oratory. To be sure, Gilbert Tennent was condemned for his "ranting, roaring Ways," and modern scholars continue to brand him as a "tub-thumper" much in the manner of Billy Sunday.[290] Yet there is also considerable evidence that Tennent was a model of elocutionary reserve whether in his own pulpit or on tour through New England. "He seemed to have no regard to please the eyes of his hearers with agreeable gestures," Thomas Prince reported, "nor their ears with delivery."[291] Eyewitness accounts of James Davenport also conflict with the customary notion of him as the most boisterous of the itinerants. Unquestionably his sermons appeared to stimulate ranting and roaring in his audiences, and this many Calvinists bewailed. But at the same time they testified there was so little unusual to Davenport's manner that one could have "expected no extraordinary effect."[292] Of course it must be remembered that nearly all "descriptions" of any phenomena of the Awakening were pieces of special pleading, on behalf not so much of persons as of principles. The opponents of the revival possibly exaggerated in order to sustain their judgment that the entire episode was the result merely of natural causes, or, as they put it, of an "artificial Working on Men's Passions."[293] The pro-revivalists were for their part disposed to overlooking and minimizing the oratorical graces of the itinerants in order that God might be given all the glory for the Awakening. Then as now not merely critical assessment of style, but what was seen and heard, depended on the larger perspective of the observer and judge.

Yet it seems almost impossible to reconcile the more hostile descriptions of evangelical preaching with the stated rhetorical theory of Calvinism, or even with the rhetorical virtues that Calvinists celebrated in their most popular and exemplary preachers. According to Finley's tribute, there was "dignity of sentiment and style" in the sermons of Samuel Davies, and "a venerable presence, a commanding voice, and emphatical delivery, concurred both to charm his audience, and overawe them into silence and attention."[294] Davies was without doubt a "rousing" preacher, but that did not mean he was necessarily a boisterous or athletic one. Clearly the evangelical ministry seemed undignified by reasonable standards, but the evidence suggests that their pulpit manner was generally as grave as the gospel they proclaimed. The most solemn of all of course was Jonathan Edwards, to whom partisans of the revival pointed for evidence that men's hearts could be touched by the most quiet of addresses. Edwards was acknowledged by his colleagues to have "the most universal character of a *good* Preacher of almost any Minister in this Age." He spoke in measured tones and just stared at the bell rope as though he would stare it off, and worked his effects, it was thought, through the sheer power of his doctrines and language.[295]

In Edwards' style was clearly reflected the Puritan notion that vision was the most godlike of man's senses and that the danger in addressing the ear was that the understanding would be distracted. In the early 1740's Edwards proposed that a "musical" tone was probably "to be avoided in public." What some of the itinerant exhorters took to be felicitous sound was to Edwards "distasteful," and the "whining tone" that characterized the Separates seemed to him "truly very ridiculous." Other Calvinists were also displeased by the "strange, unnatural *sing-*

ing tone" that Davenport—a composer of hymns—introduced into the pulpit.[296] Nor was Edwards the only Calvinist to warn against "empty sound" in a sermon. Tennent considered even the too frequent mentioning of the "Name of Christ" to be no better than the liturgical chants of Roman Catholicism—a substitution of "chimes and affected Tuning of Words" for the substance of the gospel:

> Such affections as are rais'd by Tunes and Senseless Charms of Words, without . . . Reason and Argument, are more fit for Theaters than Churches, for Children and Fools, than Men of Learning and understanding.[297]

Here again one senses the Calvinist emphasis on the primacy of the understanding and, along with it, a suspicion of that which is *merely* heard. Yet even Edwards was not averse to incantatory cadences, and, so far as music itself was concerned, encouraged the unison singing of the congregation as something of a "ravishingly beautiful" image of the final communion of the saints.[298] One suspects that the more mellifluous tones of other Calvinist ministers had not a little to do with the fact that they were seeking by one voice alone, almost as Whitman would, to bring that communion into being.

Samuel Davies was especially noted for the warmth of his voice and the use of a variety of sounds in his sermon delivery. Among the "majestic phenomena" of the latter days with which he assailed the ears of his people was "the all-alarming clangor of the last trumpet."[299] But Davies was not alone in this, however it might be that in his accents were born what was to become, through the agency of Patrick Henry, a distinctive Southern oratory. Once Joseph Bellamy had enforced his covenant on New England churches, and created thereby a situation in which mutual love presumably prevailed, the same accents were heard in his sermons kindling a "flame of holy affection" that would spread from the preacher to and through an audience.[300] In this "warm-hearted love," audibly conveyed by the minister, and then mysteriously disseminated among his audience, consisted—even according to New Englanders—"the truest sublime" in pulpit oratory.[301] Herein obviously was a source of what would come to be "romantic" oratory, which was distinguished by its assumption that music, and not pictorial art, was the primary analogue of eloquence. When Emerson in his day sought to explain eloquence in terms of the elective (and even electric) affinities of speaker and auditors, he was fulfilling a movement that began when Edwards' early emphasis on addressing the understanding gave way, among pre-Revolutionary evangelical preachers, to heart-centered and socially affectionate discourse.

In this progression all Calvinist ministers participated, so at no time were the differences among them particularly remarkable, despite their acknowledged individual gifts. Bellamy thought Davies to be slightly more "florid" than himself, and Edwards somewhat less so, but such distinctions seemed of little moment, given their common differences from the "formal" preachers of Liberalism.[302] The Calvinist minister was given, among other things, to preaching either extempore or from the sparsest of notes, on the assumption that no artist could anticipate all the "seasonable Thoughts" to which, it was believed, "the Holy Spirit frequently helps us, in the time of preaching." But even extemporaneity was resisted as a standard, largely because it was understood that pulpit talent, like any other, had to be given leave to find its own personal and even idiosyncratic mode of expression.[303] Remarkably, however, the seeming varieties of Calvinist preaching had a fairly common appeal from community to community, and even from province to province. Whitefield confessed himself "obliged, according to the Freedom and Assistance given me from above, to enlarge or make Excursions, agreeable to the People's circumstances amongst whom I was preaching."[304] But he does not seem to have correspondingly altered the manner of his delivery in any way whatever. The success of Tennent and Finley in Massachusetts and Connecticut, of the younger Tennents in Litchfield County and South Carolina, of the Long Island evangelists Jonathan Barber and Charles-Jeffrey Smith in Georgia and Virginia, suggests the degree to which the power of Calvinist eloquence was everywhere the attendant of the uniform Calvinist gospel.

Though the particular gifts of individual preachers did not go unnoticed, what was commonly noted was that which was shared. Of nearly all Calvinists it was said they had "an Almighty Power attending their Eloquence." There can be little question that in each case part of this power derived from manner no less than matter:

He had a ready and fruitful invention, a rich and lively imagination, and a clear and commanding voice, which he could vary with ease, and to great advantage. In his delivery, he spoke with proper deliberation, neither quick nor slow: and with utmost ease he could give a remarkable emphasis to his expressions, and so happily variate the manner of his pronunciation, according to the various nature of his subjects, as that his elocution was either solemn and grave, majestic and commanding, terrifying and alarming, gentle and melting, insinuating and alluring, as occasion required.[305]

Every Calvinist—Parsons, the Tennents, Buell, Wheelock, Finley, Davies, Cleaveland, Whitaker, and even Edwards—at some time inspired a comment similar to that of Spencer Roane on the "forest-born Demosthenes" who inherited the following of Whitefield and Davies: "The tones of his voice, to say nothing of his manner and gestures," recalled Roane of Patrick Henry, "were insinuated into the feelings of his hearers in a manner that baffles description."[306] The power of Calvinist preaching, like that of the Holy Spirit, was, and must remain, something of a mystery.

As the decades passed, the evangelical clergy came to comprehend some of the sources of their effectiveness, but oratory never became for them a "science." Disclaiming always their own efficacy, they refused to divest their rhetorical theory of its "transcendent" elements.[*307] They assumed that there was "an ineffable excellence" inherent in their subject, which, according to Davies, "even celestial eloquence cannot fully represent."[308] Were this excellence communicated in both its beauty and its power, this finally was the Spirit's doing.[309] The end and aim of evangelical preachers, it must be emphasized, was not any transitory effect, however remarkable, but an abiding change in the personalities of their hearers. Tennent, for one, acknowledged the power of human eloquence to touch men's hearts, but this alone was no evidence that the Word was being preached in the fullness of its power. When a preacher, Tennent observed,

> delivers divine Mysteries with Sublimity of Sentiment, beautiful Diction, and graceful Action, with what gentle Violence do such Discourses insinuate themselves into the Affections; but these natural Commotions are as transient as ineffectual.

However dazzlingly a preacher might represent the Persons of the Deity in "Points of *Light*," and however his hearer might respond to his imagery, momentary exaltation was not the ultimate test of effectual preaching. Just as men were warned not to "confide in these fading Flowers of floating, fleeting Passions," so too was a preacher's eloquence measured finally by the enduring fruits of his sermons.[310]

For Calvinists the essential mystery of eloquence was and had to be a continuing one. The effectiveness of any preaching depended, finally, on that most labyrinthine of enigmas, the human soul. Thus even when Witherspoon began to explain what was needed "to make what is called a complete orator," it was not to the science of rhetoric that he turned. He did not propose that successful eloquence derived from

---

* These were retained, for that matter, in the speculations of William Wirt on "so divine an orator" as James Waddell, the blind Virginia preacher who seemed "of a totally different nature from the rest of men." Waddell, Wirt concluded, was "a genius" whose "peculiar manner and power arose from an energy of soul which Nature could give, but which no human Being could justly copy."

familiarity with the "true sublime," but rather that it demanded and assumed above all things "a thorough knowledge of the human heart."311 If then the Calvinist ministry's contribution to the evolution of the science and art of American oratory is to be properly assessed, one returns, finally, not to their homiletic theory and practice but to that which underlay the whole of their achievement: their insight into the nature and needs of the human personality.

Such were the pulpit skills of the Calvinist ministry, however, that at one point Joseph Bellamy became troubled by the discovery he could do anything he "pleased with an audience." Bellamy, the most faithful of Edwards' disciples and possibly the best of his friends, was acknowledged, in the years after Edwards' death, to be "the most eloquent man in America."312 The tribute, from an Arminian critic (a lawyer no less) hardly touches on the myriad ways in which Bellamy employed the power of the spoken word. Suffice it here to say that he was a worker together with the Spirit, from a rostrum which, according to his biographer, was more appropriately called "a stage" than a pulpit.313 It was not, however, as a player that he supplied the drama, for Bellamy, like all the evangelical clergy, was, though vigorous and ebullient, a man of commanding dignity. He managed, as had Whitefield, to fill his sermons with heavenly dialogues which, in their vividness and often their homeliness, were to find no match in American literature until, perhaps, *The Green Pastures*. But Bellamy's drama was neither pastoral nor, surely, condescending, and his larger talent, finally, was not that merely of an interpreter of the picturesque colloquies of heaven. In the pulpit he was no less than the *régisseur* of that sublime panorama and epic, the Work of Redemption.

When toward the end of the eighteenth century Americans began to comprehend and discuss the differences between the picturesque, the beautiful, and the sublime, they would more fully appreciate the character of Calvinist preaching. The Calvinist ministry for thirty years had been seeking to avoid the picturesque, a style which, however appropriate in some circumstances, was incongruous with subjects of the "highest importance." A quite different standard emerged with the choice in 1767 of John Witherspoon as president of the College of New Jersey. Witherspoon's coming to Princeton marked the end of an era in which the intellectual life of colonial Presbyterianism had been controlled by veterans of the Awakening. Nowhere did Witherspoon more obviously betray his differences with the revivalists (and with the temper of American Calvinism) than in his lectures on oratory and eloquence. Witherspoon informed his students that the sublime was vastly overrated, and that the picturesque was probably a more engaging style, certainly a more useful one. But when Witherspoon defined "sublimity in eloquence" as embodying "not only the ideal of great force, but of carrying away every thing with it that opposes or lies in its way," he managed to capture something of the quality and the tendency of Calvinist oratory in the years between 1750 and 1765.[314]

In the years of the *Humble Attempt,* not only Edwards but the Presbyterians of the Middle Colonies were most interested in what in the critical parlance of the day would have been defined as the beautiful. Edwards, who found greater delight in the lilies of the fields—as "emanations of the sweet benevolence of Jesus Christ"—than in the cataract or the towering crag which proclaimed "His awful majesty," for the most part spared his auditors, after the Awakening, the darker aspects of God's face.[315] No more than any other Calvinist did Edwards cultivate a "delicate and flowery" style,[316] but his preaching was perhaps the first and certainly the most successful effort in America to conceive and communicate a sublimity of incredible whiteness—of a great resurrection and a Church Triumphant almost totally divested of the awe inspired by terror.

In the late 1750's, however, concurrently with the outbreak of the French and Indian War though not necessarily because of it, the Calvinist ministry would recall to their people the sublime. At the same time they would begin seeking not merely to affect the hearts of their congregations, but to activate their wills. No longer would amiable apprehensions be placed before the minds of men in order merely to induce "desire," but the more "zealous fervent Love" which Gilbert Tennent sought to arouse among his Presbyterian flock under the name of "zeal."[317] In the 1740's Edwards had come to believe that a "fierce and intemperate zeal" was inappropriate to a minister, for it was "likely to kindle the like unhallowed flame in his people." Even Gilbert Tennent in 1760 felt that the "passions" were to be "excited, and duly regulated in their Tendencies by Reason and Revelation, according to the Nature and Importance of their Objects." But the Calvinist ministers of these latter days strove to place truth before their people's understandings, not that their hearts might be touched, but so as to "strike the Passions, which are the Springs of Action,"[318] What had happened, among other things, is that the Calvinist ministry had rediscovered the monstrous beast of the Apocalypse, an object that required no little zeal to overcome.

Until that moment it was possible to distinguish, as Jonathan Mayhew thought he could, between those of the evangelical clergy whose manner was "tragical, boisterous, and outrageous," and those of a "very soft and delicate address."[319] What Mayhew was referring to was the fact that Calvinists sometimes proclaimed the moral law "in the shocking Accents of *Sinai's* dreadful Thunder" and at other moments sounded "the Jubilee Trumpet of the Gospel."[320] But in the late 1750's the sermons of Calvinism mingled the two sounds until they were barely distinguishable, and in doing so their oratory did in fact become comparable—in the words of Witherspoon—"to the voice of thunder" and "the impetuosity of a torrent."[321] No doubt it was the hope and intention of the Calvinist ministry, through the agency of their eloquence, to carry away the opposition only that the brilliant beauty of the Edwardean vision might be achieved. The Deity Himself, Joseph Bellamy explained in 1758, intended to "break to pieces the kingdoms of the earth" only in order to set up "the New Jerusalem in all her spiritual glory."[322] But what the Calvinist oratory of the decades after 1758 in fact accomplished was to instill in God's American people a taste for a kind of sublimity that made pallid, by comparison, the sweetness of the Awakening vision.

In 1758 Samuel Davies called "for the all-prevailing force of Demosthenes' oratory"—only, to be sure, to "correct" himself, and implore instead "the influence of the Lord of armies" to "fire" Virginians "into patriots and soldiers."[323] In doing so he set the Calvinist ministry on a career that would see them seeking to overcome the domestic enemies of the Kingdom and by 1775 to inspire Americans to overbear all opposition. The Calvinist discovery and communication of a new order of sublimity was successful beyond all expectation in getting the American people to exercise their wills. By 1776 the Calvinist populace, still seeking to experience exalted sensations, were to see their meetinghouses "burned as nests of rebellion," and themselves "hunted as instigators of treason." If it was not Arminianism over which they triumphed, they gained another, and perhaps a more significant, victory. For by activating the wills of their people on behalf of the ideals of Calvinism, those who were called "fanatical courting preachers" demonstrated, to the satisfaction of many who had previously scorned them, the power of ideas and language in the social affairs of mankind.[324] If they failed in their immediate hope of making America a brighter type of heaven, they left this intellectual lesson, with all its implications, as their legacy to the democratic nation that they helped to bring into existence.

PART TWO

REVOLUTION

Kings and Princes, Statesmen and Politicians, those who are influenced only by worldly Views, and whose Eyes are dazzled with earthly Grandeur and Glory, are wont to think that civil Government is the grand Object of divine Providence in this lower World—are wont to look upon Christianity as a little inferior Object, taken in, and admitted, chiefly to enlarge, fill up, and diversify the great DRAMA—to strengthen the Foundations of civil Government, and render it more permanent, perfect and glorious.

But those who rightly understand Christianity, are taught to view the Matter in quite a different Light—that the Greatness, and Glory, and Grandeur of Empires, Kingdoms, and States, are not the first and grand Object, of the divine Providence and Government; but that the Church of Christ, that little despicable Interest (as it is deemed) is, and has been, the special Design of Providence in all Ages; and will continue so to be, 'till the Consummation and final Close of all Things.

—Izrahiah Wetmore, May 13, 1773

V

THE SNARE

BROKEN

T H E Liberal clergy entered on explicit political discussion earlier than most Calvinists—largely because they happened to occupy stations that gave them something of a monopoly on the institutions and rituals that traditionally provided opportunities for clerical treatment of public issues. This was the case at least in New England, as William Smith explained in his manifesto of 1758, the notable "Letter on the Office and Duty of Protestant Ministers, and the Right of Exercising Their Pulpit Liberty; in the Handling and Treating of Civil as Well as Religious Affairs." Answering a correspondent who had rebuked him for bringing politics into the pulpit, Smith expressed admiration for the "clergy to the northward." With their Election Sermons and fast and thanksgiving days, the ministers of New England were able to engage in what Smith styled "mixing temporal with spiritual concerns." He regretted that the Anglican clergy of the Middle Colonies had not been disposed to seek the same latitude and to use it.

In practical terms, Smith's letter showed him to be no more an indiscriminate mixer than the Liberals of New England. He thought that ministers ought not "interfere any farther in civil concerns" than was necessary to defend religion or to assist the magistrate in his government of society. No civil ruler, Smith argued, could control the multitude without the assistance of some "order of men"—the "priesthood," Smith called them—who would help to "form the minds of the people to the knowledge of both law and duty."[1] Precisely this the New England clergy had been doing for a century and more—ever since the Antinomian crisis, when the ministry had been reduced in effect into the handmaids of the Massachusetts magistrates. With the exception of John Davenport (and, for a few years in the 1680's, Increase Mather and his fellow critics of moderate government) few New England preachers had publicly stood as spokesmen *against* the standing order.

The Great Awakening of course reinforced the Liberal commitment to order. In the aftermath of the revival, both Liberal and Old Light clergy were persuaded that one of the more important functions of their "special order" was that of enforcing on "Mankind, at least the Duties of Natural Religion." Such moral suasion was explicitly a contribution to the social welfare, for if men did not perform their appropriate duties, there would be, as Ebenezer Devotion explained, "no Order, Peace or Safety; Every Man must be in danger from his Neighbor."[2] Suasion was not the only, or even the preferred, technique for assuring the performance of men's duties. The rational clergy seemed disposed to achieve the peace and safety of society through the laws and institutions of the province.

Still, the principles of "natural religion" were such that the Liberal clergy necessarily had counsel to offer on the subjects of the socially good and the politically requisite. The thoughts that they articulated as opportunity arose have the virtue of being free from what might strike the modern mind as clerical obscurantism. The rationalist ministers, alone among America's pre-Revolutionary clergymen, proceeded to their discussion of civil government from the assumption that in politics, as in morality, reason was man's most salutary oracle. This belief informed their discussions of the organization and operation of civil government. Many American clergymen still contended in the 1750's that any government was, like that of the Jews, created by Divine command. But such Liberals as Jonathan Mayhew considered government "both the ordinance of God, and the ordinance of man." The social compact, Mayhew explained in 1754, might have its ultimate source in God's "original plan, and universal Providence," but "it is more immediately the result of human prudence, wisdom and concert."[3] By 1771 even so vague a Providence had all but disappeared from rationalist political speculation; "civil government," the Massachusetts Election Preacher observed in that year,

> is founded in the very nature of man, as a social being, and in the nature and constitution of things. It is manifestly for the good of society. It is the dictate of nature. It is the voice of reason, which may be said to be the voice of God.[4]

Having affirmed that God spoke in the quieter accents of reason, the Liberal ministry were able to close their ears to the thunderings of Sinai and to apply this more silent wisdom, often with reservation and seldom without inconsistency, to all their observations on political affairs.

Since the theory of social contract was, as has so often been pointed out, a translation into secular terms of the Puritan idea of the social covenant, few divines could completely forget the judicials of Moses. Though Liberals employed a Lockean vocabulary, their interpretations of the covenant were more than reminiscent of Richard Mather's commentary on the covenant established in Judea, where "the King promised to rule the people righteously, according to the will of God; and the people to be subject to a King so ruling."[5] The covenant obligations of rulers and ruled were the themes of Election Sermons well into the eighteenth century. The same ideas served as the framework for Jonathan Mayhew's *Discourse on Unlimited Submission*, which, delivered in 1750, is often called the American clergy's initial contribution to the cause of Independence. "It is evident," Mayhew began,

> that the affairs of civil government may properly fall under a moral and religious consideration, at least so far forth as it relates to the general nature and end of magistracy, and to the grounds and extent of that submission which persons of a private character ought to yield to those who are vested with authority.[6]

No clergymen of the Revolutionary period seriously questioned the crucial premise of the theory of social covenant—that magistrates were expected to rule righteously and according to the will of God. The uniquely Liberal interpretation of the covenant consisted in their judging even the will of God by reason and the nature of things, or, to use their own terms, by "the law of nature."

In expounding the magistrate's duty to govern righteously and the people's duty to obey such a governor, the Liberal clergy distinctly preferred the lessons of natural wisdom to the mandates of Scripture. Most American preachers of the pre-Revolutionary era made some effort to found their political discussions in divine revelation, where, as a preacher more orthodox than Mayhew explained in 1770, the "ends of civil government" are "clearly pointed out, the character of rulers described, and the duty of subjects asserted and explained."[7] The orthodox clergy, moreover, long and warmly opposed any effort to derive social and political wisdom merely from reason and the nature of things. Their position was most cogently stated during the Great Awakening by Solomon Williams. "There never was, nor can there be any Wisdom among men," Williams insisted in his Connecticut Election Sermon,

> but what is communicated from God; nor is there any law of Nature,

or Rule of Natural Moral Wisdom . . . but what is found in the Bible, and cultivated and improved by that Revelation.[8]

Just as strenuously did rationalists seek to subordinate the mandates of Scripture to what they considered "natural laws." In discussing the social contract, they insisted:

> A revelation, pretending to be from God, that contradicts any part of natural laws, ought immediately to be rejected as an imposture; for the Deity cannot make a law contrary to the law of nature without acting contrary to himself . . .[9]

By the late 1760's explicit Biblicism had been all but abandoned by the great majority of America's political preachers. When speculating on social issues, Calvinists too sought to derive rules of behavior from the constitution of things, but as John Cleaveland informed Mayhew in 1763, any valid law of nature had to be "a transcript of God's moral nature"; it must be "just, holy and good; it must be very pure, it must be perfect."[10]

As Calvinists sought to subject all matters to their idea of the divine excellency, Liberals attempted to make their God even more comprehensible. "God himself does not govern in an absolutely arbitrary and despotic manner," Mayhew explained in comparing Him to the constitutionally limited British monarch, but according to the "eternal laws of truth, wisdom, equity, and the everlasting tables of right reason." Charles Chauncy, always less outspoken than Mayhew, seldom found discussion of God's essential character either necessary or profitable, but he was ever ready to define the law of nature and of nature's God by the Liberal standard of reason. In affairs of government, he affirmed, all wisdom "originates in the reason of things," and the reason of things is "essentially founded on the will of God." Thus God "as truly speaks to men by the reason of things, their mutual relations to and dependencies on each other, as if he uttered his voice from the excellent glory."[11] Assured of their own capacity for discerning God's will by reason alone, Liberals were able to avoid either the mystical or the scriptural approach to the issue of pre-Revolutionary politics, and could discuss transgressions of the law of nature quite "rationally."

Though Liberals were presumably the closest of all American clergymen to the political wisdom of a Franklin or a Jefferson, they were the most laggard in arraigning King or Parliament for fundamental violations of the social contract. Their reluctance to employ the "law of nature" as anything other than abstract concept arose, in large part, from a fear that other Americans, incapable of appreciating the reasonableness of this law, would be rather immoderate in applying it to specific situations. In 1776, for instance, the Massachusetts Election Preacher invoked the law of nature in defense of the rebellion. He then turned to warn the citizenry, who, he observed, had been using natural law as an argument for a more extensive political revolution in Massachusetts. The law of nature, he exclaimed, "gives men no right to do anything that is immoral, or contrary to the will of God, and injurious to their fellow men."[12] What Liberals understood as the law of nature or the will of God was never fully clear, but something of a definition emerged in their public discourses in the thirty years preceding the Declaration, when they showed a striking preference for defining political issues in terms of the constitutional rights of British subjects and of the particular, rather than the general, guarantees of the social compact.

The first instance in which Liberals were forced to consider a ruler's violation of the social contract was the Stamp Act crisis of 1765-66. Insofar as they addressed the issue, Liberals to a man abandoned the abstractions of Locke for the charges and specifications of mercantile lawyers. In many respects their discourses on the Stamp Act are curious. All were delivered after the repeal of the tax, and all were conceived more as justification of American resistance than as indictments of those responsible for passage of the Stamp Act. Liberals were less interested in proving British transgression than in explaining why Americans might, conceivably, have taken umbrage at the tax. One such vindication of resistance was that Americans had been "fatigued and financially exhausted by a long war" and therefore, when confronted by the stamp tax, "they naturally wished to question its equity."[13]

While all Arminians indulged in some such circumlocution in 1766, Mayhew at least made an effort to defend the protests of 1765 as legitimate expressions of the right of subjects to object to violations of the social compact. Even Mayhew, however, refused to invoke the law of nature and concerned himself with the more specific Lockean principle that no man may be taxed without his consent. They "are really slaves to all intents and purposes," Mayhew reminded his audience, "who are obliged to labor and toil for the benefit of others; or, which comes to the same thing, the fruit of whose labor and industry may be lawfully taken from them without their consent."[14] Mayhew's parishioners needed no such reminder, for no Liberal minister was in grave danger of being contradicted on this point by the leading members of his congregation. The burden of the stamp tax—a levy on commercial transactions—would have fallen on the colonial merchants, most of whom held pews in the Liberal churches of the port cities.

The rationalist ministry was not, of course, alone in seeing the stamp tax as endangering American rights. Many Americans not in trade were also aroused (as they had not been by the Sugar and Navigation acts) by the threat to their religious freedom. "There was nothing we could have called our own," a Connecticut New Light declared in 1766, "not so much as our lives or our consciences." The Sons of Liberty also had a sweeping objection to the British commercial regulations, but outside the cities, and indeed wherever the clergy were cool to political argument based on calculation of income, the Stamp Act was seen as a threat to the "liberty" of the colonists. The repeal of the stamp tax, explained a rural Calvinist, was a "deliverance from *slavery*; nothing less than from vile ignominious *slavery*." To be sure, some Liberals had a few swelling words to say in 1766 about a threat to liberty, but none matched the Calvinist declaration that the "worst of all" the provisions of the Stamp Act was that which called for enforcement without jury trials.[15] In the seats of clerical rationalism a careful effort was made to limit justification of American resistance to the essential facts. The Stamp Act seemed to Liberals only an effort to deprive men of their property.

Like the lawyers of the Stamp Act Congress, the Liberal clergy defended the rights of property more as legal privileges than as natural rights. "Property" for them did not connote all that it did for Madison and Jefferson; it was not the whole product of the action of the personality upon the external world, but simply the worldly possessions gained through one's labor. Yet even so narrow an employment of Locke was avoided in the sermons of 1766, when Liberals described the affair of 1765 as a defense of "liberties"—of, that is, property rights embodied in the British constitution and colonial charters. Mayhew contended that control of one's property was a "natural right," which the British constitution and Magna Carta had "declared, affirmed, and secured to us," and which, moreover, had been "further confirmed" by various charters, "taken in their obvious sense."[16]

Charles Chauncy, who yielded to no man as a cautious Liberal, took even fewer chances in arguing the colonists' legal case. Chauncy allowed that the stamp tax had appeared at least a violation of what was thought to be the British constitution, or of what anyway had been considered the provisions of the charter given Massachusetts by William and Mary of blessed memory:

> Whether the colonists were invested with a right to these liberties and privileges which ought not to be wrested from them, or whether they were not, 'tis the truth of fact they really thought they were; all of them, as natural heirs to it by being born subjects to the British crown, and some of them by additional charter-grants, the

legality of which, instead of being contested, have all along, from the days of our fathers, been assented to and allowed of by the supreme authority at home.[17]

Concern for constitutional and charter rights was not in 1765 unique to the Liberal clergy. Sam Adams, for one, insisted (in a letter to George Whitefield) that the people of Massachusetts were "expressly declared in their Charter to be entitled to all the Libertys & Immunitys of free and natural subjects of Great Britain."[18] Where the rationalist clergy differed from many other Americans was, first, in the modesty and diffidence with which they narrowly construed the hallowed compacts. Even more noteworthy, considering the thinking and rhetoric of such as Sam Adams in 1765, was the sincere conviction of the Liberal clergy that the constitution and charter, no less than the social contract, guaranteed the inalienable right of British Americans to a profitable commerce.

As historians have pointed out, the "obvious sense" of the New England charters and the British constitution was not so self-evident in the 1760's as Jonathan Mayhew imagined. But declarations that British Americans were somehow exempt from taxation should not be read as though they were mere lawyers' briefs. They were testaments of faith, informed and warmed by the Liberal vision of American history. Liberals' admiration of constitution and charters was sincere—so sincere indeed that their sermons were unmatched in sentiments of gratitude for the privileges of British colonials. When Liberals thanked God that they were "*British* subjects, and entitled to the liberties and privileges of such,"[19] however, they spoke in confidence that their understanding of the nature of those privileges was unquestionable. This assurance was fostered by Parliament's salutary neglect of the colonies, but it was sustained by the crystallization of an image of the American experience as primarily commercial. Charles Chauncy insisted that the people of New England

imagined, whether justly or not I dispute not, that their right to the full and free enjoyment of these privileges was their righteous due, in consequence of what their forefathers had done and suffered in subduing and defending these American lands, not only for their own support, but to add extent, strength, and glory to the British crown.[20]

The prevalence of this sentiment among the Liberal clergy helps explain why John Adams could call Jeremiah Dummer's 1721 *Defence of the New-England Charters* the "handbook of the Revolution." For it was Dummer who had first positively declared that the errand of the Puritans into the wilderness had been, not to erect the city on a hill, but to make money for themselves and for the British empire.[21] By the 1770's such a version of American history was so well accepted among Masachusetts Liberals that, for an Election Preacher to defend charter privileges, it was necessary merely to allude to the "great man, Mr. Agent Dummer," as one who had placed the "services, and sufferings" of the first settlers *in a true point of light.* Many another American minister, recalling the sacrifices of America's forefathers, would attempt in the Revolutionary decade to answer the enduring question, "Why came we here?" All would conclude that the colonists had sought liberty for themselves and for posterity, but only in Liberal pulpits was it assumed that the first settlers had esteemed liberty as "their greatest glory" because this freedom permitted a plantation nominally of religion to have been, or become, one of trade.[22]

The faith that none but British Americans lived "under so happy and excellent" a form of government was enlivened by confidence that the Massachusetts charter secured more than the commercial rights of its citizens.[23] Like other eighteenth-century Americans, Liberals believed, as had John Locke, that the larger purpose of any government was "to promote the public Welfare," that it must not only secure a people's rights but see also that their happiness was pursued. Only a government seeking this goal, Liberals believed, would "coincide with the moral fitness of things" or could fulfill the purpose of a Deity who had so reasonably arranged for governments to arise naturally "from the make of man, and his circumstances in the world."[24] Within fifty years of the Stamp Act crisis partisans of the legal scheme would identify the general welfare entirely with security of property and even begin to argue that moral fitness in legislation consisted chiefly in keeping the hands of government off the economy. But pre-Revolutionary Boston Liberals, some of whom lived to see an independent "Commonwealth" of Massachusetts, were ready on occasion to urge a somewhat more energetic promotion of provincial happiness.

The specifics of the Liberals' program of welfare legislation underwent many changes in even the two decades before the Revolution. But at no point did they repudiate Dummer's definition of the sources and aims of American policy: "The only interest of the people is to thrive and flourish in their Trade."[25] Generally their praise of the constitution and charter seemed little more than celebration of the commercial blessings of the British colonial system and the privileged exemption of Americans from its burdens. But well before 1765 the Liberal clergy entertained policies and ideas that would lead to certain dilemmas in the years of the imperial crisis. Many of these were revealed in a sermon delivered by Chauncy in 1752, which also disclosed something of the scale of values that would help to determine the final allegiances of the Liberal mind.

Chauncy's sermon was a bit of special pleading on behalf of a projected linen factory in Boston. The scheme, like so many subsequent proposals for domestic industry, had its sources in the provincial sense that an unfavorable balance of trade was responsible for a shortage of a circulating medium. But Chauncy argued for the linen establishment on the basis of its larger contribution to the *"publick Good"*:

> . . . there cannot be a flourishing People, without Labour. It is by Improvement in Arts and Trade, that they must grow in Wealth, and Power, and become possessed of the various Emoluments tending to the Benefit and Pleasure of Life; and these Arts take their Rise from, and are carried on by, the Industry of particular Persons. And this is so evident, that while some Nations have increased in Riches, and Grandeur, and Power, by being Industrious, tho' great Obstacles, and discouraging Difficulties have stood in the Way; others, thro' Sloth and indolence, have been kept low, and sunk in Oblivion, tho' under great *natural Advantages* to have got into flourishing Circumstances: Or, it may be, they have become a Prey to more active and enterprising Nations, who knew how to make a better Use of their Advantages. And the Truth is, the *natural Advantages* a people are favoured with, whether for Husbandry, Navigation, Fishery, Manufactures, or any other Source of Wealth, will be, in a great Measure, lost, as it were, thrown away upon them, without Labour and Industry, in making a wise and good Use of them.[26]

One of the flaws in such an argument is that it seemed to imply that Massachusetts, or New England, or America, was a nation, when, as Liberals well knew, the colonies were part of one great and flourishing British empire. Chauncy tried to skirt this perplexity by suggesting that linen, after all, was not a leading product of British manufactures. Nevertheless his argument led him, as it was also leading Franklin, into challenging the very premises of British mercantilism.

The proposal for Boston manufacturing also raised a dilemma concerning the merchants of Boston, whose carrying trade would presumably suffer to the degree that finished goods were produced domestically instead of being imported. Chauncy suggested that the merchants of Boston were undoubtedly too public-spirited to allow such considerations to influence them. Seventy-five years later Daniel Webster, representing Boston capital, could support a protective tariff. But until then the spokesmen for Boston would object, as Thomas Hutchinson did at the close of the second volume of his *History,* to converting the happy and vigorous sailors and farmers of New England into benighted and stunted mill hands.[27] In 1752, however, Chauncy brushed aside this proto-romantic consideration, along with other "sentimental" objections to his socially constructive scheme:

> The only proper Question is, Whether this is a likely Scheme, under proper Cultivation, to counter-balance, with Advantage, the Expence necessary in order to its taking Effect?

Such hardheaded practicality was probably the quintessence of the Liberal mind, but the facts of life in pre-Revolutionary America were such that questions of "sentiment" could not be so easily put aside.

In addition to the problem of merchants' profits, there was the question whether the linen factory, as conceived by Chauncy, was not less a speculative enterprise than an investment in domestic tranquillity. It would seem that to Chauncy the primary value of the factory was that it would put the citizens of Boston to work: "Those may be employed, to good Purpose, in this Branch of Business (Children in particular) who have hitherto been suffered in a great Measure, to spend their Time too much in Idleness." There were several reasons why people should not be idle, among them that idlers were "in danger of being betrayed into Moral Disorders of every kind," including not only *"Tipling"* but even possibly underground plotting of seditious enterprises. Worst of all, these dangerous idlers had for years been subsidized, either by the provincial welfare laws or by local and individual philanthropies. Henceforth, Chauncy argued, only the hopelessly disabled should be maintained from the public coffers, and the wealthy of Boston should understand that (in the words of the sermon's title) the "idle-poor" are "secluded from the bread of charity by the Christian law."

To support this argument, Chauncy had to contend with certain fanciful notions evidently regnant among some of Boston's Christians. One was that men had more important callings in this world than temporal business, that "the Cares of Religion now, in a great Measure, supersede the Affairs of the World." This he branded a mere "specious Pretence" for idleness, since it was so clearly denied by the *"Law of Labour* given to *Adam"* and thence to all mankind as part of the "reason and justice" of the moral law. Here Chauncy digressed momentarily to explain that the law of sweated labor should not be interpreted "universally, as extending to all, the Rich as well as the Poor." Rich men, he allowed, had "no License to be lazy," but surely they might "reasonably exempt themselves from the lower and more servile Parts of Business."[28]

How to enforce the law of labor so as to put rich men to work "to some or another of the valuable Purposes of Life" was a question with which the Liberal mind would continue to wrestle. Some of the more compelling arguments were provided for pre-Revolutionary Bostonians by Jonathan Mayhew. But he too in the 1750's and 1760's was primarily concerned with stimulating the industry of the less fortunate American. His briefs on behalf of diligence in one's calling were entered as against the "lazy people, and dreaming enthusiasts" who proposed that men might "wholly neglect all worldly affairs, business and commerce, under a pretence of being heavenly-minded." Most significantly, however, the Liberal mind, in dealing with the matter of idleness, realized that with the idle poor, as distinguished from the idle rich, one did not really need to argue. The linen factory, taken together with an abrupt termination of welfare payments, would be a convincing reminder—more as stick than as carrot—to the Massachusetts proletariat: "We were made for business."[29]

On this matter Chauncy was in full agreement with Benjamin Franklin, who likewise argued in the 1750's that it was "against the order of God and Nature" to "provide encouragements for Laziness" through dispensations of charity. Franklin's arguments against compelling "the Rich to Maintain the Poor" were of universal applicability, but as it turned out they were especially pertinent to America, where an abundance of natural resources stood as an imperative to all the people of the colonies to be up and doing.[30] Similar sentiments had been voiced by the rational mind as early as Robert Beverley's *History of Virginia*. Both William Byrd and John Lawson invoked the abundance of nature as a rebuke to American "laziness," but in doing so implicitly complained that the energies of Southerners were not being devoted to the achievement of proper social goals. When after 1740 colonials outside the South began to chant the same dirge, they too revealed that behind their lamentation was the signal failure of the American populace to agree with the reasonable estimate of the promise of American life and the rational assessment of the best means of attaining it.

In 1752 Chauncy sought to portray his ideal of the American future by explicating the history of the Thessalonian Christians, among whom "Idleness was the fault too prevalent." Or at least, according to Chauncy, this seemed to have been the concern of St. Paul:

The extraordinary Charities, common in that Day, might encourage those, who were before disposed to be idle, to neglect the Business of their proper Callings. The Hope of having their Wants supplied, by the Bounties of their Christian Friends and Neighbours, might insensibly slacken their Diligence, and betray them into an indolent inactive way of Life.[31]

As it happened, Chauncy's gloss on the apostle's view of conditions at Thessalonica, like his interpretations of Christian ethics generally, stood in direct opposition to what Edwards and Calvinists generally conceived as the imperative of the "law of charity."

In the late 1740's Edwards set himself to a sustained refutation of even those who contended that the most generous interpretation of the provincial statutes could fulfill the requirements of Christian charity. After considering the scriptural and doctrinal arguments for charity, Edwards went on to observe that acts of charity are "most reasonable, considering the general state and nature of mankind":

> We are nearly allied one to another by nature. We have all the same nature, like faculties, like dispositions, like desires of good, like needs, like aversion to misery, and are made of one blood; and we are made to subsist by society and union with one another . . . Mankind in this respect are as members of the natural body, one cannot subsist alone, without an union with and the help of the rest.

For Edwards human nature, and not a reasonable prospect of American prosperity, was the starting point of social theory. A "private niggardly spirit," he declared, "is more suitable for wolves, and other beasts of prey, than for human beings."[32]

In the 1740's Edwards sought to institutionalize this insight in his Northampton church. He made it the "principal business of Deacons" to "take care of the Poor" and called on his wealthier parishioners for "frequent and liberal Contributions, to maintain a public Stock, that might be ready for the poor and necessitous members of the Church."[33] How radical was this gesture is suggested by the fact that not until the 1770's did Chauncy think to "restore" the ancient and apostolic office of deacon to Boston's First Church and to provide them with an almsgiving function. In so doing, Chauncy was obliged once more to consider the question whether the conduct of the first Christians was a pattern and exemplar to all their successors in the faith. Edwards believed that the Liberal mind—particularly when confronted with the problem of economic justice—always argued that "the case is not the same with us now, as it was in the primitive church."[34] This Edwards considered among the leading heresies of the Liberal social ethic. But the text of Chauncy's 1773 sermon, *Christian Love, as Exemplified by the First Christian Church in their Having all Things in Common, Placed in its True and Just Point of Light,* shows that Edwards erred in his estimate of the rational mentality. Chauncy, at least, was uncomfortable in the thought of so radical a discontinuity in Christian history, and his sermon was an effort to prove that the apostles looked on social questions in much the same light as proper eighteenth-century Bostonians.

Chauncy began his sermon by explaining that the passages of Scripture reporting that the primitive Christians had "all things in common" did not mean that they had "a community in everything." Most especially they could not have had a community of property. So far were the authors of the New Testament "from reducing all Christians to a level," Chauncy observed, that they frequently described the members of society "under the characters of *rich* and *poor*." Thus quite "obviously" God's own inspired penmen assumed that there always "was, and would be" a difference among men "in point of outward circumstances." The existence of such differences, Chauncy concluded, was sufficient proof that both God and good Christians considered equality to be a violation, not a fulfillment, of the law and the gospel.

Despite all this Christian history, Chauncy's argument depended much less on a demonstration that levelism was "in direct contradiction to the precepts of revelation" than on his flat assertion that such a social situation would "be an absurdity in reason." Whatever may have been the actual practice of some early Christians, any attempt to make their behavior the basis of "a law, and established rule, obligatory upon all Christians, in all ages, however differently circumstanced, would be highly absurd, and greatly hurtful in its tendencies and operation."[35] Thus Chauncy proved himself not a traditionalist but a meliorist, convinced that the law (and the gospel) must adjust to changing conditions, taking account of what would ensue from its enforcement. But however he might believe that circumstances alter cases, he would never doubt that it was reasonable for God to have given men a variety of natural abilities and advantages in order to indicate His approval of a society of rich and poor.

Chauncy's illuminating discussion of agape contained, in brief, all the essential ingredients of the argument, perfected by subsequent exponents of the legal scheme, that social classes owe little or nothing to each other. What such Liberals as Chauncy came close to arguing is that men as individuals are under no explicit obligations to their fellows. The Massachusetts rationalists differed from the Anglicans of pre-Revolutionary America in being somewhat uncomfortable with the traditional concept of a structured and interdependent society. The guiding spirit of their social thought would seem to have been an essential individualism—a disposition to believe not only that each man can and must seek his own happiness but that the community was thereby best served. "The same course of action which tends to *private* happiness, tends to *publick* also," Mayhew declared in the early months of his career. "For publick happiness is nothing but the happiness of a *number of individuals* united in society."[36] But even Mayhew never developed a social theory perfectly consistent with so atomistic a vision. His dilemma, as indeed that of later Liberals, lay in the seeming impossibility of reconciling an ethic of self-improvement with a conservative desire to preserve the ancient landmarks of the social order.

Liberal utterances on social and political questions were thus laced with evidence of the internal contradiction between an accent on individualism and a prejudice against changes in the character and structure of the community. But in the period before the Revolution the weight of Liberal argument was invariably brought to bear against those members of colonial society who thought themselves aggrieved, as individuals, by the prevailing social order. Criticisms of the revival spirit generally contained reminders that charity envieth not: "Are they richer than ourselves; it suffers us not to be uneasy."[37] Until John Adams made "emulation" a cornerstone of his social philosophy, rationalism's counsel to the disaffected remained that of admonishing men to be content with their lot. The "law of charity" as espoused by the Liberal clergy meant, for forty years and more, that "all envy of those who are wiser, richer, more virtuous, more esteemed, more prosperous,"[38] must be suppressed.

The difficulty in overcoming such "envy"—or whatever be the proper name for the attitude of the lower classes of colonial society toward their "betters"—was that Liberalism did not have a monopoly on definitions of charity. In his treatise *True Virtue* Edwards expanded and refined his earlier observations on charity into an ultimate statement of the Calvinist moral imperative. In the course of doing so, he commented on the contumacious character of one whose heart is "governed by regard to his own private interest" and is therefore disposed to "act the part of an enemy to the public." A "selfish, contracted, narrow spirit," he observed, "is generally abhorred, and is esteemed base and sordid."[39] That it was so esteemed in the America of the 1750's is something of a tribute to Edwards, Tennent, Bellamy, and a host of Calvinist ministers who publicized an interpretation of the law of love widely at variance with that of Chauncy and the Liberal clergy. That men were made poor by "a want of a natural faculty to manage affairs to advantage" was no reason for consigning them to servile labor. Such a faculty, Edwards explained,

> is a gift God bestows on some, and not on others; and it is not owing to themselves. You ought to be thankful that God hath given you such a gift, which he hath denied to the person in ques-

tion. And it will be a very suitable way for you to show your thankfulness, to help those to whom that gift is denied, and let them share the benefit of it with you.

While Liberals rejoiced in the differences among men and sought to minimize the wealthy man's obligations to his fellows, Calvinists insisted that whatever worldly substance a man happened to accrue was "an accident." It was a reason neither for pride nor for contempt of one's fellow creatures, but rather an opportunity for serving the less fortunate. The corollary of this precept was an imperative that the Calvinist clergy succeeded in fastening on the popular mind in the decades after the Awakening: "he who is all for himself, and none for his neighbors, deserves to be cut off from the benefit of human society."[40] When the American multitude began to act on the promptings of this insight, something more than the commercial faith once delivered to the Boston saints cemented Liberal affections for mother Britain. Not the least of the advantages of the empire was a power and an authority that could keep the American rabble diligent in their proper callings.

II

In 1765 the British government was tried in the balance by Liberals and found wanting—but only momentarily. No sooner was the Stamp Act repealed than Liberal spokesmen were again applauding, seemingly with even greater vigor, a constitution which "all British subjects are so happy to live under."[41] By 1770 other Americans were beginning to ask if the British constitution were indeed designed to provide for the general welfare of the colonies. Most Liberals continued to insist that the only legitimate question was whether that constitution was being legally violated by Parliament. So enamored were the Arminian clergy of the British colonial system that even in 1776 many of them could not endure the prospect of forsaking their circumstances in that world for a dangerous and untried career of independence. Still, because Chauncy, Mayhew, and other Liberal ministers had for thirty years declared themselves in favor of a government's seeking the general welfare, historians have looked on them as having prepared the American mind for revolution.

Jonathan Mayhew's 1750 *Discourse on Unlimited Submission* is generally cited as the primary source of the clergy's anticipation of the radicalism of 1776. Mayhew there declared that men are obliged to obey only that ruler who attends "continually on the good work of advancing the public welfare." Yet that the "main business" of rulers was "to seek the welfare of the people" had been a commonplace of

American political theory for nearly a century,[42] and in the eighteenth century no American clergyman thought differently. Calvinists as well as Mayhew argued that "the safety and advantage of the people is the supreme law by which the prince, and all subordinate magistrates should govern themselves," that, indeed, their entire function consisted in seeking "the good and happiness of human society."[43] The differences among the ministry, and among the populace, involved such questions as what comprised the general welfare and how it was to be achieved. The patriarchal Nathaniel Appleton (who began his career in the ministry when Increase and Cotton Mather still exercised intellectual dominion over the Boston clergy) suggested in 1766:

> Let us consider the true design of government, which is the *good of the community*; and fixing this in our mind as a firm principle, it will serve very much to direct and regulate as to all the exertions of power, as well as to our obedience and submission thereunto.[44]

Few clergymen of whatever persuasion would have faulted Appleton's generalization. But differences did emerge, in the period between the Awakening and the Revolution, on such questions as who was to decide, and by what criteria, that the public happiness was being achieved or sought, and, this decision having been made, who was to exert power and who to submit. To each of these questions the Liberal clergy offered answers that were hardly spurs to revolution. Well into the 1770's the end and aim of Liberal political thought and discourse was the preservation of the ordered tranquillity of colonial society.

From almost any perspective, it is difficult to view the Lockean arguments of Mayhew's *Discourse on Unlimited Submission* as an early espousal of the ideology of the American Revolution. His assault on the notions of the divine right of kings and passive obedience was phrased as a defense of the prevailing British constitution—and, more specifically, of the Glorious Revolution. In fact, though Mayhew was clearly familiar with Locke, the bulk of his doctrines (and much of his language) was "borrowed" from the tracts of Benjamin Hoadly, who early in the eighteenth century had contested the nonjuring bishops and their arguments on behalf of the Stuart succession. Nor is it clear that Mayhew in 1750 feared a resurgence of highflying sentiment in England, though he did note, in the course of his sermon, that the notions of divine right and nonresistance had quite recently inspired the "factions and rebellions" that were quelled at the battle of Culloden Moor. In Mayhew's view the threat lay not in Britain but in Boston, where, he believed, the Anglican clergy intended to use the anniversary of the death of Charles I for "preaching passive obedience, worshiping King Charles I, and cursing the dissenters and puritans for murdering him." There is in fact no evidence that any of the Episcopalians of Mayhew's Boston were Jacobites. Contemporary observers were certain there was no such animal in any of the colonies: "never any grew there, and if any are transported or import themselves, loss of speech always attends them."[45] Yet Mayhew's apprehensions were in part justified, and, to the degree they were, his *Discourse on Unlimited Submission* is a remarkable document, not for its political prescience but as both analysis and revelation of the provincial psychology of eighteenth-century New England.

Many of the Anglicans of Mayhew's Boston were clearly more outspoken in their Toryism than most of their counterparts at home. Just as in the nineteenth century Yankees transplanted to Ohio or South Carolina could produce "Forefathers' Day" orations and sermons filled with an officious filiopietism that incurred the resentment and wrath of the natives, so too were Mayhew's Episcopalian contemporaries capable of commemorating Charles's death with jibes directed not so much against the Puritans of an earlier day as against their New England descendants. From a salute to Charles, or a condemnation of the Puritans, it was, Mayhew believed, "natural for them to make a transition to the dissenters" of his day, and thence to stigmatizing New England Congregationalists "not only as schismatics, but as traitors and rebels, and all that is bad." In so doing, these "lofty gentlemen" were attempting, Mayhew believed, to demonstrate the superiority of those who, in the provinces, had embraced a more tasteful Anglican persuasion. They were also seeking to gain applause in England and to swell their own reputations: "every petty priest with a roll and gown thinks he must do something in imitation of his betters in lawn, and show himself a true son of the church." Mayhew's dissection and criticism of such Anglicans—"through a foolish ambition to appear considerable, they only render themselves contemptible"—are not in fact irrelevant to an understanding of his own motives. For the immediate inspiration of his *Discourse on Unlimited Submission* would seem to have been his own peculiar sensitivity, not merely to Anglican scorn, but to the applause of Englishmen, some of whom had condescendingly praised Mayhew's earlier sermons as evidence that Americans "were greatly improved in their taste."[46]

The glittering generalities of Mayhew's *Discourse* (the divine right of kings was a notion "altogether as fabulous and chimerical as transubstantiation") were thus revolutionary only in the sense that they bespoke an aching provincial pride. It was as an offended colonial that Mayhew decided to do battle with an imagined Filmerism and raised the standard of John Locke. Though on subsequent occasions Mayhew sadly neglected certain of the abstract truths of the *Second*

Treatise, Locke was indeed an appropriate philosopher for Liberals like Mayhew, who had little stomach for either Cromwell's "mal-administration" or the "reigning hypocrisy" of the 1640's. Liberals' admiration for the Whiggish gentlemen that brought William and Mary to the throne was unbounded, for they dated the liberties and happiness of British Americans from the Glorious Revolution of 1688. Mayhew's anger with those who had "the forehead to ventilate" the doctrines of passive obedience and unlimited submission produced no eulogies of the regicide judges but only hymns to "the present happy settlement of the crown."[47] Down to the Battle of Lexington, the Glorious Revolution and the Protestant succession remained leading themes for the Liberals, in part because homage to the British consti-tution was essential for the legal argument against British commercial regulations. Yet this devotion seems in larger part inspired by a fear that a new generation of diggers and levellers was at work in America. And when passed through a historical and constitutional filter, the Liberal idea of the general welfare, like the Liberal conception of natural law, served an essentially conservative purpose.

When discussing concrete political situations, Liberals so tempered their abstractions with a variety of conditions, restrictions, and pro-visos that the theory of John Locke became something of an apology for effective denial of popular participation or control in affairs of state. Down to the very moment of independence, they remained vague on such questions as what comprised tyrannical behavior and who was entitled to decide that a ruler had forfeited the allegiance due him. They were reluctant to define the crucial terms in their political creed because they knew how difficult it was to state "with precision," as one of them complained, "where submission ends and resistance may lawfully take place, so as not to leave room for men of bad minds unreasonably to oppose government, and to destroy the peace of society." Liberals were certain only that the revolution of 1688 had been legitimate, since a "majority of a whole people" had risen against a clearly unnatural and unrighteous governor. In theory they believed that a similar percentage of the population might again decide to resist a tyrant, but only as "a last resource."[48] None, however, seri-ously entertained a wish for his own society to be at the mercy of a majority of the population.

To avoid such an extremity Liberals defined tyranny so rigidly that not even nine tenths of the American population would necessarily have been justified, in their eyes, in overturning a government of which Liberals approved. Their definition of tyranny moved with the times: normally they insisted only on the negative principle that mere maladministration is not "sufficient to legitimate disobedience,"* but in moments of crisis, like 1765, they so restricted their definition of tyranny as nearly to divest it of meaning. Speaking in the year of the Stamp Act, an Election Preacher explained that a people should overlook their rulers' errors and even their vices so long as they are "not such as tend directly to overturn the state, and to bring distress and ruin on the whole community."[49] It is not impossible that the "long train of abuses" was inserted in the Declaration of Independence as much to soothe the consciences of reluctantly rebellious Liberals as to convince a candid world that Americans were right in casting off a grievous tyranny.

Another product of Liberal prudence, and their most important contribution to American political thought, was the distinction between "real" and "imaginary" grievances. Having announced that only the most heinous offenses constituted tyranny, Liberals found it necessary to add that large numbers of people often feel aggrieved by a government when they ought, indeed, to be quite happy. "A people," Mayhew admitted (though without indicating whether he meant a whole people or merely a majority), "really oppressed in a great degree by their sovereign, cannot well be insensible when they are so oppressed." Yet, Liberals emphasized, though a people "will never miss to feel and complain" of grievances "where they really are," they will sometimes, indeed often, "imagine grievances which they do not feel."[50] Whatever this distinction lacked in precision was more than made up by repetition. So long and so insistently did Liberals seek to separate imaginary grievances from real that many finally convinced themselves that every sense of oppression (save that felt by acutely sensitive Liberals) was a form of madness.

In support of their position clerical rationalists cited the psychological theory of John Locke and his followers, who had shown how easily passions distort perception and what tricks the uncultivated imagination can play. The Liberal assessment of the popular mind was reinforced, moreover, by a conviction that all societies are plagued by demagogues who both foment and exploit popular folly. In every state there are "some petulant, querulous men," Mayhew noted, "men of factious, turbulent and carping dispositions," ready always to abuse legitimate government and to instill in the people imaginary grievances. Mayhew professed to believe that such "men of contemptible character" were not too numerous in the Massachusetts of 1750,[51] but within a few years he and other Arminians discerned an alarming

* The notion that improper legislation is reason enough for turning a government out, Mayhew explained in his 1750 *Discourse*, "manifestly tends to the dissolution of government, and to throw all things into confusion and anarchy."

increase in their number. Rising to this challenge by seeking to restrain an easily misled populace, Liberals—their political faith founded
on this rock of antipopulism—might have stood for ages in defense of
constitutional legitimacy, had not both people and demagogues
expressed grievances which even Liberals eventually confessed were
real.

Liberal political theory was nevertheless deliberately contrived as
justification for restraining the people. Chauncy's first postulate was
that civil government "means the same thing" as "order and rule in
society"; his second, that the ruler's duty to seek the *"general good"*
meant, "in a word," that he was "to maintain peace and good order."[52]
Mayhew just as strongly suggested that the whole constitutional structure of Massachusetts was designed for the sole purpose of defending
the rights, persons, and property of its citizens from "lawless violence."[53] Many Americans agreed with these observations, but others
may have wondered why the Liberal political machine seemed designed, and was applied, almost exclusively for purposes of restraint.
The answer lay not in Lockean political theory, but in the experience
of the Awakening and the continuing rationalist belief that the pre-
eminent danger to society lay in the ease with which the multitude
might be inflamed.

The true measure of clerical rationalism must thus be taken from
those sermons in which Liberals were concerned with domestic affairs.
Chauncy's sermon of 1747 recalled that the despot Charles II had
once violated the peace and good order of society. But the Stuart reign,
thank God, had been ended with the accession of William and Mary,
to whom, along with the Glorious Revolution, the constitution, and
the Protestant succession, Chauncy paid fulsome tribute. This pleasant
diversion accomplished, Chauncy then turned to matters of more
immediate interest. It is "a great mistake to suppose," he informed the
General Court, that "there can be dangers only from those in the
highest stations." Another and greater danger, Chauncy affirmed, is
from

> men who strike in with the *popular* cry of liberty and *privilege,*
> working themselves, by an artful application to the fears and jealou-
> sies of the people, into their good opinion of them as lovers of their
> country [and who] are in this case, most dangerous enemies to the
> community; and may, by degrees, if not narrowly watched, arrive
> to such an height, as to be able to serve their own ends, by touching
> even the people in their most valuable rights.[54]

The remainder of Chauncy's sermon, devoted to the currency issue,
made it quite clear that this portrait of demagogues was no mere
abstraction.

These demagogues seemed just as dangerous three years later when Mayhew delivered the first of his great patriot sermons, which ended with an often slighted reminder that the revolutions of the seventeenth century held no lessons for eighteenth-century New Englanders. British Americans, Mayhew explained in the last paragraph of his sermon *Unlimited Submission,* enjoyed "all the liberty that is proper and expedient" and were therefore obliged to remain "contented and dutiful subjects." There are in this world, he continued, both those who "strike at liberty under the term licentiousness" and those who "aim at popularity under the disguise of patriotism." From these observations Mayhew deduced two suggestions as to the course which Bostonians might take in the future. We in New England, Mayhew advised, should beware both of extreme highflyers and of extreme radicals, for "extremes are dangerous." We should also realize that in Massachusetts there is at any moment far "more danger of the latter than of the former."[55] These two tenets of the creed were never again so well balanced as in 1750, since to Liberals—always eager to avoid extremes and yet equally ready to espy the dangers of demagoguery—the events of the next quarter century proved, to say the least, perplexing.

Advocates as they were of social order, Arminians were placed in a considerable dilemma during the Stamp Act crisis. It is well known that Liberals like Mayhew opposed the stamp tax, but it is often forgotten that they opposed the Sons of Liberty even more vehemently. The Liberal state of mind in 1765 was recalled by Mayhew in his sermon celebrating the act's repeal. After lauding "the mercantile part" of the community for having done "themselves much honor" in the affair, Mayhew went on to complain that other elements of the population most certainly had not:

> In this state of general disorder, approaching so near to anarchy, some profligate people, in different parts of the continent, took an opportunity to gratify their private resentments, and to get money in an easier and more expeditious way than that of labor; committing abominable excesses and outrages on the persons or property of others. What a dreadful scene was this! Who can take a cursory review of it even now, without horror, unless he is lost to all sense of religion, virtue, and good order?[56]

Mayhew's description of such fiendish looting applied, of course, to those citizens of the colonies who had seized on more direct methods for preventing the enforcement of the Stamp Act.*[57] Far from being

---

* Calvinists did not condone these depredations, but they minimized them and, indeed, went far toward excusing them. Joseph Emerson, for instance, suggested that

an agitator in 1765, Mayhew had devoted his most strenuous efforts to holding opposition to the tax within reasonable bounds. He felt so maligned by a suggestion that one of his sermons had helped incite a mob to attack Thomas Hutchinson's house that he quickly sent the lieutenant governor an abject letter of denial and apology and preached, on the next Sunday, against "the abuse of liberty."[58]

For Liberals, therefore, the repeal came as a harbinger not only of prosperity in their time, but peace, and they chanted in 1766 *jubilate deo* for an event which augured "quietness forever." Chauncy saw reason for thanksgiving in the unshackling of commerce, but he found it even more in the end of the opportunity for "evil-minded persons" to exploit the "general ferment of men's minds, in those violent outrages upon the property of others."[59] Many other Americans, also relieved by the repeal, commemorated the occasion. But only among those who believed good order the essence of both religion and virtue did the celebrations take the form (as a Rhode Island Liberal phrased it) of "a sort of joyful funeral."[60] The good news from the far country was particularly cooling to the thirsty souls of Liberals, for until it arrived they were far from sure whose obsequies they might soon be holding.

The practical significance of the legalist devotion to John Locke and constitutionalism was distinctly revealed in the Massachusetts Election Sermon of 1765. This sermon, by the Reverend Andrew Eliot of Boston, was delivered when, as Chauncy put it, the "discontent, anxiety, and perplexing solicitude" of genteel Bostonians was nearing a peak. The doctrines espoused on this occasion provide an interesting contrast to those appearing in the post-mortems of 1766, when Chauncy and his friends were again, in his words, "easy in our minds."[61] Eliot was never so outspoken a Liberal—religiously or politically—as either Mayhew or Chauncy. Not that he differed widely from his colleagues on doctrinal matters, but he was above all things an eminently prudent person. Nothing in his Election Sermon would have struck his colleagues as even mildly non-Liberal, however, for it was indeed something of an apotheosis of their political viewpoint.

Discussing the dangers of a magistrate's overstepping the law of nature or acting against the general welfare, Eliot explained that such be-

---

it was providential that "the lawless and disobedient did not in many more instances break out into the most horrid outrages"—considering the poverty and the closing of the courts in Boston. William Patten (Wheelock's son-in-law) proposed that the friends of the stamp tax might have been grateful that only their effigies had been hung. Both were rural Calvinists, inclined to suspect the motives of the urban populace generally. It is noteworthy, however, that Samuel Stillman, pastor of Boston's First Baptist Church, had nothing whatever to say about the supposed excesses of laborers, mechanics, or the Sons of Liberty.

havior should be avoided not only as contrary to the purposes of civil government but as the little spark which might ignite a holocaust. The American people, Eliot warned and complained, are acutely sensitive to attacks on their rights and privileges:

> Every attempt alarms them, makes them jealous of further designs, and often throws them into the hands of factious demagogues, who hate government, and are ever watching for opportunities to embarrass public measures, and to introduce anarchy and confusion.

Such a passage cannot be read as a threatening of the British ministry with popular reprisals, but only as a revelation of Liberal anxieties. Throughout his sermon Eliot cautiously sought to minimize the reality of American grievances. He closed his discourse with words that breathed the reasonable spirit of 1765: a hymn of praise to the Massachusetts charter and a fervent prayer that it would escape unscathed from its latest perils. Let everyone refrain from touching this seamless constitutional robe, he pleaded in conclusion, lest it be rent irreparably. "When a humour of changing once begins," was his final sigh, "no mortal can tell where it will end."62

Once the Stamp Act was repealed, Liberals simply refused to "meddle with the thorny question" of what might justify "private men, at certain extraordinary conjunctures, to take the administration of government in some respects into their hands." They were certain only that the recent "irregularities" would never again be tolerated in America and that there was "no plausible pretext" for any further measures whatsoever. Thus the theme of Mayhew's thanksgiving sermon was an invitation to all Americans to "join heart and hand in supporting the lawful, constitutional government over us, in its just dignity and vigor."63 The Liberal clergy had certainly not known in 1765 where it might all end, and in 1766, though they claimed to be once again in command of the situation, they were still evidently disturbed by the prospect before them. The urgency with which they sought to tranquilize Americans and to compose their differences suggests that to their eyes at least the Sons of Liberty loomed somewhat larger than a man's hand.

The social order cherished by Liberals and embodied in their constitution and charter was not only peaceful but harmonious; two essential elements in this harmony were hierarchy and subordination. " 'Tis unalterably right and just there should be rule and superiority in some," Chauncy had announced in 1747, "and subjection and inferiority in others." What struck Chauncy as "invariably the will of God; his will manifested by the moral fitness and reason of things,"64 was not, however, simply an argument for a ruler being stationed above what Chauncy called the "vulgar people." Heirs in part to an intellectual tradition even older than Puritanism, Liberals took special delight in what in the eighteenth century was called "the great chain of being." For them one of the beauties of nature and the glories of God was how neatly the universe displayed a "diversity of beings, duly subordinated to each other."[65]

An idea that for Alexander Pope and Bolingbroke was a source of pleasure and assurance was for the Liberal ministry the foundation of all social wisdom. Their great chain of being included not only beasts, men, angels, and God, but sub-links within each of these larger components of the chain. No Liberal, so far as is known, published a precise catalogue of the gradations of humanity—though the Boston ministers were more candid than their spiritual heirs in admitting to a suspicion that certain of their number were unusually near to the angels. They did declare, however, that some such scale of human beings existed, at least so far as man's "sociable" nature was concerned. Man in society, Chauncy explained, is necessarily comparable to "the inhabitants of the upper world," where there "seems to be a difference of *order;* as well as species; which the scripture intimates, by speaking of them in the various stile of *thrones, dominions, principalities, powers, archangels,* and *angels.*"[66] Within such a universal vision, quite obviously, a political demagogue seemed something more than a mere disturber of the peace. Rather he was a cosmic sinner who, though assigned a rank somewhat lower than the angels, aspired to the throne and challenged the standing order so he might achieve a "height" which was not properly his.

Whereas only a handful of such distempered aspirants had plagued the orderly society of Mayhew and Chauncy in 1750, this awesome disease of insubordination seemed to have reached epidemic proportions in the crisis of 1765. It appeared to Liberals that in all the excitement quite a few Bostonians, and even the residents of less favored communities, had forgotten the duties appropriate to their rank in life. "There has been a general dissipation among us for a long time," Mayhew complained in the spring of 1766,

> a great neglect and stagnation of business. Even the poor and laboring part of the community, whom I am very far from despising, have had so much to say about government and politics, in the late times of danger, tumult, and confusion, that many of them seemed to forget that they had any thing to do. Methinks, it would now be expedient for them, and perhaps for most of us, to do something more, and talk something less; every one studying to be quiet, and to do his own business.[67]

In the summings-up of 1766, Liberals all expressed a hope that the repeal would place the quietus on all such abnormal behavior. "The repeal, the repeal," Mayhew intoned, "has at once, in good measure, restored things to order," but his accents betrayed a fear that "all things that went on right before" were not, despite his insistence, "returning gradually to their proper course."[68] For Liberals it was enough that "commerce lifts up her head, adorned with golden tresses, pearls and precious stones," but this in itself was no guarantee that every American would thereafter be "contented," as Chauncy hoped, with his "condition."[69] Returning to the old course meant, as he and Mayhew saw it, that each citizen would once again be "minding his own business" and working diligently only in his "respective station."[70] And even as they stood as advocates for the great chain of Massachusetts being these partisans of the legal scheme found it hard to obscure the fact that they themselves, as well as the lawyers and merchants of America, had in the past year shown a poor example to the more vulgar part of the populace.

Beneath the constitutional cloak thrown over the "humble petitioning, and other strictly legal measures" of America's honorable men lay the glaring reality of the extralegality, by all ordinary standards, of the merchants' appeals and of the Stamp Act Congress. Also barely disguised was the substantial truth that the merchants and their spokesmen, archangels perhaps in comparison to other Americans, had themselves recently shown an inordinate desire to rise above their alloted stations. The Liberal celebrations of 1766 were in part orgies of felicitation—declarations that the gentlemen of America had proven in their response to the Stamp Act that they, as William Smith phrased it, "were worthy of having descended from the illustrious stock of Britons."[71] The rationalist clergy tried to draw a distinct line between the multitude and merchants and lawyers, but no such clear distinction existed. Mayhew's calling the Sons of Liberty "certain men of Belial" and his condemnation of the "effrontery" of those who had shown too much interest in public affairs were in a sense hysterical projections of Liberal self-knowledge.[72] The honorable resistance of 1766 was directly descended from the provincial sensitivity of 1750, and the Stamp Act crisis had given aspiring colonial gentlemen their first opportunity to claim a place in the imperial sun. Thus despite the fact that few Liberals were to be on the firing line when Independence finally dawned, there is ironic truth in the characterization of Mayhew's *Discourse on Unlimited Submission* as the "MORNING GUN OF THE REVOLUTION."[73]

III

Though America's gentlemen and its rabble were not so different as Liberals believed, one of Liberalism's basic assumptions was that

such differences existed, were recognizable, and of immense significance. The social and political theory of rationalism, like its religion
and rhetoric, rested on the assumption that the "whole creation is
diversified, and men in particular." The most significant of the diver-
sities was the "great variety" exhibited in man's "intellectual faculties." Mayhew's theory of "a continual rise or gradation" in the
"intellectual powers" of men was, not surprisingly, reflected in the
Liberal notion of precisely who was justified in interesting himself in
public affairs. Though Liberals conceded that magistrates should also
be qualified in other ways, their assumption was that wisdom was an
absolute essential. All would have to accede to "the distinguished abilities of the few," since the general welfare of society could be understood and rightly pursued only by "men of understanding and knowledge." Wisdom was necessary, and so presumably was education:
"every man is not fit to govern: there must be a genius for government,
and there must be constant study and application."[74] Participation
in public affairs they considered the prerogative only of the intelligent
and well educated.

It is readily apparent that political genius, as defined by Liberals,
consisted in the very capacities that permitted man to attain a proper
knowledge of God's will and, by conforming his conduct to that knowledge, to seek his own welfare:

> For wisdom is a just discernment of things, and such approbation of
> the mind as to determine the conduct according to it; and right
> action is, in the constitution of things, productive of happiness. . .[75]

"Happiness" was a phenomenon on which Liberals delighted to dwell,
and the thought of pursuing it was the inspiration of their political
creed as well as of natural religion. They believed that every human
being is "actuated by a desire of happiness" and accounts "every thing
more or less valuable, as it tends more or less" to its attainment. Reaching such a goal, however, depended entirely on whether "a right
estimate" were made of the stuff of which happiness is made, and the
ability to decide aright, in turn, on one's native capacities and education.[76] What this implied in terms of government is suggested by the
political theory of William Smith, the first premise of which was that
the American multitude was too much given to "an unbridled fierceness." The pursuit of the collective welfare, therefore, could be engaged in only by men capable of, and trained in, "researches" into
the "constitution of the material universe."[77] For only such men would
appreciate the degree to which security of property and social order
were writ in the very nature of things.

The ideal political man was thus, according to Liberals, the product of a liberal education. He was neither a mere political scientist nor a professional administrator, however, but a virtuous Christian gentleman. Crucial to this role, politically conceived, was the "disinterested benevolence" which increasingly flowed into Liberal moral theory in the years after the Awakening. Man was endowed, Liberals contended, "with tender and social affections, with generous and benevolent principles," which, if properly encouraged and developed, would lead him to seek the happiness of his fellow citizens.[78] The practice of such a benevolence often meant, as Edwards carefully demonstrated in the *True Virtue,* pursuing one's own happiness, or that of one's immediate family. Even in theory, Liberal benevolence, always closer in spirit to Adam Smith's moral sentiments than Hutcheson's virtue, could mean little more than sensitive expressions of concern for suffering widows and orphans.

Until the 1770's Liberals generally defined benevolence as a desire for and the pursuit of the happiness of mankind. Like Benjamin Franklin they conceived of the doer of good as emulating the Supreme Being, who they believed desired for His creatures "the greatest possible sum of happiness" that could be borne.[79] Liberals wanted no mortal to go to extremes, for they expected all benevolent endeavor to be conducted prudently and judiciously. A "principle of benevolence," wrote Chauncy of the Divine goodness,

> though of infinite *propelling force,* if not guided in its operations by *wisdom* and *intelligence,* instead of producing *nothing but good,* might, by blindly counteracting itself, produce, upon the *whole,* as the final result of its exertions, infinite confusion and disorder.[80]

Chauncy and his colleagues were equally certain that a good magistrate was not a man of infinite good will merely. He would have "the same benevolent design towards the community" that "the great Governor of the universe" had toward the "whole creation." Man was prepared "for higher and more perfect services to humanity"—even as for his own "sublime and everlasting delight and happiness"—by an education designed "to refine, improve, and exalt" his "rational powers."[81] Benevolent rule was therefore not different in terms of policy from wise and discerning rule. It meant only that a magistrate would perhaps seek "the happiness and prosperity of his people"[82] with a greater alacrity and intensity.

By introducing the concept of benevolence into social theory, Liberals managed to broaden the standard for determining who, in any society, was entitled to engage in public affairs. Though the idea of public benevolence had its source in (and was never in the pre-Revolutionary period totally separable from) the ideal of a ruler's pursuit of the general welfare, it had become even in the 1760's less a mandate than an invitation. Long before William Ellery Channing was able to advise Boston Federalists how, unaided by the Holy Spirit, they might achieve likeness to God, his spiritual predecessors were suggesting public service as a promising career.

Until the 1770's this means of resembling God and imitating "the incarnate son of God, who manifested the greatest benevolence to mankind" was offered theoretically only to such legitimately appointed or elected officials as the King and members of Parliament, or provincial governors and legislators. As late as 1768 an Election Preacher insisted that "rulers and ruled" had "different parts" to act in society, but by indicating that the efforts of all should tend, ideally, "to one grand point, the welfare of the community," he managed to enlarge somewhat the benevolent role of private persons.[83] The ranks of individuals contributing to the public welfare had long been swelling, and indeed by 1765 the colonies were overflowing with persons eager to demonstrate their benevolence by serving the community. For Harvard and the College of Philadelphia had produced far too many talented and virtuous gentlemen for the available offices, so that many would-be patriots of the Stamp Act crisis were private men.*[84]

Benevolence was, however, only one characteristic of the Liberal patriot, less important than, and severely limited by, a virtue which Liberals called "love of country." Thorough Arminians in politics as in theology, they expected no one to seek his own happiness or that of his fellows unless such happiness were well within reach. "To a generous mind," Mayhew explained, the public good is "such a noble and excellent goal" that "the prospect of attaining it will animate to the pursuit, and being attained, it will reward the pains."[85] The more reasonable public good to pursue was therefore that of the nearer community, in part because of the better chance of being rewarded there, in part because the New World was more favored with those "blessings" without which, so far as the Liberal could imagine, happiness was difficult or impossible to achieve. "Look around you!" began William Smith's summons to love of country:

Behold a country, vast in extent, merciful in its climate, exuberant in its soil, the seat of plenty, the garden of the Lord! . . . Behold

* In 1766 William Smith, celebrating the felicitous repeal of the Stamp Act, quoted long passages from his own addresses of earlier years to prove that education at the College of Philadelphia was no mere "art of furnishing the Head" and that he personally had urged benevolence, patriotism, and love of liberty on his students. "Small would have been the honour we should have derived from them," he went on to say to his alumni audience, "if you, Gentlemen, had not called those lessons forth into Action."

them exulting in their Liberty; flourishing in Commerce; the Arts and Sciences planted in them; the Gospel preached; and in short the seeds of happiness and glory firmly rooted, and growing up among them![86]

Liberal love of country, a profound love of resources more than people, was, much as the Liberal love of God, an expression for favors received or soon forthcoming.

Love of country first welled up in Liberal Americans after the Treaty of Paris, which they took as a harbinger of ascending felicity for God's most favored empire. So fascinated with the bounties of the New World were they, however, that Liberal patriotism pressed toward becoming a quasi-Americanism. Probably the Liberal mind could have continued to love the whole empire, and pursued its general welfare, had Crown and Parliament done more to hasten the growth of the plant of glory in the New World, apart even from encouraging the thriving of American happiness. But whatever the case, Liberal love of country eventually produced a movement for secession. Not, however, for revolution, so pleased were Liberals with the prevailing structure of American blessings. Their ideal patriot had to be nothing more than diligent in his calling, and to seek in little ways to further this manifest destiny by watering and fertilizing the seeds of glory. He was neither expected nor called on to reorganize society in order to achieve the greatest felicity for his country.[87] For the Liberal ministry never doubted that the manner in which blessings were distributed among Americans harmonized completely with benevolent Christianity.

Though generally dormant before the French Wars, Liberal patriotism had in those years acquired an additional component, one referred to in Liberal circles as a "love of liberty." They were usually reluctant to admit it, but Arminians loved liberty primarily in reaction to any effort "to deprive us of [our] exalted Blessings, or to circumscribe us in the possession of them."[88] Not that Liberals would have loved any country, however blessed physically, in which liberty did not dwell. Yet their love of liberty was no more in conflict with their love of country than was their benevolence, since, as Locke and British constitutional history had proven, liberty was the guarantor of property, without which security neither public nor private happiness could or would be pursued. All these strands were drawn together quite neatly by a Connecticut Old Light in the year before the Stamp Act:

Liberty is the glory of a community, the most firm and unshaken basis of public happiness. The want of this will abate the value of all the comforts of life. The embittering circumstance of precarious property . . . mars the relish of every gratification, and throws a melancholy gloom over all temporal enjoyments. But wherever public spirit prevails, liberty is secure . . . For as liberty is the source of so much happiness, he who is a patriot, and wishes well to his country, must needs be a fast friend to it.[89]

The patriotism so succinctly defined in 1764 became active in the following year. Liberal response to the Stamp Act, often expressed as a love of liberty, was in fact a love for the institutional basis of American prosperity. "We were threatened," explained David Rowland in accounting for Rhode Islanders' warm friendship to liberty in 1765, "not with instantaneous ruin, but with a gradual, if not galloping consumption, that must have wasted and destroyed us."[90] Since Liberals took the repeal of the Stamp Act as a restoration of the old basis for inevitably increasing American prosperity, they wondered why other Americans, when faced with "so fair a prospect," should have chosen to persist in a demonstrative love of liberty. Yet the rationalist clergy themselves revealed, by protesting overmuch that the repeal was "big with important blessings, not to a few individuals only, but to communities," their notion of which parts of the colonies, and which residents of its cities, were most entitled to these generous blessings.[91] Anyone whose observations led him to other conclusions, Liberals insisted, was an undiscerning, self-seeking, and hypocritical lover of liberty.

Though Liberals were ordinarily quite content with the world about them, their patriotism was in some degree a criticism of their society. Benevolence, love of country, love of liberty—all were emotions infused into or superimposed on what they publicly lauded as a rational, orderly, and harmonious universe. Expressed originally in the desires of private men to add their energies to those of magistracy in the "noble and excellent" cause of pursuing the public good, these emotions might have remained forever in the service of King and empire. But after 1765 the proponents of the legal scheme threatened to violate one of their own cardinal principles of public behavior. True patriots, they had contended, brought not the sword, but peace, and sought to strengthen, not to divide, the society and government of the imperial commonwealth.

Such were the sentiments explicitly avowed by Mayhew in his Election Sermon of 1754, one of the first colonial efforts to reinstate patriotism in the schedule of public virtues. To Mayhew, who knew how often men had served "their own base and wicked ends, under the pretext and colour" of patriotism, it came as no surprise that its "very name" had become "a jest." Observing that there are "hypocrites in politics, as well as in religion"—whether Jacobites or popular demagogues he did not specify—Mayhew quickly and confidently assured his auditors that genuine patriotism was still a possibility.[92] A true public spirit, he explained, would never produce "parties and contentions," for factions arose only from "the pursuit of separate, distinct interests, and a want of public spirit" rather than its excess. Partisans, he explained, "have always something else in view than, what they would be tho't to have, the public good," and "at the bottom" of their every venture may be found "private pique, or private interest; or a general temper and turn to wrangling." A public spirit, Mayhew propounded, embodies a spirit of liberty; but it is, far more importantly, "a spirit of union." Not liberty alone, but "union is the source of public happiness."[93]

The rationalist ministry succeeded in demonstrating the inseparability of liberty and union only so long as their ideas evolved simply in response to domestic unrest. Like all other tenets of the Liberal creed, however, this doctrine proved untenable and even embarrassing after 1765. Once they challenged Parliament, Liberals were in no inconsiderable danger of being seen as what they themselves described, when referring to sham patriots, as "evil-minded persons, desirous of novelty and change."[94] For a century Americans would continue to debate the question of the nature of true patriotism and to differ among themselves as to whether love of humanity, love of country, or love of liberty was its determining element. The Liberal definition assumed all but final form in the decade after 1765, but it was confused from the outset. For every Liberal statement on the subject of patriotism was both explicit self-commendation and implicit self-criticism.

Just as rigid constitutionalism was the reasonable resolution, in theory, of all conflicts between liberty and order, so too was the Liberal ideal of benevolent patriotism a response to the inherent contradictions and weaknesses of Arminian moral theory. The more Liberals were accused of partisanship by friends of the Crown, the more outraged grew their protestations of purely disinterested and benevolent motives. By 1775 they were fairly shouting, with William Smith, that "the sacred flame" of American patriotism was in no way "fed by the fuel of faction or party; but by pure benevolence and love of the public." Smith's very next sentence disclosed, however, that Liberals had their moments of self-awareness, though perhaps only a few. Whatever the original impulse behind patriotism, Smith averred, it "soon rises above selfish principles, refines and brightens as it rises, and expands itself into heavenly dimensions."[95]

Before Liberal philanthropists found their occupations in the pomp and circumstance of glorious war, they had to overcome severe domestic hostility to their theory and practice of morality. Liberal avowals of benevolence, though spurred by Tory jibes at American patriots, were, more importantly, the valiant efforts of Arminian divines to vindicate their religion. If public service offered a ready, and easy, opportunity to fulfill the requirements of morality, it was as patriots too that America's Liberals first successfully replied to critics of their religion. By 1775 the sincerity, and utility, of their kind of benevolent aspiration seemed fairly demonstrable, and the proof found for which legalist theologians had been looking for a half century: Liberal religion seemed at last most favorable to society, as well as to piety. Actually, it was not the proliferation of Liberal patriots in 1765 that persuaded other Americans that Arminianism was possibly consistent with benevolence, but the efforts of secular writers and orators, and of generals, whose words and deeds carried another sort of conviction than that of the rational clergy's Hutchesonian arguments.

As critics of Liberalism had charged since 1740, the Liberals' idea of patriotism, like their notion of Christian benevolence, was at best a theory of enlightened self-interest. If the efforts of gentlemen-patriots overcame some of this criticism by 1775, the Liberal ministry itself progressed in these years from the merest insinuation that the doer of good found pleasure at least in his benevolence, to a candid acknowledgment that a public-spirited citizen could not help being motivated by "a prudent regard to his own temporal happiness." Yet until perhaps 1780 Liberals shrank from a confession of the ethical premise that was necessary to sustain such a doctrine: "We all love, and we ought to love ourselves."[96] For decades Liberals blended benevolence and self-interest in their public utterances and, finally, seized on the Revolution itself as proof of their total lack of selfish regard.

In the rationalist hierarchy of motives, self-interest was officially subordinate to benevolence, but it was never wholly suppressed, even when reasons were being assigned for putting on "the most active and vigorous exertions" for furthering "the gospel scheme" of love to man and God. "Do we wish the happiness of our brethren?" asked the official spokesman of Massachusetts Liberalism in urging such an enterprise: "Do we wish our own?"[97] American Calvinists had rather different ideas of what constituted benevolence and urged that American patriotism embody their definition—a "holy love" which seemed enthusiastic nonsense to Liberals. Calvinists were similarly unimpressed by Liberal benevolence, religious or political, and were persuaded by Liberal pronouncements on the subject only if they ceased, as some at last did, to be Calvinists.

Before the Revolution, however, Arminians were far more concerned, by choice as well as by necessity, with finding an adequate and comprehensible definition of love of liberty. The extreme Calvinists, not the Liberals, forced the issue of the nature of true virtue and eventually demanded that it stand squarely at the center of American political discussion. Reluctant to join issue on this question, the Arminians tried to focus American attention on the nature, extent, and advantages of human liberty. They were most at ease so long as love of liberty could be defined as warm friendship to constitutional privileges or as a mode or correlate of love of country. But once Liberals challenged imperial hegemony in the name of vital patriotism, they found it necessary to construe love of liberty too as a more lively spirit.

Post-Awakening rationalists believed that the love of liberty was "natural," having been implanted in man by the "great and wise Author of our being." They had trouble, however, in accounting for the fact that this instinct was so often perverted, and were especially hard put to explain what in particular distinguished their own love of liberty from the spirit which they claimed to discover in the breasts of other Americans. Though they had dismissed, with a mild flourish, all conceptions of virtue but their own as insincere, unreal, and dangerous, they were nevertheless forced, in the very act of interpreting the love of liberty, to publicize their conceptions of the nature and source of sin.

Where Liberals differed from all other American Protestants of their time was in gaining a true sight of sin only through its deleterious consequences for society. Liberal treatment of love of liberty was typical of all Liberal thought, which, whatever the subject, found virtue in an order outside of man but this side of God. Their primary concern was with the mischievous effects of the passions on what was considered the best of all possible polities:

> This passion, like all other original principles of the human mind, is, in itself, perfectly innocent and designed for excellent purposes, though like them, liable through abuse of becoming the cause of mischief to ourselves and others. In a civil state, the genius of whose constitution is agreeable to it, while in its full vigor and under proper regulation, it is not only the cement of the political body, but the wakeful guardian of its interests, and the great animating spring of useful and salutary operations; and then only is it injurious to the public or to individuals, when, through misapprehension of things or by being overbalanced by self-love, it takes a wrong direction.[98]

As in so many other respects, Liberals passed through the years of imperial crisis comforted and inspired by such thoughts on the love of liberty. Untroubled by the possibility that they, and the other gentlemen of America, were engaged in any but the most salutary and useful operations, they were concerned only that some Americans, less discerning and more selfish than they, were moving in the wrong direction.

Liberals had gone a long way toward conceiving sin in purely social terms, but in the 1760's they were still contending that the corrupt human personality had certain distinguishing characteristics. Not every "pretended regard for our country or zeal for the public welfare" deserves "the name of public-spirit," one Liberal explained in 1764. "But 'tis not hard for the discerning eye to detect the imposture, and unmask the cheat." Pretended patriots, according to this same spokesman, would generally appear in the guise of "wild enthusiasts and frantic zealots."[99] Since the Great Awakening, Liberals had seldom paused to analyze the nature of enthusiasm, generally contenting themselves with ridiculing its symptoms or bewailing its effects on society. However, even in the 1740's opponents of the Awakening had read enough Locke to know something of the psychology of enthusiasm and to realize that it was somehow related to "false notions" in the mind of the enthusiast. When Liberals discovered there were enthusiasts "in patriotism and politics, as well as religion," they declaimed against diseased and visionary politicians in the same spirit as had marked their blasts against Whitefield and Davenport.[100] Yet in their more temperate moments, as when Mayhew observed that overzealous Bostonian patriots had "no two rational and consistent ideas" about politics in 1766, they implied what they had learned from Locke: the enthusiasts disturbing the social order had erred because they were naturally unable or obdurately unwilling to see the world as the Liberals did.[101]

IV

Analysis of the political enthusiasm of 1765 would not have been so troublesome to Liberals had they not themselves been enthusiasts of a sort, in politics as well as theology. Indeed it was the efforts of a few Liberal ministers to induce in their parishioners the "patriotic emotions" that embarked them on careers of political oratory. Shortly after Braddock's defeat, William Smith announced that an effort to "kindle up" the "all-enlivening flame" of love of freedom was, if properly done, an endeavor "truly worthy a preacher's character."[102] In the next decades the Liberal clergy did seek to inspire their people with political enthusiasm; yet few of them would have acknowledged that what they were about was "political oratory." Chauncy was said once to have beseeched God "never to make him an orator," a prayer which one of his friends thought had been "unequivocally granted."[103]

Jonathan Mayhew might have confessed to being an orator, but he professed to remain aloof from all "political controversy." Despite all evidence he was even convinced that in 1765-1766 he had entered on no "political consideration" of the Stamp Act. He both pleaded lack of the necessary qualifications and noted the "impropriety of minutely discussing points of this nature in the pulpit."[104]

For another fifty years rational clergymen would continue to voice indignation if accused either of orating or of engaging in politics. Their sense of outrage sprang from the limited, and invidious, meanings they attached to the words "oratory" and "politics." To the Liberal mind the first of these terms conjured up images of Whitefield, the second of factious and even seditious partisans. Liberals hoped to be neither one nor the other, but they were nonetheless political orators, if only because it became clear that neither laws nor education was adequate to the task of molding colonial society to their taste. Both Smith and the New Englanders would have preferred that their goals be attained through more orderly processes, but apparently the colonial colleges produced too few proper patriots. Jonathan Mayhew thus found it necessary to suggest that the respectable young men of his church study the works of Cicero, even before entering Harvard, so they might, by modeling themselves after this classic paradigm of patriotism, achieve a true "love of liberty, and of one's country" early in life.[105]

Whatever the reason for this rising interest among the Liberal ministry in the patriotic emotions, only Smith and Mayhew were deeply moved to encourage them. Both were in considerably better positions than other Liberals to arouse "enthusiasm," and both perhaps had personal reasons for seeking to do so. In Philadelphia, Smith was unhampered by a parish system, while Mayhew's open Arianism drove a part of his congregation toward greener and more evangelical pastures. Nor may it be entirely coincidental that in the course of their efforts to inspire love of liberty and love of country, both Smith and Mayhew gained considerable reputations as outstanding orators, if only among those British-American circles to which they looked for critical acclaim.

To the extent that Mayhew and Smith addressed themselves to the less gentlemanly parts of their community, however, they were forced to weigh their words carefully. Indeed, only when delivering discourses at collegiate exercises was Smith free of this burden. On the other hand, his sermons to such mixed audiences as regiments of colonial soldiery necessarily fell into two parts. In the first half of such sermons he inculcated "Temperance, Sobriety, Cleanliness, and Contentment," and of course "Obedience to those who are appointed to command them," as the virtues of enlisted men, while the second was always introduced with some such statement as this:

And now, gentleman officers, you will permit me to address the remainder of this discourse more immediately to you. I know you love your King and Country.[106]

Such careful contrivance was necessary, Smith once explained, because in seeking to enkindle the sublime spirit of liberty one ran the danger of all those who play with fire. The slightest spark might start a "morose and censorious" liberty-loving prairie blaze among the general populace. Smith succeeded in preventing such an event by avoiding those subjects which "might engage us in broils" or even "ruffle our tempers," and, with even greater effect, by making certain that the "spirit of freedom" he aroused kept to "that rational medium which is founded on a more enlarged and refined turn of sentiment."[107] Only in addresses to officers and gentlemen did Smith permit himself the strains of emotional elevation that gave him something of a reputation as a fervid patriotic preacher.

The image of Jonathan Mayhew as a "fiery liberal" also has every virtue except consonance with the facts. Mayhew's sermons, insofar as he found himself called on to address the populace, were if anything even more marked than Smith's by abrupt transitions. According to Chauncy (who possibly envied Mayhew this gift), he diligently and laboriously strove so "to contrive his discourses" that they would "entertain and profit the learned and illiterate, the polite and less cultivated hearer."[108] The product was a grievous disconnectedness, marked by some passages designed to arouse the more chaste affections of gentlemen and others just as obviously intended to subdue the popular passions, which too often led Mayhew's undespised poor astray. The overall effect was hardly to be compared to the flames of fire that tradition tells us leapt from the mouths of Patrick Henry and James Otis.

The formal and studied divisions of Mayhew's sermons were compounded by the curious staccato effusiveness he cultivated as a manifestation of sensibility. The eulogy of Judge Sewall, already mentioned, was an example of Mayhew's "Pulpit Effusions." They were "so unharmonious and discordant," according to Peter Oliver, that they always "grated upon the Ears of his Auditors."[109] Something of what Oliver meant is discernible in the printed text of Mayhew's celebrated "extempore" apostrophe to liberty in his sermon of 1766, *The Snare Broken*. This is the sermon celebrating the repeal of the Stamp Act that came to sustain Mayhew's literary as well as his political reputation.*[110] As with his demonstration of grief for the departed Judge Sewall, Mayhew's rise on the winged ardor of genius was followed by an apology:

> But I forget myself, whither have I been hurried by this enthusiasm, or whatever else you will please to call it? I hope your candor will forgive this odd excursion, for which I hardly know how to account myself.[111]

Analysis of the "excursion" from reason in *The Snare Broken* acquits the author of any extraordinary enthusiasm whatever. His celebration of liberty both discloses the nature of the Liberal love of liberty and demonstrates the care Mayhew took to see that none but the most cultivated members of society would share this emotion.

Mayhew's salute to liberty is in fact a recapitulation of the Liberal theory of political enthusiasm. He begins by asking indulgence to share with his listeners "a few words respecting my notions of liberty in general." He then proceeds to explain where he had first imbibed these notions and why he found them acceptable:

> Having been initiated, in youth, in the doctrines of civil liberty, as they were taught by such men as Plato, Demosthenes, Cicero and other renowned persons among the ancients; and such as Sidney and Milton, Locke and Hoadley, among the moderns, I liked them; they seemed rational.

It was only after explaining that his love of liberty and his standards for accepting or rejecting what he found in books were rational that Mayhew permitted himself the observation that his readings in Scripture had also helped him to conclude "that freedom is a great blessing." In addition to these readings, he continued, "the tender care of a good person now at rest" had helped to cultivate in him a "love of liberty, though not"—he hastened to assure his congregation—"of licentiousness." Thus nurtured, he had developed a "passion" for liberty, whose "charms, instead of decaying with time in my eyes, have daily captivated me more and more." Of course, this passion was not low or frenzied, but "chaste and virtuous."

---

* It was the failure of British critics to appreciate Mayhew's literary gifts that inspired, to some extent at least, his vigorous patriotism. Or at least Mayhew tended to identify the American cause with the literary reputations of colonials:

> And if there be some animals adapted by nature to bear heavy burdens submissively—one of which, however, is said, on a certain occasion, to have had the gift of speech, and expostulated with his master for unjustly smiting him—I hope the Americans will never be reckoned as belonging to that spiritless, slavish kind, though their 'powers of speech' should not, in the opinion of some nameless, heroic, pamphleteer-scoffers in Britain, exceed those of the other, however defective they may be in point of 'eloquence.'

Once he had certified that his love of liberty was the product of wisdom, education, and taste—and only then—did Mayhew allow himself this elevated apostrophe to liberty:

> Once more then, hail! celestial maid, the daughter of God, and, excepting his Son, the first-born of heaven! Welcome to these shores again; welcome to every expanding heart! Long mayest thou reside among us, the delight of the wise, good and brave; the protectress of innocence from wrongs and oppression, the patroness of learning, arts, eloquence, virtue, rational loyalty, religion![112]

In addition to affording Mayhew an opportunity to display his erudite culture, this outburst of "enthusiasm" demonstrated Mayhew's felt commitment to the doctrines he espoused. If Mayhew succeeded at all in communicating these feelings, only a favored few Bostonians could or should have been touched, for his excursion from reason was designed not for the multitude, but for those who, possessed of some of Mayhew's advantages, had managed to cultivate a taste for such carefully controlled entertainment.

The Liberals of 1766 were little interested, however, in reaching a popular audience, whom secular orators, even when (as Joseph Warren) they wore togas, never dared confront with such undiluted neoclassicism. Among the mass of Americans, enlightened paganism proved no surrogate for the ethical and rhetorical precepts and practices of the Christian tradition. Unconcerned, Augustan rationalists continued to affect neoclassicism that they might dissociate themselves from the orthodoxy and the vulgarity of American Protestantism. Classical virtue, and especially the virtue of patriotism, had been seized on as a way of escaping the moral confinements of the Protestant tradition. Liberals filled their sermons with references to the public spirit of Athenian heroes, Spartan matrons, and Roman statesmen because they realized that the spirit of freedom which burned "like some pure etherial flame" in the breasts of the ancients had somehow led "to deeds of virtue and renown,"[113] while the vital indwelling spirit of Jonathan Edwards seemed to have led, at best, only to deeds of virtue.

The inner dynamic of all these Liberal efforts to define nobility anew was disclosed in a discourse delivered by Provost Smith at the commencement exercises of the College of Philadelphia, held one day after news of the Stamp Act repeal reached the city. Looking back on the events of 1765 and indeed summing up an era, Smith distinguished carefully between the noble and the ignoble resistants to the stamp tax, and announced that "the unguarded sallies of intemperate zeal will soon be forgotten." But "the steadfast, the noble, the patriotic

efforts of cool men," he rejoiced, "will more and more claim the regard of all the free, in every clime and age."[114] Many Americans,
Smith and Mayhew among them, had long suspected that they were
somehow superior to the mass of their fellow citizens. The Stamp Act
crisis, when some men had been so cool as to be nearly silent, gave
substance to that faith.

The sermons in which Liberals congratulated themselves on their
achievement were among the last in which their oratorical talents
were used to enkindle the sublime spirit of liberty. As America's
gentlemen had moved toward their goal, the vulgar herd had also
developed an unanticipated interest in public life. Disturbed by this
phenomenon, the Liberal ministry turned to restrain popular aspirations and grievances, so that the total effect of the utterances of 1766
was a summoning of the American populace back to law and duty.

In this respect, the sermons of 1766 were something of an anomaly
in the history of American Liberalism, for partisans of the legal
scheme normally preferred that social order be enforced by other
means than persuasion. Chauncy's *Seasonable Thoughts,* the most
comprehensive anti-Awakening lucubration, had concluded with a
demand that the clergy of New England hold fast to the seventeenth-
century faculty psychology, without which "it can't be but People
should run into Disorders."[115] But "in order to end the irregularities,"
it became necessary to silence the evangelical clergy and to otherwise
deal with religious enthusiasm with the force of the laws.[116] No sooner
had Liberals learned how to cope with the revival, however, than they
were confronted with a new enthusiasm in the form of political agitation. Even as hand joined in hand in 1747 on the occasion of Jonathan Mayhew's ordination to celebrate the suppression of religious
enthusiasm, Chauncy confessed, in his Election Sermon, that demagogues and the citizenry generally were taking a disturbing interest
in the financial policies of the provincial government. Chauncy instructed Governor Shirley that it was the magistrate's duty to preserve
the peace of society against such factious and seditious activities, and
this remained the Liberal political program for another eighteen
years.

Again after 1779 the Liberal ministry would contend that the domestic tranquillity be secured primarily through engines of coercion—
constitutions, courts, and, when necessary, militia, and, eventually,
Federal machinery for the silencing and jailing of sedition-mongers.
But at the time of the Stamp Act crisis, torn between a belief in the
justice of American resistance to the taxing representatives of the
Crown and a concern over the behavior of the lower orders of society,

the Liberal ministry were genuinely perplexed and did not know what to ask or expect of Governor Bernard. In 1766, almost by accident, and for want of normal sanctions, they were forced to assume a primary responsibility for controlling the populace. This responsibility would never again be uniquely theirs, but since such was their lot, they stand as the grandfathers of all those American orators who in later years more often sought to persuade and exhort the people of America to inaction than to inspirit them.

Faced in 1766 with a problem not unlike that posed by the Great Awakening, Liberals could not limit themselves to the propositions and imperatives of the essentially scholastic Election Sermon. It was not enough to declare to the immoderate (as Chauncy for instance had reminded the governor and august gentlemen of the General Court in 1747) that "order and superiority" in society simply were appropriate "both to the nature of man, and his circumstances in the world."[117] Nor would it suffice to articulate a theory of social contract limited by institutions and by charter. Believers in "rational liberty," Mayhew assumed, would immediately agree that Parliament had "general jurisdiction" over the colonies and that the King's seasonable willingness to redress American grievances should end all discussion of tyranny and "give a new spring and additional vigor" to American "loyalty and obedience."[118] Such reasonable men would also be able to distinguish between reasonable and unreasonable resistance to authority, perceiving (as Mayhew phrased it in one of his more succinct expressions of the rational mentality):

> That which may be excusable, and perhaps laudable, on some very singular emergencies, would at other times be pragmatical, seditious, and high-handed presumption.[119]

The objects of Mayhew's concern in 1766 were not, however, persons to whom the truth of these propositions would have been self-evident. The elements of the populace whom he sought to render quiescent seemed to him to be in "a sort of consternation not unlike to a frenzy occasioned by a raging fever."[120] Like the enthusiasts who had confronted Chauncy during the Great Awakening, these political zealots seemed "above the force of argument, beyond conviction from a calm and sober address to their understandings."[121] It is doubtful that anyone was in 1766 so irrational as Chauncy and Mayhew believed, but many were certainly, if only by their standards, quite unreasonable. In succeeding years the more reasonable men of America slowly learned how to communicate and deal with such enthusiasts. In Virginia, where political leaders were not only reasonable but rational, the eventual solution was an alliance of the enlightened with the enthusiasts. But the Boston answer, and the Liberal answer everywhere in 1766 or 1796, was some complex pattern of public address, marked by frequent departures from the sober precepts of reason, but designed to win the unreasonable populace back to what Liberals considered a reasonably judicious course of behavior.

The result was a seasonable rhetoric, marked by an interlacing and confusion of the moral and the practical, disposed cleverly but not fraudulently into a beguiling embodiment of the Liberal faith. One of Chauncy's appeals in 1766 was an exposure and denunciation of demagogues as both sinful and socially dangerous men. His analysis of the situation began with the observation that the people of Boston were being "needlessly and unreasonably irritated" by self-appointed tribunes. To demonstrate that those whom the people thought their friends were indeed their enemies, Chauncy explained that such demagogues wanted only "to serve themselves."[122] Mayhew also entered on the kind of character analysis which among Liberals was known as unmasking the cheat. Anyone who refuses reasonable allegiance to "all persons in authority," he argued, is neither a "true friend of liberty" nor a Christian, and therefore those who take the lead in continuing to revile the dignities of Britain and Massachusetts "show that while they speak great swelling words of vanity, making liberty the pretext, they themselves are the servants of corruption, the ignoble slaves of sin."[123]

The assault on demagogues in 1766 evinced the degree to which the Liberal ministry was engaged in competition for dominion over the American mind. Victory in such a contest depended in part on which of the contending oracles the people of America considered most sinful. Hesitant to rest their claims to pre-eminence on the ground of virtue alone, Liberals were always prepared to charge that demagogues were in league with those who wished no good to American society or were at least "willing to gratify such as are our enemies" in order to serve themselves.[124] In 1766 there may have been some point to fears that further agitation would strengthen the hand of the anti-American party in London. Such fears perhaps help account for the obsessive moderation of Liberal sermons on imperial affairs in the subsequent decade.

Liberals were at all times, and in all circumstances, willing to believe and to charge that their ambitious local opponents were ready to join with the enemies of America or had, indeed, already sealed the bargain. This quaint and endearing strain of mind took one of its most absurd forms when Jonathan Mayhew accused a Calvinist, whom he considered illiterate, of tormenting him in the hope of being made an Anglican bishop. The seed planted by Mayhew and Chauncy lay nearly dormant through most of the Revolution, but it flourished once more in the 1790's and eventually brought forth its finest flower in the 1812 Federalist-Unitarian faith that all leading New England Democrats were paid henchmen of Virginia grandees, and James Madison, in turn, a hireling of Napoleon. If the substance of this faith was an inability to see that their power of persuasion had waned, it was ever sustained by a hope that the people of New England would have their sight restored and would then rally behind their traditional and natural leaders.

In 1766 Liberals posed—by way of contrast to aspiring, sinful, and divisive demagogues—as the impartial friends of social solidarity. They invoked the image of a harmonious society and called on Americans to exert themselves in the "most prudent" and "most Christian" cause of Union.[125] What had begun as an imperial affair, rousing Americans of various ranks and stations in resistance to Britain, had generated, in the course of a year, the first clearly recognizable domestic political parties. Mayhew acknowledged this fact by asking, in his thanksgiving sermon, that Bostonians "abstain from all party names," and the Election Preacher, five days later, expressed his fears that, even after the repeal, "intestine heats" threatened to prevail in Massachusetts, that all issues might "be made matter of dispute" and that the citizens of the province seemed destined to "crumble into parties."[126] The Arminian clergy, of course, pointed to the unreasonableness and inadvisability of such divisions. Are there "any valuable ends to be served by perpetuating disputes?" Mayhew asked, and immediately replied that he could not "readily conceive of any."[127]

The substance of the Liberal message was identification of political nonpartisanship with essential Christian virtue. Recalling that "one whom we all profess to reverence" had given assurance of the blessedness of peacemakers, Mayhew summoned all Americans to endeavor, in their "several stations, to promote the common good, by love serving one another."[128] Yet such nonpartisanship was quite obviously a partisan ideology. Mayhew's sermon pleaded for acquiescence in and preservation of the Liberal order. Observing that "some were blamed" as having been "too warm and sanguine" in 1765, others "too phlegmatic and indifferent in the common and noble cause of liberty," Mayhew judiciously refused to decide "how far these accusations were just or unjust on either side."[129] Such a demurrer could not, however, disguise Mayhew's commitments, for the warm and sanguine patriots of 1765 were, after all, the very persons whose excesses Mayhew bemoaned and whom he was seeking to pacify in 1766, while the phlegmatic and indifferent, on the other hand, were, like Mayhew, satisfied with a settlement which returned America to the *status quo* of 1763.

Though 1766 marked the first extensive use of such appeals in a distinctly political context, these supplications had precedent in the prayers for Christian unity uttered in the colonies ever since the Great Awakening. Ezra Stiles, whose 1760 *Discourse on the Christian Union* was one of the more famous expressions of this ideal, claimed to speak for no party, but only to seek an end to religious and social controversy. Yet when Liberals called for union, the dangerous and divisive elements in American society were inevitably those who challenged the social order from below.

There were, of course, many Americans who embraced the Liberal ideal of union in 1766. Yet some, generally those discontented with the stations assigned them, were finding more attractive a theory of the relationship of liberty and union developed by the Calvinists. These colonists were not so confident as Mayhew of the eminent virtue and utility of burying "in oblivion what is past" and "beginning our civil, political life anew, as it were, from this joyful era of restored and confirmed liberty."[130] Some believed that there was, indeed, something quite valuable to be gained by perpetuating disputes. Not everyone in America agreed that liberties, like persons, were gradable, from the most important to the insignificant; and many would not have accepted the Liberal scale of values. These incredulous Americans might not have perceived or appreciated what Chauncy once termed the danger "of losing *real* liberties, in the strife for those that are *imaginary*; or *valuable* ones, for such as are of *trifling* consideration."[131]

Liberties which Chauncy considered trifling became increasingly valuable to many Americans in the decade before the Revolution, particularly to those colonists occupying social stations also trifling by Liberal standards. They asked and pressed for a more "perfect liberty," and hearkened to those enthusiasts and demagogues who held such liberty essential if Americans were to achieve a union more harmonious and more excellent than that permitted within the organized structure of Liberal society. The ears of such should have been closed to Mayhew's invocation of Christian union, though, as in 1800, 1830, or 1850, many no doubt were hypnotized by mere words. And as throughout our history, others, realizing that Liberals were not wholly wrong in branding as selfishly depraved those who challenged the standing order, suppressed aspirations they knew to be sinful and were lulled for the moment into quiescence.

Throughout 1766 Liberals attempted to convince the populace that continued political agitation was a sinful act, and cheerful compliance with the ordinances of the powers-that-were a virtuous one. Yet Liberal sermons, designed to render Americans less restless, were paradoxically a stimulus to additional popular discontent. Liberals were themselves filled with an overwhelming conviction that the repeal of the Stamp Act was "powerfully fit," as Chauncy announced, "to excite a sense of pleasure in the breasts of all." Good men, patriots and lovers of liberty, might be "uneasy" when their country was threatened with a deprivation of the blessings which contributed to its prosperity. But when things returned to their ordinary state, all such uneasiness was to end, and those who remained uneasy knew not the things which belonged to their peace.

By discussing the crisis in terms of "uneasiness" and "pleasure," Liberals affirmed their belief that all Americans who did not see things as Liberals saw them were not only irrational, but depraved. When Chauncy likened his personal response to the repeal to the pleasure "felt by one that is athirst upon being satisfied with agreeable drink,"[132] he was implicitly insisting that everyone should be as delighted in 1766 as if he had been granted his soul's salvation.*[133] "Pleasure" and "uneasiness" were significant, perhaps central, terms in the Liberal ethical vocabulary, concepts derived from Hutcheson's theory of the moral sense. The moral sense, Mayhew believed, was an additional faculty given man by his Creator to allow him "to distinguish between moral good and evil." By means of this faculty, he explained, "moral good and evil, when they are objects to our minds, affect us in a very different manner; the first affording us pleasure, the other pain and uneasiness."[134] Thus the pleasure taken by a good man in the happiness of his country was a moral response, as was his uneasiness when its prosperity was endangered. Only if one's moral sense were depraved, rationalists concluded, would he be uneasy when confronted by a prospect that the good man found supremely pleasing.

On the basis of this theory alone Liberals were able to conclude unhesitatingly in 1766 that those Americans who remained uneasy when they had "so fair a prospect" before them were morally depraved.[135] By indicting these uneasy citizens, however, the Liberal ministry only courted a more difficult predicament. For most Americans, once under a conviction of sin, became even more uneasy and, indeed, searched for a way to relieve their anxieties. Not having read Hutcheson, they all too readily located the source of their uneasiness elsewhere than

* Chauncy's discussion of the "joy" of 1765 was informed by a belief, common to Liberals and the more rational orthodox, that pleasure and sorrow were "excited, according to the different scenes God in his providence opens to us," and that being put "into agreeable circumstances, begets a joy and gladness of heart." No Calvinist, however rational, would have suggested that this pleasure was a surrogate for the New Birth, but in 1766 there were many who found it disturbing that Americans were beginning to prefer these "human" joys to the divine pleasures of regeneration.

within themselves and endeavored, for the next ten years, not to cultivate their moral sense but to change the prospect before them.

The Liberal efforts to alleviate the uneasiness of the American people in 1766 were similarly paradoxical. That they should have tried to relieve the populace revealed the extent to which they had already assumed a defensive posture and were unwilling or unable simply to crack the skulls of the depraved in order to subdue them. Instead they attempted to portray the social situation in such terms that any American, regardless of station or aspirations, might derive gratification from the world about him. This rendition of reality was a conscious rhetorical device and the product of a confessedly selective process of observation. Liberals concluded that a man is uneasy when he should be pleased because he "fixes an eye upon the dark side of things, inattentive to the sunshine, that illuminates the other side" and thus ignores "the manifold blessings that are mixed with all the adversities of the present life."[136] To compensate for this foreboding quality of the American mind, from which few in 1766 were completely free, Liberals gave particular and perhaps undue attention to the more smiling aspects of American life.

Out of William Smith's desire to still the murmurs and complaints of the populace came some of the first literary celebrations of the glories and the promises of a prosperous America, in part, of course, the products of conviction, but the better half of pure inventiveness:

> Where ignorance and barbarity frowned over the uncultivated earth, gay fields now smile, bedecked in the yellow robe of full-eared harvest; cities rise majestic to the view; fleets too croud the capacious harbour with their swelling canvas, and swarms of chearful inhabitants cover the shore with monuments of their industry, through a long tract of two thousand miles.[137]

The difficulty with these lofty strains of celebration, however, lay in the fact that such prospects of a happy nation served also as the Liberal rhetorical technique for inducing the sublime patriotic emotion of love of country. In making their picture of the nation sufficiently selective that uneasy Americans might be satisfied, they ran the danger of departing so far from "just notions" of the general welfare that reasonable Americans would consider them visionary—and indeed of animating all sorts of Americans to the pursuit of a greater happiness than that actually provided them in 1766.

To escape from this dilemma, Liberals inevitably turned to portraying this surfeit of blessings somewhere over the horizon—but not so far over the horizon that they could not be anticipated and espied by reasonable prophets. Thus in 1766 the Massachusetts Election

Preacher called on all the citizens of the province to "look forward to a distant day" when, according to his perceptions, they would

> behold the wilderness blossoming like a rose, under the cultivation of the hand of industry. We behold our commercial interests flourishing,—the land of our original pouring in her ample stores upon us, for *convenience* and *delight,* we making as ample returns, to the increase of her *strength* and *opulence.*[138]

These visions of the future stood as promises to discontented Americans that their society would soon be so blessed that everyone, by sharing in the bounty, would be filled with the most consummate pleasure. Thus Chauncy, though he admitted in 1766 that the repeal had not brought prosperity to all, insisted that it had "laid the foundation for future prosperity" so well that few could fail to share in it.[139]

Again, such an appeal was designed as much to arouse as to subdue. In urging men to pious endeavor, for instance, it was just such "apprehensions and views" of future felicity, either heavenly or temporal, which Liberals used to inspire "a fervent zeal" and to arouse men to "the most active and vigorous exertions" to attain that felicity.[140] In 1766 they had no desire to augment the zeal of Americans or to encourage any further active exertions whatsoever, and yet, by painting these pictures of future happiness they were implicitly inviting all Americans to become patriots and to contend for the welfare of their country. Only Americans of a Liberal persuasion, however, would have found these visions appealing, for this delightful and convenient Liberal future was no more than a reasonable extrapolation from the harmonious order of 1763, and anyone who yearned for a transcendently happier society would have been no more inspired by white harbors than by yellow corn. And those who aspired to another heaven than the one promised by the Liberals were the very persons who in 1766 saw the darkness and the shadows of American life which William Smith so carefully overlooked.

Perhaps because of the inherent impossibility of subduing zealous and uneasy Americans by such devices, Liberals took recourse in 1766 to appeals based entirely on the mandates of the Scripture and called the people of America to order through a convention which, when employed by the orthodox clergy in all its rigor, comprised what has been termed the jeremiad. This sermon form reflected a belief that all difficulties came as punishments for a society's sins, that these afflictions could be removed only by repentance, and that their removal was occasion for demonstration that such repentance had been sincere. The Liberal "Jeremiahs" of 1766, were, however, quite discreet in correlating the dispensations of Providence with the obligations of American Christians.

Mayhew's thanksgiving sermon of 1766, *The Snare Broken,* opened with a reminder that on such occasions men should render "devout thanks to God, whose kingdom ruleth over all" and sing "His high praises." But after one rather hasty paragraph devoted to such homage, he quickly turned to considering the repeal as a guarantor of the "peace and prosperity" of the empire and as an event "peculiarly affecting the welfare of these colonies."[141] The remainder of his message consisted of "counsels and exhortations respecting your duty to God and man, as agreeable to the sacred oracles, to the dictates of sober reason, and adapted to the occasion."[142] Mayhew of course offered a number of more or less soberly reasonable arguments for restraint, but like other clerical rationalists he made certain that his precepts were well reinforced by oracular wisdom. When the task of subduing the disorderly was most difficult, Mayhew reminded his auditors that for "so seasonable, so signal, so important" an "appearance of divine Providence" they owed not only gratitude but "the obedience of [their] lives."[143]

Liberals were deliberately perfunctory in urging spiritual reformation on the people of New England, preferring—as good Arminians—to summon them only to moral behavior. Let each of us, concluded a Providence rationalist, "endeavor to form his conduct upon the noble maxims of Christianity, that our lives may speak the grateful sentiments of our hearts."[144] Except for this singular disdain for piety, however, their jeremiads were in theory not unusual, for they called on Americans to do "all things whatsoever it has pleased God to command" in order to testify to the sincerity of their gratitude.[145] But Christian conduct according to Scripture entailed a list of mandates no different in kind from what was found, to the Liberal satisfaction, in the nature of things.

Indeed Charles Chauncy's version of "due acknowledgments to the great Sovereign of the world" seemed only a variation of the Tory doctrines which Liberals professed to have exploded. Chauncy was by comparison to most Liberals a paragon of orthodoxy in 1766, for he devoted nearly two pages of his published text to paeans of thanksgiving, but when he turned to the obligations of Americans in consequence of their "deliverance," God's will, as Chauncy revealed it, seemed peculiarly Liberal:

> And as he has particularly enjoined us to be 'subject to the higher powers, ordained by him to be his ministers for good,' we cannot, upon this occasion, more properly express our gratitude to him than by approving ourselves dutiful and loyal to the gracious king whom he has placed over us . . . And if we should take occasion, from the great lenity and condescending goodness of those who are

supreme in authority over us, not to 'despise government,' not to 'speak evil of dignities,' not to go into any method of unseemly, disorderly conduct, but to 'lead quiet and peaceable lives in all godliness and honesty,'—every man moving in his own proper sphere, and taking due care to 'render unto Caesar the things that are Caesar's, and to God the things that are God's'—we should honor ourselves, answer the expectations of those who have dealt favorably with us, and, what is more, we should express a becoming regard to the governing pleasure of Almighty God.[146]

The ultimate weakness of the Liberal jeremiads lay in their central premise: these thanksgiving rites were festivals not of submission to the will of the Almighty but of gratitude for favors received. So heterodox indeed were prosperous Americans in their notion of man's relationship to God that David Rowland had to caution his congregation against *"Epicurean* atheism, or *Stoic* insensibility" as reactions to the repeal. Yet Rowland came as close as possible to espousing the viewpoints he officially deplored, for he argued the case for Providence solely in terms of its blessings for man. "Every event is a divine dispensation," but most events, he hastened to assure his people, are "subservient to the good of intelligent beings."[147] Though Liberals hinted that "the bonds we are under to the Lord of the universe" had something to do with His power, as well as His kindness, they were far from the piety of their forefathers. So far as Chauncy was concerned, God was to be praised in 1766 not because he was God but simply because of "the greatness of his goodness in thus scattering our fears, removing away our burdens, and continuing us in the enjoyment of our most high valued liberties and privileges."[148]

Liberal gratitude was spread, moreover, among the King of England, Parliamentary Whigs, and the merchants of London and Boston. Whatever God's role in effecting the repeal, they believed that He had clearly worked through the "instrumentality or agency of men,"[149] and that a thanksgiving service would be incomplete without considerable recognition of those "means or instruments" He had chosen to employ.[150] Although techniques for converting the thanksgiving sermon into a eulogy of the living were undeveloped and amateurish by comparison to those which evolved in America after the Revolution, their purpose was similar. If gratitude implied obedience, then grateful Americans might be expected to obey not only God and King, but the gentlemen-merchants of America whose contributions to the cause of repeal Liberals thought most efficacious.

Jonathan Mayhew reached this conclusion by making what he called the "natural transition from fearing God to honoring the king." From there he proceeded to explain how the efforts of "our friends in

Britain" laid Americans under "an additional obligation, in point of gratitude," to Pitt and the other patriots who had been "the principal means of saving Britain and her colonies from impending ruin." Chauncy was just as direct in urging "a just sense of the obligations we are under," not merely to the Crown and ministry, but to local objects of esteem—among them the "serviceable" lawyers and merchants who had set "forth the reasons they had for complaint in a fair, just and strongly convincing light, hereby awakening the attention of Great Britain."[151] More orthodox Americans, of course, had no difficulty in comprehending God's working through second causes, but they insisted that Americans must look beyond whatever instruments God "hath been pleased to make use of" and give Him all the praise. "I think too much has formerly been said," complained one evangelical clergyman in 1766, "about ministerial wisdom," and others wondered if the "illustrious patriots" and *friends of liberty* were not seeking to "rob God of his due" by taking credit for a deliverance that He alone had accomplished.[152] Among other things, the Calvinist clergy seemed to be asking why God should in any case have chosen as one of his instruments the prose style of the legal profession and of Charles Chauncy.

Whether any American felt under grateful obligations to George III, Pitt, Hancock, or even the rationalist Deity would be determined finally by what he thought the repeal had actually accomplished. Liberals were certain that it brought happiness and that all Americans, because so obviously happy, should be grateful and therefore docile. This conviction, and all the ideas which informed it, were compacted by Jonathan Mayhew into this final appeal for the Liberal program:

> Without this due regard to government and laws, we shall still be miserable, notwithstanding all that God and the king have done to make us happy. If one had wings like a dove, it were better to fly far away, and remain alone in the wilderness . . . than to live in a society where there is no order, no subordination; but anarchy and confusion reign.[153]

For Puritans the wilderness had been the region into which an angry God cast those of His people with whom He had controversy. As a metaphor it had served reasonable New England for generations (and would continue to do so for generations more) as an image of all the conceivable unhappiness in the world. In the course of the eighteenth century, however, the Canaan into which Americans had passed after trial and testing was somehow no longer the Christian garden of the early Puritans, but the Augustan civilization of America's Liberals. This reasonable paradise had not in fact brought happiness to many

Americans, some of whom were waiting in the 1760's for the dove to descend that they might be released from it, and preferred even confusion to such an infelicitous order.

In 1766 happiness came most easily to the Liberals, according to whom the entire universe worked together for good, particularly in British America. Assured of God's "wise and good Constitution of Things,"[154] Liberals were happy in the belief that God's goodness was "visible wherever we cast our eyes."[155] The source of Liberal happiness is suggested by this declaration:

> The communication of happiness being the end of creation, it will follow, from the perfections of the creator, that the whole plan of things is so adjusted as to promote the benevolent purpose; to which the immense diversity in his works, the gradation of species that we know of, and many more perhaps than we know of, and the somewhat similar gradation in the same species, arising from their make, their connections, and the circumstances they are placed in, are happily subservient.

By 1765 Liberals saw the benevolence of the Deity in the historical process. That God intended the human race to advance continuously "towards a state of perfection and happiness" was evident to them in all the "Wonderful operations of Providence." The same end should have been clear, they argued, to everyone "capable of taking notice" of all these remarkable dispensations, both in the history of past nations and in that of the society "they have lived in."[156]

Yet, even as Liberals rejoiced in these providential operations, they implicitly suggested that few Americans were sufficiently rational, temperate, and cultivated, or otherwise privileged enough to appreciate them. The "great design" of the Arminian God provided a "rational and benevolent pleasure" to its beholders, and His dispensations were "exercising and entertaining to the inquisitive." Not every person would perceive this wondrous scheme, they allowed, but only "every thoughtful person," and of these, more "especially those who have been elevated above the common level of mankind."[157] Few Americans had been prepared, by 1766, to achieve this sublime perspective; and, though Liberals realized this, they did little to mitigate the situation.*[158] They could only lament the fact that so few Americans shared this vision, for out of the distorted perceptions of the populace had arisen the false political zeal of 1765.

Liberals were forced to conclude that the unhappy Americans of 1766 were irrational, insensitive, ungrateful, and depraved asses, but

---

* "Let us all," Mayhew abjured his elite congregation, "love and honor, extol and obey the God and Father of all, whose tender mercies are over all his works; and who has been gracious and bountiful to ourselves in particular."

they genuinely wished that all Americans had been happy. Liberal concern for the happiness of their countrymen had much to do with the questions that grumbling Americans asked about the Liberal version of the workings of Providence. In answer to these questions clerical rationalists insisted that Americans ought to be happy, but their insistence only barely disguised their anxieties. "O happy *America!*" cried William Smith before differentiating between unguarded zealots and cool patriots, "if now we but knew how to prize our happiness."[159] In the next few years it began to be suggested that all Americans could indeed be happy if only God were given some assistance in diffusing the good among the members of His family. Such cavillers Liberals arraigned as deniers of the Divine pleasure. All "outward advantages," one minister explained, "that any person or people enjoy, are not casual events, but proceed from the righteous disposal of our heavenly Father."[160] If some Americans wondered whether a a righteous God really intended that urban gentry aggrandize these advantages, or use them as they had, Liberals could only counsel patience. God's "Wisdom so conducts the Eternal Scheme," according to William Smith's early *Meditation* on this very question, "that, however it may now appear to Thy short-sighted creatures, it will at last unfold itself in a perfect consistent Whole."[161]

Such notions of the Divine benevolence of the Deity working through history took some while to be codified theologically in Boston, largely because there the idea of progress was imposed so abruptly on what less than a decade earlier had been officially a dismal and abject premillenarianism. The altered vision of the promise of American life also posed new questions, for which satisfactory answers were not immediately forthcoming. When asked why the future offered no more than exaggeration of the existing arrangements of an unequal distribution of the good, the Liberal rejoinder was equivocal. Only after the Revolution, when Dudleian lecturers ceased contending that even "the meanest capacity" could discern the eternal goodness in the nature of things, were they prepared to answer promptly that a tasteful perception of the nature of Divine benevolence was probably available only to readers of the *Monthly Anthology*. But even before then they were persuaded that all reasonable, dispassionate, and cultivated men would take complacent delight in the constitution of things: "We ought not to consider its displays as they affect *individual beings only*," was Charles Chauncy's ultimate and confident explication of the mysteries of Providence, "but as they relate to the *particular system* of which they are parts."[162] To question the manner in which the goods of the world were disposed was, in sum, evidence of a sinful opposition to the Divine decree.

In the decade after the Stamp Act crisis, however, even the Liberal mind occasionally confessed that Providence could act somewhat perplexingly. Not only did the Deity witness on commercial America the plague of the Townshend duties, but those Americans who differed with the reasonable view of American society and of the individuals who controlled it began again to translate their sentiments into political action. When this occurred, God seemed less entertaining to the advocates of the legal scheme, for even the least inquisitive began to sense that in time their feet could also slide.

Rather conveniently for the later reputation of the rationalist clergy, Jonathan Mayhew died within months of the Stamp Act repeal. His life and words untroubled by the turbulent political waters of the succeeding decade, Mayhew stands serenely as the exemplary Liberal revolutionary. Chauncy's prayer at Mayhew's funeral (the first such violation of Popery-dreading tradition in the city on the hill) and the eulogies delivered by Gay and Chauncy on subsequent Sabbaths began the process whereby Mayhew has come to be remembered as "eminently a friend to liberty, both civil and religious."[163] As perpetuated and embellished by Mayhew's nineteenth-century Federalist-Unitarian memorialists, this myth has accorded Mayhew a sort of sainthood as herald not only of a "liberal faith" but of American democracy.

Yet even in 1838 Alden Bradford, author of the first book-length biography of Mayhew, found it necessary to defend his hero from the aspersions of those men of little and illiberal faith who argued that Mayhew's writings "were not important in support of the cause of civil and religious liberty."[164] These doubters showed a wisdom denied to many later historians, not all of them necessarily heirs to the Harvard tradition, who cling to a flattering image of Mayhew. Their image invariably includes speculation that had Mayhew lived he would have saved Harrison Gray—for whom he was "an oracle"—from Toryism. It is an unwise legend that ignores other possible consequences of the Mayhew-Gray friendship, and the mythmakers have also carefully avoided the painful implications of the behavior of Mayhew's respectable congregation in the first years of the Revolution. When Simeon Howard, Mayhew's successor in the West Church pulpit, returned in 1777 from Annapolis Royal (where though reputedly "a decided Whig," he had gone with his friends in 1775) he found the church so reduced in numbers—by what one chronicler of the sorry affair euphemistically styles "death, emigration, and other causes"— that thoughts of disbanding the society were seriously entertained.[165]

That the legend persists despite this record is probably testimony to the effectiveness of John Adams' reminiscences. Looking back over a half century and recalling the "awakening and revival of American principles" in the early 1760's, Adams named Mayhew as perhaps the fifth most important spokesman for those principles. Because Adams also remarked that this "enthusiasm . . . went on increasing till, in 1775, it burst out in open violence, hostility, and fury,"[166] historians have all too eagerly assumed that Mayhew, had he lived to those latter days, would have been in the first rank of the revolutionaries. To such a Tory as Peter Oliver, who was in effect competing with Adams for the allegiances of "respectable" New Englanders, Mayhew likewise seemed the most dangerous of sedition-mongers. But from another perspective it seems at least questionable that Mayhew, had he lived, would have been a zealous revolutionary in the 1770's. His Liberal colleagues, his students, and indeed nearly all the clergymen who shared Mayhew's ideology were, if rebels, then among the more reluctant and the least energetic. For Mayhew to have made a different contribution to the uprising of 1775 it would have been necessary for him to overcome his aversions to violence, revivals, awakenings, and popular enthusiasm.

Yet, far from all who proclaimed the glorious Revolution were radicals or enthusiasts. Whatever Mayhew's political allegiances, he at least exemplified that brand of libertarianism that asserts the individual's inalienable right "of thinking for himself."[167] It was in just such a vein that Robert Treat Paine (who was soon to exchange his given name, Thomas, for that of a father and lamented brother, in brave disdain for the author of *The Rights of Man*) apostrophized Mayhew at Harvard commencement in 1792:

> For this great truth he boldly led the van,
> *That private judgment is the right of man.*[168]

That Paine himself warmly saluted the Sedition Act does not necessarily detract from the merits of his eulogy, for among the New England Liberals of his day Mayhew was certainly a free thinker. Indeed he was so much the maverick that in early life he was renowned for his honesty rather than for his prudence. In this respect, as Mayhew admitted, he differed from "*many* of my own order," such as, presumably, Andrew Eliot, whose "prudence in party matters, especially in politics," earned him the sobriquet "Andrew Sly."[169]

Mayhew grew increasingly circumspect in later life and eventually succumbed to the ways of the metropolis, but not until he had publicly declared that the purpose of "speaking, especially of preaching, is to express, not to disguise a man's real sentiments."*[170] Mayhew's frank-

---

* Mayhew's relationship with other Boston Liberals was, to say the least, somewhat singular. Mayhew's frankness seems to have perplexed the other members of

ness at times verged toward exhibitionism, for his was the manner of one "born with so sumptuous a supply of self-reliance," as M. C. Tyler long ago observed, that he was "quite incapable of suspecting that his own illumination was not a match for that of all other men and of all past ages."[171] With a few minor changes, Thomas Hutchinson's characterization of John Adams would fit Mayhew quite well: he was one who "could not look with complacency upon any man who was in possession of more wealth, more honours, or more knowledge than himself."[172] Whoever surpassed Jonathan Mayhew in any of these respects (or claimed to) gained his undying enmity, and from all such tyrants he claimed his independence.*[173]

Insofar as Mayhew's *ad hominem* defiance of Kings and Popes had an element of popular appeal, he was perhaps "a sort of tribune of the people."[174] Yet his defenses of private rights, be it remembered, were as often directed against majorities as against monarchs. (It is no accident that his *Discourse on Unlimited Submission* was republished in the years when New England Federalists were trying to dignify the Hartford Convention as a successor to the Stamp Act Congress.) Mayhew's unbridled ridicule, moreover, fell far more readily on the Calvinist rabble of New England than on his betters in lawn. Mayhew's most famous declaration of intellectual independence, in fact, appeared in a 1763 reply to a Calvinist critic of his Arian doctrines—an effort which even Mayhew's most fawning admirers have never considered among his more noble productions.

The opening paragraphs of this *Letter of Reproof* to John Cleaveland contain a few sentences worth transcribing as an example of what were considered by the most liberal of Boston Liberals to be the rights of man:

> Can you possibly think it became you, an obscure person from another province, and one so unlettered as you are, an outcast from the college to which you was [sic] a disgrace? . . . Did you not show the utmost assurance, in thus setting up your little self? . . . Poor, unhappy man! You doubtless thought to emerge from your obscurity, and to appear as a person of some consequence, by this vain attempt.[175]

---

this mutual admiration society as much as their efforts to hide their heterodoxy from the public gaze amused him. Since Mayhew's near-Deism might have illumined too brightly the implications of the doctrines propounded by Chauncy and Gay, he was never asked to deliver the Dudleian Lecture on Natural Religion. Harvard honored him, however, by asking him to deliver the quadrennial discourse on "Popish idolatry," a subject which lent itself to nondoctrinal treatment.

* An antagonist in the episcopacy controversy referred to Mayhew's "invincible spleen and envy at all those that are in higher stations than himself." But Peter Oliver, hardly a populist, thought Mayhew's grossest flaw was a contempt for all those he considered inferior to himself.

Chauncy could dismiss Mayhew's antagonist as "an obscure person, without reputation," but then Chauncy was born to the purple, the grandson of a Harvard president, while Mayhew was a Nantucket boy who had perhaps too quickly made a reputation in the big city.[176] This reputation Mayhew managed to retain and augment by the easy means of flogging a dead king and inveighing against "high-church tory-principles and maxims."[177] But those who hear in that invective the true accents of American democracy mistake an *ignis fatuus* for a burning and shining light.

VI

THE WISDOM OF
GOD IN THE
PERMISSION OF SIN

I T I S easier to ascertain the ultimate form of the political thought of Calvinism than to trace the precise sequence whereby the evangelical view of society and politics impinged on the American mind. Three days after the engagements at Lexington and Concord, for instance, John Cleaveland demanded that Americans "cut off and make a final end" of the British army and of "every base Tory among us, or confine" the latter "to Simsbury mines."[1] Cleaveland's convictions were by no means surprising, considering the thrust of evangelical thinking; yet in the ten years before 1775 he had spoken only intermittently, and frequently only incidentally, on political subjects. Like the generality of the Calvinist ministry, he had been arguing not politics but theological questions, and arguing them not so much with the representatives of the empire as with the Liberal clergy of the colonies. In many respects, there was little discontinuity from the Calvinist crusade against Arminianism to its engagement in the Revolution. The manner in which Calvinists stated the case against Liberal religion in the twenty years before Independence provided their people with a definition of the "sin" against which they moved in the years of a Revolution that was not for them simply a struggle for independence from England.

The contribution of the Calvinist ministry to the formation of the Revolutionary mind is not to be discovered in the same places where

Liberals etched their record. Among other things, the Calvinist response to the public events of the era between the Awakening and the Revolution was not often registered, as was that of other elements of the "black regiment," on official days of fast and thanksgiving. The reasons for Edwards' indifference to such occasions have already been noted. Much of his thinking was shared by the other evangelical clergy, who conceived of the dispensations of Providence only as they related to God's "real saints." The course of history, as they interpreted it, largely respected the manner in which God came to "the help of his people," and not His treatment of what, in more orthodox circles, was conceived as an "externally-covenanted nation."[2] History was meaningful only as it bore some seeming relationship to the progress and improvement of the Visible Church.

Dissenter response to fast and thanksgiving days was compounded by an extreme sensitivity to civil interference with the church. Between 1765 and 1775, for instance, many Calvinist ministers, albeit good Whigs, were reluctant to acquiesce in *any* public summons to hold services on public occasions. In 1775 Eleazar Wheelock, under pressure to observe "Congress Sunday," explained that his church had already held one fast service that spring. To do so again "purely and only out of respect and obedience to the advice of Congress," he asserted, "would be an open affront to the King of Zion, unprecedented in America, and expressive of a principle abhorred by all Protestants." A day of humiliation, Wheelock reminded his congregation, was a spiritual event, meaningful only to a church "deliberating upon the moral reasons for it, and solemnly agreeing therein."[3] By so limiting their discussion of public affairs to those "special times and seasons"[4] when they felt spiritually justified in speaking, the Calvinist ministry left a discontinuous record of their response to public issues and events.*[5]

Days of praise and humiliation were truly congenial only to those American Protestants who retained the covenant theology, and insofar as Calvinists participated in such occasions they were implicitly tending to something of a reconstituted orthodoxy. Yet the metaphysics and the psychology which underlay the Calvinist theory of God's "moral government" were, as was earlier indicated, by no means retrograde concessions to inherited patterns of thought. Similarly, the manner in which Calvinist clergymen justified participation in

---

* In the late 1790's Federal fast proclamations became a burning issue in national politics, and dissenters so conspicuously refused to observe such occasions that the political attitude of their clergy in 1798 and 1799 must in most cases be deduced from the reports of hostile critics or from New Light celebrations of the "deliverance" of 1800.

fast and thanksgiving days indicates that such involvement was not necessarily symptomatic of declension from the insights of the Awakening. Rather such participation was part of the process whereby the precepts of the evangelical scheme came to be enforced on the life and thought of the colonies.

The Calvinist theory of fast days was largely a recapitulation of the evangelical refusal to accept the possibility that worldly men and nations could direct history to their purposes, rather than God's. Battles, sieges, fortunes were, according to Samuel Davies, all contingent on the working of an unseen but all-controlling Divine agency. A "nation," he explained, must be judged "in the present world," according to its "national work," unlike individuals, who would be finally rewarded or punished only in the world to come. What this implied, as Davies articulated the theory during the French and Indian War, was the absolute sovereignty of God in imperial affairs:

> The nation is thrown off from the hinge on which empire turns, and therefore must fall. The Lord of Armies is against them; and by a secret but irresistible hand, brings on their destruction.[6]

By the 1770's the notion of God's moral government of the nations had been fully translated by the Calvinist mind into its own interpretation of the course of empire. The "divine glory" was abundantly displayed, according to Samuel Buell, by the degree to which great imperial powers were prepared, even in their moment of greatest triumph, for a humbling defeat and for replacement, in the hierarchy of nations, by another:

> Mighty monarchies are but wheels rolled about, which often suddenly rush into ruin. States and kingdoms, which by strange turns and vicissitudes of earthly grandeur and glory—singing like *Babylon,* 'I sit a queen and shall see no sorrows,' in one fatal hour, sink under plagues and miseries unutterable; rise no more forever.—While *some* thus sink, others as suddenly rise, grow great in their turn, and become the terror of the world.[7]

What the Calvinist theory of Providence represented, in sum, was a conviction that neither France nor Britain could long sway the destiny of the world, that God somehow had power to control the course of history for His own more proper purposes.

The general Calvinist unwillingness to join in days of fasting derived from a belief that too often secular men wrongly interpreted the signs of the times. Wheelock's hesitancy in 1775, for instance, clearly expressed his feeling that the outbreak of the Revolution was not an affliction but probably an unadorned blessing, and that if God had a controversy with His American people it was presumably because they had delayed too long in acting on behalf of their own general welfare. Here precisely was the rationale for what eventually became the readiness of evangelical Americans to join in days of thanksgiving. Such occasions, as distinguished from days of humiliation, were a happy reminder of the Calvinist doctrine that the very nature of society prescribed collective praise, since God's earthly dispensations were, after all, communal.

By the late years of the Revolution Calvinists were urging thanksgivings in terms of "the common laws of society" that obliged all men to join in expressions of gratitude for the felicity of "communities, as collective bodies." When they concurrently allowed that on such occasions the true saint was under no coercion, but was moved to rejoice in the general welfare "from the purer springs of benevolence," Calvinists disclosed the hidden significance of their intermittent speculations on the purport and purpose of fast and thanksgiving days.[8] Over the course of thirty years they had moved from a disenchantment with the course of colonial history to a celebration of the fact that the saints, having engaged themselves in political affairs, had seemingly succeeded in imposing their moral law on American society.

Something of the process whereby this end was achieved can be followed in the record of the New Side Presbyterians, who in the 1740's found it necessary to argue for their people's participation in days of thanksgiving. That they did so at all had much to do with the fact that in New Jersey at least the evangelical party had, in Governor Jonathan Belcher, a magistrate whose person and policies identified him as one of their own. Gilbert Tennent was instrumental in having Belcher declare in 1749 the first public thanksgiving ever to be held in New Jersey. When the day arrived, Tennent found it necessary to devote much of his sermon to answering those church members who questioned the propriety of offering praise to the "King of Zion" on an occasion appointed by the state and celebrated not merely by saints but by "carnal men."

Praise awaits God, Tennent explained, only "in Zion, in his visible Church and Kingdom," but it "indeed is due to GOD from all the World."[9] In effect, Tennent was arguing the applicability of the moral law even to the unregenerate, but his more difficult task was that of demonstrating the propriety of the saints' expressing gratitude for God's kindnesses, not to the Church, but to the general society. This theme Tennent had already touched on in 1745, when he persuaded the New Side churches to celebrate the victory of Louisburg. His arguments* for the fitness and propriety of communal praise indicate that

* The first of Tennent's arguments concerned the effect of such a ritual on the

Tennent was using the occasion as but another strategy for overcoming what he considered the prevailing moral illness of the post-Awakening years: the antinomian smugness of the professing saints. Benefits "which tend to promote the publick Interest," Tennent contended, claim "peculiar acknowledgements; for surely so much more extensive any Good is, so much the more valuable it is."[10] A thanksgiving day, in sum, was a reminder that the general good was far more precious in the eyes of God than that of any particular individual—and should be likewise in the eyes of the godly.

One of Tennent's achievements during the warfare of the 1740's was to instill in his Presbyterian following a sense of the saint's obligations to society. He and the New Side clergy had of course been generally insisting that "Christ is not exalted, but dishonour'd and the Interests of His Kingdom betray'd, while any that assume the Character of His Ambassadors neglect to inculcate the Moral Law."[11] But during the 1740's he applied this insight specifically to public affairs. He strove to convince his people that the way of the Moravians and the Quakers was not to be theirs when an opportunity arose to "contribute to the Safety and Advantage of the Province."[12] In the Louisburg sermon, for instance, he declared that "Private Interest" is "no farther excellent than as it is consistent with, and conducive to the Good of the Publick, which we were born to promote."[13]

This utterance, the first of many by which Tennent roused his people to active public service under the terms of the moral law, bears comparison with the arguments advanced by Benjamin Franklin, writing over the signature of "Plain Truth," in Pennsylvania's difficult years of the mid-1740's:

> Is not the whole Province one Body, united by living under the same Laws, and enjoying the same Priviledges? Are not the People of City and Country connected as Relations both by Blood and Marriage, and in Friendships equally dear? Are they not likewise united in Interest and mutually useful and necessary to each other?[14]

Tennent's thanksgiving sermons, like his sermons of the 1740's generally, were a contribution to what Franklin took to be the war effort. But they were also trenchant and succinct demurrers from the social and political theory of the American disciples of John Locke. We are "born for *Society*," Tennent insisted, of which

> mutual *Love* is the *Band* and *Cement* . . . For Men, by the Neglect of its Exercise, and much more by its Contrary, will be tempted,

---

minds of the saints themselves. Such occasions give us "an affecting Sense of Jehovah's Excellencies," since a "long Meditation" on "the many Experiences we have had of the divine Benignity" will "fix indelible Signatures on them in our Minds."

against the *Law of Nature,* to seek a *single* and independent State, in order to secure their *Ease* and *Safety.*[15]

What Tennent was doing, even as he strove to marshal Presbyterian legions to defend Franklin's province, was entering one of the first of many Calvinist protests against the notion that society was created by contract and sustained by mutual interest. In the 1740's the proper citizens of Philadelphia could afford to overlook such disparities in aspiration and animus, so grateful were they that the preacher, once dismissed by gentlemen as "one Tennent, a fanatick,"[16] was bringing his authority and his eloquence to bear in the common cause.

The warfare of the 1740's, and the conduct of Middle Colony Presbyterians in those years, had no little to do with Franklin's discovery that Gilbert Tennent was, like himself, a doer of good. In these years also Franklin, who had once derided Whitefield as a "shaver" and even as probably an embezzler, discovered and cultivated what passed for a friendship with the grand itinerant. But a quarter-century later, when Franklin returned from London to discover that the "Irish," as he called the Scotch-Irish Presbyterians, had risen to nearly complete control of the Pennsylvania government, the differences of approach to public affairs, disclosed in the war sermons of the 1740's, seemed of greater moment. For in the same twenty-five years the followers of Gilbert Tennent, encouraged as they had been to promote the public good, had managed to discover a variety of violators of the law of nature and enemies to the public—many of whom were of the same persuasion as those who had been their "allies" in the military endeavors of the 1740's.

Tennent's pronouncements on public affairs during the 1740's do not alter the central fact that it was within the church itself that the Calvinist ministry made its chief contribution to the political thinking of colonial Americans. Not until 1762, for instance, was one of Edwards' "captains" provided an opportunity to record his theory of society and politics in a New England election sermon. Yet even before that date the Edwardean ministry had slowly been working a change in the social attitudes of their people and, by implication at least, developing the redefinition of the relationship between governors and governed in which John Adams was certain the Revolution had its sources.

Something of the Calvinist approach to political questions may be inferred from the treatment, in the election sermons of the 1740's and early 1750's, of the issues inherited from the years of currency controversy. None of the Calvinists who spoke in these years was in full sympathy with Edwards' millenarianism, nor surely with his sacramental and ecclesiastical theories. But they at least bespoke a view of the relationship of trade and religion which contrasted sharply with that offered by Liberal election preachers. Neither the somewhat orthodox Calvinists nor the Liberals espoused a specific fiscal policy. Both allowed that it made little difference whether the "*Medium,* which is current" were "coined metal or stamped paper," so long as its "true and certain *Value*" could be easily ascertained. But there was essential disagreement as to the reason and justification for legislation that stabilized the currency and *"preserv'd invariable"* its value.

Charles Chauncy argued that the government must maintain a "certain standard" so that men, assured of "the true value" of their money, could pursue with less difficulty and more confidence a career in "their Commerce," and that, of course, wise monetary legislation was to be devised by those with reasonable insights into the nature of things. The more orthodox election preachers, on the other hand, declared it the duty of magistrates to conform "all Precepts & Orders with respect to Merchandize & Trade" to the "fundamental Laws" of the "Word of God" and insisted, indeed, that all "Laws, of however minute Consequence," be so devised. They instructed the New England legislators to "take the most effectual Care" to prevent all "Fraud and Oppression" and to bring money, weights, measures and the like to such a "Standard of Justice" that a citizen would neither be "Wrong'd nor do Unjustly" in the matter of "Buying and Selling." Civil government was, quite simply, an instrument of the Divine Will, to which magistrates were to conform their conduct. Furthermore, they were to make certain that no legislation cause or tempt any member of the community to act contrary to that Will. Finally, the orthodox preachers issued the sweeping demand that no legislation, and no magistrate, bear with, countenance, or encourage any sort of "Unrighteousness" whatsoever, and warned that the cry of the "oppressed," if not hearkened to by the provincial assemblies, would be "heard on High."[17]

Even such comparatively orthodox stipulations seemed troublesome enough to Chauncy and the commercial community for which he spoke. For to Chauncy the goal of legislation was commercial stability and an efficient economy—and particularly the avoidance of the fluctuating value of incomes that came with inflation. To the orthodox mind of Calvinism the purpose of government was the perfection of a people in righteousness. When the generation of the Awakening began to develop its even more radical definition of the nature of social virtue, the results—in terms of political and economic theory—would be beyond all Liberal understanding.

The heirs of Edwards did not begin to apply their interpretation of the social contract to public affairs until the years of the imperial crisis. Then society and government were judged by the Calvinist law of nature, and God himself presented as the brightest mirror for magistrates:

> His Kingdom is a Kingdom of Holy love, and all his laws are laws of love; and, as far as they are obeyed, unite his subjects in the most cordial, happy union to each other.[18]

Well before the administration of George III came to be tried in the Calvinist balance, however, the law of love was being invoked in implicit judgment on earthly laws and governors. In 1762 Joseph Bellamy offered this portrait of the good society for the benefit and edification of Governor Fitch and the Connecticut General Assembly:

> It is not with the great Monarch of the universe, as it is many times with earthly princes. They often abuse their power and their supremacy to mischievous purposes. The thought that there is none above them to call them to account, emboldens them to cruel and barbarous deeds; and this, amidst all their external grandeur and glory, sinks their character and renders them odious and contemptible . . . For concerning God, it may be said, that great as his power is, he never used it to oppress the meanest subject in his dominions; and absolute as his sovereignty is, he never made one unwise decree. His law is holy, just, and good, like its author; perfect in beauty, without a blemish; sweeter than honey, yea, than the honey-comb; and all his conduct towards his creatures is so exactly right, and good, and wise, that it is absolutely above emendation . . . An absolutely perfect, an infinitely glorious and amiable Being![19]

Three years after Bellamy's sermon was delivered the Calvinist populace of Connecticut, faced with what they considered an unwise decree, would rise in anger against the stamp tax. In another decade they would rebel against an earthly monarch whom they found odious and contemptible. "All their royal dignity," Bellamy observed of earthly princes, "loses it lustre while they are without that moral rectitude which exalts the great Monarch of the universe." The principle on which the Connecticut rebels acted was that set forth by Bellamy at the beginning of his Election Sermon: "To view beings and things as they are, and to be affected and act accordingly, is the sum of moral virtue."[20] Yet neither in 1765 nor in 1775 were the citizens of Connecticut reacting merely to the character of the British king, but rather also to the conduct of those who, in American society, had fallen far short of fulfilling the requirements of the Calvinist moral law. The precepts of Bellamy's sermon were applicable as well to the provincial and local magistracy of the colonies, and their first service was as a commentary on laws which, for more than two decades, had grievously offended the eyes of the saints.

The prevailing evangelical opinion of colonial government was for many years largely a reflection of the fact that the rulers of colonial society, with few exceptions, had used their power to contain the Awakening and restrict the progress of the gospel. Until Jonathan Trumbull was chosen chief executive of Connecticut, only one colonial official had a reputation among Calvinists comparable to that enjoyed by Jonathan Belcher. Thomas Hutchinson's continuing concern for the religious liberties of dissenters gave him a character among Calvinists that made him, according to John Adams, perhaps the most dangerously popular figure in New England. Both Belcher and Hutchinson were known, moreover, as opponents of the land bank and other easy-money schemes. In his sermon on the death of Belcher, Aaron Burr observed that this worthy had distinguished himself by opposing all the "sordid, avaricious Methods of enriching themselves and Families" that too many governors (and too many private Americans) had employed at the expense of the "true Interest of the People."[21] Burr's sermon was the epitome of Calvinist commentary on social and political issues prior to 1760. It delineated qualities and dispositions missing from those in power but which, in the best of all possible polities, would govern the governors. Taken together with their regular treatments of the seemingly apolitical themes of experimental religion, the evangelical clergy were thereby quietly and unassumingly converting the moral law into an instrument of political action.

In June 1748, six months after publication of the *Humble Attempt,* and six months before Edwards' first public avowal that the Concert of Prayer was not succeeding in bringing in the millennium, he delivered the sermon in which Perry Miller has rightly discerned the sources of the American democratic impulse.[22] Improving the death of his uncle and protector, Colonel John Stoddard, Edwards provided the people of Northampton with a characterization of a good magistrate, which he took Stoddard ("Everything in him was great") to have been, and of a "contemptible" one. It is "peculiarly unbecoming" for rulers, Edwards observed,

> to be of a mean spirit, a disposition that will admit of their doing those things that are sordid and vile; as when they are persons of a narrow, private spirit, that may be found in little tricks and intrigues to promote their private interest. Such will shamefully defile their hands to gain a few pounds, are not ashamed to grind the faces of the poor, and screw their neighbours; and will take ad-

vantage of their authority or commission to line their own pockets with what is fraudulently taken or withheld from others.

In a sense Edwards was speaking in a mere advisory capacity and proposing only that the people of Northampton, on the next occasion for exercising the franchise, oppose such a contemptible person. It is also true that Edwards set forth qualifications for magistracy not immediately derivable from the Calvinist moral law. Stoddard "was not only great in speculative knowledge," Edwards observed, "but his knowledge was practical." Yet when Edwards remarked that Stoddard not only acted the part of a man of "public spirit," but set himself against all of a narrow, private spirit, and went on to imply that Stoddard was presumably among the elect, he had made a perhaps more formidable contribution to the American political process.[23]

When Aaron Burr, a decade later, explained that Jonathan Belcher's "noble generous Soul" had expressed itself in hostility to all wicked, designing men, and placed Belcher clearly among the saints in light, he added momentum to the ball which Edwards had set in motion. For by explaining that the virtue which had taken Belcher to the consummate felicity of the Calvinist heaven was an inner principle, "real and genuine, such as commanded his *Heart* and governed his *Life*," Burr had revealed the political implications of "experimental religion."[24] One opposed selfish men, in the final analysis, not only because they were sinners, but because by engaging in such an enterprise, one could thereby prove himself truly virtuous. This insight of Edwards, expanded by his son-in-law, was perhaps the simplest of the many simple ideas introduced by the Awakening. Yet it would prove sufficiently compelling to serve as the dynamic of the democratic political process through the era, not only of Jefferson and Jackson, but among remnants of God's people to the close of the public career of William Jennings Bryan.

It was this refusal to divest public behavior of its moral dimension that made of Calvinism, with its superficially illiberal interpretation of the social contract, a highly radical political movement. Like Tom Paine, but for somewhat different reasons, Calvinists considered government a badge of lost innocence, necessary because of "the corruption of nature by sin."[25] Their theory of government, founded in a view of human nature outlined by Edwards in the dissertation, *Original Sin,* assumed that men would "scarce be able to subsist in the world" if God had not ordained "civil government to keep men from destroying each other." Society without government, they maintained, would be "like *Hobb's* state of war," where men "would act as the wild beasts of the desert; prey upon and destroy one another."[26] Both Calvinist ministry and populace professed horror of a "state of nature," and "a state of absolute anarchy" they considered "dreadful."[27] All the petitions addressed to the Massachusetts General Court after 1776, for example, importuning the legislature to establish a constitution so the people of the commonwealth would not be left "in a state of nature," came from dissenter communities.[28] Like James Madison, Calvinists looked upon government as a means of giving men "security," of guaranteeing every man the comfort and felicity of his own vine and his own fig tree.

Edwards himself, and for that matter many of the Calvinist ministers of his generation, commenced their careers with a faith in what might be called squirearchical government. As late as the year of the death of George II, Gilbert Tennent would celebrate the institution of monarchy in such strains as to make himself seem, by comparison with a "constitutionalist" like Mayhew, a partisan of a feudal regime.[29] In the context of the eighteenth century, the Calvinist conception of the role of government was an expression of concern for what men of "superior strength or craft," if unrestrained by some higher power, might do to the weak and defenseless.[30] Government was instituted among men to preserve the persons and property of individuals from the unbridled authority of tyrants, great and small, and, in the eyes of Edwards and his followers, to restrain those who would grind the faces of the poor. With the death of the Stoddards, and with the rise of a generation of crafty men to dominion in American society, Edwards, his colleagues, and his spiritual heirs had to seek other means of accomplishing these ends. If any Calvinist ever came to the belief that government was a means of restraining, not great men, but the multitude who might wish to grind the faces of the rich, he ceased to be an Edwardean.

In the course of their careers, and particularly in the years of the Revolution, the Calvinist clergy amply demonstrated that frustrated and ineffective Tories were not the only Americans to challenge the Lockean ethos of America's Whigs. Not until the 1770's did the evangelical party officially articulate anything that might be described as a full-blown political theory, but well before then they clearly conceived of society as by no means a creature of law and contract. They considered it a "natural" organism—not, to be sure, in Edmund Burke's sense that social arrangements are the product of historic growth, but in the more radical terms of the fundamental interdependence of humanity. They differed from such semifeudal critics of a selfish and atomized society as Samuel Johnson, who espied in nature a moral law of mutual obligation:

And as all the beauty and usefulness of the natural world thus depends upon giving and receiving, so it is from hence that all the harmony and happiness of the whole moral world does in like manner derive; all depends upon a perpetual exchange of mutual good offices. Thus the parents must nourish and educate the children, and the children must return duty and obedience to the parents. The magistrate must protect and govern the subjects, and they must return honor and submission to the magistrate. The pastor must instruct and guide the flock, and they must yield reverence and subsistence to him. The master must be just and kind to the servant, and the servant must be obedient and faithful to the master. The knowing must instruct the ignorant, and they must be obsequious and generous to their instructors . . .[31]

To a degree some Calvinists shared in Johnson's view of the good society, but the evangelical mind could not, from its premises in the Edwardean law of nature, long abide a social ideal so obviously distinguished by privilege, prescription, and hierarchy.

The affinities of Calvinism were with neither Maistre nor Bonald, but rather with Rousseau. Well before the Awakening partisans of evangelical religion were arguing, on the basis of what they took to be the first principles of Protestant Christianity, that the elevation of one man over another derived "not from Nature, but from arbitrary Establishment," and that man's natural condition was one of "*Equality*, with the rest of Mankind."[32] In subsequent years this theoretical insight was given practical embodiment in what Samuel Davies called "the Rule of Equity," a rule that had its "reason or foundation" in the "natural equality of mankind." Notwithstanding "the great difference in the capacities, improvements, characters, and stations of men," Davies explained, "yet considered as men, they share in the same common nature, and are so far equal."[33] As codified in the Calvinist moral law, the "Rule of Equity" forbade "envy," not of one's "betters," for that they were not, but of the wealth and perhaps the luxury which the accidents of birth or fortune permitted men to acquire. More importantly, however, it forbade pride; we who have been "raised above the common level," insisted Gilbert Tennent, ought to remember that Providence "might have ordered us the Lot of Beggars or Ideots."[34]

In the years before the Great Awakening the Calvinist moral law, as unfolded in such utterances as Edwards' sermons, *Charity and Its Fruits*, seemed to prescribe a general contentment with the distribution of the goods of the world. Yet the evangelical ministry hardly looked with favor on the commercial bustle of the 1730's, and especially not on the eagerness of some men to "get a large Estate." Their attitude toward acquisitiveness was set forth in Tennent's observation that Scripture required of men only "a moderate careless Care for their own and their Families Support." But Tennent also made it clear that at the heart of Calvinism was a judgment on the accumulation of great wealth. The sin did not consist in the luxury—"a sort of Turk's paradise"—which men aspired to or gained, but in the ultimate motive behind the quest for riches: a desire "to be a little demigod in the World, a sort of independent Being, by having many depending on thee, courting thy Smiles, and trembling at thy frowns."[35] It was during the Awakening, however, that Calvinist spokesmen straightforwardly proclaimed a criticism of the commercial ethic. Their fundamental objection was that self-aggrandizement was an affront to the principle of human equality. The great Charleston fire of 1740, for instance, was interpreted as a rebuke to the "haughty Scorn" of merchants who "look'd over the *low* Roofs" of their "*Neighbours* Houses, and *despis'd* them who had none!"[36] The desire for wealth was not so much intrinsically meretricious, even as a symptom of indifference to spiritual things, as a revelation of the worst of sins, man's wish to be superior to his fellows.

The Calvinist moral law as preached after the Awakening stood in judgment on acquisitiveness and even strongly implied the need for redressing inequities in the division of colonial wealth. The evangelical critique of the business ethic remained at bottom a lament for society's departure from its pristine natural equality: "What is Covetousness," asked Tennent,

> but the Purveyor of Pride, that greedily seeks something to support its grandeur . . . ? Men are prodigal from the same proud Principle, with design to appear great and be talk'd of.[37]

Clearly the protest of Calvinism was not in substance economic, or social in the usual sense, but psychological. Yet even in its simplest formulations evangelical thought evinced a clear agrarian bias. The Calvinist law of charity demanded of all men something more even than "a disposition to give to the poor." The man of true charity, according to the post-Awakening Calvinist definition, was "so divested of self" that he could "readily part with any worldly good" and could not, therefore, in any sense call what he had his own.[38] Were the evangelical law of charity enforced, mankind would be restored in fact as well as in name to a full and absolute equality.

The egalitarian thrust of Calvinism might be accounted for in several ways. The poverty and distress of the 1770's undoubtedly contributed to the evangelical proposal that Americans imbibe the spirit of their Pilgrim forefathers, whose *willingness to communicate* among themselves, resembled the spirit which prevailed in the primitive church, *when no man said that ought he possessed was his own; but they had all things common* . . .[39]

The land shortage in Connecticut, manifested in the New Light party's interest in settling the Wyoming Valley, may well have helped inspire the outright agrarianism preached by Connecticut Calvinists from 1760 through the Revolution. It is necessary, observed Benjamin Trumbull in 1773, "to keep property as equally divided among the inhabitants as possible, and not to suffer a few persons to mass all the riches and wealth of the country." But already in 1741 an itinerant of the Awakening had proclaimed that the people of America were distinguished by a "near Equality."[40] The egalitarianism of the Calvinist ministry was a negative reaction to the prospering of particular individuals in the society of mid-eighteenth-century America.

Yet reinforcing all these sentiments and policies, and surely to a degree inspiring them, was Edwards' conception of the Godhead and his certainty that there was, as it were, no primogeniture in heaven. Excellency, Edwards had written long before the Awakening, "consists in the *Similarness* of one being to another"—"So much equality, so much beauty." Edwards may have retained something of the Great Chain of Being, but his notebooks show him discontent with even the traditional concept of "angelic" existences. And nowhere in his writings are to be found the descantings on the gradations among mankind that Liberals so eagerly dispensed. His hierarchy of "spiritual beings" was one of holiness and increasingly visible likeness to God: " 'tis certainly beautiful that it should be so—that in the various ranks of beings those that are nearest to the first being should most evidently and variously partake of his influence." In his published writings, culminating of course in the vision of the *Two Dissertations,* Edwards focused on the "pleasing" equality of all nature, and all art, in which the sweet concord of equals might be discerned.[41]

Edwards and his successors publicized the assumptions by portraying a "happy" Christian commonwealth in which all, except for the Supreme Being, were "stamped with the same image and superscription." Their Church Militant had but one General; the remainder, except perhaps for the "captains," were all privates. In sum, the very nature of their beatific vision prescribed as the only proper relationship for mankind "a condition of perfect *brotherhood,* as becomes beings of the same race, the offspring of one God." At the conclusion of the Revolution a Calvinist spokesman described the pleasing prospect which lay before an independent America in terms of the "happy equality" of its citizens. The words had much the same meaning for him as they had had for two earlier generations of evangelical Americans. Fifteen years later a still younger New Light was proclaiming, as against the principles and policies of Federalism, that American "happiness" depended "very essentially" on keeping all men in a *"middling condition of life,"* and that, indeed, by "bringing down the *haughty,* we restore our race to its natural order."[42] Whatever the particular grievances of Calvinists against those who in eighteenth-century America assumed or encouraged an inequality among mankind, evangelical religion found aesthetically displeasing anything but the most evident equality. In order to embrace a different social ideal it was necessary, as in so many other cases, to become something other than Edwardean Calvinists.

II

Although the ideal of equality was as instrumental as that of union in conditioning Calvinists' often intuitive response to social situations, their concern in the period between the Awakening and the Revolution was not with enforcing equality on human society, but with discovering who in their society most grievously affronted the aesthetic perceptions of the Calvinist God. Calvinist efforts to identify the children of light or of darkness were supposed to proceed from the central premise of Edwardeanism: that it was man's internal nature which made him virtuous or vicious, worthy of praise or blame. That the inner dispositions of men were to be known by the "fruit they produce" was an equally fundamental axiom of all who considered the *Religious Affections* an "excellent treatise." According to Backus' interpretation of Edwards,

> *fruits* comprehend all that men *bring forth out of their hearts,* in their principles, experience, conversation, and conduct; and hereby we are to *know* them, and to act towards them, according to the clearest light we can gain.[43]

The fruits by which a virtuous disposition was to be known might include acts of charity; but giving to the poor, or thinking "the best of others," Edwards insisted, were "only certain particular branches or fruits of that great virtue of charity which is so much insisted on throughout the New Testament." True charity, he explained, is "of much more extensive signification, than as it is used generally in common discourse," and is, in fact, a gracious *"disposition* or *affection."*[44] The nature of true virtue

> consists in a *disposition* to benevolence towards being in general; though from such a disposition may arise exercises of love to *particular* beings, as objects are presented, and occasions arise.

Through the election of 1800, when one of the major New Light criticisms of Federalists was that they were "uncharitable," Calvinists did not believe that they were judging behavior or conduct, but what they took to be the inspiration of such behavior. Such an approach to social evil was in part dictated—as was the Calvinist severance of salvation from catalogues of particular "duties"—by the rapidity with which eighteenth-century society was changing. "Formerly Vices were described by the Classes of Mankind to which they belonged," explained one of the younger Tennents in 1774,

> but we find they have spread themselves so universally among all Ranks in the *British* Empire, that we can no longer describe them in that manner.[45]

Yet the character of American society was such that when a Massachusetts dissenter in 1773 defined the anti-Christian Kingdom as simply every "unregenerate man" in the colonies, he had little difficulty in pointing out who, precisely, bore this mark. For the Calvinist ministry over the decades had compiled a rather impressive catalogue of the behavior revealing that a man's inner nature was unrenewed.

The effort to discover the inner dispositions of men—to determine whether or not they were saved, in order to know how virtuous men were to conduct themselves with respect to others—was carried out in the face of certain difficulties posed by the Calvinist ministry themselves. James Davenport in 1741, and a variety of dissenters throughout the period, thought that this judgment could be made by a "spirit of discerning." But those Calvinists who accepted the admonitions of Edwards understood, as did Samuel Buell, that men had not

> such a Spirit of Discerning that we can absolutely determine who are Godly, and who are not: For we can neither see nor feel, the internal Exercises of Grace in others.[46]

Still, Calvinist ministers urgently and probingly undertook to assess the inner dispositions of men and, even more importantly, urged their people to share in the task of separating the precious from the vile.

Something of the moral urgency of pre-Revolutionary Calvinism was attributable to a belief that as the Work of Redemption progressed, the children of light would be ever more easily distinguished from the children of darkness. At the General Judgment, Edwards explained, there would be "an everlasting separation" made between the saints and "wicked men." Their differences would, however, become "visible" even earlier, in the onset and dawning of the millennial era:

Before, they were mixed together, and it was impossible in many instances to determine their characters; but now all shall become visible; both saints and sinners shall appear in their true characters and forms.[47]

The belief that as friends and enemies ceased to be "mixed together" the more likely it was that the millennium was approaching informed the Calvinist response to the Seven Years' War. For the first time in the history of imperial wars, it seems, the light and the dark were no longer incongruously, or, as Davies would have it, "promiscuously blended."[48] In fact Calvinism found it difficult to wax enthusiastic over any contest that did not lend itself to interpretation as just such a "grand decisive conflict."

But the belief that as the millennium drew near the battle lines would be more clearly drawn could also serve, given the other premises of Calvinist thought, as an argument for distinguishing saints from sinners in order to prefigure the Kingdom and thus promote its coming. This was in part the task that Edwards set himself in the 1740's, and which, as he attempted to institutionalize it in the polity of the Northampton church, brought him dismissal in 1750. The question raised by Tennent in 1740—"Can Light Dwell with Darkness"— could not long be suppressed, however imperiously Edwards strove to bridge the divisions and temper the animosities of the Awakening. Is it not every church, Tennent asked,

> composed of Persons of the most contrary Characters? While some are sincere Servants of God, are not many Servants of Satan, under a religious Mask?[49]

Herein consisted one of the more important functions of the evangelical ministry: striking through the mask of appearances in order to disclose and discern the spiritual reality beneath.

The decades after the Awakening saw several subtle, but highly significant, shifts in the emphasis and animus of ministers' efforts to assess the spiritual state of their parishioners. In his Farewell Sermon, Edwards recalled that he had preached frequently on "the distinguishing notes of true piety, those by which persons might discover their state and most surely and clearly judge of themselves." The purpose of such preaching, he observed, was "the detecting of the deceived hypocrite, and establishing the hopes and comforts of the sincere."[50] As in the *Religious Affections*, Edwards was concerned chiefly with the evangelical hypocrite, and so nominally at least would the Calvinist ministry continue to be during the 1750's. But the evangelical ministry periodically returned to the themes of the Awakening. Gilbert Tennent, for instance, "detected the bold presumer, discovered the vanity of his confidence"—all, as Samuel Finley explained, "with admirable dexterity."[51] But Tennent also strove to expose "the formal hypocrite to his own view" and thereby focused the attention of his congregation once again on complacency rather than a misguided enthusiasm as the most suspicious of anti-Christian dispositions.

The tendency of the 1750's is clearly illustrated by the contrast between Tennent's sermon of 1749, *Irenicum,* and his pronouncement of 1760, *The Right Use of the Religious Passions.* In the former sermon Tennent, still seeking to put the quietus on the censorious spirit aroused by the Awakening, cautioned against the spiritual pride that would seek its own honor "under a Cloak of *Zeal*" for God. The ease with which men so deceive themselves, he proposed, "is a doleful dreadful *Truth,* which may justly humble the *Pride of Man,* and reasonably excite us to be as *suspicious* of *ourselves* as *cautious* and *moderate* in our *Censures* of others."[52] Such sentiments continued to fill Tennent's sermons of the 1750's, which culminated in irenic pronouncements designed to make the reunion of the Presbyterian synods palatable to his New Side followers. But in 1760 Tennent, seemingly dissatisfied with the Union of 1758, reaffirmed the essential principle of the Awakening: that it was neither policy nor polity that united the people of God, but a common response to "religious Objects."

> The *Nature* of *Holy Objects* is such, so great, so excellent, and of such transcendent and unspeakable Importance, that we cannot be sincere, in our Esteem of them, and Pursuit after them, without Zeal. . . Their Necessity, Sublimity, Value, and Duration, require and deserve all the Ardor and Vehemence, all the Vigor, the Fire, the Force, of an immortal Spirit; in its boldest *Salleys,* its widest Expansions, and most intense Operations![53]

Tennent's reaffirmation of the importance of Christian zeal was of twofold significance in the context of 1760. It marked the culmination of the Calvinist response to what was considered the "lukewarmness," the growing indifference, and the spiritual deadness of the professing saints in the 1750's. It was also a reminder that the saint was different from other men—that prudence and moderation, so close to the hearts of other Americans, were intolerable according to the premises by which Calvinists judged the character of men.

Within Calvinist doctrine itself, the 1750's witnessed something of a redefinition of Christian virtue, making "zeal" a more distinguishing affection of the regenerate soul than "love." The changing emphasis reflected the shift in focus from the heart to the will implicit in the *Religious Affections.* An emphasis on the more active constituents of sainthood was by no means inconsistent with the original Awakening faith. In 1740, for instance, Edwards insisted, "The joy of the Christian not only arises in knowing and viewing, but also in doing." Already in 1734, for that matter, he had established it as an axiom that "the most perfect rest is consistent with being continually employed." But between 1734 (when Edwards had preached on men's need of rousing up themselves "and pressing forward") and 1750 had intervened the redefinition of the Kingdom.[54] By the latter date a more appropriate rendering of the Calvinist temper was that unless men were continually employed in forwarding the earthly Kingdom they would be allowed no rest.

The activist emphasis of evangelical religion was more conspicuously revealed in the 1750's. But its sources were in the Calvinist efforts to overcome the complacency attendant on the antinomianism of the Awakening. In 1744 Tennent, addressing himself to the question of post-Awakening sloth, hymned inanimate nature as being "in a Course of constant Labour" and portrayed the angelic host as "in a Course of continual Action." God Himself, in Tennent's telling, was "a simple Act," and men should also therefore be up and doing.[55] Tennent's advice to self-centered and contentious enthusiasts was hardly a call to mere diligence in one's calling. Though he admonished men to "study their own business," his definition of that business was of a piece with the exhortations to social commitment that found expression in his public sermons of the 1740's. The various aspects of Tennent's post-Awakening thought together comprised an essential step in the intellectual process whereby the Puritan ideal of weanedness from the world was translated into an evangelical imperative to act for the good of the brethren.

In this regard, the most significant Calvinist essay of the 1740's was Edwards' *Life and Diary of David Brainerd*. Here Edwards portrayed the young missionary as no enthusiast or mystic but a Christian pilgrim whose energy and activity had not been equaled since the days of St. Paul. To the diary itself, which recorded Brainerd's career as a spiritually proud undergraduate at Yale, as a censorious itinerant, and, finally, as a tireless instrument of the expanding Kingdom among the Indians, Edwards interspersed and appended numerous noteworthy reflections on the significance of these endeavors. Edwards remarked on Brainerd's youthful dalliance with antinomianism and separatism and his growing enthusiasm, in later years, for the Concert of Prayer. In sum, the career provided Edwards an opportunity to observe the relationship between experimental religion and true virtue. Brainerd was presented as a figure in whose life might be discerned "the *nature* of *true religion* and the *manner* of its *operation* when exemplified in a *high degree* and *powerful exercise.*" Thus Edwards' first observation, one which he simply expanded in what followed, was the most succinct restatement of the doctrines of the *Religious Affections:*

> His obtaining rest of soul in Christ, after earnest striving to enter in at the strait gate, and being violent to take the kingdom of heaven, he did not look upon as putting an end to any further occasion for striving in religion; but these were continued still, and maintained constantly, through all changes, to the very end of his life. His work was not finished, nor his race ended, till his life was ended . . .[56]

In short, Brainerd's life was a reminder to all "evangelical hypocrites" that true sainthood demanded the highest pitch of active zeal on behalf of the Kingdom.

The *Life of Brainerd* was probably Edward's most popular and widely read publication. (As such it is possibly more illustrative of the eighteenth-century American temper than the *Autobiography* of Benjamin Franklin.) Its emphasis on an active pursuit of human happiness encouraged, or surely fitted, the new mood of evangelical Calvinism. To be sure, Edwards in the *Brainerd* sought largely to convey the pleasures experienced by the saint in a life of virtuous activity. A similar definition of happiness was still upheld in 1759, when Robert Smith explained to his New Side flock that "Good Men do Good with Complacency."[57] But already in 1750, when Bellamy asserted that the saint "is in his element when doing God's will,"[58] Calvinism was making action the most important ingredient, not of religion merely, but of happiness itself. In not too many years, the felicity of the heavenly saints was being portrayed as endless exercises of the will:

> In that blessed region, there is room for the most vigorous exertion; every inhabitant hath business assigned him, which will demand all his attention, thro' the whole of his endless existence.[59]

After the publication of the *Brainerd*, likeness to God became for evangelical America a state not of being but of doing.

Edwards held Brainerd's example before a ministry he assumed was primarily concerned with saving the souls of men, and before a laity to which he assigned, for the most part, only such "religious work" as secret fasting. Yet the *Brainerd* marked the beginning of something of a new era in the history of the Calvinist mind, one in which neither *Pilgrim's Progress* nor *The Saint's Everlasting Rest* would, or could, serve as the handbook for those who wished a comfortable walk with God. The *Life of Brainerd* demanded the strenuous life of all who hoped to prove that they "were not merely the children of God in name, but in truth." Such activity was more than an obligation; it was an existential necessity. For informing the *Brainerd* was, of course, the central precept of the *Religious Affections* and of experimental religion generally: "assurance is not to be obtained so much by self-examination, as by action."[60] The exemplary Christian, Brainerd, was a creature neither of meditation nor of introspection, but of endeavor—a "great and universal benevolence to all mankind, reaching all sorts of persons without distinction."[61] It was not by a probing of the inner self, but through out-reaching extensions of the will, that the would-be saint was provided the data whereby he tested his pretensions.

The full implications of experimental religion would not be revealed until the end of a half century in which numerous Calvinist saints and martyrs followed Brainerd's example and "continued pressing forward in a constant manner, forgetting the things that were behind, and reaching for the things that were before."[62] They were disclosed most conspicuously in the events that led Charles Francis Adams to observe, in 1839, that "it would appear as if the grandson of Jonathan Edwards was destined to be a striking monument to after times of the abuse of the power of 'the will.' "[63] For Burr's expedition, quite possibly conceived in Litchfield County as a means of extending the Kingdom, and almost certainly advertised as such among the awakened of Kentucky, was an experiment undertaken, not in 1800, when Burr first dedicated his talents to the good of the American people, nor in 1801, when he selflessly denied the crown which many thought was rightly his, but after 1804, when his pride had driven him to the murder of Alexander Hamilton.

Yet well before 1800 Calvinism had demonstrated the potentialities of experimental religion as a spur to action in moments, not of assurance and confidence, but of questioning one's spiritual estate. Revealingly, by the late 1750's a new importance came to be attached to the career of St. Paul, especially by those ministers who came to their calling in the years after the Awakening. Nathaniel Whitaker, for instance, pointed out how the erstwhile Saul of Tarsus had worked to prove the reality of his experience on the Road to Damascus:

> Here were dangers, unknown in their kind and degree, set before him; but whatever they might be, he, with resolution, pursues his end. He makes no account of these things; no, nor of life itself. All his aim is, to finish his course with joy, and the ministry he had received of the *Lord Jesus,* by publishing his gospel of the grace of God.[64]

But it was not quite the pure Edwardean gospel that the evangelical clergy published in the years after 1758. Ironically enough, Brainerd would be among the last of Calvinists whose heart expressed itself in universally benevolent volitions. For the zealous activity in which the evangelical ministry and populace came to engage was only in part a pursuit of social joy and mutual love. Largely it was an effort to prove to themselves that—despite an inability to love the image of God wherever it might be seen—they were still capable of proving their conformity to the Will of God by overcoming the sins of other men.

Already in 1750 Bellamy was confessing that the new light of the Awakening had dimmed among his parishioners. Over the next decade it became quite evident that many who professed a commitment to the Calvinist God were finding the world not quite so unsatisfying spiritually as the Calvinist clergy maintained. In this context the Calvinist ministry continued to detect hypocrites, always presumably as an assistance to individuals in working out their own personal salvation. Yet the separation of the precious from the vile was done, after all, in public assembly. From the first, evangelical ministers had insisted on a "right dividing of the Word," by which was meant, according to Calvinists, "a close and distinguishing and detecting method" in applying doctrines to the particular conditions of parishioners. Offering "a common *mess*," leaving each man to apply a sermon as his "*fancy* and *humour*" might direct, was, Tennent insisted, "the *bane* of preaching."[65] A "particular application" did not require the minister to thrust the spear of judgment at individuals, but neither did it leave much room for doubt as to who, precisely, were the objects of his remarks. "When we *characterize* Saints and Sinners," Davies advised,

> let us not do it in a *distant, abstract* Manner, speaking of some *Body* in the *World,* in the third Person, as tho' we were characterizing those that are *absent. . .*

To such as considered direct address "RUDE and irritating," Davies invoked, along with the example of the apostles, the orations of Demosthenes and Cicero—"*direct, immediate,* and pointed *Addresses to their Auditory.*" Do not expect, he warned, "that we should amuse you with the Character of some *vague, indefinite* individuals."[66] Like the Puritans, though in a somewhat different way, the evangelical ministers were "precisians"; they specified, largely in terms of the "classes" of young and old, and of particular callings, the character of the various members of their congregations.

Given such a theory, the social implications of Calvinist sermons were in practice far from hidden. "In every church," Davies would begin,

> there are alas! some suspicious characters; and my present design is to describe such characters, and then leave it to yourselves to judge whether there be not such among you.[67]

Herein of course lay something, at least, of an explanation of the favor in which were held the itinerants who preached in the 1740's on "the marks of the new birth," or of why, again during the revivals of the early 1760's, the most popular preaching was "the most searching and trying."[68] To one of Whitefield's admirers, the grand itinerant seemed particularly eloquent when characterizing "the graceless and the children of GOD so clearly that everyone might easily know whether he belonged to the one or to the other." Both Whitefield and his eulogist (no doubt) continued to conceive the minister's function as the offering of counsel to men "as their respective condition might render most requisite."[69] But it is not impossible that many of Whitefield's auditors were especially impressed by his descriptions of the graceless—applying them not to themselves, but to other members of their community.

The modifications of Calvinist preaching in the decades after the Awakening reflected the unleashing of the forces which in time would sustain the pervasive majoritarian tyranny that Tocqueville claimed to discover in Jacksonian America. Not until Nathanael Emmons instituted "Societies for Moral Reform" in post-Revolutionary Massachusetts and, subsequently, Lyman Beecher devised the "moral militia" of Litchfield County did this aspect of the evangelical impulse find an appropriate institutional embodiment. In being so embodied, Calvinism ceased in effect to be evangelical, except of course in the spirit of Cotton Mather's *Essays to Do Good*. The basis for such later corruptions of the Edwardean faith was laid by Edwards himself in his reconstitution of ecclesiastical polity. In his scheme, visible sainthood was to be determined, not by the minister's judgment alone, but by the "church's christian judgment"—a judgment "sanctified, regulated, and enlightened by a principle of Christian love." The trial of spirits was to be made under the counsel and direction of the minister, but the "eye of public charity" which Edwards wanted placed on church members was unmistakably the collected gaze of the Christian community.[70]

In giving the "visible saints" the power to judge the character of their neighbors, Edwards was seeking to give some form and dignity to the process that he believed had been perverted by the separatists, with their "spirit of discerning." But his strategy clearly contributed to the process whereby the ultimate power of the laity was augmented and that of the clergy diminished. Indeed, his ecclesiastical polity seems to have been partly inspired by a feeling that the censorious itinerants of the Awakening had, by their behavior, led the awakened to neglect a responsibility that rightly belonged not to any individual but to the community. Herein Edwards was joined by other Calvinists, such as Eleazar Wheelock, who admonished Davenport for his "error" of passing imperious judgment on the members of his own church and the other congregations that he visited. By calling some men "brethren" and others merely "neighbors," Davenport was in effect relieving the laity of what was after all their duty and privilege —a "mutual, zealous Christian Conversation."[71] In sum, the ecclesiastical theory of post-Awakening Calvinism was consistent with its definition of Christian virtue: men were born for society and should act as their brothers' keepers.

The "pure church" movement that arose in the late 1750's and early 1760's carried the theory of "mutual care" one step further. Critics of Calvinism were probably not mistaken when they complained that the goal of evangelicals was to force all men, in every community, to have "their conduct approved" by a self-constituted "saintly" corporation.[72] Still, it is not likely that any who clamored for an end to Stoddardeanism and to the Half-Way Covenant anticipated the uses to which the pressure of public opinion would be put in the age of Beecher, much less that of Jackson and Finney. Their avowed purpose was to keep men from presuming to righteousness so long as their hearts and wills were devoted not to God but to the things of this world. Admitting such men to communion would simply strengthen their "carnal security," or, as Jacob Green argued "flatter them with vain hopes, ease their guilty Consciences, and build them up in self-righteousness."[73] In this category were some of the awakened of the 1740's, who had not, given the principles of experimental religion, proved to be persevering saints. In arguing for exclusion and even excommunication, Isaac Backus invoked Edwards' principle: "*moral sincerity* is transient, and may be entirely lost, but a gracious principle *abides* forever."[74] The New England and Middle Colony critics of Stoddardeanism, according to which only the most scandalous behavior was reason for dismissal from church membership, likewise argued from Edwards' premises.

But the ecclesiastical struggles of the years after Edwards' death centered not so much on the awakened as on the children of the generation of 1740, who now disappointingly came on the stage of action with far from holy dispositions. We "shall hear little of their religion,"

Green complained of those who asked the seal of the covenant without regeneration, "except the offering of their children to Baptism as oft as they have them." The denial of "Rest and Relief" to such persons perhaps did serve the social purpose of identifying publicly those who were not dedicated to the "Interest of Christ."[75] But neither Bellamy nor Green, nor, for that matter, the Baptists, were seeking to induce a forced and hypocritical conformity to the Calvinist moral law. In aspiring to a pure church they did not even conceive of themselves as judging, or as urging others to judge, conduct. They were seeking to ascertain something of the inner disposition of the would-be church member. Under the Half-Way Covenant, a reasonably sincere profession of faith was sufficient for admission to the privileges of church membership. Bellamy asked something more: "we are naturally as conscious of our volitions and affections, as we are of our speculations; and therefore we are as capable of knowing what we choose and love, as what we believe."[76] What all the critics of the old polity were seeking was that whoever wished the privileges of church membership should come to a decision as to what was his primary love.

Like Theodore Frelinghuysen a generation or more earlier, the advocates of the pure church were attempting to promote an awakening through the instrument of ecclesiastical polity. One of their goals was to sustain and revive the zeal and resolution of the saints, but quite possibly they were also hoping to shatter the complacency of the obviously unregenerate with the power of the general will. It is much "more likely," Bellamy observed, that men "will be converted" if they

> live under an orthodox, pious, faithful minister, and under the watch and care of a church, whose members walk with God, and the light of whose holy examples shines all around them, than they who live under an unsound, ungodly, unfaithful minister, and in the company of carnal and loose professors, who join to hate and to blacken the true doctrines of the gospel, and to ridicule a life of strict piety.[77]

In so arguing for purity of church membership Bellamy was obviously thinking of the mysterious power of common feeling, both in itself and as underlying the efficacy of Calvinist preaching. But his words also suggest that for him the "watch and care" of the pious was simply the one force available in the America of 1760 capable of countervailing the appeal of the practical world and its religion.

The Calvinist pressure to "conformity" may have come, over time, to work against variety and individuality. But it first arose as a strategy for overcoming what seemed unthinking and easy emulation of purportedly fashionable attitudes and behavior. The crusade against "formal" church membership was an institutionalization of a long-standing Calvinist objection against a merely conventional pattern of existence. It arose almost simultaneously with what seemed, to the evangelical mind, an increase in the "madness" that led men to accede to the opinion of the "crowd." According to Samuel Finley, who in this instance was speaking in Franklin's Philadelphia, the "crowd" was not the multitude, or the majority, but the handful who set standards of "taste" and "respectability." In this sense, Finley noted, men valued the "favourable Opinion of Mankind" largely because it gave them "an Opportunity to serve their Best Interests more successfully."[78] Nor was Finley bewailing a nonexistent mode of thought; the very attitude he condemned was, by the late 1750's, being offered as ethical advice from the pulpits of Liberal churches. Jonathan Mayhew, for one, informed the youth of Boston that a reasonable religion and morality were of considerable benefit in terms of "what is commonly called worldly gain or profit." Against the tyranny of the majority, Mayhew set the patronage of the "wiser and better part" of society, men with "connexions in business," who would be most disposed to serve and befriend an aspiring but otherwise Christianly sober youth.[79]

Whether Mayhew's was the more liberal religion is less the question than what his doctrine disclosed of the tendency of the American mind in the 1750's. The Calvinist ministry in these years were contending against the appeal of a more worldly gospel, not merely among the prosperous denizens of the seaboard, but within the hearts and wills of their own parishioners. Considering the nature of the sermons delivered in these years in Calvinist churches, the preference for a more generous gospel is not surprising. When speaking to the visible saints, a Connecticut pastor would remind them to "love one another." Then he would turn to the reprobate congregation, informing them that they risked their "immortal interest" if they neglected or refused to "hear and embrace the truth."[80] The truth they were urged to embrace was, of course, the superiority of spiritual and divine things to all sources of more carnal satisfactions. Jonathan Edwards, Jr., never so radical a critic of the business ethic as his father, was nevertheless sufficiently imbued with the spirit of the Edwardean God to deliver this exemplary searching and trying discourse on the distinguishing marks of sainthood:

> Love is eminently a practical principle, towards whatever object it is directed . . . Whatever a man loves and sets his heart upon, that in proportion to the degree of his love, he pursues in his practice. For instance, those who set their hearts on riches how do they conduct as to their practice? Are they all engaged after other things, at the same time neglecting all opportunities of acquiring the wealth

which they so much love? . . . It is well known that they keep their eyes still fixed upon the one object of their pusuit, and so regulate all their conduct as tends most to secure the grand thing at which they are aiming.[81]

When some men tired of hearing that they could not serve Mammon and yet be saved, they either took membership in a more tolerant communion or sought to have their minister removed before he could succeed in enforcing his ecclesiastical polity.

That men openly embraced Arminianism or sought to impose a heretic minister on the saints helped in a way to resolve the tensions, not within each church, but within the hearts of those as yet undecided as to which of the two contending gospels was the more appealing. There were presumably many suspicious men in the churches of Calvinism. "Many in the eyes of men are reputed godly," declared Joseph Bellamy, "who in the eyes of God, as searcher of hearts, are not so."[82] The whole thrust of Calvinist ecclesiastical innovations was to expose men's hearts to public judgment, and if man reacted by signifying his preference for a more free and generous gospel, at least part of the Calvinist goal had been achieved. As in the Awakening, the Calvinists of this era found nothing less tolerable than indifference or indecisive prudence. An "open Enemy," announced Gilbert Tennent in 1760, "is like to find better Quarter than a perfidious *Neuter*."[83] Impatient with the existential dilemmas of their people, the Calvinist ministry drove resolutely toward an externalizing of the moral drama of the age. An avowal of preference for Arminianism served clearly to delineate, it seemed, the lines between the children of light and of darkness in each community.

Edwards so expounded the case against Arminianism that not only its spokesmen but all who believed it were sinners in Calvinist eyes. In this regard Joseph Bellamy possibly improved on the lessons of the master, but it was in *True Religion Delineated*, which Edwards publicly and explicitly approved, that Bellamy first stood in judgment on *all* who embraced the doctrines of "false teachers." Not merely the teachers but those who hearkened to such teachings had, according to Bellamy, "cut out a scheme in their heads to suit the religion of their hearts."[84] In subsequent years Bellamy turned his argument more directly against not so much the authors of each "false scheme of religion" as their adherents among the laity—practitioners, he called them, of "so many various kinds of idolatry."[85] What he and other evangelical preachers came to argue in the late 1750's was that since Liberal preachers designed to "amuse" a man with "a detail of his moral excellencies," whoever was so entertained was as sinful as the performer.[86] Nor were these precepts merely doctrines espoused by the Calvinist clergy; they seemed to have worked their way into the very heart of the populace. "My embracing those Wicked Doctrines," explained Joseph Hawley as he publicly recanted his youthful dalliance with Arminianism, "was owing to the natural Blindness and Pride of my heart, the Wicked and Corrupt Nature in which I was born."[87] Self-examination presumably brought Hawley to such a conclusion, but he admitted he was helped to it by a careful reading of Edwards' dissertations, *Will* and *Original Sin*. And it was in action, of course, that Hawley demonstrated, to his own satisfaction as to that of the pious, that his heart and will had truly been converted to the Edwardean gospel.

Thus in the 1750's were colonial society and the colonial mind preparing for a recapitulation of the social and moral drama of the decade before the Great Awakening. In 1756 Jonathan Parsons, commenting on a recent series of sermons by Jonathan Mayhew, complained that not only Arminianism, but Arianism, had never been "propagated with more *openness* and *resolution,* nor with *less opposition,* in our land than at this day."[88] But of course there was opposition, just as there had been in the 1730's when Edwards began preaching on the Reformation doctrine of justification by faith alone. Once again Edwards led the crusade, this time with his treatise, *Will,* wherein he again made it quite clear why it was no matter of indifference which of the schemes—legal or evangelical—triumphed in America.

> If it be indeed, as is pretended, that *Calvinistic* doctrines undermine the very foundation of all religion and morality, and enervate and disannul all rational motives to holy and virtuous practice; and that the contrary doctrines give the inducements to virtue and goodness their proper force, and exhibit religion in a rational light, tending to recommend it to the reason of mankind, and enforce it in a manner that is agreeable to their natural notions of things: I say, if it be thus, it is remarkable, that virtue and religious practice should prevail most, when the former doctrines, so inconsistent with it, prevailed almost universally: and that ever since the latter doctrines, so happily agreeing with it, and of so proper and excellent a tendency to promote it, have been gradually prevailing, vice, profaneness, luxury and wickedness of all sorts, and contempt of all religion, and of every kind of seriousness and strictness of conversation, should proportionably prevail; and that these things should thus accompany one another, and rise and prevail with one another, now for a whole age together!

Whatever the reaction of the modern temper to so positive an affirmation of the role of ideas in history, it is worthwhile to compare this declaration with the fears of the 1730's, when, as Edwards reported, the pious of the colonies feared that Arminianism was becoming so prevalent that God was about to withdraw forever the promise of His Spirit to New England. Edwards introduced his later observations with a reminder that "the tendency of doctrines" might "much more justly be argued" in the 1750's because the "general effect' of both rational and evangelical religion had been revealed, as both had "had their turn of general prevalence in our nation."[89] In the *Original Sin,* Edwards seemingly integrated this insight with the more general observation that the Work of Redemption is not continuous, but meets periodically with resistance. His perspective on history was not one of despair; rather he prepared the way once more for an advancement of the Kingdom. The power of darkness could be overthrown, he seemed almost to say, if only Arminianism were argued out of existence. Without being at the trouble of a train of reasoning, the evangelical mind seemed ready by 1756 to translate these precepts into an assault, not on Arminianism merely, but on the identifiable enemies of the Kingdom in America: the spiritually blind practitioners of the multiform idolatries of reasonable religion.

III

Already in 1750 Calvinists everywhere in the colonies were lamenting "the dreadful Increase of *Arminianism.*" From New England through Davies' Virginia and beyond they were once again sounding the trumpet call to battle against "dangerous errors in opinion."[90] As early as 1745 several of the associations which welcomed Whitefield had indicated the need for effecting "an happy *Union* and *Harmony*" of Calvinists, in opposition to the itinerant's enemies, who were, it was assumed, all crypto-Arminians.[91] Two years later Jonathan Parsons expressed the wish that all evangelicals, regardless of denomination, would work "with one Heart and Voice and Hand" to "bear down and root out the *modern* Scheme."[92] But such summonses bore little fruit, for in the late 1740's the party of the Awakening had become divided. Few were yet certain whether it was a resurgent Anglicanism or a persisting separatism that most needed to be checked, much less whether at the moment rationalism or enthusiasm was the more dangerous error.

In 1750 the "Calvinists" of America were seeking to unite, but not in every case against the new Arminianism. Tennent's *Irenicum,* part of the background of which was New Side disenchantment with Baptists and Moravians, was a symptom of the manner in which the divisions of the revival were being bridged by means of common opposition to enthusiastic "heresy." Similarly, the separatist leaders of Connecticut complained that many ministers who once held "Enthusiastick Notions" were now making common cause with "the orderly Ministers," and using the spread of separatism as an occasion for moderating the differences "between the *New-Lights* and the standing Churches," the "Opposers, and the Subjects" of the revival.[93] The decade of the 1750's witnessed other efforts to blur the doctrinal differences born of the Awakening in order to preserve or restore the unity of orthodoxy. Neither Edwards nor Bellamy was reluctant to proclaim the strictest of evangelical faiths, but such Calvinists as Solomon Williams bemoaned the degree to which divisions, between ministers and within churches, were arising over a "peculiar Explication of some non-essential Doctrine."[94] Thus one of Williams' objections to Edwards' inquiry into qualifications was that it turned Calvinist against Calvinist at the very time when all New England was threatened and distracted by "*Arminian, Independent, Antinomian* Errors."[95] Obviously, Williams' reluctance to open new breaches was consistent with his unwillingness to move, with Edwards, into acceptance of the full implications of the evangelical scheme. For Williams the unity of Calvinists was a means of reining the evangelical impulse and of establishing harmony in preserving something of the inherited intellectual and social order.

To the degree that such Calvinists as Williams did launch a crusade against Arminianism in the 1750's, they found it possible to join hands with Thomas Clap and other Old Lights whose creed was hardly the dynamic faith of the Awakening. Something of the same process occurred in the Middle Colonies, where the Presbyterians in 1757 succeeded in repairing the breaches of the Awakening on the basis of an orthodoxy that ignored the vital questions of the qualifications of ministers and church members. It bears mentioning, however, that Presbyterian reunion was by no means easily effected, despite what seemed the compelling forces leading to a muting of Old and New Side differences. For nearly a decade Tennent's *Irenicum* was "treated with great indifference by one party, and with great contempt by the other."[96] And even in Tennent's *Irenicum* there were sown the seeds of new divisions. In arguing that neither approval of the Awakening nor the experience of the New Birth was a scriptural or a Presbyterian touchstone of fellowship, Tennent had proposed "soundness of doctrine" as the only proper test.[97] On this score there was in fact no complete agreement between the Old Side clergy and the evangelical Presbyterians, and even in the moment of reunion the latter were muttering complaints against the "latitudinarian" and "easy" preaching of the Philadelphia clergy.

Still, an open battle between evangelical and rational religion was avoided by the Presbyterians in the 1750's. Nearly everywhere, in fact, it was postponed, probably because Americans had once again been asked to decide which of two wars was the more important. For the moment at least, even the most zealous Calvinists decided that they and their people were called to enlist in the struggle against the French and Indians. In Massachusetts Ebenezer Pemberton was unexpectedly called on to deliver the Artillery Sermon in 1756, the Election Sermon in the following year. Thus it was not surprising that, when Thomas Sewall tried to open the subject of Arminianism before the Massachusetts ministers' convention in 1758, the times were deemed unpropitious for such a discussion. In the same year the Synod of New York accepted reunion with the Synod of Philadelphia because—among other reasons—unity appeared essential in what seemed the "dark day" of popish invasion.

The commitment of evangelical America to the war was not without reservation. From its very outset the colonial authorities seem to have been wary of the allegiances of American dissenters. The most unlikely presses poured out copies of Whitefield's "Short Address to Persons of all Denominations, Occasioned by the Alarm of an Intended Invasion." There he warned British dissenters of the *awful infatuation,* whatever their estimate of the English ruling classes or the Establishment, of preferring "a popish pretender" to the Hanoverian succession.[98] Many New Englanders seem never to have been convinced that the war was their concern, and among the Presbyterians of the Middle Colonies and the South there was, at least at the beginning, a hearty disinterest in the pride, pomp, and circumstance of the colonial war. According to Gilbert Tennent, many Pennsylvanians not only endangered the commonwealth by their "enthusiasm" against defensive war, but brought it to the brink of civil war.[99] This pacifism, which Tennent insisted was by no means limited to Quakers, was in large part inspired by the estrangement of the awakened from their governments during the decade or more in which the rich men and great men of colonial society had had nothing "else to do," as Davies observed in remarking on Braddock's defeat, than "harrass and oppress a number of harmless dissenters."[100] Yet a French victory, so far as Finley and Davies were concerned, would be intolerable, and once again the New Light Presbyterian orators strove to arouse the wills of their people in defense of their "country" against anti-Christian invaders.

The Calvinist sermons of the French and Indian War rehearsed nearly all the rhetorical devices that the evangelical clergy employed during the greater war that began to erupt shortly after the Peace of Paris. They disclosed, moreover, the variety of tensions and anxieties within the populace that the French and Indian War did not wholly subdue and which would persist through the decade or more of the crisis leading to Independence. The success of the Presbyterian exhorters particularly in urging their people to military and other service would help to secure toleration for Davies' followers, and for all Presbyterians a new status in colonial society. Yet the war began, in the Calvinist mind, as an opportunity for preserving and fulfilling the hopes of the Great Awakening. The sermons in which the Calvinist ministry strove to enlist the American people in defense of their "evangelical ministry" and religion as against that of "hypocritical Monks, Friars, Priests, and Jesuits" are not to be confused with the pleas of William Smith or Jonathan Mayhew on behalf of colonial patriotism.[101]

The Calvinist utterances of the Seven Years' War were animated by the possibility that the struggle between papal and Protestant legions might result in the downfall of the Antichrist. Yet Calvinist ministers did not go so far as to identify the colonial militia absolutely with the Church Militant. Particularly where the influence of Edwardeanism was maintained, they were not disposed to tie the cause of Protestantism, much less the millennium, to the fortunes of war. In 1756 the New Haven New Light, Samuel Bird, faintly echoed Whitefield's blessing on the saints and martyrs of Louisburg as he beseeched the Divine Presence for the troops preparing to march on Ticonderoga. But in the subsequent years of the war Calvinists more frequently called for a redefinition of war aims that the armies of King George and his colonial people might in fact "go forth, not in our Strength, but in the name of the Lord of Hosts."[102] By 1759, when Calvinist millenarian anticipations were already focused more on the Concert of Prayer than on the war, Robert Smith informed the pietists of interior Pennsylvania that "the *Devil*, the *Pope*, and the *French King*," however "their TRIPLE ALLIANCE, to extinguish the *Protestant Lamb*" might succeed on the field of battle, could not in any case "*destroy* the Church."[103]

Such a distinction between the Kingdom of Christ and any and all earthly empires was upheld in the utterances of colonial Calvinists well into the Revolutionary decade. In November 1772, for instance, Jeremy Belknap advised the New Hampshire militia:

> Whoever understands the nature of Christ's kingdom must be sensible that an attempt to defend it by arms would be equally rash and ridiculous, it being absolutely impossible to do it. Men may defend what they call the kingdom of Christ, they may defend a form of Christianity which has been interwoven with their civil government, and makes a part of their constitution . . .

It is vain then to think of using the sword in defence of Christ's kingdom; it is so spiritual and heavenly in its nature, that no weapon formed against it shall prosper, nor can any weapon used in its defence be of the least avail: It is able to subsist in the world not only without any help from the kingdoms of the world, but even in defiance of all their art, and strength, all their malice and enmity against it.[104]

After the Revolution Belknap, increasingly attracted to the ideas of such English Unitarians as Joseph Priestley, would in part recant the teachings of Wheelock and join hands with elements of the Boston rationalist clergy. Insofar as Belknap remained firm in the belief that the Kingdom was neither to be defended nor extended by mere force of arms, he could quite legitimately maintain his intellectual descent from Edwards.*[105] In the Calvinist mind, the destiny of the Kingdom of Christ was not one with that of any nation. But on the other hand, Calvinism understood what the rhetoric of Tennent, Finley, and Davies assumed—that Zion was strengthened whenever men, confronted by what they knew to be the wrong, engaged their wills on behalf of the right.

The Presbyterian patriots of 1756-1763 all called on their people to raise their "active powers to the highest pitch of exertion."[106] The summons was phrased in the terms of the moral law and within the framework of experimental religion. Tennent's most stirring utterance of the war years simply applied his version of the moral law to the occasion. *"Brethren,"* he insisted before a militia company, "we were born not merely for ourselves, but for the *Publick Good!* which, as Members of Society we are obliged pro virili to promote!"[107] Throughout the war, whenever Calvinists addressed the troops—once they had finished lecturing the officers on their "responsibilities" and turned to offer pastoral advice to those whom they took to be "brethren"— their exhortations integrated the various concerns of evangelical religion: "Let the WELFARE of so many of your fellow subjects, the welfare of the PROTESTANT INTEREST, the welfare of the CHURCH OF CHRIST, animate your hearts."[108]

When Davies urged Virginians to be "away to the field, and prove your pretensions sincere," or Tennent called on them to "evidence in

* Unlike many erstwhile Calvinists, Belknap did not in 1798 call for a holy war against the Napoleonic Antichrist, and unlike most of the Boston rationalists he did not even summon New Englanders to a military defense of their religious institutions. He did not live long enough to hear the "rationalist" William Freeman (at Boston's 1814 "Solemn Religious Festival" for the triumph of British arms) cry ecstatically that "Babylon the Great Has fallen!"—or to hear his own successor in the Federal Street pulpit proclaiming, throughout the war, the virtues of passively resisting the sinful enterprises of James Madison and Henry Clay.

Fact the Sincerity" of their love to God and their fellow men, they had, certainly without being aware of it, compromised the rigors of the Calvinist moral law.[109] For each of these Presbyterian sermons proceeded from the premise that the Calvinist populace had not in fact for many years shown a disposition to fulfill the moral law. In seizing on the war as a means of rousing their people from spiritual lethargy, the Presbyterian ministry had unintentionally betrayed the ideas of the Awakening. They had made patriotism not merely a duty under the moral law, but a form of virtue available to the entire Calvinist populace—and perhaps too available. For if men could prove their pretensions sincere by acting on behalf of God and country, assurance might, in appropriate circumstances, be possible to all mankind.

So committed was Calvinism to the ideal of communal welfare that Tennent, Finley, and Davies seem to have entered on their own patriotic careers eagerly and in a spirit of some indifference to the sharp distinctions of the 1740's. According to Samuel Finley, for instance, Davies had shown an ability to "take under view the grand interests of his country and of religion at once," but in such a broad perspective the possible conflicts of interest were, at least for the moment, lost sight of. Similarly, Tennent lauded Finley's oratorical masterpiece, *The Curse of Meroz*, as "a SPECIMEN of a superior GENIUS (and what is still more noble) of a disinterested and undaunted ZEAL for GOD, his KING, and COUNTRY."[110] Whether the three causes were kept separate in Finley's mind is not so much the question; the zealous and eloquent blending of all in the sermons of the war opened the popular mind, at least, to the possibility of confusion, and even substitution.

Technically none of the three Presbyterians had undertaken anything more than the normal office of the Calvinist Christian ambassador. In the words of Finley's sermon on Tennent:

> Whatever appeared to him subservient to the advancement of the Redeemer's Kingdom, the salvation of souls, or the common good of mankind, he pursued with spirit; and what he did, he did with his might.[111]

Tennent, Finley recalled, had "guarded against being unministerially pragmatical."[112] But perhaps he, and Finley and Davies as well, had finally gone too far in avoiding the errors of the Old Side ministry, who, as Benjamin Franklin once complained, tried "rather to make us *Presbyterians* than *good citizens*."[113] For by 1760 the Presbyterian orators had succeeded in making so many Presbyterians good citizens that Tennent was already bemoaning the difference between their zeal for God and their zeal for their country, and Samuel Davies, called to the presidency of the College of New Jersey in that year, thought it necessary to re-establish the distinction between piety and patriotism.

Davies' sermon, *Religion and Public Spirit,* delivered in 1760 as his valedictory to the first senior class graduated under his regime, would be republished several times in the next ten years and would provide many Calvinists with their definition of patriotism through the early years of the Revolution. In the sermon Davies confronted a question which would continue to plague the mind of pietism: whether love to mankind alone could be the essence of true virtue. Davies simply struggled with the dilemma in the terms posed by the charitable endeavors of Presbyterian patriots:

> Public Spirit and Benevolence without Religion, is but a warm Affection for the Subjects, to the Neglect of their Sovereign; or a Partiality for the Children, in Contempt of their Father, who is infinitely more worthy of Love. And Religion without Public Spirit and Benevolence, is but a sullen, selfish, sour and malignant Humour for Devotion, unworthy that sacred Name.[114]

After treating at length the moral obligations of Christians to serve their society and their fellow men, Davies concluded with a declaration that unsanctified charity, under whatever name, would be "but a monstrous, atheistical Patriotism, and an uncreature-like irreligious Benevolence," and would have "no more real Goodness in it, than the instinctive fondness of a Brute for its Young."[115]

Five years later Calvinists would be provided with Edwards' formidable demonstration that patriotism might be merely the most expansive form of selfishness, love of country a product of the most grandiose calculations of self-interest. They would be better prepared for events but, in the final analysis, no more successful than Davies in holding their people to the rigors of the moral law. It was by no means fortuitous that Nathaniel Whitaker, who was soon to become the most outspoken of Calvinist Revolutionary orators, addressed in 1770 the question of the relationship between love to God and love of mankind. They who define charity merely as "benevolence to our fellow men," he argued, turn the "ten commands upside down." He "that does not love God" cannot surely love man, "whose brightest glory and sweetest beauty is but a ray from God's infinite fulness of glory." Yet the "royal law of love," Whitaker continued, "requires us to love the bodies of our neighbors as our own, and to seek their temporal felicity." Doing so "is a bright evidence of our love to God himself."[116] In sum, experimental religion contained within its own premises the possibility that men would embrace something less than the full requirements of love to Being in general in order to prove, to their own satisfaction and that of the public, an evidential love of God.

History had a way of providing Americans seemingly heaven-sent opportunities for fulfillment of the moral law. Between 1756 and 1760 Davies, Finley, and Tennent demonstrated how readily anxious Calvinists could be moved to exert themselves to remove what, in the circumstances, seemed their spiritual burdens. The Seven Years' War, in sum, had opened the possibility of Americans' achieving true virtue by means other than a recognized outpouring of the Spirit. Yet Samuel Davies unquestionably went to his death in 1761 in the firm belief that his Demosthenic performances had neither added to nor subtracted from the faith of the Awakening. Indeed, at the close of his address *Religion and Public Spirit,* Davies was able to declare that "the great foundation of true Religion and social Virtue" was none other than

> that great Change of Temper, that Extirpation of the corrupt Principles of Nature, and that Implantation of holy and supernatural Principles of Action, which the Scriptures express by such strong and significant Metaphors as *Regeneration,* a *Resurrection,* a *new Creation,* and the like . . .

For all his preservation of the principal hinge of the evangelical scheme, perhaps Davies wondered just how much the planting of Paul and the watering of Apollos had contributed to producing the rather ample harvest of Presbyterian patriots. For after urging the young Presbyterians to fulfill the moral law, Davies thought it necessary to offer this sentiment:

> Tho' I address you in the *exhortatory* Form and would *persuade* you to exert yourselves, yet I would by no Means intimate, that the Forces of mere Nature, in their utmost Exertion, can produce in you that publick Spirit and Piety I am recommending, without the Agency of the *Holy Spirit* . . .[117]

Within four months of the sermon *Religion and Public Spirit,* Davies, speaking at Princeton on the death of King George II, would improve this latest "crisis" in public affairs by reminding his students of their obligations to "King and country," and call upon them to exert their energies in their "respective spheres, to execute" all the "patriot designs" of his son and heir.[118] Few of Davies' students, of course, would persist in doing so. The graduates of the College of New Jersey in this and future years—among them Aaron Burr, James Madison, Hugh Henry Brackenridge, Philip Freneau, Benjamin Rush, and the majority of the Revolutionary chaplaincy—would find the designs of George III consistent with no one's moral law. How Davies would have responded to the events of the Revolutionary decade we can only imagine. Yet one suspects that he would have taken the same course as the Demosthenic orator who succeeded to the leadership of Davies' Virginian people and, in exhorting them to benevolent action, would have even more thoroughly confused piety with patriotism in the public mind.

At the Peace of Paris, fewer Christian ambassadors remained to remind Americans of the true sources of public spirit. Edwards, Burr, Davenport, and Davies were dead, soon to be followed by Tennent and Samuel Finley. Of the captains of the Awakening only Bellamy was to survive into the Revolutionary decade, and it was to him that not only Wheelock, Parsons, and Benjamin Pomeroy, but numerous younger Calvinist ministers, turned for guidance and direction. But to the College of New Jersey came John Witherspoon, his purpose partly that of tempering the enthusiasm of young Presbyterians. In Pennsylvania and the South, the principles of evangelical religion would be kept alive largely by Baptist exhorters and revivalists. The French and Indian War, and the brief peace that followed, wrought in sum a perceptible realignment of American religion.

In some respects the war served to heal some of the breaches in American society. To the chagrin of the survivors of the Awakening era, the close of hostilities revealed what the end of the Revolution would witness on a continental scale: a defection from the ranks of strict Calvinism. Many ministers, including some who had answered the call to chaplaincies, were by 1763 overt, or more often, covert "moderate Calvinists." Their people, spared the more "alarming" doctrines of evangelical religion, were liberated for the pursuit not merely of happiness but of the prosperity enjoyed or promised during the war years. Among the spokesmen of orthodoxy or of moderation, the goals of the war had been more avowedly secular than evangelical principles would allow. Solomon Williams, for instance, saw France as attempting to engross land legitimately owned by the British Crown, thus endangering New England investments: "'Tis vain to think of Saving, till the *French* designs are broken, and they are dispossessed of their Encroachments."[119] Most importantly, the war had raised the question among the evangelical multitude whether men who acted as Liberal religion allowed them to act were necessarily evil or would necessarily come to the unhappy end that was supposed to await all who removed their eyes from the divinity of divinity.

The contribution of the war to such declension could be traced in many ways. But none is more obvious than the manner in which the employment of the jeremiad, in these seven years as through most of the seventeenth century, disposed the Protestant mind both to a belief in the efficacy of the human will and a higher estimate of the human character (or at least the American character) than the evangelical scheme assumed. In this process even the great Presbyterian triumvirate participated, because, among other reasons, as Tennent had discovered in the late 1740's, something like a "covenant" had to be assumed if the pious populace was to be moved to concern itself with the fate of the community. In the late 1750's Davies too found it necessary to employ a modified jeremiad as part of his effort to engage the wills of Virginia Presbyterians in defense of the colony.

The implications of such preaching were laid bare in 1759, when Davies celebrated Virginia's first thanksgiving for the success of British-American arms at Crown Point, Ticonderoga, and Niagara. As if repentant for the zeal with which he had seized on the time-honored device of the jeremiad for energizing the popular will, Davies all but confessed that he had opened the public mind to the suggestion that men's endeavors had been instrumental in removing the frowns of God and, by doing so, they had proved themselves so virtuous as to have no further need of His superintending Will. "Let us suppress a proud, self-righteous spirit," Davies exclaimed, "and not once imagine that our victories are the reward of our national goodness."[120] By 1763, however, more than one erstwhile Calvinist minister was not merely indulging, but encouraging, an orgy of American self-felicitation, and thereby disposing the populace to believe they had somehow earned the right to participate in the numerous "blessings" which the coming of peace seemed to promise.

Among those blessings was, of course, the opening of the interior to settlement, and in not too many years after the Peace of Paris the popular mind would be disposed to conceive of the West, even the trans-Allegheny West, as the Christian inheritance on which they were now entitled to enter. Such a prospect challenged, among other things, the evangelical purpose of Indian conversion, and thus it was not surprising that one of Wheelock's confederates in the organization of the Lebanon Indian School was among the first to seek to recall evangelical America to its first principles. In June 1763, in a sermon at the ordination of an evangelist to Virginia, Nathaniel Whitaker proclaimed that Christians

> have done with types and figures, and have heaven set before us; the world, with all its flatteries and frowns, is dashed out of our account . . . The religion of *Christ* proposed something more divine and glorious to our view than the milk and honey of an earthly *Canaan.*[121]

With this sermon, the partisans of evangelical religion mounted what was, in effect, a counterattack on the more secular spirit aroused by the war, but the events of the next decade or so made it difficult even for Whitaker to remember Edwards' principle that the Church of Christ had nothing to do with "nations."[122] Like their more moderate brethren, Calvinists had grown impressed, during the Seven Years' War, with the special destiny, if not of the British empire, then of America itself.

Whatever the transformations of the evangelical mind in the course of the war with France, in many ways the sermons of the period served to sharpen the American's sense of his differences from other members of colonial society. According to the Presbyterian preachers, there were many residents of the colonies who "through mere Indolence, Covetousness, or other False Principles" refused to "exert themselves for the Defence of their Country." By preferring their own "private interest" to the "public Weal," they exposed themselves to the "Curse of Meroz"—"Curse ye Meroz, saith the angel of the Lord, curse ye bitterly the inhabitants thereof: because they came not to the help of the Lord against the mighty." "Let the thunder of this imprecation," cried Davies as he introduced the words of Judges 5:23, "rouse you out of your ease and security."[123]

It is not unlikely that its rousing effect derived no little from the manner in which the text provided Davies' auditors an opportunity to compare themselves with the less active citizens of the colonies. For as Finley developed the doctrine in his sermon *The Curse of Meroz,* it stood in judgment on all who were not zealously affected in a good cause:

> All who understand the Nature of *Society,* see a manifest Analogy between a *natural Body,* and a *Body politic.* Now if the natural Body be supposed in Danger of perishing, and the Hands refuse to administer proper Nourishment, or the Stomach to receive and concoct it, when administered:—If the Eyes and Feet are on contrary Sides of the Question, the former refusing to direct, and the latter to move;—is it not certain, that such recusant Members do not only hurt their respective Opponents, [*sic*] but the whole Body? Do they not expose it to Ruin, according to their several Influence and Importance, *only by standing Neuter,* and not performing each its Function?[124]

The sting of the doctrine and its application was particularly evident in Davies' sermon, *The Curse of Cowardice,* where he delineated, with the artful precision for which Calvinist preachers were noted, the character of the "sly hypocritical coward" who takes up arms "deceitfully." Such men, according to Davies, enter the service in order to enrich themselves, or to enhance their reputations.[125] As he explained in his Princeton sermon *Religion and Public Spirit,* one could be inspired with a true "Public-spirit" only out of a pure love of God. It was not the essence of benevolence, but quite the reverse, to embark on a career of patriotism to "procure Honour" or to "accomplish some interested Designs."[126] With such thoughts being instilled in the Calvinist populace, they were provided by 1763 with perhaps a modified but by no means a less compendious catalogue of sinners in their midst, and they had, moreover, once again heard Divine judgment called for on certain members of American society.

The "Curse of Meroz" occupied an honored station among the continuing themes of colonial American literature. It was invoked by Thomas Hooker even before the migration as against the "glozing neuters" of his day, and its use by Roger Williams, as applied to those who in Massachusetts Bay would not separate from the Church of England, was high on the list of reasons for his banishment. According to Gershom Bulkeley, moreover, it filled the thoughts of the Connecticut revolutionaries of 1688—their legacy from the thought of John Davenport and the regicide judges. But the Curse of Meroz was first invoked on a continental scale in the Great Awakening, by Tennent and Finley, of course, and vividly and pointedly by Jonathan Parsons:

> In vain do Men hope to shun the Censure of being against Christ, who are not *active* in his Cause: They must gather with him, or else he will have us esteem them his *Enemies.* . . And now, when this is the true State of our religious Affairs, to make any Thing serve for an Excuse to lag *behind,* is *mean* Cowardize, and a dark Sign that men don't care to engage in a *critical* Day and a *difficult* Service, when their Help is most expected. I wish such men, whether of *high* or *low* Degree, would seriously and upon their Knees before GOD, ponder those Words, *Judg.* 5. 23.[127]

It is possibly of some significance that Calvinist tradition, and that of Edwards' own family, long held that in 1735 Edwards delivered and published a sermon entitled *The Curse of Meroz.* No such publication has been discovered or acknowledged by modern bibliographers, but quite possibly Edwards' admirers had in mind his sermon, "The Unreasonableness of Indetermination in Religion," delivered in 1734, though not published until 1779. In that sermon he insisted that it is not a "matter of indifference what master we serve, whether God or Mammon," and urged his people to choose either "the service of God or the service of Baal."[128] In *The Distinguishing Marks,* however, Edwards invoked the curse explicitly, against not merely those who reproached the revival but "many who are silent and inactive, especially ministers." And in his *Thoughts on the Revival* Edwards again turned the text against indifferent men, "so prudent" that their conduct seemed "inexcusable," and those who refused to enlist in the Church Militant when Christ's banner was "displayed, and his trumpet blown."[129]

The text, used to arouse the slothful people of God in whatever operation the Calvinist ministry happened to be engaged, carefully and clearly separated the friends of Christ from His enemies in any community. Nor was the French and Indian War the last occasion on which it was found useful. It was probably the favorite text of the Calvinist ministry in the years of the Revolution, when it was used expressly to focus the animus of the people of God against, not the British, but the American Tories, and even the questionable and suspicious patriots of the colonies. But before then it was given considerable employment in the religious battles that issued from the revival of 1763, when the Calvinist ministry found that the trumpets of some clergymen supposedly enlisted under the banner of Christ gave "an uncertain sound" when the time came to continue the Work of God.[130] Several of the Calvinist calls to battle bore on their title pages the most tendentious of mottoes—"Curse ye Meroz"—and all proposed that Arminians, among the clergy or among the laity, were proper subjects of the curse, whether they stood neutral or whether they slyly and hypocritically sought to disguise their real sentiments.

The revivals of 1763 spawned throughout the colonies a variety of ecclesiastical controversies comparable to those of the 1740's. During the 1763 "awakening," which began in John Cleaveland's Ipswich congregation, Cleaveland had exchanged pulpits with other Calvinist ministers in Essex County, including the Presbyterian, Jonathan Parsons. When members of some of these churches began, soon after the revival, to request transfer to Cleaveland's church, many of those ministers who had first welcomed the revival grew noticeably cold toward Cleaveland, withdrew the right hand of fellowship, and denied their parishioners the privilege of transfer. What had happened was that many ministers who professed the Calvinist creed—among them Moses Parsons, father of the future Chief Justice of Massachusetts—had become unwilling to tolerate the consequences of religious enthusiasm, and, though also hesitant to proclaim publicly their abandonment of Calvinist doctrine and goals, were seeking to contain the revival.

Cleaveland threw down the gauntlet by declaring that all who opposed separations opposed the revival and, regardless of what creed they officially professed, were effectively supporting Arminianism.

"I wish all would consider," he insisted, that "if we have not the Spirit of Christ, we are none of his—That if we are Friends to the World, we are Enemies to God; and, That we cannot serve God and Mammon."[131] The service of both God and Mammon was precisely what the likes of Moses Parsons had learned to condone, and within a decade they would openly declare their commitment to the faith of "moderate Calvinism." This system, or lack of system, was distinguished by an avoidance in the pulpit of the more "frightening" Calvinist themes and usually by resuscitation of the theory of the covenant and of a faculty psychology. Most of its proponents were even before the Revolution in effective alliance with the Liberal founders of American Unitarianism.

The evangelical response to "moderate Calvinism" took many forms, including, once more, separations, censoring of ministers, and a drive for religious freedom. In this respect the attack on moderation was part of a more general reassertion of the principle that two cannot walk together unless they be agreed. The war with France was still in progress when Calvinist spokesmen announced that agreement "in principle, at least in the main things," was essential to the peace and unity of the church:

> To see Orthodox, Arians, Pelagians, Socinians, and even Deists, all confusedly blended together in one communion, is not seemly. This may be termed catholicism, but it is latitudinarianism. This is saying a confederacy, to which heaven will not say amen; and instead of being acceptable, is abominable to God. What fellowship hath light with darkness![132]

That something more was at isue in the early 1760's than the orthodoxy of the clergy is suggested by the degree to which the evangelical reaffirmation of "principle" was attended by the explosion of the drive for regenerate church membership. In New England the controversy generally focused on repudiation of the Half-Way Covenant, but however the issue was drawn it was evident that it was the citizens of each community, and not simply the ministry, whom strict Calvinists were unwilling to see remain in unseemly communion.

Over and again the Calvinist literature of the 1760's made the point that the unbelievers' party included not only the Arminian ministry but all who supported them in their various efforts to suppress the "faith and purity of the gospel." When Aaron Hutchinson set about exposing what he called a "Cataline's conspiracy" against Calvinism, he suggested that Arminians were "easily detected, by only observing what company they keep."[133] Calvinism in the 1760's was distinguished by a more vocal insistence on the principle that had begun to emerge in the 1750's: that subscription to Arminian tenets, openly or otherwise, was the clearest evidence of membership in the legions of Antichrist. However the world might be divided "into a great variety of sects and parties," Joseph Bellamy explained in one of the more influential pamphlets of the decade, there were but "two sorts of men, believers and unbelievers." On the one hand there were those who saw the "beauty and harmony" of Calvinism; on the other, those who, to pamper their unregenerate hearts, believed not only "one error," but a "whole system of lies."[134] The children of darkness were those whose "*hearts* were conformed to the Arminian doctrines, and influenced by the spirit of their self-righteous system."[135] Once more, it seemed, the partisans of the legal and evangelical schemes were drawn up in battle array.

The promptness with which Calvinists returned after the Peace of Paris to the doctrinal and ecclesiastical issues of the 1750's suggests that the evangelical mind had by no means fixed on the war to the exclusion of all other concerns. Indeed nothing in the literature of the period rings quite so ironically as the sermons of felicitation with which the rationalist clergy greeted the conclusion of the war. Henry Caner of Boston's King's Chapel, for instance, preached on the subject, "The Great Blessings of Stable Times," and Nathaniel Appleton sang what he called a "joyful Song" of peace and tranquillity. Yet neither was to long enjoy respite from controversy—no more than was Jonathan Boucher, who in 1763 remarked how fortunate was Virginia to have as its populace "an industrious, peaceable, and contented peasantry."[136] Within the year Virginia sectarians, rather than studying to be quiet, were boisterously mounting a crusade against Anglicanism, and in Massachusetts the spokesmen of rational religion were already in 1763 being loudly and vehemently challenged.

Throughout the war, moreover, the Concert of Prayer had enjoyed a considerable vogue among American Calvinists generally. In 1759 Robert Smith preached and published a sermon in which he told the Presbyterians of Pennsylvania that this strategy, more than the battlefield successes of British arms, promised to bring on the "brightest period of the militant Church's Glory."[137] Meanwhile, both in doctrinal sermons and even in the very orations that summoned men to combat, Calvinism was preparing the evangelical mind for a reconstitution of the earthly Church Militant.

Among the doctrines to be given new prominence in Calvinist thought was that of God's moral government and the propriety of His vindictive justice. Early in the 1750's Samuel Davies observed that "justice is not that grim, stern, tremendous attribute which is delineated by the guilty, partial examination of sinners" but is rather "infinitely amiable and lovely, as well as awful and majestic."[138] A few years later Bellamy announced that "love is the very essence of vindictive justice." When divine vengeance is "put in execution" on the Day of Judgment, Bellamy explained, it will inspire "unmixed, endless joys, among angels and saints." That the Final Judgment would "meet with universal approbation and applause from all holy beings in the universe" was a principle inherited from Edwards, who had occasionally descanted on the happiness of the saints in contemplating the punishment of the wicked. But Edwards' observations had been for the most part demonstrations, for the benefit of the people of God, that the Deity punished sinners out of the inherent goodness of his nature.[139] This remained the doctrine of Calvinism through the Revolution, when Nathaniel Whitaker, for one, consistently asserted that "God's hatred of sin, and the punishment he inflicts on the wicked, arises from his love of happiness, from the benevolence of his nature."[140] What the 1750's brought to view, however, was the possibility of this judgment being executed on earth. On whom such vengeance might be taken, who were to be its instruments, and at what time, were the crucial questions.

One answer was that offered by the Presbyterians during the French and Indian War. Both Tennent and Finley filled their sermons with demonstrations of the "Excellency and Necessity of commutative Justice," presumably in order to overcome the pacifism of those who claimed to be so filled with love of all mankind that they could not do battle for the Lord.[141] There is in such justice, Finley explained, a "fitness and Propriety" that "can never fail of the highest Approbation" when properly observed:

> They who are so highly *delighted* with the dreadful Executions of divine JUSTICE, are not turbulent, cruel, and revengeful Spirits, but Saints and Angels, full of Love to God and Men. But *Justice* has an inexpressible Excellency, and a most charming *Beauty,* to *upright Minds.* To be pleased with its Executions is only to be pleased, that Things are as they ought to be . . . But distempered Eyes cannot bear the dazzling Light of the Sun; nor can blind and guilty Minds behold the Brightness of *moral Beauty.*[142]

What the Presbyterian ministry thus provided their people during the war with France was a new and delightful means of fulfilling the moral law—as expressed in the title of Tennent's sermon, *The Happiness of Rewarding Enemies.* For these sermons were not mere exercises in doctrine, but exhortations to action. And the burden of their message was clear: whatever worldly pleasures the true saint might be expected to deny himself, he might conform his will to the Divine Will, and thus find delight, by serving God as a minister of His avenging justice.

Such a view of the Divine perfections and their imperative, given something of a dress rehearsal in the war with France, would lead the people of God to even more inexpressible delight during the Revolution, when David Avery, for one, explained on a day of thanksgiving that

> all the divine attributes are harmonious with each other; and when viewed in their connexions, they all appear *equally* amiable and glorious. One is as dear to GOD as another: he ever hath been, and still is, at immense expence to make their *respective glories shine with lustre*. His *justice,* for instance, even his *avenging* justice, (which affords so much terror to the wicked,) is *no less* an object of his *complacency* and *delight,* than is his *mercy*. And to all *holy* beings, the DEITY appears as *beautiful,* and as *lovely* in the *former,* as in the *latter*.[143]

The emergence and application of the theory of moral government in periods of war suggest that neither it nor the doctrine of the atonement to which it was hinged was, in the context of mid-eighteenth-century America, either reactionary or repressive in tendency. The evangelical ministry were seeking to energize the wills of their people by providing them at least a modicum of the "triumph and joy" that would rise to its highest flame and rapture at the Final Judgment. For Tennent, however, the "intrinsick Excellency" of commutative justice was perceivable only in the case of defensive warfare, and when he argued that it could not be wrong, in such a case, to "promote what is good," he presumably had no other target for the executors of Divine vengeance than the French and papal legions.[144] Yet the doctrine had made its appearance in the colonies independently of the imperial wars and, as it evolved, also served as the framework for the saints' dealings with their domestic enemies.

It is not difficult to appreciate why Jonathan Mayhew, in his sermon *Divine Goodness* in 1762, decided to say as little as possible about the justice of God's moral government*[145]—a theme, he had observed, of rather too *"common declamation."*[146] For even as Calvinists des-

---

* In the Mayhew-Cleaveland interchange, the issue was not merely Mayhew's Arianism but the whole question of whether God's "essence" was indivisible or his attributes capable of being conceived separately. Mayhew's position was the traditionally Liberal one; he refused "to meddle" with such questions as "the metaphysical abstract nature, or essence of the Deity." Cleaveland argued that the question was neither metaphysical nor abstract. Declaring that "the essence of God, is God," he insisted it was high time to get rid of all the orthodox "distinctions" that allowed Jonathan Mayhew, among others, to treat God as "a compound Being, made up of as many distinct self-existent qualities or parts, as he has divine attributes."

canted on a God whose "avenging justice" was consistent with his "absolute goodness," they made it perfectly obvious that the primary objects of God's wrath were those who would not see the beauty of the Calvinist Godhead.[147] Chief among the offenders were, of course, "such haughty blaspheming babblers" as Jonathan Mayhew. "I believe," John Cleaveland allowed, "if the Dr. was to suffer the punishment of hell, he would have no discovery at all, of the tender mercy of God towards him in such a terrible punishment!"[148] But by 1763 they included all who were aiding or abetting the intellectual conspiracy against the Calvinist God. That Cleaveland's theory of the atonement was, like Edwards', Anselmic, and that Bellamy's was Grotian, was a matter of minor importance in the world of 1763. Saints could find joy in the damnation of Arminians, and all that the Massachusetts Calvinists lacked was what Bellamy was busily providing his people: a view of history that could arouse the saints to experience such joy at some moment prior to the Last Judgment.

IV

A Tory historian, writing during the Revolution, was persuaded that "the REAL sources" of the "rebellion in America" lay in the attitude of the Calvinist ministry and populace toward "heretics and Arminians."[149] Since he came from Connecticut, his conviction is possibly a tribute to the special contribution of Joseph Bellamy to the formation of the American Revolutionary mind. In many respects, Bellamy's thinking during the late 1750's bespoke the disengagement of evangelical New England from the course of the French and Indian War. The war had little to do, Bellamy concluded as early as 1757, with the most distinctive sign of the times, the "great murmurings" among the Calvinist populace, "but no *reformation*." America has "had a day of great grace," he wrote to Samuel Davies, but "that is past and gone,"[150] and the question was now being asked whether the Calvinist God were indeed bent on establishing His Kingdom on earth. "The state of the world and the church" appeared "exceeding gloomy and dark," and, according to Bellamy," "still darker times are by many expected." The same view of history inspired the Presbyterian reunion; where Bellamy differed was in seeking to preserve the battle lines of the 1740's. For much of the darkness, as Bellamy saw it, had less to do with the popish threat than with the possibility of desertions from the ranks of the saintly as the millennium failed to arrive. The "tendency to apostatize," as Bellamy styled it, seemed to be taking the form of finding more attractive the gospel of Liberal religion.[151]

Even in the "towns and societies" of the Connecticut "frontier,"

339

where Bellamy had ten years earlier discovered and bewailed the rising generation's "habit of attending places of vain and fashionable amusements," the lure of Liberal culture was being felt.[152] In these circumstances, many of the Calvinist clergy of Connecticut simply bemoaned declension. In 1758, for instance, Benjamin Throop told the General Assembly of the appalling rise in popularity of Arminianism and Arianism and, with it, the prevalence of a "Pride and Vanity" that was rendering all "Men uneasy in their proper Station."[153] But Joseph Bellamy read the times, and the Connecticut mind, somewhat differently: to him, the people of God seemed above all perplexed. The Connecticut saints, it seemed, had begun to raise the cry of saints in any time: why do sinners prosper? The not-so-saintly, like their counterparts in any age, had begun to seek the secret of their neighbor's prosperity, but the saints asked their questions in forms peculiarly characteristic of post-Awakening America. Beholding the prevalence of "error and wickedness" in the colonies, their "dark and gloomy thoughts" were expressed as doubts concerning the millennial strategy and calendar of Jonathan Edwards and the ability of the Calvinist God to overcome the sinful dispositions of mankind. *The* temptation, as Bellamy saw it, was that of hearkening to the Liberal sirens who contended that Calvinism, by absurdly positing God's authorship of sin, misread both the nature and the destiny of mankind.

In this situation Bellamy prepared, delivered, and published his sermons, *The Wisdom of God in the Permission of Sin* and *The Millennium,* which, as he asserted in the preface to the former, were designed as companion doctrines that, taken together, would have a "great tendency" to make the people of God "feel right and behave well," and, indeed, "exert themselves to the utmost to promote the Redeemer's glorious cause."[154] That the people of God did not "feel right" in 1758 was to be attributed to the fact that they had long been urged to a life of self-denial as a part of their duty under the moral law, while the Arminian populace were making a profit and living a fashionable life. That they were not behaving well was a consequence of their observation that some men were diverting attention from spiritual and divine things without suffering divine punishment.

The late 1750's (in the words of the title of a Davies sermon delivered shortly before the outbreak of the French War, *A Time of Unusual Sickness*) thus betrayed the classic symptoms of a spiritual malaise which would overcome God's American people at approximately two-decade intervals for another century. The ideas expounded by Bellamy in Connecticut, and the apparent consequences of those ideas, therefore shed light, not only on the society and politics of colonial America, but on the subsequent intellectual and political history of the nation.

For Republican spokesmen in 1798-1800, as indeed Thomas Hart Benton a generation later, were no less than Bellamy dedicated to the task of holding Americans to their professions at the very moment of the greatest suspicion that "liberalism" had a more feasible program for the pursuit of happiness.

What happened in Connecticut in the period between 1756 and 1765 occurred with little attention, initially, to the foreign enemies of God. A partial explanation of the somewhat divergent history of New England generally in these years is that the Seven Years' War saw no invasion of the northern colonies. Thus comparatively few New Englanders were offered the opportunities for release from the demands of experimental religion which, south of New York, had been urged on the people of God as a matter of overwhelming necessity. Some had felt the embattled "ardor of the heart" which, according to a pious New Jersey Calvinist of 1759, could "only be understood by men of courage, who know it by experience."[155] But for the most part the people of rural New England spent the war years at home, where they, without experience, nonetheless managed to develop a taste for cavalier pleasures which, under the regimen of Bellamy and other Calvinists, they were not supposed to experience.

Unlike other areas of strong evangelical persuasion, Connecticut was far from isolated from the seeming progress and prosperity of the war years. Like those who were awakened in 1763-1764, the Calvinist populace of Connecticut had their eyes on the "rich and fashionable" of the province. But they could not, as did the Long Island parishioners of Samuel Buell, content themselves with the thought that they were geographically insulated from the enemies of the Spirit.[156] Thus the implications of the evangelical scheme were displayed, as they would not be so displayed even during the revivals of 1800, uncomplicated by any of the factors which at other times, and in other places, permitted Americans a wide choice of belief and action. For one brilliant moment at least, the social potentialities of Calvinism disclosed themselves in all their unobscured and dazzling splendor.

Joseph Bellamy's contribution to the American mind was to make explicit certain ideas present in Edwardean Calvinism, to do so without sacrificing essentials, and, in doing so, to all but proclaim to the people of God the necessity of a civil war before the millennium could begin in America. Most significant of all the lessons of the master retained by Bellamy—considering what seems to have been a tendency to Manichaeanism among the Calvinist populace in the "dark days" of the late 1750's—was a confidence that sin had no positive power of its own, but was merely the result of man's natural disposition when unaided by the power of the Spirit. Expressed as a theory of history, by Edwards as well as by Bellamy, this idea took the form of conceiving spiritual progress—the Work of Redemption—as a rhythmic series of gracious pulsations "opposing the natural current," each of them soon "overcome by a constant natural bias,"[157] then rising again to overpower the naturally sinful disposition of man. What Bellamy contributed to this theory was a greater emphasis on the fitness and beauty of the manner in which the "divine power" met and overcame "great opposition."[158]

To Edwards it seemed always clear that the happiness of man or of saints consisted "very much in beholding the glory of God appearing in the work of Redemption." But in the *End in Creation* he conceived the beauty of history almost solely as an increase in the Kingdom of Light. This had not been true in the sermons on the Work of Redemption, nor generally in the sermons of the years just previous to the Great Awakening. In 1738 he had observed that

> the beauty of good appears with the greatest advantage, when compared with its contrary evil. And the glory of that which is excellent, then especially shows itself, when it triumphs over its contrary, and appears vastly above it, in its greatest height.[159]

This note was all but abandoned, however, in his later discussions of the Work of Redemption, and it was wholly excised from the millennial theory of the *Humble Attempt*. In his private speculations, Edwards proposed but one value to darkness—and that, interestingly enough, quite consistent with his various hints that men, not children, were to inherit the earth. Seasons of darkness, the winters of the Church's discontent, allowed the Church and the saints to "come to their perfection gradually," preserving them from the withering of the summer sun in their infancy, keeping them back "from a too sudden growth and quick transition."[160]

Bellamy's millenarianism, however, proceeded from the premise that however gradually God prepared for the coming of His Kingdom, it would and must come "with celerity," and in a moment of glorious triumph of good over evil. For him the beauty of history was the bringing of light out of darkness, as when, he explained, after a storm "the sun breaks forth in his strength—an emblem of the Sun of Righteousness."[161] This, according to Bellamy, was the "wisdom in his whole grand scheme" for the redemption of mankind, a scheme so "perfect in wisdom, glory, and beauty" that it was folly "to wonder why these glorious days should be so long delayed."[162] Since "God's nature is always the same," and since it was inconceivable that He created the world only that His enemies might triumph, was it not likely, Bellamy asked, that "the infinitely wise Governor of the world" had at the beginning of time

> determined to permit the wickedness of mankind to come out and stand in so glaring a light, and to suffer Satan so long to practise and prosper; to this very purpose, that his power, wisdom and grace might be the more effectually and the more gloriously displayed, in the accomplishment of all his glorious designs?"[163]

The "grand drama" of Joseph Bellamy's Work of Redemption was perhaps less cosmic than that which Edwards had posited. As early as 1750 Bellamy had declared that the "whole world was created for a stage, on which a variety of scenes were to be opened; in and by which, God designed to exhibit a most exact image of himself."[164] But the purpose of God's permission of sin was not merely to provide the world a clearer "manifestation of himself" nor even that His "perfections" might be "most illustriously displayed."[165] Rather God wanted to give His creatures more time to "give a true specimen of themselves, that it might be known what was in their hearts." Those who would "give way to sloth and effeminacy" or "turn aside to earthly pursuits" simply because the millennium had been so long delayed, Bellamy insisted, would not be in the goodly number who would find delight in perceiving the beauty of the grand climax of the historical drama.[166] The world being a "theatre," in which events transpired "proper to raise, in intelligent beings, sublime and exalted thoughts," those who were filled with less sublime thoughts, or found pleasure elsewhere, were presumably not saints.[167] Nothing can satisfy the mind of the saint, Bellamy declared in conclusion, but "a clear view and fair prospect of Christ's final victory over all his enemies."[168]

Having made this point Bellamy called on "all the followers of Christ" to "exert themselves to the utmost, in the use of all proper means to suppress error and vice of every kind, and promote the cause of truth and righteousness in the world; and so be workers together with God." What Bellamy had accomplished was to provide a course of action for every man in Connecticut who attributed his unhappiness to the seeming prosperity of the cause of Antichrist. You have "nothing to do but your duty," Bellamy explained in 1758,

> nothing, but to attend upon the business he has marked out for you; like a faithful soldier in an army, who trusts his general to conduct affairs, while he devotes himself to the business he is set about.

All would be happy, quite simply, if they enlisted in the Church Militant, and as "volunteers" under the banner of Christ, exercised their wills to introduce that "glorious state of things" which would follow upon the overthrow of Satan's dominion.[169] They would be happy, in effect, if—being troubled or perplexed by darkness—they exerted themselves to establish the Kingdom of Light.

By 1762, the New Lights of Connecticut had attained sufficient control of the lower house of the General Assembly that they were able to appoint Bellamy Election Preacher. Since his sermon *The Millennium,* Bellamy had developed his theory of God's "moral government" of the universe and thoroughly integrated it with his conception of God's wisdom in the permission of sin. In his treatment of vindictive justice, Bellamy once more went beyond Edwards, who had offered the earthly saints no more "benevolent" action against the reprobate than excommunication.[170] But Bellamy's Election Sermon strongly implied what was abundantly clear in his other writings: that there were certain times and seasons prior to the end of the world when "executing righteous vengeance" would, if properly done, not be "a bad thing." Like Edwards, Bellamy maintained that "private revenge is altogether improper and unfit," but unlike Edwards, he went on to affirm that certain kinds of corporate justice were not necessarily so.[171]

Bellamy's Election Sermon contained a characterization of Connecticut society which made it abundantly clear where Calvinism had traveled in the years since 1750. Social conditions in 1762 nearly reproduced those of 1739; Bellamy's catalogue of errors and wickedness reads, at first glance, like a repetition of the rubrics handed down by the reforming Synod of 1679: "Sabbath profaned, family prayer neglected, hearts and hands unclean, whoredom rampant." But it was, more significantly, a commentary on the course of New England society since the glorious Awakening: "luxury, idleness, debauchery, dishonesty," "gay dressing," "extravagant high living," and, of course, "excessive law suits." Bellamy first proposed that a revival of true religion would overcome all these symptoms of sin:

> . . . pride and a luxurious disposition being mortified, those expensive and extravagant ways of living, to which our pride and luxuriousness now prompt us, would be looked upon with abhorrence, and laid aside with shame and regret . . .

Turning to the ministers of the gospel, Bellamy observed that those who upheld the faith on which Connecticut was founded "should be united as one man to bring about a universal reformation," and added, as he had in *The Millennium,* that it was their duty to preach the Calvinist gospel "whether the wicked will hear or not."

Then, as none had done in the years before the Awakening, an Election Preacher openly declared that the "rulers" of the province, however obliged to "take the lead" in reforming society, were less trustworthy than either the New Light ministry or their followers. Bellamy observed that the governor and the General Court had published a royal proclamation which required all in the realm "to exert themselves in the practice of piety and virtue." But he observed to (and of) the governor and legislators, "it is easier, you are sensible, to issue out such a proclamation than it is to act up to the true purport and spirit of it." Finally, Bellamy spoke to the "congregation in general," and, through them, to the populace of the province: "Let every man in the colony," he exhorted, join to stone sin

> with stone until it is dead—so let sin be slain. Pride, luxuriousness, contentiousness, malice, envy, idleness, dishonesty, or by whatever name it is called, it is sin, and let it die.

Of course Bellamy offered nothing tangible for the people of God to do but pray for an outpouring of the Spirit to make Connecticut a habitation of righteousness. As in *The Millennium,* he provided them with nothing but "spiritual weapons" with which to overcome their "spiritual enemies."[172] But in his very listing of the wickednesses to be overcome, he made it quite evident that, save for a disposition to "envy" among the members of the Church Militant, what needed to be overcome was the pride of the rich men and the great men of Connecticut, and indeed, of all—whether lawyers or merchants—who found the Arminian gospel more appealing.

Among the forms which "envy" had taken by 1760, it is clear, was a desire for participation in the earthly victories of the British-American armies and, presumably, a share in the honors and glory of the imperial wars. As early as 1756 Samuel Davies found it necessary to remind many Virginians that the Church Militant—being "immortal and invincible"—was actually a more impressive aggregation than any of the armies of the British King.[173] Bellamy too was aware of such a disposition among the Calvinist populace of New England, and in seeking to overcome it, ended his sermon *The Millennium* with an apostrophe to the Church Militant. "If one stood at the head of this glorious army," began Bellamy in what amounted to a revelation of the role and function of the Calvinist ministry in 1758,

> which has been in the wars above these five thousand years, and has lived through many a dreadful campaign, and were allowed to make a speech to these veteran troops upon this glorious theme, he might lift up his voice, and say,
> 'Hail noble heroes! brave followers of the Lamb!—Your General has sacrificed his life in this glorious cause, and spoiled principalities

and powers on the cross; and now he lives and reigns. He reigns on high, with all power in heaven and earth in his hands. Your predecessors, the prophets, apostles, and martyrs, with undaunted courage, have marched into the field of battle, and conquered dying, and now reign in heaven. Behold, ye are risen up in their room, are engaged in the same cause, and the time of the last general battle draws on, when a glorious victory is to be won; and, although many a valiant soldier may be slain in the field, yet the army shall drive all before them at last. And Satan being conquered, and all the powers of darkness driven out of the field, and confined to the bottomless pit, ye shall reign with Christ a thousand years;—reign in love and peace, while truth and righteousness ride triumphant through the earth. Wherefore lay aside every weight, and, with your hearts wholly intent on this grand affair, gird up your loins, and with all the spiritual weapons of faith, prayer, meditation, and watchfulness, with redoubled zeal and courage, fall on your spiritual enemies . . . And if the powers of darkness should rally all their forces, and a general battle through all the Christian world come on, O, love not your lives to the death! Sacrifice every earthly comfort in the glorious cause! Sing the triumphs of your victorious General in prisons and at the stake! And die courageously, firmly believing the cause of truth and righteousness will finally prevail.'[174]

Bellamy's celebration of the glorious Christian army, certainly among the most remarkable of perorations in the history of American public address, was apparently also one of the more effective. He first delivered this sermon in 1758, and repeated it throughout the colony an unknown number of times in the following years; his Election Sermon was given in 1762. Three years later the New Light party decided, for reasons not unconnected with their desire to achieve total control of the Connecticut government, to oppose the Stamp Act. The consequences of Bellamy's rhetoric were revealed when the New Light clergy of Connecticut called their people to action against both the tax and the instruments of its collection. They all but identified this piece of legislation with the Antichrist, burned it in effigy as "the beast," and, eventually, were able to celebrate its repeal as a victory over the *"beast, and over his mark."*[175] In doing so they disclosed how near the last general battle was imagined to be.

More importantly, however, they advised the "saints" that an "Arminian and a favorer of the Stamp Act signified the same man," that one's "Political Creed," indeed, was both "badge and Test" of his "religious Principles."[176] In 1765 New Light mobs roamed nearly at will about Connecticut, cursing, first of all, "such clergymen as rode in chaises and were above the control of God's people." They then turned to attacking both the persons and the property of "Arminians," who, according to one so attacked, were all who would "affect superiority." The saints had found release from a situation which could not have helped seeming intolerable and unbearable. In Virginia, where the "Sword" nearly ten years earlier had been "consecrated to God," Davies' Presbyterians had been given other outlets from a similar predicament, but in Connecticut the followers of Joseph Bellamy had to seize their own weapons. And even as they hurled stones through the windows of Episcopalian meeting houses and into the carriages of the fashionable, the "saints" expressed their triumph and joy by exclaiming that it was "better to live with the Church Militant than with the Church Triumphant."[177]

By early 1766 Bellamy and his colleagues, dismayed by a chaos and confusion which they had clearly neither anticipated nor intended, agreed with the Connecticut magistracy to permit the enforcement of the Stamp Act should news of its repeal not come by the next ship. In the next eight years they would seek to prevent the spread of what Bellamy called Connecticut's "civil war,"[178] first by proposing that all the citizens of the province—rich and poor, Arminians and Calvinists, but more particularly the rich and the Arminians—fulfill the moral law by manifestations of the great Christian virtue of charity. When this plea went unanswered, they sought to unite all Christians in promoting a general revival of religion, but by 1773 they were once again convinced that the saints, and the saints alone, would have to be marshaled under the banner of the coming Kingdom.

On May 13, 1773, Izrahiah Wetmore, Bellamy's lieutenant in the theological wars of the previous decade, was chosen by the General Assembly to speak the mind of God's people—not on the relationship of the colonies to the British Parliament, nor even on the questions of taxation and the rights of man in a social contract, but on the infinitely more important question of the working out of God's *grand plan* of Redemption." The "Elect," he concluded, were "not yet all gathered in," and the time was "not yet fully come," but the "glorious Day" was within sight. All "the Providences of Christ," he declared, "are now fitted and suited to this great end," and "the Period is doubtless near when the Church's *Light shall break forth as the Morning, and her Darkness be as Noon Day.*" Wetmore, and the dozens of Calvinist ministers who in the following year carried his message to their people, simply repeated the now time-honored doctrines of Joseph Bellamy. All who wished to be among the elect when God took the final steps "to advance his Church to a State of Perfection, Happiness, and compleat Honor" had best prove their right by volunteering for the Church Militant.[179] The situation of 1765 had been reproduced, and once again in early 1774 saintly mobs roamed the Connecticut countryside (in response this time to the news of the Intolerable Acts) harassing "Arminians."

In the summer of 1774, however, the Calvinist multitude was finally provided not only more effective leadership, but a more appropriate enemy. Until this moment the saints had confounded and disturbed the Calvinist ministry by all but forgetting that Christian zeal, in the words of the immortal Edwards, was "indeed a flame, but a sweet one," that there was "indeed opposition, vigorous opposition, that is an attendant of it; but is against *things,* and not *persons.*"[180] Arminianism was such a thing, and so was sin—but tyranny, of the darkest dye and deepest hue, was pre-eminently and sublimely such. Thus it was that when Israel Putnam, having heard that Admiral Graves had fired on Boston, organized forty thousand men of Litchfield and prepared to march toward Boston, Joseph Bellamy stood at the head of this glorious army, reminding the followers of the Lamb of the curse which the Lord had placed on Meroz for not coming to the aid of the mighty.[181] Unlike 1745, when Whitefield had dispatched the pious army to Louisburg, God's people were not waiting for instructions nor watchfully praying for the success of other men's designs. They were acting with vigor and dispatch—such dispatch, indeed, that Bellamy, thanking God for Putnam's "false alarm," rejoiced that he had been given the opportunity to preach his sermon to Connecticut's glorious Christian army, and never once wondered if it had been premature.[182]

A year later, when Wetmore's sermon was republished for the edification of God's embattled host, the elect seemed sufficiently gathered that their emergence, "terrible as an Army with Banners," impressed not a few Calvinists as the beginning of the last battle with the Antichrist. "The time is coming and hastening on," announced Bellamy's friend Samuel Sherwood in January of 1776, "when Babylon the great shall fall to rise no more."[183] Yet two years later Timothy Dwight would advise the people of Connecticut that the *"kingdom of the* REDEEMER" could not be expected before the end of the war, and that victory itself seemed dubious, so likely was it that America would be "ruined by its iniquities."[184] The reaction had set in—a reaction which in time would lead Dwight into the ranks of arch-Federalism and Joseph Bellamy almost at once into a mental illness from which he never recovered. By the end of the war Bellamy was advising his correspondents to read *"Mr. Edwards's History of Redemption,"* not as a handbook for the men of Issachar, but as a "map of the road" to heaven and "a glimpse" of the peace and glory it would provide for all who were weary of the "hurry and bustle," the "confusion," of American life.[185]

The Calvinism of Jonathan Edwards was dead, perhaps, from the very moment when Bellamy first called on the people of Connecticut to exert themselves in what he believed to be the Work of Redemption. So, presumably, thought Samuel Hopkins, who by 1770 was beginning to refashion the "New Divinity" into an argument for man's utter passivity in the work of his own salvation. So too many erstwhile members of the evangelical entente, most of them urban, who could not comprehend the inner logic of Bellamy's gospel. "Instead of the glad tidings of great joy which Paul was forever harping on," they complained, Bellamy and his coadjutors insisted "continually on vindictive justice, as if the Almighty's glory consisted chiefly in pouring out his wrath on sinners."[186] What they failed to understand was how well contrived was Bellamy's theology to instill the saints with the spirit necessary for overcoming the power of sin—their own as well as others'—in a moment of earthly "triumph and joy."

Bellamy's doctrines and their application represented an essential step in eighteenth-century Calvinism's commitment to what Reinhold Niebuhr has called "the necessary mechanisms of social justice." For a generation evangelical religion had struggled to evolve those instruments within the church. Failing of success, the Calvinist mind, confronted with the necessity of redeeming the larger society, had been nearly tempted into the fallacy Niebuhr describes as the assumption "that the law of love need only to be stated persuasively to overcome the selfishness of the human heart."[187] The outbreak of the imperial crisis presented American Calvinism with an opportunity to overcome, not merely the sin of Arminianism, but the selfishness implicit in the lurking perfectionism of its own doctrines. As one consequence of the Revolutionary crusade—and by no means an incidental one—Calvinists came to search for new instruments, of government as well as of suasion, for making America a land of justice no less than love.

Had Edwards lived to see the American challenge to British "tyranny," perhaps he would have strongly reminded the people of the colonies not to forget their own sins in contending for earthly justice. Given the contours of Calvinist thought, such an admonition could have only fired the hearts and wills of America to a higher and more zealous activity. Perhaps he, like Bellamy, would finally have despaired of a crusade that looked to the redemption not of the church but of society. But it should be noted that in the *End in Creation,* published in Boston in the first year of the Stamp Act crisis, Edwards had allowed that though "the church" was "now" God's chosen means for advancing the Work of Redemption, it was not impossible that He would in time reveal more effective instruments of His purpose.[188] When in 1765 God's American people had taken upon themselves the responsibility for bringing on the millennium, not a new purpose had been revealed, but only new instruments. What had begun was the long process, to be completed neither in the Revolution nor even in 1800, of making men's wills the ultimate guarantor of the collective happiness and the general welfare.

VII

THE HAPPY
EFFECTS OF UNION

NOT only in Connecticut, but throughout the colonies, Calvinists responded to the imperial crisis in a spirit clearly distinguishable from that of the Liberals. In 1765, for instance, the Calvinist ministry did not wait for merchants and lawyers to inform them that the Stamp Act threatened the commercial prosperity of the colonies. The evangelicals were not only ready for the Stamp Act, but expecting it. According to the Calvinist historian of the Revolution, they were first alerted in April of 1764, when George Whitefield informed the Calvinist divines of Portsmouth, New Hampshire, that a "deep laid plot" was being hatched in London against the "civil and religious liberties" of the colonies. In August, news of the same "plot" was sent directly from London to Joseph Bellamy, and he and one of Whitefield's confidants, the future President Langdon of Harvard, circulated its details.[1]

According to reports, the "plot" looked to an alteration of all the provincial governments, and the introduction of an Anglican bishop into America. When the news of the Stamp Act arrived, the people of New England

> saw an heavy cloud hanging over us, big with slavery and all its dreadful attendants. They looked upon it as the darkest day New-England ever saw. They considered also the near connection there is between our civil and religious privileges, and every true lover of Zion began to tremble *for the ark of God.* For they saw, while our civil liberties were openly threatened, our religious shook; after taking away the liberty of taxing ourselves, and breaking in upon our charters, they feared the breaking in upon the act of *toleration*, the taking away of liberty to choose our own ministers, and then

351

imposing whom they pleased upon us for spiritual guides, largely taxing us to support the pride and vanity of diocesan Bishops, and it may be by and by making us tributary to the See of Rome . . .[2]

Such a reaction disclosed several tendencies of the Calvinist mind. One was the concern for civil liberties which, however secondary in the minds of Calvinist preachers in 1765, came in ten years to dominate their thinking increasingly. Another was a concern for external, rather than domestic, threats to their freedom and welfare—a concern that tended to mute the internal differences among Americans.

This very competition of religious and secular concerns, of domestic and foreign issues, clearly exacerbated the response of Americans to the imperial crisis. In the year of the Stamp Act repeal a Boston Baptist lamented that the "extasy which this good News occasioned" was all out of proportion with "that awful Indifference, with which the glad Tidings of Salvation are heard by our Inhabitants in general."[3] In the next decade so many Americans became increasingly indifferent to religion, and so deeply concerned with politics, that the Calvinist ministry, lamenting what they called a "decay of vital piety," would urge men to such diligence in the affairs of the soul as would enable them to make a profession of saving faith. Those who could not, it would seem, often sought surcease from these demands, not in a life of riotous living, but in one dedicated to a love of their country. Still, the decade inaugurated by the Stamp Act was not exclusively one of interest in politics. The years saw highly articulate spiritual concern on the part of Virginia Baptists; the "work" among them, John Leland recalled, was "very noisy." Indeed this was the era when an awakening spread through Virginia, when New England Baptists witnessed a series of revivals, and when a new breed of separatists introduced the ritual of total immersion.[4]

Nevertheless, the period 1765-1775 did see an apparent flagging of American interest in religion and an increasing secular-mindedness in politics. In many New England cities, the orators of the Sons of Liberty, who in 1765 inveighed against "the Stamp Act" as *"the Beast"*—or "the sum total of all his wickedness"—and enforced this knowledge on the popular mind by reading at length from the thirteenth chapter of the Book of Revelation,[5] were by 1775 supplanted by men of Ciceronian toga and Demosthenic posture. Within a decade of the battle of Lexington, however, the vast majority of Americans would once again manifest their distaste for neoclassicism. At the opening of the next century New Lights were attacking "Heathenish Orations" in accents reminiscent of the Great Awakening.[6] In the history of American religion, as in that of American politics, the ten years before the outbreak of the Revolution were important years of transition, but in many respects they represented more an interlude than a thorough transformation of the American mind.

In the Revolutionary decade it would at times seem that Americans were tiring not only of the rigors of the Edwardean theology, but of theology itself. This was not surprising, considering how the New Divinity, as developed by Hopkins and the younger Edwards, was distinguished above all by (in the words of Edmund Morgan) its "arid doctrines."[7] What the New Divinity brought to New England seems to have been less a loss of interest in religion than a thorough and profound intellectual perplexity. It was first of all difficult to comprehend the precise meaning of Samuel Hopkins' "system of doctrines." One of the earliest Calvinist critics of the New Divinity took it to be so unremittingly insistent on God's absolute sovereignty as to verge on a passive antinomianism. (As such, the critic observed, it was probably to be explained as the consequence of an "importation" of sectarian English errors.) What seems to have scandalized the older Calvinists, even such as had followed Edwards in denigrating "preparation," was Hopkins' suggestion that the unregenerate, whose every act was worse than useless, should even be forbidden to pray. But Hopkins also succeeded in confusing many younger New England ministers, most of whom, it was said, were by the late 1760's "standing in a pause, not knowing where to fix." Even more significant, however, was the attendant distress and division of the laity: "the new divinity has raised disputes to the greatest height, divided towns, broke societies and churches, alienated affection among dead brethren, &c."[8] If such testimony be trusted, it would seem that the response to the New Divinity was not so much boredom with theology as a confusion born of a lively interest.

Undoubtedly the New Divinity helped to crystallize the desire of the pious to be done with contention. In 1768 Isaac Backus was engaged in one of the ecclesiastical debates that was nearly to be resolved in the Revolutionary decade, that between the Baptists and the spokesmen of Calvinist Congregationalism. The preface to one of his polemical tracts was almost apologetic; "some serious people," he observed, "are ready to condemn all *disputing,* as being a principal cause of all the confusions that appear in our nation and land."[9] But the disputes continued, and always to the accompaniment of lamentations that they were somehow sapping the vitality of the evangelical impulse. So likewise did Calvinist ministers express concern throughout the 1760's and 1770's over the extent to which the "subtil Speculations and scholastic Niceties" of the Hopkinsian theology were confusing the people and preventing a powerful revival of religion.[10] Given such a situation, it is not surprising that the period witnessed the beginning of a movement that would be intensified after the Revolution—the burgeoning of the Baptist Church and of other forms of straightforwardly evangelical religion: Methodism, Free-Will Baptism, Universalism, all offering the possibility of salvation without the metaphysical tortures of the New Divinity. All this is part of the intellectual history of the era, as indeed is the fact that the end of the war saw Roger Sherman debating theological questions with Hopkins.

Another response to theological perplexity was, however, the quest for existential solace in political activity. In this respect the mind of the 1770's had as its epitome the intellectual biography of Joseph Hawley. Vacillating between profound skepticism and the highest of Calvinisms, Hawley frequently gave way to despondent inertia. But he sprang easily to life when confronted by political decisions and endeavors. That he and other Calvinists poured their energies into politics makes the period, and the Revolution itself, less religious only in name. Jonathan Boucher, looking back on the Revolutionary crisis in Virginia, knew well what to call the political movement that culminated in ousting him and all representatives of the Crown from Virginia: "Instances of religious infatuation in communities are too notorious not to be acknowledged; but it seems arbitrary to limit enthusiasm to one sentiment of the human mind."[11] Beginning in 1766, when Calvinist ministers first discovered that a "wonderful spirit of patriotism" had been "infused into all orders of men," and that this spirit was "from a divine influence,"[12] they increasingly confused civic virtue with piety and, finally, political enthusiasm with the joy of conversion.

The decade that began with the Stamp Act crisis and culminated in the battle of Lexington was thus distinguished by something far more impressive than the mere application of religious doctrine to politics. The very religious life of the colonies came to center on the crisis in public affairs, and, indeed, to be defined by it and from it to derive vitality. In the summer of 1774, when Ebenezer Cleaveland preached his sermon *The Abounding Grace of God towards Notorious Sinners,* his exposition of "the conversion and call of Matthew the Publican" was given application in terms of the delight experienced by a Crown revenue officer who joined the Sons of Liberty.[13] A few months later, a rural New England clergyman announced to his church that whoever would not sign the solemn league and covenant of nonimportation was "not fit to approach" the communion table.[14] The process of redefining the principal hinge of evangelical religion was brought to fulfillment in the spring and summer of 1775, when, as one observer reported, nearly the whole country was "in perfect enthusiasm for liberty."[15] If it was not true piety but patriotism that had been brought to birth, the outbreak of the rebellion would seem to the evangelical ministry, for the moment, a far greater awakening than the first.

Through the confounding of piety with patriotic enthusiasm, evangelical America was allowed, as during the French and Indian War, to embark on a pursuit of happiness more in accord with that of the legal scheme. By the end of the Revolution the Calvinist ministry would be deploring how "fashionable" Arminianism had become among even the erstwhile people of God.[16] Actually its appeal was already being felt in the decade before the Revolution, and what the Revolutionary crisis provided was an opportunity, eagerly embraced by many members of Calvinist churches, to obscure the theological and social divisions inherited from the Awakening. Thus James Dana, in 1760 the bête noire of Connecticut New Lights, discovered in the 1770's that his preachments on behalf of the patriot cause "did much to increase his popularity" among those recently opposed to his theology. By 1775 many were "so well satisfied with his political orthodoxy" that they "came to regard his supposed Arminianism as a very pardonable offence."[17] One of the reasons for the changing estimate of Dana was what Joseph Bellamy had been preaching against since the 1750's: a general disposition among the people of Connecticut to suspect secretly that Arminianism was not all that unpardonable.

But the disposition of evangelical America to apostatize from the faith of the Awakening was only one of the factors working to obscure the differences among the people of the colonies. What is not to be overlooked is that some Liberals—clergy and laity—succeeded in gaining acceptance and in mollifying their domestic critics by engaging in ever more Whiggish activity in politics. Thus Charles Chauncy, whose *Seasonable Thoughts* had never been "vendible, except among Arminians in the colony of Connecticut," composed anti-Episcopal tracts which, in the context of the 1770's, were given a respectable, if not always enthusiastic, reading by preachers of many persuasions. He was even honored for his efforts by the College of New Jersey.[18] Each effort to encourage amity generated further pressure for independence and encouraged a revolutionary spirit. Likewise many Calvinist preachers, faced by the possibility of defections to one or more of the burgeoning "New Light" sects of the 1770's, grew more vehement in applying the dicta of experimental religion to the political issues of the day. Once again the "saints" were urged to prove their pretensions sincere by coming to the aid of the Lord against the mighty. Thus the very emergence of purely religious enthusiasm also fed the decade's tendency toward increasing political agitation.

It is not possible to trace all the developments and realignments of these years of transition—transition both in American religion and in the conduct of American politics. So far as Calvinism is concerned, however, the two major impulses of the period can be identified. Many evangelical leaders used the imperial crisis and the Revolution as occasions for continuing and in some ways winning the battles of the Awakening. This thread will be unwound in later chapters. The other tendency was one implicit in Calvinists' being drawn into alliance with men who but a few years earlier had seemed the chief vice-regents of Satan. Insofar as Calvinists embraced this as something more than a mere necessity, they relaxed their vigilance to the point where a not inconsiderable alteration was wrought in their religious purposes and commitments.

John Cleaveland, for example, emerged from the awakening of 1763 with a zealous and vehement indignation against the Massachusetts establishment. In 1767 he was holding the spirit of the "sons of liberty" before the people of Essex County as an example of the zeal with which they should contend for their "sacred Rights and Liberty."[19] Three years later, however, Cleaveland was devoting his own most spirited labors to writing a series of essays, over the signature of *Johannis in Eremo,* on the dangers of the "plot" to install an American bishop. Meanwhile he abandoned (temporarily, he thought) the battle against the Arminians and moderate Calvinists who had repressed the revival of 1763. His zealous patriotism soon earned him the accolades of some who but five years earlier had refused him the right hand of fellowship and anathematized both him and his congregation.

In 1774 the churches of Chebacco parish, Cleaveland's among them, impressed by the need for a "visible political union" among all patriotic Christians, agreed to "bury forever all former differences."[20] A year later Cleaveland entered on a chaplaincy, and, when he returned, his battle was not with Arminianism but against Baptist and Universalist exhorters. At the end of the Revolution, he would serve as the perhaps unwitting tool of his former enemies in removing from Essex County the most formidable of living Edwardeans, Nathaniel Whitaker, whom in 1770 Cleaveland had hailed as a brother in the true faith of the Awakening and who, throughout the Revolution, had fought to impose the moral law of Calvinism on an independent Massachusetts. Within a decade of the battle of Lexington, the evangelical alliance would be something of a shambles, and its members would not be regrouped until the late 1790's.

The one issue of the Revolutionary decade on which the convolutions of the American mind can be most readily traced is that of the proposed American bishop. This question, in certain respects symbolic of many others, most directly permitted a slackening of attention to domestic religious differences and quarrels. In the final analysis, however, it would seem that the Calvinist ministry and populace, though roused perhaps by what seemed an immediate threat of ecclesiastical tyranny, were disposed to rebellion by an inherited and ingrained aversion to monarchy. In the sermons of 1765 and 1766, evangelical ministers dilated on the "reigns of wicked kings" in Britain's past. They recalled to memory Charles II—"with his Andros, and Randolph, and the rest of his crew in government"—and saluted the Christian heroes who had "frighted" James II "from the throne and then voted it vacant." But even for those Calvinists who rejoiced in New England's role in the revolution of 1689, the issue was not Stuart legitimacy. If "the constitution is gone," Joseph Emerson observed in 1766, " 'tis a meer trifle whether one of the house of *Hanover* or of *Stuart,* whether an Englishman or Frenchman hold the sceptre."[21] Already in 1765 some American dissenters conveyed a distinct impression of being less than devoted to the Hanoverian succession, and over the next decade they revealed what Anglican critics had long accused them of, a lack of admiration for the very institution of kingship.

Once the Revolution had erupted, but well before the Declaration of Independence, Calvinist exhorters were defining the British constitution in a way that allowed little legitimate place to kingly authority. Tyranny, they insisted, is tyranny: "names change not the nature of things." Clearly the Calvinist ministry were "commonwealths-men" with, as it were, a vengeance. In October of 1774 an evangelical minister openly proclaimed a sentiment that one suspects nearly every pietist in New England had secretly shared since the Great Awakening:

> England was never more happy before, nor much more since, than after the head of the first Stuart was severed from his body, and while it was under the protectorship of Oliver Cromwell.[22]

Tribal memory of the Puritan Commonwealth (and possibly tribal guilt for not having come in the 1640's to the aid of the Lord against the mighty) achieved its ultimate expression shortly after the battle of Lexington, when William Stearns advised the people of Marlborough, Massachusetts, what lay in store for them if Britain gained the victory. We will be "treated as *Traitors,*" he declared, and either hung, disemboweled, or "beheaded and quartered, and our heads and quarters disposed of at the King's pleasure!"[23]

In the Tory mind the revolutionary citizens of the colonies were always identified as "congregational and presbyterian republicans." Joseph Galloway, Samuel Peters, Peter Oliver, Jonathan Boucher, and every other Loyalist traced the imperial crisis to the principles of the

Puritan Revolution and Commonwealth.[24] John Adams' critic, Daniel Leonard, warned in the *Massachusettensis Letters* of the dangers of an American "Cromwell, whom some amongst us deify and imitate in all his imitable perfections."[25] Nor was Sam Adams the only citizen of the colonies to revel in the name of Roundhead. As far south as Georgia, Governor Wright espied in the patriots "a strong tincture of Republican or Oliverian principles."[26] In Connecticut the identification with Cromwell took such forms as the religious services held by Connecticut New Lights beside the graves of the regicide justices. When it is recalled that Franklin tried to arouse American resistance in the name of one of the judges,[27] and that Ezra Stiles, soon after the Revolution, wrote a stirring history of Goffe and Whalley's near martyrdom and their exile in the wilderness, it is evident that this symbol like so many others, allowed Americans of a variety of persuasions to compose some of their inherited differences in the era of the Revolution.

Stiles's researches into the history of the Commonwealth were attended by a growing radicalism in his social and political sentiments. On the other hand, Cromwellianism served the children of the saints as a semirespectable exemption from the rigid moral law of Joseph Bellamy. Soon after the passage of the Stamp Act the young people of Connecticut composed and performed a "religious-Comic liturgy" in which the Church of England was lampooned and "Holy Cromwell" called on "to deliver us." The New Light ministry briefly tolerated this excursion into amateur theatricals but soon—perhaps remembering that buffoonery was not one of the liberal arts—forbade its further performance.[28] Apart from ritual, however, the mere recollection of Cromwell's regime allowed many Americans to substitute filiopietism for piety, and to forget or possibly atone for the fact that in the 1640's their own fathers had in fact battled only a "howling wilderness" and "savage men."[29]

Many Americans who rediscovered their "forefathers" in these years managed thereby also to conclude that Jeremiah Dummer was not wholly wrong about the settlement of America. On December 22, 1773, for instance, Charles Turner, V.D.M., told an audience at Plymouth (where an annual commemoration of the first landing had been instituted as an engine of New England patriotism) that their ancestors had had a dual purpose in migrating to New England:

> Their *design,* in coming over to this inhospitable shore, was great and honorable, to enjoy for themselves and theirs, civil and especially sacred freedom, to worship God, without molestations, agreeably to the dictates of their own consciences, to enlarge the King's dominions, and pave the way for the conversion of the heathen . . .[30]

Something less than a half-century later Daniel Webster was to succeed in reversing the Pilgrim order of worship—as John Adams, for that matter, had already effectively done in his *Dissertation on the Canon and Feudal Law*. In the 1770's Calvinists, too, were concerned with their civil as well as their religious freedoms. In the years between the Stamp Act and the Revolution the evangelical ministry often spoke in the phrases of Sam Adams—who in 1772 explained that "the religion and public liberty of a people are so intimately connected, their interests are interwoven, and cannot exist separately."[31] Not the least of the consequences of such a blending of interests and issues was that elements of the Calvinist populace were allowed to think that they were defending religion when in fact they were doing battle for civil liberties. And some, in fact, did battle for civil liberty in order to gain a freedom they would use for purposes which, in the light of the Awakening, had seemed sinful pursuits.

Still, before 1775 Calvinist spokesmen insisted that the defense of American liberty primarily involved the preservation of pure and undefiled religion from the depravations of Europe. To arouse the evangelical multitude Sam Adams found it necessary to issue periodic reminders that America's chief danger was "the utter loss of those *religious Rights*, the enjoyment of which our good forefathers had more especially in their intention, when they explored and settled this new world."[32] Meanwhile Calvinist preachers, discussing the issues of the day, continued to assert of their ancestors that "their sole motive in transporting themselves to these then uncultivated lands, was that they might plant the Gospel there, enjoy it freely while they lived, and transmit it to posterity."[33] Such a reading of seventeenth-century history was derived from Mather's *Magnalia* and, ironically enough, from the first volume of Hutchinson's *History of Massachusetts-Bay* (which the evangelical mind took to be a contribution to their side of the debate with the advocates of reasonable religion). For many Calvinists this version of the past inspired or reinforced a come-outer spirit. "Our forefathers came over into this waste and howling wilderness," Andrew Croswell explained in his critique of the Church of England's Society for the Propagation of the Gospel in Foreign Parts, "on this very *design*, that they and their posterity *might be left* to *themselves*, hoping that *that* order of men who drove them out of the old world, would never follow them into the *new*."[34] The same issue —that of American freedom from a hostile Anglican establishment— also, however, served as an occasion for an evolving alliance of evangelical Americans with those of a more rational persuasion. For Calvinists were by no means the only citizens of the colonies concerned by the "plot" to install Anglican bishops in America.

The history of the struggle against an Anglican episcopate in America has been written many times. But to understand the role of religion in the Revolution it is necessary to go over some of the same ground once more, if only briefly, in order to make clear that the divisions of the Awakening were still in existence at the moment when Britain decided to end its salutary neglect of the colonies. Too easily it is assumed that Charles Chauncy, Francis Alison, and the Liberal clergy generally spoke somehow for all Americans who opposed an Anglican establishment. Actually Samuel Johnson, speaking of the opponents of episcopacy, readily distinguished in 1764 between "such loose thinkers as Mayhew" and "such furious bitter Calvinistical enthusiasts as are really no more friends to monarchy than episcopacy."[35] At no point, not even in those moments when Americans of evangelical persuasion found it possible to embrace the Chauncys of the colonies in Christian fellowship, were the Liberal and Calvinist opposition to an American bishop identical.

It is often forgotten, not so much that Jonathan Edwards was the author of one of the first formal protests against the Society for the Propagation of the Gospel, as that his reasons for objecting to Episcopalian ventures in New England were consistent with what he conceived as the aims of evangelical religion. By admitting excommunicated persons into the Anglican Church, Edwards complained in 1734, the S.P.G. was bringing "disorder and confusion" to western Massachusetts, producing "wranglings, strifes, [and] ill names" and, most importantly, tempting men "to place religion rather in some external *observations and ceremonies* than in love to God and our neighbours."[36] So too was the opposition of Liberal ministers to episcopacy consistent with the legal scheme, and some understanding of the differences is essential both to an assessment of the contribution of each element of the ministry to the Revolution and to an appreciation of the dynamic of the American mind in the period from 1765 through the Revolution.

Unquestionably the Arminian clergy, especially those of New England, worked to inspire opposition to an American bishop. In the decades before the Revolution much of the polemical skill of New England Liberalism was spent on this question, often to the exclusion of other and possibly more vital public issues. Since Mayhew served as a leader of the anti-Episcopal forces until his death in 1766, when the mantle fell on the aging shoulders of Chauncy, admirers of reasonable religion have used this record as a springboard for "demonstrations" that the Arminian clergy made a major contribution to the patriot cause. Once again the recollections of John Adams prove useful, for he believed that the anti-Episcopal controversy contributed to spreading "a universal alarm" among the colonists by forcing them to consider the entire question of Parliamentary jurisdiction in the colonies.[37] Yet the Liberals' record on this question hardly justifies their reputations as the fiery avatars of America's Revolutionary spirit. Among other things, their contributions were part of the last public debate for nearly a century in which the written word figured far more prominently than the spoken: they did not speak to incite the multitude but wrote to convince the respectably intelligent. More importantly, the Liberal clergy in every respect approached what Mayhew liked to call "the Scheme for Sending Bishops to *America*"[38] no differently from any other issue of the period. Far from offsetting their record as political preachers, their treatment of the episcopal question only casts a more searching ray of light on their supposed achievements as molders and leaders of opinion.

The distinguishing characteristic of the Liberal attitude toward episcopacy was a frame of mind variously describable as paranoia or a disposition to "snuff the approach of tyranny in every tainted breeze." What Burke described as the American ability to augur misgovernment at a distance was, more accurately in the case of the Liberals, a notion (peculiar enough in men so insistently calm and reasonable) that the Church of England was engaged in some grand undisclosed conspiracy "to root out Presbyterianism"* from New England.[39] It was not coincidence that all the more articulate New England opponents of episcopacy were clergymen who had lost parishioners to Anglicanism and were in continual danger of losing more.

Liberals were also disturbed by the frontier activities of the Society for the Propagation of the Gospel.† What first and most furiously

---

* The use by Liberal critics of Episcopacy of the term "Presbyterian" to describe the prevailing, and traditional religion of New England is revealing. Although Massachusetts Liberals could (and did) invoke "congregational principles" against those who wished to restrict church membership to the regenerate, their own polity and practices—consociations, preventions of defections from "parish" churches, and non-exclusion from the sacraments—were much closer (insofar as seventeenth-century distinctions remained meaningful) to Presbyterianism. This was also the understanding of Isaac Backus, who, when he complained of New England "Presbyterians," was referring, not to Jonathan Parsons, but to the "standing order" of Massachusetts and Connecticut. Interestingly enough (in view of the confused ecclesiastical situation in Connecticut), Backus reserved the designation "Presbyterian" for the Old Lights of Connecticut, who, despite their dalliance, in the days of Governor Fitch, with "pure Congregational" principles, were to his mind "Presbyterians" in their conception of the church, and in their treatment of Separate and Baptist dissenters. Moreover, Backus did not see Bellamy and his followers as "Presbyterians," despite their use of ministerial councils to expose "graceless" and "heretical" ministers.

† Eventually Liberals formed their own competing Indian missionary society, but

aroused them was the activities of the Society in more settled areas. Their "great aim," Mayhew alleged, was not "the converting of Heathens to Christianity; but the converting of Christians of *other protestant denominations,* to the faith of *the church of England.*" Chauncy believed that the Society was subsidizing secessions from the Congregational churches of the larger New England towns; he complained that it was using "that charity for the propagation of Episcopacy, which was intended for the propagation of Christianity."[40]

At every point in the controversy the premise of Liberal thought was that the Church of England, unless resisted, could quickly and easily become all-powerful in the colonies. The newly formed Episcopal societies in eastern Massachusetts impressed Mayhew as "entering wedges" in a great "crusade" which would eventually bring all New England to "submit to an episcopal sovereign."[41] Liberal discussion of the subject was seldom lucid, for instead of confronting the issue directly, Mayhew and Chauncy preferred to speculate on "the true plan, and grand mystery" of the operations of the S.P.G.[42] This line of thinking soon led Mayhew to conclude that the church was plotting to install bishops in New England.

The appointment of an American bishop was actually urged at the time—by colonial Anglicans as well as by church authorities in England. The advocates of an American episcopate, however, persistently claimed that they sought such an officer only to secure the internal order and discipline of their denomination. Despite such protests, both Mayhew and Chauncy were always ready to believe that the Anglicans had "much more in design than they have been pleased to declare."[43] The Boston Liberals were not the only Americans to accuse the proponents of a bishopric of something less than candor, but the existence of such a "plot" was necessary for Liberals, for without it their predictions that Anglicanism was about to seize control of New England would have seemed incredible. If a bishop were installed, Mayhew warned, adherence to the Church of England would grow so immense that this denomination would soon control all the New England legislatures.[44] This suggestion reflected, at least in part, Liberal self-knowledge; for they knew that forms, not spirit, sustained them in their own positions of authority and determined the course of their society.

The Liberal sense of imminent disaster fed ultimately on a belief that power in any society lay with its respectable and prosperous citizens and on an appreciation of the immense appeal the Church of England had for the aspiring as well as the successful citizens of the

this endeavor was more properly a part of the Arminian counterattack on American Calvinism and of Charles Chauncy's personal effort to destroy Eleazar Wheelock.

colonies. Nor did the Old Lights of Connecticut, for instance, see Episcopalianism as attracting only a handful of emigrant merchants. The literature in which they and the Boston Liberals arraigned the Episcopal "plot" evinced a sense of panic resulting from an awareness that the children of New England were increasingly disposed to the Church of England. In 1752 the Connecticut election preacher foresaw the "unhappy day" when the Anglicans of the province would have the power "to commit our invaluable Privileges to the Flames" simply by outvoting the dissenters.[45]

The anti-Episcopal pamphlets of the rational clergy, marked as they were by a curious mixture of fascination and contempt for the "power and grandeur" of the Anglican clergy and liturgy, were themselves fairly obvious symptoms of the workings in eighteenth-century America of what might be called the inverse corollary of Weber's theory of the Protestant ethic.[*][46] The lure of Anglicanism for successful Boston merchants—while hardly so compelling then as a century later—had thus already created a considerable intellectual problem for the Liberal ministry. Slowly they were evolving the filiopietistic appeal that would eventually preserve Unitarianism from the inroads of Rome, but as critics of their own traditions they were still hard pressed to demonstrate the superiority of the New England way to a Church of England whose graces and civility were by no means unappealing. And since Liberals preached a Protestantism nearly as latitudinarian as that with which they competed, they could not and did not contend against Anglicanism by celebrating the doctrines once delivered to the Puritan saints.

The Liberal arguments against episcopacy were by no stretch of the historical imagination echoes of Cotton, much less Cartwright. Neither Chauncy nor Mayhew ever expressed his differences with Episcopalianism in militantly doctrinal terms. The quality of their commitment is suggested by Mayhew's definition of Congregationalism as "what I suppose a more scriptural way of worship."[47] Although one of Mayhew's broadsides was characterized by an Anglican critic as the "fanatic ravings of his predecessors the Oliverian holders-forth, whose

* The ambiguous attitude of the rationalist clergy to the Church of England could be detected in the literature of the Great Awakening. When they criticized Whitefield for participating in the sacraments of Congregational churches, for instance, their argument slowly but perceptibly moved away from an original outrage at his violation of Congregational principle to shock at Whitefield's disgracing his own priestly office and oath. In so attacking Whitefield for ignoring the forms of his own church the Harvard faculty showed such familiarity with High-Church standards that Whitefield's defenders were able to observe snidely that neither he nor they were *that* well "acquainted with the *subscriptions* and *canons,* and such-like trumpery of the Church of England."

spittle he hath lick'd up, and cough'd it out again, with some addition of his own filth and phlegm," he actually maintained in the debate a more moderate tone than most of his opponents. It was said of Mayhew that his zeal sometimes "betrayed him into too great severity of expression," but such expressions, as Chauncy acknowledged, were generally reserved for combat with the Cleavelands and not the East Apthorps of the colonies. In the controversy with the advocates of a bishopric the Liberal clergy generally maintained a pose of elegant urbanity, and their productions, as they insisted, were paradigms of moderation by contrast with the ugly "bigotry" of the Episcopalians. Not surprisingly, the issue according to Liberals came down finally to the question whether the Anglicans were not manifesting attitudes and using language "misbecoming a gentleman."[48]

The only real fervor betrayed by the Liberals in the course of the controversy emerged in passages of heavy-handed satire of the supposed attractions of the Church of England. "This then is the principal advantage of the Church of England," Noah Welles slyly explained in 1762, "that the religion which is generally practised by her members is perfectly agreeable to polite gentlemen; whereas no gentlemen can belong to other persuasions."[49] Welles' sermon was, not too misguidedly, attributed for a time to Mayhew, so filled was it with ridicule of the New England ministry's betters in lawn. Such modes of argument came naturally to men unwilling, or unable, to state their differences with the opposition.

The same was true of the Anglicans, from the early 1750's through the Revolutionary years of Tory pamphleteering and poetic satire. In 1753, when William Livingston opened his attack on the Anglicans of New York in the *Independent Reflector*, Chandler observed that Livingston was "peculiarly eloquent" in the language "of fish-women." There was no point in arguing with Livingston, Chandler allowed; "he should be attacked in his own way"—"I mean if he was approached with keen but pure satire, it is the only thing that would reach him to the quick."[50] Whether it did reach Livingston is of less moment than why Chandler assumed it would—or why Jonathan Odell thought satiric abuse the most appropriate vein for his Revolutionary verses. Livingston's strictures against an Anglican monopoly were clearly inspired by aspirations that the Anglican mind understood as hardly different from their own. The one issue on which Anglicans and their more urbane critics were divided was who best deserved the posts of honor and eminence in colonial society.

The Tory-patriot debate generally shows many instances of bitter polemic between men whose ideological positions were not too far removed from each other. Satire, ridicule, and personal abuse were far more characteristic of such interchanges than any reasoned statement of issues. In this regard there is probably no more comical interchange, although unintentionally so, in the history of American polemic than that between Samuel Seabury and Alexander Hamilton. Each was seeking to prove to the satisfaction of his readers his own urbanity and the other's lack of gentility; yet both meanwhile were posing as friends of the multitude, even as "rustics."

What the "farmer" debate of 1775 represented was the culmination of a process whereby a dispute between ostensible gentlemen, indifferent to the "clownish" part of the American people, was perforce transformed into a competition for the attention and allegiances of a multitude long ignored. At some point in the 1770's the debate over an Anglican episcopate was similarly transformed. Around 1770, according to Jonathan Boucher, this question was "agitated in the news-papers of Virginia and Maryland, with hardly less exertion of talents than had just before been called forth by the Stamp-Act." Such agitation was an example, again as Boucher saw it, of "that dangerous expedient, now coming into fashion, of carrying all great points of government by what is called an appeal to the people."[51] Possibly the Southern scriveners, like Mayhew and Chauncy in New England, or Livingston and Alison in New York and Philadelphia, helped to alert the "inquiring mind" to the threat of episcopacy, but if they had any influence whatsoever on the mind "of the common people" it was not that of introducing them to the evils of episcopacy.[52]

Among the evangelical populace there had never been any question that the High-Church elements of the Church of England were to be resisted in their effort to impose a hierarchy on the colonies. In 1763 Samuel Peters advised the Archbishop of Canterbury that the Calvinists of Connecticut were so "fond to a madness of these popular forms of government" that they "would dislike bishops on any footing."[53] To Boucher, similarly, it was clear that no prompting was needed to inflame the anti-Episcopal prejudices of the Presbyterian dissenters of Virginia, or the "swarms of separatists who have sprung up among us . . . under the name of anabaptists and new-lights."[54] What offended him was that the House of Burgesses, and even some Episcopal ministers, were now agitating the question. What the pamphlet disputation over an American bishop did accomplish, in sum, was to provide the evangelical populace an occasion, or an excuse, for accepting the assistance, and possibly even the leadership, of men who had long been suspicious in their eyes. The fury of Livingston and Alison against the spiritual tyranny of Lambeth was so unrestrained, for instance, that they earned "the genteel appellation of 'noisy hot-heads and pragmatical enthusiasts.'" They welcomed the charge, no doubt sincerely, and in doing so earned the admiration and perhaps even the gratitude of men who but a decade earlier had despaired of the spiritual deadness of the Old Side clergy and laity.[55]

At no point, however, was the evangelical mind dependent exclusively on Chauncy and Livingston for arguments against the proposed American bishopric. The Calvinist clergy made their own contribution to the controversy, and their response to the Episcopal "threat" was, in their minds at least, much of a piece with their longtime battle against formal religion. What Calvinists opposed was not so much the hierarchy of the Church of England as its Arminian doctrines. To be sure, in 1741 Andrew Croswell explained, by way of defending Whitefield against Commissary Garden, that the people of America had so long lived in "a freer air" than that of England that they were not likely "for several Ages" to "desire the Dominion" of a foreign or imported clergy.[56] But this observation was incidental to Croswell's attack on Garden's "Arminian" strictures against Whitefield's sermons on the New Birth. Similarly, Jonathan Dickinson, who in the 1720's and 1730's had been the colonies' most articulate defender of non-Episcopal ordination, declared, in his first rejoinder to the post-Awakening Anglican counterreformation, that his issue with the Church of England was not one of "Discipline or Ceremonies." He insisted that the dispute revolved on Arminianism, or, more precisely, on the Calvinist belief in the necessity of the New Birth—"this great Article of our Faith and Hope, which is thus subverted by some of their clergy."[57]

The Calvinist argument in subsequent decades made the same point as against Episcopal missionaries and the proposed bishop. Andrew Croswell's scathing attack on the Society for the Propagation of the Gospel in 1770 charged the Anglican clergy with advocating and preaching the "popish" doctrine of "Justification *as it were by the works of the law.*"[58] Five years later Samuel Langdon complained that the established clergy of England had "corrupted" the Westminster Catechism "into a superficial system of moral philosophy, little better than ancient Platonism," In opposing the bishopric, Calvinists were resisting "the cold, formal fashionable religion" of a country "grown old," as Langdon put it, "in vice."[59] In short, the Calvinists' opposition to Episcopalianism was companion to their more general struggle against the rational theology that was making inroads in the dissenter churches of the colonies.

Calvinist opposition to an American bishop thus rested on somewhat different grounds from Mayhew's rather antiquated notions about a highflier conspiracy. No more than Mayhew did evangelical spokesmen desire hierarchical dominion in the colonial churches. But they at least realized that Bonnie Prince Charlie was defeated and dead, and that the true threat of Episcopalianism was as an avatar and instrument of the anti-revival impulse in the colonies. As early as 1744 colonial Anglicans had begun to proselytize by boasting that their theology provided a "good Foundation" for men fearful of or weary with the emotional excess of the Awakening. Thereafter Episcopalianism throve, according to its advocates, in reaction to "the Confusions introduced by the zealous Propagators" of Calvinism. The very proposal for an American bishop was first introduced as a strategy for containing and suppressing the evangelical spirit in America.[60] Thus the Calvinist image of episcopacy—as a traditional opponent of the revival and as a haven for the excommunicate and unregenerate of other churches—was by no means identical with the one invoked by Noah Hobart and Mayhew.

In contending against Anglicanism, however, the spokesmen of evangelical religion from first to last asked only, as in their struggle with colonial establishments, that the Church of England be granted no special privileges. They insisted on religious freedom, but they were not necessarily opposed to the creation of an American bishop as an appropriate officer of one denomination among many. Indeed, in the late 1760's many Calvinists seem to have looked favorably on the idea of a bishop for the colonies, on the possibility that Whitefield might be appointed to the office. Of course even the rumor of such an appointment raised the hackles of Johnson, Chandler, and all the missionaries of the S.P.G.F.P. Whitefield had never retreated from his early persuasion that it was better that the people of America "had no minister than such as are generally sent over."[61] It is not unlikely, however, that the thought of Whitefield as the American bishop did help to energize the opposition of Boston Liberals, Connecticut Old Lights, and Old Side Presbyterians to the scheme.

Whitefield's death in 1770 removed one of the last links of American Calvinism with the Church of England. To that point it had always been assumed that any church of which the grand itinerant was officially a clergyman could not be wholly anathema. Besides, Whitefield had numerous partisans in the English Church, some of whom on occasion aided the Calvinists of the colonies. Low-Church support of the Indian School and Dartmouth College, and Wheelock's missions, were aspects of this cooperation. But after 1770 even Wheelock, who most depended on such support, was brought to confess that his allies had little authority in the church and that the hierarchy itself was probably bent on the destruction of both English and American Calvinism.

Among the sources of American discontent with the Church of England was the common knowledge that Sir William Johnson was enlisting the aid of the S.P.G. in saving the heathen of New York, and the fur trade, from the "stupid Bigots" and "independent firebrands" Wheelock was sending among them.[62] Another was the fund-raising mission of Samson Occum and Nathaniel Whitaker to England in 1766-1767. Whitaker spent most of his time in the old country arguing theology and politics with the worthies of the church; he returned to discover that Liberal America had been told he had acted like a drunkard. Also, just as Franklin and the Harvard faculty thirty years earlier had hinted that Whitefield was pocketing the money donated for his orphan asylum, so too did Anglicans and Liberals cooperate in suggesting that Whitaker and Occum had embezzled what funds they had managed to collect.

The Calvinist judgment on the British hierarchy was probably most fixed, ironically enough, by Occum's report on his return to America:

Now I am in my own country, I may freely inform you of what I honestly and soberly think of the Bishops, Lord Bishops, and Archbishops of England. In my view, they don't look like Gospel Bishops or ministers of Christ. I can't find them in the Bible. I think they a good deal resemble the Anti-christian Popes. I find the Gospel Bishops resemble, in some good measure, their good Master; and they follow Him in the example He has left them. They discover meekness and humility; are gentle and kind unto all men—ready to do good unto all—they are compassionate and merciful unto the miserable, and charitable to the poor. But I did not find the Bishops of England so. Upon my word, if I never spoke the truth before, I do now. I waited on a number of Bishops, and represented to them the miserable and wretched situation of the poor Indians, who are perishing for lack of spiritual knowledge, and begged their assistance in evangelizing these poor heathen. But if you can believe me, they never gave us one single brass farthing. It seems to me that they are very indifferent whether the poor Indians go to Heaven or Hell. I can't help my thoughts; and I am apt to think they don't want the Indians to go to Heaven with them.[63]

In 1768 Andrew Croswell informed the pious of New England that the English bishops were not merely ungenerous but venal. Episcopalianism, Croswell charged, in addition to encouraging deism and infidelity, had always "lived on money."[64] Such an argument against episcopacy suggests how the Calvinist argument for religious liberty generally came to assume more than a little of the countinghouse tone. The Calvinist clergy were quite certain they were still fighting the battles of the Awakening, and the Calvinist populace, in their quest for religious freedom, continued to proclaim their urgent need to be liberated from the compulsions of a religion with "the form only without the power."[65] Yet the very terms of the argument reflected an unconscious disposition among evangelical Americans to concern themselves with somewhat different issues, if not necessarily to worship slightly different gods. In Connecticut the cause of separatism assumed the form in the 1770's of a flight from and running battle with local taxgatherers, and in Virginia, of course, the issue was drawn on the matter of a tobacco tax. So too the argument against episcopacy; in 1774 a Boston Baptist rehearsed all the theological grievances against Anglicanism, but his pamphlet concluded with the declaration that Americans would "not give their property to support that worship which they know has not GOD for its author."[66] Slight changes of emphasis, here and there, suggested that dissenters were growing just as concerned with their property rights as with the erroneous religion of the Church of England.

The Liberal opponents of a bishopric were of course the first to call attention to the manner in which the "scheme" imperiled American property. Their battle cry was that the proposed American bishop endangered "the freedom and independence" of the colonies, civil as well as ecclesiastical.[67] The depth of Liberal commitment to these freedoms is suggested by the fact that for some time the Boston Liberals seemed receptive to a compromise, proposed by the Bishop of London, whereby bishops would be sent elsewhere but not to New England. When such an arrangement was rejected by the rectors of Boston's Episcopal churches, Mayhew and Chauncy shifted their ground, arguing that a bishop in Massachusetts would violate the hallowed charter privileges of that province.

When they ventured beyond legal arguments, the Boston Liberals inclined to see the whole question in terms of a threat to colonial pocketbooks. Mayhew complained that "a standing army of bishops" would prove to be an unbearable financial burden for the colonies. Toward the end of the debate, Chauncy tried to relate the episcopacy question to the whole issue of imperial taxation, suggesting that the levies on the colonies were necessary to provide a "large revenue for [the] grand support" of a "COMPLETE CHURCH HIERARCHY, after the pattern of that at home."[68] Again according to John Adams, Americans who feared "creeds, tests, ceremonies, and tithes" joined in resisting the Townshend duties because they understood that the Parliamentary power to tax implied a power to appoint bishops for the colonies.[69] Yet the Boston Liberals, who only belatedly declared themselves opposed to Parliamentary jurisdiction in America, did not relate the religious and economic issues exactly as Adams recalled. When they joined the two questions at all, it was to urge that Americans resist bishops in order to avoid high taxes, not taxes to prevent the arrival of bishops.

Considering its own record on the question of religious freedom, Liberalism proved somewhat embarrassed by its raising of the bishopric issue. The branch of the Presbyterian Church to which Livingston and Alison belonged was doing its utmost to subdue and even to silence advocates of the Edwardean divinity. In New England too it seemed curious to hear Mayhew and Chauncy complaining that should the Church of England succeed in its plot to establish a hierarchy in America it would allow "no other privilege to dissenters but that of toleration."[70] In the 1760's and 1770's the Liberals, as beneficiaries and executors of the church laws of Massachusetts, did not allow even that privilege to all dissenters. According to a contemporary ballad, Chauncy, the "zealous Whig." was "in Church a tyrant great," and his Whiggery must in any case be seen in the light of Chauncy's own considered judgment that an American bishop would be palatable so long as Anglican clerics would "no more depend on the STATE, and no more derive their authority from it, than our ministers do."[71]

Both Mayhew and Chauncy were professed enemies of "all human establishments in religion," but their enmity depended on rather restricted definitions of establishment and of religious freedom. Chauncy defended the standing order of Massachusetts without reservation; Mayhew thought it "perhaps, the most generous and catholic one that was ever made in any country."[72] Mayhew, for one, seemed to equate intolerance with outright persecution—fire and faggots—but he was at least willing to allow "protection" to those persons whose religion did not "directly, tend to the subversion of the government."[73] Throughout the Revolutionary decades the rationalist definition of subversive included quite a few Massachusetts dissenters, whose consciences and property rights Liberals denied were being oppressed by the church laws of the province.

Some New England Baptists and Separatists were so unimpressed by this line of argument that they at times expressed the hope that Episcopalianism would thrive in Massachusetts in order that the local tyranny might be toppled. Thomas Hutchinson, for one, sought to take advantage of such dissenter sentiment by encouraging the thought that Parliamentary authority would guarantee toleration for all sects in New England. For a moment the New England Baptists wavered. "For my part," wrote Isaac Backus to a Boston editor in 1773, "I am not able to get a pair of scales sufficient to weigh those two great bodies in, the Episcopal hierarchy and the New England Presbyterians, so as to find out exactly which is heaviest."[74] In such circumstances, the anti-Episcopal tracts of Liberal ministers only provided dissenters with quotations useful as evidence of Liberal insincerity and inconsistency; Backus was especially taken by the Bishop of Gloucester's criticism of Chauncy's free and catholic establishment. At the final reckoning, however, Backus and his followers decided that Episcopalians were not to be trusted and opted for the patriot side in the Revolutionary controversy.

Backus was confirmed in this decision by what he considered outrageous Episcopal mistreatment of southern Baptists. Like southern dissenters, and even members of the church who inclined to the warmer religion of Devereux Jarratt, Backus also recalled how Whitefield had been silenced by the Bishop of London's Charleston commissary, and how Davies had been maligned and harassed by the Virginia establishment.[75] In truth, Backus simply had little stomach for the pretensions of episcopacy. He was among the first to ridicule the Bishop of Gloucester's "discovery" that the American "savages ought to be civilized as well as Christianized." Those in England who thought that the S.P.G. had a mission among the American Indians ought, he suggested, to read the life of John Eliot and, more particularly, the life of Brainerd by the "immortal Edwards" in order to appreciate that Americans were perfectly capable of handling this matter themselves.[76] All this and more fed into what constituted the Calvinist decision, quite independent of Liberal promptings, to stand for American religion as against that of Great Britain.

It is not impossible that the episcopacy issue was something of a red herring. The whole specter of British policy, critics of the New England establishments frequently charged, was called up only to distract attention from a more tangible tyranny closer to home. Whatever the intention of Liberal and Old Light defenders of American Protestantism, the threat of episcopacy was not unrelated either in their minds or in their strategy to the possibility of overcoming the divisions of American Protestantism wrought by the Great Awakening. As Carl Bridenbaugh has indicated, the fountainhead of Liberal thought in this regard was Ezra Stiles's *Discourse on the Christian Union,* which was delivered in 1760 before the Congregational clergy of Rhode Island. Stiles invoked the specter of an Episcopal threat to the religious liberties of the colonies and summoned dissenters to join in a defensive "confederacy." But the very terms of his appeal disclosed what domestic advantages Stiles saw in such a union. "Let us be cemented together by forebearance, fellowship, union," he asked; the "universal harmony" that he hoped to bring into being was one in which men would not be concerned with such indifferent matters as whether a theology happened to be Arminian or Calvinist.[77]

Stiles's notion of religious harmony was largely conceived in terms of the old New England way, which Stiles, though otherwise a careful ecclesiastical historian, defined as pure and unmixed congregationalism. In his program, sister churches and ministers would have no control over "one another's elections and pastoral investitures." In this respect Stiles was breaking with the various political and ecclesiastical strategies devised by Old Lights (including his late father) for central control of individual churches. But in the context of 1760, it should be noted, the ideal of congregational independence could also have appealed to those who were resisting the use of associations by New Lights who wanted to ferret out Arminian heretics. (The leading Connecticut critic of New Lightism, Thomas Darling, was Stiles's teacher and friend.) Actually Stiles was genuinely committed to religious freedom, and his ideal of union without strength* seems to have been inspired not by partisanship but by an enlightened and even skeptical distaste for the bitter contentions of post-Awakening New England. Nonetheless Stiles indicated that he had no desire for fellowship with the Separates and Baptists who were springing up in Rhode Island and Connecticut, nor, quite clearly, with the spokesmen of a New Divinity which he held in such contempt as to treat it as non-existent so far as the churches of Connecticut were concerned. He bewailed the resurgence of an enthusiasm that threatened to recapitulate the scenes of the Awakening, when, as Stiles observed, "multitudes were seriously, soberly, and solemnly out of their wits."[78] In short, Stiles's appeal for unity was an explicit challenge to evangelical ideals as well as to the strategy of Joseph Bellamy.

Still, Stiles's vision was different from that which seems to have inspired the first serious proposals for an American bishop. In a sense, this scheme also had its sources in a desire for colonial harmony. Around 1750 Samuel Johnson wrote to England, describing the ecclesiastical situation in America in these words:

> their case is very deplorable among themselves since the late enthusiasm hath thrown them into so many feuds, contentions, and separations, which the awe of a bishop would we believe tend much to abate and reduce them to a better state of unity in their own way (as well as reclaim many of them). . .[79]

It was not the awe of a bishop, but the fear of one, that Stiles invoked

---

* In this respect Stiles's argument for Christian union was, as translated into political terms, something of an anticipation of the notion of state sovereignty:
The thirteen provinces on this continent subsist independent of one another as to jurisdiction and controul over one another—yet in harmony. And one church or congregation has no more power over another, than one province over another, and yet they may all subsist in union and love.

in his discourse. But the ultimate basis of American Christian union was for Stiles neither force nor fear. He opened the prospect of a "harmony" based on quiet competition, in which all Protestants were dedicated to the discovery of "resplendent and all-pervading TRUTH" and in which only "the gentle force of persuasion and truth" would bring men to one or another particular commitment.[80]

On all matters save that of compulsion the advocates of evangelical religion differed considerably from Stiles. Among other things they were not, in 1760, as disturbed as he by Episcopalianism. When the Old Light president of Yale, Thomas Clap, forbade his students to attend Anglican services, he was rebuked by the president of Princeton, Aaron Burr, who saw no "inconvenience in granting the liberty" asked for by his Episcopal students. His charter, of course, had promised "equal and exact liberties" of conscience to students of all denominations. This did not mean, however, that Burr was indifferent to men's religion, for his college had after all been founded as an engine against the doctrinal heresies of the day.[81] And here perhaps was the ultimate difference between the evangelicals and Stiles; the former were no less believers in "religious liberty" than other American Protestants, but they were not willing to forbear intellectually on differences they considered important.

The post-Awakening Calvinist mind was hardly disposed to sectarian exclusiveness. Nor was it rigidly uniformitarian; but it was not given to the kind of latitudinarianism that permitted Stiles to smooth over the doctrinal controversies of New England. As Thomas Foxcroft once reminded the readers of *A Vindication of God's Special Grace,* Jonathan Dickinson had resolutely opposed "subscription," but he had also always "boldly confronted what he took to be error." Speaking for New England Calvinists, Foxcroft went on to condemn

> that false moderation which sacrifices divine revelations to human friendships, and, under colour of peace and candour, gives up important points of gospel-doctrine, to every opposer, but still is consistent with discovering a malignity towards others that appear warm defenders and constant asserters of those evangelical truths.[82]

Though Stiles was genuinely averse to all religious rancor, few who joined in his anti-Episcopal "confederacy" were ever beyond showing contempt for the evangelicals of the colonies. And perhaps even more significantly, Foxcroft's spirit was still very much alive in the Calvinism of the 1760's and, indeed, persisted almost to the very last as a force holding it back from even defensive union with the rational and latitudinarian Protestants of America.

Something of this difference emerged in the relationship of reasonable and evangelical Americans with British dissent. First of all, there was a distinction between those with whom the Liberal clergy maintained correspondence and those in whom Calvinists found kindred spirits. Not only the New Side Presbyterians, but Edwards and the evangelical ministers of Boston, were involved with the Erskines and other Scottish revivalists. The first entry in *The Christian History* was a report on the state of religion in the Church of Scotland, which, the author noted, had been ever dear to "the intelligent and good People" of New England by virtue of the *"sound Doctrines* and *pious Spirit* express'd in the Writings of her *eminent* Divines."[83] By contrast the Boston Liberals and the Old Lights of Connecticut were in contact with the "nonconformists" of England—not evangelicals such as the Wesleys but the more affluent and urbane London dissenters. On occasion, however, representatives of both brands of American religion dealt with the English dissenters' organization. That society, as Bridenbaugh indicates, was conspicuously devoted to the cause of religious liberty—so much so that in the 1740's it rebuked the government and clergy of Connecticut for its suppression and persecution of revivalists and Separates. Samuel Davies communicated with this group when he went to England to state his case for toleration in Virginia. (Incidentally, one of the ironies of the period is that such self-anointed cosmopolitans as Jonathan Mayhew maintained their relationships with England only through correspondence, and indeed seldom left their communities, while the Calvinist ministry were frequently engaged in excursions to the other side of the water.) Davies discovered that his ideals were also questionable among English dissenters, though for different reasons. They "seemed to think," Davies reported, "that we were such rigid Calvinists, that we would not admit an Arminian into communion." Herein the English dissenters did not err, for though the branch of Presbyterianism that Davies represented was strongly opposed to subscriptionism, its method of examining candidates for the ministry required an acceptance of certain articles of the Westminster Confession deemed "essential to Christianity."[84] What the Englishmen could not comprehend was that Americans were not simply "nonconformists" and that something more was at stake in the New World than the indulgence of a variety of religious beliefs.

Even in protesting the plan to settle an American bishop, neither rationalists nor Calvinists were merely defending their right to dissent from the Church of England. Both wanted religious freedom, to be sure—but in order that they might define the character of American society and direct the course of its history. Such was likewise the hope of Anglican spokesmen, who from the 1740's onward argued that the doctrines of Calvinism and the Awakening were "well known to have a direct Tendency to Profaneness and impure living." According to James Wetmore, who first defended the Anglicans of Connecticut against the strictures of Noah Hobart, it was "easy to see that substituting" Episcopalianism "in the Room of whatever may now be said to prevail in the Country, would be the introducing *Order, Peace, Purity,* and *Happiness.*"[85] Hobart countered by complaining that Anglicanism led to the grossest immorality—not, interestingly enough, through its Arminian doctrines, but through what Hobart considered its "lack of discipline." Throughout the controversy over the bishopric the debate invariably broadened into discussion of the social consequences of allowing or preventing the ascendancy of the Church of England, with Calvinists as well as rationalists offering a judgment of the moral tendency of Episcopalianism.

In following this line of argument American dissenters displayed a divergence of approach and perspective that could not help having immense ramifications, not only in the period of the Revolution but well into the next century. The debate between Anglicans and Calvinists, as might be expected, revolved about conflicting judgments on the character of English society since the days of Cromwell. In his controversy with Jonathan Dickinson, the Connecticut missionary John Beach observed that "never was there so much Wickedness in the Nation" as in the years of "the grand Rebellion" and of the Commonwealth, when "Calvinistic" principles prevailed in England. Moses Dickinson, taking up the cudgels after his brother's death, countered with another view of English social history. The Puritan Revolution, according to Dickinson, had purged the nation of the vices encouraged by Laud's Arminianism, and it was only with the Restoration that England was struck again by a "Flood" of "open Wickedness," the "Dregs of which have not been purged off until this Day."[86] Liberal spokesmen, on the other hand, seemed reluctant to turn at all to England for evidence of the deleterious social consequences of Anglicanism. Instead Noah Hobart looked to the "plantations," particularly the American South, which he portrayed as a complete moral desert. His mode of argument was long followed by other reasonable New Englanders, who thus, even while espousing a "union" of American dissenters, sowed the seeds of disunion, or at least of Yankee particularism. The Liberal and Old Light image of the South (to which the "Cavalier myth" might well be traced) stood in sharp contrast to that of northern evangelicals. The latter, over the entire half century that began with Davies' 1750 letter to Bellamy, looked to Virginia as the one place in the New World where the Spirit seemed to be working almost without interruption.

375

With Stiles's discourse one can detect a more purely ecclesiastical purpose to rationalist arguments against the American bishop—a willingness, that is, to sacrifice certain social goals in order to preserve the liberty of the American churches. (Indeed, toward the end of the controversy Samuel Johnson indicated that he would prefer the Anglican Church to be merely one of many denominations in the colonies, rather than be destroyed by being made an engine of British policy.) Over the same years, however, the Calvinist viewpoint remained much the same—that Arminianism, by whatever denomination espoused, was a threat to the social well-being of the colonies and that the welfare of America depended on the triumph of evangelical religion. Such a perspective on the role of religion in the affairs of men inevitably stood in the way of Stiles's proposed alliance. Shortly after the *Discourse,* Stiles suggested to Francis Alison organized cooperation between New Englanders and Presbyterians. The times seemed propitious, since the reunion of New and Old Sides had been promoted by Alison, who saw their division, in the context of the French and Indian War, as fatal to "piety, morals, or liberty."[87] But already by 1760 the Presbyterian union was breaking down as a consequence of Tennent's disgust, and that of many younger ministers, with the formalism and even deadness which the more reasonable Old Side seemed to have foisted on the church. Thus Stiles's program, born of a desire to preserve on his terms the unity of the war years, was hardly rejoiced in by the evangelical ministry. Ebenezer Pemberton, for one, questioned whether anything more in the way of cooperation was possible than a correspondence, "unless the plan was very acceptable indeed." Alison immediately understood that the reluctance of Calvinists stemmed from the "easy forbearance" in matters of doctrine that Stiles espoused.[88]

In 1766, when it seemed that "delegates from every dissenting association in America" met in New Haven to devise a plan for united defense against the threat of episcopacy, partisans of the New Divinity were in fact not represented. The conclave issued a series of resolutions urging Americans to stand firmly for their "religious independence," but of course Separates and Baptists were not even invited.[89] Stiles did attempt, however, to bring stricter Calvinists into his anti-Episcopal confederation. One consequence of his efforts seems to have been to arouse the suspicions of the Boston Liberals. For by the 1770's the clergy of the Massachusetts standing order were once again obsessed with the threat of enthusiastic separation—as were also, for that matter, many of the reasonable Congregationalists of Stiles's own Rhode Island. Charles Chauncy himself was persuaded that Samuel Hopkins and other zealous opponents of the Half-Way Covenant were in fact encouraging defections to the Church of England and that the latter, in the circumstances, was possibly the less dangerous persuasion.

One encouragement to Stiles's union in the 1770's was the arrival in the colonies of John Witherspoon, or, more precisely, the reconstitution of the Presbyterian Church which his appointment brought out. Witherspoon came to Princeton as an avowed neutral in the controversies that had plagued American Presbyterianism since the Awakening. But his selection was chiefly welcomed by the New Side, and in the first years of his tenure Witherspoon made clear his opposition to "the personnel and views of the Old Side." Francis Alison, who looked on Witherspoon as an enemy and blamed him for the New Side victory that installed George Duffield in a Philadelphia pulpit, abandoned his plans to leave the College of Philadelphia. Yet it soon emerged that the independent president of Princeton was, in a "much more far-reaching way," an ally of the Old Side and that his election, resented at the time as something of a New Side coup, had, as its long-range beneficiaries, the elements of Presbyterianism for which Alison spoke.

Witherspoon's appointment was perhaps the first overt symptom of a change in American Presbyterianism—one which began around 1760, with the onset of a second great wave of immigration to the Middle Colonies—a change that would see the Presbyterian Church redefined as an exclusively Scotch-Irish institution. In acquiescing in the choice of Witherspoon, some Old Side leaders seem to have appreciated the significance of placing a Scot in the chair once occupied by Burr and Edwards, especially when, by way of concession, the New England representation on the Princeton faculty was concurrently reduced. Soon after entering office, moreover, Witherspoon effectively aligned himself with, and gave encouragement to, an anti-New England sentiment that had begun to crop up in parts of the Middle Colonies. Specifically, Witherspoon manifested a distinct "coolness" toward the New Divinity and, as Chauncy happily noted in a letter to Stiles, quickly worked "to purge it" and its partisans from the intellectual life of the college. The attack on what Witherspoon considered the "idealism" of Edwards and Bellamy contributed to a lessening of the New England influence, not in the college merely, but within Presbyterianism generally. The New Englanders of upper Jersey and Long Island began to withdraw from church councils and, as they did so, to reaffirm their affinities with Bellamy and his colleagues. What Witherspoon had helped to accomplish was a shattering of the alliance on which, since the days of Tennent and Dickinson, the power and the vitality of New Side Presbyterians had depended.[90]

The exorcising of New England influence from Presbyterianism did not result in Old Side hegemony, but clearly the balances within the church had been changed. So far as power was concerned, the reins were in fact seized by Witherspoon, but despite Alison's continual complaints, this did not represent a New Side victory. Actually, the ultimate effect of Witherspoon's strategy was to blur the differences between Old and New Sides. His counterreformation, especially his mediating philosophy, made official Presbyterian doctrine far more congenial to the Old Side than it had been in the days when Edwardean theology dominated Princeton. Witherspoon was a Calvinist, but his Calvinism was of a sort with which Alison could come to terms. Interestingly, Alison's friendly correspondents, Stiles and Chauncy, cheered Witherspoon on in his efforts to turn Presbyterianism against the New Divinity. They recognized Witherspoon (as many of his New Side admirers did not) as a moderating force contributing to a realignment, not only within Presbyterianism, but within American Protestantism generally. In 1770 the Presbyterian General Assembly asked Witherspoon to seek the cooperation of the New England clergy in resisting the Episcopal threat. He did not of course seek to woo Bellamy to the cause; rather he approached the more moderate New Englanders. With the awarding of an honorary Princeton degree to Chauncy, Witherspoon attested that even the most Liberal northern clergyman was preferable to a spokesman of the New Divinity.

Thus the stricter Calvinists of whatever denomination were effectively excluded from the operations of the anti-Episcopal entente promoted by Stiles and Alison. But in 1770 the advocates of evangelical religion were also calling for Christian union, and in doing so they made it abundantly clear that they had far different ideas of what was desirable in the way of unity. The year 1770 saw the Whitefield obsequies, and the ministers who solemnized his death made it quite clear that the unity they aspired to was among those churches only, and their members, who "appeared to befriend the inward operations of the Holy Spirit in regeneration." Whitefield was a proponent of Christian charity, Nathaniel Whitaker explained, but he had "declared in publick, as well as private, that it is a soul damning opinion that a *head* or *speculative* faith is sufficient for salvation." Any who espoused such a faith, or delighted in its preachers, were not "real christians, but quite the reverse."[91] What the admirers of Whitefield wanted was, in sum, not an alliance of all nominal Protestants, but an evangelical union—a union which would hardly embrace such critics of affectionate religion as Ezra Stiles, much less grant him a position of leadership.

III

The evangelical unionism of 1770 had its immediate inspiration in the ecclesiastical controversies engendered by the awakening of 1763-64.

Everywhere in the colonies, but especially in New England, and there particularly in Essex County, the Liberal and moderate Calvinist reaction to the revival inspired all varieties of Calvinist ministers to call for an evangelical alliance. Aaron Hutchinson, ordained and installed a Congregational minister, spoke in 1768 against the protection the New England way afforded such "hidden" enemies of God as John Tucker. Soon to take his people into Presbyterianism, Hutchinson called on "all the truly evangelical ministers" of New England to arise and contend for the truth, to abandon all their concerns "about trifling matters, or merely circumstantial things," and to unite in opposition to all who would destroy "the faith on which the Protestant church was founded."[92] This was the signal for Isaac Backus, already sympathetic by virtue of his admiration for the attacks of Pemberton and Parsons on Mayhew's Arianism, to proclaim the insignificance of differences among "true Calvinists" of the colonies. Impressed by the demands of Jacob Green and Joseph Bellamy that a "profession of saving faith was a necessary term of communion in the church,"[93] Backus urged the full participation of his Baptists in the evangelical crusade.

In 1772 Jonathan Parsons published a pamphlet which brought together all the Calvinist proposals for "rooting out heresy," each of them designed to expose and isolate those ministers who were "known to teach the doctrines which Calvinistic divines do believe are subversive of Christianity." More significantly, however, Parsons went well beyond such early proposals as John Cleaveland's for a "Consociation, or solemn explicit covenant" among "all the sound and orthodox Churches and Ministers of Christ,"[94] and proposed a popular alliance as well. Let all such members of the laity as "adhere" to Arminian preachers, he proposed, be refused "communion," and let all who are "agreed in calvinistic doctrines, heartily embrace one another." It is "being united in doctrines and their efficacy," proclaimed this surviving itinerant of the Great Awakening, "that are the closing principles."[95]

Such overtures for evangelical union anticipated David Austin's various strategies in the 1790's for inducing a "spirit of union" among Baptists, Presbyterians, and the Congregational heirs of Jonathan Edwards: the publication of *The American Preacher,* the revival of the Concert of Prayer, and the invitation to "the different denominations of Christians" to "unite together" in anticipation of the millennium.[96] In 1770, as in 1795, however, the evangelical union was being forged not so much in hope of speedy triumph as out of despair for what seemed the downward tendency of American history. It is *"high Time the Church had some faithful Warning, and something like an Alarm sounded in their Ears,*[97] cried one of the Calvinist sentinels, and another thought it high time for "us all to have done both with lukewarmness and cowardice in this cause."[98] When such Calvinists posited a "Cataline's conspiracy" against the faith once delivered to the saints, they revealed the degree to which they could not comprehend the changes in colonial life that were making reasonable religion not an aberration but something of a fixture of American civilization—one with increasing appeal. Like Bellamy a decade earlier, they were seeking to steel the churches of the faithful against defections from their own ranks.

Whatever the sources of Calvinists' discontent, their crusade did inspire purely religious revivals right down to, and even into, the Revolution. Perhaps more significantly, it drew the citizens of the colonies once more into battle array. Sermon upon sermon ridiculed the Christian charity of "Arians, Socinians, and Arminians." However "garnished with the epithet of *catholick*," such charity was manifestly un-Christian; the *"Laodicean-like"* men who espoused it, a Connecticut election preacher observed, would not "break charity with any man, upon so small a point" as the "true grace of GOD."[99] From Long Island, Samuel Buell came again to Enfield and proclaimed that "there are some *fundamental* truths which all the various denominations of professing Christians must be united in," and that it was impossible for a man to have "true religion" when his apprehension of God proved him to have "a rotten unregenerate heart."[100] The cry was raised that the "unbelievers party"—"a multitude of *worms*"—consisted not only of Arminians but of all who sought to use the power of the state in any way to deny "good men" the freedom of voluntary church membership.[101] Nor was expression of social animus limited to New England. In New Jersey Jacob Green and a group of younger New Side ministers made the same charges against the Old Side—on the basis of its nondiscriminating ordinations, its perversion of Princeton, and its unwillingness to insist on a regenerate church membership.

Once again it had been discovered that certain Americans—and this time not only the clergy—were Judases with their eyes fixed on the bag. In the opinion of Calvinists, this sin was exclusively that of the rich and fashionable Arminians. Isaac Backus, for instance, gave the lie to Liberal taunts that "a little more money would not be disagreeable" to the dissenter ministry and that the dissenter populace was unwilling to share in the burdens of state:

> And though many of us have expended ten or twenty times as much, in setting up and supporting that worship which we believe to be right, than it would have cost us to continue in the fashionable way, yet we were often accused of being covetous, for dissenting from

that way, and refusing to pay more money out of our little incomes, to uphold men from whom we receive no benefit, but rather abuse.[102]

Calvinist animosity toward seasonable Americans was proclaimed in the early 1770's in a variety of ways and in hundreds of documents, but the central doctrine was probably most succinctly stated in a 1773 sermon by Jonathan Parsons:

> Men in general seem to care but little for any thing but self. And it is an easy matter, when self is at the bottom, to make a hundred excuses to save themselves from generous distributions for the support of the poor. Besides, they make to themselves a religion which cost them nothing, and to quiet their consciences with that. One drops now and then a small matter, and wipes his mouth with a few hypocritical prayers and good words, and thinks really God is obliged to him . . . They readily join with the outside of religion, but when they hear of selling all and giving to the poor to follow Christ, they go away sorrowful.[103]

In sum, the doctrine of original sin, once theoretically an observation on human nature in general, had become a commentary on the rich and fashionable Arminians of the colonies.

In Virginia too social hostility was aroused as evangelical energies poured into the drive for religious liberty and against taxes to support the clergy of the establishment. This was especially true, according to Boucher, in "the Back Woods, near the Blue Ridge: a country which seemed to bear no faint resemblance to Ephraim; and which, like it, was over-run with sectaries." There as elsewhere dissenter animosity was translated into social terms: "the labouring classes, instead of regarding the rich as their guardians, patrons, and benefactors, now look on them as so many over-grown colossuses, whom it is no demerit in them to do wrong."[104] Further south, some of the same aggressions were manifested in the Regulator rebellion, though in the Carolinas, as probably everywhere in the colonies, resentment was strongest against the upstart nobility and the parvenu mentality of those who, having risen from the "dunghill," proceeded to look down and oppress the classes from which they sprang. Or, as Hermon Husband saw it, the wealthier citizens of North Carolina, Scotch "factors" included, were disposed to mistreat their neighbors for the simple reason that these gentry had "no religion" at all.*[105]

* It is not here argued that all the colonial unrest of the 1760's and 1770's was religiously inspired, but rather that the insurgencies gave expression to resentments that for a generation had taken theological and ecclesiastical forms. Nor can the character and vehemence of the various movements be properly understood unless they are seen as the political embodiments of older animosities. The uprising of "Paxton's Boys," for instance, had no little to do with the ancient struggle between Old and New Side Presbyterians, and with the growing strength of the Baptists in

However distinctive some of the political goals of the Regulators, they were recognized as brethren by the evangelical leadership and people of New England. There too what had once been a religious crusade took on explicit political significance as social and economic grievances were translated into demands, not for ecclesiastical freedom merely, but for a variety of laws designed to promote the general welfare and aid the "oppressed poor" in particular. Calvinist exhorters began to proclaim the example of the early communistic churches, and election preachers to hawk an outright agrarianism before the Connecticut General Assembly.

Clearly one of the problems of the 1770's was a general economic depression. So apparent were the sufferings, and so vocal the complaints, that Chauncy thought it necessary to issue his caveat against communism, *Christian Love Placed in True and Just Point of Light*, as the "Great and Thursday Lecture" to the assembled ministers and elders of Boston. This was in August of 1773, when conditions were such that Chauncy advised that the functions of deacons might include distribution of alms among at least the widows and orphans of each parish.[106] Within the year, Parliament had closed Boston Port, and it became possible to blame all of the city's poverty and distress on British policy, and for Chauncy thereby to forget many of the lessons of even his modest social enlightenment of 1773.

In 1774 Chauncy wrote and published (anonymously) a tract the title of which was something of an epitome of the Liberal Whig mind on the eve of Revolution: *A Letter to a Friend. Giving a Concise, but Just, Representation of the Hardships and Sufferings the Town of Boston is Exposed to, and Must Undergo in Consequence of the British-Parliament; which, by Shutting up It's Port, had Put a Fatal Bar in the Way of That Commercial Business on Which it Depended for It's Support*. Charitably read, the *Letter* suggests that the sufferings of the people of Boston could and did inspire somewhat mixed emotions in Chauncy. After listing all the trades and occupations economically depressed by the closure of the port, Chauncy observed that "if the multitudes . . . should act a wild and mad part," no one could be blamed but those "who were the occasional cause of it."[107] Although the crisis of empire was not seized on by Liberals merely as a means of diverting social grievances into new channels, clearly those who had long feared the wildness of the lower orders were happy to have this madness directed against another target.

---

interior Pennsylvania. As for the New York land riots of the 1760's, Cadwallader Colden immediately appreciated the importance of the fact that the most active dissidents were "independents from New England."

Chauncy's announced intention in publishing this letter was to inspire the gentlemen of America, in the ranks of which he had long numbered himself, with a flowing sympathy for Bostonians. Sympathy was a cardinal Christian virtue for Liberals, who believed that the truly benevolent man would sympathize with others "in their troubles and afflictions; bearing a part in their sorrows, and being sincerely grieved for them when they are in adversity."[108] In theory such sympathy was a response of the moral sense to a painful situation. The sense of uneasiness was heightened and sharpened by confrontation with a particular object of regard. Benevolent feeling was aroused toward individual suffering men, not for mankind in general.

To arouse sympathy, a clear idea of affliction and adversity had to be placed before the mind of the benevolent Christian. Such was Chauncy's purpose in engaging in this imaginary correspondence. Those American gentlemen who had expressed "a tender concern for the people of Boston," he began, had done so only on the basis of "a general idea" of these afflictions; but

> being at a distance, and not being distinctly acquainted with that multiplicity of ways in which this barbarous act will operate to distress us, your conception of our sufferings, by means of it, must fall vastly below the greatness of them. It will not therefore be displeasing, though it should add some degree of impetuosity to your passions, which already give you uneasiness, if I am particular in pointing out to you those avenues this horrid decree has opened to let in misery upon us.[109]

The concern which Liberals showed for their fellow Americans in the next year was of this order. Speaking at Plymouth in December of 1774, Gad Hitchcock described Christ's love of country as "a peculiar concern for the welfare of his own nation" and went on to define His benevolence as an inability to "call to mind the calamities" He knew were about to befall His nation without "the tenderest emotions of compassion and grief."[110] William Smith, always more demonstrative than his northern counterparts, observed that the opening of hostilities promised "great and deep distress" to the American people and, though knowing not what course others might take, thought it his personal duty to pause to "indulge a tear . . . over the scenes that lie before us."[111]

Smith was among the first of American clergymen to define Christian love and virtue as little more than a form of sensibility. He had prayed, in a document that he quickly published for its literary merit, that he might "feel for all my own species, *weeping* the lovely tear of sympathy for those that *weep*."[112] Eventually, of course, sensibility would become a means of salvaging the Christian ethos, if only by opening the gates of salvation to all capable of shedding a genteel tear. In the years before the Revolution, however, such a definition of virtue served to make the obligations of Christian love less onerous. Expressed as compassion or sympathy, Liberal benevolence permitted those who espoused it to pose as friends to the people and even lovers of mankind by means of feeling reactions to the plight of widows and orphans*[113]

Whether the pitiful scenes portrayed by Liberal ministers in their political sermons aided the patriot cause is questionable, since by dilating on the suffering, Liberals may well have diverted attention from its actual causes. Chauncy's letter was nevertheless a contribution to the Whig movement, even though it was no inflammatory popular harangue, but a summons to the Christian gentlemen of the colonies. Having limited his previous public efforts in the 1770's to discoursing before a group of "patriotic gentlemen," Chauncy had further restricted his local audience by choosing this epistolary form of address. Yet the old rationalist's last contribution to the literature of Revolution marked a significant departure from the tenets of Boston Liberalism—for in the fiery trials of 1774 Charles Chauncy came to realize that there were gentlemen elsewhere in America.

Such tearful sympathy for their less fortunate brethren did not, however, keep urban Liberals from seeking a settlement of imperial differences that could have left many Americans just as unhappy as they had been in 1773. Chauncy was soon to prove himself capable of turning concern for widows and orphans into a plea for a special interest, but his *Letter* of 1774 was no more devious than its central assumption—that the happiness of all would be assured by restoring the trading privileges of Boston's merchants. The Whigs of 1774, whose economic thought derived from a rather naïve version of the "filter-down" theory of prosperity espoused by their nineteenth-century descendants, were supremely confident that all American uneasiness could be alleviated by the unshackling of commerce.

Of course the Calvinist clergy thought otherwise. Their prescription for American prosperity, if not for its happiness, looked to something more than merely a return to the good old system of production and distribution. More significantly, the Calvinist mind was not about to accept either Chauncy's tender concern for the people of Boston nor the philanthropies of his deacons as evidence that the officers of the First Church were among the elect. Whoever Chauncy may have thought obliged to him for his alms and generous tears, the Calvinist

* In Mayhew's eulogy of Sewall it was observed that though the Judge gave little to charity, "a more soft and tender, a more sympathizing, or more bountiful heart, no man, perhaps, ever had."

ministry in point of fact ridiculed both these "species of modern charity." Familiar with Edwards' critique of Hutcheson and with Bellamy's observations on "natural compassion," the evangelical ministry were well prepared to examine the "charity, which seems to be in the mouths of many," consisting either in "liberal benefactions" or in the "kind of sympathy" that expresses itself in being "touched by the miseries of others." In 1772 the Connecticut election preacher suggested that the former was undoubtedly an effort "to purchase a salvation consistent with the life and power of sin," while two years later Nathaniel Niles condemned the latter as "ungodlike, unreasonable, unjust, unmanly."[114]

The cult of sensibility was clearly suspect, even remarkably ridiculous, from the moment of its introduction into American canons of taste. Jacob Duché, whose *Caspipina's Letters* represented the most contrived effort of the pre-Revolutionary mind to give literary form to "fine sensibilities" and the shedding of tears, saw himself as necessarily on the defensive. "The morose religionist" and "pretended spiritualist," he observed, might despise men, and even women, whose eyes watered at music or poetry, but what, he asked, did they have to offer in exchange but "notions and opinions, whimsical and visionary?" Actually in Duché's formulation sensibility was explicitly a strategy for rising above the petty quarrels of the imperial crisis and, finally, for fending off abuse by the vulgar. Or at least Duché hoped it would be, though his very espousal of sensibility betrayed an attitude that was hardly designed to ingratiate him with the Philadelphia multitude:

> by this he not only defeats effectually the designs of malice and envy, but (which is an infinitely more noble conquest) he triumphs over *himself,* and leads every furious frantick passion of his fallen nature in chains. --- In a word, he considers a *meek* and *quiet spirit* as one of the greatest *ornaments* of human nature, one of the grand characteristicks, by which not only the well-bred gentleman is distinguished from the untutored clown, but the *real* Christian from the *nominal* professor.[115]

In the summer of 1776 Duché's quietistic sensibilities would distinguish him from many Americans by carrying him far from the tumult and shouting—back to London, whence he bewailed the frantic passions of the Revolution.

Caspipina's Letters contained one other argument which, in the context of the 1770's, reflected the patent concern of elegant colonials over the mad levelism then seemingly rampant in the New World. Simply stated, Duché's doctrine was that whoever hungered and thirsted after righteousness had best know how truly fortunate were the poor:

Those, who earn their daily bread by the sweat of their brow, are apt to imagine, that, if they were in easy circumstances, they should have leisure to attend to their eternal concerns; but no sooner does wealth increase, than that their care and attention to it increase in proportion, and they find themselves more and more embarrassed and less at leisure than ever they had been.[116]

Thus did Duché come to something of the same wisdom that filled the pages of John Woolman's *Journal*,*[117] though probably through another line of intellectual development. Nonetheless there were probably many pious Americans—and not all of them Quakers—who, in the 1770's, thought it best not to concern themselves with loaves and fishes, and who therefore stood somewhat aloof from the economic and political issues of the day. Among them were probably the Sandemanians, whose perspective of public affairs was reflected in their prediction that the world would come to an end in 1777.

As Bellamy observed, not one Sandemanian was represented in the Putnam army of 1774, and had all American pietists believed as they or Woolman did, there might not have been any social hostility whatever in the colonies. Most evangelical Americans also probably believed that they did not lust after the riches of wealthier colonials. What did consciously concern them, however, was the iniquity as well as the inequity of Liberal ideas of social justice. The kind of charity practiced by Chauncy, for instance, like mere sensitive concern, branded its practitioners, according to Nathaniel Niles, "as enemies to the common good, and to every good and wholesome law."[118] In sum, Calvinism had developed its own views of the general welfare and social justice, and from this perspective it seemed too late in 1774 for even Chauncy to save himself and his friends from the wrath of the Calvinist God.

Yet when in 1774 Calvinist mobs roamed the Connecticut countryside, they did not spend their fury on all "Arminians." Spared were those preachers and parishes which, whatever their religion, had made clear a sympathy for the liberty of the colonies. One such group moved across the boundary into Massachusetts to execute righteous vengeance

---

* A theme—and probably *the* theme—of Woolman's writings was a quietist rejection of the world's ways as the only means of preserving the vitality of the inner life: "a way of Life, free from much Entanglement, appeared best for me . . . I saw that a humble Man, with the blessing of the Lord, might live on a little; and that where the Heart was set on Greatness, Success in Business did not satisfy the craving; but that commonly, with an Increase of Wealth, the Desire of Wealth increased." Woolman's formula represented a confession that the course of American history could not be made compatible with piety. It was of course this very concession that Edwardean religion refused to make.

on those who, in Great Barrington, had mistreated Samuel Hopkins, but they, in addition to being fashionable Episcopalians, were most of them outspoken Tories.[119] Elsewhere too the Calvinist ministry and populace, aroused against British tyranny, grew less vehement in their hostility to admirers of the Liberal gospel who happened also to be patriots. Not all the concessions of 1774, however, were made by Calvinists; Chauncy, for instance, privately confessed in that year that the merchants of Boston wanted to serve only "their own private, separate interest" and that the province's "dependence, under God," was now therefore "upon the *landed interest,* upon our free-holders and yeomanry."[120] Considering the traditional Liberal attitude toward Massachusetts rustics, this might seem one of the most absurd statements of Chauncy's life. But it was, rather, poignant testimony to his heartfelt commitment to the New England way, just as was the Calvinists' abandonment of their domestic crusade in order to defend what they were coming to call their "nation."

According to so well-informed and concerned a contemporary as General Gage, *the* turning point in American affairs was the promulgation in 1774 of the Quebec Act. Its anti-Protestant features, he believed, ended the last hope of keeping rural Calvinists docile and preventing them from uniting with those urban Americans who were struggling against British commercial regulations. The farmers, Gage observed, were strangely convinced that Britain intended to abolish their religious freedom. Once they could not "be made to believe the contrary," he wrote, "the Flame" of rebellion "blazed out in all Parts" of the countryside "at once beyond the conception of every Body."[121]

In assessing the significance of the Quebec Act, the general correctly gauged the hypersensitive and suspicious nature of American Protestantism. What Gage did not seem to appreciate, however, was that to the mind of evangelical Protestantism the Quebec Act seemed not an isolated element of British policy but the culmination, hardly unexpected, of a decade of deplorable British endeavors. The Boston Massacre, Governor Tryon's vendetta against the North Carolina Regulators, and the Intolerable Acts generally persuaded Calvinists that the government of Great Britain was bent on depriving Americans of all liberty. By 1775 the Declaratory Act of 1766 seemed, in retrospect, to have proclaimed, not Britain's right merely, but its intention, to bind America "in all cases whatsoever."

To some degree the evangelical mind partook of what by 1775 was the common intellectual property of all American Whigs: the perspective of Sidney and Hoadly on the British constitution and the projections of Burgh's *Disquisitions* as to the progressive deterioration of the government of England. Yet if Calvinists shared in what

Bernard Bailyn has characterized as a "fear of a comprehensive conspiracy against liberty throughout the English-speaking world," their view of the British administration's "corruption" had a peculiarly evangelical coloring.[122] When in 1766 Calvinists had asserted it "impossible to conceive of the many complicated evils" which might have followed the Stamp Act, their anxieties were founded not on a careful study of British history and policy but on what they believed was demonstrably the character of the human heart. Similarly, their growing conviction that "religious liberty is so blended with civil, that if one falls it is not to be expected that the other will continue," did not develop along such a legal line of argument as John Adams' tortured demonstrations of how imposition of the feudal law and enforcement of the canon law were logically congruent.[123] The organizing principle of Calvinist analysis was that articulated in a sermon before the Georgia Provincial Congress in 1775: "all laws usually wear the complexion of those by whom they were made."[124] Not British constitutional history, finally, but a sense of the degeneracy of British character, gave coherence to the various edicts and acts of the 1770's. For Calvinists the central truth of politics was the conception of "natural man" set forth in Edwards' *Original Sin*.

More specifically, the Calvinist response to the Quebec Bill reflected Edwards' conviction that the tendency of history is downward when unaided by the Holy Spirit. Such was the assumption of a commencement orator at the College of Rhode Island, who in 1774 entered "a plea for the right of private judgment in religious matters." Not a sense of the precarious balances of governments, but visions of depravity feeding on itself, enforced his conclusion that "almost every human calamity is gradually progressive."[125] Fears that the tempo of history was accelerating soon evoked expectations of worse calamities, and thus well before the text of the Quebec Bill reached the colonies, Calvinists were predicting that the next ship from England would bring the news that "we must have imposed on us, the superstitions and damnable heresies of the church of Rome."[126] When Calvinist ministers suggested in late 1774 that "depositions of the clergy, fines, imprisonment, disfranchisements, confiscations, &c." might be among the "dire attendants" of the Quebec Act, their prediction derived not from a rational analysis of the text of the edict but from what they took to be the character of those who had promulgated it. When Joseph Perry warned the civil fathers of Connecticut that the Bible commonwealth might soon be forced to exchange "the best religion in the world" for "all the barbarity, trumpery and superstition of popery; or burn at the stake, or submit to the tortures of the inquisition," he did not argue from the terms of the legislation. Rather

Perry, colleague and successor to Jonathan Edwards' father, induced the "natural tendency, complexion and effects" of the Quebec Act from the clear likelihood that "it first sprang from that original *wicked politician.*"[127] Like other pieces of legislation and other examples of British conduct, the bill merely confirmed suspicions.

In rising to the threat of popery, as in responding to that of episcopacy, the evangelical mind and will seized on issues comprehensible in terms of inherited formulas. Most Calvinists unquestionably agreed with Livingston and Alison, who had discussed the issue of an American bishop as of more importance "than the imposition of any customs, or commercial restrictions, which affect not the rights of conscience."[128] To the Calvinist mind, however, the Quebec Act seemed but further evidence of a "base, diabolical design" of British "tyranny" to "enslave" Americans.[129] Part of the threatened "slavery"—but only a part—was economic and political. By 1774 in many parishes both Calvinist ministers and people were declaring themselves "daily more and more convinced of the ambitious views of those wicked men who are attempting to parcel out our properties amongst themselves and their adherents."[130] Thus in rising to the challenge of the Intolerable Acts the evangelical mind permitted itself a slight reordering of the priority of values, and the "liberty" held so dear came to involve something more than freedom of religion.

More importantly, however, the presumed British "tyranny" allowed evangelical America to obscure, and even for the moment to forget, some of the sins of the great and rich men of colonial society. Many Calvinist ministers in 1774 tried to keep their domestic concerns and the defense against Britain distinguishable, but even the most perceptive found it difficult to do so. One of the nobler of pre-Revolutionary Calvinist utterances was Jonathan Parsons' *Freedom from Civil and Ecclesiastical Slavery.* It was delivered on March 5, 1774, on the anniversary of the Boston Massacre. (Peter Oliver rightly discerned the tendency of the period when he noted how, in Massachusetts, Guy Fawkes Day was forgotten and commemoration of the Massacre substituted in its stead.) Parsons began his sermon by reminding his people of the primary and supreme importance of their religious liberty. The bulk of what followed was a commentary on John Tucker's refusal to allow such religious freedom to the inhabitants of Newburyport. If true Christian charity were cultivated in *"all* the classes," Parsons observed, there could be no argument about the right of men to leave their parish minister. In the circumstances, however, he drew his own conclusions about "those who forcibly take away money or property from their honest neighbors, to support a minister which they cannot in conscience attend." Such men, Parsons continued, were "guilty of spiritual tyranny." But then he went on to proclaim his "great aversion" to "all enslaving measures, and a strong desire for public liberty."[131] So vehemently did Parsons denounce the British regime, its underlings and mercenaries, that his sermon constituted the most severe published American condemnation, to that point, of British "depravity."

Little more than a year later Parsons rejoiced in the outbreak of the rebellion, but he undoubtedly went to his death in the summer of 1776 uncertain as to what, precisely, had aroused his people and the other Calvinists of New England. Something of an explanation of the flame of rebellion is disclosed, however, in the central doctrine of Parsons' *Civil and Ecclesiastical Liberty*. "Equal and exact liberty granted to all denominations," he argued, "would naturally tend to beget affectionate union."[132] But the liberty without which union was impossible was not to be granted by the Massachusetts establishment; nor could it be wrested from them even by the firmest provincial evangelical alliance. So Parsons diverted his attention, instinctively as it were, to the question of what was to be done by *all* Americans should Britain persist in its design to "enslave" a whole continent. In such a case the good men of America would, he predicted, "unitedly" rise to rain righteous vengeance on their venal and bloodthirsty oppressors.

Among those oppressors, Parsons included in 1774 John Tucker and his fashionable Arminian friends, who could not possibly be true "friends to liberty," so devoted were they to local tyranny. For the moment, however, the crusade for American liberty permitted neglect of the warfare against Arminians. The process of diverted attention occurred slowly or more rapidly in each element of the evangelical party, and differently no doubt in the mind of each individual. Isaac Backus, for instance, had regularly observed in the first years of the difficulties with Britain that the very Bostonians who were most outspoken about the tyranny of taxation without representation were the leading supporters of the provincial establishments. "Can three thousand miles," he asked, "possibly fix such limits to the taxing power?"[133] But by 1775 Backus was aggrieved chiefly by the Arminians of western Massachusetts—among them the very Williams clan which had once persecuted Edwards—who continued, to the outbreak of the rebellion, their oppression of dissenters. In Hampshire and Berkshire such Arminians were more often than not Tories, and Backus entered on the Revolution convinced that the most dangerous threat to American society, and to the church, derived from the advocates of the British regime.

To be sure, Backus saw Tory policy as coming from "the same

principles, and much of it from the same persons" as had mistreated the saints, but his slight shift of focus changed his perspective on domestic affairs.[134] Something of what this implied to America generally is revealed in the career in 1775 of a rather obscure Calvinist exhorter named Elisha Rich, in whom the process of transference was greatly foreshortened. Rich began the year with a publication declaring that the Antichrist was to be discovered, not by working with the figure "666" but by espying the "mark of the beast" carried either openly or not too secretly by every "unregenerate" man in the colonies, and especially by those who, in their self-satisfied wealth, denied religious liberty to the less fashionable citizens of America.[135] No sooner, however, had Rich proclaimed the need for searching out, isolating, and overcoming the domestic enemies of the Kingdom in high and urban places than he began in April 1775 to propose that Britain, by the threat it posed to the ecclesiastical liberty of America, bore the most distinctive features of the beast. Within months Rich was composing hymns to the embattled Church Militant of Bunker Hill.[136] By focusing so intently on the apocalyptic blackness of Britain, the Calvinist mind was rendered less capable of perceiving shades of gray within the American ranks.

IV

Whatever the confusions and diversions brought about by the imperial struggle, in one respect at least Calvinism undeviatingly pursued its earlier goals. Though disposed to less churchly concerns, Calvinists continued to see the controversy with Britain as auguring success in their own local battles for religious freedom. A 1767 Baptist petition for religious liberty saw the victory over the Stamp Act as arguing "Strongly in our favour, that we shall Prevail," and "in Proportion, may be Incouraged, as our Sacred Rights are of more Importance than our Civil."[137] Throughout the decade, dissenters pointed to the incongruity of "a people, nobly struggling for *civil* Liberty," allowing foreign affairs to divert their attention from their more real domestic grievances, thus permitting themselves to be "perpetually trampled upon by the unbounded *Pride of Priests*."[138] Not even the Revolution itself quieted the Calvinist drive for religious freedom in the colonies. "While the defence of the civil rights of America appeared a matter of great importance," Backus was to recall, "our religious liberties were by no means to be neglected; and the contest concerning each kept a pretty even pace through the war."[139]

As historians have often noted, the Revolution simply added momentum to the quest for religious liberty. "Yield to the mighty current of American freedom," the younger William Tennent exhorted the

South Carolina House of Assembly in 1777, in defending a dissenter petition for an end to the establishment,

> and let our state be inferior to none on this wide continent, in the liberality of its laws, and in the happiness of its people.[140]

By 1778 this mighty current seemed to be carrying away so many of the ancient landmarks that David Avery, inspired by disestablishment in New York, was calling on Virginia, Connecticut, and Massachusetts to repeal the last restrictive ecclesiastical laws still in force, and was looking forward to the day when America would be an "asylum" for men from all over the world to "enjoy, in *full*," a complete *"Liberty of Conscience!"*[141] Throughout the war New England and Virginia dissenters continued to observe the inconsistency of a people struggling for their liberty and yet denying the most sacred of freedoms to their fellow citizens.

Considering such sentiments, neither the Calvinist reaction to the proposed bishopric nor to its presumed extension, the Quebec Act, can be set down as simple bigotry or intolerance. Though Calvinists despaired of the Church of England, or even detested it, they were not frightened by it. Instead of haunting themselves with the imagined omnipotence of an Episcopal hierarchy, they were confident that Anglicanism (or any other sterile religion of reasonableness) would remain powerless in the colonies so long as Americans were filled with the warm and enthusiastic piety of their fathers. So too were Calvinists offended by what they conceived the "open attempts" of the British government to "propagate and establish popery, that exotic plant," a religion not "native to our benign soil, nor of our Heavenly Father's planting."[142] What outraged them, though, was not so much the fear that Catholicism would spread throughout America as the fact that the British government had seen fit to establish it in any part of the New World.

Thus William Gordon observed in 1774 that he "had no objection to the Canadians being fully secured in the enjoyment of their religion, however erroneous and anti-Christian it may appear to me as a Protestant." Rather he objected "to the British legislative's not having given a universal establishment to the rights of conscience among them." The Calvinist ministry were, in fact, throughout the 1770's among the strongest advocates of religious freedom—"a universal toleration" of Catholics and deists, as well as the various shades of Protestants, and indeed, of all, "whether professors of Christianity or not."[143] Their opposition to the Quebec Act, like their resistance of an American bishop, was inspired by a desire to liberate America for free and voluntary worship of God.

If portions of the American populace were disposed to celebrate Guy Fawkes Day in the early years of the Revolution, the Calvinist clergy gave them no more encouragement in this than did Washington. Actually, the most vituperative critics of the Pope at Rome even in the years before the Revolutionary crisis were the Liberal partisans of the "free and catholic" spirit. Mayhew happily discoursed at Harvard on "Popish idolatry," and William Smith thought that "the subject of popery can never be exhausted" as a theme of pulpit discourse.[144] Old Side Presbyterians and orthodox Congregationalists were also given to this topic. But the use to which the subject of popery was put in the years after the Awakening suggests that the more reasonable Protestants of the colonies, no less than their evangelical critics, were disposed to turn from the battle lines of the Reformation.

The anti-revival literature of the 1740's was filled with pronouncements as to a similarity (and worse) between Calvinist enthusiasm and the religion of Rome. In one of his attacks on Whitefield, Alexander Garden reminded his readers that *"laying aside Reason,* is a first Doctrine of *Popery!"*

> Alas, my poor fellow Creatures! Wilfully abandoning their *Reason,* (the alone distinguishing Dignity of their Nature!) Fleeing from it as from a Serpent! And throwing themselves into the Arms of strong *Delusion!*—A Harvest indeed for *Romish* Missionaries![145]

Other critics of the revival, including the authors of "The Wandering Spirit," went even further in likening the revival spirit to that of "Popery." The Querists did not merely note that Whitefield's unreason smelled "rankly of Popery," but went on to accuse the itinerant, and the revivalists generally, of "a Design against Protestant Principles."[146] One of the more interesting suggestions of a popish plot appeared in Isaac Stiles's 1743 attack on the itinerating evangelists and the "changelings" who, in Connecticut, preferred the new preachments to the good old way. Bemoaning the extent to which "orthodox and sound" preachers were deserted and stigmatized by the awakened, and other ministers "set up, Caress'd and Canoniz'd, even such as come from the Ends of the Earth," Stiles seriously proposed that Whitefield, Tennent, Davenport, and Finley might well be *"Missionaries from the Pontificate at Rome."*[147] Whatever the ultimate ramifications of such a viewpoint (as, for instance, its serviceability in the eventual translation of anti-Catholicism in America into a provincial and conservative ideology), it established an identification, hardly wholly lost in the Revolutionary years, of Roman Catholicism with the threats of emotion and change.

A difference in opinion as to the most dangerous popish threat to

America persisted into the 1770's, when evangelical spokesmen suggested that the Massachusetts establishment was itself a form of popery. Sam Adams, however, meanwhile pointed to the anti-Protestant character of the high and fashionable life of the Boston nabobs, "deck'd" as they were "with the worst of *foreign Superfluities,* the ornaments of the *whore of Babylon,*" as evidence of the true declension of the Puritan colony toward Romanism.[148] There was thus quite possibly an undermeaning to the vehemence with which evangelical Americans responded, in 1774, to the presumed threat to the ecclesiastical liberty of the colonies. Nor would it seem merely fortuitous that the spokesmen of rational religion were the most zealous in 1774 in calling attention to the more traditional popish danger. There appears to have been a special, and even frenetic, urgency*[149] to their efforts to revive ancient prejudices by announcing that the Quebec Act—and it alone—confronted America with the possibility of the "scarlet whore" soon riding "triumphant over the heads of true Protestants, making multitudes drunk with the wine of her fornications."[150]

Following the entry of France into the war, Anglican Tory preachers such as Charles Inglis sought to play on popular anti-Catholic sentiment by ridiculing the alliance of New Jersey Presbyterians with the "popish, inveterate enemies of our nation."[151] What Inglis overlooked was the Calvinist faith in the destiny of Protestantism and in the moral stamina of the children of the Awakening—a faith which led Samuel Finley to affirm that a French victory in the Seven Years' War, and an establishment of Catholicism, would be the spiritual undoing only "of sensual, secure, and careless Protestants."[152] Thus while, during the Revolution, Liberals defended the French alliance on "political" grounds, it was John Murray, a protester among Protestants and a dissident among dissenters, who observed quietly that none but a "bigot" would refuse French aid.[153] There was always the possibility, Calvinists insisted, that the soldiers of King Louis might, in the freer air of America, be spiritually redeemed by the example of God's people. Within fifteen years, when the French people revealed that they too wished a part in the Work of Redemption, the Liberals of America would begin to bewail the overthrow of Catholicism in France so loudly that Stanley Griswold could question their "disposition to fraternize with Antichrist" and wonder if they did not have "a secret

---

* Whatever the motives, conscious or otherwise, of the vehemently anti-Catholic reasonable men of the colonies, it bears noting that Alexander Hamilton distinguished himself in 1775 (or tried to) by observing that under the terms of the Quebec Act "a superstitious, bigoted Canadian papist, though ever so profligate" was a better subject of the King than the most liberal, enlightened, virtuous New England dissenter.

willingness to introduce here something bearing some of the features of the beastly monster."[154]

The Calvinist crusade for religious freedom generally, like its response to the Quebec Act in particular, represented a convulsive and somewhat desperate effort to bring into being the pious union of the *Humble Attempt*. Freedom from the depravations of European religion, and colonial establishments, was conceived as essential to fulfillment of the latter-day glory of the Church. In Connecticut, where in 1773 the millennium seemed imminent, Izrahiah Wetmore enunciated before the General Assembly what proved to be Joseph Bellamy's final opinion on the merits of religious establishments. Let us have a church, he argued, freed from the designs of carnal men, standing "upon its own proper Gospel Foundation, regulated by its own laws, and guarded and enforced by its own Sanctions." What this involved, in the context of the 1770's, is suggested by the emphases of Levi Hart's sermon in the summer of 1774, *Liberty Described and Recommended:*

> Ecclesiastical liberty gives every member opportunity to fill up his place in acting for the general good of that great and holy society of which the true church of Christ belongs, and of which they are the part.[155]

It was just such an opportunity that Calvinists sought, in their defense of America's religious freedom, both to preserve and to fulfill. With the New Jerusalem seemingly impending, the saints could not allow their union to be interfered with by any external regulations and hierarchies whatever.

In such a context, what the Quebec Bill and the Intolerable Acts represented was evidence that the course of history was rising to a midnight darkness out of which the light might be brought:

> These violent attacks upon the woman in the wilderness, may possibly be some of the last efforts, and dying struggles of the man of sin. These commotions and convulsions in the British empire, may be leading to the fulfillment of such prophecies as relate to his downfall and overthrow, and to the future glory and prosperity of Christ's church.[156]

By 1775, over paths that had led them to consider, among other things, the westward course of empire, the ministry had arrived at the conclusion that America would be "the principal Seat of that Glorious Kingdom, which Christ shall erect upon Earth in the latter Days."[157] A favorite text—Revelation 12:6-14—concerned the "flight of the woman into the wilderness."[158] Calvinists interpreted these verses as "eminently and even literally fulfilled" when God removed His people from the depravations and ecclesiastical tyranny of Europe, that his Kingdom might be inaugurated in the western wilderness.[159] Each year of the Revolutionary War saw the date of the inauguration of the millennium further postponed, but David Avery, chaplain at Bunker Hill and Ticonderoga, predicted that so long as "pure and heavenly love" pervaded the American states, Christians of all persuasions would be joined "in the glorious interest of the REDEEMER's KINGDOM." America was certain to

> became IMMANUEL's *land*, a *Mountain of Holiness*, a *Habitation* of Righteousness! The LORD's *spiritual Empire of Love, Joy*, and *Peace* will flourish gloriously in this *Western World!*[160]

All this was to be accomplished because America had been liberated from the "arbitrary sway" of establishments and state religion, and its Christians freed for the true unity of the faithful:

> Here shall the religion of Jesus—not that falsely so called, which consists in empty words and forms, and spends its unhallowed zeal in party names and distinctions, and traducing and reviling each other—but the pure and undefiled religion of our blessed Redeemer; here shall it reign in triumph, over all opposition . . .[161]

At the end of the Revolution Timothy Dwight was proclaiming the necessity of complete religious freedom if the millennium were to begin in America. If he and the younger Jonathan Edwards eventually set themselves against such liberty in Connecticut, it was because they despaired of producing Christian union by use of the ordinary means of grace. The Calvinist principles of the Revolution, however, were those articulated in 1778 by Isaac Backus. In a pamphlet that marked the high point of his endeavors to secure religious liberty from the Massachusetts legislature, Backus undertook to explain the relationship of "GOVERNMENT and LIBERTY," which, he affirmed, involved "the greatest points of controversy, now in the world." Though Backus thought it of the greatest importance that men's "ideas be clear and just" on these points, the most compelling sections of his argument were those in which he employed the Calvinist metaphor of "streams and rivers," which, as he pointed out, "are of great use, and cause a constant flow of refreshment wherever they come." The "main obstruction to these great blessings," Backus observed, is the state's "assuming a power to govern religion." Since all the streams and rivers would, of course, tend to a single issue,

> the command of heaven is, *Let them run down;* put no obstruction in their way. No, rather be in earnest to remove every thing that hinders their free course.[162]

Throughout the 1770's and, indeed, during the Revolution itself, Arminians and Old Lights continued to argue that religious establishments were necessary, not only "to support morality," but as the only means of "holding the people together in civil society."[163] But the true Calvinists of America, their eyes on a union that transcended the petty principalities of New England, were quite ready to let the streams run down in order to feed a happier union.

In the nineteenth century evangelical Protestants would expand these early insights into a thesis that proved to be America's unique contribution to the theory of church and state: the "voluntary principle." Perhaps the first declaration of this principle appeared in an oration delivered in 1772 by a graduate of the newly formed Baptist College of Rhode Island. The granting of full religious liberty to all denominations, the orator observed, was "the grandest, surest, and best cement of the various protestant communities."[164] At almost the same time at the College of William and Mary the future bishop, James Madison, was likewise arguing for religious liberty, but his argument, like his goals, was derived more from John Locke than from Edwards.[165] So likewise was the celebration, in 1783, by Ezra Stiles of the "religious liberty" guaranteed even deists and "libertines" in the new Republic: it assured that no weapons would here be used but the gentle ones "of argument and truth."[166] Stiles's continuing insecurities were evinced by the necessity he felt to demonstrate that even the Baptist Church in America was somehow in the line of apostolic succession, but that aside, he was still conceiving of religion as a matter merely of personal enlightenment, of conscience, as divorced from the affairs of state.

Not so the spokesmen of evangelical religion in the Revolutionary era. In 1778, when a Baptist for the first time in the history of Massachusetts Bay was selected to deliver the Election Sermon, Samuel Stillman declared fervently that "a *just and equal*" liberty for all denominations was the guarantor of union and that, moreover, "union in the state is of absolute necessity to its happiness."[167] Not until the age of Jefferson would an evangelical spokesman explicitly expand this insight into a vision of a *nation* cemented by Christian liberty and love. But Stillman and his fellow Calvinists were well on the way in the 1770's to discovering that the "voluntary principle" and its concomitants were the bases not of an evangelical alliance merely but of the American Union itself.

So enamored of national union were the Calvinists of the Revolutionary era that they allowed themselves several critical modifications and "improvements" of the principles of the *Humble Attempt*. Subsequently Samuel Hopkins would seek to recall Calvinism to what he considered the first principles of the evangelical scheme and, as against the advocates of American Christian Union, invoke Edwards' distinction:

> The catholicism and love for which they plead, appears to be a *political* love and union, which may in some measure unite civil worldly societies; but has nothing of the nature of real christianity, and that union and love by which the followers of Christ are ONE.[168]

But Hopkins' appeal was not unrelated to the parochialism which his definition of benevolence tended to revive in New England, and which made his New Divinity a bulwark, not of nationalism, but of Federalism. In the late 1790's, when Hopkins insisted on the "Edwardean" definition of Christian love, his argument was not merely with reasonable men, nor even with the orthodox. For in these years evangelical exhorters were seeking to induce a "true spirit of union" among Americans—a union which, in the end, came to be identified with the national spirit of the party of Jefferson and Burr.[169]

It was during the imperial crisis that the evangelical mind glimpsed the bright prospect of uniting the people of America in affectionate union. So dazzled were many Calvinists by this possibility that in the decade before Independence they slowly abandoned the thought that none should be clasped in the embrace of Christian union but those who had "a supreme regard to God's Glory."[170] The Calvinist reaction to the Stamp Act crisis was in part a celebration of the manner in which "a whole continent" had been united in resistance to Britain, in part a rejoicing in the degree to which it had healed the religious divisions of each province. The hand of God, Benjamin Throop rejoiced, had been "very visible" in 1765 in "begetting a zeal for liberty, in all persons of every denomination; and however different our sentiments may be in other things," yet we were "universally agreed in this."[171] In the subsequent decade Calvinists would encourage defense of American liberty, not only on the merits of the case, but also because doing so provided a continuing providential opening to the visible union of God's American people.

Thus in 1774 Samuel Sherwood called for a union of "all the good *protestants* in the land" to defend "their country's welfare."[172] In the same year the Connecticut election preacher advised the people of God that, though Christians "*upon* occasion, must contend earnestly for the faith," they no longer had any "time to waste, in warm debates, about things not essential," for such issues were "apt to gender strife, and create alienation and disunion."[173] Such appeals for Christian union were not unrelated to the New Light concern, expressed most vocally in the Election Sermon of 1771, over the confusion introduced by the New Divinity.[174] In many respects, the followers of Joseph Bellamy were using the imperial crisis as a surrogate for the kind of revival which, they had hoped, would overcome the metaphysical and theological confusions of the era. It is not surprising that the very ministers who were most disturbed by the metaphysics and scholasticism of the New Divinity were among the more enthusiastic celebrants of the affective unity brought about by the Revolutionary crusade.

Still, when Calvinists called on all Christians "to forebear one another in Love, and unite" to "promote the common Good," or insisted that it was fit and becoming for God's children to fix their "attention upon the common cause," they spoke as if they had all but forgotten, not only the lessons of the French and Indian War, but the lessons of the master. For, once they began to argue that "modes of religion are not the point," and that "civil rights and liberties" were "the dear inheritance in question," they seemingly repudiated Edwards' dictum concerning the relative importance of civil and sacred affairs, indeed of the relative value of political and pious union.[175] But the irenic strains of Calvinist pronouncements in the years before the Revolution were not wholly inconsistent with the traditional Calvinist effort to promote harmony among the disparate branches of the Church of Christ. Indeed Sherwood echoed Tennent*[176] when he condemned those who would "lay unreasonable stress upon disputable points" and thus "set on foot controversies that tend to alienate people's love for each other, and to increase a party separating spirit, and sow the seeds of discord, and foment animosities."[177] The Calvinist policy of the 1770's was one with Tennent's advice to his people a generation earlier: "adopt that antient, scriptural, and rational maxim, *In Necessarius Unitas, in non necessarius Libertas, et in utrisq Charitas*."[178] The only difference lay in what the evangelicals came by 1775 to conceive as necessary and whom they managed to include in what, to them, was a charitable union of liberty-loving Americans.

Between 1774 and 1776 the Calvinist mind made at least one concession to the times. In 1774 Sherwood appealed for Christian union among all who were "actuated by evangelical principles and motives," which, he insisted, were much more likely than resasonable religions to produce both a love of liberty and such other "christian and politi-

* During the French and Indian War Tennent had urged all the Protestants of the Middle Colonies to beware of "a narrow, bitter Party-Spirit," and, however they differed "in other matters," to "agree in this common and noble Cause, the Defence of your Country, and the rather because by its excellent Constitution, it maintains your Religious Liberty inviolate!"

cal virtues" as "piety, public virtue, and a love to one's country." He made it clear that such a union could include even Episcopalians, and that every man, regardless of the communion to which he belonged, was entitled to all the "sacred rights and liberties of conscience in full."[179] Two years later Sherwood felt obliged to embrace in the arms of union all who, from New Hampshire to Georgia, had been filled with the spirit of liberty. "Where the spirit of the Lord is, there is liberty," Sherwood declared in Pauline accents, only to betray his own new commitments by proceeding to explain that the "spirit of liberty" had been "plentifully poured out," not only in the New England colonies, but likewise on his Episcopalian brethren "in the southern provinces."[180]

The spirit of liberty had replaced the vital indwelling principle of Jonathan Edwards as the chief agency of the Work of Redemption. It rose to its height among evangelical Americans in the spring of 1775, when preachers began to exclaim before their congregations that "every *kind* of love should be *absorbed* in the love of liberty, except the love of GOD, which, indeed, is connected with and involved in it."[181] That it was so connected and involved, however, was testimony to the fact that for Calvinists the spirit of 1775 was, and would continue to be, a "spirit of liberty and *union*."[182] To the evangelical mind these two were, in a manner that Daniel Webster would never come close to comprehending, one and inseparable, and the great revival of 1775 rose and prospered on an awareness that both the quest for liberty and its achievement offered America the promise of a union which, if not as pious as Edwards had hoped for, might be far more amiable.

V

It was in the cause of liberty that the evangelical mind discovered—between the death of Whitefield and the rising of Washington's star—a new sun wherewith to be inspired with affective unity. The God of liberty was largely a creature of the Calvinist imagination. To be sure, throughout the controversy with Britain, Calvinists frequently and fondly quoted the poem wherein Addison saluted "liberty" as an "object Heavenly bright." But the Calvinist creative process, which began in 1765 when the Stamp Act seemed an *"eclipse"* of the "Sun of Liberty," needed little encouragement from external sources of inspiration.[183] This was made clear when in 1772 the dissenter population was introduced to what an evangelical exhorter called "the beauties of liberty." The authorship of the *Oration on the Beauties of Liberty*, delivered as a thanksgiving sermon in 1772 in the Second Baptist Church of Boston, is a matter of dispute. Be the author Isaac

Skillman, or as is more likely, Joseph Allen, there can be no question that this discourse was the most popular public address of the years before the Revolution. It went through several editions and was, on at least one occasion, read in its entirety by James Otis to a mob on Boston Common.[184]

More interesting than the author's observations on British policy—which came down to a defense of evangelical religion against the British establishment and a series of observations on the total depravity of the British Parliament and King—was this apostrophe of liberty itself:

> LIBERTY! who would not prize it? Who would not adore it? It is the finished work of Heaven! the glory of omnipotence! the majesty of a God! the display of his power, wisdom, and perfection. All nature bespeaks it! and the whole Creation in its primeval state celebrates its praise . . . O this is Liberty divine, the unoriginated glory of the Deity. What is Liberty in all its beauties? Is it not the image of JEHOVAH? the resemblance of the GOD whom we adore? The brightness of his power, and the first blessings of love to mankind, from the womb of the morning.

That the orator saw no necessity for explaining why liberty was an "image" of the Calvinist God was understandable, for when, in the following year, he published a pamphlet calling on all Americans to unite in "the same general happiness," he explicitly proclaimed that liberty served the same function as the Calvinist Godhead. Should "not your hearts be as the heart of one man," he asked, "firmly fixed with ardor, love and affection, upon the grand object?"[185] The Calvinists of America had long been contending for liberty—liberty from the parish order of the seventeenth century, from the established churches of the provinces, from episcopacy and from popery, and finally, in the 1770's, from the British Parliament. Yet through all these contests, and whatever the particular issue, they had looked so fondly to their freedom, however they might consider it in itself a good, because the pursuit and the prize were means of encouraging and perfecting a more vital union.

In his history of the Revolution, David Ramsay looked back on the spirit of 1775, a spirit which, he acknowledged, "the interested prudence of calmer seasons can scarcely credit." His recollection of that spirit he stated in these words:

> The Governor of the Universe, by a secret influence on their minds, disposed them to union. From whatever cause it proceeded, it is certain, that a disposition to do, to suffer, and to accommodate, spread from breast to breast, and from colony to colony, beyond the reach of human calculation.[186]

In 1776 the Massachusetts election preacher too found the unity of the colonies to be much firmer than had been anticipated by those who thought Americans responsive only to appeals to their interests—so much firmer, indeed, that he likewise considered it almost providential.[187] In 1776, however, as before and after, Calvinists and Liberals were not quite agreed as to what constituted the nature of that public spirit that bound Americans in union.

From any perspective the Liberal commitment to American union showed a certain prudential wisdom. Liberals valued union primarily as a political necessity—if not merely as a reasonable coalition of mutually threatened interest groups, then because they hoped that the concerns of the lower classes would be expressed, not in disorder and subordination, but as an eager willingness to obey the mandates of the central legislature at Philadelphia. If they rejoiced in the "firm union and cement of our numerous colonies," it was generally because they hoped that the already aroused mass of Americans could somehow be persuaded to follow the lead of the Continental Congress.[188] As John Lathrop explained in the autumn of 1774, strengthening the union of the colonies required that everyone "abide by and strictly adhere to the Resolutions" of this at least semirespectable legislative body. How instrumental such Liberal appeals were in producing unionist sentiment among the American people is a matter of some doubt. Lathrop himself confessed that his audience needed none of his "arguments" to persuade them to an allegiance for which, he said, "[you are] ready even of yourselves."[189] More important is it that Liberals, ignoring the extent to which the populace had found such violent men as Sam Adams and Patrick Henry more to their liking than the wise and prudent legislators of the provincial assemblies, were blind to the implications of this unionist enthusiasm.

The nature of Liberals' unionist sentiment can be understood in terms of their favorite metaphor of the Newtonian universal machine. New England Arminians had long contended that a genuine public spirit made "men good members of the society to which they belong," by serving as the "efficacious principle" that kept them "in that place" and caused them to "move in that course, which the laws of their country have assigned them."[190] When Liberals discovered that the gravitational system of the British empire was dissipating its energy, they sought only to provide some new central orb—one which would prevent eccentricity and disorder. Such a sun in 1774 was the Continental Congress; once it was formed, Liberals moved quickly to urge on Americans their "duty to do all in our power to strengthen and perpetuate this *union*."[191] They failed to see how other Americans were taking a spiritual delight in the union of the colonial people, or why. When the time for rejoicing was past, most Liberals discovered and repented of their error. But they continued to insist that in '76 everyone was imbued with the spirit of remaining in his proper orbit.

Far different was the Union that Calvinists in the same year discovered to be of the Lord. Their belief in union was not, first of all, born of politic convictions but rather of a compelling love for intercolonial union in and of itself. It is not "*comparatively* of so much importance what method we proceed in," declared Joseph Perry in 1775, provided "as general and as strict a union" as possible be achieved and maintained, not only "in every town, and between the towns in every colony," but "between the colonies and through the whole continent."[192] Moreover, the union celebrated by Calvinists, when it emerged, was far more than a confederation. It was an "affectionate union" among the people of America, and if born, perhaps, of necessity, it immediately seemed the "natural" consequence of an "affection" among the members of "one great family"—an affection that existed long before circumstances permitted the family to discover its affinities.[193] The "people of the most distant provinces," exclaimed John Murray in one of his first sermons as Parsons' successor, have hitherto been "separated by a diversity of local prejudices, interests, and manners," but now they are "wonderfully consolidated into one body," and have become "an united band of brothers."[194] Like the inhabitants of the Calvinist heaven, Americans seemed to be possessed of "one common soul."[195]

When in after years the evangelical mind sought to account for the divisions and contentions of the years between 1783 and 1788, Calvinists would not analyze the provisions of the Article of Confederation, but the character of the American people. To them the difficulties of the postwar years were comprehensible only in terms of a spiritual declension from "that elevated and sublime virtue" which, in the glorious years of grace, had cemented the American people in the closest solidarity.[196] In early 1776 William Smith proposed to the Continental Congress an annual "Genoese *feast of union*" as the best means of "animating our virtue, and uniting ourselves more closely in the bonds of mutual friendship." In 1792 he still believed that such pagan festivals were the best way of uniting the leaders of American society. But this "wise institution," although embraced by the Society of Cincinnati and incorporated into their ritual, was hardly one to appeal to men who believed that the Lord's Supper was not a converting ordinance.[197] Communion, in whatever form expressed, was for Calvinists presumably a manifestation of a love already felt and displayed.

The American Union was confirmed, not in July of 1776, but, in the eyes of the Calvinist ministry, in July of 1775. "Congress Sunday," July 20, when churches throughout America held a day of humiliation, fasting, and prayer, long lingered in Christian memory as perhaps the most glorious moment of the Revolution, if not of American history. If the "propaganda value" of the fast did not derive from the fact that "a whole people," as some historians suggest, were "simultaneously meditating upon their wrongs" as suffered at the hands of Britain[198]— for actually they were doing no such thing, but rather, as even John Adams understood, contemplating their own sins—the significance of such a concurrent ceremony was, as Edwards had once informed the Protestant world, not to be ignored or overlooked. "My God, how important the day! How solemn the scene," cried Joseph Montgomery on Congress Sunday:

> It must strike the most inattentive observer with solemnity, when he considers that there is not, perhaps, less than two millions of intelligent beings, this day, engaged in the same public acts of religious worship.[199]

The continental fast of 1775 proved how well Edwards' warm imagination had served America. Whereas in 1743 Chauncy had belittled a fast of such extent, in 1775 some of the most vocal celebrants of American communion were Old Side Presbyterians and Old Light Congregationalists. Such preachers possibly had special reasons for rejoicing in the astounding "unanimity" of Americans, but in one respect at least they acknowledged the superior glories of the Edwardean vision.* And for the Calvinist ministry itself in 1775 it was not merely that two million Americans were united in "love and respect, as brethren engaged in, and struggling for the one and same common cause," nor even that they were joined in the pursuit of what then seemed "the best weal of Zion."[200] Rather they were impressed because the union which they had been seeking for thirty years had, for the first time in American history, become visible.

Though Calvinists throughout the war celebrated the union of "all denominations (except such as have been in opposition to all our measures)" as not the least of the war-born blessings for which America was to be grateful, it was not pious union, but a civil union. What they

---

* Montgomery was an Old Side Presbyterian, and Enoch Huntington, who discoursed in 1776 on *The Happy Effects of Union*, a nominal Old Light. What is striking about their affirmations of union is the degree to which they incorporate with the more politic (and traditional) arguments sentiments that for nearly two generations had been peculiar to evangelical religion. Their ability to do so was not, of course, unrelated to the blurring of ecclesiastical lines in Connecticut and Pennsylvania after 1775—a reorganization which saw followers of Bellamy and New Side Presbyterians (ministers as well as people) eventually move into the Baptist Church.

saw in that union, however, was something which even Edwards might well have appreciated. During the Whitefield obsequies of 1770, Jonathan Parsons had lauded the itinerant's ecumenical spirit as a belief that "differences of mode" among Christians, "like the various parts in musick, were adapted to make the greater harmony, among real christians of various denominations."[201] In the next five years Calvinists would manifest a continuing love for civil union, not only because of its good tendency, but because, quite simply, it seemed beautiful in itself. The union of 1775 was "the blessed unison of the whole American harpsichord, as now set to the tune of liberty, by the honorable great artists of the CONTINENTAL CONGRESS!"[202] Calvinists would shortly tire of legislative musicianship and find in Washington the source of a more efficient, and more affective, union. But they never forgot that union was one of the most beautiful things on earth.

That not all who entered on the Revolution saw the same beauty in liberty cannot be denied. The Loyalists, during the agitation as well as in their histories, maintained that the enthusiastic multitude, somehow dazzled by the mere word "liberty," were the unwitting dupes of ambitious and designing merchants. Something of the same distinction was drawn by David Ramsay, the Carolina dissenter, patriot, and historian of the Revolution. There were some, Ramsay explained, who for reasons of trade, or, particularly in the South, out of the hope "of honors and emoluments in administering a new government," chafed under British administration. "Though the opposition originated in the selfishness of the merchants," Ramsay recalled, and throve on the ambition of the few, the American cause triumphed only because the "great body of the people, from principles of the purest patriotism, were brought over to second their wishes."[203]

Whoever might have been the prime movers of the Revolution, it was Calvinists who, alone among the ministry in the 1770's, proclaimed the doctrine that man could only and indeed must "seek and find his happiness" in the "welfare of the whole."[204] Nor were the evangelical clergy unaware, even in the years of the gracious outpouring of the spirit of liberty and union, of the differences in patriot motives. Since 1766[*][205] they had been proclaiming that the "*true patriot,* or lover of his country, seeks the good of the whole with disinterestedness, is ready to spend his estate, his health, all his talents, yea, his very life in

* The same orator of the Sons of Liberty who saw the "Mark of the Beast" on the Stamp Act distinguished between "real patriots, who enter into and defend our interests because we are in the right," and those "whose whole religion is trade, and whose GOD is gain . . . and would model us upon a plan calculated for their own interests rather than for our welfare; it is indifferent to them whether we are freemen or slaves, so that they can pluck our feathers."

the service of his country." The "false pretender," on the contrary, seeks "himself only, and labours to promote his secular interest, tho' oftentimes under the cloak of *patriotism*."[206] From 1774 onward Calvinists developed an impressive catalogue of those who were patriots merely in "shew" but not in "reality."[207] The true patriot—such as Whitefield* had been—was filled with a spirit of the most expansive Christian benevolence. He was, moreover, a warm friend of religious liberty; otherwise his "affection" was set on "money," and his heart was "quite cold to liberty." Undoubtedly, Nathaniel Niles observed, "many visibly espouse the cause of liberty purely for the sake of rising into popularity."[208]

Throughout the rebellion, the Calvinist eye focused on all who were thought to be seeking not the good of the brethren but "precedency, honors, and profits."[209] In the years shortly before and after Lexington there was but one touchstone of genuine patriotism so far as Calvinists were concerned: "enthusiasm" or "zeal." "If we bear a true and cordial affection to our country," preacher after preacher observed, "we shall be warm and active in her cause."[210] Sermon on sermon (most of them modeled on the performances of the "late rousing preacher," Samuel Davies) invoked the "Curse of Meroz against all who were so lost to virtue, to all Sense of Liberty, to all Love of Country," as to act the part, not of Tories, but of what was far worse:

> *'Tis good to be zealously affected always in a good thing.* Indifference, at this day, is at best the bane of stupidity, and frequently of something worse; be it of either, their country loathes them, and she would they were either cold or hot; and if they continue lukewarm, would be happy, could *she spew them out of her mouth.*[211]

Full membership in the Union of 1775, in short, was reserved for those Americans whose hearts and wills were thoroughly and vitally engaged on behalf of liberty and union. Nathaniel Whitaker, the most confirmed of Edwards' disciples to mount a rostrum in the years of the Revolution, proclaimed the rebellion the fulfillment of the Awakening by demonstrating "half-way" people and "such as are ever full of their wise cautions" to be essentially un-American.[212]

Among the rashest of policies advocated by the Calvinist ministry was Independence itself. On this matter the American people were "well ahead" of the Continental Congress. Soon after the battle of Lexington a popular clamor began to be raised for independence, and by mid-April of 1776 a correspondent of John Adams informed him that the people of New England were "almost *una voce*" demanding

---

* Nathaniel Whitaker thought the repeal of the stamp tax owing "in no small measure" to Whitefield's timely intervention with the British administration.

an "immediate Declaration" of independence.[213] Late in 1776 Thomas Paine, though unwilling to argue "whether the independence of the continent was declared too soon, or delayed too long," gave as his own "simple opinion"—one which coincided with that of the troops whom he addressed—that it should have "been eight months earlier."[214] The Calvinist ministry themselves were unable to account for this "revolution in people's sentiments, making them fond of a measure that a few months before they abhorred the thought of."[215] Of course the Calvinist ministry had encouraged this revolution in sentiments, primarily with a battery of arguments—employed as early even as 1765—concerning the dangers of an unconverted British Parliament, ministry, and King, and the fact that two could not walk together unless they were agreed.

Undoubtedly some Americans wished for independence because they, like the Virginian of whom Landon Carter informed Washington in May 1776, understood it "to be a form of Government" in which "by being independ[en]t of the rich men every man would then be able to do as he pleas[e]d."[216] Yet something of the true spirit of '76 may be divined from the letters which Joseph Hawley, for months in seclusion and nearly silent as he wrestled with his conscience over the issue of independence, began writing in the spring of 1776 to Sam Adams, Elbridge Gerry, and other members of the Philadelphia Congress. Unless Congress speedily declares for independence, he informed Gerry on February 20, there "will be no abiding union," but all "will be in confusion." When Hawley argued that independence was "the only way to union and harmony, to vigour and dispatch," he propounded a thesis with which even reasonable men might have agreed. (Of course most, if not all, reasonable men in America completely disagreed in early 1776.) But when Hawley went on to explain in April that with independence "our eye will be single and our whole body full of light," his scriptural allusion touched on perceptions which perhaps only Hawley's former pastor and those who had attended to his instruction would have understood.[217]

Long before either urban merchants or Liberal ministers had ever harbored so seditious a thought as independence, the Calvinist ministry had responded to the imperial crisis as a means of forging an American union. For something over four years before the Fourth of July, 1776, they had been urging the American people "to stand, as a *band of brethren,* for their liberties," and advising them that by becoming united in such an "indissoluble bond," every "joint member" of the community might enjoy "the beauties" of the "paradise" which he pursued.[218] What Hawley and many other Americans—how many we can never know—were aspiring to in the spring of 1776 was the fullest and happiest effects of the "spirit of liberty and union" that had been rising in previous years. If independence did not bring heaven to earth, few who were then alive would forget the ample joys of the spirit of '76.

When we recall the "great Mobb" with which Hawley threatened Congress, however, it is clear that something more was at work in the movement for independence than a mere desire to unite the hearts of the American people. Hawley himself thought nothing made independence "so indispensably necessary more than cutting off traitors." Throughout the war, Calvinists continued to demand that Tories have their estates "forfeited to the justice and laws of their country," and that all who in any way endangered "the safety of the community" be removed and those who failed to contribute to its welfare punished.[219] No sooner, in fact, had the shot that was heard around the world been fired than Calvinists were invoking the moral law, not against Britons and Tories merely, but in judgment on great and rich men even if they happened to be enrolled in the ranks of the patriots.

The anti-British rhetoric of Calvinism, and its evolving political thought, will receive more detailed consideration in later chapters. But here it might be noted that to the Calvinist mind the British King and ministry, and the American Tory, were in part evocative symbols of discontent with an American society that had failed to conform to the promises of evangelical religion. Indeed, the Calvinist definition and characterization of "tyranny" generally included all of what reasonable religion and its adherents had represented in America. On the anniversary of the Massacre in 1775, for instance, a Calvinist preacher began his sermon with these words:

> Such is the accursed nature of lawless ambition, that the greatest misfortunes of kingdoms, and states, as well as of lesser communities, and individuals, have arisen from, and are owing to an insatient lust of power in men of abilities and fortunes.[220]

In rising against the Crown, Calvinists were in effect declaring war on a multitude of persons and things that without independence could not be brought under control.

At some point in the early 1770's, the evangelical mind seems to have realized that none of the goals of the Awakening could be achieved unless America were liberated from Britain. Consciously or not, it came to recognize the fact that freedom from external interference— from the power of the British government and its armies—was a necessary first step to a resolution of the domestic difficulties of the colonies.

In this regard it was by no means fortuitous that the Calvinist crusade for "liberty" took on a more urgent animus concurrently with, and often with explicit reference to, the news of the battle of Alamance. "Butcher" Tryon's suppression of the Regulators demonstrated, if nothing else, that the discontented of the colonies could not achieve a redress of their local and particular grievances so long as the power and authority of the Crown were available to interpose on behalf of the nabobs of America.

In 1774 Samuel Sherwood addressed himself to the relationship of America's internal difficulties to the resistance to British tyranny. He argued that it was necessary to secure the "liberty" of America if there were to be any solution to the problems of those who, in Connecticut as elsewhere, were groaning under poverty and distress. His sermon reveals the not-too-hidden purport of the zealous Calvinist crusade against Britain:

> Had we union and good agreement among ourselves, in the management of our civil and religious affairs; our burdens would grow lighter and easier; and the poor of the people find comfortable relief in most of their difficulties.[221]

What was implied in the Revolutionary impulse was revealed when, in 1775, another Connecticut parson explained how, through resistance to Britain, not only would "heavy taxes" be avoided and "slavery" undone, but all "sin and wickedness" brought under control. Every evil could be overcome, he contended, by good men everywhere "heartily uniting with the vastly great majority of the country."[222] Union, it seemed, was not only beautiful, but might be profitable too.

Calvinists often seemed to look backward, and express the hope that through the Revolution America would be restored to the happy government and society of the "halcyon days of settlement."[223] Yet they also looked forward to those "happy times" in which both church and state would achieve their perfection.[224] Among the "interesting and glorious" principles espoused by Calvinists in the opening years of the Revolution was the idea that free Americans could and would be governed only by "the supreme authority of the people." "We are not fighting against the name of a king," William Gordon insisted, "but the tyranny; and if we suffer that tyranny under any other name, we only change our master."[225] At the very least, the evangelical mind, as it embarked on rebellion, looked beyond King George to the time "when all wicked tyrants and oppressors shall be destroyed forever." Samuel Sherwood phrased it thus in his characterization of American war aims:

In the issue hereof, it is to be hoped, that the dragon will be wholly consumed and destroyed; that the seat of and foundation of all tyranny, persecution and oppression, may be forever demolished, that the horns may be knocked off from the beast, and his head broken; that peace, liberty and righteousness might universally prevail; that salvation and strength might come to Zion; and the kingdom of our God, and the power of his Christ might be established to all the ends of the earth.[226]

The Calvinist spirit of 1775 was one with that which would begin in 1798 to call Virginians to pray that "all the oppressed," including Negro slaves,*[227] "may enjoy the sweets of liberty,"[228] and which further expressed itself, in 1801, in the celebrations of Jefferson's election as the beginning of an epoch in which the principles of democracy would "prevail to universal emancipation."[229] The implicit premise of Revolutionary Calvinism—and often the explicit one—was that Americans, once inspired to benevolent patriotism, would persevere in the Christian warfare until all despots, great and petty, had been overthrown.

Yet in the Revolutionary era Calvinists came close to identifying King George as the single embodiment of the evil against which they strove. In 1783 George Duffield would look back on the pre-Revolutionary decade convinced that Britain had meant exactly what she said in declaring the right to bind America "in all cases whatsoever." Duffield was likewise certain that "His Brittanic Majesty," and he alone, had "formed the design" to reduce Americans into "absolute vassalage." He did not know whether the "extravagant conduct" of the British monarch had been approved by a "venal policy," nor would he decide whether it had been inspired by "a mad desire to take by compulsion what would otherwise be cheerfully given," or by an equally mad desire to "reign an absolute monarch."[230] Purposeless behavior and motiveless malignity could simply not be ascribed to one who, Calvinists were convinced, was the avatar of the counterforce to the Spirit of God.

As early as 1774 Calvinists had known that there was method in the madness of the British administration, that Parliament and the ministry were "watching to enslave" them.[231] But persistently, almost in-

---

* In the Revolutionary era too it was understood that "slavery is . . . contrary to the law of love and to the golden rule." A lay sermon in the *Boston Chronicle,* for instance, called on Americans to "break every yoke and let the oppressed go free" that all might "taste the sweets of that liberty which we so highly prize." (In the context of John Mein's journalism and political position, it is possible that such declarations were intended—like the antislavery sentiments of Timothy Dwight in "Greenfield Hill"—to focus attention on violations of the law of love at some distance from Massachusetts.)

stinctively, the evangelical mind drove, even in the months before Lexington, and between the opening of hostilities and the Declaration, to identify the King as the Prince of Darkness.

The extent to which the Revolution was conceived as a last battle with a monarchical Antichrist is disclosed in the Massachusetts Election Sermon of 1776, delivered by "Father" Samuel West, technically an Arminian, but otherwise opposed to the Boston Liberals on every issue of the day—most particularly on the merits of the Massachusetts establishment. West was, moreover, a close friend of Samuel Hopkins, with whom he had presumably discussed the thesis (which West would openly expound in December 1777) that the Revolution was certainly evidence that the millennium would soon begin in America. Americans, West insisted, were fighting for a "victory over the beast and his image—over every species of tyranny." Their ultimate enemy was Satan himself, in "whom all that undue homage and adoration centers that is given to his ministers." Yet West intently focused on the "tyrant" himself, and, as he explained, had no difficulty in finding the words with which to paint, "in lively colors, the exceeding rage, fury, and impetuosity of tyrants, in their destroying and making havoc of mankind." The tyrant of 1776, he pointed out, is

> most beautifully exhibited to view by the Apostle John in the Revelation, Thirteenth Chapter, from the first to the tenth verse, where the Apostle gives a description of a horrible wild beast.[232]

Twenty-three years later one of the Calvinist spokesmen of the Revolution, on a visit to London, would get his first glimpse of George III. In fact, Thomas Allen went out of his way to look on the King because, as he explained, he wanted to note the precise features of the man who had been, not "the father of his people," but their "destroyer."[233] Whatever the conclusions of the cultural psychologist from such evidence, the evangelical clergy had wisely and perhaps inevitably begun their crusade by seeking to topple the highest throne in Europe. The Revolutionary Church Militant began its march against a common enemy more than under a common banner, inspired not only by the divine and supernatural light of liberty but by the perception of a single and concentrated point of tyrannical blackness. Within months of the battle of Lexington the Calvinist ministry revealed how the Revolution was for them a sublime affirmation, but in the years before that engagement, as in 1739-1740, the Work of Redemption seems to have been advanced largely by the negation of negation. Like Thomas Hart Benton, the Calvinist ministry perhaps realized that few put on the whole armor of God in order to do battle with petty officials. And perhaps they also understood that only by so moving against a single incarnation of consummate evil could they find the capacity, and the organization, to act with united strength against the lesser sinners in their midst.

VIII

TRUST IN GOD

I N the decade after 1766 the rationalist clergy found it increasingly difficult to hold together the conflicting elements of their political creed. British restrictions of American commerce, they knew, had to be resisted as threats to American prosperity and happiness. Yet these very levies served to arouse the American people to a higher pitch of enthusiastic resistance, which, Liberals also knew, would be subversive of social order unless restrained. The number of Arminians able to preserve both elements of their faith in this complex situation was surprisingly few; the number of sermons on public affairs they produced, even fewer.

The Liberal attitude toward political discussion in the late 1760's was set forth succinctly by John Tucker in his address to the Massachusetts ministerial convention of 1768:

> We have little to do with politicks, farther than to exhort our people, while they maintain a just regard for their natural and civil rights and privileges, to be subject to the higher power; and to pray for kings and all in authority, that we may lead quiet and peaceable lives, in all godliness and honesty.[1]

So long as Britain refrained from interfering with what Liberals defined as American rights and privileges, this formula could be upheld. But when threatened by the Townshend duties and the enthusiastic reaction of Americans to this ostensible threat to American "liberty," the Liberal mind was bewildered.

Rationalist ministers delivered the Massachusetts Election Sermon through most of the years of the imperial crisis. In these sermons (and a few others) they expounded the same theories that Chauncy and Mayhew had set forth in the years before the Stamp Act crisis. But by oblique references to passing events, and by extraordinary emphasis on certain aspects of their theory, Liberal spokesmen disclosed how untheoretical their political concerns had become. As America moved toward Revolution and Independence, they were forced into an eminently practical dilemma: could the liberties and privileges of American commerce be preserved and defended without permitting a social and political revolution in the colonies?

From the crisis of 1765-1766 Liberals had learned to place a greater value on social order and were, in the two years following the repeal of the Stamp Act, more than ordinarily alert to symptoms of popular discontent. In the autumn of 1766 one clerical rationalist, speaking on the annual provincial thanksgiving day, warned his countrymen not to abuse their "liberty for a cloke of maliciousness or licentiousness."[2] By 1767, however, Liberals were expressing relief that the Stamp Act tempest had been stilled and that matters seemed about to go on very much as they had before that interruption. "Such convulsions there have been," the election preacher recalled with a shudder, "as have shaken the very foundations of government," but, he was able to rejoice, "things have been in a great measure appeased."[3] The preacher hinted rather darkly, nonetheless, that many citizens of Massachusetts still failed to understand the things which belonged to their peace. After listing the blessings of the province (which included the presence of a native son, Thomas Hutchinson, in the executive chair), he reminded the people that "we are more happy in these respects, than some are willing to allow."[4]

The election sermon of 1768 disclosed a growing fear that discontent with the provincial order, far from dormant, was taking a more concrete form. Daniel Shute concluded his catalogue of blessings by declaring that an elected council was so *"dear* and *sacred"* a privilege that all who had "a sense of the inestimable value of their natural and constitutional freedom" would be jubilant on election day. It is, of course, conceivable that Shute was replying to some sort of divine-right party in Massachusetts, but it is much more likely that he was chastising those ungrateful wretches who had the effrontery to suggest that an elected council was a somewhat hollow privilege*[5]—so long as the council abjectly followed the governor's lead.

By accusing these critics of "blind prejudice and sordid views," Shute revealed that those traditional bugbears of Liberals, the popular demagogues, were once again at work.†[6] There was far too much

---

* In 1766, when the Council obediently fulfilled Governor Bernard's request to provision the stormbound British troops at Fort William, James Otis, observing that he "would as soon vote for the Devil as he would for such Councellors," declared that the institution needed to be remodeled and the incumbent Council purged.

† Among the more unfavorable signs of the times, according to Shute, was a growing hostility to Harvard College. He admonished the voters not to elect "those who are unfriendly to learning, who at the most have only taken the intoxicating *draught*

"speaking *evil* of *dignities*" in Massachusetts, Shute complained, and instead of reviling the administration, the people should somehow help the governor repress the factious and disorderly.[7] "To pour contempt upon rulers," Shute advised, is "to sow the seeds of libertinism." These seeds, he explained (in what may stand as the ultimate Liberal declaration before the landing of British troops in Boston), "will soon spring up into a luxuriant growth" in a "soil so prolific as human nature."[8] Had all things proceeded reasonably, this insight into human nature— or, more precisely, into the nature of Sam Adams and his followers— might have been developed further. But the times were not propitious; neither the Townshend duties nor the events of March 5, 1770, were part of the Liberal scheme. Shute, often described as a zealous Whig, made no subsequent addition to the literature of patriotism.

The reputation of those Liberals who remained Whigs after 1770 seems largely to depend on a contrast with Ebenezer Gay, the Arminian panjandrum, who emerged as an outright Tory in the 1770's. That Shute remained on the best of terms with Gay (his theological mentor), and eulogized him on his death in 1787, suggests that in certain instances, at least, the differences between Liberal Whiggery and Massachusetts Toryism involved few burning issues. The gulf separating Gay and his Whiggish friends, so narrow that it was bridged even before the end of the Revolution, represented a difference of opinion, not of principle. Gay was simply the more consistent adherent to the Liberal postulates which had been articulated by Mayhew in 1750 and upheld thereafter by a succession of election and thanksgiving preachers. Liberal theory maintained a distinction between oppression and tyranny (which a people might justifiably resist, as in 1688) and the mere maladministration of fallible men. Should the populace manifest discontent with anything short of outright despotism, the theory ran, they were either being victimized by aspiring demagogues or were guilty of clouded perceptions.

Gay happened to believe that the Governor of Massachusetts had no more than erred in 1770, that the objections to his administration came from those who expected something more than "the best human Management of our public affairs," and that a single peccadillo—the Boston Massacre—was being exploited by demagogues in an effort to excite the people. Shute and such Liberals who remained Whigs were unhappy in 1770 and, for the moment, were even willing to grant that the untutored populace could share in the uneasiness of more generous men. Yet few of them would have found fault with Gay's con-

---

at the *pierian* spring, but have not drank so deep as to open their eyes and give them a just discernment of things, and in their patriotic phrenzy would deprive church and state of the means greatly conducive to the well-being of both."

tention that no common person should expect "the Perfection of Happiness" under any kind of administration. Nor would any of them, even while tolerating a certain amount of popular unhappiness, ever disagree with Gay's final admonition to the people of Hingham. We must never expect, he declared, "that all things will proceed according to our Minds."[9] Insofar as Liberals espoused Whiggery in the 1770's, they, in effect, tried to make certain that happiness was pursued, not by an agitated rabble, but only by America's reasonable and moderate gentlemen.

As the provincial legislatures in the early 1770's assumed a new role in public affairs, and as leadership of the colonial movement passed from the hands of the urban merchants, many rationalist ministers transferred their admiration and allegiance. Though many Liberals thereby became personally involved in politics, none was so radical as to admit that the general populace could be anything but an unwelcome distraction in affairs of state. In his election sermon of 1771, John Tucker bewailed an ominously increasing popular interest in political matters. Tucker's themes were the duty of "Rulers and People" to seek the general welfare, and the need for both to adhere to "the fundamental laws of the constitution" in doing so. "The state of the world," he remarked in a clear reference to a somewhat smaller geographical area, renders

> these observations necessary and highly important:—important and necessary as a check upon Rulers of a despotic turn; and a restraint upon the licentious among the people; that neither, by breaking over their just bounds, may disturb the peace, and injure the happiness of the state.[10]

While accusing no one of despotism, Tucker did suggest that the Townshend duties had threatened the "prosperity and happiness" of Massachusetts. Should another such threat arise, Tucker expected that the General Court—and only the General Court—would "continue to oppose, every attempt of such a nature." In urging the legislators never to "give up so rich a treasure" as the "liberty, wherewith God, and the British Constitution have made us free,"[*11] Tucker failed to indicate which particular liberty he had in mind. But his purpose

---

* It is perhaps necessary to recall at this point that in Arminian sermons references to Christian liberty were of more rhetorical than practical significance. No self-respecting Liberal believed that Christian liberty added to or conflicted with the constitutional liberty of British citizens. "Christ came to set up a kingdom, diverse, indeed, from the kingdoms of the world," was Tucker's summation of a lengthy discussion of the issue, "but it was not part of his design to put down or destroy government and rule among men."

in limiting these exhortations to the "manly Freemen" of the General Court was clear. There are in every time and nation, Tucker explained, "ambitious and designing men" who seek to "gain for themselves the names of Patriots" by calling their rulers traitors and "raising the popular cry against them." But the "wise and prudent," Tucker declared,

> will make a pause, before they enlist under such political zealots. They will judge for themselves of the faulted conduct of their rulers. They will make reasonable allowance for human frailties . . .[12]

Tucker's allusions to Sam Adams were more pointed than his comments on other current events, and he did not, apparently, consider a tax on tea a threat to either the happiness or the liberties of Massachusetts. Yet it is more than likely that his sermon was conceived in part to support the claim of the General Court to the primary right to legislate for the province.

This right the House of Representatives had demanded as a charter privilege—at least to the exclusion of ministerial decrees and royal instructions—in the summer of 1770. When the Massachusetts legislature, along with other colonial lawmaking bodies, denied even Parliamentary jurisdiction in colonial affairs, many Liberal ministers soon embraced the same opinion. Though reluctant to raise again the cry of 1766—of the tyranny of taxation without representation*[13]—they came quite close to espousing a dominion theory of empire. Whatever the motives of other Americans in contending for legislative control of colonial governors or in advancing a theory of the equality of all lawmaking bodies under the Crown, these ideas had an especial appeal to Liberals. So long as all grievances were considered and handled as jurisdictional disputes, one could rest assured that, whatever the disposition, control would remain in the hands of wise, prudent, and honorable men.

To this end the Massachusetts Liberals left the Boston Massacre to be improved by others and expressed their own displeasure only with the new British commercial regulations. Although the Whigs agreed with Ebenezer Gay that the affair of March 5 was deplorable, they did not want to arouse the populace by publicizing the horrors of that day. The Townshend duties, which they considered the pressing concern of 1770, could be treated through institutions and in an orderly manner. Charles Chauncy, speaking before a group of "Patriotic Gentlemen" a few weeks after the Massacre, and shortly before the

---

* Speaking to a group of "Gentlemen" disturbed by the Townshend duties, Chauncy refused to "incur the charge of going out of my line, by entering upon a political consideration" of the "right of taxation."

meeting of the General Court (which Lieutenant Governor Hutchinson had ordered to assemble in Cambridge), considered "taxes" the only grievance of the colony. Nor could he think of more than one way of removing this burden; we must elect, Chauncy advised his gentlemen-auditors, those who will "act up to their character, support the honor of their stations, and approve themselves invariably faithful in their endeavour to advance the common weal."[14]

So far as the greatest Liberal of all was concerned, greater trust was to be placed in men of rank and honor (and of undeclared intentions) than in an agitated populace. Within months of Chauncy's sermon a group of honorable men abrogated the Nonimportation Agreement; it took two years for the patriot cause to recover. But government, at least, was no longer (as it had seemed at the time of the Massacre) "in the hands of the Multitude."[15] Even Chauncy eventually discovered that securing the happiness of the colonies required more effort than gentlemen, merchants, or legislators alone could muster. But he never, so long as he lived, looked to the mobocracy of Boston for that assistance.*[16]

The years between 1771 and 1774 saw numerous defections, on the part of the rationalist clergy, from what was coming to be considered the "American" cause. In 1771, for instance, Eli Forbes, a moderate Calvinist, came under patriot suspicion when he seemed, in his Artillery Sermon, to credit the British regulars with all the victories in the Seven Years' War. His "capital design," however, was (as he declared in a preface to the published version of the sermon in question) to bring an end to "those dividing names, or party distinctions of British and American."[17] Forbes's conduct over the next several years was such that his congregation in 1775 accused him of Toryism and ousted him from his pastorate.[18] Nor were the Boston clergy in the early 1770's disposed to vocal support even of the provincial legislature's efforts to preserve the rights of the province. Their prevailing disposition is suggested by Sam Adams' remark, in a 1772 letter to Elbridge Gerry, that "even some of the best of them are extremely cautious of recommending (at least in their publick performances), the Rights of their Country to the protection of Heaven, lest they should give offence to the little Gods on earth."[19]

Of the Congregational clergy of the metropolis only Samuel Cooper and, to a degree, Chauncy were at all active in these years in the service of Whig patriotism. It is said that Simeon Howard, Mayhew's

---

* Beginning in 1769, when a "formidable" mob of some 2000 to 3000 persons formed in Boston (thus, according to Hutchinson, setting the stage for the confrontation of wills that issued in the Massacre) Boston Liberalism was seldom without a multitude to be disturbed by.

successor at Boston's West Church, set forth "the true grounds of dispute" on several occasions in 1772 and 1773.[20] Howard's Artillery Sermon in the spring of 1773 contained the proposition that societies are bound to "take care of their temporal happiness, and do all they lawfully can, to promote it." In the category of lawful measures Howard included neither the town meetings nor the newly formed Committees of Correspondence.[21] As it turned out, he did not even consider artillery a lawful weapon for the redress of grievances, most especially the cannon that Washington in early 1776 assembled on Dorchester Heights. For on March 17, when Boston was evacuated, Howard departed the city with many of his parishioners for the temporal happiness of Nova Scotia.

The careers of Forbes and Howard were not unique among the rationalist clergy of Massachusetts, but such conduct, however revealing, hardly provided opportunity for contribution to the pulpit literature of the Revolution. Fortunately other Liberals, likewise disturbed by the course of events, on occasion between 1770 and 1775 articulated their political beliefs. Something of a standard for Liberal political discourse in these years was set in the election sermon of 1771, delivered by that "Corypheus among the Arminians," John Tucker. His strictures typify the Liberal response to the kind of political sentiments and oratory that emerged in the colonies after the promulgation of the Townshend Act, and in Massachusetts particularly after the Boston Massacre. In the election sermon he set forth a contrast between two ideals of political discourse:

> Demosthenes and Phocion were both Statesmen and Eminent Orators at Athens, but men of very different tempers. Demosthenes, full of fire, often urged the people to bold and daring enterprizes. Phocion, calm and sedate, persuaded to methods more practical.[22]

For Tucker the distinguishing marks of a New England Phocion were a wisdom to make just and reasonable estimates of the liberties guaranteed by the charter and a willingness that the general welfare be pursued only within a constitutional framework. Having delineated the liberties thus secured to the citizens of Massachusetts, Tucker carefully avowed that he was no Demosthenes, nor was meant to be:

> I mean not, Honored Gentlemen,—I mean not, my respectable Hearers, to prove an Incendiary among you . . . Deeply penetrated, as I am, with a sense of Liberty, and ardently in love with it; and tenderly concerned for the prosperity and happiness of my native land, I abhor a licentious and factious spirit;—I detest the baneful principle.[23]

Nor was John Tucker unique in his temperate Liberalism. The

text of nearly every sermon delivered after 1770 by the leading Arminians of New England* in one way or another betrayed a fear that the spirit of liberty, rather than needing to be aroused, was threatening to assume excessive proportions among the American people. Such fears were perhaps most clearly manifested not in what rationalist preachers said but in what they so conspicuously failed to say. With few exceptions they ignored or quickly forgot the Boston Massacre: of the Boston clergy only a handful, among them Chauncy and Samuel Cooper, made special reference to the affair from their pulpits. John Lathrop, of course, preached a rather notable sermon on the following Sunday—from the text, "The voice of my brother's blood cryeth unto me from the ground"—and called on his fellow ministers "to cry aloud and not to spare." Yet Lathrop, who was to become one of New England's proto-Unitarians, retained in 1770 numerous vestiges of the Calvinism of his teachers, Samuel Davies and Eleazar Wheelock.

One indication that Lathrop's theology was in process of transformation in 1770 was his inability to decide whether to arouse moral indignation against the perpetrators of the murder or to inspire loud cries of sentimental sympathy for the victims and their families. "Who can reflect on the horrors of that night without shuddering!" was Lathrop's unsparing cry, but he neither described those horrors distinctly nor affixed the blame carefully.[24] He avoided ultimate judgment on the moral nature of the British command and contended only that the Massacre was an argument against quartering troops in the city, suggesting that an administration which could not sustain itself without such coercive measures should resign. "But we shall leave these considerations," was his final comment on this issue, "to the improvement of the politicians of the day."[25] Eight years later, on the anniversary of the Massacre, Lathrop was even more certain that it was not his duty to call his auditors "to view the ground, where the blood of our brethren was most wantonly spilled." He knew their feelings would be "sufficiently touched by the worthy Gentleman" who was about to pronounce the commemorative oration.[26] By 1778 secular orators had largely succeeded to the role once filled by the Liberal clergymen of Boston, and Lathrop's acknowledgment of their primacy was an important element in his inexorable march away from the Calvinism of his youth.

Lathrop may have delivered a sermon commemorating the first anniversary of the Massacre, but otherwise the incident was left in

* The published record indicates that through these years the Old Lights of Connecticut were not much disposed to publicizing their political views, and William Smith, so far as his collected works are an indication, did not speak on public affairs between 1766 and 1775.

Boston to the lay orators, who annually publicized the dangers of standing armies and sought to lead both the "pious and humane, of every order" to "suitable reflections."[27] Undoubtedly the Liberal ministry agreed with the first of these orators, who quoted John Dickinson's admonition that "the cause of liberty is a cause of too much dignity to be sullied by turbulence and tumult." Yet there were inhabitants of Massachusetts, not all of them demagogues, who saw in the Massacre evidence of the degeneracy of Great Britain and of the enmity of the Crown to both God and humanity. Two years before the battle of Lexington, Sam Adams blandly informed John Dickinson that the Massacre was being commemorated each year so that the citizenry would not forget the danger of quartering troops in a large city in time of peace.[28] Such a purpose the annual oration did in fact serve in Boston until 1775, when Dr. Joseph Warren (making not a single gesture in the course of his Demosthenic performance) recalled to mind the fatal night by asking, "What wretch has dared to deface the image of his God?"[29] Hereby Warren succeeded in demonstrating, among other things, a perfervid patriotism acceptable to the pious, if not to the humane. As in the case of John Hancock a year earlier (who as orator simply mouthed the words handed him by Sam Adams), Warren had managed to convert classical patriotism into a surrogate for Christian benevolence.

In the outlying communities of eastern Massachusetts commemoration of the Massacre had long inspired more than a poor opinion of martial law. In 1771 Nathaniel Whitaker of Salem celebrated the anniversary of the Massacre by praying that "the guilt of blood might be taken from the land." Those "who were hoping for peace and quietness," as Governor Hutchinson recalled, felt "a damp upon the spirit."[30] Over the next years such Calvinists left little to be improved by the politicians of the day and, in fact, entered into political discussion in order to press, not only for American liberty, but for their own peculiar local goals. Their voices, in remembrance of the events of March 5, 1770, and otherwise, were louder and less sparing than those of the Liberals. Thus on the fourth anniversary of the Massacre the venerable Jonathan Parsons delivered his discourse, *Freedom from Civil and Ecclesiastical Slavery*. He advised his people what pious men would do, should the armies of the King again venture to raise their arms against the image of God, or should the administration, for that matter, persist in its refusal to grant Americans their freedoms. "In such a case," he predicted, "the spirit of Christian benevolence would animate us to fill our streets with blood."[31]

Soon afterward John Tucker publicly and officially declared himself and Liberalism generally offended by the manner in which Parsons and other Calvinist clergymen were commemorating the Massacre. Parsons' sermon, with its strictures not only against the Crown but against the Massachusetts establishment, seemed to Tucker to reek of the baneful principle of licentiousness. Protesting that he, Tucker, was "a real and hearty friend to liberty," he qualified his friendship in those accents which, having been intoned overmuch by Liberals since 1750, had assumed the nature of a litany. Tucker was a friend to liberty, he proclaimed, only

> in its true nature and extent . . . But every man of penetration and judgment must be sensible, that liberty, like other blessings, may be abused:—It may be so, by being carried to excess, or beyond the bounds of reason.[32]

In the pages that followed, Tucker arraigned Parsons as a man of neither penetration nor judgment—as, indeed, a village Demosthenes seeking to inflame the people of Newbury parish with an unreasonable and enthusiastic zeal for liberty.

To be sure, Tucker may have feared that the Whig cause would suffer "on the other side of the water" if such radical sentiments as Parsons' were publicized. He may also have felt, with Gad Hitchcock, the election preacher in 1774, that the colonists should not "divide on little irregularities" but act in concert, both for efficiency and to present a united front to the home government. Behind Hitchcock's prayers that the people of Massachusetts be filled with "that wisdom which is profitable to direct, and distinguish between what has, and what has not, a tendency to remove our burdens" was, however, the old Liberal anxiety. Let us particularly, he concluded in his election sermon appeal, "be on our guard against a spirit of licentiousness."[33] Nor were Tucker's objections to Parsons' sermon born of an ill-defined or obscure fear. Wisely and prudently Tucker discerned that the zeal for liberty which Parsons was seeking to inspire might be directed against Tucker and his friends as well as against Governor Hutchinson. Of this kind of zeal Tucker had had more than enough; his invective against Parsons was his last sally as a writer on liberty.

What Tucker's silence bespoke was something more than an awareness that treatment of the "horrors" of March 5 was too well designed for inflaming the people with a too passionate love of liberty. This much had been clear to Liberals within weeks of the Massacre; but in those days their concern had been chiefly with the Boston mob. By 1774 they were confronted with the possibility that the crisis in imperial affairs would be converted by the Calvinist ministry of the interior into the source of another awakening. What disturbed the rationalist clergy, in brief, was the threat which this new outburst of enthusiasm bore to the institutions that Liberals had so long defended.

In 1774 the Liberal clergy began to expose and even parade their conservative social and economic allegiances, ones which they had recently tried, though seldom successfully, somewhat to disguise. But of course Chauncy's remonstrances against the Great Awakening had contained a warning that enthusiasm would always make "strong attempts to destroy all property, to make all things common."[34] By 1774 all Liberals, Chauncy among them, were once again warning that enthusiasm, whether religious or political, endangered the very basis of American happiness. In his thanksgiving sermon of 1774, Samuel Williams, for instance, defended his brand of rational Protestantism as a religion uniquely serviceable to the rich and wellborn. He insisted that the welfare of the colonies depended on its maintaining a rational religion and a rational politics, both of which, he emphasized, led "men to be looking for perfect felicity" only in "the other life." A spirit of "enthusiasm, fanaticism, and extravagance," he warned, would soon express itself in "a spirit of *levelism* and fierceness."[35] Over the next years the Calvinists of New England would prove to be more "fierce" than "leveling." But as they strove, through a revolution, to gain a less imperfect felicity this side of heaven, the rationalist clergy were more than disposed to suppress the spirit of liberty and, finally, to see that "liberal" institutions were imposed on the new nation.

II

Probably the most compelling evidence of Liberal anxieties in the years before Independence was their reluctance to swell the chorus of jeremiads that began to roll from colonial pulpits in 1770. For four years, to be sure, nearly every Massachusetts clergyman refused to act on, or even read, the thanksgiving proclamations of the royal governor. Such sermons were delivered and published in these years in other provinces, where the governors read the signs of the times in a manner more to the clergy's liking. In 1774, when General Gage refused to declare a day of fasting for the Intolerable Acts, the Massachusetts clergy ordained July 14 as a day of humiliation and prayer, but few Liberal clergymen managed to honor the occasion with a published sermon. Even the House of Burgesses, similarly disturbed by news of the Port Bill, resolved to hold a fast day in Virginia. From the spring of 1774 through the first year of hostilities, when the Continental Congress itself set a day of fasting, jeremiads thundered forth from New Hampshire to Georgia. In all this activity the Liberal clergy either failed to participate or did so only in violation of the spirit and the formula of such occasions. They seemed to dread the possibility that the religious zeal of the populace would be reinvigorated by such traditional instruments of arousing the spirits and the wills of men.

Actually the Liberal ministry should have welcomed the emergence of the jeremiad as a characteristic utterance of the Protestant clergy. As employed before and during the Revolution, the jeremiad, as Perry Miller has shown, provided yet another medium whereby the differences among Americans were obscured. In time it encouraged a nationalism defined in terms as satisfactory to Liberals as to evangelicals. By emphasizing the sins, not of individuals but of a whole society, the jeremiad gave all Americans opportunity to signify repentance of their sinful ways by participating in what at the outset seemed the cause of God but, within years, clearly revealed itself to be somewhat closer to the Liberal pursuit of happiness.[36] Insofar as Calvinists participated in this intellectual exercise, they encouraged a dilution of evangelical principles, especially by further committing themselves to a belief in God's "moral government of the nations" and, often as its corollary, the kind of passivity implicit in supplicating "the Great Governour of the world" for interpositions of his "providence to relieve us from all our difficulties and distresses."[37]

The principle from which the Jeremiahs of the Revolution proceeded in their analyses of the difficulties of the pre-Revolutionary decade was that set forth by J. J. Zubly in his celebration of the repeal of the Stamp Tax: "If ever (which GOD forbid) we should be cursed with a tyrannical oppressive government, our sins must be the cause of it."[38] Some Calvinists who like Zubly were tinged with Wesleyanism or Lutheranism converted this postulate, by 1776, into an argument against the sin of rebellion. But among those of the evangelical party for whom Edwards remained the source of inspiration, the jeremiad provided a spur to action. Whatever America's provocations in the sight of the Lord, one such evangelical minister explained, Americans were "left and shut up to the use of means, as their only refuge on earth." Divine interposition, they insisted, was not to be awaited: "we may not expect any thing properly miraculous in the course of GOD's providence."[39] The Calvinist ministry knew of only a few lessons which "Christians might learn of a Jewish school," and of these the most important was that the Lord helped the Tribes of Israel only "in a way of *means*," and sustained them only when they acted for themselves. Americans, concluded Oliver Noble in March of 1775, likewise had "no reason to expect the mighty hand of GOD working for them, while like *Asses* they crouch down, to take on them *Burdens*."[40] This lesson and others the Calvinist ministry more typically imparted in sermons cast in another framework than the jeremiad, but such utterances suggest one of the reasons why Liberals were chary of the formula.

Insofar as Calvinists employed the jeremiad in the years before Independence, they were helping to divest the evangelical scheme of much of its radical thrust. The doctrine of the covenant on which the jeremiad hinged invariably implied a less strenuous gospel. In fact, such preaching was most readily engaged in by those ministers already committed in other ways to a diluted and more conservative Calvinism. In the first year of the war, for instance, John Witherspoon delivered one of the more classic jeremiads of the era: his sermon, "The Dominion of Providence over the Passions of Men." Before the opening of hostilities, moreover, the discussion of political issues within the framework of the jeremiad was characteristic chiefly of Calvinists who in one way or another had already set themselves against both the New Light and the New Divinity.

In Connecticut, where Old Lights were in the minority by the 1770's, Calvinism itself was dividing on the issue of the "pure church." Not surprisingly the defenders of the Half-Way Covenant, conspicuous among them Moses Mather, were disposed to conceive the issues as against Britain in terms of the challenge to traditional New England institutions. Given such a formulation, the repentance demanded by the jeremiad could be defined (and was) as commitment, on the part of New Englanders, to the "privileges," ecclesiastical as well as civil, inherited from their ancestors. As was again to be made clear shortly after the Revolution, the philosophy of the covenant was uncongenial to evangelical religion. As a consequence, many of the followers of Bellamy found their way, inevitably as it were, into the Baptist Church.

Already in the years before the Revolution, moreover, it was recognized that the principles of the covenant contained a not-so-hidden conservative bias. Whether as a theory of church government or as a metaphysic for fast and thanksgiving days, the covenant emphasized both structured order and a continuity with the past. As such it found its most vocal adherents largely among the more conservatively inclined members of the "black regiment." These included ministers threatened locally by Baptist insurgents as well as those who, since the Awakening, had resisted the evangelical impulse with the weapons of orthodoxy rather than of rationalism. It was Nathaniel Appleton, for instance, who argued in 1770 (in the terms of a nearly pure seventeenth-century covenant philosophy) that "it is sin that begets the controversy between God and his people."[41] In such hands the doctrine served not as an inspiration to popular action but, as it would become during the Revolution itself, an instrument for containing and controlling the American revolutionary impulse.

The jeremiads of the early 1770's seem, according to the published record, to have emanated chiefly from urban pulpits. Yet William Smith's sermon on the Continental Fast Day of July 20, 1775, was nearly unique as a Liberal contribution to the literary output of that day. His text suggests how, to preachers of a reasonable persuasion, the jeremiad seemed intellectually barbarous. Smith's sermon evinced a thorough understanding of what was expected of a preacher on such an occasion. He admitted that many sermons would undoubtedly be delivered that day explaining the outbreak of hostilities as one of "the terrors of the Almighty" and describing the "punishments wherewith He now threatens and visits us for our past sins, and the neglect of His manifold goodness to us as a people." Yet Smith, believing that such themes would only increase the "afflictions" of his audience, flagrantly violated the spirit of the jeremiad and chose instead to animate them with "the more cheering beams of Love," hoping on this day of humiliation to "convey a dawn of comfort to their souls."[42] Smith's decision, and the embarrassment felt by all rationalist clergymen when confronted by the philosophical and practical implications of the jeremiad, reflected their inability to cope effectively with events which challenged their naïvely optimistic version of American history. Having for so long been certain that all things necessarily worked together for good—particularly in their own communities—Liberals were more than laggard in discerning what struck other Americans as signs of God's controversy with the people of the colonies.

Ebenezer Gay's Toryism, indeed, could be aptly defined as an obdurate denial that any afflictions whatsoever were befalling the land, even though in 1770 many citizens of Massachusetts, finding a different meaning in the Massacre and the Townshend Acts, insisted that a day of fasting "would have been more seasonable" than the day of thanksgiving appointed by Governor Hutchinson.[43] One index of the Liberal mentality is that even those ministers who could not agree with Gay that the Massachusetts of 1770-1774 was the best of all possible worlds, nevertheless preferred to see what the Lord was doing by enumerating the blessings of His American people. Until Smith's heterodox fast sermon of 1775, no Liberal managed to publish anything but a thanksgiving sermon.

The Liberals' difficulty in comprehending the unpleasantness after 1770 was reinforced by an intense struggle with what seemed the rhetorical absurdities of the jeremiad. Assuming as they did that generous men, at least, could be aroused to action only by visions of actual or potential felicity, even the staunchest Whigs among them chose to dilate on the bountiful future vouchsafed to America once the inconveniences of the British regulations were overcome.*[44] In 1774 John Lathrop retained enough of his older orthodoxy to imagine at least a darkened American future, though he was already sufficiently Arminian to expect that the American people could simply will to choose between *"life and death* in a political sense."* In the spring of that year, after he audaciously set two such contrasting prospects of the future before his auditors, most of his Boston colleagues and many of his parishioners complained that the darker prospect should have been excised from the sermon, since, in their opinion, such a vision could only "dishearten some good people at this time of trial."[45] Lathrop's deadly future was only a deeper commercial depression than that described in 1774 by Chauncy, just as his lively vision was only the alabaster metropolis of William Smith. But the Liberal temper simply could not appreciate—even after Americans had passed the brink of war—how God's covenant afflictions could be, as they once had been, not terrifying and disheartening but reassuring and inspiring.

The ministerial fast day of 1774 assumed, as did also that of the Continental Congress, a unanimity on the part of Americans in what they took to be the "afflictions" of their society and the "sins" that had provoked God's judgment. Actually, even in 1774 Calvinists and Liberals in their sermons offered quite differing estimates of what were the sins and the afflictions of the colonies. For instance, the younger William Tennent, speaking in Charleston, South Carolina, declared that "the prevailing Iniquities of our Country" were "the only Causes which have drawn down the Frowns of Omnipotence upon us."[46] In elaborating this statement, however, he first of all made it clear that the Divine judgment he saw falling on the land was nothing other than the base design of Britain to deprive America of its "liberty." He then proceeded to observe that, so far as the begetting sins were concerned, there were clearly certain areas and certain people who had distinguishedly caused God's countenance not to smile on the colonies:

> If *Sodom* and *Gomorrah,* if *Zeboim* and *Admah,* in the untaught Ages of the World had Showers of burning Sulphur rained down upon them, it is surely now of the Lord's Mercy that our Cities, our Nests of Iniquity, are not consumed![47]

* William Smith, for instance, sincerely believed that he could "woo and win" men to "religion and Happiness, from a consideration of what God hath promised to the Virtuous" and that "what He hath denounced against the Wicked" would only frighten and dispirit his auditors.

Needless to say, the Liberal jeremiads of the 1770's were not in full agreement with Tennent's readings of the signs of the times.

First of all, as mention of one of John Lathrop's 1774 sermons has already indicated, the Liberal mind tended to identify the colony's afflictions entirely with the interruption of the commercial activities of the ports. In the autumn Lathrop, speaking on a day of provincial thanksgiving, observed that Boston probably had little to be thankful for. In accounting for the unhappiness of the people, he echoed Chauncy's lament of the same year for the Boston poor. The "present appearance" of the city, he observed, is "quite gloomy," and the change from the previous year more than "affecting," because, as he explained, in the good old days each and every Bostonian had felt great "joy" in seeing his "capacious and safe harbour *white*" and in welcoming traders from abroad. Lathrop was annoyed that the British ministry had closed the port simply because some insignificant and "unknown" dissidents had dumped a few casks of tea into the harbor (he granted that widespread seditious behaviour would have justified closure), and hoped that Parliament would arrange "some wise or equitable plan of accommodation" so Americans and Britons might return to a relationship in which they had "maintained the most perfect harmony, and felt the purest joy in each other's happiness for more than a hundred years."[48] Such a pious wish was more than a politic gesture, for the minds of the urban Liberals were slow to accept the possibility of an America happy otherwise than through the benefits of the British system of trade. Even after the battle of Lexington some of them persisted in believing that Americans sought nothing more than return to this old course of economic felicity.[49]

Despite his nostalgia, Lathrop spoke many thoughts more revolutionary than those advanced by his colleagues in 1774. Lathrop, like those few Liberals who remained Whigs in these months, raised the issue of the extent to which Parliamentary jurisdiction of any sort posed a deadly threat to American happiness. Not only were British regulations inequitable and inexpedient, Lathrop alleged, but their very existence suggested that the British, jealous of the colonies' increasing wealth, were planning to draw off "their riches as fast as they acquire them."[50] Such an observation was all but a declaration of American independence, for according to Liberals any attempt to deprive Americans of their riches violated the fundamental spirit of their charters and of the British constitution. In an earlier sermon of 1774 Lathrop had declared that anyone making "an alteration in the established constitution" would be held guilty of "Treason of the worst kind."[51] Though as yet unprepared in the autumn of 1774 to cry treason, Lathrop was more than certain that the home government was bent on abrogating its fundamental compact with the citizens of Massachusetts.

In support of his position Lathrop explicated the law of the Commonwealth in terms expressive of the rationalist belief in the essentially commercial nature of the American experience. Here "our fathers planted themselves," he recalled in a sentence that should have disturbed the shade of John Winthrop, "that they and their posterity might prosecute those branches of trade and merchandise which give riches and strength to nations and states."[52] So far indeed did Liberals expand their conception of America as originally a plantation of trade that they all but converted the appeal to history into an appeal to nature—portraying the meaning of America as a function, not of their ancestors' errand, but of the bountiful wilderness to which they had come. "The God of nature has taught us, by the situation and uncommon advantages of the place," Lathrop observed of Boston harbor in presumably unanswerable demonstration of America's right to be let alone, "that it was designed for extensive business."[53] Within the year history, constitution, and charter all took on a single meaning for Liberals: Americans were "entitled to all the natural and improvable advantages of our situation."[54] The lessons of the Old Testament and the logic of John Locke, both once used in justification of Americans' seizure and settlement of the waste places of the New World, had at last fulfilled their destined function.

A belief in the inalienable right of Americans to exploit their natural situation was not in itself enough to convert rationalists into revolutionaries. One such nonrevolutionary Liberal was Samuel Williams of Bradford, Massachusetts, who on thanksgiving day of 1774 took stock of the physical advantages of the country to which his foresighted ancestors had come. Williams was so impressed by this bounty—congenial climate, commodious harbors, and fertile soil—that he predicted that "the perfection and happiness of mankind" would be "carried further in America, than it ever has yet in any place."[55] Williams confessed, however, that the "present difficulties" might "retard the work" of perfection, but where Lathrop had believed British regulations the only intrusion into the harmonious evolution of America's prosperity, Williams thought the retarding difficulties were of two sorts.

One was the British attempt to deprive Americans of the fruits of this abundance, but the other was American agitation to involve the colonies in a bloody and costly war with the mother country. Should either succeed, Williams lamented, the timetable of perfection would have to be revised considerably. The prospect of war, he explained, is more than frightening; but yet, to give to Britain "the management of taxes, is to give all that we have. Dreadful extremes!"[56] Torn between longings for each of the two crucial ingredients in Liberal happiness—freedom from taxation and commercial harmony with Britain—Williams, increasingly fearful of extremes, departed his pulpit (as a suspected Tory) and accepted appointment as Harvard's Hollis Professor of Mathematics and Natural Philosophy. Leaving the gates of Jerusalem to be manned by lesser men, Williams spent the war years corresponding with his friend and pupil Benjamin Thompson (Count Rumford) and sharing with his Harvard students his "sublime observations" on a serene heavenly order not given to extremes.[57]

Many Liberals, though willing for the sake of preserving American prosperity to vindicate armed resistance, blanched at independence. Of these probably the most notable was Jacob Duché, who preferred exile in Britain. Yet the career of Duché's ultraliberal instructor, William Smith, was the more significant, for Smith sufficiently reconciled himself to independence to remain in America and pour his Anglophilia into Federalism. Like Williams, Smith was a confirmed and ecstatic prophet of a glorious American future. "Ever since I was capable of reflecting on the Course of Things in this World," he recalled before the American Philosophical Society in early 1773,

> it hath been one of the most delightful Employments of my contemplative hours, to anticipate the rising Grandeur of America; to trace the Progress of the Arts, like that of the Sun, from East to West; and to look forward to that glorious Period . . . when the Regions on this Side of the Atlantic, as well as those on the other, shall enjoy their *Day* of Freedom, Light and polished Life![58]

In May of 1775 Smith, preaching to a body of troops in Philadelphia, insisted that neither Britain nor any other "human power" would be allowed to "frustrate" these "great and gracious purposes" of Providence toward the American continent. At the same time, however, he urged them to contend only for their "constitutional rights, and a final settlement of the terms on which this country may be perpetually united to the parent state."[59] Himself "ardently panting for the return of those halcyon days of harmony during which both countries so long flourished together," Smith offered terms of reconciliation that foreshadowed the foreign policy of mercantile Federalism. Dilating on how Americans and Britons had "trod the path of glory" for more than a century, "cemented by mutual love and mutual benefits," Smith observed that Americans were willing to submit to "every just regulation for appropriating to [Britain] the benefit of our trade" in order to retain such "felicity."[60] Already in December of 1775 Smith was admitting to the existence of differing opinions on "the present mighty contest," and within a few months personally adjudged its consequences so infelicitous that he tried, in his notorious "Cato" letters,*[61] to prove that Common Sense was neither prudence nor reason.[62]

As such sentiments suggest, the Liberal mind was not especially disposed to viewing events from the perspective of the jeremiad. Rather it struggled always to assess the crisis of imperial affairs "rationally" and, in doing so, to overcome the tendency of the American mind to interpret British regulations as somehow a warning voice from heaven. Another requirement of the jeremiad that Liberals found odious was the need for criticizing their own society. The only Liberal sermon delivered in these years that might be reasonably described as a formal jeremiad was Chauncy's 1770 discourse before certain "patriotic gentlemen" of Boston. The discourse was founded, in part at least, on the dark premise that "it is our lot, my hearers, to live in a time when the face of providence is angry and threatening." This "ill state of affairs," according to Chauncy, might have been ascribed to "this or the other second cause," but, he insisted, "properly speaking," the sins of the land were "the true moral cause of all that we now suffer, or have reason to fear."[63]

Most properly, therefore, Chauncy went on to explain that the only way in which the afflictions might be removed was "by an amendment of our doings which have not been right." But at no place did he offer even a hint as to which particular doings had not been right, and far from summoning the whole of Massachusetts to signify repentance by virtuous actions, his exhortation was one with the title of the sermon as published: *Trust in God, the Duty of a People in a Day of Trouble.* Chauncy's sermon undoubtedly marked a high point in his commitment to a patriotism that, by the standards of the day in Boston, was clearly radical. In glancing back over the mainstream of New England history, he allowed himself one of the strongest indictments of Laudian oppression to emanate in years from the respectable Boston pulpit:

> The deliverance of our forefathers from tyranny and oppression, by bringing them over to this distant region, is not unlike his carrying Israel of old thro' the red sea to the promised land of Old.[64]

* Considerable evidence, including attribution to Smith on the personal copies of his contemporaries, points to him as the author of the "Candidus" letters (also a confutation of Paine). Whoever he might have been, "Candidus" was one in sensibility with Smith; in an effusive introduction he proclaimed his political sentiments in these strains: "Animated and impelled by every inducement of the human heart, I love, and (if I dare to express myself) I adore my country. Passionately devoted to true liberty, I glow with the purest flame of patriotism."

Thus did Charles Chauncy contribute his mite to the re-Hebraizing of New England history in the 1770's, but as an instrument of persuasion his proper jeremiad was something less than an incitement to rebellion.

The difficulty in which Chauncy was placed in 1770 is suggested by his feeling it necessary to ask his auditors—the same gentlemen whose virtues, for Chauncy, so eminently fitted them for duty in the General Court—if they would "permit" him to state that "our sins are the worst enemies we have."[65] Presumably Chauncy would have hesitated to make this declaration if such permission had not been granted, for had he not been so eager to please these gentlemen he would not have spoken at all. His sermon—the product of a hasty day's preparation following receipt of the call—was not the outpouring of a pastoral soul concerned for the spiritual welfare of his flock, but (as he admitted by way of preface) an act of almost abject deference to those leaders of Boston society who had summoned him to this task. The jeremiad was hardly the appropriate sermon form where such a relationship between pastor and people existed, and more particularly not when the people being addressed were gentlemen. Perhaps it was because such Liberals as Chauncy intuitively realized which Americans were ripest for harvest that they were so reluctant to assert, or even to believe, that a time of reaping was about to commence.

What most disturbed the Liberals was the possible effect of a full-scale jeremiad on the general populace. Though the Liberal clergy assumed that generous men would be paralyzed by threatened adversity, they paid to the vulgar herd the high tribute of expecting them to respond far too actively to distressing situations. By portraying as divine afflictions the "difficulties which make the present, a day of trouble," Chauncy ran the danger of attaching too much significance to what Liberals considered only a "perplext situation," and of increasing thereby the uneasiness of the common people.[66] John Browne of Cohasset was one Arminian who differed from Gay in 1770 by confessing that the Massacre was sufficiently deplorable to justify the popular desire for a day of fasting. Yet in discussing this "supposed ground of uneasiness" Browne openly expressed a fear that such uneasiness could too readily lead, not to contrition and repentance, but to "thoughts of rising in Rebellion."[67]

This dilemma, which all Liberals faced after 1770, was, of course, largely of their own making. Having long asserted that the God even of the earthquake was sufficiently benevolent to leave the more substantial houses of Boston intact, they were ill-prepared to invoke once again the wrath of an inscrutable and arbitrary Jehovah. To have confessed to the existence of a fearsome Deity would, of course, have disheartened their more complacent parishioners, but far more significantly, it also would have thoroughly undermined the most effective Liberal rejoinder to the uneasy and impatient critics of their happy and prosperous world.

Liberal reluctance to employ the jeremiad was, finally, an effort to minimize popular participation in political activity. The widespread desire for fast days, for humiliation and repentance, was the expression of an inchoate desire on the part of the American people to do something—anything—to remedy the situation into which their society had fallen. Only one Arminian, old Ebenezer Gay, perfectly solved a problem which would beset the Liberal ministry for another generation: what to say to a people bent on reforming the sins of their society when repentance threatens to express itself as a radical social disturbance. By identifying both the afflictions of the land and its sins with an element of the population to which the Liberal ministry owed nothing, Gay anticipated by two decades what was to become a stock formula of Unitarian-Federalist sermons.

Gay informed those who had asked for a fast instead of a thanksgiving in 1770 that they might achieve their purpose by accompanying their gratitude with prayers for arresting "those Judgments which we labour under." But according to Gay the only discernible affliction of the land was "Disturbance of the public peace." Since, as he explained, those so ungrateful as to wish for a fast day were necessarily the same as those who wished to violate the provincial order, his suggestion amounted to a proposal that these poor sinners should spend the day petitioning that they themselves would cease to afflict their community.[68]

Whig Liberals could not, of course, adopt this strategy, but until 1774 even they refused to grant the people of America a role in relieving the afflictions of the land any larger than praying quietly that the King not hearken to evil counselors. In 1774 a few of them suggested that obedience to central authority was an appropriate (and perhaps the only truly penitent) spiritual exercise for days of humiliation and prayer. Quoting the proclamation of the Provincial Congress —"Let us humble ourselves before God on account of our sins: Let us reform whatever is amiss"—John Lathrop dismissed all other possibilities and proposed that adherence to the resolutions of the Continental Congress would be quite sufficient unto salvation, both spiritual and political.[69]

Though most Liberals placed their faith in something other than a spiritual renewal of the American people, a few of them were willing to speculate, at least, on the nature of the sins which had engendered the political calamities of the 1770's. The Liberal ministry had long felt that American society was being corrupted by "luxury, extravagance, and intemperance," more especially, as they saw it, "among the lower sort of people." In the spring of 1765 Andrew Eliot had informed the General Court of Massachusetts, "He must have little understanding of the times, who does not see that we are in more danger" from such "internal vices" than from "external impositions" like the stamp tax.[70] Liberals were fascinated by the vices of the lower orders, of course, because such behavior provided a convenient and presumably unanswerable explanation for the fact that not all in America were as happy as the rationalist God had clearly intended them to be. It was "plain to observe," Henry Cumings concluded in 1766, "that the poverty and want of most people among us, originate either from indolence, or intemperance, or some particular expensive vices to which they are addicted."[71]

Along with other colonial clergymen Liberals greeted the non-importation resolution of 1774 as a mighty moral engine as well as a stroke of policy and enjoined its fulfillment as the one act of repentance sure to remove the afflictions befalling the land. All America's calamities, Henry Cumings explained six months after the battle of Lexington, had been caused by "intemperance, prodigality and extravagance," and God, he declared, as well as the Continental Congress, was loudly calling on Americans to rid themselves of "foreign superfluities," to retrench their "extravagancies and superfluous expenses."[72]

The Revolutionary commitment of the Liberals would have been less questionable had they, in the crisis of 1774-1775, summoned everyone in America to a primitive simplicity of manners and enthusiasm for domestic industry. But habits of thought developed over generations were not to be broken in months or even years. As recently as 1763, for instance, Jonathan Mayhew had argued, as against the lower classes' wearing of "sumptuous cloathing," that such prideful presumption struck at the very heart of the New England way:

> By this means those good ends which might otherwise be answered in society, by the distinctions of dress, are in a great measure defeated; for this confounds all ranks, destroys due subordination, and even inverts the natural order of things, by setting poor people of low degree above the rich . . .[73]

Eleven years later Chauncy was explaining that God, by his threatening Providence, was trying to teach the lower orders of Boston society that they must stop putting on airs, and that they must learn "to refrain

from purchasing that merchandize, which swallows up their substance for the paultry consideration only of appearing in finery of
dress which ill becomes them."[74] Like Benjamin Franklin, who followed up his celebrated defense of linsey-woolsey America before
Parliament in 1766 by shipping silks and perfumes to his wife (along
with a confession that he himself already had enough European clothes
to last a lifetime), the Liberal ministry did not, in searching for the
moral causes of God's controversy with the colonies, look in the 1770's
much to themselves.

Surely they did not glance toward those who in colonial society
seemed in the 1770's so God-provoking to American Calvinists. In
the spring of 1775, for instance, the Calvinist clergy, speculating on
the outbreak of the rebellion, declared Americans to be possibly the
most sinful people on the face of the earth. "There is only one consideration that is very discouraging," observed David Jones in his assessment of the possibilities of American victory, "and that is the great
and many sins that prevail in our land." His catalogue, which included
"dissolute debauchery, drunkenness, pride and excess," was repeated—
and augumented—by the thousands of ministers who on July 20 participated in the first continental day of fasting, humiliation, and prayer.[75]
The Calvinist characterizations of sinful America in relation to its
latest afflictions all followed the pattern ordained by young Tennent
in 1774. The war marked the consummation of what "good men"
had been "for Years past" expecting: "some great and dismal Catas-
trophe to befal" a land given over to Arminianism and prideful
luxury.[76]

In the Boston of Charles Chauncy too, it seemed to Sam Adams,
among others, that the provoking sins of the 1770's were dalliance with
fashionable religion and the "finery" of the mercantile classes. So likewise his friend Charles Turner, whom Adams in 1773 managed to have
appointed election preacher. In listing the sins of the province, Turner
pointed particularly to the "European error, wickedness, and folly"
that distinguished those in "what is called fashionable and high life."[77]
In the course of the next decade Adams, Turner, and the Calvinist
clergy generally would discover some of these same sins among their
own followers, especially those who used liberty not merely to the
flesh but to aspire to gentility. But they never forgot the sins of the
higher orders, and surely they did not, as would Chauncy in the last
published sermon of his life, insist that all the troubles of an independent America were to be viewed as divine judgments on the "com-
moners" who were seeking, by one means or another, to rise above
their previous stations.

III

That the multitude came in the years of the Revolution to hunger after and even partake of some of the advantages once enjoyed only by their betters, was not unrelated to the changes in Liberal ideals and rhetoric in the years between 1774 and 1776. Before 1774 Liberal political sermons proceeded from the premise that popular discontent was not real*[78] and, until 1775, that the people of the colonies were already as excited as they ought reasonably to be. Yet once the war commenced, those Liberals who were still articulate made a few attempts, albeit diffident ones by comparison to the evangelical clergy, to encourage an active role in public affairs on the part of others than the recognized gentlemen of the colonies.

In the year of the Boston Port Bill a spokesman for rational religion first acknowledged that popular participation in public affairs was not a pure and unmixed evil. Perhaps the Boston town meetings and the Committees of Correspondence formed in 1773 (for the purpose, among others, of convincing the British administration that the grievances of the province were not urged by a mere discontented faction) had some effect on Liberal opinion. In any case the election preacher for 1774, Gad Hitchcock, listed "our groanings that cannot be uttered" along with "our continued complaints" as "indications of our sufferings, and the feeling sense we have of them."[79] Hitchcock's sermon is said to have filled General Gage (who had just, in the wake of the Tea Party, replaced Hutchinson as governor) "with great wrath, on account of . . . the air of defiance that pervaded it."[80]

Actually Hitchcock defied Gage in the name of the General Court, and then only after explaining that the prospect before Massachusetts was such that any reasonable man might be agitated. "Our danger is not visionary, but real—," he insisted, choosing his words quite carefully, "Our contention is not about trifles, but about liberty and property."[81] The true power of Hitchcock's sermon, however, derived not from his declaration of rights and grievances, but from his playing a trump which no Liberal spokesman had seen reason to use since 1766. "If I am mistaken in supposing plans are formed and executing, subversive of our natural and chartered rights and privileges, and incompatible with every idea of liberty," was Hitchcock's defiant thrust, *"all America is mistaken with me."*[82] That all America was so aroused by the spring of 1774 was hardly a tribute to Liberal eloquence—they had done nothing in the preceding years to encourage popular discontent. Yet now that this spirit moved Americans, and so long as it

---

* The 1772 election preacher, the moderate Calvinist Moses Parsons, remarked on "the complaints heard among us" that Americans were being deprived of happiness, but he would not admit the justice of the complaints.

served the purposes of wise and prudent men, Liberals were at last willing to grant that the unhappiness of the multitude was real.

Hitchcock was one of the handful of rural Arminians who after 1774 came into some prominence in the political discussions in Massachusetts. They seem to have been Arminians in the classic sense, having rejected Calvinism less for reasons of social policy than for what they considered its cruel fatalism. As such they were in a somewhat better position than, say, John Tucker, to argue the peculiar congeniality of Arminianism to the thriving of political liberty.*[83] They allowed that a people would readily comply with a "mild and equitable administration" of their affairs, and thus interpreted the Intolerable Acts as attempts to force Americans to obedience, rather than inducing consent through the softer persuasives of reason.[84]

Still, even in the case of these mild Arminians it is difficult to detect their precise rhetorical stance and purpose as inspirers of love of liberty. For one thing they were clearly undecided, as late as December of 1774, whether they wanted Americans to defend their legal "liberties" or be somehow inspired with a more active love of liberty. In a sermon more discursive than hortatory, Gad Hitchcock did allow that not only a condition of liberty, but a spirit of liberty, was "essential to human happiness." A "love of liberty," he declared, is requisite "to all virtuous exertions." Yet he also suggested that liberty itself was enough to assure these exertions, since it was a state of slavery that "enervates and obscures [the] faculties . . . and snaps the sinews of every exalted and virtuous design."[85] What he did not allow, however, was the possibility that a more active spirit of liberty was needed in 1774 in order to preserve or secure the status of Americans as free agents. And like any other exponent of the rationalist psychology, Hitchcock had no effective rhetorical strategy for inducing such a spirit in his auditors. Hitchcock's Arminianism seems to have disposed him to a preference for keeping the American people spectators, who, though tenacious of their right to choice, were by no means to be encouraged to be more active agents.

There is a marked contrast in both doctrine and tone between Hitchcock's sermon delivered at Plymouth in 1774 and that which had been preached a year earlier. The Plymouth commemoration, one of the many devices to emerge in the period to bring filiopietism in one form or another to the support of the patriot cause, featured in 1773 an harangue by Charles Turner, who flatly declared: "A *spirit* of liberty

* The submission God requires of man, Tucker alleged in his 1771 election sermon, is not that demanded of a slave by his tyrannical master. The "obedience we owe to civil government," similarly, "must be *free*,—a matter of choice, and not of force, driving us on against a reluctant mind."

is necessary to the preservation of the *thing*."[86] Hitchcock, even as he proclaimed his ancestors' love of liberty, was, no less than the Bostonians, full of wise cautions. Liberty, he explained, was, even when in danger of "restraint from our fellow men," still "extremely liable to abuse by ourselves."[87] He seemed unsure of himself whenever he passed beyond the merely legal argument in defense of privileges and liberties. Hitchcock argued that "the rights and liberties of the colonies" were such "important blessings" that lovers of their country should strive to "secure them to the present, and transmit them to future generations." He also proposed, at least tentatively, that Americans, in order to retain their status as free agents, should prepare to defend their "liberty." This flirtation with the idea of an extraconstitutional liberty is of some significance, in part because it stated the issue as against Britain in broader terms than most Liberals were wont to do.[88] More importantly, it stands on the record as a rebuke to the Liberal clergy of later years, who well before the Peace of Paris were swearing to a man that the Revolution had been fought only to defend the concrete inherited liberties of British citizens.

Another concession made to the times by the rural Arminians was in delineating American history as filled with an element of evangelical aspiration. Rather than seeing America as heir to Renaissance culture and the Enlightenment, they believed that "religion" was the "chief motive" in the migrations of the seventeenth century, that the gospel surpassed "happy climate and good land" as an American blessing, and that Providence had grandly designed the western continent as an asylum of "true religion."[89] Nor were these mere flourishes; at least one of these rural Liberals, Samuel West, was so lost to sweet reasonableness that he seriously speculated on the imminent fulfillment of the prophecies in America.[90] But even he fell far short of those Calvinists who were, by 1775, contending that empire was taking its course along a millennial schedule and that the Intolerable Acts had inaugurated the last chapter of the history of the Work of Redemption.

It is a question whether only ministers subscribing to some such view of American history were able to commit themselves vocally to the patriot cause in 1775-76, or whether, as in some cases seems the more likely, these flourishes of religiosity were deemed rhetorically necessary. In any case William Smith, though he continued to portray the American future as, at best, a mercantile version of the philosophers' heavenly city—a "whole continent" filled with "arts and polished life, and whatever can exalt or adorn mankind"*—insisted in 1775

---

* A similar vision appeared in Duché's *Caspipina's Letters,* together with the

that the "temporal Empire" of America was secondary to, and supported by, an "Empire of Christian Knowledge."[91] As recently as 1773, Smith had accounted for the rising grandeur of America by the "Healthfulness of our Climate, our Conveniences of Navigation, the Fertility of Soil, Variety of Produce, and Multitude of Improvements, whereof our Country is Capable." But in 1775 he declared that the most important ingredient in the rise and progress of America was its Protestant religion, more important, indeed, than "happiness and fertility of soil" or any "other blessings of nature and industry."[92]

To gauge the effectiveness of Liberal rhetoric in 1775 it is necessary to recall that these invocations of America's manifestly destined history were not merely declarations of belief but efforts to inspire Americans with love of country. Prospects of future American felicity were then, as for Liberals they had been for decades, a means of stimulating "attachment to our native country."[93] Though the "transcendent love of country" which William Smith sought to arouse in the spring of 1775 was avowedly a British-American patriotism, his depiction of the western course of the "mighty blessings" of civilization was at least implicitly divisive.[94] Whatever the precise catalogue of future blessings, these images of the future embodied a major concession— beyond even the greater religiosity—to the exigencies of the times.

The Liberal prospect of the future was by 1775 so expansive, or so blurred, that it could well have appealed to a larger segment of the populace than it had in 1766. Indeed it might have appealed to any American aspiring to the kind of happiness so long vouchsafed only to urban Liberals and their friends. By 1775 the Arminian clergy, instead of following their outbursts of cosmic optimism with admonitions about biding God's time, were strongly hinting that resistance to Britain could usher in an era of unexampled abundance and prosperity for all Americans. And, as the Liberals told the story, such happiness had all along been withheld from the average American only by the cruel oppressions of a tyrannical Parliament.

Not only did the Liberals of 1775 seemingly invite the multitude to share in this repast, but they considerably widened the path which had once led to glory and renown only for gentlemen. In December of 1775 William Smith delivered before the Continental Congress an oration honoring General Montgomery, who had fallen at the attack on Quebec. Smith characteristically intended his oration as an asser-

suggestion—characteristic of the Whig mind generally in the 1770's—that the empire of "arts and letters" was about to take its westward course, possibly to settle on the banks of the Delaware. It is necessary to distinguish, however, between the prospects as seen by Duché and Smith, and such explicitly millenarian visions as that delineated by young Philip Freneau and H. H. Brackenridge in *The Rising Glory of America*.

tion that American gentlemen had demonstrated they were not muckers. The progress of the rebellion, he gloated, had proven that though "patriotism sometimes basks in the sunshine of courts, it frequently lies hid in the shades of obscurity." In proclaiming Montgomery as worthy of "the veneration and eulogies of his country" as General Wolfe, Smith even went so far as to admit that the capability for patriotism was "confined to no class of men."[95] In a few months Smith was less certain of the advantages of provincial patriotism, for the Continental Congress refused to publish his oration, which John Adams thought "an insolent performance."[96]

The effectiveness of his oration in arousing American patriotism is questionable, since it assumed, like all of Smith's effusions of 1775, that such a "divine enthusiasm" already burned in every bosom and that he, William Smith, whose "pulpit casuistry" was "too feeble to direct or control," could do little more than offer words of encouragement.[97] Yet Smith's oration, published initially at his own expense, did enjoy some popularity throughout the colonies and was reprinted several times in the course of the year. The vogue of the oration seems testimony to Smith's wisdom in defining love of country as something other than mere gratitude for blessings received or forthcoming. Smith assured his auditors (and his readers) that the patriot was a benevolent man, aroused by the "pang" of sympathy which he felt for his "suffering country."[98] In 1775 there were more Americans than even Smith suspected who wanted to be told that glory-seeking was an act of Christian benevolence, just as those who were reaching for their share of the pie in the Liberal sky wanted reassurance that they were in actuality coming to the aid of the Lord.

New England Arminians also strove to prove the sublime disinterest of pursuing the general welfare. Sentimentalized benevolence of the sort Chauncy espoused found a place in their sermons, but they preferred to show that patriotic endeavor was motivated by a desire to secure, through present sacrifice, the happiness of posterity. "The love of our country, the tender affection that we have for our wives and children, the regard we ought to have for unborn posterity"—reads one of the more eclectic lists of objects of benevolent regard—"yea, everything that is dear and sacred, do now loudly call upon us to use our best endeavors to save our country."[99] For many reasons Liberals were fonder of New England's progeny than of its ancestors, but they nevertheless also called on Americans to defend their inheritance. Neither in asking Americans to "look forward to distant posterity" nor in urging filial obligations on the "sons and daughters" of the Puritans, did Liberals espouse or summon their auditors to a patriotism that was selfless.[100] However they related Americans to other generations, rationalist benevolence of this sort was ultimately expressed as the obligation to fulfill a contract. "A concern for them," one Liberal declared of America's children, "is a debt we owe for the care our progenitors took of us."[101]

If the rationalist clergy did not exactly contend for the faith once delivered to the saints as the only way to make certain that generations yet unborn would rise up and call the patriots of 1775 blessed, they made at least one other important bow to necessity. They included the founders of America among the "heroes of ancient times" and assured the American people that the same love of country which had "raised their names to the summit of renown" could, were it now to animate Americans, similarly permit them to be held by "future generations, conspicuous in the roll of glory."[102] The Liberals had thereby vastly swelled the ranks of potential patriots, for all Americans had forefathers and might reasonably arrange to have children. Though it is most unlikely that all who became lovers of their country did so even with such motives, it is reasonably significant that they were given the opportunity. For in a few years the Liberal clergy would profess to discover (and express horror at the very thought) that all men save them and their acquaintances had fought the good fight for selfish reasons and that too many vulgar Americans had, in the course of the war, come to unreasonable notions of their own importance.

Even as they issued so general an invitation to patriotism, however, the Liberals of 1775 did not abandon their traditional social preferences. William Smith, hardly a reckless leveler, insisted that this proliferation of patriots, however necessary and even admirable, would work no drastic changes in the structure of American society. To be sure, both the noble and the ignoble patriots of 1766 were now to be allowed within the temple:

> The tempers of men are cast in various moulds. Some are quick and feelingly alive in all their mental operations, especially those which relate to their country's weal, and are therefore ready to burst forth into flame on every alarm. Others again, with intentions alike pure, and a clear unquenchable love of their country, too steadfast to be damped by the mists of prejudice, or worked up into conflagration by the rude blasts of passion, think it their duty to weigh consequences, and to deliberate fully upon the probable means of obtaining public ends. Both these kinds of men should bear with each other; for both are friends to their country.[103]

Like most Liberal utterances, Smith's statement bears a deceptive air of moderation. Rather than conceding, Smith was actually indulging in a bit of special pleading in the very moment of capitulation.

By 1775 the men of unguarded zeal had managed to wrest colonial affairs from the hands of the more cool and dispassionate patriots. Smith was defending those who had argued, with him, that the violent men of the Second Continental Congress were moving too far and too fast in their resistance to Britain. Smith was, moreover, eager to demonstrate why such an unnatural state of affairs was inexpedient and could not continue now that the colonies were involved in war. No cause, he insisted, could succeed "without order and subordination," and every patriot would hereafter be bound "to keep the place and duty assigned him." If there were any question as to who would assume the places of leadership, and who the subordinate duties, Smith gave his personal answer by rejoicing that America had been so fortunate as to have the struggle postponed "to a period when our country is adorned with men of enlightened zeal"—men, in other words, who would coolly deliberate and both withstand and control the rude blasts of a more popular enthusiasm.[104]

When independence was declared, Smith retired from public life and reappeared only toward the end of the Revolution as the fulsome eulogist of Washington. Later he was elected chaplain of the Pennsylvania Society of the Cincinnati, an organization hardly disposed to celebrate either the passions of the multitude or the virtues of enlisted men. Still, the officers to whom Smith preached were for many reasons grateful for the general docility of the American troops during the war. Though neither Smith nor any other Liberal minister deserves credit for their obedience, rational religion made, in 1775, a fairly significant concession to the conditions of American life. As compared to his attitude at the time of the Stamp Act crisis, Smith had come to acknowledge the possibility of public spirit dwelling in the breasts of more than a chosen few. Perhaps he understood that patriots had to be enlisted rather indiscriminately if America's gentlemen were to be robed in officerial splendor.

The rationalists of rural Massachusetts eagerly embraced Independence, perhaps because, unlike such Liberals as Smith, they evaluated differently the popular temper and intelligence. All adhered to a belief in the pre-eminent utility and value of reason, but they did not consider judgment a faculty absolutely and permanently monopolized by the educated gentlemen of America. They wished for—and even considered feasible—something of a general public enlightenment, and their rationalism, though hardly Jeffersonian, verged on implicit criticism of the prevailing social order. The belief that the difference "among the several classes of mankind arises chiefly from their education" they used not as an argument for the eternal wisdom and justice of the existing class structure but for the duty of the state to "banish ignorance from among mankind"—an endeavor in which they expected the common schools of Massachusetts to prove at least as useful as Harvard College.[105]

It is possible that, having used popular discontent in vindication of legislative resistance to Britain, these Liberals were forced to accept the implications of their own arguments. It seems more likely, however, that only those nominally Arminian clergy who thought highly of the popular mind were prepared to preach Revolution. In the spring of 1776, in any case, the election preacher failed to follow his discussion of who was to decide whether the magistrate behaved tyrannically with the conventional comments about imaginary popular grievances and the dangers of demagoguery. Instead Samuel West of Dartmouth acknowledged the possible wisdom of the people:

> Great regard ought always to be paid to the judgment of the public. It is true the public may be imposed upon by a misrepresentation of facts; but this may be said of the public, which cannot always be said of individuals, viz., that the public is willing to be rightly informed, and when it has proper matter of conviction laid before it its judgment is always right.[106]

For a few years after 1776 West and some other Massachusetts rationalists affirmed what Jonathan Mayhew had never found reason to assert— that in America, and in the eighteenth century, the people themselves had rightfully made a decision that a tyrant was to be resisted.

West's sermon marked the apogee of political radicalism among Massachusetts Arminians. He argued so convincingly against tyranny that he came to the conclusion, on May 29, that the colonies were and ought to be independent of Great Britain. In view of this advanced position, it is all the more striking that less than half of West's sermon was devoted to justifying the Revolution—the greater part being a development of a traditional theme of the Liberal ministry, the dangers of excess, licentiousness, and anarchy. "I acknowledge that I have undertaken a difficult task," West frankly admitted, but "the present state of affairs loudly called for such a discourse." West's announced purpose was to discuss

> the nature and design of government, and the rights and duties both of governors and governed, that so, justly understanding our rights and privileges, we may stand firm in our opposition to ministerial tyranny, while at the same time we pay all proper obedience and submission to our lawful magistrates; and that, while we are contending for liberty, we may avoid running into licentiousness; and that we may preserve the due medium between submitting to tyranny and running into anarchy.[107]

Even West had to admit that in the spring of 1776 no one seemed to want to run into anarchy. The behavior of the people after the charter was vacated, the legislature dissolved, and the courts of justice closed in many parts of the province seemed to West admirable and no less than a work of Providence. Who "would have thought," West observed in a burst of Liberal surprise, "that in such a situation the people should behave so peaceably, and maintain such good order and harmony among themselves?"[108]

The prevailing danger of 1776, according to West, was not licentiousness, but a "seditious and factious temper" which was moving the people to impatience, suspicion, and criticism of the wise and good men who had assumed political leadership of the colonies. To counteract this disposition West employed a variety of arguments, or, more properly, modes of persuasion. There is, he began, "a wide difference" between defending our rights when "we have the strongest reason to conclude they are invaded," and "being unreasonably suspicious" of those trying to defend the constitution "only because we do not thoroughly comprehend all their designs." Such a distinction was well known throughout the colonies, but in early 1776 a number of Americans questioned West's application, and murmured of tyrants nearer home.

For these, West had the strokes of character portraiture which rationalists always found so useful rhetorically. Those who opposed British tyrants, West observed, were of "a noble and generous mind," while anyone suspicious of the colonial patriot leaders was of "a low and base spirit." As if aware that such invective was no longer an adequate mode of persuasion, West went on to explain why it was pragmatically necessary for Americans to esteem the noble and generous spirits among them. When the "unthinking herd" reviles good dignities, West declared, it "lessens their influence, and disheartens them," while, if "they are properly honored, and treated with that respect which is due to their station, it inspires them with courage and a noble ardor to serve the public."[109] Such sentiments contained, of course, a leading principle of what came to be Adams Federalism, a school of thought which could not comprehend why the people, having once so lavishly admired the leaders of Revolution, should in the late 1790's unthinkingly repeat the cavils of Jacobinic demagogues. The failures of the Adams administration, according to this same school, were inevitable; for good men, when reviled, can but sulk in their tents.

Even in early 1776 few patriot leaders were beyond suspicion, for many Americans had been inspired with an enthusiasm for liberty which neither the Continental Congress nor the provincial legislatures were ready to indulge. Although some wanted freedom from local authority as well as from Britain, their grievances subsided with the Declaration of Independence, because, among other reasons, nearly everyone agreed with "Father West" that the "political salvation" of the colonies then more than ever depended on their "being firmly united together in the bonds of love to one another." Not all, however, fully acquiesced in West's dictum that Christian love also demanded a "due submission to lawful authority,"[110] and after 1777 it became necessary to invoke the law as well as the gospel to deny overzealous Americans that liberty for which they thought they were fighting. With rare exceptions even the most Liberal of rationalist preachers grew silent, or delivered sermons clearly intended to subdue and temper this excessive zeal. Indeed the Liberal pulpit was thereafter dedicated primarily, not to inspiring Americans with Revolutionary ardor, but to defending and justifying the constitutional machinery which, in the midst of war, the rational minds of America were able to contrive.

Whether as Federalists in later years, or as Whigs justifying Revolution in the 1770's, even the most liberal of Liberals could not finally transcend the limitations of Arminian theology. The clerical Whigs of 1774 were able to welcome "the assiduous attention given to our public affairs," and not merely because the attitude of the populace impressed them more favorably than in the times when malcontents murmured against their leaders.[111] They acknowledged that government depended on the consent of the governed, and that—as in the broader Arminian scheme—every man had the right to approve or reject, depending on his judgment of the merits of an administration. In time such a principle would, to be sure, lead the Liberal mind to see rejection of John Adams' mild and equitable administration as evidence of the same obduracy that led men to reject the offers of the reasonable Arminian God. But more importantly, Arminianism granted the people no more than a passive role in political activity— the inalienable right merely to grant or withhold their consent from the operations of a government. As to the notion that a government derives its purpose and its strength from the active will of the people, this ever seemed to the Liberal mind nothing but fantastic and enthusiastic nonsense.

IV

In view of their record of anti-populism, judicious moderation, and silence, the Liberal clergy seem hardly worthy of celebration as *the* spokesmen of rebellion. Yet any estimate of their contribution to the patriot cause must take into account that their effect was felt among the more respectable and presumably most powerful elements of colonial society. Occupying a crucial social position, the preacher of

445

genteel Christianity represented, and to some extent guided, a less numerous, but also less humble, group of citizens than that reached by his Calvinist brethren. Most Liberals, indeed, made little effort to reach a truly popular audience; for their sermons, like those of the elder Thomas Barnard, "were rational and judicious, calculated for hearers of thoughtful mind," and therefore, by Liberal definition alone, lacking in all those ingredients which "give a charm to popular discourse."[112] In time these Liberals (or their successors) would find in their lack of popular appeal proof of the failure of American democracy, but in the Revolutionary decades they simply refused to admit the necessity or even propriety of speaking to the fierce democracy— save for the purpose of subduing it.

By contending against "the divine right of kings" and "the divine right of tithes" Liberals may have helped hold the line against these ostensibly resurgent beliefs among their own people. For the great mass of Americans, however, these issues were largely irrelevant, as indeed were many issues which the Liberals raised. Few Americans of the mid-eighteenth century were in any immediate danger of sliding into Catholicism, and even fewer were about to embrace the doctrines of passive obedience and nonresistance, which even Smith confessed "fully exploded."[113] Such matters seemed unworthy of discussion by the only clergyman (at that time a Calvinist) chosen to deliver the Boston Massacre oration; all Americans, he believed, had quite enough sense "to despise the insult which is offered to their understandings, by these doating absurdities."[114] If Lord Chatham can be trusted as a commentator on pre-Revolutionary America, the Liberal clergy spent their energies in tilting at windmills. "Divided as they are into a thousand forms of polity and religion, there is one point in which they all agree," ran Pitt's famous characterization of the American people: "they equally detest the pageantry of a king and the supercilious hypocrisy of a bishop."[115] Chatham viewed America, of course, from a distance that obscured for him the social situation in Boston and Philadelphia. As the subsequent history of these two communities was to prove, creeping Filmerism was an endemic disease of American society—one to which Whigs, it seemed, were hardly more immune than Tories.

Liberal exposition of the social contract helped publicize the natural right of each man to personal freedom. Yet, considering the rationalist interpretation of these ideas and the extent to which the ministry had hedged in giving them practical meaning in colonial society, it is difficult to give them much credit for the universal Lockeanism of 1775. These truths were in no sense the peculiar property of the Liberals. One reason for Joseph Warren's popularity was that he, like other Boston orators, spoke not as an oracle in these matters but as one willing to grant that these were political "truths which common sense has placed beyond the reach of contradiction."[116]

American political theory underwent few changes in the decades before the Revolution; but, as those who have canvassed the sermon literature have pointed out, the ideas were expressed in different accents after 1766. "It is true that not an idea in any sermon but had been presented through an unbroken continuity of nearly a hundred years," Alice Baldwin has observed, "but rarely with such zeal and fire."[117] If the outbreak and success of the Revolution depended on augmented zeal, those who now celebrate American Independence owe but little gratitude to the Liberals. Always more skilled in quenching fires than in igniting them, to the very last they did all they could to dampen the spirit of '75.

Only one New England Liberal came near to welcoming the enthusiasm which the American people poured into the Revolution. He, Henry Cumings of Billerica, was able to celebrate this ardor only because it seemed to him sufficiently restrained by and subordinated to the dictates of sober reason. Cumings was actually something of an anomaly among the rationalist clergy of late eighteenth-century New England and was never accorded a niche in that pantheon of heralds of a liberal faith and society which Federalism, Unitarianism, and Harvard College erected in the early years of the nineteenth century. Cumings not only refused to embrace arch-Federalism, but he numbered outright Jeffersonians among his students and broke with the Liberal Christians of Boston over the doctrine of the atonement and the questionable social uses to which it was put in the metropolis.[118]

Yet Cumings was an Arminian in the 1770's, and that party must be credited with his contributions to the cause of Revolution and its literature. A fervid Whig as early as 1773, Cumings may well have delivered political sermons even before the battle of Lexington, but his thanksgiving sermon of 1775 stands as the first—and solitary—example of a Liberal sermon designed to encourage popular enthusiasm.* Though Cumings was hardly a Demosthenes, his Revolutionary sermons are significant, if not as efforts to arouse the social passions, then as rejoicings in the fact that they had been somehow aroused. For Cumings the spirit of 1775 was an "ardent love of liberty" and its conspicuous glory the manner in which, by spreading through the

---

* Cumings' effort in this direction, rather moderate by comparison to other sermons of the day, consisted of exhortations to emulation of New England's forefathers, whose "grand motive," he declared, "in coming to the uncultivated deserts of America" had been a love of liberty.

colonies, it had inspired Virginia and Massachusetts, Carolina and Connecticut, "to unite as a band of brethren." Unlike other Liberals, Cumings was impressed not simply by the political advantages of an intercolonial league and covenant, but by the fraternal union of the people of America, who, he believed, had been inspired with "one heart and one soul" by this common spirit of liberty.[119] Though he would, quite rightly, have spurned the suggestion, Cumings came dangerously close, in 1775, to embracing the ideals of America's revivalists.

Cumings lacked the extreme social biases which so rudely informed the sermons of William Smith, but like any rationalist he could tolerate exercises of the political emotions only insofar as they were guided by the leading white steed of reason. In 1781, on the anniversary of the battle of Lexington, Cumings delivered a sermon which marked both the height of rationalist acceptance of enthusiasm and its limitations. Discussing the arrangements of Providence for overcoming the mad designs of oppressors and tyrants, Cumings allowed that Britain's own conduct after 1774 had been the very means of inspiring Americans to rise in resistance, "of stirring up a noble spirit of liberty throughout America, and kindling up into a blaze every spark of virtuous patriotism." So aroused had Americans been, Cumings recalled, that these passions had been transported "in some instances, among individuals, into criminal excesses." Having noted these excesses, however, Cumings refused to embark on the customarily elaborate and precise distinctions between liberty and license—and herein lay the difference between the rationalism of 1781 and of earlier decades.

Echoing Mayhew in an assertion that neither religion nor reason "requires the total suppression of the passions," Cumings declared that passions do become "vicious only by their exorbitancy," but, with the wisdom of experience, he observed that passions "may be indulged upon many occasions." When Cumings explained that an advantageous indulgence of the passions depended on their being "tempered with prudence and discretion, and kept within due bounds," he was not treating of the human personality, but of the operations of a whole society.[120] The "more warm and vehement" patriots, he observed, had encouraged those "more cool and sluggish," and the "calm and moderate" had served as "a curb to the more sanguine and hasty." All were balanced by a vital center "tempered with due proportions of zeal and prudence," so that, "by the mutual collision of their different tempers and passions," the American people had been able "to collect their several powers, into one combined and vigorous effort."[121]

Cumings could pass such judgment on the Revolution only because he assumed that Americans had been unanimous as to war aims. Secure in this belief, he was excused from wrestling with the question of true and false enthusiasm, and could celebrate even the most excessive passions of the war years as merely more intense expressions of differing temperaments, not of conflicting desires. If not every American had maintained the proper balance between discretion and emotion, at least the American populace, taken in its entirety, had enacted on the social stage what Liberals had all along contended was requisite to the safety and happiness of mankind.

Even while commemorating the successful outcome of this checking and balancing of the various temperamental orders of American society, however, Cumings offered a conception of the proper management of the social machine which disclosed why no rationalist, however radical he might be, could wholly escape certain prejudices. Though quite aware of the insufficiency of pure reason in politics—"patriotism without feeling or sensibility," he insisted, "is a meer name"—Cumings was actually engaged in a special plea for the enlightened and conservative patriots of America. By 1781 even such Liberals as Cumings were in a sense on the defensive politically, if only to the extent of feeling obliged to defend from popular criticism those members of the patriot party accused of having shown too little enthusiasm in their resistance to tyrants.

In answer to such complaints Cumings explained that some men could feel their country's wrongs and desire its welfare without showing "the same vehement warmth, that will discover itself in a patriot, of a more sanguine and fiery temper." Cumings was willing to admit that both the zealous and the prudent could be useful patriots, but like William Smith he believed that the latter had been the more valuable. The less passionate man, he declared, could not be "betrayed, by a fierce zeal, into imprudent and rash measures," and the mass of Americans had needed and would always "need something to restrain and direct them." Those who through the war had set proper objects before the mind of the people in order to inspire them were, so far as Cumings was concerned, the greatest of orators and preachers; the palm was awarded, not to those who had merely aroused the dormant passions of the people, but to those who had controlled as well as inspired.[122]

Cumings was no apologist for those Americans who had been so very prudent as to retire—to England, to the maritime provinces, or simply to their country estates—from the rude blasts of war; he refused to meddle with the question of receiving returning Tories. But his sermon contained all the essential ingredients of the myth, soon to develop, in which Fisher Ames and Theophilus Parsons would be portrayed as the real patriots of the Revolution. According to this legend—which many far less deserving than Cumings helped to manufacture—the heroes of the entire affair were the Romans of the Continental Congress, a commander in chief who remained, always, sublimely above the stormy passions aroused by the war, and a handful of thoughtful and dispassionate lawyers who wisely avoided military service in order to prepare themselves for concocting the fundamental charters of the new nation.

The Whig interpretation of the Revolution assumes, first of all, that members of the legal profession were instrumental, not merely in developing a case against parliamentary taxation, but in arousing the people of the colonies to revolution. Yet of all the pre-Revolutionary urban lawyers only James Otis—he of "mob-high eloquence"*[123]— and, to a lesser degree, Oxenbridge Thacher in fact brought their forensic talents directly before the public. (Alexander Hamilton's famous plea for protection of King's College and Tory property may, of course, be considered a form of popular eloquence.) The most effective urban agitators were mechanics, physicians, traders—such men as Alexander McDougall, Isaac Sears, William Molineaux, Dr. Thomas Young, and, of course, Sam Adams†[124]—none of whose public performances survive. What evidence is available suggests that those who aroused the Sons of Liberty were much more familiar with the Book of Revelation than with *Coke upon Littleton*. Of all the Boston Massacre orators, moreover, none before 1777 was a lawyer by profession,‡[125] which is not surprising, considering that somewhat more than two thirds of the practicing lawyers of Massachusetts were, by any estimate, advocates for the Crown. Yet by 1785 such younger lawyers as

* Though it is beyond the scope of this study to assess the character of the nonclerical political thought of the Revolution, it might be remarked that even a cursory glance at the writings of Otis suggests how far he was from a "rational" use of the precepts of the social contract. Rather he argues from the general welfare and comes quite close to proclaiming a corporate theory of society.

† A hint of what Adams' principles were taken to be is found in an oration published in 1776, attributed to him but in fact never delivered by anyone. The text has Adams, recalling how his Puritan "Forefathers threw off the Yoke of Popery in Religion," calling on Americans, in the spirit of Cromwell, to inaugurate the "reign of political Protestantism."

‡ The only lawyer of his generation to be chosen a Boston orator was Benjamin Hichborn, a person of such peculiar sentiments that he in 1777 defined "civil liberty" not as " 'a government by laws,' made agreeable to charters, bills of rights or compacts, but a power existing in the people at large, at any time, for any cause, or for no cause, but their own sovereign pleasure, to annihilate both the mode and essence of any former government, and adopt a new one in its stead." Hichborn's post-Revolutionary political career was such that he earned the unenviable reputation (among Boston barristers) of being "a democrat of the old school, and a warm advocate of Jefferson."

George Richards Minot were delivering the annual Fourth of July orations in Boston, and invoking the names of Cicero and Demosthenes, as well as Otis and Thacher, as evidence that lawyers could indeed be patriots.

"Did those orators," asked Benjamin Austin, "become advocates for the enemies of their country?"[126] The same question might well have been asked in Pennsylvania where, by 1778, according to President Joseph Reed, all the lawyers were "in one interest, and that not the popular one."[127] Benjamin Tilghman, the future Chief Justice of Pennsylvania, retired to his country estate in 1775 for much the same purposes as those that led Theophilus Parsons, later the Chief Justice of Massachusetts, to spend the early years of the Revolution in the family manse at Byfield. There Parsons studied law under the eminent Crown Judge, Edmund Trowbridge, who, being "accustomed to consider all questions of right or of conduct, under the light of precedent," had in 1775 moved from Boston to Byfield in order "to escape," in the judicious words of the younger Theophilus Parsons, "the consequences of neutrality in so fierce a struggle that neutrality would have been deemed hostility" to the patriot cause.[128] Similarly Fisher Ames, during these years,

> engaged in no particular business, but dwelt in the family mansion at Dedham, where he must have adorned his mind with those stores of knowledge which enabled him to give such delight to his friends, and render such eminent services to the community.[129]

Yet Parsons and Ames, Minot and Tilghman, along with Timothy Pickering, would come to be enrolled in the "family of Washington"— and, by virtue of that kinship, be permitted to affirm that they had defined and defended the true principles of the Revolution.

By 1780, in fact, the lawyers of the colonies had risen to such eminence that the Liberal clergy nearly found their occupation gone. In the year of the Massachusetts constitution, Simeon Howard, by now returned from Nova Scotia with some of the members of his (and Mayhew's) church, delivered himself of this opinion on liberty:

> The love of liberty is natural to all. It appears the first, operates the most forcibly, and is extinguished the last of any of our passions. And this principle would lead every man to pursue and enjoy everything to which he had an inclination . . . Man is not to be trusted with his unbounded love of liberty, unless it is under some other restraint than what arises from his own reason or the law of God.[130]

The restraints, of course, were provided by the new constitution, of which one of the architects was Theophilus Parsons, author of the

Essex Result. Parsons was a grandson of Charles Chauncy and, no less than he, a prophet of sweet reasonableness. Judging by the *Essex Result,* he was also a partisan of what Backus called a more powerful way of reasoning.

The *Essex Result* was, of course, an argument for constitutional checks and balances in defense of property and in opposition to majority government. Its argument, however, was distinguished by the first premise that the "idea of liberty" had "been held up in so dazzling colours" in recent years that many citizens of Massachusetts seemed unwilling to submit to a necessary "subordination."[131] The same year the *Essex Result* appeared, a lawyer in the western part of the state, lamenting withdrawal of popular confidence "from all those men of parts and learning" who had previously been "invested with any kind of civil office," complained that it had been placed instead "in a set of men who had nothing more to recommend them" than "their high pretensions to zeal in the cause of liberty."[132]

Such demagogues, according to Theophilus Parsons, "fancied a clashing of interest among the various classes" of society and, overcome with such fancies, had "acquired a thirst of power, and a wish of domination, over some of the community."[133] Such were, of course, the Reverend Thomas Allen, the Reverend Nathaniel Whitaker, the Reverend John Murray, and, for that matter, the host of Calvinist ministers who sought enforcement of the Confiscation Act (which, as Chief Justice of Massachusetts, Parsons effectively repealed). Joseph Hawley, who had mystified Thomas Hutchinson by retiring from public life in 1775, when his popularity was at its peak, had no higher opinion of the bright young men who "steered and directed" the Massachusetts Constitutional Convention than Samuel Buell had had of their light, airy, "legalist" predecessors. These "furious importunate and impetuous sticklers for a precipitous establishment of a new constitution" hoped, Hawley declared, to attain "offices and what they figure to themselves as honors."[134] The motives of the same young men in 1787, when they were similarly importunate for the establishment of a Federal Constitution, have only recently again been questioned by those historians who see in Federalism not a conservative but a parvenu impulse.

The question is not whether Ames, Parsons, and Hamilton were more ambitious than those who opposed their constitutional ventures, but why the Revolution should continue to be identified almost exclusively with the principles and policies of either the original proponents of the legal scheme or its latter-day advocates. Somehow, perhaps through their own incessant campaign of self-adulation, America's lawyers managed to create an image of the American past in which the evangelical sources of the revolutionary impulse have been effaced. Surely the spirit of 1775 was not universally one of moderation and calculated assessment of political privileges and rights. Throughout the Revolution the Calvinist clergy rejoiced in the fact that Americans had not entered the contest as "the result of cool and cautious reasoning." They were certain that God was the source of the "military enthusiasm that seized our country, and spread like a rolling flame from colony to colony." But perhaps the planting of Paul and the watering of Apollos once again had something to do with the spirit which Calvinists celebrated as from on high.[135]

Whatever the explanation for what Calvinists called the "happy rashness" of the American people, it seems somewhat inappropriate to identify the Revolution as the cause of Charles Chauncy alone. Undoubtedly many patriots of 1775-1776 agreed with Chauncy that the "affections" had to be closely watched lest men "run into Disorders," but there were others, perhaps the greater number, who followed Edwards in thinking there "can be no suitableness in the exercises of our hearts," unless they "be lively and powerful."[136] As Nathaniel Whitaker observed of Whitefield's life of benevolence and self-sacrifice, "The world may call *zeal* and *fervor* in these things, *madness* and *enthusiasm*."[137] And history is such—or perhaps not history, but the historical mind that would too easily identify rationalism as *the* American tradition—that in viewing the Revolution it tolerates a gale brewed by passion only so long as reason seems securely at the helm.

IX

THE CURSE OF
MEROZ

IN June 1775, Eleazar Wheelock observed that the members of the
New Hampshire militia seemed "to be inspired to a high degree, but
not from on high." Wheelock was one of the few Calvinist ministers
to draw so fine a distinction in that year of Revolutionary grace. Like
Bellamy, he came to grief and perplexity in the course of the Revolution, but for the moment at least he was both witness to and active
participant in one of the more profound spiritual crises in American
history. For two months Wheelock had been speaking and writing of
the "wanton butcheries" of the British troops, and already he had
embarked with fiery zeal on what amounted to a personal vendetta
against the Tories of the upper Connecticut Valley. For years, moreover, he had been telling his parishioners, friends, and students of the
value of "liberty"—not of its advantages merely, but of its "sweetness."[1] In these two themes—British depravity and the blessings of
liberty—were compacted both the doctrines of Revolutionary Calvinism and the source of its rhetorical effectiveness. By expounding
them in 1774-75, nearly to the exclusion of other matters, the evangelical ministry gave its people the opportunity, by resisting a tyrant and
promoting "liberty," to overcome their inability to perceive the excellency of the traditional Calvinist vision.

All of what Calvinism meant by liberty can probably never be com-
prehended, particularly since as early as the 1750's so outstanding a
New Light preacher as Samuel Bird was taking as his theme the
"Sweets of liberty."[2] But something of an entrance to the mind of
Revolutionary Calvinism is provided by the *Two Discourses on Liberty*
delivered in 1774 by Nathaniel Niles. The sermons were delivered in

Newburyport, though Niles himself was a minister of eastern Connecticut. He had attended Princeton during the regime of Samuel Finley and thereafter had studied with Joseph Bellamy. His very presence in Newburyport suggests the degree to which the Revolution, like the Awakening, had its itinerating evangelists, and in this case we may surmise that Niles had been dispatched to proclaim the gospel of liberty as understood by the acknowledged inheritor of Edwards' theological mantle.

Niles began his first sermon by explaining the relationship between liberty and the pursuit of happiness. As he had often explained in his doctrinal sermons, it was absurd to discuss pleasures except in terms of perceptions and sensations:

> When we would learn how anything tends to happiness, we must view it with reference to the taste of the person in whom the happiness is supposed to take place. So, the happy tendency of liberty cannot be seen, unless it be viewed as terminating on some particular disposition in him by whom it is enjoyed.[3]

Niles proceeded to remark that in a state of slavery men are possessed of a "dumb, sullen, morose melancholy" spirit, while, when man is free, his "mind is fortified on all sides, and rendered calm, resolute, and stable." In a state of "perfect liberty," he proclaimed, "a free people will enjoy composure of soul." He then listed the various "fruits of liberty," which included the flourishing of arts, sciences, trade, commerce, husbandry, and "what is infinitely more important," unadulterated Christianity.[4] Liberty was indeed "the grand fountain, under God, of every temporal blessing," but each of these blessings was to be prized, not for itself, but ultimately for its effects on the human mind.

Finally he celebrated the sensations of liberty in strains more than reminiscent of Edwards' effort to describe the effects of grace on the human personality. "The first effects of liberty, on the human mind," Niles explained,

> are calmness, serenity and pleasing hope; and all the various fruits of liberty produce the same happy effects. Thus liberty, first divides itself, as it were, into various streams; which, at length, all meet together again in soothing sensations and sweet emotion of soul . . . How great then must be the collective happiness that a community derives from a state of perfect freedom.

Thus "slavery," for Niles, was a state of inactivity and anxiety, and liberty one of joy—a joy derived not from one's personal freedom, but from living in a community having "such a system of laws, as effectually tends to the greatest felicity of a state." Niles, to be sure, went on to assert that the sinful man could not "extract and taste all the sweets of liberty." A "free spirit," he insisted, "a spirit that seeks the highest good of the community," was the only being who would "experience all the pleasures of liberty."[5] What Niles was doing, quite evidently, was urging his auditors to press into the Kingdom (or, in earthly terms, out of one), and promising them the joys of regeneration in their moment of acting to bring heaven to earth.

In celebrating the "happy effects" of liberty, Niles was not thinking of the joys of personal acquisition, but of the delights of fellowship and the benevolent union of kindred minds. Other Calvinists made the same point in other ways, and underlined it by distinguishing in their sermons between "American freedom" and "English liberty." Levi Hart, for instance, in the course of defining various kinds of liberty, proposed that the only possible meaning of the "glorious liberty of the sons of God" was not the right, but the privilege, of uniting "in the same honourable cause." To them, he continued,

> there is neither Barbarian, Scythian, Greek, or Jew, bond or free, they are all one, in one cause, and pursue it animated by one spirit; they feel how good and pleasant it is for brethren to dwell together in unity.[6]

Precisely such a situation would, according to Niles, prevail in a state of "perfect liberty," the pleasures of which condition he described in this ecstatic expression of the consummation to which the mind of Calvinism had been tending for thirty years:

> Let us then, for once, imagine a state whose members are all of a free spirit; and then attend to the glory and pleasures of liberty. The individuals are all of one mind. They unite in the same grand pursuit, the highest good of the whole . . . The good of the body will be their first aim . . . In these circumstances, there would be no room for the emotions of any of the angry painful passions; but, on the contrary, every soft and pleasing affection of every soul, would be called forth into pleasing exercise. Every individual would choose to move in his proper sphere, and that all others should move in theirs. This would at once constitute pure felicity, and exalted beauty. How *good* and how pleasant it is for brethren to dwell together in unity.[7]

Niles's state of "perfect liberty" was, to be exact, the state of millennial felicity, the happy fellowship of the heavenly saints established on earth.

What is striking about Niles's sermon is that he acknowledged how the morose and melancholy spirit of Americans was only in part due to their not enjoying perfect freedom—and then went on to suggest that they might experience the ample joys of the new birth by removing their external burdens. To understand the inner logic of Niles's sermon, as well as the existential sources of the evangelical revolutionary impulse, it is necessary to consider the sources of the Calvinist definition of liberty. It was derived neither from Locke nor Montesquieu, Harrington nor Sidney, but from Jonathan Edwards' *Careful and Strict Enquiry into the Modern Prevailing Notions of that Freedom of Will, Which is Supposed to be Essential to Moral Agency.* This treatise, so often maligned as the last desperate effort of the Calvinist mind to preserve fatalism and man's passivity, was actually the Calvinist handbook of the Revolution. More than half of Levi Hart's patriot sermon of 1774 was a recapitulation of the postulates of *Freedom of Will,* and they made their appearance in nearly every Calvinist sermon of the era, most particularly Nathaniel Whitaker's fiery invocations of the "Curse of Meroz." Edwards' doctrines, as employed in such sermons, are another reminder that the essence of Calvinism was not passivity but action.

To the Revolutionary Calvinist, the crucial precept of Edwards' *Freedom of Will* was his definition of liberty as "the ability to act as one chooses." Man is perfectly free, "according to the primary and common notion of freedom," Edwards observed, where "there is nothing in the way to hinder his pursuing and executing his will." What concerned Edwards was man's "moral ability," which consisted in having such internal dispositions as would lead him to do the will of God. The "glorified saints," Edwards observed, "have not their freedom at all diminished in any respect," because they act "in the most excellent and happy manner" from "the necessary perfection" of their internal nature.[8] The saint in heaven, as Nathaniel Niles explained in 1774, "will never be required to do any thing irksome or disagreeable, because his heart will spontaneously choose to do, whatever his sovereign will choose to command."[9] The political arrangements of such a society stood in judgment on those of pre-Revolutionary America: "The law of this nation," Edwards proclaimed, "is a law of liberty."[10]

Liberty, for Edwards as for John Winthrop, was an opportunity to act morally, while Arminian liberty, which allowed man's will to operate independently of his understanding, was "a full and perfect freedom and liableness to act altogether at random" without the "restraint or government" of anything perceived or viewed "by the understanding." The common notion of liberty, Edwards declared,

is some dignity or privilege, something worth claiming. But what dignity or privilege is there in being given up to such a wild Contingence as this, to be perfectly and constantly liable to act un-

457

reasonably, and as much without the guidance of understanding, as if we had none, and were as destitute of perception as the smoke that is driven by the wind![11]

What Edwards did not ask—for the question was beyond the purview of his concern—was what would happen if a body of men, glorified saints or no, were prevented, by some external restraint, from exercising their wills as their perceptions dictated. The answer was implicit, of course, in the very terms of Edwards' argument, for his entire discussion of what made actions "worthy of praise or blame" began by assuming men to be perfectly free of external restraint—free from such imperfect "physical liberty" as broken arms, and free from such compulsion as limited their "natural liberty." And precisely this the Calvinist ministry of the Revolutionary decade assumed to be Edwards' meaning. If men were to be wholly free to do the will of God—to do that which was good, just, and honest—"natural liberty" was an absolute necessity.

Throughout the second half of the century the Calvinist ministry confronted the possibility that the American populace, taking the Edwardean definition of liberty perhaps too literally, would seek to remove all external hindrances to their action. If one may credit the observations of the Protestant clergy—Calvinists no less than Liberals—colonial Americans were, by and large, political anarchists. As Edwards observed in his treatise *Will*, the "common people" had a "notion of liberty" as "a person's having opportunity of doing as he pleases,"[12] and in 1773 Isaac Backus, noting that the same popular notion still prevailed, went on to remark that any and all government "in the imagination of many, interferes with such liberty."[13] In the imagination of the Liberal ministry, Edwards and his successors were responsible for filling the common people with such notions, but as David Jones reminded the Baptists of Pennsylvania (shortly after the battle of Lexington), no Calvinist minister was, or ever had been, a "friend to anarchy."[14]

Within Calvinism there was, to be sure, more than a bit of the ultimate antinomian rejection of social and political compulsion as obscuring the moral visage of the church. Calvinist hostility to establishments, to "External Force" (Tennent called it *"Club-law"*) in matters of religion was, in fact, an objection to making men "accomplished hypocrites" by forcing them to "an outward compliance," rather than allowing behavior that was morally significant because voluntarily performed.[15] In the thirty years before the Revolution, Calvinists refused to apply this insight to affairs of civil government, but rather argued that the sinful dispositions of mankind require some restraint. *"Religion* is one thing, and human *society* is another," Tennent explained. It is no "matter to the state," whether its laws be obeyed freely or not; but within the church, he insisted, decisions must proceed "from love and choice" and "cannot be forced by outward violence."[16] In the course of the controversy with England, some Calvinists would continue to point out that "without law, which cements and binds" society, man's social arrangements would betray nought but "endless disorder and confusion."[17] Three weeks before the Declaration of Independence the General Association of Connecticut, remarking "a disposition to anarchy" among the citizens of that state, called on all to bow to "lawful and necessary restraint."[18] By 1783 some Calvinists would have improved this exhortation into an argument for club-law in church as well as state, but in 1775 the doctrines of Edwards and Tennent provided compelling arguments, if not for total social and political liberty, then at least for casting off the feudal law as well as the canon law.

For thirty and more years Calvinists had been urging men to leave or replace institutions that denied them "the greater good," and in the context of the 1770's this great tradition came to mean liberty from English law—in order, presumably, to come under the far more demanding, but not externally coercive, law of love. Ever since the 1740's some Calvinists had been defining liberty as "freedom from any superior Power on earth, and not being under the Will or legislative Authority of Man." They insisted, however, that such liberty was not a freedom for every one "to do what he pleased without regard to any Law," but rather a Christian liberty of having "the law of Nature (or in other Words, of its Maker) for his Rule."[19] What happened in the Revolutionary decade was that the law of nature—the "royal law of the Gospel"—became identified as the "law of liberty" as well as the law of love. Technically the law of liberty was not inconsistent with the moral law of Bellamy, nor even with the Edwardean reading of the law written in the nature of things. The "only perfect law of liberty," as Isaac Backus explained, was the will of God as revealed by Jonathan Edwards:

The true liberty of man is, to know, obey and enjoy his Creator, and to do all the good unto, and enjoy all the happiness with and in his fellow creatures that he is capable of; in order to which the law of love was written in his heart, which carries in it's nature union and benevolence to Being in general, and to each being in particular, according to it's nature and excellency, and to it's relation and connexion with the supreme Being, and ourselves. Each rational soul, as he is part of the whole system of rational beings, so it was and is, both his duty and his liberty, to regard the good of the whole in all his actions.[20]

459

Given such a definition of the law of liberty, it is not difficult to account for the Calvinist enthusiasm for liberty. All the sermons of the 1770's bespeak a pervading sense of the difference between desire and opportunity—and, indeed, of a spirit of readiness, of hammers drawn back:

> LIBERTY may be defined in general, *a power of action,* or a certain suitableness or preparedness for exertion, and a freedom from force, or hindrance from any external cause. *Liberty* when predicated of man as a moral agent, and accountable creature, is that suitableness or preparedness to be the subject of volitions, or exercises of will, with reference to moral objects; by the influence of motives, which we find belongeth to all men of common capacity, and who are come to the years of understanding.[21]

George III's attempt "to bind us in all cases whatsoever," according to Isaac Backus' recollections of the spirit of 1775, was intended to deprive Americans "both of manhood and Christianity," and had he succeeded they would no longer have been "governed by reason and Revelation," but by an external, arbitrary coercion.[22] Evangelical Americans were prepared, in brief, to throw off an unbearable yoke that they might have the opportunity to act in a manner which they, and perhaps they alone of all the people of the world, knew to be moral.

In his comments on the Declaration of Independence, Backus explained why the "greatest writer against a self-determining power in man, that our age has seen," would have had no difficulty in accounting for the failure of Pharaoh's "attempts to hold Israel in bondage," or George III's efforts to make "slaves" of the Americans. We can, Backus observed, "as easily put an end to our existence, as we can keep from choosing what we at present view or imagine to be best."[23] What Americans in 1775 imagined to be best differed not so much from colony to colony as from individual to individual. To many the Revolution seemed a heaven-sent opportunity for the people of the New World to express and declare their love for one another and for their benevolent union. Nearly all, it would seem, committed their hearts and wills to the cause of liberty without, as it were, being at the trouble of a train of reasoning.

"Liberty," however, was but one theme of Calvinist sermons in the decade between the Stamp Act and the battle of Lexington. Another was the depravity of England—its administration, aristocracy, and social temper—and, eventually, the "tyrannical" disposition of the anti-Christian British monarch. The outlines of such thinking—together with its imperatives—were sketched as early as 1765, when

Stephen Johnson, in the only Connecticut Fast Day sermon to be published, offered this explanation of the Stamp Act:

> As to the contrivers and authors of such oppressions, a most venal, covetous and arbitrary spirit of lawless ambition, is generally the accursed spring and incentive of this great wickedness. And what is the tendency of their slavish measures, carried into execution, but to add fuel to ungodly lusts; to inflame their avarice, pride, and arbitrary, boundless ambition; to plunge them into all manner of unrighteousness and oppression, debauchery, and wickedness.

Then Johnson went on to describe what acts the British administration—which had not yet "filled up the measure of its iniquity"—might be expected to commit in the future should the Stamp Act remain enforced. If "a proud, arbitrary, selfish and venal spirit of corruption, should ever reign in the British Court," Johnson predicted, there would be "left to the colonies but this single, this dreadful alternative —slavery or independency." In such a situation, he declared, Americans "will not want time to deliberate which to choose."[24]

The year of the Townshend duties, 1770, saw Johnson, as Connecticut election preacher, declaring his expectations of 1765 nearly fulfilled. Professing bewilderment over the sudden need for new revenue, Johnson explained to the Connecticut General Assembly that states are often bankrupted when "idle drones" are supported in a civil list.[25] By the spring of 1775 it was common knowledge in Calvinist circles that the "vast unnecessary expenses" of the British government had been brought about by the "enormous vices," the "waste and profligacy," of the "numberless officers," the "devouring servants," and "the avaricious courtiers of Great Britain, with their numerous train of needy dependants and hangers on, with a whole tribe of dissolute spendthrifts, and idle deboshees [sic]" surrounding the King, all of them engaged in "pursuit of pleasure and the boundless luxuries of life."[26] Perceiving "titles of dignity without virtue" and "vast public treasures continually lavished in corruption," President Langdon concluded that the British constitution (which as recently as 1769 had seemed a "happy and excellent" one to many Calvinists, and, for all, at least infinitely superior to "*Popish tyranny* and *vassalage*") was the "mere shadow" of the "ancient political system" in which loyal Americans once had gloried. The "general prevalence of vice," Langdon explained, "has changed the whole face of things in the British government."[27]

Such a view of British character was as old as the Great Awakening, and probably much older. But coupled as it now was with the question of the British constitution, it inspired several proposals for political action, some of which were clearly more come-outer in spirit than truly revolutionary. In 1773, for instance, Sam Adams' friend Charles Turner told an audience at Plymouth that their forefathers had come to this wilderness

> to remove their children, their posterity, from the snares, oppressions, and corruptions of the old world; which, however, have been permitted to follow them hither, like *a flood of waters, cast forth out of the dragon's mouth*.[28]

What Turner had in mind, quite clearly, was that the vices rampant in Britain were not unknown in his America, most particularly not in Boston. He acknowledged the "christian piety and holiness" of many New Englanders, and did not want to "exaggerate the degeneracy of the times." But he confessed himself

> unable to point out a country, founded in oeconomy industry frugality and temperance, that has arrived to such a degree of luxury, in so short a time as ours.

Then, as earlier in the year before the General Court, Turner proposed that possibly all the province's vices could be overcome if only her "*intaminating* connections" with England were severed, thus depriving the nabobs of the metropolis of, among other things, their most visible means of support.[29]

Such a proposition underlay the Calvinist flirtation, in the years of the Revolution, with what was in effect an anticipation of the philosophy of the Embargo and the American system. The "inglorious" importation of "luxury" and "tyranny" in fact inspired many Americans, including David Rittenhouse, to express the wish "that nature would raise her everlasting bars between the new and old world; and make a voyage to Europe as impracticable as one to the moon."[30] Such thoughts seemed most appealing, however, to young men like John Trumbull, who, already a budding poet in 1770, bewailed in his Yale commencement address of that year the degree to which the "effeminate manners" of Britain were coming to infect the colonies.[31] In such minds, participants as it were in some of the very changes in American society that were being condemned, the thought of separation clearly bespoke a desire to place temptation beyond reach.

II

So alluringly easy a solution to America's woes was not, however, characteristic of the Calvinist ministry generally. Throughout the Revolution they would ardently advocate American manufactures (Nathaniel Whitaker personally operated a gunpowder factory) both as a necessity of the times and as a guarantor of America's future economic and social independence. But in the 1770's, faced by the threat of moral declension within America, their answer was to demand of their people the most energetic acts of will. In part—but only in part —they embraced Sam Adams' formula:

> The Salvation of our Souls is interested in the Event: For wherever Tyranny is establish'd, Immorality comes in like a Torrent. It is in the Interest of Tyrants to reduce the People to Ignorance and Vice . . . those who are combin'd to destroy the People's Liberties, practise every art to poison their Morals. How greatly then does it concern us, at all Events, to put a Stop to the Progress of Tyranny.[32]

Evangelical thought and rhetoric stressed the consanguinity of the American temper with the selfishness that seemed inherent in the very nature of "predatory government." Its first premise was that the will of man is most readily activated when he is persuaded that he is falling short of the glory of God—and that by such action he might work out not society's salvation only, but his own.

The Calvinist clergy were in fact among the first to insist that Americans might within their "own breasts discover a disposition to" the very "covetousness" for which they upbraided the Crown and its representatives.[33] "Oppression, over-reaching, usurious contracts," along with "foppery," declared Ebenezer Chaplin in 1773: "all these things" —the "very same things we are complaining of at this day in the civil administration"—might be found, either actively or latently, in every *American* heart.[34] This irony of calling on sinners to oppose sin (or rather, not irony, but by now one of the more traditional configurations of American thought) contributed to the effectiveness of pre-Revolutionary Calvinist preaching. In the larger perspective, it revealed the degree to which the patriot crusade was mounted by Calvinism as a means of exorcising from America, not merely sinners, but the sinful spirit of selfishness itself.

The revival of the 1770's was encouraged, however, by the discovery that the enemies of American liberty were especially and profoundly sinful. The makers and movers of imperial policy, it was argued by Calvinists, were no mere indolent debauchees. In fact, after 1770 a somewhat Manichaean tone began to characterize evangelical statements on public affairs—an implication, if seldom a direct assertion, that the British ministry and Parliament were active and sedulous promoters of evil:

> O what an evil is this! But to do it with both hands, namely, with all their princely power, arbitrary authority, and united strength, this is dreadful indeed; but to do this evil *earnestly* as tho their heart was set upon it with all the intentness of desire . . . What, are

their hearts adamant? their breasts brass? their nature iron? What, can nothing awaken them?[35]

As in the 1750's, when "envy" first rose in the breasts of the Connecticut people of God, so now did they have a partial explanation, at least, for history's rising to midnight darkness.

Meanwhile election preachers introduced new emphases into their discussions of the good ruler. In 1767 a typical Calvinist utterance on this topic was that "Christ directs and regulates Rulers in their Duty" and "expects and requires that they have a principal view at his Glory." Of course, rulers must, it was observed, "exercise their authority for the Good of the Ruled,"[36] but two years later the Connecticut legislature was informed that civil government is

> not ordained for the honour and glory, the aggrandisement or enriching of rulers themselves, or for their private emolument and advantage, but for the benefit of the people; it being a maxim in which all have concurred, *Salus populi suprema Lex est.*

Instead "of being swelled and puffed up with their grandeur, and serving their own private ends," the election preacher observed, princes ought "to answer the important ends of their betrustment."[37]

All this was fairly standard doctrine, except that in Calvinist sermons such statements were not merely doctrine but exhortation. The 1769 Connecticut election preacher was an Old Light, who, having devoted several pages of his sermon to a description of "the fruits of unbridled rule," carefully observed that such tyranny existed in *"other countries,"* chiefly "Popish," but not in Britain or its empire. He did acknowledge that the British government itself had lately shown an alarming disposition to "stretches of *ministerial* power." But, he contended, this was cause neither for murmur nor complaint; it simply was a charge on the General Assembly to do all it could to resist encroachments on the colony's "essential rights and liberties."[38] After 1770, Old Lights and New were able to agree—if on nothing else—that the British administration was depraved, but it was the more strictly Calvinist clergy that openly called on all Americans, as private individuals, to resist violations of the laws of nature, love, and liberty.

The Calvinist definition of tyranny came to include anyone who, in his public actions, failed to fulfill the high standard of the Edwardean moral law. When anyone uses his "public power in any other way than by *love to serve one another*," it was urged, "he makes himself a tyrant, and acts a part, inconsistent at least with christian liberty." Herein was the touchstone by which to judge British policy: "when any laws are enacted which cross the law of nature, there civil liberty is invaded, and God and man justly offended."[39] Nor were such sentiments expressed merely on election days; in 1773 and 1774 the doctrine and its corollary were expounded from local pulpits and to such self-constituted bodies as militia companies and "minute-Men."

After the Boston Massacre, the dark features of tyranny were ever more graphically portrayed. In Calvinist sermons, however, the issue was always drawn finally on the question of the sin of a ruler's selfishness. In 1773, for instance, Charles Turner informed both the Massachusetts General Court and the people of Plymouth:

> That the civil ruler, and christian minister, should engross the wealth of the world to themselves, *as* they have done in many countries and ages, and live in pride and luxury, on spoils violently extorted, or slily drained from the people is altogether foreign to the design of God, in setting them up.[40]

In the same year Benjamin Trumbull advised the citizens of New Haven that rulers ought not to coil "themselves up in their own dirty shell" by making "self the grand end of all their pursuits."[41] In May 1774, Levi Hart asked the freemen of Farmington what "epithets of lasting infamy" were "black enough to draw the picture of the inhuman parricide, who basks in the glare of riches and grandeur, at the expense of the public welfare."[42] And in the winter of 1774-75, throughout Massachusetts, evangelical congregations, militia, and the multitude generally were being reminded that if a "Prince" should in any way oppose, or fail to serve, the welfare of "the whole body," his "sin" against the law of nature would be most "highly aggravated."[43]

Meanwhile, as early as 1765 Calvinist ministers had converted the moral law into an argument for the body of the people acting, with or without the guidance of their elected representatives and not necessarily through them, to "redress public grievances." Such action was proclaimed not a right merely, but a duty—a "duty to God and religion, to themselves, to the community."[44] Over the next decade scores of Calvinist preachers made the same point and—like Hermon Husband during the Regulator insurgency—domesticated the theme of James Murray's *Sermons to Asses:* a failure to act was itself evidence of moral shortcoming.[45] Gradually but with increasing celerity, then, the laws of love and liberty were translated into an imperative to active resistance. Rulers who were "inconsistent with liberty" were to be "detested and opposed with firmness." And what was liberty? It was the perfection of social good, a public happiness and virtue that could be achieved, it seemed, only by Americans resisting a "tyrant" who would deny them their "common happiness."[46]

Like any pre-revolutionary arguments, such sentiments betrayed a certain imprecision of thought and confused circularity. An "arbitrary despotic power in a Prince," declared the author of the *Beauties of Liberty*, was, because contrary to the "happiness" of society, to be "feared, abhorred, detested and destroyed."[47] So was all sin inconsistent with social felicity, and here precisely was *the* imperative to revolution. The great Christian virtue could be fulfilled, or at least displayed, through "irreconcilable disgust to arbitrary measures," and in endeavors devoted to the overthrow of "tyranny—the illegitimate offspring of pride."[48] Somehow Americans could prove their moral right to freedom by pursuing a general welfare which the government of Britain seemed woefully disposed to deny.

Between 1770 and 1775, moreover, it was the Calvinist exhorters, and they alone among the colonial clergy, who sought to inspire Americans—all Americans—with what was called "a high relish" for the "national felicity" of the colonies. Their premise was not the unconstitutionality of taxes merely, nor even the venality of the British administration; rather Calvinists were pointing toward a new concept of the nature and sources of the general welfare. Addressing those whom he called his "dear associates in life, and friends of liberty," the author of the *Beauties of Liberty* told New Englanders that

> the natural body is only in health, and vigour, when every organ is disposed to act its part. So the body politic can only be in health, and prosper, when every member unites regularly, and ardently, to preserve the privileges of the whole.[49]

The "privileges" of which he spoke, and the "encroachments" which Americans were called on in these years to resist, were not the immunities of British citizens nor the errant policies of a misguided Parliament. To the Calvinist mind, the crusade for "American freedom" and against the "tyranny" of the Crown was, finally, no less than a common pursuit of the "common happiness." The resistance to Britain, in sum, was an opportunity both for revitalizing and giving new meaning to what for thirty and more years had been the social goals of the evangelical scheme.

Of the pre-Revolutionary Calvinist sermons, two at least deserve particular consideration, revealing as they do something of the existential sources of the revolutionary impulse. One is the 1773 sermon by Ebenezer Chaplin, already mentioned as one in which the social good was defined ultimately in the Edwardean terms of a "harmony" like that shadowed forth in nature. Chaplin's title disclosed another of his legacies from the typological and metaphorical world of the Awakening: *The Civil State Compared to Rivers, All Under God's Controul, and What People Have to do When Administration is Grievous.*

Chaplin's sermon contained a thought characteristic of the Calvinism of the 1770's:*[50] "there are many bitter things in the stream of *civil* administration, that we are very loath to drink." For this distasteful water Chaplin had also a common explanation: "the multitude of placemen" in the British administration had embittered the streams of government. "The springs and streams must be mended," he insisted, "before the great river is likely to be pure." The question was how to purify the waters, and the answer lay in what Chaplin conceived to be the sources of the civil waters. The people, he insisted, were the spring and fountain of all the "multitude of branches and springs" which make up the power and administration of civil society. If the water which flows from them and toward the magistrate returns embittered, it is not merely the fault of placemen, but of the people, whose sins pollute the whole society.

What then was Chaplin's improvement of so curious a doctrine? In normal times, Chaplin observed, all the streams of society run smoothly; they are "gentle, easy and delightsome." At other times, however, the streams become "rapid; then all becomes noise and roaring, foaming, and confusion." Such sublimely cascading streams, he concluded, are very useful to society, for they "stir up people; and by the severe schools of such tryals, they are brought to understand the nature of society, and the genuine common rights of mankind." The imperial crisis, like Calvinist rhetoric itself, was designed to rouse the populace from their chiefest sin: a lack of "concern" for the community. By making them thereby more "serviceable to the great ends of the community,"[51] the very agitation of the times, whoever its author, would recall Americans to what had been and should be the first love of God's people. By attending to matters of common concern, they would be purged of the covetousness, pride, and selfishness that had allowed them to neglect the great and last end of God's creation of both the universe and civil society.

Another notable sermon was the second of the *Two Discourses on Liberty,* in which Nathaniel Niles applied his doctrine of the sweet and happy effects of liberty and union directly to the question of civil government. "When we see the body of a community plundered," Niles explained,

> for the sake of indulging individuals in pride, luxury, idleness and debauchery,—when we see thousands rewarded with pensions, or having either devised, or attempted to execute some scheme for

---

* In the same year Charles Turner observed that too many people in high places in Massachusetts government and society called "that by the name of *light,* which the people rationally perceive to be *darkness;* and give that the denomination of *sweetness,* which the people know to be *bitter.*"

plundering a nation, and establishing despotism, we cannot be in doubt whether some horrid attack is made on liberty.[52]

But Americans, he continued, should neither revel in the prospect of such sinners receiving final damnation at the hands of God, nor, especially, console themselves with their comparatively saintly way of life. We too, he insisted, have forgotten the beauty of spiritual and divine things, and "it is high time for us to reform." In what reformation consisted was not so important, in the spring of 1774, as the absolute obligation of all to exert themselves to the utmost:

> Ages are composed of seconds, the earth of sands, and the sea of drops, too small to be seen by the naked eye. The smallest particles have their influence. Such is our state, that each individual has a proportion of influence on some neighbour at least; he, on another, and so on; as in a river, the following drop urges on that which is before, and every one through the whole length of the stream has the like influence. We know not, what individuals may do. We are not at liberty to lie dormant until we can, at once, influence the whole. We must begin with the weight we have.[53]

Perhaps because the Calvinist populace of New England was convinced of these truths, all the streams and rivers came hurtling down in the spring of 1775.

In any case, Calvinist preachers sought to engage their people's wills on behalf of liberty and their "country," not by flattering them as to their peculiar virtue, but by insisting that any one who would not defend his "birthright" of freedom must himself be a violator of the law of nature. Their sermons all followed a similar pattern, one which began with pointing to the least "infringement" of "American freedom" as a violation of the "first law of nature," and ended with a proclamation of the obligation of all men to remedy such a situation.[54] What this involved is suggested by the sermon *The Love of Country* delivered on Thanksgiving Day of 1774 by the uncle of Joseph Story:

> As to the duty, it is founded on the grand law of love. The command is, thou shalt love thy neighbour as thyself . . . and that shall prompt thee to wish his welfare and pursue it, as opportunities permit, and his needs and circumstances shall require . . . If this be our love to an individual, how great must be our regard to a community. If we are to love a neighbour *as* ourselves, we ought to love the public *better* than self. And, of consequence, we ought to be ready, when the exigencies of the State require it, to expose our reputation, our interest, and our lives for its good.[55]

Such a definition of patriotism permitted, in the context of the 1770's, at least a temporary mediation between the disparate branches into which Edwardean theology was flowing. Endeavor so selfless was consistent both with Bellamy's gospel, which called on men to exert their wills in order to prove their benevolence, and with the scheme that Samuel Hopkins was slowly developing, in which the nature of true benevolence would be defined as a willingness to be damned, if necessary, to satisfy the needs of Being in general. Hopkins' argument seemed to imply the total passivity of man, to the point where ministers and people alike became perplexed over the age-old dilemma of Calvinism: "Why had he not Just as good lie still and do nothing?"[56] After the Revolution, such questions would be given new and vital theological answers, but in the 1770's one solution, at least, to psychological torment was self-sacrificing patriotism, in which the active engagement of the will seemed not inconsistent with the most selfless commitment to the general good.

Patriotism was also a confutation of all who, from whatever theological perspective, saw the people of New England as declining from an earlier virtue, piety, and zeal. In a sense, the Calvinist definition of patriotism, as it emerged in 1774-75, was an effort to avoid and undo the perplexities into which Samuel Davies had fallen in the Seven Years' War. No sentiment expressed in the Revolutionary years was wholly inconsistent with the Edwardean definition of charity. In 1771 Mark Leavenworth delivered a sermon, the doctrines and language of which suggest he may have had access to Edwards' as yet unpublished sermons, *Charity and Its Fruits*. There Leavenworth recommended charity as the only internal principle that could truly "actuate" men to "pursue the Public Good" with overwhelming "Force and Alacrity." Nothing else, he insisted, would so effectively

> engage and dispose us to love our Neighbour as ourselves, to pursue the public Happiness as our own, and greatly to deny ourselves, from a Generous and Ardent Desire to promote the Good of Mankind.[57]

Where later sermons differed was, first, in the note of impending martyrdom, even of atonement. Not unexpectedly, in the sermons of 1774 likeness to God became no mere weeping over Jerusalem but a readiness to die on behalf of the community. "We, and all we have, belong to the community," Niles for one affirmed. "Whenever the common cause requires it, we should, like Paul, be ready to lay down our lives for the brethren."[58] What such sermons also assumed is that the requirements of the common cause were to be rejoiced in as a means by which men might either prove their pretensions sincere or even discover within themselves a disposition to benevolence that they till then had suspected was missing.

The clarity with which it was explained that self-sacrificing action on behalf of the community could not in any case be a violation of the moral law but, more likely, evidence of its fulfillment is possibly not unrelated to the events that transpired at Lexington and Concord in the spring of 1775. In any case, the minutemen of Massachusetts were on more than one occasion reminded of how an opportunity might soon present itself in which they could prove, by experiment and trial, whether they possessed a proper spirit. Joseph Hawley did it in terms, not merely of the Edwardean definition of true virtue, but of the "piety" and "zeal" of New England's forefathers:

> I have no inclination to raise your vanity as if men inherited all the good qualities of their progenitors; or if valor was hereditary. You will show by your future conduct whether you are worthy to be called offspring of such men.[59]

The formula of the jeremiad, properly employed, drove resolutely to the same conclusion as the more directly exhortatory Calvinist sermons. For in these years the evangelical ministry, whenever they touched on New England's history, called on their people, not to preserve the institutions[*][60] of their forefathers, but to seize whatever opportunity offered itself to emulate their "zeal and virtue."[61]

What was needed, of course, was an opportunity in which such zeal and virtue could be displayed and not left open to question. The raw nerves of the people of God were revealed already in the spring of 1774, when one preacher, observing that Britons "stigmatize us with the opprobrious names of hipocrites and enthusiasts," suggested that the evangelical populace simply accept the designation given them by such scoffers: "saints."[62] But this, he observed, merely revealed the

---

* This distinction is of some importance, not only as it was inherited from the seventeenth century, but as a legacy of eighteenth-century Calvinism to the Fourth of July oratory of later years. In the 1770's the Old Light ministry recalled their "noble ancestors" as one means of identifying the patriot cause with defense of the New England way. Their concern was with a heritage to be preserved—a heritage which for these Jeremiahs generally included, quite explicitly, the Half-Way Covenant. Such Jeremiahs were following a formula developed in the era of Increase Mather and employed by his son in the *Magnalia* and elsewhere. But just as Cotton Mather on many occasions sought to rekindle the "piety" of his forebears among the people of his day, so too did Calvinists in the 1770's speak, not of the institutions nor even of the liberties of the Puritans, but of their "integrity and uprightness." Similarly in the period after the Revolution, when the patriots of 1775 and 1776 became the paradigms of civic virtue, Democrats would call on Americans to recapture the spirit of '76, Whigs to preserve the constitutional rights for which the Revolution was presumably fought.

true character of those who reviled Americans and did not necessarily guarantee the virtue of the people of New England.[63] On the anniversary of the Massacre, Parsons did explain what circumstances might allow them to express a spirit of Christian benevolence. And Bellamy, of course, assumed these circumstances had arrived when he expounded "The Curse of Meroz" to Putnam's troops, reminding them, presumably, of the beautiful consistency of vindictive justice with divine benevolence: "Love itself is a consuming fire with respect to sin."[64]

On March 5, 1775, a Calvinist exhorter, after discussing at some length "the influence of minions, and court parasites" and the prostitution of authority in England to the "iniquitous, and low purpose of aggrandizing individuals, instead of the good of the whole," proceeded to rehearse the horrors of the Boston Massacre.[65] Nor was he alone among the preachers, patriarchs as well as youths, who on this day recalled to mind the sum of British depravity. The atmosphere in the late winter and early spring of 1774-1775 is well described (allowing for a language and perspective that hardly does justice to the evangelical creed and crusade) by Peter Oliver:

> Boys who had just thrown away their satchels and who could scarcely read English mounted the pulpit and ventured to decide on matters which had puzzled the sages of the law. Nay they could not be contented to decide controversies of law, in their harangues to the Supreme Being, telling him who had been guilty of murder where the law had pronounced the supposed crime to be only self-defense, and some of them even debased the sacred character, by setting on the rabble in the public streets, to insult a person who was obnoxious to the leaders of the mob.[66]

But it was not just the rabble that such sermons set on, nor was the target merely a Tory gentleman or two. "Awake, arise, and stand for your life," was the exhortation to all "Americans":

> You have a grant to so do, against all that *assault* you, from the King of Heaven; from NATURE and from NATURE's GOD.[67]

In the same month, March of 1775, John Adams was busy composing and preparing for publication his "Novanglus" essays, in one of which he sought to explain why the friends of American liberty had adopted recently a less legalistic argument against British policy:

> If the people are capable of understanding, seeing, and feeling the difference between true and false, right and wrong, virtue and vice, to what better principle can the friends of mankind apply, than to this sense of the difference?[68]

Adams would live to hear the friends of mankind appeal to the popular sense of a difference between virtue and vice in a context which led him to doubt the propriety of such "political warfare," but in April of 1775 his justification of American political rhetoric was cut short by the firing of the shot heard round the world.

Adams might have anticipated such consequences of the moral approach to public affairs, for it was he who in the autumn of 1774 had furtively circulated among the members of the Continental Congress the celebrated "Broken Hints" of Joseph Hawley. Disposing of the various iniquities of the British administration in a few words, Hawley set the controversy in a light which any evangelical American would understand: "It is evil against right." Yet of all the members of the Congress (many of whom were appalled by these observations) only one, according to Adams, spontaneously and in a "rapturous burst of approbation" responded to Hawley's hints: "By God," Patrick Henry exclaimed, "I am of that man's mind!" And Hawley's opening words, of course, were, "We must *fight*."[69]

Commemorating the battle of Lexington in 1776, Jonas Clark, in a sermon entitled *The Fate of Blood-Thirsty Oppressors, and God's Tender Care of his Distressed People,* confessed himself unequal to a description of "the distress, the *horror* of that *awful morn.*" He was certain, however, that the first shot was not fired by any citizen of the colonies and that the battle was, indeed, wholly unprovoked. Farmers and villagers, he insisted, had been cut down, "not by the sword of an open enemy," but by the hands of those who took such great delight in shedding "innocent blood" that they acted with a "cruelty and barbarity, which would have made the most hardened savage blush."[70] Within months of the engagement, in fact, Calvinists had a common account of the events of the ever-memorable nineteenth of April. "That the *Lexington* battle was *begun* by the *British* troops," one of them explained on July 20, "is what with us admits of *no* doubt."[71]

Already, on May 31, however, Samuel Langdon (the first to have heard and circulated Whitefield's report of the British "plot") had proposed that the minutemen had had at least as much right to fire first (albeit they didn't) as any man who, under terror of instant death, kills another who was armed "to commit a robbery."[72] By 1777 Nathaniel Whitaker would be observing that though, "in our contest with the tyrant of Britain, we did not, indeed, commence the war," yet even had King George "withheld his hand from shedding our blood," his contemptuous violations of the law of nature "were fully sufficient to justify us in the sight of God, and all wise men, had we begun the war, and expelled his troops from our country by fire and sword."[73]

Perhaps if the battle of Lexington had not occurred, Calvinists would have invented it as well as the royal brute, for the smoke of battle had barely lifted when John Cleaveland was addressing General Gage in these accents:

> Without speedy repentance, you will have an aggravated damnation in hell. You are not only a wicked robber, a murderer, and usurper, but a wicked Rebel: A wicked rebel, against the authority of truth, law, equity . . . and humanity itself.[74]

No Calvinist, surely, supposed that the utter depravity of any soul was revealed in a single day; it took longer than that for Cleaveland to decide what punishment lay in store for Mayhew. What they did believe, however (and especially those who recalled the Great Awakening), was that men might, in appropriate circumstances, be saved in the twinkling of an eye.

III

That Calvinists were in the months before and after Lexington the most prolific of preachers and pamphleteers does not of itself necessarily derogate from either the services or the patriotism of the Liberal ministry. There is a difference in kind, however, between sermons delivered before respectable Bostonians and published, not for the edification of the populace, but for their possible impact on English opinion, and a Calvinist sermon, printed at the preacher's own expense, not to establish a "literary reputation" but for "the best service of the people." In a moment when the "minds of all" were in a ferment, Calvinists strove to give Americans a "clear, distinct knowledge" of the issues of the day, and then brought down the whole weight of the moral law on the side of Revolution and Independence.[75]

Moreover, the Calvinist sermons of the years and months before the Revolution assumed that the multitude had somehow taken over responsibility for defining America's goals and that the task at hand was to remind the more favored, and more prudent, members of American society of their duty and obligation to the general welfare. Isaac Story, for instance, was certain that "superior abilities, and more advantageous circumstances, whether possessed by birth or accident, ought to be considered as noble prerogatives, designed by heaven to promote the good of the species." Whoever derived any other interpretation of the moral law, he declared, "either from the constitution of human nature, or the fitness of things," was "reduced to a glaring absurdity."[76] It was not necessarily absurdity to which the better-advantaged members of colonial society were reduced, but as late as the summer of 1775 some of the Liberal clergy were repeating Mayhew's classic precept: a "being," whether King or God, is worthy of allegiance, confidence, and love so long as he provides "what we want."[77]

Thirty years earlier Edwards had declared that they "whose affection to God is founded first on his profitableness to them" begin "at the wrong end."[78] The same truth was maintained at the beginning of the Revolution by Calvinists describing the "moral beauty" of the good society, and how and why it was to be loved. "The public welfare," proclaimed Connecticut's election preacher in the spring of 1776, demands "the attention of all." He assumed, moreover, that the merest consideration of the nature of society, not of its benefits but of its promised glories, would "inspire and invigorate" everyone's "best efforts for its advancement," and that all would "pursue the public good" with "inextinguishable ardour."[79] That many Americans were doing so in 1776 as they had in 1775 was hardly a tribute to the counsels of sweet reason. Had the voice of Liberalism prevailed, war, revolution, and dissolution of the British empire might have been avoided, and the admirers of the legal scheme assured, eventually, of an abundance of what they wanted. But the spirit of 1775-76 would not have risen to such flame and rapture had not prudent Americans so long denied that the multitude had no clear and distinct idea of how to pursue happiness, nor the capacity to engage in the pursuit.

It was said by David Ramsay, in his retrospect of the Revolution, that among "the active instruments" of the Revolution, most "were self-made, industrious men." In "these times of action," he recalled, "classical education was found of less service than good natural parts, guided by common sense and sound judgment."[80] Whatever the validity of this observation as applied to the members of the Continental Congress, or to Washington's staff, the fact is that the Calvinist ministry happily embodied all of the characteristics Ramsay thought serviceable, as well as some that he did not. In the spring of 1776 the Reverend Peter Thacher, friend of Jacob Green and admirer of Whitefield (who, impressed by Thacher's eloquence, had publicly anointed him "the young Elijah"), was selected to deliver the oration on the anniversary of the Boston Massacre. Thacher commenced his oration by explaining that the "ambition of princes" caused them to practice the "arts of bribery and corruption" (with easy success in the case of "mitred hypocrites, and cringing, base souled priests") and that the "king" had found "means to corrupt the other branches of the legislature." So much for "the righteous administration of the righteous king George the third," concluded the only clergyman appointed to deliver a Massacre oration, and the only Boston orator, it would seem, to have perused the ancients carefully enough to know how to compose a philippic.[81]

When the time came for action, moreover, the Calvinist ministry were first and longest in the field; at the age of seventy-one, Benjamin Pomeroy sped east to serve at the battle of Bunker Hill. Mayhew once remarked that it would be "as much out of character for a gentleman" to debate with John Cleaveland "as it would be for a general of an army to accept a challenge from a subaltern,"[82] and yet in 1775 it was Cleaveland, and none of Mayhew's gentlemanly colleagues, who served in Washington's headquarters. Yet of all the Calvinists of the Revolutionary era, only Thomas Allen, whom Washington Irving described in the *Life of Washington* as "a belligerent parson, full of fight,"[83] has received the honor that is rightly his.

Most of them remain unsung—even David Avery, second only to Allen in the eyes of Calvinists contemporaries as a Christian hero of the Revolution. Avery had been converted at the age of twenty under Whitefield's preaching, studied with Eleazar Wheelock, served as a missionary among the Oneidas, and took leave of his congregation early in the war. Present at Bunker Hill, Ticonderoga (where a musket ball passed through his eye), and the surrender of Burgoyne, Avery was the paradigm of the Revolutionary clergy. To the end of his life he was "an Edwardean in sentiment, and a Whitefieldian in warmth of manner."[84] He was also in the profoundest sense one in spirit with Edwards, who at the beginning of his adult life had resolved "to do whatever I think to be my *duty,* and most for the good and advantage of mankind in general," to do so "whatever *difficulties* I meet with, how many soever, and how great soever," and "to live with all my might, while I do live."[85] The Calvinists of the Revolution shared his spirit. David Jones, for instance, a graduate of Isaac Eaton's Hopewell School (the Log College of the Pennsylvania Baptists) narrowly escaped death at the hands of New Jersey's Tories, moved to Pennsylvania and served with St. Clair's regiment from early 1776 through Yorktown, and was severely wounded in the Paoli massacre. In 1775 Jones believed that his duty to God and man called him to serve his country, and he believed it again in 1812, when at the age of seventy-six he enlisted for his second war with Britain.[86]

Perhaps Cleaveland and the other Calvinist ministers who rushed into service in 1775 were seeking—as modern historiography would suggest—a status in colonial society from which they had declined or to which they aspired. Yet clearly their own anticlericalism and their insistence on the superior rights and privileges of the laity had undermined something of their inherited authority in the churches. If George Duffield, an eloquent New Side preacher whom Old Side strategists had fought in court as well as in church councils, was by 1776 a chaplain of the Continental Congress, he had achieved that eminence by virtue of his popular reputation for eloquence and fearless defiance of the Philadelphia city fathers. The expressed desire of the Calvinists who urged their people to combat, who entered the army as private soldiers as well as chaplains, and who remained, many of them, in the service through the surrender of Cornwallis, was to "give God all the glory, if he enables me to throw even a mite into the offering to aid the great American cause against tyranny and wicked usurpation."[87]

Undoubtedly the Calvinists of the Revolution were deceiving themselves when they thought they had put on the whole armor of God in the battle against tyranny. Surely the ministry were in error when they identified the friends of American freedom as "the children of light; who always act above ground and are open and fair in their proceedings, and do the thing that is lawful and right," or when they confidently described Britain's purpose as "glaringly the cause of the devil."[88] Revolutionary Calvinism betrayed the same dualism that historians have recently posited as the essence of Jacksonian Democracy and Populism, including a disposition in the brethren to sin against the very commandments which they were sure only the devil's children would violate—to be, as it were, "at once the judges and the judged."[89]

The anxiety of self-judgment was a vital source, however, of Calvinist patriotic enthusiasm. Because they consciously believed that "all the true friends of virtue," as well as "the God of truth and justice," were on their side, Calvinists easily concluded that "a calm concern is inconsistent with true patriotism."[90] Similarly, they were able to scorn the desire to be "esteemed among the BEST MEMBERS of the STATE" and to enjoy "the Benefits of Victory" that characterized those who "stood NEUTERS, while their Nation was engaged in War."[91] Thus the evangelical clergy were able to pass some measure of judgment on those who spent the early war years "skulking as behind the door, and undetermined on which side they can serve themselves to the best advantage,"[92] as well as on such "enlightened" Americans as "Colonel Benjamin Thompson, a native of Massachusetts, and the same man who was afterwards created by the Duke of Bavaria, and known to the world as Count Rumford." The acts of this "redoubtable commander" of a Tory regiment gave him, among Calvinists and their descendants, "an immortality, which all his military exploits, philosophical disquisitions, and scientific discoveries will never secure to him."[93] As one of Jackson's more astute admirers was to ask, who will be judge if the judge himself is brought to the bar?

In the spring of 1775 whole Calvinist congregations, often in response to a single sermon, followed their preachers into battle, and for eight years members of the household of faith served at Valley Forge and Bennington, at Cowpens and Eutaw Springs. Their spirit was that of the ministers who reminded them, as before the gates of Ticonderoga, to "rejoice that you have an opportunity to contribute your whole might for the deliverance of your country from the disturbers of the common peace, and robbers of the rights of mankind." Throughout these years they were certain that God was in their midst, and owned their righteous cause. "What then, though the waters roar and tremble," they exclaimed, "our God shall help us and that right early."[94] Perhaps their God helped them most signally by providing them an image of the British Prince of Darkness, for what they were providing was, in part at least, only a corollary of Edwards' definition of *True Virtue:* if "there be any being statedly and irreclaimably opposite and an enemy to Being in general," Edwards had written, "then consent to Being in general will induce the truly virtuous heart to forsake that being, and to oppose it."[95]

Actually, the course of history was such that Americans had an opportunity to oppose their enemy before making the decision to forsake him. But given the perspective from which the evangelical mind viewed public affairs, it is not surprising that the same animus that triggered the muskets on Lexington Green built almost concurrently into a desire for independence. The outbreak of open hostilities seems to have added little to the Calvinist catalogue of evidence of the depraved character of Britain and its leadership. In New England especially, "THE EVER MEMORABLE NINETEENTH OF APRIL, 1775" (as a preacher styled it on May 11, 1775) was a day on which merely "new bloody scenes were opened to our view." The carnage at Lexington had simply fulfilled what, it was said, had been expected since

THE FATAL FIFTH OF MARCH, 1770; when Beelzebub broke loose, and with infernal train, joined with the scarlet throng, with George's livery, by name of the xxxixth.[96]

Within days of the skirmish John Cleaveland was publishing, in the *Essex Gazette,* sentiments for which his readers and parishioners were not entirely unprepared:

Great Britain, Adieu! No longer shall we honor you as our mother; you are become cruel; you have not such bowels as the sea monsters towards their young ones . . . By this stroke you have broken us off from you and effectually alienated us from you . . . King George III, adieu! . . . you have dissolved our allegiance to your crown and government.[97]

What Calvinists thought they had been doing was testing British character according to the principles of experimental religion; carefully, that is, following Edwards' principle that "a steady effect argues a steady cause." A disposition to view each element of British policy and conduct, as it unfolded, as evidence of motive and intention, was implicit even in such reasonable documents as Dickinson's *Letters of a Pennsylvania Farmer* and Jefferson's *Summary View*. Something closer even to the strict Calvinist viewpoint, however, informed the immensely popular *Declaration of the Causes and Necessity of Taking up Arms* issued by the Continental Congress in July of 1775. The British Parliament, according to that pronouncement, "stimulated by an inordinate Passion" for money and power, had "in their intemperate Rage for unlimited Domination" used every means "to effect their cruel and impolitic Purpose of enslaving these colonies by Violence."[98]

To the evangelical mind, such a pronouncement was an imperative to Independence, if only as a summons to separation from a dangerously unconverted British ministry. In May 1776, in fact, an "honest farmer" of Pennsylvania published a tract in which he claimed to have heard "a voice, as if an angel from heaven proclaimed, 'come out from among them, and be ye separate from them.'"[99] A month earlier William Henry Drayton, the South Carolina judge who happened also to be one of that province's more outstanding dissenter laymen, advised his grand jurors that all allegiance to the Crown was ended. He listed the long "train" of "dishonorable machinations" that gave "nothing less than absolute proof" that "British tyranny" was "capable of attempting to perpetrate whatever is infamous," and clearly intended to do so.[100] His conclusion was echoed by the anonymous Pennsylvania pamphleteer who, scarcely attempting to distinguish among minions, ministers, and kings, declared that Britain was "so basely, so cruelly, so industriously, and obstinately, bent on our destruction" that there was no point in holding out the olive branch.[101]

But it was a Calvinist minister, Jacob Green, who in the very first months of 1776 produced what were probably the most resounding of counterstatements to such temporizing essays as those published in early 1776 by William Smith. Green's *Observations on the Reconciliation of Great-Britain and the Colonies* was a point-by-point application of Calvinist doctrine to political affairs. His statement that if "a kingdom, or a house, be divided against itself, it cannot stand" echoed not merely Scripture but Green's own arguments, less than a decade earlier, for a "pure" church. His opinions on the question of improvement in the conduct of British policy were likewise informed by what Calvinists thought to be expected of "natural" men, even the most "sincere." It would be the "greatest absurdity in nature," Green contended, to expect anyone in the British government to "be what they ought to be—wholly for the good of the people."[102] Then Green passed judgment on the suggestion that Britain, after all, had shown remarkable moderation in its treatment of the colonies. Actually, he observed, the Crown had made every effort "to crush us, and expected what she has done would have accomplished it." And even if England had not so acted, went Green's final, and to Calvinists unanswerable, argument, it was not "for want of will and disposition" that "she does not proceed against us to the utmost."[103] In sum, Green was arguing for independence from no other principle than that of Edwards: "moral evil, with its desert of dislike and abhorrence" consists in "certain dispositions of the heart, and acts of the will."[104]

Many years later John Adams, seeking to minimize the importance of Tom Paine's *Common Sense,* recalled that the "temper and wishes of the people supplied every thing at that time"; such phrases as "The Royal Brute of England, 'the blood upon his soul,' and a few others of equal delicacy, had as much weight with the people as his arguments."[105] That they had such weight is perhaps explained by the fact that the Calvinist ministry were just as familiar as Paine with the words of Milton: "never can true reconcilement grow where wounds of deadly hate have pierced so deep." The Calvinist ministry, long accustomed to employing the same phrase in their discussion of the irreconcilable hatred of the carnal mind for an excellent Deity, were now equally ready to apply it in treating the benevolent soul's aversion to political powers of blackness. The doctrine, as applied to public affairs, had been a staple of the sermons of the French and Indian War, when Samuel Finley declared it impossible that *"Light* and *Darkness* may be *reconciled."* (And in a few years more, Milton's words would be invoked by Nathaniel Whitaker in explaining why Americans might "as well hope for Satan's cordial friendship to mankind, as for that of the tories to these states.") But in 1776 the sense that Americans and Britons were "direct *Contradictories"* made independence necessary if for no other reason than assuring the lovers of liberty that whoever could not dwell with darkness was a child of light indeed.[106]

British "tyranny" and "depravity" served as, if nothing else, a compelling vindication of the great Christian doctrine of original sin. On the day that General Gage and his troops evacuated Boston, Elijah Fitch explained that the various "atrocities" of the British were proof

> that there is a rooted hatred and enmity in the hearts of the ungodly against both God and his people: There is that in them, which is contrary to holiness, righteousness and purity; for this reason they are said to be of their father the devil, whose works they do.[107]

In May 1776, John Witherspoon used the various fruits of the British disposition—the "ravages of lawless power"—in answering Tom Paine's effort to impugn the doctrine of human depravity in his attack on hereditary succession. Throughout the war Calvinists, in whatever else they might have differed, could agree that the British character proved human sin no mere fancy but a quite obvious and substantial fact.[108]

Meanwhile David Rittenhouse, feeling it bliss to be alive when so many Americans were sacrificing and dying on behalf of the community, wondered aloud if possibly his Baptist ancestors' doctrine of sin were universally true. Something of the same disposition was disclosed in sermons wherein the friends of liberty were identified as "the children of light." Each of these tendencies—the one focusing on human depravity, the other emphasizing the easiness of election— built what, in the course of the Revolution, would become a Calvinist house divided against itself.*[109] It was not such theologies, however, that provided the impetus of the Revolution, but those of the Awakening and of Edwards, of Bellamy, Tennent, Finley, and Davies. Though the Revolution witnessed a resurgence of a new Arminianism and a new antinomianism, the evangelical scheme seemed intact at the outset of the war. In the summer of 1775, for instance, a Baptist exhorter echoed the strains that for nearly two decades had succeeded in exercising the wills of the Calvinist multitude:

> There is another objection, which good people make against war of any kind, viz. 'That war is not agreeable to the disposition of souls newly converted to the knowledge of CHRIST: Then we long for the salvation of souls, and have a tender regard for all men: Surely martial engagements do not suit a meek and loving disciple of JESUS.' I confess, no objection to me is of equal importance to this. It is a solemn consideration: . . . The reason why a defensive war seems so awful to good people, is, they esteem it to be some kind of murder: but this is a very great mistake: for it is no more murder than a legal process against a criminal. The end is the same, the mode is different. In some cases it is the only mode left to obtain justice. And surely that religion is not from heaven, which is against

---

* The theological consequences of the Revolution—among them the stimulus provided by energetic American virtue to such evangelical forms of Arminianism as Methodism and Free-Will Baptism—were immense. A few will be touched on in the course of the succeeding narrative, but what cannot be treated is the degree to which secular thought and writers took on themselves, in the Revolution, both the doctrines and the functions of the Edwardean clergy. One example must suffice: that of Philip Freneau, the more evocative of whose war poems gave coherence to both the doctrine of original sin and the notion of America's spiritual potentialities. It was also Freneau who in the 1790's had to remind the field preachers of that day that the millennium would come to pass only if men remembered that depravity and tyranny were as much a social and political reality as the ability and willingness of men to love each other.

justice on earth. Remember all men are not converted; if they were, there could be no necessity of war in any sense.[110]

Given such rhetoric, John Adams may well have been right in suggesting that Paine contributed little to the arousing of enthusiasm for independence. Joseph Hawley, for one, observed at the time that *Common Sense* expressed only what most citizens of his area had felt for a long time. It was in western Massachusetts, of course, that Edwards had written that a "great degree of holiness" would render "a man unable to take complacence in wicked persons or things."[111] Bellamy had expanded the thought, possibly on the basis of his own experience with the people of Connecticut: "when natures are in perfect contrariety, the one sinful, and the other holy, the more they are known to each other, the more is mutual hatred stirred up, and their entire aversion to each other becomes sensible."[112] The question is how and why Americans came in 1775-1776 to be so convinced of the absolute contrast in American and British character. If there be any answer, it is probably not contained in the stated doctrines of Calvinism, but in its warnings against the infinite capacity of the human soul for self-deception. For in his heart of hearts the evangelical American knew, or sensed, that beneath his zealous opposition to tyranny lay an anxious awareness that, were something not done to change the course of history, the American character, his own included, might well not prove to be completely different from that of the British tyrant whom he opposed.

IV

The evangelical Revolutionary impulse, like that of the Great Awakening, represented a counterthrust to the seeming tendency of American history. Many Calvinists seem to have agreed with Joseph Hawley that, unless Britain were resisted, "twenty years" would "make the number of Tories on this continent equal to the number of Whigs."[113] By Tories Hawley meant not merely defenders of royal prerogative or of antirepublican political principles but advocates and practitioners of an acquisitive and prideful social ethic. The Revolution for him and for others who shared his faith represented an effort to check a rising capitalist culture. It was born of the sense, not merely that wealth was being wrongly and inequitably accumulated in the New World, but that the land was threatened by the worst of all ills: the hastening decay of its moral manhood. The Calvinist Revolutionary crusade had many particular goals, but at its center was the hope of nipping in the bud, as it were, an ethos which, if allowed to thrive, would produce in America all manner of unvirtuous fruits.

As once before in American history, however, the religious violence of an awakening was seen also as the necessary first step of pressing into a more joyful kingdom. If "the principles on which the present civil war is carried on by the American colonies," one Calvinist announced, "were universally adopted and practiced by mankind, they would turn a vale of tears, into a paradise of God."[114] The "cause of liberty," as Calvinists saw it, was "the grand cause of the whole human race." It was one about which God was "incapable of changing his mind."[115] In sum, it was the good old cause of the Work of Redemption, being forwarded now by the spirit of liberty and union rather than by the Spirit of God:

> It is the cause of truth, against error and falsehood, the cause of righteousness against iniquity; the cause of the oppressed against the oppressor; the cause of pure and undefiled religion, against bigotry, superstition, & human inventions. It is the cause of the reformation, against arbitrary power; of benevolence, against barbarity, and of virtue against vice. It is the cause of justice and integrity, against bribery, venality, and corruption. In short it is the cause of heaven and against hell—of the kind Parent of the universe, against the prince of darkness, and the destroyer of the human race.[116]

In the field, such a definition of issues allowed, among other things, a summons to be of good cheer, to despair not in the face of adversity or numbers: "Be not afraid of them, because they are engaged in a wicked and unrighteous cause, which the righteous Lord abhorreth." Elsewhere it allowed the Calvinist ministry to try, at least, to enforce their definition of the purpose of the Revolution on the less "righteous" people of America.

The Revolution opened as what seemed a continuation of the pious mainstream of eighteenth-century history. In the summer of 1775 a Pennsylvania militia company, for instance, was exhorted in the accents which once had aroused the followers of Gilbert Tennent against a papal invasion:

> Equip yourselves, and be equipt for this warfare—put on, Gentlemen, the gospel armoury—*have your feet shod with its preparation* —for your *helmet salvation*—for your *shield* faith—and be *girt with truth*—this, Sirs, is a gospel uniform, that well becomes the Christian soldier—and thus go forth in the name of the Lord of Hosts.[117]

In New England the crusade recalled 1745, and the Louisburg expedition. Once Benedict Arnold had assembled from Massachusetts, Connecticut, and Rhode Island the troops for the assault on Quebec, they marched to Newburyport, where two hundred bateaux had been collected to carry troops and provisions. There they remained over the Sabbath, in order to hear the counsel of Samuel Spring, late of Princeton and now official chaplain to the brigade. All "the officers and as many of the soldiers as could be crowded on to the floor" of Jonathan Parsons' church heard Spring preach on the very theme that had emblazoned the banner of the pious army thirty years before.

"*I preached over the grave of Whitefield*," the chaplain later recalled. Then Spring performed a ritual that he could never forget. Along with some of the officers, Spring descended into the tomb and took the lid from Whitefield's coffin, removed Whitefield's collar and wrist bands, cut them in small pieces, and divided them among the officers. That one of the recipients of those talismans was Arnold, another the younger Aaron Burr, Spring would remember to the end of his days. Only later would he wonder if his prayer—"If thy spirit go not with us, carry us not up hence"—had not been answered, in the winter of 1775, by a Lord of Battles who, outraged by such blasphemous, un-Protestant conduct, carried New England's army only within sight of the Plains of Abraham.[118]

Possibly Spring's most un-Protestant error (in Calvinist terms) was his lavishing of special attention on the officers of the expedition. It may have been that he hoped, by providing them with such mementos, to commit them to the Calvinist crusade as Whitefield had once succeeded in encouraging the multitude to perform the tasks assigned them by carnal officers and gentlemen. Whatever his motives, Spring's gesture was inconsistent with a long tradition of Calvinist chaplains, whose concern and whose eloquence had long centered on the enlisted men. Throughout the war, younger Calvinists preserved this tradition, most strikingly in such discourses as Hugh Brackenridge's *Eulogium of the Brave Men Who Have Fallen in the Contest with Great Britain*, which was, in effect, one of the first Fourth of July orations.*[119] To be sure, Brackenridge ended the war not a Calvinist clergyman but a republican pamphleteer and editor. His decision, like that of Joel Barlow and Aaron Burr (once a candidate for the ministry and a student of Joseph Bellamy), may not have been wholly unrelated to the course on which Spring and other ministers, after the completion of their chaplaincies if not already during them, were pointing the evangelical scheme.

* In this regard, Brackenridge's *Six Political Discourses Founded on the Scripture* (1778), designed as they were for what seemed a woefully corrupt civilian population, represent a major transition in the republican-Calvinist mind. It is interesting, however, that in the 1790's Brackenridge saw reason to republish, not these *Discourses*, but his more explicitly evangelical sermons to the army just after the Declaration of Independence and just before the battle of Brandywine.

A breakdown of the evangelical synthesis is evident at nearly every point where the necessities of the war against Britain impinged on the Calvinist mind. One of the more compelling sources of intellectual change was the effort of evangelical chaplains to suppress among the soldiers what was clearly a dark suspicion of the inner motives of many higher-echelon patriots. In a sermon before a brigade of Virginia militia, for instance, one John Hurt in 1777 advised the troops to be less critical of their officers and the Continental Congress. That certain people seemed to be harvesting a rather immoderate portion of glory and fame, he insisted, was no "sort of derogation to the benevolence of their character." The love of fame, he explained, "is so connected with virtue that it seems scarcely possible to be possessed of the latter without some degree of the former." But Hurt immediately added—almost as if he were frightened by how close he had come to making self-interest an essential ingredient of true virtue—that the crucial question is the manner in which one comes by glory:

> A good man feels a pleasure from the reputation he acquires by serving his country, because he loves it; but he does not love it for the sake of that pleasure; the passion did not spring from the expectation of the delight, but the delight was the consequence of the passion.[120]

Since the Awakening, America had been offered many ready formulas for confounding piety with what Cotton Mather (among the earliest to contribute to the confusion) had called the "old *Heathen* Virtue of PIETAS IN PATRIAM, or LOVE TO ONE'S COUNTRY."[121] Yet Hurt, good post-Awakening pietist that he was, proved, by seeking to provide the sufferers in the Jersey campaign with a definition of the "quintessence" of patriotism, that even in 1777 the new light had not entirely dimmed. Hurt's sermon was essentially an application of the doctrines of experimental religion to the affairs in which Americans of the day were primarily engaged. In the first part of his sermon he endeavored "to explain the nature and obligation of love to our country," and in the second, to delineate "that conduct which seems requisite to testify the sincerity of this affection."

Hurt began by looking at the simplest argument for patriotism, one which often exhausted the stock of many orators of the day: the notion that "the public is, as it were, one great family." Admitting that he might enlarge on this, and on the pleasures of social intercourse, and "from thence show the reasonableness of an affectionate attachment to the community," Hurt chose instead to "point out the obligations to this associating virtue as they arise from higher and more interesting principles." One such principle was the injustice of failing to contribute to the common good at least the equivalent of one's share in "the benefits of society"; the "public good," he insisted, "is, as it were, a common bank."

Many items (though not this last one) in Hurt's rather eclectic inventory of motives to patriotic endeavor might have been found in the sermons of the Liberal ministry and in the secular addresses of the day. For the authors of such discourses, as for the "heathens" from whom "all their beautiful lectures, and pompous declamations, on the love of their country" were derived, Hurt had nothing but contempt. "Indisputable proofs, indeed," he insisted, "of their eloquence, but not so of their humanity." Hurt's commitment to Calvinist principles* emerged most vividly in his declaration that there was but one quintessential patriotic spirit:

> But still, the more noble motive to a generous soul, is that which springs from a benevolent desire of diffusing the joys of life to all around him. There is nothing, he thinks, so desirable as to be the instrument of doing good; and the further it is extended, the greater is the delight, and the more glorious his character. Benignity to friends and relations is but a narrow-spirited quality compared with this, and perhaps as frequently the effect of caprice, or pride, as of a benevolent temper. But when our flow of good-will spreads itself to all the society . . . when charity rises into public spirit, and partial affection is extended into general benevolence—then it is that man shines in the highest lustre, and is the truest image of his Divine Maker.

Still, Hurt's doctrines provided Americans (if not necessarily the veterans of Valley Forge whom he addressed) a rather wide margin for error in conceiving the nature of true virtue. His statement that the "Creator has connected our interest with our duty, and made it each man's happiness to contribute to the welfare of his country" was literally no more than Nathaniel Niles's principle that the joys of the new birth might be achieved by something other than the spirit of God. But his declaration that enlisted men ought to tolerate the public services of less saintly men permitted, however unwittingly, a reinterpretation of the nature of interest and happiness. By repeating Davies' adage—"as there can be no real virtue in that breast which is not susceptible of the love of the public, there can be no genuine love of

---

* Little is known of Hurt's denominational affiliation, since he spent most of his active career as a chaplain (1776-1784 and 1791-1794). He was ordained in 1775, presumably as an Episcopalian, but in all likelihood as one committed to the evangelical principles of Devereux Jarratt. Hurt's one published sermon (other than his address to the Virginia troops) was a Masonic funeral discourse, in which were asserted the strictest Calvinist definitions of sainthood and benevolence.

the public where virtue is wanting"—he and other Revolutionary chaplains granted, if nothing else, a definition of true virtue which, in the context, all but forgot that no man was able to fulfill the law of nature unless renewed by the Spirit of God.[122]

In the course of the war, Calvinists offered the military what was, in effect, a theology of justification by works. Some told their auditors that by serving as patriots in the cause of the earthly Jerusalem, they were preparing to "be received as true sons and citizens of that Jerusalem which is above."[123] Others called on the military to be "such good soldiers in the temporal militia, as that, at last, they may be raised to, and mingled with the CHURCH TRIUMPHANT in heaven."[124] In these years of Revolutionary grace, each such abandonment of the principal hinge of the evangelical scheme seemed of little moment, and possibly was. For if those who listened to Calvinist counsel were persuaded that America was to be, not merely an independent nation, but—as Hurt's doctrines made clear—literally a commonwealth, then Americans were surely opening a new chapter in the Work of Redemption. Summoned to battle against temporal powers of darkness, they were being informed, more explicitly than ever before, that happiness and salvation were to be found in dedication to the welfare, not of one's person, but of the community.

Although the social goals of Revolutionary Calvinism were proclaimed throughout America, analysis of the thought and rhetoric of the clergy with respect to noncombatants must perforce concentrate primarily on New England. From 1776 to 1779 only the northern states were firmly in the hands of the American army. This circumstance helps to explain why many of the evangelical clergy who were not on active duty took refuge in these years in the land of the Puritans. It may also account for the extremity, in New England, of the social and economic crisis which preachers were forced to consider.

Clearly evangelical spokesmen were active elsewhere; in Virginia, as in Massachusetts, the Baptists were pursuing, in cooperation with Thomas Jefferson, their goal of religious liberty. In the Carolinas, the spokesmen of Calvinism were assigned a somewhat unique task—that of attempting to bring over to the patriot side the people of the back country. The bitterness lingering from the Regulator years made it seem advisable to send among the evangelical populace William Tennent III and William Henry Drayton. One spoke on the millenarian prospects of America opened by the Revolution, the other on the guarantees of religious freedom implicit in the cause of liberty.[125] But except for Tennent's plea for ecclesiastical liberty in the South Carolina Assembly of 1777, the sermons and addresses delivered in these years in the South seem not to have been published. A plausible explanation is that for most of the first four years of the war the printing presses of Boston were the only ones available to patriot spokesmen.

It was in New England that there was first and foremost revealed among the civilian populace what Charles Chauncy called *The Accursed Thing*—an "inordinate love of money."[126] Obviously the currency crisis was not unique to New England, so in many respects the response of the northern clergy to this situation was representative of the manner in which American Protestantism generally met the chief domestic challenge of the war years. To the New England clergy, the problem of depreciated currency posed moral as well as economic issues. Which was emphasized, and how, depended in part on inherited doctrine, though many ministers reacted in a manner that marked something of a reconstruction of the creed professed before the Revolution. Chauncy's response was the simplest and most traditional. Ever the enemy of inflation, he issued a demand for regulation of the currency—in order to relieve, as he phrased it, *"the poor, the fatherless, and the widow."*[127] Isaac Backus*[128] immediately interpreted Chauncy's program as a directive to the General Court to help the established "ministers about their salaries, which the depreciation of our currency had greatly lessened."[129] Others, however, were less interested in melioristic devices for preserving the value of vested capital, and even Chauncy, standing for the last time as a Jeremiah (albeit a reasonable one), summoned the acquisitive wretches of New England to repentance of their sinful ways: *The Accursed Thing Must be Taken Away from among a People, if They Would Reasonably Hope to Stand before Their Enemies.*

On March 5, 1778, John Lathrop sought to employ other devices to "exterminate that meanness of spirit—that criminal selfishness," which, as he saw it, was interfering with the prosecution of the war. What was needed, he declared, was "magnanimity of soul," and this alone would end the embarrassments into which the war effort had fallen:

> How ardently then is this noble affection—this enthusiasm for the public good to be desired! May it kindle up in some favorite breast. May it catch from soul to soul, till the inhabitants of this land in general, feeling the irresistible influence, shall unite in one vigorous effort against the enemies of our civil and religious liberties and put an end to their existence in this part of the world.

---

* Possibly Backus was reading Chauncy's sermon in the light of his recollection of the 1747 election sermon, in which Chauncy had attacked bills of credit as "a cruel engine of oppression," the "pernicious influence" of which was most felt by "men of *nominal salaries*"—though *"widows* and *orphans"* were, to be sure, as "much to be pitied."

What distinguished Lathrop's sermon from many others delivered in 1778 (and, in fact, clearly revealed his final departure from the ways of his Calvinist mentors) was that it was not Christian benevolence that he hoped to see rekindled, but "Roman patriotism." Moreover, as Lathrop himself confessed, he had no rhetorical strategy available to inspire such patriotism except a reminder to the merchants and other commercially minded men of Boston that their new wealth would be of little use if Britain should win the war![130]

The avowed Calvinists among the clergy took a somewhat different approach to the same economic and social changes. When Samuel Spring returned from the siege of Quebec he delivered before his Newburyport congregation a sermon which captured to a considerable degree the Calvinist view of the spirit of post-1776. No sooner had Americans declared their independence of Britain, he observed, than "selfishness" had taken

> the rule, and dispatched her whole force of pride, prodigality, contention, extortion, and oppression against the publick good. The wheels of publick interest did but just move, while those of private interest were rattling all over the country. Publick spirit was a common expression, but few traces of the thing were to be found.[131]

So appalled was Spring by the change of affairs since his departure for Quebec that he saw his immediate task as that of summoning his congregation back to virtue. He grew so concerned with the spiritual declension of his parishioners that, like many other Calvinists, he preached for the remainder of the war largely on doctrinal subjects—to the exclusion of direct treatment of public affairs.

Spring's concern for the state of his people took such a form, however, that by the turn of the century he would be one of the most violent and most outspoken of Massachusetts clerical Federalists. As an opponent of Republicanism and of the War Hawks, his sermons were filled with lamentations, not for the public's falling short of Edwardean true virtue, but for the departed spiritual glories of New England. Actually Spring turned to the jeremiad already in 1778, when his thanksgiving sermon was phrased as a prediction of judgments impending on a people who had fallen off from the public spirit of 1776. If in time such preaching came to encourage (or revive) a sense of New England's special destiny, during the Revolution it promoted to some degree one Calvinist goal: a feeling of kinship among all the American people.

The Jeremiahs of the middle years of the war helped to create an American identity based not on the peculiar virtue of a whole people, nor even on their spiritual potentialities, but on a seemingly continent-wide selfishness. Those Calvinists who employed such a formula showed themselves, like Spring, to be (with few exceptions) more students of Witherspoon than heirs of Whitefield. Its use represented then, as in the seventeenth century, an encouragement or at least a toleration of the acquisitiveness it bewailed. For even in 1778, Samuel Spring summoned his people to repentance largely that the God of the covenant would grant them entrance into a Canaan more distinguished by its prosperity than by its religion.

Already in 1774, to be sure, Calvinists when contemplating the future of America predicted, as a consequence of the struggle with Britain, a New World "far more glorious, wealthy, and populous than ever." However, they identified the cause of American liberty with something more than the "riches, arts, and sciences" that comprised William Smith's visions of the future, and insofar as they defined the American cause in terms of security of property as well as "liberty," the prospect before them was hardly one of rampant acquisition.[132] Indeed, as delineated by one young Calvinist in the first sermon honoring the Declaration of Independence, the picture of American felicity was something of an evangelization of Crèvecoeur's ideal physiocracy, or the counterpart of Jefferson's subsistence-farming "chosen people":

> We are ready to anticipate those happy times, when these days of tribulation shall be at an end; when our brethren shall return from the high places of the field, when we with them, shall sit under our own vines and fig-trees quietly enjoying the . . . fruits of our own hard labor, and honest industry, and have none to make us afraid. Safe from the enemy of the wilderness; safe from the griping hand of arbitrary sway, and cruel superstition; here shall be the late founded seat of peace and freedom. Here shall arts and sciences, the companions of tranquillity and *liberty* flourish. Here shall dwell uncorrupted faith, the pure worship of God, unawed, uninterrupted.[133]

The Calvinist Jeremiahs of the Revolution did not so much alter this picture as retouch it, coloring more splendidly, especially by 1783, the gloriously prosperous future which America—perhaps even without repentance—was now to enjoy. There is no need to trace the contours of this changing Calvinist rhetoric, for the whole process, both as it took place in the minds of the ministers and as it impinged on the minds of their auditors, had already been summed up in 1777. Then a Connecticut minister, a student of both Bellamy and Hopkins, contrasted the "goodness of God towards these colonies" with "the foul sins and abominations of this highly privileged land." He was "at once struck," and was sure his people would also be, "with the description of Israel, as being a most perfect resemblance of these American Colonies."[134] For twenty and more years ministers (among them Andrew Lee, who in 1776 preached on "The Curse of Meroz") would observe, both before their congregations and on election, fast, and thanksgiving days, that "what was said of Canaan" in the Old Testament "will apply to these States."[135] Whether impressed by the sins of Americans, or by the dispensations of Providence toward God's most favored nation, such ministers had committed the most unforgivable sin in the Edwardean catalogue: the confusion of the type with the trope.

Probably many of the Calvinists who coupled the United States with the Tribes of Israel thought they were indulging themselves in no more than a metaphor. But if so, the history of the American mind in the course of the Revolution can be defined as the increasing failure of their auditors to apprehend their meaning, or quite possibly as an insistence on misconstruing it. The "Jewish nation," Bellamy had explained in contrasting their expectations with those of his sermon on the millennium,

> longed for a Messiah to set them at liberty, to make them victorious, rich, and honorable; a Messiah in the character of a temporal prince, even such a one as they expected, would have suited their hearts to perfection, and so have naturally appeared a glorious Messiah; and the news of his coming, of his victories, and of his rising, spreading Kingdom, would have been glorious news . . . Had he thus come into his own, his own would have received him with all their hearts, joyfully enlisted under his banner, and followed him to battles, to victories, to universal empire; the very thing their hearts desired.[136]

In the years between 1765 and 1775 no Calvinist articulated such aspirations, but after 1776 many ministers, some of them once accepted as members of the evangelical alliance, forgot that "Israel, in the Egyptian bondage," was, as Bellamy had put it, only "a designed type of the fallen world under the dominion and tyranny of Satan."[137] Trying to hasten the passage of Americans through the moral wilderness of the war years, and at the same time to free them from the tyranny of a British Pharaoh, they seem to have succeeded often in inspiring the American people with many of the desires that Bellamy thought unworthy of a Christian.

Bellamy's illness, like the confusion and despair that overcame both Wheelock and Hawley after 1776, was not unrelated to this rhetorical revolution. The fragmentation of evangelical religion generally was likewise a consequence of the variety of responses of Americans, people and pastors alike, to the moral and political phenomena of the middle years of the war. What Calvinism needed in the years after the Declaration of Independence was, quite obviously, another Edwards, some-one who could put all the varieties of beliefs and behavior spawned by the Revolution into coherent perspective, and, by doing so, perhaps once again give the people of God the capacity to act with united strength. But so great was the confusion and disorder—so seemingly incapable of being given a single meaning—that the partisans of the evangelical scheme divided into numerous streams and branches and, finally, worked clearly at cross-purposes.

There were many Calvinist preachers, however, who responded to what they called the "extortion" of 1777 and after in a manner clearly consistent with the inherited doctrines of the Awakening. "I am ready to think," one observed,

> that the especial design of Heaven, in the present war, is to manifest the *real character* of the present generation in America; and that in the course of events, every class of men will be tried so far as to manifest the temper of their hearts, either in one way or another.[138]

In such a statement, as in the many wherein Calvinists improved the words, "These are the times that try men's souls," with a literalness that possibly even their author did not appreciate, was disclosed what was quite likely one of the unconscious impulses behind the Calvinist drive for "liberty." As Nathaniel Whitaker observed, "external force," by preventing man "from acting as he chooses or wills to act," made him less than "a moral, accountable creature" and therefore neither clearly nor demonstrably "worthy of praise or blame."[139] Freedom to America was essential so it might be discovered just who was capable of fulfilling the law of love. In 1777-1779, Calvinists even seemed to rejoice in the opportunity provided by a depreciating currency to test American character: "some will conceal what is within, until a proper temptation draw it forth."[140] In such minds the economic behavior of these years was an occasion for undoing at least one of the implications of the jeremiad—the indistinguishability of Americans in point of sinfulness.

If nothing else, the revelations of American character in 1777 served to put in a proper light the years immediately preceding the Revolution. One minister allowed that he did "not imagine the sin of covetousness rages at this day, so much above what it has in years past, as the price of goods is enhanced." But, he added, the "peculiar circumstances of the day, afford abundant occasion for manifestation of this sin."[141] Such observations could be, for obvious reasons, as much an excuse as an explanation, and could lead, among other things, to proposals for social and economic legislation designed to place the

American people out of the way of temptation. What truly distinguished among preachers, then as at any time, was not merely their interpretation of social phenomena, but how, in terms both of doctrine and rhetoric, they decided to cope with it.

Thus "the *depreciation* of the paper currency," as a friend of David Avery called it, provided a "trial of the spirit" for ministers as well as for their people. According to Avery, the economic situation had "a most wonderful and extensive influence, to bring out the inward springs of action, of almost every class of people."

> The covetousness and dishonesty of church members, which had long been lurking under a *religious profession* and *sober face,* appear without a covering. And men, generally, begin to *appear* as they *really are;* both with regard to *christianity* and *public spirit.*

As economic pressure and temptation revealed the true character of the people, the ministry would be forced to disclose its own principles and commitments: "We of the *clergy* are now in some measure, brought to the *test,* whether we preach in the *love of gain,* or for the interest of the *Redeemer's kingdom.*"[142] But of course the homiletic options available to Calvinists were actually many more than two, and their responses to the financial crisis were more complex than Avery suggested. No avowed Calvinist overtly preached the love of gain, but all had to make the more important decision of whether it was Christianity or public spirit that they sought to revive. Depending on this judgment, there was the further question of how precisely to preach the Redeemer's Kingdom—in purely ecclesiastical terms or, as was the choice of some, a more expressly socially conscious version of the Work of Redemption.

To unfold all the roads taken by the evangelical clergy is beyond the scope of this study. The modifications of the Edwardean vision in the course of the Revolution were such that the evangelical impulse was thereafter divided into two discernible streams—one flowing toward the nineteenth-century revival, and the other into Jeffersonian and Jacksonian democracy. In the middle years of the war, however, the distinction emerged largely as one of mere emphasis. Avery himself, for instance, preached a modified version of the old gospel, centered in part on ecclesiastical liberty, but also on the "pure and heavenly love" that was essential were "the glorious interest of the REDEEMER'S KINGDOM" to flourish "in this *Western* World." Avery made it quite clear, moreover, that Christian benevolence had nothing in common with, in fact was the very contrary of, the avaricious spirit of the war years. But he did not, except in passing, relate this insight directly to the social and political goals of the Revolution.[143]

Other Calvinists offered even less conclusive theories on the tendency and necessities of history. During the Revolution Timothy Dwight, for one, seemed to argue that the most pressing danger was a secular spirit, and that, in sum, the Church was and must always be the exclusive instrument of God's attainment of His End in Creation. But by the end of the war he was proposing rather secular mechanisms for forwarding the Work of Redemption. Hereby he was preparing for the curiously divided vision of clerical Federalism and of Hopkinsian Calvinism—both of which bemoaned worldliness as the reigning sin of America and yet offered a prospect of the chiliad distinguished by a graphic portrayal of its economic plenty.

After the outbreak of the French Revolution, such Calvinists as Dwight would redefine the Work of Redemption as a counterthrust to the forces of the Goddess of Reason, and even as a repudiation of the Enlightenment itself. But in the early 1780's intellectual progress seemed to them wholly consistent with—indeed a necessary prelude to—the spiritual advancement of the race. Such a faith produced, at the close of the Revolution, a variety of millenarian schemes, some less consistent than others with either Edwards' vision or the mystique of 1775-76. In 1783, for instance, Charles Turner proposed that those who had made immense fortunes during the war distribute their increase among the veterans and the poor, and that the state devote all its income to the education of youth in "christian practical godliness, public spirit and virtue." If "all the youth were educated in the manner we recommend," Turner predicted, the *"Kingdom of God* would appear to have *come."*[144] Turner's proposal was hardly a confutation of the Awakening vision, but it did to a degree assume what Joel Barlow and others were to make explicit: that it was possible to redeem society through the manufacturing of virtuous men.

Actually Turner by 1783 was preparing to leave the ministry and embark on an avowedly political career—a course by no means peculiar to him among the Calvinist patriots of the 1770's. Among those who remained in the pulpit, probably the one to preserve the old vision in its perfection, while still adapting it to the changing circumstances of the new America, was George Duffield:

> Here, if wisdom guide our affairs, shall a happy equality reign; and joyous freedom bless the inhabitants wide and far, from age to age . . . here shall the husbandman enjoy the fruits of his labor; the merchant trade, secure of his gain; the mechanic indulge his inventive genius; and the sons of science pursue their delightful employment, till the light of knowledge pervade yonder, yet uncultivated, wilds . . . Here also, shall our JESUS go forth conquering and to conquer; and the heathen be given him for an inheritance; and

these uttermost parts of the earth, a possession. Zion shall here lengthen her cords, and strengthen her stakes; and the mountain of the house of the Lord be gloriously exalted on high. . . Vice and immorality shall yet here, become ashamed and banished; and love to God, and benevolence to man, rule the hearts and regulate the lives of men. Justice and truth shall here yet meet together, and righteousness and peace embrace each other: And the wilderness blossom as the rose, and the heart rejoice and sing. And here shall the various ancient promises of rich and glorious grace begin their compleat divine fulfillment; and the light of divine revelation diffuse its beneficent rays, till the gospel of Jesus have accomplished its day, from east to west, around our world. . .

That Duffield, chaplain to the Continental Congress, should have preserved such a "transporting" prospect through the war was in itself no small achievement.*[145] What distinguished his portrait of the rising glories of America was not, moreover, his discovery that the Revolution had opened the passage to India (for that wisdom would likewise be vouchsafed to Timothy Dwight), nor even his celebration of the dawning enlightenment. What mattered, after all, was that the three chief ingredients of the millenarian impulse of the Awakening were all retained; Duffield's new America was one in which liberty, equality, and fraternity would all somehow come to their fulfillment.[146]

V

What differentiated the ministers who spoke at the close of the Revolution was not the kind of blessings which they anticipated. All who were Calvinists emphasized the spiritual glories to come, but all likewise prophesied more tangible felicities. The more important question to their minds was how the favors of God were to be received —and how they were to be distributed among the American populace. The evangelical clergy granted men only the fruits of their labor and what Dwight in "Greenfield Hill" would call a "happy competence."[147] As during the Revolution, they indicated that the genuinely American spirit (like that of Calvinism) could not abide unbounded avarice and selfish acquisition. But the even more impressive difference among Calvinists—express or implied—was whether Americans, when faced with economic inequity, should, as Dwight was also to insist, take comfort in their own "contentment" rather than actively pursue the general welfare.

* In the early years of the Revolution, Duffield (like many other evangelical clergymen) justified American Independence from the example of the "separation of the Jewish tribes." As William Gordon's 1777 sermon on this theme (commemorating the first anniversary of Independence) suggests, the very terms of the argument offered a strong temptation to dilution and even corruption of the evangelical vision.

494

For many ministers the "sin of oppression" that emerged during the Revolution served as an occasion for reaffirming certain of the fundamental principles of Calvinism. In 1777, for example, Nicholas Street, observing men "striving for the highest price for every article they have to part with," saw the selfishness of Americans as a rebuke to the spirit of self-exaltation which then, as in the war with France, seemed rising in so many American breasts. "If this disposition had not appeared upon the trial, we should have been self-righteous and trusted in ourselves."[148] Street then called on his own people for repentance, but he also proposed a number of measures for dealing with those who would "sell their country" for "a little worldly pelf." To Street the seeming "analog" of Americans and the children of Israel was thus neither consolation nor reason for speaking in the muted accents of the jeremiad. It was a reminder that Americans, were theirs to be a Christian nation, must recapture the evangelical spirit of 1775 and enforce its principles.

Much the same was true of Jacob Green, who in 1778 delivered a fast sermon in New Jersey. Green proposed that God was, through the instrumentality of Great Britain, rebuking and correcting Americans for their "vices and sins." His catalogue of vices was not, however, lengthy; and in this respect Green did not fall prey to the confusion that characterized many sermons of the middle years of the Revolution. Many preachers were disposed to compile an exhaustive list of the variety of "vices" to which independent Americans showed themselves disposed. In fixing on such items of behavior as "dancing,"[*][149] they concerned themselves (as also had the "Reforming Synod" of 1679) with symptoms rather than with what, according to strict definition, was only so many poisonous streams flowing from the single fountain of selfishness. To Green, however, all the attempts of patriots to qualify for good breeding were the fruits merely of a single and sinful disposition. To him all sin, and all vices, could be summed up as a violation of the law of love:

> Selfishness, avarice, and extortion abound, and cry to Heaven against us.—The selfishness I mean is that which is opposite to public spiritedness and general benevolence. This is really the root of all vices in the world. . . But instead of a public spirit which should have been the moving principle in us all, there has in many appeared the most insatiable avarice, and a greedy grasping at every

---

* Calvinism's "open and vigorous war with all the vices and sinful diversions of the age" seems to have been fought mostly in those cities where the withdrawal of British troops immediately spawned attempts to ape the manners and costume of one's departed betters. Charleston, and, at the close of the war, New York, seemed in Calvinist eyes singularly infamous for this not wholly unexpected mode of behavior.

thing within their reach; endeavouring, at the expence of the public, to draw every thing possible into the narrow circle of self.[150]

Green's sermon represented an effort to remind Americans that it was their "cause," and not their character, that was in God's eyes virtuous. He was likewise attempting to restate a principle that many of the sermons of 1775 and 1776 had obscured: that mankind's original sin was not "tyranny" (or "brutality") but the selfishness that inspired and underlay it. The preoccupation with the sins of Britons— the pride and arrogance of administrators and generals—had helped to vitiate the dynamic of Calvinism. From this heresy the Calvinist populace was being recalled as early as 1777, when ministers reminded them that "selfishness" was universal and that American behavior, not British, proved the doctrine of human depravity to be no speculative abstraction. It was not fortuitous, however, that the most ringing indictments of American "selfishness" came from preachers already inclined to Hopkinsianism.[151] One of the intellectual consequences of the economic misbehavior of the late 1770's was the seeming confirmation it gave to Hopkins' reading of human nature and the stimulus it provided to his negative conception of true benevolence.

By the end of the Revolution Hopkins and his followers would have defined virtue in terms of repression both of the self and of the will. In their formulation the more affirmative aspects of the Edwardean theology nearly disappeared, and the way was prepared for making this brand of Calvinism, at least, an instrument of Federalism's policy of encouraging the passivity of the populace. Where Green, for one, differed from the Hopkinsians (at least in the 1770's) was in indicting something less than the whole body of the American people and in tying his analysis of sinfulness, finally, to a social and political imperative. Those who did not consider their neighbors "a part of the same body" with themselves, he argued, were "not fit to be members of civil society." Furthermore, they were to be treated accordingly by all Americans who were still moved by a public spirit—or who wished to prove themselves capable of general benevolence.[152]

It was one thing, however, to state Green's propositions, and another to enforce them. How close they came to enforcement in New Jersey is suggested by the manner in which the Calvinist clergy rose to ascendancy in the legislature in 1776, leading even the pious Elias Boudinot to question the propriety of ministers entering so vigorously on political careers. In April 1776, Jonathan Sergeant reported to John Adams that "all the great & mighty ones in the Colony" were "preparing to make their last Stand against" the "levelling" principles that seemed to be prevailing in New Jersey.[153] The stand was successful, and for many of the same reasons that made Adams and Theophilus Parsons the architects of the Massachusetts constitution rather than the evangelical advocates of liberty and the general welfare. Among these reasons, and perhaps the foremost, was the fact that the nature and purposes of the Revolution were hardly definable by Calvinism alone.

Yet the evangelical clergy had courted and embraced that Revolution as their own. Their enthusiasm for rebellion had been based more on potentiality, it would seem, than on actuality, and they had read into America's war aims not the stated goals of 1775 but their own expectations. Their subsequent pronouncements were inevitably registers of disappointment with an independent America that refused to conform to what the evangelical mind had assumed were the only promises of the Revolution. The readiest objective symbol of their frustrations was the apparent decline of Americans from public virtue, and to this subject they turned in the sermons of the war years almost to the exclusion of all others.

That Calvinists saw the future through the eye of faith in 1775 does not, however, necessarily mean that their later observations on American life were sheer imaginings. To the evangelical clergy of New England (many of them refugees from the Middle Colonies) was granted, among other things, the same keenness of perception that had allowed Edwards to explain, in his sermons on charity, what kind of persons particularly were of "a mean spirit." Thus in Connecticut and Massachusetts the Calvinist clergy were given to expounding the parable of the camel and the needle's eye and, in the years of "extortion," to condemning most of all the greed of the "rich" and the "mighty."[154] In December of 1776 a Connecticut New Light thought it clear to "any observing person" that the "rich merchant" and the "great men" of the state were primarily responsible for the advancement of "price upon the necessary articles of life,"[155] and that, indeed,

> as affairs are now going on, the common soldiers have nothing to expect, but that if America maintain her independency, they must become slaves to the rich. It seems as if our rich men, like so many hard millstones, had got the poor people between them, and had agreed to grind them to death.

These were indeed the times that tried men's souls, and one cannot help wondering what the Virginia troops thought when John Hurt told them, in 1777, about the "common bank" of society. If a man were given "a good understanding," Hurt argued, he was to contribute to the community his "advice and counsel," if strength, his "labor," and, "in short," each was to direct "his talents to the proper ends." For Hurt this included "liberality" on the part of all gifted with wealth, particularly (as he strongly hinted) if it were but recently acquired.[156] Perhaps the soldiers thought it enough that they, at least, were not sunshine patriots, except that two years later the army too were asking what their country would do for them. In 1779 the young Calvinist Israel Evans (who at Yorktown would harangue probably the largest audience gathered in America between the triumphs of Whitefield and Webster's first address at Bunker Hill) posed these questions to the western army:

> . . . whither fled that patriotic zeal which first warmed your disinterested breasts? Whither that public spirit, which made you willing to sacrifice not only your fortunes but also your lives in defence of Liberty? Whither is fled that happy union of sentiment in the great service of your country?[157]

All over America, it seemed, the light kindled in 1775 had grown dim.

Still, it is not likely that in the late 1770's—any more than in previous eras of declension—a universal darkness covered and penetrated all. This at least was the assumption of the many Calvinist preachers who were not seduced into an indiscriminate bewailing of the new antinomianism. In their sermons the distinguishing marks of evil, if not always of good, continued to be brought vividly to mind. It is "mournful to see most men eagerly pursuing gain, and heaping up unrighteous mammon," they observed. But they also went on to note how and at whose expense gain was being eagerly pursued—"by cruel oppression and grinding the faces of the poor."[158] Nor were such Calvinists simply mourning the fall from grace of the civilian populace. They were proposing policy both to the people and to their governments.

For Abraham Keteltas, late of New Jersey, the law of nature contained, in the circumstances of 1777, both an absolute standard by which to judge economic misbehavior, and an imperative. Selfish acquisition was "directly contrary to the love of mankind, and all those generous virtues enjoined upon christians." It was likewise

> a shameful reverse of the example of the primitive christians at Jerusalem, who sold their estates, and distributed the money arising from the sales, to supply the wants of their distressed brethren. All that believed (says the sacred Historian) had all things common, and sold their possessions and goods, and parted them to all men, as every man had need.[159]

From this point on through the end of the war, the Calvinist clergy proposed to the legislature of Massachusetts a variety of laws seeking to implement and enforce such insights. But it was discovered that the civil authorities were not about to conform their legislation to what seemed the obvious dictates of the evangelical law of love.

In 1779 Jonathan Parsons' successor at Newburyport, John Murray, delivered a sermon entitled *Nehemiah, or the Struggle for Liberty Never in Vain, When Managed with Virtue and Perseverance.* The sermon opened with a description of how such a struggle would ideally be managed; with each man, that is, contributing his all according to his abilities and opportunities. Such, according to Murray, was the conduct of the Tribes of Israel in the days of Nehemiah:

> See! with what unanimity they pursue their plan! How cordially each works to the hand of the other! Nor watching—nor building— nor fighting is shunned when the common cause requires it. Every man exerting his utmost for the good of the whole—and influencing all within his reach to join their endeavors for effecting the purpose.[160]

Like the conservative Jeremiahs of the war years, Murray had apparently forgotten that Nehemiah was, after all, only a "type" of Christ. Even so, he seems to have preserved, more fully than many "Calvinists," what thirty years earlier Gilbert Tennent had proclaimed as the Christ-exalting moral law.

For Murray, as for Tennent, Nehemiah was something of an exemplary political leader. What Murray took to be the prophet's role emerged in the course of a lament for the failure of the civil governments of the 1770's to make certain that the actions of all men conspired to the public good. It is "truly discouraging," Murray allowed, when magistrates "are found first in the crime" of selfishly prospering while their country goes to ruin. In such circumstances, the Presbyterian preacher announced, "corrosive remedies must be applied." There is "a power in the public which no individual is able to withstand—to that power recourse must be had when all other fails." And in 1779 there was no question in Murray's mind as to how, finally, this power had to be used:

> Nehemiah was led by the Spirit of God. And what were his measures in so great a tryal? . . . The patriot's anger was kindled against them—their crimes were censured by public rebuke, but his authority failing to influence them to their duty, the assembly of the people were called on the case—modern language would say *Nehemiah headed a Mob!*[161]

In point of fact, mobs were organized in New England in the late 1770's, sometimes under the direct leadership of Calvinist ministers like Murray. Among their purposes was preventing, by physical force if necessary, the return of the Tories, and agitating against the resumption of political rights by the "refugees." But the issues of banishment, confiscation, and proscription were, in the Calvinist mind, symbolic of a more general discontent with the manner in which the cause of liberty, of patriotism and the general welfare, had been betrayed. And what Murray discovered, finally, was the difficulty, even the impossibility, of arousing the will of the public on behalf of the general welfare when, as it turned out, the multitude no less than the visibly Tory-hearted were no longer capable of the patriotic love and zeal which to Calvinism had defined the spirit of 1776.

The intellectual and moral history of the Revolutionary years is most strikingly epitomized in the career and eloquence of Nathaniel Whitaker of Salem. Of all Calvinist ministers, Whitaker most conspicuously applied Calvinist principles to the political and social issues of the day, and in doing so he brilliantly displayed both the power and the pathos of the evangelical scheme in the context of independent America. To appreciate Whitaker's sermons of the war years, and the Salem reaction to them, it is first of all necessary to set forth something of his career and reputation in the years before the Revolution. In the 1770's his fame (or notoriety) was not merely that of a zealous patriot who preached and prayed on the subject of the Boston Massacre. He was also an articulate defender of evangelical doctrine, not only in his sermon on the death of Whitefield but in his study, *Doctrine of Reconciliation* (also published in 1770). The latter was probably the supreme embodiment of the latter-day Calvinist effort to defend, as against such critics of the doctrine of original sin as William Hart, the first principles of the Edwardean theology. Indeed Whitaker's sermons show him closer to Edwards, in spirit as well as doctrine, than any of the multitude of theologians who, in these years, claimed to have inherited his mantle.

At the same time Whitaker was involved in one of the more bitter ecclesiastical disputes to rack New England in the 1770's. Whitaker had come to Salem soon after the completion of his fund-raising tour of Europe. The Third Church, itself an offshoot of the Great Awakening, installed him as minister, largely because, according to historians of the church, of their "peculiar liking" for his doctrines and manner, "his preaching in particular."[162] Within a year of his installation, Whitaker sought to alter the ecclesiastical polity of the church, imposing on it what was called "Presbyterianism" but what was in fact no more than a denial of church membership or its privileges to the visibly unregenerate. His repudiation of the Half-Way Covenant seems to have been the occasion for a new edition, in 1773, of John Wise's *Vindication of Congregationalism*—a document subscribed to by the leading Liberal, moderate Calvinist, and orthodox ministers of the province and such arch-democrats as Peter Oliver, Jr.*

In the Third Church itself the critics of Whitaker were such "respectable" members as Timothy Pickering, whose claims to Christian virtue Whitaker would not recognize. In 1773 Pickering and his friends demanded that Whitaker return the church to "the solid basis of pure and unmixed Congregationalism." To force him to do so, Whitaker's opponents summoned a purely Congregational ministerial council from among the neighboring churches.[163] In the course of these proceedings, Whitaker published a *Confutation* of Wise in which he criticized Wise's "boasted form of government" as, above all, ingenuous. Whitaker's observations on the manner in which wealthy but unsanctified members could corrupt a democratic church—observations which proceed throughout from his experience with the character of respectable citizens of Salem—anticipated by several years the judgment of John Adams on the role of "men of considerable influence" in popular assemblies.[164] The effectiveness of Whitaker's enemies in the 1770's seems not, however, to have been very great, for Whitaker, declaring himself a "Presbyterian" and therefore beyond the purview of a Congregational council, was sustained by the vast majority of his church. The battle seemingly over, Whitaker returned to the work at hand, which included, among other things, the construction of a new church edifice, called "The Tabernacle" in memory of Whitefield.

It was against such a background that Whitaker began to preach his patriot sermons. In the circumstances, it is not surprising that the two he published were both on the text of Judges 5:23—"The Curse of Meroz." His first sermon, delivered in 1777, began with a recapitulation of the central doctrines of Edwards' theology: "The sum of the law of nature, as well as of the written law, is love." Whitaker then proceeded to demonstrate how all who oppose "the happiness" of mankind betray an "enmity to the Creator." Every member of society, he argued, is obliged therefore to fulfill both the positive and negative imperatives of the law of love. Tyranny "is a violation of the law of nature, which requires all to exert themselves to promote happiness among mankind," and one might so promote happiness by serving as an instrument of divine justice in resisting and punishing violators of the law of nature. "God himself hates sin with a perfect hatred from the essential holiness of his nature," Whitaker proclaimed, and "so the greater our conformity to Him is, the greater will be our abhorrence of those persons and actions which are opposite to the divine

---

* The republication of Wise probably also reflected the efforts of Calvinists in the western part of the state, among them Hopkins, to undo the Half-Way Covenant.

law." When such "characters" as spread ruin and unhappiness among mankind "present themselves to our view," he proclaimed,

> if we are possessed with the spirit of love required in the law and gospel, we must feel a holy abhorrence of them. Love itself implies hatred to malevolence, and the man who feels no abhorrence of it, may be assured he is destitute of a benevolent temper, and ranks with the enemies of God and man . . . True benevolence, is therefore, exercised in opposing those who seek the hurt of society . . .[165]

As Whitaker saw it, the reaction to British tyranny could be the means of restoring mankind to its primeval beauty—a social paradise where everything was in a "state of perfect freedom and happiness" until men sinfully and wilfully made civil government necessary. Just as every child of Adam is equally culpable in the sight of God, so too is every man responsible for upholding the law of love. The war against tyranny is an opportunity to exert one's will, confirm one's benevolence, and thus add to the number of those on earth who are conformed to the image of God. Confrontation with the archenemy of American happiness, the "monster in nature" who has violated the law of love, Whitaker explained,

> surely must animate every man, inspired with the benevolent temper of the gospel—which disposes to the greatest advancement of human happiness, and to relieve the miserable and oppressed—to vigorous exertions . . . Would you, my friends, count it an honor to be employed by God to restore peace and happiness to the oppressed and miserable? do you wish to perform acts of love and kindness to mankind, and therein be like your Creator and Redeemer? . . . Are these the objects of your desire and pursuit? I know they are if the love of God and your neighbor rules in your hearts. Well, then, here is an opportunity presented to you, to manifest your love, by coming to the help of the Lord against the mighty. The cause we are engaged in is the cause of God; and you may hope for his blessing and fight under his banner. In supporting and defending this cause, you may, you ought to seek for glory and honor; even that glory and honor which come from God and man for acts of benevolence, goodness and mercy, for the performance of which the fairest opportunity now offers.[166]

In offering the people of Salem such an opportunity, Whitaker may momentarily have forgotten all of what was involved in the great Christian virtue of charity. Its duties presumably could be performed only by those whose hearts were already ravished by the excellence of the Deity, and whose wills were already disposed to fulfilling the law of love. What Whitaker did not forget, however (and herein lay both his glory and his grief) was that many citizens of the colonies were acting as "patriots" from far other motives than consent to Being in general.

The very title of Whitaker's sermon, *An Antidote against Toryism,* indicates his animus and the purport of his invocation of the "Curse of Meroz." Since 1774, when Bellamy preached on this text to the Connecticut army, Judges 5:23 had been the favored text of evangelical preachers who wished to condemn those who would not come to the aid of the Lord against the mighty—or who did so "luke-warmly" or without a proper spirit. From 1775 to 1777 scores of sermons were delivered in which Tories and neutrals, profit seekers and glory seekers, and men who aspired either to honors or to offices, were cursed as "execrable Parricides" by the Lord's avenging angel.[167] But of all such employments of "The Curse of Meroz," Whitaker's is the most fascinating, in part because he chose to mount his domestic crusade in the one ostensibly patriot city most infested with Tories, Tory sympathizers, and war profiteers. Even more impressively, Whitaker persevered in the Christian warfare long after other Calvinist ministers had seemingly abandoned the cause of pure patriotism as hopeless.

The text of *An Antidote against Toryism* disclosed that Whitaker had by no means permitted the outbreak of the rebellion to change his opinion of the Timothy Pickerings of America. His catalogue of all who did "anything against" or neglected to "assist all in their power, this glorious cause of freedom," reads, indeed, like a roster of the first families of Salem and of those who would later be officers of the Society of the Cincinnati. The immediate purpose of his sermon was to divest the citizens of Salem of the various disguises they had put on to hide their true character from the community—"to bring such contemptible characters to view, and expose them to the curse they deserve."[168] Whitaker's catalogue of the "marks" by which such violators of the law of nature might be known represented the ultimate perfection of the oratorical techniques developed by Calvinist preachers over the decades. For even Samuel Davies had offered only a general portrait of the selfish and the cowardly, leaving it for "others to judge, whether the original of this ugly picture is to be found anywhere in the universe."[169] Whitaker, however, left little to the imagination of his auditors; no citizen of Salem was left wondering who, precisely, deserved the curse of Whitaker's God and the punishment of His people.

Whitaker had lived long enough in New England to realize there particularly the outward and the inward man were not necessarily the same. As Nathaniel Niles observed in 1773, when speaking of the terms of church communion, the "art of counterfeiting, is like all others, gradually acquired."[170] The people of New England had had considerable training, as it were, in the method. Since the 1630's and especially after the adoption of the Half-Way Covenant, the very conditions of admission to church membership had tolerated and even encouraged hypocrisy. One purpose of Edwards' revisions in church polity, in fact, had been to discourage the disposition to masquerade inherent in the old system. Bellamy's attack on the Half-Way Covenant was similarly inspired. Thus Whitaker's sermon, though his focus might have shifted, was a recapitulation, in political terms, of all the Calvinist utterances that lay in the great tradition of Tennent's unmasking of the children of darkness in *The Danger of an Unconverted Ministry*. Whitaker insisted that for the true and counterfeit patriot to be distinguished, men must be first of all "stript of their vizards." This Whitaker proceeded to do:

> There are other pretended friends whose countenance betrays them. When things go ill with our army, they appear with a cheerful countenance, and assume airs of importance, and you'll see them holding conferences in one corner or another. The joy of their hearts, on such occasions, will break through all their disguises, and discover their real sentiments; while their grief and long faces in a reverse of fortune, are a plain index pointing to the end at which they really aim.[171]

There were many in Salem whose inner principles were not even so well hidden. "How provoking in the sight of God," Whitaker cried, "is it to see some quite unconcerned for the good of public, rolling in ease, amassing wealth to themselves, and slyly plotting to assist our enemies." Whatever "motives influence men at this day," Whitaker concluded, "whether a desire of ease, hope of power, honor, or wealth," if not outright treachery, they and every "idle spectator" and every "over-prudent" man equally deserve the curse of Meroz. They are to be "considered and treated as confederates and abettors" of the enemy of God and man, "and partakers in his crimes." Such men were simply the "images" of the more ingloriously deformed: "Pharaoh, Saul, Manasseh, Antiochus, Julian, Charles I, of blessed memory, and George III, who vies with the chief in the black catalogue, in spreading misery and ruin round the world."[172] Whoever in civil society presents such a visage is "an enemy not only to his country, but to all mankind," and

> every member of the body politic is bound, by the eternal law of benevolence, to set himself against him, and if he persists, the whole must unite to root him from the earth, whether he be high or low, rich or poor, a king or subject.[173]

In 1777 Whitaker proposed no such drastic policy as literally rooting the overtly tory and the over-prudent from the earth. He urged merely that virtuous men ought, at least, avoid "intimacy" with them, disarm them, confiscate their estates, apply the proceeds to the cost of war, disfranchise them, and then banish—or, more accurately, excommunicate*[174] them—"from these states."[175] In this early year of the war Whitaker looked to the Massachusetts General Court, to the Congress of the Confederacy, and the Commander in Chief for action, meanwhile advising the people to signify by their votes in the next election their approval or disapproval of the actions of the legislature.

Within a year, however, Whitaker despaired of seeing confiscation enforced, and by 1780 he saw ships arriving from Nova Scotia and Bermuda, depositing their cargo of returning Tories on the city piers. In these circumstances, Whitaker undertook a course of action that added to and spread his already considerable reputation. He was "usually called Dr. Meroz in America," it was reported, "from his constantly applying the twenty-third verse of the fifth chapter of Judges to the poor refugees"—as those who had kept the waters clean about them in the snug harbors of Halifax and London chose to call themselves. Whitaker also followed the example of Nehemiah; he began to act, and not just preach, against the return of the Tories: "on the wharves as well as in the desk," as one exile complained.[176]

Whitaker, in sum, headed a mob, and his partisans were called to action not only against the refugees but in opposition to all who aided or tolerated their return. To be a Tory, Whitaker declared, it was not necessary to have left America during the Revolution. Others, having "tory hearts," had used "LIBERTY for their motto, in order to deceive," and had spent the war "speculating in trade" or seeking "some post in the army or State." Not surprisingly, according to Whitaker, such "half-way" and perverse "patriots" were more than ready even before the end of hostilities, to welcome back the offending exiles—and their prestige and wealth.[177]

These observations appeared in the second of Whitaker's published revolutionary sermons, *The Reward of Toryism*, which was delivered in May 1783 as part of Salem's celebration of the treaty of peace. In

---

* Whitaker's argument for the banishment of Tories and Tory sympathizers was simply an application of Edwardean ecclesiastical principles to civil society. "Common sense teaches all mankind," Edwards had observed in defending his requirements for communion, "in admission of members into societies, at least societies formed for very great and important purposes, to admit none but those concerning whom there is an *apparent probability,* that they are the hearty friends of the society, and of the main designs and interests of it; and especially not to admit such concerning whom there is a greater probability of their being habitual fixed enemies."

this sermon Whitaker clearly revealed what for him, as others, now seemed to be the principal hinge of the evangelical scheme. There is "too much reason to suspect," Whitaker observed, that the "conversion" of many from "open toryism" or lukewarmness to "patriotism" was "owing to a view of profit." Finally he disclosed the full implications of his argument, in relating what was to become of an independent America should the Tories and Tory-hearted be allowed to remain:

> It is manifest that the state cannot be safe while the tories remain among us, unless their principles are changed, and their whole man renewed, which we have not the least reason to hope for, as no new arguments have been offered, and no new principles can be supposed to have taken place in them.[178]

Within a year of this declaration, Whitaker was removed from his Salem pulpit in a drama which saw him re-enacting, almost as if he had memorized the script, an earlier banishment from Northampton. "Large bribes," character-assassination, the calling of a consociation, and, concurrently, appeals to the traditional New England right of congregational control, all saw service in Whitaker's defeat at the hands of the subtle, and crafty, and the prudent. His ouster was clearly desired, and, if the letters of the Tory Samuel Curwen are any evidence, planned and promoted by the "refugees."[179] But it had its sources also in the ancient struggle, with Timothy Pickering and others, over questions of ecclesiastical polity.

On the issue of church polity, Whitaker was the victim, not only of his avowed and traditional enemies, but of such evangelical ministers as John Cleaveland, the brother of Whitaker's one-time colleague in the supervision of Wheelock's Indian missions. Cleaveland, once a separatist pariah in the eyes of the Massachusetts standing order, was a member of the council that ousted Whitaker. In the course of the proceedings, Cleaveland arraigned Whitaker for failing to understand the meaning of "liberty" and "democracy" in the church.[180] The same questions had been raised in 1778, by an enthusiastic dissenter who published a lengthy critique of Whitaker's confutation of Wise. Whitaker's critics displayed the most simplistic of Congregational spirits: the "legislative power, is lodged in the Common People, and they may chuse a Brother to represent them, to have things according to their own mind, the major ruling the minor."[181]

No less than Whitaker, the people of New England were struggling to ascertain the meaning of the Revolution to church government. By the end of the war the dissenter populace throughout the colonies were insisting that Christian ministers must be in all cases subject to "the will of the people whom they serve."[182] This principle the

Calvinist ministry, including Whitaker, had long espoused and defended—but not without admonitions as to which elements of the "people," in any church or parish, were entitled to the congregational keys. For many reasons, these caveats were forgotten or dismissed by the ecclesiastical democrats of independent America. Perhaps because they were unsuccessful in enforcing the counterpart of church democracy on the political institutions of the new nation, they were unyieldingly suspicious of church constitutions that did not acknowledge the superior "will of the people." In Massachusetts especially, the frame of civil government adopted in 1780 hardly represented a vindication of the principles of democracy invoked to justify the removal of Nathanial Whitaker from his Salem pulpit.

Actually, many of Whitaker's church members, probably the majority, remained loyal to him throughout the controversy. This despite the charges that Whitaker was "a frequenter of Stews" and had "debauched the young women of his congregation under the pretence of converting them"—accusations that even William Bentley, who scoffed at Whitaker's Calvinism and his sermons on the curse of Meroz, considered ludicrous if not slanderous. If the blackening of Whitaker's character was to any degree instrumental in effecting his ouster, this was testimony to the changing taste of Americans—not of the critics of Calvinism but of the people.*[183] It is more than likely that some of Whitaker's parishioners were disposed by 1783 to worry more about "beastly lusts" than about what Edwards had called the "devilish ones." Still, in order for Whitaker to be ousted, it was necessary to create a majority from outside his church membership. For Congregationalism to be vindicated, Whitaker's opponents had to restore church privileges to those whom he had excommunicated in 1773—and indeed as many Half-Way descendants of the original membership as could be found.

When the time came for a final reckoning, moreover, it was not John Cleaveland whom the worthies of Salem called in to explain to the people of the Tabernacle why Whitaker had to be removed. The spokesman for the council (and "consociated congregationalism") was Eli Forbes, of late a suspected Tory, and always a most moderate Calvinist. "Pray for the peace of Jeru-Salem," Forbes intoned.

They shall prosper, that love thee. Peace be within thy walls, and prosperity within thy palaces.[184]

* Ever since the Awakening similar charges had been brought against Calvinist ministers by Liberal critics and disaffected parishioners. But as one Liberal complained, ministers of the worst character were "not only protected but applauded by the giddy Multitude, because they look'd upon their *Zeal* and *Orthodoxy* to be sufficient Excuse for *their Chambering and Wantonness.*"

The prosperity of the war years had fallen not only to Timothy Pickering, but to many others who now preferred dwelling in pleasant palaces
(or aspiring to do so), to being reminded of the nature of true virtue.
This Whitaker seems to have understood, when he confessed that it
was not the "threats, promises, or rewards" of the Tories that brought
about his downfall, but the spiritual degeneracy of many of the very
people on whom he had counted for support:

> I really believe, and on good grounds, that had I preached smooth
> things; and promised heaven to works of natural men; been delicate
> and modest in reproving the fashionable vices of the times: in a
> word, if I had studied and preached people's tempers more, and my
> Bible less . . . I should have been, this hour, as quiet, reputable,
> and esteemed in the world, at least, as common, and *the crimes
> charged* [against] *me would not have been mentioned.*[185]

Of course Whitaker had, as a Revolutionary preacher, in one respect
at least all but promised heaven to the works of natural men—by
giving his people the opportunity to enlist under the banner of liberty
and godlike benevolence. It may well be that many of the Salem
patriots, even the most dedicated, were by their wartime services so
persuaded of their virtue that they no longer thought it necessary to
work out their salvation in fear and trembling.

Yet in the final analysis Whitaker's downfall seems to have stemmed
less from his seemingly antiquated doctrine than from the clarity and
vigor with which he displayed the new imperatives of the moral law.
After Whitaker's departure, the pulpit of the Tabernacle was filled by a
brother of Samuel Hopkins, whose gospel was, doctrinally at least,
no more generous than Whitaker's. It may be that the debacle in
Salem was a consequence, finally, of a failure of aesthetic perception.
Even as Whitaker summoned his people to a continuing warfare
against the covetousness and petty tyranny in their midst, he admitted
that the "monster" of selfishness had "shown its odious head" in Salem
"in open day-light," and only "few, very few," were able to see it for
what it was.[186] Whitaker's vision had remained unimpaired. The inhabitants of heaven, he asserted in the last published sermon of his
life, do not behave "as ambitious, sinful, aspiring mortals do," and
their "order and government is beautiful, sweet and glorious." The
merest perception of that beautiful order, he affirmed, "should animate
us to a cheerful imitation."[187] Whatever the perceptions of the people
of Salem in 1784, many listened attentively, and possibly with joy on
their countenances, as Forbes advised them to look on Whitaker and
all such Christian ambassadors "as eccentric planets, that have broken
loose from their orbits, and will sooner or later, occasion some disorder
in the system."[188]

By 1799 Eli Forbes was held in such esteem by the ministers of the Massachusetts establishment that he was called on to deliver the keynote address of the annual convention. There he explained—to the edification, presumably, of the many young men about to embark on careers in Unitarianism, Federalism, and literature—the means of a minister's achieving an "innocent, and inoffensive conduct."[189] Meanwhile Whitaker had entered the wilderness of Maine, where he gathered a church that throve until he ran into difficulty with land speculators. After a brief stay in Taunton, where once again Whitaker saw a "Presbyterian" church restored to Congregationalism, he went, finally, to a region of America where even in the 1790's the evangelical scheme still had its adherents. He died in Hampton, Virginia, on January 21, 1795, a few years too early to witness the next pulsation advancing the Work of Redemption.[190] In 1813, when the Republicans of New England looked back to the Revolution for a testament of first principles, it was no lawyer's tract they republished, nor even a sermon of Jonathan Mayhew's, but Nathaniel Whitaker's *Reward of Toryism*. And thus did the first orator of American Democracy come finally into his rightful inheritance.

X

THE PEOPLE, THE BEST GOVERNORS

O THER Calvinists joined Whitaker in redefining the great end of preaching during the Revolution, and many experienced at least some of his difficulties. By the end of the war the very preachers who had trumpeted both sedition and salvation in the 1770's heard complaints from their parishioners that their sermons were "too highly charged with politics." Of the octogenarian Benjamin Pomeroy, itinerant of the Great Awakening and chaplain of the Revolution, it was murmured that his zeal on behalf of the Kingdom had turned into a rather too intense and pointed enthusiasm for social justice.[1] Not all Calvinists, however, responded to the Revolution in the same spirit as Pomeroy, and of those who did, few made the great leap forward so easily as Whitaker.

Clearly evangelical America did not march uniformly into the new era. A difference of opinion as to the relative importance of politics and religion was expressed, not only among the clergy, but within each community. In marked contrast to Pomeroy's experience was that of Robert Smith, a graduate of the Log College, who in 1781 complained that his parishioners were too disposed to listen only to "political" discourses. Smith proposed that they might better hearken, once again, to some of the fundamental truths of evangelical religion.[2] Similarly, Baptist preachers, and the spokesmen of the many new evangelical sects that proliferated during the war, devoted their pulpit and polemic energies to theology, or, more often, to the question of religious freedom.

Still, it cannot be gainsaid that the tendency of the Revolutionary era was toward a greater interest in politics on the part of both ministers and people. In 1773, for instance, Nathaniel Niles had twice discoursed, in arguing for strict church membership, on the "proficiency" of Connecticut people in the "black art of deception." Speaking of the "whited sepulchre" in religion, Niles thought to illustrate his doctrine with the example of two men, one a "hearty friend" to his country, the other "in heart a traitor," both of whom undertook to serve their country—the latter only, in a time of trial and temptation, to betray it.[3] Five years later, once again speaking on the Lord's Supper, Niles acknowledged that what had only a short while ago been a source of simile was now probably the chief concern of American Christians: "The present times abundantly prove to *us,* that mankind universally views political hypocrisy as the greatest imaginable sin."[4]

In this respect, the change was more in the focus of evangelical thought than in its quality and character. As in Whitaker's case, the question was still one of morality and judgment—of allegiance and commitment—and the perspective was still that of experimental religion. The subject, however, was not the perseverance of the saints, but of patriots. In some minds, *the* issue of the Revolution was the public virtue of Americans, and on this question all "political" matters ultimately centered. But for many Calvinists the Revolutionary crusade was not merely a moral one, and the disappointment of the war years was not simply derived from the failure of the American people to maintain in its purity the public spirit of the early 1770's. Calvinism had also entered on the Revolution with something of a political theory—even with a notion of the best form of government for an independent America. Had their institutional goals been achieved, some of the frenzy and the frustration of Whitaker, Murray, and other Calvinists might well have been avoided.

To comprehend the political expectations of Calvinism in the years and months before the Revolution is no easy task. Few ministers, caught up as they were in the exigencies of the times, managed to publish anything that strictly fulfills the criteria for what, to the modern mind, constitutes a treatise on political theory. In 1773 Isaac Backus, in the course of a plea for religious liberty, set forth what seems to have been the reigning Calvinist doctrine of the form of government. He asserted that God had not, "by the light of nature" or "any positive declarations of his will, infallibly directed" mankind to any particular "form of society" or "prescribed any one species of civil government." Rather, Backus explained, God had left every community to "choose that which they apprehend to be most perfect in its nature and kind, and best suited to their state, situation, and circumstances." What was certain was that God wanted men to "unite and combine" into society "for their mutual benefit."[5] Beyond this Backus did not elaborate his argument, for his purpose, like that of so many Calvinists, was simply to indict the existing governments— both British and American—for their failure to fulfill the purposes of society.

Even so inconclusive a discourse on government reveals, however, that the evangelical ministry were not prepared to make those careful distinctions between social and political theory which are, presumably, the mark of a philosopher. In their thought, the purposes of society and of government were one, and their very terms of discussion evinced the urgency with which all their thinking drove to the question of the "general good." This perspective alone would have distinguished them from John Adams or from the author of the *Essex Result,* who believed that to "determine what form of government, in any given case, will produce the greatest possible amount of happiness to the subject, is an arduous task, not to be compassed perhaps by any human powers."[6] Evangelical religion assumed that the happiness of one citizen ("subject" he was not called by the Calvinists, even in the early 1770's) was not separable from that of the whole. In so believing, the spokesmen of Calvinism did not trouble themselves with the train of reasoning, or the elaborate inquiries into the mechanics of past polities, that distinguished, among other essays of the age, Alexander Hamilton's contributions to the *Federalist* papers.

Still, inspired as they were by the imperial crisis to investigate the first principles of government, the Calvinist ministry did, both before and during the war, publish a number of discourses at least as deserving of the historian's attention as any of the declamations of Jonathan Mayhew. To the student of American political thought, indeed, or to anyone who would understand the fullness of the Revolutionary mind, they are possibly as useful as any of the pamphlets of Alexander Hamilton. For not only did the evangelical preachers so reformulate the Lockean theory of civil government that they in effect contravened its fundamental axioms, but in so doing they clearly revealed that, however Calvinists happened to agree with Chauncy and Hamilton that Britain was to be resisted, they embarked on the Revolution in a rather different frame of mind.

The evangelicals of the 1770's made it clear, first of all, that it was not simply a corrupt British administration against which they were fighting. Neither a change of ministry, they declared, nor even a purging of the British constitution would, or could, improve the situation. When one set of "old Harpies, are ousted," Oliver Noble declared, "the public gets nothing by the change; a new set of the same character and conduct succeed, *ut unda supervenit undam.*"7 Like so much Calvinist rhetoric of the period, this seems a mere negative statement, but behind it was the conviction, first, that the function of all governors was to serve the public welfare, and, in political terms, that all rulers were or should be literally engaged in the public service. "Kings and Governors," a Baptist pamphleteer declared, are "the people's servants, to be made and unmade by them and answerable only to them."8 Perhaps the most incisive phrasing of this precept (and one frequently quoted in other Calvinist publications of the day) was that provided by Charles Turner in his 1773 Election Sermon. The notion that the "servants of the publick, should not be responsible to the publick, is popery, either in religion or politics."

Whenever the people decide that it is "necessary for the publick salvation," Turner continued, they may "give the servants of society a dismission."9 But even Turner did not capture the Calvinist mood so felicitously as Nathaniel Niles, who simply declared that when a "king" becomes "an obstacle in the way of the public good, he is to be removed like other common nuisances."10 What such Calvinists were driving at is not to hard to discover; they were asserting the principle that not the king, nor any other public official, is the state, but the people themselves. "Kings can't do any thing more than other men considered merely in their own persons," Ebenezer Chaplin explained,

> it is the united and social force of the whole people for mutual happiness and protection, is what is the king; and the centering of that force in one particular man is what makes that man go by the name of the king.11

When Chaplin proceeded to define the king as no different from a "treasurer" of a joint-stock company, he was declaring that society and government are one. Both as community and as polity, the ideal was that of a mutually interdependent commonwealth, governed and sustained by the virtue and energy of the multitude.

In the years before Lexington and Concord, most Calvinist utterances on the subject of government were perforce characterized by an abundance of negative propositions. Chaplin, for instance, proclaimed in 1773 that

> any state, society or government not formed with that natural connection, dependency, and subserviency of all the parts with, upon and for each other is not a creature of God's making . . . but are some of the broken cisterns of man's invention, and hewing out.12

But such sentiments, taken together with the urgent efforts of Calvinists in the 1770's to energize the wills of the multitude, suggest the more positive goals underlying their resistance to British "tyranny."

They seemed bent on replacing the common nuisance with the purest of democracies—possibly of the kind that Nehemiah evolved, but certainly one distinguished by full popular participation in the affairs of state, the will of the people constantly guiding an administration which it made and unmade, likewise at will.

Fortunately, these primitive essays in political thought do not represent the whole of Calvinist speculation on the nature of state and society in the years before the Revolution. Nathaniel Niles's *Two Discourses on Liberty,* which undoubtedly represented, as has been noted, the political gospel according to Joseph Bellamy, exhibit a theoretical argument and formal structure lacking in the more topical and exhortatory sermons. They provide the key—if not to the Revolution, then at least to what was the social and political theory in 1774 of many of the heirs of Edwards. They are likewise interesting in view of Niles's subsequent career, which included, during the Revolution, not only itinerant preaching but the composition of a hymn that helped sustain the Connecticut people of God through eight years of war. In 1779, however, Niles entered the legislature of the state, and at the close of hostilities he, like so many ministers of his persuasion, left the active ministry. He remained an outstanding theologian and immensely popular preacher to the end of his life, but after 1783 his main career was politics. His activities included membership in the legislatures of Connecticut and of Vermont (and the speakership of the latter in 1784), a judgeship on the Vermont Supreme Court, and, in the 1790's, service in the national Congress, where he voted against the Hamiltonian program. In 1796 and five times thereafter he was a Republican presidential elector. Just as John Leland's career joins the world of Devereux Jarratt to that of Andrew Jackson, so does Niles's represent the continuity from the thought of Samuel Finley and Joseph Bellamy—and of Edwards—to that of America's first truly triumphant democracy.[13]

Other Calvinist preachers of the period between 1773 and 1783 anticipated or echoed Niles's leading sentiments—though few expressed them so clearly and eloquently or with so little immediate attention to the particulars of the controversy with Great Britain. The most striking section of Niles's sermons is that in which he examines Locke's theory of social contract. So disdainful of this theory was Niles that he relegated the better part of his criticism to a footnote. That he saw fit to publish his opinions, however, is a cause for rejoicing, since this future judge of the Vermont Supreme Court thereby disclosed how sharply evangelical republicanism could diverge from the more reasonable and legalist Whiggery of the day.

Civil governments, Niles observed, have theoretically been formed by the acts of a despot, on the basis of conquest, or by the members of a community entering into contract for protection against the "inconveniences" of a state of nature. But to Niles, for whom there was nothing "romantic" in the idea of the millennium, the notion of a social contract was a fiction—a dangerous fiction. The principles of Locke's *Second Treatise,* Niles declared, are no better than those demolished in the *First.* "Both of these" forms of government, Niles insisted, arise from sin, for "there were no private interests antecedent to compact, but such as had been taken by usurpation." The notion of government as an instrument for mutual defense of individual property "is the maxim on which pirates and gangs of robbers live in a kind of unity."[14]

Any rational theory of goverment must assume, according to Niles, that men enter society, not to conserve their private interests, but to seek and serve the common good. Precisely such a premise underlay all the Calvinist essays in political theory during the Revolutionary period:

> God cements mankind into society for their greater good, while each, consenting to submit his exercise of the several powers with which he is vested to the cognizance of the whole body, agrees to deny himself such gratifications as are deemed incompatible with the felicity of the rest . . .[15]

What concerned Niles in 1774, however, was not what had happened in the past (if indeed it had) but the form of government for which, in the future, Christians ought to contend. His sermons were not simply disquisitions or exhortations on imperial questions, but projections of Calvinist principles into the era of independence which he quite obviously expected would soon begin.

If "government is first founded on private interest," Niles explained, "it cannot be reasonably expected, that the superstructure will stand." A legitimate government must be founded on principles consistent with the Edwardean law of nature. "Every individual is to have his part assigned to him, and so long as he fills his place well, he is to be rewarded for his services by the community." But "he is not to have any separate interest assigned him," Niles continued, "for this would tend to detach him from the community." At this point Niles sustained his view of commonwealth with an analysis of human nature that revealed, in all their glory, the social implications of the Edwardean thesis that men by nature are totally depraved:

> Just so far as his affection is turned on private interest, he will become regardless of the common good, and when he is detached from the community in heart, his services will be very precarious

at best, and those will not be expected at all which imply self-denial. He is only to enjoy it at the will of the community, which is to be regulated by the interest of the whole.

The radical political thrust of this doctrine of government by the will of the people for the general welfare emerged in the text of Niles's sermon:

Every one must be required to do all he can that tends to the highest good of the state: For the whole of this is due to the state, from the individuals of which it is composed. Every thing, however trifling, that tends, even in the lowest degree, to disserve the interest of the state must also be forbidden.[16]

The state, in sum, was to take over the function which for years had been that of the clergy and the church membership: enforcement of the moral law. Indeed, the community was to judge men by the same standards that Edwards had set as the test of visible sainthood. Every individual was to be considered and treated by the state as "a good or bad member as he uniteth to, or counteracteth the interest of the body."[17]

The question of who were to serve, in such a state, as the ministers of social justice Niles answered by dismissing as well the notion of a political covenant. His magistrates were not to be "rulers," empowered, like John Winthrop's, to pursue the general welfare according to their own lights, nor even, like John Locke's, bound only by specific requirements of a contract. "The several offices in the government," Niles declared, are "so many parts of the common good, or stock," and, like "other parts of the common inheritance," they are "committed to individuals by the body" to be "improved for the company of proprietors."[18] Public officials were like anyone else merely the stewards of the community, subject to continual judgment and instruction, and removable by the sovereign will of the people whenever, for whatever reason, a society decided its servants were not fulfilling the purposes of the community.

In explaining how and by whom social policy was to be made, Niles expressed both the reasoned conclusions and the felt expectations of a Calvinism preparing to make America safe for democracy. The "voice of a majority," he affirmed, is "much more likely" in any given circumstance to decide what is best for the state and whether the ministering servants of society are seeking the general good. Niles's defense of this proposition discloses the latter-day function of the evangelical scheme in colonial America. His doctrine was not that the rulers of society have to be intelligent, but that they must be virtuous—and his application, that the few great men are rarely virtuous and that God must favor the common people because he made so many of them. His argument for majority rule proceeded from the premise that "private interest is the great idol of the human mind." In any and all circumstances, therefore, the majority will better appreciate "the general interests of the body" than "any minority whatever," since the views of any minority are, by definition, more partial. A majority would even have "a more general and distinct knowledge of the circumstances, and exigencies of a state than a minority," for its attention would not, like that of great men, be riveted on selfish concerns. A majority would also be "more able to judge of what is to be done" because it would be more widely dispersed about a state (and not concentrated in a trading town or two). The majority is, finally, in the very nature of things, more virtuous. The affairs of society must be in the hands of persons of "a disinterested benevolent spirit," Niles declared, and there

> is reason to believe that by far the greater part of these are to be found among the lower classes of mankind, and that a very small proportion of them are among the great.[19]

Niles did not believe that a majority would "necessarily, nor invariably" seek the highest good of the community, but only that they, rather than some minority, would bring society to the "highest degree" of felicity "that can possibly be expected in earthly states."[20] The will of the majority, to be right, had to be, not reasonable, but conformable to the law of nature. It was not that a majority would infallibly and consistently fulfill the moral law, but simply that any number less than the majority was all the more likely to violate it. Niles was asserting, in short, that 51 per cent of the populace, while not necessarily free from error, would, in any state short of perfection, have to be considered the closest approximation of the right.

If Niles's *Discourses* have no other significance, they at least indicate why it was that the writings of Jean Jacques Rousseau were so little perused in late eighteenth-century America. From the 1770's through the election of 1800, when rural Jeffersonians vehemently denied that the government of the United States had been created through "contract" or "covenant" and just as confidently insisted that the "general will" of "the sovereign people" was the only determinant of social and political right, the spokesmen of a radical democracy had little need to turn to the Genevan philosopher.[21] In 1774, Levi Hart declared that "the welfare and prosperity of the society is the *common good*," that "everything transacted in society is to be regulated by this standard," and that all men, at every moment, must act to fulfill the common happiness and to see that nothing is done to inter-fere with it.[22] To Hart these principles seemed the logical extensions of the doctrines recapitulated in the opening section of his discourse: those of Edwards' *Will*. The most radical of democratic theories was derivable, in sum, from another, and perhaps the greatest, of the students of John Calvin.

Already in 1774 American Calvinists were seeking to enforce their notions on the communities of America, and throughout the war they strove to uphold them as the social and political goals of the Revolution. In 1774, William Gordon recalled, any citizen who ex-pressed dissatisfaction over the discontinuance of importations from Britain was "considered as selfish, preferring private interest to the good of the country." In many communities the multitude would "apply singular punishments" to individuals who defied "the general sense of the community."[23] Once the war began, Calvinists even more urgently invoked, in word as well as deed, their curious political prin-ciples. The "general will," declared a Connecticut New Light, must be considered "to be the nature of a law."[24] But not all Americans—nor even all who proclaimed the glorious revolution—agreed. As the reader of John Trumbull's *M'Fingal* readily appreciates, the more reasonable patriots were distressed, not merely by mob rule, but by the very notion that they might be given over to the government of a rude and unwashed multitude.

Shortly after independence had been declared, John Adams, who for more than a decade had been arguing that the "people" needed to be aroused as a "control" on arbitrary government, proposed that, so far as the constitutions of independent America were concerned, the first need was a check on the power of the multitude.[25] For many reasons his theories of government more readily found their way into the fundamental charters of the period than Nathaniel Niles's simpler formula. One was that the American multitude, by its dismally selfish conduct in 1776-1778, had seemingly forfeited the right to rule. In fact, more than one political theory or program took as its first prem-ise what the Calvinist ministry discovered, during the war, to be the character of the American people. "We may preach till we are tired of the theme," affirmed Alexander Hamilton in his first proposal for a stronger confederacy, "the necessity of disinterestedness in re-publics, without making a single proselyte."[26] With somewhat differ-ent ends in view, and perhaps out of a somewhat different experience, Thomas Jefferson argued the need for establishing religious liberty during the Revolution, while Americans were still capable of public-spirited behavior. At the end of the war, Jefferson predicted in his *Notes on Virginia,*

They will forget themselves, but in the sole faculty of making money, and will never think of uniting to effect a due respect for their rights.[27]

The emergence of the issues of bills of rights and of internally checked-and-balanced governments, and the nature of the constitutions drawn up and ratified in the 1770's and 1780's, cannot deny, however, the fact that many Americans began the Revolution with somewhat happier, and simpler, thoughts of government. In many evangelical minds it seemed possible, once men were aroused to put "forth a helping hand for the common cause," to prolong the spirit of 1775 so that Americans would create a society and form a government in which the general good would be achieved by the general will—not only, as Andrew Lee put it, "at the present," but "in all future ages."[28] The thought and rhetoric of Calvinism during the war, as in fact its mobs, were attempts to preserve these hopes. But it proved not enough to declare, merely, that "all may, one way or another, put to a helping hand" in promoting the social good, especially not when, as Whitaker and Murray discovered, the general will became, in Calvinist terms, both palsied and perverse.[29] Nor is it surprising that, in the intellectual confusion of the Revolutionary years, the spokesmen of Calvinism, divided as they were among themselves as to the ills of American society, met less than successfully the political challenges of the age and, in the aftermath, seemed to leave the governments of America, once again, in the hands of "other men."

II

The precise contribution of the Calvinist ministry in the constitutional debates of the period after the Declaration of Independence is difficult to determine. In the first heady years of the Revolution, young preachers seriously propounded the *theological* doctrine that "the voice of the people is the voice of God," and many, either because rebuked or because impatient, thereafter embarked on unrecorded careers as itinerant political exhorters.[30] Something of their role, as well as that of such unofficial evangelical tribunes as Whitaker and Murray, may be inferred, however, from the lament of William Whiting, who complained during the constitutional discussion of 1778 that the people of Massachusetts "appeared to pay a much greater regard to the person speaking than to the argument he offers."[31] Their arguments may likewise be seen as reflected in such documents as the *Essex Result,* in which Theophilus Parsons bewailed the many curious notions about majority rule that were misleading the people of Massachusetts in their political thinking.

Obviously not every spokesman of political democracy in the 1770's was an evangelical exhorter. Nor was every Calvinist in those days persuaded of the truths of Niles's sermons. Many Calvinist ministers, deeply affected by the selfish avarice of the period, were preparing their own minds, as well as those of their people, for a Federalism even less democratic than that of the latter-day apostles of "reasonableness." In addition to those Calvinists who were turning against the sinful multitude, there were others who, despite their abiding faith in the people, had abandoned much of their pre-Revolutionary enthusiasm for a positive majority government. Profoundly impressed with the fact that there were "tyrants enough at heart" working to construct and control the new American governments, some evangelical theorists seemed willing to settle for constitutional provisions (such as equal representation for all communities) that would preserve each rural town and village from the power of the seaboard cities.[32] Finally, the evangelical mind was thrown into considerable confusion by the perplexing question of the relationship of church and state. In Massachusetts as in Virginia, Calvinist attention was devoted to this issue to the exclusion of nearly all others, and in both places the evangelical populace were thoroughly torn among and even against themselves on the questions of establishment, toleration, and religious freedom.

The fixation on the issue of church-state relations bespoke the difficulties Calvinists experienced in defining the manner in which their principles were to be applied in the public life of an independent America. Their disagreements reflected the fragmentation of the evangelical party during the Revolution, and the intellectual disarray into which every element had fallen. For many reasons—not the least among them the revival's historic indifference, even hostility, to institutional solutions—the evangelical mind was simply ill-prepared to grapple wth the problem of deciding what formal political structure was most consistent with its inherited ideals. Beyond these generalizations, few conclusions can be drawn as to the evangelical role in the formation of the state constitutions. The published literature of the debates is less than abundant, and the scholarly studies of the period of constitution-making are not sufficiently comprehensive to make less than formidable the task of tracing and assessing the constitutional theory of evangelical Americans. In any case, the subject lies, at least in its details, outside the scope and intention of the present study. Still, there are a few identifiably evangelical contributions to the constitutional controversies that seem worthy of attention—many of them from Massachusetts, where the debates over a new charter have been often and thoroughly studied.[33] From them may be extracted something of the intellectual contours of the later

1770's and some inferences as to the continuing relevance of evangelical principles to the politics of post-Revolutionary America.

First of all, the evangelical participants in the constitutional discussion seem to have assumed that the task of drawing up the fundamental charters of an independent commonwealth did not require a search for elaborate checks on the excesses of representative democracy. On the contrary, Calvinist utterances agreed (as a pamphleteer of the "College Party" in New Hampshire—probably Eleazar Wheelock's son—put it) that the task of embodying the "fundamental principle of free government" required no more than deciding the "mode of representation."[34] According to an anonymous tract of 1776, *The People, the Best Governors* (with which the Dartmouth party expressed its essential agreement), most of the forms of government proposed to that point seemed "rather too arbitrary." In fact, the author advanced his arguments as "against the sly insinuations and proposals of those of a more arbitrary turn," including some who had argued the need for a council independent of the legislature and empowered to veto its actions. A council, the pamphleteer insisted, might be useful in an advisory capacity, but there must be no constitutional check on the power of a majority of the people's representatives to decide for the welfare of the community.[35] Something of the same position was upheld by Peter Thacher in the Massachusetts Constitutional Convention. Thacher first argued that the Commonwealth ought to have no executive independent of the legislature. When overruled, Thacher distinguished himself (as did the Calvinist mind generally perhaps too often in these years) by raising a symbolic objection—"to connecting with the office the title of *Excellency*."[36]

Another issue raised in *The People, the Best Governors* was that of a property qualification for holding office. On this question the evangelical position was both traditional and, in a sense, well ahead of the times:

> So sure as we make interest necessary in this case, as sure we root out virtue; and what will then become of the genuine principle of freedom. This notion of an interest has the directest tendency to set up the avaricious over the head of the poor, though the latter are ever so virtuous.[37]

Convinced that virtue and not interest was the fundamental principle of a republic, Calvinists argued—as would John Taylor of Caroline a generation and more later—that it was worse than folly, not merely to permit the flourishing of evil "moral principles" in a state but, through the very structure of government, seemingly to give them encouragement.

Of course the Massachusetts draft constitution proposed a property qualification for officeholders and (as Parsons argued it must) for the franchise. The notion that allegiance to the community derived from a "stake" in society was most resoundingly and scathingly attacked by Joseph Hawley. If one asked who "deserved" the franchise, Hawley observed, the very question revealed the mistaken thinking of those who thought wealth was entitled to special privilege. The notion that the rich somehow deserved the vote more than the poor was a damnable (and, like Arminianism, implicitly self-condemnatory) heresy. "He who is willing to enslave his brother," he exclaimed, "is if possible less deserving of liberty than he who is content to be enslaved."[38] The remark was an expression of what some citizens of Massachusetts took to be Hawley's "obsession" with the role of "Tories" in the Massachusetts convention and government*[39] and of his conclusion that those who had been least willing, or zealous, to defend the cause of liberty in 1775 were now among the most eager to deny the franchise to men who had served the glorious cause throughout the war:

> Shall we who have property, when God shall have full secured it to us, be content to see our brethren, who have done their full share in procuring that security, shall we be content and satisfied, we say, to see those, our deserving brethren on election days, standing aloof and sneaking into corners and ashamed to show their heads, in the meetings of free men; because by the constitution of the land they are deemed intruders, if they should appear at such meetings?[40]

Hawley's subsequent "Protest" against the constitution of 1780 differed from his first "Letter" in that he no longer urged amendments but simply threatened the solons of the Commonwealth with what might be expected as the consequence of failing to consider experience and human nature in constructing a government for the new Commonwealth. Only if every man in society has a vote, Hawley declared, could there be "general content, satisfaction, and acquiescence" in the constitution. Otherwise "upon short experience, your State,

---

* Hawley also gave way to his "obsession" in arguing against a property qualification for officeholding. A "freehold in the state of the annual income of three pounds," he declared, "will attach a man to the State as much at least as 200 value in all estate," particularly as many whose income exceeded the latter amount had no "real or personal estate," but only such capital as could be "transferred from place to place." What Hawley had in mind, of course, was such capital as could be, and had been, transferred from Boston or Salem to Halifax and London and then back again. It bears remarking that the continuing strength of the Federalist party in eastern Massachusetts was not unrelated to the fact that there, as distinguished from the other parts of the colonies, even the most rigidly enforced confiscation act could not have reached commercial capital. The solution, as both Hawley and Whitaker realized, was banishment and/or proscription.

commonwealth, country, or whatever you are pleased to call it, will be filled with murmurs and discontent." However cleverly devised a constitution, if the people believe that the government does not intend their happiness and welfare, or is designed to benefit a few at the expense of the many, they will be "discouraged," and conclude that they have found "a pitiful compensation" for their "drudgeries" and "hazards." The success of a government, Hawley insisted (in accents echoed a few years later by Madison), depends on its being supported enthusiastically and joyfully, not feebly or "with reluctance."[41]

Within six years the citizens of western Massachusetts, outraged by what they believed the indifference of the General Court to their petitions, fulfilled the fears, or threats, of Joseph Hawley by rebelling.*[42] That they rebelled had as much to do with a desire for a more equitable distribution of the property their arms had secured in the Revolution as with their feeling that the Massachusetts government could not possibly be responsive to their needs. In this regard, Hawley's complaint of 1780—let us "never more be puzzled and plagued with the jargon of virtual representation"[43]—was a recapitulation of the first political premise of Revolutionary Calvinism. A government that did not provide for the active participation of the people would, by its very structure, even apart from the question of unredressable grievances, breed alienation and disaffection.

The evangelical notion of the "supremacy" of the people[44] culminated in John Leland's demand, shortly after the election of 1800, that judges, as well as governors and legislators, not be "independent" of the people—that the nation and all the states should have an "elective judiciary."[45] The same principle had been invoked in Mas-

---

* Neither Hawley nor Thomas Allen approved Shays' Rebellion, but their stand was not to be confused with that of Fisher Ames, who entered on his career as the most eminent New England spokesman for the legal scheme by writing a series of essays in which he explained that "government does not subsist by making proselytes to sound reason, or by compromise or arbitration with its members, but by the power of the community compelling the obedience of individuals." During the abortive Ely uprising, Hawley had written Governor Hancock that the situation had arisen because of the unnecessary secrecy of the General Court and was to be remedied, not by force, but by the government attending to the very real grievances of the Berkshire populace. (Hawley also reported that most of the citizens of western Massachusetts who disapproved the rebellion were unwilling to take arms against those whom they had long considered their "brethren unto blood and death.") That the rebellion occurred at all, Hawley was convinced, was a consequence of a constitution devised by "uninspired men," and a government that did not merit the confidence and allegiance of the people. Ames's answer was that "the reality of grievances is no kind of justification of rebellion," and that the people of Berkshire were in any case the victims of their own imaginations.

sachusetts during the Revolution, except that it was not yet understood how complicated was the system of independent and balanced branches of government that was about to be imposed on the commonwealth. John Murray, for instance, conceived all officers of government as representatives, recallable at will by the "people, with whom the original of all power does reside." When the people perceive their magistrates failing to promote the common good, Murray declared, they may and must "discard the unworthy incumbents from office" and "proceed in the work of the Lord without them."[46] The assumption was that no government could be properly constituted that had within it a vested power distinct from and not immediately answerable to the people.

Actually, the very nature of the Massachusetts constitution, as adopted, contributed to a feeling, among evangelicals, that the entire government of the commonwealth was an institution detached from the work of worthy men. This situation arose in part out of the confusion into which the evangelical mind was thrown by the perplexing question of the relationship of the state to religion. Whether by conscious manipulation or not, the authors and promoters of the Massachusetts constitution succeeded in embodying in that document a formula which could not help dividing the Calvinist populace, half satisfying some while completely alienating others. As in Virginia, where the Presbyterians for a time wanted religion established (but no particular religion) and the Baptists wanted a complete separation of church and state, so too in New England the Calvinist mind seemed undecided whether Erastianism or an establishment was the chief danger.*[47] The result was a curious compromise the actual significance of which would be argued out, in court decisions and in local parishes, for another half-century. The address published at the conclusion of

* The evangelical ministry insisted on the one hand that religion was never "in more danger of degenerating into a raree-show" than when "modelled to the taste of the state," and yet some of the same men insisted that a Christian commonwealth could not tolerate a constitution that showed "no symptom of difference between them and a society of pagans and infidels." Out of this confusion, born in part of the misguided hope that possibly the government might become the instrument of evangelical religion, came petitions from Massachusetts demanding both that religion not be corrupted by "being mixt with the civil government" and that the constitution stipulate that "not only the governor, but all executive, legislative, and military officers shall be of the Protestant religion."

According to Madison, Sam Adams was in 1787 expected to oppose the Federal Constitution unless it contained a similar provision, while at the same time it was only by promising John Leland what was to be the First Amendment that Madison was able to overcome dissenter opposition to the Constitution in Virginia. Needless to say, Leland represented the future of American religion and, in 1787, its majority, but it was by perplexing themselves with the establishment issue that evangelical Americans were rendered as politically ineffective in the 1780's as they would be active and significant in the 1790's.

the Massachusetts Convention of 1780 justified the provisions for public support of "religion" in these words:

> Surely it would be an affront to the People of Massachusetts Bay to labour to convince them, that the Honor and Happiness of a people depend upon Morality; and that the Public Worship of God has a tendency to inculcate the Principles thereof, as well as to preserve a People from forsaking Civilization and falling into a state of savage barbarity.[48]

This address was convincing, by 1780, not only to Liberals but to those moderate Calvinists who defended the establishment as necessary for keeping alive "a sense of moral obligation" in the people. It was acceptable to all, according to the Massachusetts election preacher of 1778, but those who would leave "the subject of public worship to the humors of the multitude." It was neither infidels nor enlightened rationalists against whom this speaker inveighed, however, but "persons of a gloomy, ghostly, and mystic cast, absorbed in visionary scenes," who, he insisted, deserved "but little notice in matters either of religion or government."[49] Just such a person was Joseph Hawley, who in 1780 immediately protested that the provision of the Massachusetts constitution requiring men to support religious teachers was inconsistent with "the unalienable rights of conscience."[50]

It was not this provision of the constitution, however, that most aroused Hawley's indignation, but that requiring all officers of the government to profess their belief in the Christian religion. The possible appeal of such a requirement to the Calvinist mind is suggested by the argument of *The People, the Best Governors*: that no one should hold public office "except he possesses a belief of one only invisible God, that governs all things; and that the bible is his revealed word; and that he be also an honest moral man."[51] What was desired, quite clearly, was not a denominational test, but a standard—unfortunately one of the few available to Calvinism in 1776—for assuring the virtue of those elected to office. But the Massachusetts constitution did not contain a provision guaranteeing the magistrate's conformity to the moral law. Rather it demanded an oath of Christian belief—a narrower and, at the same time, a less rigorous requirement, given the varieties of Christian faiths available in post-Awakening New England.

It was because the constitution asked such a profession that Hawley, elected and re-elected to the state senate by his Berkshire admirers, as many times refused to serve. His words of protest upon first declining deserve quotation if only as an expression of the attitude of perhaps the most gloomy, ghostly, and visionary of all the spokesmen of the Revolutionary generation:

Be the person ever so immaculate and exemplary a Christian; altho' he has in his proper place, that is, in the Christian Church, made a most solemn, explicit, and public profession of the Christian Faith, tho' he has a hundred times, and continues perhaps every month in the year, by participating in the Church of the body and blood of Christ practically recognized and affirmed the sincerity of that Profession, yet by the Constitution he is held, before he may be admitted to execute the duties of his office to make and subscribe a profession of the Christian Faith on Declaration that he is Christian. Did our Father Confessors imagine, that a man who had not so much fear of God in his heart, as to restrain him from acting dishonestly and knavishly in the trust of a Senator or Representative would hesitate a moment to subscribe to that declaration.[52]

Hawley's departure from Massachusetts politics was, considering his age, probably not an irreparable loss to the Calvinist populace. Yet in 1821, when Massachusetts once again held a constitutional convention, it was observed that not only Hawley, but a "great number" of Massachusetts citizens had refused to participate in the government on these very grounds.[*][53]

The withdrawal of enthusiasts like Hawley from active service in the government was a symptom of what seems to have been a general disaffection from politics among post-Revolutionary evangelicals. Over the next decades there were many who decided that the governments of America were largely institutions for the adjudication of secular differences among the ungodly. As a result, the political process was hardly as representative of the general populace as it had been in the Revolutionary years. Not until the late 1790's was the evangelical community aroused from self-imposed indifference to politics. When that awakening was complete, fifty dissenter ministers would have seats in the Massachusetts General Court, and New Jersey would send as one of its representatives to Congress an exhorter who interpreted Jefferson's election as "conclusive evidence, that the prophecies con-

---

* In that convention Daniel Webster explained that the religious test did not "require the declaration of that *faith,* which is deemed essential to personal salvation," but merely "a general assent to the truth of the Christian revelation, and, at most, to the supernatural occurrences which establish its authority." A Boston minister, serving in the convention of 1821, followed Webster by observing that Hawley's refusal was somewhat mystifying, seeing that "his zeal in support of the cause of christianity almost bordered on an undue enthusiasm," and went on to explain that everyone should realize that Christianity does not depend on a profession of faith but—as the Liberal minister William Shute had pointed out in the Massachusetts ratifying convention of 1788—merely "on the performance of moral and social duties." Had Hawley agreed with this last proposition, or with Webster's Unitarian definition of the nature of religious faith, he would not, of course, have been the Joseph Hawley who in 1760 repented of the wicked Arminian doctrines he had once embraced out of the depravity of his heart.

tained in sacred writ, will be fulfilled, and that their final accomplishment is near at hand."[54]

Meanwhile "Lawyers," as an early visitor to the United States observed, invariably took "the most active part" in the state assemblies.[55] Most such lawyers were by no means Joseph Hawleys, disposed either to enthusiasm or to the foolishness of preaching. Their ideal was closer to that of Alexander Hamilton, to whom politics was largely the science of administration. To the legal mind it would ever seem evident that the multitude, having neither the "time for, nor the means of furnishing themselves with proper information," ought to seek guidance from those of their "fellow subjects" who did. Theophilus Parsons, after a series of observations on the danger of hearkening to the "artful demagogue," who speaks in the voice of "false patriotism," went on to observe that in forming constitutions, as in administering governments, the necessary information should be derived from

> men of education and fortune. From such men we are to expect genius cultivated by reading, and all the various advantages and assistances, which art, and a liberal education aided by wealth, can furnish.

The knowledge which Parsons considered essential included a familiarity with the history and politics of the nations of antiquity, with the "produce and manufacture," the "exports and imports," of this country and those with which it traded,[56] and, in short, all that mine of general information which Hamilton in addition to Parsons believed few in America would ever attain.

The Calvinist ministry, however, were in the same years proposing a task for men of genius and cultivation that few of the order of which Parsons was a member would ever agree to undertake. "May courts be purged," asked John Murray in 1783, "and voluminous laws curtailed into a plain compend, which the common people, of plain sense, may understand."[57] Among the hopes of the Revolution for many Americans, including such lawyers as Thomas Jefferson, was the codification, or at least the clarification, of the British common law, its "many technical terms," and its "obscure and barbarous Latin that was so much used in the ages of popish darkness and superstition."[58] Ezra Stiles, who had himself studied law before deciding on a ministerial career, in 1783 listed a purging of the common law and a rationalizing of the mysterious science of jurisprudence as among the hoped-for intellectual consequences of independence.

Enlightened as he was, Stiles seemingly could not avoid attaching more importance to the rise of a recognizable American genius than to the social advantages of a simplified code of law. In contemplating the future glory and honor of the United States, Stiles looked forward to the day when "American systems of jurisprudence" would rise

> to the highest purity and perfection—especially if hereafter some Fleta, Bracton, Coke, some great law genius, should arise, and, with vast erudition, and with the learned sagacity of a Trebonianus, reduce and digest all into one great jural system.[59]

The closest to such a "law genius" to arise in America was perhaps Stiles's own pupil James Kent. But whatever Kent may have learned during his years at Yale, he was afterward hardly a friend to a digested code. Nor was he an admirer of any who suggested that American laws and institutions should and could be less complicated than those of Europe. If not exactly a friend to popish darkness and superstition, Kent in later years ridiculed Stiles's post-Revolutionary proposal for an American government modeled after Cromwell's "excellent" commonwealth. So simplistic a government Kent considered a "Utopia"— one in its visionary excess with Stiles's celebration of the regicide justices.[60] Quite clearly, with its learning and sagacity the legal mind was unwilling to tolerate even Stiles's modest concessions to the new light of the Revolutionary era.

Had the Calvinist ministry had their way in 1783, Kent might have found his occupation gone even before he entered on his career as teacher and commentator on American law and as chancellor of New York. Actually, much of the achievement of the legal profession in Kent's lifetime consisted in devising defenses—both intellectual and institutional—against the persisting evangelical disposition to "unmask" and arraign the "vice" of both the common law and the bar.[61] At the heart of such criticisms was not merely an inherited conception of the nature and sources of public virtue but a definition of the role of the intellect in public affairs that would never cease to haunt the advocates of law and reason.

To the evangelical preachers of Revolutionary America forms of government were not the only question, nor administration or legislation the only means whereby intellectual abilities could be put to the service of the public. They were first of all certain that the form without the spirit is nothing, or worse than nothing. In 1783, for instance, Charles Turner expressed the hope that in days to come a "*true* spirit of liberty," so necessary to the thriving of the commonwealth and its government, might inspire both magistrates and people. Turner defined this spirit as no other than that of "true christianity, considered as extending itself into, and operating in reference to matters of civil and ecclesiastical government."[62] Turner's thinking was not an anticipation of the argument of conservative jurists who, beginning with Jacob Rush in the 1790's, argued that for reasons of social order Christianity must be considered a part of the common law. Rather Turner was asserting the more vital truth which Benjamin Rush (Jacob's brother) would proclaim to his friend Thomas Jefferson. Christianity, Dr. Rush wrote in 1800, was a *"strong ground* of republicanism," because its "precepts" had as their objects "republican liberty and equality." More importantly, Rush affirmed, it seemed impossible to "produce political happiness by the solitary influence of human reason." Reason, Rush acknowledged,

> produces, it is true, great and popular truths, but it affords *motives* too feeble to induce mankind to act agreeably to them. Christianity unfolds the same truths and accompanies them with *motives*, agreeable, powerful, and irresistible.[63]

In sum, reason was not enough to bring the heavenly city into being—because reason provided no more than an oracle. What was needed was not merely truths, but a spirit capable of translating doctrine into lively activity.

Like other enlightened Calvinists, Turner proposed in 1783 that a spirit of liberty and Christianity might be inculcated in the rising generation through a remodeling of Harvard College and an intensive program of free public education. But he had also another theory of how the essential spirit of free government could be revived and spread through Massachusetts. Ministers "have a right, *at least*, to preach the Gospel," he insisted,

> and, if they might be the means of its being universally propagated, and practically regarded; to the suppression of the exorbitant pride, ambition, covetousness, lust of dominion, and other *vile affections*, which now reign among men, all the curious, exalted, wicked and formidable machinery of papal and anti-republican despotism, would instantly be precipitated headlong to the ground, and dashed to pieces; and, if ministerial endeavours might be blessed, for the *continuance* of such universal, pure christianity, the Hydra-monsters of civil, and ecclesiastical tyranny, would no more erect their horrendous terrific heads, to the abuse and destruction of the human race, and to the dishonor of God, and usurpation of his sacred throne, but would be forever banished from this world.[64]

In 1783 the more reasonable minds of Massachusetts were certain that the political services of the black regiment were no longer needed, now that constitutions had been erected and governments established by and of men of leisure and wisdom. But Turner knew, among other things, that for any society or government to fulfill its purpose it was essential that the people, and not merely their rulers, have their heads stored—and, most importantly, their hearts touched.

In sum, the evangelical clergy understood that one of the most important roles of the intellectual—even in purely political terms—was that of persuasion. In "a free state," John Murray insisted in one of the more confident portions of his 1783 thanksgiving sermon, "where the instructions of Constituents direct legislators," the "people may have any law that they please." There is therefore "no surer way to obtain good regulations," Murray declared, "than to convince the people of the necessity of them."[65] What Murray considered good regulations and something of what he conceived to be the best means of persuading people of their necessity are suggested by the form in which he cast his political platform—not as a series of demands, but by way of prophecy:

> Should any AMERICAN ever be so unhappy as to be reserved for a time when the public credit should have failed . . . when government has lost its energy and the laws their force—when the confederation is weakened or broken—the union dissolved—the constitutions of particular states corrupted, and their civil governments, torn by factions, totter on the brink of anarchy;—or when AGRARIAN LAWS cannot be obtained; or must pass unexecuted—when individuals are permitted to purchase or possess such enormous tracts of land as may gradually work them up to an influence, dangerous to the liberty of the state:—when commerce, which ought to be open and extensive as the ocean which laves our shores, is in-bayed and swallowed up in the narrow gulf of partial monopolies—when real estates are publicly known and permitted to be sold, or conveyed to known enemies of the country's peace—when inveterate and persisting tories are suffered to mix with its free citizens, or to rise to places of power among them. . .

Murray's catalogue of political afflictions went on for pages, but what chiefly distinguished it was not the particular ills he thought unbearable, but the one which he listed as both affliction and, as it were, the procuring sin:

> when the people at large shall become inured to the opinion that the business of the state is too mysterious for them to look into, and so shall have forgotten the important duty of watching their rulers.

Here was indeed a jeremiad, but one of a peculiar and novel order. For Murray's doctrine was, in sum, that if the rulers of America should ever come to "consider themselves masters of the people," this would represent not merely the sin of the legislators, but of the people, who, lost to the first of republican virtues, suffered them to do so.[66]

Nor was Murray's democratic jeremiad all that new, considering how it had served the exhorters of the early 1770's as one device in arousing Americans from what they considered both a spiritual and a political lethargy. The original social and political sin, according to Ebenezer Chaplin, was the

> natural disposition of mankind to *slavery* or *tyranny*, which ever induces them to put their common power or force out of their hands, as that they can't regularly reassume it, whenever they see their rights embezzled.[67]

To Chaplin this was an argument for Americans' overcoming their depravity by regaining at least a constitution that would not place an administration beyond the will of the people. But to him also, as to other Calvinist agitators of the day, it was a reminder that no government, however well-contrived, could serve the welfare of a people who had renounced interest and concern in its conduct. "We are too ready to fancy," Niles observed in 1774,

> that when once we have appointed legislators, we need give ourselves no farther concern about it. But this is not our whole duty. We are all stewards, to whom the God of nature has committed this talent. The design of appointing a few individuals to government, is not to free the rest from their obligations . . . Communities ought therefore to keep an impartial and watchful eye on government. They are urged to do so, by a consideration of the avaricious, and aspiring dispositions of mankind in general, and the peculiar opportunities and temptations that Governors have to indulge them.[68]

Almost the same thoughts were to be voiced, by Jefferson and Freneau among others, in the party battles of the late 1790's. Until then, however, the evangelical mind was seldom reminded, and was disposed to forget, who, after all, were responsible for "ruling" America. In his 1791 New Hampshire election sermon, ex-chaplain Israel Evans explained that citizens should vote for magistrates who were "actuated by principles of love and obedience to God, and animated by a generous benevolence to mankind."[69] Washington, it was assumed, was a supreme embodiment of such virtue, and because he was, evangelical Americans gave over into his hands responsibility for their government. With Washington's retirement, a great debate ensued over whether Adams or Jefferson had the virtue necessary in a ruler. The issue was finally resolved only with the discovery that the very question was, or should be, of secondary importance in America. Washington's death in December 1799 seems to have served as a reminder that the American people could not expect some Federal head to fulfill the responsibilities of civic virtue. In the next election year enough evangelical Americans recalled who must, in the last analysis, "rule" their nation, and the democratic impulse of the Revolution resumed its proper channel.

Thus it was probably not so much any of Murray's particular policies (though these too had their appeal) that led the Republicans of New England to republish his Revolutionary sermon on the occasion of Jefferson's first inaugural. Rather it served as a reminder that the American people had suffered the spiritual and political darkness of the Federalist era because of their own failure to fulfill the demands of Christian and Republican citizenship. What was called the "great deliverance" of 1800 was not, to be sure, merely a freeing of the American mind from its own shackles—any more than either the Massachusetts constitution or the ouster of Whitaker is to be understood as the consequence of nought but intellectual confusion and spiritual lethargy. When in the 1790's Jefferson set about inducing in the American people what he termed a "resurrection of their republican spirit," he called attention to both the repressive policies of Federalism and the "dupery" of the public practiced by its spokesmen.[70] But whatever the devices of other men, and whatever their part in creating the conditions Jefferson hoped to undo, the "Republican revival" of 1800 derived from a people's conviction that they, having failed in their own political duties, were themselves responsible for the seemingly oppressive burden of Federalism.

III

There were many factors in the 1800 revival of Republican spirit, and many sources to which it can be traced. Many of them were quite remote from the course of American politics, and some antedated the Alien and Sedition laws, Jay's Treaty, or even Hamilton's program to fund American debt. One of the remoter—for it was undertaken in a conscious rejection of political strategies—was the effort of the evangelical clergy to bring about another religious "awakening" in America. The need for a religious revival was proclaimed throughout the Revolution, but the summons grew in volume only with the close of the war. In 1783, amidst the general self-felicitations, a few voices were raised pointing to the difficulties Americans were experiencing and reminding Americans that their troubles had much to do with their own self-delusions. In his thanksgiving sermon John Murray confessed it "amazing" that America, "marked out for singular favors" by Divine Providence, should be at the same time "a land swarming with the most audacious classes of gospel-sinners."[71] To this paradox (the key to the wholesale confusion of the Calvinist ministry at the close of the Revolution) Murray turned in another of his publications of 1783: *Bath Kol, a Voice from the Wilderness. Being an Humble Attempt to Support the Sinking Truths of God against Some of the Principal Errors Raging at this Time.* This document—the official lament of New England Presbyterianism for the spiritual and political declension of the years after 1776—called particular attention to the spread of strange theological opinions—both Arminian and antinomian—in independent America. But many of its pages were devoted to description and analysis of what, in evangelical eyes, were the conspicuous social sins of the American states. "The love of money," it was observed,

> by whatever means obtained, rages universally: Extortion is become an avowed practice, that sordid covetousness which is idolatry, rears its front without shame, and defies the beams of noon: Fraud and dishonesty in the way of trade, is considered as expertness in business and passed over with a smile.

That such was the American character in 1783 was not the fault merely of Arminians, but of evangelical pastors and people who had too long spent their energies exclusively "investigating the natural or political springs of our troubles." Had any inquired into the "moral causes," they had assumed that all was "to be ascribed to the luxury, venality, tyranny and injustice and other crimes of England alone— and as if nobody in America had any hand in its present woes, unless the tories and traitors who have abetted the measures of our iniquitous oppressors."[72] In sum, hopefully pious Americans would have to look to themselves, and on this assumption Murray, along with many other evangelical ministers of the day, concluded that what was needed in the new nation was, above all things, a powerful revival of true religion.

The same conclusion was reached over other paths by the Baptists of America. During the Revolution they, in the South as well as in New England, struggled to achieve their religious liberty. In Virginia they succeeded, only to discover, as their historian (himself a participant) recalled, that perhaps "persecution was more favorable to vital piety than unrestrained liberty." No sooner were they "unshackled," he observed, than they seemed to have "abated in their zeal." But this "chill to their religious affections," he was sure, might well have subsided with the close of the war had not the reopening of trade "served as a powerful bait to entrap professors who were in any degree inclined to pursuit of wealth." From the experience of the Revolution and from the early years of the Confederation, the Baptists came to an insight into the nature and destiny of man which, though hardly new, apparently had to be relearned by each generation of Americans:

> Nothing is more common than for the increase of riches to produce a decrease of piety. Speculators seldom make warm Christians.[73]

The last sentence may well stand as something of a universal truth, but the other proved, in the uneven prosperity of the Federalist years, to be something of a fallacy. For the close of the eighteenth century witnessed a resurgence of piety that probably overmatched—in intensity and in number of participants—the Great Awakening of the 1740's.

The "Second Great Awakening" of 1800-1801 is a familiar episode in the chronicles of American religion. It is remembered for the "barking" and "jerking," and other "primitive traits," with which the nineteenth-century American revival has come to be identified. To this awakening is traced the reorganization and reorientation of evangelical religion—the implicit "Arminianizing" of its theology, and a democratization of the church. In the evangelical impulse of the frontier are discerned rough parallels to the rise of a democratic spirit in American society and politics in the first half of the nineteenth century. Actually, the explosion of religious energy in 1800 was an overt expression of social discontent and political aspiration. The spirit of the Kentucky revival, according to a participant (and its first historian) was one of "zeal for liberty" and "indignation against the old aristocratic spirit." The church that emerged from the revival was seen as a "new republic," its members marshaled "under the standard of liberty and equality." Nor was the "warm democratic zeal" of the awakening of 1800 confined to religious exercises, for the revival did not consist merely of the camp-meetings of the frontier, nor even of these together with the brooding concern that overcame the churchgoers of New England at the same time.[74] Throughout the United States, though most conspicuously in the East, the religious energies of Americans were released directly into politics—and, specifically, as enthusiasm for the election of Jefferson and Burr.

The "Republican revival" of 1800-1801 is one of the most neglected significant episodes in American intellectual and political development. A full account of this crisis, of its background and aftermath, cannot be written here. The political-religious explosion of 1800 represented the culmination of a full generation of intellectual turbulence in which the American mind underwent some of the most intricate convolutions in its entire history. To unravel the many fine threads in this fabric would require as many words as it has taken to carry the story from the Great Awakening to the Revolution. The 1790's alone offer enough material for a major study, and a fascinating one, since in this decade the religious and political concerns of Americans impinged on each other more directly, and also in many more subtle ways, than at nearly any other moment in our past. The result was a transformation in the American mind that set the terms of much of the thought and action of the nineteenth century. What follows here, therefore, is of necessity but the slightest of sketches, in which are provided glimpses of the intellectual history of the Federalist-Republican era—or, more precisely, of questions and areas of investigation that need to be confronted before the outlines of that period can be drawn. It is tendered by way of epilogue to what has gone before, as an attestation of the continuing relevance of the religious aspirations of pre-Revolutionary America.

It is a commonplace of history that Timothy Dwight and Jedidiah Morse, among other Calvinist spokesmen, were rabid Federalists. Morse's reports of an "Illuminatist" plot against Christianity and Dwight's fearful prospects of ravished Connecticut virgins helped give New England orthodoxy the mold of defensive ecclesiasticism in which it was to remain nearly frozen for a quarter century. But their crusade against Jacobin and Republican infidelity was only one ingredient in the heady intellectual brew of the 1790's and, so far as partisan politics were concerned, probably not the most substantial. Of profounder significance in the rise of Calvinist Federalism were the efforts of Hopkins and Nathaniel Emmons to define true virtue in ever more passive terms, their insistence that Christian love must find its objects in the local community (because charity could not be comprehended beyond), and a return to premillenarianism among clergymen perplexed and then frightened by the course of the French Revolution.

However, such translations of the "New England theology" into a socially conservative ideology were not universally or uniformly welcomed by the pious multitude of America. Even in the land of steady habits, the new religious scheme met resistance among those who faithfully preserved an evangelical faith, and throughout the United States there were Calvinists who resisted the conversion of their religion into an engine of Federalist partisanship. It "is important, if we would make sense" out of the developments at the turn of the century, "to insist that by no means all the religious—call them Calvinist, Evangelical, or simply Orthodox—went with Hamilton against Jefferson."[75] There were many preachers—many more than historians allow—who avidly and vocally supported the Republican party, and did so in the conviction that Republicanism embodied the first principles of evangelical Christianity. One such was Thomas Allen, who in the late 1790's indicted Federalism in these phrases:

> Federalism consists in the love of arbitrary power . . . It is hostile to the character of Jehovah, and the love of our Neighbour. It is a leprosy on the body politic, destructive of peace, order, and happiness. Self is its idol. It essentially consists in selfishness.[76]

In such accents the affinities of Edwardean Calvinism with Republican politics are clear. The relationship is also evident in the multitude of discourses in which evangelical preachers assailed Federalist "tyranny" and "aristocracy" as violations of the "liberty" and "equality" demanded by the moral law. Together they constituted an attack on the Hamiltonian program and spirit that helps explain why and how many pious Americans could finally commit themselves to support of Jefferson and Burr. To Christians tormented by the economic temptations of the Federalist years, such rhetoric comprised an invitation, not unlike that which had been offered in the 1770's, to prove their own virtue by resisting, and overcoming, the sinful selfishness of other men.

The process of summoning and restoring elements of Calvinist America to "Republican virtue" was by no means a simple one, for the evangelical mind, and indeed the American mind generally, was torn in the 1790's between conflicting oracles. These were years of profound ethical confusion, of personal and social dilemmas which, as the protagonist of Brockden Brown's *Arthur Mervyn* discovered, were not quickly resolvable either in deliberation or through action. In politics too the American mind appears to have made its way, not along one direct and well-marked path, but through what at the time must have seemed a dark and elaborate maze. For many Americans, all the more important steps were taken in a single year, or even in a few dizzying months of 1800, when the sharpening political confrontation offered a ready and practical opportunity to break out into enlightenment. But for others nearly the whole decade was one of intellectual bewilderment, of abrupt alternations and curious inversions in their perspectives and judgments on a changing American life.

The intellectual volatility of the 1790's was perhaps nowhere more crazily displayed than in the ideas of the one Calvinist preacher who possibly did the most to bring piety to bear on the election of the Republican ticket: David Austin. In 1791 Austin edited and published the first volume of *The American Preacher*, a collection of sermons by "sound" divines, designed to revive the "union" of all American evangelicals. Three years later Austin strove to further encourage such unity by republishing Edwards' *Humble Attempt* and Bellamy's *The*

Millennium, together with a prefatory declaration that the times seemed propitious for the fulfilling of the prophecies of an earlier generation. To this point Austin conceived of his ventures as, among other things, incidental supports to the government and administration of George Washington. But in 1795 Austin commenced the series of intellectual maneuvers that saw him break, at first reluctantly, then violently, with his "Federalist brethren." By 1798 Austin had passed through what he called his "political conversion" and was embarked on a career of itinerant Republican exhortation that struck his critics as sheer lunacy.

To a degree the charge seems justified. Austin delivered one of his harangues while riding a horse, which he spurred and reined so as to add emphasis to his oratorical cadences. Indeed there was an antic quality to the whole of Austin's political career—one that culminated in his delivering a series of discourses in 1801 in the new Hall of Representatives in Washington, where this self-appointed first "Chaplain to the Republic" celebrated the beginning of what he called "the Republican millennium." But it would be a mistake to dismiss Austin as a mere eccentric, or to overlook the efforts of this evangelical orator to apply the doctrines of the old faith to the public issues of the late 1790's. Austin, who proudly described himself as "the last charge shot out of that great gun of the gospel, Dr. Bellamy," was not conceivably a representative of Enlightenment rationalism. Nor, for that matter, were the multitudes who, after listening to the discourses of Austin and other evangelicals, then "mightily bestirred themselves" on behalf of the election of Jefferson and Burr. These "honest men"—"baptists, methodists, seceders & dissenters of every sort," and even New England Congregationalists—were of quite another breed. They were, to use Austin's phrase, "spiritual republicans," whose very existence, apart even from their numbers, challenges the accepted view of the dynamic and significance of the election of 1800.[77]

There is some evidence that the primary object of the attention and affection of many such Republican enthusiasts was "that darling of the Presbyterians," Aaron Burr. However, none seem to have begrudged Jefferson the election, and even in 1800 most evangelical spokesmen praised him as the Republican party's recognized candidate for the Presidency. Jefferson acknowledged such support, even encouraged it, and did so because he appreciated the difference between the joyful and liberating exuberance of enthusiasts and the fear-filled and repressive "bigotry" of New England's "priesthood." This is not to suggest that Jefferson, or any of his more enlightened associates, partook of the vagaries of the "spiritual Republicans." Still, the

Republican spokesmen of the Enlightenment and of enthusiasm shared several interests, grievances, and even attitudes in 1800. They were joined in common objection to the "standing order" of the New England churches, and in mutual fear of what Jefferson, no less than John Leland and other dissenter preachers, conceived to be a Federalist "plot" for a nationally established religion. Jefferson's animus against establishments was known, and understood, among dissenters, though it was not quite on Jeffersonian principles that evangelical Republicans were aroused against what they called "Federal religion." In many pious minds, the cause of religious freedom was bound up with prospects of "the millennial estate" and the persuasion that "the only way in which preparation for that happy event can be made" was by removing from America the "rubbish" of a church-state connection. Of course Jefferson never echoed such sentiments, or suggested, as his enthusiastic partisans did, that there was a remarkable resemblance between John Adams and the toe of Nebuchadnezzar's image.[78] Nevertheless Jefferson did brood over a dark crisis in American affairs, which, once passed, would open the United States to the possibility of unending enlightened felicity. Perhaps it was something more than a mere community of interest that joined him in 1800 with the heirs of Edwards.

To explore the profounder affinities of Jeffersonianism and evangelical thought would require a reassessment of the American Enlightenment generally, in its Revolutionary as well as in its Republican manifestations. Without entering on such an investigation, it surely bears re-emphasis that the Enlightenment, as it came to America, was a far different faith from that of the pre-Revolutionary rationalist clergy. Indeed, it might even be argued that the American Enlightment represented something of a translation into secular terms of the goals, and even the spirit, of the Awakening impulse. Even to begin such an argument, and surely to determine the degree of conscious strategy, it would be necessary to probe deeply into such matters as the early lives of many enlightened Americans—among them Jefferson himself—who were the children of piety, and the intellectual life of the College of New Jersey in the 1760's and early 1770's. Whatever the inner mechanisms of the process, America's true Age of Reason unfolded, especially in its post-Revolutionary phase, more as a reaffirmation of evangelical principle than as repudiation. An instance is the chief of American Deists, Elihu Palmer, who, educated at Dartmouth and called to the Baptist ministry, in his later career abjured the formulas merely, but not the ethical and social aspirations of his early faith. Indeed, Palmer turned to "the religion of nature" expressly as a means of reclaiming and revitalizing ideals he believed had been forgotten by a clergy who had relapsed into dogmatic Scripturalism. It may even be (as many enthusiastic Christians surmised at the time) that the late-century vogue of Deism generally was an expression of religious concern—of impatience particularly with the divisions and contentions of a Christianity that had once promised to inspire social as well as ecclesiastical unity. In any event, the reception and spread of the "infidel philosophy" did not represent simply what Timothy Dwight held it to be: an exotic intrusion on America's Christian heritage. Rather it served many Americans as a new bottle in which to preserve an older native wine.

The intellectual biography of Dwight's cousin, Aaron Burr, is one of the more graphic illustrations of the difficulty of assigning any single significance to the appropriation, by the Republican mind, of the radical intellectual dispensations that accompanied and followed the French Revolution. Burr seems to have received and interpreted William Godwin as, in substance, a millenarian philosopher, whose ethical theories closely approximated the ancestral formulations. Nor is it easy to sort out precise lines of "influence" in the period, since Godwin, for instance, was apparently disabused of an early Sandemanian premillenarianism by, among other things, his own reading in Jonathan Edwards. Such questions apart, however, it should be noted that the architecture of the Republicans' heavenly cities was not all that different from what had been envisioned in the philosophy of Edwards. Joel Barlow's *Advice to the Privileged Orders* was in fact expressly cast as a program for achieving through legislation and environmental change what "good men," the Christian ministry, had failed to accomplish through exhortation. "I am not preaching a moral lecture on the use of riches," Barlow explained in the course of his attack on the funding system, "or the duty of charity; I am endeavouring to point out the means by which the necessity for such lectures may be superceded."[79]

Actually Barlow was "preaching," as was also, in the 1790's, the leading Jeffersonian publicist, Philip Freneau. For whatever their enlightened faith in education, the practicalities of American political life demanded something more than a program of instruction. Republican polemicists may not have assailed the ears of the populace, or sought to touch their hearts, but they clearly came to adopt many of the rhetorical strategies of the evangelical ministry. Merely by addressing themselves to the minds, as well as to the needs, of the people, the Republican spokesmen set themselves apart from all but one of the leading rationalist clergy of the period. The exception was the gifted William Bentley, who, once he revealed his Jeffersonian sympathies, was anathematized by the Liberal ministers of Massachusetts.

By their Federalist lights Bentley was a heretic; he carried reason, not only to extremes, but, like Jefferson, to the multitude. Conversely, one of the more plausible explanations for the popularity of Republicanism among the pious lay in its leaders' seeming fulfillment of the evangelical definition of the role and responsibility of the intellectual.

Precisely here, in fact, is to be found possibly the most compelling evidence of the affinities of eighteenth-century Calvinism and enlightened Republicanism. David Ramsay, for instance, had this to say of George Whitefield:

> As to wealth, power, pleasure, honor, or the ordinary pursuits of the vulgar great, he soared above their influence. All his popularity, and all his powers, as the greatest pulpit orator of the age, were employed by him in the capacity of an itinerant preacher for advancing the present and future happiness of mankind . . .[80]

Ramsay was shot to death before he could complete a history of the United States that, to judge by its projected title, might have read like an application of Condorcet's notion of progressive enlightenment to the history of the American mind. Yet what "progress" actually meant to Ramsay—or even, for that matter, "light"—may well have had less to do with the theories of the *philosophes* than with the precepts, as well as the examples, of an earlier generation of American enlighteners. The same possibility should be entertained for most of the philosophers of enlightened Republicanism, if only to account for the feeling of pious Americans that Jeffersonian "reason" embodied a spirit kindred to their own.

The peculiar qualities of Republican thought also serve to suggest that there was possibly more than one avenue over which the perspectives and the commitments of eighteenth-century religion were carried into the subsequent intellectual life of the United States. Generally the continuities of American thought are confined to the preservation of older religious ideals in the nineteenth-century evangelical movement. Yet there is considerable evidence that the American church was by no means the only legitimate heir of the evangelical scheme of the Awakening. One piece is the curious moral urgency in the political thought of John Taylor of Caroline—a source of the evangelical quality that historians have detected in "the Jacksonian persuasion." Even more striking are the indications, in the literature of the "Republican revival" of 1800, that nineteenth-century American Democracy was a lineal descendant of the evangelical party—probably even the truest avatar of the Awakening impulse.

To be sure, the campaign of 1800 clearly marked the beginning of a more secular era in American politics. With it began an era in which the lay orator, rather than the preacher, increasingly took over the task of expounding public issues for and to the popular mind. During the War of 1812 there were numerous Liberal and orthodox ministers who inveighed against Madison and his "unholy alliance" with Bonaparte, and there were at least an equal number of evangelical preachers who added to the volume of Republican rhetoric and to the intensity of war-hawk sentiment. But in the aftermath of the war, the clergy seemed to retreat into a self-imposed ecclesiastical exile, thus completing a transition that had begun, even before the war, with the rise of lay spokesmen to eminence in American political life.

Religion and politics were never again so closely intertwined as at the very beginning of the nineteenth century. In the years after 1801, the two evolved as separate, and by no means equal, competitors for the interest and allegiance of the American mind. However, the two spheres were by no means so rudely divorced as in the 1780's, nor did the emergence of a secular politics necessarily represent an abrupt discontinuity in American intellectual life. It bears recalling that the chief of the new political breed, Henry Clay, was the son of a Baptist elder, and himself a flower of the awakened western wilderness. In his speeches were sharply etched and loudly echoed many of the ideals and the slogans—not the least of them an overwhelming "love of union"—of the evangelical heritage. In other cases, particularly on the local political level, the transition was so gradual, so undramatic, that it was often achieved merely through a change in vocation. Many of the clergymen who in the period of Republican ascendancy found their way into state legislatures simply failed to resume their clerical callings, while others mingled the two careers, generally with their people's understanding that Republican politics was an appropriate channel for the expression and achievement of evangelical goals.

One example is the Reverend Stanley Griswold of New Milford, Connecticut. In a sense, Griswold was a clerical Republican even before the party was founded or named. Throughout the 1790's he preached almost ceaselessly on the expansive "benevolence universally and strenuously inculcated in the gospel," and on "the glory of the Millennial period." His sermons were designed to free the minds of his parishioners from the vise of Hopkinsianism, but he occasionally applied his doctrines to such political questions as the progress of the French Revolution and the rise of "infidelity," which, he advised his people, was far from the most dangerous intellectual development in America. Griswold argued against the rigidities of the new orthodoxy of New England, and against the establishment itself. In 1798, in sermons touching on the Alien and Sedition laws, Griswold reminded his listeners that the fullest of religious and intellectual freedom was necessary were the American people to achieve the harmony and unity to which they had once aspired. In arguing with the Federalist prophets of political apocalypse, Griswold evolved, somewhat less frenetically than Austin, his own vision of a "Republican millennium." His discourses, whether or not directly concerned with the issues involved in the Republican challenge to Federalism, invariably closed with an exhortation to all men to rouse themselves to "endeavours to hasten this wished-for time." In 1800 he devoted his own energies to speaking, throughout Connecticut, on behalf of the Republican ticket. After the triumph of Jefferson, Griswold was often featured as the preacher at Connecticut's "Republican festivals."

Within a few years of the election, however, Griswold began his slow drift* out of the ministry and into an avowedly secular career in politics. By 1803 he was devoting as much of his time to the editorship of a Republican journal as to his parish duties. Eventually Griswold moved to Ohio, which state he represented as a Republican Senator in Congress, and he closed his life as a Federal judge in the Illinois Territory. But his new callings brought no sudden transformation in his thinking, and surely little perceptible change in the content of his public addresses. In 1812 Griswold, exhorting the Ohio militia to enlist in the warfare against the enemies of America, thundered against the British and Federalist Antichrists in the traditional accents of his religion. Griswold understood, as presumably did also many whom he addressed, that the political life and institutions of the United States were now the most appropriate instrument for achieving the promises of American life. But those promises, he insisted, were nothing new; in fact he sometimes defined the felicitous American future as a return to the "happy old order of things," an era of prelapsarian American simplicity in which all citizens were

---

* Griswold was harassed by the ministerial association of Litchfield County, in part for his political activity (and specifically, his Republicanism), but nominally and probably primarily as a preacher of "Arminianism." Griswold's sermons attest that he was in fact no more heterodox on this score than Joseph Bellamy had been, but of course by 1800 his efforts to energize his people's wills was, from the perspective of the new orthodoxy, heretical. It should be noted, however, that there was some validity to the charge against Griswold, at least to the extent that his accusers had put their finger on the intellectual revolution wrought in the revival of 1800. Griswold's political activism was the counterpart of the free-will doctrines of the Methodists who with the Second Great Awakening came to dominate and even to typify the American evangelical spirit. Though the revival of 1800 began among people who thought themselves Calvinists, its aftermath brought a foreswearing of the more rigid denials of human efficacy. In the larger perspective, however, the new evangelical scheme simply carried to conclusion the tendencies of Bellamy's sermons and of the Revolutionary utterances of the Calvinist ministry.

supposedly guided by the principles of liberty, equality, and benevolence. And these "Republican principles" Griswold identified, explicitly and closely, with the first premises of an evangelical religion that had been violated by Federalist theologians no less than by Federalist politicians.[81]

Griswold's career is a particularly striking illustration of the intellectual continuities of the period of transition from religion to politics. It was atypical only in the respect that Griswold shifted to his new role belatedly by comparison to many of his evangelical contemporaries. Already in 1800 there were several Republican exhorters who had once served in the ministry, and many others who, though never enrolled in the ranks of the clergy, delivered addresses that clearly bespoke their evangelical lineage and function. Not surprisingly these lay preachers appeared in, and itinerated through, areas where the official clergy had largely neglected, or even sought to repress, evangelical aspirations and ideals. One such orator was James Sloan, the mentor and leader of the "democratic republicans" of New Jersey, who in 1802 was elected representative to Congress from a district that had once been awakened by the Tennents. Sloan's numerous partisan addresses, delivered during and immediately after the campaign of 1800, suggest how and why the new political persuasion came to appeal to the pious as a reaffirmation of the evangelical scheme. Phrased in 1800 as a challenge to Federalism, Sloan's "democratic" creed was, in practical application, a summons and inspiration to common endeavors against violations of the common good: "Let every class of Christians rise in a mass, and unite in the suppression of every species of tyranny and oppression, of luxury [and] pride."

The further, and possibly greater, value of Sloan's discourses lies in their eloquent testimony to the persistence, in the concepts and language of the evolving political faith, of nearly all the more vital meanings and imperatives of the older dispensation. In 1801 Sloan hailed Jefferson's victory as no less than presumptive evidence that the millennial day was about to dawn. In Sloan's historical vision, the American Revolution was a "prelude to the commencement of the Millennium," and the Kingdom of God would come in its fullness when "all earthly governments are democratic." Such a revelation was far from a simplistic secularization of the millenarian vision on which it drew. For to Sloan "democracy" was much more than merely a form of government. It was a comprehensive faith, "calculated to promote the complete happiness of mankind." Sloan's "perfect system of democracy" embodied principles of "virtue and morality" identical, in his mind, to those of evangelical Christianity. The "genuine spring of democracy" was, according to Sloan, "the love of God and man," and its end and aim, the continuing fulfillment of the fuller promise of the Work of Redemption:

> Let us persevere in this blessed warfare until oppression and tyranny are exterminated from the earth, and equal liberty and justice substituted in their place; until the original harmony of the creation of God be restored, and white robed peace, and universal love, pervade all the human race.

Republican Democracy, as Sloan understood and expounded it, represented a resumption of the unfinished business, not of the Revolution merely, but of the Great Awakening.[82]

The "revolution" of 1800–1801 reawakened the evangelical hope of the great community. When Sloan exhorted the "democratic republican" faithful to "unite in the sacred cause of liberty," that cause, like the one espoused by Calvinists during the Revolution, consisted of far more than national independence and political freedom. Sloan rejoiced in "the rising of that glorious sun of liberty, which will never set again," because its benign and cheering rays revealed and illuminated the fullness of a "democratic" prospect: a nineteenth century in which humanity's social arrangements would be perfected. To the enthusiastic participants in the revival as well, the very experience of the "divine light" of democratic freedom seemed a foretoken and pledge of the good society that it was expected would come into being in the new era. In the frontier awakening it was discovered that Christians would see the "coming of the Lord's kingdom with power," not when the Pope was deposed, but when everywhere "the power of the government was considered in the body of the people." But democracy, as defined in the ecstatic exercises at Cane Ridge, was not a political abstraction; it was a felt experience of radical brotherly communion: "old and young, male and female, black and white, had equal privilege." So too at the eastern counterparts of the Kentucky camp meetings, the Republican political rallies of 1800-1801. These gatherings, which Federalists condemned in phrases more than reminiscent of the diatribes sixty years earlier against Whitefield's "mass assemblies," were an expression of the prevailing spirit of the Republican revival—a felt need to renew and reaffirm fraternal equality.

In the first years of the century, the evangelical Republican seized many opportunities—the anniversary of Jefferson's inaugural and the Fourth of July among them—to sustain and manifest his sense of solidarity. On such occasions the orator restated the hostility of the "democratic principle" to "exclusive honours" and to any American who would "usurp ascendancy." Then, speaking always in the first person plural, he gave voice to the soul and sense of the democratic multitude: "We are but part of the common mass—Man is our brother. We revere the sovereignty and majesty of the people." Like the new light of an earlier awakening, that of 1800-1801 also dimmed in time, and the democratic spirit ebbed, but no participant in these acts of shared public experience was allowed to forget completely the social goals of which his party and his government were expected to be the instruments.[83]

Throughout the United States the Second Great Awakening was recognized, by its enthusiastic subjects, as a carrying forward of the impulse of 1740. The sense of continuing heritage was expressed in many ways. At one of the eastern "Republican festivals," David Austin traced the evolution explicitly, while sharing the platform with the orator of the day and the Connecticut Republican leader, Pierpont Edwards, the last surviving son of Jonathan Edwards. Nor was such symbolism fortuitous, for the new democratic ideology attested, by its retention of the more vital elements of the inherited faith, its profound indebtedness to the philosopher of the Great Awakening. Republican orators often proclaimed a lineage and a heritage that began long before the era of Jonathan Edwards—with the "first Republicans," Christ and his Apostles. Nevertheless, even they espoused a Democracy that had, as its most prominent feature, one ideal that was clearly a legacy handed down for no more than two generations. "Our Christian brethren love the nation," it was affirmed; "they love the constitution." But above all, Republican spokesmen invariably and without exception emphasized, they loved "the union."[84] The spirit and doctrine of the new Democracy did not consist solely in a nay-saying to the tyrannical oppressions of an upstart Federalist aristocracy. Rather it was pre-eminently distinguished by a warm and resounding American nationalism.

Whatever the local discontents and particular grievances out of which the Republican revival was born, it expressed itself ultimately as a consummate realization of the nationalistic strivings awakened in 1740. So overwhelming did such evangelical nationalism come to be that in 1800 it made nearly irrelevant to the pious the presumed states-rights proclivities of the more rational Republican leaders. The Virginia and Kentucky Resolutions were interpreted, not as attacks on the central government, but as stratagems for circumventing the Sedition Laws in direct appeals to the people—even as the voices of the citizens of two states to their brethren elsewhere, alerting all to their common concerns, and thus arousing their mutual affections. For not surprisingly, the union beloved by the evangelical Republican was one defined, and bound together, by the heart-felt love of its citizenry. Later (approximately at the time of Madison's succession to the Presidency), the evangelical notion that "love" was "the only efficacious cement of our Union" came to inform the highest deliberations of the party and the government.[85] In the era of National Republicanism, and of Clay's American System, it contended for hegemony with the more mechanical nationalism of the Enlightenment heritage. Eventually, of course, the warmer nationalism of the evangelical tradition infused the ideology of Jacksonian Democracy and, with its corollary definition of patriotism as fraternal affection, helped to distinguish the Democratic persuasion from the more legal (and allegedly self-interested) scheme of Whiggery.

The evangelicals' distinctive love of union was not suddenly or unexpectedly first revealed in the last years of the eighteenth century. A remarkable unionist fervor had filled the Calvinist utterances of the Revolution, and in at least one instance had issued in a radical proposal for the most thorough nationalization of America's political life and institutions. In his thanksgiving sermon of 1783, John Murray announced that the "truest policy" for the confederated states was to "grow together, as one living body, animated by ONE living soul," and

> cast their government into such a mould, as to demolish all divisional lines between state and state—and reduce all (as might easily be done, without either danger or disorder) into ONE GREAT REPUBLIC, WITH ONE TREASURY—ONE CODE OF LAWS—ONE MILITARY FORCE—ONE FORM OF ADMINISTRATION—ONE INTEREST—ONE END—ONE HEART AND ONE LIFE.[86]

Murray's projection probably reflected his belief that a sovereign Massachusetts was not in fact a free state, and an assumption that the American people needed a more perfect instrument of government through which to act with united strength. Yet whatever his reasons, Murray's visionary proposal clearly derived from evangelical premises, and from his driving them relentlessly to what he realized were their appropriate conclusions. And thus did the anointed successor of Jonathan Parsons, three years before the Annapolis Convention, and five years previous to Hamilton's elaborate defense of "consolidated" government, call for, not a Federal Constitution merely, but a radically national American government.

The Constitution actually adopted in 1787-1788 held, like the Revolution, different meanings for various elements of the American population. Master Masons such as Christopher Gore, already impressed with the "sublimity of the idea" of a Massachusetts constitutional "temple" (not unlike Solomon's), duly responded to the craftsmanship of the architects and builders of Federal union. Other Americans seem to have reacted in terms of the evangelical principle that each "particular State" must in any case be conceived as "a member of the great national body." For in the period of the Articles of Confederation evangelical exhorters were incessantly reminding their people of this truth, and urging them, as individuals, to always "consider themselves as members one of another."[87] Thus once Calvinists were persuaded that the Philadelphia Convention had planned no restriction of religious liberty, they were among the most ardent advocates of the Constitution—not because they were so much impressed by the Hamiltonian predictions of national grandeur as because Washington and Madison somehow succeeded in touching the mystic chords of union, and, in the latter case, the wellsprings of American guilt for having declined from what pious Americans, like Madison, remembered as the fraternal spirit of '76.

Throughout the post-Revolutionary years the evangelical mind had continued to interpret the progress of millenarian history in the light of "the events which have taken place in America." America's achievement of its place among the independent countries of the world was, of course, a significant epoch in mankind's movement toward "the glory of the latter day." In each of the early years of the 1780's, however, the millennium seemed to retreat further into the future. Then, on the occasion of New Jersey's thanksgiving for the ratification of the Constitution, a Calvinist minister (for the first time since Edwards had so hinted in the ecstasies of the Great Awakening) advised his people to "look around, and see if it do not already dawn."[88] Whatever else had been achieved through the Revolution, or whatever other promises remained unfulfilled, Americans had now apparently established the most perfect of earthly unions.

So it seemed for the moment—and possibly until the people of back-country Pennsylvania complained that none of the governments then constituted were responsive to the popular will,* and were forcibly reminded that the Federal administration was not about to redress their grievances.[89] Soon after the Whiskey Rebellion, though for many other reasons as well, the evangelical mind was gradually

* It is interesting, in the light of the Pennsylvania insurrection, that some Calvinist ministers continued, well after the close of the Revolution, to identify the principles of American republicanism with the unalienable right and duty of active resistance to unjust laws. In 1789, for instance, Oliver Hart, celebrating the new Federal Constitution, reminded his hearers that further rebellion would be called for should any "corrupt legislature" pass "oppressive" laws. With heavy irony Hart noted that even a "polite preacher (not over friendly to the American Revolution)"—William Smith—had acknowledged the validity of this doctrine. Hart's sermon, delivered at Hopewell, New Jersey, was published in 1791 in Philadelphia.

persuaded that a "SECOND REVOLUTION, which is inward and spiritual," was necessary to complete the "Federal temple" erected and occupied by Washington and Hamilton. It was not so much that the Constitution needed to be remodeled—though even here several dissenters urged a more genuinely national "fabric" of government—as that America's national identity seemed unattainable through forms alone. Only by inducing a "true spirit of union" in the hearts of the American people, political evangelists argued, could this "first-born" of the earth's true nations be made to realize the full meaning and potential of its creation. The American states had to be united in reality as well as in name if the new republic, so uniquely constituted, were not to fall back toward the outworn models of Europe.[90]

The evangelical nationalism that rose to crescendo in 1800 represented, like Jeffersonian Republicanism itself, a foreswearing of direct involvement in European affairs. It preserved the vision of America as "a bright and excellent example for the oppressed inhabitants of the Old World to follow," but it offered only comfort, not outright aid, to revolutionary France. However, evangelical Republicanism defined itself as a repudiation of what seemed the profounder isolationism of Federalism. The alien law was for pious Republicans a denial of the New World's traditional role as a haven for the victims of ecclesiastical and political oppression. It was also viewed as a symptom and symbol of what seemed the worst of Federalist heresies —a perverse ethic that limited the scope of Christian benevolence by forbidding its extension to "those outside our own circle and country." But the Federalist restriction of Christian love (sustained and even inspired, of course, by the Hopkinsian theology) chiefly offended, not by its provincialism, but by what evangelical Republicans took to be its narrow and dangerous parochialism. Federalist policy, Jay's Treaty in particular, was arraigned as designed to make America once more a dependency of Britain, but evangelical emotions were even more aroused by the program's service to the local, even selfish, interests of commerce. To the evangelical Republican, Federalism seemed, in sum, not simply dedicated to a less than general welfare, but disloyal in spirit to the very idea of an American nation.[91]

As early as 1799 evangelical spokesmen were condemning the Federalist leadership for separatist inclinations and ambitions, and even hinting darkly of secessionist "plots." Thus it was that Jefferson's election could be celebrated by pious Republicans as the victory of a national spirit over those who had tried to "dissolve" the bonds that united the American people. Concurrently, however, Jefferson's critics were either, with Timothy Dwight, seeking to inspire a "come-outer" spirit of sectionalism among the New England orthodox, or,

in the case of the Essex Junto, embarking on those apparently disunionist ventures, later recorded by Henry Adams, that persuaded his
ancestors to withdraw from the Federalist Party. Multitudes of Adams
Federalists seem to have been rallied to the Republican banner by
Burr's "conspiracy"—which, incidentally, the Jefferson administration
so exploited as to ensure the decaying of the lingering attachment of
the pious to Edwards' grandson. But somehow other evidence of Federalist disloyalty managed to filter its way into the evangelical mind,
as witness the sharp phrasing of one New England Baptist elder's
celebration of Jefferson's second inauguration:

> The unity in our government is not a bare name; it is a reality.
> The strength of it has been tried by foreign foes, and domestic
> juntos. Every plan has been laid to dissolve this union; but all
> human exertions are vain; this union is of the *Lord,* and will stand.
> The *anti-christs under different names, are defeated in every* DIS-
> CORDANT *plan they have laid.*

To the evangelical Republican, the re-election of Jefferson was the
ultimate vindication of America's true nationhood. For him the
"democratic republican" party was the embodiment of national spirit,
and his partisan faith was defined as a continuing pledge that the
American union must and would be preserved.[92]

Throughout the first half of the nineteenth century, the American
Democrat remained dedicated not merely to unity in government but
to the heartfelt union of the American people. So glorious a "union"
was, however, though never unreal, nevertheless also very much a
name—a slogan even, and as such, possibly the most pleasing shape
assumed by the Antichrist of the Democracy. Indeed, no sooner had
Jefferson's first election been announced than many evangelical Republicans were hastening to soothe the angrier passions of 1800 and
to compose the differences that had, in the campaign, divided Americans. Like Jefferson himself, the spiritual Republican prized "that
harmony and affection without which liberty and life itself are but
dreary things." Like him also, they viewed the election of 1800 as not
so much a victory of party as a triumph over the demon of partisan
discord. They too hoped (and perhaps it was by looking inward that
the enthusiastic Republican sustained the belief) that Americans were
at heart all Republicans, all Federalists, and that there could and
should be "but *one soul in the nation.*" Thus even the most ardent
democrats called on Americans, as had Jefferson, to "unite with one
heart and one mind" in "common efforts for the common good." Increasingly they argued that there were, in "this good land," none of
those permanent and unyielding conflicts that divided the peoples

of Europe—or, at least, that Americans could gain nothing by encouraging divisions or perpetuating a sense of discord. "Let us spread a broad mantle of charity over the petty animosities, which have too long divided us," evangelical exhorters pleaded, particularly after the overwhelming Republican victory of 1804. Such magnanimous appeals were not simply efforts to woo the Federalist remnant to political virtue, although the evangelical Republican did seem to believe that nearly all Americans were potential converts to the democratic faith. The doctrine of conciliation was more clearly the expression of an abiding hope and faith in America as "a land of charity," where, in politics as in religion, "all HONEST men" of whatever "denomination" might harmonize by forgetting their differences on "non-essentials."[93]

Somewhat rudely, in the embargo years and afterward, the Democratic Republican was forced to acknowledge that his hopes, founded as they were on an unconfirmed reading of the realities of American life, were not so easily fulfilled. Yet shortly after the news of the Treaty of Ghent reached America, a New England Republican arose to ask once again that all Americans cherish "a sincere desire of union." Whatever "differences of opinion we may have entertained," he advised, "let every honest heart beat to harmony of sentiment." This self-proclaimed "democrat" went on to insist that his fellow-patriots should sacrifice "no vital principle" of their political creed. But perhaps in desiring and encouraging union he did more violence to democratic principle than had all the barking of the Essex kennel, more even than the recently disbanded Hartford Convention. For it was not union alone that had been proclaimed in the glorious Revolution, nor in the elections that had seemed, at the time, the final conflicts with Federalism. And though the greatest of Christian virtues was surely charity, the god, as it were, of evangelical democracy had once been triune: a republic of Americans "all *free,* all *equal,* all *united.*"[94] Possibly the dazzling prospect of national unity had blinded men to the other details of the vision. What is more likely, however, is that the desire for union served, once again, as an occasion, even an excuse, for neglecting the other two vital principles of evangelical democracy.

On the day John Adams and Thomas Jefferson died, orators throughout the nation were celebrating the fiftieth anniversary of American Independence. Most of them were deeply impressed, even inspired, by the unanimity of principles and purposes to which the whole nation had seemingly come in the half-century since the Revolution. To this salute to felicitous concord there was, however, at least one exception, for on July 4, 1826, John Leland shared these thoughts with his people:

It is now called a day of good feeling, in which party strife and religious bigotry flee away before the dawn of correct principles. The former contentions that have been between monarchs and vassals—tyranny and slavery—Whig and Tory—Federalists and Republicans, is now turned into union and friendship. And all classes of Christians, Papists and Protestants—Calvinists and Arminians—Trinitarians and Socinians, have all become one . . .

If the same spirit of amalgamation and good feeling continues and progresses, we shall lament every reform of religion that has taken place from the introduction of Christianity to the present time, and brand all reformers, the apostles not excepted, with the mark of ignorant, illiberal enthusiasts, for disturbing the peace of the world. And all those men, who have sought to ameliorate the state of society, by destroying absolute tyranny, and supporting rational liberty, will lose their names, and their unprofitable works will be forgotten . . .

But I check my roving fancy. Satan is not yet bound. The strong man armed keeps his place. Men are under the influence of pride, covetousness, envy and ambition, and will continue to do so as they have done. The sea is somewhat calm, but let the sailors be awake, looking out for the breakers. The next presidential election is hastening on. . .[95]

In the campaign of 1828 Leland's faith was amply confirmed—more so even than was, in almost the same year, that of the less politically inclined clergy who had also grown disturbed by Americans' indiscriminate blending of the faith once delivered to the saints and more reasonable forms of Christianity. What vindicated Leland was not simply that his favorite, the "Christian candidate," Andrew Jackson, was elected, but that in the process the political American experienced an awakening of mind and spirit more impressive than the religious revival that fired the "Burned Over District." The Jacksonian challenge to the civilized and tranquil political order and outlook of the 1820's shook the popular mind from its complacency in the quality and direction of American public life. In the decade and more of partisan strife that followed, Americans of whatever affiliation were engrossed by a struggle, not between different programs merely, but of opposing ideologies. It might even be said that in the intellectual confrontations of the Age of Jackson—of Benton and Bancroft, Story and Webster—there was resumed much of the century-old contest between the "evangelical scheme" and the "legal." But it is hardly necessary to press the point in order to see that one of the most significant consequences of the Jacksonian impulse was its recalling Americans to the knowledge that there were and ought to be essential differences among them.

To be sure, there were even in the 1830's many public figures—by no means all of them Whigs—who insisted that there was no issue so vital that it should be allowed to impair the harmony of American life, or interfere with the common prosperity. It was such a conciliatory doctrine, and not either Democratic principles or Whig, that came to prevail, by 1840, for the American majority. The fuller promises of the Jacksonian revolution remained, like others before, unfulfilled. But neither were the goals of Jacksonian democracy wholly disavowed; nor were the lessons of the 1830's allowed to pass completely from the memory of the American Democrat. One truth that was not forgotten was that it had hardly been in an era of consensus that one aspect, at least, of the democratic revolution had been completed. For it was in a context of partisan strife that, sometime in the early 1830's, John Leland's Calvinistic Deity of unconditional election had been irrevocably transformed into what Melville was to call the "great democratic God" that raised Andrew Jackson higher than a kingly throne. In Melville's time, the question remained whether democracy could maintain its progress, or even long endure, were all Americans persuaded it was their nature and their destiny to deify harmonious concord as the norm of political life. No final answer has yet been provided, and herein may consist our most important legacy from the eighteenth century. Neither Edwards' Calvinism nor Chauncy's Liberal religion can be made to speak meaningfully and directly to the social circumstances and the public needs of the modern American. But the confrontation of the two schemes tells us clearly what can be accomplished, in government as well as in the realm of ideas, when the American people is brought to realize that it does indeed matter how its goals are defined, and that there is more than one spirit in which to pursue them.

BIOGRAPHICAL
GLOSSARY

SOURCES

NOTES

INDEX

BIOGRAPHICAL
GLOSSARY

ALISON, FRANCIS, 1705-1779. Born, Leck, Ireland. Studied under Bishop of Raphoe and at University of Glasgow. Licensed, May 25, 1737; first parish, New London, Pennsylvania. Vice-Provost, College of Philadelphia, 1752-1779. Pastor, First Presbyterian Church, Philadelphia. Died, Philadelphia.

ALLEN, THOMAS, 1743-1810. Born, Northampton, Mass. (Father, Joseph Allen, supported Edwards in controversy over church membership.) Harvard, 1762. Ordained first minister, Pittsfield, 1764. Chaplain, 1776, 1777. Died, Pittsfield.

APPLETON, NATHANIEL, 1693-1784. Born, Ipswich, England. (Nephew of President Leverett of Harvard.) Harvard, 1712; graduate studies through 1716. Ordained, Cambridge, Mass., 1717. Died, Cambridge.

AUSTIN, DAVID, 1759-1831. Born, New Haven. Yale, 1779. Studied with Bellamy. Ordained, Presbyterian Church, Elizabeth, New Jersey, 1788. Pastor, Congregational Church, Bozrah, Conn., 1815. Died, Bozrah.

AVERY, DAVID, 1746-1817. Born, Norwich, Conn. Studied at Lebanon School; Yale, 1769. Studied with Wheelock; missionary to Oneida Indians, 1769-1773. Installed, Gagetown (Windsor), Vt., 1773. Chaplain, 1777-1780. Pastor, Bennington, Vt., 1780, 1783; Wrentham, Mass., 1786-1794. Preached intermittently in "vacant places" and on missionary tours in New York and Maine. Died, Shepardstown, Va.

BACKUS, ISAAC, 1724-1806. Born, Yantic, Conn. No formal education. Awakened, 1742, and 1746 withdrew from church with other members to form Separate church. 1746, felt call to preach and began to itinerate. 1749, ordained minister of Separate conventicle at Titicut, Mass. After controversy over infant baptism withdrew and formed Baptist church in Middleborough, Mass., 1756. Member of Massachusetts convention for ratifying Federal Constitution. Died, Middleborough.

BELLAMY, JOSEPH, 1719-1790. Born, New Cheshire, Conn. Yale, 1735. Studied with Edwards. Licensed, 1737. Pastor, Bethlehem, Conn., 1738. Conducted school for graduate training in divinity. Died, Bethlehem.

BLAIR, SAMUEL, 1712-1751. Born, Ulster. Studied at Log College. Licensed, Philadelphia, 1733. Pastor, 1734, at Middletown and Shrewsbury, N.J. 1740, installed New Londonderry, Chester County, Pa. Conducted school for education of ministerial candidates. Died, New Londonderry.

BOUCHER, JONATHAN, 1737/8-1804. Born, Blencogo, Cumberland, England. Studied in school at St. Bees until emigration to America in 1759. Ordained Church of England, 1762; pastor, St. Anne's, Annapolis, Maryland. M.A., King's College, New York. Chaplain, lower house of Maryland Assembly. 1764, Queen Anne's parish, Prince George County, Maryland. September 1775, left America. Died, Epsom, England.

BRAINERD, DAVID, 1718-1747. Born, Haddam, Conn. Entered Yale, 1739; expelled, 1742. Licensed at Danbury, Conn., July 1742 and appointed missionary to Indians. 1743-1744, Kaunaumeek in western Massachusetts; 1744-1746, Easton, Pa., and Freehold, N.J. Died, Northampton (in home of Edwards).

BUELL, SAMUEL, 1716-1798. Born, Coventry, Conn. Yale, 1741. Licensed by Fairfield East Association, 1741. Itinerated 1741; ordained November 1742 in New Fairfield as evangelist. Installed East Hampton, Long Island, 1746. Died, East Hampton.

BURR, AARON, 1715/16-1757. Born, Fairfield, Conn. Yale, 1734. Licensed, 1736. After short pastorates at Greenfield, Mass. and Hanover, N.J., installed First Presbyterian Church, Newark, N.J., 1736. (Son-in-law of Jonathan Edwards.) Elected president, College of New Jersey, 1748. Died, Princeton, N.J.

BYLES, MATHER, 1706/07-1788. Born, Boston. (Nephew of Cotton Mather.) Harvard, 1725; A.M., 1728. Ordained, Hollis Street Church, Boston, 1732. Removed from pulpit 1776 after end of British occupation. Died, Boston.

CHAPLIN, EBENEZER, 1733-1822. Born, Pomfret, Conn. Yale, 1763. Installed, 1764, Millbury, Mass. (Second Parish, Sutton, originally a Separate Congregation). Member, Massachusetts Constitutional Convention, 1779. Dismissed from pastorate during controversy over baptism by "immersion," 1792. Died, Hardwick, Mass.

CHAUNCY, CHARLES, 1705-1787. Born, Boston. Harvard, 1721; A.M., 1724. Ordained, 1727, First Church, Boston (colleague of Thomas Foxcroft until 1749). Died, Boston.

CLAP, THOMAS, 1703-1767. Born, Scituate, Mass. Harvard, 1722. Ordained, Windham, Conn., 1726. Elected Rector of Yale, 1739. Resigned, 1766. Died, New Haven.

CLEAVELAND, JOHN, 1722-1799. Born, Canterbury, Conn. Entered Yale, 1741; expelled, 1745. Pastor to groups of Boston Separates, 1745-46. Ordained, Chebacco parish (Separate), Ipswich, Mass., 1747. Chaplain, 1758, 1759, 1775, 1776. Died, Ipswich.

COLMAN, BENJAMIN, 1673-1747. Born, Boston. Harvard, 1692; occupied pulpit in Medford, Mass., for six months. A.M., Harvard, 1695. To England, 1695, where preached at Bath; ordained by Presbytery of London, 1699, for new Brattle Street Church, Boston. Returned to Boston, 1699. Died, Boston.

COOPER, WILLIAM, 1694-1743. Born, Boston. Harvard, 1712. Ordained colleague pastor (to Benjamin Colman) at Brattle Street Church, 1716. (Son-in-law of Samuel Sewall.) Died, Cambridge.

CROSWELL, ANDREW, 1708/09-1785. Born, Charlestown, Mass. Harvard, 1728; A.M., 1731. Ordained, Second Church, Groton, Conn., 1736. 1741/42, itinerated; 1746 asked dismission from parish. 1748, installed Eleventh Church, Boston. Died, Boston.

CUMINGS (or Cummings), HENRY, 1737-1823. Born, Tyngsboro, Mass. Spent youth in Hollis, N.H. Harvard, 1760. Ordained, Billerica, Mass., 1763. Delegate, Massachusetts Constitutional Convention. Died, Billerica.

DANA, JAMES, 1735-1812. Born, Cambridge, Mass. Harvard, 1753. Called to Wallingford, Conn., 1758, and ordained after extended controversy. Installed, First Church, New Haven, 1789. Voted into retirement, 1805. Died, New Haven.

DARLING, THOMAS, 1719/20-1789. Born, Newport, R.I. Yale, 1740. Licensed, New Haven, 1743. Tutor at Yale, 1743-45. Resigned to marry and become merchant. Justice of the Peace, 1758; Judge of County Court, 1760; deputy to General Assembly, 1774. Died, Woodbridge, Conn.

DAVENPORT, JAMES, 1716-1757. Born, Stamford, Conn. Yale, 1732. Licensed, 1735; ordained, Southhold, Long Island, 1738. 1740-42, itinerated with Whitefield and then alone. 1742, tried and transported by Connecticut General Court, and declared insane in Boston trial. 1743, dismissed from Southhold church. Subsequently pastor in several churches in New York and New Brunswick presbyteries, and evangelist in Virginia. Died, Hopewell, N.J.

DAVIES, SAMUEL, 1723-1761. Born, New Castle County, Delaware. Studied with elder Abel Morgan and with Samuel Blair. Licensed, 1746; ordained as evangelist, 1747, and sent to Virginia. 1753, to Britain with Gilbert Tennent to raise funds for College of New Jersey and plead for toleration of dissent in Virginia. 1759, President, College of New Jersey. Died, Princeton.

DICKINSON, JONATHAN, 1688-1747. Born, Hatfield, Mass. Yale, 1706. Ordained, Elizabethtown, N.J., 1709. First President, College of New Jersey, at Elizabethtown. Died just before college was to move to Princeton. (Brother of Moses Dickinson, 1695-1778.)

DUCHÉ, JACOB, 1737/38-1798. Born, Philadelphia. College of Philadelphia, 1757. Studied, Cambridge University, England, 1758, and returned to Philadelphia, 1759 with deacon's orders. Taught oratory, College of Philadelphia, and served as assistant rector, Christ Church and St. Peter's. 1762, ordained in London. 1775, Chaplain to Continental Congress; 1776, declared loyalty to Crown; 1777, to England, where became chaplain of orphan asylum. 1792, returned to America. Died, Philadelphia.

DUFFIELD, GEORGE, 1732-1790. Born, Lancaster County, Pa. College of New Jersey, 1752. Studied with Robert Smith at Pequea School. Tutor, College of New Jersey. Licensed, New Castle, N.J., 1756. (Son-in-law of Samuel Blair.) Pastor, 1757-1769, Big Spring, and 1757-1772, Carlisle. Installed, Third Street Church, Philadelphia, 1772. Chaplain, Pennsylvania militia and to Continental Congress. First clerk, Pennsylvania General Assembly. Died, Philadelphia.

DWIGHT, TIMOTHY, 1752-1817. Born, Northampton, Mass. (Grandson of Jonathan Edwards.) Yale, 1769. Principal, Hopkins Grammar School, New Haven. 1771, Tutor at Yale. A.M., 1772. Licensed, 1777; chaplain to Connecticut Continental Brigade. Resigned, 1779. Established school at Northampton. Represented Northampton in county conventions and state legislature, 1781-1782. 1783, ordained, Greenfield Hill, Conn., where he again founded a school. Elected President of Yale, 1795. Died, New Haven.

EDWARDS, JONATHAN, 1703-1758. Born, East Windsor, Conn. (Grandson of Solomon Stoddard.) Yale, 1722; studied theology in New Haven for two years. August 1722—May 1723, minister of Presbyterian Church, New York City. 1724-25, Tutor at Yale. 1726, installed colleague pastor (to Stoddard) at Northampton. Dismissed, 1750. Beginning August 1751, pastor to Indians at Stockbridge, Mass. Elected President, College of New Jersey after death of Aaron Burr. Took office, January 1758; died of smallpox, March 22, 1758, Princeton.

EDWARDS, JONATHAN, JR., 1745-1801. Born, Northampton. College of New Jersey, 1765. Studied with Bellamy. Tutor, College of New Jersey, 1767-69. 1769, installed, White Haven Church, New Haven. Dismissed, 1795. 1796, installed, Colebrook, Conn. 1799, President, Union College. Died, Schenectady, N.Y.

ELIOT, ANDREW, 1718-1778. Born, Boston. Harvard, 1737; A.M., 1740. Ordained, New North, Boston, 1742. Died, Boston.

ELIOT, JARED, 1685-1763. Born, Guilford, Conn. (Grandson of John Eliot, "apostle to the Indians.") Yale, 1706. Pastor, Killingworth, Conn., 1708. Studied medicine and later taught it. Member, Royal Society, London. Died, Killingworth.

EVANS, ISRAEL, 1747-1807. Born, Tredyffrin, Pa. Princeton, 1772; A.M., 1775. Ordained as Chaplain, 1776; served with New Hampshire Brigade, 1777-1783. Installed, Concord, N.H., 1789; resigned, 1797. Died, Concord.

FINLEY, SAMUEL, 1715-1766. Born, County Armagh, Ireland. Emigrated, 1734; studied at Log College. Licensed, 1740; ordained, 1742; itinerated, 1740-1743. Installed, Milford, Conn., 1743, but expelled from colony. 1744, installed, Nottingham, Pa. 1761, President, College of New Jersey. Died, Philadelphia.

FOXCROFT, THOMAS, 1696/97-1749. Born, Boston. Harvard, 1714. Ordained, First Church, Boston, 1716/17. Died, Boston.

FROTHINGHAM, EBENEZER, 1719-1798. Born, Cambridge, Mass. One of original Wethersfield Separates, 1741-42; ordained their pastor, 1747. Jailed, 1748. Moved with parishioners to Middletown, Conn., 1754; served as their pastor until dismissal in 1788. Died, Middletown.

GARDEN, ALEXANDER, c. 1685-1756. Born in England. Ordained Church of England before coming to America in 1719. Elected Rector of St. Philip's, Charleston on arrival; resigned, March 1754. Died, Charleston.

GAY, EBENEZER, 1696-1787. Born, Dedham, Mass. Harvard, 1714. Taught grammar schools, Hadley and Ipswich, Mass., until called to First Parish, Hingham, Mass. Ordained, 1718. Died, Hingham.

GORDON, WILLIAM, 1728-1807. Born, Hitchin, Hertfordshire, England. Installed, Independent Church, Ipswich, England, 1752. Quarreled over church membership and left for Old Gravel Lane Church, Southwark; 1770, resigned and emigrated to America. 1772, ordained, Third Church, Roxbury. 1775, chaplain to Provincial Congress; dismissed for attacks on proposed constitution. Returned to London, 1786; died, Ipswich, England.

GREEN, JACOB, 1722-1790. Born, Malden, Mass. Harvard, 1744. Licensed, 1745; ordained, Presbyterian Church, Hanover, N.J., 1746. 1758-59, Vice-President, College of New Jersey. Member, Provincial Congress, 1776; chairman of committee to draft New Jersey Constitution. Died, Hanover.

GRISWOLD, STANLEY, 1763-1815. Born, Torrington, Conn. Served in militia during Revolution. Yale, 1786; studied theology with Bellamy. Installed, New Milford, Conn., 1790. Expelled 1797 by Litchfield South Association, but his congregation insisted on retaining him. 1802, moved to Walpole, N.H., where edited *The Political Observatory*. 1805, appointed Secretary, Michigan Territory. 1808, moved to Ohio; U.S. Senator, 1809-1810. 1810, appointed judge, Illinois Territory. Died, Shawneetown.

BIOGRAPHICAL GLOSSARY

HART, LEVI, 1738-1808. Born, Southington, Conn. Yale, 1760. Studied with Joseph Bellamy, whose daughter he married. Ordained Preston (Griswold), Conn., 1762. Helped found Connecticut Missionary Society, and involved in formation of Presbyterian-Congregational Union of 1801. Member, Dartmouth Corporation, 1784-1788, and Yale Corporation, 1791-1807. Died, Griswold.

HAWLEY, JOSEPH, 1723-1788. Born Northampton, Mass. (Grandson of Stoddard and cousin of Edwards.) Yale, 1742; probably studied theology with Edwards. Chaplain in Louisburg Expedition, 1745. Admitted to bar, 1749. Elected to Massachusetts General Court, 1751, 1754, 1755, 1766. Died, Northampton.

HITCHCOCK, GAD, 1718/19-1803. Born, Springfield, Mass. Harvard, 1743. Ordained, Tunk (Pembroke), Mass., 1748. Died, Tunk.

HOBART, NOAH, 1705/06-1773. Born, Hingham, Mass. Harvard, 1724; A.M., 1729. Ordained, Fairfield, Conn., 1732/33. Died, Fairfield.

HOPKINS, SAMUEL, 1721-1803. Born, Waterbury, Conn. Yale, 1741. Licensed, 1742; studied with Edwards. 1743, ordained, Great Barrington, Mass.; dismissed, 1769. Installed, First Congregational Church, Newport, R.I., 1770. Died, Newport.

HOWARD, SIMEON, 1733-1804. Born, Bridgewater, Mass. Harvard, 1758. Taught school, and preached two years at Cumberland, Nova Scotia. 1765, returned to Harvard; appointed tutor, 1766. Ordained, 1767, West Church, Boston. 1775-1777, preached at Halifax, Nova Scotia. Died, Boston.

HUSBAND (or Husbands), HERMON, 1724-1795. Born Cecil County, Maryland (?). Farmer; moved back and forth from Maryland to Carolina. 1769, elected to North Carolina Assembly; expelled in 1770, and jailed in 1771. After Battle of Alamance, outlawed in North Carolina. Fled to Pennsylvania; leader in Whiskey Rebellion.

JOHNSON, SAMUEL, 1696-1772. Born, Guilford, Conn. Yale, 1716; appointed Tutor. Ordained, 1720, Congregational Church, West Haven, Conn. 1722, to England, for ordination in Church of England; appointed missionary to Stratford, Conn., where took office, 1724. First president, King's College, 1754. Resigned, 1763, and returned to Stratford parish. Died, Stratford.

JOHNSON, STEPHEN, 1724-1786. Born, Newark, N.J. Yale, 1743. Ordained, First Church, Lyme, Conn., 1746 (as successor to Jonathan Parsons). Chaplain, 1775. Died, Lyme.

LANGDON, SAMUEL, 1723-1797. Born, Boston. Harvard, 1740. Taught school; chaplain in Louisburg expedition, 1745. Assisting pastor, Portsmouth, N.H.; pastor, 1747-1774. Elected president of Harvard, 1774; resigned, 1780. Pastor at Hampton Falls, N.H., until his death.

LATHROP, JOHN, 1740-1816. Born, Norwich, Conn. College of New Jersey, 1763. Taught at Lebanon Indian School. Ordained, 1768, Old North, Boston. 1775-76, pastor in Providence; 1777, installed colleague pastor (to Ebenezer Pemberton) at New Brick; and merged it with Old North. Died, Boston.

LELAND, JOHN, 1754-1841. Born, Grafton, Mass. Licensed as Baptist preacher, 1774, and assigned to Mount Poney, Va. 1776, installed as pastor, Orange, Va. Delegate to Virginia convention for ratification of Federal Constitution. 1791, moved to Cheshire, Mass. Elected as Republican to Massachusetts legislature, 1811. Died, Cheshire.

LIVINGSTON, WILLIAM, 1723-1790. Born, Albany, N.Y. Yale, 1741. Studied law and admitted to bar, New York City, in 1748. 1752, editor, *The Independent Reflector*. 1772, moved to Elizabethtown, New Jersey. Delegate to First and

Second Continental Congress. In June 1776, took command of New Jersey militia; first governor, until his death at Elizabethtown.

MAYHEW, JONATHAN, 1720-1766. Born, Chilmark, Martha's Vineyard, Mass. Harvard, 1744. Installed, West Church, Boston, 1747. Died, Boston.

MORGAN, ABEL, 1713-1785. Born, Welsh Tract, Pa. (Nephew of Abel Morgan, 1673-1722, the patriarch of Pennsylvania Baptists, at whose school studied several of the awakeners.) Educated at Thomas Evans' academy at Pencander. Ordained, 1734; installed, Middletown, N.J., 1738. Died, Middletown.

MURRAY, JOHN, 1742-1793. Born, County Antrim, Ireland. Educated, Edinburgh; emigrated to Pennsylvania, 1763. Installed, Second Presbyterian Church, Philadelphia (as successor to Gilbert Tennent). Dismissed for having questionable credentials; settled Boothbay, District of Maine, where organized "Presbytery of the Eastward." 1774, invited to Newburyport by Jonathan Parsons; declined, but installed as Parsons' successor, 1781. Member, Provincial Congress. Died, Newbury. (Not to be confused with John Murray, 1741-1815, who came to the colonies in 1770, settled eventually in Gloucester, Mass., and is considered the founder of American Universalism.)

NILES, NATHANIEL, 1741-1828. Born in South Kingston, R.I. (Son of Samuel Niles, 1674-1762, author of *Vindication of Divers Important Doctrines*.) Attended Harvard for one year; graduated, College of New Jersey, 1766. Studied with Bellamy. Invited to numerous pulpits but never ordained; settled in Norwich, Conn., for a time. Connecticut Legislature, 1779-1781. Moved to West Fairlee, Vt., 1782. Speaker, Vermont House of Representations, 1784; Member of Federal Congress, 1791-1795; 6 times Presidential Elector; Judge of Vermont Supreme Court to 1814.

OCCUM (or Occom), SAMSON (or Sampson), 1723-1792. Born, Mohegan, Conn. 1743-1747, studied with Wheelock. 1749, appointed schoolmaster and minister to Montauk tribe, Long Island. Ordained, 1759; missionary to Oneidas, upper New York, 1761-1764. To England with Nathaniel Whitaker to raise funds for Lebanon Indian School, 1765-1768. On return, became itinerant preacher. 1789, installed pastor to Indians at Brothertown, N.Y. Died, Brothertown.

PARSONS, JONATHAN, 1705-1776. Born, West Springfield, Mass. Yale, 1729. Ordained, 1730/31, First Church, Lyme, Conn. Resigned, 1745, and installed in new church (Separate, later proclaimed Presbyterian) at Newbury, Mass., 1745/46. Died, Newburyport.

PEMBERTON, EBENEZER, 1704/05-1777. Born, Boston. (Son of Ebenezer Pemberton, 1671-1717, pastor of Old South Church.) Harvard, 1721; appointed chaplain of the harbor castle, 1723. Ordained Boston, 1727, to become pastor of Wall Street Presbyterian Church, New York City. Resigned at request of members, 1753, and became minister, New Brick, Boston, 1754. Entered into semi-retirement, 1774; died, Boston.

PETERS, SAMUEL, 1735-1826. Born, Hebron, Conn. Yale, 1757; M.A., 1760. In 1759, went to England where was ordained in Church of England. 1760, rector, Hebron, Conn. 1774, left for England; returned to United States in 1805. Died, New York City.

POMEROY, BENJAMIN, 1704-1784. Born, Suffield, Conn. Yale, 1733. Ordained, Hebron, Conn., 1735. Arraigned with Davenport, 1742; tried by Connecticut Assembly, 1744. (Brother-in-law of Eleazar Wheelock.) One of original Dartmouth Trustees. Died, Hebron.

PRINCE, THOMAS, 1697-1758. Born, Sandwich, Mass. Harvard, 1709. Traveled two years in West Indies and Europe; accepted ministry at Coombs, Suffolk, England. Returned to Boston, 1717; installed colleague pastor (to Joseph Sewall) at Old South, 1718. Died, Boston.

RAMSAY (or Ramsey), DAVID, 1749-1815. Born, Lancaster County, Pa. College of New Jersey, 1765. Tutored in Maryland for two years; studied medicine with Benjamin Rush. M.D., College of Pennsylvania, 1772. Practiced medicine a year in Maryland; in 1773, moved to Charleston. Throughout Revolution represented Charleston in state legislature, and thereafter held numerous state offices until 1796. Died, Charleston.

SHERWOOD, SAMUEL, 1730-1783. Born, Fairfield, Conn. Yale, 1749. Tutor at Princeton, 1750-1752, where studied theology with his uncle, Aaron Burr. Ordained, Nor[th]field, Conn., 1757. Died, Northfield.

SLOAN, JAMES, d. 1811. Born, New Jersey. Farmer; county assessor. Member of Congress, March 4, 1803—March 3, 1809.

SMITH, ROBERT, 1723-1793. Born, Londonderry, Ireland. Awakened by Whitefield in first month of American tour, 1739. Studied with Samuel Blair; licensed, 1749. 1750, married Blair's sister and called to churches in Pequea and Leacock, Pa. Founded school for instruction in languages. (Father of Samuel Stanhope Smith.)

SMITH, WILLIAM, 1727-1803. Born, Aberdeen, Scotland. University of Aberdeen (A.M.), 1747. Tutor in New York City, 1751-1753. Returned to England and ordained, Church of England. 1754, teacher at Philadelphia Academy; 1756, Provost, College of Philadelphia. 1757-58, editor, *The American Magazine.* Rector, Chester Parish, Maryland, 1779, after revocation of college charter; returned as Provost with restoration of charter in 1789. Died, Philadelphia.

SPRING, SAMUEL, 1746-1819. Born, Northbridge, Mass. Princeton, 1771; studied with Bellamy and with Hopkins. Licensed, 1774; chaplain, 1775-1776. Ordained, Newburyport, Mass., 1777. Among the founders of Andover Theological Seminary. Died, Newburyport.

STILES, EZRA, 1727-1795. Born, New Haven, Conn. (Son of Isaac Stiles.) Yale, 1746. Licensed to preach; appointed Yale Tutor, 1749. Studied law and admitted to bar, 1753. Ordained, 1755, Second Congregational Church, Newport, R.I. Pastor, 1777, First Church, Portsmouth, N.H. Elected president of Yale, 1777. Died, New Haven.

STILES, ISAAC, 1697-1760. Born, Windsor, Conn. Prepared for college by Timothy Edwards, father of Jonathan, Yale, 1722; studied theology with Edward Taylor and married his daughter. Licensed, Westfield, and ordained, North Parish, New Haven, 1724. Died, North Haven.

STILLMAN, SAMUEL, 1737-1807. Born, Philadelphia. Ordained Baptist minister, Charleston, 1759; preached two years at James Island, S.C. Supplied churches in New Jersey until in 1763 was installed pastor, First Baptist Church, Boston. Delegate to Massachusetts Constitutional Convention. Died, Boston.

STREET, NICHOLAS, 1730-1806. Born, Wallingford, Conn. Yale, 1751; ordained, East Haven, Conn., 1755. Uncle (by marriage) of David Austin.

TENNENT, GILBERT, 1703-1764. Born, County Armagh, Ireland. (Son of William Tennent, and brother of John Tennent, 1706-1732, and William Tennent II, 1705-1777.) Educated, Log College, where he also taught; A.M., Yale, 1725. Licensed by Presbytery of Philadelphia, 1725. Briefly pastor, Newcastle, Delaware; installed, 1726, New Brunswick, N.J.; installed, 1743, "Free Church," Philadelphia. 1753, to England with Samuel Davies to raise funds for College of New Jersey. Died, Philadelphia.

TENNENT, WILLIAM, 1673-1746. Born, Ireland. University of Edinburgh, 1695;

ordained, Church of Ireland, 1706. 1716 or 1717, emigrated to America; admitted to Presbyterian ministry, 1718. 1720, pastor, Bedford, Pa.; 1726, Neshaminy, Pa. There founded Log College. Died, Neshaminy.

TENNENT, WILLIAM, III, 1740-1777. Born, Freehold, N.J. (Son of William Tennent II.) Princeton, 1758; M.A., Harvard, 1763. Licensed 1761; ordained, Presbytery of New Brunswick, 1762, and appointed to serve in Hanover Presbytery, Va. Installed, Norwalk, Conn., 1765; dismissed, 1772, to accept call to Independent Church, Charleston, S.C. Member, South Carolina Legislature. Died, Santee, S. C.

THACHER, PETER, 1752-1802. Born, Milton, Mass. Harvard, 1769. Ordained, Malden, Mass., 1770. Became pastor of Brattle Street Church, Boston, 1785. Died, Savannah, Ga.

TRUMBULL, BENJAMIN, 1735-1820. Born, Hebron, Conn. Yale, 1759. Studied with Eleazar Wheelock. 1760, ordained, Congregational Church, North Haven, Conn. Died, North Haven.

TUCKER, JOHN, 1719-1792. Born, Amesbury, Mass. Harvard, 1741. Ordained, First Church, Newbury, 1745. Died, Newbury.

TURNER, CHARLES, d. 1796. Harvard, 1752. Pastor, Duxbury, Mass. 1775, requested dismission and moved to Scituate. 1776, member, Massachusetts General Court; subsequently member of Senate. Retired to farm at Cumberland, Maine, where he died "at an advanced age."

WELLES, NOAH, 1718-1776. Born, Colchester, Conn. Yale, 1741; studied theology and directed Hopkins Grammar School. 1745-46, Tutor at Yale. Ordained, Stamford, Conn., 1746. Died, Stamford.

WEST, SAMUEL, 1730-1807. Born, Yarmouth, Mass. (Parents "zealous New Lights.") Harvard, 1754; schoolmaster at Falmouth, Mass., 1756. Ordained, Dartmouth, Mass., 1761. Chaplain, 1775. Delegate to Massachusetts Constitutional Convention and convention to ratify Federal Constitution. Retired, 1803; died, Tiverton, R. I.

WHEELOCK, ELEAZAR, 1711-1779. Born, Windham, Conn. Yale, 1733. Licensed, 1734, and ordained, Second Society, Lebanon, Conn., 1735. Itinerated, 1740-1742; began tutoring Indians, 1743. Founded Dartmouth College and moved to Hanover to serve as its first president, 1770. Died, Hanover.

WHITAKER, NATHANIEL, 1730-1795. Born, Huntington, Long Island. College of New Jersey, 1752. Ordained, Presbyterian Church, Woodbridge, N.J., 1755. 1760, began work with Eleazar Wheelock and installed, Sixth Parish, Norwich, Conn. 1765-68, in England with Samson Occum to raise money for Indian School. 1769, called to Third Church, Salem, Mass.; removed, 1784. Minister of Presbyterian Church, Skowhegan, Maine, 1785-1790, and Taunton, Mass., 1791-92. Died, Hampton, Va.

WHITEFIELD, GEORGE, 1714-1770. Born, Gloucester, England. Ordained deacon, a month before graduating Oxford, 1736. 1737, departed for Georgia to join the Wesleys. In America, May-September, 1738. Returned to England and ordained priest, 1739, to supply church of Savannah, Ga. First field-preaching, Feb. 17, 1739; in July, preached to audiences of 10,000 to 20,000. In America, Oct. 30, 1739—Jan. 6, 1741; Oct. 26, 1744—February 1748. Appointed domestic chaplain to Countess of Huntingdon, 1748. In America, November 1751—April 1752; May 26, 1754—March 1755; September 1763—June 1765; Nov. 30, 1769—Sept. 30, 1770, when he died at Newburyport, Mass.

WILLIAMS, SOLOMON, 1700-1776. Born, Hatfield, Mass. (Grandson of Solomon Stoddard; cousin of Jonathan Edwards.) Harvard, 1719. Directed Hadley

Grammar School for a year. Ordained, 1722, Lebanon, Conn. Died, Lebanon.

WINTHROP, JOHN, 1714-1779. Born, Boston. Harvard, 1732. Appointed Hollis Professor of Mathematics and Natural Philosophy, 1738. Fellow of Royal Society, 1766. (Son-in-law of Charles Chauncy.) Died, Boston.

WITHERSPOON, JOHN, 1723-1794. Born, Yester, Scotland. Edinburgh, 1743. Licensed, 1743; ordained, 1745, Beith, Ayrshire. 1768, president, College of New Jersey. In Continental Congress, 1776 to 1782. Died on his farm, "Tusculum," New Jersey.

ZUBLY, JOHANN JOACHIM, 1724-1781. Born, St. Gall, Switzerland. Ordained, 1744, German Church, London. Emigrated to South Carolina; minister, Independent Presbyterian Church, Savannah, 1760. Delegate to First Continental Congress. Died, Savannah.

SOURCES

PRIMARY

A full listing of the eighteenth-century sermons, tracts, and other pamphlets read in the course of preparing this study would correspond roughly with all the entries in Charles Evans' *American Bibliography* for the years 1730-1801. Evans, together with the addenda published by various scholars and libraries, was the essential bibliography; it lists, with locations, the titles of all American publications for these years. Additional bibliographical assistance, supplementing Evans or correcting its minor inaccuracies, was provided by the listing in Henry M. Dexter, *The Congregationalism of the Last Three Hundred Years as Seen in its Literature* (New York, 1880), and by the bibliographies in Gaustad, Goen, Love, and Trinterud. (See below, under secondary sources.) The chronological lists of titles by individual minister-authors in William B. Sprague, *Annals of the American Pulpit* (8 vols., New York, 1859-1865), provided a particularly convenient aid.

Wherever possible I have used collected editions of the writings of the period. The works of only one major eighteenth-century religious leader have been collected in the twentieth century: *Samuel Johnson. His Career and Writings,* edited by Herbert and Carol Schneider (4 vols., New York, 1929). This edition, which includes letters and other material not published during Johnson's lifetime, expresses Columbia University's respect to the founder of King's College. Other institutions have not manifested a similar interest in the writing of their earlier leaders. *The Works of William Smith, D.D. Late Provost of the College and Academy of Philadelphia* (2 vols., Philadelphia, 1803), was hastily assembled shortly after Smith's death. It contains only published material and is even in that respect far from complete.

The writings of Jonathan Dickinson and the other early presidents of the College of New Jersey have never been published in collected form. Samuel Davies, *Sermons on Important Subjects,* was several times reprinted in the nineteenth century; I have used the fourth edition (3 vols., New York, 1845). This collection of sermons is by no means the full record of Davies' publications. His unpublished series of letters, *Charity and Truth* (1755), was edited by Thomas Clinton Pears, Jr., for the *Journal of the Department of History of the Presbyterian Church in the U.S.A.,* vol. XIX (1941), numbers 5-7. *The Works of the Rev. John Witherspoon* appeared in four volumes (Philadelphia, 1801); I have used the second edition (1802).

Otherwise the writings of the Presbyterian leaders have seldom seen the light since the eighteenth century. *Sermons and Essays by the Tennents and Their Contemporaries* (Philadelphia, 1855) includes utterances by Blair, Finley, and Robert Smith. A few of the documents of the Awakening era appear in Maurice W. Armstrong, *et al.,* eds., *The Presbyterian Enterprise; Sources of American Presbyterian History* (Philadelphia, 1956). Finley's preface to the 1759 edition of Jonathan Edwards' *Original Sin* was reprinted as "A Contemporaneous Account of Jonathan Edwards," *Journal of the Presbyterian Historical Society,* II (1903), 125-135. Abridgments of Tennent's *Danger of an Unconverted Ministry* and Davies' *Curse of Cowardice* appear in H. Shelton Smith, *et al.,* eds., *American Christianity: An Historical Interpretation with Representative Documents,* Volume I: 1607-1820 (New York, 1960).

Of the writings of the New England divines, collected editions include *The Works of Joseph Bellamy, D.D.* (2 vols., Boston, 1850); *The Works of Samuel Hopkins, D.D.* (3 vols., Boston, 1852); and *The Works of Jonathan Edwards, D.D. Late President of Union College* (2 vols., Andover, 1842). Selections from Bellamy, Hopkins, and Timothy Dwight appear in Smith, *American Christianity,* as do excerpts from one of Charles Chauncy's anti-revival sermons and from one of his later theological volumes, and an abbreviated version of Mayhew's *Discourse Concerning Unlimited Submission.* The last has been frequently anthologized; a nearly complete text can be found in Perry Miller and Thomas H. Johnson, eds., *The Puritans* (New York, 1938; revised paper edition, 2 vols., Harper Torchbooks, 1963). But the writings of the two most important Liberal thinkers have never been collected. Alden Bradford, *Memoir of the Life and Writings of Rev. Jonathan Mayhew, D.D.* (Boston, 1838), contains lengthy excerpts from his doctrinal discourses as well as from his political sermons.

The works of Jonathan Edwards have, of course, often been published. A register of editions, and of material published separately, is Thomas H. Johnson, *The Printed Writings of Jonathan Edwards,*

1703-1758 (Princeton, 1940). I have used what seemed a convenient and generally accessible edition, that edited by E. Hickman (10th ed., 2 vols., London, 1865). (Neither the London edition nor the Worcester, on which other nineteenth-century editions were based, is particularly precise in its rendering of Edwards; and though quotations and citations in the text of the present volume refer to the London edition, I have checked each one with the language of the original publications.) A new and superbly accurate (though "modernized") edition of Edwards' *Works* is in process. The first two volumes, which appeared under the general editorship of Perry Miller, have here been used and cited: *The Freedom of the Will,* edited by Paul Ramsey (New Haven, 1957), and *Religious Affections,* edited by John E. Smith (New Haven, 1959).

A listing of other recent publications of writings by Edwards is provided in the bibliography in Clarence H. Faust and Thomas H. Johnson, eds., *Jonathan Edwards: Representative Selections* (revised edition, American Century paperback, New York, 1962). This remains the most tasteful and scholarly anthology of Edwards; Virgilius Ferm, ed., *Puritan Sage: Collected Writings of Jonathan Edwards* (New York, 1953), contains some hitherto unpublished material, but the text is unsystematically modernized and the selections are not dated or identified with precision. Portions of Edwards' unpublished "Miscellanies" appear in Harvey G. Townsend, ed., *The Philosophy of Jonathan Edwards. From His Private Notebooks* (Eugene, Oregon, 1955). Perry Miller collected and edited some of Edwards' more significant unpublished writing in *Images or Shadows of Divine Things* (New Haven, 1948); "Jonathan Edwards on the Sense of the Heart," *Harvard Theological Review,* XLI (1948), 123-145; and "Jonathan Edwards' Sociology of the Great Awakening," *New England Quarterly,* XXI (1948), 50-77.

For Whitefield, the bibliography in Henry (see below) indicates some of the numerous editions of the sermons and other writings. *George Whitefield's Journals. A New Edition Containing Fuller Material* (London, 1960) contains a few items never before published. It also prints, as an appendix, an excerpt from the "Spiritual Travels" of Nathan Cole (manuscript, Connecticut Historical Society) describing Whitefield's first appearance at Middletown, Connecticut. This has also been published in *The William and Mary Quarterly,* 3 ser. VII (1950), 590-591. Other primary materials of the Awakening years are to be found in *The General Magazine and Historical Chronicle for All the British Plantations in America. Published by Benjamin Franklin. Reproduced from the Original Edition Philadelphia, 1741* (New York, 1938).

William K. Boyd, ed., *Some Eighteenth Century Tracts Concerning North Carolina* (Raleigh, N.C., 1927), contains Hermon Husband's published record of his spiritual pilgrimages of the revival years: *Some Remarks on Religion*. The frequently reprinted *Life and Diary of David Brainerd*, which of course appears in any edition of Edwards' works, was separately edited (in a condensed and modernized text) by Philip E. Howard, Jr. (Chicago, 1949). A few of the central documents of the Awakening and subsequent years are abridged in Richard Hofstadter and Wilson Smith, eds., *American Higher Education: A Documentary History*, vol. I (Chicago, 1961). Smith, *American Christianity*, devotes full sections to the revival and to the emergence of rational religion. Some material relevant to the religious history of the eighteenth century appears in Williston Walker, *The Creeds and Platforms of Congregationalism* (New York, 1893; Pilgrim Paperbound, 1960). Another useful collection is Charles F. James, *Documentary History of the Struggle for Religious Liberty in Virginia* (Lynchburg, Va., 1900). For the Awakening however, Tracy (see below) remains the single most valuable source of original material, much of it otherwise unavailable. Portions of *The Christian History* (Boston, 1744, 1745) were occasionally reprinted in the nineteenth century, but there has not been a modern or scholarly anthology of the literature of the revival. *The Great Awakening*, edited by Alan Heimert and Perry Miller, is scheduled to appear almost concurrently with the present volume.

Several early studies are valuable both as documents of the era and for the sources they reprint or quote extensively. Morgan Edwards, *Materials toward a History of the American Baptists* (Philadelphia, 1770), consists largely of outline histories, but a few major documents are excerpted. Source material is also to be found in Benjamin Trumbull, *A Complete History of Connecticut, Civil and Ecclesiastical* (2 vols., New Haven, 1818); David Ramsay, *The History of the Independent or Congregational Church in Charleston, South Carolina* (Philadelphia, 1815); and Robert B. Semple, *A History of the Rise and Progress of the Baptists in Virginia* (Richmond, Va., 1810). A monument in nearly every respect is Isaac Backus, *A History of New England. With Particular Reference to the Denomination of Christians Called Baptists;* I have used the second edition, with notes by David Weston (2 vols., Newton, Mass., 1871).

With one exception, that of the Stanley Griswold manuscripts (Houghton Library, Harvard University), I have not ventured deeply into unpublished material. Sources that are not properly part of the "public" thought of the eighteenth century have, however, been consulted wherever appropriate. The various editions of writings by religious spokesmen include, either in the body of the collection or by way of introduction, letters, diary excerpts, and reminiscences. Other private material has appeared in the collections of historical societies, as cited in the notes to this volume. Sprague's *Annals* is especially useful, not only as a mine of biographical and bibliographical information, but for the excerpts it offers from journals and correspondence. Other material, chiefly the letters and reports of colonial Anglican clergymen, are collected in Francis L. Hawks and William S. Perry, eds., *Documentary History of the Protestant Episcopal Church . . . Connecticut* (2 vols., New York, 1863-1864), and in Perry, ed., *Historical Collections Relating to the American Colonial Church* (4 vols., Hartford, Conn., 1870-1878), which contains similar material for Maryland, Pennsylvania, Delaware, Virginia, and Massachusetts.

For the years of the Revolution the available sources are more numerous and, at the same time, often less immediately pertinent to my interests in the present volume. I have consulted the writings of secular spokesmen and statesmen both for commentary on the religion of the period and for evidence of relationships between religious ideas and political thought and expression. Among the secular writings, one item directly relevant to the religious mind is *The Independent Reflector, or Weekly Essays on Sundry Important Subjects . . . by William Livingston and Others,* ed. Milton M. Klein (Cambridge, Mass., 1963). Boyd, *Eighteenth Century Tracts,* contains the major Regulator utterances and a sermon delivered and published during the crisis. Some of the political sermons of the imperial debate, including the full text of Mayhew's 1750 *Discourse,* were assembled by John Wingate Thornton in *The Pulpit of the American Revolution* (Boston, 1860). Thornton's selections are consistent with his Bostonian (and generally Unitarian) view of the Revolution. On the other hand, [Frank Moore, ed.], *The Patriot Preachers of the American Revolution* (New York, 1862), is heavily weighted with evangelical sermons of the Revolution. Volume I of Bernard Bailyn's superb edition of *Pamphlets of the American Revolution, 1750-1776* (Cambridge, Mass., 1965) reprints only one sermon: Mayhew's *Discourse on Unlimited Submission.* However, his list of "Pamphlets to Appear in Subsequent Volumes" includes several sermons, orations, and tracts essential to an appreciation of the role of the clergy, and of religious ideas, in the forming of the Revolutionary mind.

Excerpts from other clerical statements of the period appear in the appendices to Baldwin (see below). Brackenridge's *Eulogium* and a few other preachments are made available in Hezekiah Niles, ed., *Principles and Acts of the Revolution,* which also provides the texts of the Boston Massacre Orations. (I have used the Centennial Edition,

New York, 1876.) The fast and thanksgiving proclamations of the Revolution are lavishly excerpted in B. F. Morris, *Christian Life and Character of the Civil Institutions of the United States. Developed in the Official and Historical Annals of the Republic* (Philadelphia, 1864). The complete text of *The People, the Best Governors* is given as an appendix to Frederick Chase, *A History of Dartmouth College and the Town of Hanover, New Hampshire,* vol. I, edited by John K. Lord (Cambridge, Mass., 1891). Some evidence of the role of the clergy and of religious ideas in the constitutional debates is provided in the standard editions of the convention debates and in Robert J. Taylor, ed., *Massachusetts, Colony to Commonwealth. Documents on the Formation of its Constitution* (Chapel Hill, N.C., 1961). For my purposes the single most valuable collection proved to be Mary Catherine Clune, ed., "Joseph Hawley's Criticism of the Constitution of Massachusetts," *Smith College Studies in History,* III (1917), 5-55.

Nearly all the eighteenth-century writers of history made some observations on the American religious scene. Two histories were written almost concurrently with the impact of the Awakening: William Stith, *The History of the First Discovery and Settlement of Virginia* (Williamsburg, 1747; reprinted, 1865), and William Douglass, *Summary, Historical and Political, of the First Planting, Progressive Improvements, and Present State of the British Settlements in North America,* which came out in installments beginning in 1747. (I have used the two-volume edition, London, 1752.) Particularly useful traveler's accounts include Dr. Alexander Hamilton's *Itinerarium,* the record of a journey undertaken during the revival years, which has been reprinted as *Gentleman's Progress,* edited by Carl Bridenbaugh (Chapel Hill, N.C., 1948). Another is *The Carolina Backcountry on the Eve of the Revolution; the Journal and other Writings of Charles Woodmason, Anglican Itinerant,* edited by R.J. Hooker (Chapel Hill, N.C., 1953).

An Anglican voice of the Revolution is Jonathan Boucher, *A View of the Causes and the Consequences of the American Revolution* (London, 1797). This contains, in addition to thirteen of Boucher's sermons on public affairs, a retrospective commentary on dissenter sedition. Boucher's "Autobiography" is available as *Reminiscences of an American Loyalist, 1738-1789,* edited by his grandson, Jonathan Boucher (Boston, 1925). Samuel Peters, *A General History of Connecticut* (2nd ed., London, 1782; reprinted, 1877) is, despite its embittered satire and inaccuracies (Trumbull called them "lies"), an invaluable report on the attitudes of Connecticut's revolutionary Calvinists. The lawyer-politician Joseph Galloway more calmly measures the religious dimension of the Revolution in his *Historical and Political Reflections on the Rise and Progress of the American Rebellion* (London, 1780). The most notable contemporary account of the role and significance of religion in the Revolution is, however, that in which the phrase "black regiment" was first turned: Peter Oliver's manuscript history of the revolutionary movement in Massachusetts. Long consulted and alluded to by historians, the full text has only recently been published as *Peter Oliver's Origin and Progress of the American Revolution. A Tory View,* edited by Douglass Adair and John A. Schutz (San Marino, Calif., 1961).

To balance the judgment of the Tory commentators, if not necessarily to correct their facts, Trumbull and Backus are essential. Ramsay's various histories, cited in the notes to this volume, pay careful attention to the evangelical quality of the Revolutionary impulse. The most extensive Calvinist history of the Revolution is William Gordon, *The History of the Rise, Progress, and Establishment of the Independence of the United States of America* (4 vols., London, 1788). Gordon's *History,* much maligned for its plagiarism and inaccuracies, reflects his bitterness at being in effect exiled from Massachusetts for his criticisms of its constitution, and his suspicion that Alexander Hamilton, in particular, was a dubious patriot. (The letters in which Gordon originally made his charges against Hamilton are printed in *The Papers of Alexander Hamilton,* Volume II: 1779-1781, edited by Harold C. Syrett and Jacob E. Cooke [New York, 1961].)

SECONDARY

In the course of developing and refining my thoughts about religion in eighteenth-century America I have been led for illumination and inspiration to numerous studies remote from my immediate subject: histories and interpretations of early Christian dogma and Reformation doctrine, analyses of philosophical systems, literary history and criticism, sociological studies, and interpretations of the relationship of ideologies to political behavior at other times and in other places. Perhaps the most helpful of such works have been recent English reexaminations of the Puritan revolution and reconsiderations by American scholars of the Jacksonian era and the Populist movement. I have also read through innumerable surveys of the history, intellectual or otherwise, of the eighteenth century generally. One in particular deserves special mention, for it served to crystallize and reinforce my thinking as to the broad intellectual forces at work in the society and the politics of the period: R. R. Palmer, *The Age of the Democratic Revolution. A Political History of Europe and America, 1760-1800. The Challenge* (Princeton, N.J., 1959).

I have also used numerous denominational histories, the annals of individual colonial churches, state and local histories, and, for the

Revolution itself, what seems in retrospect to have been every monograph and article in the pertinent sections of Oscar Handlin, *et al., Harvard Guide to American History.* All were of some assistance at particular moments during my investigation, as were a variety of articles and books on American literature and thought in the eighteenth century. I list below, however, only those items which proved most immediately relevant to my concerns, and of those only the ones I consider to have been essential to me—or of promised value to anyone who decides to pursue further the subject of religion and the eighteenth-century American mind.

Akers, Charles W. *Called unto Liberty; a Life of Jonathan Mayhew, 1720-1766.* Cambridge, Mass., 1964.

Andrews, W. G. "The Parentage of American High Churchmanship," *Protestant Episcopal Review,* XII (1899), 196-221.

Anglo-American Cultural Relations in the Seventeenth Century: Papers Delivered . . . at the Fourth Clark Library Seminar. Los Angeles, 1958.

Armstrong, Maurice Whitman. "Religious Enthusiasm and Separatism in Colonial New England," *Harvard Theological Review,* XXXVIII (1945), 111-140.

Bainton, Roland H. *Yale and the Ministry. A History of Education for the Christian Ministry at Yale from the Founding in 1701.* New York, 1957.

Balch, Thomas. *Calvinism and American Independence.* Philadelphia, 1909.

Baldwin, Alice M. *The New England Clergy and the American Revolution.* New York, 1958.

Birdsall, Richard D. "Ezra Stiles versus the New Divinity Men," *American Quarterly,* XVII (Summer, 1965), 248-258.

———— "The Reverend Thomas Allen: Jeffersonian Calvinist," *New England Quarterly,* XXX (1957), 147-165.

Blaikie, Alexander. *A History of Presbyterianism in New England.* Boston, 1887.

Brasch, Frederick E. "The Newtonian Epoch in the American Colonies, 1680-1783," *Proceedings of the American Antiquarian Society,* n.s. XLIX (1939), 314-332.

Breed, William Pratt. *Presbyterians and the Revolution.* Philadelphia, [1876].

Bridenbaugh, Carl. *Cities in Revolt. Urban Life in America. 1743-1776.* New York, 1955.

———— *Mitre and Sceptre: Transatlantic Faiths, Ideas, Personalities, and Politics, 1689-1775.* New York, 1962.

Brigance, William Norwood, ed. *A History and Criticism of American Public Address,* vol. I. New York, 1943.

Brown, E. Francis. *Joseph Hawley. Colonial Radical.* New York, 1931.

Brown, Robert E. *Middle-Class Democracy and the Revolution in Massachusetts, 1691-1780.* Ithaca, 1955.

Brydon, G. MacLaren. "The Clergy of the Established Church in Virginia and the Revolution," *Virginia Magazine of History and Biography,* XLI (1933), 11-18.

Brynestad, Lawrence E. "The Great Awakening in New England and the

Middle Colonies," *Journal of the Presbyterian Historical Society*, XIV (1930), 80-91, 104-141.

Butterfield, Lyman H. "Elder John Leland, Jeffersonian Itinerant," *Proceedings of the American Antiquarian Society*, n.s. LXII (1952), 155-242.

Cathcart, William. *The Baptists and the American Revolution*. Philadelphia, 1876.

Christie, Francis Albert. "The Beginnings of Arminianism in New England," American Society of Church History, *Papers*, 2 ser. III (1912), 153-172.

Craven, Wesley Frank. *The Legend of the Founding Fathers*. New York, 1956.

Cross, Arthur L. *The Anglican Episcopate and the American Colonies*. New York, 1902.

Davidson, Philip. *Propaganda and the American Revolution, 1763-1783*. Chapel Hill, 1941.

Dorfman, Joseph. *The Economic Mind in American Civilization: 1606-1865*. New York, 1946. Volume I.

Douglass, Elisha P. *Rebels and Democrats. The Struggle for Equal Rights and Majority Rule during the American Revolution*. Chapel Hill, 1955.

Eckenrode, Hamilton J. *Separation of Church and State in Virginia. A Study in the Development of the Revolution*. Richmond, 1910.

Eggleston, Percy C. *A Man of Bethlehem, Joseph Bellamy, D.D., and His Divinity School*. New London, Conn., 1908.

Faust, Clarence H. "The Decline of Puritanism," in Harry H. Clark, ed., *Transitions in American Literary History*. Durham, N.C., 1953.

Foster, Frank Hugh. "The Eschatology of the New England Divines," *Bibliotheca Sacra*, XLIII (1886), 6-19.

────── *A Genetic History of the New England Theology*. Chicago, 1907.

Gambrell, Mary L. *Ministerial Training in Eighteenth-Century New England*. New York, 1937.

Gaustad, Edwin Scott. *The Great Awakening in New England*. New York, 1957.

Gewehr, Wesley M. *The Great Awakening in Virginia, 1740-1790*. Durham, N.C., 1930.

Gifford, Frank Dean. "The Influence of the Clergy on American Politics from 1763 to 1776," *Historical Magazine of the Protestant Episcopal Church*, X (1941), 104-123.

Goen, C. C. "Jonathan Edwards: A New Departure in Eschatology," *Church History*, XXVIII (1959), 25-40.

────── *Revivalism and Separatism in New England, 1740-1800*. New Haven, 1962.

Greene, M. Louise. *The Development of Religious Liberty in Connecticut*. Boston, 1905.

Hall, Thomas C. *The Religious Background of American Culture*. Boston, 1930.

Haroutunian, Joseph. *Piety versus Moralism: the Passing of the New England Theology*. New York, 1932.

Hartz, Louis. *The Liberal Tradition in America*. New York, 1955.

Hayes, Samuel P. "An Historical Study of the Edwardean Revivals," *American Journal of Psychology*, XIII (1902), 550-574.

Headley, Joel T. *The Chaplains and Clergy of the Revolution*. New York, 1864.

Henry, Stuart C. *George Whitefield: Wayfaring Witness*. New York, 1957.

Hofstadter, Richard. *Anti-Intellectualism in American Life*. New York, 1963.

Hooker, Richard J. "John Dickinson on Church and State," *American Literature*, XVI (1945), 82-98.

Hornberger, Theodore. "Samuel Johnson of Yale and King's College. A Note on the Relation of Science and Religion in Provincial America," *New England Quarterly*, VIII (1935), 378-397.

———— "The Science of Thomas Prince," *New England Quarterly*, IX (1936), 26-42.

Jernegan, Marcus W. *Laboring and Dependent Classes in Colonial America, 1607-1783*. Chicago, 1931.

Jones, Howard Mumford. "American Prose Style: 1700-1770," *Huntington Library Bulletin*, No. 6 (November 1934).

———— *The Pursuit of Happiness*. Cambridge, Mass., 1953.

Koch, G. Adolph. *Republican Religion*. New York, 1933.

Labaree, Leonard W. *Conservatism in Early American History*. New York, 1948.

———— "The Conservative Attitude toward the Great Awakening," *William and Mary Quarterly*, 3 ser. I (1944), 331-352.

Longeley, R. S. "Mob Activities in Revolutionary Massachusetts," *New England Quarterly*, VI (1933), 98-130.

Love, W. DeLoss. *The Fast and Thanksgiving Days of New England*. Boston, 1895.

Maclear, James F. "The Birth of the Free Church Tradition," *Church History*, XXVI (1957), 99-131.

Magoun, G. F. "President Edwards as a Reformer," *Congregational Quarterly*, n.s. I (1869), 259-274.

Mampoteng, Charles. "The New England Clergy in the American Revolution," *Historical Magazine of the Protestant Episcopal Church*, IX (1940), 267-304.

Matthews, Albert T. "The Term Pilgrim Fathers and the Early Celebrations of Forefathers' Day," *Publications of the Colonial Society of Massachusetts*, XVII (1915), 293-391.

Maxson, C. H. *The Great Awakening in the Middle Colonies*. Chicago, 1920.

Mead, Sidney E. "The American People: Their Space, Time, and Religion," *Journal of Religion*, XXXIV (1954), 244-255.

———— "American Protestantism during the Revolutionary Epoch," *Church History*, XXII (1953), 279-297.

———— "Denominationalism: the Shape of Protestantism in America," *Church History*, XXIII (1954), 291-320.

———— "The Rise of the Evangelical Conception of the Ministry in America (1607-1850)," in H. Richard Niebuhr and Daniel D. Williams, eds., *The Ministry in Historical Perspective*. New York, 1956.

Metzger, Charles H. *The Quebec Act: a Primary Cause of the American Revolution*. New York, 1937.

Meyer, Jacob Conrad. *Church and State in Massachusetts from 1740 to 1833*. Cleveland, 1938.

Miller, John C. "Religion, Finance and Democracy in Massachusetts," *New England Quarterly*, VI (1933), 29-58.

Miller, Perry. *Errand into the Wilderness*. Cambridge, Mass., 1956.

———— "From the Covenant to the Revival," in James Ward Smith and A. Leland Jamison, eds., *The Shaping of American Religion*. Religion in American Life, vol. I. Princeton, 1961.

—— "The Great Awakening from 1740 to 1750," *Encounter* (The Divinity School, Duke University, March 1956).

—— "The Insecurity of Nature. Being the Dudleian Lecture for the Academic Year 1952-1953," *Harvard Divinity School Bulletin: Annual Lectures and Book Reviews.* Official Register of Harvard University, LI, No. 13, Cambridge, Mass., [1954].

—— *Jonathan Edwards.* New York, 1949.

—— *The New England Mind: From Colony to Province.* Cambridge, Mass., 1953.

—— *The New England Mind: The Seventeenth Century.* Cambridge, Mass., 1954.

Mitchell, Mary Hewitt. *The Great Awakening and Other Revivals in the Religious Life of Connecticut.* New Haven, 1934.

Morgan, Edmund S. "The American Revolution Considered as an Intellectual Movement," in Arthur M. Schlesinger, Jr., and Morton White, eds., *Paths of American Thought.* Boston, 1963.

—— *The Gentle Puritan: A Life of Ezra Stiles, 1727-1795.* New Haven, 1962.

—— *The Stamp Act Crisis. Prologue to Revolution.* Chapel Hill, 1953.

Niebuhr, H. Richard, *The Kingdom of God in America.* New York, [1959].

Schafer, Thomas A. "Jonathan Edwards' Conception of the Church," *Church History,* XXIV (1955), 51-66.

—— "Jonathan Edwards and Justification by Faith," *Church History,* XX (1951), 55-67.

Schlesinger, Arthur M. *The Colonial Merchants and the American Revolution. 1763-1776.* New York, 1918.

—— *Prelude to Independence. The Newspaper War on Britain, 1764-1776.* New York, 1958.

Shipton, Clifford K. "The New England Clergy of the 'Glacial Age,' " *Publications of the Colonial Society of Massachusetts,* XXXII (1936), 24-54.

Sklar, Robert. "The Great Awakening and Colonial Politics: Connecticut's Revolution in the Minds of Men," *Connecticut Historical Society Bulletin,* XXVIII (1963), 81-95.

Smith, H. Shelton. *Changing Conceptions of Original Sin: A Study in American Theology Since 1750.* New York, 1955.

Stokes, Anson Phelps. *Church and State in the United States.* 3 vols. New York, 1950.

Stowe, Walter H. "A Study in Conscience; Some Aspects of the Relations of the Clergy to the State," *Historical Magazine of the Protestant Episcopal Church,* XIX (1950), 301-323.

Suter, Rufus. "The Strange Universe of Jonathan Edwards," *Harvard Theological Review,* LIV (1961), 125-128.

Taylor, Robert J. *Western Massachusetts in the Revolution.* Providence, 1954.

Tolles, Frederick B. "Quietism versus Enthusiasm: The Philadelphia Quakers and the Great Awakening," *Pennsylvania Magazine of History and Biography,* LXIX (1945), 26-49.

Tracy, Joseph. *The Great Awakening. A History of the Revival of Religion in the Time of Edwards and Whitefield.* Boston, 1841.

Trinterud, Leonard J. *The Forming of an American Tradition. A Re-Examination of Colonial Presbyterianism.* Philadelphia, 1949.

—— "The New England Contribution to Colonial Presbyterianism," *Church History,* XVII (1948), 32-43.

SECONDARY SOURCES

Tucker, Louis Leonard. *Puritan Protagonist. President Thomas Clap of Yale College.* Chapel Hill, 1962.

Turnbull, Ralph G. *Jonathan Edwards the Preacher.* Grand Rapids, Mich., 1958.

Tyler, Moses C. *A History of American Literature, 1687-1765.* Ithaca, N.Y., 1949.

—— *The Literary History of the American Revolution, 1763-1783.* 2 vols. New York, [1957].

Van Tyne, Claude H. "Influence of the Clergy, and of Religious Sectarian Forces, on the American Revolution," *American Historical Review,* XIX (1913), 44-64.

Walker, George L. *Some Aspects of the Religious Life of New England.* Boston, 1897.

Weeks, Stephen D. *The Religious Development in the Province of North Carolina.* Baltimore, 1892.

White, Eugene E. "Decline of the Great Awakening in New England: 1741 to 1746," *New England Quarterly,* XXIV (1951), 35-52.

—— "The Preaching of George Whitefield during the Great Awakening in America," *Speech Monographs,* XV (1948), 33-43.

—— "The Protasis of the Great Awakening in New England," *Speech Monographs,* XXI (1954), 10-20.

Winslow, Ola Elizabeth. *Meetinghouse Hill, 1630-1783.* New York, 1952.

Wright, Conrad. *The Beginnings of Unitarianism in America.* Boston, 1955.

NOTES

INTRODUCTION

1. "Observations on the Support of the Clergy," *American Museum*, VIII (1790), 254.

2. Jonathan Mayhew, *The Snare Broken . . . May 23d, 1766*, in [Frank Moore, ed.], *The Patriot Preachers of the American Revolution* (New York, 1862), p. 23.

3. Charles Chauncy, *Seasonable Thoughts on the State of Religion in New-England* (Boston, 1743), p. 55.

4. *Some Thoughts Concerning the Present Revival of Religion in New England*, in *The Works of Jonathan Edwards* (10th ed., London, 1865), I, 422.

5. Perry Miller, "Jonathan Edwards and the Great Awakening," *Errand into the Wilderness* (Cambridge, 1956), pp. 156-157.

6. Edwin S. Gaustad, *The Great Awakening in New England* (New York, 1957).

7. Quoted, *George Whitefield's Journals. A New Edition Containing Fuller Material* (London, 1960), p. 19n.

8. Edwards, *Introduction to Five Discourses*, in *Works*, I, 620.

9. Gilbert Tennent, *A Sermon upon Justification. Preach'd at New-Brunswick . . . in August, Anno 1740* (Philadelphia, 1741), p. 17.

10. Perry Miller, "The Insecurity of Nature. Being the Dudleian Lecture for the Academic Year 1952-1953," *Harvard Divinity School Bulletin: Annual Lectures and Book Reviews*, 1954, p. 31.

11. Ebenezer Gay, *Natural Religion as Distinguish'd from Revealed* (Boston, 1759), pp. 10-11.

12. Edwards, *A Careful and Strict Enquiry into the Modern Prevailing Notions of that Freedom of Will, Which is Supposed to be Essential to Moral Agency*, Paul Ramsey, ed. (New Haven, 1957), p. 131.

13. Samuel Hopkins, *The Life of the Late Reverend, Learned and Pious Mr. Jonathan Edwards* (Boston, 1765), p. 41.

14. Jacob Green, *An Inquiry into the Constitution and Discipline of the Jewish Church* (New York, 1768), p. iii; Nathaniel Whitaker, *A Funeral Sermon, on the Death of the Reverend George Whitefield* (Salem, Mass., 1774), p. 13.

15. Hopkins, *Edwards*, p. 41.

16. David Bostwick, in Francis Alison and David Bostwick, *Peace and Union Recommended; and Self Disclaimed and Christ Exalted,* in *Two Sermons, Preached at Philadelphia, before the Reverend Synod* (Philadelphia, 1758), p. 47; Joseph Bellamy, *A Careful and Strict Examination of the External Covenant,* in *The Works of Joseph Bellamy, D.D.* (Boston, 1850), II, 70; Isaac Backus, *True Faith will Produce Good Work* (Boston, 1767), p. 68; Bellamy, *An Essay on the Nature and Glory of the Gospel,* in *Works,* II, 418.

17. Ebenezer Frothingham, *A Key to Unlock the Door* (n.p., 1767), p. 33.

18. Gilbert Tennent, in David Bostwick, *Self disclaimed, and Christ exalted* (London, 1759), pp. 31n-32n.

19. Harvey G. Townsend, ed., *The Philosophy of Jonathan Edwards. From His Private Notebooks* (Eugene, Oregon, 1955), p. 200.

20. Samuel Buell, in William B. Sprague, *Annals of the American Pulpit* (New York, 1859-1865), III, 105.

21. David McGregore, *The Spirits of the Present Day Tried. A Sermon at the Tuesday Evening Lecture in Brattle-Street, Boston, Nov. 3. 1741* (Boston, 1742), p. 19.

22. Nathaniel Appleton, *Faithful Ministers of Christ, the Salt of the Earth, and the Light of the World. Illustrated in a Sermon Preach'd before the Ministers of the Massachusetts-Bay . . . at their Annual Convention . . . May 26. 1743* (Boston, 1743), pp. 20-21.

23. Isaac Backus, *A History of New England* (2 vols., 2nd ed., Newton, Mass., 1871), II, 134; Gilbert Tennent, *A Persuasive to the Right Use of the Passions in Religion* (Philadelphia, 1760), p. 21.

24. John C. Miller, "Religion, Finance and Democracy in Massachusetts," *New England Quarterly,* VI (1933), 29.

25. Edward Holyoke, *The Duty of Ministers of the Gospel to guard against the Pharisaism and Sadducism, of the present Day . . . Preach'd at the Convention of Ministers . . . May 28. 1741* (Boston, 1741), p. 24.

26. Edwards, *Works,* I, ciii.

27. Quoted, Alan Simpson, *Puritanism in Old and New England* (Chicago, 1955), p. 59.

28. Perry Miller, ed., "Jonathan Edwards' Sociology of the Great Awakening," *New England Quarterly,* XXI (1948), 72.

29. Richard Mosier, *The American Temper* (Berkeley, 1952), p. 76.

30. H. Richard Niebuhr, *The Kingdom of God in America* (New York, [1959]), pp. 110-111.

31. Edwards, *A Faithful Narrative of the Surprising Work of God,* in *Works,* I, 348.

32. Edwards, *Five Discourses,* in *Works,* I, 646.

33. Samuel Johnson to the Secretary of the S.P.G., March 25, 1742, in Herbert and Carol Schneider, eds., *Samuel Johnson. His Career and Writings* (New York, 1929), III, 231.

34. Isaac Backus, *An Appeal to the Public for Religious Liberty* (Boston, 1773), p. 50.

35. Quoted, Leonard W. Labaree, *Conservatism in Early American History* (New York, 1948), pp. 66-67.

36. Quoted, Edmund Morgan, *The Stamp Act Crisis. Prologue to Revolution* (Chapel Hill, 1953), p. 228.

37. Quoted, Wesley M. Gewehr, *The Great Awakening in Virginia, 1740-1790* (Durham, N.C., 1930), p. 89.

38. Edwards, *Thoughts on the Revival,* in *Works,* I, 366.

39. John Gillies, *Memoirs of Rev. George Whitefield* (Middletown, Conn., 1838), p. 105.

40. Samuel Davies, "The Happy Effects of the Pouring out of the Spirit," *Sermons on Important Subjects* (4th ed., New York, 1845), I, 345.

41. Samuel Buell, *The Best New-Year's Gift for Young People . . . January 1st, 1775* (New London, n.d.), p. 53.

42. Edwards, *Thoughts on the Revival,* in *Works,* I, 390.

43. Noah Benedict, *Preparation for Death. A Sermon, Delivered at the Funeral of Rev. Joseph Bellamy* (New Haven, 1790), p. 19.

44. Aaron Burr, *A Discourse Delivered at New-Ark in New-Jersey, January 1, 1755. Being a Day set apart for solemn Fasting and Prayer* (New York, 1755), p. [1].

45. Edward Eels, *Christ, the Foundation of the Salvation of Sinners, and of Civil and Ecclesiastical Government: . . . Preached . . . on the Day of the Anniversary Election* (Hartford, [1767]), p. 25.

46. Robert Ross, *A Sermon, in which the Union of the Colonies is Considered and Recommended* (New York, 1776), p. 9.

47. Bellamy, *Election Sermon* (1762), in *Works,* I, 596.

48. Mark Leavenworth, *Charity Illustrated and Recommended . . . a Sermon Delivered . . . on the Day of . . . Election* (New London, [1772]), p. 31.

49. Edwards, "Farewell Sermon," *Works,* I, ccxlv.

50. William Gordon, *A Discourse Preached December 15th, 1774,* in John Wingate Thornton, ed., *The Pulpit of the American Revolution* (Boston, 1860), p. 197.

51. Douglass Adair and John A. Schutz, eds., *Peter Oliver's Origin and Progress of the American Revolution. A Tory View* (San Marino, Calif., 1961), *passim.*

52. Ebenezer Bridge, *A Sermon Preached . . . May 27th, 1767. Being the Anniversary for the Election* (Boston, 1767), p. 14.

53. [Elisha Williams], *The Essential Rights and Liberties of Protestants. A Seasonable Plea for the Liberty of Conscience* (Boston, 1744), p. 5.

54. Nathan Fiske, *The Importance of Righteousness to the Happiness, and the Tendency of Oppression to the Misery of a People* (Boston, 1774), p. 10.

55. [Moses Mather], *America's Appeal to the Impartial World* (Hartford, 1775), p. 3.

56. [Jacob Green], *Observations: on the Reconciliation of Great-Britain, and the Colonies* (Philadelphia, 1776), pp. 19-20.

57. Perry Miller, "From the Covenant to the Revival," *The Shaping of American Religion,* Religion in American Life, vol. I, James W. Smith and A. Leland Jamison, eds. (Princeton, 1961), p. 343.

58. Edwards, *Thoughts on the Revival,* in *Works,* I, 426.

59. Quoted, Morgan, *Stamp Act Crisis,* p. 228.

60. John Wise, *A Word of Comfort to a Melancholy Country,* quoted, Perry Miller, *The New England Mind: From Colony to Province* (Cambridge, 1953), p. 232.

61. Quoted, Joseph Dorfman, *The Economic Mind in American Civilization: 1606-1865* (New York, 1946), I, 161.

62. Charles E. Jorgensen and Frank Luther Mott, eds., *Benjamin Franklin: Representative Selections* (New York, 1936), p. 203.

63. Alexander Garden, *Take Heed How Ye Hear. A Sermon . . . July 13, 1740 . . . With a Preface Containing Some Remarks on Mr. Whitefield's Journals* (Charleston, 1741), Preface, p. 13.

64. James Sproutt, *A Discourse, Occasioned by the Death of the Reverend George Whitefield* (Philadelphia, 1771), p. 17.

65. William McGilchrist to Secretary of S.P.G., December 7, 1770, in William Stevens Perry, ed., *Historical Collections Relating to the American Colonial Church*, Volume III, Massachusetts ([Hartford], 1873), p. 555.

66. Benjamin Lord, *Religion and Government Subsisting Together in Society, Necessary to Their Compleat Happiness and Safety* (New London, 1751), p. 42.

67. William L. Saunders, ed., *The Colonial Records of North Carolina*, Volume IX, 1771 to 1775 (Raleigh, 1890), p. 1086.

I. THE NATURE AND NECESSITY OF
THE NEW BIRTH

1. John Webb, *The Duty of a Degenerate People to Pray for the Reviving of God's Work. A Sermon Preach'd June 18. 1734* (Boston, 1734), p. 24; cf. Joseph Sewall, *The Holy Spirit Convincing the World of Sin* (Boston, 1741), pp. 16-17.

2. Jonathan Parsons, "Account of the Revival of Religion at Lyme West Parish," in Thomas Prince, Jr., ed., *The Christian History, Containing Accounts of the Revival and Propagation of Religion . . . For the Year 1744* (Boston, 1745), pp. 122ff.

3. Gilbert Tennent, *The Espousals* (New Brunswick, 1741), p. 15.

4. Ebenezer Pemberton, *Practical Discourses on Various Texts* (Boston, 1741), p. 185

5. Thomas Symmes, *Good Soldiers Described, and Animated. A Sermon Preached before the Honourable Artillery Company* (Boston, 1720), p. 2.

6. Samuel Wigglesworth, *An Essay for the Reviving of Religion. A Sermon Delivered . . . May 30th. MDCCXXXIII. Being the Anniversary for the Election* (Boston, 1733), p. 25.

7. Gilbert Tennent, *A Solemn Warning to the Secure World from the God of Terrible Majesty* (Boston, 1735), p. 86.

8. Tennent, Preface to *The Unsearchable Riches of Christ*, in *Sermons on Sacramental Occasions by Divers Ministers* (Boston, 1739), pp. ii-iii; *Solemn Warning*, p. 102.

9. Edwards, *Works*, I, 681.

10. Miller, "Edwards' Sociology," pp. 71-73.

11. Holyoke, *Duty of Ministers*, pp. 24-25.

12. Edwards, *Images or Shadows of Divine Things*, Perry Miller, ed. (New Haven, 1948), p. 102.

13. Miller, "Edwards' Sociology," p. 55; Edwards, *Works*, II, 293.

14. *Three Letters to the Reverend Mr. George Whitefield* (Philadelphia, 1739), p. 6; *Whitefield's Journals*, pp. 343, 357.

15. *Whitefield's Journals*, p. 371.

16. Benjamin Colman and William Cooper, Preface to Josiah Smith, *The Character, Preaching, &c. of the Rev. Mr. Whitefield* (Boston, 1740).

17. Edwards, *Copies of the Two Letters cited by the Rev. Mr. Clap* (Boston, 1745), p. 13.

18. Samuel Niles, *Tristitae Ecclesiarum; or, a Brief and Sorrowful Account of the Present State of the Churches in New England* (Boston, 1745), p. 4.

19. Samuel Blair, *A Particular Consideration of a Piece, Entitled, The Querists* (Philadelphia, 1741), p. 3.

20. Jonathan Ashley, *The Great Duty of Charity . . . a Sermon, Preached at the Church in Brattle-Street, Boston . . . November 28, 1742* (Boston, 1742), p. 2; *The Testimony and Advice of a Number of Laymen Respecting Religion, and the Teachers of It* (Boston, 1743), p. 3.

21. Garden, *Take Heed,* Preface, p. 19; *Whitefield's Journals,* pp. 400-403.

22. Garden, *Regeneration, and the Testimony of the Spirit. Being the Substance of Two Sermons . . . Occasioned by Some Erroneous Notions of Certain Men Who Call Themselves Methodists* (Charleston, 1740; reprinted Boston, 1741), pp. 13-14.

23. Josiah Smith, *Sermon on Whitefield,* in Whitefield, *Fifteen Sermons Preached on Various Important Subjects* (New York, 1794), p. 12.

24. *A Letter from the Reverend Mr. Whitefield, to Some Church Members of the Presbyterian Persuasion* (Boston, 1740), p. 13.

25. *Testimony and Advice of Laymen,* p. 3.

26. Whitefield, *The Nature and Necessity of Our New Birth in Christ Jesus* (3rd ed., London, 1737), p. 21.

27. J. Smith, *Character of Whitefield,* p. 8.

28. Dickinson, *The Nature and Necessity of Regeneration* (New York, 1743), p. 3; cf. Gilbert Tennent, *The Danger of an Unconverted Ministry . . . Preached at Nottingham in Pennsylvania, March 8. Anno 1739, 40* (2nd ed., Philadelphia, 1740), p. 10.

29. *Three Letters wrote from Boston in New-England to a Correspondent in the Gorbels of Glasgow* (Glasgow, 1741), p. 7; Thomas Prince, John Webb, and William Cooper, Preface to McGregore, *Spirits of the Present Day Tried.*

30. Josiah Smith, *Success a Great Proof of St. Paul's Fidelity. Sacred to the Memory of the Reverend George Whitefield* (Charleston, 1770), p. 4.

31. William Cooper, "Preface to the Reader," in Edwards, *The Distinguishing Marks of a Work of the Spirit of God,* in *Works,* II, 258.

32. Perry Miller, "The Great Awakening from 1740 to 1750," *Encounter* (The Divinity School, Duke University, March 1956), p. 9.

33. Chauncy, *Seasonable Thoughts,* p. 199.

34. Miller, "Great Awakening," *Encounter,* p. 9.

35. Dickinson, *The Witness of the Spirit. A Sermon Preached at Newark in New-Jersey, May 7th. 1740 . . . On Occasion of the Wonderful Progress of Converting Grace in These Parts* (Boston, 1740), pp. 4-9, 20-21.

36. Edwards, *Works,* II, 81.

37. *Ibid.,* p. 266.

38. Hermon Husband, *Some Remarks on Religion, with the Author's Experience in Pursuit Thereof,* in William K. Boyd, ed., *Some Eighteenth Century Tracts Concerning North Carolina* (Raleigh, N.C., 1927), p. 221.

39. *Three Letters to Glasgow,* p. 7.

40. Prince, *Christian History for 1744,* p. 242.

41. Whitefield, *New Birth,* p. 8.

42. *The Querists, Part III. Or, an Extract of Sundry Passages Taken Out of Mr. G. Tennent's Sermon* (Philadelphia, 1741), p. 141.

43. *The Testimony of a Number of New-England Ministers Met at Boston, Sept. 25, 1745* (Boston, 1745), p. 4.

44. *The Works of the Reverend George Whitefield* (6 vols., London, 1771-72), V, 369.

45. Perry Miller, *Jonathan Edwards* (New York, 1949), p. 177.

46. Jonathan Parsons, *To Live is Christ, to Die is Gain. A Funeral-Sermon on the Death of the Reverend Mr. George Whitefield* (Portsmouth, N.H.,

[1770]), p. 24; Edwards, *A Treatise Concerning Religious Affections,* John E. Smith, ed. (New Haven, 1959), p. 95.

47. Edwards, *Religious Affections,* pp. 208, 272ff.

48. Edwards, *Works,* I, cclxxi; Jonathan Parsons, "The Knowledge of Christ Improved," *Sixty Sermons on Various Subjects* (2 vols., Newburyport, Mass., 1779-1780), I, 148; Nathaniel Niles, *The Perfection of God the Fountain of Good. Two Sermons . . . December 21st, 1777* (Elizabethtown, N.J., 1791), p. 6.

49. John Bass, *A True Narrative of an Unhappy Contention in the Church of Ashford* (Boston, 1751), p. 3; cf. Samuel Niles, *A Vindication of Divers Important Gospel-Doctrines* (Boston, 1752), p. 95.

50. Joseph Huntington, *The Vanity and Mischief of Presuming on Things beyond our Measure* (Norwich, Conn., 1774), pp. 26-27.

51. Husband, *Some Remarks,* in Boyd, *Eighteenth Century Tracts,* p. 212.

52. Edwards, *Works,* II, 625.

53. Samuel Buell, *A Faithful Narrative of the Remarkable Revival of Religion in the Year of Our Lord 1764* (New York, 1766), p. iii; Aaron Burr, *A Servant of God Dismissed from Labour to Rest. A Funeral Sermon, Preached at the Interment of His Late Excellency Jonathan Belcher* (New York, 1757), p. 11; Bellamy, *Works,* II, 437; Edwards, *Works,* II, 448; Buell, *Best New-Year's Gift,* p. 12.

54. Leonard J. Trinterud, *The Forming of an American Tradition* (Philadelphia, 1949), pp. 185-186.

55. Davies, "God is Love," *Sermons,* I, 319.

56. Bellamy, *Works,* I, xxx.

57. William Cooke, *The Great Duty of Ministers, to Take Heed to Themselves and Their Doctrine. A Sermon Preach'd in a New Township, Narragansett, No. 2. October 20. 1742* (Boston, 1742), p. 23.

58. Benjamin Doolittle, *An Enquiry into Enthusiasm* (Boston, 1743), p. 21.

59. William Hart, *A Discourse Concerning the Nature of Regeneration, and the Way Wherein it is Wrought* (New London, 1742), p. 36.

60. William Hobby, *Self-Examination, in it's Necessity and Advantages Urged and Applied in Sundry Sermons* (Boston, 1746), p. 97.

61. John Caldwell, *An Impartial Trial of the Spirit Operating in this Part of the World . . . A Sermon Preached at New London-derry, October 14th, 1741* (Boston, 1742), p. 38.

62. Samuel Quincy, "The Nature and Necessity of Regeneration," *Twenty Sermons . . . Preach'd in the Parish of St. Philip, Charles-Town, South-Carolina* (Boston, 1750), p. 289.

63. Josiah Stearns, *A Sermon, Preached at Epping, in New Hampshire . . . September 19, 1779* (Exeter, N.H., 1780), p. 15; N. Niles, *The Remembrance of Christ. A Sermon . . . October 31, 1771* (Boston, 1773), p. 21.

64. Johnson, *Writings,* II, 373.

65. Edwards, *Works,* II, 91; N. Niles, *Perfection of God,* p. 6; Stearns, *Sermon at Epping,* p. 15; Samuel Buell, *A Spiritual Knowledge of God in Christ* (New London, 1771), p. 40.

66. Gad Hitchcock, *Natural Religion Aided by Revelation and Perfected in Christianity* (Boston, 1779), p. 20.

67. Charles Chauncy, *Five Dissertations on the Scripture Account of the Fall* (London, 1785), pp. 173ff.

68. Andrew Eliot, *A Discourse on Natural Religion Delivered in the Chapel of Harvard College* (Boston, 1771), p. xii.

69. Chauncy, *Five Dissertations*, p. 23.

70. Jonathan Mayhew, *Seven Sermons . . . Preached at a Lecture in the West Meeting House in Boston . . . in August, 1748* (Boston, 1749), pp. 29-32.

71. Jonathan Mayhew, *Christian Sobriety* (Boston, 1763), p. 25.

72. Johann Joachim Zubly, *The Wise Shining as the Brightness of the Firmament . . . A Funeral Sermon . . . on the Much Lamented Death of the Rev. George Whitefield* (Savannah, 1770), p. 22.

73. Whitaker, *Funeral Sermon on Whitefield*, pp. 19-20; Miller, "Edwards' Sociology," p. 70.

74. John Tucker, *Observations on the Doctrines, and Uncharitableness, &c of the Rev. Mr. Jonathan Parsons* (Boston, 1757), p. 32; Miller, "Edwards' Sociology," pp. 70-71.

75. Whitaker, *Two Sermons: on the Doctrine of Reconciliation* (Salem, Mass., 1770), Appendix, p. 75.

76. Davies, "Things Unseen to be Preferred to Things Seen," *Sermons*, I, 203.

77. Bellamy, *Millennium*, in *Works*, I, 456; *Four Sermons on the Wisdom of God in the Permission of Sin*, in *Works*, II, 55n.

78. Stearns, *Sermon at Epping*, pp. 14-15.

79. Buell, *Revival of 1764*, pp. 76-77.

80. Jonathan Greenleaf, "Memoir of the Rev. Jonathan Parsons, M.A.," *American Quarterly Register*, XIV (1841), 115.

81. Abel Stevens, *The History of the Religious Movement of the Eighteenth Century, Called Methodism* (3 vols., New York, 1858-1861), I, 467.

82. John Tucker, *Remarks on a Sermon of the Rev. Aaron Hutchinson* (Boston, [1767]), p. 47.

83. "To the Honourable the People's Council, and the House of Representatives, of the Province of the Massachusetts-Bay," appended to [Joseph Allen?], *The American Alarm, or the Bostonian Plea, for the Rights, and Liberties, of the People* (Boston, 1773), pp. 12-13.

84. Tennent, *Right Use of Passions*, pp. 29-30.

85. Samuel Davies, *Charity and Truth United, or the Way of the Multitude Exposed. In Six Letters to the Rev. Mr. William Stith, A.M.* (1755), Thomas Clinton Pears, Jr., ed. (Philadelphia, 1941), pp. 210-211.

86. William Serjeant to Secretary of S.P.G., October 17, 1768, in Perry, *Historical Collections, Massachusetts*, p. 543.

87. Nathaniel Henchman, *A Letter to the Reverend Mr. William Hobby* (Boston, 1745), p. 12.

88. Aaron Hutchinson, *A Reply to the Remarks of the Rev. Mr. John Tucker* (Boston, 1768), p. 13.

89. William Smith, quoted, Trinterud, *Forming of American Tradition*, pp. 140-141.

90. Edwards, *Thoughts on the Revival*, in *Works*, I, 426.

91. Bellamy, *Nature and Glory of the Gospel*, in *Works*, I, 128.

92. Whitaker, *Funeral Sermon on Whitefield*, p. 13n; *Sermons on Reconciliation*, pp. 27, 69n.

93. Benjamin Colman, *Souls Flying to Christ Pleasant and Admirable to Behold. A Sermon Preach'd . . . October 21. 1740* (Boston, 1740), p. 12.

94. Edwards, *A Dissertation Concerning the Nature of True Virtue*, in *Works*, I, 128.

95. Stearns, *Sermon at Epping*, pp. 14-15.

96. Lyman H. Butterfield, "Elder John Leland, Jeffersonian Itinerant," *Proceedings of the American Antiquarian Society,* LXII (1952), 155-242.

97. Leland, "The Virginia Chronicle," quoted, Charles F. James, *Documentary History of the Struggle for Religious Liberty in Virginia* (Lynchburg, 1900), p. 86.

98. Patrick Tailfer, *et al., A True Historical Narrative of the Colony of Georgia,* Clarence L. Ver Steeg, ed. (Athens, Ga., 1960), p. 11.

99. Quoted, Labaree, *Conservatism,* p. 81.

100. William Douglass, *A Summary, Historical and Political . . . of the British Settlements in North-America* (2 vols., London, 1760), I, 249n.

101. Oliver Hart, *America's Remembrancer . . . A Sermon, Delivered in Hopewell, New Jersey . . . November 26, 1789* (Philadelphia, 1791), p. 23.

102. Smith, *Character of Whitefield,* p. 12.

103. Boston *Weekly News-Letter,* October 2, 1740, quoted, Eugene E. White, "The Protasis of the Great Awakening in New England," *Speech Monographs,* XXI (March, 1954), 15.

104. Tucker, *Observations on Jonathan Parsons,* p. 32.

105. Jonathan Dickinson, *A Defence of the Dialogue, Intitled, A Display of God's Special Grace* (Boston, 1743), p. 35.

106. Tennent, *Unconverted Ministry,* p. 9.

107. Ebenezer Pemberton, *A Sermon Preached . . . May 25th, 1757. Being the Anniversary for the Election* (Boston, 1757), p. 15; Jacob Johnson, *Honours Due to the Memory and Remains of Pious and Good Men at Death . . . Preached at the Funeral of Col. Christopher Avery* (New London, 1768), p. 26.

108. Tennent, *Unconverted Ministry,* p. 4.

109. Burr, *Servant of God,* p. 14.

110. Backus, *An Address to the Inhabitants of New-England, Concerning the Present Bloody Controversy Therein* (Boston, 1787), pp. 3-7.

111. Jonathan Dickinson, *A Call to the Weary & Heavy Laden to Come unto Christ for Rest. A Sermon Preached at Connecticut Farms in Elizabeth-Town Dec. 23. 1739* (New York, 1740), p. 9.

112. McGregore, *Spirits of the Present Day Tried* (2nd ed., Boston, 1742), Appendix, p. iii.

113. Henchman, *Letter to Hobby,* p. 8; Chauncy, *A Letter to the Reverend Mr. George Whitefield, Vindicating Certain Passages he has Excepted Against, in a Late Book Entitled, Seasonable Thoughts* (Boston, 1745), p. 37; Samuel Finl[e]y, *A Letter to a Friend* (n.p., [1740]), pp. 2-4.

114. Edwards, *Thoughts on the Revival,* in *Works,* I, 374, 387.

115. *Ibid.,* p. 424; Edwards, *Images or Shadows,* p. 102.

II. THE WORK OF REDEMPTION

1. C. C. Goen, "Jonathan Edwards: A New Departure in Eschatology," *Church History,* XXVIII (1959), 26.

2. Edwards, *Thoughts on the Revival,* in *Works,* I, 377.

3. Edwards, *A History of the Work of Redemption,* in *Works,* I, 613.

4. Robert Ross, *A Plain Address to the Quakers, Moravians, Separatists, Separate-Baptists, Rogerenes, and Other Enthusiasts* (New Haven, [1762]), p. 45.

5. Richard McNemar, *The Kentucky Revival; or, a Short History of the Late Extraordinary Outpouring of the Spirit of God in the Western States of America* ([2nd ed.], New York, 1846), p. 12.

6. John White, *New England's Lamentations* (Boston, 1734), pp. 7-9; Ebenezer Pemberton, *Sermons on Several Subjects. Preach'd at the Presbyterian Church in the City of New York* (Boston, 1738), pp. 79-83; Boston *Weekly News-Letter*, quoted, Chauncy, *Seasonable Thoughts*, p. 97.

7. Edwards, "Personal Narrative," *Works*, I, clxxxix.

8. Edwards, *Work of Redemption*, in *Works*, I, 584.

9. *Ibid.*, pp. 539, 605.

10. Niebuhr, *The Kingdom of God in America*, p. 143.

11. Smith, *Character of Whitefield*, p. 20.

12. Edwards, *Distinguishing Marks*, in *Works*, II, 272; *Thoughts on the Revival*, in *Works*, I, 380.

13. Edwards, "The Church's Marriage to Her Sons and to Her God. Preached at the Instalment of the Rev. Samuel Buell . . . September 19, 1746," *Works*, II, 25.

14. *The Christian History . . . for the year 1743* (Boston, 1744), pp. 106ff; Thomas Foxcroft, *A Seasonable Momento for New Year's Day* (Boston, 1747), pp. 54-57.

15. Edwards, *Will*, p. 246.

16. Miller, "The End of the World," *Errand*, p. 235; Edwards, *The Great Christian Doctrine of Original Sin Defended*, in *Works*, I, 218; Edwards, *Will*, p. 246.

17. Edwards, *Humble Attempt*, in *Works*, II, 295.

18. Levi Hart, *The Christian Minister, or Faithful Preacher of the Gospel Described* (New London, 1771), pp. 13-14; N. Niles, *The Remembrance of Christ*, p. 27.

19. Edwards, "An Essay on the Trinity," in Clarence H. Faust and Thomas H. Johnson, eds., *Jonathan Edwards: Representative Selections* (New York, 1935), p. 379.

20. Buell, *Revival of 1764*, pp. iii-iiii.

21. Davies, *The Religious Improvement of the Late Earthquakes*, in *Sermons*, III, 187.

22. Edwards, *Work of Redemption*, in *Works*, I, 617.

23. Townsend, ed., *Philosophy of Edwards*, pp. 207-208.

24. Edwards, *True Virtue*, in *Works*, I, 127.

25. Edwards, *Will*, pp. 255-256.

26. Edwards, *Work of Redemption*, in *Works*, I, 614; *Humble Attempt*, in *Works*, II, 289.

27. Miller, *Errand*, p. 235.

28. Edwards, *Work of Redemption*, in *Works*, I, 605.

29. Edwards, *Humble Attempt*, in *Works*, II, 299.

30. Edwards, "True Saints, when Absent from the Body, are Present with the Lord. A Sermon, Preached at the Funeral of the Rev. David Brainerd," *Works*, II, 30.

31. Edwards, *Work of Redemption*, in *Works*, I, 616.

32. Edwards, *Images or Shadows*, p. 76.

33. Edwards, *Work of Redemption*, in *Works*, I, 617.

34. Davies, "The Success of the Ministry of the Gospel, Owing to a Divine Influence," *Sermons*, II, 522-523.

35. Edwards, "Church's Marriage," *Works*, II, 25.

36. Jonathan Parsons, *Good News from a Far Country* (Portsmouth, N.H., 1756), p. 168.

37. Edwards, *Humble Attempt,* in *Works,* II, 281, 287, 310.

38. Edwards, *Works,* I, cxxviii; Ralph G. Turnbull, *Jonathan Edwards the Preacher* (Grand Rapids, Mich., 1958), p. 43.

39. Edwards, *Humble Attempt,* in *Works,* II, 289.

40. Parsons, *Good News,* p. 168.

41. For example, *Questions & Answers to the prophetic numbers of Daniel and John Calculated . . . By an aged gentleman* (Boston, 1759).

42. Jonathan Mayhew, *The Expected Dissolution of All Things, a Motive to Universal Holiness. Two Sermons Preached . . . Nov. 23, 1755; Occasioned by the Earthquakes* (Boston, 1755), pp. 39-40.

43. Charles Chauncy, *The Earth Delivered from the Curse to which it is, at Present, Subjected* (Boston, 1756), pp. 25-26.

44. Jared Eliot, *Essays upon Field Husbandry in New England,* Harry J. Carman and Rexford G. Tugwell, eds. (New York, 1934), pp. 96-97.

45. Townsend, *Philosophy of Edwards,* pp. 207-208; [Timothy Dwight], *A Sermon, Preached at Northampton, on the Twenty-Eighth of November, 1781* (Hartford, [1781]), p. 31; Samuel Hopkins, *The System of Doctrines . . . to which is Added, a Treatise on the Millennium* (2 vols., Boston, 1793), II, 69-72 (separate pagination).

46. John Winthrop, *A Lecture on Earthquakes; Read in the Chapel of Harvard-College . . . November 26th, 1755* (Boston, 1755), pp. 29-31.

47. *Ibid.,* p. 29n.

48. Joseph Morgan, Letter to Nathan Prince, December 28, 1726, in Richard Schlatter, ed., *The History of the Kingdom of Basaruah* (Cambridge, 1941), p. 169; "To the author of the *General Magazine,*" June 2, 1741, in Benjamin Franklin (pub.), *The General Magazine* (Philadelphia, 1741; facsimile edition, New York, 1938), pp. 340-341.

49. Miller, *Jonathan Edwards,* pp. 121-122.

50. Davies, "The Religious Improvement of the Late Earthquakes," *Sermons,* III, 179; Robert Smith, *A Wheel in the Middle of a Wheel: or, the Harmony and Connexion of the Various Acts of Divine Providence* (Philadelphia, 1759), pp. 10-11.

51. Whitaker, *Funeral Sermon on Whitefield,* p. 8n.

52. Samuel Buell, *Intricate and Mysterious Events of Providence, Design'd to Display Divine Glory* (New London, [1770]), pp. 11-12, 37; Parsons, *To Live is Christ,* pp. 23-24.

53. Edwards, *Will,* p. 256.

54. Davies, "The Signs of the Times," *Sermons,* III, 102; William Torrey, *A Brief Discourse Concerning Futurities* (Boston, 1757), pp. 19, ii.

55. Buell, *Intricate and Mysterious Events,* p. 12.

56. N. Niles, *Perfection of God,* p. 23.

57. Edwards, *Will,* p. 246.

58. Edwards, *Humble Attempt,* in *Works,* II, 289.

59. Edwards, *Will,* p. 266.

60. Edwards, *A Dissertation Concerning the End for Which God Created the World,* in *Works,* I, 120.

61. Edwards, *Images or Shadows,* p. 76.

62. Edwards, *Work of Redemption,* in *Works,* I, 617.

63. R. Smith, *Wheel in the Middle,* pp. 9-10; Buell, *Intricate and Mysterious Events,* pp. 12-13.

64. Buell, *Intricate and Mysterious Events*, p. 12; Davies, "The Success of the Ministry," *Sermons*, II, 519-522.

65. Parsons, *To Live is Christ*, pp. 22-25.

66. Samuel Blair, *The Doctrine of Predestination*, in *Works* (Philadelphia, 1754), p. 234.

67. Thomas Allen, *Particular Providence a Source of Comfort* (Pittsfield, Mass., [1801]), p. 15.

68. McNemar, *Kentucky Revival*, pp. 59, 69.

69. Edwards, *Thoughts on the Revival*, in *Works*, I, 387; *Work of Redemption*, in *Works*, I, 617-618.

70. Edwards, "True Saints, when Absent from the Body," *Works*, II, 30.

71. Edwards, *Work of Redemption*, in *Works*, I, 605.

72. Edwards, "Church's Marriage," *Works*, II, 24.

73. Eleazar Wheelock, *A Sermon Preached . . . June 30, 1763. At the Ordination of the Rev. Mr. Charles-Jeffry Smith . . . To which is Added, a Sermon Preached by Nathaniel Whitaker, D.D., after the Said Ordination* (London, 1767), p. 3.

74. Israel Evans, *A Discourse, Delivered at Easton, on the 17th of October, 1779* (Philadelphia, 1779), p. 12; William Gordon, *The Separation of the Jewish Tribes . . . Applied to the Present Day, in a Sermon, Delivered on July 4th, 1777*, in Moore, *Patriot Preachers*, p. 160.

75. Edwards, *Humble Attempt*, in *Works*, II, 310.

76. *Ibid.*

77. William Tennent II, quoted, "History of Revivals of Religion," *American Quarterly Register*, V (1833), 212.

78. R. Smith, *Wheel in the Middle*, p. 26.

79. David Austin, *The Voice of God to the People of These United States* (Elizabethtown, N.J., 1796), pp. 40-41.

80. Thomas Baldwin, *A Sermon, Delivered . . . April 2, 1799; at a Quarterly Meeting of Several Churches for Special Prayer* (Boston, 1799), p. 23.

81. Austin, *The Millennium . . . Shortly to Commence* (Elizabethtown, N.J., 1794), pp. v-vi; *The Millennial Door Thrown Open, or the Mysteries of the Latter Day Glory Unfolded in a Discourse, Delivered at East-Windsor, State of Connecticut, July Fourth, 1799* (East Windsor, Conn., 1799), *passim*.

82. Edwards, *Works*, I, cxxiv.

83. [Nathaniel Whitaker], *A Brief Narrative of the Indian Charity-School* (London, 1766), p. 15.

84. Thomas Prince, *Extraordinary Events the Doings of God, and Marvellous in Pious Eyes . . . a Sermon . . . Occasion'd by Taking the City of Louisburg* (Boston, 1745), p. 35.

85. William Foster, *True Fortitude Delineated. A Sermon, Preached at Fags Manor Februrary 18th, 1776* (Philadelphia, 1776), p. 17.

86. Buell, *Revival of 1764*, p. 87.

87. Prince, *Extraordinary Events*, pp. 11-17.

88. Edwards, *Humble Attempt*, in *Works*, II, 294; Prince, *Extraordinary Events*, p. 23; Backus, *True Faith*, p. 62.

89. Gilbert Tennent, *Sermon Preach'd at Philadelphia, January 7. 1747-8 . . . a Day of Fasting and Prayer* (Philadelphia, 1748), p. 18.

90. Parsons, *Good News*, p. 168.

91. Davies, *Charity and Truth*, pp. 320-322.

92. Davies, "The Crisis," *Sermons*, III, 76-77.

93. Burr, *1755 Fast*, p. 36.

94. John Bolles, *The Following Treatise, Containes, a Brief Account of Persecutions* ([New London], 1758), p. 9.

95. Edwards, *Humble Attempt,* in *Works,* II, 299.

96. Edwards, *Works,* I, cxxiii.

97. Edwards, *Work of Redemption,* in *Works,* I, 607; *Humble Attempt,* in *Works,* II, 309n.

98. Abraham Keteltas, *The Religious Soldier: or, the Military Character of King David* (New York, 1759), p. 15.

99. Davies, "The Crisis," *Sermons,* III, 76-77.

100. Davies, "The Mediatorial Kingdom and Glories of Jesus Christ," *Sermons,* I, 197.

101. Burr, *The Watchman's Answer to the Question, What of the Night* (2nd ed., Boston, 1757), pp. 20, 22, 27n.

102. Bellamy, *Millennium,* in *Works,* I, 450, 459.

103. Austin, *Millennial Door Thrown Open,* pp. 35-36.

104. McNemar, *Kentucky Revival,* p. 69; James Sloan, *An Oration, Delivered at a Meeting of the Democratic Association of the County of Gloucester . . . on the Fourth Day of March, 1802.* (Trenton, 1802), p. 6.

105. Charles Brockwell to Secretary of S.P.G., Feb. 18, 1741/2, in Perry, *Historical Collections, Massachusetts,* pp. 353-354.

106. *The Wonderful Narrative: or, a Faithful Account of the French Prophets* (Boston, 1742), Appendix, p. 106; A——Z. (pseud.), *Mr. Parsons Corrected. Or, an Addition of Some Things to His Late Sermon* (Boston, 1743), p. 10; Chauncy, *Seasonable Thoughts,* p. 209; Philemon Robbins, *A Plain Narrative of the Proceedings of the Reverend Association and Consociation of New-Haven County* (Boston, 1747), pp. 19-22; Samuel Finley, *Clear Light Put Out in Obscure Darkness* (Philadelphia, 1743), p. 72.

107. Edwards, "Christ Exalted: or, Jesus Christ Gloriously Exalted Above All Evil in the Work of Redemption," *Works,* II, 216; *Distinguishing Marks,* in *Works,* II, 273, 276, 288; *Thoughts on the Revival,* in *Works,* I, 387.

108. Edwards, *Humble Attempt,* in *Works,* II, 299; cf. *Works,* I, cxxiii.

109. Edwards, "Miscellaneous Observations," *Works,* II, 474-475.

110. Edwards, "Church's Marriage," *Works,* II, 474; "True Grace Distinguished from the Experience of Devils," *Works,* II, 42.

111. Edwards, *Humble Attempt,* in *Works,* II, 281-282.

112. Quoted, Joseph Tracy, *The Great Awakening* (6th ed., Boston, c1841), p. 322.

113. Douglass, *Summary,* I, 249n.

114. Carl Bridenbaugh, *Cities in Revolt. Urban Life in America, 1743-1776* (New York, 1955), p. 151.

115. Quoted, Sprague, *Annals,* III, 91.

116. Robbins, *Plain Narrative,* p. 19.

117. *General Magazine,* p. 414; Chauncy, *Seasonable Thoughts,* p. 373.

118. Garden, *Regeneration,* p. 24; Edward Wigglesworth, *A Letter to the Reverend Mr. George Whitefield, By Way of Reply to His Answer to the College Testimony* (Boston, 1745), pp. 3-4.

119. Chauncy, *Seasonable Thoughts,* pp. 372-374; *Enthusiasm Describ'd and Caution'd Against* (Boston, 1742), p. 15.

120. Jonathan Todd, *Civil Rulers the Ministers of God, for Good to Men . . . a Sermon Preach'd . . . the Day of Election* (New London, 1749), p. 74n.

121. Tennent, *Right Use of Passions,* pp. 29-30.

122. Edwards, *Thoughts on the Revival,* in *Works,* I, 371.

587

123. Chauncy, *Enthusiasm Describ'd*, p. 16.

124. Alexander Craighead, *A Discourse Concerning the Covenants* (Philadelphia, 1742), p. 18; Samuel Finley, *Satan Stripp'd of his Angelick Robe. Being the Substance of Several Sermons Preach'd at Philadelphia, January 1742-3* (Philadelphia, [1743]), p. vi.

III. THE BEAUTY AND GOOD TENDENCY OF UNION

1. Edwards, *Humble Attempt*, in *Works*, II, 295.

2. *Whitefield's Journals*, p. 363; Dickinson, *The True Scripture-Doctrine Concerning Some Important Points of Christian Faith* (Boston, 1741), Preface, p. ii.

3. Edwards, *Thoughts on the Revival*, in *Works*, I, 381-382.

4. John Witherspoon, "The Dominion of Providence over the Passions of Men," *The Works of the Rev. John Witherspoon* (2nd ed., Philadelphia, 1802), III, 25.

5. Edwards, *Thoughts on the Revival*, in *Works*, I, 382.

6. John Cleaveland, *A Short and Plain Narrative of the Late Work of God's Spirit at Chebacco* (Boston, 1767), and *A Reply to Dr. Mayhew's Letter of Reproof* (Boston, 1765), p. 95; Buell, *Revival of 1764*, pp. 23-25, 49-50, 77; Johnson, *Honours Due to the Memory*, p. 28; Backus, *Evangelical Ministers Described, and Distinguished from Legalists* (Boston, 1772), p. 36; Backus, *History of New England*, II, 98.

7. Samuel Sherwood, *The Church's Flight into the Wilderness: An Address . . . Delivered on a Public Occasion, January 17, 1776* (New York, 1776), pp. 22-23.

8. Chauncy, *Seasonable Thoughts*, p. 372n.

9. Robert Sklar, "The Great Awakening and Colonial Politics: Connecticut's Revolution in the Minds of Men," *Connecticut Historical Society Bulletin,* XXVIII (1963), 85.

10. Edwards, *Work of Redemption*, in *Works*, I, 610.

11. Edwards, *Original Sin*, in *Works*, I, 167.

12. Edwards, "Sermon VIII," *Works*, II, 898.

13. Edwards, *Original Sin*, in *Works* I, 168, 218; Bellamy, *Millennium*, in *Works*, II, 448.

14. James Sloan, *An Address, Delivered at a Meeting of the Democratic Association* (Trenton, [1801]), p. 23.

15. Edwards, *Humble Attempt*, in *Works*, II, 288.

16. Edwards, *Work of Redemption*, in *Works*, I, 610.

17. Edwards, *End in Creation*, in *Works*, I, 101.

18. Edwards, "The Future Punishment of the Wicked Unavoidable and Intolerable," *Works*, II, 81; "The Final Judgment," *Works*, II, 197-198; "Miscellaneous Observations," *Works*, II, 620-628. Cf. Davies, "The General Resurrection," *Sermons*, I, 345.

19. Edwards, *Works*, I, cclxxi; *True Virtue*, in *Works*, I, 141.

20. Edwards, *Works*, I, cclxxi.

21. Edwards, "Covenant of Redemption: 'Excellency of Christ,'" in Faust and Johnson, *Edwards Selections*, p. 374; "Sermon VIII," *Works*, II, 898.

22. Edwards, "Miscellaneous Observations," *Works*, II, 621.

23. Nathaniel Niles, *Two Discourses on Liberty* (Newburyport, Mass., 1774), p. 27; Ebenezer Pemberton, *A Sermon Preached to the Ancient and Honourable Artillery Company* (Boston, 1756), p. 8.

24. Edwards, "Church's Marriage," *Works*, II, 25.

25. Parsons, "The Beatific Vision," *Sixty Sermons*, II, 193.

26. Edwards, *True Virtue*, in *Works*, I, 141.

27. Edwards, *Images or Shadows*, p. 135.

28. Edwards, "Sermon XI," *Works*, II, 926.

29. Edwards, "Covenant of Redemption," in Faust and Johnson, *Edwards Selections*, p. 373.

30. Quoted, Turnbull, *Jonathan Edwards*, p. 77.

31. Edwards, *True Virtue*, in *Works*, I, 127-128.

32. Townsend, *Philosophy of Edwards*, p. 65.

33. Bellamy, *Wisdom of God*, in *Works*, II, 4, 29; Bellamy, *Nature and Glory of the Gospel*, in *Works*, II, 277-278; Samuel Buell, *Christ the Grand Subject of Gospel-Preaching* (New York, 1755), p. 11; Levi Hart, *The Excellence of Scripture-Arguments to Persuade Men to Repentance* (New London, 1775), p. 17.

34. Edwards, "Types of the Messiah," *Works*, II, 674.

35. Samuel Davies, *Miscellaneous Poems, Chiefly on Divine Subjects* (Williamsburg, 1751), p. 56.

36. Ebenezer Chaplin, *The Civil State Compared to Rivers* (Boston, 1773), p. 24.

37. Austin, *The Voice of God*, pp. 40-41.

38. Sprague, *Annals*, II, 49.

39. Perry Miller, Introduction to Edwards, *Images or Shadows*, p. 20.

40. Mayhew, *Christian Sobriety*, p. 54.

41. Appleton, *Faithful Ministers*, p. 39; Isaac Stiles, *A Looking-Glass for Changlings. A Seasonable Caveat* (New London, 1743), pp. 26-27.

42. Daniel Shute, *A Sermon Preached . . . May 25th, 1768. Being the Anniversary For the Election* (Boston, 1768), pp. 33-34.

43. Henry Cumings, *A Sermon Preached . . . May 28, 1783. Being the Anniversary of General Election* (Boston, 1783), p. 15.

44. Edwards, *Images or Shadows*, p. 48.

45. Miller, Introduction to Edwards, *Images or Shadows*, p. 20.

46. Edwards, *Works*, I, cclxxi.

47. Edwards, *End in Creation*, in *Works*, I, 120.

48. Samuel E. McCorkle, *A Sermon on the Comparative Happiness and Duty of the United States of America* (Halifax, N.C., 1795), p. 41.

49. Edwards, *Works*, I, cclxxi.

50. Bellamy, *True Religion Delineated*, in *Works*, I, 242; Gilbert Tennent, *Brotherly Love Recommended, by the Argument of the Love of Christ* (Philadelphia, 1748), p. 13.

51. *Brotherly Love*, p. 3; Tennent, *The Divinity of the Sacred Scriptures Considered; and the Danger of Covetousness Detected* (Boston, 1739), p. 155; Tennent, *Charity Recommended*, in *Two Sermons Preached at New Brunswick, in the Year 1741* (Boston, 1743), p. 35.

52. Wheelock, *Sermon at Ordination of Smith*, p. 11.

53. Edwards, *True Virtue*, in *Works*, I, 123, 128-129.

54. Isaac Stiles, *A Prospect of the City of Jerusalem in It's Spiritual Building, Beauty, and Glory, Shewed in a Sermon Preached at Hartford at the Election* (New London, 1742), p. 58; Ministers of Providence, R.I., Preface to 1763

edition of Jonathan Dickinson, *A Display of God's Special Grace,* quoted, Backus, *History of New England,* II, 138.

55. Buell, *Revival of 1764,* pp. 76-77.

56. Ross, *Plain Address to the Quakers,* p. 89n.

57. Edwards, *Religious Affections,* p. 200.

58. Edwards, *Will,* p. 137.

59. Cf. Whitefield, "Christ the Believer's Wisdom," in Gillies, *Memoirs of Whitefield,* p. 369.

60. Parsons, "On Regeneration," *Sixty Sermons,* II, 10-11; Chauncy, *Enthusiasm Describ'd,* p. 5.

61. Bellamy, *True Religion Delineated,* in *Works,* I, 14.

62. Edwards, "True Saints, when Absent from the Body," *Works,* II, 31.

63. Tennent, *Brotherly Love,* p. 13.

64. Edwards, *True Virtue,* in *Works,* I, 123.

65. Solomon Williams, *Vindication of the Gospel-Doctrine of Justifying Faith* (Boston, 1746), p. 43; Tennent, *Brotherly Love,* p. 13; Gilbert Tennent, *Love to Christ a Necessary Qualification in Order to Feed His Sheep* (Philadelphia, 1744), p. 7; Buell, *Spiritual Knowledge,* p. 7.

66. Davies, *Poems,* p. 56.

67. Tennent, *Love to Christ,* p. 7; Edwards, *True Virtue,* in *Works,* I, 133.

68. Edwards, *Will,* p. 147.

69. Parsons, "Shewing Wherein the Specific Difference Lies," *Sixty Sermons,* II, 585.

70. Parsons, "The Nature of Regeneration," *Sixty Sermons,* II, 55.

71. Edwards, *Works,* I, cclxxii.

72. Edwards, *Religious Affections,* p. 365. Bellamy, *True Religion Delineated,* in *Works,* I, 361; Burr, *Servant of God,* p. 11; John Cleaveland, *An Essay, to Defend Some of the Most Important Principles . . . of Christianity* (Boston, 1763), p. 31; Davies, "The Tender Anxieties of Ministers for Their People," *Sermons,* II, 323.

73. N. Niles, *The Remembrance of Christ,* p. 36.

74. Edwards, *True Virtue,* in *Works,* I, 133.

75. *Ibid.,* p. 122.

76. Edwards, *Charity and Its Fruits* (New York, 1854), *passim;* Virgilius Ferm, ed., *Puritan Sage: Collected Writings of Jonathan Edwards* (New York, 1953), p. 333; Leavenworth, *Charity Illustrated,* p. 15.

77. Davies, "God is Love," *Sermons,* I, 316.

78. Burr, *Watchman's Answer,* p. 34.

79. Bellamy, *Election Sermon,* in *Works,* I, 590.

80. *Ibid.,* p. 583.

81. Nathaniel Niles, *Two Discourses on I. John I. 9* (Newport, 1773), p. 46n; cf. David Avery, *The Lord To Be Praised for the Triumphs of His Power* (Norwich, Conn., 1778), p. 8; Hopkins, *System of Doctrines,* I, 91; Davies, "God is Love," *Sermons,* I, 316.

82. Channing, "Christian Worship," in *The Works of William E. Channing* (Boston, 1894), pp. 427-428.

83. Edwards, "A Divine and Supernatural Light," *Works,* II, 13; Bellamy, *Election Sermon,* in *Works,* I, 585.

84. Edwards, *Humble Attempt,* in *Works* II, 289; cf. *Works,* I, cxxviii.

85. Benedict, *Preparation for Death,* p. 20.

86. Bellamy, *Election Sermon,* in *Works,* I, 585; N. Niles, *Two Discourses on Liberty,* p. 27.

87. Parsons, "The Beatific Vision," *Sixty Sermons,* II, 193.

88. Edwards, *Humble Attempt,* in *Works,* II, 295-297.

89. Edwards, *Thoughts on the Revival,* in *Works,* I, 427, 429.

90. Edwards, *Humble Attempt,* in *Works,* II, 297.

91. Witherspoon, "Lectures on Eloquence," *Works,* III, 498.

92. Parsons, "Wherein the Difference between Common, and Saving Knowledge, Consisteth," *Sixty Sermons,* II, 456-457.

93. James Sloan, "A Discourse on Government and Laws," *Proceedings of the Democratic Association of Gloucester County, New Jersey: at Several Meetings Held in the Month of March, 1801* (n.p., n.d.), p. 20.

94. Buell, *The Excellence and Importance of the Saving Knowledge of the Lord Jesus Christ in the Gospel-Preacher* (New York, [1760]), p. 11.

95. Whitaker, *Sermons on Reconciliation,* pp. 57-58.

96. Edwards, "Church's Marriage," *Works,* II, 22-23.

97. Davies, *Charity and Truth,* pp. 260, 312; "The General Resurrection," *Sermons,* I, 349; "The Universal Judgment," *Sermons,* I, 360.

98. Parsons, "Christ is Resolutely Determined, that All His People be with Him," *Sixty Sermons,* II, 667.

99. Boston *Evening Post,* quoted, Chauncy, *Seasonable Thoughts,* p. 150.

100. *An Examination and Refutation of Mr. Gilbert Tennent's Remarks upon the Protestation . . . by Some Members of the Synod* (Philadelphia, 1742), p. 30.

101. Tennent, *Unconverted Ministry,* pp. 25, 27.

102. *A Short Reply to Mr. Whitefield's Letter Which He Wrote in Answer to the Querists* (Philadelphia, 1741), p. 30; *Querists III,* pp. 63, 70, 111; John Cotton, *An Earnest Exhortation to Seek the Lord* (Boston, 1741), p. 64.

103. Edwards, *Works,* I, ci.

104. William Shurtleff, *A Letter to Those of His Brethren who Refuse to Admit the Rev. Mr. Whitefield into their Pulpits* (Boston, 1745), p. 4.

105. Francis L. Hawks and William S. Perry, eds., *Documentary History of the Protestant Episcopal Church . . . Connecticut* (New York, 1863-64), I, 210-211.

106. *The Testimony of the President, Professors . . . of Harvard College . . . Against the Rev. Mr. George Whitefield* (Boston, 1744), p. 14.

107. Noah Welles, *The Divine Right of Presbyterian Ordination Asserted* (New York, 1763), p. 78.

108. Noah Hobart, *A Second Address to the Members of the Episcopal Separation* (Boston, 1751), p. 160; *Ministers Fellow-Workers . . . A Sermon at the Ordination of Noah Welles* (Boston, 1747), p. 20; *A Serious Address to the Members of the Episcopal Separation* (Boston, 1748), p. 72.

109. Chauncy, *Seasonable Thoughts,* p. 175; *Christian Love, as Exemplified by the First Christian Church in Their Having All Things in Common, Placed in Its True and Just Point of Light* (Boston, 1773), p. 10.

110. Tucker, *Remarks on a Discourse of the Rev. Jonathan Parsons . . . Delivered on the 5th of March Last* (Boston, 1774), pp. 18-21.

111. Backus, *History of New England,* II, 57.

112. Stiles, *Looking-Glass,* p. 4.

113. *Observations upon the Plan of Church Government . . . by the Convention of the Ministers of the Province* (Boston, 1773), p. 20.

114. Reuben Fletcher, *The Lamentable State of New-England* (Boston, 1772), p. 21.

115. For example, *Some Serious Remarks in Reply to Rev. Mr. Jonathan*

Todd's Faithful Narrative of the Proceedings Relative to Mr. James Dana's Call and Settlement (New Haven, 1759), esp. p. 50.

116. Eleazar Wheelock, *Liberty of Conscience; or, No King but Christ in His Church* (Hartford, [1776]), pp. 16, 26.

117. Charles Chauncy, *Civil Magistrates Must Be Just . . . A Sermon Preached . . . May 27. 1747. Being the Anniversary for the Election* (Boston, 1747), p. 37.

118. *Examination and Refutation of Tennent's Remarks,* p. 62; *Querists III,* p. 35.

119. William Hobby, *An Inquiry into the Itinerancy, and the Conduct of the Rev. Mr. George Whitefield* (Boston, 1745), p. 7.

120. Rev. Mr. Ellington, "Funeral Sermon on Whitefield," Savannah, Ga., November 11, 1770, quoted, Gillies, *Memoirs of Whitefield,* p. 231.

121. Parsons, *Freedom from Civil and Ecclesiastical Slavery, the Purchase of Christ* (Newburyport, [1774]), p. 13.

122. Tennent, *The Blessedness of Peace-Makers Represented; and the Danger of Persecution Considered; in Two Sermons . . . Preach'd at Philadelphia, the 3d Wednesday in May, 1759* (Philadelphia, 1765), p. 36.

123. Stiles, *Prospect of City of Jerusalem,* p. 58.

124. Robert Cross, *et al., A Protestation Presented to the Synod of Philadelphia, June 1, 1741* (Philadelphia, 1741), p. 6; Samuel Blair, *A Vindication of the Brethren Who Were Unjustly and Illegally Cast out of the Synod of Philadelphia* (Philadelphia, 1744), pp. 57-58; Trinterud, *Forming of American Tradition,* p. 180,

125. Samuel Finley, *A Charitable Plea for the Speechless: or, the Right of Believers-Infants to Baptism* (Philadelphia, 1746), Preface.

126. Edwards, *An Humble Inquiry into the Rules of the Word of God, Concerning the Qualifications Requisite to a Complete Standing and Full Communion in the Visible Christian Church,* in *Works,* I, 432.

127. Tucker, *Observations on Jonathan Parsons,* p. 62; [David S. Rowland], *Catholicism: or Christian Charity* (Providence, 1772), p. 68.

128. Edwards, *Works,* I, clx.

129. Edwards, "Farewell Sermon," *Works,* I, ccxl.

130. C. C. Goen, *Revivalism and Separatism in New England, 1740-1800* (New Haven, 1962), pp. 209-210.

131. Edwards, *Humble Inquiry,* in *Works,* I, 461; "Sermon VIII," *Works,* II, 898; *Work of Redemption,* in *Works,* I, 610.

132. Tennent, *Unconverted Ministry,* p. 25.

133. Gilbert Tennent, *The Righteousness of the Scribes and Pharisees Considered* (Boston, 1741), p. 3.

134. Backus, *Evangelical Ministers,* p. 31; *History of New England,* II, 158; David McGregore, *Christian Unity and Peace Recommended* (Boston, 1765), p. 23.

135. Edwards, *Humble Inquiry,* in *Works,* I, 461.

136. Solomon Williams, *The True State of the Question Concerning the Qualifications Necessary to Lawful Communion* (Boston, 1751), p. 134.

137. Edwards, *Humble Inquiry,* in *Works,* I, 467-468.

138. Edwards, "Church's Marriage," *Works,* II, 18ff.

139. Cf. N. Niles, *The Remembrance of Christ,* p. 6.

140. Edwards, "Church's Marriage," *Works,* II, 26.

141. Edwards, *Thoughts on the Revival,* in *Works,* I, 393, 428-429.

142. Edwards, *Work of Redemption*, in *Works*, I, 610; *Humble Inquiry*, in *Works*, I, 435.

143. Solomon Williams, *The Relations of God's People to Him, and the Engagements and Obligations They are Under to Praise Him . . . A Thanksgiving Sermon, on Occasion of the Smiles of Heaven on the British Arms in America* (New London, 1760), pp. 15-16.

144. Edwards, "Sermon XIII," *Works*, II, 945.

145. Edwards, *Humble Inquiry*, in *Works*, I, 463.

146. John Rogers, *An Epistle Sent from God to the World* (New York, 1757), pp. 24-25; Edwards, *Distinguishing Marks*, in *Works*, II, 268.

147. Whitaker, *A Confutation of Two Tracts . . . Written by the Reverend John Wise* (Boston, 1774), p. 15.

148. Ebenezer Frothingham, *The Articles of Faith and Practice, with the Covenant that is Confessed by the Separate Churches* (Newport, R.I., 1750), p. 328; Solomon Paine, *A Short View of the Difference between the Church of Christ, and the Established Churches of the Colony of Connecticut* (Newport, R.I., 1752), p. 60; John Rogers, *A Servant of Jesus Christ, to Many of the Flock of Christ that May be Scattered among the Churches of New-England, Greeting* (3rd ed., Newport, R.I., 1754), *passim*; Bolles, *The Following Treatise*, pp. 29-30.

149. Abel Morgan, *Anti-Paedo-Rantism; or Mr. Samuel Finley's Charitable Plea for the Speechless Examined and Refuted* (Philadelphia, 1747), p. 13; *Anti-Paedo-Rantism Defended* (Philadelphia, 1750), p. vii.

150. Frothingham, *Articles*, p. 355.

151. Williams, *Vindication*, Preface, p. v; Ross, *Plain Address to the Quakers*, p. 87.

152. Williams, *Vindication*, p. 43.

153. Edwards, *Religious Affections*, Related Correspondence, p. 502.

154. Andrew Croswell, *A Second Defence of the Old Protestant Doctrine of Justifying Faith* (Boston, 1747), *passim*.

155. Edwards, *Religious Affections*, p. 87.

156. Bellamy, *True Religion Delineated*, in *Works*, I, 196; Edwards, *Religious Affections*, p. 151; John Caldwell, *The Nature, Folly, and Evil of Rash and Uncharitable Judging* (Boston, 1742), p. 5.

157. Edwards, *Religious Affections*, p. 398.

158. Edwards, *Misrepresentations Corrected, and Truth Vindicated, in a Reply to the Rev. Mr. Solomon Williams's Book . . . Concerning the Qualifications Necessary to Lawful Communion*, in *Works*, I, 490-491.

159. Charles Chauncy, *Breaking of Bread in Remembrance of the Dying Love of Christ . . . Five Sermons on the Lord's Supper* (Boston, 1772), p. 106.

160. Bellamy, *True Religion Delineated*, in *Works*, I, 396.

161. Edwards, *Humble Inquiry*, in *Works*, I, 474.

162. Edwards, *Religious Affections*, pp. 450-452.

163. Johnson, *Honours Due to the Memory*, p. 7.

164. Edwards, *Religious Affections*, p. 365.

165. *Ibid.*, p. 236.

166. *Ibid.*, pp. 417, 437.

167. *Ibid.*, p. 410.

168. *Works*, I, cxxi-cxxx; *Thoughts on the Revival*, in *Works*, I, 426.

169. Bellamy, *True Religion Delineated*, in *Works*, I, 361; cf. *Nature and Glory of the Gospel*, in *Works*, II, 329n, 447n.

170. Edwards, *Life of Brainerd*, in *Works*, II, 447.

171. For example, Tennent, *Solemn Warning*, p. 30.
172. Bellamy, *True Religion Delineated*, in *Works*, I, 35.
173. Tennent, *Brotherly Love*, p. 3.
174. Bellamy, *Nature and Glory of the Gospel*, in *Works*, II, 296ff.
175. Tennent, *The Late Association for Defence, Farther Encourag'd* (Philadelphia, [1748]), p. 2.
176. Edwards, *Religious Affections*, p. 284.
177. Bellamy, *True Religion Delineated*, in *Works*, I, 288.
178. Parsons, "The Uses of the Moral Law to the Unregenerate," *Sixty Sermons*, I, 426; *The Doctrine of Justification by Faith Asserted* (Boston, 1748), pp. 60, 62.
179. Backus, *A Discourse, Concerning the Materials . . . of the Church of Christ* (Boston, 1773), p. 23.
180. Backus, *True Faith*, p. 29.
181. Backus, *Appeal to the Public*, p. 4.
182. Parsons, "The Uses of the Moral Law to the Regenerate," *Sixty Sermons*, I, 463; Bellamy, *Nature and Glory of the Gospel*, in *Works*, II, 431.
183. Quoted, Ola E. Winslow, *Meetinghouse Hill, 1630-1783* (New York, 1952), pp. 232-233.
184. N. Niles, *The Remembrance of Christ*, p. 6.
185. Dickinson, *Witness of the Spirit*, p. 13.
186. Dickinson, "On Serving God," *Sixty Sermons*, I, 577.
187. Edwards, *Religious Affections*, pp. 159ff, 382, 386-388.
188. "An Address to the Anabaptists Imprisoned in Caroline County, August 8, 1771," quoted, Gewehr, *Great Awakening in Virginia*, p. 130.
189. Tennent, *The Necessity of Religious Violence in Order to Obtain Durable Happiness* (New York, [1735]), p. 43.
190. William Cooper, Preface to Isaac Chanler, *New Converts Exhorted to Cleave to the Lord* (Boston, 1740).
191. Robbins, *Plain Narrative*, p. 4.
192. Foxcroft, *An Apology in Behalf of the Revd. Mr. Whitefield* (Boston, 1745), p. 20.
193. *The Querists*, p. 20.
194. Blair, *Particular Consideration*, p. 46.
195. *Querists' Short Reply to Whitefield*, p. 60.
196. *Querists III*, p. 100.
197. Backus, *History of New England*, II, 239.
198. Davies, "The Apostolic Valediction Considered and Applied. A Farewell Sermon," *Sermons*, III, 486; Backus, *True Faith*, p. 93.
199. [Jonathan Parsons], *Communion of Faith Essential to Communion of the Churches* (Salem, 1770), p. 11.
200. Cleaveland, *Short and Plain Narrative*, p. 38.
201. Whitaker, *Funeral Sermon on Whitefield*, p. 27; Whitefield, "Spiritual Baptism," *Eighteen Sermons . . . Taken Verbatim in Short-hand, and Faithfully Transcribed by Joseph Gurney* (Newburyport, 1797), p. 249.
202. Whitaker, *Funeral Sermon on Whitefield*, pp. 27-28.
203. Zubly, *The Wise Shining*, p. 23; Gillies, *Memoirs of Whitefield*, p. 231.
204. *Virginia Gazette*, no. 1015, quoted, Stuart C. Henry, *George Whitefield: Wayfaring Witness* (New York, 1957), p. 152.
205. Ebenezer Pemberton, *Heaven the Residence of the Saints. A Sermon Occasioned by the . . . Death of the Rev. George Whitefield* (London, 1771), p. 17.

206. Henry, *Whitefield*, p. 152.

207. Zubly, *The Wise Shining*, p. 23.

208. Tennent, *Espousals*, pp. 19-20; *Three Letters to Whitefield*, p. 9;

209. Tennent, *Love to Christ*, pp. 17-18.

210. [Aaron Burr], *The Supreme Deity of our Lord Jesus Christ* (Boston, 1757); Tennent, Preface to Bostwick, *Self Disclaimed*, pp. 3-4.

211. N. Niles, *The Remembrance of Christ*, pp. 26-27.

212. Edwards, *Religious Affections*, pp. 149, 211-213; *Life of Brainerd*, in *Works*, II, 448.

213. Nathaniel Appleton, *Evangelical and Saving Repentance . . . Distinguished from a Legal Sorrow. In a Sermon . . . Preach'd at Newton, August 9th 1741* (Boston, 1741), p. 22; Joseph Fish, *The Church of Christ a Firm and Durable House* (New London, 1767), p. 136n.

214. Cotton Mather, *Thaumatographia Christiana . . . A Brief Recapitulation of many Wonderful Mysteries, in our Lord Jesus Christ* (Boston, 1701), p. 26; Edward Taylor, *Christographia*, Norman S. Grabo, ed. (New Haven, 1962), esp. p. 245.

215. Benjamin Colman, *Practical Discourses upon the Parable of the Ten Virgins* (London, 1707), p. 15.

216. Tennent, *The Solemn Scene of the Last Judgment*, in *Sermons on Sacramental Occasions*, p. 224; *Necessity of Religious Violence*, p. 8; *A Funeral Sermon Occasion'd by the Death of the Reverend Mr. John Rowland* (Philadelphia, 1745), p. 7.

217. Jonathan Dickinson, *Familiar Letters to a Gentleman upon a Variety of Seasonable and Important Subjects in Religion* (1745; 4th ed., Edinburgh, 1784), p. 26.

218. Whitaker, *Confutation of Wise*, p. 15.

219. Edwards, "Sermon VIII," *Works*, II, 898; "The True Excellency of a Gospel Minister," *Works*, II, 956-957.

220. *Works*, II, 959; *End in Creation*, in *Works*, I, 219.

221. Whitefield, "The Lord Our Light," Gillies, *Memoirs of Whitefield*, Appendix, p. 563.

222. Edwards, "Church's Marriage," *Works*, II, 22.

223. Whitaker, *Funeral Sermon on Whitefield*, p. 5.

224. John Foster, *An Oration, Pronounced . . . on the Fourth of July, 1808* (n.p., 1808), pp. 9-10.

225. Joseph Hawley to Samuel Adams, April 1, 1776, quoted, John C. Miller, *Origins of the American Revolution* (Boston, 1943), p. 485.

226. Dr. Jonathan Elmer, Address, Bridgetown, J.J., 1776, quoted, John H. Hazelton, *The Declaration of Independence. Its History* (New York, 1906), p. 246; cf. William Tudor, "Oration, Delivered at Boston, March 5, 1779," in *Orations, Delivered . . . to Commemorate the Evening of the Fifth of March, 1770* (2nd ed., Boston, 1807), p. 117.

227. John Murray, *Nehemiah, Or the Struggle for Liberty Never in Vain* (Newbury, 1779), p. 23.

228. S. Niles, *Vindication*, p. 113.

229. Whitefield, *The Necessity and Benefits of Religious Society* (Boston, 1740), pp. 11-12.

230. Gillies, *Memoirs of Whitefield*, p. 105.

231. Dickinson, *Defense of Dialogue*, p. 36.

232. Parsons, *Wisdom Justified of Her Children* (Boston, 1742), p. 49; A——— Z., *Mr. Parsons Corrected*, p. 14.

233. Tennent, *The Necessity of Studying to be Quiet, and Doing our Own Business* (Philadelphia, [1744]), p. 38.

234. Tennent, *Irenicum Ecclesiasticum, or a Humble Impartial Essay upon the Peace of Jerusalem* (Philadelphia, 1749), pp. 10-11.

235. Edwards, "God's Awful Judgment in the Breaking and Withering of the Strong Rods of the Community. Preached . . . June 26, 1748, on the Death of the Honourable John Stoddard, Esq.," *Works*, II, 38.

236. Edwards, "Christ the Example," *Works*, II, 963.

237. Quoted, Sprague, *Annals*, I, 395.

238. Eliphalet Wright, *The People Ripe for an Harvest. A Sermon Delivered . . . on a Day of Public Thanksgiving* (Norwich, Conn., [1776]), p. 7.

239. Joseph Adams, *The Necessity and Importance of Rulers . . . Sermon at Newington, March 13, 1769* (Portsmouth, n.d.), p. 10.

240. Edwards, *Thoughts on the Revival*, in *Works*, I, 425.

241. *Ibid.*, p. 410.

242. *Ibid.*, p. 387.

243. Edwards, *Religious Affections*, p. 315.

244. Edwards, *Humble Attempt*, in *Works*, II, 198, 310; *Works*, I, cxxviii.

245. Edwards, *Religious Affections*, pp. 350-353.

246. Edwards, *Thoughts on the Revival*, in *Works*, I, 408-410.

247. *Ibid.*, p. 407.

248. Edwards, *Religious Affections*, p. 331.

249. Edwards, *Thoughts on the Revival*, in *Works*, I, 407.

250. Solomon Williams and Eleazar Wheelock, *Two Letters . . . to the Rev. Mr. Davenport* (Boston, 1744), p. 18.

251. *The Declaration of the Rector and Tutors of Yale-College in New-Haven Against the Reverend Mr. George Whitefield* (Boston, 1745), p. 8; S. Niles, *Tristitae*, p. 5.

252. Edwards, "Christ the Example," *Works*, II, 963.

253. Solomon Stoddard, *The Presence of Christ with the Ministers of the Gospel* (Boston, 1718), "Examination of the Power of the Fraternity," pp. 10-11.

254. Edwards, "Sermon XIII," *Works*, II, 945.

255. Edwards, *Thoughts on the Revival*, in *Works*, I, 427.

256. Chauncy, *Seasonable Thoughts*, p. 410.

257. Edwards, *Thoughts on the Revival*, in *Works*, I, 427.

258. Ezra Stiles, *A Discourse on the Christian Union: The Substance of Which was Delivered before the Reverend Convention of the Congregational Clergy in the Colony of Rhode-Island* (Boston, 1760), p. 97.

259. Carl Bridenbaugh, *Mitre and Sceptre: Transatlantic Faiths, Ideas, Personalities, and Politics, 1689-1775* (New York, 1962), p. 114.

260. Quoted, *ibid.*

261. Tennent, *Blessedness of Peace-makers*, p. 36.

262. Edwards, *Humble Attempt*, in *Works*, II, 295; Tennent, *The Divine Government over All Considered* (Philadelphia, [1752]), p. 45.

IV. THE DANGER OF AN UNCONVERTED MINISTRY

1. Appleton, *The Great Apostle Paul Exhibited and Recommended as a Pattern of True Gospel Preaching* (Boston, 1751), p. 6.

2. Bellamy, *True Religion Delineated*, in *Works*, I, 163.

3. Chauncy, *The Gifts of the Spirit to Ministers Consider'd in Their Diversity . . . A Sermon Preach'd . . . Decemb. 17. 1741* (Boston, 1742), pp. 8, 15.

4. Husband, *Some Remarks*, in Boyd, *Eighteenth Century Tracts*, p. 211; Zubly, *The Wise Shining*, p. 23.

5. Parsons, *To Live is Christ*, pp. 33-34.

6. Foxcroft, *Some Seasonable Thoughts on Evangelic Preaching . . . Occasioned by the Late Visit, and Uncommon Labours . . . of the Rev. Mr. Whitefield* (Boston, 1740), p. 43; Miller, "Great Awakening," *Encounter*, p. 5; Sidney E. Mead, "The Rise of the Evangelical Conception of the Ministry in America (1607-1850)," in H. Richard Niebuhr and Daniel D. Williams, eds., *The Ministry in Historical Perspective* (New York, 1956), p. 246.

7. Timothy Walker, *The Way to Try All Pretended Apostles* (Boston, 1743), p. 5.

8. Tennent, *Unconverted Ministry*, p. 9.

9. *Ibid.*, pp. 26-27.

10. Bellamy, *A Letter to Scripturista*, in *Works*, I, 608.

11. Tennent, *Unconverted Ministry*, p. 6.

12. Wheelock, *The Preaching of Christ an Expression of God's Great Love to Sinners* (Boston, 1761), p. 25.

13. Jonathan Ashley, *A Letter . . . to the Reverend Mr. William Cooper. In Answer to his Objections to Mr. Ashley's Sermon* (Boston, 1743), p. 5; Tucker, *Remarks on a Discourse of Parsons*, p. 17.

14. *Ibid.*, p. 18.

15. Sprague, *Annals*, VIII, *passim*.

16. Edwards, "Church's Marriage," *Works*, II, 26.

17. *Ibid.*, pp. 20, 25.

18. Edwards, "True Excellency of Gospel Minister," *Works*, II, 958.

19. Edwards, *Life of Brainerd*, in *Works*, II, 381-383.

20. Quoted, Trinterud, *Forming of American Tradition*, p. 186.

21. *Ibid.*, p. 210.

22. George Gillespie, *A Sermon against Divisions* (Philadelphia, 1740), p. 3; Cooke, *Great Duty of Ministers*, p. 21.

23. Gilbert Tennent, *The Danger of Spiritual Pride Represented* (Philadelphia, 1745), p. 23; Bellamy, *True Religion Delineated*, in *Works*, I, 83-84.

24. Thomas Arthur, *Sermon Preached at the Ordination of Daniel Thane* (New York, 1750), p. 9.

25. Quoted, Anson Phelps Stokes, *Church and State in the United States* (New York, 1950), I, 422; Backus, *Discourse Concerning Materials of Church*, p. 128.

26. Tennent, *Unconverted Ministry*, p. 4.

27. Edwards, *Work of Redemption*, in *Works*, I, 601.

28. Ebenezer Pemberton, *The Knowledge of Christ Recommended, in a Sermon Preach'd in the Public Hall at Yale-College* (New London, 1741), p. 22.

29. Foxcroft, Preface to Dickinson, *True Scripture-Doctrine;* Tennent, *Unconverted Ministry*, p. 6.

30. Edwards, *Will*, p. 437.

31. Backus, *Spiritual Ignorance Causeth Men to Counter-Act their Doctrinal Knowledge* (Providence, 1763), pp. 16, 83.

32. Backus, *A Fish Caught in His Own Net. An Examination on Nine Sermons . . . by Mr. Joseph Fish of Stonington* (Boston, 1768), p. 121.

33. Edwards, "Christian Knowledge; or, the Importance and Advantage of a Thorough Knowledge of Divine Truth," *Works*, II, 160.

34. Chauncy, *Seasonable Thoughts,* p. 362.

35. Bass, *Narrative of Unhappy Contention,* p. 3n.

36. John Eliot to Jeremy Belknap, July 31, 1779, *Collections of the Massachusetts Historical Society,* 6th ser., vol. IV (1891), 145.

37. John Cotton, in Appendix to John Porter, *A Vindication of a Sermon Preached at Braintree . . . December 25th, 1749* (Boston, 1751), pp. 35, 44n.

38. Bellamy, *Law Our Schoolmaster,* in *Works,* I, 389.

39. Garden, "To the Inhabitants of Charleston," *Regeneration,* p. ii.

40. Quincy, *Twenty Sermons,* p. 365.

41. *A Word to the Well-Wishers of the Good Work of God in this Land* (Boston, 1742), pp. 4-6.

42. Chauncy, *The Out-Pouring of the Holy Ghost. A Sermon Preach'd . . . May 13, 1742* (Boston, 1742), p. 19.

43. Jonathan Mayhew, *Sermons upon the Following Subjects. viz. On Hearing the Word* (Boston, 1755), p. 291.

44. *General Magazine,* p. 105; Gilbert Tennent, *The Examiner, Examined* (Boston, 1743), p. 121; *A Letter from the Rev. Mr. James Davenport, to Jonathan Barber* ([Philadelphia, 1744]), p. 3; Trinterud, *Forming of American Tradition,* pp. 224-225.

45. Thomas Foxcroft, *Ministers, Spiritual Parents, or Fathers in the Church of God. A Sermon Preach'd at the Ordination of the Reverend Mr. John Lowell* (Boston, 1726), p. 6.

46. Increase Mather, *A Discourse Concerning the Maintenance Due to those that Preach the Gospel* (Boston, 1706), p. 10.

47. Alison, *Peace and Union,* p. 24.

48. Thomas Barnard, *Tyranny and Slavery in Matters of Religion, Caution'd Against; and True Humility Recommended to Ministers and People* (Boston, 1743), p. 23.

49. Mayhew, *Christian Sobriety,* p. 244.

50. For example, Davies, "On the Defeat of General Braddock," *Sermons,* III, 222.

51. Alexander Hamilton, *Gentleman's Progress: the Itinerarium,* Carl Bridenbaugh, ed. (Chapel Hill, 1948), pp. 185-186.

52. Jonathan Boucher, "On the Revenue of the Clergy," *A View of the Causes and Consequences of the American Revolution* (London, 1797), p. 233.

53. Johnson, *Writings,* III, 8, 37.

54. Quoted, Bridenbaugh, *Mitre and Sceptre,* p. 139.

55. Francis Alison to Ezra Stiles, September 17, 1757, in Franklin B. Dexter, ed., *Extracts from the Itineraries . . . of Ezra Stiles* (New Haven, 1916), p. 422.

56. [William Smith], *A Letter from a Gentleman in London, to his Friend in Pennsylvania; with a Satire* (London, 1756), p. 5.

57. Sprague, *Annals,* III, 145.

58. Davies, *Poems,* Preface, pp. vii, xi-xii; *The Duties, Difficulties and Reward of the Faithful Minister. A Sermon, Preached . . . Nov. 12, 1752* (Glasgow, 1754), p. 46n.

59. Richard Pateshall, *Pride Humbled, or Mr. Hobby Chastised* (Boston, 1745), p. 9.

60. Huntington, *Vanity and Mischief,* p. 22.

61. Edwards, Preface to Bellamy, *True Religion Delineated,* in Bellamy, *Works,* I, 6; Edwards, *Five Discourses on Important Subjects,* in *Works,* I, 621.

62. James Finley, *An Essay on the Gospel Ministry* (Wilmington, 1763), p. 34.

63. Bostwick, in *Peace and Union, and Self Disclaim'd,* p. 25.

64. J. Finley, *Essay on Gospel Ministry,* p. iv.

65. Mayhew, *Christian Sobriety,* p. 159.

66. Buell, *Excellence and Importance of Saving Knowledge,* p. 23.

67. Quoted, Trinterud, *Forming of American Tradition,* p. 202.

68. Davies, "Defeat of Braddock," *Sermons,* III, 222.

69. Charles Chauncy, *Ministers Exhorted . . . to Take Heed to Themselves* (Boston, 1744), p. 18.

70. Bellamy, *True Religion Delineated,* in *Works,* I, 163.

71. Davies, "The Love of Souls, a Necessary Qualification for the Ministerial Office," *Sermons,* III, 372.

72. Finley, *Clear Light,* p. 4.

73. Blair, *Works,* p. 162.

74. Nathaniel Eels, *A Letter to the Second Church and Congregation in Scituate . . . Shewing Some Reasons why he Doth Not Invite . . . Whitefield into his Pulpit* (Boston, 1745), p. 14.

75. Mayhew, *Seven Sermons,* p. 39.

76. Smith, *Letter from a Gentleman,* pp. 12-13.

77. Backus, *Discourse Concerning Materials of Church,* p. 128.

78. Lemual Briant, *Some Friendly Remarks on a Sermon Lately Preach'd at Braintree* (Boston, 1750), p. 27.

79. Hutchinson, *Reply to Remarks of Tucker,* pp. 6. 7n.

80. S. Niles, *Vindication,* p. 4; John Porter, *Superlative Love to Christ a Necessary Qualification of a Gospel-Minister* (Boston, 1748), p. 27.

81. Leavenworth, *Charity Illustrated,* pp. 31-32.

82. Andrew Croswell, *Brief Remarks on the Satyrical Drollery at Cambridge, Last Commencement Day* (Boston, 1771), pp. 6-7.

83. *Ibid.,* pp. 8, 11.

84. Boucher, "On Schisms and Sects," *View,* p. 77.

85. Jonathan Elliot, ed., *The Debates in the Several State Conventions, on the Adoption of the Federal Constitution* (4 vols., 2nd ed., Washington, 1836), III, 296.

86. Quoted, Richard D. Birdsall, "The Reverend Thomas Allen: Jeffersonian Calvinist," *New England Quarterly,* XXX (1957), 156.

87. [William Whiting], *An Address to the Inhabitants of the County of Berkshire. Respecting Their Present Opposition to Civil Government* (Hartford, [1778]), p. 7.

88. *American Museum,* III (1787), 132.

89. Backus, *Address to the Inhabitants of New-England,* p. 3. The articles to which Backus referred were those by Benjamin Austin, reprinted in pamphlet form as *Observations on the Pernicious Practice of the Law . . . by Honestus* (Boston, 1819).

90. Quoted, Birdsall, "Thomas Allen," p. 157.

91. Eels, *Christ, the Foundation,* p. 26.

92. [Joseph Allen], *An Oration on the Beauties of Liberty, or the Essential Rights of the Americans. Delivered at the Second Baptist-Church in Boston . . . Dec. 3d, 1772* (3rd ed., Boston, 1773), p. xvi; J. C. Miller, *Origins of Revolution,* p. 320; William L. Saunders, ed., *The Colonial Records of North Carolina,* Volume VIII, 1769 to 1771 (Raleigh, 1890), p. 520.

93. *General Magazine,* p. 51; *The Querists,* p. 27.

94. James Parker to Charles Stewart, April 6, 1775, in *Magazine of History,* III (1900), 158.

95. The text of Hawley's letter is given in Edwards, *Works*, I, clxvii-clxix.

96. Thomas Hutchinson, *The History of the Province of Massachusetts Bay, from the Year 1750, until June, 1774* (London, 1828), p. 296.

97. John Stewart to Hawley, November 18, 1761, quoted, E. Francis Brown, *Joseph Hawley, Colonial Radical* (New York, 1931), p. 57.

98. Bellamy, *Election Sermon*, in *Works*, I, 584.

99. Backus, *True Faith*, p. 62.

100. Edwards, "Dishonesty; or, the Sin of Theft and Injustice," *Works*, II, 222.

101. J. Johnson, *Honours Due to the Memory*, pp. 26-27.

102. Andrew Croswell, *What is Christ to Me, if He is Not Mine?* (Boston, 1745), p. 8.

103. Nathan Whiting to Jared Ingersoll, in *Papers of the New Haven Colony Historical Society*, vol. IX (New Haven, 1918), p. 303.

104. Edwards, *Thoughts on the Revival*, in *Works*, I, 424.

105. [Benjamin Gale], *The Present State of the Colony of Connecticut Considered. In a Letter from a Gentleman in the Eastern Part of Said Colony* (n.p., 1755), p. 9.

106. Richard Peters, *A Sermon on Education, Wherein Some Account is Given of the Academy, Established in the City of Philadelphia* (Philadelphia, 1751), pp. 3-4.

107. William Smith, "College of Mirania," *The Works of William Smith, D.D.* (Philadelphia, 1803), I (pt. II), 195.

108. Alison to Stiles, in Ezra Stiles, *Extracts from Itineraries*, p. 428.

109. Smith, "College of Mirania," *Works*, I (pt. II), 180.

110. Mayhew, *A Discourse Occasioned by the Death of the Honourable Stephen Sewall, Esq.* (Boston, 1760), pp. 23, 25ff.

111. Smith, "The Hermit, No. I" (*American Magazine*, October 1757), *Works*, I (pt. II), 97.

112. Smith, "College of Mirania," *Works*, I (pt. II), 190-195.

113. Smith, "Sermon XII," *Works*, II, 233.

114. Mayhew, *Christian Sobriety*, p. 159.

115. Johnson, "Raphael," *Writings*, II, 566.

116. Simeon Howard, *A Sermon Preached . . . May 31, 1780. Being the Anniversary for the Election*, in Thornton, *Pulpit of Revolution*, p. 367.

117. Smith, "Discourse VI," *Discourses on Public Occasions in America* (2nd ed., London, 1762), p. 164.

118. [Samuel Peters], *A General History of Connecticut* (London, 1782), pp. 334-335.

119. Edwards, *Thoughts on the Revival*, in *Works*, I, 426; Eels, *Christ, the Foundation*, p. 26; cf. Howard, *Election Sermon*, in Thornton, *Pulpit of Revolution*, p. 392.

120. John Murray, *Jerubbaal, or Tyranny's Grove Destroyed* (Newburyport, Mass., 1783), p. 73.

121. Charles Turner, *Due Glory to be Given to God. A Discourse Containing Two Sermons Preached in Cambridge May 15, 1783* (Boston, 1783), p. 31.

122. Davies, "The Rejection of Gospel-Light the Condemnation of Men," *Sermons*, II, 555; cf. Edwards, "True Grace Distinguished from the Experience of Devils," *Works*, II, 43.

123. Buell, *Spiritual Knowledge*, p. 19.

124. Quoted, Winslow, *Meetinghouse Hill*, p. 235.

125. Samuel Finley, *Christ Triumphing, and Satan Raging. A Sermon on*

Matth. XII. 28. Wherein is Proved, That the Kingdom of God is Come unto Us at This Day (Philadelphia, 1741; reprinted Boston, 1742), p. 25.

126. Backus, *Fish Caught*, Preface, p. ix.

127. S. Finley, *The Approved Minister of God. A Sermon Preach'd at the Ordination of the Reverend Mr. John Rodgers . . . March 16, 1749* (Philadelphia, n.d.), p. 6.

128. Edwards, *Thoughts on the Revival,* in *Works*, I, 410.

129. Edwards, *Works*, I, cxliv.

130. Edwards, "Christian Knowledge," *Works*, II, 157-158.

131. For example, Jonathan Dickinson, *Observations on that Terrible Disease Vulgarly Called the Throat Distemper* (Boston, 1740).

132. Davies, "Religion the Highest Wisdom, and Sin the Greatest Madness and Folly," *Sermons*, II, 203.

133. Hopkins, *System of Doctrines,* II (separate pagination for *Treatise on the Millennium*), 69.

134. J. Finley, *Essay on Gospel Ministry*, p. 46.

135. L. Hart, *Christian Minister Described*, p. 10; J. Finley, *Essay on Gospel Ministry*, p. 46.

136. John Leland, *A Blow at the Root, Being a Fashionab[l]e Fast Day Sermon* (Suffield, 1801), pp. 35-36.

137. Croswell, *A Testimony against the Profaneness of Some of the Public Disputes, on the Last Commencement Day* (Boston, 1760), p. 16.

138. *Ibid.*

139. [Thomas Prentice], *A Letter to the Reverend Andrew Croswell; Occasioned by His Brief Remarks on the Satyrical Drollery* (Boston, 1771), pp. 20, 36.

140. Croswell, *Brief Remarks on the Satyrical Drollery*, p. 14.

141. Croswell, *Testimony against Profaneness*, p. 16n.

142. Gilbert Tennent, *Remarks upon a Protestation Presented to the Synod of Philadelphia, June 1. 1741* (Philadelphia, 1741), p. 24.

143. Blair, "Last Advice," *Works*, p. 365.

144. Edwards, "True Excellency of Gospel Minister," *Works*, II, 958.

145. Adams to Jefferson, November 15, 1813, *The Adams-Jefferson Letters*, Lester J. Cappon, ed. (2 vols., Chapel Hill, 1959), II, 397.

146. Samuel Johnson, Preface to John Beach, *A Second Vindication of God's Sovereign Free Grace Indeed, in a Fair and Candid Examination of the Last Discourse of the Late Mr. Dickinson* (Boston, 1748).

147. Dickinson, *True Scripture-Doctrine*, p. 150.

148. Edwards, *Will*, p. 463.

149. *Ibid.,* p. 428.

150. Dickinson, *True Scripture-Doctrine*, p. 83.

151. Bellamy, *Wisdom of God*, in *Works*, II, 91.

152. Conrad Wright, *The Beginnings of Unitarianism in America* (Boston, 1955), pp. 93-94; [James Dana], *An Examination of the Late Reverend President Edwards's 'Enquiry on Freedom of Will'* (Boston, 1770), pp. 82-83; John Tucker, *Remarks on a Sermon of the Rev. Aaron Hutchinson* (Boston, [1767]), p. 16n.

153. Bellamy, *True Religion Delineated*, in *Works*, I, 156.

154. Timothy Stone, *The Nature, and Evil, of Selfishness Considered and Elustrated [sic]. In a Sermon Preached . . . September 21st, 1777* (Norwich, Conn., 1778), p. 27.

155. Parsons, "Evidence of Regeneration," *Sixty Sermons*, II, 94-95; Davies,

"The Religious Improvement of the Late Earthquakes," *Sermons,* III, 179; A. Hutchinson, *Reply to Remarks of Tucker,* p. 24.

156. Edwards, *Original Sin,* in *Works,* I, 233.

157. Edwards, *Religious Affections,* p. 300.

158. Appleton, *Faithful Ministers,* p. 31; cf. Appleton, *The Great Blessings of Good Rulers* (Boston, 1742), p. 56.

159. Croswell, *Testimony against Profaneness,* p. 16n.

160. Nathaniel Whitaker, *A Sermon Preached on the 30th of June, 1763; after the Ordination of the Rev. Charles-Jeffry Smith* (London, 1767), p. 37 (paged continuously with Wheelock, *Sermon at Ordination of Smith*); L. Hart, *Christian Minister,* p. 10.

161. Lemuel Briant, *The Absurdity and Blasphemy of Depreciating Moral Virtue* (Boston, 1749), p. 6.

162. Chauncy, *Christian Love,* p. 13.

163. Edwards, *Religious Affections,* p. 301.

164. Tucker, *Remarks on Sermon of Hutchinson,* p. 21; Bellamy, *True Religion Delineated,* in *Works,* I, 349; Ross, *Plain Address to the Quakers,* p. 109.

165. Paine, *Short View,* p. 68.

166. J. Finley, *Essay on Gospel Ministry,* p. 40.

167. Bellamy, *Nature and Glory of the Gospel,* in *Works,* II, 275.

168. William Balch, *A Vindication of Some Points of Doctrine* (Boston, 1746), p. 5.

169. Foxcroft, Preface to Dickinson, *True Scripture-Doctrine,* pp. vi-vii.

170. Dickinson, *Reflections upon Mr. Wetmore's Letter in Defence of Dr. Waterland's Discourse of Regeneration* (Boston, 1744), p. 10.

171. Jedidiah Mills, *A Vindication of Gospel Truth, and Refutation of Some Dangerous Errors* (Boston, 1747), p. 37.

172. John Porter, *The Absurdity and Blasphemy of Substituting the Personal Righteousness of Men in the Room of the Surety-Righteousness of Christ* (Boston, 1750), p. 22.

173. Edwards, *Brainerd,* in *Works,* II, 454.

174. Townsend, *Philosophy of Edwards,* p. 138.

175. *Christian History for 1743,* pp. 155-156.

176. *The Testimony of an Association or Club of Laymen, Conven'd at Boston Respecting the Present Times* (Boston, 1745), pp. 7-8.

177. [John Cleaveland], *The Chebacco Narrative Rescu'd from the Charge of Falshood and Partiality* (Boston, 1738 [sic, 1748]), p. 20.

178. Parsons, *Wisdom Justified,* Preface, p. v.

179. S. Niles, *Vindication,* p. 14.

180. Edwards, *Works,* I, cxciv.

181. Finley, *Clear Light,* pp. 62-63.

182. Tennent, Preface to James Davenport, *The Faithful Minister Encouraged. A Sermon Preached at the Opening of the Synod of New-York . . . October 1, 1755* (Philadelphia, 1756), p. iv; *ibid.,* p. 27.

183. Quoted, Charles Hodge, *The Constitutional History of the Presbyterian Church* (2 vols., Philadelphia, 1839-40), II, 306.

184. Noah Hobart, *An Attempt to Illustrate and Confirm the Ecclesiastical Constitution of the Consociated Churches* (New Haven, 1765), p. 44.

185. [Thomas Darling], *Some Remarks on Mr. President Clap's History and Vindication of the Doctrines of the New-England Churches* (New Haven, 1757), p. 68.

186. John Moorhead, Jonathan Parsons, and David McGregore, *A Fair Narrative of the Proceedings of the Presbytery of Boston* (Boston, 1756).

187. Bellamy, *Letter to Scripturista*, in *Works*, I, 608-609.

188. Benjamin Trumbull, *A Complete History of Connecticut, Civil and Ecclesiastical* (New Haven, 1818), II, 519n.

189. Tucker, *Remarks on a Sermon of Hutchinson*, pp. 39-40; *Remarks on a Discourse of Parsons*, p. 4.

190. Tucker, *Remarks on a Discourse of Parsons*, pp. 9-11.

191. John Tucker, *A Brief Account of an Ecclesiastical Council, So Called, Convened in the First Parish of Newbury, March 31, 1767* (Boston, [1767]), pp. 16, 24.

192. Backus, *Appeal to the Public*, p. 29.

193. Frothingham, *Key to Unlock Door*, p. 59.

194. Quoted, Backus, *History of New England*, II, 266.

195. Samuel Davies, *The State of Religion among the Protestant Dissenters in Virginia; in a Letter to the Rev. Mr. Joseph Bellamy* (Boston, 1751), pp. 4-5.

196. Quoted, Elisha P. Douglass, *Rebels and Democrats. The Struggle for Equal Political Rights and Majority Rule during the American Revolution* (Chapel Hill, 1955), p. 147.

197. [John Cleaveland], *A Plain Narrative of the Proceedings which caused the Separation . . . in Ipswich* (Boston, 1747), p. 5.

198. Davies, *Duties and Difficulties*, Dedication, p. 7.

199. McGregore, *Christian Unity*, p. 22.

200. Trumbull, *History of Connecticut*, II, 340.

201. John Searl, *The Character and Reward of a Good and Faithful Servant of Jesus Christ. A Funeral Sermon, Occasioned by the Death of the Rev. Jonathan Parsons* (published as introduction to volume I of Parsons' *Sixty Sermons*), p. xxix.

202. Edwards, *Thoughts on the Revival*, in *Works*, I, 391.

203. Bellamy, *Works*, I, xvii; Trumbull, *History of Connecticut*, II, 159.

204. Chauncy, *Diversity of Gifts*, p. 8.

205. Chauncy, *Seasonable Thoughts*, p. 302.

206. Chauncy, *Enthusiasm Describ'd*, p. 20; Ebenezer Gay, *The Evangelical Preacher. A Sermon at the Ordination of the Rev'd Bunker Gay* (Boston, 1763), p. 19.

207. Appleton, *Great Apostle Paul*, pp. 11-12; Ebenezer Devotion, *An Answer of the Pastor & Brethren of the Third Church in Windham, to . . . Its Separating Members* (New London, 1747), pp. 5ff; Devotion, *The Mutual Obligation upon Ministers, and People, to Hear, and Speak, the Word of God* (New London, 1750), p. 12.

208. Mayhew, *Seven Sermons*, p. 95.

209. Mayhew, *Christian Sobriety*, p. 211.

210. Mayhew, *Seven Sermons*, pp. 152-154.

211. *Ibid.*, p. 94.

212. Smith, "Sermon VIII," *Works*, II, 171n.

213. Mayhew, *Seven Sermons*, p. 95.

214. Mayhew, "Sermon XVI," *Works*, II, 332.

215. Mayhew, *Christian Sobriety*, p. 54.

216. Smith, "College of Mirania," *Works*, I (pt. II), 190-195.

217. Smith, "Philosophical Meditation," *Works*, I (pt. II), 157.

218. Smith, "The Hermit, No. VIII," *Works*, I (pt. II), 148-149.

219. Smith, "Sermon XVI," *Works*, II, 334.

220. Mayhew, *Death of Sewall,* pp. 6-7.

221. Smith, "Sermon XVI," *Works,* II, 335.

222. *Ibid.,* p. 332.

223. Quoted, Kenneth B. Murdock, ed., *Selections from Cotton Mather* (New York, 1926), p. xxxvii.

224. Quoted, Perry Miller, *The New England Mind: The Seventeenth Century* (Cambridge, 1954), p. 354.

225. Mather Byles, quoted, Moses C. Tyler, *A History of American Literature, 1607-1765* (Ithaca, New York, 1949), p. 429.

226. *Life of Devereux Jarratt* (Baltimore, 1806), p. 88.

227. William Livingston, April 26, 1753, in *The Independent Reflector,* Milton M. Klein, ed. (Cambridge, 1963), p. 208.

228. George B. Bohman, "The Colonial Period," in William Norwood Brigance, ed., *A History and Criticism of American Public Address* (2 vols., New York, 1943), I, 19.

229. Walker, *Way to Try Apostles,* p. 23.

230. *Mr. [Ebenezer] Turell's Direction to his People with Relation to the Present Times* (3rd ed., Boston, 1742), p. 10.

231. Smith, "Philosophical Meditation," *Works,* I (pt. II), 157.

232. Henry Caner, *The True Nature and Method of Christian Preaching, Examined and Stated* (Newport, R.I., 1745), p. 6.

233. Perry Miller and Thomas H. Johnson, eds., *The Puritans* (New York, 1938), pp. 689-691.

234. Chauncy, *Seasonable Thoughts,* p. 218.

235. John Thomson, *The Government of the Church of Christ* (Philadelphia, 1741), Appendix, p. 127; William Hooper, *The Apostles Neither Imposters nor Enthusiasts* (Boston, 1742), pp. 28-29.

236. A ——— Z., *Parsons Corrected,* p. 4; Samuel Johnson, Preface to John Beach, *A Calm and Dispassionate Vindication of the Professors of the Church of England . . .* (Boston, 1749), p. iii.

237. Quoted, Tyler, *History of American Literature,* p. 429.

238. Gay, *Evangelical Preacher,* p. 19.

239. Quoted, Sprague, *Annals,* III, 145.

240. Channing, "Remarks on National Literature," *Works,* p. 128.

241. Smith, "Sermon VII," *Works,* II, 143-144, 215.

242. "A Speech against the Immoderate Use of Spirituous Liquors, Delivered by a Creek Indian, in a National Council, on the Breaking Out of a War, about the Year 1748," in Smith, *Works,* II, 214-224.

243. Hugh Henry Brackenridge, *Modern Chivalry,* Claude M. Newlin, ed. (New York, 1937), pp. 56-57.

244. Quoted, Sprague, *Annals,* III, 194.

245. Buell, "A Letter to the Rev. Mr. David Bostwick," in *Excellence and Importance of Saving Knowledge,* pp. viii-ix.

246. "Notes on the State of Virginia," *The Writings of Thomas Jefferson,* Paul Leicester Ford, ed. (10 vols., New York, 1892-1899), III, 157.

247. Buell, "Letter to Bostwick," in *Excellence and Importance of Saving Knowledge,* p. ix.

248. Miller and Johnson, *The Puritans,* p. 694.

249. Edwards, Preface to *Five Discourses,* in *Works,* I, 621; Buell, *Excellence and Importance of Saving Knowledge,* pp. 12-13; J. Finley, *Essay on Gospel Ministry,* pp. 43-44; L. Hart, *Christian Minister,* p. 11.

250. Buell, *Christ the Grand Subject of Gospel-Preaching*, p. 24n.

251. Searl, *Character and Reward*, p. xxii.

252. J. Finley, *Essay on Gospel Ministry*, p. 43.

253. Quoted, Turnbull, *Edwards the Preacher*, p. 127.

254. Zubly, *The Wise Shining*, p. 22 .

255. Buell, *Christ the Grand Subject of Gospel-Preaching*, p. 24.

256. Davies, *Charity and Truth*, pp. 237, 255, 292.

257. "The Manifestation of Truth, the End of Preaching. Preached November 5, 1783, at the Ordination of the Reverend Mr. Timothy Dwight," *The Works of Jonathan Edwards, D.D.* (2 vols., Andover, 1842), II, 61.

258. Trinterud, *Forming of American Tradition*, p. 177; S. Finley, *Approved Minister of God*, p. 6.

259. Perry Miller, *Errand*, p. 181.

260. Quoted, Trinterud, *Forming of American Tradition*, p. 177.

261. Parsons, *To Live is Christ*, p. 17; cf. Searl, *Character and Reward*, p. xlix,

262. Edwards, *A Divine and Supernatural Light*, in *Works*, II, 14.

263. Buell, *Spiritual Knowledge*, p. 40.

264. Benedict, *Preparation for Death*, p. 20.

265. Backus, *Fish Caught*, p. 33.

266. *The Sad State of the Unconverted* (Boston, 1736), p. 47.

267. John Rowland, "Narrative of the Revival," with Tennent, *Funeral Sermon*, p. 54.

268. Tennent, *Necessity of Religious Violence*, p. 27.

269. Tennent, Preface to Whitefield, *Five Sermons* (Philadelphia, 1746), p. ix.

270. Edwards, "Christian Knowledge," *Works*, II, 158.

271. Finley, *Approved Minister of God*, p. 7.

272. Tennent, *Love to Christ*, p. 16; Wheelock, *Preaching of Christ*, p. 25.

273. L. Hart, *Christian Minister*, p. 10.

274. Searl, *Character and Reward*, p. xxii.

275. Edwards, "Christian Knowledge," *Works*, II, 157.

276. Isaac Backus, *All True Ministers of the Gospel, are Called into that Work by the Special Influences of the Holy Spirit* (Boston, 1754), p. 70.

277. Edwards, *End in Creation*, in *Works*, I, 106, 199.

278. Buell, *Christ the Grand Subject of Gospel-Preaching*, p. 24; Hopkins, *Edwards*, p. 47.

279. John Lawson, *Lectures Concerning Oratory* (3rd ed., Dublin, 1760), pp. 153-154.

280. L. Hart, *Excellence of Scripture-Arguments*, p. 23.

281. Buell, *Christ the Grand Subject of Gospel-Preaching*, p. 24.

282. Edwards, *Religious Affections*, p. 115.

283. Edwards, *Thoughts on the Revival*, in *Works*, I, 391.

284. Thomas Sheridan, *A Course of Lectures on Elocution. A New Edition* (Providence, 1796), p. vii.

285. Garden, *Take Heed*, Preface, p. 13; Chauncy, *Seasonable Thoughts*, p. 303; Garden, "To the Inhabitants," *Regeneration*, p. [i]; Nathaniel Henchman, *Reasons offered . . . for Declining to Admit Mr. Whitefield to His Pulpit* (Boston, 1745), p. 7.

286. Eugene E. White, "The Preaching of George Whitefield during the Great Awakening in America," *Speech Monographs*, XV (1948), 42.

287. Quoted, Trumbull, *History of Connecticut,* II, 149.

288. Davies, "The Love of Souls," *Sermons,* III, 372.

289. Edwards, *Reply to Williams,* in *Works,* II, 523-524.

290. *Examination and Refutation of Tennent's Remarks,* p. 74; Richard Hofstadter, *Anti-Intellectualism in American Life* (New York, 1963), p. 67.

291. *Christian History for 1744,* p. 387.

292. *Christian History for 1743,* p. 205.

293. *Querists' Short Reply to Whitefield,* p. 42.

294. Sprague, *Annals,* III, 145.

295. Hopkins, *Edwards,* p. 47; Finley, Preface to Edwards, *The Great Christian Doctrine of Original Sin Defended* (Boston, 1758).

296. Roland H. Bainton, *Yale and the Ministry* (New York, 1957), p. 54; Fish, *Church of Christ,* p. 117.

297. Tennent, *Unsearchable Riches,* p. 26.

298. Edwards, *Thoughts on the Revival,* in *Works,* I, 420.

299. Davies, "The Universal Judgment," *Sermons,* I, 382.

300. Finley on Davies, quoted, Sprague, *Annals,* III, 145; Bellamy, *A Careful and Strict Examination of the External Covenant,* in *Works,* II, 572; John Searl, *Revelation a Guide to Reason; or, the Word of God Our Supreme Rule in Religion* (Boston, 1773), p. 27.

301. L. Hart, *Christian Minister,* p. 16.

302. Bellamy, *Works,* I, xxiii.

303. Buell, *Excellence and Importance of Saving Knowledge,* p. 12; Whitefield, "The Pharisee and the Publican," in Gillies, *Memoirs of Whitefield,* Appendix, p. 381; Hopkins, *Edwards,* p. 48; J. Finley, *Essay on Gospel Ministry,* p. 33.

304. George Whitefield, Preface to *Nine Sermons* (2nd ed., Boston, 1743), pp. i-ii.

305. Searl, *Character and Reward,* pp. xlix-l.

306. Spencer Roane, "Memorandum," in George Morgan, *The True Patrick Henry* (Philadelphia, 1907), Appendix B, p. 445.

307. [William Wirt], *The British Spy* (Newburyport, Mass., 1804), pp. 56-57.

308. Davies, "God is Love," *Sermons,* I, 316.

309. Parsons, *Sixty Sermons,* I, 581; II, 41.

310. Tennent, *Solemn Warning,* pp. 27-28.

311. Witherspoon, "Lectures on Eloquence," *Works,* III, 479.

312. Bellamy, *Works,* I, lx.

313. *Ibid.,* pp. lxii-lxiii.

314. Witherspoon, "Lectures on Eloquence," *Works,* III, 481, 513-514.

315. Edwards, "Covenant of Redemption," in Faust and Johnson, *Edwards Selections,* p. 373.

316. Searl, *Character and Reward,* p. xlvi.

317. Tennent, *Right Use of Passions,* p. 24.

318. Edwards, "True Excellency of Gospel Minister," *Works,* II, 958; Tennent, *Right Use of Passions,* pp. 5-6; Buell, *Christ the Grand Subject of Gospel-Preaching,* p. 25.

319. Mayhew, *Christian Sobriety,* p. 208.

320. Buell, *Excellence and Importance of Saving Knowledge,* pp. 12-13.

321. Witherspoon, "Lectures on Eloquence," *Works,* III, 513.

322. Bellamy, *Millennium,* in *Works,* I, 447.

323. Davies, "The Curse of Cowardice, Preached to the Militia of Hanover County," *Sermons,* III, 91.

324. C. H. Maxson, *The Great Awakening in the Middle Colonies* (Chicago, 1920), p. 150; Enoch Huntington, *A Sermon, Delivered at Middletown, July 20th, A.D. 1775* (Hartford, [1775]), p. 20.

V. THE SNARE BROKEN

1. Smith, *Works*, II, 5-7.
2. Devotion, *Mutual Obligation*, p. 4.
3. Mayhew, *A Sermon Preach'd . . . May 29th, 1754. Being the Anniversary for the Election* (Boston, 1754), p. 2.
4. John Tucker, *A Sermon Preached at Cambridge . . . May 29th, 1771, Being the Anniversary for the Election* (Boston, 1754), p. 12.
5. Quoted, Miller, *New England Mind*, p. 415.
6. Mayhew, *Unlimited Submission*, in Thornton, *Pulpit of Revolution*, p. 53.
7. Samuel Cooke, *A Sermon Preached at Cambridge . . . May 30th, 1770. Being the Anniversary for the Election,* in Thornton, *Pulpit of Revolution,* p. 157.
8. Solomon Williams, *A Firm and Immoveable Courage to Obey God, and an Inflexible Observation of the Laws of Religion, the Highest Wisdom and Certain Happiness of Rulers* (New London, 1741), p. 18.
9. Samuel West, *A Sermon Preached before the Honorable Council . . . May 29th, 1776. Being the Anniversary for the Election,* in Thornton, *Pulpit of Revolution,* p. 272.
10. Cleaveland, *Essay, to Defend,* p. 25.
11. Mayhew, *Unlimited Submission,* in Thornton, *Pulpit of Revolution,* p. 95; Chauncy, *Civil Magistrates,* pp. 9-10.
12. West, *1776 Election Sermon,* in Thornton, *Pulpit of Revolution,* p. 271.
13. David S. Rowland, *Divine Providence Illustrated and Improved. A Thanksgiving Discourse, Preached in the Presbyterian, or Congregational Church in Providence* (Providence, [1766]), p. 18.
14. Mayhew, *Snare Broken,* in Moore, *Patriot Preachers,* p. 20.
15. Benjamin Throop, *A Thanksgiving Sermon, upon the Occasion of the Glorious News of the Repeal of the Stamp-Act* (New London, 1766), p. 11; Joseph Emerson, *A Thanksgiving Sermon Preached at Pepperell . . . on the Account of the Repeal of the Stamp-Act* (Boston, 1766), p. 9.
16. Mayhew, *Snare Broken,* in Moore, *Patriot Preachers,* p. 12.
17. Chauncy, *A Discourse on 'the good News from a far Country.' Delivered July 24th. A Day of Thanks-giving . . . on Occasion of the Repeal of the Stamp Act,* in Thornton, *Pulpit of Revolution,* p. 128.
18. "To Reverend G——— W———," November 11, 1765, *The Writings of Samuel Adams,* Harry Alonzo Cushing, ed. (4 vols., New York, 1904-1908), I, 28.
19. Mayhew, *Two Sermons on the Nature, Extent and Perfection of the Divine Goodness. Delivered December 9, 1762. Being the Annual Thanksgiving* (Boston, 1763), p. 72.
20. Chauncy, *Good News,* in Thornton, *Pulpit of Revolution,* p. 128.
21. Miller, *New England Mind: From Colony to Province,* pp. 389-390.
22. Moses Parsons, *A Sermon Preached at Cambridge . . . May 27th, 1772. Being the Anniversary for the Election* (Boston, 1772), p. 25; Chauncy, *Good News,* in Thornton, *Pulpit of Revolution,* p. 129.

23. Mayhew, *Divine Goodness*, p. 72.

24. Chauncy, *Civil Magistrates*, pp. 8, 13.

25. Jeremiah Dummer, *A Defence of the New-England Charters* (London, 1721), p. 40.

26. Chauncy, *The Idle-Poor Secluded from the Bread of Charity by the Christian Law. A Sermon Preached in Boston, before the Society for Encouraging Industry and Employing the Poor, Aug. 12, 1752* (Boston, 1752), pp. 11-12.

27. Thomas Hutchinson, *The History of the Colony and Province of Massachusetts-Bay*, Lawrence S. Mayo, ed. (3 vols., Cambridge, 1936), II, 391.

28. Chauncy, *Idle-Poor*, pp. 7, 19-20, 13.

29. Mayhew, *Christian Sobriety*, p. 204; Chauncy, *Idle-Poor*, p. 7.

30. Letters to Richard Jackson, May 5, 1753, and to Peter Collison, May 9, 1753, *The Writings of Benjamin Franklin*, Albert Henry Smyth, ed. (10 vols., New York, 1905-1907), III, 134ff.

31. Chauncy, *Idle-Poor*, p. 6.

32. Edwards, "Christian Charity: or, the Duty of Charity to the Poor, Explained and Enforced," *Works*, II, 164-165.

33. Hopkins, *Edwards*, p. 45.

34. Edwards, "Christian Charity," *Works*, II, 173.

35. Chauncy, *Christian Love*, pp. 12-15, 21.

36. Mayhew, *Seven Sermons*, p. 11.

37. Ashley, *Great Duty of Charity*, p. 9.

38. Simeon Howard, *A Sermon on Brotherly Love Preached . . . Before the Most Ancient and Honorable Society of Free and Accepted Masons* (Boston, [1778]), p. 9.

39. Edwards, *True Virtue*, in *Works*, I, 126.

40. Edwards, "Christian Charity," *Works*, II, 172, 164.

41. Daniel Shute, *1768 Election Sermon*, pp. 23-24.

42. Miller and Johnson, *The Puritans*, p. 237.

43. Fiske, *Importance of Righteousness*, p. 10.

44. Nathaniel Appleton, *A Thanksgiving Sermon on the Total Repeal of the Stamp Act* (Boston, 1766), pp. 31-32.

45. Bernard Bailyn, ed., *Pamphlets of the American Revolution, 1750-1776*, Volume I, 1750-1765 (Cambridge, 1965), pp. 205-206, 696-697: Mayhew, *Unlimited Submission*, in Thornton, *Pulpit of Revolution*, p. 84.

46. Mayhew, *Unlimited Submission*, in Thornton, *Pulpit of Revolution*, p. 102; Bailyn, *Pamphlets*, p. 205.

47. Mayhew, *Unlimited Submission*, in Thornton, *Pulpit of Revolution*, pp. 96-97, 102; *1754 Election Sermon*, p. 20.

48. Andrew Eliot, *A Sermon Preached . . . May 29th, 1765. Being the Anniversary for the Election* (Boston, 1765), pp. 34-35; Smith, "An Earnest Exhortation to Religion, Brotherly Love, and Public Spirit," *Works*, II, 35-36.

49. Mayhew, *Unlimited Submission*, in Thornton, *Pulpit of Revolution*, p. 87n; Eliot, *1765 Election Sermon*, p. 35.

50. Mayhew, *Unlimited Submission*, in Thornton, *Pulpit of Revolution*, p. 87; Smith, "Earnest Exhortation," *Works*, II, 36.

51. Mayhew, *Unlimited Submission*, in Thornton, *Pulpit of Revolution*, p. 87n.

52. Chauncy, *Civil Magistrates*, p. 13.

53. Mayhew, *1754 Election Sermon*, p. 7.

54. Chauncy, *Civil Magistrates*, pp. 34-35.

55. Mayhew, *Unlimited Submission,* in Thornton, *Pulpit of Revolution,* p. 104.

56. Mayhew, *Snare Broken,* in Moore, *Patriot Preachers,* p. 26.

57. Emerson, *1766 Thanksgiving Sermon,* pp. 12-13; William Patten, *A Discourse Delivered at Hallifax . . . July 24th 1766 on the Day of Thanksgiving . . . for the Repeal of the Stamp-Act* (Boston, 1766), pp. 18-20; Samuel Stillman, *Good News from a Far Country. A Sermon Preached at Boston, May 17, 1766. Upon the . . . Repeal of the Stamp-Act* (Boston, 1766), pp. 33-34.

58. Andrew Eliot, quoted, Alice M. Baldwin, *The New England Clergy and the American Revolution* (New York, 1958), p. 92n.

59. Chauncy, *Good News,* in Thornton, *Pulpit of Revolution,* p. 104.

60. Rowland, *Divine Providence,* p. 10.

61. Chauncy, *Good News,* in Thornton, *Pulpit of Revolution,* pp. 133, 137.

62. Eliot, *1765 Election Sermon,* pp. 15, 42.

63. Mayhew, *Snare Broken,* in Moore, *Patriot Preachers,* pp. 46-47.

64. Chauncy, *Civil Magistrates,* p. 8.

65. Chauncy, *The Benevolence of the Deity, Fairly and Impartially Considered* (Boston, 1784), p. 191.

66. Chauncy, *Civil Magistrates,* p. 8.

67. Mayhew, *Snare Broken,* in Moore, *Patriot Preachers,* p. 46.

68. *Ibid.,* p. 29.

69. Chauncy, *Good News,* in Thornton, *Pulpit of Revolution,* p. 137.

70. *Ibid.;* Mayhew, *Snare Broken,* in Moore, *Patriot Preachers,* p. 46.

71. Smith, "An Eulogium, on the Delivery of Mr. Sargent's Prize-Medal at the Public Commencement," *Four Dissertations, on the Reciprocal Advantages of a Perpetual Union between Great Britain and Her American Colonies* (Philadelphia, 1766), p. 10.

72. Mayhew, *Snare Broken,* in Moore, *Patriot Preachers,* p. 14.

73. Thornton, *Pulpit of Revolution,* p. 43.

74. Daniel Shute, *A Sermon Preached to the Ancient and Honorable Artillery Company . . . June 1, 1767* (Boston, 1767), p. 29; Howard, *1780 Election Sermon,* in Thornton, *Pulpit of Revolution,* p. 367; Eliot, *1765 Election Sermon,* p. 12.

75. Shute, *1767 Artillery Sermon,* p. 28.

76. Smith, "Sermon XVII . . . the Anniversary Commencement, May 1761," *Works,* II, 339.

77. Smith, "Philosophical Meditation," *Works,* I (pt. II), 155-157.

78. West, *1776 Election Sermon,* in Thornton, *Pulpit of Revolution,* p. 267.

79. Smith, "Philosophical Meditation," *Works,* I (pt. II), 154.

80. Chauncy, *Benevolence of Deity,* p. vii.

81. John Tucker, *Ministers Considered as Fellow-Workers, Who Should be Comforters to Each Other . . . A Sermon Preached before the Ministers of the Province . . . at Their Annual Convention* (Boston, 1768), p. 23.

82. Bridge, *1767 Election Sermon,* p. 33.

83. *Ibid.;* Shute, *1768 Election Sermon,* p. 43.

84. Smith, "Eulogium," *Four Dissertations,* pp. 4-5.

85. Mayhew, *1754 Election Sermon,* p. 12.

86. Smith, "Sermon VIII," *Works,* II, 172.

87. Mayhew, *Divine Goodness,* p. 72.

88. Smith, "Sermon VIII," *Works,* II, 172.

89. Noah Welles, *Patriotism Described and Recommended, in a Sermon*

Preached . . . on the Day of the Anniversary Election, May 10th, 1764 (New London, 1764), p. 16.

90. Rowland, *Divine Providence,* p. 2.

91. Mayhew, *Snare Broken,* in Moore, *Patriot Preachers,* p. 44; Chauncy, *Good News,* in Thornton, *Pulpit of Revolution,* p. 120.

92. Mayhew, *1754 Election Sermon,* p. 12.

93. *Ibid.,* p. 45.

94. Mayhew, *Death of Sewall,* p. 14.

95. Smith, *An Oration, in Memory of General Montgomery . . . Delivered . . . at the Desire, of the Honorable Continental Congress; Philadelphia, February 19, 1776,* in *Works,* I (pt. II), 17.

96. Howard, *1780 Election Sermon,* in Thornton, *Pulpit of Revolution,* pp. 370-371.

97. Tucker, *Ministers Fellow-Workers,* p. 23.

98. Tucker, *1771 Election Sermon,* p. 23.

99. Welles, *Patriotism Described,* p. 14.

100. *Ibid.*

101. Mayhew, *Snare Broken,* in Moore, *Patriot Preachers,* p. 23.

102. Smith, "Duty of Protestant Ministers," *Works,* II, 5-7.

103. William Emerson, *An Historical Sketch of the First Church in Boston* (Boston, 1812), p. 184.

104. Mayhew, *Snare Broken,* in Moore, *Patriot Preachers,* p. 11.

105. Mayhew, *Christian Sobriety,* Dedication, p. ix.

106. Smith, "Sermon VIII," *Works,* II, 168-169.

107. Smith, "Duty of Protestant Ministers," *Works,* II, 8-15.

108. Chauncy, *A Discourse Occasioned by the Death of the Reverend Jonathan Mayhew, D.D. . . . Delivered the Lord's Day after His Decease* (Boston, 1766), p. 31.

109. Oliver, *Origin and Progress,* p. 43.

110. Mayhew, *Snare Broken,* in Moore, *Patriot Preachers,* p. 43.

111. *Ibid.,* p. 40.

112. *Ibid.,* pp. 40-41.

113. Smith, "Duty of Protestant Ministers," *Works,* II, 9; "Address to the Colonies," *Works,* II, 22; Rowland, *Divine Providence,* p. 9; Mayhew, *Snare Broken,* in Moore, *Patriot Preachers,* p. 24.

114. Smith, "Eulogium," *Four Dissertations,* p. 10.

115. Chauncy, *Seasonable Thoughts,* p. 422.

116. Ebenezer Gay, *The Alienation of Affections, from Ministers Consider'd and Improv'd. A Sermon Preach'd at the Ordination of the Reverend Mr. Jonathan Mayhew* (Boston, 1747), pp. 15, 19.

117. Chauncy, *Civil Magistrates,* p. 10.

118. Mayhew, *Snare Broken,* in Moore, *Patriot Preachers,* pp. 29-31.

119. *Ibid.,* p. 47.

120. *Ibid.,* p. 23.

121. Chauncy, *Enthusiasm Describ'd,* p. 5.

122. Chauncy, *Good News,* in Thornton, *Pulpit of Revolution,* p. 139.

123. Mayhew, *Snare Broken,* in Moore, *Patriot Preachers,* p. 47.

124. Chauncy, *Good News,* in Thornton, *Pulpit of Revolution,* p. 139.

125. Edward Barnard, *A Sermon Preached . . . May 28th, 1766. Being the Anniversary for the Election* (Boston, 1766), p. 36.

126. Mayhew, *Snare Broken,* in Moore, *Patriot Preachers,* p. 44; Barnard, *1766 Election Sermon,* pp. 37-38.

127. Mayhew, *Snare Broken*, in Moore, *Patriot Preachers*, p. 44.

128. *Ibid.;* cf. Barnard, *1766 Election Sermon*, p. 37.

129. Mayhew, *Snare Broken,* in Moore, *Patriot Preachers,* p. 44.

130. *Ibid.,* p. 45.

131. Chauncy, *Civil Magistrates*, pp. 33-34.

132. Chauncy, *Good News*, in Thornton, *Pulpit of Revolution*, pp. 119-121.

133. Appleton, *Thanksgiving Sermon for Repeal*, p. 14.

134. Mayhew, *Seven Sermons*, p. 97.

135. Mayhew, *Snare Broken*, in Moore, *Patriot Preachers*, p. 10.

136. Henry Cumings, *A Thanksgiving Sermon Preached at Billerica, November 27, 1766* (Boston, 1767), p. 15.

137. John Morgan, "Dissertation on the Reciprocal Advantages," in Smith, *Four Dissertations*, p. 6.

138. Barnard, *1766 Election Sermon*, p. 26.

139. Chauncy, *Good News*, in Thornton, *Pulpit of Revolution*, p. 136.

140. Tucker, *Ministers Fellow-Workers*, p. 23.

141. Mayhew, *Snare Broken*, in Moore, *Patriot Preachers*, p. 10.

142. *Ibid.,* p. 11.

143. *Ibid.,* p. 29.

144. Rowland, *Divine Providence*, p. 29.

145. Chauncy, *Good News*, in Thornton, *Pulpit of Revolution*, p. 143.

146. *Ibid.,* pp. 143-144.

147. Rowland, *Divine Providence*, p. 19.

148. Chauncy, *Good News*, in Thornton, *Pulpit of Revolution*, pp. 140-142.

149. Mayhew, *Snare Broken*, in Moore, *Patriot Preachers*, p. 47.

150. Chauncy, *Good News*, in Thornton, *Pulpit of Revolution*, p. 140.

151. Mayhew, *Snare Broken*, in Moore, *Patriot Preachers*, pp. 29, 36-37; Chauncy, *Good News,* in Thornton, *Pulpit of Revolution,* pp. 141-144.

152. Emerson, *1766 Thanksgiving Sermon*, p. 18; Throop, *Thanksgiving on Stamp-Act*, p. 6; Elisha Fish, *Joy and Gladness: A Thanksgiving Discourse . . . Occasioned by the Repeal of the Stamp-Act* (Providence, 1767), p. 13.

153. Mayhew, *Snare Broken*, in Moore, *Patriot Preachers*, p. 57.

154. Gay, *Natural Religion*, pp. 10-11.

155. Chauncy, *Benevolence of Deity*, p. 77.

156. Shute, *1768 Election Sermon*, p. 6.

157. Bridge, *1767 Election Sermon*, pp. 5-6; Rowland, *Divine Providence*, p. 5; Samuel Williams, *A Discourse on the Love of Our Country* (Salem, 1775), p. 5.

158. Mayhew, *Divine Goodness*, p. 90.

159. Smith, "Eulogium," *Four Dissertations*, p. 9.

160. Cumings, *1766 Thanksgiving Sermon*, p. 9.

161. Smith, "Philosophical Meditation," *Works*, I (pt. II), 154-155.

162. Chauncy, *Benevolence of Deity*, p. 57.

163. Chauncy, *Death of Mayhew*, p. 27.

164. Alden Bradford, *Memoir of the Life and Writings of Rev. Jonathan Mayhew, D.D.* (Boston, 1838), p. 276.

165. Sprague, *Annals*, VIII, 65-66.

166. John Adams, *Works*, X, 284.

167. Chauncy, *Death of Mayhew*, p. 29.

168. "The Nature and Progress of Liberty," *The Works, in Verse and Prose, of the Late Robert Treate Paine, Jun. Esq.* (Boston, 1812), p. 74.

169. Quoted, Sprague, *Annals*, I, 420.

170. Mayhew, *On Hearing the Word,* Dedication, p. iii.
171. M. C. Tyler, *The Literary History of the American Revolution, 1763-1783* (2 vols., New York, [1957]), I, 124.
172. Hutchinson, *History of Massachusetts, 1750-1774,* p. 297; cf. J. Adams, *Works,* II, 86.
173. [Arthur Browne], *Remarks on Dr. Mayhew's Incidental Reflections, Relative to the Church of England* (Portsmouth, N.H., 1763), p. 24; Oliver, *Origin and Progress,* p. 43.
174. Tyler, *History of American Literature,* p. 432.
175. Mayhew, *A Letter of Reproof to Mr. John Cleaveland of Ipswich, Occasioned by a Defamatory Libel Published under His Name* (Boston, 1764), p. 4.
176. Chauncy, *Death of Mayhew,* p. 30.
177. Mayhew, *Remarks on an Anonymous Tract. Intitled an Answer to Dr. Mayhew's Observations* (Boston, 1764), p. 67.

VI. THE WISDOM OF GOD
IN THE PERMISSION OF SIN

1. John Cleaveland, *Essex Gazette,* April 18, 25, 1775, in Baldwin, *New England Clergy,* Appendix A, p. 179.
2. Parsons, "God's ancient dispensations towards his people, designed for future improvement of his Church," *Sixty Sermons,* II, 508-509.
3. Wheelock, *Liberty of Conscience,* p. 21.
4. William Gordon, *A Discourse Preached December 15th, 1774,* in Thornton, *Pulpit of Revolution,* p. 197.
5. For instance, Leland, *A Blow at the Root.*
6. Davies, "The Crisis," *Sermons,* III, 78-79.
7. Buell, *Intricate and Mysterious Events,* pp. 7-8.
8. Robert Smith, *The Obligations of the Confederate States of America to Praise God . . . Two Sermons. Preached at Pequea, December 13th, 1781* (Philadelphia, 1782), p. 1.
9. Tennent, *A Sermon Preached at Burlington in New-Jersey, November 23, 1749. Being the Day Appointed . . . for a Provincial Thanksgiving* (Philadelphia, 1749), p. 5.
10. Tennent, *The Necessity of Praising God for Mercies Receiv'd. A Sermon Occasion'd by the Success of the Late Expedition* (Philadelphia, [1745]), pp. 7, 20.
11. Tennent, *Funeral Sermon,* p. 7.
12. Samuel Finley, *The Successful Minister of Christ Distinguish'd in Glory. A Sermon Occasion'd by the Death of . . . Gilbert Tennent* (Philadelphia, 1764), p. 20.
13. Tennent, *Necessity of Praising God,* p. 7.
14. Smyth, *Writings of Franklin,* II, 342.
15. Tennent, *Brotherly Love,* p. 3.
16. Hamilton, *Gentleman's Progress,* p. 22.
17. Chauncy, *Civil Magistrates,* p. 22; Nathanael Hunn, *The Welfare of Governments Considered. A Sermon Preached before the General Assembly of Connecticut* (New London, 1747), pp. 11-13; Benjamin Lord, *Religion and Government,* pp. 59-60; Samuel Phillips, *Political Rulers Authoris'd and Influenc'd by God Our Saviour, to Decree and Execute Justice* (Boston, 1750), p. 14.

18. Hart, *Excellence of Scripture-Arguments*, p. 15.

19. Bellamy, *Election Sermon*, in *Works*, I, 580.

20. *Ibid.*, p. 578.

21. Burr, *Servant of God*, p. 14.

22. Miller, "Jonathan Edwards and the Great Awakening," *Errand*, pp. 153-166.

23. Edwards, *God's Awful Judgment*, in *Works*, II, 37-39.

24. Burr, *Servant of God,* pp. 14-16.

25. Nathaniel Whitaker, *An Antidote Against Toryism, or the Curse of Meroz*, in Moore, *Patriot Preachers*, p. 198.

26. Eliphalet Williams, *A Sermon, Preached in the Audience of the General Assembly, . . . on the Day of Their Anniversary Election* (Hartford, [1769]), p. 11; John Carmichael, *A Self-Defensive War Lawful. Proved in a Sermon, Preached at Lancaster, . . . June 4, 1775* (Philadelphia, 1775), p. 11; Emerson, *1766 Thanksgiving Sermon*, p. 31.

27. Samuel Langdon, *Government Corrupted by Vice, and Recovered by Righteousness*, in Thornton, *Pulpit of Revolution*, p. 250.

28. Cf. Wheelock to Governor Trumbull, December 1, 1775, in Frederick Chase, *A History of Dartmouth College*, vol. I, John K. Lord, ed. (Cambridge, 1891), p. 348.

29. Tennent, *A Sermon on 1 Chronicles XXIX. 28. Occasioned by the Death of King George the Second* (Philadelphia, 1761). Cf. Davies, "On the Death of His Late Majesty, King George II, Delivered in Nassau-Hall, Jan. 14, 1761," *Sermons*, III, 32, 34.

30. Williams, *1769 Election Sermon*, p. 11.

31. Johnson, "A Sermon of the Blessedness of Giving Beyond That of Receiving," *Writings*, III, 461-462.

32. Ebenezer Pemberton, Sr., quoted, Davenport, *Faithful Minister*, p. 13n.

33. Davies, "The Rule of Equity," *Sermons*, II, 65.

34. Tennent, *Danger of Spiritual Pride*, p. 23.

35. Tennent, *Solemn Warning*, pp. 56, 59.

36. Josiah Smith, *The Burning of Sodom, with It's Moral Causes, Improv'd in a Sermon, Preach'd at Charlestown, South-Carolina, after a Most Terrible Fire* (Boston, 1741), p. 12.

37. Tennent, *Danger of Spiritual Pride*, p. 18.

38. Ferm, *Puritan Sage*, p. 333; Parsons, *To Live is Christ*, p. 26.

39. Charles Turner, *A Sermon, Preached at Plymouth, December 22d, 1773* (Boston, 1774), p. 14.

40. Benjamin Trumbull, *A Discourse, Delivered at the Anniversary Meeting of the Freemen of the Town of New-Haven, April 12, 1773* (New Haven, 1773), pp. 30-31; Andrew Croswell, *An Answer to the Rev. Mr. Garden's Three First Letters to the Rev. Mr. Whitefield* (Boston, 1741), p. 59.

41. Edwards, *Works*, I, cclxxi; Townsend, *Philosophy of Edwards*, pp. 65, 259.

42. Parsons, "Christ is Resolutely Determined," *Sixty Sermons*, II, 667; George Duffield, *A Sermon Preached in the Third Presbyterian Church in the City of Philadelphia, on December 11th, 1783*, in Moore, *Patriot Preachers*, p. 360; Stanley Griswold, Sermons 399 and 500, in "Griswold Manuscript Sermons," Houghton Library, Harvard University.

43. Nathaniel Whitaker, *The Trial of the Spirits . . . Preached at Newent, in Norwich, March 17, 1762* (Providence, 1752 [sic]), p. 24; Backus, *True Faith*, p. 75.

44. Edwards, *Charity and Its Fruits, passim; True Virtue,* in *Works,* I, 123.

45. William Tennent [III], *An Address, Occasioned by the Late Invasion of the Liberties of the American Colonies by the British Parliament, Delivered in Charles-Town, South-Carolina* (Philadelphia, 1774), p. 13.

46. Buell, *Revival of 1764,* p. 80.

47. Edwards, *Work of Redemption,* in *Works,* I, 612.

48. Davies, "The Crisis," *Sermons,* III, 76-77.

49. Tennent, *Unconverted Ministry,* p. 25.

50. Edwards, "Farewell Sermon," *Works,* I, ccxlvi.

51. Finley, *Successful Minister,* p. 23.

52. Tennent, *Irenicum Ecclesiasticum,* p. 100.

53. Tennent, *Right Use of Passions,* pp. 24-25.

54. Edwards, "Discourse II. Pressing into the Kingdom of God," *Works,* I, 657; "Sermon VIII" and "Sermon X," *Works,* II, 890, 913.

55. Tennent, *Necessity of Studying to be Quiet,* pp. 27-28.

56. Edwards, *Brainerd,* in *Works,* II, 446.

57. R. Smith, *Wheel in the Middle,* p. 16.

58. Bellamy, *True Religion Delineated,* in *Works,* I, 132.

59. Benedict, *Preparation for Death,* p. 13.

60. Edwards, *Religious Affections,* p. 195.

61. Edwards, *Brainerd,* in *Works,* II, 453.

62. *Ibid.,* p. 446; Bellamy, *Law our Schoolmaster,* in *Works,* I, 396.

63. [Charles Francis Adams], "Davis's *Memoirs and Journal of Burr,*" *North American Review,* XLIX (1839), 160.

64. Whitaker, *Sermon after Ordination of Smith,* pp. 29-30.

65. Tennent, Preface to John Tennent, *The Nature of Regeneration Opened* (Boston, 1735), p. ix.

66. Davies, *Duties and Difficulties,* pp. 42-43.

67. Davies, "The Tender Anxieties of Ministers," *Sermons,* II, 312.

68. William Cooper, "Preface to the Reader," in Edwards, *Distinguishing Marks,* in *Works,* II, 258; Cleaveland, *Short and Plain Narrative,* p. 19.

69. Zubly, *The Wise Shining,* p. 22.

70. Edwards, *Humble Inquiry,* in *Works,* I, 435; *Reply to Williams,* in *Works,* I, 490.

71. Williams and Wheelock, *Two Letters to Davenport,* p. 27.

72. Ross, *Plain Address to the Quakers,* p. 202.

73. Green, *Inquiry into Constitution,* p. vii.

74. Backus, *Fish Caught,* p. 57.

75. Green, *Inquiry into Constitution,* p. vii.

76. Bellamy, *Examination of External Covenant,* in *Works,* II, 658.

77. *Ibid.,* p. 572.

78. S. Finley, *The Madness of Mankind* (Philadelphia, [1754]), p. 29.

79. Mayhew, *Christian Sobriety,* p. 260.

80. L. Hart, *Christian Minister,* pp. 20-21.

81. Edwards, Jr., "Grace Evidenced by Its Fruits," *Works,* II, 395.

82. Bellamy, *There is But One Covenant,* in *Works,* II, 507.

83. Tennent, *Right Use of Passions,* p. 39.

84. Bellamy, *True Religion Delineated,* in *Works,* I, 349.

85. Bellamy, *Nature and Glory of the Gospel,* in *Works,* II, 275.

86. Parsons, *Good News,* p. 13n; Bellamy, *Nature and Glory of the Gospel,* in *Works,* II, 272.

87. Quoted, Brown, *Hawley,* p. 21.

88. Parsons, *Good News*, p. iii.

89. Edwards, *Will*, p. 422.

90. Porter, *Absurdity and Blasphemy*, p. [31].

91. *The Testimony of a Number of Ministers Convened at Taunton . . . in Favour of the Rev. Mr. Whitefield* (Boston, 1745), p. 12.

92. Parsons, *Doctrine of Justification*, p. 94.

93. Paine, *Short View*, pp. 32-33.

94. Solomon Williams, *The Sad Tendency of Divisions and Contentions in Churches* (Newport, [1751]), p. 10.

95. Williams, *True State of the Question*, Preface, p. i.

96. Alison, *Peace and Union*, p. 52.

97. Tennent, *Irenicum Ecclesiasticum*, p. 80.

98. Gillies, *Memoirs of Whitefield*, p. 623.

99. Tennent, *The Happiness of Rewarding the Enemies of Our Religion and Liberty* (Philadelphia, 1756), p. 20.

100. Davies, "Defeat of Braddock," *Sermons*, III, 227.

101. S. Finley, *The Curse of Meroz; or, the Danger of Neutrality, in the Cause of God, and Our Country* (Philadelpia, 1757), p. 25.

102. Burr, *Servant of God*, p. 22.

103. R. Smith, *Wheel in the Middle*, p. 40.

104. Jeremy Belknap, *A Sermon on Military Duty. Preached at Dover, November 10, 1772* (Salem, 1773), pp. 14-15.

105. Sprague, *Annals*, VIII, 174; William Ellery Channing, *A Sermon Preached in Boston, July 23, 1812, the Day of the Public Fast* (Boston, 1812), esp. pp. 19-20; *A Discourse at the Solemn Festival in Commemoration of the Goodness of God in Delivering the Christian World from Military Despotism, June 15, 1814* (Boston, 1814), esp. p. 10; *A Sermon, Delivered in Boston, September 18, 1814* (Boston, 1814), esp. pp. 18-19. (Channing's wartime sermons appear in his *Complete Works* only in expurgated form, under the title: "Duties of the Citizen in Times of Trial or Danger.")

106. Davies, "Religion and Patriotism the Constituents of Good Soldiers," *Sermons*, III, 51.

107. Tennent, *Happiness of Rewarding*, p. 21.

108. Keteltas, *Religious Soldier*, p. 15.

109. Davies, "Curse of Cowardice," *Sermons*, III, 94; Tennent, *Happiness of Rewarding*, p. 20.

110. Sprague, *Annals*, III, 145; Tennent, Preface to Finley, *Curse of Meroz*, p. iii.

111. Sprague, *Annals*, III, 40.

112. Finley, *Successful Minister*, p. 19.

113. Franklin, *The Autobiography . . . and Other Papers* ([New York, 1936]), p. 102.

114. Samuel Davies, *Religion and Public Spirit. A Valedictory Address to the Senior Class, Delivered in Nassau Hall, September 21, 1760* (n.p., 1761), p. 5.

115. *Ibid.*, p. 11.

116. Whitaker, *Funeral Sermon on Whitefield*, pp. 13-14, 16.

117. Davies, *Religion and Public Spirit*, p. 12.

118. Davies, "On the Death of George II," *Sermons*, III, 40.

119. Solomon Williams, *The Duty of Christian Soldiers, when Called to War, to Undertake it in the Name of God* (New London, 1755), pp. 33-34.

120. Davies, "Thanksgiving Sermon," *Sermons*, III, 267.

121. Whitaker, *Sermon after Ordination of Smith*, p. 31.

122. Edwards, *Qualifications for Communion*, in *Works*, I, 462-463.

123. Davies, "Curse of Cowardice," *Sermons*, III, 94.

124. Finley, *Curse of Meroz*, pp. 13-14.

125. Davies, "Curse of Cowardice," *Sermons*, III, 86.

126. Davies, *Religion and Public Spirit*, p. 11.

127. Tennent, *The Necessity of Holding Fast the Truth* (Boston, 1743), p. 64; *Examination and Refutation of Tennent's Remarks*, p. 150; Parsons, *Wisdom Justified*, pp. 35-36.

128. Edwards, *Works*, II, 58-59.

129. Edwards, *Distinguishing Marks*, in *Works*, II, 273; *Thoughts on the Revival*, in *Works*, I, 384, 387.

130. Aaron Hutchinson, *Valor for the Truth. In a Sermon . . . Preached in the Presbyterian Congregation at Newbury-port, April 23d, 1767* (Boston, 1767), p. 20.

131. Cleaveland, *Short and Plain Narrative*, p. 83.

132. McGregore, *Christian Unity*, p. 6.

133. Hutchinson, *Valor for Truth*, pp. 24, 51.

134. Bellamy, *Nature and Glory of the Gospel*, in *Works*, II, 451.

135. Whitaker, *Funeral Sermon on Whitefield*, p. 27.

136. Henry Caner, *The Great Blessing of Stable Times, together with the Means of Procuring It* (Boston, 1763); Benjamin T. Spencer, *The Quest for Nationality: An American Literary Campaign* (Syracuse, 1957), p. 15; Boucher, "On the Peace in 1763," *View*, p. 28.

137. R. Smith, *Wheel in the Middle*, p. 56.

138. Davies, "God is Love," *Sermons*, I, 322.

139. For example, Edwards, "The Future Punishment of the Wicked Unavoidable and Intolerable," *Works*, II, 82.

140. Whitaker, *Antidote Against Toryism*, in Moore, *Patriot Preachers*, p. 188.

141. Tennent, *Happiness of Rewarding*, p. 5.

142. S. Finley, *Curse of Meroz*, p. 20.

143. David Avery, *The Lord is to be Praised for the Triumphs of His Power* (Norwich, 1778), p. 8.

144. Tennent, *Happiness of Rewarding*, p. 5.

145. Cleaveland, *Essay, to Defend*, pp. 48, 62-63, 80; Mayhew, *On Hearing the Word*, p. 269n.

146. Mayhew, *Divine Goodness*, p. 88.

147. Cleaveland, *Essay, to Defend*, p. 48.

148. Parsons, *Good News*, p. 76n; Cleaveland, *Essay, to Defend*, p. 80.

149. [Samuel Peters], *A General History of Connecticut . . . to Which is Added, an Appendix, wherein New and True Sources of the Present Rebellion in America are Pointed Out* (2nd ed., London, 1782), pp. 121, 383.

150. Quoted, Davies, "Time of Unusual Sickness," *Sermons*, III, 157.

151. Bellamy, *Wisdom of God*, in *Works*, II, 5.

152. Bellamy, "Early Piety Recommended," *Works*, I, 551.

153. Benjamin Throop, *Religion and Loyalty, the Duty and Glory of a People; Illustrated in a Sermon . . . on the Day of the Anniversary Election* (New London, 1758), p. 17.

154. Bellamy, *Wisdom of God*, in *Works*, II, 5, 8.

155. Keteltas, *Religious Soldier*, p. 4.

156. Buell, *Revival of 1764, passim.*

157. Edwards, *Original Sin*, in *Works*, I, 170.

158. Cf. Edwards, "The Wisdom of God, Displayed in the Way of Salvation," *Works*, II, 144.

159. Edwards, "Christ Exalted: or, Jesus Christ Gloriously Exalted above All Evil in the Work of Redemption," *Works*, II, 217.

160. Edwards, *Images or Shadows*, p. 104; cf. *Works*, I, cxxiii.

161. Bellamy, *The Wisdom of God in the Permission of Sin, Vindicated*, in *Works*, II, 129.

162. Bellamy, *Millennium*, in *Works*, I, 459; *Wisdom of God*, in *Works*, II, 27-28.

163. Bellamy, *Millennium*, in *Works*, I, 452.

164. Bellamy, *True Religion Delineated*, in *Works*, I, 29.

165. *Ibid.*, p. 304; Bellamy, *Wisdom of God*, in *Works*, II, 22.

166. Bellamy, *Millennium*, in *Works*, I, 460.

167. Bellamy, *Wisdom of God*, in *Works*, II, 43.

168. Bellamy, *Millennium*, in *Works*, I, 445.

169. *Ibid.*, p. 459; Bellamy, *Wisdom of God*, in *Works*, II, 95.

170. Edwards, "The Nature and End of Excommunication," *Works*, II, 119.

171. Bellamy, *Nature and Glory of the Gospel*, in *Works*, II, 344.

172. Bellamy, *Election Sermon*, in *Works*, I, 590-596.

173. Davies, "The Mediatorial Kingdom and Glories of Jesus Christ," *Sermons*, I, 194.

174. Bellamy, *Millennium*, in *Works*, I, 459-460.

175. Peters, *General History of Connecticut*, pp. 396-397.

176. Quoted, Morgan, *Stamp Act Crisis*, p. 234.

177. Peters, *General History of Connecticut*, p. 347n.

178. Bellamy, *Works*, I, xl.

179. Izrahiah Wetmore, *A Sermon, Preached before the Honorable Assembly . . . on the Day of Their Anniversary Election, May 13th, 1773* ([Hartford, 1773]), pp. 19-21.

180. Edwards, *Religious Affections*, pp. 352-353.

181. Peters, *General History of Connecticut*, pp. 416-417.

182. *Ibid.*, p. 417.

183. Sherwood, *Church's Flight into the Wilderness*, p. 49.

184. [Timothy Dwight], *A Sermon, Preached at Stamford . . . upon the General Thanksgiving, December 18th, 1777* (Hartford, 1778), pp. 15-16.

185. Bellamy, *Works*, I, xlii.

186. Andrew Croswell, *Free Justification thro' Christ's Redemption . . . in Which the New Gospel Contained in the Writings of Messrs Bellamy and Cuming . . . is Weigh'd in the Ballance* (Boston, 1765), p. 14.

187. Reinhold Niebuhr, *An Interpretation of Christian Ethics . . . with a New Preface by the Author* (New York, 1956), pp. 154-155.

188. Edwards, *End in Creation*, in *Works*, I, 101.

VII. THE HAPPY EFFECTS OF UNION

1. William Gordon, *The History of the Rise, Progress, and Establishment of the Independence of the United States of America* (4 vols., London, 1788), I, 143-145; Charles W. Baird, "Civil Status of the Presbyterians in the Province of New York," *Magazine of American History*, III (1879), 617.

2. Emerson, *1766 Thanksgiving Sermon*, pp. 11-12.

3. Stillman, *Good News,* p. 4.

4. Gewehr, *Great Awakening in Virginia,* p. 110; Backus, *History of New England,* II, 198-199.

5. *A Discourse, Addressed to the Sons of Liberty, at a Solemn Assembly, near Liberty-Tree, in Providence, February 14, 1766* (Providence, [1766]), pp. 5-6.

6. For example, Daniel Humphreys, *A Plain Attempt to Hold up to View the Ancient Gospel* (Portsmouth, N.H., 1800) and *Recent Proofs of a Defection from the Christian Religion . . . and Remarks on Several Late Popular Publications; Certain Heathenish Practices, Sentiments and Effusions* (Portsmouth, N.H., 1802).

7. Edmund Morgan, "The American Revolution Considered as an Intellectual Movement," in Arthur M. Schlesinger, Jr. and Morton White, eds., *Paths of American Thought* (Boston, 1963), pp. 19-20.

8. Jedidiah Mills, *An Inquiry Concerning the State of the Unregenerate under the Gospel; . . . Containing Remarks on . . . the Rev'd Mr. Samuel Hopkins's Late Answer to Doctor Mayhew's Sermon on Striving to Enter in at the Strait Gate* (New Haven, 1767), pp. ii, vii, 67, 121-124.

9. Backus, *Fish Caught,* Preface, p. [iii].

10. James Cogswell, *A Sermon, Preached before the General Assembly . . . on the Day of Their Anniversary Election, May 9th, 1771* (New London, 1771), pp. 43-44.

11. Boucher, *View,* Preface, p. [50].

12. Emerson, *1766 Thanksgiving Sermon,* pp. 15-16.

13. Ebenezer Cleaveland, *The Abounding Grace of God Towards Notorious Sinners, Illustrated in a Sermon, upon the Conversion and Call of Matthew the Publican . . . Preached . . . July 31, 1774* (Salem, 1775).

14. Oliver, *Origin and Progress,* p. 104.

15. Quoted, Edward Frank Humphrey, *Nationalism and Religion in America, 1774-1789* (Boston, 1924), p. 20.

16. [John Murray, *et al.*], *Bath Kol, a Voice from the Wilderness* (Boston, 1783), *passim.*

17. Sprague, *Annals,* I, 566.

18. Eleazar Wheelock, quoted, Gaustad, *Great Awakening,* p. 128.

19. Cleaveland, *Short and Plain Narrative,* p. 64.

20. Quoted, Winslow, *Meetinghouse-Hill,* p. 292.

21. Peters, *General History of Connecticut,* p. 338; Patten, *Stamp Act Thanksgiving,* p. 17; Emerson, *1766 Thanksgiving Sermon,* pp. 30-31, 14.

22. David Jones, *Defensive War in a Just Cause Sinless. A Sermon, Preached on the Day of the Continental Fast, at Tredyffryn, in Chester County* (Philadelphia, 1775), p. 16; Dan Foster, *A Short Essay on Civil Government. The Substance of Six Sermons, in Windsor, October 1774* (Hartford, 1775), p. 71.

23. William Stearns, *A View of the Controversy Subsisting between Great-Britain and the American Colonies. A Sermon, Preached . . . May 11, 1775* (Watertown, 1775), p. 20.

24. Joseph Galloway, *Historical and Political Reflections on the Rise and Progress of the American Rebellion* (London, 1780), p. 20.

25. *Novanglus and Massachusettensis; or, Political Essays, Published in the Years 1774 and 1775* (Boston, 1819), p. 163.

26. Quoted, Arthur M. Schlesinger, *The Colonial Merchants and the American Revolution, 1763-1776* (New York, 1918), p. 380n.

27. *The Papers of Thomas Jefferson.* Volume I. 1760-1766 (Princeton, 1950), Appendix II, "Bradshaw's Epitaph: The Source," pp. 677-679.

28. Peters, *General History of Connecticut*, p. 340.

29. Wesley Frank Craven, *The Legend of the Founding Fathers* (New York, 1956), pp. 23-50.

30. Turner, *A Sermon, Preached at Plymouth, December 22d, 1773 . . . in Commemoration of the Landing of the Fathers There. A.D. 1620* (Boston, 1774), pp. 15-16; cf. Turner, *A Sermon Preached . . . May 26th, 1773. Being the Anniversary for the Election* (Boston, 1773), p. 37.

31. S. Adams, *Writings*, II, 232.

32. Article signed "A Puritan," *Boston Gazette*, April 4, 1768, *ibid.*, I, 201.

33. Patten, *Stamp Act Thanksgiving*, p. 37; O. Hart, *America's Remembrancer*, p. 4.

34. Andrew Croswell, *Observations on Several Passages in a Sermon Preached by William Warburton, Lord Bishop of Gloucester* (Boston, 1768), p. 21.

35. Johnson to Archbishop Secker (of Canterbury), September 20, 1764, *Writings*, I, 346.

36. "Hampshire Address," September 10, 1734, Perry, *Historical Collections, Massachusetts*, pp. 299-302.

37. Adams, *Works*, X, 288; Arthur Lyon Cross, *The Anglican Episcopate and the American Colonies* (New York, 1902), p. 140.

38. Mayhew, *Remarks on an Anonymous Tract*, Title page.

39. Jonathan Mayhew, *Observations on the Charter and Conduct of the Society for the Propagation of the Gospel in Foreign Parts* (Boston, 1763), p. 103; Charles Chauncy, *A Letter to a Friend, Containing Remarks on a Sermon Preached, by the Right Reverend Father in God, John Lord Bishop of Llandaff* (Boston, 1767), p. 51.

40. Sprague, *Annals*, VIII, 23; I, 375-376, 461-462; Mayhew, *1754 Election Sermon*, p. 33n; Chauncy, *Death of Mayhew*, p. 27.

41. Mayhew, *Observations on the Charter*, p. 47.

42. *Ibid.*

43. Charles Chauncy, *The Appeal to the Public Answered, in Behalf of the Non-Episcopal Churches of America* (Boston, 1768), p. 201.

44. Mayhew, *Remarks on an Anonymous Tract*, pp. 62-64.

45. Ashbel Woodbridge, *A Sermon Delivered before the General Assembly . . . May 14th, 1752* (New London, 1753), p. 7.

46. *The Sentiments and Resolution of an Association of Ministers (Convened at Weymouth, Jan. 15th. 1744,5) Concerning the Reverend Mr. George Whitefield* (Boston, 1745), p. 7; *A Vindication of the Reverend Mr. George Whitefield . . . By a Lover of Good Men* (Boston, 1745), p. 15.

47. Mayhew, *Remarks on an Anonymous Tract*, p. 77.

48. Chauncy, *Death of Mayhew*, p. 27; Browne, *Remarks on Dr. Mayhew's Reflections*, p. 24; Charles Chauncy, *A Reply to Dr. Chandler's Appeal Defended* (Boston, 1770), Introduction, p. vi.

49. [Noah Welles], *The Real Advantages which Ministers and People May Enjoy, Especially in the Colonies, by Conforming to the Church of England . . . in a Letter to a Young Gentleman* (n.p., 1762), pp. 5-6.

50. Thomas Bradbury Chandler to Samuel Johnson, February 26, 1753, Johnson, *Writings*, I, 166.

51. Boucher, *View*, pp. 148, 221.

52. J. Adams, *Works*, X, 185.

53. F. L. Hawks and W. S. Perry, eds., *Documentary History of the Protestant Episcopal Church . . . Connecticut* (New York, 1863-1864), II, 193.

54. Boucher, *View*, pp. 100-103.

55. Quoted, Cross, *Anglican Episcopate*, p. 200.

56. Croswell, *Answer to Garden*, p. 59.

57. Dickinson, "Remarks on a Discourse of Dr. Waterland's," with *Regeneration*, p. 65.

58. Croswell, *Observations on Sermon by Gloucester*, p. 14.

59. Samuel Langdon, *Government Corrupted by Vice*, in Thornton, *Pulpit of Revolution*, p. 242.

60. James Wetmore, "A Prefatory Address to the Gentlemen of America," in Edward Weston, *The Englishman Directed in the Choice of his Religion. Reprinted for the Use of English Americans* (Boston, 1748), p. [5]; Wetmore, *A Letter Occasioned by Mr. Dickinson's Remarks upon Dr. Waterland's Discourse of Regeneration* (New York, 1744), p. 3.

61. *Whitefield's Journals*, p. 389.

62. Quoted, Miller, *Origins of Revolution*, p. 190.

63. Quoted, Sprague, *Annals*, III, 193-194.

64. Croswell, *Observations on Sermon by Gloucester*, p. 8.

65. Wheelock, *Liberty of Conscience*, p. 28.

66. Allen, *American Alarm*, p. 4.

67. Cross, *Anglican Episcopate*, p. 140.

68. Chauncy, *Appeal to the Public Answered*, p. 202.

69. J. Adams, *Works*, X, 288.

70. Chauncy, *Appeal to the Public Answered*, p. 202.

71. *Ibid.*, p. 151.

72. Chauncy, *Death of Mayhew*, p. 29; Mayhew, *A Defence of the Observations of the Charter and Conduct of the Society* (Boston, 1763), p. 60.

73. Mayhew, *1754 Election Sermon*, p. 10.

74. Letter to Draper, Oct. 14, 1773, in Backus, *History of New England*, II, 179.

75. *Ibid.*, pp. 197ff.

76. Backus, *Fish Caught*, Preface, p. viii.

77. Stiles, *Christian Union*, p. 54.

78. *Ibid.*, pp. 30, 43-45, 50.

79. Johnson, *Writings*, III, 240-241.

80. Stiles, *Christian Union*, p. 97.

81. Johnson, *Writings*, I, 191.

82. Foxcroft, Preface, Dickinson, *Second Vindication of God's Sovereign Free Grace*, in Dickinson, *Familiar Letters*, Preface, p. iv.

83. *Christian History for 1743*, p. 3.

84. William H. Foote, *Sketches of Virginia* (2 vols., Philadelphia, 1850-1855), I, 257.

85. James Wetmore, *A Vindication of the Professors of the Church of England in Connecticut. Against the Invectives Contained in a Sermon ... by Mr. Noah Hobart* (Boston, 1747), p. 34.

86. Moses Dickinson, *An Inquiry into the Consequences both of Calvinistic and Arminian Principles* (Boston, 1750), p. 39.

87. Bridenbaugh, *Mitre and Sceptre*, p. 114.

88. *Ibid.*

89. Peters, *General History of Connecticut*, pp. 336-337; Humphrey, *Nationalism and Religion*, p. 71.

90. Trinterud, *Forming of American Tradition*, pp. 221-225.

91. Whitaker, *Funeral Sermon on Whitefield*, pp. 27, 33.

92. A. Hutchinson, *Reply to Remarks of Tucker,* p. 52; James Chandler, sermon delivered June 23, 1767, quoted, Tucker, *Brief Account,* pp. 4-5.

93. Backus, *History of New England,* II, 239.

94. Cleaveland, *Short and Plain Narrative,* p. 84.

95. Parsons, *Communion of Faith,* pp. 5-10.

96. Austin, *Voice of God,* p. 90.

97. Green, *Inquiry into Constitution,* p. vii.

98. Backus, *Fish Caught,* pp. 65n-66n; *True Faith,* p. 93.

99. Hutchinson, *Valor for Truth,* pp. 6-7; Leavenworth, *Charity Illustrated,* pp. 31-32.

100. Buell, *Spiritual Knowledge,* p. 50.

101. Backus, *True Faith,* p. 93.

102. Tucker, *Remarks on a Discourse of Parsons,* p. 17; Backus, *Appeal to the Public,* p. 30.

103. Parsons, "The Blessedness of Christian Liberality," *Sixty Sermons,* II, 620.

104. Boucher, "Schisms and Sects," *View,* p. 46; "On Fundamental Principles," *ibid.,* p. 309.

105. Quoted, Labaree, *Conservatism,* p. 63; Charles Woodmason, *The Carolina Backcountry on the Eve of the Revolution* (Chapel Hill, 1953); George Sims, "An Address to the People of Granville County," Boyd, *Eighteenth Century Tracts,* p. 189; Hermon Husband, *A Fan for Fanning, and a Touch-Stone for Tryon* (Boston, 1771), in Boyd, *ibid.,* p. 343.

106. Chauncy, *Christian Love,* p. 21.

107. [Charles Chauncy], *A Letter to a Friend . . . Giving a Concise, but Just, Representation of the Hardships and Sufferings the Town of Boston is Exposed to . . . by T.W. a Bostonian* (Boston, 1774), p. 9.

108. Howard, *Sermon on Brotherly Love,* p. 16.

109. Chauncy, *Letter to Friend,* pp. 3-4.

110. Gad Hitchcock, *A Sermon Preached at Plymouth, December 22nd, 1774* (Boston, 1775), p. 32.

111. Smith, "Sermon XIV. On the Present Situation of American Affairs; Preached in Christ-Church, June 23, 1775," *Works,* II, 276.

112. Smith, "Philosophical Meditation," *Works,* I (pt. II), 161.

113. Mayhew, *Death of Sewall,* p. 46.

114. Leavenworth, *Charity Illustrated,* pp. 30-31; N. Niles, *Perfection of God,* pp. 15-16.

115. [Jacob Duché], *Caspipina's Letters; Containing observations on a variety of subjects, literary, moral, and religious. Written by a Gentleman who resided some Time in Philadelphia* (2 vols., Bath, England, 1777), I, 119-120; II, 60-61.

116. *Ibid.,* I, 90.

117. John Woolman, *The Journal, with Other Writings,* Vida D. Scudder, ed. (New York, 1922), p. 29.

118. N. Niles, *Perfection of God,* p. 16.

119. Peters, *General History of Connecticut,* pp. 396-397.

120. Chauncy to Richard Prince, May 30, 1774, in *Proceedings of the Massachusetts Historical Society,* 2nd ser. vol. XVII (Boston, 1903), 267.

121. Quoted, Miller, *Origins of Revolution,* p. 376.

122. Bailyn, *Pamphlets,* p. x.

123. Throop, *1766 Thanksgiving Sermon,* p. 11; Turner, *1773 Election Sermon,* p. 39.

124. J. J. Zubly, *The Law of Liberty. A Sermon on American Affairs, Preached at the Opening of the Provincial Congress of Georgia, 1775,* in Moore, *Patriot Preachers,* pp. 117-121.

125. Barnabas Binney, *An Oration Delivered at the Late Public Commencement at Rhode-Island College in Providence, September 1774* (Boston, 1774), p. 39.

126. Israel Holly, *God Brings about His Holy and Wise Purpose or Decree . . . a Sermon, Preached at Suffield, December 27, 1773* (Hartford, 1774), p. 21.

127. Joseph Perry, *A Sermon, Preached before the General Assembly . . . on the Day of Their Anniversary Election, May 11, 1775* (Hartford, 1775), p. 9.

128. Quoted, Cross, *Anglican Episcopate,* pp. 199-200.

129. [William Henry Drayton], *A Letter from Freeman of South-Carolina, to the Deputies of North-America* (Charleston, 1774), p. 7.

130. "Letter from Hatfield. To Mr. Sam'l Adams," *Collections of the Massachusetts Historical Society,* 4th ser., vol. IV (Boston, 1858), 243; cf. Joseph Lyman, *A Sermon Preached at Hatfield December 15th, 1774* (Boston, 1775).

131. Parsons, *Freedom from Civil and Ecclesiastical Slavery,* pp. 7-8.

132. *Ibid.,* p. 15.

133. Backus, *Appeal to the Public,* p. 54.

134. Backus, *History of New England,* II, 198-199.

135. Elisha Rich, *The Number of the Beast Found Out by Spiritual Arithmetic* (Chelmsford, Mass., 1775), p. 2.

136. Elisha Rich, *A Sermon on Ecclesiastical Liberty. Preached Soon after the Civil War . . . in the Year 1775* (Concord, 1776); *A Poem on the Bloody Engagement That Was Fought on Bunker's Hill . . . Together with Some Remarks on the Cruelty and Barbarity of the British Troops* ([Chelmsford, Mass., 1775]).

137. Quoted, Baldwin, *New England Clergy,* p. 80n.

138. John Murray, *An Appeal to the Impartial Public, in Behalf of the Oppressed* (Portsmouth, N.H., 1768), pp. 36-37.

139. Backus, *History of New England,* II, 199.

140. William Tennent [III], "Speech on the Dissenting Petition, Delivered in the House of Assembly, Charleston, South-Carolina, Jan. 11, 1777," in David Ramsay, *The History of the Independent or Congregational Church in Charleston* (Philadelphia, 1815), p. 71.

141. Avery, *Lord to be Praised,* p. 47.

142. Sherwood, *Church's Flight into the Wilderness,* p. 16.

143. Gordon, *Discourse, Dec. 15, 1774,* in Thornton, *Pulpit of Revolution,* p. 216n.

144. Smith, "An Eulogium," *Four Dissertations,* p. 10.

145. Garden, *The Doctrine of Justification According to the Scriptures . . . In a Letter to Mr. A. Croswell of Groton, in New-England* (Charleston, 1742), p. 66.

146. *Querists III,* p. 4.

147. Stiles, *Looking-Glass,* p. 15.

148. Adams, *Writings,* I, 202.

149. *The Works of Alexander Hamilton,* H. C. Lodge, ed. (10 vols., New York, 1904), I, 196.

150. Henry Cumings, *A Sermon, Preached in Billerica, on the 23d of November, 1775 . . . a Public Thanksgiving* (Worcester, 1775), p. 12n.

151. [Charles Inglis], *The Duty of Honouring the King, Explained and Recommended* (New York, 1780), p. 26.

152. S. Finley, *The Curse of Meroz*, p. 25.

153. Murray, *Nehemiah*, p. 50.

154. Stanley Griswold, *Infidelity, Not the Only Enemy of Christianity, or, Hypocrisy and Antichrist Exposed* (New Haven, 1803), p. 20.

155. Hart, *Liberty Described and Recommended; in a Sermon, Preached to the Corporation of Freemen in Farmington . . . September 20, 1774* (Hartford, 1775), p. 14.

156. Sherwood, *Church's Flight into the Wilderness*, p. 49.

157. Ebenezer Baldwin, *The Duty of Rejoicing under Calamities and Afflictions, Considered and Improved in a Sermon, Preached at Danbury, November 16, 1775* (New York, 1776), p. 38.

158. Foster, *True Fortitude Delineated*, p. 17.

159. R. Smith, *Obligations of Confederate States*, p. 27n.

160. Avery, *Lord to be Praised*, pp. 45-46.

161. Duffield, *Sermon Preached December 11th, 1783*, in Moore, *Patriot Preachers*, pp. 360-361. Cf. David Tappan, *A Discourse Delivered at the Third Parish in Newbury . . . Occasioned by the Ratification of a Treaty of Peace* (Salem, [1783]), pp. 12-13.

162. Backus, *Government and Liberty Described; and Ecclesiastical Tyranny Exposed* (Boston, [1778]), pp. 3-4.

163. John Devotion, *The Duty and Interest of a People to Sanctify the Lord of Hosts. A Sermon, Preached before the General Assembly* (Hartford, 1777), p. 31n.

164. Binney, *Oration Delivered at Commencement*, p. 39.

165. James Madison, *An Oration in commemoration of the founders of William and Mary College, August 15, 1772*, in *Bulletin of the College of William and Mary in Virginia*, vol. 31, no. 7 (November 1937).

166. Ezra Stiles, *The United States Elevated to Glory and Honor. A Sermon, Preached . . . at the Anniversary Election, May 8th, 1783*, in Thornton, *Pulpit of Revolution*, p. 471.

167. Samuel Stillman, *A Sermon Preached before the Honorable Council . . . May 26th, 1779*, in Moore, *Patriot Preachers*, p. 281.

168. Hopkins, *System of Doctrines*, II (separate pagination), 64n.

169. David Austin, *The National "Barley Cake," or the "Rock of Offence" into a "Glorious Holy Mountain,"* in *Discourses and Letters* (Washington, 1802), p. 24; Stanley Griswold, "How Far Men May Set up Authority over Each Other's Opinions. A discourse Delivered at New Milford October 5th and 12th 1800," Griswold Manuscripts; Griswold, *Truth Its Own Test and God Its only Judge . . . A Discourse, Delivered at New-Milford, October 12th, 1800* (Bridgeport, 1800), esp. p. 19; *Overcoming Evil with Good. A Sermon, Delivered at Wallingford, Connecticut, March 11, 1801, before a Numerous Collection of the Friends . . . of Thomas Jefferson, President, and of Aaron Burr, Vice-President, of the United States* (Hartford, 1801), p. 9; *The Good Land We Live in. A Sermon, Delivered at Suffield (Connecticut) . . . July 7th, 1802* (Suffield, 1802), p. 18.

170. Green, *Inquiry into the Constitution*, p. vi.

171. Throop, *1766 Thanksgiving Sermon*, p. 16.

172. Sherwood, *A Sermon, Containing, Scriptural Instructions to Civil Rulers, and All Free-born Subjects . . . Delivered on the Public Fast, August 31, 1774* (New Haven, n.d.), p. 41.

173. Samuel Lockwood, *Civil Rulers an Ordinance of God, for Good to*

Mankind. A Sermon, Preached before the General Assembly (New London, 1774), p. 36.

174. Cogswell, *1771 Election Sermon,* pp. 43-44.

175. Lockwood, *Civil Rulers,* p. 36; J. Allen, *American Alarm,* p. 40.

176. Tennent, *Happiness of Rewarding,* p. 28.

177. Sherwood, *Scriptural Instructions,* pp. 39-41.

178. Tennent, *Right Use of Passions,* p. 21; *Blessedness of Peace-Makers,* p. 36.

179. Sherwood, *Scriptural Instructions,* preface, p. ix.

180. Sherwood, *Church's Flight into the Wilderness,* Introduction.

181. Oliver Noble, *Some Strictures upon the Sacred Story Recorded in the Book of Esther* (Newburyport, 1775), p. 18n.

182. Turner, *1773 Plymouth Sermon,* p. 42.

183. Fish, *Joy and Gladness,* pp. 9-10.

184. James Spear Loring, *The Hundred Boston Orators* (Boston, 1852), p. 23.

185. [Joseph Allen?], *An Oration on the Beauties of Liberty, or the Essential Rights of the Americans. Delivered at the Second Baptist-Church in Boston. Upon the Last Annual Thanksgiving, Dec. 3d, 1772* (3rd ed., Boston, 1773), pp. 30-31; *American Alarm,* pp. 28-29.

186. David Ramsay, *The History of the American Revolution* (2 vols., London, 1791), I, 145-146.

187. West, *1776 Election Sermon,* in Thornton, *Pulpit of Revolution,* p. 303.

188. Hitchcock, *1774 Plymouth Sermon,* p. 42.

189. John Lathrop, *A Discourse Preached, December 15th, 1774. Being the Day Recommended by the Provincial Congress* (Boston, 1775), p. 40.

190. Williams, *Love of Our Country,* p. 13.

191. Lathrop, *1774 Thanksgiving Sermon,* p. 40.

192. Perry, *1775 Election Sermon,* pp. 10-11.

193. Isaac Mansfield, *A Sermon, Preached in the Camp at Roxbury, November 23, 1775* (Boston, 1776), p. 21; John Hurt, *The Love of Country. A Sermon Preached before the Virginia Troops in New Jersey, 1777,* in Moore, *Patriot Preachers,* p. 146.

194. Murray, *Nehemiah,* p. 23.

195. Enoch Huntington, *The Happy Effects of Union, and the Fatal Tendency of Divisions, Shown in a Sermon Preached . . . April 8, 1776* (Hartford, 1776), p. 16.

196. Samuel Stanhope Smith, *The Divine Goodness to the United States of America. A Discourse . . . Delivered in the Third Presbyterian Church in Philadelphia, on Thursday the 19th of February, 1795* (Philadelphia, 1795), p. 12.

197. Smith, "An Oration, in Memory of General Montgomery," *Works,* I (pt. II), 13.

198. Arthur M. Schlesinger, *Prelude to Independence. The Newspaper War on Britain 1764-1776* (New York, 1958), p. 31.

199. Joseph Montgomery, *A Sermon, Preached at Christiana Bridge and Newcastle, the 20th of July 1775* (Philadelphia, 1775), pp. 7, 9.

200. John Carmichael, *Self-Defensive War,* pp. 28-29.

201. Parsons, *To Live is Christ,* p. 30.

202. Carmichael, *Self-Defensive War,* p. 29.

203. Ramsay, *American Revolution,* I, 97, 340.

204. L. Hart, *Liberty Described*, p. 11.

205. *Discourse to the Sons of Liberty*, p. 6.

206. Emerson, *1766 Thanksgiving Sermon*, p. 28.

207. Whitaker, *Funeral Sermon on Whitefield*, p. 33.

208. N. Niles, *Two Discourses on Liberty*, p. 58.

209. Andrew Lee, *Sin Destructive of Temporal and Eternal Happiness: and Repentance, Trust in God, and a Vigorous, Harmonious, and Persevering Opposition, the Duty of a People* (Norwich, Conn., 1776), p. 32.

210. Hurt, *Love of Country*, in Moore, Patriot Preachers, p. 152.

211. Lee, *Sin Destructive of Happiness*, Preface, p. 4; *ibid.*, p. 32.

212. Whitaker, *Antidote Against Toryism*, in Moore, *Patriot Preachers*, p. 214.

213. Benjamin Hichborn to John Adams, April 20, 1776, quoted, Hazelton, *Declaration of Independence*, p. 52.

214. *The Selected Works of Tom Paine*, Howard Fast, ed. (New York, 1945), p. 135.

215. William Gordon, *The Separation of the Jewish Tribes*, in Moore, *Patriot Preachers*, p. 178.

216. Quoted, Hazleton, *Declaration of Independence*, p. 52.

217. Hawley to Gerry, in Peter Force, comp., *American Archives*, 4th ser., vol. IV (Washington, 1843), 1219; Hazleton, *Declaration of Independence*, p. 50.

218. Allen, *Beauties of Liberty*, p. 63; *American Alarm*, p. 28.

219. Hawley to Gerry, July 17, 1776, in Hazleton, *Declaration of Independence*, p. 224.

220. Noble, *Strictures on Esther*, p. 5.

221. Sherwood, *Scriptural Instructions*, pp. 40-41.

222. Ross, *Union of Colonies Recommended*, pp. 20-21.

223. Murray, *Nehemiah*, p. 55.

224. Abraham Keteltas, *God Arising and Pleading His People's Cayse . . . a Sermon Preached October 5th, 1777 . . . in the Presbyterian Church in Newbury-Port* (Newburyport, 1777), p. 19.

225. Gordon, *Separation of Jewish Tribes*, in Moore, *Patriot Preachers*, pp. 183-184.

226. Sherwood, *Church's Flight into the Wilderness*, pp. 48-50.

227. *Boston Chronicle*, Feb. 27, March 2, 1769.

228. David Barrow, *Circular Letter* (Norfolk, Va., [1798]), p. 12.

229. Ebenezer Wheelock, *An Oration, Delivered at Middlebury . . . The Republican Trumpet, like That of the Gospel, Sounds Peace and Goodwill to Man* (Bennington, Vt., 1801), p. 12.

230. Duffield, *Sermon on Restoration of Peace*, in Moore, *Patriot Preachers*, pp. 350-351.

231. Parsons, *Freedom from Civil and Ecclesiastical Slavery*, p. 16.

232. West, *1776 Election Sermon*, in Thornton, *Pulpit of Revolution*, pp. 316-317; cf. West, *An Anniversary Sermon, Preached at Plymouth, December 22d, 1777* (Boston, 1778).

233. Quoted, Birdsall, "Thomas Allen," p. 153.

VIII. TRUST IN GOD

1. Tucker, *Ministers Fellow-Workers*, p. 17.
2. Cumings, *1766 Thanksgiving Sermon*, p. 22.
3. Bridge, *1767 Election Sermon*, p. 4.
4. *Ibid.*, pp. 15, 45.
5. Miller, *Origins of Revolution*, p. 238.
6. Shute, *1768 Election Sermon*, p. 56.
7. *Ibid.*, pp. 55, 63-64.
8. *Ibid.*, p. 46.
9. Ebenezer Gay, *The Devotions of God's People Adjusted to the Dispensations of His Providence. A Sermon Preached in the First Parish of Hingham, December 6, 1770* (Boston, 1771), p. 22.
10. Tucker, *1771 Election Sermon*, p. 4.
11. *Ibid.*, p. 56.
12. *Ibid.*, pp. 34-35.
13. Charles Chauncy, *Trust in God, the Duty of a People in a Day of Trouble. A Sermon Preached, May 30th, 1770. At the Request of a Great Number of Gentlemen, Friends to the Liberties of North-America* (Boston, 1770), p. 24.
14. *Ibid.*, p. 34.
15. Quoted, Miller, *Origins of Revolution*, p. 295.
16. R. S. Longeley, "Mob Activities in Revolutionary Massachusetts," *New England Quarterly*, VI (1933), 98-130.
17. Eli Forbes, *The Dignity and Importance of the Military Character Illustrated. A Sermon Preached to the Ancient and Honorable Artillery Company, in Boston, New-England, June 3d, 1771* (Boston, 1771), p. i.
18. Sprague, *Annals*, I, 493-495.
19. S. Adams, *Writings*, II, 349.
20. Baldwin, *New England Clergy*, p. 119n.
21. Simeon Howard, *A Sermon Preached to the Ancient and Honorable Artillery Company . . . June 7th, 1773* (Boston, 1773), p. 32.
22. Tucker, *1771 Election Sermon*, p. 53.
23. *Ibid.*, pp. 56-57.
24. John Lathrop, *Innocent Blood Crying to God from the Streets of Boston. A Sermon Occasioned by the Horrid Murder . . . on the Fifth of March, 1770, and Preached the Lord's-Day Following* (Boston, 1771), pp. 19-20.
25. *Ibid.*, p. 7.
26. Lathrop, *A Discourse, Preached on March the Fifth, 1778* (Boston, 1778), p. 2.
27. James Lovell, *Oration, Delivered at Boston, April 2, 1771*, in *Orations, Delivered at the Request of the Inhabitants of the Town of Boston, to Commemorate the Evening of the Fifth of March, 1770* (2nd ed., Boston, 1807), p. 3.
28. S. Adams, *Writings*, II, 104.
29. Joseph Warren, *Oration, Delivered at Boston, March 6, 1775*, in *Orations to Commemorate the Fifth of March*, p. 63.
30. Hutchinson, *History of Massachusetts, 1750-1774*, p. 335.
31. J. Parsons, *Freedom from Civil and Ecclesiastical Slavery*, p. 16.
32. Tucker, *Remarks on a Discourse of Parsons*, p. 3.
33. Gad Hitchcock, *A Sermon Preached . . . May 25th, 1774. Being the Anniversary of the Election* (Boston, 1774), p. 55.

34. Chauncy, *Enthusiasm Describ'd*, p. 15.

35. Williams, *Love of Our Country*, p. 14.

36. Miller, "From the Covenant to the Revival," in Smith and Jamison, *Shaping of American Religion*, pp. 322-344.

37. John Browne, *A Discourse Delivered on the Day of the Annual Provincial Thanksgiving, December 6, 1770* (Boston, 1771), p. 13; Thaddeus Maccarty, *Praise to God, a Duty of Continual Obligation. A Sermon, Preached at Worcester, Thursday, November 23rd, 1775* (Worcester, [1776]), p. 16.

38. Zubly, *The Stamp-Act Repealed: a Sermon, Preached in the Meeting at Savannah in Georgia, June 25th, 1766* (Savannah, 1766), p. 27.

39. [Stephen Johnson], *Some Important Observations, Occasioned by, and Adapted to, the Publick Fast, Ordered by Authority, December 18, A.D. 1765* (Newport, R.I., 1766), p. 24; Maccarty, *Praise to God*, p. 23.

40. Noble, *Strictures on Esther*, p. 19.

41. Nathaniel Appleton, *The Right Method of Addressing the Divine Majesty in Prayer . . . Two Discourses on April 5, 1770. Being the Day of General Fasting and Prayer* (Boston, 1770), p. 55.

42. Smith, "Sermon V," *Works*, II, 119.

43. Gay, *Devotions of God's People*, p. 16.

44. Smith, "Sermon V," *Works*, II, 119.

45. Lathrop, *A Sermon Preached to the Ancient and Honorable Artillery Company, in Boston . . . June 6th, 1774* (Boston, 1774), p. 28n.

46. Tennent, *Address, Occasioned by Late Invasion of Liberties*, p. 11.

47. *Ibid.*, p. 15.

48. Lathrop, *A Discourse Preached, December 15th, 1774. Being the Day Recommended by the Provincial Congress* (Boston, 1775), pp. 37-39.

49. Smith, "Sermon XIV. On the Present Situation of American Affairs," *Works*, II, 272.

50. Lathrop, *1774 Thanksgiving Sermon*, p. 25.

51. Lathrop, *1774 Artillery Sermon*, pp. 23-24.

52. Lathrop, *1774 Thanksgiving Sermon*, p. 36.

53. *Ibid.*

54. Smith, "Sermon XIV," *Works*, II, 271.

55. Williams, *Love of Our Country*, pp. 23-25.

56. *Ibid.*, p. 26.

57. Sprague, *Annals*, I, 595-597.

58. Smith, *An Oration, Delivered, January 22, 1773, before the Patron, Vice-Presidents and Members of the American Philosophical Society* (Philadelphia, 1773), pp. 5-6.

59. Smith, "Sermon XIV," *Works*, II, 280, 283.

60. *Ibid.*, p. 280.

61. Smith, "Candidus," (pseud.), *Plain Truth: Addressed to the Inhabitants of America. Containing Remarks on a Late Pamphlet, Intitled Common Sense* (Philadelphia, 1776), Introduction. (The crucial sections of the Cato letters are shown in the Appendix to this tract.)

62. Smith, *An Oration in Memory of General Montgomery, and of the Officers and Soldiers,* in *Works*, I (pt. II), 14.

63. Chauncy, *Trust in God*, p. 22.

64. *Ibid.*, p. 13.

65. *Ibid.*, pp. 28-29.

66. *Ibid.*, p. 24.

67. Browne, *1770 Thanksgiving Discourse*, p. 13.

68. Gay, *Devotions of God's People*, pp. 16-21.

69. Lathrop, *1774 Thanksgiving Sermon*, p. 39.

70. Eliot, *1765 Election Sermon*, pp. 44-46.

71. Cumings, *1766 Thanksgiving Sermon*, p. 11.

72. Cumings, *1775 Thanksgiving Sermon*, pp. 26-27.

73. Mayhew, *Christian Sobriety*, p. 152.

74. Chauncy, *Letter to a Friend*, p. 29.

75. Jones, *Defensive War*, p. 25.

76. Tennent, *Address, Occasioned by Late Invasion of Liberties*, p. 11.

77. Charles Turner, *1773 Election Sermon*, p. 36.

78. M. Parsons, *1772 Election Sermon*, p. 19.

79. Hitchcock, *1774 Election Sermon*, p. 47.

80. Sprague, *Annals*, VIII, 30.

81. Hitchcock, *1774 Election Sermon*, p. 47.

82. *Ibid.*

83. Tucker, *1771 Election Sermon*, p. 37.

84. Shute, *1768 Election Sermon*, p. 65.

85. Hitchcock, *1774 Plymouth Sermon*, p. 32.

86. Turner, *1773 Plymouth Sermon*, p. 38.

87. Hitchcock, *1774 Plymouth Sermon*, p. 11.

88. *Ibid.*, p. 41.

89. Hitchcock, *1774 Plymouth Sermon*, p. 36; West, *1776 Election Sermon*, in Thornton, *Pulpit of Revolution*, p. 311.

90. West, *1777 Plymouth Sermon*, pp. 46-48.

91. Smith, "Sermon V. A Fast Sermon Preached . . . July 20, 1775," *Works*, II, 124.

92. Smith, *Oration before Philosophical Society*, p. 7; "Sermon V," *Works*, II, 124.

93. Williams, *Love of Our Country*, p. 22.

94. Smith, "Sermon XIV," *Works*, II, 276.

95. Smith, *Oration on Montgomery*, in *Works*, I (pt. II), 17.

96. John Adams to Abigail Adams, April 28, 1776, in Charles Francis Adams, ed., *Familiar Letters of John Adams and His Wife Abigail Adams, during the Revolution* (New York, 1876), p. 167.

97. Smith, "Sermon XIV," *Works*, II, 280.

98. Smith, *Oration on Montgomery*, in *Works*, I (pt. II), 17.

99. West, *Election Sermon*, in Thornton, *Pulpit of Revolution*, p. 267.

100. Lathrop, *1774 Artillery Sermon*, p. 28.

101. Howard, *1773 Artillery Sermon*, p. 33.

102. Smith, "Sermon XIV," *Works*, IX, 282.

103. *Ibid.*, II, 284.

104. *Ibid.*, p. 283.

105. West, *Election Sermon*, in Thornton, *Pulpit of Revolution*, pp. 297-298.

106. *Ibid.*, p. 285.

107. *Ibid.*, p. 303.

108. *Ibid.*, pp. 303-304.

109. *Ibid.*, p. 302.

110. *Ibid.*, p. 314.

111. Hitchcock, *1774 Plymouth Sermon*, p. 41.

112. John Eliot, *A Biographical Dictionary, Containing a Brief Account of*

the First Settlers, and other Eminent Characters . . . *in New-England* (Salem, 1809), p. 46.

113. Smith, "Sermon XIV," *Works*, II, 280.

114. Peter Thacher, *Oration, Delivered at Watertown, March 5, 1776*, in *Orations to Commemorate the Fifth of March*, p. 72.

115. Humphrey, *Nationalism and Religion*, p. 24.

116. Warren, *1775 Oration*, in *Orations to Commemorate the Fifth of March*, pp. 55-56.

117. Baldwin, *New England Clergy*, p. 89.

118. Sprague, *Annals*, VIII, 57-59.

119. Cumings, *1775 Thanksgiving Sermon*, pp. 11, 14.

120. Henry Cumings, *A Sermon Preached at Lexington, on the 19th of April, 1781* . . . (Boston, 1781), pp. 26-27.

121. *Ibid.*, p. 29.

122. *Ibid.*, pp. 26-29.

123. James K. Hosmer, *The Life of Thomas Hutchinson* (Boston, 1896), p. 104; E. L. Magoon, *Orators of the American Revolution* (2nd ed., New York, 1848), p. 92; Charles F. Mullett, comp., *Some Political Writings of James Otis*, The University of Missouri Studies, vol. IV, no. 3 (July 1929), esp. *The Rights of the British Colonies Asserted and Proved* (1764), p. 52.

124. "Samuel Adams," (pseud.), *An Oration, Delivered at the State-House, in Philadelphia, to a very Numerous Audience; on Thursday the 1st of August, 1776* (London, 1776), pp. 2-3.

125. Loring, *The Hundred Boston Orators*, p. 132; Benjamin Hichborn, *Oration, Delivered at Boston, March 5, 1777*, in *Orations to Commemorate the Fifth of March*, pp. 83-84.

126. Austin, *Observations by Honestus*, p. 33.

127. William B. Reed, *Life and Correspondence of Joseph Reed* (2 vols., Philadelphia, 1847), II, 39.

128. Theophilus Parsons, *Memoir of Theophilus Parsons, Chief Justice of the Supreme Judicial Court of Massachusetts* (Boston, 1859), p. 29.

129. Eliot, *Biographical Dictionary*, p. 27.

130. Howard, *1780 Election Sermon*, in Thornton, *Pulpit of Revolution*, p. 362.

131. "Essex Result," in *Memoir of Parsons*, p. 364.

132. Whiting, *Address to Berkshire*, p. 7.

133. "Essex Result," in *Memoir of Parsons*, p. 364.

134. "Protest to the Constitutional Convention of 1780," in Mary Catherine Clune, ed., "Joseph Hawley's Criticism of the Constitution of Massachusetts," *Smith College Studies in History*, III: 1 (October 1917), 49.

135. Israel Evans, *A Discourse, Delivered at Easton, on the 17th of October, 1779* (Philadelphia, 1779), p. 20.

136. Edwards, *Religious Affections*, pp. 99-100.

137. Whitaker, *Funeral Sermon on Whitefield*, p. 19.

IX. THE CURSE OF MEROZ

1. Chase, *History of Dartmouth*, pp. 326-327.

2. Samuel Bird, *The Importance of the Divine Presence with Our Host. A Sermon Delivered in New-Haven, April 27th 1759* (New Haven, 1759), p. 16; John Rodgers, quoted, Bridenbaugh, *Mitre and Sceptre*, p. 281.

3. Niles, *Two Discourses on Liberty*, pp. 23-24.

4. *Ibid.*, pp. 23-25; cf. Abraham Keteltas, *God Arising*, pp. 22-23.

5. Niles, *Two Discourses on Liberty*, pp. 24-28.

6. L. Hart, *Liberty Described*, p. 22.

7. Niles, *Two Discourses on Liberty*, pp. 26-27.

8. Edwards, *Will*, pp. 164, 364, 377.

9. N. Niles, *Two Discourses on Liberty*, p. 53.

10. Edwards, "Sermon XIII," *Works*, II, 945.

11. Edwards, *Will*, p. 272.

12. *Ibid.*, p. 358.

13. Backus, *Appeal to the Public*, p. 9.

14. Jones, *Defensive War*, p. 12.

15. Ebenezer Pemberton, *A Sermon, Preached . . . at the Ordination of Mr. David Brainerd*, in Edwards, *Works*, II, 444; Tennent, *Right Use of Passions*, p. 16.

16. Tennent, *Blessedness of Peace-Makers*, p. 32.

17. J. J. Zubly, *The Law of Liberty*, in Moore, *Patriot Preachers*, p. 117.

18. Quoted, Humphrey, *Nationalism and Religion*, p. 64.

19. Williams, *Essential Rights and Liberties*, pp. 2-3.

20. Backus, *Appeal to the Public*, p. 4.

21. L. Hart, *Liberty Described*, p. 9.

22. Backus, *Address Concerning the Bloody Controversy*, p. 5.

23. Backus, *Truth is Great, and Will Prevail* (Boston, 1781), pp. 6-7.

24. S. Johnson, *Some Important Observations*, p. 20.

25. Stephen Johnson, *Integrity and Piety the Best Principles of a Good Administration of Government, Illustrated, in a Sermon Preached . . . the Day of . . . Election* (New London, 1770), p. 20.

26. Langdon, *Government Corrupted*, in Thornton, *Pulpit of Revolution*, p. 246; Huntington, *Happy Effects of Union*, p. 25.

27. Langdon, *Government Corrupted*, in Thornton, *Pulpit of Revolution*, pp. 243-244; E. Williams, *1769 Election Sermon*, p. 12.

28. Turner, *1773 Plymouth Sermon*, pp. 15-16; cf. *1773 Election Sermon*, p. 37.

29. Turner, *1773 Plymouth Sermon*, p. 36.

30. David Rittenhouse, *An Oration, Delivered February 24, 1775, before the American Philosophical Society* (Philadelphia, 1775), p. 20.

31. [John Trumbull], *An Essay on Use and Advantages of Fine Arts. Delivered at the Public Commencement* (New Haven, [1770]), p. 12.

32. Samuel Adams, "Valerius Poplicola," *Writings*, II, 336.

33. David Brooks, *The Religion of the Revolution. A Discourse, Delivered at Derby, Conn., 1774* (Rochester, New York, 1854), pp. 9-10.

34. Chaplin, *Civil State*, p. 22.

35. Allen, *Beauties of Liberty*, pp. 41-42.

36. Eels, *Christ, the Foundation*, p. 15.

37. E. Williams, *1769 Election Sermon*, pp. 5, 12.

38. *Ibid.*, pp. 27-29, 34-35.

39. Whitaker, *Antidote Against Toryism*, in Moore, *Patriot Preachers*, p. 199.

40. Turner, *1773 Election Sermon*, p. 8.

41. L. Hart, *Liberty Described*, p. 13.

42. Trumbull, *Discourse at New Haven*, p. 33.

43. Elisha Fish, *A Discourse, Delivered . . . March, 28th, 1775* (Worcester, 1775), p. 14.

44. S. Johnson, *Some Important Observations*, pp. 26-27.

45. Hermon Husband, *An Impartial Relation of the First Rise and Cause of the Recent Differences* (1770), in Boyd, *Eighteenth Century Tracts*, pp. 312-331.

46. Chaplin, *Civil State*, p. 6.

47. Allen, *Beauties of Liberty*, p. 59.

48. Leavenworth, *Charity Illustrated*, pp. 22-23.

49. Allen, *American Alarm*, p. 21.

50. Turner, *1773 Election Sermon*, p. 19.

51. Chaplin, *Civil State*, pp. 10-11, 21-22.

52. N. Niles, *Two Discourses on Liberty*, pp. 18-19.

53. *Ibid.*, pp. 34-35.

54. For example, Allen, *Beauties of Liberty*, pp. 5ff.

55. Isaac Story, *The Love of Our Country Recommended and Enforced. In a Sermon from Psalm CXXII. 7* (Boston, 1775), p. 7.

56. Quoted, Morgan, "The American Revolution Considered as an Intellectual Movement," in Schlesinger and White, *Paths of American Thought*, p. 21.

57. Cogswell, *1771 Election Sermon*, pp. 18, 22.

58. Niles, *Two Discourses on Liberty*, p. 18n.

59. Hawley, "Address to the Minute-Men," *Magazine of American History*, XXII (1889), 493.

60. Amos Adams, *Religious Liberty an Invaluable Blessing . . . Preached at Roxbury Decr 3, 1767* (Boston, 1768), p. 53; Emerson, *1766 Thanksgiving Sermon*, pp. 30-31.

61. Judah Champion, *A Brief View of the Distresses, Hardships and Dangers Our Ancestors Encounter'd* (Hartford, 1770), Preface.

62. Timothy Hilliard, *The Duty of a People under the Oppression of Man, to Seek Deliverance from God* (Boston, 1774), p. 11.

63. Cf. Langdon, *Government Corrupted*, in Thornton, *Pulpit of Revolution*, p. 256.

64. Bellamy, *Nature and Glory of the Gospel*, in *Works*, II, 343-344.

65. Noble, *Strictures on Esther*, pp. 8, 28.

66. Oliver, "An Address to the Soldiers. For the *Massachusetts-Gazette*," in *Origin and Progress*, pp. 163-164.

67. Noble, *Strictures on Esther*, p. 28.

68. J. Adams, *Works*, IV, 14.

69. Hawley, "Broken Hints to be Communicated to the Committee of Congress for the Massachusetts," in Hezekiah Niles, ed., *Principles and Acts of the Revolution in America* (Centennial Edition, New York, 1876), p. 107.

70. Jonas Clark, *The Fate of Blood-Thirsty Oppressors, and God's Tender Care of His Distressed People. A Sermon, Preached at Lexington, April 19, 1776* (Boston, 1776), p. 27.

71. Ezra Sam[p]son, *A Sermon Preached at Roxbury-Camp, before Col. Cotton's Regiment; on the 20th of July* (Watertown, 1775), p. 19.

72. Langdon, *Government Corrupted*, in Thornton, *Pulpit of Revolution*, p. 235.

73. Whitaker, *Antidote Against Toryism*, in Moore, *Patriot Preachers*, pp. 208-209.

74. Quoted, Baldwin, *New England Clergy*, p. 157.

75. Sherwood, *Scriptural Instructions*, p. xiv; Carmichael, *Self-Defensive War*, p. 6; Lyman, *Sermon at Hatfield*, p. [5]; Josiah Stearns, *Two Sermons, Preached at Epping, in the State of New-Hampshire, January 20th, 1777* (Newburyport, 1777), p. 26.

76. Story, *Love of Our Country Recommended*, p. 10.

77. Mayhew, *A Sermon Preached at Boston . . . May 26, 1751. Occasioned by the Much-Lamented Death of His Royal Highness, Frederick, Prince of Wales* (Boston, 1751), pp. 9-10.

78. Edwards, *Religious Affections*, p. 243.

79. Judah Champion, *Christian and Civil Liberty Considered and Recommended. A Sermon . . . on the Day of . . . Election* (Hartford, 1776), p. 23.

80. Ramsay, *American Revolution*, I, 316.

81. Thacher, *1776 Oration,* in *Orations to Commemorate the Fifth of March,* pp. 71-75.

82. Cleaveland, *A Reply to Dr. Mayhew's Letter of Reproof,* p. 1.

83. Washington Irving, *Life of George Washington* (3 vols., New York, 1859), III, 177.

84. Sprague, *Annals,* I, 697n.

85. Edwards, *Works,* lxii.

86. Sprague, *Annals,* VI, 85-89.

87. *Ibid.,* III, 229-230.

88. Elijah Fitch, *A Discourse, the Substance of Which was Delivered at Hopkington, . . . Following the Precipitate Flight of the British Troops from Boston* (Boston, 1776), p. 7; Keteltas, *God Arising,* p. 47.

89. Marvin Meyers, *The Jacksonian Persuasion. Politics and Belief* (Stanford, Calif., 1957), p. 106.

90. Carmichael, *Self-Defensive War,* p. 53; Hurt, *Love of Country,* in Moore, *Patriot Preachers,* p. 152.

91. S. Finley, *Curse of Meroz,* p. 8.

92. Sherwood, *Scriptural Instructions,* p. ix.

93. Quoted, Sprague, *Annals,* III, 33.

94. Fitch, *Discourse Following Precipitate Flight,* p. 30.

95. Edwards, *True Virtue,* in *Works,* I, 123.

96. W. Stearns, *View of the Controversy,* p. 27.

97. Quoted, Baldwin, *New England Clergy,* pp. 178-179.

98. *The Papers of Thomas Jefferson,* I, 213.

99. "Speech of an Honest Farmer," in H. Niles, *Principles and Acts,* p. 222.

100. Drayton, "The Charge to the Grand Jury," in H. Niles, *Principles and Acts,* p. 221.

101. "Speech of an Honest Farmer," in H. Niles, *Principles and Acts,* p. 221.

102. Green, *Observations,* p. 24.

103. *Ibid.,* p. 13.

104. Edwards, *Will,* p. 339.

105. J. Adams, *Works,* II, 509.

106. S. Finley, *Curse of Meroz,* p. 15; Nathaniel Whitaker, *The Reward of Toryism. A Discourse on Judges V. 23 . . . Delivered at the Tabernacle in Salem, May, 1783* (Boston, 1812), p. 19.

107. Fitch, *Discourse Following Precipitate Flight,* pp. 6-7.

108. Witherspoon, "The Dominion of Providence over the Passions of Men," *Works,* III, 23n.

109. "The Millennium" (1797), *The Poems of Philip Freneau,* H. H. Clark, ed. (3 vols., Princeton, 1907), III, 147-148.

110. Jones, *Defensive War,* p. 5.

111. Edwards, *Will,* p. 160.

112. Bellamy, *True Religion Delineated,* in *Works,* I, 16.

113. Hawley, "Broken Hints," in H. Niles, *Principles and Acts,* p. 107.

114. Keteltas, *God Arising,* pp. 19-20; Murray, *Nehemiah,* pp. 17-18.

115. Murray, *Nehemiah,* p. 55; Keteltas, *God Arising,* p. 19.

116. *Ibid.,* pp. 30-31.

117. Carmichael, *Self-Defensive War,* p. 33.

118. Joel T. Headley, *The Chaplains and Clergy of the Revolution* (New York, 1864), pp. 92-93.

119. "Fragment of a Sermon Delivered to a Section of the American Army, after the Declaration of Independence at Morristown, New-Jersey, in 1776," and "Sermon, Delivered to the American Army in the Capacity of Chaplin [sic] a Few Days before the Battle of Brandywine," in Hugh H. Brackenridge, *Gazette Publications* (Carlisle, Pa., 1806), pp. 265-268, 125-132.

120. Hurt, *Love of Country,* in Moore, *Patriot Preachers,* p. 154.

121. Murdock, *Selections from Cotton Mather,* p. 174.

122. Hurt, *Love of Country,* in Moore, *Patriot Preachers,* pp. 144-157; *A Funeral Sermon on the Death of Mr. Daniel Kellogg* (Augusta, Ga., 1788), esp. p. 4.

123. Hurt, *Love of Country,* in Moore, *Patriot Preachers,* p. 156.

124. W. Stearns, *View of the Controversy,* p. 32.

125. Headley, *Chaplains and Clergy,* pp. 118-119.

126. Chauncy, *The Accursed Thing Must be Taken Away from among a People, if They Would Reasonably Hope to Stand before Their Enemies. A Sermon Preached at the Thursday-Lecture in Boston, September 3, 1778* (Boston, 1778), p. 9; Lathrop, *Discourse March 5, 1778,* p. 22.

127. Chauncy, *Accursed Thing,* p. 16.

128. Chauncy, *Civil Magistrates,* p. 63.

129. Backus, *History of New England,* II, 224.

130. Lathrop, *Discourse March 5, 1778,* pp. 22-23.

131. Samuel Spring, *A Sermon Delivered at the North Congregational Church in Newburyport . . . November 20th, MDCCLXXVII* (Newburyport, 1778), pp. 18-19.

132. William Gordon, *Discourse Preached December 15th, 1774,* in Thornton, *Pulpit of Revolution,* p. 225.

133. Peter Whitney, *American Independence Vindicated. A Sermon Delivered September 12, 1776. At a Lecture Appointed for Publishing the Declaration of Independence* (Boston, 1777), p. 53.

134. Nicholas Street, *The American States Acting over the Part of the Children of Israel . . . or, the Human Heart Discovering Itself under Trials. A Sermon, Preached at East-Haven, 1777* (New Haven, n.d.), pp. 33-34.

135. Cyprian Strong, *God's Care of the New-England Colonies . . . a Sermon Preached in the First Society of Chatham* (Hartford, [1777]), p. 5; Andrew Lee, *A Sermon Preached before His Excellency, Samuel Huntington . . . May 14, 1795* (Hartford, 1795), pp. 33-34.

136. Bellamy, *Nature and Glory of the Gospel,* in *Works,* II, 416-417.

137. Bellamy, *Millennium,* in *Works,* I, 447.

138. Avery, *Lord to be Praised,* p. 36n.

139. Whitaker, *Antidote Against Toryism,* in Moore, *Patriot Preachers,* p. 198; cf. L. Hart, *Liberty Described,* p. 9.

140. Street, *American States,* p. 17.

141. John Devotion, *The Duty and Interest of a People to Sanctify the Lord of Hosts. A Sermon, Preached before the General Assembly* (Hartford, 1777), p. 25n.

142. Avery, *Lord to be Praised,* p. 36n.

143. *Ibid.,* pp. 45-46.

144. Turner, *Due Glory to God,* p. 29.

145. Gordon, *The Separation of the Jewish Tribes,* in Moore, *Patriot Preachers,* esp. pp. 180-181.

146. Duffield, *Sermon Preached December 11th, 1783,* in Moore, *Patriot Preachers,* pp. 360-361.

147. Joseph Huntington, *God Ruling the Nations for the Most Glorious End. A Sermon, Preached . . . at Hartford, May 13th, 1784* (Hartford, 1784), p. 12; Samuel MacClintock, *A Sermon Preached before the Honorable the Council . . . of the State of New-Hampshire, June 3, 1784. On Occasion of the Commencement of the New Constitution . . .* (Portsmouth, N.H., 1784), p. 46; Tappan, *1783 Discourse,* pp. 12-13; David Osgood, *Reflections on the Goodness of God in Supporting the People of the United States through the Late War* (Boston, 1784), p. 17; Nathan Strong, *The Agency and Providence of God Acknowledged, in the Preservation of the American States* (Hartford, 1780), p. 9.

148. Street, *American States,* pp. 17-18, 22.

149. Oliver Hart, *Dancing Exploded. A Sermon Showing the Unlawfulness, Sinfulness, and Bad Consequences of Balls, Assemblies, and Dances in General; Delivered in Charleston, S.C., 1778,* in Moore, *Patriot Preachers,* pp. 235, 252; cf. Israel Evans, *A Discourse, Delivered in New-York, before a Brigade of Continental Troops, and a Number of Citizens, Assembled in St. George's Chapel, on the 11th December* (New York, [1783]), and John Rodgers, *The Divine Goodness Displayed in the American Revolution,* in Moore, *Patriot Preachers,* p. 339.

150. Jacob Green, *A Sermon Delivered at Hanover (in New-Jersey) April 22d, 1778* (Chatham, 1779), pp. 9-10.

151. Stone, *Nature and Evil of Selfishness,* p. 37.

152. Green, *Sermon at Hanover,* p. 10.

153. Quoted, Hazelton, *Declaration of Independence,* p. 58.

154. Abraham Keteltas, *Reflections on Extortion, Shewing the Nature, Malignity, and Fatal Tendency of That Sin to Individuals and Communities* (Newburyport, 1778), p. 15.

155. E. Wright, *People Ripe for Harvest,* pp. 9-10.

156. Hurt, *Love of Country,* in Moore, *Patriot Preachers,* p. 148.

157. Israel Evans, *Discourse at Easton,* p. 28.

158. Whitaker, *Antidote Against Toryism,* in Moore, *Patriot Preachers,* p. 211.

159. Keteltas, *God Arising,* pp. 10-11.

160. Murray, *Nehemiah,* p. 19; cf. Joseph Huntington, *A Discourse, Adapted to the Present Day, on the Health and Happiness, or Misery and Ruin, of the Body Politic, in Similitude to That of the Natural Body* (Hartford, 1781), p. 12.

161. Murray, *Nehemiah,* pp. 38-39.

162. *The Claims of the Tabernacle Church, to be Considered the Third*

Church in Salem (Salem, 1747), pp. 51-54; John Cleaveland, *The Reverend Dr. N. Whitaker's Neighbour is Come, and Searcheth Him* (Salem, 1784), p. 26.

163. *Claims of the Tabernacle Church,* pp. 52-54.

164. Whitaker, *Confutation of Wise,* pp. 53, 87.

165. Whitaker, *Antidote Against Toryism,* in Moore, *Patriot Preachers,* pp. 187-188.

166. *Ibid.,* pp. 228-229.

167. Lee, *Sin Destructive of Happiness,* pp. 21-22, 32; Ebenezer Baldwin, *Duty of Rejoicing,* pp. 22-23.

168. Whitaker, *Antidote Against Toryism,* in Moore, *Patriot Preachers,* p. 212.

169. Davies, *Curse of Cowardice,* in *Sermons,* III, 95.

170. N. Niles, *Remembrance of Christ,* p. 8; *Secret Prayer Explained and Inculcated* (Boston, 1773), pp. 35n-36n.

171. Whitaker, *Antidote Against Toryism,* in Moore, *Patriot Preachers,* pp. 212-213.

172. *Ibid.,* pp. 216-219.

173. *Ibid.,* pp. 206-207.

174. Edwards, *Reply to Williams,* in *Works,* I, 501.

175. Whitaker, *Antidote Against Toryism,* in Moore, *Patriot Preachers,* pp. 228-230.

176. George A. Ward, ed., *Journal and Letters of the Late Samuel Curwen* (New York, 1842), pp. 382-383.

177. Whitaker, *Reward,* Preface.

178. *Ibid.,* pp. 13-14.

179. Ward, *Journal of Curwen,* p. 383.

180. Cleaveland, *Whitaker's Neighbour, passim.*

181. Samuel Gatchel, *A Contrast to the Reverend Nathaniel Whitaker, D.D. His Confutation of the Reverend John Wise, A.M.* (Danvers, Mass., 1778), p. 6.

182. Presbytery of Hanover, quoted, Stokes, *Church and State,* I, 378; cf. Ebenezer Chaplin, *A Second Treatise on Church-Government* (Boston, 1773), p. 61.

183. *The Diary of William Bentley* (4 vols., Salem, 1905-1914), I, 34-35; Lemuel Briant, *Some More Friendly Remarks on Mr. Porter & Company* (Boston, 1751), p. 26.

184. Eli Forbes, *The Christian Ambassador. A Sermon, Preached in the Tabernacle of Salem, Thursday, 26th of February, 1784, after Which, the Annexed Result of an Ecclesiastical Council, Then Setting, was Publickly Read* (Salem, 1784), p. 22.

185. Nathaniel Whitaker, *A Brief History of the Settlement of the Third Church in Salem, in 1769; and Also of the Usurpation and Tyranny of an Ecclesiastical Council, in 1784* (Salem, 1784), pp. 24-25.

186. Whitaker, *Reward,* p. 25.

187. Whitaker, *The Mutual Care the Members of Christ's Body Owe to Each Other. A Sermon, Preached at the Opening of the Reverend Presbytery of Salem at Groton, June 9, 1784* (Salem, [1785]), p. 6.

188. Forbes, *Christian Ambassador,* p. 20.

189. Forbes, *The Inoffensive Ministry Described, in a Sermon, Delivered before the Convention of the Clergy of Massachusetts, May 30, 1799* (Charlestown, 1799), p. 5.

190. Chase, *History of Dartmouth,* p. 60n; Bentley, *Diary,* II, 136, 298; *American Quarterly Register,* VII (1834), 260.

X. THE PEOPLE, THE BEST GOVERNORS

1. Sprague, *Annals*, I, 396.
2. R. Smith, *Obligations of Confederate States*, p. 2.
3. Niles, *Secret Prayer Explained*, pp. 35n-36n.
4. Niles, *The Substance of Two Sermons, Delivered in the Second Society in Norwich, . . . July 12, 1778* (Norwich, 1779), p. 37.
5. Sherwood, *Scriptural Instructions*, p. 11.
6. "Essex Result," in *Memoir of Parsons*, p. 363.
7. Noble, *Strictures on Esther*, p. 8.
8. Allen, *American Alarm*, p. 20n.
9. Turner, *1773 Election Sermon*, pp. 30-31.
10. Niles, *Two Discourses on Liberty*, p. 15n.
11. Chaplin, *Civil State*, p. 5.
12. *Ibid.*, pp. 19-20.
13. Sprague, *Annals*, I, 716-717.
14. Niles, *Two Discourses on Liberty*, pp. 11n-12n.
15. Murray, *Nehemiah*, p. 7.
16. Niles, *Two Discourses on Liberty*, pp. 9, 12n-13n.
17. L. Hart, *Liberty Described*, p. 11.
18. Niles, *Two Discourses on Liberty*, p. 13n.
19. *Ibid.*, pp. 44-45.
20. *Ibid.*, p. 45.
21. Anthony Haswell, *An Oration, Delivered at Bennington, Vermont, August 16th, 1799* (Bennington, 1799), pp. 8-9.
22. L. Hart, *Liberty Described*, p. 11.
23. Gordon, *History of Rise of Independence*, I, 126.
24. Street, *American States*, p. 17.
25. J. Adams, *Works*, III, 453; IV, 195.
26. "The Continentalist," No. VI, July 4, 1782, *The Papers of Alexander Hamilton*, Volume III: 1782-1786, Harold C. Syrett and Jacob E. Cooke, eds., (New York, 1962), 103.
27. Jefferson, *Writings*, III, 266.
28. Lee, *Sin Destructive of Happiness*, p. 27.
29. Whitaker, *Antidote Against Toryism*, in Moore, *Patriot Preachers*, p. 211.
30. Alexander Blaikie, *A History of Presbyterianism in New England* (Boston, 1887), p. 211.
31. Whiting, *Address to Berkshire*, p. 5.
32. Chase, *History of Dartmouth*, p. 431.
33. Robert J. Taylor, ed., *Massachusetts, Colony to Commonwealth. Documents on the Formation of Its Constitution, 1775-1780* (Chapel Hill, 1961).
34. Chase, *History of Dartmouth*, p. 431.
35. *The People, the Best Governors: Or a Plan of Government Founded on the Just Principles of Natural Freedom*, in Appendix, Chase, *History of Dartmouth*, pp. 662-663.
36. Sprague, *Annals*, I, 721.
37. *The People, the Best Governors*, in Chase, *History of Dartmouth*, pp. 659-660.
38. "The Amendments to the Constitution of Massachusetts, Suggested by the Town of Northampton, June 5, 1780," in Clune, "Hawley's Criticism," p. 28.

39. *Ibid.,* pp. 15-16.

40. *Ibid.,* p. 28.

41. "Protest to the Constitutional Convention of 1780," in Clune, "Hawley's Criticism," pp. 49-50.

42. "Lucius Junius Brutus," *Works of Fisher Ames* (Boston, 1809), p. 5; Hawley, "Amendments," in Clune, "Hawley's Criticism," p. 18; Hawley to Hancock, June 14, 1782, in Brown, *Hawley,* p. 188.

43. Hawley, "Protest," in Clune, "Hawley's Criticism," p. 50.

44. Joseph Barker, *An Address [Delivered in] . . . Plymouth County . . . in Halifax, July 4th, 1803* (Boston, [1803]), pp. 12-13.

45. John Leland, *An Elective Judiciary, with Other Things, Recommended in a Speech, Pronounced at Cheshire, July 4, 1805* (Pittsfield, 1805), pp. 4, 19, 23.

46. Murray, *Nehemiah,* pp. 22-23.

47. *Ibid.,* pp. 43-44; Douglass, *Rebels and Democrats,* pp. 202-203; Madison to Edmund Randolph, October 7, 1787, *The Writings of James Madison,* Gaillard Hunt, ed. (9 vols., New York, 1900-1910), V, 8.

48. *An Address of the Convention for Framing a New Constitution of Government for the State of Massachusetts Bay to Their Constituents* (Boston, 1780), p. 10.

49. Phillips Payson, *A Sermon Preached before the Honorable Council . . . May 27, 1778,* in Thornton, *Pulpit of Revolution,* pp. 336-340.

50. Hawley, "Protest," in Clune, "Hawley's Criticism," p. 41.

51. *The People, the Best Governors,* in Chase, *History of Dartmouth,* p. 661.

52. Hawley, "Reasons for Declining to Serve as Senator," in Clune, "Hawley's Criticism," p. 53.

53. *Journal of Debates and Proceedings in the Convention . . . to Revise the Constitution of Massachusetts, Begun and Holden at Boston, November 15, 1820* (Boston, 1821), pp. 85-86.

54. Sloan, *Oration, Fourth of March, 1802,* p. 4.

55. Johann D. Schoepf, *Travels in the Confederation,* A. J. Morrison, ed. (2 vols., Philadelphia, 1911), II, 56.

56. "Essex Result," in *Memoir of Parsons,* pp. 368-369.

57. Murray, *Jerubbaal,* p. 71.

58. West, *1776 Election Sermon,* in Thornton, *Pulpit of Revolution,* p. 321.

59. Stiles, *The United States Elevated to Glory and Honor,* in Thornton, *Pulpit of Revolution,* p. 424.

60. Stiles, *A History of Three of the Judges of King Charles I* (Hartford, 1794), p. 253; Kent, *An Address, Delivered at New Haven, before the Phi Beta Kappa Society, September 13, 1831* (New Haven, 1831), p. 44.

61. P. W. Grayson, *Vice Unmasked, an Essay: Being a Consideration of the Influence of Law upon the Moral Essence of Man* (1830), in Perry Miller, ed., *The Legal Mind in America* (Garden City, N.Y., 1961), esp. p. 198.

62. Turner, *Due Glory to God,* p. 29.

63. Jacob Rush, *Charges and Extracts of Charges, on Moral and Religious Subjects* (New York, 1804), esp. p. 97; *Letters of Benjamin Rush,* L. H. Butterfield, ed. (2 vols., Princeton, 1951), II, 799, 820-821.

64. Turner, *Due Glory to God,* pp. 32-33.

65. Murray, *Jerubbaal,* p. 71.

66. *Ibid.,* pp. 56-57.

67. Chaplin, *Civil State,* p. 6.

68. Niles, *Two Discourses on Liberty,* pp. 30-31.

69. Israel Evans, *A Sermon, Delivered at Concord, before the Hon. General Court* (Concord, N.H., 1791), p. 19.

70. Letter to Edmund Pendleton, January 29, 1799, in *The Life and Selected Writings of Thomas Jefferson,* Adrienne Koch and William Peden, eds. (New York, 1944), p. 548.

71. Murray, *Jerubbaal,* p. 69.

72. Murray, *Bath Kol,* pp. vi, xiii.

73. Robert B. Semple, *A History of the Rise and Progress of the Baptists in Virginia* (Richmond, 1810), p. 147.

74. McNemar, *Kentucky Revival,* p. 59.

75. Miller, "Covenant to Revival," *Shaping of American Religion,* p. 351.

76. Quoted, Birdsall, "Thomas Allen," p. 163.

77. Sprague, *Annals,* II, 202; Austin, *The National "Barley Cake,"* pp. 23-24; [David Austin], *Republican Festival, Proclamation, and New Jerusalem, New Haven, March 9th, A.D. 1803* (n.p., n.d.).

78. Tracy, *Great Awakening,* pp. 419-420, 420n; Austin, *Voice of God,* pp. 11, 90; *Republican Festival,* p. 9; [David Austin?], *The Dance of Herodias, through the Streets of Hartford* (n.p., 1799), p. 16; Stanley Griswold, *Truth Its Own Test,* p. 19.

79. *The Political Writings of Joel Barlow* (New York, 1796), pp. 137-138.

80. David Ramsay, *History of South Carolina* (2 vols., Charleston, 1809), II, 15.

81. Sermon 280, Griswold Manuscript Sermons, Houghton Library, Harvard University; Griswold, *Overcoming Evil,* p. 9.

82. James Sloan, Address, September 6, 1800, and "A Discourse on Government and Laws," in *Proceedings of the Democratic Association of Gloucester County, New Jersey, at Several Meetings Held in the Month of March, 1801* (n.p., n.d.), pp. 6, 15-17; *Oration, Fourth of March, 1802,* p. 6.

83. Sloan, *Oration, Fourth of March, 1802,* p. 24; McNemar, *Kentucky Revival,* p. 31; David A. Leonard, *An Oration, Pronounced at Raynham, Monday, July 5, 1802* (Boston, 1802), pp. 26-27.

84. Austin, *The National "Barley Cake,"* p. 23.

85. *Annals of Congress,* 9th Congress, 1st Session, pp. 801-802.

86. Murray, *Jerubbaal,* p. 59.

87. Christopher Gore, *An Oration: Delivered . . . before the Ancient and Honourable Society of Free and Accepted Masons* (Boston, [1783]), p. 8; Thomas Barnard, *A Sermon, Preached at the Request of the Ancient and Honourable Artillery Company* (Boston, 1789), p. 23; MacClintock, *Sermon on New Hampshire Constitution,* pp. 43-44.

88. John Woodhull, *A Sermon for the Day of Public Thanksgiving . . . November 26, 1789* (Trenton, 1790), p. 25.

89. O. Hart, *American Remembrancer,* p. 22.

90. Austin, *Dance of Herodias,* p. 6; *The National "Barley Cake,"* pp. 21-22; *Republican Festival,* pp. 6-9; *A Discourse Delivered on the Fourth of July, 1804, at Rahway, Nigh to Elizabeth-Town* (Elizabethtown, N.J., n.d.), p. 13; Sloan, *Proceedings of the Democratic Association,* p. 18.

91. Griswold, *Infidelity, Not the Only Enemy,* p. 17; Sloan, *Oration, Fourth of March, 1802,* p. 24.

92. Elias Smith, *The Whole World Governed by a Jew . . . Delivered March 4, 1805* (Exeter, N.H., 1805), p. 29.

93. William Fancher, *An Oration, Delivered at Poundridge [N.Y.], on the 20th December, 1801, before the Republican Society* (n.p., n.d.), pp. 7-8;

Austin, *The National "Barley Cake,"* p. 24; Barnabas Bidwell, *A Summary, Historical and Political Review of the Revolution, the Constitution and Government of the United States* (Pittsfield, Mass., 1805); Griswold, *The Good Land We Live In,* p. 18.

94. Sherman Leland, *An Oration, Pronounced at Dorchester, July 4, 1815* (Boston, 1815), p. 14; E. Smith, *Whole World,* p. 26.

95. John Leland, "Part of a Speech, delivered at Suffield Connecticut, on the First Jubilee of the United States," *The Writings of Elder John Leland* (New York, 1845), pp. 522-523.

INDEX

with Scotch Presbyterians, 374; role in Revolution, 473-476; goals in Revolution, 482, 486, 511-515, 519. *See also under subject headings*
Cambridge Platform, 98
Cane Ridge, *see* revivals of 1799-1801
Caner, Henry, 216; *The Great Blessings of Stable Times*, 336
Carter, Landon, 407
Cartwright, Thomas, 363
Chain of Being: in Liberal social theory, 261-262, 288; Edwards spiritualizes, 307
Causation, 73-78
Chandler, Thomas Bradbury, 196n, 364, 367
Chanler, Isaac, "Advice to New Converts," 168n
Channing, William Ellery, 76, 113-114, 144, 173, 197, 212, 218n, 266, 326n
Chaplin, Ebenezer, *The Civil State Compared to Rivers*, 105, 463, 466-467, 513, 531
Charity: Joel Barlow on, 539
Calvinist conceptions: economic justice, 32, 93, 306, 497-498; love or benevolence, 112, 308; not latitudinarianism, 123, 380; and typology, 125, 132; law of, 164; Edwards' critique of Liberal notions, 250; selflessness, 252-253; and equality, 306; as disposition, 308; in judging church members, 316; not benefactions, sympathy, or tears, 385; and religious freedom, 389-390; ecumenical, 399; as patriotism, 469; lacking in Federalists, 536; as political harmony, 550
Liberal conceptions: forbids separations, 119; as benefactions, 213, 384n; Chauncy on, 248-251; forbids envy, 252; as sympathy, 383-386
Charles I, 254-255, 504
Charles II, 258, 357
Charters, New England: and religious freedom, 121; and commercial privileges, 244-246, 429; and issue of American Bishop, 369
Chauncy, Charles: Liberal spokesman, 5; uses Locke's *Understanding*, 44, 110n, 177, 209; encourages manufactures, 70, 247-248; opposes separations, 119; Backus on, 120, 252, 487; evasiveness and imprecision, 168; defends Harvard, 184; use of jeremiad, 285-286, 487; awarded degree by College of New Jersey, 355, 378; reputation, 355, 370; animus against Wheelock, 362n;

applauds Witherspoon's assault on New Divinity, 377; restores office of deacon, 382; patriot activities, 383, 418; puts hope in farmers, 387
writings: *The Accursed Thing Must be Taken Away*, 487; *Christian Love, as Exemplified by the First Christian Church*, 250, 382; *Election Sermon* (1747), 258, 277-278, 487n; *Good News from a Far Country*, 285-286; *The Idle-Poor*, 247-249; *A Letter to a Friend*, 382-384; *The Mystery Hid from Ages and Generations*, 166, 226-227; *Seasonable Thoughts*, 92, 119-120, 152, 166, 177, 209, 277, 355; *Trust in God, the Duty of a People in a Day of Trouble*, 431-432
doctrines and ideas: benevolence, 265; charity, 119, 249-251; conception of church, 131; political theory, 258, 277, 418; premillenarianism, 69-70; Providence, 289; psychology, 110n, 209, 216, 277-278; law of nature in reason and revelation, 242; rhetorical theory, 209; interpretation of Scripture, 197, 250; social criticism, 434-435; social theory, 249-251, 261-262, 278, 435; universal salvation, 47
on: religious parties, 2, 8; Whitefield, 57, 160; Edwards, 92, 109-110; notion of millennium, 92-93; enthusiasm, 93, 177, 278, 423, 453; communism, 93, 197, 250-251, 382, 423; notion of millennium in America, 98; itinerants, 118, 163; Concert of Prayer, 156, 404; preaching styles, 160-161; status and prerogatives of clergy, 166; evangelical preaching, 175, 217; *Paradise Lost*, 198; Stamp Act, 244-245; right of taxation, 244-245, 417n; New England history, 245; American future, 247, 284; idleness and charity, 248; demagogues, 258, 279; Stamp Act repeal, 260, 263, 282, 287; orators and oratory, 272; Mayhew, 274, 290, 364; real and imaginary liberties, 281; Cleaveland, 293; currency, 300, 487n; American Bishop, 355, 369-370; Society for the Propagation of the Gospel, 362; opponents of Half-Way Covenant, 376-377; sufferings of Bostonians, 383; inflation in Revolution, 487
mentioned: 16, 45, 72, 91, 141, 292n, 360, 365, 371, 386, 427, 440, 452, 512, 552
Chiliasm, 60-61, 64-65, 68, 128-129, 493. *See also* Premillenarianism

INDEX

INDEX

Bishop, American; Society for the Propagation of the Gospel

Equality: in colonies, 170; Calvinist ideal of, 305-308; of saints, 146, 155, 307-308; in Calvinist image of post-Revolutionary future, 493-494; in revivals of 1799-1801, 534, 544; as evangelical Republican ideal, 550. *See also* Communism

Equity, rule of, 305

Erskine, Ebenezer, 374

Erskine, Ralph, 374

Eschatology, Calvinist, 63-64, 101; and Calvinist eloquence, 114-115. *See also* Church Triumphant; Millennium; Work of Redemption

Essex Gazette, 477

Essex Junto, 549-550

Evangelical religion: defined, 3-5; as Edwardeanism, 6-7; appeal of, 49-50; focus on New Birth, 42-43; doctrines as instrumental truths, 199-200; not quietism, 386n; held most favorable to patriotism, 399-400; affinities with American Enlightenment, 537-540. *See also* Calvinism; Experimental religion

Evangelical Republicans, *see* Republican revival

Evans, Israel, 498, 531

Excellence, and excellency: central to all Calvinist thought, 41-42; perceived in regeneration, 41; source of happiness, 49, 102n; definitions, 52, 102, 104; not known by reasoning, 134, 224; determines action, 194-195; effort to communicate in preaching, 224, 233

of: American union, 117, 405; art and literature, 104, 198; Christ, 31, 144-146, 163n; Church Triumphant, 116; communion of saints, 111, 231; Deity, 103, 145-146, 298n; doctrines, 199, 224, 336; equality, 307-308; eloquence, 116; free communion, 140; good society, 101-103, 456, 474; heaven, 146, 508; history, 65-66, 79, 101, 153, 342-343; law of nature, 242; liberty, 400-401; millennium, 101; minister, 163n; moral law, 134; nature, 103; saints, 111, 132, 146; Scripture, 134, 196-198; union, 52, 95, 104, 404-405; vindictive justice, 337-338

Experimental religion: distinctively American, 42; defined, 131-133; millenarian context, 137; redefinition of virtue and morality, 137-139; basis of

evangelical union, 142; and examination of clergy, 202; political implications, 303, 309, 328-329; social implications, 308-309, 314-315; emphasis on action, 311-315; and qualifications for church membership, 317-318; in Calvinist sermons of Seven Years War, 326-327; and Calvinist response to British policy, 477-478; and post-Revolutionary politics, 511. *See also* Evangelical religion

Faculty psychology, 44-46, 109n-110n, 113n, 194, 209-210, 215-216, 277, 335

Familism, 136

Fast days, Calvinist reluctance to participate, 295-297

Fast sermons, *see* Jeremiad

Federal theology, *see* Covenant theology

Federalism: Adams, 444, 549; Calvinist, 348, 488, 493, 520, 534; New England, 292; Unitarian, 266, 280, 433, 447, 509, 539-540; evangelical critique, 78, 105, 308-309, 532, 535-536, 543, 548; commercial policy anticipated in 1770's, 430; reassessed, 452; and Tories, 522n; Jefferson on, 532

Federalist, The, 512

Fénelon, François, 144

Filmer, Robert, 255, 446

Finley, James, 175, 199

Finley, Samuel, proclaims arrival of millennium, 61; preaches to Baptists, 122, 140; criticizes Moravians, 122; debates with Abel Morgan, 129-130; criticizes Baptists and Covenanter Presbyterians, 130; removed from Connecticut, 141; *The Curse of Meroz,* 327, 332, 479; president, College of New Jersey, 455; death, 330; mentioned, 326, 333, 393, 480, 514

on: Whitefield's role in history, 57; anti-revivalists, 88; evangelical cooperation, 122, 140; Davies, 173, 218, 230, 327; Old Side modes of argument, 176; qualifications of clergy, 189, 202; preaching style, 226; Tennent, 310-311, 327; fashionable religion, 319; clergy's role in society, 327; vindictive justice, 337; danger of Catholic victory in Seven Years War, 394

Finney, Charles G., 182, 194, 209, 317

Fitch, Elijah, 479

Fitch, Thomas, 203, 301, 361n

Flavel, John, 167; *Husbandry Spiritualized,* 105

6 5 1

INDEX

fectionate religion, 210-213, 275-276; social theory, 252, 434; political theory, 253-254, 275; patriotism, 268-269; moral sense, 282; divine goodness, 288n
on: parties in Stamp Act crisis, 1, 280; preaching politics, 15, 273; intercolonial confederacy, 157; learned professions, 175, 186; enthusiasm, 177, 249, 275-276; distinguished families and original sin, 185n; religious freedom, 206, 291, 370; Calvinist manner of address, 235-236; taxation, 243-244; New England charters, 245; idleness and laziness, 249; Boston Anglicans, 254-255; Cromwell and Puritan Commonwealth, 256; right of revolution, 257, 278; demagogues, 257, 259; Sons of Liberty, 259-260, 263; popular involvement in public affairs, 262-263; political enthusiasts, 272, 278; education of patriots, 273; liberty, 275; false patriots, 279; need for unity in 1766, 280-281; gratitude to Stamp Act opponents, 286-287; wilderness and anarchy, 287; worldly advantages of religion, 319; American Bishop, 360-364, 369-370; Society for the Propagation of the Gospel, 362; Congregationalism, 363; Massachusetts establishment, 370; charity and sympathy, 384n; allegiance, 473
mentioned: 16, 72, 97, 304, 321, 325, 365-367, 448, 509, 512
Means, doctrine of: 29; interconnections of, 83-84; in Stamp Act sermons, 286-287; in Calvinist sermons of Revolution, 424-425
Mein, John, 410n
Melville, Herman, 188, 426, 552; *Moby-Dick*, 116
Meroz, Curse of: in Seven Years War, 332-334; in seventeenth century, 333; in Great Awakening, 333-334; in revival of 1763-1764, 334; in Revolution, 334, 348, 406, 471, 490, 503; Whitaker on, 501-507
Methodists, 137, 354, 537, 542n
Meyers, Marvin, 476, 540
Migrations, purpose of, 358-359, 429, 438, 447, 462. *See also* Forefathers
Millennium: in Calvinist theory of history, 62-66, 101-103; characteristics, 49, 62-65, 70-71, 98-191, 309-310, 456, 482, 493-529; and revivals, 80-81; and Calvinist redefinition of virtue, 130, 133-134, 137; and union, 152-153; and Armageddon, 235-236; Bellamy on, 340-

345; and religious freedom, 395-396; secularized, 493, 529
in America, 95-98, 108, 395-396, 411, 438, 486, 492, 494, 547
expectations: in 1730's, 61; in Great Awakening, 59-62, 66-67; in 1740's, 90-91, 130; in Seven Years War, 84-86, 325; in 1750's, 340; in 1770's, 97-98, 395-396, 410; in Revolution, 347-348, 409-410, 482, 486; in 1780's, 547; in 1790's, 81, 379, 537-538, 548; in election of 1800, 526, 538, 543-544
Liberals on, 69, 92, 98, 113; in secular literature, 439n, 480n; Republican, 537, 541-542
See also Premillenarianism; Work of Redemption
Miller, John C., 9
Miller, Perry, 3, 5, 18, 38-39, 62, 73, 105-107, 223, 302, 424, 535
Milton, John, 174, 188, 193, 206, 275, 479; *Paradise Lost*, 188, 198
Minot, George Richards, 451
Mobs, 259-260, 346-348, 386, 401, 408, 418, 471, 499, 505
Moderate Calvinism, 8, 208, 330, 334-335, 356, 436, 525; within Presbyterianism, 378
Molineaux, William, 450
Montcalm, Louis, 86
Montesquieu, Charles Louis, 457
Montgomery, Joseph, 404
Montgomery, Richard, 439-440
Monthly Anthology, The, 175, 289
Moral government: doctrine of, 336, 338; of nations, 80, 296, 424; in history, 295, 342-344
Moral law, Calvinist definition: 133-136, 298, 305; millenarian context, 134-136; and courts, 182; and thanksgiving days, 297-298; applied to politics, 297-298, 302-304; magistrates judged by, 301; applied to economic activity, 305-306; in sermons of Seven Years War, 326-327; in sermons of Revolution, 408; tyranny as violation, 464, 501-502; in Calvinist political theory, 516-517
Separates and Baptists on, 135-136; Liberals on, 137-138; Episcopal interpretation as law of mutual obligation, 304-305
Moral sense, in Liberal social and political thought, 282; and Liberal definition of virtue, 383. *See also* Sentiment
Moravians, 122, 127, 129, 298, 322
Morgan, Abel, 128

INDEX

Morgan, Edmund, 353
Morgan, Joseph, 73; *The History of the Kingdom of Basaruah*, 31, 60
Morse, Jedidiah, 535
Mosier, Richard B., 10
Murray, James: *Sermons to Asses*, 465
Murray, John: on Washington, 148; on anti-Catholicism, 394; on union in Revolution, 403; *Nehemiah, or the Struggle for Liberty Never in Vain*, 499; on need for cooperation in Revolution, 499; urges and leads mob, 499-500; *Bath-Kol*, 533; mentioned, 452, 511, 519
   1783 thanksgiving sermon: on sovereignty of people, 524; on codification, 527; as democratic jeremiad, 530-531; republished, 532; urges unitary national government and society, 546
Music, and preaching, 228-231; and sensibility, 385

Nationalism, 14, 94, 545-550. *See also* Independence; Union, American
Natural religion: emerges in colonies, 5; as anti-Calvinist ideology, 240-241; and Deism, 538-539
Nature: as metaphor and type, 103-107, 120, 130-131, 132n, 396, 402, 466-467, 508
   law of: in political sermons, 16-17; in Liberal political theory, 241-243; Calvinist definition, 108, 242, 459; in Calvinist political theory, 501, 515. *See also* Moral law
   laws of, *see* Newtonian physics
   state of, 304
Navigation Acts, 244
Neoclassicism, and rationalism, 191; in education, 185; in Liberal discourse, 222; in moral theory, 191, 196; in Episcopal doctrine, 366; in poetry, 173-174; in political sermons, 276; in oratory, 352, 485; in sermon form, 219, 227
New Birth: focus of Calvinism, 38-39, 42-43, 53, 200, 366; criticized, 37; and happiness, 39-43; as communal experience, 52; Tennent rejects as fundamental of doctrine, 323; Dickinson defends against Episcopalians, 366
New Divinity, 349, 353-354, 372, 377-378, 398-399, 425
New England sectionalism, 117, 375, 398, 548-549
New Jersey, College of: 171, 188, 455, 538; revival at, 81; New Side–New England cooperation in founding, 142; Bellamy's writings suppressed at, 168n; purpose of founding, 184, 373; reorganized under Witherspoon, 234, 330, 377-378; influential graduates, 329-330; awards degree to Chauncy, 355, 378; religious freedom at, 373; New Side criticisms of, 380
New Lights, pro-Awakening party in Connecticut, 2; as Edwardeans, 6; argue with Separates, 8; achieve power in legislature, 12-13; interest in western lands, 82, 220; efforts to suppress, 151; influence at Yale, 183; reorganization in 1750's, 203, 323; appoint Bellamy as election preacher, 344; oppose Stamp Act, 346-347; honor regicide judges, 358
   in 1770's, 355, 365; in Virginia, 365; in 1800, 352
New Side, pro-Awakening party in Presbyterian Church, 2; identify opponents as Antichrist, 88; define goals of Awakening, 93-94; conception of church, 122; cooperation with New Englanders, 140, 142; debates with Baptists, Covenanter Presbyterians, and Moravians, 8, 122, 128, 322; disposition to reunion with Old Side, 150; discontent with reunion, 150, 380; influence at College of New Jersey, 142, 377; position on examination of clergy, 193, 202; involvement in public affairs, 297; New England influence in, 377-378. *See also* Log College Party
Newton, Isaac, 49, 117. *See also* Newtonian physics
Newtonian physics, 41-42, 49, 61, 73, 78, 106-108, 146, 155, 191, 402
Niebuhr, H. Richard, 10, 61
Niebuhr, Reinhold, 349
Niles, Nathaniel: conception of Deity, 63n; divine attributes, 113n; composer of hymns, 174; derides notion of charity as tearful sympathy, 385-386; on self-seeking patriots, 406; career, 454-455, 514; *Two Discourses on Liberty*, 454-457, 467-468, 513-517; effects of liberty on the mind, 455-456; perfect liberty as millennial commonwealth, 456-457; on freedom of heaven, 457; on avarice of British administration, 467-468; on need for all to act, 468; on self-sacrificing patriotism, 469; on hypocrisy, 503-504; on political hypocrisy, 511; on rulers as servants of people, 513; political theory, 514-517;

INDEX

Priestley, Joseph, 191, 326
Prince, Thomas, 69, 72, 75
Prince, Thomas, Jr., 115
Princeton College, *see* College of New Jersey
Property: Liberals on, 244; Calvinists on, 304, 389; qualification for office and franchise in Massachusetts, 521-523
Prophet, The, 221
Providence: Calvinist doctrine, 66-67, 72, 74-78, 80, 82-84, 97-98, 105, 295-296, 347, 424-425; Liberal interpretation, 71-72, 240, 284-289, 431. *See also* History; Work of Redemption
Psychology: faculty, *see* Faculty psychology; Lockean, 41-42, 44-46, 177, 206, 209, 228, 257, 272
    Calvinist theory: 41-44, 109-111, 131n, 195; and rhetorical theory, 227, 234; political implications, 455; Hopkins recasts, 113
    Liberal theory: 44-46, 109n, 131n, 194, 277; and rhetorical theory, 209-212, 215-216, 437; political implications, 255, 272, 437, 445; in interpretations of Revolution, 448-449, 453
Public spirit, *see* Patriotism
Puritan Commonwealth: specter during Great Awakening, 92; view of American Episcopalians, 254; Mayhew on, 256; Calvinist image, 357; contrasting images in Calvinist-Episcopal debate, 375; Stiles on, 528. *See also* Cromwell, Oliver
Puritanism: intellectual balance, 3; rationalism in, 5; doctrine of means, 79; ecclesiastical theory, 124; status of clergy, 169; interpretation of Scripture, 198, 225; plain style, 214, 222, 224, 226; sermon form, 216, 227; on vision and hearing, 230; image of wilderness, 287; weaned affections, 312. *See also* Covenant theology; Faculty psychology; Preparation; Puritan Commonwealth
Putnam, Israel, 348

Quakers, 27, 177, 298, 324, 386n
Quebec Act, response to, 387-389, 391-392, 394-396
Querists, The, 140-141, 176, 393
Quincy, Samuel, 167
Quintilian, 215

Ramsay, David, 191, 401, 405, 474, 540
Ramus, Petrus, 225, 227
Randolph, Edward, 357

Rationalism: distinguished from Enlightenment, 3, 278, 537; defined, 4-6; in American Puritanism, 5; as anti-evangelical ideology, 5-6; not politically inspiring, 18; appeal of, 50-51. *See also* Arminianism
Reconciliation with Britain: Liberal desires for, 384, 428, 430, 478; Calvinist opposition to, 478-479
Red Jacket, 220
Reed, Joseph, 451
Regulators, 180, 381-382, 387, 409, 465, 486
Religious freedom: partisan issue in Connecticut and Virginia, 13; issue in Great Awakening, 36; dynamic of evangelical crusade for, 120-122, 458-459; contrasting Calvinist and Liberal conceptions of, 200-207, 370, 373-374, 525; threatened by Stamp Act, 244, 351-352; issue in revival of 1763, 334; British "plot" against, 351; and civil liberty, 352, 356, 358-359, 388-390; struggle for, 1765-1775, 356, 380-381, 389-391; and property rights, 368-369; not latitudinarianism, 373-374; at College of New Jersey, 373; and social hostility, 380-381; threatened by Quebec Act, 387-389; and taxation, 389-390; opponents called false patriots, 390, 406; struggle for, during Revolution, 391-392, 486, 518, 533; and American union, 395-397; and millennium, 396, 538; issue in constitutional debates, 524-526, 547; issue in 1798-1801, 295n, 537-538. *See also* Bishop, American; Voluntary principle
Republican festivals, 542, 544-545
Republican revival, 78, 81, 97, 100-101, 105, 116, 148, 191, 194, 398, 410, 526-527, 532, 540-544
Revival: as Calvinist goal, 13; and nationalism, 14; and millennium, 67, 79-80; promoted by ecclesiastical strategy, 318; as goal in 1770's, 347, 398; hindered by New Divinity, 353; need for proclaimed, at end of Revolution, 532-533
Revivals: in 1720's, 27-28, 92; of 1734-1735, 2, 4, 28-29, 34, 61; at College of New Jersey, 81; of 1763-1764, 49-50, 81, 83, 97, 142, 334-335, 341, 378-379; in 1770's, 97, 352, 380; in Virginia, 139, 352; of 1799-1801, 60, 78, 81, 87, 191, 534, 542; in 1820's, 551. *See also* Great Awakening; Republican revival; Revolution

FOLIOTHÈQUE

Collection dirigée par
Bruno Vercier
Maître de conférences
à l'Université de
la Sorbonne-Nouvelle-Paris III

Albert Camus

Le Premier Homme

par Pierre-Louis Rey

Pierre-Louis Rey

commente

Le Premier Homme

d'Albert Camus

Gallimard

Pierre-Louis Rey est professeur émérite à l'Université de Paris III-Sorbonne nouvelle. Sur Camus, il a écrit notamment *Camus. Une morale de la beauté*, SEDES, 2000, et *Camus. L'homme révolté*, coll. « Découvertes », Gallimard, 2006. Il a édité *Caligula*, *Le Malentendu*, *L'État de siège* et *Les Justes* (sous presse) dans la collection « Folio Théâtre ». Il collabore à l'édition des *Œuvres complètes* de Camus dans la « Bibliothèque de la Pléiade ».

Les indications de pages données entre parenthèses renvoient à l'édition du *Premier Homme* (*PH*) dans la collection « Folio », n° 3320, Gallimard, 2000.

Pour les autres œuvres de Camus, les notes renvoient, jusqu'en 1948, aux *Œuvres complètes* (édition en cours), « Bibliothèque de la Pléiade », Gallimard (abréviation : *OC*, t. I ou II) ; après 1948, à *Théâtre, récits, nouvelles* ou aux *Essais*, « Bibliothèque de la Pléiade », ainsi qu'aux *Carnets II* et *III*, Gallimard. Pour plus de détails, voir Bibliographie, p. 211 et suivantes.

I   PRÉSENTATION

UN MANUSCRIT TROUVÉ

Quand Camus mourut dans un accident d'auto, le 4 janvier 1960, on trouva à proximité du véhicule le manuscrit inachevé d'un roman autobiographique de cent quarante-quatre pages, *Le Premier Homme*. En tête, Camus avait inscrit une dédicace à sa mère illettrée : « Intercesseur : Vve Camus. À toi qui ne pourras jamais lire ce livre. » La première partie du roman retrace une « recherche du père ». À quarante ans, Jacques Cormery (masque transparent de l'auteur) se rend en effet sur la tombe de son père, Henri Cormery, tué au début de la guerre de 14-18 et enterré à Saint-Brieuc. Jacques prend alors brusquement conscience qu'il est aujourd'hui plus âgé que ne l'était son père au moment de sa mort. Cette révélation bouleverse en lui l'ordre du temps. À l'image des colons qui l'avaient précédé en Algérie, Henri Cormery était le « premier homme »; Jacques, à son tour, devient le « premier homme ». Faute de témoignages suffisants, cette « recherche du père » se révélera décevante. Mais elle permettra à Jacques de recomposer l'univers de son enfance, de confesser ses fautes à sa mère, et d'ouvrir son esprit et son cœur à un passé lointain, celui des premiers temps de la colonisation. Jamais, depuis sa première œuvre, *L'Envers et l'En-*

11

1. « Absence du sens historique chez les Grecs. [...] Les Grecs, peuple heureux, n'ont pas d'histoire » (*Carnets*, *OC*, t. II, p. 845).

droit (1937), Camus ne s'était livré avec autant d'intimité sur lui-même et sur ses proches. Surtout, après avoir soutenu que les peuples heureux, à l'image des Grecs, n'ont pas d'histoire[1], puis bataillé contre les intellectuels de son temps parce qu'ils soumettaient leur pensée au sens de l'Histoire, le voici curieux, dans son dernier ouvrage, de remonter et d'expliquer le passé de sa terre natale.

De ce manuscrit souillé, peu lisible et négligemment ponctué, Francine, l'épouse de Camus, fit une première dactylographie, que retravailla sa fille, Catherine Camus. L'inachèvement du texte ne se signale pas par sa dernière phrase, qui pourrait trompeusement sonner comme une conclusion (« [...] des raisons de vieillir et de mourir sans révolte », p. 307). Il ressort en premier lieu de l'usage des noms propres : en principe dissimulés, les noms réels (de lieux ou de personnes) réapparaissent souvent par inadvertance. Le bouleversement du temps, inscrit dans le programme du roman, déconcerte d'autant plus le lecteur qu'il s'accompagne d'incohérences appelées à être rectifiées. Le critique doit suspendre son jugement devant certaines audaces de style : les points de suspension du « Il pouvait... » (p. 37) qui clôt un paragraphe expriment-ils l'infinie rêverie de Jacques ou l'incapacité provisoire du romancier à achever sa phrase ? On ignore enfin si certaines phrases extraordinairement longues, plus longues que

1. Voir
notamment
dans le dernier
chapitre,
« Obscur à
soi-même ».

les plus longues phrases de Proust[1], auraient été conservées dans leur état, parfois déstructuré, ou si Camus les aurait réduites pour les rendre plus conformes à ses habitudes de style.

C'est en 1994 seulement que *Le Premier Homme* fut publié chez Gallimard, dans la collection des « Cahiers Albert Camus », avant d'être repris en 2000 dans la collection « Folio ». L'édition donne la partie rédigée du texte avec, en bas de page, les notes marginales (parfois sibyllines) de Camus, signalant les ajouts à faire, les morceaux à retrancher, les incohérences à rectifier. À la suite sont reproduits, d'une part des feuillets qu'il avait insérés dans le manuscrit ou placés à sa suite, d'autre part des « notes et plans » consignés dans un petit carnet sur lequel il avait écrit : *Le Premier Homme*. Ainsi prend-on une idée approximative de la voie dans laquelle aurait été poursuivi le roman et de son dénouement. Mais le chantier était immense. Il aurait fallu à Camus des mois, plus vraisemblablement des années, pour mener à bien ce qui s'annonçait comme son ouvrage le plus volumineux et peut-être le plus original.

« Le livre *doit être* inachevé », lit-on dans le petit carnet (p. 333). Cette note ne doit pas consoler de l'interruption du manuscrit. Même si la confession faite à la mère se profile dans les « notes et plans » au terme de l'itinéraire du héros, Camus envisageait de donner à son roman une fin qui eût ouvert la perspective d'un recommencement. Cette forme d'inachèvement aurait été le fruit d'un dessein médité, non d'un hasard malheureux. Le titre de l'ouvrage, au moins, ne souffre pas d'incertitude. De grands romans inachevés ont été légués à la postérité sans titre (*Jean Santeuil*, de Proust) ou avec plusieurs titres possibles (*Lucien Leuwen*, de Stendhal); l'éditeur n'a d'autre choix, en pareil cas, que d'intituler l'ouvrage du nom de son héros. Rien de tel ici. Du moment où il a commencé d'écrire son roman et jusque sur son carnet de notes, Camus l'a toujours appelé *Le Premier Homme*. Ce titre signale un début plutôt qu'un achèvement. Les allusions à la Bible imposent d'y lire une référence à Adam. Mais certains accents évangéliques laissent supposer que le « premier homme » est aussi un avatar du « fils de l'homme ».

L'ÉTAGE DE L'AMOUR

1. Voir dès 1947, dans les *Carnets*, *OC*, t. II, p. 1084-1085.

2. *Carnets III*, p. 187. Les projets de « Don Juan » et de « Némésis » reviennent plusieurs fois dans les *Carnets*.

Camus a tendu la perche aux historiens de la littérature qui découpent par cycles les carrières des écrivains[1]. Lui-même parle plus volontiers d'« étages ». Il y aurait eu l'étage de l'absurde, puis celui de la révolte. En 1956, il annonce : « Le troisième étage, c'est l'amour : le Premier Homme, Don Juan. Le mythe de Némésis. / La méthode est la sincérité[2]. » L'inspiration du *Premier Homme* est confirmée par cette note du petit carnet : « En somme, je vais parler de ceux que j'aimais. Et de cela seulement. Joie profonde » (p. 357). On croit lire ici un écho au « Joie, joie, joie, pleurs de joie » du « Mémorial » de Pascal. Pascal, « le plus grand de tous, hier et aujourd'hui », note Camus à l'automne de 1956[1]. Séparé par la foi du philosophe des *Pensées*, il le rejoint dans une exigence supérieure d'amour. C'est une large ouverture du cœur que devrait en effet permettre l'élan d'affection pour les proches : en aimant mieux les siens, Jacques comprend qu'il aurait dû mieux aimer aussi « tant de créatures qui méritaient de l'être » (p. 145). Ainsi prend tout son sens la qualité d'« intercesseur » conférée à la mère dans la dédicace : elle est celle qui permet d'accéder, non à Dieu, mais à ce qu'il y a de meilleur en l'homme.

Les trois étages de l'œuvre de Camus offrent des « hauteurs » à peu près égales, soit sept à neuf ans. 1) L'absurde, formulé dès 1934 dans les ébauches de *L'Envers et l'Endroit*, lui a inspiré *Caligula* (première version : 1941), *L'Étranger* et *Le Mythe de Sisyphe* (1942)[2]. 2) La révolte, nommée en 1942 dans les *Carnets* (projet d'un « essai sur la révolte »), a été illustrée par *Le Malentendu* (1944), *La Peste* (1947), *L'État de siège* (1948) et *Les Justes* (1949), avant d'être analysée dans *L'Homme révolté* (1951). 3) L'année 1953 s'ouvre en janvier avec « Retour à Tipasa », recueilli dans *L'Été* (1954). Alors que *La Peste* pouvait se résumer par la formule « Il y a chez les

1. *Ibid.*, p. 177.

2. « Les trois Absurdes », comme les appelle Camus (*Carnets*, *OC*, t. II., p. 920).

1. *Ibid.*, p. 991.

2. « Retour à Tipasa », *L'Été, Essais*, p. 873.

hommes plus de choses à admirer qu'à mépriser[1] », Camus souhaite désormais « aimer et admirer », et il met l'accent sur le premier des deux termes : « Il y a du malheur à ne point aimer. Nous tous, aujourd'hui, mourons de ce malheur[2]. » Quelques mois plus tard, il commence à composer *Le Premier Homme*. Mais son ouvrage sera loin d'être achevé en 1960. Seule une fatalité navrante a donc empêché la troisième étape de son œuvre de déborder en durée les deux précédentes.

Cette périodisation de l'œuvre en étages successifs admet d'autres nuances. Dès 1942, la révolte donnait sens à la mort du héros de *L'Étranger*; à l'inverse, l'absurdité de l'existence continue de peser, en 1947, sur les « exilés » de *La Peste*. Enfin, trois ans après avoir commencé *Le Premier Homme*, Camus publie un récit qui en est le négatif : Clamence, le « juge-pénitent » de *La Chute* (1956), a en effet choisi de se séparer du genre humain pour prêcher le désespoir. Les titres des deux ouvrages affichent leur contraste : selon la Genèse, le premier homme, après avoir été créé par Dieu, a succombé à la Chute. « Avant le troisième étage : nouvelles d'"un héros de notre temps". Thème du *jugement et de l'exil* », a

3. *Carnets III*, p. 187. Le pluriel de « nouvelles » s'explique difficilement.

noté Camus dans ses *Carnets* en 1956[3], comme si le lancement du troisième étage était décidément retardé.

Le cloisonnement tient moins encore quand on constate que Camus n'a jamais renoncé à l'inspiration de *L'Envers et l'En-*

droit. « S'il est vrai que les seuls paradis sont ceux qu'on a perdus, je sais comment nommer ce quelque chose de tendre et d'inhumain qui m'habite aujourd'hui. Un émigrant revient dans sa patrie. [...] Et si j'aimais alors en me donnant, enfin j'étais moi-même puisqu'il n'y a que l'amour qui nous rende à nous-mêmes[1]. » Il a vingt-quatre ans quand il publie ces lignes qu'on croirait lourdes d'expérience. De 1942 à 1946, ses *Carnets* portent la trace d'un projet de roman, « L'enfance pauvre », qui relaie *L'Envers et l'Endroit*. Enfin, après avoir inventé à l'automne de 1951 la formule du *Premier Homme* (le fils qui, sur la tombe de son père, s'aperçoit qu'il est devenu « l'aîné »[2]), il va intégrer à son roman les éléments destinés à « L'enfance pauvre ». De sa fidélité à *L'Envers et l'Endroit* témoigne la préface à la réédition du recueil (1958) : « il y a plus de véritable amour dans ces pages maladroites que dans toutes celles qui ont suivi[3] », et aussi : « [...] le jour où l'équilibre s'établira entre ce que je suis et ce que je dis, ce jour-là peut-être, et j'ose à peine l'écrire, je pourrai bâtir l'œuvre dont je rêve. Ce que j'ai voulu dire ici, c'est qu'elle ressemblera à *L'Envers et l'Endroit*, d'une façon ou de l'autre, et qu'elle parlera d'une certaine forme d'amour[4]. » Le troisième étage de l'œuvre serait donc moins la découverte de l'amour que sa mise en forme. S'éloignant de son point de départ (une recherche du père plus ou moins vouée à l'abstraction),

1. « Entre oui et non », *L'Envers et l'Endroit*, *OC*, t. I, p. 47.

2. On trouvera toutes ces étapes dans le Dossier, p. 158 et suiv.

3. *OC*, t. I, p. 31-32.

4. *Ibid.*, p. 37.

Le Premier Homme trouvera sa vérité dans le retour vers des proches qu'on peut mieux aimer parce qu'on les a connus.

En somme, l'œuvre de Camus est cyclique en ce sens que, après la quarantaine, il réussit à écrire une œuvre qui renoue avec la veine de sa jeunesse. Lui-même le signifie en 1955 quand, au lieu de diviser son œuvre en étages, il la voit évoluer « selon une sorte de spirale où la pensée repasse par d'anciens chemins sans cesser de les surplomber[1] ». *Le Premier Homme* surplombe *L'Envers et l'Endroit*. Entre ces deux ouvrages, Camus a vécu, aimé et souffert. Il a sans doute appris à mieux aimer, mais aussi à mieux écrire.

1. Lettre à André Nicolas, citée dans André Nicolas, *Camus*, Seghers, 1966, p. 148.

RETOUR À LA « CRÉATION »

Pourquoi la préface à *L'Envers et l'Endroit* publiée en 1958 parle-t-elle au futur du *Premier Homme*, auquel Camus travaille depuis plus de quatre années ? Parce que, ébauchée dès 1950[2], elle a été pour l'essentiel achevée en octobre 1953, mois de naissance du *Premier Homme*[3]. À Maria Casarès, Camus confiera qu'une nuit, sans doute celle du samedi 17 au dimanche 18 octobre, « il fut pris d'insomnie et se leva à quatre heures du matin pour fixer le thème de son prochain roman[4] ». Cette nuit inaugure, croit-il, une période où il va enfin se consacrer pleinement à la création littéraire. Ce n'est pas la première fois qu'il nourrit cette illusion. « Après *L'Homme*

2. *Carnets II*, p. 297-298 et *III*, p. 13 et 18.

3. Voir Yosei Matsumoto, « Année 1953 : le tournant décisif », *Études camusiennes*, n° 7, 2006, p. 73.

4. Confidence rapportée par Herbert R. Lottman, *Albert Camus*, p. 538.

1. *Carnets II*,
p. 324.

2. *Carnets III*,
p. 103.

3. *Carnets, OC*,
t. II, p. 795.

révolté, la création en liberté », s'était-il déjà promis en mai 1950[1]. La polémique née de la publication de l'essai et les affaires du monde ne lui ont guère laissé de répit. Il réitère sa résolution deux ans et demi plus tard, quand il commence *Le Premier Homme* : « Octobre 1953. Publication d'*Actuelles II*. L'inventaire est terminé — le commentaire et la polémique. Désormais, la création[2]. » La création avancera cahin-caha au fil des années suivantes. Elle sera troublée non seulement par ses activités politiques (à *Actuelles II* succède en 1958 *Actuelles III*), mais par de graves soucis familiaux. Ce n'est qu'en 1959 qu'une série de séjours à Lourmarin, ainsi qu'un court voyage en Algérie où il se documentera sur son passé familial, lui permettront de travailler avec continuité à son manuscrit.

Se consacrer enfin à la « création », c'était, pour Camus, retrouver un chemin trop souvent oublié depuis sa jeunesse. « À mauvaise conscience, aveu nécessaire. L'œuvre d'art est un aveu, il me faut témoigner. Je n'ai qu'une chose à dire, à bien voir. C'est dans cette vie de pauvreté, parmi ces gens humbles ou vaniteux, que j'ai le plus sûrement touché ce qui me paraît le vrai sens de la vie. Les œuvres d'art n'y suffiront jamais. L'art n'est pas tout pour moi. Que du moins ce soit un moyen[3]. » Ces mots sont écrits en mai 1935, à la première page des *Carnets*. La vie de pauvreté que Camus a menée parmi les siens, la mauvaise conscience qu'il éprouve de l'avoir trahie, l'aveu qu'il en fera à sa mère : on croirait qu'il trace ici, déjà, un premier projet de son dernier roman. *Le Premier Homme* n'est donc pas pour Camus un simple retour à l'amour : il répond à une mission définie à l'orée de son œuvre, même si, de l'art d'abord conçu comme un simple « moyen », il se fera en 1950 une idée « bien trop haute pour consentir à le soumettre à rien[1] ».

En 1937, un projet de préface (demeuré inachevé) à *L'Envers et l'Endroit* a résumé d'avance l'ensemble de son œuvre : « C'est vrai que les pays méditerranéens sont les seuls où je puisse vivre, que j'aime la vie et la lumière ; mais c'est aussi vrai que le tragique de l'existence obsède l'homme et que le plus profond de lui-même y reste attaché[2]. » Du contraste entre l'envers et l'endroit, illustré par le « sourire sur les lèvres désespérées d'un homme[3] », naît l'ironie. « Toute mon œuvre est ironique », notera-t-il dans ses *Carnets*[4]. Loin de s'opposer, le bonheur et le malheur se nourrissent l'un de l'autre. C'est parce qu'elle est sans cesse menacée que la vie est précieuse, le tragique vivifiant la lumière et réciproquement. Dès 1934, dans « L'Hôpital du quartier pauvre », Camus évoquait son séjour parmi d'autres tuberculeux qui évaluaient leurs chances de s'en tirer. Des fous rires ponctuaient leurs réflexions fatalistes (« Un peu plus tôt, un peu plus tard[5] »). La digne attitude du malade — de

1. *Carnets II*, p. 329.

2. *OC*, t. I, p. 73.

3. *Ibid.*

4. *Carnets II*, p. 317.

5. *OC*, t. I, p. 75.

l'être humain en général — face à l'ironie de la vie se résume par un mot : « le courage ». Ainsi devait s'intituler le dernier récit de *L'Envers et l'Endroit* (finalement appelé « L'Envers et l'Endroit », comme l'ensemble du recueil). « Le grand courage, c'est encore de tenir les yeux ouverts sur la lumière comme sur la mort », y écrivait Camus[1]. Au héros du *Premier Homme* et à sa famille, réduits à la pauvreté, le courage tiendra lieu de morale.

Son roman aurait-il, s'il avait été poursuivi, approché mieux encore l'inspiration des premières années ? Un des feuillets insérés dans le manuscrit (Feuillet IV), sur « le thème de la comédie » et ce qu'il faut attendre des autres, reproduit à la lettre une des toutes premières pages des *Carnets*[2].

1. *Ibid.*, p. 71.

2. Voir *PH*, p. 318-319, et *Carnets*, *OC*, t. II, p. 797-798.

RETOUR À L'ALGÉRIE

L'expérience des pays méditerranéens, invoquée par Camus dans le projet de préface à *L'Envers et l'Endroit*, se limite alors presque exclusivement à l'Algérie. Un court séjour aux îles Baléares, terre d'origine de sa mère (septembre 1935), le retour par l'Italie d'un voyage en Europe centrale (fin de l'été 1936), c'était peu pour décider des pays où il pouvait vivre. L'expérience ne s'élargira guère ensuite : son premier voyage en Grèce, long de trois semaines à peine, il ne le fera qu'à qua-

21

rante-deux ans. Une fois les hommages rendus à la douceur des paysages italiens et aux ruines du berceau de la tragédie, le royaume, pour cet exilé de la métropole, demeurera toujours l'Algérie natale. Abus du biographisme ? Quand, dans *Le Malentendu*, Martha évoque avec nostalgie les « rivages heureux », aucun spectateur ne doute qu'elle aspire à rejoindre la patrie de l'auteur.

Après avoir baigné les paysages de *Noces*, la lumière de l'Algérie vire au tragique dans *L'Étranger* (lumière noire à force d'être aveuglante, qui fait du héros un meurtrier). À cette ironie de la géographie correspond celle de l'Histoire. Ce pays où des jeunes gens s'enivrent des joies du soleil et de la mer est le même dont Camus, envoyé en reportage par le journal *Alger républicain*, découvre en 1939 (l'année de *Noces*) la « détresse indicible ». « La Grèce évoque irrésistiblement une certaine gloire du corps et de ses prestiges. Et dans aucun pays que je connais, le corps ne m'a paru plus humilié que dans la Kabylie[1]. » À la beauté des paysages, Camus consacre quelques lignes à peine, à la fin de son article ; sans doute jugerait-il indécent de développer davantage. Aucun sourire ne vient attendrir les visages de ce peuple qui crie famine. Si toute l'œuvre de Camus est ironique, alors il faut admettre que le reportage en Kabylie ne fait pas, à proprement parler, partie de son œuvre.

L'injustice faite aux indigènes sur cette

1. « La Grèce en haillons », 5 juin 1939, *OC*, t. I, p. 653.

terre de bonheur, Camus la gardera présente au cœur et à l'esprit. Mais *Le Premier Homme* surprendra les lecteurs du reportage en Kabylie. C'est que, en germe dès les ébauches de *L'Envers et l'Endroit*, régulièrement nourri par les notes des *Carnets*, le roman est pour l'essentiel rédigé à une époque où, dans une Algérie meurtrie par la guerre, se profile de plus en plus l'éventualité de l'indépendance du pays. Les victimes du système colonial algérien ne sont plus seulement les indigènes, mais la population d'origine européenne, frappée par le terrorisme, calomniée par la métropole et menacée d'être chassée d'une terre à laquelle elle a droit. Après la publication en juin 1958 de ses *Chroniques algériennes (Actuelles III)*, Camus ne s'est presque pas exprimé dans la presse au sujet de l'Algérie. La tragédie, pensait-on, l'avait réduit au silence. Qu'il s'exprimât en composant *Le Premier Homme*, peu de gens le savaient. Le paradoxe est que ce roman d'un écrivain à vocation tragique, écrit alors que son pays vivait une tragédie, échappe pour finir au tragique.

AUTOBIOGRAPHIE ET ROMAN

ORDRE DU TEMPS, ORDRE DU LIVRE

La substitution du fils au père comme figure du « premier homme » est la clé du roman. Du moment où Jacques a vu la tombe d'Henri Cormery, les années ont cessé de « s'ordonner suivant ce grand fleuve qui coule vers sa fin. Elles n'étaient plus que fracas, ressac et remous » (p. 35). Ce bouleversement conditionne une complexité chronologique sur laquelle Camus n'en finit pas de s'interroger dans les marges du manuscrit et sur son carnet. « Quand, près de la tombe de son père, il sent le temps se disloquer — ce nouvel ordre du temps est celui du livre » (p. 362). Ce ferme principe, qu'il formule dans les ébauches après l'avoir mis en doute quatre feuillets plus tôt (« Si finalement je choisis l'ordre chronologique... », p. 358), se traduit par des hésitations renouvelées sur la succession des chapitres ou des épisodes (« mettre avant », « mettre après »...). S'ajoutent à ces incertitudes des incohérences dues à l'inachèvement de l'ouvrage. Subsistent enfin, dans la trame d'ensemble du récit que Camus avait projeté, d'immenses lacunes que l'imagination du lecteur évalue sans pouvoir les combler.

PETITE CONTRIBUTION
À UNE CHRONOLOGIE DU RÉCIT

Un regard d'ensemble sur la partie achevée du récit aidera à la fois à y fixer des repères chronologiques et à relativiser leur valeur.

Première partie : « Recherche du père »

1. Nous donnons aux deux premiers chapitres une numérotation qui est absente du manuscrit. Cette absence signifie-t-elle l'hésitation de Camus sur l'ordre à donner finalement à son récit ? Les chapitres suivants seront plus ou moins numérotés, sans grande rigueur.

Chapitre 1[1]. Arrivée d'Henri Cormery et de sa femme à Mondovi. Naissance de Jacques. *Novembre 1913.*

Chapitre 2 : « Saint-Brieuc. » Visite de Jacques sur la tombe de son père. *Printemps 1953.*

Chapitre 3 : « Saint-Brieuc et Malan (J. G.). » Visite à son ancien « maître » (les initiales sont celles de Jean Grenier, professeur de philosophie de Camus). *Soir de la même journée.*

Chapitre 4 : « Les jeux de l'enfant. » On remonte d'un présent du narrateur non daté (Jacques adulte se rend en bateau à Alger) jusqu'à l'époque de l'enfance.

Chapitre 5 : « Le père. Sa mort. La guerre. L'attentat ». Retour au présent du narrateur. Jacques, arrivé à Alger, rend visite à sa mère et il l'interroge sur son père, en particulier sur la date à laquelle il est né. Comme il a pu lire cette date sur la tombe, on en déduit que cette visite est antérieure au pèlerinage à Saint-Brieuc (1953). Jacques raconte pourtant bientôt à sa mère qu'il a vu des fleurs sur la tombe, et la suite de sa visite est troublée par l'explosion d'une bombe, dans la rue. Nous voici donc, contre toute attente, à l'époque du terrorisme à Alger, plus précisément en 1957.

« La bombe avait explosé dans le poteau électrique qui se trouvait près de l'arrêt [du tramway] » (p. 88). Le 3 juin 1957, trois bombes furent en effet placées dans des socles de lampadaires qui servaient d'arrêts d'autobus près de la Grande Poste, au bas de la rue Hoche et au carrefour de l'Agha, causant de vrais carnages (voir Yves Courrière, *La Guerre d'Algérie*, « Bouquins », Robert Laffont, t. I, 1990, p. 854-855). Dans *Le Premier Homme*, c'est vraisemblablement un de ces attentats que Camus situe à Belcourt.

Chapitre 6 : « La famille. » Il semble que se poursuive le récit de la même visite à la mère. En réalité, c'est d'une autre visite qu'il s'agit, sans doute postérieure : Jacques revient, en effet, d'un voyage à Solférino[1]. La visite permet d'enchaîner sur de nouveaux souvenirs familiaux.

Chapitre non numéroté : « Étienne. » Suite du récit des souvenirs, centrés cette fois sur la figure de l'oncle, auquel est aussitôt restitué son vrai prénom, Ernest. L'absence de numérotation de ce chapitre s'explique par une note marginale où Camus se demande s'il faudra placer l'oncle *avant* ou *après*. L'Étienne d'aujourd'hui (commentateur des attentats terroristes) y est confronté à celui dont Jacques enfant partageait les distractions (bains de mer, parties de chasse...) et dont la famille subissait l'humeur querelleuse. Les épi-

1. Camus écrit d'abord « Solférino », puis « Solferino ». Nous unifions en « Solférino ».

26

sodes y étant racontés à la queue leu leu, on suppose qu'ils suivent un ordre chronologique; les marges du texte en prévoient pourtant le bouleversement (« l'amener bien avant », « mettre tonnellerie avant colères », p. 138, 139), preuve que Camus s'interroge non seulement sur l'ordre de ses chapitres, mais sur celui des éléments qui les composent.

Chapitre 6 bis : « L'école. » Comme dans le chapitre précédent, une figure du présent (M. Bernard, l'instituteur âgé auquel Jacques rend visite) est confrontée à ce qu'elle était jadis (l'instituteur qui lui traça la voie).

Chapitre 7 : « Mondovi : La colonisation et le père. » On lit enfin le récit de cette visite au lieu de naissance (appelé ici de son vrai nom) à laquelle faisait allusion le début du chapitre 6. C'est la « recherche du père » que Jacques était allé y poursuivre. Mais les souvenirs qu'il a recueillis auprès des derniers témoins de cette époque se sont révélés incertains. La première partie du roman est bouclée. Ainsi que le lui avait laissé pressentir Malan, c'est dans une quête décevante que s'est lancé Jacques.

Deuxième partie :
« Le fils ou le premier homme »

Chapitre 1 : « Lycée. » Ce chapitre enchaîne sur le chapitre « L'école » de la première partie.

Deux chapitres non numérotés : « Le

poulailler et l'égorgement de la poule » et
« Jeudis et vacances ». Les jeudis, jours des
jeux, mais aussi des visites à la bibliothèque
du quartier, marquent une étape décisive
dans la formation de Jacques. Quant à ses
vacances, elles sont consacrées en majeure
partie aux deux emplois (deux étés) qu'il
a dû occuper pour faire entrer de l'argent
à la maison. Le deuxième de ces chapitres
nous conduit jusqu'à la période de l'adolescence (« l'enfant en effet était mort dans cet
adolescent maigre et musclé... », p. 298).

Chapitre 2 : « Obscur à soi-même. »
Méditation globale sur le passé (années
d'école, de lycée, de jeunesse et de maturité), qu'on lira comme une ébauche des
pages non écrites, une réflexion sur soi-
même, en même temps que comme une
ouverture vers l'avenir.

Le manuscrit couvre donc deux
époques :

1) celle de la maturité de Jacques Cormery, entrevue uniquement à l'occasion
de ses voyages à Saint-Brieuc, à Alger et
sur son lieu de naissance (Solférino ou
Mondovi).

2) celle de son enfance et de son adolescence à Alger, qu'on peut au contraire
reconstituer (même si les indications chronologiques sont rares et souvent marginales) presque année par année.

L'interruption du récit au moment où
Jacques parvient à l'adolescence est acci-
dentelle. « Le *ménage* Ernest, Catherine
après la mort de la grand-mère », avait noté

1. Camus
appelle ici
« ménage » le
couple que for-
meront le frère
et la sœur après
la mort de leur
mère.

Camus, en marge du manuscrit (p. 135)[1].
Il n'aura, en fait, pas le temps d'évoquer
ces années où, privés de leur mère, le frère
et la sœur se mettent à former une sorte
de couple. Si l'on réfère la vie de Jacques
à celle d'Albert Camus, cette période
aurait débuté en 1931 (date de la mort
de la grand-mère de l'auteur), c'est-à-dire
lorsque Jacques a dix-huit ans. L'allusion
à Hitler et aux persécutions anti-juives
(p. 113-114) fait dès lors l'effet d'une
intrusion anachronique dans le récit.
Quant au « ménage », le lecteur ne le
découvrira que vieillissant, dans la seconde
époque du roman, c'est-à-dire celle de la
maturité de Jacques.

Entre le moment où nous quittons
Jacques adolescent et celui où nous le
retrouvons sur la tombe de son père,
manque la totalité de ces années de jeunesse qui devaient être celles de ses engagements. Une ébauche de plan prévoit
en effet de traiter l'« action politique » de
l'« homme » en Algérie, mais aussi dans
« la Résistance », en miroir avec les gestes
de l'« adolescence » (p. 351). Quant à la
période de la maturité, elle aurait également été étoffée : « Récupérer Michel
[oncle de Jacques] pendant le tremblement
de terre d'Orléansville », lit-on dans une
marge. Ce tremblement de terre ayant eu
lieu le 9 septembre 1954, on en conclut
que l'expérience de Jacques quadragénaire
ne se serait pas limitée à ces va-et-vient
entre la métropole et l'Algérie qui, dans le

1. *Carnets*, *OC*, t. II, p. 1043.

2. « Oh non, oh non, disait-elle dans les larmes, j'aime tant l'amour » (*PH*, p. 305) reproduit les *Carnets* : « Mi à qui je parle miriant mi-sérieux de l'extrême vieillesse où c'en est fini de l'envolée des choses, de la jubilation des sens, etc., éclate en sanglots, "j'aime tant l'amour" » (*Carnets III*, p. 272).

3. Le bégaiement du texte doit sans doute ici à l'inachèvement du manuscrit.

manuscrit, semblent suffire à ses occupations. Jeunesse et maturité eussent enfin été nourries par les amours de Jacques, en particulier pour la mystérieuse Jessica. Ce prénom était inscrit dans les *Carnets* dès 1946 (« Roman d'amour : Jessica[1] ») avant de masquer « Mi », une jeune étudiante danoise qu'il connut dans les toutes dernières années de sa vie[2].

Le flou persiste à plus forte raison sur la date à laquelle eût abouti le récit. Nous apprenons qu'après avoir retrouvé son vieil instituteur en 1945, Jacques va le voir « chaque année depuis quinze ans » (p. 177). La date de 1960 aussitôt déduite par le lecteur relève du hasard : le présent du narrateur nous aurait évidemment conduits au-delà.

INCOHÉRENCES ET HARDIESSES

Complexe et lacunaire, la chronologie est brouillée par une pratique équivoque de l'imparfait, en particulier au chapitre 5 : Camus y raconte-t-il *une* scène de retrouvailles de Jacques avec sa mère ou une série de scènes semblables ? Enchaînant avec le voyage en bateau de Jacques, l'imparfait de « Il la serrait dans ses bras » (p. 66) exprime vraisemblablement la longueur de l'étreinte filiale. Réitérant son récit à la page suivante[3], Camus en confirme, par l'usage du passé simple, la singularité : « Quand il arriva devant la porte, sa mère l'ouvrait et se jetait dans ses bras » (p. 68), les imparfaits de la proposition principale traduisant ici la concomitance de l'élan maternel avec l'arrivée *ce jour-là* de Jacques devant sa porte. Mais on est perplexe quand, Jacques ayant lancé à sa mère : « Papa? », le romancier écrit : « Elle le regardait et devenait attentive » (p. 73). « Regardait » et, à plus forte raison, « devenait » expriment à l'évidence le comportement habituel de la mère chaque fois que son fils lui parlait, non sa réaction ponctuelle à une soudaine interpellation. À l'inverse, l'interrogatoire serré sur le père auquel a préludé « Papa? » se déroulera ensuite, non comme un rituel de leurs rencontres, mais comme un moment unique des relations du fils à la mère, indispensable à la conduite de la « recherche du père ». Une phrase a donc suffi pour faire planer, sur l'ensemble du chapitre, un flou chronologique. On ne s'étonne plus trop, dès lors, que cet entretien qui devrait logiquement précéder le pèlerinage à Saint-Brieuc comporte des éléments qui le situent après. À l'aune de ces doutes, on relit le chapitre 5 depuis son début, et on remet en question les hypothèses formulées sur les imparfaits qui l'ouvraient.

Ce chapitre illustre une réflexion valable pour l'ensemble des souvenirs d'enfance et d'adolescence : Camus n'avait pas nettement articulé, au moment où la mort a interrompu son manuscrit, les passages évoquant la permanence du foyer maternel avec les épisodes ponctuels qui y prendraient place (interrogatoire sur le père, attentats terroristes...). Au plan de la technique du récit et de ses incidences chronologiques, il est resté à mi-chemin entre la méditation traversant les années qui lui avait inspiré *L'Envers et l'Endroit* et les exigences temporelles appelées par l'intrigue d'un roman qui, à le prendre sous son aspect le plus extérieur, a pour sujet la conduite d'une enquête.

1. *Mes pensées, Œuvres complètes,* Gallimard, « Pléiade », t. I, p. 1220.

Les surprises réservées par le montage du manuscrit ne doivent pas toujours aux aléas de l'inachèvement. « Pour bien écrire, il faut sauter les idées intermédiaires », disait Montesquieu[1]. Camus supprime, pour composer son roman, des scènes intermédiaires. Ainsi, alors que Jacques se trouvait à l'endroit où a explosé la bombe de l'attentat, c'est-à-dire à l'arrêt du tramway, le paragraphe suivant débute par : « Il s'était retourné vers sa mère » (p. 88). Comprenons qu'il est, entre-temps, remonté dans l'appartement. Le « Papa ? », trouant la rêverie de Jacques sur les objets du foyer, trouve un écho dans le « Maman » qui ramène au réel après la reconstitution de la scène où le maire vint apprendre à Catherine la mort de son mari (p. 84).

L'Envers et l'Endroit offrait des exemples comparables de rupture du récit.

« Être un homme, c'est ce qui compte. Sa grand-mère mourra, puis sa mère, lui.

La mère a sursauté. Elle a eu peur. [...] » (*OC*, t. I, p. 50).

Point d'attentat ici. Le texte n'indique pas de quoi la mère a eu peur.

Soucieux de ruptures, Camus se révèle néanmoins, dans trois notes marginales, attentif aux transitions (p. 34, 69 et 96). Signale-t-il ainsi des transitions faites ou à trouver ? On ne saurait dire. Il en a en tout cas réussi d'autres. Ainsi, de l'éclat d'obus qui frappa Henri Cormery et que la mère a pieusement conservé, le texte enchaîne sur la patrouille de parachutistes qui passe dans la rue, image de la guerre dont souffre aujourd'hui l'Algérie (p. 85). On parlerait au cinéma de fondu enchaîné. Et d'une scène où Jacques est l'élève de M. Bernard, on passe aussi à celle où, adulte, il lui rend visite ; entre ces deux époques distantes de trente ans, « petit » assure le lien. « Allons petit, allons petit », lui disait son maître quand il était en classe ; « Attends, petit », lui dit-il aujourd'hui (p. 167). Aux yeux de ses aînés, Jacques est demeuré un enfant.

L'HORIZON ROMANESQUE

L'EFFACEMENT DES CONFIDENCES

Nous avons sans excès de scrupules utilisé la biographie de Camus pour éclairer des points obscurs de la vie de Jacques Cormery. De même utilise-t-on sans façons *Vie de Henry Brulard* pour connaître en détail la vie d'Henri Beyle. Le parallèle ne peut être poussé trop loin : si Beyle utilise un pseudonyme (il en a utilisé d'autres) pour raconter sa vie, il présente du moins son récit comme une autobiographie, alors que Camus a dès l'origine désigné son ouvrage comme un roman. L'étiquette vaut contrat de lecture. Surtout, même si rien n'interdit à un autobiographe de faire interférer les époques, la priorité donnée dans *Le Premier Homme* à un ordre expressif du temps relève bien d'un souci de composition propre aux techniques du roman. Jusqu'à présent, Camus s'était signalé comme un romancier de la linéarité. Pour cette raison autant peut-être qu'à cause de leur brièveté, les critiques qualifient souvent de « récits » *L'Étranger* et *La Chute*, tandis que la chronique tenue par le docteur Rieux, dont elle n'est pourtant que l'écrin, confère à *La Peste* elle-même l'étiquette de « chronique[1] ». Pour la première fois, avec *Le Premier Homme*, Camus conçoit une fiction qui exprime par sa composition le bouleversement du temps ; mais pour la première fois aussi depuis *L'Envers et l'Endroit*, il donne forme littéraire à une expression intime du moi. Ainsi, alors qu'il mérite, aux yeux des spécialistes des genres, la qualité de roman pour ses vertus formelles, *Le Premier Homme* soulève un doute d'une autre nature : le public peut-il lire comme une fiction le récit authentifié de la vie d'un personnage célèbre sous prétexte que les noms y ont été plus ou moins déguisés et l'ordre des épisodes modifié ?

« Cette rédaction initiale a un caractère autobiographique qui aurait sûrement dis-

1. « Recueil de faits historiques, rapportés dans l'ordre de leur succession » (Grand Robert). La première édition des œuvres de Camus dans la Pléiade comporte deux volumes : I. *Théâtre, récits, nouvelles.* II. *Essais.* Il n'aurait donc pas écrit de romans ?

paru dans la version définitive du roman »,
lit-on sur la quatrième page de couverture
de l'édition « Folio ». Au moins Camus
aurait-il unifié les transpositions des noms
propres. D'abord appelée Lucie, la mère
retrouve bientôt son vrai prénom, Catherine, se démasquant même une fois comme
la «Vve Camus » (p. 224). L'oncle Étienne
(exceptionnellement Émile) est le plus
souvent Ernest, prénom de l'oncle de
Camus. Son instituteur Louis Germain,
baptisé M. Bernard, retrouve lui aussi deux
fois son identité (p. 164 et 190). Mondovi,
appelé Solférino, redevient ensuite Mondovi. Il arrive, à l'inverse, que Camus
donne spontanément leurs vrais noms à
ses personnages. « Attention, changer les
prénoms » (p. 121), s'enjoint-il en marge
après avoir nommé « Daniel » et « Pierre »
les deux camarades d'atelier de son oncle.
C'est dire que tantôt il s'applique à la fiction (les noms sont uniformément déguisés dans le premier chapitre, que ne nourrit aucun souvenir personnel), tantôt il se
laisse aller au récit autobiographique,
remettant les transpositions à plus tard.
Prend-on plus facilement ses distances
avec soi-même qu'avec les êtres chers ? Un
seul « moi » vient, au plan formel, troubler
la cohérence du personnage de « Jacques
Cormery » : « La Méditerranée séparait en
moi deux univers » (p. 214). L'autre première personne du manuscrit est celle d'un
narrateur qui, de l'extérieur, introduit un
commentaire au sein du récit : « et les eth-

nologues me font bien rire qui cherchent la raison de tant de rites mystérieux » (p. 130). Comme elle est unique, cette occurrence sonne comme une incongruité.

Camus pouvait-il, mieux que par de fragiles changements de noms, gommer ou voiler les événements et les lieux de son enfance, qui sont la chair même du récit ? L'autobiographie serait de toute façon demeurée transparente. « La méthode est la sincérité », écrivait-il quand il programmait l'« étage » de l'amour[1]. Il est vrai que la sincérité s'accommode volontiers de pseudonymes, alors que la fidélité à la lettre peut être l'alibi du mensonge. Mais du moment que Camus avait décidé de livrer le fond de son cœur (« En somme, je vais parler de ceux que j'aimais... »), l'exercice du déguisement se révélait précaire.

L'avenir proprement romanesque du *Premier Homme* se devine toutefois grâce aux ébauches. « Faire parler de J., l'amener, le présenter par les autres et par le portrait contradictoire qu'à eux tous ils brossent », prévoit Camus (p. 329), autant dire : changer en personnage de roman le sujet du récit autobiographique. Il résume du reste son projet dans la même page : « Faire ainsi *grandir* le personnage ». Son entourage étoffera le roman : « Se servir alors de Pierre comme repère et lui donner un passé, un pays, une famille, une morale (?) — Pierre — Didier ? » (p. 324). Pierre Fassina, le meilleur copain de Jacques, était donc destiné à assurer, au

1. Voir *supra*, p. 14, note 2.

détriment de l'authenticité des faits, une fonction romanesque qui l'aurait rendu interchangeable avec le personnage de Didier, copain de lycée venu de la métropole, qui impressionne Jacques par la riche mémoire que sa famille a gardée de son propre passé et de celui de sa patrie. « Pierre serait l'artiste ? » se demande Camus un peu plus loin (p. 326), puis « Pierre avocat » (p. 327), l'orientant vers d'autres fonctions possibles. Jessica surtout, évoquée par allusions dans le manuscrit et promise à un bel avenir dans les ébauches, aurait sans doute transposé des aventures amoureuses pour lesquelles Camus était, moins que pour ses amitiés d'école ou de lycée, disposé aux confidences.

OÙ JACQUES S'ÉLOIGNE D'ALBERT

L'examen de la conformité de la vie de Jacques Cormery avec celle d'Albert Camus est un exercice malaisé parce qu'il recourt à deux approches d'essences différentes : d'une part, il met à contribution les biographies de Camus (critique extérieure au texte), d'autre part, il nous impose d'imaginer pour quelles raisons littéraires le romancier a menti, oublié ou transposé (critique interne, mais hasardeuse).

À coup sûr, certains écarts entre le roman et la réalité ne sont pas intentionnels. L'origine alsacienne attribuée à la famille paternelle de Jacques (p. 80), Camus la croyait vraiment sienne : dans son Avant-

propos à *Actuelles III. Chroniques algériennes*
(mars-avril 1958), il se compte à l'évidence
parmi ces hommes « dont les grands-
parents, par exemple, ont opté pour la
France en 1871 et quitté leur terre
d'Alsace pour l'Algérie, dont les pères sont
morts en masse dans l'est de la France en
1914 [...][1] ». Il est vrai que « les mairies
d'Algérie *n'ont pas d'archives* la plupart du
temps » (p. 314). Il se trompe encore, s'il
entend refléter le destin de sa famille,
quand il prétend que la guerre a chassé
les Cormery de la ferme de Saint-Apôtre
(p. 76) : Lucien Camus était résolu, avant
même la déclaration de la guerre, à revenir à Alger pour épargner à sa famille les
piqûres des moustiques de la vallée de
la Seybouse. Camus a-t-il, comme Jacques,
fait sa première communion à l'église
Saint-Charles, située au centre-ville ? Dès
la publication du roman, des lecteurs atten-
tifs jugèrent qu'il n'y avait aucune vraisemblance que sa grand-mère se fût adressée à cette paroisse huppée plutôt qu'à
celle du quartier de Belcourt, l'église Saint-
Bonaventure. Mais l'« affreuse bâtisse en
gothique moderne » (p. 185) désigne à
coup sûr l'imposante église Saint-Charles,
non la frêle et modeste église Saint-Bona-
venture. La démarche de la grand-mère
restera donc un mystère.

D'autres écarts doivent à l'invention
romanesque. D'abord, Camus devait bien
savoir que Lucien Camus s'était dès le
printemps de 1913 installé à Mondovi, où

1. *Essais*, p. 897.
« Rarement
légende familiale
aura été aussi
erronée que dans
le cas d'Albert
Camus »,
écrit Herbert
R. Lottman
(*Albert Camus*,
p. 20), qui
est remonté
jusqu'à l'origine
bordelaise
de la famille
paternelle.

il avait été envoyé par la maison Ricome pour gérer un domaine viticole. Sa femme Catherine, enceinte, l'y ayant rejoint en septembre, Albert put naître en novembre dans des conditions moins périlleuses que Jacques Cormery. « En voilà un qui commence bien, dit la patronne de la cantine. Par un déménagement » (p. 27). En inventant cet accouchement précipité, le romancier a placé son héros sous le signe de l'errance. Plus imaginatif que la vie, le roman autorise à multiplier les symboles : figure de pionnier toujours prêt pour un nouveau départ, Jacques, né à la va-vite, éclaire idéalement la destinée de Camus qui, par nécessité matérielle, refus de l'embourgeoisement ou indépendance sentimentale, connut jusqu'à la fin de sa vie un nombre incalculable de domiciles[1].

Ensuite, alors que Camus avait un frère aîné (né en 1910 et prénommé Lucien comme son père), c'est à peine, a-t-on envie de dire, si Jacques en a un. Le « petit garçon de quatre ans » qui dort dans la carriole contre sa mère (p. 15) devient vite problématique : « Le petit garçon », se contente de noter Camus, en marge, un peu plus loin (p. 17), puis, dans une parenthèse : « (Il prit le petit garçon?) » (p. 19). Enfin, à la question du docteur : « C'est votre premier ? », le père de Jacques contredit les brèves indications qui précèdent en répondant : « Non, j'ai laissé un garçon de quatre ans à Alger chez ma belle-mère » (p. 24). Bref, ce frère, Camus paraît ne

1. « Naissance dans un déménagement », a prévu Camus dès qu'il a conçu son roman. Voir Dossier, p. 159.

savoir qu'en faire. Dans la suite du récit, nous saurons que les deux enfants partagent le même lit, que tous deux subviennent aujourd'hui aux besoins de la mère (p. 72), qu'ils interprétaient en duo la *Sérénade* de Toselli (p. 105)[1]; l'instituteur, enfin, rend hommage à la grand-mère et à la mère d'avoir élevé « deux bons garçons » (p. 179). Mais le frère aîné ne prend vraiment consistance que pour s'effacer devant Jacques quand il faut aller dans l'obscurité chercher la poule dans le poulailler. En somme, la seule scène du roman qui établisse fortement sa présence consacre sa couardise. L'ensemble du texte fait implicitement de Jacques le préféré de la famille : on ne surprend aucun geste d'affection de la mère pour son fils aîné, et du moment que les deux enfants couchent dans le même lit, puisque l'un se réveille à l'aube pour suivre l'oncle à la chasse, l'autre devrait être réveillé aussi (p. 118); peine perdue, Jacques seul aura le privilège de ces journées qui comptent parmi les plus belles de son enfance. Le Christ, pareillement, n'a pas eu de frères. Ou s'il en a eu, comme l'affirment à la lettre les Évangiles[2], les exégètes ont préféré l'en débarrasser. Les héros de roman en général n'ont pas de frères, ou ils les relèguent dans l'ombre. Après avoir inscrit le nom de son frère Robert sur les premiers brouillons d'*À la recherche du temps perdu*, Proust en a délesté le parcours du héros-narrateur, fils unique et chéri d'une mère dont la figure est redoublée par celle de la grand-mère.

---

1. En cette occasion, le frère est (logiquement) prénommé Henri, comme le père. Il sera aussi prénommé Louis (p. 250).

2. « Il parlait encore aux foules, lorsque survinrent sa mère et ses frères qui, se tenant dehors, cherchaient à lui parler » (saint Matthieu, 13, 46), « Sa mère et ses frères arrivent [...] » (saint Marc, 3, 31).

Nous savons que Jacques, à partir de 1945, rend chaque année visite à son ancien instituteur, M. Bernard, donc à sa mère puisqu'elle habite dans la même ville. *Le Premier Homme* dessine peut-être un fils plus attentif ou assidu que ne put l'être Camus, dont les séjours à Alger furent souvent commandés par l'état de santé de sa mère. Mais nous avons appris à ne pas dénombrer trop exactement ces retours au foyer. Effet d'une mémoire embellissante : Jacques donne, dans le texte, l'impression de ne cesser d'aller voir sa mère, au point que les séjours se chevauchent ou se confondent.

La visite rendue par Jacques à son ancien maître, retiré à Saint-Brieuc, entretient un lien avec la réalité : ancien professeur de philosophie de Camus devenu son ami, Jean Grenier (désigné par ses initiales dans le titre du chapitre) était, en effet, breton, et s'il ne prit pas sa retraite dans sa région natale, une carte adressée à Camus de Trébeurden en juillet 1953 atteste qu'il y séjourna l'année où Jacques Cormery fait son pèlerinage à Saint-Brieuc. C'est bien « son vieux maître » (p. 33) que Jacques décide de revoir à l'occasion du pèlerinage sur la tombe de son père. Il reste que, même si un maître n'est pas obligatoirement un enseignant, la révélation que Malan est un ancien administrateur des douanes (p. 39) surprend. À l'exception des moustaches (à moins que Jean Grenier en ait porté à une époque de sa vie), la des-

1. Voir Albert
Camus-Jean
Grenier,
Correspondance,
lettre du 1ᵉʳ août
1958, p. 221.
Jean Grenier
sollicite de
Camus un prêt
parce que, son
traitement ayant
été augmenté,
il doit payer plus
d'impôts.

2. C'est aussi
l'avis de Jean
Sarocchi, *Le
Dernier Camus
ou « Le Premier
Homme »*, qui y
voit « un des
morceaux les
plus faibles du
roman » (p. 72).

cription physique de Malan concorde avec les photos que nous avons conservées du vrai maître. Quant à « l'air d'un Chinois » (p. 41) prêté au personnage, on le soupçonne de devoir au goût de Grenier pour les philosophies d'Extrême-Orient. Le sens de l'économie enfin, cette « peur de manquer », que Jacques reproche à Malan (p. 43), une lettre de Grenier lui donne crédit[1]. « Chapitre à écrire et à supprimer », a noté Camus en marge du titre (p. 39). « Supprimer, puis réécrire », attendrait-on plutôt. On comprend, en tout cas, qu'avec ses plats effets de réel (le fromage de chèvre, la salade de fruits, la suspension à l'ancienne...) et ses dialogues qui sombrent pour finir dans un humanisme exagérément sentimental, ce chapitre n'ait pas satisfait Camus[2].

LA MISE EN ŒUVRE DU ROMAN

L'HOMME ET LE FILS DE L'HOMME

Le Premier Homme étant, à l'exception du premier chapitre, tributaire de la conscience et de l'expérience de Jacques Cormery, Camus aurait pu écrire presque tout son roman, comme il l'avait fait pour *L'Étranger*, à la première personne. Choisir la troisième, c'était accuser une distance, au moins formelle, avec son héros. C'était surtout s'autoriser à lui prêter une portée symbolique magnifiante, qu'aurait difficilement assumée un « je ». Autant, en effet, la conscience de Meursault est étroite, autant celle de Jacques vise à une forme d'intelligence et d'amour universels. C'est le lecteur de *L'Étranger* qui, guidé par le titre du roman, donne au héros une valeur symbolique (jamais Meursault n'articule : je suis un étranger). Dans *Le Premier Homme*, il revient, au contraire, au héros de justifier lui-même le titre de l'ouvrage. Et s'il n'y aurait rien d'incongru à ce que Camus écrivît « je suis le premier homme » plutôt que « il est le premier homme » pour marquer une simple antériorité, la formule « je suis un nouvel Adam », qui se lit en filigrane derrière cette information chronologique, ne pouvait être prononcée sans emphase et ridicule par un individu ordinaire.

***

Dans *La Peste*, le docteur Rieux est un citoyen parmi d'autres. Son héroïsme, sa douceur, son attention aux autres (il aide un enfant à traverser la rue), suscitent l'admiration et l'attendrissement du lecteur. Mais du moment où celui-ci apprend, à la fin du roman, que le docteur a tenu lui-même cette chronique écrite à sa gloire, il est saisi de gêne. On est ému au spectacle de Sisyphe roulant son rocher. Mais imaginez que Sisyphe vous dise lui-même : « Admirez comme je roule mon rocher avec grâce » ? L'idée *a priori* intéressante d'une chronique de l'héroïsme écrite par le héros lui-même contribua sans doute, après la publication de *La Peste*, à donner de Camus l'image d'un juste auto-proclamé. Il fallait que Jacques Cormery, être d'amour et de bonté, accédât, au-delà de sa ressemblance avec l'écrivain, à un statut exemplaire et quasiment mythique de « premier homme » pour que l'erreur de *La Peste* ne fût pas renouvelée.

Le parallélisme des présentations du père (le « premier homme ») et de Jacques (appelé à devenir à son tour le « premier homme ») contribue, dans les deux premiers chapitres, à élever la figure de Jacques au-dessus de celle d'un individu ordinaire. Camus raconte, dans le cas d'Henri comme de Jacques, l'histoire d'un « homme » (p. 14 et 29). Si le père est un personnage de roman, Jacques en sera un autre. Rien de plus traditionnel que l'ouverture du récit : une carriole sur la route et, brossés à grands traits, le cadre et le temps qu'il fait. L'« homme », sommairement décrit ainsi que son épouse et le conducteur de la voiture, sera le héros de cette aventure dans le bled algérien. Après cette entrée *in medias res*, Camus fait retour sur la date de l'événement (« une nuit de l'automne 1913 ») et sur les circonstances du voyage. À l'exemple des romanciers qui, par souci de la vraisemblance, se font simples spectateurs quand débute l'histoire[1], il appelle son héros de façon répétitive l'« homme » jusqu'à ce que celui-ci révèle son identité : « Je m'appelle Henri Cormery » (p. 23). Du trio de voyageurs, décrits d'abord avec une égale attention, l'« homme » avait progressivement émergé sans focaliser toutefois la perspective. « On le vit surgir, de dos, portant un matelas » (p. 20), « On distinguait » (p. 22) : il n'était qu'un personnage dans le tableau.

1. « En 1829, par une jolie matinée de printemps, un homme âgé d'environ cinquante ans [...] » (Balzac, *Le Médecin de campagne*). « Un jeune homme de dix-huit ans, à longs cheveux [...] » (Flaubert, *L'Éducation sentimentale*).

Dès qu'il est nommé Henri Cormery, son regard conduit le récit : on n'aperçoit pas le nouveau-né du moment que le docteur le masque à ses yeux (p. 26) ; la pièce où sont couchés la femme et l'enfant est ensuite telle qu'il la voit ; le chapitre s'achève enfin au moment où il ferme les yeux (p. 28).

Quelques mois plus tard, les yeux d'Henri Cormery se fermeront pour toujours. Mais le récit s'en tient pour l'instant à ce sommeil mérité au soir d'une dure journée, qui l'a vu devenir père pour la seconde fois. Une ellipse de quarante ans, enjambant deux guerres mondiales, sépare, en effet, le voyage en carriole vers Solférino du voyage en train vers Saint-Brieuc ; ce sont les témoignages personnels fournis à Jacques sur son père, non des documents historiques, qui permettront de reconstituer ce début de la guerre de 14-18 où celui-ci a perdu la vie.

À l'image d'Henri Cormery, le passager du train est « un homme ». Au « regard clair » d'Henri (p. 24) répond son « regard bleu et droit » (p. 29). En signe de fidélité sans doute à la pauvreté de son milieu familial, Jacques voyage, comme son père jadis, en troisième classe (p. 17 et 30). Son âge : « la quarantaine ». Comme dans les romans d'aventures qui exhibent malicieusement leurs ficelles, le lecteur a compris : cet homme, c'est donc... Durant trois paragraphes, il sera pourtant désigné obstinément comme « le voyageur ». Au lecteur qui ne l'aurait pas reconnu, son patronyme sera révélé du moment où il indiquera au gardien du cimetière le nom de son père. À la page suivante, il recevra aussi un prénom, Jacques, sans qu'aucune précaution narrative ait justifié ce complément d'identité. Rude gaillard dont la personnalité s'exprimait par l'autorité naturelle ou par de pudiques gestes de tendresse, Henri Cormery semblait imperméable à l'analyse psychologique ; la « recherche du père » s'est donc présentée, dès l'origine, comme une tâche difficile. Jacques, à l'inverse, est transparent dans ses moindres intentions. Et tandis que son père avait la gravité du chargé de famille, son fils regrette, l'air badin, de rater l'occasion que lui a offerte un échange de sourires avec une voyageuse : « Dommage » (p. 30). Les deux hommes ont un point commun : Henri a été sensible à « l'odeur de fumée » qui se dégageait des vêtements du vieil Arabe (p. 27) et à « l'odeur puissante » qui émanait de la terre quasi déserte (p. 28) ; Jacques, à l'odeur de transpiration du gardien du cimetière (p. 32), puis à « l'odeur des fleurs mouillées » (p. 34). L'acuité du sens olfactif est donc un trait héréditaire.

La suite du roman confirmera à quel point Jacques est le fils d'Henri. La mère de Jacques, qui se souvient si peu, se souvient au moins du visage de son époux : « Oui, c'était toi tout craché. Il avait les yeux clairs. Et le front, comme toi » (p. 74). La filiation ne se limite pas à cette ressemblance physique. C'est encore la mère qui témoigne : « "Il avait de la tête." Elle le regardait. "Comme toi" » (p. 75-76) ; et, quasiment muet, l'oncle dit tout de même l'essentiel au sujet de Jacques : « L'a la bonne tête, celui-là. [...] Comme son père » (p. 114). La distinction de principe qu'on voudrait maintenir entre Camus et son héros est ici difficile à tenir. Dans *L'Envers et l'Endroit*, la mère exprimait au fils sa ressemblance avec le père en des termes identiques :

« C'est vrai que je ressemble à mon père ?

— Oh, ton père tout craché[1]. »

1. *OC*, t. I, p. 53.

Si, à vingt ans d'intervalle, Camus remploie les mêmes expressions, on y verra le signe, non qu'il réutilise ses textes, mais que, à travers les époques, le vocabulaire de la mère n'a pas varié, et que *Le Premier Homme* reflète sans transposition des souvenirs personnels.

Henri Cormery avait de la tête, mais aussi du cœur. Il a rejeté, quand il combattait en 1905 au Maroc, l'idée que la guerre autorise les hommes à commettre des atrocités : « Non, un homme ça s'empêche » (p. 78). Il répondait ici aux arguments de Levesque, aux yeux de qui tous les moyens sont bons pour des hommes qui défendent leur terre. La position d'Henri Cormery préfigure celle que défendra Camus pendant la guerre d'Algérie : on n'a pas le droit de servir une cause qu'on croit juste en recourant à la torture ou au terrorisme. À sa façon, avec son vocabulaire fruste, il formule plus généralement la philosophie camusienne de la « limite ». Les mots lui ont manqué, en revanche, le jour où il est rentré du spectacle de l'exécution de Pirette : il a seulement vomi. Saisi de nausée à la seule évocation de cette horreur, Jacques prend le relais de l'indignation paternelle (p. 95). Ainsi se simplifient en rejets physiques les arguments de Camus contre la peine de mort. Si, enfin, l'infirmière qui a assisté à la mort d'Henri a cru bon d'écrire à sa veuve qu'il s'était montré « bien courageux » (p. 85), il s'agit d'une formule convenue, mais Jacques la prendra pour argent comptant : on le voit, à la page suivante, s'exalter à « des histoires d'honneur et de courage » (p. 86), dont Camus saura lui-même tirer les leçons. La « recherche du père », c'est donc pour Jacques la recherche d'un double de soi en même temps que d'un modèle. Le fils aura en grandissant les moyens de formuler une morale dont le père lui avait, d'instinct, transmis les valeurs. Ces valeurs, ce sont celles sur lesquelles Camus a édifié sa pensée.

La notion de la limite, formulée dès *L'Envers et l'Endroit* (« Je sais bien que j'ai tort, qu'il y a des limites à se donner », *OC*, t. I, p. 68) et qu'on retrouve au cœur de la « pensée de midi » (dernier chapitre de *L'Homme révolté*), guide la pensée de Camus sur la révolution bien avant la guerre d'Algérie. Dans *Les Justes*, par exemple, à Dora qui lui dit : « Même dans la destruction, il y a un ordre, il y a des limites », Stepan, le révolutionnaire fanatique, réplique : « Il n'y a pas de limites » (acte II).

La scène de l'exécution de Pirette s'éclaire grâce au passage de *La Peste* où Tarrou raconte comment il prit en dégoût son père magistrat le jour où celui-ci obtint grâce à une plaidoirie brillante la tête d'un inculpé (*La Peste*, Quatrième partie, *OC*, t. II, p. 205-207). Son hostilité personnelle à la peine de mort, Camus l'a formulée notamment dans *Réflexions sur la peine capitale*, ouvrage écrit en collaboration avec Arthur Koestler où son texte est intitulé *Réflexions sur la guillotine* (Calmann-Lévy, 1957).

Les portraits parallèles des deux hommes sont tracés sur des fonds de pays différents. Si les « petites maisons sans étages, toutes semblables » (p. 22), du paysage algérien n'appellent pas de commentaire du romancier, celles de la métropole sont « laides » (p. 29), « banales » avec de « vilaines tuiles rouges » (p. 31). La carriole d'Henri Cormery s'aventurait dans un pays « sans nom », étendu comme à l'infini de l'Atlantique à la mer Tyrrhénienne, l'Algérie se fondant dans l'immense territoire du Maghreb ; c'est au contraire un pays « étroit » que traverse le train de Saint-Brieuc. « Pendant des millénaires » les empires et les peuples sont passés par le Maghreb sans, dirait-on, y laisser de traces ; « depuis des siècles » les prés et les champs de la métropole sont cultivés « jusqu'au dernier mètre carré ». À une terre de pionniers et de défricheurs s'oppose donc un pays où les hommes peuvent se contenter de relayer ceux qui leur ont légué un héritage. On n'ouvrait sa porte qu'avec précautions, à Solférino, à cause des « bandits », mais dès que l'étranger avait été reconnu, l'hospitalité y était cordiale et généreuse, et les offres de service désintéressées; les voyageurs du train sont surpris, eux, que Jacques les salue avant de quitter le compartiment, et il faut un pourboire pour amener de la sympathie sur le visage de la femme de chambre de l'hôtel. Avec leurs « joues pleines » ou leur visage « poupin » (p. 22 et 23), l'aubergiste et le docteur de Solférino offraient un air avenant; Jacques, au contraire, est condamné à voyager en face d'un individu à la digestion difficile qui, contrairement à lui (demeuré mince malgré sa quarantaine), paraît plus que son âge. On vieillit avec élégance en Algérie; en métropole, c'est le contraire. Un « enfant roux au visage éteint et fade » (p. 30), « un groupe de voyageurs aux vêtements sombres et au teint brouillé » (p. 31) complètent le tableau du train. Pourquoi faut-il enfin que la femme de chambre de Saint-Brieuc ait « une figure de pomme de terre » (p. 31) et que le gardien du cimetière sente la transpiration? Un voyageur a toute liberté pour préférer l'habitat algérien à celui de la métropole; et un romancier plus de liberté encore pour accabler les gens qui vivent du mauvais côté de la Méditerranée. Le manichéisme de Camus n'en est pas moins comique ou touchant[1]. On ne combat pas les partis pris : le regard de Jacques, dans le train, était d'emblée « désapprobateur » (p. 29).

1. « On aura l'occasion de s'apercevoir de la supériorité réelle de l'Algérien sur le Français, c'est-à-dire de sa générosité sans limites et de son hospitalité naturelle », écrivait-il, non sans humour il est vrai, dans *L'Été* (*Essais*, p. 850). Voir aussi son discours d'ancien du R.U.A., Dossier, p. 149.

Il se peut que Camus ait aussi voulu marquer l'écart qui sépare deux époques en faisant résonner, aux dernières lignes du deuxième chapitre, le bruit d'un avion qui franchit le mur du son. On n'est décidément plus, comme en 1913, au temps des carrioles. Mais cette observation n'a aucune valeur polémique : elle s'appliquerait également aux deux pays.

LES LIMITES DE L'AUTOPORTRAIT

Le portrait ingénument flatteur de Jacques dans le train de Saint-Brieuc (mince dans son imperméable malgré la quarantaine, les cheveux coupés ras, dégageant une impression d'aisance et d'énergie) est celui de Camus. Sa personnalité s'éclairera à partir du troisième chapitre où le lecteur est, comme dans le premier, introduit *in medias res*. Que, dès la première phrase du chapitre, Malan attaque sa deuxième tranche de gigot sert moins, en effet, à signifier son appétit qu'à saisir l'action en cours de repas. Les apostrophes du vieux maître : « Toujours aussi sobre ! » (p. 42), « Oh ! vous êtes doué » (p. 43), « Vous êtes généreux » (p. 44), « Vous aimez la vie » (p. 45), contribuent au portrait moral de Jacques. Aimer la vie, nous avons deviné que c'était, entre autres plaisirs, aimer les femmes. Un monologue intérieur, ébauché à la fin du troisième chapitre, se poursuit en marge de façon incertaine. Il n'y en aura pas d'autre dans la suite du roman, sauf en cette fin de chapitre (« Mondovi ») où un « moi » fait bizarrement irruption dans le texte.

D'autres détails de la vie et des habitudes de Jacques seront révélés au fil du récit : son aisance matérielle, qui lui permet désormais d'éviter à sa mère de travailler (p. 72), sa manie de fumer, qui ajoute, lors de ses visites au domicile familial, un cendrier aux rares objets de la maison (p. 73), sa passion pour le football (p. 99), son amour des chiens (p. 119)... Chaque fois, des photos de Camus (cigarette aux doigts, en tenue de footballeur...) se présentent à l'esprit du lecteur. On croit pouvoir déduire, d'après la scène de la plage, qu'à l'âge de neuf ans Albert ne savait pas encore nager (p. 115) et on le crédite spontanément de la petite taille qu'il prête à Jacques, au moins jusqu'à l'âge de quinze ans (p. 98 et 118) ; c'est elle qui lui vaut, de la part de son instituteur, le surnom de « moustique[1] ». En vertu du contrat romanesque, le lecteur devrait oublier la figure de l'écrivain pour composer peu à peu dans son imagination le personnage de Jacques, héros de l'histoire. Avouons que, peu prodigue de transpositions romanesques, Camus ne lui facilite pas la tâche.

Et pourtant, qu'on y lise une confession ou un roman, cet « autoportrait » souffre de lacunes étonnantes, qu'on mettra difficilement au compte de l'inachèvement. Jacques a été victime dans un passé récent d'une grave maladie (p. 52). Laquelle ?

1. On croit deviner cette petite taille grâce à la photo de couverture du « Folio », où il a pourtant déjà seize ou dix-sept ans. Adulte, Camus mesurera 1,76 m.

Vit-il ordinairement à Paris? Son aisance matérielle, d'où lui est-elle venue? Quel est son métier? Rien ne suggère qu'il soit, à l'image de l'auteur, un écrivain. Orchestrées par Camus autour du thème de la « recherche du père », les expériences de Jacques à Saint-Brieuc, à Alger et à Solférino ne sont pas destinées, au sein de la fiction, à la composition d'un livre. À Camus (en l'occurrence plus différent de Jacques que Proust ne l'est du héros de la *Recherche*), il reviendra ensuite de leur donner une forme, mais cet horizon littéraire n'est pas intégré au roman. Jalonné d'apprentissages, le récit de l'enfance de Jacques demeure d'ailleurs discret sur ses succès scolaires. Au poids des livres qu'il rapporte de la distribution des prix, on le suppose brillant élève, mais son histoire n'est pas celle d'un prix Nobel en puissance. Il est vrai que Camus dédiera à son ancien instituteur ses *Discours de Stockholm*, mais *Le Premier Homme* aide à comprendre que sa reconnaissance envers M. Germain allait au-delà des lauriers académiques que celui-ci lui avait permis de conquérir.

Jacques aime les femmes : le sourire d'une passagère, croisée dans le train, en a d'emblée informé le lecteur. Est-il marié? A-t-il des enfants? Nous n'en saurons rien. Le récit de son adolescence s'achève sur le premier baiser qu'il ait goûté sur les lèvres d'une jeune fille, ouvrant vers d'autres amours sur lesquelles le dernier chapitre (« Obscur à soi-même ») ainsi que les

« notes et plans » lèvent à peine le voile. Mais le manuscrit est muet sur l'éducation sexuelle approximative que reçoivent tous les adolescents avant de vivre leur première expérience. Des genoux et des cuisses entrevus sous les jupes d'une collègue de bureau (p. 291), un bâton de rouge à lèvres dérobé que respirent tour à tour les collégiens (p. 304), figurent les seules brèches vers le monde interdit de la femme (p. 304). Camus avait remis à plus tard (dans le texte ou dans la vie de Jacques ?) l'évocation d'approches plus troublantes ou moins fétichistes. Le pensionnat de jeunes filles proche de la bibliothèque municipale y aurait pourvu : « C'est dans ce quartier, si près et si loin du leur, que Jacques et Pierre connurent leurs émotions les plus profondes (dont il n'est pas encore temps de parler, dont il sera parlé, etc.) » (p. 267). En fait, on sautera directement à ce premier baiser, si allusivement évoqué, qui fera comprendre à Jacques qu'il est entré dans sa vie d'homme. C'est le portrait d'un héros étonnamment chaste que dresse, somme toute, la partie rédigée du roman.

Quelle que soit l'intimité partagée par le lecteur avec les pensées et les sentiments de Jacques, son individualité est donc délestée de ce qui contribue ordinairement à l'épaisseur d'un personnage de roman. Tenu à distance plus qu'il n'était nécessaire pour l'empêcher de servir à une confession personnelle, il est appelé « l'enfant » (sept fois aux pages 50-52, à nouveau

p. 54 ou p. 187), ou encore « le bébé » (p. 83) dans la scène où la mère et la grand-mère apprennent le décès d'Henri Cormery. Jacques ayant assisté à une rixe qui a ensanglanté le trottoir de son quartier, Camus écrit au dénouement du récit que « l'enfant soudain plein d'angoisse courait vers la maison misérable pour y retrouver les siens » (p. 151). Au-delà de l'effroi personnel de Jacques, c'est une scène fondamentale qui est donnée ici à lire, dont le pouvoir est renouvelé à travers les âges : la première confrontation de l'enfant avec la violence. Ces catégories générales, sinon abstraites, sont cohérentes avec un titre qui n'énonce pas, suivant la tradition romanesque, un état civil ou une profession propres à un individu, mais une nouvelle figure d'Adam. L'expression « l'homme », par laquelle était désigné le passager du train, n'exprimait donc pas seulement la feinte ignorance du narrateur : une fois révélée l'identité de Jacques, le genre humain tout entier se profile derrière son individualité. Aussi, quand, prenant un recul temporel par rapport à l'anecdote qu'il rapporte, Camus écrit : « (et toute sa vie ce fut la bonté et l'amour qui le firent pleurer, jamais le mal ou la persécution qui renforçaient son cœur et sa décision au contraire) » (p. 187-188), sa formule ne sonne pas comme un témoignage d'auto-satisfaction, mais comme un message d'espoir dans les vertus du cœur humain.

55

S'il évite de réduire Jacques au sujet d'une autobiographie, c'est aussi pour mieux en faire un sujet de l'histoire. Cette histoire ne sera pas seulement celle de sa famille et de son pays. La force épique des éléments qui, dès la première page du roman, déferlaient sur le continent africain l'avait fait pressentir : c'est à l'histoire universelle des hommes qu'appartient le héros du livre. « Souverain humble et fier de la beauté de la nuit », note Camus en marge afin de caractériser Jacques quand celui-ci penche sa tête sur l'épaule de sa mère (p. 150). Appliquée à un personnage ordinaire ou à un sujet réel, la formule ferait sourire. Son emphase ne se justifie que si elle couronne un héros mythique dont le royaume a chance d'être aussi le nôtre.

L'homme, au sens le plus accompli du terme, aurait fait la matière du roman à écrire : le manuscrit ne nous laisse entrevoir que par éclairs, à l'occasion de ses voyages, ce qu'il est devenu aujourd'hui. À le considérer dans l'état où il nous est parvenu, *Le Premier Homme* raconte d'abord l'histoire d'une formation interrompue à l'âge de l'adolescence. Le premier mouvement de révolte de Jacques marque le terme de cette formation : il arrache des mains de sa grand-mère le nerf de bœuf avec lequel elle avait l'habitude de le frapper (p. 298), mouvement pareil à celui de l'esclave qui, au début de *L'Homme révolté*, affirme sa dignité contre le maître qui l'opprime : « Qu'est-ce qu'un homme révolté? Un homme qui dit non. [...] Quel est le contenu de ce "non"? Il signifie, par exemple : "les choses ont trop duré", "jusque-là oui, au-delà non", "vous allez trop loin", et encore, "il y a une limite que vous ne dépasserez pas"[1] ». Jacques se sent désormais un homme, capable de résister à une autorité abusive, parce que trois événements, presque simultanés, ont marqué son existence : il a apporté son premier salaire au foyer, il est devenu gardien de but titulaire de l'équipe de football, il a pour la première fois embrassé une jeune fille (p. 298). (L'irruption de la fatalité, sous la forme de la maladie, ce sera pour bientôt.) De même Henry Brulard connaît-il à vingt-quatre heures d'intervalle, alors qu'il est âgé de dix-sept ans, le baptême du feu (au passage du Grand-Saint-Bernard) et celui de l'amour. Le souvenir de ces moments de sublime bonheur mettait un terme, chez Stendhal, au récit autobiographique : « On gâte des sentiments si tendres à les raconter en détail[2]. » Que Camus suspende la partie narrative de son récit au même point que Stendhal est une coïncidence : jamais il n'a exprimé l'impossibilité de dire le bonheur, et la mort seule ici l'en a empêché. Rien ne nous autorise, enfin, à décider si cette triple expérience de Jacques reflète exactement ou transpose celle de Camus. Ou plutôt, puisqu'il est hors de doute que chacune des trois s'est produite, s'il n'a pas cédé à la tentation de

1. *L'Homme révolté, Essais,* p. 423.

2. *Vie de Henry Brulard,* dans Stendhal, *Œuvres intimes,* Gallimard, « Bibliothèque de la Pléiade », t. II, p. 959.

composer son roman en les unissant miraculeusement dans un espace de temps aussi restreint.

Moins de dix pages plus loin, Jacques voit se dessiner le temps où il trouvera « des raisons de vieillir et de mourir sans révolte » (p. 307). Le court chapitre qui clôt le manuscrit, « Obscur à soi-même », récapitulant (ou anticipant dans le texte?) le récit de l'existence de Jacques, l'aura donc fait passer de l'étage de la révolte à celui d'un amour apaisé, entrevu sinon encore déjà vécu. « Que croyez-vous que les critiques français aient négligé dans votre œuvre? » demandait à Camus un critique anglais quinze jours avant sa mort. Réponse de Camus : « La part obscure, ce qu'il y a d'aveugle et d'instinctif en moi[1]. » L'élucidation de la part obscure de Jacques était l'avenir du *Premier Homme*. Mais il restait à Camus à élucider sa propre obscurité pour approfondir celle de son personnage. On se dit parfois qu'il s'était décidément engagé dans un roman sans fin.

MÉMOIRE ET IMAGINATION

Aux souvenirs de Jacques s'ajoutent ceux qu'il a collectés auprès de proches et qui, parfois, se mêlent aux siens. Aux événements qu'il n'a pas personnellement vécus et sur lesquels il n'a pu recueillir de témoignage, il faudra le renfort de l'imagination. Que l'écrivain mêle sans crier gare le souvenir et l'invention est encore un

1. « Dernière interview d'Albert Camus (20 décembre 1959) », *Essais*, p. 1925.

indice du genre romanesque du *Premier Homme*.

L'ouverture du récit précède les souvenirs de Jacques puisqu'elle précède sa naissance. Mais quand George Sand attend le septième chapitre de la Deuxième partie d'*Histoire de ma vie* pour annoncer sa venue au monde, l'événement a été précédé d'une longue chronique des ancêtres, et les gestes et les paroles dont le texte accompagne sa naissance s'inscrivent, suppose-t-on, dans une tradition familiale qu'il suffisait à l'écrivain de rapporter. Rien de tel dans la famille Cormery où, comme chez tous les pionniers, on démarre chaque fois de zéro. Aucun survivant ne sera en mesure de commémorer la naissance de Jacques. Le romancier est libre, dès lors, de composer à la manière d'une scène de Nativité la venue au monde de ce fils de l'homme, né à la hâte d'une mère dont le visage est celui des « innocents » (p. 15) dans une ferme appelée Saint-Apôtre[1]. L'ouverture du troisième chapitre le célébrera de ses seules initiales : « J. C. ». « Je vais naître, comme dit Tristram Shandy », parodiait Stendhal[2]. « Je vais naître », pourrait s'intituler le premier chapitre du *Premier Homme*, mais la solennité de la déclaration ne se teinterait pas ici d'ironie. « Dieu soit loué », dit l'Arabe à Henri Cormery. « Tu es un chef » (p. 27). Le miracle s'est produit. Henri peut dormir tranquille.

Au-delà du chapitre d'ouverture, Jacques devra recourir encore à l'imagination pour

1. Transposition emphatique de Saint-Paul, localité située à 8 km de Mondovi parmi les vignobles. Le domaine que géra Lucien Camus s'appelait plus prosaïquement le Chapeau-de-gendarme.

2. *Vie de Henry Brulard*, éd. citée, t. II, p. 909. Voir le chapitre VI de *Vie et opinions de Tristram Shandy*, de Laurence Sterne, où la venue au monde du héros est célébrée avec une emphase amusée.

recomposer, dans la suite du récit, certaines phases de son existence. « Le temps perdu ne se retrouve que chez les riches. Pour les pauvres, il marque seulement les traces vagues du chemin de la mort » (p. 93). Dans une « famille française moyenne » comme celle de son ami Didier, on conserve « les lettres de la famille, des souvenirs, des photos » (p. 225-226). Du passé familial, le foyer de Jacques n'a gardé que l'éclat d'obus dont son père fut victime. La mémoire, chez lui, manque à tous (p. 134). « Il y a longtemps », dit la mère (p. 74), ou encore : « C'est vieux, tout ça » (p. 75). Afin de composer une histoire familiale, Jacques devra relier à l'aide de l'imagination les hasardeux fragments de souvenirs qu'on lui a légués : « Et il essayait d'imaginer, avec le peu qu'il savait par sa mère, le même homme neuf ans plus tard, marié, père de deux enfants, ayant conquis une situation un peu meilleure et rappelé à Alger pour la mobilisation » (p. 78-79). L'essai se révèle concluant : il débouche sur un vrai tableau du père en partance pour la guerre, en gare de Bône, « dans son beau costume multicolore » (p. 81). On devine que, dans sa naïveté, la mère dut l'apercevoir ainsi. À Jacques revient de reconstituer la scène telle qu'elle s'offrait à ses yeux. Et le maire venu annoncer aux deux femmes occupées à trier des lentilles qu'Henri Cormery était mort au champ d'honneur, comment Jacques s'en souviendrait-il, lui qui suçait ce jour-là une carotte pleine de

bave dans une petite corbeille à linge
(p. 83) ? Il fallait pourtant célébrer l'événement, avec des effets de réel qui inscrivent
ce tableau imaginaire au même rang que
les souvenirs les plus intensément vécus.
À cette guerre dont aucun membre de sa
famille ne lui a jamais parlé, *Les Croix de
bois* donnent enfin une profondeur historique. Alors que le pèlerinage sur la tombe
de Saint-Brieuc ou la visite à la ferme de
Mondovi aboutissent à un résultat déce-
vant, le roman de Dorgelès aide Jacques
à inscrire son père parmi les hommes de
sa génération. En lui faisant don de cette
œuvre de fiction qui l'avait ému aux larmes
quand il était enfant, M. Bernard contribue
à perpétuer dans sa mémoire la figure du
héros.

C'est toutefois en priorité par les souvenirs personnels de Jacques qu'est assu-
rée la continuité entre l'enfant et l'adulte.
La mémoire du corps qui lui a permis,
de retour au foyer, de monter « l'escalier
quatre à quatre, d'un seul élan infaillible,
sans manquer une marche » (p. 67), ou qui
le fait maintenant tourner « comme autrefois autour de la table centrale » (p. 92),
lui offre, autant que l'immobilité de sa
mère veillant à sa fenêtre, la rassurante
certitude que rien n'a vraiment changé.
« S'il est vrai que les seuls paradis sont ceux
qu'on a perdus », écrivait Camus, paro-
diant Proust, dans *L'Envers et l'Endroit*,
avant d'évoquer ces détails grâce auxquels
l'émigrant retrouve sa patrie : « une odeur

1. *OC*, t. I, p. 46. « Les vrais paradis sont les paradis qu'on a perdus » (Proust, *Le Temps retrouvé*, Gallimard, coll. « Folio », 1990, p. 177).

de chambre trop longtemps fermée, le son singulier d'un pas sur la route[1] ». La « douce odeur » de la mère (p. 68) rapatrie Jacques au foyer. Le passé resurgit soudain, sans que la volonté y ait de part, ou alors il s'insinue à la faveur d'une rêverie. Ainsi du « A benidor » qui, revenant flotter dans la mémoire de Jacques à moitié assoupi sur la couchette du bateau qui le ramène vers Alger, lui fait revivre l'espace d'un instant ces après-midi de sieste que lui imposait sa grand-mère quand il était enfant (p. 49).

Il faut faire la part de ces moments proustiens ou nervaliens du *Premier Homme*. Ils permettent de rêver à un roman que Camus eût déroulé tout entier en arabesques à la manière de *Sylvie*, au point que le lecteur eût perdu pied, ne sachant plus faire la part du réel et du rêve. Mais *Le Premier Homme* a été conçu, pour l'essentiel, dans un esprit différent. C'est à un effort volontaire et même méthodique que s'y applique d'abord Camus.

À travers les zigzags imposés par la construction de l'ouvrage se reconstitue le parcours année par année des expériences de Jacques. La recomposition des souvenirs débute à l'école maternelle, « dont il ne gardait aucun souvenir, sinon celui d'un lavabo de pierre sombre qui occupait tout le fond du préau couvert et où il avait atterri un jour tête la première, pour se relever couvert de sang » (p. 155). Une fois le texte du roman délesté de la part d'invention qui y meuble les vides, tel est le premier souvenir authentique de Jacques, empreint d'une violence dont on ne tirera aucune conséquence tant le premier accident reste souvent gravé comme une initiation à la vie. L'étonnant est que Jacques ait gardé ce seul événement en mémoire de toute la période qui l'a mené à sa quatrième année. À cet âge le petit Brulard avait déjà plusieurs bûches à son actif. De cette supériorité, Stendhal fournit l'explication : « Je me figure l'événement, mais probablement ce n'est pas un souvenir direct, ce n'est que le souvenir de l'image que je me formai de la chose fort anciennement et à l'époque des premiers récits qu'on m'en fit[1]. » Qui pouvait raconter à Jacques ce qui lui arrivait quand il était tout petit ? Sa mémoire de la prime enfance est une mémoire de pauvre.

Du moment où elle ne doit qu'à lui-même, elle est extraordinaire. « Mémoire prodigieuse du petit Tolstoï », note Paul Morand. « Vingt-quatre ans plus tard, quand il écrit *Enfance*, il se souvient de tout, du moindre détail de l'habillement de son précepteur allemand[2]. » La description de la tonnellerie de l'oncle, des boutiques de la rue Bab-Azoun, le récit de la distribution des prix, les portraits des conducteurs de tramways ou du marchand de beignets sont tout aussi stupéfiants. Parfois, on devine Jacques attaché à un devoir de mémoire. Exposer par le menu les règles de la canette *vinga*, le rituel des « donnades » ou le savant travail de Galoufa l'attrapeur de chiens,

1. *Vie de Henry Brulard,* édition citée, t. II, p. 578.

2. Paul Morand, *Journal inutile,* Gallimard, t. I, 2001, p. 28. Sur Tolstoï, voir Dossier, p. 200.

concourt moins à une sociologie du folklore algérois qu'à une reconstitution fidèle de la mentalité de l'enfance, dont les priorités ont de quoi surprendre par leur frivolité les adultes oublieux. C'était surtout pour Camus rendre hommage à l'univers des enfants pauvres, qui n'ont d'autres trésors que le théâtre de la rue et les objets qu'on y ramasse. « Je veux donner l'idée d'un divertissement innocent », écrivait Baudelaire[1]. Au pauvre, son joujou offre une joie qui vaut celle de l'enfant riche. Camus s'ingénie, dirait-on, à le faire comprendre au lecteur.

Cette prodigieuse mémoire admet pourtant des hésitations, des erreurs corrigées au fur et à mesure de la composition de l'ouvrage. Reconstituant l'épisode de la pièce de monnaie que Jacques fait semblant d'avoir égarée, Camus annule en marge la première explication donnée par l'enfant à sa grand-mère : « Non. C'est parce qu'il avait déjà prétendu avoir perdu l'argent qu'il est obligé de trouver une autre explication » (p. 102). Ainsi le lecteur est-il placé, comme dans le « nouveau roman », au carrefour d'interprétations différentes : « Au-dessus de la commode une gravure encadrée de bois noir est fixée... Non. Non. Non. [...] comme si l'ensemble était monté sur un rail et tiré en arrière par une ficelle. Non[2]. » C'est l'année où Camus rédige l'essentiel de son manuscrit qu'Alain Robbe-Grillet se livre à ces variations. Cette même année encore, on inter-

1. « Le joujou du pauvre », *Le Spleen de Paris (Petits poèmes en prose)*.

2. Alain Robbe-Grillet, *Le Labyrinthe*, Éditions de Minuit, 1959, p. 96-97.

roge Camus sur les rapports qu'il entretient avec le « nouveau roman » : « Les romanciers dont vous parlez ont raison de défricher de nouveaux chemins. Personnellement, toutes les techniques m'intéressent et aucune ne m'intéresse en elle-même. [...] L'erreur de l'art moderne est presque toujours de faire passer le moyen avant la fin, la forme avant le fond, la technique avant le sujet[1]. » Les « non » marginaux du *Premier Homme* ne sont pas des exercices. Camus l'a dit en programmant l'étage de l'amour : « La méthode est la sincérité. » Que l'imagination supplée parfois à l'authenticité des souvenirs ne déroge pas à l'exigence de sincérité : l'art avait ici pour mission de rendre leur mémoire aux pauvres.

1. « Dernière interview d'Albert Camus (20 décembre 1959) », *Essais*, p. 1927.

III   L'UNIVERS DE L'ENFANCE

LES PARADIS PERDUS

LES VOYAGES DE JACQUES

2. « Quand mon père fut appelé sous les drapeaux, il n'avait jamais vu la France. Il la vit et fut tué » (p. 324).

Comme la plupart des Français d'Algérie de condition modeste, Camus était déjà un adulte quand il aborda pour la première fois en métropole. Au moins ne fut-ce pas, comme son père, pour y faire la guerre[2].

De toute son enfance, il ne quitta guère Alger. *Le Premier Homme* traduit la curiosité de Jacques pour les paysages de campagne que lui donnent à découvrir les parties de chasse de l'oncle Ernest. Les descriptions de facture très classique offertes en cette occasion par le roman recomposent après coup les souvenirs d'enfance plutôt qu'elles ne les reflètent dans leur naïveté. Étonnant passage où s'ébauche une sorte de roman autonome, au point que le texte prend en charge les pensées non seulement des chasseurs, mais des chiens dont le sommeil lourd est « traversé de rêves sanguinaires » (p. 128). C'est le romancier qui nomme les « chênes nains » et les « genévriers » qu'un enfant de la ville n'aurait pas su reconnaître (p. 124).

Quoiqu'il se trouve à l'intérieur d'Alger, le Jardin d'Essai offre le dépaysement d'un voyage. Camus ne nomme pas les essences rares dont il était planté. Mais cette réserve ne vise pas à respecter l'ignorance de Jacques et de ses camarades quand ils allaient y jouer : une note marginale (« dire le nom des arbres », p. 60) indique que, menée à terme, la description du jardin aurait offert des noms beaucoup plus exotiques que ceux de simples genévriers[1]. Il a pris le temps, à l'inverse, de nommer les arbres et les fleurs de la « jungle parfumée » (p. 262) de la Maison des invalides de Kouba. Pour l'enfant des villes qu'est Jacques, cette proche banlieue représente déjà la campagne. Le parc et le plateau

1. Ces noms sont donnés par Montherlant. Voir Dossier, p. 185.

« bouillonnant d'arbres, sous le ciel traversé à toute vitesse par d'énormes nuages » (p. 265), qui rappelle l'évocation géologique de la première page du roman, ont aux yeux de Jacques les couleurs de l'aventure.

On supposera les découvertes géographiques de Jacques modelées sur celles de Camus. Celui-ci n'aura qu'après l'adolescence, par exemple, la révélation des ruines de Tipasa, absentes du roman. Ouled-Fayet, lieu de naissance du père, ou Solférino, il semble que Jacques y aille dans le récit pour la première fois de sa vie, seulement motivé par son enquête. Camus, qui se rendit à Ouled-Fayet en mars 1959, en avait-il été curieux auparavant ? Si lui aussi n'est allé que sur le tard à Mondovi, cette visite a dû lui suffire pour reconstituer sans grande difficulté son village de naissance : les villages d'Algérie n'avaient guère changé en quarante ans. « Mais ça a dû changer depuis que tu ne l'as pas vu », dit pourtant Jacques à sa mère (p. 92). Il est vrai que, sur la route parcourue jadis par la carriole, on croise désormais « des jeeps hérissées de fusils » (p. 195). Et la maison natale de Jacques n'existe plus : « Ici, on ne garde rien. On abat et on reconstruit », dit le colon Veillard (p. 197). Mais la physionomie générale du village (son kiosque à musique, son unique rue bordée de maisons basses, hangars et vignes aux alentours) avait dû demeurer suffisamment la même pour que l'ouverture du roman ne nécessitât pas un grand effort d'imagination. Tout au plus les champs de vignes se sont-ils étendus.

ALGER, VILLE DE SYMBOLES

Le lieu principal du roman est ce que Camus, par commodité sans doute, appelle ici comme dans *L'Étranger* le « faubourg » (p. 50). Belcourt était en réalité un quartier d'Alger (« on disait "aller à Alger" quand on allait dans le centre », p. 220), « quartier pauvre » évoqué dans les ébauches de *L'Envers et l'Endroit*[1], à nouveau dans le texte du recueil intitulé « Entre oui et non » (« Je pense à un enfant qui vécut dans un quartier pauvre. Ce quartier, cette maison ! Il n'y avait qu'un étage et les escaliers n'étaient pas éclairés[2] »), puis dans *La Mort heureuse*, où le nom de Belcourt figure en toutes lettres[3], enfin dans *L'Étranger* où le lecteur l'identifie grâce à la rue de Lyon, qui le traverse[4]. Pour composer le décor du foyer, Camus aurait pu reprendre mot pour mot, dans *Le Premier Homme*, les pages écrites une vingtaine d'années plus tôt. L'appartement de trois pièces où vivent la mère, la grand-mère, deux enfants et l'oncle Ernest n'appelle pas de longues descriptions parce que s'y trouve seulement l'essentiel, et Jacques a beau fouiller dans les tiroirs (« "Tu fouilles toujours", dit sa mère », p. 72), aucun objet n'apporte de surprise. Un ajout marginal témoigne de l'effort de Camus pour pousser plus loin

1. Voir « L'Hôpital du quartier pauvre » et « Les Voix du quartier pauvre », *OC*, t. I, p. 73-85.

2. *L'Envers et l'Endroit, ibid.*, p. 48.

3. « Arrivé à Belcourt, Mersault descendit avec Emmanuel qui chantait », *ibid.*, p. 1109.

4. On peut voir le vieux Salamano et son chien « le long de la rue de Lyon », *ibid.*, p. 156.

l'inventaire (« Une armoire, une table de toilette en bois au dessus de marbre [...] », p. 51), comme s'il s'appliquait à son devoir de mémoire ; le butin sera plutôt maigre.

C'est vers la rue que la veuve désoccupée dirige obstinément ses regards. À la faveur du beau temps, les vieux installent leurs chaises sur le trottoir, l'investissant comme un second domicile. Dans *L'Étranger* déjà : « Sur le trottoir d'en face, le marchand de tabac a sorti une chaise, l'a installée devant sa porte et l'a enfourchée en s'appuyant des deux bras sur le dossier[1]. » Puisque, au fil des années, rien n'a changé au domicile de la veuve, c'est dans la rue que Jacques guette les manifestations du temps qui passe. Les roseaux creux du rideau du buraliste, qui avaient remplacé des perles multicolores (p. 80), ont euxmêmes fait place à des lanières de plastique (p. 86) : indice de modernité assez minuscule pour prouver à quel point rien n'a vraiment changé non plus dans le quartier pauvre. Les « lourds tramways rouges » (p. 69), qui offraient à Meursault accoudé à son balcon l'essentiel du spectacle de la rue[2], sont eux aussi demeurés les mêmes. Pour Jacques, dont le lycée se situait à l'autre extrémité de la ville, ils ont été le symbole de sa promotion chez les grands. C'est à l'endroit précis où vient d'être placée la bombe de l'attentat qu'il guettait leur passage quand il était adolescent (p. 88). La patrouille de parachutistes, qui fait désormais partie du décor, se prome-

1. *Ibid.*, p. 153.

2. *Ibid.*

nait avec assez de nonchalance pour qu'on ne pût redouter l'imminence d'un danger. Que le sang coule, soudain, dans une ville qui semble ignorer la guerre, en un lieu qui est demeuré immuable et familier, signifie l'étrangeté de ce conflit.

Identifié dans *La Mort heureuse* (roman raté), mais non dans les autres récits, Belcourt ne sera nommé dans *Le Premier Homme*, comme par inadvertance, qu'à un point où le fil du récit s'en est détourné (p. 246). Cette discrétion a sa raison d'être. De son lieu d'enfance, Camus a choisi de faire un symbole ; mieux vaut que Belcourt soit, dans l'esprit du lecteur, « le quartier pauvre » plutôt qu'un lieu dont l'appellation arbitraire rétrécirait la signification. « Ce vieux quartier », écrit aussi Camus et, plutôt que de nommer la rue de Lyon, il préfère évoquer « la rue principale du quartier » (p. 154). Le boulevard où a été installée la bibliothèque municipale, et que le lecteur familier des lieux identifie comme le boulevard Auguste-Comte, sépare plus ou moins, dans son anonymat, le quartier pauvre et les abords d'un quartier riche[1]. La rue Prévost-Paradol, perpendiculaire à la rue de Lyon, doit à sa fontaine un traitement particulier (p. 54). Plus loin, au lieu d'appeler d'emblée par son nom le quartier de Bab-el-Oued, à l'entrée duquel se trouve le Grand Lycée, Camus commence par parler d'« un quartier autrefois opulent et morne, et devenu, par la vertu de l'immigration espagnole, un des plus popu-

1. Il semble que le « pensionnat Sainte-Odile », qu'entourent les villas du quartier, soit en réalité le pensionnat Sainte-Chantal.

laires et des plus vivants d'Alger » (p. 191).
Le centre-ville n'est guère plus précisément traité. Si le quartier de l'Agha est en
vertu d'une coïncidence de la vie trois
fois cité (lieu de rendez-vous des chasseurs, p. 121 ; adresse de la quincaillerie,
p. 285 ; port marchand où Jacques se rend
en commissionnaire, p. 293), le « boulevard Front-de-mer », préféré aux noms
des deux boulevards qui le composaient[1],
doit à sa simplicité évocatrice de figurer
dans le texte (p. 292). Monumentale tenta-
tive d'accommodation de l'art mauresque
à la civilisation occidentale et point traditionnel de rendez-vous des amoureux, la
Grande Poste est ravalée, affublée de lettres
minuscules, à un lieu générique[2] (p. 289).
Quant au « large boulevard qui montait du
port jusqu'au sommet des collines où la
ville était construite » (*ibid.*), son tracé ano-
nyme et sommaire ne satisfera pas les amateurs de précisions topographiques. Que
le général de Gaulle ait lancé sur ce boulevard Laferrière le fameux « Je vous ai
compris » n'aurait aucune pertinence dans
la perspective du récit. C'est à une histoire
plus ancienne et à certains égards mythique
que se réfère *Le Premier Homme* : celle de
l'immigration de pauvres gens, en partie
espagnols, venus s'installer dans une ville
présentée au départ comme une « forêt de
ciment et de fer » emprisonnée dans un
« splendide décor » (p. 53) et bâtie comme
un « amphithéâtre » (p. 62). Le roman, à sa
parution, risquait de décevoir ceux qui

1. Voir Dossier,
p. 169.

2. C'est un peu
comme si, dans
une description
de Paris, on
écrivait non
l'« Arc de
Triomphe »,
mais l'« arc de
triomphe ».

espéraient alimenter leur « nostalgérie[1] »
grâce à une onomastique aux résonances
affectives. Il ne conviendra pas davantage
à ceux qui y chercheraient un guide touristique. Cet effort vers la généralité était
encore plus sensible dans *L'Étranger* :
Camus avait, autant qu'il était possible,
dépouillé son roman des idiomes et des
traits du folklore algériens, afin de le rendre
universellement lisible. C'est à ce prix qu'il
fut, à brève échéance, considéré comme un
« classique ».

Les autres œuvres romanesques de Camus
confirment le soin qu'il met à faire de chaque
lieu un symbole. Ainsi, dans *La Peste*, Oran, qui
tourne le dos à la mer, est-elle durant l'épidémie un lieu d'enfermement, tandis que dans *La
Chute* Clamence a choisi de résider à Amsterdam
parce que, avec son réseau concentrique de
canaux, la ville figure à ses yeux l'enfer de Dante.

Avec la prudence qu'ordonne l'inachèvement du texte, on étendra à d'autres dénominations l'effort du romancier vers le
général ou le symbolique. Les « tramways
rouges » qui passent rue de Lyon ne recevront que plus loin leur identité : ils appartiennent aux C.F.R.A. [Chemins de fer sur
route d'Algérie], par opposition aux tramways verts des T.A. [Tramways algériens]
(p. 241). Peut-être Camus s'est-il, dans un
premier temps, tenu à l'impression naïve
de l'enfant, attentif à la seule couleur des
wagons[2]. Plus tard, en fonction de la destination des lignes, les wagons rouges seront

ceux des pauvres ; les verts, ceux des riches. De même le « cinéma proche » du domicile de Jacques (p. 59) n'est-il que plus tard nommé le « Musset » (p. 87). « Le cinéma de quartier se trouvait à quelques pas de la maison et il portait le nom d'un poète romantique comme la rue qui le longeait », écrit pourtant Camus de façon évasive quelques pages après l'avoir nommé[1] (p. 107). Aurait-il, s'il avait mené son roman à bien, gommé le nom du cinéma « Musset » ou la périphrase qui le désigne ensuite ? Le symbolisme fait mouche ici dans les deux cas. Les éventaires d'Arabes vendant des cacahuètes devant une enseigne qui célèbre un dandy de la littérature française, c'est, autant que les souliers Louis XV des femmes arabes (p. 86), une de ces images incongrues de l'Algérie coloniale, dont le texte, au-delà parfois des intentions de l'auteur, porte témoignage.

Que *Le Premier Homme* réduise à de rares indices les éléments de reconnaissance du centre-ville (le quartier des riches), nous trouverons d'autres motifs pour l'expliquer. Le paradoxe est que le quartier pauvre de Bab-el-Oued, situé à l'ouest d'Alger, soit en fin de compte décrit avec de meilleures précisions topographiques que Belcourt, quartier est, où Camus vécut sans discontinuer jusqu'à vingt ans. Le nom même de Bab-el-Oued apparaît dans le texte du moment que l'enfant ne se rend pas au lycée seulement pour y passer son examen d'entrée en sixième, mais quoti-

1. Rue Alfred-de-Musset, perpendiculaire à la rue de Lyon.

73

1. Voir Dossier,
p. 189.

diennement (p. 239). Il apparaîtrait plus souvent si Camus n'avait baptisé « rue Bab-Azoun », dans le chapitre « Lycée », ce qui était en réalité la rue Bab-el-Oued[1]. L'église Sainte-Victoire avec son offertoire fleuri, la succession des boutiques sous les arcades, sont mieux données à voir que l'architecture de la rue de Lyon. Il est vrai que les souvenirs de lycée sont, dirait M. de La Palice, plus frais que ceux de l'école. Mais Camus revint souvent, jusqu'à la fin de sa vie, dans sa maison de Belcourt. À moins que la mémoire ne grave mieux les lieux qu'on doit inventorier (Jacques redécouvre chaque jour cette « rue Bab-Azoun » qu'il ne devait guère connaître auparavant) que ceux dans lesquels on a vécu depuis la naissance. Si fortement présent par son atmosphère, sa couleur locale et ses odeurs, le quartier de Belcourt resterait ainsi une sorte de point aveugle du récit, se confondant pour Jacques « à la longue avec le soir, le sommeil, le rêve » (p. 272). Il constitue son élément naturel.

UN MONDE D'ODEURS

Henri Cormery avait un sens olfactif développé. Du moins le romancier du *Premier Homme* en a-t-il décidé ainsi : que son père fût courageux, des témoins l'ont rapporté à Jacques, mais qu'il eût le nez fin, qui aurait pu le lui apprendre ? Quoiqu'il appartienne à l'autre branche familiale, l'oncle a, lui aussi, les narines en éveil. « Comme beaucoup de sourds, Ernest avait l'odorat très développé », écrit Camus en préambule à une scène à laquelle l'imparfait confère un caractère répétitif (p. 128-130). L'oncle ayant décelé une odeur d'œuf sur son assiette, la mère, au « nez délicat », et la grand-mère, de mauvaise foi puisqu'elle a fait la vaisselle, se livrent à un reniflage collectif qui fera dégénérer la soirée en drame. Ainsi cette famille où les mots manquent pour aboutir à des disputes trouve-t-elle dans le seul raffinement que lui ait accordé la nature un moyen rituel de se déchirer.

Camus semble avoir situé dans les ténèbres du soir l'arrivée de la carriole à Solférino afin que le paysage se révèle grâce aux « odeurs d'herbes brûlées » et à la « forte odeur d'engrais » (p. 16). Il a oublié cette contingence du récit deux pages plus loin, puisque les voyageurs peuvent voir, derrière les hangars, les premières rangées des champs de vigne. N'importe : la « forte odeur de moût » s'impose à son tour. Dans l'ensemble du manuscrit, le nombre de notations d'odeurs dépassera la soixantaine. À la sensibilité olfactive que Jacques a héritée de son père et de sa famille s'ajoutent d'autres facteurs : la simplicité du décor familial libère chez l'enfant d'autres sens que la vue, la chaleur qui règne en Algérie rend plus intense le parfum des fleurs, et la pauvreté du domicile et du quartier se signale entre autres par les mauvaises odeurs.

Rien ne pouvait empêcher qu'au domicile de Jacques la puanteur des cabinets « débordât jusque dans l'escalier » (p. 102). Mais existe-t-il de mauvaises odeurs pour un enfant ? Le narrateur d'*À la recherche du temps perdu*, dont l'appartement familial est à l'abri de tout soupçon, respire avec délices l'odeur du chalet d'aisance des Champs-Élysées[1]. Sort-il de chez lui, Jacques se plaît à jouer avec ses copains dans une « cave puante et mouillée » (p. 58). Il n'apprendra que plus tard à apprécier, tel le voyageur de *Noces* pris à la gorge par les absinthes de Tipasa[2], les entêtantes odeurs des jasmins ou des « plantes parfumées qui croissaient vigoureusement sur les pentes humides et chaudes d'Alger » (p. 267).

Les odeurs du *Premier Homme* se mélangent de façon parfois incongrue : les cafés sentent « l'anisette et la sciure de bois » (p. 117) ; au domicile de Pierre, « l'odeur pharmaceutique du dentifrice se mêlait à celle du café au lait » (p. 229) ; par la fenêtre ouverte de la classe enfin, « l'odeur des seringas et des grands magnolias venait noyer les parfums plus acides et plus amers de l'encre et de la règle » (p. 245). Leur attrait s'augmente d'impressions visuelles ou morales. Ainsi le bassin de la rue Prévost-Paradol sent-il « l'urine et le soleil » (p. 56), les maisons du quartier où habite M. Bernard sentent « à la fois les épices et la pauvreté » (p. 154) et la quincaillerie sent « le fer et l'ombre » (p. 288) avant que son « odeur de papier et de colle » ne devienne pour Jacques « l'odeur même

1. Voir Proust, *À l'ombre des jeunes filles en fleurs*, Gallimard, coll. « Folio », 1998, p. 63.

2. *OC*, t. I, p. 106.

de l'ennui » (p. 289). À défaut de voyager beaucoup, il respire dans chaque cargo du port l'odeur spécifique d'un pays lointain (p. 293). La métropole elle-même a son parfum, celui du beurre, insolite dans un pays où on cuisine à l'huile (p. 284).

Plonger dans le passé pour tenter d'en dissiper l'obscurité sera, en priorité, récapituler les odeurs qui l'ont composé. La liste dressée dans le dernier chapitre (p. 303-304) se substitue à ce que serait, pour un tempérament plus visuel, un album de photos. Que s'y ajoute le parfum d'un bâton de rouge à lèvres signifie que l'éducation de Jacques vient de franchir une étape. Chèvrefeuille ou cabinets : les odeurs ne s'ordonnent pas selon un indice d'agrément ou de raffinement. Toutes ont également concouru à la personnalité de Jacques. Élucider ce qu'il est devenu ne sera pas choisir entre elles, mais comprendre quelles zones de sa sensibilité elles ont touchées.

FAMILLE, JE VOUS AIME

LA MÈRE

« Je suis trop vieille. Peut-être que je sens mauvais » (p. 91), dit la mère pour déplorer sa solitude. Elle doit pourtant à « la douce odeur de sa peau » (p. 68) que son fils la reconnaisse aussi bien. Figure centrale d'« Entre oui et non » (*L'Envers et l'Endroit*), la mère hantait, à l'insu du héros, toute l'intrigue de *L'Étranger* : survenue juste avant l'ouverture du récit, sa mort a fait perdre à Meursault ses repères moraux avant qu'il ne trouve, sur le point d'être exécuté, une forme de salut en communiant avec son souvenir. La piété de Camus envers sa mère sert de fil conducteur à ses biographes. Plus ou moins en filigrane, la mère est présente tout au long de son œuvre ; elle entretient, parfois, une confusion dommageable entre l'homme et l'artiste. En centrant *Le Premier Homme* en priorité sur la recherche du père, figure jusqu'alors quasi absente de l'œuvre, et en le dédiant à sa mère, Camus paraît rétablir une forme d'équilibre dans le couple parental. Mais, soit qu'il l'ait d'emblée médité, soit que la pente du roman l'y incline, l'équilibre est rompu, dans les ébauches, en faveur de la mère.

Dédicataire du *Premier Homme,* la « veuve Camus », qui ne sait pas lire, succède dans ce rôle à des « maîtres », Jean Grenier (*L'Envers et l'Endroit*) et Louis Germain (*Discours de Stockholm*), ou à des amis lettrés, Pascal Pia (*Le Mythe de Sisyphe*) ou René Char (*L'Homme révolté*). *Le Premier Homme* n'est décidément pas un livre comme les autres. « Intercesseur », comme l'indique la dédicace, la mère paraît l'être d'abord dans la mesure où le héros s'adresse à elle pour retrouver la trace du père. Silencieuse et dépourvue de mémoire, elle sera pourtant incapable d'accomplir son office. Elle en remplira un autre, tellement plus précieux : dans son silence ou ses paroles à peine murmurées, grâce à de simples gestes aussi, Jacques découvre en elle le plus sûr chemin vers l'amour. Il ne renonce pas pour autant à la pourvoir de ce passé qui est inconnu d'elle : à force de l'interroger sur le père, il lui apprend, par le contenu même de ses questions, des choses qu'elle n'a jamais sues de lui, ou qu'elle a oubliées. Plus étonnant : alors qu'elle « ne pouvait même pas avoir idée de l'histoire ou de la géographie » (p. 79) et qu'elle ignorait jusqu'à sa propre date de naissance (p. 74), les ébauches du roman prévoient que Jacques, dans la « dernière partie », lui expliquera « la question arabe, la civilisation créole, le destin de l'Occident. "Oui, dit-elle, oui." Puis confession complète et fin » (p. 351). Du moment où Jacques se mue lui-même en « maître », les fruits de l'enseignement apparaissent dérisoires en comparaison du lien qui l'unit à l'élève.

La première page des *Carnets*, datée de mai 1935, ne parlait pas d'amour, mais du « sentiment bizarre » que le fils porte à sa mère[1]. Le sentiment filial n'est pas vraiment clarifié dans *L'Envers et l'Endroit* (« Entre oui et non ») : « Parce que ce sont ses enfants, elle les aime bien. Elle les aime d'un égal amour qui ne s'est jamais révélé à eux », et plus loin : « Il a pitié de sa mère, est-ce l'aimer[2] ? » Elle se contente, à la fin d'un échange avec son fils, d'exprimer son inquiétude : «Tu reviendras ? dit-elle. Je sais

1. *OC*, t. II, p. 795.

2. *L'Envers et l'Endroit*, *OC*, t. I, p. 49.

bien que tu as du travail. Seulement, de temps en temps[1]... » Mais le fils n'élucidera jamais la signification de sa propre « pitié ». Un autre passage d'« Entre oui et non » laisse mieux percer ses sentiments : « Plus tard, bien plus tard, il devait se souvenir de cette odeur mêlée de sueur et de vinaigre, de ce moment où il avait senti les liens qui l'attachaient à sa mère[2]. » Que désigne ce « bien plus tard » ? L'époque où il n'est plus un enfant et compose sa première œuvre ? Ou un avenir sur lequel il anticipe ? Dans les deux hypothèses, le terme « liens » paraît tiède ou pudique. Il n'y a pas, dans *L'Envers et l'Endroit*, de « révélation » de l'amour de la mère.

Dans *Le Premier Homme*, cette révélation se produit un jour où Jacques et son frère ont donné un de ces duos musicaux que leur imposait la grand-mère. Au compliment adressé à Jacques par une des tantes, la mère a répondu : « "Oui, c'était bien. Il est intelligent", comme si les deux remarques avaient un rapport. Mais, en se retournant, il comprit le rapport. Le regard de sa mère, tremblant, doux, fiévreux, était posé sur lui avec une telle expression que l'enfant recula, hésita et s'enfuit. "Elle m'aime, elle m'aime donc", se disait-il dans l'escalier, et il comprenait en même temps que lui l'aimait éperdument, qu'il avait souhaité de toutes ses forces d'être aimé d'elle et qu'il en avait toujours douté jusque-là » (p. 106). La révélation de l'amour maternel provoque par contrecoup, telle une illumination, celle de l'amour filial. Une forme de pudeur l'empêche toutefois d'aller, pour le moment, jusqu'à l'aveu.

« Il a toujours eu sur le bout des lèvres l'envie de lui dire qu'elle était belle, et il n'a jamais osé » (p. 71). Les ébauches du *Premier Homme* font supposer que Jacques attendra le dénouement du roman pour lui dire qu'il l'aime. Ainsi, dans le seul livre qui représente l'« étage de l'amour », l'amour qui unit une mère et son fils n'est toujours pas une certitude acquise. Il faut une occasion favorable pour qu'il vous soit révélé, et qu'un long chemin s'accomplisse encore pour qu'il parvienne à s'exprimer. L'occasion est caractéristique de la bonte de Jacques. N'importe quel enfant, soucieux pour soi-même et vis-à-vis des autres d'éprouver de l'estime pour ses parents, aurait rougi que sa mère mélange l'intelligence et le sens musical, et c'est à ce penchant que cède ailleurs Jacques, quand il préfère à son amour le « jugement du monde » ; il s'accuse alors d'avoir un « mauvais cœur » (p. 222). Cette fois, devinant que toutes les confusions lui sont bonnes pour porter son fils au pinacle, il apprécie sa mère sans préjugé. Il n'aime pas sa mère parce qu'elle est bête, mais sa bêtise lui a révélé l'étendue de sa tendresse. Les demi-habiles s'offusqueront que la dédicace du livre officialise un illettrisme qu'on dissimule d'ordinaire comme une tare. Comprenons que Camus signifie ainsi qu'il est attaché à sa mère par un lien plus secret et plus fort que celui que tisseraient les vertus de l'intelligence. À la communion des esprits est préférée celle des cœurs.

La mère est entrée dans le récit à la suite de la grand-mère (chapitre 4), comme dans son ombre. De cet instant, c'est elle qui, silencieusement, y régnera. Quand Camus écrit sans autre précision « Il la serrait dans ses bras » (p. 67), « la » désigne la mère, comme « elle », dans *L'Éducation sentimentale*, désignait sans ambiguïté la femme aimée. Elle avait assumé dans *L'Envers et l'Endroit*, à cinquante ans à peine, le « rôle d'une vieille femme pauvre[1] »; veuve à trente-deux ans, la mère de Camus dut, en effet, selon la coutume espagnole, prendre le deuil pour ne plus le quitter. Comme elle est restée « la même que trente ans auparavant » (p. 70), Jacques admire en elle, dans *Le Premier Homme*, « une jeune femme » (p. 68). L'amour, enfin révélé, a-t-il opéré ce renversement? Ses expressions préférées sont demeurées les mêmes : ce « tu sais... », répété déjà dans *L'Envers et l'Endroit*, comme si elle ne connaissait que ces deux mots, à moins qu'ils ne suffissent à résumer le lien qui l'unissait à son fils : « Il est son fils, elle est sa mère. Elle peut lui dire : "Tu sais"[2]. » Dans *Le Premier Homme* à nouveau : « Oui, tu sais, tu arrivais » (p. 70). Quand « elle disait oui, c'était peut-être non » (p. 93) : elle est bien « la femme qui ne pensait pas », la première des « Voix du quartier pauvre[3] », origine du récit intitulé « Entre oui et non ». N'a pas

1. *Ibid.*

2. *Ibid.*, p. 52.

3. *Ibid.*, p. 75.

1. On trouve
une autre
« pomme
d'Adam » dans
le texte ; c'est
une poule cette
fois qui appelle
l'expression :
« [...] elle
l'égorgeait
ensuite lentement
à la place où se
trouve chez
l'homme la
pomme d'Adam »
(p. 253).

changé non plus la maigreur du cou qui, dans ce roman au titre adamique, lui vaut l'unique et bizarre privilège d'avoir une « pomme d'Adam[1] » (p. 68). Les chapitres 4, 5 et 6 du roman donnent l'impression de vagues successives, nous ramenant invariablement au même point. Un chapitre suit (ou précède ?) le pèlerinage à Saint-Brieuc, un autre marque le retour de Solférino ; toujours on se retrouve au même endroit, avec la mère guettant à sa fenêtre. Elle figure pour le voyageur le havre rassurant et pour l'exilé un point d'ancrage.

Avant de boucler *L'Envers et l'Endroit*, Camus avait imaginé que le fils, ne se résignant plus à la demi-surdité physique et intellectuelle de sa mère, lui expliquerait « bien des choses » et lui confesserait ses fautes. Ainsi se lit, dans les brouillons de *L'Envers et l'Endroit*[2], une première mouture de la confession que Jacques Cormery va, « pour finir », « écrire » (lapsus ou début de transposition romanesque ?) à sa mère illettrée (p. 363). Étonnante destinée de cette page que Camus ajourne à l'époque où il compose son premier recueil, qu'il élargit pour en faire la conclusion du *Premier Homme*, et que le destin nous oblige à lire, à nouveau, à l'état d'ébauche, comme si la charge d'émotion la rendait indicible.

L'ONCLE

Et si le vrai « premier homme », c'était lui ? Il est le seul, en tout cas, que Camus cré-

83

dite d'une « innocence adamique » (p. 117).
Après avoir été présenté anonymement
comme « l'oncle à demi muet » (p. 51),
il est aussi le seul personnage du roman à
être appelé de trois prénoms différents :
Émile (p. 68), Étienne (en tête de chapitre)
et, le plus souvent, Ernest (son prénom
dans la réalité). Promis à de longs développements par les brouillons de « Louis
Raingeard », esquisse d'un roman autobiographique contemporaine de *L'Envers et
l'Endroit,* mais à peine mentionné dans le
recueil, il occupe dans *Le Premier Homme*
la presque totalité d'un chapitre qui est, à
deux pages près, le plus long du roman. Il
est vrai que, alors que la mère et la grand-
mère sont, à l'exception des séances de
cinéma, toujours confinées au foyer, l'oncle
procure à Jacques la plupart de ses sorties :
bains à la plage des Sablettes, parties de
chasse, visites à la tonnellerie... Sous le titre
« Étienne » figure en outre le rituel de la
mouna[1], dont l'initiateur est cette fois
l'oncle Michel, mais que Camus égrène,
selon une logique échappant au titre du
chapitre, parmi les festivités familiales. Les
sorties avec l'oncle Ernest offrent au
roman ses pages les plus allègres, les plus
chaleureuses. On reste perplexe quand on
lit en marge du récit si travaillé de la partie
de chasse : « chasse ? on peut supprimer »
(p. 120). On ne pouvait pas. Parions que
Camus se serait ravisé. L'oncle est aussi le
boute-en-train de la famille et du groupe
de ses amis. Sans lui, les repas familiaux

1. Voir
Dossier, p. 196.

auraient été sinistres. Tant pis si ses plaisanteries se résument à une exhibition naïve des plaisirs corporels.

Dans *Noces* (« L'Été à Alger »), Camus opposait à l'exaltation cérébrale et compliquée des plaisirs du corps par Gide la simplicité de Vincent, personnage éphémère qui doit sans doute beaucoup à l'oncle : « Mon camarade Vincent, qui est tonnelier et champion de brasse junior, a une vue des choses encore plus claire. Il boit quand il a soif, s'il désire une femme cherche à coucher avec, et l'épouserait s'il l'aimait (ça n'est pas encore arrivé). Ensuite, il dit toujours : "Ça va mieux" — ce qui résume avec vigueur l'apologie qu'on pourrait faire de la satiété » (*OC*, t. I, p. 119). L'oncle accompagnait d'un « Bon, bon [...] toutes les sensations agréables, entre lesquelles il ne faisait pas de différence, qu'elles fussent d'excrétion ou de nutrition » (*PH*, p. 115).

Les écrits de caractère autobiographique de Camus ne dégagent pas une idée très cohérente de la personnalité de l'oncle. « Louis Raingeard » nous apprend qu'il s'était montré à l'égard de sa sœur « méchant et despote[1] ». Évinçant à coups de poing son prétendant, il la plongera dans le désespoir : « Elle avait trop peur de son frère pour le quitter. Elle le haïssait trop pour l'oublier. Elle le tuerait un jour, c'était sûr[2]. » En un autre endroit du texte, elle le quitte pour aller s'installer dans une petite chambre sans air d'un autre quartier[3] ; un peu plus loin, il est écrit qu'elle reviendra tout de même vers ce « frère méchant et brutal[4] ». Dans *Le Premier*

1. *OC*, t. I, p. 88.

2. *Ibid.*, p. 94.

3. *Ibid.*, p. 88.

4. *Ibid.*, p. 94.

Homme, la bagarre entre hommes n'est pas moins violente, mais Jacques, après en avoir gardé rancune à son oncle, lui trouve des excuses en raison de sa pauvreté (p. 135 et suiv.). On ne trouve pas d'indice que Mme Camus ait, fût-ce provisoirement, quitté son domicile de Belcourt. « Louis Raingeard » en prenait donc à son aise, déjà, avec les données de la vie réelle... Sans doute la prolongation de l'existence menée par le « ménage » frère-sœur après la mort de la grand-mère, et projetée en marge du manuscrit du *Premier Homme*[1], aurait-elle reflété plus exactement la réalité. Une interview de Camus explique ces deux versions contradictoires : « [...] mon oncle que j'admirais (sans l'estimer tout à fait, parce qu'il buvait). Je n'ai pas supporté longtemps son goût de la domination[2] ». Dans « Louis Raingeard », Camus a donc donné libre cours à ses réticences envers son oncle, en dramatisant les conséquences de ses écarts de conduite. Dans *Le Premier Homme*, l'habitude d'Ernest de fréquenter les cafés (ordinaire chez les célibataires) ne tourne pas au vice, et on ne trouve pas à redire au godet d'anisette et au rosé rafraîchi dont il partage le plaisir avec ses compagnons de chasse. Physiquement aussi, le portrait flotte un peu. Dans « Louis Raingeard », « il avait trente ans, était petit, assez beau[3] »; dans *Le Premier Homme*, vêtu de frais, il suscite chez la grand-mère un regard de tendresse qu'il ne lui avait jamais vu : c'est qu'il lui est apparu

1. Voir *supra*, p. 29, note 1.

2. « Notes pour le futur biographe d'Albert Camus », par Carl A. Viggiani, dans « Autour de *L'Étranger* », *Revue des Lettres modernes*, Minard, 1968, p. 205.

3. *OC*, t. I, p. 88.

« pour ce qu'il était, c'est-à-dire très beau » (p. 131). Roman de l'amour, *Le Premier Homme* euphémiserait en somme la figure de l'oncle.

L'oncle a offert au jeune Camus une caricature de ce peuple qui « ne peut être accepté de tous. Ici [en Algérie], l'intelligence n'a pas de place comme en Italie. Cette race est indifférente à l'esprit. Elle a le culte et l'admiration du corps ». Pourtant, « ces barbares qui se prélassent sur des plages, j'ai l'espoir insensé qu'à leur insu peut-être, ils sont en train de modeler le visage d'une culture où la grandeur de l'homme trouvera enfin son vrai visage[1] ». Par son indifférence complète aux vertus de l'esprit, ses dons d'athlète et son goût de la plage, Ernest apparaît comme un rejeton exemplaire de la race algérienne. On doute pourtant que ses instincts véritablement animaux lui donnent une chance de modeler le visage d'une culture. Il est bien vrai que sa morale est celle de son pays. Ce peuple a « sa morale, et bien particulière. On ne "manque" pas à sa mère. On fait respecter sa femme dans les rues[2] ». Le respect d'Ernest pour sa mère est sans faille (« Toi t'y es comme le bon Dieu pour moi ! », p. 135), et, faute d'avoir pu trouver une épouse, il juge qu'un homme manque au respect dû à sa sœur s'il se risque seulement à l'approcher. Mais, aussi adouci soit-il dans *Le Premier Homme*, son instinct tyrannique porte à son comble l'ordinaire machisme méditerranéen. Sa

1. *Noces*, « L'Été à Alger », *ibid.*, p. 123-124.

2. *Ibid.*, p. 122.

1. « Tu m'as manqué, tu m'as manqué », dit Sintès à sa « protégée » (*ibid.*, p. 161).

façon primitive de « protéger » le sexe faible trouve sa version crapuleuse avec Sintès, le proxénète de *L'Étranger*[1].

Le fil du récit tend à faire oublier sa surdité totale. « T'as peur, disait [l'oncle] aussitôt. — Non, mais reviens » (p. 115). Comment, accroché au cou de son oncle qui l'entraîne vers le large, Jacques peut-il bien formuler sa prière? En lui passant le doigt devant le visage? Ces contingences de l'échange ne tourmenteront qu'un lecteur vétilleux ; mais on souligne, en les relevant, que s'élabore avec des gestes, des mimiques, des bribes de phrases (encore faut-il que le sourd lise sur les lèvres...) une communication que borne le faible quotient intellectuel de l'oncle plutôt que son handicap physique. Le travail pédagogique de Jacques sur la nocivité d'Hitler, ou sur la distinction à établir entre les bons et les mauvais Arabes, suppose une ingéniosité difficile à concevoir.

Sa demi-surdité a condamné la mère au silence ; sa surdité complète rend le demi-muet Ernest extraordinairement bavard. Se lance-t-on plus hardiment dans la conversation du moment qu'on n'entend rien et que, admirateurs ou curieux de la performance, les autres évitent de vous interrompre? Le talent de mime de l'oncle accompagne, en effet, de vraies histoires, qui ravissent ses copains. Il est vrai que, « heureux de se sentir flanc à flanc, de partager la même chaleur », les chasseurs jouissent d'une communion qui ne se limite pas à

la parole. Et c'est dans un style aux résonances bibliques que Camus commente :
« Jacques apprit dans ces dimanches que
la compagnie des hommes était bonne et
pouvait nourrir le cœur » (p. 122). Ainsi,
unissant hommes et bêtes dans un même
amour de la nature, les parties de chasse
font-elles du *Premier Homme* un roman du
retour à l'origine. Mais cette dimension
épique, il faut au sein du récit un interprète
pour l'exalter. De la grandeur primitive de
la chasse, l'oncle est sacré « grand aède »
(p. 126). Le mot ne raille pas avec légèreté
l'infirmité d'Ernest : le romancier ne fait
que magnifier, au plan littéraire, le compliment spontanément formulé par les chasseurs : « Ton oncle, c'est un as ! » (p. 123).
Qu'un demi-muet chante idéalement les
plaisirs ancestraux de l'homme est ironique ; mais cette ironie est moins un
trait d'esprit surimposé au récit par un
esprit malicieux qu'une de ces surprises de
l'existence qu'il revenait à l'écrivain de
refléter.

LA GRAND-MÈRE

Catherine Marie Cardona, la grand-mère
maternelle d'Albert Camus, née dans l'île
de Minorque en 1857, avait épousé en
1874 Étienne Sintès. L'onomastique de
Camus, volontiers familiale, réserve décidément des surprises : dans *L'Étranger*,
la grand-mère de Camus donne son nom
à la belle jeune fille qui suscite le désir de

Meursault ; la mère donne le sien à un proxénète (Raymond Sintès).

« À soixante-dix ans, la grand-mère dominait encore tout ce monde », écrit Camus dans « Louis Raingeard » après avoir fait le tour du cercle familial. « Il [Louis] n'était jamais allé sur sa tombe. Mais cette femme par ses brutalités et ses outrances avait tenu une place trop grande dans sa vie pour qu'il pût s'en tenir là[1]. » Le trait s'accuse dans *L'Envers et l'Endroit*. Selon « L'Ironie », cette femme qui avait fait neuf enfants « ne manquait pas de qualités », mais elle avait, pour mieux se poser en victime, un détestable penchant à jouer la comédie[2]. Et elle est peinte dans « Entre oui et non » comme une femme « rude et dominatrice qui sacrifiait tout à un amour-propre de bête susceptible et qui avait long-temps dominé l'esprit faible de sa fille ». Qu'elle élève les enfants à la cravache, le lecteur du *Premier Homme* ne le sait que trop, mais « Entre oui et non » suggérait, au-delà de la sévérité des châtiments, des formes d'une violence indigne : « Quand elle frappe trop fort, sa fille lui dit : "Ne frappe pas sur la tête." » Le texte l'appelle « la vieille », sans que probablement le mot soit insultant : il pourrait être aussi bien une marque de respect ou d'affection[3].

Pas plus que la mère, la grand-mère n'a droit dans *Le Premier Homme* à un chapitre spécial. Elle le déborderait largement. À peine s'il a été fait mention, au premier chapitre, de la « belle-mère » d'Henri Cor-

1. *Ibid.*, p. 86.

2. *L'Envers et l'Endroit, ibid.*, p. 45.

3. *Ibid.*, p. 49.

mery : pendant le voyage du couple à Solférino, elle garde, à Alger, l'encombrant frère aîné du héros (p. 24). Quand Jacques navigue vers Alger, c'est la figure de la grand-mère et son « A benidor » qui, les premiers, déclenchent ses souvenirs d'enfance. Entre la belle-mère d'Henri, que Jacques n'a pu connaître, et la vieille femme qui tyrannisa plus tard le foyer, le récit assure une forme de continuité : elle est là pour assister sa fille quand le maire vient leur annoncer la mort d'Henri (p. 83) et c'est elle encore qui prend la première la mesure de l'événement : « Et la grand-mère, droite, les cheveux blancs tirés en arrière, les yeux clairs et durs : "Ma fille, il va falloir travailler" » (p. 76). Son indifférence à la religion et son insensibilité devant la mort en font une représentante typique des Français d'Algérie tels que Camus les a depuis longtemps définis. « Le pauvre, il ne chantera plus », dit-on là-bas, selon *Noces*, à l'annonce d'un décès[1]. « Bon, [...] il ne pétera plus », dit la grand-mère, qui a du tempérament (p. 181-182).

1. *Noces* (« L'Été à Alger »), *OC*, t. I, p. 123.

Sur le passé familial, elle offre à Jacques, bien qu'elle ne soit guère portée aux confidences, une source d'informations moins désespérément vide que l'oncle ou que la mère. Ainsi apprend-il grâce à elle comment son père avait réagi à l'exécution de Pirette, même si elle ignore pour quelle raison le condamné avait tué (p. 94). Elle n'est pas toujours une source fiable : qu'une typhoïde soit à l'origine de la demi-

surdité de sa fille, Jacques en doute (p. 93).
A-t-elle transmis à sa famille le souvenir de
la geste qui, avant 1848, exila des Baléares
en Algérie toute une tribu de petits Sintès ?
Comment Jacques en aurait-il été informé,
sinon par elle ? Au moins Camus donne-
t-il à l'aventure un tour picaresque qui
ne relève sûrement pas du génie de la
grand-mère. Doux rêveur pris à tort pour
un galant, l'ancêtre Sintès avait été, en
des temps lointains, descendu d'un coup
de fusil par un mari jaloux. Sa mort rédui-
sit à la misère et à l'exode en Algérie toute
sa progéniture. Ainsi Catherine Marie Cardona, qui venait elle-même des Baléares,
en serait-elle venue à épouser tout près
d'Alger un petit-fils du rêveur (p. 96). Le
jaloux eût-il raté son coup, jamais Camus/
Cormery n'aurait vu le jour.

Cette femme d'exception avait besoin
qu'on lui concédât aussi une forme de
grandissement épique. Chantre incertaine
du passé, elle se mue en « prophétesse »
(p. 96), et bientôt en « Cassandre » (p. 99).
Quel malheur prédit-elle au juste ? Aucun
en particulier : elle est seulement la figure
qui rappelle en toutes circonstances à ses
proches que l'existence est un chemin de
Croix, particulièrement pour les pauvres.
Comme dans le cas de l'oncle, *Le Premier
Homme* s'ingénie à infléchir en sa faveur
un jugement qui, à l'exposé brut des événements, ne devrait pas s'atténuer d'indulgence. Son avarice, qui n'en est pas vraiment une (p. 98), reçoit de la misère où elle

se débat son absolution, et Jacques, qui avait au cinéma l'obligation de lui lire à haute voix les panneaux des films muets, est submergé de remords un jour où la tâche s'est révélée trop ardue : c'est lui, la victime hebdomadaire, qui finit par pleurer, « bouleversé à l'idée qu'il avait gâché l'un des rares plaisirs de la malheureuse et le pauvre argent dont il avait fallu le payer » (p. 110). « En somme, je vais parler de ceux que j'aimais. » Oui, il a aimé son oncle, il a aimé sa grand-mère. Ce ne dut pas être toujours facile. À Saint-Brieuc, avant d'énumérer ses « très gros défauts », il avait dit tout à trac au vieux Malan : « Je vous aime » (p. 43). On devine que *Le Premier Homme* obéit à ces actes d'aveuglement que commande l'amour, gommant les aspérités pour aller à l'essentiel.

Il est vrai qu'en une occasion au moins, Cassandre s'est muée en déesse bienfaitrice. Après avoir refusé à Jacques le droit de poursuivre ses études, elle a cédé le lendemain, au bout d'une heure, aux arguments de l'instituteur. Cette scène donne lieu à son unique élan d'affection pour son petit-fils : « Et pour la première fois elle lui serrait la main, très fort, avec une sorte de tendresse désespérée » (p. 181). Camus/Cormery, qui a dû sa présence au monde à l'adresse d'un tireur jaloux, se serait retrouvé en apprentissage à dix ans si l'ambassade de son maître avait échoué. Cette heure de délibération, à laquelle on l'a prié de ne pas assister, a été cruciale dans son existence.

« Celui-là n'avait pas connu son père »
(p. 153). C'est en fonction du principe
romanesque énoncé dans le titre de la
partie « Recherche du père » que débute le
chapitre « L'école », consacré pour l'essentiel à l'instituteur et fondé sur une confrontation à laquelle le lecteur est désormais
habitué : les êtres chers tels qu'ils étaient au
temps de l'enfance, tels qu'ils sont aujour-
d'hui. Le fil narratif reste lâche, toutefois :
le chemin de l'école fait une longue place
aux mésaventures de Galoufa.

M. Bernard fait partie de la famille. S'il
n'a pas connu Henri Cormery, il l'a remplacé. Appelé deux fois dans le chapitre
de son vrai nom, Louis Germain, il offre
le portrait édifiant d'un maître à l'ancienne. Qu'on aborde *Le Premier Homme*
par ses aspects les moins spécifiques, on
y lira au moins un document sur la vie
d'une classe dans l'école de la IIIe République, où les enfants calculaient mentale-
ment combien font 1 267 + 691 (p. 162).
« Allonger et faire exaltation de l'école
laïque », a noté Camus en marge du
manuscrit (p. 164).

Jean Grenier, son autre maître, Camus
ne le découvrit qu'en classe de philosophie. Il ne pouvait donc trouver place dans
la chronologie du manuscrit. Mais on
s'étonne que l'apprentissage des premières
classes du lycée[1] y occupe une place si inférieure à celui de l'école primaire. Aussi
bien les livres que Jacques adolescent

1. On dirait
aujourd'hui :
du collège.

emprunte à la bibliothèque valent-ils moins par leur contenu (« Ce que contenaient ces livres au fond importait peu », p. 269) que par leur odeur. Des piles d'ouvrages qu'il reçoit aux distributions des prix, un seul titre émergera, tardivement noté en marge par le romancier : « *Les Travailleurs de la mer* » (p. 277). On doute que son accession aux classes supérieures du lycée eût corrigé le déséquilibre. En déguisant Jean Grenier sous les traits d'un douanier en retraite, Camus s'interdisait la possibilité de lui dédier un portrait symétrique de celui de Louis Germain. La multiplicité des professeurs, qui changent selon les matières, explique en priorité cette préférence : « Un instituteur, de ce point de vue, est plus près d'un père, il en occupe presque toute la place » (p. 240). Mais on se rappellera aussi que Jacques Cormery n'a pas de profession déclarée. Camus n'ayant pas choisi d'illustrer l'histoire d'un écrivain, mais d'un homme, le maître qui lui a appris, en le tirant de la pauvreté, les vertus du courage et de l'honnêteté compte plus, dans la perspective du *Premier Homme*, que ceux qui ont développé son intelligence.

CE SECRET D'UNE PAUVRETÉ CHALEUREUSE

Le Premier Homme rend hommage à la pauvreté. Ainsi s'explique qu'y figure à peine l'autre oncle de Camus, Gustave Acault, riche boucher établi près de la rue Michelet (au centre d'Alger) et mari de sa tante maternelle, Marie-Antoinette. « On le ramena chez l'oncle qui l'avait soigné », lisait-on dans « Louis Raingeard[1] ». Chez l'oncle Acault, dont le logement était plus confortable que celui de Belcourt, Camus passa, en effet, sa convalescence après sa première atteinte pulmonaire et il découvrit à cette occasion la fabuleuse bibliothèque de cet admirateur des « Lumières », lecteur de Hugo, de Gide et d'Anatole France. L'événement est un peu postérieur au point de l'adolescence où s'arrête le manuscrit du *Premier Homme*. Mais comment imaginer que cette intimité familiale se soit nouée tout d'un coup, à l'occasion de la maladie d'Albert ?

Le cas est ordinaire dans les familles : la richesse des uns ne profite guère aux autres (sinon, au mieux, aux ascendants et aux descendants directs). Les biens de l'oncle lettré n'auraient pas préservé le petit Albert des servitudes de l'apprentissage si la grand-mère avait persisté dans son refus. La place faite à Gustave Acault dans *Le Premier Homme* est plus que dis-

1. *OC*, t. I, p. 88.

crète. Pour une fois associé à son frère, Jacques reçoit un peu d'argent quand ils consentent à « rendre une visite à un oncle commerçant et une tante bien mariée. Pour l'oncle, c'était facile car ils l'aimaient bien. Mais la tante avait l'art de faire sonner sa richesse relative, et les deux enfants préféraient rester sans argent et sans les plaisirs qu'il procure plutôt que de se sentir humiliés » (p. 100). Auparavant, Camus avait déjà expliqué que contrairement aux maisons des pauvres, où les objets sont désignés par des noms communs, les maisons des riches (« chez son oncle... ») sont celles où on recourt à des noms propres : « le grès flambé des Vosges », « le service de Quimper » (p. 73). L'oncle riche n'a pourtant droit lui-même à aucun nom propre dans le roman ; l'oncle pauvre, lui, en a trois.

Le monde des pauvres est un « monde refermé sur lui-même comme une île dans la société mais où la misère tient lieu de famille et de solidarité » (p. 194), et c'est « l'île pauvre du quartier » qui sera à nouveau évoquée dans « Obscur à soi-même » (p. 299). Camus répète (recopie ?) dans *Le Premier Homme*, presque mot pour mot, ce qu'il écrivait dans les ébauches de « Louis Raingeard » : « Le monde des pauvres est un des rares sinon le seul qui soit replié sur lui-même et qui soit une île dans la société. » Il ajoutait seulement alors : « C'est à peu de frais qu'on peut y jouer les Robinson[1] ». On supposera que le symbole de l'île lui était inspiré par le recueil de Jean Grenier,

1. *Ibid.*, p. 89.

Les Îles (1933), ouvrage dont il redit en 1959 l'« ébranlement » qu'il en reçut, l'« influence » qu'il exerça sur lui[1]. Entrer dans l'écriture fut en premier lieu, pour Camus, découvrir la capacité de s'exprimer par symboles. Si l'île offre un symbole géographique à ce monde où on est coupé des autres, la mère y est elle-même une figure symbolique de ses valeurs. « Quelque chose dormait au fond de son âme, qui était fait du parfum de cette pauvreté infinie, qui recelait des phrases entendues il y a très longtemps, des attitudes de sa mère, des destinées perdues de vue. C'était cela qui valait à ses yeux. Et de tout cela sa mère était le vivant symbole[2]. » De ce monde, Camus, de la première à la dernière ligne de son œuvre, a voulu témoigner. En décembre 1934, épousant une jeune fille riche, il lui dédiait, comme pour la prévenir qu'il ne renoncerait pas aux valeurs qui étaient les siennes, le manuscrit des « Voix du quartier pauvre ». « Ajouter signes de pauvreté », note-t-il en marge du *Premier Homme* (p. 110). Tel est bien, décidément, le thème central de son roman. Aux souvenirs recueillis pour « L'enfance pauvre[3] » s'en ajouteront d'autres, qui augmenteront la portée du témoignage. Et, pour lui qui mène désormais une existence de nanti, les voyages à Alger signifient « revenir à l'enfance dont il n'avait jamais guéri, à ce secret de lumière, de pauvreté chaleureuse qui l'avait aidé à vivre et à tout vaincre » (p. 53).

1. Voir Dossier, p. 156.

2. « Louis Raingeard », *OC*, t. I, p. 90.

3. Voir *supra*, p. 17.

Camus n'idéalise pas la pauvreté. C'est elle qui attise les querelles familiales (ces « microtragédies », p. 130) : « Ils se faisaient du mal les uns aux autres sans le vouloir et simplement parce qu'ils étaient chacun pour l'autre les représentants de la nécessité besogneuse et cruelle où ils vivaient » (p. 139). La pauvreté découvre à l'enfant l'humiliation : celle d'accepter des dons qui lui semblent des aumônes (p. 100 et 184). Reçoit-on, à la veille d'une fête, des « parents plus fortunés », encore une fois estompés du texte par l'anonymat, il faut à la fois les honorer et les « tromper, par décence, sur la situation réelle de la famille » (p. 250). Il arrive que Jacques se découvre encore plus pauvre que les pauvres : la famille de son copain Pierre est un peu moins démunie que la sienne. Quand quatre élèves « méritants » sont choisis par M. Bernard, pour se présenter au concours des bourses, peu s'en faut que Jacques ne soit le seul à être trop pauvre pour tenter cette épreuve destinée aux pauvres. Enfin, il se sent « le plus misérable des enfants » quand, aux vacances, on se débarrasse de lui pour l'envoyer en colonie de vacances (p. 163). Nulle part ailleurs, dans le roman, Camus n'exprime aussi crûment la misère de l'enfant ; nulle part il ne glisse aussi rapidement sur un épisode. On le croirait, lui qui raconte en détail les moindres sorties de Jacques, atteint ici d'un trou de mémoire. Aurait-il atteint un point où le malheur est indicible ? Il arrive aussi que l'humour ou le détachement ne puissent masquer tout à fait la cruauté du réel. Car enfin, qu'un enfant n'ait même pas le droit de s'épanouir dans son royaume (p. 99 et 244), entendez de jouer au football dans la cour d'école sans recevoir, quand il rentre à la maison, des coups de cravache sous prétexte qu'il y a usé ses semelles (p. 99-100), voilà qui nourrirait, si Camus n'avait fait le choix de l'amour, le plus larmoyant des romans naturalistes.

« Presque tous les écrivains français qui prétendent aujourd'hui parler au nom du prolétariat sont nés de parents aisés ou fortunés », remarquait Camus en 1948, dans un texte qui servira en 1953 de préface à *La Maison du peuple*, roman de son ami Louis Guilloux (1899-1980). « Ce grand écrivain, parce qu'il a fait ses classes à l'école de la nécessité, a appris à juger sans embarras de ce qu'est un homme. [...] L'enfance pauvre, avec ses rêves et ses révoltes, lui a fourni l'inspiration de son premier et de ses derniers livres » (*Essais*, p. 1111-1112).

À l'époque de *L'Envers et l'Endroit*, Camus regrettait que son livre eût été lu comme un message de tristesse. À son ami Jean de Maisonseul, il écrivait le 8 juillet 1937 : « [...] l'accueil qu'on a fait à ces pages a été inespéré. Mais je lisais chez ces gens les mêmes phrases qui revenaient : amertume, pessimisme, etc. Ils n'ont pas compris — et je me dis parfois que je me suis mal fait comprendre[1]. » Apprendre à faire une œuvre, ce sera témoigner que la foi domine

1. *Ibid.*, p. 97.

en lui les atteintes du malheur. Alors que *Le Premier Homme* se réfère aux mêmes réalités personnelles et sociales que *L'Envers et l'Endroit*, on n'y relève nulle trace d'amertume ou de pessimisme. « Je n'ai pas eu une enfance malheureuse, la pauvreté réelle où j'ai vécu ne m'a jamais été réellement pénible », écrivait Camus à Jean Grenier le 18 septembre 1951[1]. Sans doute obéit-il par cette laborieuse dénégation à une forme d'honneur castillan (« son côté espagnol », p. 330) et au refus de trahir les richesses que lui ont apportées les siens. Le bonheur de Jacques Cormery relèverait ainsi d'un parti pris. Mais il se nourrit aussi de la comédie que chacun se donne et donne aux autres dès qu'il met son malheur en mots ou en spectacle. « Important aussi le thème de la comédie. [...] Le bonheur souvent n'est que le sentiment apitoyé de notre malheur », écrit Camus sur ce feuillet qu'il reprend textuellement de ses *Carnets* de jeunesse[2] (p. 318). Cette note ancienne est la seule du *Premier Homme* où s'entrevoient les sources de la vocation théâtrale de Camus. Le comédien, dont les compositions incluent celle de son propre personnage, fait partie de ces créateurs qui ont choisi la voie de l'art pour corriger le réel et lutter ainsi contre l'absurdité du monde[3]. Dans le domaine du genre romanesque, Proust a expliqué comment « l'œuvre est signe de bonheur[4] ». Placé sous le signe de la généralité, le malheur s'y exprime en effet avec des tonalités peu

1. Albert Camus-Jean Grenier, *Correspondance*, p. 180.

2. Voir *supra*, p. 21.

3. Voir *Le Mythe de Sisyphe*, « L'Homme absurde. La comédie ».

4. Proust, *Le Temps retrouvé*, Gallimard, coll. « Folio », 1990, p. 211.

différentes de celles du bonheur, le sujet du livre s'estompant, pour finir, derrière le bonheur de l'écriture. Ce que Camus exprime à sa manière : « Au centre de notre œuvre, fût-elle noire, rayonne un soleil inépuisable[1]. »

1. *L'Été*, *Essais*, p. 865.

VERTUS DE LA PAUVRETÉ

« La pauvreté ne [se] choisit pas » (p. 78). Mais du moment qu'elle vous a été donnée en partage, on l'acceptera comme sa patrie. Ainsi, hors de cette île où « la misère tient lieu de famille et de solidarité », le pauvre s'aventure-t-il dans un « monde inconnu » (p. 194). Une fois le voyage accompli, sa fidélité à la patrie de la pauvreté demeure chez Camus aussi indéfectible, aussi têtue que sa fidélité à la patrie algérienne. Se vouloir pauvre et Algérois, c'est pour lui tout un et, dans l'une et l'autre origines, il puise des motifs d'énergie. C'est même « à force de pauvreté » (p. 300) qu'il se libérera un jour des contraintes de l'argent.

La pauvreté lui a d'abord appris le courage. Cette vertu, nous savons qu'il la revendiquait comme un héritage paternel[2]. Elle était celle des pionniers de l'Algérie coloniale, et leurs descendants ont continué d'en faire « la vertu principale de l'homme » (p. 182). Adulte, Jacques revoit sa propre vie « folle, courageuse, lâche, obstinée » (p. 35), et le courage figure à nouveau dans la liste chaotique des vertus et défauts qu'il se reconnaît (p. 36).

2. Voir *supra*, p. 48.

Tout petit déjà, en accomplissant « son devoir d'homme » face à Munoz qui l'avait provoqué, il avait fait honneur à sa race (p. 172). Le courage est demeuré, dans ce peuple dépourvu d'héritage, la vertu des pauvres. L'univers de la misère tendant à faire un luxe de l'échelle habituelle des valeurs (« Personne en vérité n'avait jamais appris à l'enfant ce qui était bien ou ce qui était mal », p. 101), Jacques doit apprendre en priorité par quels moyens une famille subvient aux besoins de l'existence : « Mais c'était là leçon de courage, non de morale » (p. 102). Assez courageux à l'école pour affronter plus grand que lui, il est enfin consacré dans sa famille grâce au rite solennel de l'égorgement de la poule (variante de la scène du seau de Cosette dans *Les Misérables*). L'épreuve l'oblige à affronter l'obscurité, symbole de celle qu'il affrontera plus tard pour se trouver lui-même. « Il a le courage », décrète l'oncle quand il s'est dévoué pour accomplir la mission. « Tu es courageux », lui dit la mère. Avare en compliments, la grand-mère met l'accent sur la peur du frère qui s'est dérobé (p. 254-255). Au fond de lui-même, Jacques sait bien quelle est la vraie nature de son courage. Lui qui avait affronté Munoz en « serrant les fesses », il analyse moins comme du courage que comme « une volonté de courage » la résolution qui lui a fait braver l'obscurité et l'horreur de la bête à égorger. Mais le vrai courage ne réside pas dans l'ignorance du danger :

il consiste au contraire à en prendre la mesure et à surmonter ses faiblesses.

Bon sang ne saurait mentir : digne fils d'Henri, Jacques est aussi le fils de sa mère. Après l'attentat qui a ébranlé tout le quartier, Catherine présente à Jacques, le premier moment d'émotion passé, « son beau sourire vaillant. Elle avait grandi, comme toute sa race, dans le danger, et le danger pouvait lui serrer le cœur, elle l'endurait comme le reste » (p. 88-89).

La pauvreté a pour autre vertu d'enseigner les « vraies richesses ». C'est à cette enseigne que Raymond Charlot, l'ami et premier éditeur de Camus (*L'Envers et l'Endroit, Noces*), vendait et publiait des livres, rue Charras, à Alger. Sa boutique faisait référence à un ouvrage tout récent (1936) de Giono. Pour Camus existent d'abord les richesses du cœur, celles de la nature et celles du corps vivant en harmonie avec elle. Profitant de la générosité du soleil et de la mer, les enfants qui se partagent les miettes d'un cornet de frites sont « comme des seigneurs assurés de leurs richesses irremplaçables » (p. 64). Richesse aussi celle que procure la communauté des hommes. « Le plus misérable des enfants » (quand sa famille le reléguait en colonie de vacances) « se sentait le plus riche des enfants » les dimanches où il pouvait, à la chasse, connaître avec son oncle et ses amis une authentique chaleur humaine (p. 126). On s'explique ainsi qu'Ernest, le pauvre, soit spontanément plus généreux que son frère Joséphin : « La prodigalité est toujours plus facile dans le dénuement. Rares sont ceux qui continuent d'être prodigues après en avoir acquis les moyens. Ceux-là sont les rois de la vie, qu'il faut saluer bas » (p. 133), conclut Camus d'une de ces formules morales d'allure évangélique qui élargissent souvent le récit. « Heureux, vous les pauvres, car le Royaume de Dieu est à vous. [...] Mais malheur à vous, les riches ! Car vous avez votre consolation » (saint Luc, 6, 20-24). Dans son royaume, qui est de ce monde[1], Camus laisse aux riches une voie de passage vers le salut, mais on la devine aussi étroite que le chas d'une aiguille.

La pauvreté des élus n'est pas seulement matérielle. « Heureux les pauvres en esprit, car le Royaume des Cieux est à eux », annonce le Christ au début du Sermon sur la montagne (saint Matthieu, 5, 3). La simplicité et le dénuement de langage sont, chez l'oncle ou chez la mère, à l'image de leur humilité devant la vie. « Chapitres alternés qui donneraient une voix à la mère. Le commentaire des mêmes faits mais avec son vocabulaire de 400 mots », avait prévu Camus (p. 356). Elle ignore par exemple les mots « domestique » (p. 222), « patrie » (p. 226) ou « bibliothèque » (p. 271). « Elle n'a jamais employé un subjonctif » (p. 91), lit-on en marge[2]. Le projet des chapitres alternés n'a pas vu le jour, mais, tant que le manuscrit se borne à l'horizon domestique, il en respecte la pau-

1. « À cette heure, tout mon royaume est de ce monde » (*L'Envers et l'Endroit, OC*, t. I, p. 71). Il reprendra la même formule deux ou trois fois, avec de légères variantes.

2. « Et puis je suis contente que tu sois allé à sa tombe », dit-elle pourtant (p. 85).

vreté d'expression. Les rares mots savants relèvent de l'univers du travail : les « bourrettes » (p. 120), les « douelles » (p. 141) ou, en attendant de trouver le terme technique, le « hachoir » (p. 140) sont familiers aux ouvriers de la tonnellerie[1]. Il est logique que Jacques parle de « connaissements » (p. 292) du moment qu'il travaille chez un courtier maritime. Dans *L'Étranger*, qui offrait un exemple voisin d'une langue modelée par le romancier sur la simplicité de culture et d'esprit de son héros, le seul mot rare était déjà « connaissement » (c'est-à-dire : reçu des marchandises expédiées par voie maritime) : « Il y avait un tas de connaissements qui s'amoncelaient sur ma table et il a fallu que je les dépouille tous » (*OC*, t. I, p. 155). On se rappelle que Meursault était lui aussi employé chez un courtier maritime.

POURQUOI JACQUES EST UN MONSTRE

Le monde des pauvres, Jacques Cormery s'accuse (ou il est accusé par le romancier) de l'avoir trahi. Ainsi faut-il entendre cette « monstruosité » présente une seule fois dans le manuscrit, où le souvenir de Jacques est donné comme celui de « l'homme monstrueux et [banal] » (p. 215), mais que les marges et les ébauches promettaient à d'amples développements. On lit en effet dans les marges : « Dès le début, il faudrait marquer plus le monstre

1. « Vérifier le nom de l'outil », s'est enjoint Camus en marge (p. 140) après avoir parlé d'« un instrument assez semblable à un hachoir ».

chez Jacques » (p. 29), « mais au fait ce sont des monstres ? (non c'était lui le m.) » (p. 149), « présentation de l'adulte monstre » (p. 219) ; puis dans les ébauches : « Je vais raconter l'histoire d'un monstre » (p. 344) et enfin : « Elle semblable à ce que la terre porte de meilleur, et lui tranquillement monstrueux » (p. 352). « Un peu monstrueux », avait seulement écrit Camus dans le premier plan du roman[1].

1. Voir Dossier, p. 160.

« Qu'on peut avoir — sans romantisme — la nostalgie d'une pauvreté perdue », lit-on dans les *Carnets* à la date de « mai 1935. [...] De là, pour qui s'en aperçoit, une reconnaissance et donc une mauvaise conscience[2] ». La confession que Camus envisage, vers la même époque, de prêter au jeune héros de *L'Envers et l'Endroit* pour soulager cette mauvaise conscience aurait pris un autre poids dans *Le Premier Homme* du moment que Jacques, pleinement adulte, se serait éloigné depuis longtemps de son « île » d'origine. L'entrée au lycée, monde « inassimilable » qui fait grandir le silence entre sa famille et lui (p. 221), est déjà dans le roman une première trahison. « Tu ne mangeras pas de l'arbre de la connaissance », dit Dieu au premier homme dans la Genèse. Le plus grave était à venir. Après avoir longuement évoqué les soins que la mère de Jacques porte au linge de la famille, Camus accorde une seule ligne à l'« autre univers », celui « des femmes qui ne lavent ni ne repassent » (p. 70-71). Sans doute cet univers aurait-il

2. *OC*, t. II, p. 795.

été peuplé par des développements non encore écrits. Y auraient pris place ces femmes de la société parisienne qui préfèrent les discussions philosophiques au silence de leurs cuisines. Ainsi s'explique et s'adoucit le machisme parfois rebutant de Camus : il a dû chercher, dans les femmes qu'il rencontrait, quelque chose qui fît écho à l'humble soumission de sa mère. « Non, je ne suis pas un bon fils : un bon fils est celui qui reste. Moi j'ai couru le monde, je l'ai trompée avec les vanités, la gloire, cent femmes » (p. 362). Les retours de Jacques à Alger, chaotiques dans leur multiplicité, corrigent les visites peut-être plus espacées que Camus consentit à sa mère, mais ils n'atténuent pas son remords.

Le lecteur se doute, même si le manuscrit fait silence sur ses activités professionnelles, que Jacques a « réussi » dans la vie. Constater qu'il n'a pu « vivre au niveau de cette patience aveugle, sans phrases, sans autre projet que l'immédiat » (p. 214-215), c'est exprimer la nostalgie de cette ivresse du présent qui faisait le bonheur du narrateur de *Noces*, dans « Le Vent à Djémila » : « Que signifient ici les mots d'avenir, de mieux-être, de situation? [...] Si je refuse obstinément tous les "plus tard" du monde, c'est qu'il s'agit aussi bien de ne pas renoncer à ma richesse présente[1]. » À Tipasa déjà, Camus avait compris face à l'innocence du monde « ce qu'on appelle gloire : le droit d'aimer sans mesure[2] ». Ses proches

1. *Noces*, *OC*, t. I, p. 113.

2. *Ibid.*, p. 107.

1. Catherine Sellers, par exemple, a déclaré qu'il avait eu alors la tentation du suicide (*Albert Camus [1913-1960]. Une tragédie du bonheur.* Voir Filmographie, p. 214).

2. *Carnets, OC,* t. II, p. 1027.

3. *Ibid.,* p. 810.

4. Voir *Carnets III,* p. 63.

ont témoigné de l'amertume que lui infligea l'attribution du prix Nobel[1]. Elle a dû nourrir les remords de Jacques.

La « gloire » de Jacques elle-même, dont les ébauches laissent parfois supposer qu'elle lui a été apportée par la création artistique, s'annonce donc comme une forme de trahison. « Révolte : Créer pour rejoindre les hommes ? Mais peu à peu la création nous sépare de tous et nous rejette au loin sans l'ombre d'un amour[2]. » Ce scepticisme, confirmé par une première ébauche : « Se libérer de tout souci d'art et de forme. Retrouver le contact direct, sans intermédiaire, donc l'innocence. Oublier l'art ici, c'est *s'oublier* » (p. 343), est corrigé par une seconde : « Et ce qui m'a soutenu c'est d'abord la grande idée, la très grande idée que je me fais de l'art. / Non qu'il soit pour moi au-dessus de tout, mais parce qu'il ne se sépare de personne » (p. 366). Ainsi l'art vaut-il à condition de répondre, non à une ambition esthétique intellectuelle et solitaire, mais à l'exigence de rejoindre par ses voies la communauté des hommes. « Intellectuel = celui qui se dédouble. Ça me plaît. Je suis content d'être les deux », notait Camus en mai 1936[3]. Il écrivait ces mots avant de découvrir en métropole la « jungle[4] » des intellectuels parisiens. Désormais, il aspire moins à un dédoublement qu'à la simplicité et à l'innocence qui le rapprocheront des siens. De cette forme supérieure de l'art, *Le Premier Homme* était destiné à témoigner.

L'enfant pauvre aurait donc pour devoir de demeurer à vie dans son île. Fragmentairement, dans l'état où il nous est parvenu, *Le Premier Homme* est l'histoire d'un homme qui a trahi par ses aventures, par des amours dont aucun ne valait celui qui l'unissait à sa mère, par une soif d'une connaissance orgueilleuse du monde à laquelle son milieu était étranger. La confession du monstre de retour au bercail s'offrait comme le seul dénouement possible du roman. De même le fils prodigue se repent-il à l'heure où il regagne le foyer. « Père, j'ai péché contre le Ciel et contre toi, je ne mérite plus d'être appelé ton fils » (saint Luc, 15, 21). Le fils prodigue des Évangiles a, pour courir le monde, renoncé à la fortune familiale ; Jacques, lui, a déserté la pauvreté du foyer, mais c'est d'elle que venait sa richesse. « Le sentiment des richesses perdues », écrivait Camus en 1935 à la première page de ses *Carnets* pour désigner sa mauvaise conscience d'avoir déserté son milieu[1].

1. *OC*, t. II, p. 795.

Le fils prodigue est une figure du « premier homme ». « Les Pères ont mis tout leur amour dans l'interprétation de cette scène. Pour eux, le fils prodigue est l'image de l'homme par excellence, de l'"Adam" que nous sommes tous, cet Adam à la rencontre duquel Dieu est allé et qu'il a à nouveau accueilli dans sa maison » (Joseph Ratzinger-Benoît XVI, *Jésus de Nazareth*, Flammarion, 2007, p. 230-231).

À l'époque où il dirigeait le Théâtre de l'Équipe, plus précisément au début de 1938,

Camus avait adapté pour la scène *Le Retour de l'enfant prodigue*, d'André Gide. Lui-même tenait le rôle de l'enfant prodigue.

Une note des ébauches va compliquer un peu l'inspiration évangélique du roman en magnifiant le rôle d'intercesseur dévolu à la mère dans la dédicace : « Sa mère *est* le Christ » (p. 328). Au moins n'altère-t-elle pas, pour l'essentiel, le sens du mouvement qui conduira finalement le monstre à demander pardon.

IV   HOMMAGE À LA « PATRIE »

UNE MÉMOIRE D'AFRICAIN

L'océan Atlantique à l'ouest, la mer Tyrrhénienne à l'est, la Méditerranée au nord, le désert du Sahara au sud : le Maghreb se présente à l'ouverture du roman comme un continent autonome, une « sorte d'île immense » (p. 13). Au cœur de cette île sera située l'« île pauvre du quartier ». La savante fresque géographique du romancier anticipe sur la vision naïve de la mère, qui « ne savait même pas ce qu'était une île puisqu'elle n'en avait jamais vu », mais qui ne conçoit pas autrement l'Algérie que comme une terre isolée de tous ces pays dont elle sait à peine prononcer les noms

(p. 80). La lointaine métropole n'inspire à sa bonté christique que générosité. « Les Français sont bien braves », dit-elle à Jacques quand elle apprend que la tombe d'Henri Cormery est fleurie (p. 85). Ils ont pris la vie à son mari ; en échange, la relique de l'éclat d'obus et quelques bouquets de fleurs. De quoi fondre de reconnaissance, en effet.

À l'anonymat du monde des pauvres devait aussi préluder d'emblée l'anonymat de la terre qui les a accueillis. « (Ajouter anonymat géologique. Terre et mer) », a noté Camus en marge de la dédicace du roman. Les strates du continent nord-africain seront aussi difficiles à distinguer et à nommer que les strates de la mémoire des pauvres. Plus tard, à l'occasion de son voyage à Mondovi, Jacques découvrira de ses yeux ce pays aux « contours imprécis » et il constatera que sur le marécage qui le couvrait autrefois s'étendent aujourd'hui « jusqu'à la mer au nord » des « champs de vigne tirés au cordeau » (p. 200). En attendant de modeler peut-être un jour une culture où se reconnaîtra la grandeur de l'homme, les gens ignorants et courageux qu'on a envoyés, souvent contre leur gré, sur des terres ingrates et hostiles y ont construit les bases d'une civilisation.

Pour Jacques enfant aussi bien que pour sa mère, la France est « une absente » dont son camarade métropolitain Didier lui donne une vague idée (p. 226), mais dont les images rapportées dans les livres figurent à ses yeux « l'exotisme même » (p. 162). Après y avoir abordé et fait sa vie, il continuera de considérer l'Algérie comme sa terre d'attache. Si, dans le cimetière de Saint-Brieuc, il respire « la senteur salée qui venait en ce moment de la mer lointaine et immobile » (p. 34), on se doute qu'il retrouve ses impressions d'enfance quand, sur la route de Sidi-Ferruch, il était sensible à l'odeur vanillée « mêlée à l'odeur d'embrun qui de la mer parvenait jusque sur la route du littoral » (p. 147). Il sait bien, par expérience, que les « Français » sont moins braves que l'imagine sa mère. La mauvaise humeur que lui inspire chaque visage dans le train ou à l'hôtel de Saint-Brieuc fait même tache dans cet ouvrage tout entier voué à l'amour du prochain. Elle n'aura pas de suite, pour la simple raison qu'à l'exception de Didier (qui a l'excuse de l'âge) on ne rencontrera plus, après ce deuxième chapitre, l'ombre d'un métropolitain. « Si j'avais le malheur de ne pas connaître l'amour et si je voulais me donner le ridicule de m'en instruire, ce n'est pas à Paris ou dans les gazettes que je viendrais faire mes classes », écrivait-il dans les *Carnets* à la fin de 1949[1]. Le meilleur moyen d'être tout amour est encore d'ignorer les gens qu'on n'aime pas.

Le devoir de mémoire que nous avons reconnu dans l'écriture des souvenirs d'enfance de Jacques s'inscrit dans un devoir de mémoire plus vaste, celui de l'histoire de sa terre natale. La tâche était ardue. Dépour-

1. *Carnets II*, p. 300.

vues d'archives[1], les mairies d'Algérie sont aussi peu prodigue d'informations sur le passé du pays que la mère sur celui de la famille. Et tandis que sur la tombe d'Henri Cormery figuraient au moins ses dates de naissance et de mort, « les dalles usées et verdies des petits cimetières » de la colonisation sont « devenues illisibles ». On interprétera comme une fatalité l'« immense oubli » qui s'étend sur cette terre où les temples eux-mêmes sont détruits, puisque y contribuent à la fois la lumière du soleil, où s'évapore l'histoire des hommes, et la nuit qui noie tout, « morts et vivants » (p. 210-212).

La mémoire qu'entreprend de se donner Jacques est à ce point une mémoire d'Africain que (piété filiale oblige) il considère la Première Guerre mondiale du point de vue de ces « vagues d'Algériens arabes et français » qui furent alors sacrifiés, laissant « dans tous les coins d'Algérie, arabes et français, fils et filles sans père qui devraient ensuite apprendre à vivre sans leçon et sans héritage » (p. 82-83). Ainsi la situation de l'orphelin, dans tous les cas cruelle, est-elle aggravée du moment qu'il est, après le décès de son père, condamné à vivre sur une terre à laquelle les traditions morales et historiques font défaut. Au fil du récit s'inscrivent pourtant des pans de l'histoire de l'Algérie. Les aventures du poète mahonais, dont la mort tragi-comique aboutit à l'implantation d'une « nichée d'analphabètes » (p. 96-97), éclairent d'un jour pittoresque les ascendances familiales ; elles offrent en même temps une page d'histoire illustrée sur une source parmi tant d'autres de l'implantation coloniale. L'oncle Ernest lance-t-il « Lui Mzabite » pour qualifier un avare, le romancier saisit la phrase au bond pour dérouler une leçon d'histoire à propos de cette « tribu d'hérétiques » que les persécutions de l'Islam spécialisèrent dans l'épicerie (p. 132-133). Profiter d'une anecdote ou d'un bon mot pour instruire sur des sujets sérieux, le procédé témoigne d'un sens pédagogique éprouvé.

Inspirée par la « recherche du père », la visite à Mondovi ouvre à Jacques de nouveaux horizons sur l'histoire de son pays. Au moment où il se rend à l'invitation à déjeuner du docteur, dernier témoin de l'époque de sa naissance, le lecteur s'attend à une sorte de dénouement de l'enquête. Or, curieusement, coupant à cet endroit le fil narratif du récit, Camus enchaîne directement sur le retour en avion de Jacques. « Plus tard, dans l'avion qui le ramenait à Alger, Jacques essayait de mettre en ordre les renseignements qu'il avait recueillis. À vrai dire, il n'y en avait qu'une poignée, et aucun ne concernait directement son père » (p. 202). C'est que, si elle a échoué au plan personnel, l'enquête n'aura pas été vaine au plan historique. Et, plutôt que d'être égrenée au fil d'une conversation, mieux valait qu'elle fût récapitulée, décantée, méditée par Jacques sur le chemin du retour. La fondation de Solférino (à nouveau appelée ainsi) par des quarante-hui-tards au nombre desquels Veillard compte des ancêtres, *Le Labrador* judicieusement nommé qui conduit vers une chaleur d'enfer une population hébétée, le calvaire des arrivants à qui on n'offre pour gîte que des baraques où ils seront dévorés par les moustiques : de son voyage à Mondovi, Jacques rapporte une épopée en raccourci, petit western auquel ne manque même pas le violoneux qui fait danser les couples à la veillée, mais où font cruellement défaut les troupeaux qui nourriraient tout ce monde. Leurs moyens de subsistance, les pionniers d'Algérie durent les inventer sur place. « Où était son père en tout ceci ? » (p. 204). Il n'est nulle part, puisque c'est une histoire antérieure à la naissance d'Henri Cormery qu'ont ressuscitée Veillard et le docteur ; il est partout, parce que d'autres vagues de pionniers ont succédé à celles de 1830, de 1848, de 1871, et que, en 1913 encore, les moustiques de la vallée de la Seybouse menaçaient les gens qu'on y expédiait.

L'épopée de la conquête avait vocation à s'étoffer. Il restait à Camus à y intégrer les informations qu'il avait accumulées sur les feuillets séparés ou sur son carnet : le taux de mortalité des colons envoyés en Algérie en 1831, les cultivateurs-soldats de Boufarik (p. 313), les « mariages au tambour » qui peuplèrent la commune de Fouka, la colonisation de Cheraga[1] par des horticulteurs de Grasse (p. 314), le déve-

1. Voir Dossier, p. 161.

loppement de Mondovi de 1840 à 1913, programmé sans commentaire (p. 330), puis déroulé en phrases brèves, voire télégraphiques, comme en vue d'écrire un chapitre d'histoire, même si deux prénoms (Rosine et Eugène) visent sans doute à donner chair à l'exposé, voire à ébaucher un petit roman de la colonisation du lieu (p. 345-347). Un dialogue imaginaire se réfère aux raisons qui poussèrent Camus, à l'automne de 1937, à quitter le parti communiste (p. 358). Pour obéir à l'Union soviétique, qui avait conclu des accords avec le gouvernement de Pierre Laval, les communistes avaient, en effet, freiné les revendications des nationalistes algériens, jusqu'à aider le gouvernement français à les mettre en prison. Sur cet épisode mal connu, *Le Premier Homme* aurait apporté des lumières. La perspective du roman promet même de s'élargir à la Russie. L'année 1905 est à la fois celle de la guerre du Maroc, qu'a faite Henri Cormery, et celle du « dimanche rouge », à la suite duquel Kaliayev[1] exécutera le Grand-Duc (p. 360). Comment Camus aurait-il fondu dans la pâte du roman ces statistiques, ces éléments d'archives, qu'il a été obligé de chercher ailleurs que dans les mairies, ces considérations de géopolitique ? Assurément, il était loin du terme.

1. Kaliayev est le héros des *Justes* (1949), pièce où Camus met en scène les scrupules des terroristes russes.

LES DEUX « RACES »

Les étapes de la colonisation ont créé une population composite, où le sang de Mahonais miséreux s'est mêlé à celui d'Alsaciens partis de chez eux pour rester Français (p. 210). Quant aux descendants des quarante-huitards ou des communards, pour qui l'exil en Algérie avait été une alternative à la prison, les voici soupçonnés par la mère patrie de s'être changés en exploiteurs du peuple. À moins que, par leur résistance à l'armée française qui les expulse aujourd'hui pour les protéger des rebelles, ils prouvent qu'ils ont de qui tenir ? Le père Veillard, qui vient de saccager sa propriété en conseillant aux Arabes de prendre le maquis, comptait parmi ses ancêtres des héros de 1848. « C'est pour ça que le vieux est une graine de révolutionnaire », conclut son fils (p. 202).

De ce mélange d'immigrants est née une race, celle des Français d'Algérie[1]. En gardant son sang-froid lors de l'attentat, la mère de Jacques a montré qu'elle savait, « comme toute sa race », endurer le danger (p. 89). « Je savais que tu étais de la bonne race », déclare M. Bernard à Jacques (p. 177). Cette race de souche européenne est, à une époque où la nation algérienne n'a pas encore vu le jour, celle des « Algériens[2] » (p. 182). Elle s'oppose à celle que les Européens appellent, faisant fi de la minorité berbère, la race des Arabes. « Sale race ! Quelle sale race ! » s'indignait Henri

1. Jamais Camus n'emploie l'expression « pieds-noirs », qui ne se répandit qu'après sa mort.

2. Dans L'Été, Camus parlait de la « race algérienne » pour saluer sa « franchise » (Essais, p. 825). Voir aussi Dossier, p. 173.

Cormery devant les exactions de nationalistes marocains (p. 78). Un ouvrier qui a assisté à l'attentat de Belcourt lui fait écho : « Cette sale race » (p. 87). Les inégalités sociales des deux races ne sont pas occultées par *Le Premier Homme*. Jacques, qui avait des camarades arabes à l'école communale, n'en a plus au lycée, parce qu'ils y sont l'exception (p. 221), et le spectacle des Arabes et des Mauresques « faméliques » qui fouillent dans les poubelles, « trouvant encore à prendre dans ce que des familles pauvres et économes dédaignaient assez pour le jeter » (p. 156), prouve que les indigènes d'Alger ne le cèdent guère en misère à ceux du bled. « Par un petit matin, j'ai vu à Tizi-Ouzou des enfants en loques disputer à des chiens kabyles le contenu d'une poubelle », écrivait Camus en 1939, à l'occasion d'une enquête en Kabylie pour le journal *Alger républicain*[1].

Le Premier Homme ne fait pas désespérer de l'entente des deux races. L'union sacrée que noue entre communautés la naissance de Jacques est certes ambiguë : la froideur autoritaire d'Henri Cormery et la complaisance trop soumise de l'Arabe affichent surtout la supériorité morale du colonisateur. Au cinéma, spectateurs « arabes et français » vibrent d'émotion devant les mêmes films (p. 108). Dans les années 1950 encore, les jeunes indigènes, friands de westerns, applaudissaient avec une belle inconscience les exploits de pionniers venus dépouiller les Indiens de leurs terres.

1. *Actuelles III, Essais*, p. 907-908.

Hommage à un héros mythique de la civilisation occidentale : de jeunes commissaires politiques du F.L.N. « ont pris pour nom de guerre Tarzan » (p. 365). Enfin, si une famille arabe promène un enfant déguisé en parachutiste (p. 86), elle témoigne assurément moins d'un désir de fraternité que d'une aliénation aux forces d'oppression.

D'autres signes réchauffent davantage le cœur. Dès qu'ils se retrouvent de l'autre côté de la Méditerranée, Arabes et Français partagent la même nostalgie du pays : « Rencontre avec l'Arabe à Saint-Étienne. Et cette fraternité des deux exilés en France » (p. 324). Que les colons soient prêts à crever sur place, personne ne peut le comprendre à Paris.

« À part nous, vous savez ceux qui sont seuls à pouvoir le comprendre ?

— Les Arabes.

— Tout juste. On est fait pour s'entendre » (p. 199).

Ce pathétique acte de foi est prononcé par Veillard alors que sa ferme est quasiment assiégée par les fellaghas. Aux pires moments enfin, il arrive que le devoir d'hospitalité efface les antagonismes. À l'instar de Daru, l'instituteur de « L'hôte » (*L'Exil et le Royaume*), et alors qu'il « est déjà contre le terrorisme », Jacques « accueille S[addok], le droit d'asile étant sacré ». Ce militant du F.L.N. s'incline alors devant sa mère : « Elle est ma mère, dit-il. La mienne est morte. Je l'aime et la

respecte comme si elle était ma mère. »
Peut-on détester un homme qui aime à
égalité votre mère et la sienne ? Cette communauté profonde sera inintelligible aux
lecteurs de la métropole. Ensuite, du
moment où Saddok est menacé d'être
arrêté par les forces de l'ordre, Jacques
l'invite à rester chez lui (p. 325).

« LES RAISONS DE L'ADVERSAIRE »

On jugera ces lueurs d'espoir bien faibles
dans le climat de violence qui règne en
Algérie. Mais Jacques n'a pas attendu
l'éclatement du conflit pour en faire l'expérience. Une image de son enfance a sur-
vécu à toutes les autres : celle d'un homme
étendu, une balle dans la tempe, sur ce
trottoir de Belcourt où les habitants du
quartier, peu de temps auparavant, pre-
naient le frais[1] (p. 150-151). Le règlement
de comptes n'impliquait aucun Arabe : il a
seulement appris à l'enfant que la violence
pouvait surgir n'importe quand, en des
heures qu'on aurait cru paisibles. Un autre
jour, un Arabe est sorti tel un canard
égorgé de la boutique d'un coiffeur maure.
Il ne s'agissait pas, cette fois encore, d'un
affrontement de races. La chaleur, qui
« rendait fou presque tout le monde »
(p. 282), expliquait seule ce meurtre sans
mobile. La chaleur accablante est aussi
la vraie responsable de l'acte de Meursault, dans *L'Étranger*. Cette fois, il s'agit
du meurtre d'un Arabe par un Français.

1. Camus avait
noté cette scène
dès 1935 dans
ses *Carnets* (*OC*,
t. II, p. 798).

Camus a-t-il voulu lui donner une valeur symbolique? À son corps défendant peut-être, certains critiques liront le roman comme une fable de l'oppression coloniale. Qu'une bombe explose, dans *Le Premier Homme*, sur ce même trottoir de Belcourt où Jacques a vu pour la première fois le sang répandu, est-ce le signe d'une violence éternelle ou le symptôme d'une guerre dont *L'Étranger* offrait un raccourci précurseur? On peut faire l'histoire de la violence entre les hommes « ... et alors on remonte au premier criminel, vous savez, il s'appelait Caïn, et depuis c'est la guerre, les hommes sont affreux, surtout sous le soleil féroce » (p. 209). Ainsi a raisonné le vieux docteur pour conclure ses réflexions sur les affrontements qui, bien avant que n'éclate la guerre d'Algérie, ont opposé Arabes et Français. « Il y a toujours eu la guerre, dit Veillard. Mais on s'habitue vite à la paix. Alors on croit que c'est normal. Non, ce qui est normal c'est la guerre » (p. 201).

Jacques est un enfant et une victime de la guerre, terminée depuis cinq ans à peine quand il entre à l'école communale. Elle lui est moins révélée par des témoignages directs que grâce au roman de Dorgelès que son instituteur lit pieusement aux élèves. Ses conséquences, il les voit de ses yeux en allant jouer dans le parc de la Maison des invalides de Kouba, où la mère de son copain Pierre est lingère en chef. Mais cette expérience ne lui inspire aucune horreur : à force d'y côtoyer d'anciens combattants amputés, il en conclut que la guerre est une époque où on perd les bras et les jambes. « C'est pourquoi cet univers d'éclopés n'était nullement triste pour les enfants » (p. 260). Jacques aussi pourrait trouver, en somme, que la guerre est la condition « normale » du genre humain.

Il n'en est rien. Il a beau se battre courageusement, à l'école, contre plus grand et plus fort que lui, le « visage déconfit » de son adversaire ne lui inspire aucun sentiment de triomphe. Après avoir créé l'univers, puis l'homme et la femme, Dieu déclara que « cela était bon » (Genèse). *Le Premier Homme* suggère que la première faille de la Création est moins le péché originel que le meurtre d'Abel par Caïn[1]. « Et il [Jacques] connut ainsi que la guerre n'est pas bonne, puisque vaincre un homme est aussi amer que d'en être vaincu » (p. 173). À la différence du vieux docteur, il ne se résignera jamais au forfait de Caïn.

Aux pires moments du conflit algérien, il s'obstine à comprendre (pour reprendre le titre d'un de ses articles) « les raisons de l'adversaire[2] ». Mais, du moment qu'il s'oppose également au terrorisme et au contre-terrorisme, les adversaires sont dans les deux camps. Opposé, après l'attentat de Belcourt, à la violence aveugle d'Européens prêts à lyncher un innocent, Jacques s'attire une réplique — « Va là-bas et tu parleras quand tu auras vu la bouillie » (p. 88) — qui absout, à défaut de la légiti-

1. « [...] le crime de Caïn (et non celui d'Adam qui, à côté, fait figure de péché véniel) a épuisé nos forces et notre amour à vivre » (*Carnets* [1942], *OC*, t. II, p. 971).

2. (28 octobre 1955), *ibid.*, p. 978-980.

mer, la réaction injuste qu'a suscitée l'injustice. De même l'atroce description du carnage dont Pirette s'est rendu coupable risque-t-elle de persuader le lecteur qu'à une telle extrémité, il n'est d'autre solution que la guillotine (p. 94). Camus s'attache à comprendre, enfin, les motifs de la xénophobie plutôt que de la condamner. « Cela expliquait que ces ouvriers, chez Pierre comme chez Jacques, qui toujours dans la vie quotidienne étaient les plus tolérants des hommes, fussent toujours xénophobes dans les questions de travail, accusant successivement les Italiens, les Espagnols, les Juifs, les Arabes et finalement la terre entière de leur voler leur travail — attitude déconcertante certainement pour les intellectuels qui font la théorie du prolétariat, et pourtant fort humaine et bien excusable » (p. 279). Pareillement, comment l'intelligentsia parisienne comprendrait-elle les sentiments exaspérés ou angoissés du petit peuple que, au nom du sens de l'Histoire, elle confond avec quelques gros colons ? À force d'écouter les raisons de l'adversaire, Camus lui fournit des armes. Il se fait objectivement son allié. On se retrouve comme au début des années 1950, quand il était accusé par l'équipe des *Temps modernes* de servir objectivement la bourgeoisie. « Conversation sur le terrorisme. [...] Ne dis plus objectivement ou je te frappe » (p. 323). Les ébauches du *Premier Homme* promettaient un prolongement du débat.

La dernière prise de position politique

de Camus est l'Avant-propos, composé en mars-avril 1958, au volume *Actuelles III. Chroniques algériennes*. L'« Appel en faveur d'une trêve civile », lancé le 22 janvier 1956 à Alger, était pathétique parce que, en réclamant que fussent épargnés au moins les civils innocents, il entérinait implicitement les raisons qu'avaient Français et nationalistes algériens de poursuivre leur combat au plan militaire[1]. Deux ans plus tard, sa position est aussi balancée, non pas en vertu d'une quelconque modération, mais parce qu'elle résulte, au contraire, d'une tension entre d'égales exigences adressées aux deux partis en présence.

1. Voir Dossier, p. 153.

UN ROMAN POLITIQUE ?

Aux yeux des partisans de l'Algérie française, la France, après une résistance locale qui survécut une vingtaine d'années à la conquête de 1830, a assuré à l'Algérie un développement économique et social ainsi que des libertés démocratiques que celle-ci n'aurait jamais connus sans elle. Des troubles sporadiques ont contrarié la grande entreprise coloniale, en particulier les révoltes, sévèrement matées, survenues dans le Constantinois en 1945. Appuyée par des puissances étrangères, une poignée de nationalistes a rallumé en 1954 des hostilités qu'on ne saurait désigner sous le nom de « guerre » puisque l'Algérie est, depuis longtemps, constituée de trois départements français. Sans doute ces « événements » s'expliquent-ils en partie par les imperfections de l'œuvre coloniale. Il convient donc de pacifier le pays afin de poursuivre et d'améliorer cette œuvre. En dernier ressort, les partisans de l'Algérie française envisageront d'accorder aux indigènes, en vertu d'une politique dite d'intégration, une nationalité française de plein exercice qui leur avait été refusée jusqu'alors.

Aux yeux des nationalistes algériens, la France a conquis en 1830, au nom de la loi du plus fort, un pays sur lequel elle n'avait aucun droit, et dépossédé de leurs terres leurs propriétaires légitimes. Les populations indigènes n'ont jamais admis cette usurpation : quoi qu'en dise la propagande officielle, elles n'ont pas cessé de mener, dans la limite de leurs moyens, la guerre contre l'occupant. Privés de tout droit syndical et de l'essentiel des droits civiques, réduits à la pauvreté par le système d'exploitation coloniale, reconnus comme pleinement Français aux seules heures où on les obligeait à se sacrifier pour la « patrie », les Algériens se sont progressivement forgé une conscience nationale qui s'est révélée avec éclat en 1945 et a trouvé, après des années de maturation, sa pleine expression dans le soulèvement de 1954. L'armée qui combat la France est une armée de libération nationale. Aucune négociation n'est envisageable avec l'armée d'occupation française si elle n'inclut pas le principe de l'indépendance du pays. Les Français installés en Algérie pourront continuer d'y vivre, à condition de se soumettre aux lois du nouvel État.

Jamais Camus ne reproche aux Français d'avoir conquis l'Algérie. À ses yeux, l'Histoire s'étant constituée depuis ses origines par des conquêtes successives, aucun peuple ne saurait affirmer sa possession exclusive d'un pays sous prétexte qu'il l'a envahi avant un autre. Ainsi serait-il « vain de condamner plusieurs siècles d'expansion européenne, absurde de comprendre dans la même malédiction Christophe Colomb et Lyautey[1] ». Quant aux pionniers qui se sont établis sur le sol algérien, ils ont mérité par leur courage et leur travail d'avoir échappé (et fait échapper leurs enfants) à la misère qui les avait, pour la plupart, poussés à l'exil. Mais la France n'a pas su transformer sa conquête coloniale en une œuvre de justice. Militant communiste pendant deux ans, homme de gauche jusqu'à la fin, Camus a dénoncé dès avant la guerre la privation de droits dont étaient victimes les populations indigènes et la misère où le système colonial les avait réduites. « C'est la force infinie de la justice, et elle seule, qui doit nous aider à reconquérir l'Algérie et ses habitants », écrit-il encore en mai 1945, en conclusion d'une série d'articles publiés dans *Combat* à la suite des émeutes du Constantinois[2]. Quand le conflit éclate en novembre 1954, il est mieux placé que quiconque pour en

1. *Essais*, p. 897-898.

2. *Ibid.*, p. 959.

comprendre les racines. Il ne peut pourtant adhérer aux objectifs du F.L.N. parce qu'il n'y a jamais eu, à ses yeux, de nation algérienne. On ne saurait envisager l'avenir du pays sans admettre qu'il est composé de « deux peuples ». Rappelant, dans les colonnes de *L'Express*, que « l'Algérie n'est pas la France », mais qu'elle compte un million de Français, il met ses espoirs dans une solution fédérale qui assurerait la justice à l'ensemble de ses habitants.

Inaudible pour les Français d'Algérie, qui refusent qu'on accorde des « raisons » à un adversaire qui use d'un terrorisme aveugle pour les chasser de chez eux, la position de Camus, formulée pour l'essentiel dans l'Avant-propos d'*Actuelles III*, apparaît comme une chimère à ceux, de plus en plus nombreux, qui voient dans l'indépendance du pays la seule issue à une guerre où la France compromet ses intérêts et son honneur. Ainsi Raymond Aron, auteur un an plus tôt d'un livre intitulé *La Tragédie algérienne*, écrit-il quelques mois après la publication d'*Actuelles III* : « En dépit de sa volonté de justice, de sa générosité, M. Albert Camus n'arrive pas à s'élever au-dessus de l'attitude du colonisateur de bonne volonté. À aucun moment, il ne semble comprendre l'essence de la revendication nationale et la légitimité de cette revendication[1]. »

Dans ses écrits, Camus analyse les solutions qui ont chance de sortir l'Algérie de la crise. En privé, son discours est différent.

1. Raymond Aron, *L'Algérie et la République*, Plon, 1958, p. 107-108.

À Jean Grenier, il confie le 4 août 1958, trois mois après la fraternisation artificielle qui a uni Français et Arabes sur le forum d'Alger : « Je crois comme vous qu'il est sans doute trop tard pour l'Algérie. Je ne l'ai pas dit dans mon livre parce que lo peor no es siempre seguro (*sic*) — parce qu'il faut laisser ses chances au hasard historique — et parce qu'on n'écrit pas pour dire que tout est fichu. Dans ce cas-là, on se tait. Je m'y prépare[1]. » De ce moment en effet, et jusqu'à sa mort, il ne publiera rien qui prétende concourir à une solution politique. Mais, tout au long de l'année 1959, il avance dans la composition du *Premier Homme*, qui aborde d'une autre façon la crise algérienne.

De même que la mère est toujours assise à la même place, près de sa fenêtre, quand Jacques vient la retrouver, de même la situation de l'Algérie paraît-elle immuable au lecteur du roman. En novembre 1913, on n'ouvrait sa porte qu'avec précaution, à Solférino, parce qu'on avait peur des « bandits ». « Les portes mettent du temps à s'ouvrir au pays de l'hospitalité », constate pareillement Veillard, une quarantaine d'années plus tard, quand il frappe à celle du vieux Tamzal (p. 201). « Je ferme maintenant à cause des bandits », dit aussi la mère quand on frappe à sa porte (p. 143). « C'est pour les bandits », a-t-elle prévenu Jacques (qui s'en serait douté tout seul) en apercevant la patrouille de parachutistes qui surveille la rue (p. 85). Surprenante

1. Albert Camus-Jean Grenier, *Correspondance*, p. 222 (traduction : « Le pire n'est pas toujours sûr », comme dit Paul Claudel dans *Le Soulier de satin*).

expression pour qui se souvient de la guerre d'Algérie : on n'appelait jamais « bandits », mais « terroristes » les rebelles qui opéraient en ville et « fellaghas » (ou « fellouzes ») ceux qui combattaient dans le bled. Suggérer que rien n'a changé depuis le début du siècle pourrait apporter de l'eau au moulin des nationalistes, pour qui la France n'a jamais véritablement pacifié l'Algérie. Mais traiter les militants armés comme des criminels de droit commun, c'est nier à l'inverse l'inspiration nationaliste de leur action. « Dis, les bandits, c'est bien ? » interroge l'oncle. « Non, dit Jacques, les autres Arabes oui, les bandits non » (p. 145). La réponse exprime un refus camusien du recours au terrorisme. « Objectivement », elle cautionne aussi la propagande officielle qui prétend isoler d'une poignée de meneurs irresponsables une population qui n'aspirerait qu'à vivre tranquille.

N'ont pas varié non plus, depuis les temps héroïques de la conquête, le courage et l'esprit d'entreprise de ceux qui sont venus peupler ce pays. La geste des pionniers, amorcée dans le manuscrit et promise à une vaste amplification par les ébauches, n'aurait pu être reçue autrement que comme un plaidoyer à une époque où les Français d'Algérie étaient couramment considérés comme des exploiteurs. Le titre d'inspiration biblique du roman prend à ce point une signification politique. Si, à une époque où la présence française en Algérie est menacée, Jacques est le « premier homme », on l'interprétera comme un acte de foi dans les possibilités qu'il incarne d'un renouveau dont l'exemple de ses ancêtres lui donne la force. Et c'était comme si tout recommençait. En somme, à une époque où Raymond Aron analyse la « tragédie algérienne », Camus, auteur tragique, rêve magiquement d'une Algérie réconciliée où, en dépit des signes d'une violence qui ne date pas d'hier, il serait possible de croire à une forme d'innocence. Faut-il s'étonner qu'après avoir orienté toute sa pensée contre la tyrannie de l'Histoire, il recoure aux archives pour recomposer le passé de son pays ? Nullement, puisque c'est vers une Histoire toujours répétée, voire figée, que semble conduire son enquête.

La foi ne suppose pas forcément l'inconscience. Si, contrairement au rêve entretenu par le roman, il se confirme qu'« il est trop tard pour l'Algérie », *Le Premier Homme* en aura donné des signes précurseurs. Malgré les vagues promesses du F.L.N., l'indépendance accentuera un exode des Européens qui a déjà commencé : le père de Veillard tourne en rond dans sa chambre, à Marseille (p. 199). « Les maisons édifiées en *54* », note Camus (p. 348), soupir désabusé sur ces Européens qui, au début de la guerre (et encore après), ont continué de bâtir comme s'ils devaient rester ici à jamais. « Viens avec moi en France », propose Jacques à sa mère après l'attentat de Belcourt (p. 89). Dans une ébauche abandonnée du roman, elle s'installe définitivement en France ; dans une autre, postérieure, elle suit le conseil de son fils, mais regagne bientôt son quartier de Belcourt[1]. Dans le manuscrit, elle refuse catégoriquement de partir. Comment se cacher, désormais, qu'il faudra sans doute un jour consentir à l'exil ?

« Il est bien connu que la patrie se reconnaît toujours au moment de la perdre », écrivait Camus dans *Noces*, précisant aussitôt qu'il appelait « patrie » le « pays natal[2] ». Il confirme dans *L'Été* : « En ce qui concerne l'Algérie, j'ai toujours peur d'appuyer sur cette corde intérieure qui lui correspond en moi et dont je reconnais le chant aveugle et grave. Mais je puis bien dire au moins qu'elle est ma vraie patrie et qu'en n'importe quel lieu du monde je reconnais ses fils et mes frères à ce rire d'amitié qui me prend devant eux[3]. » Henri Cormery a été sacrifié à une patrie abstraite, puisque c'est « loin de sa patrie de chair » (p. 212) que sa mort s'est produite. Avant de la perdre, Camus se devait de célébrer cette patrie de chair, mais aussi ceux qui méritaient d'y vivre puisqu'ils avaient contribué à la construire. Au moins va-t-il les célébrer grâce à une patrie que personne ne lui enlèvera : « Oui, j'ai une patrie : la langue française[4]. »

1. Voir Dossier, p. 165-166.

2. *OC*, t. I, p. 125.

3. *L'Été, Essais*, p. 850.

4. *Carnets II* [1950], p. 337.

CONCLUSION

Il vaut mieux, sans doute, que *Le Premier Homme* n'ait pas été publié à la hâte, aussitôt après la mort de Camus. Ceux qui l'accusaient alors de se prendre pour un « juste » (titre auquel il n'a jamais prétendu) auraient trouvé dans l'autoportrait lisible à travers la figure de Jacques Cormery un argument supplémentaire à leurs préventions, et son éloge des Français d'Algérie, prononcé à une époque où la guerre n'était pas terminée, aurait eu mauvaise presse.

Selon une confidence faite à Jean Grenier, il aurait aimé garder « la qualité du style de Stendhal, mais acquérir quelque chose du style de Chateaubriand[1] ». Il s'approche peut-être de son idéal avec *Le Premier Homme*, dont les accents sentimentaux auraient provoqué les sarcasmes de Stendhal, mais que sa fidélité scrupuleuse aux détails de la mémoire apparente à la *Vie de Henry Brulard*. Aurait-il conservé ces phrases interminables et éperdues, différentes par essence de la période proustienne dans laquelle s'accumulent ou s'emboîtent causes, conséquences et comparaisons, mais proches parfois des élans lyriques de Chateaubriand ? Comment le savoir ?

Au moins son travail de mémoire est-il à l'opposé de celui des *Mémoires d'outre-tombe*. « Ma mémoire oppose sans cesse mes voyages à mes voyages, montagnes à montagnes, fleuves à fleuves, forêts à forêts,

1. *Albert Camus. Souvenirs*, p. 100.

1. *Mémoires d'outre-tombe*, édition de J.-Cl. Berchet, Classiques Garnier, t. IV, 1998, p. 147.

et ma vie détruit ma vie », écrivait Chateaubriand[1]. Camus s'ingénie, lui, à superposer le présent au passé pour ressourcer sa vie. Et alors que l'un et l'autre sont témoins de la disparition d'un ancien régime, Chateaubriand en contemple avec mélancolie l'effondrement, tandis que Camus en rêve l'impossible survivance.

De l'égotisme de Stendhal et de celui de Chateaubriand, Camus s'est tenu également éloigné. La reconstitution de son passé intime ne vise à faire du moi ni un individu singulier, ni un sujet privilégié de l'Histoire. « Les œuvres d'un homme retracent souvent l'histoire de ses nostalgies ou de ses tentations, presque jamais sa propre histoire, surtout lorsqu'elles prétendent à être autobiographiques », écrivait-il en 1950[2]. S'efforçant, non sans peine, d'affranchir *Le Premier Homme* de l'autobiographie, il recourt à ses nostalgies et se repent de ses tentations afin de composer un rêve qui n'aura de portée qu'à condition de dépasser son cas individuel. On pourrait croire le titre du *Premier Homme* bouffi d'orgueil ; il affiche au contraire l'aspiration à une généralité que la Bible, vie du Christ incluse, avait chance de rendre intelligible à l'Occident. La référence ne doit pas prêter au malentendu. Après la publication de *La Chute*, certains s'imaginèrent que Camus se rapprochait, sinon du dogme, du moins de l'esprit des chrétiens. « Rien vraiment ne les y autorise », répondit Camus. « J'admire la façon

2. *L'Été*, *Essais*, p. 864.

1. Interview au *Monde* (31 août 1956), *Théâtre, récits, nouvelles*, p. 1881.

2. Nietzsche, *Ainsi parlait Zarathoustra*, Quatrième partie, « La fête de l'âne ».

3. *Ibid.*, « Notes et aphorismes », n° 226.

4. *Ibid.*, n° 216.

dont il [le Christ] a vécu, dont il est mort. Mon manque d'imagination m'interdit de le suivre plus loin[1]. » À la fable du *Premier Homme*, la croyance chrétienne a seulement offert une imagerie idéale, comme Sisyphe ou Prométhée avaient illustré l'absurde ou la révolte.

Détaché de toute origine céleste, l'homme camusien n'est pas pour autant un surhomme. « Nous ne voulons pas du tout entrer dans le royaume des cieux : nous sommes devenus des hommes, — aussi voulons-nous le royaume de la terre » : ces paroles de Zarathoustra[2] pourraient être reprises par celui qui proclame : « Tout mon royaume est de ce monde. » Mais jamais Camus ne dira avec le héros de Nietzsche : « Que l'homme soit le point de départ de quelque chose qui n'est plus l'homme[3]. » « Le contraire du *surhomme* est le *"dernier homme"*. J'ai créé en même temps l'un et l'autre », déclare encore Zarathoustra[4]. En créant le « premier homme », Camus a imaginé un héros dont les faiblesses rassurent, parce que, lui faisant pardonner celles de son entourage, elles lui permettent d'accéder à l'amour.

DOSSIER

I. REPÈRES BIOGRAPHIQUES

1913   *7 novembre* : Albert Camus naît à Mondovi (Algérie). Son père, Lucien Camus, y a été envoyé avec sa femme Catherine (née Sintès) pour gérer une exploitation viticole. Albert a un frère aîné de trois ans, prénommé Lucien comme son père.

1914   *Août* : à la déclaration de la guerre, Catherine Camus s'installe à Alger chez sa mère avec ses deux enfants. *11 octobre* : Lucien Camus, blessé en septembre à la bataille de la Marne, meurt à l'hôpital militaire de Saint-Brieuc. Sa veuve devra faire des ménages pour subvenir aux besoins de sa famille.

1921   Installation dans un appartement du quartier de Belcourt. Catherine Camus y finira ses jours.

1924   Grâce à l'attention et aux cours particuliers de son instituteur, Louis Germain, Camus est reçu au concours des bourses et entre en sixième au Grand Lycée d'Alger (quartier de Bab-el-Oued).

1930   En classe de philosophie, il suit les cours de Jean Grenier et s'illustre comme gardien de but de l'équipe du Racing Universitaire d'Alger. *Décembre* : premières atteintes de la tuberculose.

1931   Mort de la grand-mère.

1932   Classe de première supérieure préparatoire (hypokhâgne).

1934   Premier mariage, avec Simone Hié. Le couple se défera au bout de deux ans. Il occupe de petits emplois temporaires.

1935	Il adhère au parti communiste, qu'il quittera deux ans plus tard, et fonde le Théâtre du Travail, devenu ensuite Théâtre de l'Équipe. Il adapte des pièces, les met en scène et y joue parfois lui-même.
1936	Sa première pièce (œuvre collective), *Révolte dans les Asturies*, est interdite de représentation par le maire d'Alger. Voyage en Europe centrale (Salzbourg, Prague...) et retour par l'Italie.
1937	*L'Envers et l'Endroit*, chez Charlot (Alger). Il travaille à *La Mort heureuse*, roman qu'il laissera inachevé. Voyage dans le midi de la France et en Italie.
1938	Ayant dû, pour raison de santé, renoncer à préparer l'agrégation, il fait ses débuts dans le journalisme à *Alger républicain*.
1939	*Noces*, chez Charlot. Enquête pour *Alger républicain* sur « la misère en Kabylie ». *Septembre* : à la suite de la déclaration de la guerre, *Alger républicain* suspend sa parution et cède la place à *Soir républicain*.
1940	Parti pour Paris, Camus travaille quelques mois à *Paris-Soir*. *Décembre* : il se remarie avec Francine Faure.
1942	*L'Étranger* et *Le Mythe de Sisyphe*, chez Gallimard, qui éditera désormais toutes ses œuvres majeures. Il séjourne au Panelier, dans le Forez. *Novembre* : la zone dite « libre » étant occupée par les Allemands, il est séparé jusqu'à la fin de la guerre de sa femme, demeurée à Alger.
1943	Début de l'amitié avec Sartre. Il entre dans le

réseau de résistance « Combat » et participe à son journal clandestin.

1944   Création du *Malentendu*. À la libération de Paris, *Combat* paraît au grand jour. Camus y donnera de nombreux éditoriaux jusqu'en juin 1947.

1945   Création de *Caligula*. Naissance de ses jumeaux, Jean et Catherine.

1946   Voyage aux États-Unis et au Canada.

1947   *La Peste*, qui connaît un immense succès.

1948   Création de *L'État de siège*, qui est, selon son expression, « un four ».

1949   Voyage en Amérique du Sud. Création des *Justes*, un « demi-succès ».

1950   *Actuelles, chroniques 1944-1948*. Il achète un appartement à Paris, 29, rue Madame (VIe arrondissement).

1951   *L'Homme révolté*. Cet essai, où il condamne la terreur soviétique, déclenchera de vives polémiques et le brouillera définitivement avec Sartre.

1953   *Actuelles II. Automne* : ébauche du *Premier Homme*.

1954   *L'Été. Novembre* : début de la guerre d'Algérie.

1955   Voyage en Grèce. *Mai* : début de sa collaboration à *L'Express*, qu'il interrompra en février 1956.

1956   *Janvier* : il lance à Alger un appel pour une trêve civile. *La Chute*. Adaptation et mise en scène de *Requiem pour une nonne*, d'après Faulkner.

1957   *L'Exil et le Royaume. Réflexions sur la peine capitale. Juin* : festival d'Angers, avec la reprise de *Caligula* et sa mise en scène du *Chevalier d'Olmedo*, adapté d'après Lope de Vega. *Octobre* : le prix Nobel de littérature lui est décerné.

1958   *Discours de Suède. Actuelles III, chroniques algériennes (1939-1958)*. Voyage en Grèce. Il achète une maison à Lourmarin (Vaucluse).

1959   Création de son adaptation des *Possédés*, d'après Dostoïevski. Il passe une grande partie de l'année à Lourmarin et travaille au *Premier Homme*.

1960   *4 janvier* : au retour de Lourmarin, il est tué dans un accident d'automobile. Il est enterré à Lourmarin. Sa mère ne lui survivra que quelques mois.

II. CAMUS AVANT *LE PREMIER HOMME*

LA VEUVE ET SON AMOUREUX

La veuve Cormery du *Premier Homme* est en âge d'avoir un amoureux, mais son frère, l'« oncle Étienne » (plus souvent appelé de son vrai prénom, « Ernest »), lui impose une impitoyable tutelle ; l'assiduité d'un prétendant va provoquer la colère de l'oncle (*PH*, p. 135 et suiv.). Cette scène du *Premier Homme* est préfigurée dans un roman esquissé par Camus vers 1935, « Louis Raingeard » (anagramme approximative de Louis Germain, son instituteur), fondu ensuite dans *L'Envers et l'Endroit* (1937). Sur la comparaison des deux scènes, voir *supra*, p. 84 et suiv.

Et voici que ce soir sa mère pleurait devant lui. Il faisait de la musique[1], écoutait une romance populaire naïve et banale comme un grand élan de jeune homme qui n'a pas encore connu la vie. Et sa mère était entrée dans cette immense et sotte mélancolie. Tout de suite elle avait pleuré et puis parlé. Son malheur ne laissait aucun doute. Elle vivait avec son frère qui était sourd, muet, méchant et bête. C'était bien sûr par pitié qu'elle restait avec lui. C'était aussi par crainte. Car si encore il l'avait laissée vivre à sa guise ! Mais il l'empêchait de voir l'homme qu'elle aimait. À leur âge pourtant ça n'avait plus grande importance. Lui aussi, lui qu'elle aimait était empê-

Appendices de
L'Envers et l'Endroit.
Œuvres complètes,
Pléiade, t. I,
p. 93-94.

1. Même si, dans *Le Premier Homme*, Jacques s'essaie à la chansonnette (p. 104), « faire de la musique » doit sans doute s'entendre ici dans une acception populaire, au sens d'en écouter. « Joue-moi de l'électrophone », chantait Charles Trenet. Quand l'expression « faire de la musique » a son sens habituel (appliquée à une jeune fille venue de la métropole), elle est placée entre guillemets (*PH*, p. 225).

ché. Il était marié. Depuis des années sa femme buvait et n'arrangeait pas ses affaires. Alors il gardait une tendresse rugueuse pour ce qui était exceptionnel dans sa vie. Il apportait à son amie des fleurs qu'il avait cueillies dans les haies de la banlieue, des oranges et des liqueurs qu'il gagnait à la foire. Certes il n'était pas beau. Mais la beauté ne se mange pas en salade et il était si brave. Pour elle aussi c'était l'Aventure. Elle tenait à lui qui tenait à elle. Est-ce autre chose l'amour. Elle lui lavait son linge et tâchait de le tenir propre. Il avait l'habitude de porter des mouchoirs « pliés » en triangle et noués autour du cou : elle lui faisait des mouchoirs bien blancs et c'était une de ses joies.

Mais l'autre, le frère, ne voulait pas qu'elle reçoive son ami. Il lui fallait le voir en secret. Elle l'avait reçu aujourd'hui. Surpris, ç'avait été une affreuse rixe. Et elle était venue chez son fils pour pleurer. Que faire vraiment. Son malheur était certain. Elle avait trop peur de son frère pour le quitter. Elle le haïssait trop pour l'oublier. Elle le tuerait un jour, c'était bien sûr. Et tout cela d'une voix morne, maintenant pleine de larmes. Cette femme se pénétrait du sentiment de son abandon et s'offrait aux blessures dont Dieu orne ceux qu'il préfère. « Qu'est-ce qu'il faut faire. Je finirai par prendre un poison un jour, au moins je serai tranquille. »

Son fils maintenant la sentait très loin. Sa décision lui donnait la résignation. Sans doute ne l'accomplirait-elle jamais. Mais l'avoir arrêtée, s'en croire capable, prendre conscience que son malheur était assez important pour lui donner de telles idées lui apportait le calme. Puisque somme toute il y avait une issue.

Son fils n'a encore rien dit. Mais cela n'a plus

beaucoup d'importance. Elle va partir. Elle enfonce gauchement son chapeau et ses lèvres sourient, un pauvre sourire émouvant. Elle reviendra dit-elle. Son fils, étranger, la contemple. Corps déchiré, osseux et laid, corps sans grâces, il voudrait pleurer sur lui.

Louis a remis la même mélodie après son départ. Maintenant il la devine respirant sans hâte, s'acheminant régulièrement par des rues dont elle sait le nom vers le frère méchant et brutal qui l'attend. Son dîner est à faire, d'autres soucis encore. Elle tourne au coin d'une rue et c'est comme une fenêtre qui se ferme sur le bruit d'une ville.

CONFESSION À LA MÈRE

La même ébauche nous fait lire un peu plus loin une confession à la mère qui préfigure le dénouement que Camus prévoyait pour *Le Premier Homme* (voir « Confession à la mère pour finir », p. 363).

Mère, tu vois, je suis très calme. Mais quand les journaux rendent compte d'une exécution capitale ils disent quelquefois que le condamné a fait impression par son calme et sa résignation. C'est que le journaliste lui savait qu'il devait coucher dans son lit le soir. Le condamné savait que c'était impossible. Impossible, tu comprends. Il ne triche pas. Il sait bien qu'il ne va pas « payer sa dette à la société » mais qu'on va lui couper le cou. Ça n'a l'air de rien. Mais ça fait une petite différence. Et moi aussi je suis calme.

Je voudrais t'expliquer bien des choses, Mère. Et d'abord que je suis un malheureux. [La suite est

Ibid., p. 95.

d'une écriture différente à l'encre bleue.] Je sais bien que ça n'a pas beaucoup d'importance. Je sais bien que les tramways marchent quand même dans les rues. Mais c'est un fait qu'il faut bien dire. Et qu'on est toujours seul à souffrir ou à être bête. Mère, j'ai cru que c'était arrivé ; quand j'avais raison contre la vie — et la vie m'a giflé à tour de bras. Il faut bien croire qu'elle a raison. J'ai cru à l'amour et qu'amour et foi ne faisaient qu'un. Je sais maintenant que la vraie vie est la santé et que le corps est un moyen de connaissance. Je ne peux plus maintenant rétablir l'équilibre. Mère, je suis un malheureux. Un grand élan m'habitait et je sais maintenant ce que veut dire absurdité. Me voilà nu et désemparé, éloigné de tout, indifférent à tous et à moi-même et c'est vers toi que je me tourne. Bien plutôt dans ce que tu représentes, cette pauvreté, ce dénuement auxquels je veux revenir. Mère, tu es pure comme un cristal. Tu n'as rien, ni beauté, ni richesse, ni complication de l'esprit. Ton cœur, ton corps, ton esprit, tout se confond car tu n'es qu'indifférence du cœur, indifférence de l'âme, indifférence du corps. Je ne suis pas sûr de t'aimer. Je ne suis pas sûr de t'avoir bien aimée. Mais quelle place est la tienne et quel rôle joues-tu sans t'en douter.

LES SOIRÉES À BELCOURT

Dans *L'Envers et l'Endroit*, que Camus publie en mai 1937 aux éditions Charlot (Alger), plusieurs pages très autobiographiques préfigurent celles du *Premier Homme.* Ainsi cette évocation des soirées dans le quartier pauvre (Belcourt), le portrait de la mère de l'enfant (elle a conservé l'éclat d'obus qui a tué son mari) et

celui de la terrible « vieille » (la grand-mère), qui fait régner l'ordre dans la maison.

Les soirs d'été, les ouvriers se mettent au balcon. Chez lui, il n'y avait qu'une toute petite fenêtre. On descendait alors des chaises sur le devant de la maison et l'on goûtait le soir. Il y avait la rue, les marchands de glaces à côté, les cafés en face, et des bruits d'enfants courant de porte en porte. Mais surtout, entre les grands ficus, il y avait le ciel. Il y a une solitude dans la pauvreté, mais une solitude qui rend son prix à chaque chose. À un certain degré de richesse, le ciel lui-même et la nuit pleine d'étoiles semblent des biens naturels. Mais au bas de l'échelle, le ciel reprend tout son sens : une grâce sans prix. Nuits d'été, mystères où crépitaient des étoiles ! Il y avait derrière l'enfant un couloir puant et sa petite chaise, crevée, s'enfonçait un peu sous lui. Mais les yeux levés, il buvait à même la nuit pure. Parfois passait un tramway, vaste et rapide. Un ivrogne enfin chantonnait au coin d'une rue sans parvenir à troubler le silence.

La mère de l'enfant restait aussi silencieuse. En certaines circonstances, on lui posait une question : « À quoi tu penses ? — À rien », répondait-elle. Et c'est bien vrai. Tout est là, donc rien. Sa vie, ses intérêts, ses enfants se bornent à être là, d'une présence trop naturelle pour être sentie. Elle était infirme, pensait difficilement. Elle avait une mère rude et dominatrice qui sacrifiait tout à un amour-propre de bête susceptible et qui avait longtemps dominé l'esprit faible de sa fille. Émancipée par le mariage, celle-ci est docilement revenue, son mari mort. Il était mort au champ d'honneur, comme on dit. En bonne place, on peut voir dans un cadre

L'Envers et l'Endroit,
Œuvres complètes,
op. cit., t. I, p. 48-50.

doré la croix de guerre et la médaille militaire. L'hôpital a encore envoyé à la veuve un petit éclat d'obus retrouvé dans les chairs. La veuve l'a gardé[1]. Il y a longtemps qu'elle n'a plus de chagrin. Elle a oublié son mari, mais parle encore du père de ses enfants. Pour élever ces derniers, elle travaille et donne son argent à sa mère. Celle-ci fait l'éducation des enfants avec une cravache. Quand elle frappe trop fort, sa fille lui dit : « Ne frappe pas sur la tête[2]. » Parce que ce sont ses enfants, elle les aime bien. Elle les aime d'un égal amour qui ne s'est jamais révélé à eux. Quelquefois, comme en ces soirs dont lui se souvenait, revenue du travail exténuant (elle fait des ménages), elle trouve la maison vide. La vieille est aux commissions, les enfants sont encore à l'école. Elle se tasse alors sur une chaise et, les yeux vagues, se perd dans la poursuite éperdue d'une rainure du parquet. Autour d'elle, la nuit s'épaissit dans laquelle ce mutisme est d'une irrémédiable désolation. Si l'enfant entre à ce moment, il distingue la maigre silhouette aux épaules osseuses et s'arrête : il a peur. Il commence à sentir beaucoup de choses. À peine s'est-il aperçu de sa propre existence. Mais il a mal à pleurer devant ce silence animal. Il a pitié de sa mère, est-ce l'aimer ? Elle ne l'a jamais caressé puisqu'elle ne saurait pas. Il reste alors de longues minutes à la regarder. À se sentir étranger, il prend conscience de sa peine. Elle ne l'entend pas, car elle est sourde. Tout à l'heure, la vieille rentrera, la vie renaîtra : la lumière ronde de la lampe à pétrole, la toile cirée, les cris, les gros mots. Mais maintenant, ce silence marque un temps d'arrêt, un instant démesuré. Pour sentir

1. Voir *PH*, p. 76.
2. Voir *ibid*., p. 100.

cela confusément, l'enfant croit sentir dans l'élan qui l'habite, de l'amour pour sa mère. Et il le faut bien parce qu'après tout c'est sa mère.

Elle ne pense à rien. Dehors, la lumière, les bruits ; ici le silence dans la nuit. L'enfant grandira, apprendra. On l'élève et on lui demandera de la reconnaissance, comme si on lui évitait la douleur. Sa mère toujours aura ces silences. Lui croîtra en douleur. Être un homme, c'est ce qui compte. Sa grand-mère mourra, puis sa mère, lui.

La mère a sursauté. Elle a eu peur. Il a l'air idiot à la regarder ainsi. Qu'il aille faire ses devoirs. L'enfant a fait ses devoirs. Il est aujourd'hui dans un café sordide. Il est maintenant un homme. N'est-ce pas cela qui compte ? Il faut bien croire que non, puisque faire ses devoirs et accepter d'être un homme conduit seulement à être vieux.

UN RUAÏSTE CÉLÈBRE NOUS PARLE DE SA « BELLE ÉPOQUE »

Sous ce titre paraît en 1953, dans le *Journal du R.U.A.* (Racing Universitaire d'Alger), le texte d'un discours que Camus a prononcé au siège du club, à l'occasion d'un séjour effectué en Algérie au début de l'année. Au mois d'octobre suivant, il commence à écrire *Le Premier Homme*. « R.U.A. Bonheur de cette simple amitié dont j'ai vécu », note-t-il le 25 février 1955 dans ses *Carnets*. Jacques Cormery considère comme son « royaume » (*PH*, p. 99) la cour de l'école, puis celle du lycée, où il joue au football. Le R.U.A. consacra les talents de gardien de but de Camus. La photo figurant en couverture du *Premier Homme* (collection « Folio ») a été prise en 1929 ou 1930.

Oui, j'ai joué plusieurs années au R.U.A. Il me semble que c'était hier. Mais lorsqu'en 1940 j'ai remis les crampons, je me suis aperçu que ce n'était pas hier. Avant la fin de la première mi-temps, je tirais aussi fort la langue que les chiens kabyles qu'on rencontre à deux heures de l'après-midi au mois d'août, à Tizi-Ouzou. C'était donc il y a long-temps : 1928 et la suite je crois. J'avais débuté à l'Association sportive de Montpensier, Dieu sait pourquoi puisque j'habitais Belcourt, et que Belcourt et Mustapha, c'est le Gallia[1]. Mais j'avais un ami, un velu, qui nageait au port avec moi, et qui faisait du water-polo à l'A.S.M. C'est comme ça que se décident les vies. L'A.S.M. jouait le plus souvent au Champ-de-Manœuvres, sans raison visible là encore[2]. Le terrain avait plus de bosses qu'un tibia d'avant-centre en visite au stade d'Alenda (Oran). J'appris tout de suite qu'une balle ne vous arrivait jamais du côté où l'on croyait. Ça m'a servi dans l'existence et surtout dans la métropole où l'on n'est pas franc du collier[3]. Mais au bout d'un an d'A.S.M. et de bosses, on m'a fait honte au lycée : un « universitaire » devait être au R.U.A. À cette époque le velu avait disparu de ma vie. Nous n'étions pas fâchés mais il allait nager à Padovani où l'eau était impure. Pour tout dire, ses raisons n'étaient pas pures non plus. Moi, je trouvais que sa raison était charmante, mais qu'elle dansait mal[4].

Où en étais-je ? Oui, le R.U.A. Je voulais bien y entrer ; l'essentiel pour moi était de jouer. Je piéti-

1. Gallia Sport d'Alger.

2. Le Champ-de-Manœuvres était un quartier de l'est d'Alger, proche de Belcourt ; Montpensier, un quartier de l'ouest, proche de Bab-el-Oued.

3. Sur la « franchise » de la race algérienne, voir *supra*, p. 118, note 2.

4. Forme d'humour familière à Camus. Dans *L'Été*, un boxeur oranais défend son honneur : « Son plaidoyer a un vice de forme : il manque d'allonge » (*Essais*, p. 822).

nais d'impatience du dimanche au jeudi, jour d'entraînement, et du jeudi au dimanche, jour de match. Alors va pour les universitaires. Et me voilà gardien de but de l'équipe junior. Oui, cela paraissait tout simple. Mais je ne savais pas que je venais de contracter une liaison qui allait durer des années, à travers tous les stades du département, et qui n'en finirait plus. Je ne savais pas que vingt ans après, dans les rues de Paris ou même de Buenos-Aires (oui, ça m'est arrivé), le mot R.U.A. prononcé par un ami de rencontre me ferait encore battre le cœur le plus bêtement du monde. Et puisque j'en suis aux confidences, je puis avouer qu'à Paris, par exemple, je vais voir les matches du Racing-Club de Paris, dont j'ai fait mon favori, uniquement parce qu'il porte le même maillot que le R.U.A., cerclé de bleu et de blanc. Il faut dire d'ailleurs que le Racing a un peu les mêmes manies que le R.U.A. Il joue « scientifiquement », comme on dit, et scientifiquement il perd les matches qu'il devrait gagner. Il paraît que ça va changer (d'après Lefebvre[1]), au R.U.A. du moins. Il faut en effet que ça change, mais pas trop. Après tout, c'est pour cela que j'ai tant aimé mon équipe, pour la joie des victoires, si merveilleuses, lorsqu'elle s'allie à la fatigue qui suit l'effort, mais aussi à cette envie de pleurer les soirs de défaite.

J'avais pour arrière « le Grand », je veux dire Raymond Couard. Il avait fort à faire, si mes souvenirs sont bons. On jouait dur, avec nous. Des étudiants, fils de leurs pères, ça ne s'épargne pas. Pauvres de nous, à tous les sens, dont une bonne moitié étaient fauchés comme les blés. Il fallait donc

1. Sans doute le nom d'un dirigeant (peut-être du président) du R.U.A. Champion d'Afrique du Nord en 1935 et 1939, le R.U.A. était devenu, après la guerre, une équipe d'un modeste niveau.

faire face. Et nous devions jouer à la fois « correcte-
ment », parce que c'était la règle d'or du R.U.A., et
« virilement » parce que enfin, un homme est un
homme. Difficile conciliation ! Ça n'a pas dû changer, j'en suis sûr. Le plus dur, c'est l'Olympique
d'Hussein-Dey. Le stade est à côté du cimetière. Le
passage était direct ; on nous le faisait savoir, sans
charité.

Quant à moi, pauvre gardien, on me travaillait au
corps. Sans Roger[1], j'aurais souffert. Il y avait Boufarik[2] aussi, et cette espèce de gros avant-centre
(chez nous on l'appelait Pastèque) qui atterrissait
de tout son poids régulièrement sur mes reins, sans
compter le reste : massage des tibias aux coups
de crampons, maillot retenu à la main, genou dans
les parties nobles, sandwich contre le poteau, etc.
Bref, un fléau. Et à chaque fois, Pastèque s'excusait
d'un « Pardon, fils », avec un sourire franciscain.

Je m'arrête. J'ai passé déjà les limites fixées par
Lefebvre. Et puis je m'attendris. Oui, même Pastèque avait du bon. Du reste, soyons francs : nous
lui avons rendu son compte. Mais sans tricher, car
c'était la règle qu'on nous enseignait. Et je crois
bien qu'ici je n'ai pas envie de plaisanter. Car, après
beaucoup d'années où le monde m'a offert beaucoup de spectacles, ce dont finalement je suis le
plus sûr sur la morale et les obligations des
hommes, c'est au sport que je le dois, c'est au
R.U.A. que je l'ai appris. C'est pourquoi en effet le
R.U.A. ne peut pas périr[3]. Gardez-le-nous. Gardez-

1. Roger Couard, frère du précédent.
2. L'A.S. Boufarik. Boufarik, qui comptait alors 20 000 habitants, est située à 35 kilomètres au sud-ouest d'Alger.
3. « Ils hurlaient et chantaient à pleins poumons que leur club ne périrait pas » (*L'Étranger*, *OC*, t. I, p. 153).

nous cette grande et bonne magie de notre adolescence. Elle veillera aussi sur la vôtre.

« APPEL POUR UNE TRÊVE CIVILE EN ALGÉRIE »

« On est fait pour s'entendre », déclare Veillard, le colon dont la ferme est quasiment assiégée par les rebelles nationalistes (*PH,* p. 199). Abrupte et, avec le recul, tragiquement dérisoire, cette formule trouve un écho dans l'appel lancé par Camus à Alger, le 22 janvier 1956, aux deux communautés. Même si Français et Arabes devaient poursuivre leur lutte, dit-il, que celle-ci épargne du moins les innocents. Le discours de Camus fut prononcé au Cercle du Progrès, près de la place du Gouvernement, devant une assistance composée en majorité de musulmans, sous la menace d'une foule de Français de souche qui stationnaient à l'extérieur. Nous en donnons ici deux extraits.

[...] Si sombre qu'il soit, l'avenir algérien n'est pas encore tout à fait compromis. Si chacun, Arabe ou Français, faisait l'effort de réfléchir aux raisons de l'adversaire, les éléments, au moins, d'une discussion féconde pourraient se dégager. Mais si les deux populations algériennes, chacune accusant l'autre d'avoir commencé, devaient se jeter l'une contre l'autre dans une sorte de délire xénophobe, alors toute chance d'entente serait définitivement noyée dans le sang. Il se peut, et c'est notre plus grande angoisse, que nous marchions vers ces horreurs. Mais cela ne doit pas, ne peut pas se faire, sans que ceux d'entre nous, Arabes et Français, qui refusent les folies et les destructions du nihilisme, aient lancé un dernier appel à la raison.

La raison, ici, démontre clairement que sur ce

Essais, Gallimard, Pléiade, édition de R. Quilliot, 1965, p. 994-997.

point, au moins, la solidarité française et arabe est inévitable, dans la mort comme dans la vie, dans la destruction comme dans l'espoir. La face affreuse de cette solidarité apparaît dans la dialectique infernale qui veut que ce qui tue les uns tue les autres aussi, chacun rejetant la faute sur l'autre, et justifiant ses violences par la violence de l'adversaire. L'éternelle querelle du premier responsable perd alors son sens. Et pour n'avoir pas su vivre ensemble, deux populations, à la fois semblables et différentes, mais également respectables, se condamnent à mourir ensemble, la rage au cœur.

Mais il y a aussi une communauté de l'espoir qui justifie notre appel. Cette communauté est assise sur des réalités contre lesquelles nous ne pouvons rien. Sur cette terre sont réunis un million de Français établis depuis un siècle, des millions de musulmans, Arabes et Berbères, installés depuis des siècles, plusieurs communautés religieuses, fortes et vivantes. Ces hommes doivent vivre ensemble, à ce carrefour de routes et de races où l'histoire les a placés. Ils le peuvent, à la seule condition de faire quelques pas les uns au-devant des autres, dans une confrontation libre. Nos différences devraient alors nous aider au lieu de nous opposer. Pour ma part, là comme partout, je ne crois qu'aux différences, non à l'uniformité. Et d'abord, parce que les premières sont les racines sans lesquelles l'arbre de liberté, la sève de la création et de la civilisation, se dessèchent. Pourtant, nous restons figés les uns devant les autres, comme frappés d'une paralysie qui ne se délivre que dans les crises brutales et brèves de la violence. C'est que la lutte a pris un caractère inexpiable qui soulève de chaque côté des indignations irrépressibles, et des passions qui ne laissent place qu'aux surenchères. [...]

Mais nous pouvons agir au moins sur ce que la lutte a d'odieux et proposer, sans rien changer à la situation présente, de renoncer seulement à ce qui la rend inexpiable, c'est-à-dire le meurtre des innocents. Le fait qu'une telle réunion mêlerait des Français et des Arabes, également soucieux de ne pas aller vers l'irréparable et la misère irréversible, lui donnerait des chances sérieuses d'intervenir auprès des deux camps.

Si notre proposition avait une chance d'être acceptée, et elle en a une, nous n'aurions pas seulement sauvé de précieuses vies, nous aurions restitué un climat propice à une discussion saine qui ne serait pas gâtée par d'absurdes intransigeances, nous aurions préparé le terrain à une compréhension plus juste et plus nuancée du problème algérien. En provoquant, sur un point donné, ce faible dégel, nous pourrions espérer un jour défaire, dans son entier, le bloc durci des haines et des folles exigences où nous sommes tous immobilisés. La parole serait alors aux politiques et chacun aurait le droit de défendre à nouveau ses propres convictions, et d'expliquer sa différence.

C'est là, en tout cas, la position étroite sur laquelle nous pouvons, pour commencer, espérer de nous réunir. Toute plate-forme plus vaste ne nous offrirait, pour le moment, qu'un champ de discorde supplémentaire. Nous devons être patients avec nous-mêmes.

Mais à cette action, à la fois limitée et capitale, je ne crois pas, après mûre réflexion, qu'aucun Français ni aucun Arabe puisse refuser son accord. Pour bien nous en persuader, il suffira d'imaginer ce qui adviendrait si cette entreprise, malgré les précautions et les limites étroites où nous la renfermons, échouait. Ce qui arrivera, c'est le divorce définitif, la destruction de tout espoir, et un malheur dont nous n'avons encore qu'une faible idée. Ceux de nos amis arabes qui se tiennent courageusement auprès de nous dans ce « no man's land » où l'on est menacé des deux côtés et qui, déchirés eux-mêmes, ont déjà tant de difficultés à résister aux surenchères, seront forcés d'y céder et s'abandonneront à une fatalité qui écrasera toute possibilité de dialogue. Directement ou indirectement, ils entreront dans la lutte, alors qu'ils auraient pu être des artisans de la paix. L'intérêt de tous les Français est donc de les aider à échapper à cette fatalité. [...]

« CETTE SOUMISSION ENTHOUSIASTE »

À partir d'octobre 1930, Camus suit en classe de philosophie les cours du philosophe Jean Grenier (1898-1971). *Les Îles,* recueil de courts textes publié par celui-ci en 1933, vont jouer un rôle décisif dans sa vocation d'écrivain. En 1959, il en préface la réédition. Le maître, devenu un ami, est curieusement transposé au chapitre III du *Premier Homme* dans le personnage d'un administrateur des douanes en retraite, Victor Malan. « [...] vous vous êtes tourné vers moi, et vous m'avez ouvert sans y paraître les portes de tout ce que j'aime en ce monde », déclare Jacques Cormery à Malan (*PH,* p. 43).

À l'époque où je découvris *Les Îles,* je voulais écrire, je crois. Mais je n'ai vraiment décidé de le faire qu'après cette lecture. D'autres livres ont contribué

Préface de Camus à Jean Grenier, *Les Îles*, 1933 (1959 pour la Préface) ; rééd. « L'Imaginaire », Gallimard, 1977, p. 13-14.

à cette décision. Leur rôle achevé, je les ai oubliés. Celui-ci, au contraire, n'a pas cessé de vivre en moi, depuis plus de vingt ans que je le lis. Aujourd'hui encore, il m'arrive d'écrire ou de dire, comme si elles étaient miennes, des phrases qui se trouvent pourtant dans *Les Îles* ou dans les autres livres de son auteur. Je ne m'en désole pas. J'admire seulement ma chance, à moi qui, plus que quiconque, avais besoin de m'incliner, de m'être trouvé un maître, au moment qu'il fallait, et d'avoir pu continuer à l'aimer et à l'admirer à travers les années et les œuvres.

Car c'est une chance en effet que de pouvoir, une fois au moins dans sa vie, connaître cette soumission enthousiaste. Parmi les demi-vérités dont s'enchante notre société intellectuelle figure celle-ci, excitante, que chaque conscience veut la mort de l'autre. Aussitôt, nous voilà tous maîtres et esclaves, voués à nous entre-tuer. Mais le mot maître a un autre sens qui l'oppose seulement au disciple dans une relation de respect et de gratitude. Il ne s'agit plus alors d'une lutte des consciences, mais d'un dialogue, qui ne s'éteint plus dès qu'il a commencé, et qui comble certaines vies. Cette longue confrontation n'entraîne ni servitude, ni obéissance, mais seulement l'imitation, au sens spirituel du terme. À la fin, le maître se réjouit lorsque le disciple le quitte et accomplit sa différence, tandis que celui-ci gardera toujours la nostalgie de ce temps où il recevait tout, sachant qu'il ne pourrait jamais rien rendre. L'esprit engendre aussi l'esprit, à travers les générations, et l'histoire des hommes, heureusement, se bâtit sur l'admiration autant que sur la haine.

Si les *Carnets* portent trace dès 1942 (peut-être dès 1940) d'éléments qui nourriront *Le Premier Homme*, le roman ne sera vraiment ébauché qu'à partir d'octobre 1953.

[*Avril 1940*]

Œuvres complètes, op. cit., t. II, p. 912.

À cette date, Camus désigne déjà « l'homme » par un troublant « J. C. » (voir *supra*, p. 59).

Roman (2ᵉ partie — conséquences).

L'homme (J. C.) s'est fixé tel jour pour mourir — assez rapproché. Son étonnante et immédiate supériorité sur toutes les forces sociales et autres.

[*Entre août et octobre 1942*]

Ibid., p. 958.

Enfance pauvre. L'imperméable trop grand — la sieste. La canette Vinga — les dimanches chez la tante. Les livres — la bibliothèque municipale. Rentrée le soir de Noël et le cadavre devant le restaurant. Les jeux dans la cave (Jeanne, Joseph et Max). Jeanne ramasse tous les boutons, « c'est comme ça qu'on devient riche ». Le violon du frère et les séances de chant — Galoufa.

[*Décembre 1942*]

Ibid., p. 973.

Enfance pauvre. Différence essentielle quand j'allais chez mon oncle : chez nous les objets n'avaient pas de nom, on disait : les assiettes creuses, le pot qui est sur la cheminée, etc. Chez lui : le grès flambé des Vosges, le service de Quimper, etc. — Je m'éveillai au choix.

Ibid., p. 1069.

Roman. Enfance pauvre. J'avais honte de ma pauvreté et de ma famille (Mais ce sont des monstres!). Et si je puis en parler aujourd'hui avec simplicité c'est que je n'ai plus honte de cette honte et que je ne me méprise plus de l'avoir ressentie. Je n'ai connu cette honte que lorsqu'on m'a mis au lycée. Auparavant, tout le monde était comme moi et la pauvreté me paraissait l'air même de ce monde. Au lycée, je connus la comparaison. [...]

Oui, j'avais mauvais cœur, ce qui est commun. Et si, jusqu'à l'âge de 25 ans, je n'ai supporté qu'avec rage et honte le souvenir de ce mauvais cœur, c'est que je refusais d'être commun. Tandis que je sais maintenant que je le suis et, ne le trouvant plus ni bon ni mauvais, je m'intéresse à autre chose...

J'aimais ma mère avec désespoir. Je l'ai toujours aimée avec désespoir.

[1951. Automne?]

Carnets III, p. 27-28.

À 35 ans le fils va sur la tombe de son père et s'aperçoit que celui-ci est mort à 30 ans. Il *est devenu l'aîné*.

[Octobre 1953]

Ibid., p. 96-97.

Roman. 1ʳᵉ partie. Recherche d'un père ou le père inconnu. La pauvreté n'a pas de passé. « Le jour où dans le cimetière de province... X découvrit que son père était mort plus jeune qu'il n'était lui-même à ce moment-là... que celui qui était couché là était son cadet depuis 2 ans bien qu'il y eût 35 ans qu'il fût étendu là... Il s'aperçut qu'il ignorait tout de ce père et décida de le retrouver... »

Naissance dans un déménagement.

2e partie. L'enfance (ou mêlée à la première partie). Qui suis-je?

3e partie. L'éducation d'un homme. Incapable de s'arracher aux corps. Ah! L'innocence des premiers actes! Mais les années passent, les êtres se lient et chaque acte de chair ligote, prostitue, engage de plus en plus.

Il ne veut pas être jugé (il juge peu à vrai dire), mais on ne peut pas ne pas l'être.

Deux personnages:

1) L'indifférent: élevé dans un milieu familial. Sans père. La mère singulière. Se débrouille seul. Un peu hautain, quoique poli. Marche seul toujours. Va aux matches de boxe et de football. N'aime rien que l'instant de pointe. Oublie le reste. En même temps réclame des autres la tendresse dont il est incapable. A le mensonge facile mais des accès terribles de vérité. Un peu monstrueux. Secret jusqu'à la limite, parce qu'il oublie des grandes parties de sa vie, parce que peu de choses l'intéressent — Artiste par ses défauts mêmes.

2) L'autre, sensible et généreux.

Ils se rejoignent à la fin (et c'est le même) près de la mère.

[*Automne 1953*]   *Ibid.*, p. 100-101.

Le Premier Homme.

Plan?

1) Recherche d'un père.

2) Enfance.

3) Les années de bonheur (malade en 1938). L'action comme une surabondance heureuse. Puissant sentiment de libération quand c'est fini.

4) Guerre et résistance (Bir Hakeim et journal clandestin alternés).

160

5) Femmes.

6) Mère.

L'indifférent. Un homme complet. Esprit d'envergure, corps adroit et rompu aux plaisirs. Il refuse d'être aimé par impatience, et par sentiment exact de ce qu'il est. Doux et bon dans l'illégitime. Cynique et terrible dans la vertu.

Il peut tout faire parce qu'il a décidé de se tuer. Cyanure. Il entre donc dans la résistance d'où son incroyable audace. Mais le jour où il doit se servir du cyanure, *il s'en prive*.

Le Premier Homme.

Recherche d'un père.

L'hôpital. La mère (et ce papier de la mairie qu'on apporte aux deux femmes analphabètes qui pèlent des pommes de terre sur le palier, et il faut faire entrer l'adjoint au maire et lui rendre le papier pour qu'il le lise[1]), la presse, Cheragas[2], etc. Il voit se dessiner un peu le père. Puis tout s'efface. En définitive, il n'y a rien.

C'était toujours ainsi sur cette terre, où, il y a 50, 70 ans[3]...

[*Avant août 1954*]   *Ibid.*, p. 114.

Le Premier Homme : les étapes de Jessica[4] : La petite fille sensuelle. La jeune amoureuse éprise d'absolu. L'amoureuse vraie. L'accomplissement hors de l'équivoque des débuts.

« Quand je l'aimais le plus, quelqu'un au fond de moi la détestait pour ce qu'elle avait fait, vu, et subi.

---

1. Voir *Le Premier Homme*, p. 83.
2. Cheraga, commune d'Algérie dans la région du Sahel (note de l'éditeur).
3. Suite illisible (note de l'éditeur).
4. Voir *Le Premier Homme*, p. 343, 354, 356.

Subi surtout. Je la haïssais de ne m'avoir pas attendu, morte, jusqu'à l'heure du bon matin. Et je la haïssais en présence de quelqu'un d'autre qui, en moi, riait de cette dérisoire prétention. »

[*6 décembre 1954*]   *Ibid.*, p. 142.

Roman.
Le Premier Homme refait tout le parcours pour découvrir son secret : il n'est pas le premier. Tout homme est le premier homme, personne ne l'est. C'est pourquoi il se jette aux pieds de sa mère.

[*Décembre 1954* ?]   *Ibid.*, p. 148-150.

Le Premier Homme. L'ambition le faisait rire. Il ne voulait pas avoir, il ne voulait pas posséder, il voulait être. Pour cela la seule obstination.

Dès l'instant où la vie privée est jetée en montre, expliquée, à des tas de gens, elle est la vie publique et il est vain de vouloir s'y maintenir.

Cette vie-là (vide) des villes et des jours insupportables sans l'amour.

Elle est ce qui depuis dix ans m'a le plus intéressé au monde.

Le Premier Homme. « Et pensant à tout ce qu'il avait fait sans le vouloir vraiment, que d'autres avaient voulu ou plus simplement parce que d'autres avaient fait ainsi dans des circonstances assez semblables, tout cela dont l'accumulation pourtant avait fini par faire une vie, celle qu'il partageait avec tous les hommes qui pour finir meurent de n'avoir pas su vivre ce qu'ils voulaient réellement vivre. »

Le Premier Homme. Thème de l'énergie : « Je dominerai, mais sans compromission. Le compromis, l'hypocrisie, le désir bas de la puissance, tout cela est trop facile. Mais je dominerai vraiment, sans faire un geste pour posséder ou avoir. »

La seule loi de l'être c'est d'être et de se surpasser. [...]

Le Premier Homme. Thème de l'amitié.

M. sans grande culture et entrant de plain-pied dans les grandes œuvres. Incapable de s'attarder, même par paresse, au médiocre, et d'instinct discernant la grandeur.

Le Premier Homme. Thème de l'angoisse (cf. Connaissance de l'homme. Adler p. 156[1]). Le moteur des personnages : le désir de puissance, psychologiquement parlant. [...]

Premier Homme. Avec Simone. Il ne peut la prendre pendant un an. Et puis la fuite. Elle pleure et cela déclenche tout.

Tout vient de mon impossibilité congénitale à être un bourgeois et un bourgeois content. La moindre apparence de stabilité dans ma vie me terrifie.

Pour finir ma grande supériorité sur les tricheurs est que je n'ai pas peur de mourir. J'ai pour la mort horreur et dégoût. Mais je n'ai pas peur de mourir. [...]

[*19 février 1955*]   *Ibid.*, p. 153.

Camus ébauche à cette date un dialogue de Jacques avec sa mère, proche du texte du manuscrit (*PH*, p. 73 et suiv.).

---

1. Alfred Adler (1870-1937), médecin et psychologue autrichien, qui étudia le sentiment d'infériorité chez l'homme et sa compensation grâce à la volonté de puissance. Auteur notamment de *La Connaissance de l'homme* (1927).

Premier Homme. « Bien des années après, quand, abandonnés à des fatigues différentes, il nous arrivait de nous séparer le soir avec cette légère déception de ne pas nous être vraiment aimés ce jour-là, le petit geste de victoire qu'elle me faisait devant sa porte, quand j'attendais au volant de ma voiture qu'elle disparût, reliait cette journée apparemment perdue au fil solide de notre amour obstiné et le sauvait alors de toute amertume. »

Id. Dureté de Jessica dans les ruptures. La perte de l'amour est la perte de tous les droits alors qu'on les avait tous.

Premier Homme. L'ami Saddok.

1) Jeune militant — Mon camarade — crise de 36.

2) Ami — Revient à la coutume musulmane puisque l'autre l'a trahi. Se marie selon la volonté de son père. Craint de manquer sa femme inconnue.

3) Terroriste[1].

Plus tard un ami européen a sa femme violée et tuée. Le premier homme et cet ami se précipitent sur leurs armes, arrêtent un complice, le torturent puis se jettent à la poursuite du coupable, le surprennent et le tuent. Sa honte, après. L'histoire c'est le sang. [...]

Premier Homme. Pierre, militant, Jean[2], dilettante. Pierre est marié. Ils rencontrent tous les deux Jessica. Jean et Jessica comme la vieille maîtresse. Dans un des intervalles, elle a Pierre qu'elle quitte et

1. Voir *Le Premier Homme*, p. 357-358.
2. Camus prévoit ici de prénommer son héros « Jean » plutôt que « Jacques ». Voir également l'ébauche donnée dans *PH*, p. 324. Dans les deux cas, le héros est « J.C. » (voir *supra*, p. 59).

blesse, et qui fera souffrir sa femme. Il apprend ainsi, loin des meetings, ce qu'est réellement la justice. Jean au contraire apprend à aimer Jessica et par ce biais va vers les hommes. Pierre meurt près de Jean (guerre, résistance) qui l'a détesté de jalousie. Et il l'assiste de tout son cœur. Il est l'homme qu'elle a aimé au moins un peu.

Id. Découverte de l'amour. Fascination M.A.

Le terrorisme n'a pas encore frappé Alger quand Camus imagine que la mère de Jacques vient vivre avec son fils en Provence, où elle finit ses jours.

[*Entre le 22 août et le 24 octobre 1955*]   *Ibid.*, p. 182.

Premier Homme. La mère obligée de fuir l'Algérie finit sa vie en Provence, dans la campagne achetée pour elle par le fils. Mais elle souffre d'exil. Son mot : « C'est bien. Mais il n'y a pas d'Arabes. » C'est là qu'elle meurt et qu'il comprend[1].

Titre : Le Père et la Mère ?

[*27 janvier 1956*]   *Ibid.*, p. 183.

Premier Homme. X. qui déclare que *seul* le P.C. a fait ce qu'il fallait toujours pour les camarades. Différence des générations. Ils ont tout à apprendre aussi.

L'ébauche suivante est écrite par Camus peu après que les premiers attentats terroristes ont frappé Alger (20, 21, 22 juin 1956). Jacques a obtenu que sa mère le rejoigne en France, mais elle retourne bientôt chez elle. Dans le manuscrit, elle refuse de quitter Belcourt (voir *PH*, p. 89).

---

1. Quand le terrorisme gagna Alger, Camus envisagea de demander à sa mère de venir s'installer en métropole, sans doute à Lourmarin (voir Olivier Todd, *Albert Camus. Une vie*, p. 618).

Roman-fin. Maman. Que disait son silence. Que criait cette bouche muette et souriante. Nous ressusciterons.

Sa patience à l'aérodrome, dans ce monde de machines et de bureaux qui la dépasse, à attendre sans un mot, comme depuis des millénaires des vieilles femmes dans le monde entier, attendent que le monde passe. Et puis toute petite, un peu cassée, sur l'immense terrain, vers les monstres hurlants, retenant d'une main ses cheveux bien peignés... [...]

Roman (fin). Elle repart vers l'Algérie où l'on se bat (parce que c'est là-bas qu'elle veut mourir). On empêche le fils d'aller dans la salle d'attente. Il reste à attendre. Ils se regardent à vingt mètres l'un de l'autre, à travers trois épaisseurs de verre, avec de petits signes de temps en temps. [...]

Roman. Après quinze ans d'amour avec Jessica il rencontre une jeune danseuse, qui a, avec des différences, les mêmes dons, la même flamme que J. Et quelque chose naît en Jean qui ressemble à l'amour qu'il a eu pour J. Comme s'il était encore capable de recommencer (et comme M.H., sur les mêmes lieux, avait aimé Jessica sans le dire). Mais il est vieux, elle est jeune, il aime toujours Jessica et l'amour qu'il a eu pour elle. Il se tait. Renonce. La vie ne recommence pas. À peine avait-il découvert ou cru découvrir qu'il l'aimait que terrifié il décidait de ne jamais porter les mains sur elle. On voudrait que ceux qu'on commence d'aimer vous aient connu tel que vous étiez avant de les rencontrer, pour qu'ils puissent apercevoir ce qu'ils ont fait de vous.

III. L'ALGÉRIE COLONIALE

ALGER VERS LA FIN DU XIXᵉ SIÈCLE

« Alger, et avec elle certains lieux privilégiés comme les villes sur la mer, s'ouvre dans le ciel comme une bouche ou une blessure » (« L'Été à Alger », *Noces*). La splendeur de la baie, les restes de la « vieille ville musulmane » abîmée par les constructions européennes, les rues (Bab-Azoun et Bab-el-Oued) qui donnent sur la place du Gouvernement : on reconnaît dans ce texte de 1887 l'essentiel de la ville décrite dans *Le Premier Homme*. Mais à l'époque de Camus, le « cœur d'Alger » s'est éloigné de la Casbah. Il ne se trouve plus place du Gouvernement, mais du côté de la Grande Poste, où Jacques va faire des courses pour le quincaillier qui l'a employé (voir *PH*, p. 289). Sur le pourtour de la baie s'est développée cette « cité nouvelle » que Maurice Wahl appelait de ses vœux. Mais les dégâts déplorés par les « amateurs de pittoresque » étaient irréversibles.

Une large échancrure du rivage arrondie en demi-cercle presque régulier ; une enceinte de collines boisées où les maisons blanches brillent dans la verdure sombre ; à droite, des masses rocheuses violemment découpées par la mer ; à gauche, derrière le profil amoindri des hauteurs qui s'abaissent, le poudroiement lumineux d'une grande plaine, et, surgissant au fond, les hautes montagnes souvent coiffées de neige ; un air léger, vibrant, qui dessine nettement les contours et où les couleurs s'harmonisent dans la lumière : telle apparaît la baie d'Alger, moins vaste, mais aussi belle que les baies vantées

Maurice Wahl, « Les Villes de l'Algérie », 1887 ; recueilli dans *L'Algérie*, choix de textes, Paris, Renouard, 1931, p. 117-118.

de Naples ou de Rio[1]. La ville est bâtie dans la partie nord-ouest, sur les dernières pentes du Sahel ; resserrée dans un espace étroit, elle s'offre tout entière au regard, d'un seul bloc, avec son port à ses pieds, son monumental boulevard bordé d'arcades[2], ses rues montantes où s'étagent les terrasses mauresques. Et le spectacle est divers, mais d'un charme égal, soit qu'on la découvre de la mer ou des hauteurs voisines, baignée dans l'éclatant soleil de midi ou dormant sous les étoiles.

Il est regrettable qu'au lendemain de la conquête on n'ait pas pris le parti de respecter la vieille ville musulmane et de construire à côté, dans la plaine de Mustapha, une cité nouvelle qui aurait eu, pour se développer à l'aise, tout le pourtour de la baie. Les artistes et les simples amateurs de pittoresque n'auraient pas eu à déplorer tant de constructions barbares. L'ancienne Alger serait debout avec ses curieux édifices, ses intérieurs mystérieux, avec la physionomie étrange et colorée que lui faisaient la masse blanche des maisons, les teintes hardies des minarets polychromes et les taches de verdure des jardins dansant dans la lumière. La ville européenne, aménagée selon les convenances d'une population civilisée, aurait grandi librement, sans être gênée dans sa croissance par les accidents du terrain ou les servitudes militaires. Mais qui donc aurait pu, en 1830 et dans les années qui suivirent, jeter les grandes lignes d'un plan d'ensemble ? Comment penser à l'avenir quand on était exposé à plier bagage le lendemain ? En attendant il fallait loger les troupes, installer les services ; les émigrants civils

1. « L'espace immense du golfe qui s'étendait jusqu'aux grandes montagnes bleutées au fond de l'horizon » (*PH*, p. 232).
2. « Le boulevard Front-de-mer » (*PH*, p. 292).

arrivaient et se faisaient leur place ; on achetait, vendait, démolissait, bâtissait, des intérêts se créaient avec lesquels on dut compter plus tard. C'est ainsi que s'est faite au jour le jour, sous l'inspiration changeante du moment, au hasard des besoins, des spéculations, des caprices, la ville moderne d'Alger. Telle qu'elle est, malgré les erreurs de goût, des disparates choquantes, avec ce qui lui reste d'originalité, dans le cadre merveilleux que lui met la nature, elle demeure l'un des coins les plus attrayants du monde.

Le centre, le cœur d'Alger est la place du Gouvernement[1]. Qu'on se figure un rectangle long dont trois faces sont formées par de hautes maisons à arcades, garnies de magasins, d'étalages, de cafés, coupées de passages et de rues. Le quatrième côté rompt la symétrie ; c'est d'abord une mosquée, la Djema-el-Djedid, toute blanche, aux murs dentelés de merlons, élançant au-dessus de sa coupole et de ses dômes la fine silhouette du minaret, puis une large échappée se découvre avec le port, la mer, les lointains monts kabyles et toute l'ampleur de l'horizon.

Autour de la place, par les rues Bab-Azoun, Bab-el-Oued, par le boulevard de la République[2], roulent des galops de calèches, des cahotements criards de corricolos[3], de pesants départs de diligences. Les terrasses des cafés débordent, des appels sonores éclatent parmi le brouhaha des conversations à pleine voix, dans l'exubérance de mimiques méridionales. Sous la longue allée de platanes qui fait face à la mosquée, des groupes de promeneurs

1. Voir *Le Premier Homme*, p. 232.
2. Le boulevard Carnot et le boulevard de la République formaient le « boulevard Front-de-mer ».
3. Sorte de tilbury d'origine napolitaine.

vont lentement, se suivent, se croisent, se mêlent. On déplie les journaux frais imprimés, on échange les nouvelles du jour, on commente les dépêches de France, on discute les questions locales, on négocie les affaires de commerce ; c'est la Bourse et c'est le Forum. À deux pas de cette agitation, assises dans le bosquet de palmiers de la Régence, des femmes font cercle ; des vieillards, des malades respirent l'air doux ; des oisifs laissent flotter leur rêverie solitaire. Et là-bas, au pied de la statue équestre du duc d'Orléans[1], les petits décrotteurs biskris[2], les petits marchands d'allumettes juifs, toute la plèbe enfantine des Ouled-plaça[3] se gourme et se chamaille avec des cris aigus, tandis que de grands vagabonds arabes étalent nonchalamment leurs guenilles au soleil.

« CE PEUPLE ATTACHÉ À LA GLÈBE »

La geste des pionniers de l'Algérie française, à laquelle Camus promettait d'amples développements (voir *PH*, p. 345 et suiv.), fut célébrée sur un ton très officiel, en 1930, dans un album commémorant le Centenaire de la colonisation. Charles Hagel exprime la même admiration que Camus pour ces hommes et ces femmes dont beaucoup payèrent leur audace de leur vie, et le même ressentiment contre les autorités de la métropole qui, après les avoir abandonnés à leur sort, tirèrent gloire et profit de leur dévouement.

1. Voir *PH*, p. 232, et *L'Été* : « Je recommande au voyageur sensible, s'il va à Alger [...], de s'asseoir par terre, au pied de la statue du duc d'Orléans, place du Gouvernement (ce n'est pas pour le duc, c'est qu'il y passe du monde et qu'on y est bien) » (*Essais*, p. 849).
2. Originaires de Biskra (sud de l'Algérie).
3. Terme obscur. On appelait les enfants arabes (souvent cireurs de chaussures) des *ya-ouled*.

Ce miracle, qu'on ne peut attribuer à la France réunie dans ses conseils et représentée par ses gouvernants, non plus qu'à l'administration française, dont l'attitude fut surtout mobile et variable, les décisions alternativement noires et blanches et en lignes brisées, le mérite en revient aux Français. Non pas à tous les Français dont la grande masse resta au moins indifférente quand elle ne fut pas hostile et qui, aujourd'hui même, cent ans après, ne sait rien d'autre de l'Afrique du Nord que c'est un vague pays, situé quelque part de l'autre côté de l'eau, mais aux quelques milliers de Français qui, du jour de la conquête à celui où nous sommes, vinrent s'y fixer et y travailler.

L'administration militaire ou civile, à part quelques exceptions, ne fit rien de particulier pour les aider, trop souvent se complut à les gêner et se contenta surtout d'éluder les difficultés et de gagner son argent le plus facilement qu'elle put. À ces Français, il faut joindre les éléments étrangers venus s'agglomérer à eux, les sobres travailleurs de l'Espagne, défricheurs de la première heure, et les robustes ouvriers de l'Italie. Dès 1871, le dernier effort militaire accompli que les circonstances imposaient, c'est à ce peuple algérien, fondu, brassé par les mariages mixtes[1], resté fidèle à la langue et à l'esprit français, qu'on est redevable du labeur accompli. Le second Empire, et plus tard la République, pourront à loisir y déléguer au commandement et à la tête des affaires leurs favoris, leurs fils à papa ou leurs personnages consulaires indésirables à Paris, c'est ce peuple attaché à la glèbe, ces colons, ces marchands dont le panégyrique n'est pas à refaire ni

Charles Hagel, dans *Le Centenaire de la colonisation algérienne (1830-1930)*, Éditions d'Alger, 1930, p. 22-23.

1. Mixité entre Européens s'entend : les barrières culturelles et religieuses autant que les préjugés racistes empêchèrent toujours que la mixité s'étendît aux populations indigènes.

le martyrologe à redire, qui effectuera la mise en valeur, créera la prospérité et trouvera par l'usage, empiriquement, les formules et méthodes que les bureaux à la suite et les autorités à la remorque n'auront qu'à consacrer. Composés, pour la France, des éléments les plus aventureux et les plus énergiques du pays, et pour l'Espagne et l'Italie de pauvres gens chassés par la misère et farouchement empressés à se pourvoir, ces immigrants jouaient leur va-tout et développèrent pour réussir une incroyable activité. Contre l'entourage hostile, le climat meurtrier, la terre avare, ce fut une bataille épique dont on voit bien les magnifiques rendements mais dont il convient que l'on n'oublie point les drames et les désastres. Tout autant que ceux des soldats, les ossements de ces pionniers ont parsemé ce sol aujourd'hui couvert de moissons et de vignobles, traversé de routes et parsemé d'heureux villages. Les vaincus retombaient à la nuit du silence et de l'oubli, mais d'autres continuaient, et cet assaut du travail civilisateur contre les forces barbares et la nature marâtre se poursuivait comme l'assaut des vagues au long des plages. L'effort de ceux qui échouaient ne restait pas inutile, chacun avait apporté son coup de pioche, son coup de hache dans la barrière à faire sauter, sa pierre à l'édifice en construction. *Farà da se*, cette formule que Cavour inventa pour l'Italie s'applique merveilleusement à l'Algérie où par-dessus tout c'est le triomphe des forces et de la vie qu'il faut saluer. *Farà da se*, elle s'est faite elle-même par la force des choses, contre vents et marées et avec le plus parfait mépris des voies qu'on lui assignait, par le seul travail accumulé des gens qui vinrent s'y fixer dans l'évidente volonté de vivre et non celui d'y mourir.

« LA FORMATION DE LA RACE »

Ainsi Émile-Félix Gautier (1864-1940), explorateur et géographe, intitule-t-il le chapitre d'un opuscule publié également à l'occasion du Centenaire de la colonisation. Camus aussi parle de la « race » des Européens d'Algérie (*PH,* p. 89). Avant eux, André Gide (1869-1951) a eu, en arrivant à Alger, conscience de la naissance d'« une race nouvelle » : « Cela semble tenir de l'Andalou, du Basque, du Provençal, du Corse, du Sicilien, du Calabrais : c'est l'Algérien » (*Journal,* Gallimard, « Pléiade », t. I, 1996, p. 381). Sur un ton moins emphatique que Charles Hagel, E.-F. Gautier évoque les souffrances des premiers colons et l'importance de cette quinine « qui se vendait dans les cafés de Bône et dans la cantine de Mondovi » (*PH,* p. 208). « La quinine est vendue dans les cafés comme une consommation », a encore noté Camus sur un feuillet (*PH,* p. 313). E.-F. Gautier analyse enfin la notion de « créole », qui surgit curieusement, une seule fois, dans les ébauches du roman (p. 351).

L'Algérie était à peu près inculte. En particulier les plaines du littoral, qui font aujourd'hui la richesse du Tell, étaient des marais, défendus par des milliards d'anophèles, c'est-à-dire par la malaria.

La Mitidja, aux portes d'Alger, avec sa capitale Boufarik, est un exemple excellent.

Bien entendu les colons sont les premiers frappés. D'autant qu'il faut songer à ce que fut longtemps leur installation : « couchés sur une poignée de foin », dit Trumelet.

Pendant longtemps on a dit d'un visage rendu livide par la fièvre : c'est une figure de Boufarik. Ce point avait une telle réputation d'insalubrité, que les militaires ou les voyageurs qui étaient obligés de le

Émile-Félix Gautier, *L'Évolution de l'Algérie de 1830 à 1930,* Publications du Comité national métropolitain du Centenaire de l'Algérie [sans date], p. 16-19.

traverser, le faisaient le plus rapidement possible, en se voilant le visage, ou en se bouchant le nez, dans la crainte d'aspirer son air pestilentiel.

Chez les marchands de goutte de Boufarik, quand un client demandait « une consommation », sans préciser davantage, tout le monde savait ce que signifiait, dans l'argot local, cette expression humoristique. Il ne s'agissait ni d'anisette, ni de cognac : le patron servait, sans hésitation, un cachet de quinine.

Malgré la quinine et l'hôpital, la mortalité était énorme. Le seul mois d'octobre 1840 emporte 48 fiévreux sur 400 habitants ; à peu près un quart en un mois.

L'administration a renoncé plusieurs fois à tenir le coup. À diverses reprises elle a voulu abandonner l'expérience de Boufarik.

À la fin de 1839 le projet est si avancé, que l'ordre est donné d'évaluer la valeur des constructions pour indemniser les colons évacués. [...]

Évidemment ce sont les colons qui se sont cramponnés à leur tâche meurtrière. On n'a pu les en arracher.

Naturellement on s'est préoccupé dès le premier moment d'assainir Boufarik et à partir de 1842 le génie militaire d'abord, les Ponts et Chaussées ensuite, travaillent systématiquement.

Assainir, cela signifiait drainer le marais, transformer les eaux stagnantes en eaux courantes. Besogne terrible.

Il faut songer aussi au progrès de l'installation. Les colons n'habiteront plus des gourbis en branchage. Ils se construisent des maisons en pierre, et ils couchent dans des lits.

En 1843 déjà, au dire de Toussenel, « le chiffre des décès n'atteignit que 42, c'est-à-dire le 1/17e ».

En 1843, pourtant, il était un peu tôt pour chanter victoire. Il faudra bien plus de temps que ça : il faudra une vingtaine d'années, pour arriver à l'époque que chante Trumelet, où l'on voit à Boufarik « des cultivateurs à muscles d'acier et à visages dorés de santé par le hâle... une fourmilière de beaux enfants bâtis à chaux et à sable... de nombreux centenaires... le temps où la profession de médecin sera une sinécure, et où l'excellent Dr George se verra dans l'obligation de consommer lui-même sa quinine, s'il tient absolument à écouler ce fébrifuge ».

Cette bataille contre le climat, qui se livrait à Boufarik, n'avait pas un intérêt simplement local. Boufarik battait, il est vrai, en Algérie, tous les records d'insalubrité, mais il n'en avait pas le monopole. Jusque sous le second Empire des gens très sérieux ont établi scientifiquement, statistiques en mains, qu'une race « créole » n'avait aucun avenir en Algérie. Vous entendez bien que ce mot de créole, complètement mort aujourd'hui dans la littérature algérienne, comportait une assimilation entre le climat méditerranéen de l'Algérie, et celui de la zone tropicale, où toute colonisation blanche était impossible.

COLONS DES VILLAGES, COLONS DU BLED

Si on observe la distinction proposée par ce texte, c'est dans une ferme isolée, mais à proximité d'un village, Mondovi, que s'était installé le père d'Albert Camus. À son époque la situation des colons s'était améliorée

par rapport à celle des pionniers évoquée ici. Les premiers colons dansaient, dit Veillard, pour s'échauffer le sang, suer et éviter ainsi le choléra (*PH,* p. 207). Marc Baroli confirme que ce n'est pas là une légende, même si la fête pouvait n'être pas seulement thérapeutique. Quant aux « consommations » dont parlait E.-F. Gautier (voir *supra*), il faut croire qu'elles ne se résumaient pas à la ration de quinine.

Si le tableau de Daudet montrant tous les colons dans les cafés en train de boire de l'absinthe et discutant des projets de réforme et de constitution est quelque peu caricatural[1], on relève cependant des chiffres inquiétants. À Boufarik il y avait, en 1841, dix-huit cabarets et dix auberges, et il est difficile de croire qu'on n'y vendait que de la quinine. Il est vrai que Boufarik est un lieu de passage et un camp. Mais Draria comptait à la même époque huit cabarets pour quarante-deux feux, jusqu'à l'intervention de Bugeaud qui n'en autorisa que trois.

À partir de 1848, date à laquelle les arrivées par familles entières se firent plus nombreuses, on dansa beaucoup dans les villages, et pas seulement pour éviter le choléra. On danse à Novi, aussi bien qu'à Mondovi, et aussi à Assi ben Okba, où le premier mariage a lieu en 1850 et la première naissance en 1852.

Les colons ne sont, en général, guère religieux et l'on note en divers endroits qu'ils passent le dimanche soit à travailler, soit à voisiner. Il semble que la messe soit plus fréquentée là où il y a des militaires et qu'elle constitue surtout une cérémonie sociale.

Marc Baroli, *Algérie, terre d'espérances. Colons et immigrants (1830-1914)*, L'Harmattan, 1992 (première édition : Hachette, 1976), p. 54-57.

---

1. Allusion probable à *Tartarin de Tarascon*, où le héros aperçoit « la brave figure tannée de maître Barbassou, le capitaine du *Zouave*, qui prenait l'absinthe en fumant sa pipe sur la porte d'un petit café » (II, 12).

La vie privée, elle, se déroule dans le cadre des maisons de colonisation toutes semblables dans leur alignement monotone. Très souvent, surtout en 1848, elles sont jumelées et comportent deux pièces par famille. Les cloisons intérieures de chaque logement sont en planches, le sol carrelé, parfois boursouflé par des racines de palmiers nains quand le défrichement n'a pas été poussé. Le mobilier, en principe apporté par le colon, reste rare. Les lits sont parfois de simples planches sur des tréteaux, les matelas presque toujours bourrés de foin.

Les colons sont arrivés avec des vêtements aussi peu adaptés que possible au climat et au genre de vie qu'ils allaient mener. Tous ceux qui les avaient précédés en Algérie se sont gaussés des robes de soie des « colonnes » de 48. Les robes de soie se sont usées très vite et il n'a pas été facile de les remplacer. La ville était loin et l'argent manquait. Une fois de plus, l'armée a pourvu à tout ; elle a habillé les colons et même leurs femmes. L'on a vu des Parisiennes affublées de vieilles capotes et de pantalons rouges ou portant, en guise de chemises, des sacs à orge sur lesquels on lisait d'un côté « Campement » et de l'autre « Fourrage ». Au printemps de 1858 encore, dix ans après la fondation de Millesimo, Flaubert y voit des femmes sarcler et labourer en veste et chapeau d'homme[1].

Carteron[2] est frappé en 1866 de l'air las des femmes hâlées, visiblement fatiguées et dont les vêtements européens font tache dans le paysage, de la tristesse de ces villages bas entourés d'un

1. « MILLESIMO. Village atroce, tout droit », et, à propos de ces femmes : « portières de Paris, transportées au pays des Moresques, la crasse de la banlieue dans le soleil d'Afrique » (Flaubert, *Voyage à Carthage, Œuvres complètes*, Le Seuil, t. II, 1964, p. 719). Millesimo se trouve, comme Mondovi, dans la vallée de la Seybouse.

2. Collaborateur de l'*Encyclopédie moderne*.

petit mur d'enceinte ; mais, tout autour, les hommes sont au travail des champs et les blés commencent à lever.

Si la vie était dure dans les villages, elle semble l'avoir été plus encore dans les fermes isolées et, à cet égard, il apparaît que les organisateurs de la colonisation avaient fait un bon choix.

Par fermes isolées, il ne faut pas entendre les grandes concessions comme celle de Jules du Pré de Saint-Maur, par exemple, qui constituaient, en fait, d'importants villages privés, souvent plus prospères que ceux de la colonisation officielle. Quelques colons riches venus de la métropole avec des capitaux et parfois des hommes, quelques anciens officiers qu'une bonne concession avait récompensés de leurs services menaient sur leurs terres une véritable vie de seigneurs, entourés de travailleurs européens nombreux, et se livraient souvent à des expériences agronomiques qui ont parfois assuré leur fortune, mais, quelquefois aussi, fait avancer l'agriculture de la colonie à leurs dépens. « Je ne viens pas faire fortune, disait du Pré de Saint-Maur, je viens risquer une partie de la mienne. »

Mais il y avait aussi dans le bled de tout petits colons et les descriptions s'accordent longtemps à nous les montrer misérables. La plupart du temps, ils s'abritent d'abord dans un gourbi, puis dans une baraque en planches. Il leur faut plusieurs années pour construire une petite maison. Mais souvent, entre-temps, la terre n'a pas produit suffisamment ou la maladie est arrivée ; il faut donc abandonner. Le premier colon chassé, un autre vient parfois le remplacer et poursuivre son œuvre dans de moins mauvaises conditions.

Ceux qui choisissent de s'installer ainsi, loin de tout, sont de toutes origines. Il y a des militaires libérés d'un long service et qui tiennent à rester sur cette terre où ils se sont longtemps battus ; il y a des Espagnols qui ont commencé à travailler comme fermiers ou comme manœuvres à la ville et sont parvenus à amasser un petit pécule ; il y a aussi des Français partis de chez eux, sur la foi de récits vagues et mirobolants, et qui, débarqués à Alger ou à Oran sans un sou vaillant ou presque, ont attendu longtemps et fini par obtenir dans des conditions plus ou moins régulières une mauvaise terre dont la propriété leur sera sans doute contestée plus tard.

Sur ces concessions isolées, il faut trouver de l'eau, puis défricher à la hâte, avant même de bâtir, pour récolter et payer les dettes, car le pire ennemi ce n'est pas la nature, mais l'usurier. Quand la terre ne produit pas suffisamment et assez vite, l'usurier s'en saisit en paiement et tout est dit. Mais quand elle produit convenablement, le colon est tenté de s'agrandir ; c'est en général possible dans le cas de concessions isolées. Il accroît alors son patrimoine en s'endettant, mais n'améliore pas son existence. On le retrouve souvent plusieurs années après avec le lit de fer de ses débuts, un seul costume et du linge mal tenu.

IV. LA « NOSTALGÉRIE »

« Nostalgérie » est le titre d'un poème publié dans les années 1930 par Marcello Fabri (de son vrai nom Marcel-Louis Faivre) : « *Alger je t'ai rêvée ainsi qu'une amoureuse, toi parfumée, et soleilleuse, et pimentée; tu es plus belle encore d'être si loin, la pluie d'ici, la pluie habille comme une magie le gris du ciel, avec tout l'or de ton soleil.* » Ce mot-valise désigne aujourd'hui la nostalgie des Français rapatriés après l'indépendance de l'Algérie (3 juillet 1962); on le trouve, par exemple, sur la couverture d'un « numéro pour l'histoire » du *Figaro Magazine* (16 octobre 2004). Camus est mort trop tôt pour connaître l'exode massif de ses compatriotes, mais il sait, à l'époque où il compose *Le Premier Homme,* que l'Algérie ne sera plus jamais comme avant. Nous donnons ici quelques pages d'écrivains ou d'historiens qui font écho aux souvenirs de Camus.

« CES VENDANGES QUI S'ANNONÇAIENT »

Tandis que la guerre et le terrorisme dévastent l'Algérie, Jean Pélégri (1920-2003), fils d'un colon de la Mitidja, raconte comment il a jadis rêvé de poursuivre l'œuvre de son père.

Autrefois, au temps où l'adolescence me plongeait en rêverie, quand je me promenais le soir sur les chemins blancs de l'été, entre les vignes et les caroubiers verts, il m'arrivait, dans ce couchant aux couleurs d'enluminure, de penser à tout ce que mon père avait planté, labouré, construit, à cette belle terre qu'avec le travail des Arabes il avait fait naître d'un sol inculte et marécageux.

Olivier Pélégri,
« Les Oliviers
de la justice »,
*dans Algérie.
Un rêve de fraternité,*
Omnibus, 1997,
p. 826-827
(1ʳᵉ édition :
Gallimard, 1959).

Et j'étais fier de l'œuvre de mon père.

J'étais fier, et je le suis encore! Chaque fois que j'arrive en avion à Alger, chaque fois qu'avant de se poser l'avion survole dans un grand virage la plaine de la Mitidja et que je devine au loin la ferme de mon père, chaque fois je suis ému par la beauté fertile de cette plaine — ma plaine, mon paysage! Je suis ému par la netteté géométrique des vignes et des chemins clairs, par la blancheur des maisons et des caves. C'est chaque fois comme un beau tableau qui m'est offert, où les carrés verts des vignes, les rectangles jaunes des moissons viennent s'appuyer sur le rouge soutenu des tuiles neuves, le cercle gris des puits — un beau tableau aux lignes modernes où je retrouve le compas, l'équerre et les pendules de mon père.

Mais autrefois rien n'était encore venu dénaturer, corrompre, cette œuvre. Aussi, lorsque dans le bonheur du crépuscule je marchais le long des terres fraîchement labourées, le long des feuilles bleues de sulfate qui cachaient les jeunes récoltes, il m'arrivait souvent de me demander : « Et moi, qu'aurai-je à faire, plus tard, pour être digne de mon père. Quelles seront mes vendanges ? »

Alors, pour me rassurer, je me disais que la moitié seulement du travail était fait... Certes, ici, et depuis longtemps, presque toutes les fermes, si on en cachait les gourbis, étaient déjà des fermes modèles : elles étaient déjà toutes prêtes, toutes équipées, pour le bonheur futur de l'homme. Mais, pour ce bonheur, il fallait encore autre chose. Il ne suffit pas, en effet, qu'il y ait des blés et des vignes pour qu'un paysage devienne un pays. Il faut encore de jolies fontaines et des parcs, des écoles et des stades, des églises et des mosquées, et puis des arbres et des monuments qui ne servent à rien mais qui sont aussi utiles pour l'homme que le pain. Et, architecte rêveur, je me lançais dans des projets de construction. Ce serait là ma part dans le paysage. Ah! que ma plaine alors serait belle!

Je songeais aussi au bonheur que m'avaient procuré tous les livres que mon père n'avait pas eu le temps de lire, que Bouaza, ni Boralfa son fils, par notre faute, ne pouvaient lire. Que ce serait bon, plus tard, d'en discuter avec les fils de Boralfa, surtout si ces livres parlaient de notre pays, et apprenaient à l'aimer! Surtout s'ils étaient écrits par des Musulmans. En classe, étais-je jaloux quand un petit Arabe était premier en français? Sa copie, quand le professeur la lisait, ne me faisait-elle pas découvrir, sous une autre lumière, nombre de choses très évidentes, très familières que je n'avais pas su regarder?

Pourquoi je n'écrirais pas, moi, un livre comme ça? Ah oui, le travail n'allait pas manquer — même pour les paresseux! Qu'elles étaient belles les vendanges qui s'annonçaient!

« JE SUIS NÉ À ROVIGO »

Camus est né en 1913 à Mondovi; Jules Roy, son « cher Julius », en 1907 à Rovigo. Rythmée par les vendanges et les accès de paludisme, l'enfance de Jules Roy est celle qu'aurait connue Camus si, avant même que la guerre ne soit déclarée, son père n'avait décidé de rapatrier à Alger sa famille menacée par les moustiques de la vallée de la Seybouse. Auteur de *La Guerre d'Algérie,* parue quelques mois après la mort de Camus, Jules Roy se révélera au grand public grâce à sa grande saga de la colonisation de l'Algérie, *Les*

Chevaux du soleil (1968-1975, 6 vol.). Peu avant de mourir (2000), il fera un pèlerinage sur la tombe de sa mère à Sidi-Moussa.

Je suis né à trente kilomètres au sud d'Alger, le 22 octobre 1907, à six heures du soir, dans un petit village de colonisation qui porte le nom d'une victoire du premier Empire : Rovigo. Mon père était originaire du Doubs. Quelles circonstances l'avaient conduit à devenir gendarme ? Je ne l'ai jamais su. Il mourut quelques mois après ma naissance et on ne me parla jamais de lui. J'ai un frère, de dix-sept ans mon aîné ; lui aussi a toujours gardé le silence à ce sujet.

Mon origine profonde s'enracine à quelques kilomètres de là, à Sidi-Moussa, un autre village de colonisation construit sur un carrefour de routes, avec son église minuscule, son bistrot, son école, sa poste, ses maisons en tuiles rondes et ses gourbis. La ferme est à deux kilomètres au nord, au milieu des vignes : c'est là que j'ai passé une grande partie de mon enfance avec ma mère, ma grand-mère, mon oncle Jules et les Arabes. En ce temps-là, on ne les appelait pas encore les ratons, mais les troncs de figuiers, sans doute parce qu'ils aiment s'asseoir au pied des arbres. Après la guerre de 14-18, on commença à leur donner le nom de bicots.

Le plus vieil ouvrier de la ferme s'appelait Meftah. Il habitait avec sa famille une hutte de paille et de torchis près du bassin et du potager. Il n'a jamais eu d'âge. Un jour, j'ai appris qu'il était mort après avoir, pendant trente ou quarante ans, fait la litière du bétail que nous avions, conduit les voitures et les attelages, porté plusieurs arrosoirs d'eau par jour du puits à la maison. À cette nouvelle, j'ai pleuré

Jules Roy, « La Guerre d'Algérie », dans *Algérie. Un rêve de fraternité*, Omnibus, 1997, p. 679-681 (1ᵉ édition : Julliard, 1960).

parce que je l'aimais bien. Je l'accompagnais souvent à son travail. Au retour, il me hissait sur les chevaux et quelquefois me prenait sur son dos. Ma mère n'aimait pas cela. Elle disait que j'allais attraper des poux.

Le vieux Meftah, on a dû l'emporter au cimetière musulman de la tribu voisine. Il n'y a pas de beaux tombeaux et des chapelles de marbre comme à Sidi-Moussa, mais de simples pierres dressées, jusqu'à ce que le temps les couche sur le sol. Aujourd'hui, ses os doivent être confondus avec la terre. Déjà, de son vivant, son visage en avait la couleur, les sillons et les craquelures.

Des autres ouvriers, je me souviens plus. Il y en avait beaucoup, des Kabyles surtout, qui descendaient des montagnes pour venir s'engager, en troupes, au moment des travaux saisonniers. [...]

En septembre, c'étaient les vendanges. Les chariots étaient gluants de sucre ; les baquets des raisins se déversaient dans les pressoirs, l'odeur du moût envahissait la ferme. Ma mère avait grand-peur que je ne tombe dans les cuves où je me penchais, fasciné par le bouillonnement du vin.

C'est pourquoi, moi qui les ai toujours vus travailler, je me suis toujours étonné d'entendre dire que les Arabes ne faisaient rien. Le soir, bien sûr, ils s'arrêtaient. Ils allumaient les feux, faisaient cuire leur soupe rouge de piments et leurs galettes d'orge pétries avec un peu d'huile et chantaient. Quelques-uns jouaient de leurs flûtes de roseaux.

Ce que je savais parce qu'on me le répétait, c'était qu'ils étaient d'une autre race que moi, inférieure à la mienne. Nous étions venus défricher leurs terres et leur apporter la civilisation. Et, à la vérité, des marécages dont j'avais entendu parler, et dont il existait encore quelques témoins sur des parcelles qui appartenaient aux tribus voisines, mes grands-parents et mon oncle avaient fait des vignes semblables à celles de Chanaan, de puissantes terres à céréales ou des orangeraies. En s'amusant? Dans la famille de ma mère, on est mort de travail et de paludisme. J'ai connu mon oncle Jules régulièrement abattu par les fièvres et moi-même, tout enfant, j'ai été la proie de ces crises qui terrassaient subitement, faisaient grelotter en plein été malgré bouillottes et couvertures, puis assommaient. La fièvre prenait à la ferme la régularité d'un rite.

LE JARDIN D'ESSAI

Le Jardin d'Essai, situé dans le quartier du Ruisseau, à l'est de Belcourt, offre aux errances de Jacques Cormery ses dédales d'arbres aux essences rares (voir *PH,* p. 60 et suiv.). André Gide l'avait évoqué en 1903 : « Jardin d'Essai, le soir. Allée de bambous déjà sombre... Je m'y suis promené le soir, à l'heure où, dans l'avenue des platanes, à peine on distinguait du tronc des arbres l'épais enveloppement des lianes... » (*Journal,* Gallimard, Pléiade, t. I, 1996, p. 367). Henry de Montherlant (1895-1972) en découvre à son tour les mystères en 1928, avant de regretter dans une note, cinq ans plus tard, que des jardiniers sans goût l'aient systématiquement détérioré. « Dire le nom des arbres », a noté Camus en marge de sa description. Le livre de Montherlant aurait pu l'aider.

Je trouvais là tour à tour, avec parfois une échappée sur la mer, les hauts ombrages des allées nobles et les retraites les plus écartées. Allée des bambous, allée de dragonniers des Canaries, centenaires, aux

Henry de Montherlant, *Il y a encore des paradis. Images d'Alger (1928-1931),* P. & G. Soubiron, Alger, 1935, p. 74-76.

troncs pâles, majestueuse avenue des figuiers d'Australie, dont les racines adventives se sont collées au tronc, le rendant énorme et lui donnant, avec sa teinte grise, une apparence de pachyderme. Et puis, resserrée dans un espace de vingt mètres carrés, une « Société des Nations » d'arbres, des arbres des cinq continents, mais dont les feuillages ne se mangent pas entre eux. Plus droites que les troncs, les racines adventives des figuiers de l'Inde, descendant des branches jusqu'au sol, sous forme de lianes ou bien déjà ignifiées, font à cette assemblée une architecture de colonnades. Et je regarde, troublé, ces racines qui croissent toujours dans la direction de l'eau, se poussent vers elle en contournant les obstacles à la façon d'un serpent, puis, sitôt qu'elles ont trouvé une citerne, quittent l'horizontale pour y plonger, à angle droit avec elles-mêmes, se laissent tomber comme un boa qui pend d'une branche, et boivent. L'esprit le plus rassis se pose un « Qu'est-ce que la vie ? » à regarder cette matière insensible poursuivre son but avec une telle apparence d'intelligence. Et moi, je suis profondément touché, en voyant comme elle s'efforce vers son bonheur. Elle a soif! Soif comme j'ai soif. Soif comme a soif le rossignol dont Kazwini, naturaliste arabe, nous dit qu'à cause de l'ardeur qui le brûle il est de tous les oiseaux le plus altéré.

Tandis que je les contemple, un oiseau, pour m'étonner, se suspend les pattes en l'air, comme les mouches qui marchent au plafond. Mais, j'y songe, certainement, étant oiseau, cet oiseau voudrait une mouche. Et il joue à faire la mouche.

Il y a aussi des lieux plus secrets : la plantation de strelizia (Afrique centrale), à tournures de plantes énormes, qui vous séparent du monde comme un bosquet sacré ; le toit de verdure qui sur une large étendue abrite les palmiers nains, si bas qu'en certains endroits on le touche de sa tête. Le matin, de bonne heure, on dirait que là-dessous l'ombre est verte, et le soleil la crible d'ocelles. Et je songe que si nos âmes, selon la croyance de tant de peuples, se retrouvent après la mort dans un jardin, cela doit être dans un lieu couvert semblable à celui-ci, tout irréel avec son toit de feuilles rapproché comme un plafond de caveau funèbre, avec sa glauque lumière sépulcrale, où les taches de soleil mettent pourtant une gaîté apaisée : à la fois mélancolique et gracieux, comme doit l'être, si l'on en croit les poètes, un séjour des âmes.

Roland Bacri (né à Alger en 1926), qui signa longtemps dans *Le Canard enchaîné* la chronique du « petit poète », offre du jardin une vision voisine de celle de Montherlant. Si on s'étonne du titre de son ouvrage, *Et alors ? Et oilà !*, on se reportera à l'entretien du fils et de la mère dans *L'Envers et l'Endroit* : « Alors, maman. — Alors, voilà. — Tu t'ennuies ? Je ne parle pas beaucoup ? — Oh, tu n'as jamais beaucoup parlé » (*OC*, t. I, p. 52), et aussi au *Premier Homme* : « "Eh bien voilà", disait Jacques. Et voilà en effet, il se retrouvait entre eux deux […] » (p. 144).

Vous descendez du tram après Belcourt mais avant le Stade Municipal, au Ruisseau. Une entrée somptueuse ! C'est la principale pasqu'y en a plusieurs des entrées, il est tellement immense, le Jardin d'Essai. C'est le seul dans le monde de cette importance. Nous, en Algérie, on bénéficie d'un climat qui permet d'acclimater la plupart des essences d'arbres qu'y a partout.

Roland Bacri,
Et alors ? Et oilà !,
Edmond Nalis, Paris,
1968, p. 83-85.

Des cèdres du Liban au magnolia du Kentucky, de l'hévéa du Sénégal au sycomore de l'Hindoustan, du séquoia géant au palmier nain, du palétuvier de l'Oubangui au platane de l'Ardèche en passant par l'arbre à beurre et le pin de Gênes, vous aviez tous les plants, toutes les greffes, toutes les souches.

Et je vous parle pas de toutes les fleurs en massifs, en serres, en plates-bandes, en parterres qu'on avait plantées que pour garnir !

Ce Jardin d'Essai, c'était vraiment quéque chose mais c'est idiot, c'est toujours comme ça : au lieu de bien admirer, de s'instruire en même temps, on allait là-bas le dimanche que pour prendre le frais, courir dans les allées, acheter une glace vanille-chocolat, passer l'après-midi.

On disait : « Tiens, un paulownia très rare ou un goyavier de je sais pas où ! » que quand on était caché derrière trop longtemps qu'on regardait l'étiquette, quand on jouait à la cachette, que Marco comme d'habitude il était allé demander dix sous à tata Fifi, sa mère, pour une limonade !

Vers cinq heures, on sortait du Jardin d'Essai par en bas pour aller voir le lion de l'Atlas[1].

Il était vieux !!! Tout triste. Le gardien (de la porte) y disait qu'il avait vu la Conquête d'Alger. Mon père y disait que c'était toujours comme ça : les anciens combattants c'est tous des lions.

LE TRAMWAY DE LA RUE BAB-AZOUN

Face au square Bresson, où Jacques assiste parfois avec son oncle au concert public (*PH,* p. 117), a été bâti en 1853 l'Opéra d'Alger, que le père de Gabriel Audisio

---

1. Le parc zoologique est contigu au Jardin d'Essai.

dirigea à deux reprises. L'Opéra est relié à la place du Gouvernement par la rue Bab-Azoun. Au-delà de la place, c'est la rue Bab-el-Oued, élargie en son centre par l'église Notre-Dame-des-Victoires, qui mène jusqu'au Grand Lycée. Dans *Le Premier Homme* (p. 233 et suiv.), la rue Bab-el-Oued est baptisée par erreur rue Bab-Azoun. Peu importe : les souvenirs de G. Audisio (1900-1978) ont beau être d'une dizaine d'années antérieurs à ceux de Camus, la perche de la motrice des tramways verts des T.A. apparaît aussi instable que celle des tramways rouges des C.F.R.A. (Chemin de fer sur route d'Alger. Voir *PH,* p. 231 et 241).

La rue Bab-Azoun est rectiligne, mais brusquement elle fait un écart à gauche avant d'entrer sur la place du Gouvernement. Cet angle est du plus haut intérêt pour un gamin. Il y a là, en faction, un employé des T.A. (tramways algériens). Il est coiffé d'une chéchia, mais vêtu d'un costume européen d'uniforme, en fil à fil à rayures bleues et blanches : le même tissu de mes culottes, ce que les amies algéroises de ma mère trouvent indigne d'un jeune Français. Tant pis. L'employé manipule un disque alternativement vert et rouge, recto-verso, qui fait soleil en haut d'une longue tige pivotant dans un anneau fixé à un pilier d'arcade, au coin de la pâtisserie. Pourquoi ? Parce que la rue Bab-Azoun est trop étroite pour tolérer deux paires de rail. Quand un tram s'engage à l'un des deux bouts, le disque présente sa face rouge à celui de l'autre bout, qui attend pour s'élancer à son tour.

   La manœuvre était artisanale, du travail à la main, d'autant plus plaisante qu'une fois sur deux, quand le tram prenait le virage, la perche de la motrice sautait. Alors l'employé se livrait à un long jeu d'adresse pour replacer la roulette de la perche

Gabriel Audisio,
L'Opéra fabuleux,
Julliard, 1970,
p. 47-49.

sur le câble électrique. On appréciait très bien la manipulation chez le docteur Rouquet, avec ses fils, mes condisciples, au coin de la rue Sainte, au-dessus de la pharmacie Brenta.

D'autres fois, des chevelures de serpentins multicolores, accrochées aux fils électriques, flottaient au vent. C'était pendant le carnaval. Du balcon la vue plongeait sur la foule bariolée qui engorgeait le boyau de la rue Bab-Azoun, piétinait des monticules de confetti, en soulevait des tourbillons. Sous les déguisements et les masques, déchaînés, garçons et filles des faubourgs se livraient à des bousculades où régnait une obscénité familière. Où était le tram, à ce moment-là? Je ne sais plus. Englouti peut-être par quelque monstre des Lupercales.

Dès qu'il avait fait surface, à son bruit on devinait son arrivée, la motrice traînant deux jardinières. Ce bruit des T.A. d'il y a un demi-siècle, il est aussi évocateur, pour un ancien enfant d'Alger, que la bouchée de madeleine ou l'odeur des aubépines pour Proust. Bruit à nul autre pareil, il m'éveillait au milieu de la nuit quand j'habitais rue de Richelieu, pourtant loin de la ligne, en contrebas : crissement métallique, fusée jaillissante, qui me retournait dans mon lit à mesure que le tram décrivait sa courbe vers le haut de la rue Michelet. Je me levais, j'allais à la fenêtre ; au fond ténébreux de l'impasse un mitron achevait de scander les claquements de la pâte à pétrir en gueulant un refrain d'hymne au drapeau rouge, « rouge du sang de l'ouvrier ». Des cafards volants s'échappaient des vapeurs du fournil. Avant de fermer la fenêtre je guettais encore le bruit d'un tram, le dernier. Comme un long pan de soie, du haut en bas, il déchirait la nuit et l'abandonnait déserte au silence des étoiles.

Là j'étais un homme. Mais rue Bab-Azoun, dans mon enfance, c'était avec un terrible bruit de ferraille que le tram s'annonçait en brinquebalant ses deux baladeuses. Les gamins n'avaient pas peur de s'accrocher aux marchepieds. Pourtant, lancé à toute vitesse il était redoutable, il frôlait les piliers des arcades. Un jour, le tram a écrasé le docteur Henri Aboulker, qui débouchait distraitement de la galerie.

Mais retournons sur les pas du petit garçon de 1910. S'il n'a pas pris, rue Bab-Azoun, le côté des riches mais celui du tram homicide, il voit des boutiques de vêtements, d'étoffes, les mêmes ou les héritières de celles où sa mère s'était fait injurier pendant les troubles antijuifs. Mais il ne le saura que plus tard.

LE TRAMWAY, DÉCIDÉMENT...

On hésite à parler de la « nostalgérie » de Rachid Boudjedra, romancier et poète algérien né à Aïn El-Beïda (Constantinois) en 1941, connu notamment pour *La Répudiation* (1969). Boudjedra a lutté, dans les rangs du F.L.N., pour l'indépendance de l'Algérie, c'est-à-dire pour l'abolition de cet État colonial dont les injustices embellissent la mémoire de certains Européens. Au moins arrive-t-il que les nostalgies de l'enfance unissent Français et indigènes. Comme Camus, comme Audisio, Rachid Boudjedra se rappelle les perches rebelles des tramways algérois.

Rachid Boudjedra, « Périples urbains », dans *Alger. Une ville et ses discours*, Praxiling, Université Paul Valéry, Montpellier III, 1996, p. 183-184.

J'ai connu Alger à une époque où il y avait encore des tramways et j'en éprouve encore de la nostalgie. Lorsque j'étais petit, je prenais les tramways en marche et j'en descendais en marche, non seulement pour le plaisir de la voltige mais pour ne pas payer parce que je n'avais pas d'argent. J'ai fait la même chose à Constantine d'autant plus que le tramway passait dans la rue où se trouvait la maison de mes parents. J'ai une relation particulière avec le tramway. Cette fascination vient du fait que c'était de vieux tramways déglingués, électriques, à perche — et souvent la perche sortait de ses rails. Il y avait dans chaque tramway un préposé chargé, lorsque la perche quittait les rails, de descendre et de remettre la perche à sa place. Ce n'était pas facile. Avec mes frères, mes amis, nos copains de quartier, c'était un moment formidable que de regarder cette remise dans les rails des choses. Ma vraie histoire avec le tramway, c'est qu'un de ces tramways avait écrasé une vieille tante : c'est ça la littérature ; ce n'est pas plus que ça. Le tramway avait écrasé une bonne qu'on appelait la vieille tante ; elle était chez nous avant la naissance de mon père ; elle est morte centenaire. Le malheur, c'est que j'étais avec elle lorsqu'elle a été écrasée. Je l'ai vue mourir, ça a été une longue agonie sous le tramway avec tout ce que l'on peut imaginer de sang, de pompiers... J'avais sept ans. Ma fascination pour le tramway doit tenir à l'imbrication des rails. À Alger, la gare de marchandises est toute proche du port et ces rails rentrent dans le port ; sortent du port. Il y a, en dehors de la complexité de l'urbanisme, une sorte de poétique des rails à Alger. Certains quartiers ont même gardé les pavés à cause des rails des tramways et des trains. Quand j'étais adolescent, je prenais un tramway qui a disparu. Il longeait la côte d'Alger du port jusqu'à la Madrague vers l'est et à une dizaine de kilomètres de Tipasa vers l'ouest. Je crois que Camus a pris ce tramway parce qu'il parle de l'arrivée à Tipasa en tramway[1]. Ces choses-là n'existent que dans les villes.

LA VIE DE LA RUE

Les vives couleurs et les odeurs entêtantes des fleurs, les cris des martinets, les échoppes des marchands : une autre présentation du spectacle de la rue évoqué dans *Le Premier Homme*. Où nous trouvons de précieux compléments d'information sur Galoufa (voir *PH*, p. 157).

En Algérie, la rue est beaucoup plus qu'une voie de circulation, elle est un lieu où l'on vit. Et si chacune a sa particularité, du fait de sa situation géographique ou de la nature des constructions qui la bordent, elles ont toutes la même « âme », faite de couleurs, de parfums et de bruits qui éclatent littéralement au long des cinq mois que dure l'été algérien. Aussi, celui qui déambule dans une rue ou, simplement, la traverse, pénètre dans un halo de sensations qui s'expriment en puissants mélanges. Les jardins exhalent des senteurs de glycine, de jasmin, de chèvrefeuille, dans l'alternance de leurs grappes violines et de leur feuillage piqueté de fleurs blanches ou ocre. Ici et là, les bougainvilliers dressent des murs rouges ou mauves. Partout des flaques d'ombre alternent avec des plages de lumière blonde et coupante. La poussière y danse, soulevée par un souffle intermittent, faible ou rageur

Pierre Mannoni,
Les Français d'Algérie. Vie, mœurs, mentalités.
L'Harmattan, 1993, p. 153-154.

---

1. À la première page de « Noces à Tipasa » (*Noces*, 1939), Camus arrive à Tipasa en autobus. Tipasa est située à 68 kilomètres d'Alger ; il est très douteux que les tramways algérois soient jamais allés jusque-là. Quand il y retourne (« Retour à Tipasa », *L'Été*, texte écrit en 1953), c'est à nouveau par la route (sans doute en automobile).

suivant les cas. De lourds nuages s'amoncellent parfois très rapidement et éclatent en « bafounes » ou orages surprenants de brutalité. Les dernières gouttes à peine tombées cependant, le soleil réapparaît et, du sol mouillé, montent bientôt de forts effluves où se mêlent en s'exaspérant des senteurs d'oranger, de caroubier ou d'eucalyptus. Il faut plisser les yeux pour regarder les façades des maisons, blanches pour la plupart. Tandis que l'air vrombit de l'incessant vol des mouches et autres insectes, le ciel est traversé des martinets qui se poursuivent et, de temps à autre, par le caquetage d'une cigogne. Et l'on peut apercevoir le grand oiseau dressé sur son nid au sommet d'un toit, qui renverse sa tête pour claquer du bec. Quant aux hommes, ils donnent à la rue son animation typique.

[...] D'autres personnages retiennent l'attention. Ils appartiennent à des couches sociales très modestes, tantôt Européens, tantôt Arabo-Berbères. Installés au milieu de la chaussée dont ils font leur échoppe, leurs boîtes ou leurs couffins leur tiennent lieu de vitrine et leur voix d'enseigne. Minuscules héros d'un univers picaresque dont on trouve d'autres variantes dans d'autres pays, ils sont les modestes, mais nécessaires constituants du quotidien. Car, aussi bien, de la fresque colorée qu'ils composent se dégage le véritable génie de la rue algérienne. Même les plus misérables d'entre eux véhiculent encore une certaine poésie, triviale certes, mais confinant aussi, par certains côtés, au légendaire, si tant est, comme le note Joëlle Hureau[1], que « l'ordinaire alimente inlassablement le

1. *La Mémoire des pieds-noirs*, Orban, 1987, p. 231 (note de l'auteur).

mythique ». En eux se mêlent vulgarité et grandeur, matérialité et spiritualité. Et les passants sont, bon gré mal gré, les témoins et interlocuteurs, obligés en quelque sorte, de ces démons du pavé.

[...] Tous les *fourachaux*[1] d'Alger connaissent, dans les années 1920, Marie-Anisette, ainsi nommée parce que la pauvre femme ne boit pas que du thé. Personnage misérable, vêtue de loques et traînant la savate, hâve et décoiffée, elle vagabonde en roulant des yeux fiévreux, toujours à la recherche d'un verre. Proie toute désignée des petits *ouallilounes*[2] qui la harcèlent, elle poursuit son chemin de somnambule en leur crachant quelques « sales bâtards ! » qui sont autant d'encouragements à la poursuivre. Dans les mêmes rues circule une autre malheureuse petite vieille aux vêtements noirs et râpés, qui furent élégants, chapeau enfoncé sur la tête. Portant toujours serrée contre elle une gamelle, la pauvresse erre le soir avec les chiens à qui elle dispute des reliefs de poubelle, tandis que les impitoyables gamins se précipitent sur ses talons dès qu'ils l'aperçoivent, histoire de faire avec son nom des rimes douteuses : « Y-a du bon rata, Madame Bourata ? »

Autre héros générique, aux multiples visages couverts par l'originel patronyme, « Galoufa » est « l'attrapeur de chiens », de Bône à Alger tout au moins. Quel que soit par ailleurs son véritable nom d'état civil, l'employé de la fourrière le quitte pour endosser, bon gré mal gré, celui de Galoufa attaché à la fonction *sub specie æternitatis*, comme l'écrit Paul Achard qui, augurant d'une façon plaisante

1. Le *fourachaux*, comme le *salaouètche*, est un Français d'Algérie d'origine modeste, plus ou moins vagabond.

2. Sorte de poulbot indigène.

ce que l'avenir pourra introduire comme nouveauté, se demande si on ne verra pas « un ramasseur de chiens automatique, qui opérera à la façon d'un aspirateur. Nous verrons sans doute le Galoufa-automobile, le Galoufa-électrique, le Galoufa-robot, peut-être le Galoufa-volant, aérien, l'aviateur Galouféen[1] ». Tâche ingrate au demeurant, exposée aux quolibets et à la réprobation que celle du pauvre employé municipal parcourant les rues, rivé à sa charrette sur laquelle est installée une cage à barreaux. Par ailleurs, les proverbes algériens le présentent comme symbole tout à fait inattendu de « goinfre ». « Quel Galoufa! », dira-t-on de celui qui s'empiffre.

LA MOUNA DU LUNDI DE PÂQUES

Le lundi de Pâques, le petit Jacques Cormery monte dans la carriole de l'oncle Michel pour aller « faire la mouna » dans la forêt de Sidi-Ferruch (*PH*, p. 146). Celle-ci est située en aplomb de la plage où les troupes françaises avaient débarqué en 1830.

La Mouna se fête partout, dans les villes comme dans les villages. C'est, à l'origine, un gâteau espagnol, une sorte de brioche couronnée d'un œuf retenu par un croisillon de pâte et qui durcit pendant la cuisson. Dans la deuxième moitié du XIXᵉ siècle, l'habitude s'est répandue chez tous les Européens d'Algérie d'aller en bande manger la Mouna au-dehors, le lundi de Pâques, et le phénomène a très vite pris une grande ampleur. Toute la fin de la semaine sainte est consacrée aux préparatifs. Chez

Marc Baroli, *La Vie quotidienne des Français en Algérie (1830-1914)*, Hachette, 1967, p. 206-207.

1. Paul Achard, *Salaouètches*, Balland, 1972, p. 127 (note de l'auteur).

Cagayous[1] on met des objets au mont-de-piété pour couvrir les frais de la journée ; les femmes n'admettent de faire aucun travail ; elles préparent trois sortes de gâteaux que l'on porte au four du boulanger, chez qui il faut avoir retenu son tour longtemps à l'avance. Les hommes préparent des tentes, se procurent des instruments de musique, remettent en état de vieilles charrettes.

Le grand jour venu, on part très tôt à pied, en charrette ou en tram vers le coin de plage ou de forêt choisi plusieurs jours à l'avance et que les plus vaillants sont parfois allés occuper en pleine nuit, et toute la journée on mange, on danse et on se baigne.

Mais, au fond, l'importance de la Mouna vient de ce qu'elle ouvre les plaisirs de la belle saison avec les longues soirées au grand air et les dimanches à la mer. En Algérie, la belle saison, c'est le printemps ; en été, les villes commencent à se dépeupler, du moins à partir de 1905.

Dès juin ou juillet, une partie de la société algéroise prend le même chemin que les hivernants, rentrés chez eux avant Pâques. Mais les bateaux ont beau être pleins, cela ne fait pas encore beaucoup de monde, et les fonctionnaires auxquels le passage est assuré gratuitement un an sur deux forment la majorité des passagers.

CINÉMAS DE QUARTIER

Parmi les « petits cinés de quartier » d'Alger, Montherlant se rappelle « l'*Alfred-de-Musset* » (en réalité le *Musset*) où Jacques Cormery se rend avec sa grand-

---

1. Auguste Robinet, sous le pseudonyme de Musette, a écrit vers 1900 les aventures de Cagayous, héros populaire algérois. Voir Gabriel Audisio, *Cagayous. Ses meilleures histoires*, Gallimard, 1931.

mère (voir *PH.* p. 106 et suiv., ainsi que p. 87). Il était situé à Belcourt, à l'angle de la rue de Lyon et de la rue Alfred-de-Musset, tout près du domicile des Camus. Le *Bijou* se trouvait à Bab-el-Oued.

Les petits cinés de quartier, le *Bijou*, le *Plateau*, le *Minor*, l'*Alfred-de-Musset*, ont tangué toute l'après-midi sur les vagues de pluie (la pluie d'Alger! divinité-épouse du mistral de Marseille), comme des rafiots courant au naufrage, emportant leur cargaison de jeunes mâles surexcités et hagards, saouls de ce gros vin de l'écran avec lequel le peuple s'est refait son opium. Les avez-vous vus, ces petits cinés de quartier, quand on y embarque par une pluie battante, en corps de chemise (car il fait chaud, malgré la pluie), et que la pluie vous colle la chemise sur le torse, vous dessine sur le torse le « drapé mouillé » des statues grecques, et qu'on est fumant comme des jeunes étalons ? Le contrôleur, à l'entrée, serre toutes les mains, comme un « monsieur de la famille ». « Pourquoi que tu lui as pas gardé le 32, à Mme Guigui ? Tu sais bien qu'elle veut toujours le 32. » Dans l'obscurité, on dialogue d'une extrémité à l'autre de la salle : « Ô Garcia ! Ta mère elle cherche les clefs. » — « Oïe oïe oïe, si elle a pas les clefs, elle me tue[1] ! » Ma voisine, quand le documentaire commence, me fait des yeux hors de la tête : « C'est le drâme ? C'est le drâme ? » Aucun « drame », pourtant, n'est annoncé sur l'affiche. Quand on projette le titre du nouveau film, qui est un film comique, elle sursaute et dit à son fils, avec un air de plus en plus égaré : « Va dire à tata Clo que le drâme y va commencer. » Et lui, avec le ton de supériorité de la robe prétexte, posant l'index sur la

Henry de Montherlant, *Il y a encore des paradis. Images d'Alger (1928-1931)*, *op. cit.*, p. 91-92.

---

1. « Si tu te noies, ta mère elle te tue » (*Le Premier Homme*, p. 64).

tempe droite, pour faire signe que sa mère démé-
nage : « Oh! le drâme tu dis ?... Tu vois pas que
c'est un rigolo ? » Cependant sur l'écran passent des
fantômes de films, la pellicule si usée que bientôt on
ne reconnaît plus le héros du traître, découpée au
hasard, les légendes interchangées ou cul sur tête,
des films qui sont devenus quelque chose qui n'a
de nom dans aucune langue, mais ne peuvent surprendre pour cela un public habitué à voir Charlot
voler dans les airs, ou Mickey se diviser en deux ;
la féerie continue, pour de magnifiques garçons, si
ravis — soit dans le film, soit dans la conversation
avec leurs cousines — que vous leur passeriez une
aiguille à travers le bras sans les faire broncher.

V. RÉCITS D'ENFANCE

LE SOURIRE D'UNE MÈRE

Dans ses _Carnets_, vers le début de l'année 1948 (_OC_, t. II, p. 1109), Camus copie deux citations d'_Enfance_, récit autobiographique de Tolstoï. « Un fort vent d'ouest soulevait en colonnes la poussière des routes et des champs, penchait les sommets des hauts tilleuls et des bouleaux du jardin, et emmenait au loin les feuilles jaunes qui tombaient. » Coïncidence ? Un vent d'ouest souffle aux premières lignes du _Premier Homme_. Et puis : « S'il m'était donné encore dans les heures douloureuses de la vie de revoir ce sourire [de sa mère] ne fût-ce qu'un instant, je ne connaîtrais pas la douleur. » Quel rapport entre l'enfance choyée de Tolstoï, qui grandit dans l'aisance aux côtés de ses deux parents et de son précepteur (Karl Ivanovitch), et celle de Jacques Cormery ? Seul, peut-être, le sourire de la mère : « Je demanderai pardon sans autre explication et tu me souriras... » (_PH._, p. 363).

Lorsque maman souriait, aussi beau que fût son visage, il devenait incomparablement plus beau, et tout autour d'elle paraissait se réjouir. Si, dans les moments difficiles de mon existence, j'avais pu fût-ce une seconde apercevoir ce sourire, j'aurais ignoré ce qu'était le chagrin. Il me semble que le sourire à lui seul fait ce qu'on appelle la beauté d'un visage ; si le sourire ajoute de la grâce au visage, le visage est beau : s'il ne le transforme pas, il est ordinaire, s'il l'abîme, il est laid.

En me disant bonjour, maman prit ma tête entre ses mains et la pencha en arrière, puis elle me regarda avec insistance et me dit :

Tolstoï, _Souvenirs et récits_ (trad. Sylvie Luneau), Gallimard, Pléiade, 1960, p. 22.

— Tu as pleuré aujourd'hui ?

Je ne répondis pas. Elle m'embrassa sur les yeux et me demanda en allemand :

— Pourquoi as-tu pleuré ?

Lorsqu'elle prenait avec nous le ton de l'amitié, elle usait toujours de cette langue qu'elle possédait à la perfection.

— C'est en rêve que j'ai pleuré, maman, lui dis-je en me remémorant tous les détails de mon rêve imaginaire et en frémissant à cette pensée.

Karl Ivanovitch confirma mes dires, mais il passa le songe sous silence. Après avoir échangé plusieurs phrases sur le temps (conversation à laquelle se mêla Mimi), maman posa sur le plateau six petits morceaux de sucre pour les visiteurs de marque, se leva et se dirigea vers son métier à broder, installé devant la fenêtre.

— Eh bien, allez maintenant voir papa, enfants, et dites-lui qu'il passe me voir sans faute avant de partir pour l'enclos de battage.

La musique, l'énoncé des temps et les regards menaçants recommencèrent et nous allâmes chez papa. Après avoir traversé la pièce qui depuis l'époque de mon grand-père avait gardé le nom d'OFFICE nous entrâmes dans son cabinet.

L'ENFANCE D'UN « PETIT MONSTRE »

« Lisez, dans *Devenir !*, le portrait du père Mazerelles et de sa femme », écrit Camus au début de sa Préface aux *Œuvres complètes* de Roger Martin du Gard. À ses yeux, l'« épaisseur » de ce portrait suffirait à situer Martin du Gard dans la lignée de Tolstoï, alors que la littérature contemporaine se réclame plutôt de Dostoïevski. On s'attardera ici sur le portrait de l'enfant,

André Mazerelles, dont les dons précoces émerveillent ses parents. *Devenir!* (Ollendorff, 1908) est la première œuvre de Martin du Gard ; il était alors âgé de vingt-sept ans. À sa façon, Jacques Cormery est lui aussi un « monstre » (voir *supra*, p. 106).

Il était né avec une part estimable d'intelligence, et semblait placé dans des conditions favorables pour en faire un emploi normal ; mais, dès le plus jeune âge, il l'avait appliquée à contredire obstinément ce qu'il entendait et voyait autour de lui.

Sa prime enfance avait été celle des petits monstres. Primesautier, observateur, indiscipliné d'esprit, il s'appliquait à paraître « étonnant pour son âge », en formulant ce que les autres enfants pensent peut-être et ne disent pas. Il tirait adroitement parti de son précoce cabotinage. Sa mère, sa sœur aînée, se paraient de lui : on citait ses mots ; il les répétait, avec une feinte ingénuité, devant des amis. Dès qu'il fut en âge de lire, le livre l'attira : c'était un vice de nature. Il y trouvait de quoi alimenter son besoin de parade. Les expressions qu'il y recueillait étonnaient sur ses lèvres de mioche : « On ne sait pas où il va chercher ça... »

À onze ans il eut un gros registre où il copiait des poésies préférées : *Le Petit Savoyard*, *Les Deux Cortèges*, *Le Crucifix*... Il eut aussi un cahier de moleskine bleu tendre, où il calligraphiait ses œuvres personnelles : puérils pastiches des morceaux choisis dans lesquels on lui taillait ses leçons. Le soir, quand il était couché, sa mère portait en cachette ces rimailles à M. Mazerelles, et tous deux, souriants, haussaient les épaules et s'enorgueillissaient.

De jour en jour, ses habitudes de contradiction s'affirmaient et rendaient plus difficile la vie de famille. Tout ce que ses parents pensaient ou fai-

Roger Martin du Gard, *Œuvres complètes*, préface d'Albert Camus, Gallimard, Pléiade, 1955, t. I, p. 6-7.

saient, était le contraire de ce qu'il fallait penser ou faire. Il ne songeait pas à s'étonner que ce fût justement lui, leur descendant, qui s'en rendît compte, et n'y relevait aucun avertissement de sa présomption ; il en éprouvait même plus fortement la conviction qu'il appartenait à une autre race qu'eux. Il s'attribuait exclusivement le domaine des hautes pensées, des sentiments nobles ; et, en fait, l'élan qui le soulevait était peut-être légitime : n'était-ce pas le flambeau des générations jeunes, qu'il brandissait à sa manière.

UNE VEUVE DE GUERRE ET SON FILS

En 1932, Jean Grenier fait lire à Camus un roman d'André de Richaud, *La Douleur*. « Je ne connais pas André de Richaud. Mais je n'ai jamais oublié son beau livre, qui fut le premier à me parler de ce que je connaissais : une mère, la pauvreté, de beaux soirs dans le ciel. Il dénouait au fond de moi un nœud de liens obscurs, me délivrait d'entraves dont je sentais la gêne sans pouvoir les nommer » (Camus, « Rencontres avec André Gide », *Hommage à André Gide,* Gallimard, 1951, p. 223). *La Douleur* raconte la souffrance infligée à un enfant par le déshonneur qui pèse sur sa mère : ayant perdu son mari, tué au front, celle-ci est tombée amoureuse d'un prisonnier allemand. La veuve Camus n'eut pas à affronter ce genre de soupçon, mais on devine, au début du roman, combien le jeune Albert pouvait se sentir proche du héros d'André de Richaud.

En août 1914, lorsque le capitaine avait été mobilisé, elle était venue là[1], seule avec son fils, à attendre la fin de la guerre. Elle ne s'était pas instal-

André de Richaud, *La Douleur*, Grasset, 1931 ; réédition « Les Cahiers rouges », 1988, p. 16-17.

1. Dans une maison isolée, près de la Sorgue.

lée, pensant que cette guerre ne durerait pas. Les grandes malles d'osier restèrent longtemps entrebâillées dans le vestibule sombre. Peu à peu, leur contenu alla se ranger aux places habituelles : dans le buffet, dans les armoires. Au bout de quelques mois, elles allèrent au grenier, retrouver leurs sœurs qui ne voyagent plus et quand toutes les choses furent à leurs places, lorsque Thérèse Delombre eut renoncé à l'espoir d'aller encore habiter à la ville, elle reçut l'avis de décès de son mari. Elle était engourdie par la solitude, par la tristesse des lieux où elle vivait et le choc fut violent mais bref. Elle pleura huit jours dans les cheveux de son fils et puis, comme elle se demandait ce qu'elle allait devenir toute seule, l'enfant eut la rougeole.

Quand il se leva, amaigri, grandi, Thérèse Delombre avait presque oublié le capitaine. Son avenir lui était dicté par toutes les femmes qui étaient venues voir le petit malade : elle vivrait là, dans l'ombre, jusqu'à sa mort ; pour son Georget...

Elle s'émerveillait du pathétique de la situation ; elle se sentait devenir l'héroïne de quelque grand roman d'abnégation et de courage.

AU TEMPS DU CINÉMA MUET

Sartre était de huit ans plus âgé que Camus. Tous deux ont connu, dans leur enfance, les charmes du cinéma muet, où les accents du (de la) pianiste soulignaient les moments tragiques de l'action (voir *PH,* p. 108).

Le spectacle était commencé. Nous suivions l'ouvreuse en trébuchant, je me sentais clandestin ; au-dessus de nos têtes, un faisceau de lumière blanche

Jean-Paul Sartre, *Les Mots*, Gallimard, 1964, p. 98-100.

traversait la salle, on y voyait danser des poussières, des fumées ; un piano hennissait, des poires violettes luisaient au mur, j'étais pris à la gorge par l'odeur vernie d'un désinfectant. L'odeur et les fruits de cette nuit habitée se confondaient en moi : je mangeais les lampes de secours, je m'emplissais de leur goût acidulé. Je raclais mon dos à des genoux, je m'asseyais sur un siège grinçant, ma mère glissait une couverture pliée sous mes fesses pour me hausser ; enfin je regardais l'écran, je découvrais une craie fluorescente, des paysages clignotants, rayés par des averses ; il pleuvait toujours, même au gros soleil, même dans les appartements ; parfois un astéroïde en flammes traversait le salon d'une baronne sans qu'elle parût s'en étonner. J'aimais cette pluie, cette inquiétude sans repos qui travaillait la muraille. Le pianiste attaquait l'ouverture des *Grottes de Fingal* et tout le monde comprenait que le criminel allait paraître : la baronne était folle de peur. Mais son beau visage charbonneux cédait la place à une pancarte mauve : « Fin de la première partie. » C'était la désintoxication brusquée, la lumière. Où étais-je ? Dans une école ? Dans une administration ? Pas le moindre ornement : des rangées de strapontins qui laissaient voir, par en dessous, leurs ressorts, des murs barbouillés d'ocre, un plancher jonché de mégots et de crachats. Des rumeurs touffues remplissaient la salle, on réinventait le langage, l'ouvreuse vendait à la criée des bonbons anglais, ma mère m'en achetait, je les mettais dans ma bouche, je suçais les lampes de secours. Les gens se frottaient les yeux, chacun découvrait ses voisins. Des soldats, les bonnes du quartier ; un vieillard osseux chiquait, des ouvrières en cheveux riaient très fort : tout ce monde n'était pas de notre monde ; heureusement, posés de loin en loin sur ce parterre de têtes, de grands chapeaux palpitants rassuraient. [...]

Ma mère s'enhardit jusqu'à me conduire dans les salles du Boulevard : au Kinérama, aux Folies Dramatiques, au Vaudeville, au Gaumont Palace qu'on nommait l'Hippodrome. Je vis *Zigomar* et *Fantômas, Les Exploits de Maciste, Les Mystères de New York* : les dorures me gâchaient le plaisir. Le Vaudeville, théâtre désaffecté, ne voulait pas abdiquer son ancienne grandeur : jusqu'à la dernière minute un rideau rouge à glands d'or masquait l'écran ; on frappait trois coups pour annoncer le commencement de la représentation, l'orchestre jouait une ouverture, le rideau se levait, les lampes s'éteignaient. J'étais agacé par ce cérémonial incongru, par ces pompes poussiéreuses qui n'avaient d'autre résultat que d'éloigner les personnages ; au balcon, au poulailler, frappés par le lustre, par les peintures du plafond, nos pères ne pouvaient ni ne voulaient croire que le théâtre leur appartenait : ils y étaient reçus. Moi, je voulais voir le film *au plus près*. Dans l'inconfort égalitaire des salles de quartier, j'avais appris que ce nouvel art était à moi, comme à tous. Nous étions du même âge mental : j'avais sept ans et je savais lire, il en avait douze[1] et ne savait pas parler. On disait qu'il était à ses débuts, qu'il avait des progrès à faire ; je pensais que nous grandirions ensemble.

1. Sartre date donc de 1900 les débuts du cinéma. Les premiers films des frères Lumière remontent en fait à 1895.

PARDAILLAN, HÉROS DÉMOCRATIQUE

Sartre trouva dans les livres ou les journaux qu'achetait sa famille les récits qui façonnèrent son imagination ; Camus les découvrit grâce à la bibliothèque municipale de son quartier. Ils ont eu un héros en commun : le Pardaillan de Michel Zévaco (voir *PH*, p. 266).

J'étais sans-culotte et régicide, mon grand-père m'avait prévenu contre les tyrans, qu'ils s'appelassent Louis XVI ou Badinguet[1]. Surtout, je lisais tous les jours, dans *Le Matin*, le feuilleton de Michel Zévaco : cet auteur de génie, sous l'influence de Hugo, avait inventé le roman de cape et d'épée républicain. Ses héros représentaient le peuple ; ils faisaient et défaisaient les empires, prédisaient dès le XIVe siècle la Révolution française, protégeaient par bonté d'âme des rois enfants ou des rois fous contre leurs ministres, souffletaient les rois méchants. Le plus grand de tous, Pardaillan, c'était mon maître : cent fois, pour l'imiter, superbement campé sur mes jambes de coq, j'ai giflé Henri III et Louis XIII. Allais-je me mettre à leurs ordres, après cela ? En un mot, je ne pouvais ni tirer de moi le mandat impératif qui aurait justifié ma présence sur cette terre ni reconnaître à personne le droit de me le délivrer. Je repris mes chevauchées, nonchalamment, je languis dans la mêlée ; massacreur distrait, martyr indolent, je restais Grisélidis[2], faute d'un tsar, d'un Dieu ou tout simplement d'un père.

Ibid., p. 109.

1. Surnom donné à Napoléon III.
2. Personnage de petite paysanne soumise au marquis qui l'a épousée. Cette légende de Boccace, reprise par de nombreux écrivains, a fait aussi le sujet d'un opéra de Massenet (1901).

Claude Simon (1913-2005) est né la même année que Camus ; il a reçu le prix Nobel vingt-huit ans après lui, en 1985. Comme Camus, il se souvient du prestige imposé par le conducteur de tramways, machiniste souverain à qui il était défendu d'adresser la parole (voir *PH*, p. 230-231), et il l'évoque dans un roman très auto-biographique, son dernier paru. Le tramway relie ici Nantes à la plage.

Rester dans la cabine (par où il fallait d'ailleurs passer pour pénétrer dans le tramway) au lieu d'aller s'asseoir à l'intérieur sur les banquettes, semblait être une sorte de privilège non seulement pour mon esprit d'enfant mais aussi, à l'évidence, de ceux des deux ou trois voyageurs qui, méprisant de même les banquettes, s'y trouvaient régulièrement, non pas sans doute pénétrés comme moi de l'importance du lieu, mais, simplement, parce qu'il était permis d'y fumer, à l'exemple du conducteur apparemment taciturne — ou contraint au silence, comme en témoignait dans un franco-anglais approximatif l'inscription : « Défense de parler au wattman » qui faisait en quelque sorte de lui un personnage à la fois assez misérable, d'une caste inférieure, condamné à une muette solitude, en même temps que nimbé d'une aura de pouvoir, comme ces rois ou ces potentats de tragédie auxquels il était interdit par un sévère protocole (et parfois sous peine de mort) d'adresser directement la parole, statut (ou position — ou fonction) qu'il assumait avec gravité, l'œil toujours fixé sur les rails qui venaient au-devant de lui, comme absorbé par le poids de sa responsabilité, se bornant aux arrêts, en attendant le coup de sonnette libérateur

Claude Simon,
Le Tramway,
Éditions de Minuit,
2001, p. 12-15.

du receveur, de rallumer au moyen d'un briquet de fer le mégot collé à sa lèvre inférieure d'un bout du trajet à l'autre (ce qui, de la plage à la ville, demandait, arrêts compris, environ trois quarts d'heure), petit tube ventru, grisâtre, dont l'enveloppe de mince papier imbibée de salive et rendue transparente laissait entrevoir la couleur brune du tabac maladroitement enrobé, bosselé parfois, presque crevé, par quelque brin (une « bûche ») trop gros ou mal tassé.

Il me semblait voir cela, y être, me trouver parmi les deux ou trois privilégiés admis à se tenir debout dans l'étroit habitacle d'environ deux mètres sur deux pourvu qu'ils ne parlent ni ne gênent l'homme silencieux vêtu d'une chemise de flanelle grise au col sans cravate mais fermé, d'un complet fatigué, gris lui aussi, et dont le pantalon élimé tombait sur une paire d'espadrilles aux semelles de corde non pas exactement élimées mais comme moustachues, effilochées, sur lesquelles il se tenait, les pieds légèrement écartés, personnage quasi mythique à la cigarette éteinte, à l'impassible visage, et dont les gestes — du moins à mes yeux d'enfant — semblaient avoir quelque chose d'à la fois rituel et sacré, qu'il poussât de ses petits coups de paume la manivelle des vitesses, se baissât pour actionner le volant du frein ou appuyer à coups pressés de son pied droit le champignon du timbre avertisseur lorsque le tramway s'engageait dans une courbe sans visibilité ou presque continuellement quand, une fois passé l'octroi, la motrice pénétrait dans la ville, descendait d'abord la longue pente qui menait au jardin public, longeait le mur de celui-ci, tournait sur la gauche à hauteur du monument aux morts et, suivant le boulevard du Président-Wilson, ralentissait peu à peu le long de l'Allée des Marronniers pour s'immobiliser en fin de course, presque au centre-ville, en face du cinéma à l'entrée protégée par une marquise de verre et aux aguichantes affiches qui, dans des couleurs violentes, proposaient aux éventuels spectateurs les gigantesques visages de femmes échevelées, aux têtes renversées et aux bouches ouvertes dans un cri d'épouvante ou l'appel d'un baiser.

Pour un rapprochement moins anecdotique entre Camus et Claude Simon, voir Pierre Schoentjes, « *Le Premier Homme* et *L'Acacia* », dans *Europe,* numéro spécial « Albert Camus », octobre 1999, p. 154-166.

VI. BIBLIOGRAPHIE

Le Premier Homme, publié pour la première fois chez Galli-
    mard en 1994 (série des « Cahiers Albert Camus », n° 7), a
    été réédité en 2000 dans la collection « Folio ».

AUTRES ŒUVRES DE CAMUS

Œuvres complètes, édition de Jacqueline Lévi-Valensi, Galli-
    mard, Bibliothèque de la Pléiade, t. I (1931-1944) et II
    (1944-1948), 2006 (abrégé en *OC*).
Pour les œuvres postérieures à 1948, on se référera à :
Théâtre, récits, nouvelles, édition de Roger Quilliot, Gallimard,
    Bibliothèque de la Pléiade, 1962.
Essais, édition de Roger Quilliot, Gallimard, Bibliothèque de la
    Pléiade, 1965.
Carnets II (janvier 1942-mars 1951), Gallimard, 1964.
Carnets III (mars 1951-décembre 1959), Gallimard, 1989.
Voir aussi :
Albert Camus-Jean Grenier, *Correspondance (1932-1960)*,
    édition de Marguerite Dobrenn, Gallimard, 1981.
Albert Camus-René Char, *Correspondance (1946-1959)*,
    édition de Franck Planeille, Gallimard, 2007.

BIOGRAPHIES, TÉMOIGNAGES

Daniel, Jean, *Avec Camus. Comment résister à l'air du
    temps*, Gallimard, 2006.
Grenier, Jean, *Albert Camus. Souvenirs*, Gallimard, 1968.

Lottman, Herbert R., *Albert Camus*, trad. française : Le Seuil, 1978.

Rey, Pierre-Louis, *Camus. L'homme révolté*, Gallimard, coll. « Découvertes », 2006.

Rondeau, Daniel, *Camus ou les Promesses de la vie*, Société des éditions Mengès, 2005.

Todd, Olivier, *Albert Camus. Une vie*, Gallimard, 1996.

Vircondelet, Alain, *Albert Camus. Vérités et légendes*, Éditions du Chêne, 1998.

ÉTUDES :

Albert Camus et le lyrisme, textes réunis par J. Lévi-Valensi et Agnès Spiquel, SEDES, 1997 (études sur *Le Premier Homme* de Raymond Gay-Crosier et de Pierre Grouix).

Camus et la politique, textes réunis par Jeanyves Guérin, L'Harmattan, 1986.

Chabot, Jacques, *Albert Camus*, « *la pensée de midi* », Édisud, Aix-en-Provence, 2002.

Chaulet-Achour, Christiane, *Albert Camus*, *Alger*, Biarritz, Atlantica, 1998, et Séguier, 1999.

Grenier, Jean, *Albert Camus. Souvenirs*, Gallimard, 1968.

Grenier, Roger, *Albert Camus. Soleil et ombre*, Gallimard, 1987 (« Folio », 1991).

Guérin, Jeanyves, *Camus. Portrait de l'artiste en citoyen*, François Bourin, 1993.

Lévi-Valensi, Jacqueline, *Albert Camus ou la Naissance d'un romancier (1930-1942)*, Gallimard, 2006.

Mailhot, Laurent, *Albert Camus ou l'Imagination du désert*, Presses de l'Université de Montréal, 1973.

Rey, Pierre-Louis, *Camus. Une morale de la beauté*, SEDES, 2000.

REVUES

« Albert Camus : parcours méditerranéens », sous la direction de Fernande Bartfeld et David Ohana, *Perspectives. Revue de l'Université hébraïque de Jérusalem*, n° 5, 1998.
Europe, octobre 1999.
Le Magazine littéraire, mai 2006.

ÉTUDES PARTICULIÈRES SUR *LE PREMIER HOMME*

Inada, Harutoshi, « *Le Premier Homme*, roman ou autobiographie ? », *Études camusiennes*, n° 2, Seizansha, 1996.
Matsumoto, Yosei, « Année 1953 : le tournant décisif », *Études camusiennes*, n° 7, Seizansha, 2006.
Sarocchi, Jean, *Le Dernier Camus ou « Le Premier Homme »*, Nizet, 1995.
Takatsuka, Hiroyuki, « *Le Premier Homme* comme perpétuelle quête du secret », *Études camusiennes*, n° 3, Seizansha, 1998.

« *Le Premier Homme* » *d'Albert Camus*, études réunies par Christian Morzewski, avant-propos d'Yves Baudelle et Ch. Morzewski, *Roman 20-50*, 1999.
« *Le Premier Homme* en perspective », textes réunis et présentés par Raymond Gay-Crosier, *Revue des Lettres modernes*, série « Albert Camus », n° 20, Lettres modernes Minard, 2004.

FILMOGRAPHIE :

Albert Camus (1913-1960). Une tragédie du bonheur, film de Jean Daniel et Joël Calmettes, d'après des archives de l'IMEC, production : CKF/IMEC/France 3. « Un siècle d'écrivains », coll. dirigée par Bernard Rapp, 1999.

TABLE

DANS LA MÊME COLLECTION

Composition CMB graphic.
Impression Bussière à Saint-Amand (Cher),
le 5 février 2008.
Dépôt légal : février 2008.
Numéro d'imprimeur : 080298/1.
ISBN 978-2-07-034099-6./Imprimé en France.